2021

Income Tax
FUNDAMENTALS

GERALD E. WHITTENBURG

STEVEN L. GILL

San Diego State University

CENGAGE

Australia • Brazil • Canada • Mexico • Singapore • United Kingdom • United States

Income Tax Fundamentals, **2021 Edition**
Gerald E. Whittenburg and Steven L. Gill

Senior Vice President, Higher Ed Product, Content, and Market Development: Erin Joyner

Product Director: Jason Fremder

Associate Product Manager: Jonathan Gross

Senior Content Manager: Tricia Hempel

Product Assistant: Margaret Russo

Marketing Manager: Chris Walz

Senior Digital Project Manager: Tim Richison

Production Service: MPS Limited

Designer: Chris Doughman

Cover Images:

donatas1205/Shutterstock.com;
iStock.com/gerenme

Special page images:

Zhukov Oleg/Shutterstock.com;
ILYA AKINSHIN/Shutterstock.com

Intellectual Property

Analyst: Ashley Maynard
Project Manager: Carly Belcher

For product information and technology assistance, contact us at
Cengage Customer & Sales Support, 1-800-354-9706.
For permission to use material from this text or product,
submit all requests online at **www.cengage.com/permissions.**
Further permissions questions can be emailed to
permissionrequest@cengage.com.

Tax forms reproduced courtesy of the Internal Revenue Service (**www.irs.gov**).

Library of Congress Control Number: 2020919760

ISBN: 978-0-357-14136-6

Cengage
200 Pier 4 Boulevard
Boston, MA 02210
USA

Cengage is a leading provider of customized learning solutions with employees residing in nearly 40 different countries and sales in more than 125 countries around the world. Find your local representative at **www.cengage.com.**

To learn more about Cengage platforms and services, register or access your online learning solution, or purchase materials for your course, visit **www.cengage.com.**

Printed in the United States of America
Print Number: 01   Print Year: 2020

CONCISE, CURRENT, & PRACTICAL!

Income Tax Fundamentals'
Winning Forms Approach Is Time-Tested

*I*ncome Tax Fundamentals 2021 Edition is designed as a self-contained book for an introductory course in individual income taxation. We take pride in the concise, current, and practical coverage of the income tax return preparation process. *Income Tax Fundamentals* continues to be the **market-leading textbook** with a tax forms-based approach that is a reliable choice, with an experienced author team that offers a commitment to accuracy. The workbook format of the textbook presents materials in practical sections with multiple examples and review problems. The presentation of the material does not assume that the reader has taken a course in accounting, making it appropriate for use as a self-study guide to federal income tax. *Income Tax Fundamentals* adopters tell us:

> Great text. I have used it for years mostly because of its simple and straightforward approach to the basic income tax elements.
>
> — Jerold K. Braun, Daytona State College

> This text provides an excellent overview for community tax classes. The software gives these students good hands-on experience with the concepts.
>
> — Jay Wright, New River Community College

> I love this book with all its comprehensive problems that progress from easy to difficult.
>
> — LoAnn Nelson, PhD, CPA, Lake Region State College

> The layout of the chapters is well-thought out.
>
> — James Hromadka, San Jacinto College

> I enjoy using the Whittenburg text...it is the best I have found.
>
> — Jana Hosmer, Blue Ridge Community College

Whittenburg and Gill's hallmark "**Forms Approach**" allows students to practice filling out tax returns right in the book while also having the option to download tax forms online. *Income Tax Fundamentals* has been redesigned to follow the new Form 1040 and supporting Schedules 1 through 3. Every attempt to align the concepts with the schedules has been made so students can follow from the detailed form to the schedule and eventually to Form 1040.

intuit.
Accountants

ProConnect™ Tax

Each individual tax form required to complete the problems in the textbook is included within *Income Tax Fundamentals* and within the complimentary ProConnect Tax software. ProConnect Tax is an industry-leading tax preparation software that is hosted on the cloud and provides robust tax content and easy navigation. The ProConnect Tax website offers community and knowledge-based content, view alerts, and FAQ articles. All of the 2020 individual income tax return problems in the textbook may be solved using the ProConnect Tax software, or students may prepare the tax returns by hand.

Income Tax Fundamentals

Evolves Each Year to Benefit You

NEW TO THIS EDITION

Many Changes to Tax Law

In the past year, the tax law has experienced a number of significant changes. In December 2019, the Taxpayer Certainty and Disaster Tax Relief Act of 2019 (TCDTR Act) was enacted as part of an omnibus spending package. In what has become typical "extender's bill" fashion, this law extended several tax provisions that had expired, or were going to expire, at the end of 2019. That same month, December 2019, the Setting Every Community Up for Retirement Enhancement Act (SECURE Act) was passed, making changes to the way in which retirement savings contributions and distributions are taxed. In response to the COVID-19 pandemic, The Families First Coronavirus Response Act was passed in March 2020 and made only a few changes to the tax law, such as extending the 2019 tax year individual filing deadline from April 15, 2020 to July 15, 2020. Shortly thereafter, the Coronavirus Aid, Relief, and Economic Security (CARES) Act was passed. The CARES Act included extensive economic impact programs, including loan forgiveness and small-business relief through grants and loans, unemployment insurance, and a bevy of payroll tax deferrals and credits. The CARES Act also contained individual tax relief, some of which had provisions that were retroactively applied to 2019 or prior. To the extent these provisions significantly affect individual income taxpayers (for example, the $1,200 economic impact payment and related recovery rebate credit), they have been included in this edition. Because many of the COVID-related relief provisions are temporary and will end with tax year 2020, discussions of provisions that are expected to end include "with and without COVID provisions" examples, self-study problems, and end-of-chapter problems, so that the instructor can determine which level of coverage is appropriate.

Introduction of Additional Real-life Source Documents

We continue to include commonly used source documents in the exercises and tax return problems, such as Form W-2, a myriad of forms 1099, Form 1095-A, and additional accounting schedules, such as trial balances and income statements in an effort to replicate the tax return preparation process. Information that is extraneous to the problem is included to encourage students to use analytical and critical-thinking skills to deal with less structured problems.

Additions to Content

To address pending state legislation, a new section regarding the classification of an employee versus an independent contractor has been added. Given the increased probability of cancellation of debt due to the economic downturn, the topic of forgiveness of debt income has been added.

UPDATED CUMULATIVE SOFTWARE PROBLEM

The cumulative software problem included as Group 5 questions at the end of Chapters 1–8 have been updated to include more source documents (Forms W-2, 1099, etc.), current COVID-related events, and extraneous information to encourage students to think more critically about the relevance of certain items when preparing tax returns.

A COMPLETE LEARNING SYSTEM—CENGAGENOWv2

CengageNOWv2 for Taxation takes students from motivation to mastery. It elevates thinking by providing superior content designed with the entire student workflow in mind. Students learn more efficiently with a variety of engaging assessments and learning tools. For instructors, CengageNOWv2 provides ultimate control and customization and a clear view into student performance that allows for the opportunity to tailor the learning experience to improve outcomes.

Motivation

Many instructors find that students come to class unmotivated and unprepared. To help with engagement and preparedness, CengageNOWv2 for Whittenburg offers the following feature:

Self-Study Questions based on the information presented in the textbook help students prepare for class lectures or review prior to an exam. Self-Study Questions provide ample practice for the students as they read the chapters, while providing them with valuable feedback and checks along the way, as the solutions are provided conveniently in Appendix E of the textbook.

Application

Students need to learn problem-solving skills in order to complete taxation problems on their own. However, as students try to work through homework problems, sometimes they become stuck and need guidance. To help reinforce concepts and keep students on the right track, CengageNOWv2 for Whittenburg offers the following:

- **End-of-chapter homework: Group 1 and 2 problems**

- **Algorithmic versions:** End-of-chapter homework is available for at least 10–15 problems per chapter.

- **Detailed feedback for each homework question:** Homework questions include enhanced, immediate feedback so students can learn as they go. Levels of feedback include an option for "check my work" prior to submission of an assignment. Then, after submitting an assignment, students receive even more extensive feedback explaining why their answers were incorrect. Instructors can decide how much feedback their students receive and when, including providing the full solution, if they wish.

- Built-in **Test Bank:** Provides online assessment.

- CengageNOWv2's **Adaptive Study Plan:** Complete with quizzes, an eBook, and more, it is designed to provide assistance for students who need additional support and prepare them for the exam.

Mastery

Finally, students need to make the leap from memorizing concepts to critical thinking. They need to be able to connect multiple topics and master the material. To help students grasp the big picture of taxation, tax return preparation, and achieve the end goal of mastery, CengageNOWv2 for Whittenburg offers the following:

- **Comprehensive Problems:** Allow students to complete the tax return problems by entering the relevant information on tax forms and schedules in the ProConnect Tax software or by manually preparing the tax forms and schedules provided within each chapter.

Cengage Learning Testing Powered by Cognero®

Cognero® is a flexible, online system that allows instructors to:

- author, edit, and manage test bank content from multiple Cengage Learning solutions
- create multiple test versions in an instant
- deliver tests from your LMS, your classroom or wherever you want

Cognero® possesses the features necessary to make assessment fast, efficient, and effective:

- **Simplicity at every step:** A desktop-inspired interface features drop-down menus and familiar, intuitive tools.
- **Full-featured test generator:** Choose from 15 question types (including true/false, multiple choice, and essay). Multi-language support, an equation editor, and unlimited metadata help ensure your tests are complete and compliant.
- **Cross-compatible capability:** Import and export content into other systems.

CL Testing Powered by Cognero® is accessible through the instructor companion site, **www.cengage.com/login.**

Key Terms

Key Terms with page references are located at the end of all of the chapters and reinforce the important tax terms introduced and discussed in each chapter.

Key Points

Following the Key Terms is a brief summary of the learning objective highlights for each chapter to allow students to focus quickly on the main points of each chapter.

RELIABLE INSTRUCTOR RESOURCES ARE CONVENIENT

Solutions Manual

The manual, located on the instructor companion website: **www.cengage.com/login**, contains detailed solutions to the end-of-chapter problems in the textbook, Chapter Outlines and Suggested Minimum Assignments, and the solutions for the Additional Comprehensive Problems are located in Appendix D.

Comprehensive Instructor Companion Website

This password-protected site contains instructor resources: the Solutions Manual, the Test Bank, Cognero® testing tools, Solutions to the Cumulative Tax Return Problems, ProConnect Tax software solutions and instructions, PowerPoints, and more: **www.cengage.com/login**.

AS WE GO TO PRESS

To access tax law information after the publication of this textbook, please visit **www.cengage.com**. At the home page, input the ISBN of your textbook (from the back cover of your book). This will take you to the product page where free companion resources are located.

Step-by-Step Format
Builds Student Confidence

The practical, step-by-step format in *Income Tax Fundamentals 2021 Edition* builds from simple to complex topics. The authors are careful to lead students down a path of understanding rather than overwhelming them with excessive detail and multiple Internal Revenue Code references.

- Helpful examples within each chapter provide realistic scenarios for students to consider.

EXAMPLE Scott provides all of the support for an unrelated family friend who lives with him for the entire tax year. He also supports a cousin who lives in another state. The family friend can qualify as Scott's dependent, but the cousin cannot. The family friend meets the member of the household test. Even though the cousin is not considered a relative, he could have been a dependent if he met the member of the household part of the test. ◆

- The short Learning Objective sections within each chapter offer numerous examples, supported by the "Self-Study Problems" throughout. The Self-Study Problems encourage students to answer a series of short questions in a fill-in-the-blank or multiple-choice format. The solutions to the Self-Study Problems are provided at the end of the textbook, offering immediate solutions to students to help build confidence.

- The Quick Tax Reference Guide on the inside of the back cover of the textbook includes the Tax Equation.

MARRIED FILING JOINTLY OR QUALIFYING WIDOW(ER)		
$0		
$19,750	$19,750	
$80,250	$80,250	
$100,000	$100,000	
$171,050	$171,050	10% of taxable income *
$326,600	$326,600	$1,975.00 + 12% of the excess over $19,750 *
$414,700	$414,700	$9,235.00 + 22% of the excess over $80,250 *
$622,050	$622,050	$9,235.00 + 22% of the excess over $80,250
		$29,211.00 + 24% of the excess over $171,050
MARRIED FILING SEPARATELY		$66,543.00 + 32% of the excess over $326,600
$0		$94,753.00 + 35% of the excess over $414,700
$9,875	$9,875	$167,307.50 + 37% of the excess over $622,050
$40,125	$40,125	
$85,525	$85,525	
$100,000	$100,000	10% of taxable income *
$163,300	$163,300	$987.50 + 12% of the excess over $9,875 *
$207,350	$207,350	$4,617.50 + 22% of the excess over $40,125 *
$311,025	$311,025	$14,605.50 + 24% of the excess over $85,525 *
		$14,605.50 + 24% of the excess over $85,525
HEAD OF HOUSEHOLD		$33,271.50 + 32% of the excess over $163,300
		$47,367.50 + 35% of the excess over $207,350
		$83,653.75 + 37% of the excess over $311,025

10% of tax...

LEARNING OBJECTIVES

After completing this chapter, you should be able to:

LO 1.1 Explain the history and objectives of U.S. tax law.

LO 1.2 Describe the different entities subject to tax and reporting requirements.

LO 1.3 Apply the tax formula for individuals.

LO 1.4 Identify individuals who must file tax returns.

LO 1.5 Determine filing ... understand the calculation of tax according to filing

- Learning Objectives help organize information and are referenced by the end-of-chapter exercises.

Real-World Applications Keep Students Engaged

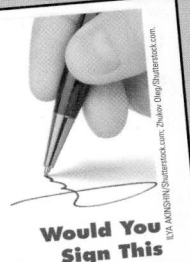

- Real-world examples within Tax Break segments provide actual, effective examples of tax-planning strategies that clearly illustrate the concepts discussed throughout the book and cover nearly every basic tax-planning technique used by tax preparers.

- The "Would You Sign This Tax Return?" feature places readers in the office of a tax preparer with interesting and sometimes humorous real-world tax ethics questions that will intrigue students. Many of these features are inspired by the authors' own experiences working with various clients in tax preparation. As part of each scenario, students decide if they would sign the tax return. The instructor can use the cases to spark group discussions on basic tax preparation ethics.

Would You Sign This Tax Return?

Your client, William Warrant, was hired for a management position at an Internet company planning to start a website called "indulgedanimals.com" for dogs, cats, and other pets. When he was hired, William was given an incentive stock option (ISO) worth $500,000, which he exercised during the year. Exercise of the ISO creates a tax preference item for alternative minimum tax (AMT) and causes him to have to pay substantial additional tax when combined with his other tax items for the year. He is livid about the extra tax and refuses to file the AMT Form 6251 with his tax return because the AMT tax is "unfair" and "un-American" according to him. Would you sign this tax return?

TAX BREAK

Divorcing couples may save significant taxes if one or both of the spouses qualify as an "abandoned spouse" and can use the head of household filing status. The combination of head of household filing status for one spouse with married filing separately filing status for the other spouse is commonly seen in the year (or years) leading up to a divorce. In cases where each spouse has custody of a child, the separated taxpayers may each claim head of household status.

Would You Believe?

The following quotation is often attributed to Albert Einstein: "The hardest thing in the world to understand is the income tax."

- Interesting tax facts within "Would You Believe?" sections grab students' attention with interesting asides, including captivating facts and stories about tax laws and preparation.

- New Tax Law boxes throughout the textbook draw students' attention to specific areas affected by new tax legislation.

New Tax Law!

The CARES Act allows higher education institutions to support students by using emergency financial aid grants which may be used for unexpected expenses, unmet financial need, or expenses related to the disruption of campus operations on account of the COVID-19 pandemic, such as unexpected expenses for food, housing, course materials, technology, health care, or childcare. These payments are considered grants and are excluded from income.

Income Tax Fundamentals
Delivers Proven End-of-Chapter Strengths

- The pages are perforated, allowing students to complete end-of-chapter problems and submit them for homework. Students can also tear out tax forms as needed.

- Several question types ensure a variety of assignment options:
  - Multiple-Choice Questions
  - Problems
  - Writing Assignments
  - Comprehensive Problems
  - The Cumulative Software Problem provided in Chapters 1–8 gives students the flexibility to use multiple resources, such as the tax forms within the book, ProConnect Tax or alternative tax preparation software. The problem evolves with each succeeding chapter's content, allowing students to build on their comprehension of various tax topics.
  - Additional Comprehensive Tax Return Problems located in Appendix D.

Digital Tools Enhance Student Understanding

CengageNOWv2 is a powerful online homework tool. This online resource includes an interactive eBook, end-of-chapter homework, detailed student feedback and interactive quizzing, that covers the most challenging topics, a lab guide for using the ProConnect Tax software, flashcards, and much more. The student companion website offers—*at no additional costs*—study resources for students. Go to **www.cengage.com**, and input the ISBN number of your textbook (from the back cover of your book). This will take you to the product page where free companion resources are located.

---

intuit.
Accountants

ProConnect™ Tax

ProConnect Tax access is included with each textbook. A detailed reference lab guide will help the student use the tax software for solving end-of-chapter problems.

For students who are new to the ProConnect Tax software product, we have placed tips throughout the textbook providing guidance to assist students with the transition from a paper form to using the tax software.

Note to Students: Maximize Your Reading Experience

This textbook includes many examples to help illustrate learning objectives. After reading each section, including the examples, answer the corresponding Self-Study Problems. You can find the solutions to the Self-Study Problems at the end of the textbook in Appendix E to check your accuracy. Use your performance to measure your understanding, and re-read the Learning Objectives section if needed. Many key tax terms are defined in each chapter, which will help improve your overall comprehension.

USING TAX SOFTWARE

Numerous tax return problems in the textbook can be solved using either the online tax preparation software or hand preparation. The popular software, ProConnect Tax, is available with the textbook. Helpful tips for using ProConnect Tax have been placed throughout the book so that students can more easily train on the software and prepare the tax returns included in each of the first eleven chapters. A student guide to ProConnect Tax is provided at the companion website. Your college may offer additional tax preparation software, but remember that you can always prepare the solutions manually on the chapter-provided tax forms, schedules and worksheets.

USING THE "WOULD YOU SIGN THIS TAX RETURN?" FEATURE

A practitioner who knows when to say "I cannot sign this tax return," even if it means losing a client, is exercising the most basic ethical wisdom. Most chapters contain a "Would You Sign This Tax Return?" case reflecting a common client issue. Each issue corresponds to an obvious concept illustrated in the previous section. However, the approach to advise the client is not always obvious nor easy. The art of explaining tax rules to a client who does not understand them, or, worse, wants to break them, requires not only a good understanding of the rules, but also good interpersonal skills and sometimes the gift of persuasion. The news in the last several years has shown reports of respected CPA firms with members who failed to say the simple words, "I cannot sign this tax return," demonstrating that simple ethical practice is not always easy. We hope instructors will use these cases to spark group discussions or contemplation, and, perhaps, add examples from their own experience.

USING THE CUMULATIVE SOFTWARE PROBLEM

The Cumulative Software Problem can be found at the end of Chapters 1–8. The case information provided in each chapter builds on the information presented in previous chapters, resulting in a lengthy and complex tax return by the conclusion of the problem in Chapter 8. Your instructor may have you work in groups to prepare each of the tax returns. The groups can follow the real-world accounting firm model using a preparer, a reviewer, and a firm owner who takes responsibility for the accuracy of the return and signs it. All of the issues in the problem are commonly seen by tax preparers and are covered in the textbook. The full return is difficult to prepare by hand, so tax software is recommended. If the problem is prepared using tax software, the data should be saved so the additional information in the succeeding chapters can be added without duplicating input from previous chapters.

ABOUT THE AUTHORS

Gerald E. Whittenburg On March 8, 2015, we unexpectedly lost our dear friend and co-author Gene Whittenburg. As the original author of *Income Tax Fundamentals*, Gene was critical in designing the forms-based approach that the book has used successfully for over two decades. Gene started his life in a small town in Texas, entered the Navy, served his country in Vietnam, earned a Bachelor's, Master's, and PhD degrees, and served as a distinguished faculty at San Diego State University for almost 40 years. We intend to continue to honor Gene by committing to uphold his standard of publishing excellence.

Steven L. Gill is an associate professor of accounting and taxation in the Charles W. Lamden School of Accountancy at San Diego State University. He also serves as the Director of Graduate Programs at the Fowler College of Business at SDSU. Steve received a BS in Accounting from the University of Florida, an MS in Taxation from Northeastern University, and a PhD in Accounting from the University of Massachusetts. Prior to entering academia, he worked for almost 12 years in the field of tax and accounting, including roles in public accounting, internal audit, corporate accounting, and, ultimately, vice president of finance. Although currently in inactive status, Steve holds a Certified Public Accountant designation. He has published a wide variety of articles in various academic and practitioner journals, and has taught at both the undergraduate and graduate levels, including taxation and financial and management accounting. Steven also serves as an author on Cengage's Federal Tax Research series.

REVIEWERS

Janice Akao, *Butler Community College*

Sandra Augustine, *Hilbert College*

George Barbi, *Lanier Technical College*

Lydia Botsford, *DeAnza College*

Mike Bowyer, *Montgomery Community College*

Jerold Braun, *Daytona State College*

Lindy Byrd, *Augusta Technical College*

Greg Carlton, *Davidson County Community College*

Diana Cescolini, *Chaffey College*

John Chappell, *Northland Community and Technical College*

Marilyn Ciolino, *Delgado Community College*

Diane Clugston, *Cambria-Rowe Business College*

Tonya Coates, *Western Piedmont Community College*

Thomas Confrey, *SUNY Orange*

Amy Conley, *Genesee Community College*

Eric DaGragnano, *Western Governors University*

Geoffrey Danzig, *Miami Dade College – Hialeah Campus*

Richard Davis, *Susquehanna University*

Susan Davis, *Green River Community College*

Vaun Day, *Central Arizona College*

Ken Dennis, *San Diego City College*

Kerry Dolan, *Great Falls College Montana State University*

Vicky C. Dominguez, *College of Southern Nevada*

Lisa Farnam, *College of Western Idaho*

John Fasler, *Whatcom Community College*

Brian Fink, *Danville Area Community College*

Brenda Fowler, *Central Carolina Community College*

George Frankel, *San Francisco State University*

Alan Fudge, *Linn-Benton Community College*

Gregory Gosman, *Keiser University*

Nancy Gromen, *Blue Mountain Community College*

Jeffery Haig, *Copper Mountain College*

Tracie Hayes, *Randolph Community College*

Michael Heath, *River Parishes Community College*

Cindy Hinz, *Jamestown Community College*

Rob Hochschild, *Ivy Tech Community College*

Japan Holmes, Jr., *Savannah Technical College*

Jana Hosmer, *Blue Ridge Community College*

James Hromadka, *San Jacinto College*

Carol Hughes, *Asheville Buncombe Technical Community College*

Norma Hunting, *Chabot College, Hayward, California*

Adrian Jarrell, *James Sprunt Community College*

Paul Johnson, *Mississippi Gulf Coast Community College*

Jessica Jones, *Mesa Community College*

Dieter Kiefer, *American River College*

Christopher Kinney, *Mount Wachusett Community College*

Angela Kirkendall, *South Puget Sound Community College*

Mark Klamrzynski, *Phoenix College*

Raymond Kreiner, *Piedmont College*

William Kryshak, *University Wisconsin-Stout*

Linda Lane, *Walla Walla Community College*

Christie Lee, *Lanier Technical College*
Anna Leyes, *Ivy Tech Community College*
Jeannie Liu, *Rio Hondo College*
Susan Logorda, *Lehigh Carbon Community College*
Heather Lynch, *Northeast Iowa Community College*
Diania McRae, *Western Carolina University*
Deanne Michaelson, *Pellissippi State Community College*
Jennifer Morton, *Ivy Tech Community College*
Sharon O'Reilly, *Gateway Technical College*
Mike Prockton, *Finger Lakes CC*
John Ribezzo, *Community College of Rhode Island*
Lance Rodrigues, *Ohlone College*
Hanna Sahebifard, *Golden West College*
Larry Sayler, *Greenville University*
James Shimko, *Jackson Community College*
Barry Siebert, *Concordia University–Saint Paul*
Kimberly Sipes, *Kentucky State University*
Amy Smith, *Pearl River Community College*
Thomas Snavely, *Yavapai College*

Joanie Sompayrc, *UT-Chattanooga*
Barbara Squires, *Corning Community College*
Todd Stowe, *Southwest Florida College*
Gracelyn Stuart-Tuggle, *Palm Beach State College*
Robert L. Taylor, *C.P.A., Lees-McRae College*
Teresa Thamer, *Brenau University*
Craig Vilhauer, *Merced College*
Stan Walker, *Georgia Northwestern Technical School*
Teresa Walker, *Greensboro College*
Joe Welker, *College of Western Idaho*
Jean Wells, *Howard University*
Mary Ann Whitehurst, *Southern Crescent Technical College*
Sharon Williams, *Sullivan University*
Douglas Woods, *Wayne College*
Patty Worsham, *Chaffey College*
Jay Wright, *New River Community College*
Douglas Yentsch, *South Central College*
James Zartman, *Elizabethtown PA College*
Jane Zlojutro, *Northwestern Michigan College*

ACKNOWLEDGMENTS

The authors wish to thank all of the instructors who provided feedback for the 2021 edition via surveys as well as the following supplement authors and verifiers for their most valuable suggestions and support:

D. Elizabeth Stone Atkins—*High Point University, High Point, NC*
David Candelaria—*Mt. San Jacinto College, Menifee, CA*
Jim Clarkson—*San Jacinto College South, Houston, TX*

Pennie Eddy—*Appalachian Technical College, Jasper, GA*
Paul Shinal—*Cayga Community College, Auburn, NY*

In addition, gratitude is expressed to Susan Gill, Kathleen Smith, and Steve Smith for their expert assistance reviewing chapters of this textbook. We would also like to thank Janice Stoudemire, Tracy Newman, and Wendy Shanker on their work of reviewing and verifying the content in CengageNOWv2, including the end-of-chapter items, and Test Bank problems. We would also like to extend our thanks to the Tax Forms and Publications Division of the Internal Revenue Service for their assistance in obtaining draft forms each year.

We appreciate your continued support in advising us of any revisions or corrections you feel are appropriate.

Steven L. Gill

THE ANNOTATED 1040 MAP

The annotated 1040 map is an expanded tax formula, illustrating where each piece of the tax formula is covered in the textbook. The 1040 map helps you understand how all of the elements of the textbook and the tax formula fit together. Use this as a reference and bookmark this page.

Form **1040** Department of the Treasury—Internal Revenue Service (99)
U.S. Individual Income Tax Return **2020** OMB No. 1545-0074 IRS Use Only—Do not write or staple in this space.

Filing Status
Check only one box.
☐ Single ☐ Married filing jointly ☐ Married filing separately (MFS) ☐ Head of household (HOH) ☐ Qualifying widow(er) (QW) **LO 1.5**

If you checked the MFS box, enter the name of your spouse. If you checked the HOH or QW box, enter the child's name if the qualifying person is a child but not your dependent ▶

Your first name and middle initial	Last name	Your social security number
If joint return, spouse's first name and middle initial	Last name	Spouse's social security number

Home address (number and street). If you have a P.O. box, see instructions. | Apt. no.

Presidential Election Campaign Check here if you, or your spouse if filing jointly, want $3 to go to this fund. Checking a box below will not change your tax or refund.

City, town, or post office. If you have a foreign address, also complete spaces below. | State | ZIP code

Foreign country name | Foreign province/state/county **LO 1.8** | Foreign postal code

☐ You ☐ Spouse

At any time during 2020, did you receive, sell, send, exchange, or otherwise acquire any financial interest in any virtual currency? ☐ Yes ☐ No

Standard Deduction
Someone can claim: ☐ You as a dependent ☐ Your spouse as a dependent
☐ Spouse itemizes on a separate return or you were a dual-status alien **LO 1.6, 7.1**

Age/Blindness You: ☐ Were born before January 2, 1956 ☐ Are blind **Spouse:** ☐ Was born before January 2, 1956 ☐ Is blind

Dependents (see instructions):
If more than four dependents, see instructions and check here ▶ ☐

(1) First name Last name	(2) Social security number	(3) Relationship to you	(4) ✔ if qualifies for (see instructions): Child tax credit	Credit for other dependents
			☐	☐
			☐	☐
			☐	☐
			☐	☐

Attach Sch. B if required.

1	Wages, salaries, tips, etc. Attach Form(s) W-2		**1**	LO 2.2
2a	Tax-exempt interest	**2a** LO 2.10	**b** Taxable interest	**2b** LO 2.9
3a	Qualified dividends	**3a** LO 2.9	**b** Ordinary dividends	**3b** LO 2.9
4a	IRA distributions	**4a** LO 5.3	**b** Taxable amount	**4b** LO 5.3
5a	Pensions and annuities	**5a** LO 2.7	**b** Taxable amount	**5b** LO 2.7
6a	Social security benefits	**6a** LO 2.16	**b** Taxable amount	**6b** LO 2.16

Standard Deduction for—
• Single or Married filing separately, $12,400
• Married filing jointly or Qualifying widow(er), $24,800
• Head of household, $18,650
• If you checked any box under *Standard Deduction,* see instructions.

7	Capital gain or (loss). Attach Schedule D if required. If not required, check here ▶ ☐	**7**	LO 4.1 to 4.6
8	Other income from Schedule 1, line 9	**8**	
9	Add lines 1, 2b, 3b, 4b, 5b, 6b, 7, and 8. This is your **total income** ▶	**9**	
10	Adjustments to income:		
a	From Schedule 1, line 22	**10a**	
b	Charitable contributions if you take the standard deduction. See instructions	**10b** LO 5.9	
c	Add lines 10a and 10b. These are your **total adjustments to income** ▶	**10c**	
11	Subtract line 10c from line 9. This is your **adjusted gross income** ▶	**11**	
12	**Standard deduction or itemized deductions** (from Schedule A)	**12**	LO 1.8, 5.6 to 5.10
13	Qualified business income deduction. Attach Form 8995 or Form 8995-A	**13**	LO 4.10
14	Add lines 12 and 13	**14**	
15	**Taxable income.** Subtract line 14 from line 11. If zero or less, enter -0-	**15**	

For Disclosure, Privacy Act, and Paperwork Reduction Act Notice, see separate instructions. Cat. No. 11320B Form **1040** (2020)

Form 1040 (2020)   Page **2**

16	**Tax** (see instructions). Check if any from Form(s): **1** ☐ 8814 **2** ☐ 4972 **3** ☐ _____		16	LO 1.5, 2.9, 4.4, 6.4
17	Amount from Schedule 2, line 3		17	
18	Add lines 16 and 17		18	
19	Child tax credit or credit for other dependents		19	LO 1.8, 7.1
20	Amount from Schedule 3, line 7		20	
21	Add lines 19 and 20		21	
22	Subtract line 21 from line 18. If zero or less, enter -0-		22	
23	Other taxes, including self-employment tax, from Schedule 2, line 10		23	
24	Add lines 22 and 23. This is your **total tax** ▶		24	
25	Federal income tax withheld from:			
a	Form(s) W-2	25a	LO 2.2, 9.1	
b	Form(s) 1099	25b	9.1	
c	Other forms (see instructions)	25c		
d	Add lines 25a through 25c		25d	
26	2020 estimated tax payments and amount applied from 2019 return		26	
27	Earned income credit (EIC)	27	LO 7.2	
28	Additional child tax credit. Attach Schedule 8812	28	LO 7.1	
29	American opportunity credit from Form 8863, line 8	29	LO 7.5	
30	Recovery rebate credit. See instructions	30	LO 1.7	
31	Amount from Schedule 3, line 13	31		
32	Add lines 27 through 31. These are your **total other payments and refundable credits** ▶		32	
33	Add lines 25d, 26, and 32. These are your **total payments** ▶		33	

- If you have a qualifying child, attach Sch. EIC.
- If you have nontaxable combat pay, see instructions.

Refund	34	If line 33 is more than line 24, subtract line 24 from line 33. This is the amount you **overpaid**	34
	35a	Amount of line 34 you want **refunded to you.** If Form 8888 is attached, check here ▶ ☐	35a
Direct deposit? See instructions.	▶ b	Routing number ▶ c Type: ☐ Checking ☐ Savings	
	▶ d	Account number	
	36	Amount of line 34 you want **applied to your 2021 estimated tax** ▶ 36	

Amount You Owe	37	Subtract line 33 from line 24. This is the **amount you owe now** ▶	37
For details on how to pay, see instructions.		**Note:** Schedule H and Schedule SE filers, line 37 may not represent all of the taxes you owe for 2020. See Schedule 3, line 12e, and its instructions for details.	
	38	Estimated tax penalty (see instructions) ▶ 38	

Third Party Designee	Do you want to allow another person to discuss this return with the IRS? See instructions ▶ ☐ **Yes.** Complete below. ☐ **No**
	Designee's name ▶ _____ Phone no. ▶ _____ Personal identification number (PIN) ▶ _____

Sign Here	Under penalties of perjury, I declare that I have examined this return and accompanying schedules and statements, and to the best of my knowledge and belief, they are true, correct, and complete. Declaration of preparer (other than taxpayer) is based on all information of which preparer has any knowledge.
Joint return? See instructions. Keep a copy for your records.	Your signature _____ Date _____ Your occupation _____ If the IRS sent you an Identity Protection PIN, enter it here (see inst.) ▶ _____
	Spouse's signature. If a joint return, **both** must sign. _____ Date _____ Spouse's occupation _____ If the IRS sent your spouse an Identity Protection PIN, enter it here (see inst.) ▶ _____
	Phone no. _____ Email address _____

Paid Preparer Use Only	Preparer's name _____ Preparer's signature _____ Date _____ PTIN _____ Check if: ☐ Self-employed
	Firm's name ▶ _____ Phone no. _____
	Firm's address ▶ _____ Firm's EIN ▶ _____

Go to *www.irs.gov/Form1040* for instructions and the latest information.   Form **1040** (2020)

SCHEDULE 1
(Form 1040)

Department of the Treasury
Internal Revenue Service

Additional Income and Adjustments to Income

▶ Attach to Form 1040, 1040-SR, or 1040-NR.
▶ Go to *www.irs.gov/Form1040* for instructions and the latest information.

OMB No. 1545-0074

2020

Attachment
Sequence No. **01**

Name(s) shown on Form 1040, 1040-SR, or 1040-NR

Your social security number

Part I — Additional Income

1	Taxable refunds, credits, or offsets of state and local income taxes	**1**	LO 5.7
2a	Alimony received	**2a**	LO 2.13
b	Date of original divorce or separation agreement (see instructions) ▶		
3	Business income or (loss). Attach Schedule C	**3**	Chapter 3
4	Other gains or (losses). Attach Form 4797	**4**	LO 8.8
5	Rental real estate, royalties, partnerships, S corporations, trusts, etc. Attach Schedule E	**5**	LO 4.7, 4.8
6	Farm income or (loss). Attach Schedule F	**6**	
7	Unemployment compensation	**7**	LO 2.15
8	Other income. List type and amount ▶	**8**	LO 2.6, 2.12
9	Combine lines 1 through 8. Enter here and on Form 1040, 1040-SR, or 1040-NR, line 8	**9**	

Part II — Adjustments to Income

10	Educator expenses	**10**	LO 5.5
11	Certain business expenses of reservists, performing artists, and fee-basis government officials. Attach Form 2106	**11**	LO 5.5
12	Health savings account deduction. Attach Form 8889	**12**	LO 5.1
13	Moving expenses for members of the Armed Forces. Attach Form 3903	**13**	LO 5.5
14	Deductible part of self-employment tax. Attach Schedule SE	**14**	LO 6.6
15	Self-employed SEP, SIMPLE, and qualified plans	**15**	LO 5.4
16	Self-employed health insurance deduction	**16**	LO 5.2
17	Penalty on early withdrawal of savings	**17**	LO 2.9
18a	Alimony paid	**18a**	LO 2.13
b	Recipient's SSN ▶		
c	Date of original divorce or separation agreement (see instructions) ▶		
19	IRA deduction	**19**	LO 5.3
20	Student loan interest deduction	**20**	LO 5.8
21	Tuition and fees deduction. Attach Form 8917	**21**	
22	Add lines 10 through 21. These are your **adjustments to income.** Enter here and on Form 1040, 1040-SR, or 1040-NR, line 10a	**22**	

For Paperwork Reduction Act Notice, see your tax return instructions.   Cat. No. 71479F   Schedule 1 (Form 1040) 2020

DRAFT AS OF AUGUST 18, 2020 DO NOT FILE

SCHEDULE 2
(Form 1040)
Department of the Treasury
Internal Revenue Service

Additional Taxes

▶ Attach to Form 1040, 1040-SR, or 1040-NR.
▶ Go to *www.irs.gov/Form1040* for instructions and the latest information.

OMB No. 1545-0074

2020

Attachment
Sequence No. **02**

Name(s) shown on Form 1040, 1040-SR, or 1040-NR | Your social security number

Part I — Tax

1	Alternative minimum tax. Attach Form 6251	1	LO 6.5
2	Excess advance premium tax credit repayment. Attach Form 8962	2	LO 7.4
3	Add lines 1 and 2. Enter here and on Form 1040, 1040-SR, or 1040-NR, line 17 . .	3	

Part II — Other Taxes

4	Self-employment tax. Attach Schedule SE	4	LO 6.6
5	Unreported social security and Medicare tax from Form: **a** ☐ 4137 **b** ☐ 8919 .	5	
6	Additional tax on IRAs, other qualified retirement plans, and other tax-favored accounts. Attach Form 5329 if required	6	
7a	Household employment taxes. Attach Schedule H	7a	LO 6.7
b	Repayment of first-time homebuyer credit from Form 5405. Attach Form 5405 if required	7b	
8	Taxes from: **a** ☐ Form 8959 **b** ☐ Form 8960		
	c ☐ Instructions; enter code(s)_____	8	LO 6.8
9	Section 965 net tax liability installment from Form 965-A . . . [9]		
10	Add lines 4 through 8. These are your **total other taxes.** Enter here and on Form 1040 or 1040-SR, line 23, or Form 1040-NR, line 23b	10	

For Paperwork Reduction Act Notice, see your tax return instructions. Cat. No. 71478U **Schedule 2 (Form 1040) 2020**

SCHEDULE 3
(Form 1040)
Department of the Treasury
Internal Revenue Service

Additional Credits and Payments

▶ Attach to Form 1040, 1040-SR, or 1040-NR.
▶ Go to *www.irs.gov/Form1040* for instructions and the latest information.

OMB No. 1545-0074

2020

Attachment
Sequence No. **03**

Name(s) shown on Form 1040, 1040-SR, or 1040-NR | Your social security number

Part I — Nonrefundable Credits

1	Foreign tax credit. Attach Form 1116 if required	1	LO 7.6
2	Credit for child and dependent care expenses. Attach Form 2441	2	LO 7.3
3	Education credits from Form 8863, line 19	3	LO 7.5
4	Retirement savings contributions credit. Attach Form 8880	4	LO 7.9
5	Residential energy credits. Attach Form 5695	5	LO 7.8
6	Other credits from Form: **a** ☐ 3800 **b** ☐ 8801 **c** ☐ _____	6	
7	Add lines 1 through 6. Enter here and on Form 1040, 1040-SR, or 1040-NR, line 20	7	

Part II — Other Payments and Refundable Credits

8	Net premium tax credit. Attach Form 8962	8	LO 7.4
9	Amount paid with request for extension to file (see instructions)	9	LO 1.4
10	Excess social security and tier 1 RRTA tax withheld	10	LO 9.3
11	Credit for federal tax on fuels. Attach Form 4136	11	
12	Other payments or refundable credits:		
a	Form 2439 . . . . [12a]		
b	Qualified sick and family leave credits from Schedule(s) H and Form(s) 7202 . . . . [12b] LO 6.6, 6.7		
c	Health coverage tax credit from Form 8885 . . . . [12c]		
d	Other: _____ [12d]		
e	Deferral for certain Schedule H or SE filers (see instructions) . [12e] LO 6.6		
f	Add lines 12a through 12e	12f	
13	Add lines 8 through 12f. Enter here and on Form 1040, 1040-SR, or 1040-NR, line 31	13	

For Paperwork Reduction Act Notice, see your tax return instructions. Cat. No. 71480G **Schedule 3 (Form 1040) 2020**

TABLE OF CONTENTS

Glow Images/Getty Images

Pgiam/iStock Unreleased/Getty Images

QUESTIONS

Please contact the Cengage Learning Taxation publishing team if you have any questions:

Jonathan Gross, Associate Product Manager: jonathan.gross@cengage.com
Chris Walz, Marketing Manager: chris.walz@cengage.com
Tricia Hempel, Senior Content Manager: patricia.hempel@cengage.com

The Individual Income Tax Return

After completing this chapter, you should be able to:

LO 1.1 Explain the history and objectives of U.S. tax law.

LO 1.2 Describe the different entities subject to tax and reporting requirements.

LO 1.3 Apply the tax formula for individuals.

LO 1.4 Identify individuals who must file tax returns.

LO 1.5 Determine filing status and understand the calculation of tax according to filing status.

LO 1.6 Define qualifying dependents.

LO 1.7 Determine the tax impact of the economic impact payment and the recovery rebate credit.

LO 1.8 Calculate the correct standard or itemized deduction amount for taxpayers.

LO 1.9 Compute basic capital gains and losses.

LO 1.10 Access and use various Internet tax resources.

LO 1.11 Describe the basics of electronic filing (e-filing).

OVERVIEW

This chapter introduces the U.S. individual income tax system. Important elements of the individual tax formula are covered, including the tax calculation, who must file, filing status, and the interaction of itemized deductions and the standard deduction. The chapter illustrates all of the steps required for completion of a basic Form 1040. There is also a discussion of reporting and taxable entities.

An introduction to capital gains and losses is included to provide a basic understanding of capital transactions prior to the detailed coverage in Chapter 4. An overview of tax information available at the Internal Revenue Service (IRS) website and other helpful tax websites is also provided. A discussion of the process for electronic filing (e-filing) of an individual tax return completes the chapter.

Learning Objective 1.1

Explain the history and objectives of U.S. tax law.

1-1 HISTORY AND OBJECTIVES OF THE TAX SYSTEM

1-1a Tax Law History and Objectives

The U.S. income tax was established on March 1, 1913 by the Sixteenth Amendment to the Constitution. Prior to the adoption of this amendment, the U.S. government had levied various income taxes for limited periods of time. For example, an income tax was used to help finance the Civil War. The finding by the courts that the income tax law enacted in 1894 was unconstitutional eventually led to the adoption of the Sixteenth Amendment. Since adoption of the amendment, the constitutionality of the income tax has not been questioned by the federal courts.

Many people inaccurately believe the sole purpose of the income tax is to raise sufficient revenue to operate the government. The tax law has many goals other than raising revenue. These goals fall into two general categories—economic goals and social goals—and it is often unclear which goal a specific tax provision was written to meet. Tax provisions have been used for such economic motives as reduction of unemployment, expansion of investment in productive (capital) assets, and control of inflation. Specific examples of economic tax provisions are the limited allowance for expensing of capital expenditures and the bonus depreciation provisions. In addition to pure economic goals, the tax law is used to encourage certain business activities and industries. For example, an income tax credit encourages businesses to engage in research and experimentation activities, the energy credits encourage investment in solar and wind energy businesses, and a special deduction for soil and water conservation expenditures related to farm land benefits farmers.

Social goals have also resulted in the adoption of many specific tax provisions. The child and dependent care credit, the earned income credit, and the charitable contributions deduction are examples of tax provisions designed to meet social goals. Social provisions may influence economic activities, but they are written primarily to encourage taxpayers to undertake activities to benefit themselves and society.

An example of a provision that has both economic and social objectives is the provision allowing the gain on the sale of a personal residence up to $250,000 ($500,000 if married) to be excluded from taxable income. From a social standpoint, this helps a family afford a new home, but it also helps achieve the economic goal of ensuring that the United States has a mobile workforce.

The use of the income tax as a tool to promote economic and social policies has increased in recent years. Keeping this in mind, the beginning tax student can better understand how and why the tax law has become so complex.

1-1b The Tax Cuts and Jobs Act of 2017

Although the tax laws often change in some way each year, significant overhauls of the tax code are actually quite rare. However, in December 2017, The Tax Cuts and Jobs Act or TCJA (PL 115-97) was signed into law. For budgetary reasons, many of the provisions of the tax law are set to expire over the next decade. Many of the more important expiring provisions are listed below along with the chapter in this textbook in which they are discussed.

Summary of Major Tax Provisions Scheduled to Expire

TCJA Provision	Expires	Chapter
Reduction of individual tax rates	2025	1
Increased standard deduction	2025	1
Suspension of personal exemptions	2025	1
Qualified business income deduction	2025	4
Suspension of itemized deduction phase-out	2025	5
Temporary cap on state and local taxes	2025	5
Suspension of miscellaneous itemized deductions subject to 2 percent floor	2025	5
Suspension of moving expense deduction	2025	5
Reduced limits on mortgage interest deduction	2025	5

TCJA Provision	Expires	Chapter
Restrictions on personal casualty losses	2025	5
Increased AMT exemption and phase-out	2025	6
Changes to kiddie tax	2025	6
Increased child tax credit	2025	7
100 percent bonus depreciation	Phases out starting 2023	8

It remains uncertain whether these provisions will be extended or made permanent; however, when appropriate, the textbook includes background on the pre-TCJA law in the event those provisions return.

Due to the COVID-19 pandemic, a series of additional temporary tax provisions were enacted or administratively put in place. These included the Families First Coronavirus Response Act of 2020 and the Coronavirus Aid, Relief, and Economic Security Act of 2020 (CARES Act). Some of the more significant provisions are listed below.

Provision	Chapter
Educational assistance plans	2
Qualified tuition plans	2
Net operating losses	4 & 11
Distributions from retirement plans	5
Charitable contributions deduction	5 & 11
Recovery rebate credit	1
Payroll tax deferral	9
Employee retention credit	9
Sick and family leave credit	9
Paycheck Protection Program	9

Self-Study Problem 1.1   *See Appendix E for Solutions to Self-Study Problems*

Which of the following is not a goal of the income tax system?

a. Raising revenue to operate the government.

b. Providing incentives for certain business and economic goals, such as higher employment rates, through business-favorable tax provisions.

c. Providing incentives for certain social goals, such as charitable giving, by allowing tax deductions, exclusions, or credits for selected activities.

d. All the above are goals of the income tax system.

1-2 REPORTING AND TAXABLE ENTITIES

1.2 Learning Objective

Describe the different entities subject to tax and reporting requirements.

Under U.S. tax law, there are five basic tax reporting entities. They are individuals, corporations, partnerships, estates, and trusts. The taxation of individuals is the major topic of this textbook; an overview of the taxation of partnerships and corporations is presented in Chapters 10 and 11, respectively. Taxation of estates and trusts is a specialized area not covered in this textbook.

1-2a The Individual

The most familiar taxable entity is the individual. Taxable income for individuals generally includes income from all sources such as wages, salaries, self-employment earnings, rents, interest, and dividends. Most individual taxpayers file Form 1040.

The Form 1040 has undergone only minor changes for 2020. The Form 1040-SR (for taxpayers age 65 and over) remains available for 2020 and has been redesigned in a way that largely increases the size of the form from two to four pages.

Schedules 1-3 remain more or less the same:

Schedule	Primary Purpose
1	Additional forms of income other than wages, interest, dividends, distributions from qualified retirement plans such as IRAs and pensions, Social Security benefits, and capital gains and losses, along with many of the deductions for adjusted gross income
2	Additional taxes beyond the basic income tax such as the alternative minimum tax, repayments of excess advance premium tax credit, self-employment taxes, and household employment taxes
3	Credits and payments other than withholding including education credits, the credit for child and dependent care expenses, residential energy credit, estimated tax payments, excess Social Security taxes withheld, and the net premium tax credit

In addition to Schedules 1–3, certain types of income and deductions must be reported on specific schedules that are included with the Forms 1040 or 1040-SR.

Schedule	Primary Purpose
A	Itemized deductions such as medical expenses, certain taxes, certain interest, charitable contributions, and other miscellaneous deductions
B	Interest income (over $1,500) or ordinary dividend income (over $1,500)
C	Net profit or loss from a sole proprietor trade or business, other than farm or ranch activities
D	Capital gains and losses
E	Rental, royalty, and pass-through income from partnerships, S corporations, estates, and trusts
F	Farm or ranch income

These tax forms and schedules and some less common forms are presented in this textbook.

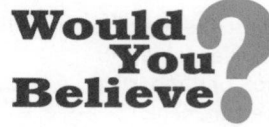

The origin of the Form 1040 has been rumored to be associated with the year 1040 B.C. when Samuel warned his people that if they demanded a king, the royal leader would be likely to require they pay taxes. However, in the early 1980s, the then-Commissioner of the IRS, Roscoe Eggers indicated that the number was simply the next one in the control numbering system for federal forms in 1914 when the form was issued for taxpayers for the tax year 1913. About 350,000 people filed a 1040 for 1913. All the returns were audited. In 2019, less than 1 percent of the approximately 150 million individual tax returns were audited.

1-2b **The Corporation**

Corporations are subject to the U.S. income tax and must report income annually on Form 1120. Corporations are taxed at a flat rate of 21 percent for all corporations regardless of income level.

Some corporations may elect S corporation status. An S corporation does not generally pay regular corporate income taxes; instead, the corporation's income passes through to the shareholders and is included on their individual returns. S corporations must report tax information annually on Form 1120S. Chapter 11 covers the basics of corporate taxation, including a discussion of S corporations.

1-2c **The Partnership**

The partnership is not a taxable entity; instead it is a reporting entity. Generally, all income or loss of a partnership is included on the tax returns of the partners. However, a partnership must file Form 1065 annually to report the amount of the partnership's total income or loss and show the allocation of the income or loss to the partners. The partners, in turn, report their share of ordinary income or loss on their tax returns. Other special gains, losses, income, and deductions of the partnership are reported and allocated to the partners separately, since these items are given special tax treatment at the partner level. Capital gains and losses, for example, are reported and allocated separately, and the partners report their share on Schedule D of their income tax returns. See Chapter 10 for a discussion of partnerships, including limited partnerships and limited liability companies.

SUMMARY OF MAJOR TAX FORMS AND SCHEDULES

Form or Schedule	Description
1040	Individual income tax return
Schedule 1	Additional income and adjustments to income
Schedule 2	Additional taxes
Schedule 3	Additional credits and payments
Schedule A	Itemized deductions
Schedule B	Interest and dividend income
Schedule C	Profit or loss from business (sole proprietorship)
Schedule D	Capital gains and losses
Schedule E	Supplemental income and loss (rent, royalty, and pass-through income from Forms 1065, 1120S, and 1041)
Schedule F	Farm and ranch income
1041	Fiduciary (estates and trusts) tax return
1120	Corporate tax return
1120S	S corporation tax return
1065	Partnership information return
Schedule K-1 (Form 1065)	Partner's share of partnership results

All of the forms listed here, and more, are available at the IRS website (**www.irs.gov**).

Self-Study Problem 1.2   *See Appendix E for Solutions to Self-Study Problems*

Indicate which is the most appropriate form or schedule(s) for each of the following items. Unless otherwise indicated in the problem, assume the taxpayer is an individual.

ITEM	Form or Schedule
1. Bank interest income of $1,600 received by a taxpayer who itemizes deductions	_____
2. Capital gain on the sale of AT&T stock	_____
3. Income from a farm	_____
4. Estate income of $850	_____
5. Partnership reporting of an individual partner's share of partnership income	_____
6. Salary of $70,000 for a taxpayer under age 65 who itemizes deductions	_____
7. Income from a sole proprietorship business	_____
8. Income from rental property	_____
9. Dividends of $2,000 received by a taxpayer who does not itemize deductions	_____
10. Income of a corporation	_____
11. Partnership's loss	_____
12. Charitable contributions deduction for an individual who itemizes deductions	_____
13. Single individual, age 67, with no dependents whose only income is $18,000 (all from Social Security) and who does not itemize deductions or have any credits	_____

Learning Objective 1.3

1-3 THE TAX FORMULA FOR INDIVIDUALS

Apply the tax formula for individuals.

Individual taxpayers calculate their tax in accordance with a tax formula. Understanding the formula is important, since all tax determinations are based on the result. The formula is:

Gross Income
− Deductions for Adjusted Gross Income
= Adjusted Gross Income
− Greater of Itemized Deductions or the Standard Deduction
− Qualified Business Income Deduction
= Taxable Income
× Tax Rate (using appropriate tax tables or rate schedules)
= Gross Income Tax Liability and Additional Taxes
− Tax Credits and Prepayments
= Tax Due or Refund

Would You Believe?

According to the 2019 Comprehensive Taxpayer Attitude Survey, 87 percent of American taxpayers continue to say that it is "not at all" acceptable to cheat on taxes. Ninety-five percent agree that it is every American's civic duty to pay their fair share of taxes. However, about 30 percent of taxpayers do not trust the IRS to fairly enforce the tax laws and to help taxpayers understand their tax obligations. Trust is especially lower among the more educated and high-income taxpayers.

1-3a Gross Income

The calculation of taxable income begins with gross income. Gross income includes all income, unless the tax law provides for a specific exclusion. The exclusions from gross income are discussed in Chapter 2. Gross income from wages, interest, dividends, pensions, Social Security, and capital gains and losses are reported directly on Form 1040 (interest and dividends and capital gains and losses may first flow through Schedules B and D, respectively). All other forms of income are reported on Schedule 1.

1-3b Deductions for Adjusted Gross Income

The first category of deductions includes the deductions for adjusted gross income. These deductions include certain trade or business expenses, certain reimbursed employee business expenses paid under an accountable plan, pre-2019 alimony payments, student loan interest, the penalty on early withdrawal from savings, contributions to qualified retirement plans, and certain educator expenses. Later chapters explain these deductions in detail. Deductions for gross income are reported on Schedule 1.

1-3c Adjusted Gross Income (AGI)

The amount of adjusted gross income is sometimes referred to as the "magic line," since it is the basis for several deduction limitations, such as the limitation on medical expenses. A taxpayer's adjusted gross income is also used to determine limits on certain charitable contributions and contributions to certain individual retirement accounts.

Talk Show Host Stephen Colbert's Tax Tip: Be extremely wealthy…all kinds of breaks for guys like that!

Colbert Report, April 3, 2006

1-3d Standard Deduction or Itemized Deductions

Itemized deductions are personal expense items that Congress has allowed as tax deductions. Included in this category are medical expenses, certain interest expenses, certain taxes, charitable contributions, certain casualty losses, and a small number of miscellaneous items. Taxpayers should itemize their deductions only if the total amount exceeds their standard deduction amount. The following table gives the standard deduction amounts for 2020.

Filing Status	Standard Deduction
Single	$ 12,400
Married, filing jointly	24,800
Married, filing separately	12,400
Head of household	18,650
Qualifying widow(er)	24,800

Taxpayers who are 65 years of age or older or blind are entitled to an additional standard deduction amount. For 2020, the additional standard deduction amount remains unchanged at $1,650 for unmarried taxpayers and $1,300 for married taxpayers and surviving spouses. Taxpayers who are both 65 years of age or older and blind are entitled to two additional standard deduction amounts. See LO 1.8 for a complete discussion of the basic and additional standard deduction amounts.

1-3e Exemptions

Prior to the TCJA, taxpayers received a deduction called an exemption for themselves, spouse (if married filing jointly), and dependents. Exemptions were suspended by the TCJA starting in 2018. The suspension is scheduled to expire at the end of 2025.

1-3f The Gross Tax Liability

A taxpayer's gross tax liability is calculated by referencing the tax table or by using a tax rate schedule. Tax credits and prepayments are subtracted from gross tax liability to calculate the net tax payable to the government or the refund to the taxpayer.

TAX BREAK

Taxpayers may provide information with their individual tax return authorizing the IRS to deposit refunds directly into their bank account. Taxpayers with a balance due may also pay their tax bill with a credit card, subject to a fee.

Self-Study Problem 1.3   *See Appendix E for Solutions to Self-Study Problems*

Bill is a single taxpayer, age 27. In 2020, his salary is $29,000 and he has interest income of $1,500. In addition, he has deductions for adjusted gross income of $2,200 and he has $6,500 of itemized deductions. Calculate the following amounts:

1. Gross income $_____
2. Adjusted gross income $_____
3. Standard deduction or itemized deduction amount $_____
4. Taxable income $_____

Learning Objective 1.4

Identify individuals who must file tax returns.

1-4 WHO MUST FILE

Several conditions must exist before a taxpayer is required to file a U.S. income tax return. These conditions primarily relate to the amount of the taxpayer's income and the taxpayer's filing status. Figures 1.1 through 1.3 summarize the filing requirements for taxpayers in 2020. If a taxpayer has any nontaxable income, the amount should be excluded in determining whether the taxpayer must file a return.

Taxpayers are also required to file a return if they have net earnings from self-employment of $400 or more, or owe taxes such as Social Security taxes on unreported tips. When a taxpayer is not required to file but is due a refund for overpayment of taxes, a return must be filed to obtain the refund.

A taxpayer who is required to file a return should electronically file the return or mail the return to the appropriate IRS Campus Processing Site listed on the IRS website (**www.irs.gov**). Generally, individual returns are due on the fifteenth day of the fourth month of the year following the close of the tax year. For a calendar year individual taxpayer, the return due date is generally April 15. If the 15th falls on a weekend or holiday, returns are due the next business day. However, there are two exceptions: (1) In Maine and Massachusetts, Patriots' Day is celebrated on the third Monday of April. When Patriots' Day is on April 15 or the first business day after April 15, the tax filing deadline is deferred for an additional day for residents of Maine and Massachusetts. (2) The second exception is a result of Emancipation Day, a holiday observed in the District of Columbia. Emancipation Day is

FIGURE 1.1 WHO MUST FILE

Chart A—For Most People

IF your filing status is . . .	AND at the end of 2020 you were* . . .	THEN file a return if your gross income** was at least . . .
Single	under 65 65 or older	$12,400 14,050
Married filing jointly***	under 65 (both spouses) 65 or older (one spouse) 65 or older (both spouses)	$24,800 26,100 27,400
Married filing separately	any age	$5
Head of household	under 65 65 or older	$18,650 20,300
Qualifying widow(er)	under 65 65 or older	$24,800 26,100

*If you were born on January 1, 1956, you are considered to be age 65 at the end of 2020. (If your spouse died in 2020 or if you are preparing a return for someone who died in 2020, see Pub. 501.)

**Gross income means all income you received in the form of money, goods, property, and services that isn't exempt from tax, including any income from sources outside the United States or from the sale of your main home (even if you can exclude part or all of it). Don't include any social security benefits unless (a) you are married filing a separate return and you lived with your spouse at any time in 2020, or (b) one-half of your social security benefits plus your other gross income and any tax-exempt interest is more than $25,000 ($32,000 if married filing jointly). If (a) or (b) applies, see the instructions for lines 6a and 6b to figure the taxable part of social security benefits you must include in gross income. Gross income includes gains, but not losses, reported on Form 8949 or Schedule D. Gross income from a business means, for example, the amount on Schedule C, line 7, or Schedule F, line 9. But, in figuring gross income, don't reduce your income by any losses, including any loss on Schedule C, line 7, or Schedule F, line 9.

***If you didn't live with your spouse at the end of 2020 (or on the date your spouse died) and your gross income was at least $5, you must file a return regardless of your age.

FIGURE 1.2

Chart B—For Children and Other Dependents (See Who Qualifies as Your Dependent, later.)

If your parent (or someone else) can claim you as a dependent, use this chart to see if you must file a return.

In this chart, **unearned income** includes taxable interest, ordinary dividends, and capital gain distributions. It also includes unemployment compensation, taxable social security benefits, pensions, annuities, and distributions of unearned income from a trust. **Earned income** includes salaries, wages, tips, professional fees, and taxable scholarship and fellowship grants. **Gross income** is the total of your unearned and earned income.

Single dependents. Were you **either** age 65 or older **or** blind?

☐ **No.** You must file a return if **any** of the following apply.
- Your unearned income was over $1,100.
- Your earned income was over $12,400.
- Your gross income was more than the **larger** of—
  - $1,100, or
  - Your earned income (up to $12,050) plus $350.

☐ **Yes.** You must file a return if **any** of the following apply.
- Your unearned income was over $2,750 ($4,400 if 65 or older **and** blind).
- Your earned income was over $14,050 ($15,700 if 65 or older **and** blind).
- Your gross income was more than the **larger** of—
  - $2,750 ($4,400 if 65 or older **and** blind), or
  - Your earned income (up to $12,050) plus $2,000 ($3,650 if 65 or older **and** blind).

Married dependents. Were you **either** age 65 or older **or** blind?

☐ **No.** You must file a return if **any** of the following apply.
- Your unearned income was over $1,100.
- Your earned income was over $12,400.
- Your gross income was at least $5 and your spouse files a separate return and itemizes deductions.
- Your gross income was more than the **larger** of—
  - $1,100, or
  - Your earned income (up to $12,050) plus $350.

☐ **Yes.** You must file a return if **any** of the following apply.
- Your unearned income was over $2,400 ($3,700 if 65 or older **and** blind).
- Your earned income was over $13,700 ($15,000 if 65 or older **and** blind).
- Your gross income was at least $5 and your spouse files a separate return and itemizes deductions.
- Your gross income was more than the **larger** of—
  - $2,400 ($3,700 if 65 or older **and** blind), or
  - Your earned income (up to $12,050) plus $1,650 ($2,950 if 65 or older **and** blind).

FIGURE 1.3

Chart C—Other Situations When You Must File

You must file a return if any of the seven conditions below apply for 2020.
1. You owe any special taxes, including any of the following. **a.** Alternative minimum tax. **b.** Additional tax on a qualified plan, including an individual retirement arrangement (IRA), or other tax-favored account. But if you are filing a return only because you owe this tax, you can file **Form 5329** by itself. **c.** Household employment taxes. But if you are filing a return only because you owe this tax, you can file **Schedule H** by itself. **d.** Social security and Medicare tax on tips you didn't report to your employer or on wages you received from an employer who didn't withhold these taxes. **e.** Write-in taxes, including uncollected social security and Medicare or RRTA tax on tips you reported to your employer or on group-term life insurance and additional taxes on health savings accounts. See the instructions for Schedule 2, line 8. **f.** Recapture taxes. See the instructions for line 16 and Schedule 2, lines 7b and 8.
2. You (or your spouse, if filing jointly) received health savings account, Archer MSA, or Medicare Advantage MSA distributions.
3. You had net earnings from self-employment of at least $400.
4. You had wages of $108.28 or more from a church or qualified church-controlled organization that is exempt from employer social security and Medicare taxes.
5. Advance payments of the premium tax credit were made for you, your spouse, or a dependent who enrolled in coverage through the Marketplace. You or whoever enrolled you should have received Form(s) 1095-A showing the amount of the advance payments.
6. Advance payments of the health coverage tax credit were made for you, your spouse, or a dependent. You or whoever enrolled you should have received Form(s) 1099-H showing the amount of the advance payments.
7. You are required to include amounts in income under section 965 or you have a net tax liability under section 965 that you are paying in installments under section 965(h) or deferred by making an election under section 965(i).

observed on April 16; however, when the 16th is a Saturday, the holiday is celebrated on the prior Friday and when the 16th is Sunday, the holiday is celebrated on the following Monday. In 2021, April 15 is a Thursday, Patriots' Day is Monday the 19th and Emancipation Day is Friday the 16th, thus the filing deadline will be Thursday, April 15th.

TAX BREAK Due to the COVID-19 pandemic, the 2019 individual income tax return due date was deferred until July 15, 2020. Note however that the extended due date remained October 15.

A six-month extension of time to file may be requested on Form 4868 by the April due date. Regardless of the original filing deadline, the extension is until October 15 unless that day falls on a weekend or holiday in which case the extended due date is the following business day. However, all tax due must be paid by the April due date or penalties and interest will apply. Due to the COVID-19 pandemic, income tax returns and payments that would have been due April 15, 2020, were extended to July 15, 2020.

Self-Study Problem 1.4   *See Appendix E for Solutions to Self-Study Problems*

Indicate by a check mark whether the following taxpayers are *required* to file a return for 2020 in each of the following independent situations:

	Filing Required?	
	Yes	**No**
1. Taxpayer (age 45) is single with income of $10,000.	_____	_____
2. Husband (age 67) and wife (age 64) have an income of $25,000 and file a joint return.	_____	_____
3. Taxpayer is a college student with a salary from a part-time job of $6,500. She is claimed as a dependent by her parents.	_____	_____
4. Taxpayer has net earnings from self-employment of $4,000.	_____	_____
5. Taxpayers are married with income of $15,900 and file a joint return. They expect a refund of $600 from excess withholding.	_____	_____
6. Taxpayer is a waiter and has unreported tips of $450.	_____	_____
7. Taxpayer is a qualifying widow (age 48) with a dependent son (age 18) and income of $22,800.	_____	_____

5 reporting entities   *5 filing status*

1-5 FILING STATUS AND TAX COMPUTATION

> **1.5 Learning Objective**
>
> Determine filing status and understand the calculation of tax according to filing status.

An important step in calculating the amount of a taxpayer's tax liability is the determination of the taxpayer's correct filing status. The tax law has five different filing statuses: single; married filing jointly; married filing separately; head of household; and qualifying widow(er). A tax table that must be used by most taxpayers, showing the tax liability for all five statuses, is provided in Appendix A. The tax table must be used unless the taxpayer's taxable income is $100,000 or more or the taxpayer is using a special method to calculate the tax liability. If taxpayers cannot use the tax table to determine their tax, a tax rate schedule is used. Each filing status has a separate tax rate schedule as presented in Appendix A.

1-5a Single Filing Status

A taxpayer who does not meet the definition of married, qualifying widow(er), or head of household status must file as single. This status must be used by any taxpayer who is unmarried or legally separated from his/her spouse by divorce or separate maintenance decree as of December 31 of the tax year. State law governs whether a taxpayer is married, divorced, or legally separated. If a taxpayer's spouse dies during the year, the taxpayer's status is married for that year.

1-5b Married Filing Jointly

Taxpayers are considered married for tax purposes if they are married on December 31 of the tax year. Also, in the year of one spouse's death, the spouses are considered married for the full year. In most situations, married taxpayers pay less tax by filing jointly than by filing separately. Married taxpayers may file a joint return even if they did not live together for the entire year.

TAX BREAK Head of Household is a filing status that can be difficult to understand but comes with some substantial tax benefits if a taxpayer qualifies. Single parents should carefully analyze their situation since Head of Household provides lower tax rates and higher standard deductions than Single filing status. This benefit is not just limited to single parents. All unmarried taxpayers that maintain a household and provide support for another person should consider whether they qualify for this tax-advantageous status.

1-5c Married Filing Separately

Married taxpayers may file separate returns and should do so if it reduces their total tax liability. They may file separately if one or both had income during the year. If separate returns are filed, both taxpayers must compute their tax in the same manner. For example, if one spouse itemizes deductions, the other spouse must also itemize deductions. Each taxpayer reports his or her income, deductions, and credits and is responsible only for the tax due on their return. If the taxpayers live in a community property state, they must follow state law to determine community income and separate income. The community property states include Arizona, California, Idaho, Louisiana, Nevada, New Mexico, Texas, Washington, and Wisconsin. See Chapter 2 for additional discussion regarding income and losses from community property.

A legally married taxpayer may file as head of household (based on the general filing status rules) if he or she qualifies as an abandoned spouse. A taxpayer qualifies as an abandoned spouse only if *all* of the following requirements are met:

1. A separate return is filed,
2. The taxpayer paid more than half the cost (rent, utilities, etc.) to maintain his or her home during the year,
3. The spouse did not live with the taxpayer at any time in the last 6 months of the year, and
4. For over 6 months during the year the home was the principal residence for a dependent child, stepchild, or adopted child. Under certain conditions, a foster child may qualify as a dependent.

In certain circumstances, married couples may be able to reduce their total tax liability by filing separately. For instance, since some itemized deductions, such as medical expenses and casualty losses, are reduced by a percentage of adjusted gross income (discussed in Chapter 5), a spouse with a casualty loss and low separate adjusted gross income may benefit from filing separately.

1-5d Head of Household

If an unmarried taxpayer can meet special tests or if a married taxpayer qualifies as an abandoned spouse, they are allowed to file as head of household. Head of household tax rates are lower than rates for single or married filing separately. A taxpayer qualifies for head of household status if both of the following conditions exist:

1. The taxpayer was an unmarried or abandoned spouse as of December 31 of the tax year, and
2. The taxpayer paid more than half of the cost of keeping a home that was the principal place of residence of a dependent child or other qualifying dependent relative. An unrelated dependent or a dependent, such as a cousin, who is too distantly related, will not qualify the taxpayer for head of household status. If the dependent is the taxpayer's parent, the parent need not live with the taxpayer. In all cases other than dependent parents, who may maintain a separate residence, the qualifying dependent relative must actually live in the same household as the taxpayer. A divorced parent who meets the above requirements, but has signed an IRS form or a qualifying legal agreement shifting the dependency deduction to his or her ex-spouse, may still file using head of household status.

Divorcing couples may save significant taxes if one or both of the spouses qualify as an "abandoned spouse" and can use the head of household filing status. The combination of head of household filing status for one spouse with married filing separately filing status for the other spouse is commonly seen in the year (or years) leading up to a divorce. In cases where each spouse has custody of a child, the separated taxpayers may each claim head of household status.

TAX BREAK

1-5e Qualifying Widow(er) with Dependent Child

A taxpayer may continue to benefit from the joint return rates for 2 years after the death of a spouse. To qualify to use the joint return rates, the widow(er) must pay over half the cost of maintaining a household where a dependent child, stepchild, adopted child, or foster child lives. After the 2-year period, these taxpayers often qualify for the head of household filing status.

1-5f Tax Computation

For 2020, there are seven income tax brackets (10 percent, 12 percent, 22 percent, 24 percent, 32 percent, 35 percent, and 37 percent). Individuals with taxable income below $100,000 are required to use the tax tables presented in Appendix A. Taxpayers with income equal to or more than $100,000 use the tax rate schedules (also presented in Appendix A). An example of the single tax rate schedule is presented below. Certain high-income taxpayers are subject to additional taxes discussed in Chapter 6.

Single Tax Rate Schedule

If taxable income is over–	But not over–	The tax is:
$ 0	$ 9,875	10% of the taxable income
9,875	40,125	$987.50 + 12% of the excess over $9,875
40,125	85,525	$4,617.50 + 22% of the excess over $40,125
85,525	163,300	$14,605.50 + 24% of the excess over $85,525
163,300	207,350	$33,271.50 + 32% of the excess over $163,300
207,350	518,400	$47,367.50 + 35% of the excess over $207,350
518,400	----------	$156,235 + 37% of the excess over $518,400

The tax rates applicable to net long-term capital gains currently range from 0 percent to 31.8 percent depending on the taxpayer's tax bracket and the kind of capital asset. The calculation of the tax on capital gains is discussed in detail in Chapter 4, and the applicable tax rates are discussed in this chapter.

The tax rates for qualifying dividends, discussed in detail in Chapter 2, range from 0 percent to 23.8 percent in 2020.

EXAMPLE Carol, a single taxpayer, has adjusted gross income of $120,000 and taxable income of $105,000 for 2020. Her tax is calculated using the 2020 tax rate schedule from Appendix A as follows:

$19,279.50 = $14,605.50 + [24% × ($105,000 − $85,525)] ♦

EXAMPLE Meg is a single taxpayer during 2020. Her taxable income for the year is $27,530. Using the tax table in Appendix A, her gross tax liability for the year is found to be $3,106. ♦

TAX BREAK

Taxpayers considering marriage may be able to save thousands of dollars by engaging in tax planning prior to setting a wedding date. If the couple would pay less in taxes by filing as married rather than as single (which will frequently happen if one spouse has low earnings for the year), they may prefer a December wedding. They can take advantage of the rule that requires taxpayers to file as married for the full year if they were married on the last day of the year. On the other hand, if filing a joint return would cause the couple to pay more in taxes (which frequently happens if both spouses have high incomes), they may prefer a January wedding.

Self-Study Problem 1.5   *See Appendix E for Solutions to Self-Study Problems*

Indicate the filing status (or statuses) in each of the following independent cases, using this legend:

A – Single
B – Married, filing a joint return
C – Married, filing separate returns
D – Head of household
E – Qualifying widow(er)

Case	Filing Status
1. The taxpayers are married on December 31 of the tax year.	_____
2. The taxpayer is single, with a dependent child living in her home.	_____
3. The taxpayer is unmarried and is living with his girlfriend.	_____
4. The taxpayer is married and his spouse left midyear and has disappeared. The taxpayer has no dependents.	_____
5. The unmarried taxpayer supports her dependent mother, who lives in her own home.	_____
6. The taxpayer's wife died last year. His 15-year-old dependent son lives with him.	_____

ProConnect™ Tax TIP

In ProConnect, much of the input is controlled by the left-hand margin. Filing status is part of Client Information under the General heading. By clicking on Filing Status, a dropdown appears in the main window to allow the preparer to select the taxpayer's filing status. For married filing jointly and separately statuses, the Live With Spouse box should be checked if it applies.

Learning Objective 1.6

Define qualifying dependents.

1-6 QUALIFYING DEPENDENTS

1-6a Dependents

Prior to 2018, taxpayers were able to deduct approximately $4,000 each for themselves, their spouse (if married filing jointly), and any dependents. The TCJA eliminated the personal and dependency exemptions in lieu of a larger standard deduction; however, dependents remain important for other reasons. For example, head of household filing status, the child tax credit, and the earned income tax credit all require having a qualified dependent. Lastly, the suspension of personal and dependency exemptions is scheduled to expire after 2025 which means, exemptions may yet return. A dependent is an individual who meets the tests discussed on the following page to be considered either a *qualifying child* or a *qualifying relative*.

The IRS started requiring the disclosure of Social Security numbers for each dependent claimed by a taxpayer to stop dishonest taxpayers from claiming extra dependents or even claiming pets. Before this change, listing phony dependents was one of the most common forms of tax fraud. Reportedly, 7 million dependents disappeared from the tax rolls after Congress required taxpayers to include dependents' Social Security numbers on tax returns.

1-6b Qualifying Child

For a child to be a dependent, he or she must meet the following tests:

1. **Relationship Test**

   The child must be the taxpayer's child, stepchild, or adopted child, or the taxpayer's brother or sister, half-brother or half-sister, or stepsibling, or a descendant of any of these. Under certain circumstances, a foster child can also qualify. The taxpayer must be older than the child unless the child is permanently disabled.

2. **Domicile Test**

   The child must have the same principal place of abode as the taxpayer for more than half of the taxable year. In satisfying this requirement, temporary absences from the household due to special circumstances such as illness, education, and vacation are not considered.

3. **Age Test**

   The child must be under age 19 or a full-time student under the age of 24. A child is considered a full-time student if enrolled full-time for at least 5 months of the year. Thus, a college senior graduating in May or June can qualify in the year of graduation.

4. **Joint Return Test**

   The child must not file a joint return with his or her spouse. If neither the spouse nor the child is required to file, but they file a return merely to claim a refund of tax, they are not considered to have filed a return for purposes of this test.

5. **Citizenship Test**

   The dependent must be a U.S. citizen, a resident of the United States, Canada, or Mexico, or an alien child adopted by and living with a U.S. citizen.

6. **Self-Support Test**

   A child who provides more than one-half of his or her own support cannot be claimed as a dependent of someone else. Support includes expenditures for items such as food, lodging, clothes, medical and dental care, and education. To calculate support, the taxpayer uses the actual cost of the above items, except lodging. The value of lodging is calculated at its fair rental value. Funds received by students as scholarships are excluded from the support test.

In the event that a child satisfies the requirements of dependency for more than one taxpayer, the following tie-breaking rules apply:

- If one of the individuals eligible to claim the child is a parent, that person will be allowed to claim the dependent.
- If both parents qualify (separate returns are filed), then the parent with whom the child resides the longest during the year prevails. If the residence period is the same or is not ascertainable, then the parent with the highest AGI (Adjusted Gross Income) prevails.
- If no parents are involved, the taxpayer with the highest AGI prevails.

EXAMPLE   Bill, age 12, lives in the same household with Irene, his mother, and Darlene, his aunt. Bill qualifies as a dependent of both Irene and Darlene. Since Irene is Bill's mother, she has the right to claim Bill as a dependent. The tie-breaking rules are not necessary if the taxpayer who can claim the dependent does not claim the dependent. Hence, Darlene can claim Bill as a dependent if Irene does not claim him. ◆

In the case of divorced or legally separated parents with children, the ability to claim a qualifying child belongs to the parent with whom the child lived for more than 6 months out of the year. The opportunity to claim the child as a dependent can be shifted to the noncustodial parent if the custodial parent signs IRS Form 8332, and the form is attached to the noncustodial parent's tax return.

Figure 1.4 illustrates the interaction of the qualifying child dependency tests described on the previous page.

1-6c Qualifying Relative

A person who is not a qualifying child can be a qualifying relative if the following 5-part test is met. A child of a taxpayer who does not meet the tests to be a qualifying child can still qualify as a dependent under the qualifying relative tests described below.

1. **Relationship or Member of Household Test**

   The individual must either be a relative of the taxpayer or a member of the household. The list of qualifying relatives is broad and includes parents, grandparents, children, grandchildren, siblings, aunts and uncles by blood, nephews and nieces, "in-laws," and adopted children. Foster children may also qualify in certain circumstances. If the potential dependent is a more distant relative, additional information is available at the IRS website (**www.irs.gov**). For example, cousins are not considered relatives for this purpose.

   In addition to the relatives listed, any person who lived in the taxpayer's home as a member of the household for the entire year meets the relationship test. A person is not considered a member of the household if at any time during the year the relationship between the taxpayer and the dependent was in violation of local law.

   EXAMPLE   Scott provides all of the support for an unrelated family friend who lives with him for the entire tax year. He also supports a cousin who lives in another state. The family friend can qualify as Scott's dependent, but the cousin cannot. The family friend meets the member of the household test. Even though the cousin is not considered a relative, he could have been a dependent if he met the member of the household part of the test. ♦

2. **Gross Income Test**

   The individual cannot have gross income equal to or above the exemption amount ($4,300 in 2020). Although exemptions are no longer deductible, the exemption amount will continue to be updated by the IRS. Gross income does not include any income exempt from tax (for example, tax-exempt interest or exempt Social Security benefits).

3. **Support Test**

   The dependent must receive over half of his or her support from the taxpayer or a group of taxpayers (see multiple support agreement below). Unlike the gross income test, income exempt from tax and earned by the potential dependent is considered for the support test.

4. **Joint Return Test**

   The dependent must not file a joint return unless it is only to claim a refund of taxes.

5. **Citizenship Test**

   The dependent must meet the citizenship test discussed above.

   EXAMPLE   A taxpayer has a 26-year-old son with gross income less than the exemption amount and receives more than half of his support from his parents. The son fails the test to be a qualifying child based on his age, but passes the test to be a dependent based on the qualifying relative rules. ♦

Figure 1.5 illustrates the qualifying relative tests described above.

As long as the dependency tests are met, a person who was born or died during the year, such as a baby born before or on December 31, can be claimed as a dependent. Taxpayers must provide a Social Security number for all dependents.

If a dependent is supported by two or more taxpayers, a multiple support agreement may be filed. To file the agreement, the taxpayers (as a group) must provide over 50 percent of the support of the dependent. Assuming that all other dependency tests are met, the group may give the dependent to any member of the group who provided over 10 percent of the dependent's support.

FIGURE 1.4   DEPENDENCY TESTS FLOW CHART FOR QUALIFYING CHILD

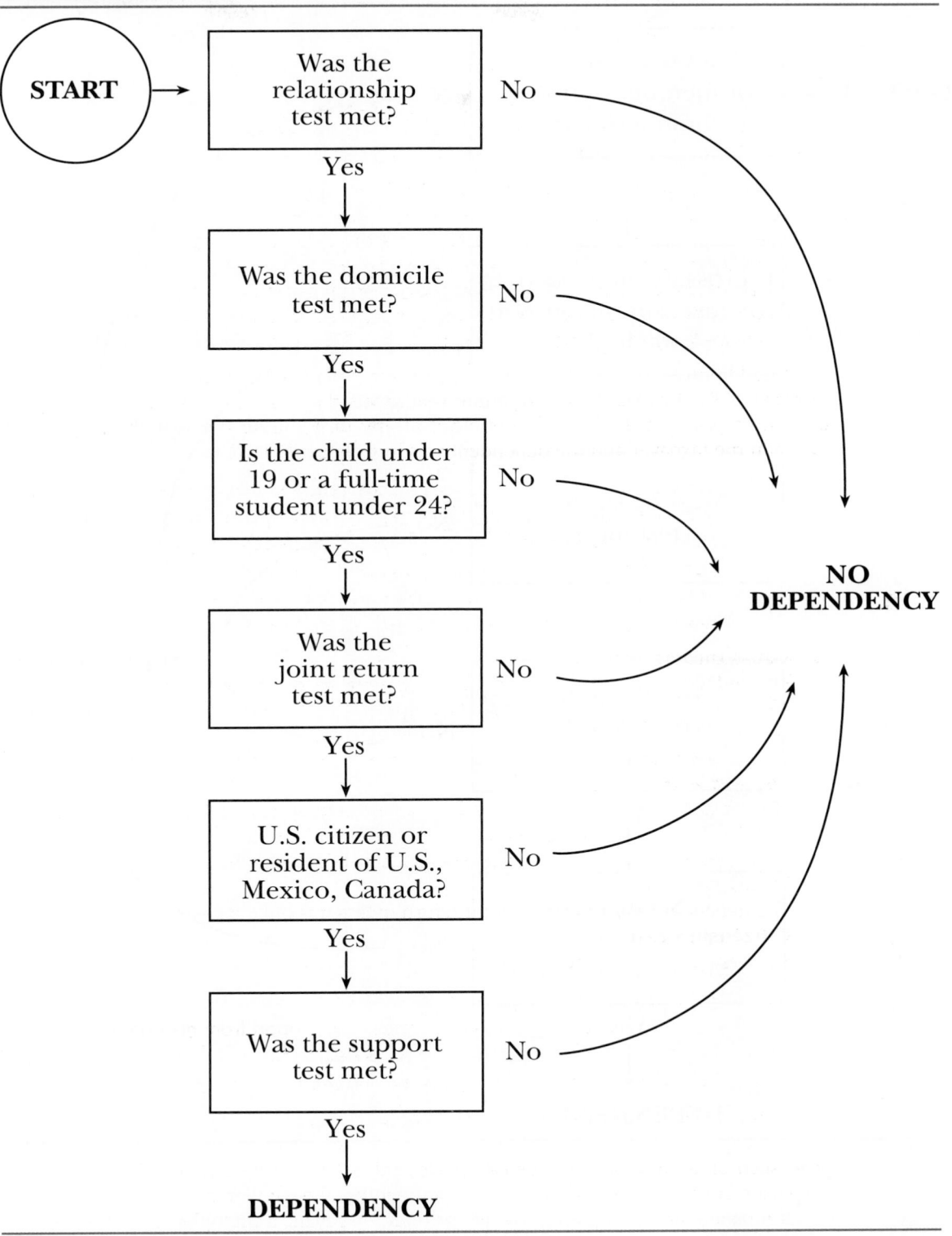

FIGURE 1.5 DEPENDENCY TESTS FLOW CHART FOR QUALIFYING RELATIVE

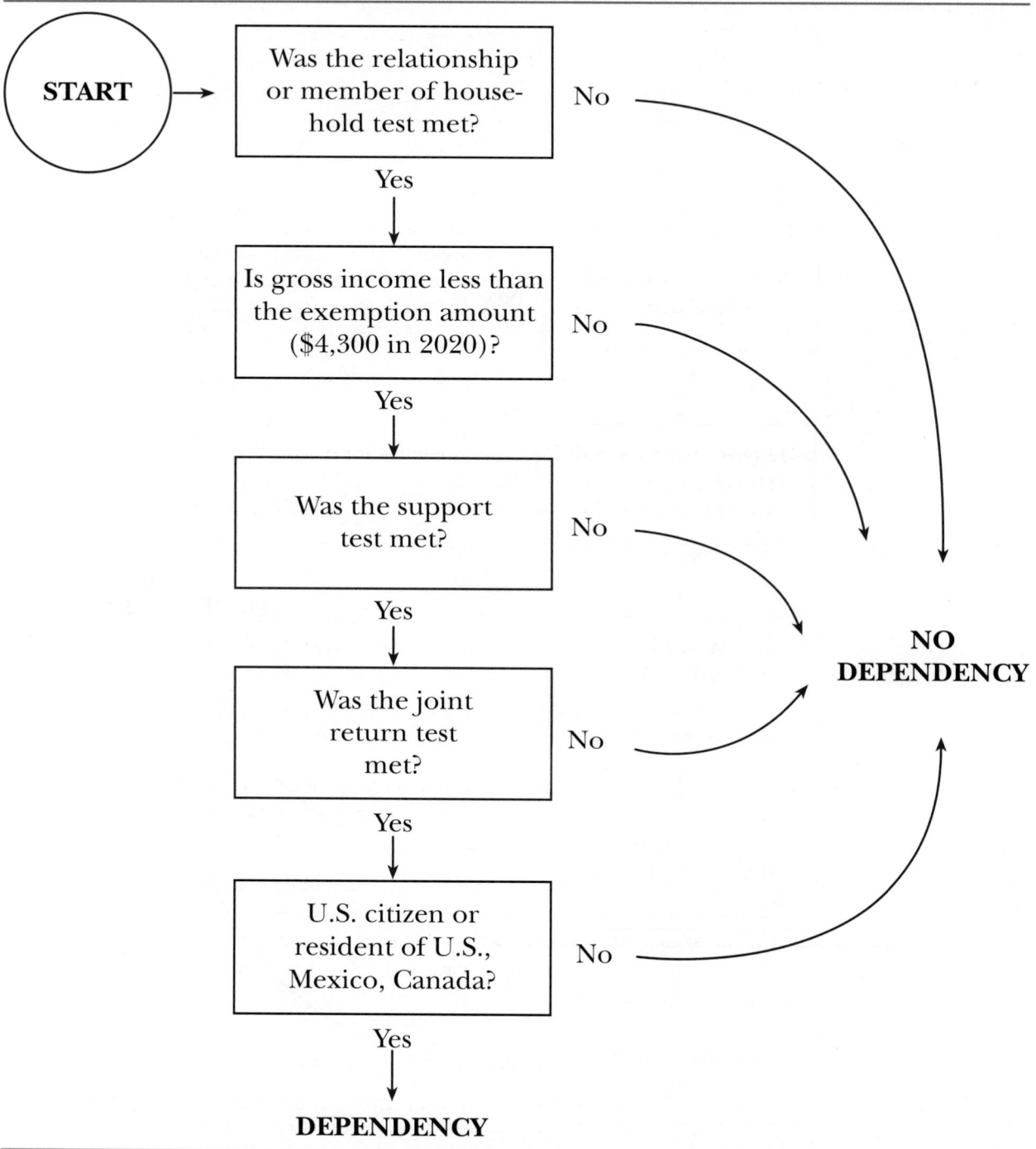

ProConnect™ Tax

TIP

Spouse information is entered under Client Information and is just under Taxpayer Information on the left-hand margin. Dependents are a category under General. Be sure and input date of birth and other fields. Typically, the Child Tax Credit and the Earned Income Credit should be set to When Applicable to permit the software to make the correct determination based on input. New dependents can be added by clicking the [+] tab at the top of the main window for Dependents.

1-6d Credits for Dependents

Although deductions for personal exemptions are no longer permitted from 2018 through 2025, dependent status is important for claiming a number of individual tax credits such as the child tax credit, the credit for other dependents, and the earned income tax credit. Many of these tax credits are covered in Chapter 7; however, due to the relatively large number of taxpayers that are eligible for the child tax credit and the credit for other dependents, an overview is provided here.

A tax credit differs from a tax deduction. A tax deduction serves to lower the taxable income of the taxpayer.

EXAMPLE   Emily's adjusted gross income is $50,025. She is eligible for a $12,400 standard deduction. This lowers her taxable income to $37,625 ($50,025 − $12,400). If Emily is single, her 2020 tax liability is $4,318. ◆

A tax credit lowers the tax liability dollar for dollar. A credit is generally more advantageous than a deduction.

EXAMPLE   Emily (from the previous example) is also eligible for a $500 tax credit. Rather than reduce her taxable income, the tax credit reduces the tax itself to $3,818 ($4,318 − $500). ◆

In 2020, the child tax credit is $2,000 per child. To qualify for the credit, the child must be a qualifying child under the age of 17 and have a Social Security number at the time the tax return is filed. Additional requirements are covered in Chapter 7.

The credit for other dependents is $500 per dependent. An "other dependent" need not be a child but must qualify as either a qualifying child or qualifying dependent. Additional requirements are covered in Chapter 7.

EXAMPLE   Bruce and Demi Mehr have two children, Anna (age 12) and Clark (age 18). Both Anna and Clark qualify as qualifying children under the dependent rules. Assuming all other requirements are met, the Mehrs may claim a $2,000 child tax credit for Anna and a $500 other dependent credit for Clark (as he is not under age 17). ◆

ProConnect™ Tax

TIP

ProConnect is designed to automatically compute the child tax credit and other dependent credit based on the information input in the Dependent window. If no such credit is being shown, it could be due to missing information (for example, birthdate) or the credits were inadvertently suppressed in the Dependent window. The child tax credit and other dependent credit can be overridden under Credits/EIC, Residential Energy, Oth Credits in the left-hand margin but this is generally not a good idea.

Self-Study Problem 1.6   *See Appendix E for Solutions to Self-Study Problems*

Indicate in each of the following situations whether the taxpayer has a dependent in 2020.

	Yes	No
1. Betty and Bob, a married couple, had a new baby in December 2020.	_____	_____
2. Charlie, age 25, supports his 26-year-old brother, who is not a full-time student. His brother lives with Charlie all year. His brother's gross income is $4,500 from a part-time job.	_____	_____
3. Donna and her sister support their mother and provide 60 percent of her support. If Donna provides 25 percent of her mother's support and her sister signs a multiple support agreement, can Donna claim the mother as a dependent?	_____	_____
4. Frank is single and supports his son and his son's wife, both of whom lived with Frank for the entire year. The son (age 20) and his wife (age 19) file a joint return to get a refund, reporting $2,500 ($2,000 earned by the son) of gross income. Both the son and daughter-in-law are full-time students.	_____	_____
5. Gary is single and provides $5,000 toward his 19-year-old daughter's college expenses. The remainder of her support is provided by a tax-exempt $9,500 tuition scholarship. The daughter is a full-time student.	_____	_____
6. Helen is 50 years old and supports her 72-year-old mother, who is blind and has $5,000 of Social Security benefits that are not taxable.	_____	_____

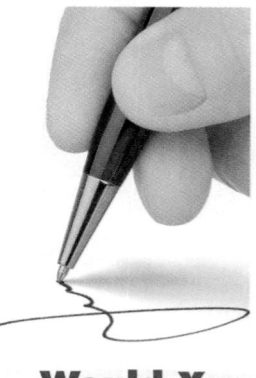

Would You Sign This Tax Return?

Sign Here	Under penalties of perjury, I declare that I have examined this return and accompanying schedules and statements, and to the best of my knowledge and belief, they are true, correct, and complete. Declaration of preparer (other than taxpayer) is based on all information of which preparer has any knowledge.			
Joint return? See instructions. Keep a copy for your records.	Your signature	Date	Your occupation	If the IRS sent you an Identity Protection PIN, enter it here (see inst.) ▶
	Spouse's signature. If a joint return, **both** must sign.	Date	Spouse's occupation	If the IRS sent your spouse an Identity Protection PIN, enter it here (see inst.) ▶
	Phone no.		Email address	
Paid Preparer Use Only	Preparer's name	Preparer's signature	Date	PTIN	Check if: ☐ Self-employed
	Firm's name ▶			Phone no.	
	Firm's address ▶			Firm's EIN ▶	

Your clients, Adam and Amy Accrual, have a 21-year-old daughter named April. April is single and is a full-time student studying for her bachelor's degree in accounting at California Poly Academy (CPA) in Pismo Beach, California, where she lives with her roommates year-round. Last year, April worked at a local bar and restaurant four nights a week and made $18,000, which she used for tuition, fees, books, and living expenses. Her parents help April by sending her $300 each month to help with her expenses at college. This is all of the support given to April by her parents. When preparing Adam and Amy's tax return, you note that they claim April as a dependent for tax purposes. Adam is insistent that they can claim April because of the $300 per month support and the fact that they "have claimed her since she was born." He will not let you take April off his return as a dependent. Would you sign the Paid Preparer's declaration (see example above) on this return? Why or why not?

1-7 ECONOMIC IMPACT PAYMENT AND RECOVERY REBATE CREDIT

1.7 Learning Objective

Determine the tax impact of the economic impact payment and the recovery rebate credit.

The economic impact payment (EIP) and recovery rebate credit (RRC) are designed to be integrated one-time actions in response to the economic impact of the COVID-19 pandemic. The EIP is a direct payment to certain taxpayers authorized by the CARES Act. The amount of the EIP starts at $1,200 ($2,400 for married filing jointly) with an additional $500 for each qualifying child. Taxpayers that were claimed as a dependent are not eligible for an EIP. The EIP phases out 5 percent of the taxpayer's AGI that exceeds $150,000 for married filing jointly, $75,000 for single, and $112,500 for head of household.

Example: Aisha is a head of household taxpayer with a 13-year-old qualifying child. Her 2019 AGI was reported as $138,050. Aisha's EIP before any phase out would be $1,700 ($1,200 for herself plus $500 for the qualifying child). However, her income exceeds the phase-out threshold by $25,550 ($138,050 − $112,500). The phase out is $1,278 ($25,550 × 5 percent) leaving an EIP of $422 ($1,700 − $1,278).

A qualifying child is a child that would have otherwise qualified for the child tax credit (a dependent child under the age of 17 *as of the time of filing a 2018 or 2019 tax return*).

Example: Tina and Than are married filing jointly taxpayers in 2018 with a child that was 16 years of age at the end of 2018. Their 2018 income was below the phase-out threshold. They had not yet filed a 2019 tax return and thus received an EIP of $2,900 ($2,400 for married filing jointly plus $500 for the qualifying child). Despite the child turning 17 in 2019 and thus being ineligible for the additional $500, the EIP was based on 2018 information and therefore will include a payment for the child.

The payment amount was based on either the taxpayers' 2019 tax returns (if filed) or 2018 (if filed). If no tax returns were filed, the IRS used Social Security, Veteran's or Railroad Retirement benefits to determine eligibility. Lastly, if no returns were filed and no such benefits were received, the taxpayer could self-report their information to the IRS to obtain an EIP. Because of the speed at which the payments were designed to be issued, the actual amount of the EIP may not actually match the taxpayer's situation at the time of the payment. For example, if the taxpayer had filed taxes for 2018 but not 2019, and had children born in 2019 or 2020, these children would not have been considered in the EIP calculation.

The EIP is not considered gross income; however, it does interact with the RRC, but in a very taxpayer favorable way. The RRC is a credit that is designed to account for situations when the EIP was not representative of the taxpayer's 2020 tax position. The RRC is a 2020 refundable tax credit much like the Earned Income Credit. The RRC is the same amount as the EIP (e.g., $1,200 for a single taxpayer), and has the same phase-out limits. The way in which the RRC and EIP interact, is that the EIP is considered an advanced refund of the RRC. When the EIP and RRC are equal, they offset and there is no effect on the tax liability of the taxpayer. When the EIP exceeds the RRC, the taxpayer is *not* required to pay back any excess. If, on the other hand, the EIP is less than the RRC, the excess RRC may be claimed as additional refundable credit.

Example: Helga, a single taxpayer receives a $1,200 EIP in 2020. At the time of preparing her 2020 tax return, Helga calculates a $1,200 RRC. The amounts are equal and offsetting and will not affect her tax payments or tax refund.

Example: Georgia and Floyd, married filing jointly taxpayers with two children, received an EIP of $3,400. By the end of 2020, one of the children had reached age 17; thus, the RRC claimed on their 2020 tax return was only $2,900. Although the EIP reduces the RRC, it does not do so below zero and thus, the income tax refund or payment due for 2020 is not affected.

Example: Florida and James are married taxpayers with one qualifying child in 2019 and received a $2,900 EIP in 2020. They adopted a child in 2020 and thus finished the year with 2 qualifying children. Their RRC was $3,400. They will reduce the RRC by $2,900 and claim the additional refundable credit of $500 on their 2020 tax return.

Taxpayers that received an EIP and were not eligible (e.g., non-residents or an incarcerated taxpayer) are required to return the EIP payment to the IRS.

Self-Study Problem 1.7   *See Appendix E for Solutions to Self-Study Problems*

What is the net effect of the EIP and RRC on each of the following taxpayers:

1. Mirka and Liam are married and file jointly with AGI of $97,000 in 2020. In 2020 they received an EIP of $2,900 based on their filing status and having a dependent child that was age 14 at the end of 2019.

   $_____

2. Phoebe was a dependent taxpayer in 2018 and had not filed a tax return. In 2020, she failed to request and did not receive an EIP, although she was no longer a dependent and had AGI of $28,000 as a single taxpayer.

   $_____

3. Mahima received a $1,200 EIP in 2020. Due to the birth of her son in 2020, Mahima was classified as a head of household taxpayer with AGI of $47,000.

   $_____

Learning Objective 1.8

Calculate the correct standard or itemized deduction amount for taxpayers.

1-8 THE STANDARD DEDUCTION

The standard deduction was placed in the tax law to provide relief for taxpayers with few itemized deductions. The amount of the standard deduction is subtracted from adjusted gross income by taxpayers who do not itemize their deductions. If a taxpayer's gross income is less than the standard deduction amount, the taxpayer has no taxable income. The 2020 standard deduction amounts are presented below:

Filing Status	Standard Deduction
Single	$ 12,400
Married, filing jointly	24,800
Married, filing separately	12,400
Head of household	18,650
Qualifying widow(er)	24,800

1-8a **Additional Amounts for Old Age and Blindness**

Taxpayers who are 65 years of age or older or blind are entitled to an additional standard deduction amount. For 2020, the additional standard deduction amount remains unchanged at $1,650 for unmarried taxpayers and $1,300 for married taxpayers and qualifying widows or widowers. Taxpayers who are both at least 65 years old and blind are entitled to two additional standard deduction amounts. The additional standard deduction amounts are also available for the taxpayer's spouse, but not for dependents. An individual is considered blind for purposes of receiving an additional standard deduction amount if:

1. Central visual acuity does not exceed 20/200 in the better eye with correcting lenses, or
2. Visual acuity is greater than 20/200 but is limited to a field of vision not greater than 20 degrees.

EXAMPLE   John is single and 70 years old in 2020. His standard deduction is $14,050 ($12,400 plus an additional $1,650 for being 65 years of age or older). ♦

EXAMPLE   Bob and Mary are married in 2020 and file a joint return. Bob is age 68, and Mary is 63 and meets the test for blindness. Their standard deduction is $27,400 ($24,800 plus $1,300 for Bob being 65 years or older and another $1,300 for Mary's blindness). ♦

1-8b **Individuals Not Eligible for the Standard Deduction**

The following taxpayers cannot use the standard deduction, but must itemize instead:

1. A married individual filing a separate return, whose spouse itemizes deductions
2. Most nonresident aliens
3. An individual filing a short-period tax return because of a change in the annual accounting period

EXAMPLE   Ann and Ed are married individuals who file separate returns for 2020. Ann itemizes her deductions on her return. Ed's adjusted gross income is $12,000, and he has itemized deductions of $900. Ed's taxable income is calculated as follows:

Adjusted gross income	$ 12,000
Itemized deductions	(900)
Taxable income	$ 11,100

Since Ann itemizes her deductions, Ed must also itemize deductions and is not entitled to use the standard deduction amount. ♦

1-8c **Special Limitations for Dependents**

The standard deduction is limited for the tax return of a dependent. The total standard deduction may not exceed the greater of $1,100 or the sum of $350 plus the dependent's earned income up to the basic standard deduction amount in total (e.g., $12,400 for single taxpayers), plus any additional standard deduction amount for old age or blindness. The standard deduction amount for old age and blindness is only allowed when a dependent files a tax return. It is not allowed to increase the standard deduction of the taxpayer claiming the dependent.

EXAMPLE   Penzer, who is 8 years old, earned $17,000 as a child model during 2020. Penzer is claimed as a dependent by his parents on their tax return. Penzer is required to file a tax return, and his taxable income will be $4,600

($17,000 less $12,400, the standard deduction amount). If Penzer had earned only $9,000, his standard deduction would be $9,350 [the greater of $1,100 or $9,350 ($9,000 + $350)], and he would not owe any tax or be required to file a return. ♦

EXAMPLE Geoffrey, who is 4 years old and claimed as a dependent on his parents' tax return, earned $6,500 of interest income on a large bank account left to him by his grandmother. He had no earned income. His standard deduction is $1,100 (the greater of $1,100 or $350). His taxable income will be $5,400 ($6,500 less $1,100, the standard deduction amount). Dependent children may be taxed at trust income tax rates when their taxable income is made up of unearned income, such as interest. The special "kiddie tax" calculations are covered in Chapter 6. ♦

Self-Study Problem 1.8   *See Appendix E for Solutions to Self-Study Problems*

Indicate in each of the following independent situations the amount of the standard deduction the taxpayers should claim on their 2020 income tax returns.

———— 1. Adam is 45 years old, in good health, and single.

———— 2. Bill and Betty are married and file a joint return. Bill is 66 years old, and Betty is 60.

———— 3. Charlie is 70, single, and blind.

———— 4. Debbie qualifies for head of household filing status, is 35 years old, and is in good health.

———— 5. Elizabeth is 9 years old, and her only income is $3,600 of interest on a savings account. She is claimed as a dependent on her parents' tax return.

———— 6. Frank and Frieda are married with two dependent children. They file a joint return, are in good health, and both of them are under 65 years of age.

Learning Objective 1.9

Compute basic capital gains and losses.

1-9 A BRIEF OVERVIEW OF CAPITAL GAINS AND LOSSES

When a taxpayer sells an asset, there is normally a gain or loss on the transaction. Depending on the kind of asset sold, this gain or loss will have different tax consequences. Chapter 4 of this textbook has detailed coverage of the effect of gains and losses on a taxpayer's tax liability. Because of their importance to the understanding of the calculation of an individual's tax liability, a brief overview of gains and losses will be discussed here.

The amount of gain or loss realized by a taxpayer is determined by subtracting the *adjusted basis* of the asset from the *amount realized*. Generally, the adjusted basis of an asset is its cost less any depreciation (covered in Chapter 8) taken on the asset. The amount realized is generally what the taxpayer receives from the sale (e.g., the sales price less any cost of the sale). The formula for calculating the gain or loss can be stated as follows:

Gain (or loss) realized = Amount realized − Adjusted basis

Most gains and losses realized are also recognized for tax purposes. Recognized gains and losses are those that are included in the taxpayer's taxable income. The exceptions to this general tax recognition rule are discussed in Chapter 4.

EXAMPLE Lisa purchased a rental house a few years ago for $100,000. Total depreciation to date on the house is $25,000. In the current year she sells the house for $155,000 and receives $147,000 after paying selling expenses of $8,000. Her gain on the sale is $72,000, calculated as follows:

Amount realized ($155,000 − $8,000)	$ 147,000
Adjusted basis ($100,000 − $25,000)	(75,000)
Gain realized	$ 72,000

This gain realized will be recognized as a taxable gain. ◆

1-9a **Capital Gains and Losses**

Gains and losses can be either *ordinary* or *capital*. Ordinary gains and losses are treated for tax purposes just like other items of income such as salaries and interest, and they are taxed at ordinary rates. Capital gains and losses receive special tax treatment.

A capital gain or loss arises from the sale or exchange of a capital asset. In general, a capital asset is any property (either personal or investment) held by a taxpayer, with certain exceptions as listed in the tax law (see Chapter 4). Examples of capital assets held by individual taxpayers include stocks, bonds, land, cars, boats, and other items held as investments or for personal use. Typical assets that are not capital assets are inventory and accounts receivable.

The tax rates on long-term (held more than 12 months) capital gains are summarized as follows:

Income Level	2020 Long-term capital gains rate*
Married filing jointly	
$0–$80,000	0%
$80,001–$496,600	15%
>$496,600	20%
Single	
$0–$40,000	0%
$40,001–$441,450	15%
>$441,450	20%
Head of household	
$0–$53,600	0%
$53,601–$469,050	15%
>$469,050	20%
Married filing separately	
$0–$40,000	0%
$40,001–$248,300	15%
>$248,300	20%

*Special higher rates for "high-income" taxpayers are covered in Chapter 6.

Gain from property held 12 months or less is deemed to be short-term capital gain and is taxed at ordinary income rates. Capital gains from the sale of assets that have been depreciated, or capital gains from "collectibles," may be taxed at higher rates as discussed in Chapter 4.

EXAMPLE   In the current year, Chris, a single taxpayer, sells AT&T stock for $25,000. He purchased the stock 5 years ago for $15,000, giving him an adjusted basis of $15,000 and a long-term gain of $10,000. Chris' taxable income without the sale of the stock is $140,000, which puts him in the 24 percent ordinary tax bracket. The tax due on the long-term capital gain would be $1,500 (15% × $10,000) instead of $2,400 (24% × $10,000) if the gain on the stock were treated as ordinary income. ♦

When calculating capital gain or loss, the taxpayer must net all capital asset transactions to determine the nature of the final gain or loss (see Chapter 4 for a discussion of this calculation). If an individual taxpayer ends up with a net capital loss (short-term or long-term), up to $3,000 per year can be deducted against ordinary income. The net loss not used in the current year may be carried forward and used to reduce taxable income in future years (see Chapter 4 for a discussion of capital losses). Losses from capital assets held for personal purposes, such as a nonbusiness auto or a personal residence, are not deductible, even though gains on personal assets are taxable.

TAX BREAK

Taxpayers may wish to postpone the sale of capital assets until the holding period is met to qualify for the preferential long-term capital gains rate. Of course, there is always the risk that postponing the sale of a capital asset such as stock may result in a loss if the price of the stock decreases below its cost during volatile markets. The economic risks of a transaction should always be considered along with the tax benefits.

EXAMPLE   Amy purchased gold coins as an investment. She paid $50,000 for the coins. This year she sells the coins to a dealer for $35,000. As a result, Amy has a $15,000 capital loss. She may deduct $3,000 of the loss against her other income this year. The remaining unused loss of $12,000 ($15,000 − $3,000) is carried forward and may be deducted against other income in future years. Of course, the carryover is subject to the $3,000 annual limitation in future years. ♦

TAX BREAK

Volunteer Income Tax Assistance (VITA) Program

The Volunteer Income Tax Assistance (VITA) program offers free tax help to people who generally make $55,000 or less, persons with disabilities, the elderly and limited English-speaking taxpayers who need assistance in preparing their own tax returns. IRS-certified volunteers provide free basic income tax return preparation with electronic filing to qualified individuals. VITA sites are generally located at community and neighborhood centers, libraries, schools, shopping malls, and other convenient locations across the country.

Many universities and colleges operate VITA sites in conjunction with their accounting programs. This is a small but vital part of the VITA program run by the IRS. The majority of the VITA sites are not run by schools, but rather by community groups, such as churches, senior groups (AARP), military bases, etc. If a student has a chance to participate in a VITA program, they should do so if at all possible. The experience provides valuable insight into preparing tax returns for others. Please see the IRS website **www.irs.gov** to locate the nearest VITA site and for more information.

Self-Study Problem 1.9 *See Appendix E for Solutions to Self-Study Problems*

Erin purchased stock in JKL Corporation several years ago for $8,750. In the current year, she sold the same stock for $12,800. She paid a $200 sales commission to her stockbroker.

1. What is Erin's amount realized? $_____
2. What is Erin's adjusted basis? $_____
3. What is Erin's *realized* gain or loss? $_____
4. What is Erin's *recognized* gain or loss? $_____
5. How is the gain or loss treated for tax purposes (if any)?

_____

_____

_____

The IRS recommends considering the following when getting married:

- Social Security numbers on the tax return need to match the Social Security Administration's (SSA) records. Be sure and report any name changes to the SSA.
- Taxpayers may want to consider changing their withholding, especially if both spouses work.
- Marriage is likely to trigger a "change in circumstance" if a taxpayer is receiving advance payments on the premium tax credit. The appropriate health insurance marketplace should be notified.
- Change of address with the U.S. Postal Service (online) and with the IRS (Form 8822).
- Change in filing status to married filing jointly or separately should be considered.

TAX BREAK

1-10 TAX AND THE INTERNET

1.10 Learning Objective

Access and use various Internet tax resources.

Taxpayers and tax practitioners can find a substantial amount of useful information on the Internet. Government agencies, businesses, organizations, and groups (e.g., the IRS, AICPA, and Cengage) maintain sites that contain information of interest to the public.

The information available on various websites is subject to rapid change. Discussed below are some current Internet sites that are of interest to taxpayers. Taxpayers should be aware that the locations and information provided on the Internet are subject to change by the site organizer without notice.

1-10a The IRS Website, www.irs.gov

One of the most useful websites containing tax information is the one maintained by the IRS. The IRS site has a search function to assist users in locating information. A number of common tasks are available at the home page such as refund status or making a tax payment. The Forms and Publications search function is particularly useful and allows the user to locate and download almost any tax form, instructions, or publication available from the IRS. A Help function is available to aid users of the IRS website. Online and telephone assistance from the IRS is provided for users who have questions or want to communicate with the IRS. The IRS also has a YouTube channel, a podcast, a Twitter account, and a Linkedin, Instagram, and Facebook page. The YouTube channel has numerous educational videos covering a number of tax-related topics, including how to check on a refund and how to file a tax return extension. The IRS offers various news feeds on Twitter, including @IRSnews, which are good sources of tax information. The IRS also offers IRS2GO—a mobile phone application.

A 2020 screenshot of the IRS website (**www.irs.gov**) is presented in Figure 1.6.

FIGURE 1.6 IRS WEBSITE

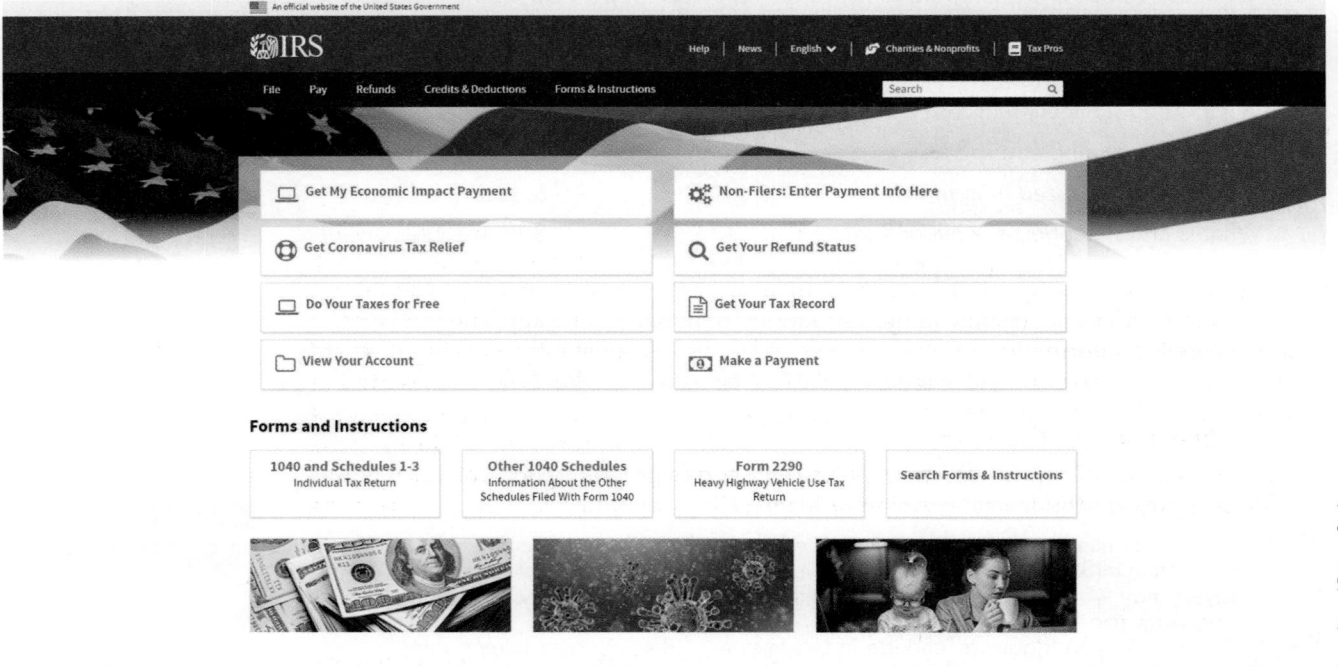

Source: Internal Revenue Service

1-10b Intuit's ProConnect Tax Online

Intuit offers a line of tax preparation products such as ProConnect Tax, Lacerte, and the well-known Turbo Tax. Many of the Intuit products have training and support available online at no charge. You can find ProConnect help at **https://proconnect.intuit.com/community/support/**.

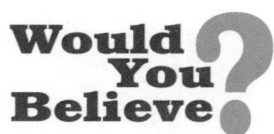

The IRS issues warnings to taxpayers each year about identity theft scams via e-mail known as "phishing" scams. The e-mails look official and may even have a link to a bogus website that looks almost identical to **www.irs.gov** (and may even mention USA.gov or IRS.gov). The fake e-mails may also appear to have been sent by the IRS Taxpayer Advocate's Office. Taxpayers who get these messages should not respond to the e-mail or click on the links. Although the IRS maintains Twitter and Facebook accounts, the IRS does not initiate contact with taxpayers by e-mail, texting, or any social media.

Self-Study Problem 1.10 *See Appendix E for Solutions to Self-Study Problems*

Indicate whether the following statements are true or false by circling the appropriate letter.

T F 1. Taxpayers can download tax forms and IRS publications from the IRS website.

T F 2. A help function is available to aid users of the IRS website.

T F 3. The IRS has a mobile phone app.

1-11   **ELECTRONIC FILING (E-FILING)**

1.11 Learning Objective

Describe the basics of electronic filing (e-filing).

Electronic filing (e-filing) is the process of transmitting federal income tax return information to the IRS Service Center using a device with Internet access. For the taxpayer, electronic filing offers faster processing and generally a faster refund. The fastest refund can be obtained through a direct deposit to the taxpayer's bank account (however, the taxpayer can also choose to be paid by check). IRS statistics show an error rate of less than 1 percent on electronically filed returns, compared with more than 20 percent on paper returns.

Two methods of e-filing of individual income tax returns are available with the IRS. The first e-filing method is using an Internet-connected device and tax preparation software such as Intuit's ProConnect Tax Online, which is included as part of this textbook. Individual taxpayers may transmit their returns from their homes, workplaces, libraries, retail outlets, or, in some limited situations, a mobile phone app. The IRS website contains detailed information on this process as the IRS is constantly working to make e-filing more user-friendly and widely available. The IRS provides free tax preparation and e-filing software to individuals with income below certain thresholds (see **www.irs.gov/freefile**). Individuals with higher income may still e-file free, using IRS fill-in forms (see **www.freefilefillableforms.com**). The fillable forms program performs calculations but will not provide the tax preparation guidance that standard tax software programs provide.

The second e-filing option is to use the services of a tax professional, including certified public accountants, tax attorneys, IRS-enrolled agents, and tax preparation businesses qualifying for the IRS tax professional e-filing program.

Electronic filing represents a significant growth area in computerized tax services. More than 90 percent of all individual taxpayers now e-file. Mandatory electronic filing is currently in the process of being phased in for the professional tax return preparation industry. In the future, electronic filing will likely be required for most tax returns filed.

Self-Study Problem 1.11   *See Appendix E for Solutions to Self-Study Problems*

Indicate whether the following statements are true or false by circling the appropriate letter.

T   F   1. Compared to paper returns, electronic filings significantly reduce the error rate for tax returns filed.

T   F   2. Individuals may not use electronic filing for their own personal tax returns, but must engage a tax professional if they wish to e-file.

T   F   3. Taxpayers who e-file generally receive faster refunds.

T   F   4. Taxpayers who e-file can only request their refund in the form of a check.

KEY TERMS

individual, 1-3
Form 1040, 1-3
corporation, 1-5
partnership, 1-5
tax formula for individuals, 1-6
gross income, 1-7
adjusted gross income, 1-7
standard deductions, 1-7
itemized deductions, 1-7

exemptions, 1-8
single filing status, 1-11
married filing jointly, 1-11
married filing separately, 1-12
abandoned spouse, 1-12
head of household, 1-12
qualifying widow(er), 1-13
dependent, 1-14
qualifying child, 1-15
qualifying relative, 1-16

tax deduction, 1-19
tax credit, 1-19
economic impact payment (EIP), 1-21
recovery rebate credit (RRC), 1-21
adjusted basis, 1-24
amount realized, 1-24
ordinary gains and losses, 1-25
capital gains and losses, 1-25
capital assets, 1-25
e-filing, 1-29

KEY POINTS

Learning Objectives	Key Points
LO 1.1: Explain the history and objectives of U.S. tax law.	• The income tax was established on March 1, 1913 by the Sixteenth Amendment to the U.S. Constitution. • In addition to raising money to run the government's programs, the income tax is used as a tool for enacting economic and social policies. • Examples of economic tax provisions are the limited allowance for expensing capital expenditures and bonus depreciation provisions. The child and dependent care credit, earned income credit, and the charitable contributions deduction are examples of social tax provisions. • The Tax Cuts and Jobs Act (TCJA) of 2017 has a number of significant individual tax provisions that expire in 2025. • A number of temporary tax provisions were enacted in 2020 to assist taxpayers affected by the COVID-19 pandemic.
LO 1.2: Describe the different entities subject to tax and reporting requirements.	• Individual taxpayers file Form 1040 or 1040-SR (if age 65 or older) and any supplemental schedules required. • Corporations must report income annually on Form 1120 and pay taxes at a flat rate of 21 percent. • An S corporation generally does not pay regular corporate income taxes; instead, the corporation's income or loss passes through to its shareholders and is included in their individual tax returns. S corporations file on Form 1120S. • A partnership files Form 1065 to report the amount of partnership income or loss and to allocate the items of income, loss, deduction, and credit to the partners. Generally, all income or loss of a partnership is included in the tax returns of the partners.
LO 1.3: Apply the tax formula for individuals.	• AGI (adjusted gross income) is gross income less deductions for adjusted gross income. • AGI less the larger of itemized deductions or the standard deduction and less the qualified business income deduction equals taxable income. • Appropriate tax tables or rate schedules are applied to taxable income to calculate the gross tax liability. • The gross income tax liability plus additional taxes less credits and prepayments equals the tax due or refund.
LO 1.4: Identify individuals who must file tax returns.	• Conditions relating to the amount of the taxpayer's income must exist before a taxpayer is required to file a U.S. income tax return. • Taxpayers are also required to file a return if they have net earnings from self-employment of $400 or more, or owe taxes such as Social Security taxes on unreported tips.

LO 1.5: Determine filing status and understand the calculation of tax according to filing status.	• There are five filing statuses: single; married filing jointly; married filing separately; head of household; and qualifying widow(er). • Tax is calculated using the appropriate tax table or tax rate schedule for the taxpayer's filing status.
LO 1.6: Define qualifying dependents.	• Personal exemptions were suspended by the TCJA for tax years 2018–2025. • Dependents are still important for determining filing status and certain credits. • A dependent is an individual who is either a qualifying child or qualifying relative.
LO 1.7: Determine the tax impact of the economic impact payment and the recovery rebate credit.	• Taxpayers with income below certain thresholds were eligible for an economic impact payment (EIP) of $1,200 per taxpayer and $500 for each qualifying dependent. • The EIP is an advanced refund of the recovery rebate credit (RRC) of an equal amount for the tax year 2020 only. • For most taxpayers, the EIP and the RRC will be equal and offsetting amounts.
LO 1.8: Calculate the correct standard or itemized deduction amount for taxpayers.	• The standard deduction was placed in the tax law to provide relief for taxpayers with few itemized deductions. • For 2020, the standard deduction amounts are: Single $12,400; Married, filing jointly $24,800; Married, filing separately $12,400; Head of household $18,650; Qualifying widow(er) $24,800. • Taxpayers who are 65 years of age or older or blind are entitled to additional standard deduction amounts of $1,650 for unmarried taxpayers and $1,300 for married taxpayers and surviving spouses in 2020.
LO 1.9: Compute basic capital gains and losses.	• The amount of gain or loss realized by a taxpayer is determined by subtracting the adjusted basis of the asset from the amount realized. • Gains and losses can be either ordinary or capital. • Ordinary gains and losses are treated for tax purposes like other items such as salary and interest. • Capital gains and losses result from the sale or exchange of capital assets. • Common capital assets held by individual taxpayers include stocks, bonds, land, cars, boats, and other items held as investments. Typical assets that are not capital are inventory and accounts receivable. • Gain from property held 12 months or less is deemed to be short-term capital gain and is taxed at ordinary income tax rates. • Gain from property held more than 12 months is deemed to be long-term capital gain and is taxed at preferential income tax rates. • The long-term capital gain rates for 2020 vary between 0, 15, and 20 percent, depending on the taxpayer's income. • If an individual taxpayer ends up with a net capital loss (short-term or long-term), up to $3,000 per year can be deducted against ordinary income. Any excess capital loss is carried forward to subsequent tax years. Losses from personal-use assets are not deductible.
LO 1.10: Access and use various Internet tax resources.	• Taxpayers and tax practitioners can find a substantial amount of useful information on the Internet. • Useful websites containing tax information include the IRS (**www.irs.gov**) and the Intuit websites.
LO 1.11: Describe the basics of electronic filing (e-filing).	• Electronic filing (e-filing) is the process of transmitting federal income tax return information to the IRS Service Center using a device with Internet access. • Electronic filing offers a faster refund through a direct deposit to the taxpayer's bank account or the taxpayer can request the refund be sent by check.

QUESTIONS and PROBLEMS

GROUP 1:
MULTIPLE CHOICE QUESTIONS

LO 1.1
1. Which of the following recent tax changes is *not* scheduled to expire after 2025?
   a. Suspension of personal exemptions
   b. General lowering of individual tax rates
   c. Restrictions on the deduction of casualty and theft losses
   d. Reduction of corporate tax rates to 21 percent

LO 1.1
2. Which of the following tax forms are used by individuals in 2020?
   a. 1040A
   b. 1040-EZ
   c. 1040-SR
   d. 1120

LO 1.2
3. Typical corporate income is reported on:
   a. Form 1040
   b. Form 1120
   c. Form 1040X
   d. Form 1065

LO 1.2
4. On which of these would capital gain income be reported?
   a. Schedule 1
   b. Schedule 2
   c. Schedule 3
   d. Form 1040

LO 1.3
5. Which of the following is a deduction for adjusted gross income in 2020?
   a. Personal casualty losses
   b. Medical expenses
   c. Student loan interest
   d. Mortgage interest
   e. None of the above

LO 1.3
6. All of the following are itemized deductions in 2020 *except*:
   a. Charitable contributions
   b. Deductible IRA contributions
   c. State and local taxes
   d. Medical expenses
   e. All of the above are itemized deductions

LO 1.3
7. Ramon, a single taxpayer with no dependents, has adjusted gross income for 2020 of $98,000 and his itemized deductions total $9,000. What taxable income will Ramon show in 2020?
   a. $74,950
   b. $85,800
   c. $79,000
   d. $85,600
   e. $89,000

LO 1.4
8. Ben is a single taxpayer with no dependents and is 32 years old. What is the minimum amount of income that he must have to be required to file a tax return for 2020?
   a. $4,200
   b. $12,400
   c. $12,000

d. $12,200

e. None of the above

LO 1.5

9. Joan, who was divorced in 2020, had filed a joint tax return with her husband in 2019. During 2020, she did not remarry and continued to maintain her home in which her five dependent children lived. In the preparation of her tax return for 2020, Joan should file as:

a. A single individual

b. A qualifying widow(er)

c. Head of household

d. Married, filing separately

e. None of the above

LO 1.5

10. Glenda, a single taxpayer from Kansas, paid for more than one-half of the support for her mother, Dorothy. Dorothy did not live with Glenda in Kansas, but rather has lived in a nursing home in an adjacent state since Dorothy's husband died three years ago. Glenda's filing status should be:

a. Single

b. Married filing separately

c. Qualifying widower

d. Head of household

e. Parental dependent

LO 1.6

11. Margaret and her sister support their mother and together provide 85 percent of their mother's support. If Margaret provides 40 percent of her mother's support:

a. Her sister is the only one who can claim their mother as a dependent.

b. Neither Margaret nor her sister may claim their mother as a dependent.

c. Both Margaret and her sister may claim their mother as a dependent.

d. Margaret and her sister may split the dependency exemption.

e. Margaret may claim her mother as a dependent if her sister agrees in a multiple support agreement.

LO 1.6

12. Kardi, age 65, and Kanye, age 62, are married with a 23-year-old daughter who lives in their home. They provide over half of their daughter's support, and their daughter earned $4,600 this year from a part-time job. Their daughter is not a full-time student. The daughter can/cannot be claimed as a dependent because:

a. She can be claimed because she lives in their household for 12 months.

b. She can be claimed because she is a qualifying child.

c. She can be claimed because she is a qualifying relative.

d. She cannot be claimed because she fails the gross income test.

LO 1.6

13. Yasmine and her spouse Carlos, who file married filing jointly, provide all the support for their 16-year-old son, Miguel. If Miguel qualifies as a qualifying child under the dependent rules, Yasmine and Carlos will be able to claim

a. $0

b. $500

c. $1,000

d. $2,000

e. $2,500

LO 1.6

14. Lakota and Dominique file married filing jointly and have a 13-year-old daughter. They also provide 25 percent of the support for Lakota's 82-year-old mother, who lives in a nursing home nearby. The amount of the combined child tax credit and other dependent credit for Lakota and Dominique is:

a. $0

b. $1,000

c. $1,500

d. $2,000

e. $2,500

LO 1.7

15. Which of the following taxpayers is *not* eligible for an economic impact payment in 2020?
    a. Savannah, a married taxpayer with no children, and has AGI of $75,000 in 2020
    b. Blake, a single taxpayer with no income in 2020, and who was incarcerated
    c. Kaylee, a 24-year old single individual (not a dependent) who did not file a tax return in either 2018 or 2019 as her income was below the filing threshold
    d. Ava, a married taxpayer that had a child in 2020. Her joint AGI in 2020 was $76,000.

LO 1.7

16. As a married couple, Yihong and Kaylee's EIP was $2,400. In 2020, they computed their recovery rebate credit as $2,900 due to the birth of a child in 2020. The 2020 net impact of the EIP and RRC will be to:
    a. increase their income
    b. decrease their tax liability by $500
    c. increase their tax liability by $500
    d. have no impact on their tax liability

LO 1.8

17. Morgan is 65 years old and single. He supports his father, who is 90 years old, blind, and has no income. What is Morgan's standard deduction?
    a. $12,400
    b. $14,050
    c. $20,300
    d. $18,650
    e. $20,000

LO 1.8

18. Taxpayers who are 65 or older get the benefit of:
    a. An additional exemption
    b. An additional amount added to their standard deduction
    c. An additional amount added to their itemized deductions
    d. None of the above

LO 1.8

19. Taxpayers who are blind get the benefit of:
    a. An additional exemption
    b. An additional amount added to their standard deduction
    c. An additional amount added to their itemized deductions
    d. None of the above

LO 1.9

20. Which of the following is *not* a capital asset to an individual taxpayer?
    a. Stocks
    b. A 48-foot sailboat
    c. Raw land held as an investment
    d. Inventory in the taxpayer's business
    e. All of the above are capital assets

LO 1.9

21. Joyce purchased General Electric stock 4 years ago for $10,000. In the current year, she sells the stock for $25,000. What is Joyce's gain or loss?
    a. $15,000 long-term gain
    b. $15,000 short-term gain
    c. $15,000 ordinary loss
    d. $15,000 extraordinary gain
    e. No gain or loss is recognized on this transaction

LO 1.9

22. Alex purchased a rental house 4 years ago for $270,000. Her depreciation at the time of the sale is $40,000. Due to a decrease in real estate prices, she sells the house for only $240,000 in 2020. What is her gain or loss for tax purposes?
    a. $0
    b. $10,000 loss
    c. $10,000 gain
    d. $35,000 loss
    e. $25,000 gain

LO 1.9   23. Dorit, a single taxpayer, has a long-term capital loss of $7,000 on the sale of bonds in 2020 and no other capital gains or losses. Her taxable income without this transaction is $43,000. What is her taxable income considering this capital loss?
   a. $40,000
   b. $36,000
   c. $43,000
   d. $55,000
   e. Some other amount

LO 1.10   24. Access the Internet and go to **www.irs.gov** and select "Search Forms & Instructions." Enter "4868" into the search box. What is Line 5 of the Form 4868?
   a. Total payments
   b. Balance due
   c. Your name
   d. Estimate of total tax liability
   e. Your social security number

LO 1.10   25. Access the Internet and go to **www.irs.gov** and select "News" in the upper right hand corner (on mobile devices, select "Menu" in the upper right hand corner and select "News"). Select "IRS Guidance" (on mobile devices, hit the plus on "more News," then scroll down until you see "IRS Guidance") and then select "IRS Guidance in Plain English." Which of the following is a public pronouncement that has only immediate or short-term value?
   a. Private letter ruling
   b. Revenue ruling
   c. Revenue procedure
   d. Notice
   e. Announcement

LO 1.11   26. Electronically filed tax returns:
   a. May not be transmitted from a taxpayer's home computer
   b. Constitute more than 90 percent of the returns filed with the IRS
   c. Have error rates similar to paper returns
   d. Offer larger refunds than paper returns

GROUP 2:
PROBLEMS

LO 1.1   1. List three major purposes the tax system is meant to serve:
   a. _Fund the Gov_
   b. _Economic Change_
   c. _Social Change_

LO 1.3   2. Rahul and Ruby are married taxpayers. They are both under age 65 and in good health. For 2020 they have a total of $42,000 in wages and $300 in interest income. Rahul and Ruby's deductions for adjusted gross income amount to $6,000 and their itemized deductions equal $18,700. They have two children, ages 32 and 28, that are married and provide support for themselves.
   a. What is the amount of Rahul and Ruby's adjusted gross income?

   $ _____

   b. What is the amount of their itemized deductions or standard deduction?

   $ _____

   c. What is their taxable income?

   $ _____

LO 1.3

3. Xialu is a single taxpayer who is under age 65 and in good health. For 2020, she has a salary of $25,000 and itemized deductions of $7,000. Leslie allows her mother to live with her during the winter months (3–4 months per year), but her mother provides all of her own support otherwise.

   a. How much is Leslie's adjusted gross income?

      $ _____ 25k ✓

   b. What amount of itemized or standard deduction(s) should she claim?

      $ _____ Sh. will take 12,400

   c. What is the amount of Leslie's taxable income?

      $ _____ 12,600

LO 1.3
LO 1.9

4. In 2020, Manon earns wages of $54,000. She also has dividend income of $2,800. Manon is single and has no dependents. During the year, Manon sold silver coins held as an investment for a $7,000 loss. Calculate the following amounts for Manon:

   a. Adjusted gross income

      $ _____ 53,800 ✓

   b. Standard deduction

      $ _____ 12,400 ✓

   c. Taxable income

      $ _____ A - B ✓

LO 1.3
LO 1.5
LO 1.8

5. Diego, age 28, married Dolores, age 27, in 2020. Their salaries for the year amounted to $48,000. They had dividend income of $2,500. Diego and Dolores' deductions for adjusted gross income amounted to $3,000, their itemized deductions were $16,000, and they have no dependents.

   a. What is the amount of their adjusted gross income?

      $ _____ 47,500

   b. What is the amount of their itemized deductions or standard deduction?

      $ _____ 24,800

   c. What is the amount of their taxable income?

      $ _____ 23,700

   d. What is their tax liability for 2020?

      $ _____ 2,332

LO 1.3
LO 1.5
LO 1.8

6. Marco and Tatiana are married and file separate returns for 2020. Tatiana itemizes her deductions on her return. Marco's adjusted gross income was $18,000, his itemized deductions were $2,400. Neither have any dependents. Calculate Marco's income tax liability assuming the couple does not live in a community property state.

      $ _____ 18 - 2,400
                           1,678

LO 1.3
LO 1.5
LO 1.8

7. Alicia, age 27, is a single, full-time college student. She earns $13,200 from a part-time job and has taxable interest income of $1,450. Her itemized deductions are $845. Calculate Alicia's taxable income for 2020. (Please note: Chapter 6 will cover the computation of tax credits for dependent college students under age 24.)

      $ _____ 14,625
                    - 12,400

LO 1.3
LO 1.5
LO 1.8

8. Jonathan is a 35-year-old single taxpayer with adjusted gross income in 2020 of $47,000. He uses the standard deduction and has no dependents.
   a. Calculate Jonathan's taxable income. Please show your work.

   _____

   _____

   b. When you calculate Jonathan's tax liability are you required to use the tax tables or the tax rate schedules, or does it matter?

   _____

   c. What is Jonathan's tax liability?

   _____

LO 1.3
LO 1.5
LO 1.8

9. Brock, age 50, and Erin, age 49, are married with three dependent children. They file a joint return for 2020. Their income from salaries totals $50,000, and they received $8,000 in taxable interest, $5,000 in royalties, and $3,000 in other ordinary income. Brock and Erin's deductions for adjusted gross income amount to $2,500, and they have itemized deductions totaling $19,250. Calculate the following amounts:
   a. Gross income

   $ _____

   b. Adjusted gross income

   $ _____

   c. Itemized deduction or standard deduction amount

   $ _____

   d. Taxable income

   $ _____

   e. Income tax liability (Do not consider the alternative minimum tax covered in Chapter 6 or any credits.)

   $ _____

LO 1.3
LO 1.5
LO 1.6
LO 1.8

10. Jackson, age 35, and Peggy, age 34, are married and file a joint income tax return for 2020. Their salaries for the year total $85,000 and they have dividend income of $4,000. They have no deductions for adjusted gross income. Their itemized deductions are $24,900. Jackson and Peggy do not have any dependents.
    a. What is the amount of their adjusted gross income?

    $ _____

    b. What is their deduction for personal exemptions?

    $ _____

    c. What is the amount of their taxable income?

    $ _____

LO 1.3
LO 1.5
LO 1.8

11. Wanda is a single 50-year-old taxpayer with no dependents. Her only income is $41,000 of wages. Calculate her taxable income and her tax liability. Please show your work.

    _____

    _____

    _____

LO 1.4

12. Nicoula is a server at a La Jolla restaurant. Nicoula received $1,200 in unreported tips during 2020 and owes Social Security and Medicare taxes on these tips. Her total income for the year, including the tips, is $4,300. Is Nicoula required to file an income tax return for 2020? Why or why not?

_____

_____

_____

LO 1.4

13. For each of the following situations (none of the taxpayers claim dependents), indicate whether the taxpayer(s) is (are) required to file a tax return for 2020. Explain your answer.

a. Helen is a single taxpayer with interest income in 2020 of $8,750.

_____

b. Joan is a single college student who is claimed as a dependent by her parents. She earned $1,550 from a part-time job and has $1,150 in interest income.

_____

c. Leslie, age 64, and Mark, age 66, are married and file a joint return. They received $17,800 in interest income from a savings account.

_____

d. Ray, age 60, and Jean, age 57, are married and file a joint tax return. Their only income is $14,700 in interest income.

_____

_____

e. Harry, a 19-year-old single taxpayer, had net earnings from self-employment of $1,500.

_____

LO 1.5

14. Determine from the tax table in Appendix A the amount of the income tax for each of the following taxpayers for 2020:

Taxpayer(s)	Filing Status	Taxable Income	Income Tax
Allen	Single	$21,000	$_____
Boyd	MFS	24,545	$_____
Caldwell	MFJ	35,784	$_____
Dell	H of H	27,450	$_____
Evans	Single	44,999	$_____

LO 1.5

15. For each of the following cases, indicate the filing status for the taxpayer(s) for 2020 using the following legend:

    A—Single   **D**—Head of household

    B—Married filing a joint return   **E**—Qualifying widow(er)

    C—Married filing separate returns

Case   Filing Status

a. Linda is single and she supports her mother (who has no income), including paying all the costs of her housing in an apartment across town.   _____

b. Frank is single and he has a dependent child living in his home.   _____

c. Arthur is single and he supports his 30-year-old brother, who lives in his own home.

d. Leslie's final decree of divorce was granted on June 18, 2020. She has no dependents.

e. Tom and Carry were married on December 31, 2020.

LO 1.5 16. Melissa and Whitney are married taxpayers with taxable income of $106,000.

a. When you calculate their tax liability, are you required to use the tax tables or the tax rate schedules, or does it matter? _Yes over 100k_

b. What is their 2020 tax liability? _106 – 24,800_

LO 1.5 17. Jessica and Carl were married on July 1, 2020. What are their options for filing status for their 2020 taxes? _Must file married – joint or seperate_

LO 1.5 18. Maggie is single and supports her 85-year-old parents who have no income and live in a home rented for them by Maggie. What is Maggie's filing status and why? _Head of household. Parents may live elsewhere_

LO 1.5 19. List each alternative filing status available to unmarried individual taxpayers and the circumstances under which the alternatives can be used. _Single, Head of Household, Qualifying widow_

LO 1.5 LO 1.6 20. Marquez is single and supports his 30-year-old son who has income of $2,000 and lives in his own apartment.

a. Can Marquez claim his son as a dependent? _Yes_

b. Can Marquez claim head of household filing status? Why or why not? _No Son must live in same Home_

LO 1.6 21. In each of the following situations, determine whether the taxpayer(s) has/have a dependent and if so, the total amount of child tax credit and other dependent credit (assuming no limitations apply).

	Dependent? (Yes/No)	Total Child and Other Dependent Credit
a. Donna, a 20-year-old single taxpayer, supports her mother, who lives in her own home. Her mother has income of $1,350.	Y	$500
b. William, age 43, and Mary, age 45, are married and support William's 19-year-old sister, who is not a student. The sister's income from a part-time job is $4,300.	NO Too much income	$0
c. Devi was divorced in 2019 and receives child support of $250 per month from her ex-husband for the support of their 8-year-old son, John, who lives with her. Devi is 45 and provides more than half of her son's support.	Y	$2,000 child
d. Wendell, an 89-year-old single taxpayer, supports his son, who is 67 years old, lives with him, and earns no income.	Yes	$500
e. Wilma, age 65, and Morris, age 66, are married. They file a joint return.	NO	$0

LO 1.6   22. What is the total dollar amount of personal and dependency exemptions which a married couple with two children (ages 11 and 14, both of which are qualified children) and $80,000 of adjusted gross income would deduct in 2020? What is the total child and other dependent credit that could be claimed (before any limitations)

[handwritten: $0 2018-2025]

[handwritten: $4,000]

LO 1.6   23. If Charles, a 16-year-old child model, earns $50,000 a year and is completely self-supporting even though he lives with his parents, can his parents claim him as a dependent? Why or why not?

[handwritten: 2k per kid]

[handwritten: N - income/self supporting]

LO 1.6   24. Marc's brother, Phillip, who is a 20-year-old French citizen, lives in France for the full year. Marc supports Phillip while he attends college. Can Marc claim Phillip as a dependent? Why or why not?

[handwritten: N - not citizen]

LO 1.7   25. Luke and Vanessa have been married since 2016 and have filed jointly each year since then. Their 2019 EIP was based on their 2019 tax return that was filed in early February 2020. In May 2020, they celebrated the adoption of a child. If their AGI was never greater than $120,000, what was their EIP and RRC in 2020?

EIP $ *[handwritten: 2,400]*
RRC $ *[handwritten: 2,900]*

LO 1.8   26. Describe the difference between the standard deduction and itemized deductions. How should a taxpayer decide whether to take the standard deduction or claim itemized deductions?

[handwritten: RRC?]

[handwritten: which one is more]

LO 1.10   27. Go to the IRS website (**www.irs.gov/newsroom**) and note the name of the most recent news release.

LO 1.10   28. Go to the IRS website (**www.irs.gov**) and print out a copy of the most recent *Schedule F* of *Form 1040*.

LO 1.10   29. Go to the Turbo Tax Blog (**http://blog.turbotax.intuit.com/**) and search the blog for an article on the deduction of student loan interest. What is the maximum deduction that can be taken in a year?

[handwritten: $2,500 student interest limit deduction]

GROUP 3:
WRITING ASSIGNMENTS

RESEARCH

1. Jerry, age 23, a full-time student and not disabled, lives with William and Sheila Carson. Jerry is William's older brother. Jerry is single, a U.S. citizen, and does not provide more than one-half of his own support. William and Sheila are both 21 and file a joint return. Can William and Sheila claim Jerry as a qualifying child?

   Required: Go to the IRS website (**www.irs.gov**) and review Publication 501. Write a letter to William and Sheila stating if they can claim Jerry as a qualifying child.

ETHICS

2. Jason and Mary Wells, friends of yours, were married on December 30, 2020. They know you are studying taxes and have sent you an e-mail with a question concerning their filing status. Jason and Mary would each like to file single for tax year 2020. Jason has prepared their taxes both as single and married filing jointly, and he has realized that the couple will get a larger combined refund if they each file single. Jason argues "that it's not as if we were married for very long in 2020." Prepare an e-mail to respond to Jason and Mary's inquiry.

GROUP 4:
COMPREHENSIVE PROBLEMS

> **Instructions for working all Group 4 Comprehensive Tax Return Problems in this textbook are as follows:**
>
> **Birthdays:** If using the tax software, create birthdates for taxpayers and dependents. Adult taxpayers should have ages between 25 and 64 unless a different age is specified.
>
> **Wages:** Assume the wages subject to income tax in the problems are the same as Social Security wages and Medicare wages unless presented otherwise. Create employer names and other information which may be required by your tax software package.
>
> **Missing Data:** Please make realistic assumptions about any missing data. Decide whether taxpayers contribute to the Presidential Election Campaign, which does not affect tax liability. No taxpayers will have traded virtual currency unless specific details are provided. All taxpayers request a refund of any overpaid tax unless otherwise indicated.
>
> **Tax Forms:** Tax forms to complete the problems are found at the end of each chapter. Additional copies can be found on the IRS website (**www.irs.gov**).

1A. Maria Tallchief is a single taxpayer (birthdate May 18, 1993) living at 543 Space Drive, Houston, TX 77099. Her Social Security number is 466-33-1234. For 2020, Maria has no dependents, and her W-2, from her job at a local restaurant where she parks cars, contains the following information:

a Employee's social security number 466-33-1234	OMB No. 1545-0008	Safe, accurate, FAST! Use	IRS e~file	Visit the IRS website at www.irs.gov/efile

b Employer identification number (EIN) 33-1235672	1 Wages, tips, other compensation 20,250.34	2 Federal income tax withheld 1,196.69
c Employer's name, address, and ZIP code Burger Box 1234 Mountain Road Houston, TX 77099	3 Social security wages 20,250.34	4 Social security tax withheld 1,255.12
	5 Medicare wages and tips 20,250.34	6 Medicare tax withheld 293.63
	7 Social security tips	8 Allocated tips
d Control number	9	10 Dependent care benefits
e Employee's first name and initial Last name Suff. Maria Tallchief 543 Space Drive Houston, TX 77099	11 Nonqualified plans	12a See instructions for box 12
	13 Statutory employee Retirement plan Third-party sick pay	12b
	14 Other	12c
		12d
f Employee's address and ZIP code		

15 State Employer's state ID number TX	16 State wages, tips, etc.	17 State income tax	18 Local wages, tips, etc.	19 Local income tax	20 Locality name

Form **W-2** Wage and Tax Statement   **2020**   Department of the Treasury—Internal Revenue Service

Copy B—To Be Filed With Employee's FEDERAL Tax Return.
This information is being furnished to the Internal Revenue Service.

These wages are Maria's only income for 2020. Maria received a $1,200 EIP in 2020.

Required: Complete Form 1040 for Maria Tallchief for the 2020 tax year.

1B. Using the information from Problem 1A, assume Maria's birthdate is May 18, 1953 and complete Form 1040-SR for Maria Tallchief for the 2020 tax year.

2A. Hardy and Dora Knox are married and file a joint return for 2020. Hardy's Social Security number is 466-47-3311 and her birthdate is January 4, 1976. Dora's Social Security number is 467-74-4451 and her birthday is July 7, 1975. They live at 143 Maple Street, Knoxville, TN 37932. For 2020, Hardy did not work, and Dora's W-2 from her teaching job showed the following:

a Employee's social security number 467-74-4451	OMB No. 1545-0008	Safe, accurate, FAST! Use	IRS e~file	Visit the IRS website at www.irs.gov/efile

b Employer identification number (EIN) 33-0711111	1 Wages, tips, other compensation 51,020.40	2 Federal income tax withheld 3,052.87
c Employer's name, address, and ZIP code Knoxville Unified School District 1700 Harding Valley Street Knoxville, TN 37932	3 Social security wages 51,020.40	4 Social security tax withheld 3,163.26
	5 Medicare wages and tips 51,020.40	6 Medicare tax withheld 739.80
	7 Social security tips	8 Allocated tips
d Control number	9	10 Dependent care benefits
e Employee's first name and initial Last name Suff. Dora Knox 143 Maple Street Knoxville, TN 37932	11 Nonqualified plans	12a See instructions for box 12
	13 Statutory employee Retirement plan Third-party sick pay	12b
	14 Other	12c
		12d
f Employee's address and ZIP code		

15 State Employer's state ID number TN	16 State wages, tips, etc.	17 State income tax	18 Local wages, tips, etc.	19 Local income tax	20 Locality name

Form **W-2** Wage and Tax Statement   **2020**   Department of the Treasury—Internal Revenue Service

Copy B—To Be Filed With Employee's FEDERAL Tax Return.
This information is being furnished to the Internal Revenue Service.

Hardy and Dora have a son named Fort (birthdate December 21, 2000, Social Security number 552-52-5552), who is a dependent living with them, is not a full-time student, and generates $5,200 of gross income for himself. Hardy and Dora received a $2,400 EIP in 2020.

Required: Complete Form 1040 for Hardy and Dora for the 2020 tax year.

2B. Abigail (Abby) Boxer is a single mother (birthdate April 28, 1982) working as a civilian accountant for the U.S. Army. Her Social Security number is 676-73-3311 and she lives at 3456 S Career Avenue, Sioux Falls, SD 57107. Helen, Abby's 18-year-old daughter (Social Security number 676-73-3312 and birthdate April 16, 2002), is a dependent child living with her mother, and she does not qualify for the child tax credit due to her age but does qualify for the other dependent credit of $500. Abby's Form W-2 from the U.S. Department of Defense shows the following:

a Employee's social security number 676-73-3311	OMB No. 1545-0008	Safe, accurate, FAST! Use IRS e~file	Visit the IRS website at www.irs.gov/efile	
b Employer identification number (EIN) 31-1575142		1 Wages, tips, other compensation 59,664.57	2 Federal income tax withheld 4,993.32	
c Employer's name, address, and ZIP code		3 Social security wages 59,664.57	4 Social security tax withheld 3,699.20	
DFAS Cleveland Center PO Box 998002 Cleveland, OH 44199		5 Medicare wages and tips 59,664.57	6 Medicare tax withheld 865.14	
		7 Social security tips	8 Allocated tips	
d Control number		9	10 Dependent care benefits	
e Employee's first name and initial Last name Suff.		11 Nonqualified plans	12a See instructions for box 12	
Abigail Boxer 3456 S. Career Avenue Sioux Falls, SD 57107		13 Statutory employee Retirement plan Third-party sick pay	12b	
		14 Other	12c	
			12d	
f Employee's address and ZIP code				
15 State Employer's state ID number SD	16 State wages, tips, etc.	17 State income tax	18 Local wages, tips, etc.	19 Local income tax	20 Locality name

Form **W-2** Wage and Tax Statement   **2020**   Department of the Treasury—Internal Revenue Service

Copy B—To Be Filed With Employee's FEDERAL Tax Return.
This information is being furnished to the Internal Revenue Service.

Abby also has taxable interest from Sioux Falls Savings and Loan of $127 and tax-exempt interest from bonds issued by the state of South Dakota of $300. Abby received a $1,700 EIP in 2020.

Required: Complete Form 1040 for Abigail for the 2020 tax year.

GROUP 5:
CUMULATIVE SOFTWARE PROBLEM

1. Albert Gaytor and his wife Allison are married and file a joint return for 2020. The Gaytors live at 12340 Cocoshell Road, Coral Gables, FL 33134. Captain Gaytor is a charter fishing boat captain but took 6 months off from his job in 2020 to train and study for his Masters Captain's License.

   In 2020, Albert received a Form W-2 from his employer, Coconut Grove Fishing Charters, Inc.:

a Employee's social security number 266-51-1966	OMB No. 1545-0008	Safe, accurate, FAST! Use	IRS e~file	Visit the IRS website at www.irs.gov/efile

b Employer identification number (EIN) 60-3456789		1 Wages, tips, other compensation 67,254.70	2 Federal income tax withheld 5,588.17

c Employer's name, address, and ZIP code	3 Social security wages 67,254.70	4 Social security tax withheld 4,169.79
Coconut Grove Fishing Charters, Inc. 2432 Bay Blvd. Coconut Grove, FL 33133	5 Medicare wages and tips 67,254.70	6 Medicare tax withheld 975.19
	7 Social security tips	8 Allocated tips

d Control number	9	10 Dependent care benefits

e Employee's first name and initial Last name Suff.	11 Nonqualified plans	12a See instructions for box 12
Albert T. Gaytor 12340 Cocoshell Road Coral Gables, FL 33134	13 Statutory employee ☐ Retirement plan ☐ Third-party sick pay ☐	12b
	14 Other	12c
		12d
f Employee's address and ZIP code		

15 State Employer's state ID number	16 State wages, tips, etc.	17 State income tax	18 Local wages, tips, etc.	19 Local income tax	20 Locality name
FL					

Form **W-2** Wage and Tax Statement   2020   Department of the Treasury—Internal Revenue Service

Copy B—To Be Filed With Employee's FEDERAL Tax Return.
This information is being furnished to the Internal Revenue Service.

Name	Social Security Number	Date of Birth
Albert T. Gaytor	266-51-1966	09/22/1971
Allison A. Gaytor	266-34-1967	07/01/1972
Crocker Gaytor	261-55-1212	12/21/2003
Cayman Slacker	261-11-4444	03/13/2002
Sean Slacker	344-23-5656	05/01/2001

The Gaytors have a 17-year-old son, Crocker, who is a full-time freshman at Brickell State University. The Gaytors also have an 18-year-old daughter, Cayman, who is a part-time student at Dade County Community College (DCCC). Cayman is married to Sean Slacker, who is 19 years old and a part-time student at DCCC. Sean and Cayman have a 1-year-old child, Wanda Slacker (Social Security number 648-99-4306). Sean, Cayman, and Wanda all live in an apartment up the street from Albert and Allison during the entire current calendar year. Sean and Cayman both work for Sean's wealthy grandfather as apprentices in his business. Their wages for the year were a combined $50,000, which allowed them to pay all the personal expenses for themselves and their daughter. The Gaytors received a $2,900 EIP in 2020.

Albert and Allison have a savings account and received the following Form 1099-INT for 2020:

☐ CORRECTED (if checked)

PAYER'S name, street address, city or town, state or province, country, ZIP or foreign postal code, and telephone no. Vizcaya National Bank 9871 Coral Way Miami, FL 33134	Payer's RTN (optional)	OMB No. 1545-0112 20**20** Form **1099-INT**	**Interest Income**
	1 Interest income $ 348.19		
	2 Early withdrawal penalty $		Copy B
PAYER'S TIN **60-7654321** RECIPIENT'S TIN **266-51-1966**	3 Interest on U.S. Savings Bonds and Treas. obligations $		For Recipient
RECIPIENT'S name Albert T. Gaytor	4 Federal income tax withheld $	5 Investment expenses $	This is important tax information and is being furnished to the IRS. If you are
Street address (including apt. no.) 12340 Cocoshell Road	6 Foreign tax paid $	7 Foreign country or U.S. possession	required to file a return, a negligence penalty or other sanction may be
City or town, state or province, country, and ZIP or foreign postal code Coral Gables, FL 33134	8 Tax-exempt interest $	9 Specified private activity bond interest $	imposed on you if this income is taxable and the IRS determines that it has
FATCA filing requirement ☐	10 Market discount $	11 Bond premium $	not been reported.
	12 Bond premium on Treasury obligations $	13 Bond premium on tax-exempt bond $	
Account number (see instructions)	14 Tax-exempt and tax credit bond CUSIP no.	15 State 16 State identification no.	17 State tax withheld $ $

Form **1099-INT**   (keep for your records)   www.irs.gov/Form1099INT   Department of the Treasury - Internal Revenue Service

Required: Use a computer software package such as Intuit ProConnect to complete Form 1040 for Albert and Allison Gaytor for 2020. Be sure to save your data input files since this case will be expanded with more tax information in later chapters. Make assumptions regarding any information not given.

Form **1040**
Department of the Treasury—Internal Revenue Service   (99)
U.S. Individual Income Tax Return   20**20**   OMB No. 1545-0074   IRS Use Only—Do not write or staple in this space.

Filing Status
Check only one box.

☐ Single ☐ Married filing jointly ☐ Married filing separately (MFS) ☐ Head of household (HOH) ☐ Qualifying widow(er) (QW)

If you checked the MFS box, enter the name of your spouse. If you checked the HOH or QW box, enter the child's name if the qualifying person is a child but not your dependent ▶

Your first name and middle initial	Last name	Your social security number

If joint return, spouse's first name and middle initial	Last name	Spouse's social security number

Home address (number and street). If you have a P.O. box, see instructions.		Apt. no.

Presidential Election Campaign
Check here if you, or your spouse if filing jointly, want $3 to go to this fund. Checking a box below will not change your tax or refund.
☐ You ☐ Spouse

City, town, or post office. If you have a foreign address, also complete spaces below.	State	ZIP code

Foreign country name	Foreign province/state/county	Foreign postal code

At any time during 2020, did you receive, sell, send, exchange, or otherwise acquire any financial interest in any virtual currency?   ☐ Yes ☐ No

Standard Deduction
Someone can claim: ☐ You as a dependent ☐ Your spouse as a dependent
☐ Spouse itemizes on a separate return or you were a dual-status alien

Age/Blindness **You:** ☐ Were born before January 2, 1956 ☐ Are blind **Spouse:** ☐ Was born before January 2, 1956 ☐ Is blind

Dependents (see instructions):
If more than four dependents, see instructions and check here ▶ ☐

(1) First name Last name	(2) Social security number	(3) Relationship to you	(4) ✔ if qualifies for (see instructions):	
			Child tax credit	Credit for other dependents
			☐	☐
			☐	☐
			☐	☐
			☐	☐

Attach Sch. B if required.

1	Wages, salaries, tips, etc. Attach Form(s) W-2	1	
2a	Tax-exempt interest . . .	2a	**b** Taxable interest	2b	
3a	Qualified dividends . . .	3a	**b** Ordinary dividends	3b	
4a	IRA distributions	4a	**b** Taxable amount	4b	
5a	Pensions and annuities . .	5a	**b** Taxable amount	5b	
6a	Social security benefits . .	6a	**b** Taxable amount	6b	
7	Capital gain or (loss). Attach Schedule D if required. If not required, check here . . . . . ▶ ☐	7	
8	Other income from Schedule 1, line 9	8	
9	Add lines 1, 2b, 3b, 4b, 5b, 6b, 7, and 8. This is your **total income** . . . . ▶	9	
10	Adjustments to income:		
a	From Schedule 1, line 22	10a	
b	Charitable contributions if you take the standard deduction. See instructions	10b	
c	Add lines 10a and 10b. These are your **total adjustments to income** . . . . ▶	10c	
11	Subtract line 10c from line 9. This is your **adjusted gross income** . . . . . ▶	11	
12	**Standard deduction or itemized deductions** (from Schedule A)	12	
13	Qualified business income deduction. Attach Form 8995 or Form 8995-A	13	
14	Add lines 12 and 13	14	
15	**Taxable income.** Subtract line 14 from line 11. If zero or less, enter -0-	15	

Standard Deduction for—
- Single or Married filing separately, $12,400
- Married filing jointly or Qualifying widow(er), $24,800
- Head of household, $18,650
- If you checked any box under Standard Deduction, see instructions.

For Disclosure, Privacy Act, and Paperwork Reduction Act Notice, see separate instructions.   Cat. No. 11320B   Form **1040** (2020)

Form 1040 (2020)   Page **2**

16	**Tax** (see instructions). Check if any from Form(s): **1** ☐ 8814 **2** ☐ 4972 **3** ☐ _____ . .		**16**	
17	Amount from Schedule 2, line 3		**17**	
18	Add lines 16 and 17		**18**	
19	Child tax credit or credit for other dependents		**19**	
20	Amount from Schedule 3, line 7		**20**	
21	Add lines 19 and 20		**21**	
22	Subtract line 21 from line 18. If zero or less, enter -0- . . .		**22**	
23	Other taxes, including self-employment tax, from Schedule 2, line 10		**23**	
24	Add lines 22 and 23. This is your **total tax** . . . . . . ▶		**24**	
25	Federal income tax withheld from:			
a	Form(s) W-2	**25a**		
b	Form(s) 1099	**25b**		
c	Other forms (see instructions)	**25c**		
d	Add lines 25a through 25c		**25d**	
26	2020 estimated tax payments and amount applied from 2019 return . .		**26**	
27	Earned income credit (EIC)	**27**		
28	Additional child tax credit. Attach Schedule 8812	**28**		
29	American opportunity credit from Form 8863, line 8	**29**		
30	Recovery rebate credit. See instructions	**30**		
31	Amount from Schedule 3, line 13	**31**		
32	Add lines 27 through 31. These are your **total other payments and refundable credits** . . ▶		**32**	
33	Add lines 25d, 26, and 32. These are your **total payments** . . . . . . ▶		**33**	

Left margin note beside lines 26–31: • If you have a qualifying child, attach Sch. EIC. • If you have nontaxable combat pay, see instructions.

Refund	34	If line 33 is more than line 24, subtract line 24 from line 33. This is the amount you **overpaid**	**34**	
Direct deposit? See instructions.	35a	Amount of line 34 you want **refunded to you**. If Form 8888 is attached, check here . . . ▶ ☐	**35a**	
	▶ b	Routing number ☐☐☐☐☐☐☐☐☐ ▶ **c** Type: ☐ Checking ☐ Savings		
	▶ d	Account number ☐☐☐☐☐☐☐☐☐☐☐☐☐☐☐☐☐		
	36	Amount of line 34 you want **applied to your 2021 estimated tax** . . ▶	36	
Amount You Owe	37	Subtract line 33 from line 24. This is the **amount you owe now** . . . . ▶	**37**	
For details on how to pay, see instructions.		**Note:** Schedule H and Schedule SE filers, line 37 may not represent all of the taxes you owe for 2020. See Schedule 3, line 12e, and its instructions for details.		
	38	Estimated tax penalty (see instructions) . . . . ▶	38	

Third Party Designee	Do you want to allow another person to discuss this return with the IRS? See instructions . . . . ▶ ☐ **Yes.** Complete below. ☐ **No**
	Designee's name ▶ _____ Phone no. ▶ _____ Personal identification number (PIN) ▶ ☐☐☐☐☐

Sign Here	Under penalties of perjury, I declare that I have examined this return and accompanying schedules and statements, and to the best of my knowledge and belief, they are true, correct, and complete. Declaration of preparer (other than taxpayer) is based on all information of which preparer has any knowledge.

	Your signature	Date	Your occupation	If the IRS sent you an Identity Protection PIN, enter it here (see inst.) ▶ ☐☐☐☐☐☐
Joint return? See instructions. Keep a copy for your records.	Spouse's signature. If a joint return, **both** must sign.	Date	Spouse's occupation	If the IRS sent your spouse an Identity Protection PIN, enter it here (see inst.) ▶ ☐☐☐☐☐☐
	Phone no.		Email address	

Paid Preparer Use Only	Preparer's name	Preparer's signature		Date	PTIN	Check if: ☐ Self-employed
	Firm's name ▶				Phone no. ▶	
	Firm's address ▶				Firm's EIN ▶	

Go to *www.irs.gov/Form1040* for instructions and the latest information.   Form **1040** (2020)

Form **1040-SR** Department of the Treasury—Internal Revenue Service (99) **2020** U.S. Tax Return for Seniors | OMB No. 1545-0074 | IRS Use Only—Do not write or staple in this space.

Filing Status
Check only one box.

☐ Single ☐ Married filing jointly ☐ Married filing separately (MFS)
☐ Head of household (HOH) ☐ Qualifying widow(er) (QW)

If you checked the MFS box, enter the name of your spouse. If you checked the HOH or QW box, enter the child's name if the qualifying person is a child but not your dependent ▶

Your first name and middle initial	Last name		Your social security number
If joint return, spouse's first name and middle initial	Last name		Spouse's social security number
Home address (number and street). If you have a P.O. box, see instructions.		Apt. no.	**Presidential Election Campaign**
City, town, or post office. If you have a foreign address, also complete spaces below.	State	ZIP code	Check here if you, or your spouse if filing jointly, want $3 to go to this fund. Checking a box below will not change your tax or refund. ☐ You ☐ Spouse
Foreign country name	Foreign province/state/county	Foreign postal code	

At any time during 2020, did you receive, sell, send, exchange, or otherwise acquire any financial interest in any virtual currency? . . . . ▶ ☐ Yes ☐ No

Standard Deduction

Someone can claim: ☐ You as a dependent ☐ Your spouse as a dependent
☐ Spouse itemizes on a separate return or you were a dual-status alien

Age/Blindness { You: ☐ Were born before January 2, 1956 ☐ Are blind
Spouse: ☐ Was born before January 2, 1956 ☐ Is blind

Dependents (see instructions):

(1) First name Last name	(2) Social security number	(3) Relationship to you	(4) ✔ if qualifies for (see instructions):	
			Child tax credit	Credit for other dependents
If more than four dependents, see instructions and check here ▶ ☐			☐	☐
			☐	☐
			☐	☐
			☐	☐

Attach Schedule B if required.

1	Wages, salaries, tips, etc. Attach Form(s) W-2	**1**	
2a	Tax-exempt interest . **2a**	**b** Taxable interest . . **2b**	
3a	Qualified dividends . . **3a**	**b** Ordinary dividends . **3b**	
4a	IRA distributions . . . **4a**	**b** Taxable amount . . **4b**	
5a	Pensions and annuities **5a**	**b** Taxable amount . . **5b**	
6a	Social security benefits . **6a**	**b** Taxable amount . . **6b**	
7	Capital gain or (loss). Attach Schedule D if required. If not required, check here . . . . ▶ ☐	**7**	
8	Other income from Schedule 1, line 9	**8**	
9	Add lines 1, 2b, 3b, 4b, 5b, 6b, 7, and 8. This is your **total income** . . ▶	**9**	
10	Adjustments to income:		
a	From Schedule 1, line 22 . . . . **10a**		
b	Charitable contributions if you take the standard deduction. See instructions **10b**		
c	Add lines 10a and 10b. These are your **total adjustments to income** ▶	**10c**	
11	Subtract line 10c from line 9. This is your **adjusted gross income** . . ▶	**11**	

For Disclosure, Privacy Act, and Paperwork Reduction Act Notice, see separate instructions. Cat. No. 71930F Form **1040-SR** (2020)

Form 1040-SR (2020)   Page **2**

Standard Deduction See *Standard Deduction Chart* on the last page of this form.	**12**	**Standard deduction or itemized deductions** (from Schedule A) . . .	**12**	
	13	Qualified business income deduction. Attach Form 8995 or Form 8995-A	**13**	
	14	Add lines 12 and 13	**14**	
	15	**Taxable income.** Subtract line 14 from line 11. If zero or less, enter -0- .	**15**	
	16	**Tax** (see instructions). Check if any from:		
		1 ☐ Form(s) 8814 **2** ☐ Form 4972 **3** ☐ _____	**16**	
	17	Amount from Schedule 2, line 3	**17**	
	18	Add lines 16 and 17	**18**	
	19	Child tax credit or credit for other dependents	**19**	
	20	Amount from Schedule 3, line 7	**20**	
	21	Add lines 19 and 20	**21**	
	22	Subtract line 21 from line 18. If zero or less, enter -0-	**22**	
	23	Other taxes, including self-employment tax, from Schedule 2, line 10 . .	**23**	
	24	Add lines 22 and 23. This is your **total tax** . . . . ▶	**24**	
	25	Federal income tax withheld from:		

	a	Form(s) W-2	**25a**	
	b	Form(s) 1099	**25b**	
	c	Other forms (see instructions)	**25c**	
	d	Add lines 25a through 25c	**25d**	

	26	2020 estimated tax payments and amount applied from 2019 return . .	**26**	
• If you have a qualifying child, attach Sch. EIC. • If you have nontaxable combat pay, see instructions.	**27**	Earned income credit (EIC)	**27**	
	28	Additional child tax credit. Attach Schedule 8812 . .	**28**	
	29	American opportunity credit from Form 8863, line 8 .	**29**	
	30	Recovery rebate credit. See instructions	**30**	
	31	Amount from Schedule 3, line 13	**31**	
	32	Add lines 27 through 31. These are your **total other payments and refundable credits** . . . . ▶	**32**	
	33	Add lines 25d, 26, and 32. These are your **total payments** . . . . . ▶	**33**	

Go to *www.irs.gov/Form1040SR* for instructions and the latest information.   Form **1040-SR** (2020)

Form 1040-SR (2020)   Page **3**

Refund   **34**   If line 33 is more than line 24, subtract line 24 from line 33. This is the amount you **overpaid** . . . . | **34** |

35a   Amount of line 34 you want **refunded to you.** If Form 8888 is attached, check here . . . . ▶ ☐ | **35a** |

Direct deposit?   ▶**b**   Routing number | | | | | | | | | ▶ **c** Type: ☐ Checking ☐ Savings
See instructions.   ▶**d**   Account number | | | | | | | | | | | | | | | |

36   Amount of line 34 you want **applied to your 2021 estimated tax** . . . . ▶ | **36** |

Amount You Owe   **37**   Subtract line 33 from line 24. This is the **amount you owe now** . . . ▶ | **37** |

For details on how to pay, see instructions.

Note: Schedule H and Schedule SE filers, line 37 may not represent all of the taxes you owe for 2020. See Schedule 3, line 12e, and its instructions for details.

38   Estimated tax penalty (see instructions) . . . . . ▶ | **38** |

Third Party Designee   Do you want to allow another person to discuss this return with the IRS? See instructions . . . . ▶   ☐ **Yes.** Complete below.   ☐ **No**

Designee's name ▶   Phone no. ▶   Personal identification number (PIN) ▶ | | | | | |

Sign Here   Under penalties of perjury, I declare that I have examined this return and accompanying schedules and statements, and to the best of my knowledge and belief, they are true, correct, and complete. Declaration of preparer (other than taxpayer) is based on all information of which preparer has any knowledge.

Joint return? See instructions. Keep a copy for your records.

Your signature	Date	Your occupation	If the IRS sent you an Identity Protection PIN, enter it here (see inst.)						
Spouse's signature. If a joint return, **both** must sign.	Date	Spouse's occupation	If the IRS sent your spouse an Identity Protection PIN, enter it here (see inst.)						
Phone no.		Email address							

Paid Preparer Use Only

Preparer's name	Preparer's signature	Date	PTIN	Check if: ☐ Self-employed
Firm's name ▶			Phone no.	
Firm's address ▶			Firm's EIN ▶	

Go to *www.irs.gov/Form1040SR* for instructions and the latest information.   Form **1040-SR** (2020)

Student Name _____

Class/Section _____

Date _____

KEY NUMBER TAX RETURN SUMMARY

CHAPTER 1

Comprehensive Problem 1A

Adjusted Gross Income (Line 11) _____

Taxable Income (Line 15) _____

Total Tax (Line 24) _____

Tax Refund (Line 35a) _____

Comprehensive Problem 1B

Adjusted Gross Income (Line 11) _____

Standard Deduction or Itemized Deductions (Line 12) _____

Total Tax (Line 24) _____

Tax Refund (Line 35a) _____

Comprehensive Problem 2A

Adjusted Gross Income (Line 11) _____

Standard Deduction or Itemized Deductions (Line 12) _____

Total Tax (Line 24) _____

Amount Overpaid (Line 34) _____

Comprehensive Problem 2B

Adjusted Gross Income (Line 11) _____

Standard Deduction or Itemized Deductions (Line 12) _____

Credit for Other Dependents (Line 19) _____

Total Tax (Line 24) _____

Amount Overpaid (Line 34) _____

Gross Income and Exclusions

LEARNING OBJECTIVES

After completing this chapter, you should be able to:

LO 2.1   Apply the definition of gross income.

LO 2.2   Describe salaries and wages income reporting and inclusion in gross income.

LO 2.3   Explain the general tax treatment of health insurance.

LO 2.4   Determine when meals and lodging may be excluded from taxable income.

LO 2.5   Identify the common employee fringe benefit income exclusions.

LO 2.6   Determine when prizes and awards are included in income.

LO 2.7   Calculate the taxable and nontaxable portions of annuity payments.

LO 2.8   Describe the tax treatment of life insurance proceeds.

LO 2.9   Identify the tax treatment of interest and dividend income.

LO 2.10   Describe the tax treatment of municipal bond interest.

LO 2.11   Identify the general rules for the tax treatment of gifts and inheritances.

LO 2.12   Describe the elements of scholarship income that are excluded from tax.

LO 2.13   Describe the tax treatment of alimony and child support.

LO 2.14   Explain the tax implications of using educational savings vehicles.

LO 2.15   Describe the tax treatment of unemployment compensation.

LO 2.16   Apply the rules governing inclusion of Social Security benefits in gross income.

LO 2.17   Distinguish between the different rules for married taxpayers residing in community property states when filing separate returns.

LO 2.18   Describe the inclusion and exclusion of cancellation of debt income.

OVERVIEW

This chapter starts with the definition of gross income. Tables 2.1 and 2.2 list the common inclusions in and exclusions from gross income. Detailed coverage is provided for inclusions and exclusions that may present unique issues for taxpayers. The coverage includes the special tax treatment for interest and dividends, alimony, prizes and awards, annuities, life insurance proceeds, and gifts and inheritances. Coverage of exclusions from gross income includes scholarships, accident and health insurance benefits, certain meals and lodging, municipal bond interest, and the special treatment of Social Security benefits. The elements of gross income discussed here represent much of what is included in the first line of the individual tax formula.

Learning Objective 2.1

Apply the definition of gross income.

2-1   THE NATURE OF GROSS INCOME

Gross income is the starting point for calculating a taxpayer's tax liability. The tax law states that gross income is:

> … all income from whatever source derived, including (but not limited to) the following items:

- Compensation for services, including fees, commissions, fringe benefits, and similar items
- Gross income derived from business
- Gains derived from dealings in property
- Interest
- Rents
- Royalties
- Dividends
- Annuities
- Income from life insurance and endowment contracts
- Pensions
- Income from discharge of indebtedness
- Distributive share of partnership gross income
- Income in respect of a decedent
- Income from an interest in an estate or trust

The definition of gross income as **"all income from whatever source derived"** is perhaps the most well-known definition in the tax law. Under this definition, unless there is an exception in the law, the U.S. government considers all income taxable. Therefore, prizes and awards, cash and noncash payments for goods and services, payments made in trade or *barter* (such as car repairs traded for tax preparation services), and illegal income not generally reported to the IRS are all still taxable income.

Table 2.1 provides an expanded list of items that are included in gross income. When in doubt, the general rule is that everything a taxpayer receives must be included in gross income unless specifically excluded. Any noncash items must be included in gross income at the fair market value of the items received.

The tax law provides that certain items of income are exempt from taxation; these items are referred to as *exclusions*. The exclusions include items such as life insurance proceeds, gifts, and veterans' benefits. A more complete list of exclusions from gross income is provided in Table 2.2.

The CARES Act allows higher education institutions to support students by using emergency financial aid grants which may be used for unexpected expenses, unmet financial need, or expenses related to the disruption of campus operations on account of the COVID-19 pandemic, such as unexpected expenses for food, housing, course materials, technology, health care, or childcare. These payments are considered grants and are excluded from income.

New Tax Law!

TABLE 2.1	2020 INCLUSIONS IN GROSS INCOME—PARTIAL LIST

Alimony (excluded after 2018)
Amounts recovered after being deducted
    in prior years
Annuities
Awards
Back pay
Bargain purchase from employer
Bonuses
Breach of contract damages
Business income
Clergy fees
Commissions
Compensation for services
Contributions received by members
    of the clergy
Damages for nonphysical personal injury
Death benefits
Debts forgiven
Directors' fees
Dividends
Embezzled funds
Employee awards (except certain service awards)
Employee benefits (except certain fringe benefits)
Employee bonuses
Employee stock options
Estate and trust income
Farm income
Fees
Gains from illegal activities

Gains from sale of property
Gambling winnings
Group-term life insurance premiums paid by
    employer for coverage over $50,000
Hobby income
Incentive awards
Interest income
Jury duty fees
Living quarters, meals (unless furnished for employer's convenience, etc.)
Military pay (unless combat pay)
Notary fees
Partnership income
Pensions
Prizes
Professional fees
Punitive damages
Rents
Retirement pay
Rewards
Royalties
Salaries
Scholarships (room and board)
Severance pay
Strike and lockout benefits
Supplemental unemployment benefits
Tips and gratuities
Unemployment compensation
Virtual currency (such as Bitcoin) paid for services
Wages

TABLE 2.2	2020 EXCLUSIONS FROM GROSS INCOME—PARTIAL LIST

Accident insurance proceeds
Alimony (excluded after 2018)
Annuities (to a limited extent)
Bequests
Casualty insurance proceeds
Child support payments
Damages for physical personal injury
    or sickness
Disability benefits (generally,
    but not always)
Gifts
Group-term life insurance
    premiums paid by employer
    (coverage not over $50,000)
Health insurance proceeds

Inheritances
Life insurance proceeds
Meals and lodging (furnished for
    employer's convenience, etc.)
Military allowances (including G.I. bill benefits)
Minister's dwelling rental value allowance
Municipal bond interest
Olympic medals and cash awards given
    to athletes
Relocation payments
Scholarships (tuition and books)
Social Security benefits (with limits)
Veterans' benefits
Welfare payments
Workers' compensation

Self-Study Problem 2.1   *See Appendix E for Solutions to Self-Study Problems*

Indicate whether each of the items listed below should be included in gross income or excluded from gross income in 2020.

	Included	Excluded
1. Prizes and awards	_____	_____
2. Embezzled funds	_____	_____
3. Child support payments	_____	_____
4. Alimony	_____	_____
5. Pensions	_____	_____
6. Inheritances	_____	_____
7. Welfare payments	_____	_____
8. Bequests	_____	_____
9. Jury duty fees	_____	_____
10. Royalties	_____	_____
11. Life insurance proceeds paid at death	_____	_____
12. Hobby income	_____	_____
13. Rewards	_____	_____
14. Partnership income	_____	_____
15. Casualty insurance proceeds	_____	_____
16. G.I. Bill benefits	_____	_____
17. Scholarships for room and board	_____	_____
18. Business income	_____	_____
19. Gifts	_____	_____

New Tax Law

In 2020, the federal government issued economic impact payments (EIPs) of up to $1,200 per individual to millions of Americans. The EIP is excluded from income via the new Recovery Rebate credit that is fully discussed in Chapter 7.

Learning Objective 2.2

Describe salaries and wages income reporting and inclusion in gross income.

2-2 SALARIES AND WAGES

Serving as an employee of a company is the most common way to earn income in the United States. More than 80 percent of all individual income tax returns include some amount of wage income, and wages represent approximately 70 percent of the adjusted gross income reported. Payments in almost any form, including salaries and wages, from an employer to an employee are considered income. The primary form of reporting wages to an employee is through Form W-2. An employee should receive a Form W-2 from an employer providing information about the wages paid to that employee during the year (the employer's responsibilities with Form W-2 are examined in Chapter 9). Figure 2.1 presents a Form W-2 for 2020.

Box 1 of Form W-2 is where employers should report taxable wages, salary, bonuses, awards, commissions, and almost every other type of taxable compensation. In most instances, the amount in Box 1 is reported directly on Line 1 of Form 1040, Wages, salaries, tips, etc. If

FIGURE 2.1 FORM W-2

a Employee's social security number 791-51-4335			OMB No. 1545-0008	**Safe, accurate,** **FAST! Use** IRS *e-file*	Visit the IRS website at www.irs.gov/efile	

b Employer identification number (EIN) 12-3456789		1 Wages, tips, other compensation 131,080.00	2 Federal income tax withheld 15,190.00

c Employer's name, address, and ZIP code Ivy Technologies, Inc. 436 E. 35 Avenue Gary, IN 46409	3 Social security wages 137,700.00	4 Social security tax withheld 8,537.40
	5 Medicare wages and tips 138,380.00	6 Medicare tax withheld 2,006.51
	7 Social security tips	8 Allocated tips

d Control number	9	10 Dependent care benefits 5,000.00

e Employee's first name and initial Last name Suff. Eric Hayes 555 E. 81st Street Merrillville, IN 46410	11 Nonqualified plans	12a See instructions for box 12 DD 11,567.00
	13 Statutory employee ☐ Retirement plan ☒ Third-party sick pay ☐	12b C 130.00
	14 Other	12c D 7,300.00
f Employee's address and ZIP code		12d

15 State Employer's state ID number IN 00122231001	16 State wages, tips, etc. 131,080.00	17 State income tax 4,900.00	18 Local wages, tips, etc. 131,080.00	19 Local income tax 927.00	20 Locality name LAKE

Form **W-2** Wage and Tax Statement   2020   Department of the Treasury—Internal Revenue Service

Copy B—To Be Filed With Employee's FEDERAL Tax Return.
This information is being furnished to the Internal Revenue Service.

a taxpayer receives more than one Form W-2 or is jointly filing with a spouse having their own Form W-2, the amounts in Box 1 are combined before entering on Line 1 of Form 1040.

EXAMPLE Bonnie and Clyde are married and file jointly. In 2020, Bonnie received two Forms W-2 from two separate employers reporting $34,000 of wages on one and $16,500 on the other. In addition, Clyde also received a Form W-2 reporting wages of $23,000 in Box 1. Bonnie and Clyde should report $73,500 ($34,000 + $16,500 + $23,000) on Line 1 of Form 1040 (or Form 1040-SR, if Bonnie or Clyde are age 65 or older). ◆

Box 2 of Form W-2 reports the amount of federal income tax withheld from the taxpayer's wages by the employer for the year. This amount is reported on Line 25a of Forms 1040 and 1040-SR.

Boxes 3 through 6 report information related to the amount of wages subject to Social Security and Medicare taxes and the related taxes withheld. The amounts generally do not impact the income tax reporting by a taxpayer, although as discussed in Chapter 9, when a taxpayer has multiple employers and the amount of Social Security tax withheld exceeds the annual limits of Social Security taxable wages, the excess is treated as an additional tax payment. Note that the amounts in Box 1 and Boxes 3 and 5 often agree but they are not always the same for all taxpayers. For example, if an employee contributes part of their salary to a qualified retirement plan such as a 401(k) plan, the contribution is not generally subject to income tax but is subject to employment taxes. The amount of taxable wages in Box 1 would be lower than the amounts reported in Boxes 3 and 5 by the retirement plan contribution amount. In addition, wages are subject to Social Security tax up to a limit ($137,700 in 2020) and therefore, Box 3 will not exceed the annual limit.

Box 8 reports allocated tips for amounts not included in Box 1 taxable wages. Box 10 is where flexible spending contributions to a dependent care program are reported (see LO 2.5 for more information). Box 12 is for reporting a variety of different forms of compensation such as reimbursed parking, health care premiums paid by the employer, and other fringe benefits. The type of compensation is identified by the code provided adjacent to the amount in Box 12, as described in the instructions to the Form W-2. Commonly used codes are:

Code	Explanation
C	Taxable group life insurance
D	Elective deferral into 401(k) plans
E	Elective deferral into 403(b) plans
G	Elective deferral into 457(b) plans
V	Income from nonstatutory stock options
W	Contributions to a health savings account
DD	Cost of employer-sponsored health care

The retirement plan box in Box 13 will be checked if the taxpayer is eligible to participate in a retirement plan [and thus may limit the amount of deductible IRA (individual retirement account) contributions]. Box 14 is designated to report other forms of compensation as needed.

State and local tax information is reported at the bottom of Form W-2 in Boxes 15 through 20. This includes the taxable wages for state tax purposes and the amount of state income tax withheld which is generally part of the state and local tax itemized deduction (see Chapter 5).

LO 2-2a **Employee versus Independent Contractor**

Business owners are required to correctly determine whether the individuals providing services to their business are employees or independent contractors. Many taxpayers view this as a decision, when in fact, the classification is a function of law and not a choice on the part of either the employer or employee. Potential employees most often accept the choice made by the employer since attempting to negotiate this classification may prevent acquisition of the work. This classification makes a great deal of difference. Generally, an employer must withhold income taxes, withhold and pay Social Security and Medicare taxes, and pay unemployment tax on wages paid to an employee (see Chapter 9). A business does not generally have to withhold or pay any taxes on payments to independent contractors and will generally only have to provide an informational return such as the Form 1099-NEC (Chapter 9). The differences extend beyond just payroll tax liability and processing. For example, employees are far more restricted in deducting employee-related business expenses. Independent contractors are generally not provided benefits and are required to pay self-employment taxes. Because the outcomes differ greatly and the guidance is less well understood, the subject of employee versus independent contractor also tends to be an area of tax controversy.

A potential source of confusion is that the tax code itself does not define employee in any meaningful way. Instead, regulations and court cases have over time congealed into a more-or-less acceptable common law definition that relies heavily on the degree of control and independence between the individual and the business. Characteristics that provide evidence of the degree of control and independence fall into three categories:

1. *Behavioral:* Does the business control or have the right to control what and how the worker does his or her job?
2. *Financial:* Are the business aspects of the worker's job controlled by the payer (how the worker is paid, whether expenses are reimbursed, who provides tools/supplies, etc.)?
3. *Relationship:* Are there written contracts or employee benefits (i.e. pension plan, insurance, vacation pay, etc.)? Will the relationship continue and is the work performed a key aspect of the business?

The IRS released a list of 20 factors to consider in classifying a worker as an employee or an independent contractor. The degree of importance for each factor can vary and no single factor is controlling.

Behavioral Factors

1. Instruction: Employees are more likely to be required to comply with when, where and how the work is to be done.
2. Training: Employees are trained to perform the work.
3. Personally Rendered: Employees must generally perform the work themselves and cannot subcontract the work.
4. Hiring, Supervising and Paying Assistants: Independent contractors have the ability to hire, supervise, and pay assistants and are primarily responsible for the end result.
5. Continuing Relationship: Continuing relationships (even at infrequent intervals) are more common with employees.
6. Work Hours: Independent contractors are more likely to set their own work hours.
7. Time required: Employees work full-time for an employer.
8. Workplace: Employees are generally required to perform work on premises.
9. Sequence of Work: Employees follow the business entity sequence of work.
10. Reports: Employees will be required to submit regular reports whereas an independent contractor's main goal is to deliver results.

Financial Control Factors

11. Payment timing: Employees are paid by time period (hour, week, month). Contractors are paid based on project completion.
12. Travel/Business Expenses: Employees' travel and business expenses are controlled and covered by the employer.
13. Tool and Materials: Furnishing of tools, equipment, or an office indicates employee.
14. Investment: Contractors make a significant investment in the facilities where the work is performed.
15. Profit or loss: Employee generally bear no liability for loss.

Relationship Factors

16. Integration: Employees are more likely to be integrated into business operations.
17. Multiple Engagements: Contractors work for multiple unrelated businesses.
18. Availability of Services: Contractors make their services available to the general public.
19. Right to Discharge: Employees are subject to firing by the business
20. Right to Quit: Employees can quit without breeching any agreements.

EXAMPLE Tabitha works at Pizza Cabana as a cashier. Her manager sets her schedule each week and she was trained by the company's Pizza Cabana University on her job duties and responsibilities. She is naturally expected to perform her role at the restaurant. Tabitha works at Pizza Cabana full time, is paid hourly, and participates in the company's retirement plan. This job is the primary source of Tabitha's income. She can quit at any time but is likely to provide customary two-week notice. Tabitha appears to be under the behavioral, financial, and relationship control of Pizza Cabana and is an employee. ◆

EXAMPLE Tracy drives her own vehicle for a number of different shared delivery services. She tends to drive for Flying Food on the weekends because they are connected to restaurants that have more customers during the weekends. She also delivers food for Snax Car and Mobile Munchies. She checks to see which service seems to have more demand at a particular date or time and logs on to work with that company. Tracy is paid by the delivery and mile by the shared services companies and through tips from customers. She only delivers when she feels like it or really needs the money. All the operating expenses, maintenance, and repairs on her vehicle are her costs to bear. Tracy has more of the characteristics associated with an independent contractor. ♦

The classification of a worker from a federal tax perspective has become more complex with the advent of certain states (for example, California) implementing labor laws designed to classify more workers as employees. Technically, these state-level laws would not control federal tax classification, but from a pragmatic perspective, most businesses would classify workers the same for state and federal purposes.

Self-Study Problem 2.2   *See Appendix E for Solutions to Self-Study Problems*

a Employee's social security number 232-11-4444	OMB No. 1545-0008	Safe, accurate, FAST! Use IRS e-file Visit the IRS website at www.irs.gov/efile

b Employer identification number (EIN) 12-9876543	1 Wages, tips, other compensation 56,000.00	2 Federal income tax withheld 3,456.00
c Employer's name, address, and ZIP code QBI Company 4512 Lake Drive Grand Rapids, MI 49503	3 Social security wages 61,000.00	4 Social security tax withheld 3,782.00
	5 Medicare wages and tips 61,000.00	6 Medicare tax withheld 884.50
	7 Social security tips	8 Allocated tips
d Control number	9	10 Dependent care benefits
e Employee's first name and initial Last name Suff. Summer Sandborne 134 Bostwick Ave NE Grand Rapids, MI 49503	11 Nonqualified plans	12a See instructions for box 12 D	5,000.00
	13 Statutory employee ☐ Retirement plan ☒ Third-party sick pay ☐	12b DD	8,700.00
	14 Other	12c	
		12d	
f Employee's address and ZIP code		

15 State Employer's state ID number MI	16 State wages, tips, etc. 56,000.00	17 State income tax 1,145.00	18 Local wages, tips, etc.	19 Local income tax	20 Locality name

Form **W-2** Wage and Tax Statement   **2020**   Department of the Treasury—Internal Revenue Service

Copy B—To Be Filed With Employee's FEDERAL Tax Return.
This information is being furnished to the Internal Revenue Service.

Based on Summer's Form W-2, determine the following amounts:

a. Taxable wages to report on Line 1 of Form 1040   _____

b. Federal tax payments withheld to report on Line 25a of Form 1040   _____

c. The amount that Summer contributed to her company's 401k plan   _____

ProConnect™ Tax
TIP

Entering wages from a Form W-2 is one of the most common data entry points for a tax preparer. Predictably, wages are entered under the Income section, more specifically, under Wages, Salaries, Tips (W-2). When selecting the Wages subheading, the entire entry screen for the W-2 is presented in the main window. The subheadings on the left-hand margin slide the entry form up and down for easier entry. Any additional W-2s can be added using the [+] tab at the top of the main window. Although the fictional textbook employers do not have import access, using ProConnect, many W-2s can be imported directly from an employer's payroll system. Enter the employer's identification number and click the circular arrow to import wages data.

2-3 ACCIDENT AND HEALTH INSURANCE

Many taxpayers are covered by accident and health insurance plans. These plans pay for the cost of medical care of the taxpayer and any dependents who are insured under the plan. The taxpayer may pay the total premiums of the plan, or his or her employer may pay part or all of the premiums. Taxpayers are allowed liberal exclusions for payments received from these accident and health plans. The taxpayer may exclude the total amount received for payment of medical care. This exclusion applies to any amount paid for the medical care of the taxpayer, his or her spouse, or dependents. The payment may be made to the doctor, the hospital, or the taxpayer as reimbursement for the payment of the expenses. In addition, any premiums paid by a taxpayer's employer are excluded from the taxpayer's income, and the premium payments may be deducted by the employer.

Most accident and health care policies also pay fixed amounts to the insured for loss of the use of a member or function of the body. These amounts may also be excluded from income. For example, a taxpayer who receives $25,000 because he or she is blinded in one eye may exclude the $25,000 from income.

EXAMPLE Bob is a married taxpayer. His employer pays a $750 per month premium on a policy covering Bob and his family. Jean, Bob's wife, is sick during the year and her medical bills amount to $6,500; the insurance company paid $6,000 for the bills. Bob and Jean may exclude from income the $750 per month premium paid by Bob's employer and the $6,000 paid by the insurance company. The $500 not paid by the insurance company is deductible on Bob and Jean's return, subject to the medical expense deduction limitations (see Chapter 5). ♦

Self-Study Problem 2.3 *See Appendix E for Solutions to Self-Study Problems*

Marjorie, a single taxpayer, is an employee of Big State Corporation. Big State Corporation pays premiums of $3,000 on her health insurance for the current year. Also, during the current year, Marjorie has an operation for which the insurance company pays $5,000 to her hospital and doctor. Of the above amounts, how much must Marjorie include in her gross income?

$_____

2-4 MEALS AND LODGING

2.4 Learning Objective

Determine when meals and lodging may be excluded from taxable income.

If certain tests are met, employers may exclude the value of meals and lodging from an employee's taxable income. The exclusion is granted for any meals and lodging furnished by the employer for the convenience of the employer, but only if:

1. The meals are furnished on the business premises of the employer during working hours because the taxpayer must be available for emergency calls or the employer limits the employee to short meal periods, and
2. The lodging is on the business premises and must be accepted as a requirement for employment.

To exclude the value of lodging provided by the employer, the employee must be required to accept the lodging to perform the duties of the job properly. For example, a taxpayer who receives lodging on an offshore oil rig may exclude the value of the lodging from income, since the employee cannot go home at night. The exclusion for lodging also includes the value of utilities such as electricity, water, heat, gas, and similar items that make the lodging habitable.

The value of meals or lodging provided by the employer in other situations, and cash allowances for meals or lodging, must be included in the employee's gross income. Starting in 2018, the business that pays the costs for meals provided for the convenience of an employee may only deduct 50 percent of those costs (the deduction is eliminated after 2025).

Self-Study Problem 2.4   *See Appendix E for Solutions to Self-Study Problems*

In each of the following independent cases, indicate whether the value of the meals or lodging should be included in or excluded from the taxpayer's income.

	Included	Excluded
1. A waiter is required to eat lunch, furnished by his employer, on the premises during a busy lunch hour.	_____	_____
2. A police officer receives a cash allowance to pay for meals while on duty.	_____	_____
3. A worker receives lodging at a remote construction site in Alaska.	_____	_____
4. A taxpayer manages a motel and, although the owner does not require it, she lives at the motel rent free.	_____	_____
5. A bank teller is furnished meals on the premises to limit the time she is away during busy hours.	_____	_____

Learning Objective 2.5

Identify the common employee fringe benefit income exclusions.

2-5 EMPLOYEE FRINGE BENEFITS

The tax law provides that all fringe benefits must be included in the employee's gross income, unless specifically excluded by law. The primary types of fringe benefits that may be excluded from gross income are described below.

2-5a Flexible Spending Accounts

Many employers create formal plans that allow employees to contribute pre-tax money to a special account from their wages to pay for one or more of the expenses listed below. If all the requirements of the plan are met and the employee provides receipts for the expenses incurred, the full amount of expenses reimbursed out of the employee's account will be treated as a tax-free reduction in salary. These accounts may provide significant tax savings for employees, with only a small administrative cost to employers.

EXAMPLE   In 2020, Dina has wage income of $43,000 and elects to defer $2,000 into a health care flexible spending account. She uses all $2,000 of the money for qualifying medical expenses in 2020. Dina's taxable income will be $41,000. The $2,000 is excluded from her income as long as she uses the funds for qualifying medical expenses. ◆

Employees must be aware, however, of the "use-it-or-lose-it" rule for flexible spending accounts (e.g., any balance remaining in the employee's account at December 31 is lost). For health care flexible spending accounts, employers have the option to allow $550 of the unused medical spending account to carry over to 2021 or to offer a $2\frac{1}{2}$-month grace period after year-end to incur additional medical expenses before the employee loses the balance in the account. For flexible spending accounts that permit a grace period, a temporary COVID-19 provision was passed that would allow the grace period to extend to December 30, 2020.

EXAMPLE   Allie contributed $2,700 in 2019 to her health FSA. Her employer typically allows a 2.5-month grace period to pay expenses (through March 15, 2020). Due to COVID-19, Allie was unable to have her orthodontics work done in early 2020 and had to postpone the services until July 2020. Allie's employer is permitting employees a grace period through December 31, 2020 and thus Allie will have her costs paid in July covered by the FSA. ◆

Dependent Care Flexible Spending Accounts

Employers may offer dependent care flexible spending accounts (FSAs) in which employees may set aside up to $5,000 of their salary each year to cover the costs of caring for a dependent child or aging parent. Such costs may include day care, day camp, in-home care and preschool. Dependent care benefits paid will be reported in Box 10 of Form W-2 and are reported on Form 2441 with the Child and Dependent Care Credit. See Chapter 7 for more information.

Health Care Flexible Spending Accounts

Employers may offer health care flexible spending accounts in which employees can set aside up to $2,750 from their 2020 salary to cover medical expenses that they anticipate incurring during the year. These expenses may include eyeglasses, laser-eye surgery, necessary dental work, and health insurance copayments. Amounts used from a health care FSA may not also be deducted as an itemized deduction for medical expenses (see Chapter 5). Health care FSAs should not be confused with Archer medical spending accounts (MSAs) or health savings accounts (HSAs) which are covered in Chapter 5.

Starting in 2020, over-the-counter medicines without a prescription and menstrual care products are both considered medical expenses for purposes of health savings accounts, and health care flexible spending accounts. This extension of the definition of medical expenses does not apply to medical expenses as defined for the itemized deduction (Chapter 5).

Public Transportation, Parking at Work, and Bicycle Commuting

Employees can exclude from gross income payments from employers of up to $270 per month in 2020 (the maximum exclusion is adjusted for inflation) to cover the cost of public transportation to, or parking for, work. However, employers may not deduct these payments to the extent they excluded from the employee's income; thus effectively removing transportation and parking as a qualified fringe benefit. In cases where the employee is being reimbursed transportation or parking costs that are necessary to ensure the safety of the employee, those costs remain deductible. The bicycle commuter fringe is suspended until 2025. Employers may continue to establish a plan whereby an employee's own pre-tax salary is used to pay for public transportation costs and parking up to the exclusion limits. By doing so, these costs are paid for by the employee using pre-tax dollars as the withheld wages used to cover these costs are not subject to income or employment taxes.

2-5b **Group Term Life Insurance**

Employers may pay for up to $50,000 of group term life insurance for employees as a tax-free fringe benefit. Providing group term life insurance to employees must not favor officers, shareholders, or highly compensated personnel.

Internal Revenue Code §79 was first passed in 1964 and provided the exclusion of employer paid group term life insurance premiums up to $50,000. The $50,000 limit has not been adjusted since originally passed into law. In today's dollars, you would need almost $400,000 to equal $50,000 in 1964. The National Funeral Directors Association estimated the median cost of a funeral in 1965 as $790 and over $7,600 in 2019.

2-5c **Education Assistance Plans**

Employers may provide up to $5,250 of excludable annual tuition assistance under an educational assistance plan. The exclusion requires an employer to have a written plan and the educational assistance can be paid to an employee or former employee. Assistance over $5,250 is included in the taxpayer's wages unless otherwise excludable as a working condition benefit that would have been deductible as a business expense (see Chapter 3). For 2020, as part of the COVID-19 relief provisions, payments from an education assistance plan can also be excluded if paid to an employee or lender if the payments are applied toward the employee's student loans.

> **EXAMPLE** Ahmaud's employer offers an education plan that Ahmaud had been taking advantage of every year. Unfortunately, the cost of Ahmaud's college education exceeded $5,250 each year and he was required to take out student loans. Ahmaud graduated in 2019. Before 2021, Ahmaud's employer may pay his student debt up to $5,250 and Ahmaud is not required to include the payment in his income. ♦

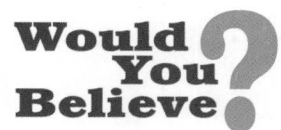

Section 127 of the Code introduced the education assistance plan in 1979. In 1985, the $5,000 exclusion limit was increased to $5,250. According to the College Board, average tuition and fees for a public four-year college in the 1985–1986 school year was $1,318. In 2019–2020, that amount had increased to $10,440. Today's exclusion is about one semester of college tuition. Source: **www.collegeboard.org**

2-5d No-Additional-Cost Services

This category of fringe benefits includes services that are provided to employees and their families at little or no additional cost to the employer, and which would otherwise have remained unused. An airline employee who is allowed to fly at no cost on a standby basis is an example. The value of the airfare may be excluded from the employee's gross income.

Employees are only allowed to receive tax-free services in the major line of business in which they are employed. For example, if an airline company also owns a rental car agency, the employees working in the airline division would not be entitled to the tax-free use of rental cars.

2-5e Qualified Employee Discounts

The value of employee discounts may be excluded from gross income if the discounts are available on a nondiscriminatory basis. That is, the discounts must be available to substantially all full-time employees. The item being discounted must be from the line of business in which the employee is engaged. The discount exclusion also does not apply to discounts on real estate or personal property held for investment. For services provided at a discount, the exclusion is limited to 20 percent of the typical customer price. For merchandise, the exclusion is limited to the employer's gross markup on the goods.

> **EXAMPLE** R.J. works for an auto parts store chain. R.J. purchases a new water pump for her car at the employee discounted price of $26. Normally, the part would be sold for $41. R.J.'s employer's cost for the part is $26. Because R.J.'s cost is not less than the cost of the part to her employer, the discount is within the exemption and is not taxable to R.J. ♦

2-5f Working Condition Fringe Benefits

An employee may exclude the value of property or services provided by an employer to the extent that the cost of the property or services would be a deductible expense of the employee. Examples of this type of exclusion include the use of a company car for business (not personal) purposes and a subscription to a tax journal paid for by a CPA firm.

The working condition fringe benefit rules also allow several expenses which would not be deductible if paid by the employee. These include the value of certain employer-provided education and certain use of demonstrator autos by automobile salespeople.

2-5g De Minimis Fringe Benefits

The value of small fringe benefits may be excluded from an employee's gross income if accounting for the benefits would be impractical. Examples of this type of exclusion include occasional personal use of an office copy machine, personal letters typed by a company administrative assistant, a company picnic for the employees, and small non-cash holiday gifts provided to employees (e.g., a holiday turkey).

If an employer provides a subsidized lunchroom for its employees, the value of the meals may be excluded from the employees' income if (1) the facility is on or near the employer's place of business, (2) the revenue from the lunchroom normally exceeds direct operating costs, and (3) the meals are provided without discrimination to all employees. Starting in 2018, the tax law limits the employer's deduction related to the eating facility to only 50 percent of the cost. Upon the expiration of the provision in 2025, the tax law permits no deduction for such costs.

Cell phones provided to employees primarily for business purposes are considered tax-free de minimis fringe benefits. Examples of cell phones which qualify include those provided to allow employees to communicate with clients, or to allow employers to contact employees in the field or at home.

2-5h Tuition Reduction

All employees of educational institutions may exclude from their income the value of a tuition reduction, if the plan is for an undergraduate education and available to all employees. The exclusion applies to the employees, their spouses, and their dependents. The value of a graduate education tuition reduction plan may only be excluded by graduate students of the institution who are teaching or doing research at that institution.

2-5i Athletic Facilities

Employees may exclude from gross income the value of the use of an athletic facility located on the premises of their employer. The facility must be used primarily by employees.

2-5j Retirement Planning Fringe Benefit

Qualified retirement planning services constitute a fringe benefit that is excluded from income. This change was made to encourage employers to provide retirement planning services for their employees to assist them in preparing for retirement. Qualified retirement planning services are any retirement planning services provided to an employee and his or her spouse by an employer maintaining a "qualified employer plan." The exclusion also applies to advice and information on retirement income planning for an individual and his or her spouse, including how the employer's plan fits into the individual's overall retirement income plan. The exclusion, however, does not apply to services that may be related to tax preparation, accounting, legal, or brokerage services.

EXAMPLE   As part of its qualified plan, Linda's employer provides retirement planning services. Linda has a meeting with a financial planner to review her retirement plan. The cost of the meeting ($600) is paid for by her employer's qualified plan. The $600 is not income to Linda and is deductible to the employer. ◆

A summary of various fringe benefits is provided in Table 2.3.

TABLE 2.3	SUMMARY OF FRINGE BENEFITS	
Type of Fringe	**Summary of Treatment**	**Learning Objective**
Accident and Health Benefits	Exempt except for long-term care provided through a flexible spending arrangement	2.3, 2.5
Achievement Awards	Exempt up to $1,600 for qualified plan awards ($400 for nonqualified)	2.6
Adoption Assistance	Exempt up to $14,300	7.7
Athletic Facilities	Exempt if substantially all use is by employees and families and operated on employer's premises	2.5
De Minimis Benefits	Exempt if property or service provided to employee has so little value that accounting for it would be unreasonable or administratively impracticable (never cash and cash equivalents)	2.5
Dependent Care Assistance	Exempt up to $5,000	2.5
Educational Assistance	Exempt up to $5,250	2.5
Employee Discounts	Exempt with certain limits	2.5
Employee Stock Options	Beyond scope of textbook	
Employer-provided cell phones	Exempt if primarily for business purposes	2.5
Group-term Life Insurance	Exempt up to $50,000	2.5
Health Savings Accounts (HSA)	Exempt up to certain limits	5.1
Lodging on Business Premises	Exempt if for convenience as a condition of employment	2.4
Meals	Exempt if furnished on premises for convenience or de minimis	2.4
Moving Expenses	Exempt if otherwise deductible and related to military service	5.5
No-additional-cost Services	Exempt	2.5
Retirement Planning Services	Exempt	2.5
Transportation (Commuting) Benefits	Exempt up to $270 per month for parking and transit passes and exempt if de minimis	2.5
Tuition Reduction	Exempt if undergraduate or if graduate and employee performs teaching or research	2.5
Working Condition Benefits	Exempt	2.5

Source: Adapted from IRS Publication 15-B.

Self-Study Problem 2.5 *See Appendix E for Solutions to Self-Study Problems*

Indicate in each of the following cases whether the value of the employee fringe benefit is included (I) in or excluded (E) from the employee's gross income.

_____ 1. An employee of a railroad receives a free train-trip pass.

_____ 2. An employee of a department store receives a 25 percent discount on a shirt. The department store's markup is 15 percent.

_____ 3. An employee attends a New Year's party paid for by her employer.

_____ 4. An employee of a stock brokerage firm receives a subscription to a financial newsletter paid for by his employer.

_____ 5. An employee's spouse regularly uses a company car to go shopping.

_____ 6. An airline employee receives a 50 percent discount at a hotel chain owned by her employer while traveling on vacation. The hotel chain has a 30 percent profit margin on rooms.

_____ 7. An employee uses the company's employee fitness room.

Learning Objective 2.6

Determine when prizes and awards are included in income.

2-6 PRIZES AND AWARDS

Prizes and awards are taxable income to the recipient. Winnings from television or radio shows, door prizes, lotteries, and other contest winnings are income to taxpayers. In addition, all other awards are generally taxable, even if they are awards given for accomplishments and with no action on the part of the taxpayer. Even a Nobel prize is taxable. If the prize or award is received in property instead of cash, the fair market value of the property is included in the taxpayer's income. For example, the gift bags given to the attendees at the Academy Awards include items such as expensive jewelry and vacations worth more than $100,000. The value of these gift bags is included in taxable income. Taxpayers may refuse a prize and exclude its value from income.

An exception is provided for certain employee achievement awards in the form of tangible personal property, such as a gold watch for 25 years of service. If the award is made in recognition of length of service or safety achievement, the value of the property may be excluded from income. Generally, the maximum amount excludable is $400. However, if the award is a "qualified plan award," the maximum exclusion is increased to $1,600. The definition of tangible personal property with respect to employee achievement awards excludes cash, cash equivalents, gift cards, gift coupons, gift certificates, vacations, meals, lodging, tickets to theater or sporting events, stocks, bonds, other securities, and other similar items.

EXAMPLE Van enters a drawing and wins a new automobile. The automobile has a sticker price of $20,200. The fair market value of the prize should be included in Van's gross income, but the fair market value is probably not the sticker price; instead, it is the price at which a similar car normally would be sold. ◆

Self-Study Problem 2.6 | *See Appendix E for Solutions to Self-Study Problems*

For each of the following independent cases, indicate the amount of gross income that should be included on the taxpayer's return.

Gross Income

1. Helen enters a radio contest and wins $2,000. $_____

2. Professor Deborah wins an award of $10,000 for a book on literature she published 4 years ago. The award was presented in recognition of her past literary achievements. $_____

3. Bill is a professional baseball player. Because he has hit 50 home runs this season, he was given a new wrist watch worth $2,500. $_____

4. John is an employee of Big Corporation. He is awarded $5,000 for a suggestion to improve the plant layout. $_____

5. Martha received a desk clock worth $350 from her employer in recognition of her 15 years of loyal service as an employee. $_____

2-7 ANNUITIES

2.7 Learning Objective

Calculate the taxable and nontaxable portions of annuity payments.

When taxpayers consider retirement, they often purchase annuities. An annuity is a type of investment in which the taxpayer purchases the right to receive periodic payments for the remainder of his or her life. The amount of each periodic payment is based on the annuity purchase price and the life expectancy of the annuitant. Standard mortality tables, based on the current age of the annuitant, are used to calculate the annuity amount.

2-7a **The Simplified Method**

Individual taxpayers generally must use the "simplified" method to calculate the taxable amount from an annuity for annuities starting after November 18, 1996. Nonqualified plan annuities and certain annuitants age 75 or older must still use the general rule discussed below.

To calculate the excluded amount, the IRS provides the following worksheet.

SIMPLIFIED METHOD WORKSHEET

1. Enter total amount received this year.   1. ___8,000___

2. Enter cost in the plan at the annuity starting date.   2. ___4___

3. Age at annuity starting date

	Enter
55 or under	360
56–60	310
61–65	260
66–70	210
71 or older	160

3. _____

4. Divide line 2 by line 3.   4. _____

5. Multiply line 4 by the number of monthly payments this year. If the annuity starting date was before 1987, also enter this amount on line 8, and skip lines 6 and 7. Otherwise, go to line 6.   5. _____

6. Enter the amount, if any, recovered tax free in prior years.   6. _____

7. Subtract line 6 from line 2.   7. _____

8. Enter the smaller of line 5 or 7.   8. _____

9. Taxable amount this year: Subtract line 8 from line 1. Do not enter less than zero.   9. _____

Note 1: The denominators provided in step 3 above are effective for annuity starting dates after November 18, 1996. For annuity starting dates prior to November 18, 1996, see the IRS website.

Note 2: When annuity benefits with starting dates after 1997 are paid over two lives (joint and survivor annuities), a different set of denominators must be used in step 3.

Combined Age of Annuitants	Number of Payments
110 or under	410
111–120	360
121–130	310
131–140	260
141 or older	210

EXAMPLE Joey, age 67, began receiving benefits under a joint and survivor annuity to be paid over the joint lives of himself and his wife Jody, who is 64. He received his first annuity payment in March of the current year. Joey contributed $38,000 to the annuity and he had no distributions from the plan before the current year. The monthly payment to Joey is $1,700.

Joey must use the simplified method to calculate his taxable amount. Using the worksheet, Joey's taxable amount for the current year would be:

SIMPLIFIED METHOD WORKSHEET

1. Enter total amount received this year.   1. _$17,000.00_

2. Enter cost in the plan at the annuity starting date.   2. _$38,000.00_

3. Combined age at annuity starting date

	Enter
110 or under	410
111–120	360
121–130	310
131–140	260
141 or older	210

3. _____260_____

4. Divide line 2 by line 3.   4. $____146.15____

5. Multiply line 4 by the number of monthly payments this year.   5. $ _1,461.50_

6. Enter the amount, if any, recovered tax free in prior years.   6. $____0.00____

7. Subtract line 6 from line 2.   7. _$38,000.00_

8. Enter the smaller of line 5 or 7.   8. $ _1,461.50_

9. Taxable amount this year: Subtract line 8 from line 1. Do not enter less than zero. ◆   9. _$15,538.50_

The exclusion ratio (the result on line 4 of the Simplified Method Worksheet) is calculated at the start of the annuity and remains constant. For annuities starting after 1986, the maximum amount excludable is limited to the taxpayer's investment in the annuity. After the taxpayer's investment is recovered, all additional amounts received are fully taxable. If the taxpayer dies before the entire investment is recovered, any unrecovered amount is permitted as a miscellaneous itemized deduction (not subject to the 2 percent floor) at the time of the annuitant's death. For annuities starting before 1987, the exclusion ratio is used for the life of the annuitant, even after full recovery of the investment. For these earlier annuities, if the annuitant dies prior to recovering the entire investment, the unrecovered portion is lost.

2-7b **The General Rule**

Prior to implementation of the Simplified Method discussed above, the General Rule was used for most annuities. Rather than use the denominators provided in Step 3 of the Simplified Method Worksheet, the life expectancy of the annuitant was determined based on mortality tables provided by the IRS. The excluded amount under the general rule can be calculated as follows:

$$\text{Amount Excluded} = \frac{\text{Investment in Contract}}{\text{Annual Payment} \times \text{Life Expectancy}} \times \text{Amount Received}$$

2-7c Employee Annuities

Many employees participate in retirement plans organized by their employers. Employers generally make periodic payments to the plans on behalf of their employees. If the payments are made to qualified retirement plans, contributions by the employer are not taxable to the employees in the current year. Since the contributions are not taxable when made, they are not considered part of the employee's investment in the contract when calculating the exclusion ratio.

Self-Study Problem 2.7   *See Appendix E for Solutions to Self-Study Problems*

Part a

Phil retired in January 2020 at age 63. His pension is $1,500 per month from a retirement plan to which Phil contributed $42,500. Phil's life expectancy is 21 years, and this year he received eleven payments for a total pension income of $16,500. Calculate Phil's taxable income from the annuity in the current year, using the general rule.

$_____

Part b

Calculate Phil's taxable income using the following Simplified Method Worksheet.

SIMPLIFIED METHOD WORKSHEET

1. Enter total amount received this year.   1. __16,500__
2. Enter cost in the plan at the annuity starting date.   2. __42,500__
3. Age at annuity starting date

	Enter
55 or under	360
56–60	310
61–65	260
66–70	210
71 or older	160

3. _____

4. Divide line 2 by line 3.   4. _____
5. Multiply line 4 by the number of monthly payments this year. If the annuity starting date was before 1987, also enter this amount on line 8, and skip lines 6 and 7. Otherwise, go to line 6.   5. _____
6. Enter the amount, if any, recovered tax free in prior years.   6. _____
7. Subtract line 6 from line 2.   7. _____
8. Enter the smaller of line 5 or 7.   8. _____
9. Taxable amount this year: Subtract line 8 from line 1. Do not enter less than zero.   9. _____

2-8 LIFE INSURANCE

Life insurance proceeds are excluded from gross income based on the premise that it would be inappropriate in a time of need to tax the proceeds from a life insurance policy. Therefore, a major exclusion from gross income is provided for life insurance proceeds. To be excluded, the proceeds must be paid to the beneficiary by reason of the death of the insured. If the proceeds are taken over several years instead of a lump sum, the insurance company pays interest on the unpaid proceeds. The interest is generally taxable income.

Early payouts of life insurance, also called accelerated death benefits or viatical settlements, are excluded from gross income for certain terminally or chronically ill taxpayers. The taxpayer may either collect an early payout from the insurance company or sell or assign the policy to a viatical settlement provider. A terminally ill individual must be certified by a medical doctor to have an illness which is reasonably expected to cause death within 24 months. A chronically ill individual must be certified by a medical doctor as unable to perform daily living activities without assistance. Chronically ill taxpayers may only exclude gain on accelerated death benefits to the extent proceeds are used for long-term care.

If an insurance policy is transferred to another person for valuable consideration, all or a portion of the proceeds from the life insurance policy may be taxable to the recipient. For example, taxable proceeds result when a policy is transferred to a creditor in payment of a debt. When a transfer for value occurs, the proceeds at the death of the insured are taxable to the extent they exceed the cash surrender value of the policy at the time it was transferred, plus the amount of the insurance premiums paid by the purchaser. There is an exception to the rule that policies transferred for valuable consideration result in taxable proceeds. Transfers to a partner of the insured, a partnership in which the insured is a partner, or a corporation in which the insured is an officer or a shareholder do not cause the policy proceeds to be taxable.

EXAMPLE Howard dies on January 15, 2017, and leaves Wanda, his wife, a $50,000 insurance policy, the proceeds of which she elects to receive as $10,000 per year plus interest for 5 years. In the current year, Wanda receives $12,200 ($10,000 + $2,200 interest). She must include the $2,200 of interest in income. ♦

EXAMPLE David owns a life insurance policy at the time he is diagnosed with a terminal illness. After his diagnosis, he sells the policy to Viatical Settlements, Inc., for $100,000. David is not required to include the gain on the sale of the insurance in his gross income. ♦

EXAMPLE Amy transfers to Bill an insurance policy with a face value of $40,000 and a cash surrender value of $10,000 for the cancellation of a debt owed to Bill. Bill continues to make payments, and after 2 years Bill has paid $2,000 in premiums. Amy dies and Bill collects the $40,000. Since the transfer was for valuable consideration, Bill must include $28,000 in taxable income, which is equal to the $40,000 total proceeds less $10,000 value at the time of transfer and $2,000 of premiums paid. If Amy and Bill were partners in the same partnership, the entire proceeds ($40,000) would be tax free. ♦

Self-Study Problem 2.8   *See Appendix E for Solutions to Self-Study Problems*

On March 19, 2015, Karen dies and leaves Larry an insurance policy with a face value of $100,000. Karen is Larry's sister, and Larry elects to take the proceeds over 10 years ($10,000 plus interest each year). This year Larry receives $13,250 from the insurance company. How much income must Larry report for the current year?

$_____

Learning Objective 2.9

Identify the tax treatment of interest and dividend income.

2-9 INTEREST AND DIVIDEND INCOME

Any interest or dividend income a taxpayer receives or that is credited to his or her account is taxable income, unless it is specifically exempt from tax such as state or municipal bond interest (discussed further in LO 2.10). If the interest or dividends total more than $1,500, the taxpayer is required to file Schedule B of Form 1040, which instructs the taxpayer to list the amounts and sources of the income.

The fair market value of gifts or services a taxpayer receives for making long-term deposits or opening accounts in savings institutions is also taxable interest income. Interest is reported in the year it is received by a cash basis taxpayer.

TAX BREAK

Taxpayers may defer reporting interest income on a bank certificate of deposit (CD) if the CD has a maturity of 1 year or less and there is a substantial penalty for early withdrawal. For example, assume an investor purchases a 6-month CD on September 1, 2020, which matures on March 1, 2021, and the bank charges a penalty equal to 2 months of interest in the event of early withdrawal. In this case, the 4 months of interest earned on the account during 2020 will not have to be reported until the investor's 2021 tax return is filed.

When a taxpayer withdraws funds early from a CD and must pay a penalty as described above, the full amount of the interest is reported as income and the penalty may be deducted on Form 1040 as a deduction for adjusted gross income.

2-9a U.S. Savings Bonds

The U.S. government issues three basic types of savings bonds to individuals: Series EE Bonds, Series HH Bonds, and Series I Bonds. Series EE Bonds, whether sold at a discount (before 2012) or at face value, increase in value over their life, and the increase in redemption value is generally taxable when the bond is redeemed and the interest is paid. The second type of savings bond, Series HH Bond, was issued at face value and pays interest twice a year. Interest on Series HH Bonds is reported in the year received by a cash basis taxpayer. (Note: As of August 31, 2004, the Treasury stopped issuing Series HH bonds. HH bonds sold before August 31, 2004, are still outstanding and paying interest.) Series I Bonds, like Series EE Bonds, do not pay interest until maturity, but earnings are adjusted for inflation on a semiannual basis.

Cash basis taxpayers report the increase in redemption value (interest) on a Series EE Bond or a Series I Bond using one of the following methods:

1. The interest may be reported in the year the bonds are cashed or in the year they mature, whichever is earlier (no election is required to use this method), or
2. The taxpayer may elect to report the increase in redemption value each year.

If the taxpayer wants to change from method (1) to method (2), he or she may do so without the permission of the IRS. In the year of change, all interest earned to date and not previously reported must be reported on all Series EE Bonds and Series I Bonds held by the taxpayer. Once method (2) is selected, the taxpayer must continue to use it for all Series EE Bonds currently held or acquired in the future. Taxpayers cannot change back to method (1) without permission of the IRS.

Would You Believe?

Schedule B of Form 1040 has been around for a long time—the first version appeared as part of the Form 1040 in 1950. The dollar threshold of interest or dividends to require a Schedule B was at $400 in 1974. It was changed to $1,500 in 2002 and remains at that same amount today. Using the Consumer Price Index Inflation Calculator (**www.bls.gov/data/inflation_calculator.htm**), you would need about $2,200 to equal the purchasing power of $400 in 1974.

2-9b **Dividends**

Dividends are a type of distribution paid to a shareholder by a corporation. Taxpayers may receive the following types of distributions from a corporation:

1. Ordinary and qualified dividends
2. Nontaxable distributions
3. Capital gain distributions

Ordinary dividends are by far the most common type of corporate distribution. They are paid from the earnings and profits of the corporation. Ordinary dividends are also qualifying dividends if the stock is held for a certain amount of time (generally 60 days) and the dividend is issued by a U.S. corporation. If the ordinary dividends are not qualifying dividends, then instead of being taxed at the lower long-term capital gains rate, they will be taxed at the ordinary income rate. Corporations issuing dividends and brokerage companies holding stock investments for taxpayers are required to classify and report the amount of qualifying dividends to investors.

Nontaxable distributions are a return of invested capital and are not paid from the earnings and profits of the corporation. They are considered a return of the taxpayer's investment in the corporation and are not included in the taxpayer's income. Instead, the taxpayer's basis in the stock is reduced by nontaxable distributions until the basis reaches zero.[1] After the stock has reached a zero basis, distributions that represent a return of capital are taxed as capital gains. Capital gain distributions are reported on Line 7 of Forms 1040 or 1040-SR or Schedule D, Line 13 (if required otherwise).

2-9c **Current Tax Rates for Dividends**

For years, experts have argued that corporate dividends are taxed twice, once when the corporation pays tax on profits, and once when the dividend is received by the shareholder. To provide some tax relief for individual taxpayers who receive corporate dividends, the tax rates on qualifying dividends are lower than the rates for ordinary income.

Income level	Qualified dividends and long-term capital gains rates*
Married filing jointly	
$0–$80,000	0%
$80,001–$496,600	15%
>$496,600	20%
Single	
$0–$40,000	0%
$40,001–$441,450	15%
>$441,450	20%
Head of household	
$0–$53,600	0%
$53,601–$469,050	15%
>$469,050	20%

*An additional 3.8 percent Medicare tax on net investment income, including qualifying dividends, applies to high-income taxpayers with income over certain thresholds. Please see Chapter 6 for further details.

---

[1]A taxpayer's basis in an investment is usually the cost of the investment. The basis is used to determine the gain or loss when the investment is sold.

Note that the break points between 0 and 15 percent for qualified dividends and long-term capital gains rates are similar to but not the same as the ordinary rate brackets for the same filing status. For example, the single ordinary income rate bracket breaks between 12 and 22 percent at $40,125; whereas the dividend/capital gain rate breaks at $40,000.

EXAMPLE Sandra is a single taxpayer with wage income of $42,200 and qualified dividends of $1,000 in 2020. Assume Sandra has no other deductions or income except the standard deduction. Sandra's taxable income is:

Wage income	$42,200
Qualified dividends	1,000
Standard deduction	(12,400)
Exemption (suspended by TCJA)	0
Taxable income	$30,800

Sandra's income now must be separated into the ordinary and qualified dividends portions:

Taxable income	$30,800
Qualified dividends	(1,000)
Ordinary income	$29,800

The 2020 tax on $29,800 of ordinary income is $3,382. As Sarah's taxable income of $30,800 including the qualified dividend is below $40,000, the threshold for 0 percent qualified dividend and long-term capital gains for a single taxpayer in 2020, her dividend tax rate is 0 percent and thus her total tax liability is $3,382. ◆

EXAMPLE Dee is a single taxpayer with wage income of $45,000 and qualified dividends of $8,000 in 2020. Assume Dee has no other deductions or income except the standard deduction. Dee's taxable income is

Wage income	$45,000
Qualified dividends	8,000
Standard deduction	(12,400)
Exemption (repealed by TCJA)	0
Taxable income	$40,600

Dee's income now must be separated into the ordinary and qualified dividend and long-term capital gain portions:

Taxable income	$40,600
Qualified dividends	(8,000)
Ordinary income	$32,600

The 2020 tax on $32,600 of ordinary income is $3,718. Dee's taxable income without the qualified dividends is below the 15 percent threshold of $40,000 for a single taxpayer in 2020, but her taxable income with qualified dividends of $40,600 is above the threshold; thus a part of the qualified dividend will be taxed at 0 percent and a part at 15 percent. Of her $8,000 qualified dividends, $7,400 is below the $40,000 threshold and is taxed at 0 percent while $600 is above the $40,000 threshold and is taxed at 15 percent for an additional tax of $90 to bring Dee's total tax liability to $3,808. The treatment of Dee's ordinary and qualified dividend income is presented in Figure 2.2.

| FIGURE 2.2 | **TAX RATES FOR QUALIFIED DIVIDENDS AND LONG-TERM CAPITAL GAINS** |

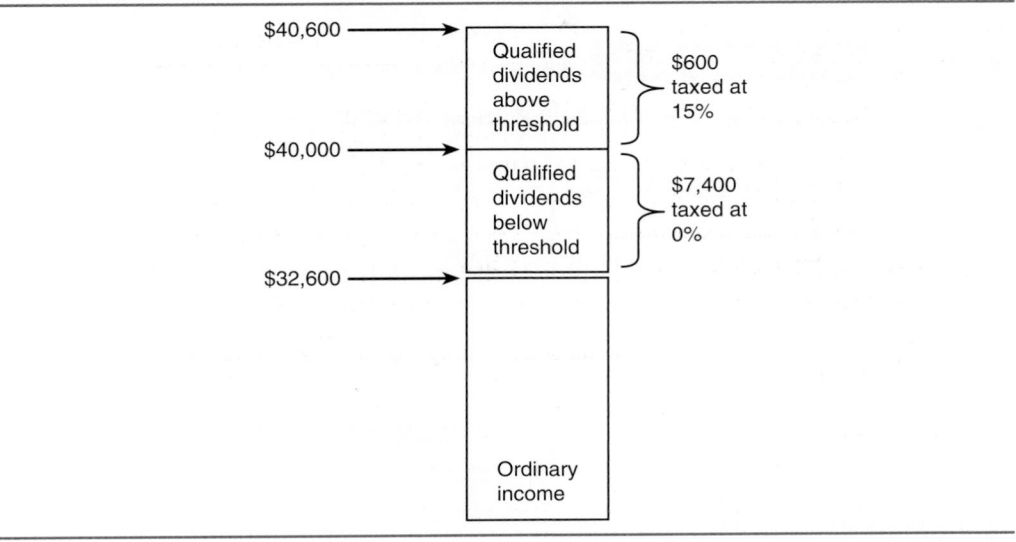

In order to assist with the calculation of preferential taxes on qualified dividends and long-term capital gains, the IRS provides the Qualified Dividends and Capital Gain Tax Worksheet as part of the Form 1040 instructions. This worksheet is presented on Page 2-26. ♦

2-9d Reporting Interest and Dividend Income

Generally, interest or dividend income in amounts greater than $10 must be reported by the payor to the recipient on a Form 1099-INT or Form 1099-DIV. These two forms are presented as part of Self-Study Problem 2-9.

On the Form 1099-INT, most taxable interest is reported in Box 1. The penalty for early withdrawal from a deposit account is reported in Box 2 and is generally deductible as a for AGI deduction (see Chapter 5). Because states may not tax interest from U.S. government obligations such as Treasury Bills, Treasury Bonds, and U.S. savings bonds, interest from these items is reported in Box 3. Tax-exempt interest is reported in Box 8 and to the extent the payor withheld income tax, that amount is reported in Box 4 and should be included on Line 25b of Form 1040. Taxable interest from each payor is reported on Schedule B (shown on Page 2-25) if interest totals more than $1,500 or is simply totaled on Line 2b of Form 1040. Tax-exempt interest is reported on Line 2a of Form 1040 (but not on Schedule B).

Form 1099-DIV reports total ordinary dividends in Box 1a. Box 1b reports the amount of qualified dividends included in Box 1a. These amounts are entered on to Schedule B (if more than $1,500 in total) or directly on to Lines 3a and 3b of Form 1040. Mutual fund investments, and to a lesser degree, corporate stock investments, can also pay capital gain dividends, which are reported in Box 2a of Form 1099-DIV. Unlike ordinary and qualified dividends which are reported by the taxpayer on Schedule B or Form 1040 as described above, capital gain dividends are reported on Schedule D of Form 1040 (see Chapter 4) or if a taxpayer has *only* capital gain distributions reported on Form 1099-DIV, the amount can be reported on Line 7 of Form 1040.

Self-Study Problem 2.9   *See Appendix E for Solutions to Self-Study Problems*

Victor and Grace Alito received the following Forms 1099-INT and 1099-DIV during 2020:

☐ CORRECTED (if checked)

PAYER'S name, street address, city or town, state or province, country, ZIP or foreign postal code, and telephone no. Mango Savings and Loan 600 Tausick Way Walla Walla, WA 99362	Payer's RTN (optional) — OMB No. 1545-0112 — **2020** Form **1099-INT** — **Interest Income**

1 Interest income $ 1,780.00

2 Early withdrawal penalty $

Copy B

PAYER'S TIN 13-2122333   **RECIPIENT'S TIN** 313-44-5454

3 Interest on U.S. Savings Bonds and Treas. obligations $

For Recipient

RECIPIENT'S name Victor Alito

4 Federal income tax withheld $ **5 Investment expenses** $

6 Foreign tax paid $ **7 Foreign country or U.S. possession**

Street address (including apt. no.) 1112 Constitution Ave., NW

8 Tax-exempt interest $ **9 Specified private activity bond interest** $

City or town, state or province, country, and ZIP or foreign postal code Washington, DC 20224

10 Market discount $ **11 Bond premium** $

This is important tax information and is being furnished to the IRS. If you are required to file a return, a negligence penalty or other sanction may be imposed on you if this income is taxable and the IRS determines that it has not been reported.

FATCA filing requirement ☐

12 Bond premium on Treasury obligations $ **13 Bond premium on tax-exempt bond** $

Account number (see instructions)

14 Tax-exempt and tax credit bond CUSIP no.   **15 State   16 State identification no.   17 State tax withheld** $ / $

Form **1099-INT**   (keep for your records)   www.irs.gov/Form1099INT   Department of the Treasury - Internal Revenue Service

☐ CORRECTED (if checked)

PAYER'S name, street address, city or town, state or province, country, ZIP or foreign postal code, and telephone no. Grape Large Cap Index Fund 21251 Stevens Creek Rd. Cupertino, CA 95014	**1a Total ordinary dividends** $ 1,658.00 — OMB No. 1545-0110 — **2020** Form **1099-DIV** — **Dividends and Distributions**

1b Qualified dividends $ 1,600.00

2a Total capital gain distr. $ 200.00   **2b Unrecap. Sec. 1250 gain** $

Copy B
For Recipient

PAYER'S TIN 24-1234567   **RECIPIENT'S TIN** 313-44-5454

2c Section 1202 gain $ **2d Collectibles (28%) gain** $

RECIPIENT'S name Victor and Grace Alito

3 Nondividend distributions $ **4 Federal income tax withheld** $

5 Section 199A dividends $ **6 Investment expenses** $

Street address (including apt. no.) 1112 Constitution Avenue, NW

7 Foreign tax paid $ **8 Foreign country or U.S. possession**

This is important tax information and is being furnished to the IRS. If you are required to file a return, a negligence penalty or other sanction may be imposed on you if this income is taxable and the IRS determines that it has not been reported.

City or town, state or province, country, and ZIP or foreign postal code Washington, DC 20224

9 Cash liquidation distributions $ **10 Noncash liquidation distributions** $

FATCA filing requirement ☐

11 Exempt-interest dividends $ **12 Specified private activity bond interest dividends** $

Account number (see instructions)

13 State   14 State identification no.   15 State tax withheld $ / $

Form **1099-DIV**   (keep for your records)   www.irs.gov/Form1099DIV   Department of the Treasury - Internal Revenue Service

In addition, the Alitos also received $400 of tax-exempt interest. The Alitos file jointly and have taxable income, including interest and dividends of $42,000.

Complete Schedule B of Form 1040 and the Qualified Dividends and Capital Gain Tax Worksheet on Pages 2–25 and 2–26 for the Alito's 2020 tax year.

Self-Study Problem 2.9

SCHEDULE B (Form 1040)	Interest and Ordinary Dividends	OMB No. 1545-0074
Department of the Treasury Internal Revenue Service (99)	▶ Go to *www.irs.gov/ScheduleB* for instructions and the latest information. ▶ Attach to Form 1040 or 1040-SR.	20**20** Attachment Sequence No. **08**

Name(s) shown on return | Your social security number

Part I

Interest

(See instructions and the instructions for Forms 1040 and 1040-SR, line 2b.)

Note: If you received a Form 1099-INT, Form 1099-OID, or substitute statement from a brokerage firm, list the firm's name as the payer and enter the total interest shown on that form.

1 List name of payer. If any interest is from a seller-financed mortgage and the buyer used the property as a personal residence, see the instructions and list this interest first. Also, show that buyer's social security number and address ▶

	Amount
	1

2 Add the amounts on line 1 . . . . | **2** |

3 Excludable interest on series EE and I U.S. savings bonds issued after 1989. Attach Form 8815 . . . . | **3** |

4 Subtract line 3 from line 2. Enter the result here and on Form 1040 or 1040-SR, line 2b . . . . ▶ | **4** |

Note: If line 4 is over $1,500, you must complete Part III.

Part II

Ordinary Dividends

(See instructions and the instructions for Forms 1040 and 1040-SR, line 3b.)

Note: If you received a Form 1099-DIV or substitute statement from a brokerage firm, list the firm's name as the payer and enter the ordinary dividends shown on that form.

5 List name of payer ▶

	Amount
	5

6 Add the amounts on line 5. Enter the total here and on Form 1040 or 1040-SR, line 3b . . . . ▶ | **6** |

Note: If line 6 is over $1,500, you must complete Part III.

Part III

Foreign Accounts and Trusts

Caution: If required, failure to file FinCEN Form 114 may result in substantial penalties. See instructions.

You must complete this part if you **(a)** had over $1,500 of taxable interest or ordinary dividends; **(b)** had a foreign account; or **(c)** received a distribution from, or were a grantor of, or a transferor to, a foreign trust.

		Yes	No
7a	At any time during 2020, did you have a financial interest in or signature authority over a financial account (such as a bank account, securities account, or brokerage account) located in a foreign country? See instructions		
	If "Yes," are you required to file FinCEN Form 114, Report of Foreign Bank and Financial Accounts (FBAR), to report that financial interest or signature authority? See FinCEN Form 114 and its instructions for filing requirements and exceptions to those requirements		
b	If you are required to file FinCEN Form 114, enter the name of the foreign country where the financial account is located ▶		
8	During 2020, did you receive a distribution from, or were you the grantor of, or transferor to, a foreign trust? If "Yes," you may have to file Form 3520. See instructions		

For Paperwork Reduction Act Notice, see your tax return instructions. | Cat. No. 17146N | Schedule B (Form 1040) 2020

Self-Study Problem 2.9

Qualified Dividends and Capital Gain Tax Worksheet—Line 16

Before you begin:	✓ See the earlier instructions for line 16 to see if you can use this worksheet to figure your tax.
	✓ Before completing this worksheet, complete Form 1040 or 1040-SR through line 15.
	✓ If you don't have to file Schedule D and you received capital gain distributions, be sure you checked the box on Form 1040 or 1040-SR, line 7.

1. Enter the amount from Form 1040 or 1040-SR, line 15. However, if you are filing Form 2555 (relating to foreign earned income), enter the amount from line 3 of the Foreign Earned Income Tax Worksheet . . . . **1.** _____

2. Enter the amount from Form 1040 or 1040-SR, line 3a* . . . . **2.** _____

3. Are you filing Schedule D?*

   ☐ **Yes.** Enter the **smaller** of line 15 or 16 of Schedule D. If either line 15 or 16 is blank or a loss, enter -0-.

   ☐ **No.** Enter the amount from Form 1040 or 1040-SR, line 7. } **3.** _____

4. Add lines 2 and 3 . . . . **4.** _____

5. If filing Form 4952 (used to figure investment interest expense deduction), enter any amount from line 4g of that form. Otherwise, enter -0- . . . . **5.** _____

6. Subtract line 5 from line 4. If zero or less, enter -0- . . . . **6.** _____

7. Subtract line 6 from line 1. If zero or less, enter -0- . . . . **7.** _____

8. Enter:

   $40,000 if single or married filing separately,

   $80,000 if married filing jointly or qualifying widow(er), $53,600 if head of household. } . . . . **8.** _____

9. Enter the smaller of line 1 or line 8 . . . . **9.** _____

10. Enter the smaller of line 7 or line 9 . . . . **10.** _____

11. Subtract line 10 from line 9. This amount is taxed at 0% . . . . **11.** _____

12. Enter the smaller of line 1 or line 6 . . . . **12.** _____

13. Enter the amount from line 11 . . . . **13.** _____

14. Subtract line 13 from line 12 . . . . **14.** _____

15. Enter:

    $441,450 if single,
    $248,300 if married filing separately,
    $496,600 if married filing jointly or qualifying widow(er),
    $469,050 if head of household. } . . . . **15.** _____

16. Enter the smaller of line 1 or line 15 . . . . **16.** _____

17. Add lines 7 and 11 . . . . **17.** _____

18. Subtract line 17 from line 16. If zero or less, enter -0- . . . . **18.** _____

19. Enter the smaller of line 14 or line 18 . . . . **19.** _____

20. Multiply line 19 by 15% (0.15) . . . . **20.** _____

21. Add lines 11 and 19 . . . . **21.** _____

22. Subtract line 21 from line 12 . . . . **22.** _____

23. Multiply line 22 by 20% (0.20) . . . . **23.** _____

24. Figure the tax on the amount on line 7. If the amount on line 7 is less than $100,000, use the Tax Table to figure the tax. If the amount on line 7 is $100,000 or more, use the Tax Computation Worksheet . . . . **24.** _____

25. Add lines 20, 23, and 24 . . . . **25.** _____

26. Figure the tax on the amount on line 1. If the amount on line 1 is less than $100,000, use the Tax Table to figure the tax. If the amount on line 1 is $100,000 or more, use the Tax Computation Worksheet . . . . **26.** _____

27. **Tax on all taxable income.** Enter the **smaller** of line 25 or 26. Also include this amount on the entry space on Form 1040 or 1040-SR, line 16. If you are filing Form 2555, don't enter this amount on the entry space on Form 1040 or 1040-SR, line 16. Instead, enter it on line 4 of the Foreign Earned Income Tax Worksheet . . . . **27.** _____

If you are filing Form 2555, see the footnote in the Foreign Earned Income Tax Worksheet before completing this line.

This worksheet adapted from the 2019 worksheet.

2-10 MUNICIPAL BOND INTEREST

In 1913 when the Sixteenth Amendment was enacted, Congress questioned the constitutionality of taxing the interest earned on state and local government obligations. Congress provided an exclusion from taxpayers' income for the interest on such bonds. To qualify for the exclusion, the interest must be from an obligation of a state, territory, or possession of the United States, or a political subdivision of the foregoing or of the District of Columbia. For example, Puerto Rico bonds qualify for the exclusion. Federal obligations, such as treasury bills and treasury bonds, do not qualify.

The interest exclusion allows high-income taxpayers to lend money to state and local governments at lower interest rates (discounts).

EXAMPLE Rigby is considering two different bond investments. This first option is a corporate taxable bond that yields a pre-tax return of 8.4 percent. The second option is a tax-exempt municipal bond that yields 6.5 percent. If Rigby is in the 35 percent tax bracket, the after-tax return of the taxable bonds can be computed as:

$$\text{After-tax return} = \text{Pre-tax return} \times (1 - \text{tax rate})$$
$$5.46\% = 8.4\% \times (1 - 0.35)$$

Since the tax-exempt bond is not subject to tax, the after-tax return is 6.5 percent and thus is preferable. Using a re-arranged version of the same formula can determine what the equivalent yield on a taxable bond would need to be to make Rigby indifferent between the two bonds (all other terms being equal):

$$\text{After-tax return} = \text{Tax-free return} / (1 - \text{tax rate})$$
$$10.0\% = 6.5\%/(1 - 0.35) \; \blacklozenge$$

Typically, interest rates on municipal bonds reflect the after-tax return that compensates for higher income tax rates (35 or 37 percent) and thus tax-exempt bonds will often have a lower after-tax yield than a taxable bond in the hands of a lower-income investor.

EXAMPLE Mordecai is also considering the same bonds as Rigby in the previous example; however, Mordecai is in the 22 percent tax bracket. The after-tax return on the corporate bond is 6.55 percent [8.4% × (1 − 0.22)]. In Mordecai's situation, the after-tax return on the taxable corporate bond is greater than the tax-exempt return of 6.5 percent on the municipal bond. ♦

Taxpayers in low tax brackets are likely to find that they earn a higher overall return investing in taxable bonds rather than comparable tax-free municipal bonds. This is because the smaller tax benefit from the municipal bonds does not make up for the reduced interest rate paid on municipal bonds. Municipal bonds are also generally not appropriate investments for IRAs or other retirement accounts since income on these accounts is excluded from tax until withdrawn.

TAX BREAK

Self-Study Problem 2.10   *See Appendix E for Solutions to Self-Study Problems*

Calculate the taxable interest rate that will provide the equivalent after-tax return in the cases that follow.

1. A taxpayer is in the 24 percent tax bracket and invests in a San Diego City Bond paying 7 percent. What taxable interest rate will provide the same after-tax return?

_____%

2. A taxpayer is in the 32 percent tax bracket and invests in a New York State Bond paying 6.5 percent. What taxable interest rate will provide the same after-tax return?

_____%

ProConnect™ Tax

TIP

Interest and dividends are both common forms of income in addition to wages. The way the two items are reported is slightly different and not always intuitive. Tax-exempt interest (which is entered on Line 2a of Form 1040) is not included as part of taxable interest (Line 2b). Qualified dividends (line 3a), however, are included as part of ordinary dividends (Line 3b). Interest and Dividends are both located in ProConnect under Income and have a Quick Entry and a 1099 entry screen (with Box numbers presented) available. Quick Entry handles most Forms 1099-INT and Forms 1099-DIV; however, should one wish to use the detailed entry screens, they will appear in the left-hand margin when Quick Entry is open. One can always return to Quick Entry using the link at the top of the detail entry form (especially if there is a need to enter additional Forms 1099).

Learning Objective 2.11

Identify the general rules for the tax treatment of gifts and inheritances.

2-11 GIFTS AND INHERITANCES

Taxpayers are allowed to exclude from income the fair market value of gifts and inheritances received, but income received from the property after such a transfer is generally taxable. Normally, the gift tax or estate tax is paid by the donor or the decedent's estate; such property is, therefore, usually tax free to the person receiving the gift or inheritance.

One tax problem that may arise concerning a gift is the definition of what constitutes a gift. The courts define a gift as a voluntary transfer of property without adequate consideration. Gifts made in a business setting are suspect since they may be disguised payments for goods or services. The courts are likely to rule that gifts in a business setting are taxable income, even if there was no obligation to make the payment. Also, if the recipient renders services for the gift, it will be presumed to be income for the services performed.

EXAMPLE   In January of the current year, Richard inherits shares of Birch Corporation stock worth $22,000. After receiving the stock, he is paid $1,300 in dividends during the current year. His gross income from the inheritance in the current year would be $1,300. The $22,000 fair market value of the stock is excluded from gross income. ♦

Self-Study Problem 2.11   *See Appendix E for Solutions to Self-Study Problems*

Don is an attorney who supplied a list of potential clients to a new attorney, Lori. This list aided in the success of Lori's practice. Lori was very pleased and decided to do something for Don. In the current year, Lori gives Don a new car worth $40,000. Lori was not obligated to give this gift to Don, and she did not expect Don to perform future services for the gift. How much income, if any, should Don report from this transaction? Explain your answer.

Income $_____

Explain _____

_____

2-12 SCHOLARSHIPS

2.12 Learning Objective

Describe the elements of scholarship income that are excluded from tax.

A scholarship is an amount paid or awarded to, or for the benefit of, a student to aid in the pursuit of his or her studies. Scholarships granted to degree candidates are taxable income, with the exception of amounts spent for tuition, fees, books, and course-required supplies and equipment. Therefore, scholarship amounts received for items such as room and board are taxable to the recipient.

EXAMPLE In 2020, Diane receives a $5,000 scholarship to study accounting at Big State University. Diane's expenses for tuition and books amount to $1,200 during the fall semester; therefore, she would have taxable income of $3,800 ($5,000 − $1,200) from the scholarship. ♦

Payments received by students for part-time employment are not excludable; they are taxable as compensation. For example, students in work–study programs must include their compensation in gross income. Some scholarships will be reported on Form 1098-T. This form is discussed further in Chapter 7.

Self-Study Problem 2.12   *See Appendix E for Solutions to Self-Study Problems*

Indicate whether each item below would be included in or excluded from the income of the recipient in 2020.

	Included	*Excluded*
1. A $2,000 National Merit Scholarship for tuition	_____	_____
2. A basketball scholarship for room and board	_____	_____
3. Payments under a work–study program	_____	_____
4. Salary for working at Beech Research Laboratory	_____	_____
5. A scholarship for $10,000 to cover qualified costs of $7,600.	_____	_____
6. Payment received from an employer while on leave working on a research project	_____	_____

2-13 ALIMONY

2.13 Learning Objective

Describe the tax treatment of alimony and child support.

The term alimony, for income tax purposes, includes separate maintenance payments or similar periodic payments made to a spouse or former spouse. Payments must meet certain requirements to be considered alimony.

1. The payments must be in cash and must be received by the spouse (or former spouse).
2. The payments must be made under a decree of divorce or separate maintenance or under a written instrument incident to the divorce.
3. The payor must have no liability to make payments for any period following the death of the spouse receiving the payments.
4. The payments must not be designated in the written agreement as anything other than alimony.
5. If the parties are divorced or legally separated, they must not be members of the same household at the time the payments are made.

Disguised child support payments may not be treated as alimony. Payments contingent on the status of a child, such as the age or marital status of the child, are not considered alimony.

EXAMPLE   Under a 2014 divorce agreement, Sam has agreed to pay his former spouse, Silvia, $1,000 per month. The payments meet all the tests for classification as alimony, but they will be reduced to $600 per month when their child, in Silvia's custody, becomes 18 years of age. In this situation, $400 of each payment must be treated as nondeductible child support and cannot be considered alimony. ♦

Under previous tax law, alimony was deductible by the payer and includable in income by the recipient. However, the alimony provisions were repealed and these amounts are neither includable nor deductible for divorce and separation agreements entered after December 31, 2018. For alimony paid pursuant to a divorce or separation instrument executed on or before December 31, 2018, alimony is deductible by the payor and included by the recipient unless the agreement is modified and the modification expressly provides that the new tax law applies to such modification.

EXAMPLE   Brad and Jen were married in 2015. The relationship did not work out and they divorced in 2016. The divorce decree required Brad to pay Jen alimony of $1,000 per month. Because this divorce was effective prior to 2019, the alimony is deductible by Brad and is gross income to Jen. ♦

EXAMPLE   Miley and Liam were married in 2018. The relationship did not work out and they divorced in 2020. Miley is required to pay Liam alimony of $1,000 per month. The alimony is neither deductible to Miley nor included in Liam's gross income. ♦

2-13a Property Transfers

A spouse who transfers property in settlement of a marital obligation is not required to recognize any gain as a result of the property's appreciation. Thus, if in a divorce settlement, a wife transfers property with a fair market value of $10,000 and a tax basis of $3,000 to her husband, she will not be required to recognize the gain of $7,000 ($10,000 − $3,000). Of course, the husband would be required to assume the wife's tax basis ($3,000) in the property. The transfer of property in settlement of a divorce is not considered alimony and there is no deduction by the spouse who transfers the property, nor is it income to the recipient.

2-13b Child Support

Payments made for child support are not deductible by the taxpayer making them, nor are they income to the recipient. However, they may be an important factor in determining which spouse is entitled to claim the dependent child (see Chapter 1). Child support payments must be up to date before any amount paid may be treated as alimony. That is, if a taxpayer is obligated to pay both child support and alimony, he or she must first meet the child support obligation before obtaining a deduction for alimony payments (for divorce agreements prior to 2019). Payments for child support include payments designated as such in the marital settlement agreement, plus any alimony payments that are contingent upon the status of a child.

EXAMPLE   Jim is required under a 2013 divorce decree to pay $400 in alimony and $250 in child support per month. Since the decree separately states that $250 is child support, only $400 per month is deductible by Jim and counts as income to his ex-wife. ♦

ProConnect™ Tax

TIP

Income from alimony, when applicable, is reported in the Income section under SS Benefits, Alimony, Misc. Income (SS Bene., Misc. Inc.). Once this heading is clicked, Alimony and Other Income will be presented as a subheading. Deductible alimony paid, when applicable, is reported under Deductions. Once Adjustments to Income is clicked, a series of subheadings is presented including Alimony Paid.

Self-Study Problem 2.13   *See Appendix E for Solutions to Self-Study Problems*

A taxpayer (payor ex-spouse) is required to pay an ex-spouse (recipient ex-spouse) alimony of $12,000 per year. Determine how much alimony is deductible by the payor ex-spouse and how much alimony is recognized as income by the recipient ex-spouse based on the following information:

Details	*Deductible by payor*	*Includable by recipient*
a. The payments are made in 2020 as part of a divorce decree executed in 2018. The divorce decree is modified in 2020 to explicitly apply the provisions of the TCJA.	_____	_____
b. The payments are made in 2020 as part of a divorce decree executed in 2016.	_____	_____
c. The payments are made in 2020 as part of a divorce decree executed in 2020.	_____	_____

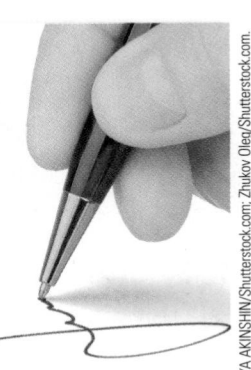

Sign Here	Under penalties of perjury, I declare that I have examined this return and accompanying schedules and statements, and to the best of my knowledge and belief, they are true, correct, and complete. Declaration of preparer (other than taxpayer) is based on all information of which preparer has any knowledge.			
	Your signature	Date	Your occupation	If the IRS sent you an Identity Protection PIN, enter it here (see inst.) ▶
Joint return? See instructions. Keep a copy for your records.	Spouse's signature. If a joint return, **both** must sign.	Date	Spouse's occupation	If the IRS sent your spouse an Identity Protection PIN, enter it here (see inst.) ▶
	Phone no.	Email address		
Paid Preparer Use Only	Preparer's name	Preparer's signature		Date	PTIN	Check if: ☐ Self-employed
	Firm's name ▶			Phone no.
	Firm's address ▶			Firm's EIN ▶

Would You Sign This Tax Return?

For the last 10 years, you prepared the joint tax returns for Dominic (husband; age 40) and Dulce (wife; age 35) Divorcio. In 2018, they got a divorce and remained as your separate tax clients. Under the dissolution decree, Dominic has to pay Dulce $2,500 per month alimony, which he does for the current year. You have completed Dominic's tax return for the current year and you deducted the required alimony payments to Dulce on Dominic's Form 1040. Dulce came in to have you prepare her tax return and refused to report her alimony received as income. She stated, "I am not going to pay tax on the $30,000 from Dominic." She views the payments as "a gift for putting up with him for all those years of marriage." Dulce will not budge on excluding this alimony from income. Would you sign the Paid Preparer's declaration (see example above) on this return? Why or why not?

Learning Objective 2.14	2-14 **EDUCATIONAL INCENTIVES**

Explain the tax implications of using educational savings vehicles.

2-14a Qualified Tuition Programs (QTP)

A Qualified Tuition Program (more commonly referred to as a Section 529 tuition plan) allows taxpayers (1) to buy in-kind tuition credits or certificates for qualified higher education expenses (a prepaid tuition plan) or (2) to contribute to an account established to meet qualified higher education expenses (a savings-type plan). Such Section 529 plans may be sponsored by a state government or a private institution of higher learning. Section 529 plans permit tax-free distributions if the distribution is used for qualified higher education expenses. Qualified higher education expenses include tuition, fees, books, supplies, and equipment required for the enrollment or attendance at an eligible educational institution. In addition, reasonable room and board costs, subject to certain limitations, are also qualified expenses allowed to be paid from the Section 529 tuition plan. Qualified higher education expenses also include tuition in connection with enrollment or attendance at an elementary or secondary public, private, or religious school. The use of the specific term "tuition" excludes other types of qualifying education expenses such as books, supplies, and equipment for elementary or secondary students. The maximum exclusion for elementary or secondary education (i.e., K-12) is $10,000 per beneficiary per year.

EXAMPLE   Walt and Skyler Blanco have two children, Jesse and Jane, and established 529 plans for both of them many years ago. Jesse is now in his second year of college at Albuquerque Community College and Jane is a junior at Albuquerque High School for Math and Science, a private high school. In 2020, the Blancos have $3,500 distributed from the 529 plan with Jesse as the named beneficiary to pay for his community college tuition, books, and course-related supplies. Jane's private school tuition is much higher and the Blancos distribute $12,000 from the 529 plan for which she is the beneficiary. $11,000 of the distribution is used to pay for tuition, $550 for books, and $450 for her private school uniforms. The Blancos may exclude $13,500 of the distributions. Jesse's $3,500 distribution meets the definition of qualified higher education expenses. Only $10,000 of Jane's distribution meets the definition of qualified higher education expenses. The remaining $1,000 of Jane's tuition is in excess of the annual limit and her books and uniform costs do not qualify. ♦

The definition of qualified higher education costs that are eligible for exclusion from income when distributed from a Section 529 plan was expanded retroactively to the start of 2019. Distributions of up to $10,000 used to pay student loan principal or interest for the plan beneficiary or a sibling are also now excluded from gross income. The student loan distributions can be made for the benefit of the plan's beneficiary or for the benefit of the beneficiary's sibling(s), or both. However, the $10,000 limit related to student loan principal or interest payments is a lifetime limit for any single beneficiary.

EXAMPLE   Breonna graduated college in 2019 and has a remaining student loan debt balance in 2020 of $13,000. Breonna's brother Christian is a current college student and is the beneficiary of Section 529 qualified tuition plan. In 2020, a $16,000 distribution is made to Christian to pay for his qualified higher education expenses. In addition, the same plan makes a $10,000 distribution to Breonna to pay her student loans. Neither Breonna nor Christian will be required to include the distribution in income. Breonna will not be eligible for any additional exclusion on Section 529 distributions for loans in the future as she has met her lifetime limit; however, if Christian finishes college with student loan debt, his $10,000 lifetime limit remains available. ♦

Taxpayers may not exclude student loan interest under these provisions and also deduct the same interest as a for AGI student loan interest deduction (Chapter 5). In an additional expansion of qualified higher education costs, 529 distributions used to pay for costs for apprenticeship programs which are registered and certified are now eligible to be excluded from income. The U.S, Department of Labor certifies such programs.

The earnings portion of 529 plan distributions that are not used for qualified tuition expenses are includable in the distributee's gross income under the annuity income rules and are subject to a 10 percent early withdrawal penalty.

Unlike Educational Savings Accounts, discussed later in this section, there is no income limit on the amount of contributions to a Section 529 plan. Like an Educational Savings Account, however, the contributions are not deductible. Any contributions are gifts, and thus subject to the gift tax rules. In addition, most programs impose some form of overall maximum contribution for each beneficiary based on estimated future higher education expenses.

EXAMPLE Bill has AGI of $275,000 and has two children. He chooses to contribute $9,000 (he is allowed to contribute any amount up to the limit imposed by his state's law) to a QTP for each of his children in 2020, even with his high AGI. The $18,000 is not deductible to Bill. Any earnings on the contribution accumulate tax free and are excluded from gross income if used for future qualified higher education expenses. ♦

A taxpayer may claim an American Opportunity credit or lifetime learning credit (discussed in detail in Chapter 7) for a tax year and exclude from gross income amounts distributed (both the principal and the earnings portions) from a qualified tuition program on behalf of the same student. This is true as long as the distribution is not used for the same expenses for which a credit was claimed. However, the amount of qualified higher education expenses for a tax year for purposes of calculating the exclusion from income must be reduced by scholarships, veterans' benefits, military reserve benefits, employer-provided educational assistance amounts, and the tuition amounts used to generate the American Opportunity and lifetime learning credits.

EXAMPLE In 2020, Sammy receives $15,000 from a qualified tuition program. He uses the funds to pay for his college tuition and other qualified higher education expenses. Sammy also claims an American Opportunity credit of $1,500 for the year, using the expenses paid from the Section 529 plan funds. For purposes of the Section 529 plan exclusion calculation, the $15,000 must be reduced to $13,500 ($15,000 − $1,500). ♦

The tax law provides that if the total distributions from a Section 529 plan and from an educational savings account exceed the total amount of qualified higher education expenses, the taxpayer will have to allocate the expenses among the distributions for purposes of determining how much of each distribution is excludable.

If Section 529 funds are used to pay for qualified higher education expenses that are then refunded because of classes being canceled or university housing closing, and if those funds are redeposited within 60 days of the refund, the tax and 10 percent penalty are waived.

TAX BREAK

2-14b Educational Savings Accounts

Taxpayers are allowed to set up educational savings accounts, also known as Coverdell Education Savings Accounts, to pay for qualified education expenses. The maximum amount a taxpayer can contribute annually to an educational savings account for a beneficiary is $2,000. Contributions are not deductible and are subject to income limits. Contributions cannot be made to an educational savings account after the date on which the designated beneficiary becomes 18 years old. In addition, contributions cannot be made to a beneficiary's educational savings account during any year in which contributions are made to a qualified state tuition program (such as a 529 saving plan) on behalf of the same beneficiary. The educational savings account exclusion for distributions of income is available in any tax year in which the beneficiary claims the American Opportunity credit or the lifetime learning credit (see Chapter 7), provided the distribution is not used for the same expenses for which the credit was claimed.

Contributions to educational savings accounts are phased out between AGIs of $95,000 and $110,000 for single taxpayers and $190,000 and $220,000 for married couples who file a joint return (these limits are not adjusted annually for inflation). Like regular and Roth IRAs, contributions applied to the current tax year must be made by April 15 (or the next business day, if April 15 falls on a weekend or holiday) of the following year.

EXAMPLE Joe, who is single, would like to contribute $2,000 to an educational savings account for his 12-year-old son. However, his AGI is $105,000, so his contribution is limited to $667, calculated as follows:

$$\frac{(\$110,000 \text{ upper limit} - \$105,000 \text{ AGI})}{\$15,000} \times \$2,000 = \$667 \text{ contribution}$$

$15,000 is the difference between the upper ($110,000) and lower ($95,000) phase-out limits. ◆

TAX BREAK

For parents with income above the allowable limit, a gift may be made to a child and the child may make the contribution to an educational savings account. There is no requirement that the contributor have earned income as there is for IRAs.

Amounts received from an educational savings account are tax free if they are used for qualified education expenses. Qualified education expenses include tuition, fees, books, supplies, and related equipment for private, elementary, and secondary school expenses as well as for college. Room and board also qualify if the student's course load is at least 50 percent of the full-time course load. If the distributions during a tax year exceed qualified education expenses, part of the excess is treated as a return of capital (the contributions), and part is treated as a distribution of earnings. The distribution is presumed to be pro rata from each category. The exclusion for the distribution of earnings is calculated as follows:

$$\frac{\text{Qualified education expenses}}{\text{Total distribution}} \times \text{Earnings} = \text{Exclusion}$$

EXAMPLE Amy receives a $2,000 distribution from her educational savings account. She uses $1,800 to pay for qualified education expenses. Immediately prior to the distribution, Amy's account balance is $5,000, $3,000 of which are her contributions. Because 60 percent ($3,000/$5,000) of her account balance represents her contributions, $1,200 ($2,000 × 60%) of the distribution is a tax-free return of capital and $800 ($2,000 × 40%) is a distribution of earnings. The excludable amount of the earnings is calculated as follows:

$$\frac{\$1,800}{\$2,000} \times \$800 = \$720 \text{ is excludable (thus, the amount taxable is \$80,}$$
$$\text{or } \$800 - \$720).$$

Amy's adjusted basis for her savings account is reduced to $1,800 ($3,000 − $1,200). ◆

2-14c Higher Education Expenses Deduction

The higher education expense deduction had expired at the end of 2017 but was retroactively restored through the end of 2020.

Taxpayers are allowed a for AGI or "above-the-line" deduction for qualified tuition and related expenses incurred during the tax year. The deduction is allowed for qualified tuition and related expenses for enrollment at an institution of higher education during the tax year. In addition, the deduction is allowed for qualified expenses paid during a tax year if those expenses are in connection with an academic term beginning during the tax year or during the first 3 months of the next tax year. The tuition expense deduction is currently scheduled to expire at the end of 2020.

EXAMPLE Jerry pays $2,000 for his son's college tuition in November 2020 for the spring 2021 term. The spring term starts in January 2021. The $2,000 is deductible in 2020, even though it is for education provided in a later tax year. ◆

The deduction cannot exceed a specified annual amount. The deduction is $4,000 for single and head of household taxpayers with modified AGI below $65,000 and for married filing jointly taxpayers with modified AGI below $130,000. The amount is $2,000 for single taxpayers with modified AGI between $65,000 and $80,000 and for married joint filers with modified AGI between $130,000 and $160,000. Taxpayers with AGI exceeding the limits are not allowed a deduction.

Self-Study Problem 2.14   *See Appendix E for Solutions to Self-Study Problems*

a. Abby has a distribution of $10,000 from a qualified tuition program, of which $3,000 represents earnings. The funds are used to pay for her daughter's qualified higher education expenses. How much of the $10,000 distribution is taxable to the daughter?

$_____

b. During 2020, Henry (a single taxpayer) has a salary of $85,000 and interest income of $4,000. Henry has no other income or deductions. Calculate the maximum contribution Henry is allowed for an educational savings account.

$_____

c. In 2020, Esther, a single taxpayer, paid graduate tuition and fees of $3,500 for the spring semester and $4,300 for the fall semester at the University of State. Esther's AGI in 2020 is $70,000. How much can Esther deduct as a tuition deduction in 2020?

$_____

2-15 UNEMPLOYMENT COMPENSATION

2.15 Learning Objective

Describe the tax treatment of unemployment compensation.

Unemployment compensation payments are fully taxable. Unemployment compensation is generally reported on a Form 1099-G.

EXAMPLE Genny was unemployed for several months during 2020 and received unemployment compensation of $4,000. The $4,000 is included in Genny's taxable income for 2020. ◆

The taxation of unemployment is not a new tax provision; however, given the number of people that received unemployment in 2020 due to the COVID-19 pandemic, the IRS is emphasizing the taxability of unemployment benefits and reminding taxpayers that they can request income tax withholding as part of their unemployment.

New Tax Law!

Self-Study Problem 2.15   *See Appendix E for Solutions to Self-Study Problems*

Anthony was unemployed during part of 2020 and received the following Form 1099-G:

☐ CORRECTED (if checked)		

PAYER'S name, street address, city or town, state or province, country, ZIP or foreign postal code, and telephone no.	1 Unemployment compensation	OMB No. 1545-0120	
Florida Dept. of Economic Opportunity 107 E. Jefferson St. Tallahassee, FL 32399	$ 3,000.00	**2020**	**Certain Government Payments**
	2 State or local income tax refunds, credits, or offsets $	Form **1099-G**	

PAYER'S TIN 12-7654321	RECIPIENT'S TIN 313-22-1212	3 Box 2 amount is for tax year	4 Federal income tax withheld $ 0.00	Copy B For Recipient
RECIPIENT'S name Anthony Starky		5 RTAA payments $	6 Taxable grants $	This is important tax information and is being furnished to the IRS. If you are required to file a return, a negligence penalty or other sanction may be imposed on you if this income is taxable and the IRS determines that it has not been reported.
Street address (including apt. no.) 103 Brickell Ave.		7 Agriculture payments $	8 If checked, box 2 is trade or business income ▶ ☐	
City or town, state or province, country, and ZIP or foreign postal code Miami, FL 33101		9 Market gain $		
Account number (see instructions)		10a State	10b State identification no.	11 State income tax withheld $ $	

Form **1099-G**   (keep for your records)   www.irs.gov/Form1099G   Department of the Treasury - Internal Revenue Service

How much unemployment compensation is included in Anthony's gross income?

$ _____

Learning Objective 2.16

2-16 SOCIAL SECURITY BENEFITS

Apply the rules governing inclusion of Social Security benefits in gross income.

Some taxpayers may exclude all of their Social Security benefits from gross income. However, most middle-income and upper-income Social Security recipients may have to include up to 85 percent of their benefits in gross income. The formula to determine taxable Social Security income is based on *modified adjusted gross income* (MAGI). Generally, MAGI is the taxpayer's adjusted gross income (without Social Security benefits) plus any tax-free interest income. On rare occasions, taxpayers will also have to add back unusual items such as the foreign earned income exclusion, employer-provided adoption benefits, or interest on education loans. If MAGI plus 50 percent of Social Security benefits is less than the base amount shown below (base amounts are not adjusted for inflation), benefits are excluded from income.

Base Amounts	*Applies To*
$32,000	Married filing jointly
0	Married taxpayers who did not live apart for the entire year and still filed separate returns
25,000	All other taxpayers

The formula for calculating the taxable amount of Social Security is complex and time-consuming. Many taxpayers rely on tax-preparation software to perform the calculation. For preparation by hand, the Form 1040 Instructions include a full-page worksheet that takes taxpayers through the calculation one step at a time.

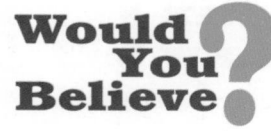

Would You Believe?

Originally, Social Security benefits were not taxed; however, starting in 1984, a portion of Social Security benefits became taxable using the now familiar $25,000 and $32,000 base amounts. At the time, the explanation used to support the change was that one-half of the tax was paid by employers and employees were not taxed on that benefit. The base amounts have not changed since 1984. Using the Consumer Price Index Inflation Calculator (**www.bls.gov /data/inflation_calculator.htm**), you would need more than $63,000 to equal the purchasing power of $25,000 in 1984. As a result, a much larger percentage of taxpayers are paying tax on their Social Security benefits.

EXAMPLE For the 2020 tax year, Nancy, a single taxpayer, receives $7,000 in Social Security benefits. She has adjusted gross income of $20,000, not including any Social Security income, and receives $10,000 of tax-exempt municipal bond interest. Nancy must include $3,500 of her Social Security benefits in gross income as determined as follows:

SIMPLIFIED TAXABLE SOCIAL SECURITY WORKSHEET (FOR MOST PEOPLE)

1. Enter the total amount of Social Security income.	1.	$ 7,000
2. Enter one-half of line 1.	2.	3,500
3. Enter the total of taxable income items on Form 1040 except Social Security income.	3.	20,000
4. Enter the amount of tax-exempt interest income.	4.	10,000
5. Add lines 2, 3, and 4.	5.	33,500
6. Enter all adjustments for AGI except for student loan interest, the domestic production activities deduction, and the tuition and fees deduction.	6.	–0–
7. Subtract line 6 from line 5. If zero or less, stop here, none of the Social Security benefits are taxable.	7.	33,500
8. Enter $25,000 ($32,000 if married filing jointly; $0 if married filing separately and living with spouse at any time during the year).	8.	25,000
9. Subtract line 8 from line 7. If zero or less, enter –0–.	9.	8,500

Note: If line 9 is zero or less, stop here; **none of your benefits are taxable.** Otherwise, go on to line 10.

10. Enter $9,000 ($12,000 if married filing jointly; $0 if married filing separately and living with spouse at any time during the year).	10.	9,000
11. Subtract line 10 from line 9. If zero or less, enter –0–.	11.	–0–
12. Enter the **smaller** of line 9 or line 10.	12.	8,500
13. Enter one-half of line 12.	13.	4,250
14. Enter the **smaller** of line 2 or line 13.	14.	3,500
15. Multiply line 11 by 85% (.85). If line 11 is zero, enter –0–.	15.	–0–
16. Add lines 14 and 15.	16.	3,500
17. Multiply line 1 by 85% (.85).	17.	5,950
18. **Taxable benefits.** Enter the **smaller** of line 16 or line 17.	18.	$ 3,500

◆

EXAMPLE Linda, a widow, is retired and receives Social Security benefits of $14,000 in 2020. She has MAGI of $47,000. Linda must include $11,900 of her Social Security benefits in gross income as determined as follows:

SIMPLIFIED TAXABLE SOCIAL SECURITY WORKSHEET (FOR MOST PEOPLE)

1. Enter the total amount of Social Security income.	1.	$14,000
2. Enter one-half of line 1.	2.	7,000
3. Enter the total of taxable income items on Form 1040 except Social Security income.	3.	47,000
4. Enter the amount of tax-exempt interest income.	4.	–0–
5. Add lines 2, 3, and 4.	5.	54,000

6. Enter all adjustments for AGI except for student loan interest, the domestic production activities deduction, and the tuition and fees deduction.

6.   –0–

7. Subtract line 6 from line 5. If zero or less, stop here, none of the Social Security benefits are taxable.

7. 54,000

8. Enter $25,000 ($32,000 if married filing jointly; $0 if married filing separately and living with spouse at any time during the year).

8. 25,000

9. Subtract line 8 from line 7. If zero or less, enter –0–.

9. 29,000

Note: *If line 9 is zero or less, stop here;* **none of your benefits are taxable.** *Otherwise, go on to line 10.*

10. Enter $9,000 ($12,000 if married filing jointly; $0 if married filing separately and living with spouse at any time during the year).

10. 9,000

11. Subtract line 10 from line 9. If zero or less, enter –0–.

11. 20,000

12. Enter the **smaller** of line 9 or line 10.

12. 9,000

13. Enter one-half of line 12.

13. 4,500

14. Enter the **smaller** of line 2 or line 13.

14. 4,500

15. Multiply line 11 by 85% (.85). If line 11 is zero, enter –0–.

15. 17,000

16. Add lines 14 and 15.

16. 21,500

17. Multiply line 1 by 85% (.85).

17. 11,900

18. **Taxable benefits.** Enter the **smaller** of line 16 or line 17.

18. $11,900

◆

A summary of the tax treatment of Social Security benefits is presented in Table 2.4.

TABLE 2.4   SOCIAL SECURITY INCOME INCLUSION FORMULAS

Filing Status	MAGI + 50% SS	Amount of SS That Is Included in Taxable Income
Single, HOH, Surviving Spouse, MFS (Living apart)	Under $25,000	No SS benefits included in taxable income
	$25,000–$34,000	The lesser of: 50% of SS benefits, or 50% of (MAGI + 50%SS, over $25,000)
	Over $34,000	The lesser of: 85% of SS benefits, or (lesser of box above or $4,500) + 85% of (MAGI + 50%SS, over $34,000)
Married Filing Jointly	Under $32,000	No SS benefits included in taxable income
	$32,000–$44,000	The lesser of: 50% of SS benefits, or 50% of (MAGI + 50%SS, over $32,000)
	Over $44,000	The lesser of: 85% of SS benefits, or (lesser of box above or $6,000) + 85% of (MAGI + 50%SS, over $44,000)

Note: The Social Security income inclusion formulas in the table above are shown for information only. No problems in the textbook will require the use of these formulas.

Social Security benefits are entered under the same heading in Income as alimony discussed in LO 2.13.

Self-Study Problem 2.16 *See Appendix E for Solutions to Self-Study Problems*

For the 2020 tax year, Kim and Edward are married and file a joint return. They have Social Security benefits of $13,000 and their adjusted gross income is $20,000, not including any Social Security income. They also receive $30,000 in tax-free municipal bond interest. How much, if any, of the Social Security benefits should Kim and Edward include in gross income? Use the worksheet below to compute your answer.

$_____

SIMPLIFIED TAXABLE SOCIAL SECURITY WORKSHEET (FOR MOST PEOPLE)

1. Enter the total amount of Social Security income.   1. $_____
2. Enter one-half of line 1.   2. _____
3. Enter the total of taxable income items on Form 1040 except Social Security income.   3. _____
4. Enter the amount of tax-exempt interest income.   4. _____
5. Add lines 2, 3, and 4.   5. _____
6. Enter all adjustments for AGI except for student loan interest, the domestic production activities deduction, and the tuition and fees deduction.   6. _____
7. Subtract line 6 from line 5. If zero or less, stop here, none of the Social Security benefits are taxable.   7. _____
8. Enter $25,000 ($32,000 if married filing jointly; $0 if married filing separately and living with spouse at any time during the year).   8. _____
9. Subtract line 8 from line 7. If zero or less, enter –0–.   9. _____

   Note: *If line 9 is zero or less, stop here;* **none of your benefits are taxable.** *Otherwise, go on to line 10.*

10. Enter $9,000 ($12,000 if married filing jointly; $0 if married filing separately and living with spouse at any time during the year).   10. _____
11. Subtract line 10 from line 9. If zero or less, enter –0–.   11. _____
12. Enter the **smaller** of line 9 or line 10.   12. _____
13. Enter one-half of line 12.   13. _____
14. Enter the **smaller** of line 2 or line 13.   14. _____
15. Multiply line 11 by 85% (.85). If line 11 is zero, enter –0–.   15. _____
16. Add lines 14 and 15.   16. _____
17. Multiply line 1 by 85% (.85).   17. _____
18. **Taxable benefits.** Enter the **smaller** of line 16 or line 17.   18. $_____

Distinguish between the different rules for married taxpayers residing in community property states when filing separate returns.

2-17 COMMUNITY PROPERTY

When married couples file separate income tax returns, a special problem arises. Income derived from property held by a married couple, either jointly or separately, as well as wages and other income earned by a husband and wife, must be allocated between the spouses. State law becomes important in making this allocation.

The law in nine states is based on a community property system of marital law. In these states, the property rights of married couples differ from the property rights of married couples residing in the remaining common law states. The nine states that are community property states are:

Arizona	Louisiana	Texas
California	Nevada	Washington
Idaho	New Mexico	Wisconsin

Note: In Alaska, spouses may elect to treat income as community income.

Under the community property system, all property is deemed to be either separate property or community property. Separate property includes property acquired by a spouse before marriage or received after marriage as a gift or inheritance. All other property owned by a married couple is presumed to be community property. For federal income tax purposes, each spouse is automatically taxed on half of the income from community property.

The tax treatment of income from separate property depends on the taxpayer's state of residence. In Idaho, Louisiana, Texas, and Wisconsin, income from separate property produces community income. Thus, just as each spouse is taxed on half of the income from community property, each spouse is also taxed on half of the income from separate property. In the other five community property states, income on separate property is separate income and is reported in full on the tax return of the spouse who owns the property. Income such as nontaxable dividends or royalties from mineral interests assumes the classification of the asset from which the income is derived. Capital gains also retain their classification based on the classification of the property from which the gain arises.

EXAMPLE John and Marsha are married and live in Texas. John owns, as his separate property, stock in AT&T Corporation. During the year, John receives dividends of $4,000. Assuming John and Marsha file separate returns, each of them must report $2,000 of the dividends. On the other hand, if John and Marsha lived in California, John would report the entire $4,000 of the dividends on his tax return and Marsha would not include any of the dividend income on her tax return. ♦

In all of the community property states, income from salary and wages is generally treated as having been earned one-half by each spouse.

EXAMPLE Robert and Linda are married but file separate tax returns. Robert receives a salary of $30,000 and has interest income of $500 from a savings account which is in his name. The savings account was established with salary earned by Robert since his marriage. Linda collects $20,000 in dividends on stock she inherited from her father. The amount of income which Linda must report on her separate income tax return depends on the state in which Robert and Linda reside. Three different assumptions are presented below:

State of Residence

Linda's Income:	Texas	California	Common Law States
Salary	$15,000	$15,000	$ 0
Dividends	10,000	20,000	20,000
Interest	250	250	0
Total	$25,250	$35,250	$20,000

◆

2-17a Spouses Living Apart

To simplify problems that could arise when married spouses residing in a community property state do not live together, the tax law contains an exception to the above community property rules. Under this special provision, a spouse will be taxed only on his or her actual earnings from personal services. For this provision to apply, the following conditions must be satisfied:

1. The individuals must live apart for the entire year,
2. They must not file a joint return, and
3. No portion of the earned income may be transferred between the spouses.

EXAMPLE Bill and Betty, both residents of Nevada, are married but live apart for the entire year. Bill has a salary of $30,000 and Betty has a salary of $35,000. Normally, Bill and Betty would each report $32,500. However, if the required conditions are met, Bill and Betty would each report their own salary. If Bill and Betty had any unearned income, such as dividends or interest, the income would be reported under the general community property rules. The special provision applies only to earned income of the spouses. ◆

Another provision addresses the problem of spouses who fail to qualify for the above special exception because they do not live apart for the entire year. In certain cases, a spouse who fails to include in income his or her share of community income, as required by the community property laws, may be relieved of any liability related to this income. To be granted relief, the taxpayer must not know of or have reason to know of the omitted community property income.

Self-Study Problem 2.17 *See Appendix E for Solutions to Self-Study Problems*

Tom and Rachel are married and living together in California. Their income is as follows:

Tom's salary	$40,000
Rachel's salary	30,000
Dividends (Tom's property)	5,000
Dividends (Rachel's property)	3,000
Interest (community property)	4,000
Total	$82,000

a. If Rachel files a separate tax return, she should report income of:

$_____

b. If Tom and Rachel lived in Texas, what should Rachel report as income?

$_____

Learning Objective 2.18

Describe the inclusion and exclusion of cancellation of debt income.

2-18 FORGIVENESS OF DEBT INCOME

The cancellation of debt represents an economic benefit to the taxpayer that receives the debt relief. Unsurprisingly, the broad definition of gross income generally treats the amount forgiven as income to the taxpayer. This can also be referred to as forgiveness of debt income or discharge of indebtedness income.

EXAMPLE Howard borrowed funds from Usury National Bank so he could start a small business. Unfortunately, Howard's business failed and he was unable to pay back the entire loan balance. Howard and the bank agreed to settle Howard's $50,000 outstanding debt for only $40,000. Howard has $10,000 of cancellation of debt income. ♦

There are a number of provisions provided to exclude forgiveness of debt from gross income including:

- The taxpayer is bankrupt or insolvent at the time the debt is cancelled or reduced
- The debt is qualified real property business debt
- The debt is qualified principal residence debt
- The debt is certain types of student loan debt that is forgiven under certain conditions

If a taxpayer's debt has been discharged in a bankruptcy, the tax law recognizes that requiring a bankrupt individual to pay taxes on debt that was required to be forgiven because the taxpayer lacks the ability to repay the debt would not make economic sense. As a result, this cancellation of debt income is generally excluded from gross income.

EXAMPLE Sharon borrowed funds from Usury National Bank so she could start a small business. Unfortunately, Sharon's business failed and her entire debt was discharged in a bankruptcy proceeding. Sharon may exclude the debt discharged. ♦

Often times debt is associated with the acquisition of real property, for example, land, a building used in business, or a house; and that property serves as collateral on the debt. If that property is qualified business property or the taxpayer's principal residence, an exclusion of the cancellation of debt income may apply. In the case of business property, the debt generally must have been incurred with respect to the acquisition, construction, or a substantial improvement to real property used in a trade or business.

EXAMPLE Heidi's small business purchased a warehouse to store inventory. The acquisition was funded by a loan from a local bank. The loan is secured by the building. Heidi found herself unable to make the loan payments and the bank agreed to cancel $15,000 of the loan. Heidi will be able to exclude the cancellation of debt income under the qualified real property business debt provisions. ♦

Similarly, debt incurred by a taxpayer to purchase, build, or substantially improve the taxpayer's principal residence is afforded similar treatment when forgiven. To qualify, the debt must be secured by the principal residence. The provision to exclude qualified principal residence debt forgiven currently is scheduled to expire at the end of 2020.

EXAMPLE Tyra acquired a new principal residence for $250,000 using a $200,000 mortgage that was secured by the home. In 2020, when the balance of the loan was $190,000, Tyra lost her job and was struggling to continue to make mortgage payments. The bank agreed to lower Tyra's loan principal to $160,000. Tyra may exclude the $30,000 of cancellation of debt income. ♦

When cancellation of debt income is excluded under the qualified business property and principal resident provisions, the basis in the underlying property is adjusted to reflect that exclusion amount.

EXAMPLE   In 2020, Muffy was required to renegotiate the mortgage on her principle residence. Although Muffy was solvent at the time, she was unable to make mortgage payments due to losing her job. The mortgage balance was $100,000 and she was able to reduce the balance to only $75,000, which in turn reduced her monthly mortgage payments. The $25,000 cancellation of mortgage debt will be excluded from Muffy's gross income. Accordingly, Muffy will need to reduce her basis in the home by the $25,000 of debt forgiven. ◆

The amount of excludable income under the qualified principal residence exception is limited to $2 million ($1 million for married taxpayers filing separately).

Because taxpayers that exclude cancellation of debt income under any of these provisions are often bankrupt, insolvent, or both, the tax rules require that the cancellation be attributed first to bankruptcy, if that applies and next to insolvency, if that applies.

In order to encourage students to pursue careers in certain occupations or locations that have unmet needs, the cancellation of certain student loans is also excluded from income. The student loan generally must be issued by a university or government agency.

EXAMPLE   Yousef attended Grays Medical University to become a pediatrician. Due to the cost of medical education, Yousef incurred substantial student loan debt. When Yousef graduated, he entered Grays Native American Loan Repayment Program. This program will refinance Yousef's existing student loans and then cancel Yousef's debt if he agrees to serve as a pediatrician for five years at a Native American reservation hospital. ◆

More broadly, student loans discharged before 2026 because of the student's death or total and permanent disability are also excluded from income.

Loans issued and forgiven under the Paycheck Protection Program may also be excluded. See Chapter 9 for more details.

The rules related to the exclusion of cancellation of debt can be complex and this section provides only a basic overview. Taxpayers report exclusions from bankruptcy, insolvency, and qualified business or principal residence property on Form 982.

Self-Study Problem 2.18   *See Appendix E for Solutions to Self-Study Problems*

In 2020, Stuart loses his job when his employer closes due to the COVID-19 pandemic. Because Stuart is struggling to pay his monthly expenses, he arranges a decrease in his mortgage from $160,000 to $120,000 with his mortgage lender. His basis in the home is $200,000 and the fair market value at the time of the mortgage reduction is $250,000.

a. What amount of the cancellation of debt must Stuart include in his income in 2020?

$_____

b. What is Stuart's basis in his home after applying exclusion provisions (if any)?

$_____

KEY TERMS

gross income, 2-2
barter, 2-2
inclusions – gross income, 2-3
exclusions – gross income, 2-3
Form W-2, 2-4
employee, 2-6
independent contractor, 2-6
employee fringe benefits, 2-10
flexible spending accounts, 2-10
dependent care flexible spending
    accounts, 2-11
health care flexible spending
    accounts, 2-11
group term life insurance, 2-11
education assistance plans, 2-11
no-additional-cost services, 2-12
qualified employee discounts, 2-12
working condition fringe benefit, 2-12

de minimis fringe benefits, 2-13
tuition reduction, 2-13
retirement planning fringe benefit, 2-13
qualified plan award, 2-15
tangible personal property, 2-15
annuities, 2-15
the simplified method, 2-16
the general rule, 2-17
exclusion ratio, 2-17
employee annuities, 2-18
accelerated death benefits, 2-19
viatical settlements, 2-19
interest income, 2-20
Schedule B, 2-20
U.S. savings bonds, 2-20
dividends, 2-21
municipal bond interest, 2-27
gift, 2-28

scholarship, 2-29
alimony, 2-29
property transfers, 2-30
qualified tuition programs
    (Section 529 tuition plan), 2-32
educational savings account
    (Coverdell Education Savings
    Accounts), 2-33
modified adjusted gross income
    (MAGI), 2-36
community property, 2-40
separate property, 2-40
cancellation of debt income, 2-42
qualified real property business debt,
    2-42
qualified principal residence debt,
    2-42

KEY POINTS

Learning Objectives	Key Points
LO 2.1: Apply the definition of gross income.	• Gross income means "all income from whatever source derived." • Gross income includes everything a taxpayer receives unless it is specifically excluded from gross income by the tax law.
LO 2.2: Describe salaries and wages income reporting and inclusion in gross income.	• The primary form of reporting wages to an employee is through Form W-2. • Employers should report the employee's taxable wages, salary, bonuses, awards, commissions, and almost every other type of taxable compensation in Box 1 of the Form W-2. • If a taxpayer receives more than one Form W-2 or is jointly filing with a spouse having their own Form W-2, the amounts in Box 1 are combined before entering the total on Line 1 of the Form 1040. • Other Form W-2 information such as federal taxes paid will also be reported by the taxpayer on the Form 1040. • Employees and independent contractors are subject to income and employment taxes differently. • The classification of a worker as an employee or independent contractor depends on the degree of control and independence between the individual and the business.
LO 2.3: Explain the general tax treatment of health insurance.	• Taxpayers may exclude health insurance premiums paid by their employer. • Taxpayers are allowed an exclusion for payments received from accident and health plans. The taxpayer may exclude the total amount received for payment of medical care, including any amount paid for the medical care of the taxpayer, his or her spouse, or dependents.

LO 2.4: Determine when meals and lodging may be excluded from taxable income.	• Meals and lodging are excluded from gross income provided they are for the convenience of the employer and they are furnished on the business premises. Lodging must be a condition of employment to be excluded.
LO 2.5: Identify the common employee fringe benefit income exclusions.	• Certain fringe benefits provided to employees may be excluded from the employees' gross income. These include dependent care and health care flexible spending accounts, group term life insurance (up to $50,000), education assistance plans, and others.
LO 2.6: Determine when prizes and awards are included in income.	• Amounts received from prizes and awards are normally taxable income unless refused by the taxpayer. • Certain small prizes (generally under $400) for length of service and safety achievement are excluded from gross income. If the award is a "qualified plan award," then up to $1,600 of the value of the award may be excluded.
LO 2.7: Calculate the taxable and nontaxable portions of annuity payments.	• Annuity payments received by a taxpayer have an element of taxable income and an element of tax-free return of the original purchase price. • The part of the payment that is excluded from income is the ratio of the investment in the contract to the total expected return. • The total expected return is the annual payment multiplied by the life expectancy of the annuitant, based on mortality tables provided by the IRS. • Individual taxpayers generally must use the "simplified" method to calculate the taxable amount from a qualified annuity starting after November 18, 1996.
LO 2.8: Describe the tax treatment of life insurance proceeds.	• Life insurance proceeds are generally excluded from gross income. If the proceeds are taken over several years instead of in a lump sum, any interest on the unpaid proceeds is generally taxable income. • Early payouts of life insurance are excluded from gross income for certain terminally or chronically ill taxpayers. • All or a portion of the proceeds from a life insurance policy transferred to another person for valuable consideration may be taxable to the recipient.
LO 2.9: Identify the tax treatment of interest and dividend income.	• Interest income is taxable except for certain state and municipal bond interest. • Interest or dividend income exceeding $1,500 per year must be reported in detail on Schedule B of Form 1040. • Series EE and Series I Savings Bond interest is taxable in the year the bonds are cashed unless a taxpayer elects to report the interest each year as it accrues. • Series HH Savings Bond interest is taxable each year as it is paid to the taxpayer. • Ordinary dividends are taxable in the year received. • Qualified dividends are taxed at rates ranging from 0 percent to 20 percent and possibly included in the 3.8 percent net investment income tax for high-income taxpayers.
LO 2.10: Describe the tax treatment of municipal bond interest.	• Interest from an obligation of a state, territory, or possession of the United States, or of a political subdivision of the foregoing, or of the District of Columbia, is excluded from gross income.
LO 2.11: Identify the general rules for the tax treatment of gifts and inheritances.	• The receipt of gifts and inheritances is usually excludable from gross income. Income received from the property after the transfer may be taxable to the recipient.
LO 2.12: Describe the elements of scholarship income that are excluded from tax.	• Scholarships granted to degree candidates are excluded from gross income if spent for tuition, fees, books, and course-required supplies and equipment. Amounts received for items such as room and board are taxable to the recipient.

LO 2.13: Describe the tax treatment of alimony and child support.	• Alimony paid in cash is taxable to the person who receives it and is deductible to the person who pays it, for divorce agreements dated prior to January 1, 2019. • Alimony is neither included in nor deducted from taxable income beginning with divorce or separation agreements after December 31, 2018. • Child support is not alimony and is not taxable when received, nor deductible when paid. • A spouse who transfers property in settlement of a marital obligation is not required to recognize any gain as a result of the property's appreciation. The receiving spouse assumes the tax basis of the property.
LO 2.14: Explain the tax implications of using educational savings vehicles.	• A Qualified Tuition Program (Section 529 plan) allows taxpayers (1) to buy in-kind tuition credits or certificates for qualified higher education expenses (a prepaid tuition plan) or (2) to contribute to an account established to meet qualified higher education expenses (a savings-type plan). Distributions from the account are not taxable if the proceeds are used for qualified higher education expenses. • Qualified higher education expenses include tuition, fees, books, supplies, and equipment required for the enrollment or attendance at an eligible educational institution. In addition, taxpayers are allowed reasonable room and board costs, subject to certain limitations. • The maximum exclusion for elementary or secondary education (K-12) for tuition only, is $10,000 per beneficiary per year. • Starting in 2019, distributions from a Section 529 plan may be used for student loan payments up to a lifetime limit of $10,000 per beneficiary or beneficiary's siblings.
LO 2.15: Describe the tax treatment of unemployment compensation.	• Unemployment compensation is taxable.
LO 2.16: Apply the rules governing inclusion of Social Security benefits in gross income.	• Taxpayers with income under $25,000 ($32,000 for Married Filing Jointly) exclude all of their Social Security benefits from gross income. • Middle-income and upper-income Social Security recipients, however, may have to include up to 85 percent of their benefits in gross income. • Calculating the taxable amount of Social Security is complex and most easily performed using a worksheet, such as the one provided in this chapter, or by using a tax program such as Intuit ProConnect Tax Online.
LO 2.17: Distinguish between the different rules for married taxpayers residing in community property states when filing separate returns.	• Income derived from community property held by a married couple, either jointly or separately, as well as wages and other income earned by a married couple, must be allocated between the spouses, if filing separately. • Nine states use a community property system of marital law. These states are Arizona, California, Idaho, Louisiana, Nevada, New Mexico, Texas, Washington, and Wisconsin. In Alaska, spouses may elect to treat income as community property. • In general, in a community property state, income is split one-half (50 percent) to each spouse. There are exceptions for certain separate property (e.g., property owned prior to marriage, inherited property, etc.).
LO 2.18: Describe the inclusion and exclusion of cancellation of debt income.	• Generally, cancellation of debt results in taxable income. • Income from the cancellation of debt due to bankruptcy, insolvency, associated with qualified real business property or a qualified primary residence, and certain student loan debt can be excluded from gross income.

QUESTIONS and PROBLEMS

LO 2.1   1. The definition of gross income in the tax law is:
   a. All items specifically listed as income in the tax law
   b. All cash payments received for goods provided and services performed
   c. All income from whatever source derived
   d. All income from whatever source derived unless the income is earned illegally

LO 2.1   2. Which of the following is not taxable for income tax purposes?
   a. Prizes
   b. Severance pay
   c. Gifts
   d. Partnership income
   e. All of the above are taxable

LO 2.1   3. All of the following items are taxable to the taxpayer receiving them, *except*:
   a. Life insurance proceeds
   b. Unemployment compensation
   c. Embezzled funds
   d. Prizes
   e. Gambling winnings

LO 2.1   4. Which of the following types of income is tax exempt?
   a. Unemployment compensation
   b. Income earned illegally
   c. Dividends from foreign corporations
   d. Municipal bond interest
   e. Dividends from utility corporations' stock

LO 2.1   5. Which of the following is included in gross income?
   a. Loans
   b. Scholarships for room and board
   c. Economic impact payments in 2020
   d. Health insurance proceeds
   e. None of the above

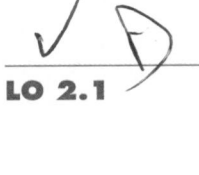

LO 2.2   6. The classification of a worker as an employee or an independent contractor is:
   a. Made by the employer
   b. Made by the employee
   c. Based on a negotiation between the employer and employee
   d. Based on a set of common law factors related to control and independence

LO 2.2   7. Which of the following is likely to indicate classification of a worker as an employee:
   a. The worker must provide their own tools and equipment.
   b. The worker can provide services at a location they choose.
   c. The worker receives benefits like health care.
   d. The worker makes their services available to the general public.

LO 2.3
LO 2.4
LO 2.11
LO 2.12   8. Which of the following items would be included in the gross income of the recipient?
   a. Insurance payments for medical care of a dependent child
   b. Insurance payments for loss of the taxpayer's sight
   c. Season tickets worth $2,000 given to a son by his father
   d. Payments to a student for working at the student union food court
   e. Lodging provided to a worker on a remote oil rig

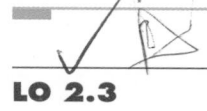

LO 2.3 9. Malin is a married taxpayer and has three dependent children. Malin's employer offers health insurance for employees and Malin takes advantage of the benefit for her entire family (her spouse's employer also offers health insurance but they opt out). During the year, Malin paid $1,200 toward her family's health insurance premiums through payroll deductions while the employer paid the remaining $9,200. Malin's family visited health care professionals numerous times during the year and made total co-payments toward medical services of $280. Malin's daughter had knee surgery due to a soccer injury and the insurance company paid the hospital $6,700 directly and reimbursed Malin $400 for her out-of-pocket health care expenses related to the surgery. How much gross income should Malin recognize related to her health insurance?

    a. $0
    b. $9,200
    c. $14,020 ($9,200 + $6,700 − $1,200 − $280 − $400)
    d. $8,000 ($9,200 − $1,200)
    e. None of the above

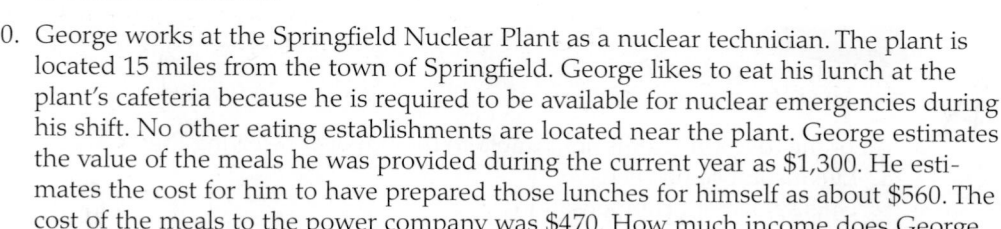

LO 2.4 10. George works at the Springfield Nuclear Plant as a nuclear technician. The plant is located 15 miles from the town of Springfield. George likes to eat his lunch at the plant's cafeteria because he is required to be available for nuclear emergencies during his shift. No other eating establishments are located near the plant. George estimates the value of the meals he was provided during the current year as $1,300. He estimates the cost for him to have prepared those lunches for himself as about $560. The cost of the meals to the power company was $470. How much income does George need to recognize from the meals?

    a. $1,300
    b. $560
    c. $470
    d. $830 ($1,300 − $470)
    e. None of the above

LO 2.5 11. Which of the following is a fringe benefit excluded from income?

    a. A mechanic at Denise's employer, a car rental company, provides $1,000 of repair services to Denise's personal car for free
    b. Alfa-Bet, a high-tech corporation, pays for each employee's membership at the 24 Hour Biceps Gym closest to each Alfa-Bet office
    c. Quickchat Inc. gives each employee a $10 giftcard to the local coffee shop on National Coffee Day
    d. Hedaya, a doctoral student at Ivy University, receives a full tuition waiver while serving as research assistant

LO 2.5 12. Which of the following will result in the recognition of gross income?

    a. Gail's employer allows her to set aside $4,000 from her wages to cover the cost of daycare for Gail's four-year-old daughter. Gail's daycare costs are $4,300 for the year.
    b. Hannah purchases a new sofa from her employer, Sofas-R-Us, for $1,200. The cost of the sofa to the furniture store is $1,100 and the sofa normally sells for $1,700.
    c. Jayden's employer purchases her commuting pass for the subway at a cost of $325 per month.
    d. Havana is a lawyer. The law firm she works for pays for her subscription to Lawyer's Weekly, a trade magazine for attorneys.
    e. None of the above will result in recognition of gross income.

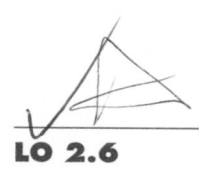

LO 2.6 13. Which of the following prizes or awards is *not* taxable?

    a. A crystal paperweight worth $125 given to an employee for achieving 10 years of service to the company
    b. Prizes from a television game show
    c. Awards for superior performance on the job

d. A $100 gift card received as a prize in a raffle run by the local school parent-teacher organization

e. All of the above are taxable

LO 2.6

14. Huihana receives 4 tickets to the local professional football game for achieving 20 years of employment with her employer. The tickets cost the employer $390 and have a market value of the same on the date awarded. Huihana is in the highest tax bracket for single taxpayers. How much gross income will Huihana recognize on the receipt of the tickets?

a. $390

b. $200

c. $25

d. $0

e. $50 or $59.50 including the net investment income tax

LO 2.7

15. A 67-year-old taxpayer retires this year and receives the first payment on an annuity that was purchased several years ago. The taxpayer's investment in the annuity is $94,500, and the annuity pays $1,000 per month for the remainder of the taxpayer's life. Based on IRS mortality tables, the taxpayer is expected to live another 20 years. If the taxpayer receives $4,000 in annuity payments in the current year, the nontaxable portion calculated using the simplified method is:

a. $0

b. $1,500

c. $1,800

d. $4,000

e. None of the above

LO 2.7

16. Amara has an annuity and over time has recovered her entire investment but it continues to pay her $450 per month. Amara should recognize how much of each monthly payment as gross income?

a. $0

b. Some amount greater than $450

c. Some amount between $0 and $450

d. $450

LO 2.8

17. Which of the following might result in life insurance proceeds that are taxable to the recipient?

a. A life insurance policy in which the insured is the son of the taxpayer and the beneficiary is the taxpayer

b. A life insurance policy transferred by a partner to the partnership

c. A life insurance policy transferred to a creditor in payment of a debt

d. A life insurance policy purchased by a taxpayer insuring his or her spouse

e. A life insurance policy purchased by a corporation insuring an officer

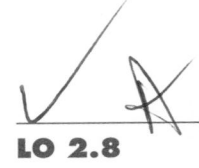

LO 2.8

18. Lupita dies in 2020 but has a $1 million life insurance policy that lists her spouse, M'Baku as the beneficiary. M'Baku elects to receive all $1 million in a lump sum and spends $200,000 immediately on a new yacht. M'Baku's gross income from the life insurance is:

a. $0

b. $200,000

c. $800,000

d. $1,000,000

LO 2.9

19. Nomi is in the highest individual tax bracket and receives $375 in qualified dividends from Omega Corp. Nomi's tax liability (not including any net investment income tax) with respect to these dividends is:

a. $0

b. $277.20

c. $100.00

d. $75.00

e. $50.00

LO 2.9   20. Rebecca, a single taxpayer, owns a Series I U.S. Savings Bond that increased in value by $46 during the year. She makes no special election. How much income must Rebecca recognize this year?

    a. $0

    b. $46

    c. $23

    d. $0 if in first 5 years or $46 thereafter

LO 2.10   21. Interest from which of the following types of bonds is included in federal taxable income?

    a. State of California bond

    b. City of New Orleans bond

    c. Bond of the Commonwealth of Puerto Rico

    d. U.S. Treasury Bond

    e. All of the above are excluded from income

LO 2.11   22. Which of the following gifts would probably be taxable to the person receiving the gift?

    a. One thousand dollars given to a taxpayer by his or her father

    b. An acre of land given to a taxpayer by a friend

    c. A car given to a loyal employee by her supervisor when she retired to recognize her faithful service

    d. A Mercedes-Benz given to a taxpayer by his cousin

    e. An interest in a partnership given to a taxpayer by his or her uncle

LO 2.12   23. Kelly receives a $40,000 scholarship to Ivy University. She uses $35,000 on tuition and books and $5,000 for rent while at school. Kelly will recognize _____ gross income.

    a. $0

    b. $5,000

    c. $10,000

    d. $30,000

    e. $40,000

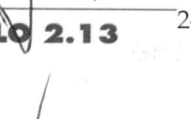

LO 2.13   24. Hillary gets divorced in 2019 and is required to pay her ex-spouse $200 per month until her son reaches 18 years of age in 7 years and $120 per month thereafter. How much of her 2020 payments are deductible as alimony?

    a. $0

    b. $2,400

    c. $1,440

    d. $960

LO 2.13   25. Donald and Michelle are divorced in the current year. As part of the divorce settlement, Michelle transfers a plot of land in Long Island, NY to Donald. Michelle's basis in the property was $20,000 and the market value of the property was $250,000 when transferred. Donald holds the property through the end of the year and in hopes of building a residence on it. How much income do Michelle and Donald recognize in the current year?

    a. $0 for Michelle and $20,000 for Donald

    b. $230,000 for Michelle and $20,000 for Donald

    c. $230,000 for Michelle and $0 for Donald

    d. $0 for both Michelle and Donald

    e. $0 for Michelle and $250,000 for Donald

LO 2.14   26. Gina receives a $2,900 distribution from her educational savings account. She uses $1,500 to pay for qualified higher education expenses and $1,400 on a vacation. Immediately prior to the distribution, Gina's account balance is $5,000, $3,000 of which is her contributions. What is Gina's taxable income (after any exclusion) from the distribution?

    a. $1,400

    b. $560

    c. $840

    d. $0

    e. Some other amount

LO 2.14
27. Which of the following is correct for Qualified Tuition Programs (Section 529 plans)?
   a. Contributions are deductible, and qualified educational expense distributions are tax free.
   b. Contributions are not deductible, and qualified educational expense distributions are tax free.
   c. Contributions are deductible, and qualified educational expense distributions are taxable.
   d. Contributions are not deductible, and qualified educational expense distributions are taxable.

LO 2.14
28. In 2020, Amy receives $8,000 (of which $3,000 is earnings) from a qualified tuition program. She uses the funds to pay for tuition and other qualified higher education expenses. What amount is taxable to Amy?
   a. $0
   b. $8,000
   c. $3,000
   d. $11,000

LO 2.14
29. For married taxpayers filing a joint return in 2020, at what AGI level does the phase-out limit for contributions to Section 529 plans start?
   a. $110,000
   b. $190,000
   c. $220,000
   d. There is no phase-out limit on Section 529 plan contributions

LO 2.14
30. Which of the following is true with respect to education incentives?
   a. The contributions to qualified tuition programs (Section 529 plans) are deductible.
   b. The contributions to educational savings accounts (Coverdell ESA) are deductible.
   c. Tuition paid by a taxpayer earning $300,000 of income is deductible.
   d. Married taxpayers have no income limit to contribute to a qualified tuition program (Section 529 plan).

LO 2.14
31. During 2020, Carl (a single taxpayer) has a salary of $91,500 and interest income of $11,000. Calculate the maximum contribution Carl is allowed for an educational savings account.
   a. $0
   b. $400
   c. $1,000
   d. $2,000
   e. Some other amount

LO 2.14
32. Wendy is a single taxpayer and pays tuition of $7,800 in 2020. Her 2020 AGI is $66,000. What is the amount of Wendy's tuition deduction?
   a. $0
   b. $7,800
   c. $4,000
   d. $2,000
   e. $3,733.33

LO 2.15
33. Alicia loses her job part way through 2020. Her employer pays her wages of $15,450 up through her date of termination. After that, she received $1,600 of unemployment compensation from the state until she gets a new job for which she is paid wages of $1,400 through year end. Based on this information, Alicia's gross income for 2020 is:
   a. $15,450
   b. $16,850
   c. $17,050
   d. $18,450
   e. $21,850

LO 2.16

34. For 2020, the maximum percentage of Social Security benefits that could be included in a taxpayer's gross income is:
    a. 0%
    b. 25%
    c. 50%
    d. 75%
    e. 85%

LO 2.16

35. Generally, when calculating the taxable portion of Social Security benefits, modified adjusted gross income (MAGI) is adjusted gross income (without Social Security benefits):
    a. Plus tax-exempt interest
    b. Less personal and dependency exemptions
    c. Less itemized deductions
    d. Less tax-exempt interest plus any foreign income exclusion
    e. Less tax-exempt interest income

LO 2.17

36. Dana and Larry are married and live in Texas. Dana earns a salary of $45,000 and Larry has $25,000 of rental income from his separate property. If Dana and Larry file separate tax returns, what amount of income must Larry report?
    a. $0
    b. $22,500
    c. $25,000
    d. $47,500
    e. None of the above

LO 2.17

37. Which of the following conditions need *not* be satisfied in order for a married taxpayer, residing in a community property state, to be taxed only on his or her separate salary?
    a. The husband and wife must live apart for the entire year.
    b. A minor child must be living with the spouse.
    c. The husband and wife must not file a joint income tax return.
    d. The husband and wife must not transfer earned income between themselves.
    e. All of the above must be satisfied.

LO 2.18

38. Jack borrows $13,000 from Sawyer Savings and Loan and uses the proceeds to acquire a used car. When the loan balance is $12,000, Jack loses his job and is unable to make payments for three months. When Jack gets a new job, the bank agrees to forgive the missed principal payments and reduces his loan to $11,500. Jack remains solvent even when unemployed. How much cancellation of debt income does Jack have?
    a. $0
    b. $500
    c. $1,500
    d. $2,000

LO 2.18

39. Kate acquires a principal residence in 2016 for $200,000 secured by a $180,000 mortgage. In 2020, Kate catches the coronavirus and misses work for 3 months. Her employer stops paying her after 10 days. In 2020 when the mortgage balance is $170,000, Kate and the bank revise her terms and lower the loan balance to $150,000. The market value of the home remains above $200,000. How much cancellation of debt income will Kate recognize?
    a. $0
    b. $20,000
    c. $10,000
    d. $150,000
    e. $170,000

GROUP 2:
PROBLEMS

LO 2.1

1. Indicate whether each of the items listed below would be included (I) in or excluded (E) from gross income for the 2020 tax year.
   - a. Welfare payments
   - b. Commissions
   - c. Hobby income
   - d. Scholarships for room and board
   - e. $300 set of golf clubs, an employee award for length of service
   - f. Severance pay
   - g. Ordinary dividend of $50
   - h. Accident insurance proceeds received for personal bodily injury
   - i. Inheritances
   - j. Gifts
   - k. Tips and gratuities

LO 2.1

2. Jane is a roofing contractor. Jane's friend needed a new roof but did not have the cash to pay. Jane's friend instead paid with a used truck that Jane could use in her roofing business. The truck had originally cost the friend $17,500 but it was gently used and only worth $6,000. Jane did not actually need the truck and ended up selling it to a used car dealer for $5,200 a few months later. Explain what amount of gross income Jane must recognize as a result of the truck payment and why. _____

_____

_____

_____

LO 2.1

3. Larry is a tax accountant and Sheila is a hairdresser. Larry prepares Sheila's tax return for free and Sheila agrees to style Larry's hair six times for free in return for the tax return. The value of the tax return is approximately $300 and the hair styling work is approximately $300.
   - a. How much of the $300 is includable income to Larry? Why? _____

   _____

   _____

   - b. How much of the $300 is includable income to Sheila? Why? _____

   _____

   _____

LO 2.1

4. Kerry and Jim have a successful marijuana farm in the woods around Humboldt County, California. Growing marijuana is illegal for federal purposes. Are Kerry and Jim required by law to report the income from their farm on their tax return? Why? _____

_____

_____

LO 2.2

5. Kristen, a single taxpayer, receives two 2020 Forms W-2 from the two employers she worked for during the year. One Form W-2 lists her wages in Boxes 1, 3, and 5 as $18,700. Her other employer's Form W-2 has $43,000 in Box 1 but only $46,500 in both Box 3 and Box 5. Kristen participated in the second employer's 401(k) plan. She also received health care from her second employer. Lastly, her second employer provided $30,000 of group term life insurance to Kristen.
   - a. What amount should Kristen report as taxable wages in 2020?
   - b. What could explain the difference between Box 1 wages and Boxes 3 and 5 on her second employer's W-2?

LO 2.2   6. List four behavioral factors that could be used to classify a worker as either an employee or an independent contractor and provide a brief example.

_____

_____

_____

_____

LO 2.3   7. Skyler is covered by his company's health insurance plan. The health insurance costs his company $9,500 a year. During the year, Skyler is diagnosed with a serious illness and health insurance pays $100,000 for surgery and treatment. How much of the insurance and treatment payments are taxable to Skyler? _____

_____

LO 2.3   8. Ellen is a single taxpayer. Ellen's employer pays $150 per month ($1,800 this year) for her health insurance. During the year, Ellen had medical expenses of $3,500 and the insurance company paid $2,000 of the expenses. How much of the above amounts, if any, must be included in Ellen's gross income?

$ _____

Why? _____

_____

LO 2.4   9. a.   Milton is a nurse whose employer provided meals for him on the employer's premises, since he is given only 30 minutes for lunch. Is the value of these meals taxable income to Milton?
Explain _____

_____

b.   Mary is a San Diego ambulance driver. The city provides Mary with meals while she is working so she will be available for emergencies. Is the value of these meals taxable income to Mary?
Explain _____

_____

c.   Indigo is the head of security at a casino. The casino operator frequently provides meals from the casino buffett to Indigo as a gesture of goodwill for the great job she is doing. Is the value of these meals taxable income to Indigo?
Explain _____

LO 2.5   10. Linda and Richard are married and file a joint return for 2020. During the year, Linda, who works as an accountant for a national airline, used $2,100 worth of free passes for travel on the airline; Richard used the same amount. Linda and Richard also used $850 worth of employee discount coupons for hotel rooms at the hotel chain that is also owned by the airline. Richard is employed at State University as an accounting clerk. Under a tuition reduction plan, Richard saved $4,000 in tuition fees during 2020. He is studying for a master's degree in business at night while still working full-time. Richard also had $30 worth of personal typing done by his administrative assistant at the University. What is the amount of fringe benefits that should be included in Linda and Richard's gross income on their 2020 tax return?

$ _____

LO 2.5   11. Ellen's tax client, Tom, is employed at a large company that offers health care flexible spending accounts to its employees. Tom must decide at the beginning of the year whether he wants to put as much as $2,750 of his salary into the health care flexible spending account. He expects that he will have to pay for at least $8,000 of medical expenses for his family during the year since his wife is seeing a psychiatrist every week and his daughter and son are both having their teeth straightened. Tom does not itemize deductions. Should Ellen recommend that Tom put the maximum amount in his health care flexible spending account, and if so, why? _____

_____

_____

_____

LO 2.6

12. How much of each of the following is taxable?
    a. Cheline, an actress, received a $6,400 gift bag for attending the Academy Awards Ceremony during 2020.
    b. Jon received a gold watch worth $660 for 25 years of service to his accounting firm (not a qualified award).
    c. Kerry won $1,000,000 in her state lottery.
    d. Deborah is a professor who received $30,000 as an award for her scientific research from the university that employs her.

LO 2.6
LO 2.12

13. For each of the following independent cases, indicate the amount of gross income that must be included on the taxpayer's 2020 income tax return.
    a. Malchia won a $4,000 humanitarian award.

    $ _____

    b. Rob won a new automobile (with a sticker price of $15,700 and a market value of $14,500) for being the best junior tennis player in 2020.

    $ _____

    c. George received a $3,500 tuition and fees scholarship to attend Western University.

    $ _____

LO 2.7

14. Lola, age 67, began receiving a $1,000 monthly annuity in the current year upon the death of her husband. She received seven payments in the current year. Her husband contributed $48,300 to the qualified employee plan. Use the Simplified Method Worksheet below to calculate Lola's taxable amount from the annuity.

SIMPLIFIED METHOD WORKSHEET

1. Enter total amount received this year.   1. _____

2. Enter cost in the plan at the annuity starting date.   2. _____

3. Age at annuity starting date

	Enter
55 and under	360
56–60	310
61–65	260
66–70	210
71 and older	160

3. _____

4. Divide line 2 by line 3.   4. _____

5. Multiply line 4 by the number of monthly payments this year. If the annuity starting date was before 1987, also enter this amount on line 8, and skip lines 6 and 7. Otherwise, go to line 6.   5. _____

6. Enter the amount, if any, recovered tax free in prior years.   6. _____

7. Subtract line 6 from line 2.   7. _____

8. Enter the smaller of line 5 or 7.   8. _____

9. Taxable amount this year: Subtract line 8 from line 1. Do not enter less than zero.   9. _____

LO 2.8

15. Sharon transfers to Russ a life insurance policy with a cash surrender value of $27,000 and a face value of $100,000 in exchange for real estate. Russ continues to pay the premiums on the policy until Sharon dies 7 years later. At that time, Russ has paid $12,000 in premiums, and he collects the $100,000 face value. How much of the proceeds is taxable to Russ?

$ _____

Why? _____

_____

LO 2.8

16. Greg died on July 1, 2020, and left Lea, his wife, a $45,000 life insurance policy which she elects to receive at $9,000 per year plus interest for 5 years. In the current year, Lea receives $9,500. How much should Lea include in her gross income?

$ _____

LO 2.8

17. David is certified by his doctor as terminally ill with liver disease. His doctor certifies that he cannot reasonably be expected to live for more than a year. He sells his life insurance policy to Viatical Settlements, Inc., for $250,000. He has paid $20,000 so far for the policy. How much of the $250,000 must David include in his taxable income? _____

_____

LO 2.8

18. Helen receives a $200,000 lump sum life insurance payment when her friend Alice dies. How much of the payment is taxable to Helen? _____

_____

LO 2.9

19. How are qualified dividends taxed in 2020? Please give the rates of tax which apply to qualified dividends, and specify when each of these rates applies. _____

_____

_____

LO 2.9

20. Describe the methods that an individual taxpayer that holds Series I Bonds can use to recognize interest.

_____

_____

LO 2.9

21. Sally and Charles Heck received the following Form 1099-DIV in 2020:

☐ CORRECTED (if checked)		

PAYER'S name, street address, city or town, state or province, country, ZIP or foreign postal code, and telephone no.	1a Total ordinary dividends	OMB No. 1545-0110	
Devona Corporation 33133 Hilltop Drive Alpine, CA 91901	$ 850.00	2020	**Dividends and Distributions**
	1b Qualified dividends		
	$ 694.00	Form **1099-DIV**	
	2a Total capital gain distr. $	2b Unrecap. Sec. 1250 gain $	**Copy B**
PAYER'S TIN 27-1234567	RECIPIENT'S TIN 313-13-1313	2c Section 1202 gain $	2d Collectibles (28%) gain $	**For Recipient**
RECIPIENT'S name Sally Heck	3 Nondividend distributions $	4 Federal income tax withheld $ 0.00	This is important tax information and is being furnished to the IRS. If you are required to file a return, a negligence penalty or other sanction may be imposed on you if this income is taxable and the IRS determines that it has not been reported.
Street address (including apt. no.) 1420 Pasadena Blvd.	5 Section 199A dividends $	6 Investment expenses $	
	7 Foreign tax paid $	8 Foreign country or U.S. possession	
City or town, state or province, country, and ZIP or foreign postal code Carrollton, TX 75007	9 Cash liquidation distributions $	10 Noncash liquidation distributions $	
	FATCA filing requirement ☐	11 Exempt-interest dividends $	12 Specified private activity bond interest dividends $	
Account number (see instructions)	13 State 14 State identification no. $	15 State tax withheld $	

Form **1099-DIV**   (keep for your records)   www.irs.gov/Form1099DIV   Department of the Treasury - Internal Revenue Service

The Hecks also received the following dividends and interest in 2020 (Forms 1099-DIV not shown):

	Sally	Charles	Jointly
Qualifying dividends:			
Altus Inc.	$2,000		
Buller Corp.		$350	
Gene Corporation			$3,100
Interest:			
Porcine Bank			1,245
River Bank			650
City of New York Bonds		100	

a. Assuming the Hecks file a joint tax return, complete Schedule B of Form 1040 (on Page 2-59) for them for the 2020 tax year.

b. What amounts are reported on Lines 2a and 2b of Form 1040?

2a $ _____

2b $ _____

c. What amounts are reported on Lines 3a and 3b of Form 1040?

3a $ _____

3b $ _____

LO 2.10

22. Vandell is a taxpayer in the 22 percent tax bracket. He invests in Otay Mesa Water District Bonds that pay 4.5 percent interest. What interest on a taxable bond would provide the same after-tax return to Vandell?

_____ %

LO 2.10

23. Karen is a wealthy retired investment advisor who is in the 35 percent tax bracket. She has a choice between investing in a high-quality municipal bond paying 5 percent or a high-quality corporate bond paying 7 percent. What is the after-tax return of each bond and which one should Karen invest in? Explain your answer.

_____

_____

_____

LO 2.11

24. In June of 2020, Kevin inherits stock worth $125,000. During the year, he collects $5,600 in dividends from the stock. How much of these amounts, if any, should Kevin include in his gross income for 2020?

$ _____

Why? _____

_____

LO 2.11

25. Gwen is a tax accountant who works very hard for a large corporate client. The client is pleased and gives her a gift of $10,000 at year-end. How much of the gift is taxable to Gwen? _____

_____

LO 2.11

26. Charlene receives a gift from her boyfriend of $10,000. He knows she is having financial problems and wants to help her. How much of the gift is taxable to Charlene? _____

_____

SCHEDULE B
(Form 1040)

Department of the Treasury
Internal Revenue Service (99)

Interest and Ordinary Dividends

▶ Go to *www.irs.gov/ScheduleB* for instructions and the latest information.
▶ Attach to Form 1040 or 1040-SR.

OMB No. 1545-0074

2020

Attachment
Sequence No. **08**

Name(s) shown on return

Your social security number

				Amount
Part I **Interest** (See instructions and the instructions for Forms 1040 and 1040-SR, line 2b.) **Note:** If you received a Form 1099-INT, Form 1099-OID, or substitute statement from a brokerage firm, list the firm's name as the payer and enter the total interest shown on that form.	**1**	List name of payer. If any interest is from a seller-financed mortgage and the buyer used the property as a personal residence, see the instructions and list this interest first. Also, show that buyer's social security number and address ▶	**1**	
	2	Add the amounts on line 1	**2**	
	3	Excludable interest on series EE and I U.S. savings bonds issued after 1989. Attach Form 8815	**3**	
	4	Subtract line 3 from line 2. Enter the result here and on Form 1040 or 1040-SR, line 2b . . . . ▶	**4**	

Note: If line 4 is over $1,500, you must complete Part III.

				Amount
Part II **Ordinary Dividends** (See instructions and the instructions for Forms 1040 and 1040-SR, line 3b.) **Note:** If you received a Form 1099-DIV or substitute statement from a brokerage firm, list the firm's name as the payer and enter the ordinary dividends shown on that form.	**5**	List name of payer ▶	**5**	
	6	Add the amounts on line 5. Enter the total here and on Form 1040 or 1040-SR, line 3b . . . . ▶	**6**	

Note: If line 6 is over $1,500, you must complete Part III.

Part III **Foreign Accounts and Trusts** **Caution:** If required, failure to file FinCEN Form 114 may result in substantial penalties. See instructions.	You must complete this part if you **(a)** had over $1,500 of taxable interest or ordinary dividends; **(b)** had a foreign account; or **(c)** received a distribution from, or were a grantor of, or a transferor to, a foreign trust.	Yes	No
	7a At any time during 2020, did you have a financial interest in or signature authority over a financial account (such as a bank account, securities account, or brokerage account) located in a foreign country? See instructions		
	If "Yes," are you required to file FinCEN Form 114, Report of Foreign Bank and Financial Accounts (FBAR), to report that financial interest or signature authority? See FinCEN Form 114 and its instructions for filing requirements and exceptions to those requirements		
	b If you are required to file FinCEN Form 114, enter the name of the foreign country where the financial account is located ▶		
	8 During 2020, did you receive a distribution from, or were you the grantor of, or transferor to, a foreign trust? If "Yes," you may have to file Form 3520. See instructions		

For Paperwork Reduction Act Notice, see your tax return instructions.   Cat. No. 17146N   **Schedule B (Form 1040) 2020**

DRAFT AS OF July 8, 2020 DO NOT FILE

LO 2.12

27. Robbie receives a scholarship of $20,000 to an elite private college. $8,000 of the scholarship is earmarked for tuition, and $12,000 covers his room and board. How much of the scholarship, if any, is taxable to Robbie? _____

_____

LO 2.13

28. Answer the following questions:

a. Under a 2017 divorce agreement, Joan is required to pay her ex-husband, Bill, $700 a month until their daughter is 18 years of age. At that time, the required payments are reduced to $450 per month.

   1. How much of each $700 payment may be deducted as alimony by Joan?

      $ _____

   2. How much of each $700 payment must be included in Bill's taxable income?

      $ _____

   3. How much would be deductible/included if the divorce agreement were dated 2020?

      $ _____

b. Under the terms of a property settlement executed during 2020, Jane transferred property worth $450,000 to her ex-husband, Tom. The property has a tax basis to Jane of $425,000.

   1. How much taxable gain must be recognized by Jane at the time of the transfer?

      $ _____

   2. What is the amount of Tom's tax basis in the property he received from Jane?

      $ _____

LO 2.13

29. Arlen is required by his 2020 divorce agreement to pay alimony of $2,000 a month and child support of $2,000 a month to his ex-wife Jane. What is the tax treatment of these two payments for Arlen? What is the tax treatment of these two payments for Jane?

Arlen _____

_____

Jane _____

_____

LO 2.13

30. As part of the property settlement related to their divorce, Cindy must give Allen the house that they have been living in, while she gets 100 percent of their savings accounts. The house was purchased for $90,000 20 years ago in Southern California and is now worth $700,000. How much gain must Cindy recognize on the transfer of the house to Allen? What is Allen's tax basis in the house for calculating tax on any future sale of the house?

Cindy _____

_____

Allen _____

_____

LO 2.14

31. Jose paid the following amounts for his son to attend Big State University in 2020:

Tuition	$6,400
Room and board	4,775
Books	772
A car to use at school	1,932
Student football tickets	237
Spending money	4,000

How much of the above is a qualified higher education expense for purposes of his Section 529 plan?

$ _____

LO 2.14

32. In 2020, Van receives $20,000 (of which $4,000 is earnings) from a Section 529 plan. He uses the funds to pay for his college tuition and other qualified higher education expenses. How much of the $20,000 is taxable to Van?

$ _____

LO 2.15

33. Lydia, a married individual, was unemployed for a few months during 2020. During the year, she received $3,250 in unemployment compensation payments. How much of her unemployment compensation payments must be included in gross income?

$ _____

LO 2.16

34. During the 2020 tax year, Brian, a single taxpayer, received $7,400 in Social Security benefits. His adjusted gross income for the year was $14,500 (not including the Social Security benefits) and he received $30,000 in tax-exempt interest income and has no for AGI deductions. Calculate the amount of the Social Security benefits that Brian must include in his gross income for 2020.

SIMPLIFIED TAXABLE SOCIAL SECURITY WORKSHEET (FOR MOST PEOPLE)

1. Enter the total amount of Social Security income.   1. _____
2. Enter one-half of line 1.   2. _____
3. Enter the total of taxable income items on Form 1040 except Social Security income.   3. _____
4. Enter the amount of tax-exempt interest income.   4. _____
5. Add lines 2, 3, and 4.   5. _____
6. Enter all adjustments for AGI except for student loan interest, the domestic production activities deduction, and the tuition and fees deduction.   6. _____
7. Subtract line 6 from line 5. If zero or less, stop here, none of the Social Security benefits are taxable.   7. _____
8. Enter $25,000 ($32,000 if married filing jointly; $0 if married filing separately and living with spouse at any time during the year).   8. _____
9. Subtract line 8 from line 7. If zero or less, enter –0–.   9. _____

Note: If line 9 is zero or less, stop here; **none of your benefits are taxable.** Otherwise, go on to line 10.

10. Enter $9,000 ($12,000 if married filing jointly; $0 if married filing separately and living with spouse at any time during the year).   10. _____
11. Subtract line 10 from line 9. If zero or less, enter –0–.   11. _____
12. Enter the **smaller** of line 9 or line 10.   12. _____
13. Enter one-half of line 12.   13. _____
14. Enter the **smaller** of line 2 or line 13.   14. _____
15. Multiply line 11 by 85% (.85). If line 11 is zero, enter –0–.   15. _____
16. Add lines 14 and 15.   16. _____
17. Multiply line 1 by 85% (.85).   17. _____
18. **Taxable benefits**. Enter the **smaller** of line 16 or line 17.   18. _____

LO 2.16 35. Please answer the following questions regarding the taxability of Social Security:

a. A 68-year-old taxpayer has $20,000 in Social Security income and $100,000 in tax-free municipal bond income. Does the municipal bond income affect the amount of Social Security the taxpayer must include in income? _____

_____

b. A 68-year-old taxpayer has $20,000 in Social Security income and no other taxable or tax-free income. How much of the Social Security income must the taxpayer include in taxable income? _____

_____

_____

c. A 68-year-old taxpayer has $20,000 in Social Security income and has significant other taxable retirement income. What is the maximum percentage of Social Security that the taxpayer might be required to include in taxable income? _____

_____

_____

LO 2.18 36. In 2020, Son loses his job and becomes insolvent. His debts are worked out in bankruptcy and he is able to reduce his mortgage debt by $30,000. Explain how much cancellation of debt income Son will recognize and what exception provision might apply, if any.

GROUP 3:
WRITING ASSIGNMENT

RESEARCH   1. Vanessa Lazo was an amazing high school student and so it was no great surprise when she was accepted into Prestige Private University (PPU). To entice Vanessa to attend PPU, the school offered her a reduced tuition of $13,000 per year (full-time tuition would typically be $43,000 per year). PPU also has a scholarship program thanks to a large donation from William Gatos. Vanessa was the Gatos Scholarship winner and will receive a scholarship for $20,000. Vanessa is required to use the scholarship first to pay her $13,000 tuition and the remainder is to cover room and board at PPU. Lastly, PPU also offered Vanessa a part-time job on the PPU campus as a student lab assistant in the Biology Department of PPU for which she is paid $1,500.

Required: Go to the IRS website (**www.irs.gov**) and locate Publication 970. Review the section on Scholarships. Write a letter to Vanessa Lazo stating how much of the PPU package for Vanessa is taxable.
(An example of a client letter is available at the website for this textbook, located at **www.cengage.com**.)

GROUP 4:
COMPREHENSIVE PROBLEMS

1. Beverly and Ken Hair have been married for 3 years. Beverly works as an accountant at Cypress Corporation. Ken is a full-time student at Southwest Missouri State University (SMSU) and also works part-time during the summer at Cypress Corp. Ken's birthdate is January 12, 1994 and Beverly's birthdate is November 4, 1996. Bev and Ken's earnings and income tax withholdings are reported on the following Forms W-2:

a Employee's social security number 465-74-3321	OMB No. 1545-0008	Safe, accurate, FAST! Use	IRS e-file	Visit the IRS website at www.irs.gov/efile

b Employer identification number (EIN) 31-1238967	1 Wages, tips, other compensation 51,100.00	2 Federal income tax withheld 4,610.00
c Employer's name, address, and ZIP code Cypress Corp. 1234 E. Chestnut Pkwy. Springfield, MO 65802	3 Social security wages 51,100.00	4 Social security tax withheld 3,168.20
	5 Medicare wages and tips 51,100.00	6 Medicare tax withheld 740.95
	7 Social security tips	8 Allocated tips
d Control number	9	10 Dependent care benefits
e Employee's first name and initial Last name Suff. Beverly Hair 3567 River Street Springfield, MO 63126	11 Nonqualified plans	12a See instructions for box 12
	13 Statutory employee ☐ Retirement plan ☐ Third-party sick pay ☐	12b
	14 Other	12c
		12d
f Employee's address and ZIP code		

15 State Employer's state ID number MO	16 State wages, tips, etc. 51,100.00	17 State income tax 690.00	18 Local wages, tips, etc.	19 Local income tax	20 Locality name

Form **W-2** Wage and Tax Statement   **2020**   Department of the Treasury—Internal Revenue Service

Copy B—To Be Filed With Employee's FEDERAL Tax Return.
This information is being furnished to the Internal Revenue Service.

a Employee's social security number 465-57-9934	OMB No. 1545-0008	Safe, accurate, FAST! Use	IRS e-file	Visit the IRS website at www.irs.gov/efile

b Employer identification number (EIN) 31-1238967	1 Wages, tips, other compensation 2,750.00	2 Federal income tax withheld 0.00
c Employer's name, address, and ZIP code Cypress Corp. 1234 E. Chestnut Pkwy. Springfield, MO 65802	3 Social security wages 2,750.00	4 Social security tax withheld 170.50
	5 Medicare wages and tips 2,750.00	6 Medicare tax withheld 39.88
	7 Social security tips	8 Allocated tips
d Control number	9	10 Dependent care benefits
e Employee's first name and initial Last name Suff. Ken Hair 3567 River Street Springfield, MO 63126	11 Nonqualified plans	12a See instructions for box 12
	13 Statutory employee ☐ Retirement plan ☐ Third-party sick pay ☐	12b
	14 Other	12c
		12d
f Employee's address and ZIP code		

15 State Employer's state ID number MO	16 State wages, tips, etc. 2,750.00	17 State income tax 0.00	18 Local wages, tips, etc.	19 Local income tax	20 Locality name

Form **W-2** Wage and Tax Statement   **2020**   Department of the Treasury—Internal Revenue Service

Copy B—To Be Filed With Employee's FEDERAL Tax Return.
This information is being furnished to the Internal Revenue Service.

The Hairs have interest income of $956 on City of St. Louis bonds. Beverly and Ken also received the following Form 1099-INT and 1099-DIV:

☐ CORRECTED (if checked)		
PAYER'S name, street address, city or town, state or province, country, ZIP or foreign postal code, and telephone no. Boatman's Bank 300 City Avenue Springfield, MO 63126	Payer's RTN (optional) **1** Interest income $ 656.62	OMB No. 1545-0112 20**20** Form **1099-INT**	**Interest Income**
	2 Early withdrawal penalty $		**Copy B**
PAYER'S TIN 33-1234566	RECIPIENT'S TIN 465-74-3321	**3** Interest on U.S. Savings Bonds and Treas. obligations $	**For Recipient**
RECIPIENT'S name Beverly and Ken Hair	**4** Federal income tax withheld $	**5** Investment expenses $	This is important tax information and is being furnished to the IRS. If you are required to file a return, a negligence penalty or other sanction may be imposed on you if this income is taxable and the IRS determines that it has not been reported.
Street address (including apt. no.) 3567 River Street	**6** Foreign tax paid $	**7** Foreign country or U.S. possession	
	8 Tax-exempt interest $	**9** Specified private activity bond interest $	
City or town, state or province, country, and ZIP or foreign postal code Springfield, MO 63126	**10** Market discount $	**11** Bond premium $	
FATCA filing requirement ☐	**12** Bond premium on Treasury obligations $	**13** Bond premium on tax-exempt bond $	
Account number (see instructions)	**14** Tax-exempt and tax credit bond CUSIP no.	**15** State **16** State identification no.	**17** State tax withheld $ $

Form **1099-INT**   (keep for your records)   www.irs.gov/Form1099INT   Department of the Treasury - Internal Revenue Service

☐ CORRECTED (if checked)		
PAYER'S name, street address, city or town, state or province, country, ZIP or foreign postal code, and telephone no. Green Corporation 900 South Orange Ave. Springfield, MO 62126	**1a** Total ordinary dividends $ 302.00	OMB No. 1545-0110 20**20**	**Dividends and Distributions**
	1b Qualified dividends $ 302.00	Form **1099-DIV**	
	2a Total capital gain distr. $	**2b** Unrecap. Sec. 1250 gain $	**Copy B** **For Recipient**
PAYER'S TIN 33-1122334	RECIPIENT'S TIN 465-57-9934	**2c** Section 1202 gain $	**2d** Collectibles (28%) gain $
RECIPIENT'S name Ken Hair	**3** Nondividend distributions $	**4** Federal income tax withheld $	This is important tax information and is being furnished to the IRS. If you are required to file a return, a negligence penalty or other sanction may be imposed on you if this income is taxable and the IRS determines that it has not been reported.
	5 Section 199A dividends $	**6** Investment expenses $	
Street address (including apt. no.) 3567 River Street	**7** Foreign tax paid $	**8** Foreign country or U.S. possession	
City or town, state or province, country, and ZIP or foreign postal code Springfield, MO 63126	**9** Cash liquidation distributions $	**10** Noncash liquidation distributions $	
FATCA filing requirement ☐	**11** Exempt-interest dividends $	**12** Specified private activity bond interest dividends $	
Account number (see instructions)	**13** State **14** State identification no.	**15** State tax withheld $ $	

Form **1099-DIV**   (keep for your records)   www.irs.gov/Form1099DIV   Department of the Treasury - Internal Revenue Service

Ken is an excellent student at SMSU. He was given a $1,750 scholarship by the university to help pay educational expenses. The scholarship funds were used by Ken for tuition and books.

Last year, Beverly was laid off from her former job and was unemployed during January 2020. She was paid $1,847 of unemployment compensation until she started work with her current employer, Cypress Corporation.

Ken has a 4-year-old son, Robert R. Hair, from a prior marriage that ended in divorce in 2015. During 2020, he paid his ex-wife $300 per month in child support. Robert is claimed as a dependent by Ken's ex-wife.

During 2020, Ken's aunt died. The aunt, in her will, left Ken $15,000 in cash. Ken deposited this money in the Boatman's Bank savings account.

Beverly and Ken received a $2,400 EIP in 2020.

Required: Complete the Hairs' federal tax return for 2020 on Form 1040, Schedule 1, and the Qualified Dividends and Capital Gain Tax Worksheet.

2A. Ray and Maria Gomez have been married for 3 years. Ray is a propane salesman for Palm Oil Corporation and Maria works as a city clerk for the City of McAllen. Ray's birthdate is February 21, 1992 and Maria's is December 30, 1994. Ray and Maria's earnings are reported on the following Forms W-2:

a Employee's social security number 469-21-5523	OMB No. 1545-0008 Safe, accurate, FAST! Use IRS e-file — Visit the IRS website at www.irs.gov/efile

b Employer identification number (EIN) 21-7654321	**1** Wages, tips, other compensation 30,660.00	**2** Federal income tax withheld 2,996.00
c Employer's name, address, and ZIP code Palm Oil Corporation 11134 E. Pecan Blvd. McAllen, TX 78501	**3** Social security wages 30,660.00	**4** Social security tax withheld 1,900.92
	5 Medicare wages and tips 30,660.00	**6** Medicare tax withheld 444.57
	7 Social security tips	**8** Allocated tips
d Control number	**9**	**10** Dependent care benefits
e Employee's first name and initial Last name Suff. Ray Gomez 1610 Quince Avenue McAllen, TX 78701	**11** Nonqualified plans	**12a** See instructions for box 12
	13 Statutory employee ☐ Retirement plan ☐ Third-party sick pay ☐	**12b**
	14 Other	**12c**
		12d
f Employee's address and ZIP code		
15 State Employer's state ID number TX	**16** State wages, tips, etc.	**17** State income tax	**18** Local wages, tips, etc.	**19** Local income tax	**20** Locality name

Form **W-2** Wage and Tax Statement   2020   Department of the Treasury—Internal Revenue Service

Copy B—To Be Filed With Employee's FEDERAL Tax Return.
This information is being furnished to the Internal Revenue Service.

a Employee's social security number 444-65-9912	OMB No. 1545-0008 Safe, accurate, FAST! Use IRS e-file — Visit the IRS website at www.irs.gov/efile

b Employer identification number (EIN) 23-4444321	**1** Wages, tips, other compensation 32,500.00	**2** Federal income tax withheld 2,654.00
c Employer's name, address, and ZIP code City of McAllen 1300 W. Houston Ave. McAllen, TX 78501	**3** Social security wages 32,500.00	**4** Social security tax withheld 2,015.00
	5 Medicare wages and tips 32,500.00	**6** Medicare tax withheld 471.25
	7 Social security tips	**8** Allocated tips
d Control number	**9**	**10** Dependent care benefits
e Employee's first name and initial Last name Suff. Maria Gomez 1610 Quince Avenue McAllen, TX 78701	**11** Nonqualified plans	**12a** See instructions for box 12
	13 Statutory employee ☐ Retirement plan ☐ Third-party sick pay ☐	**12b**
	14 Other	**12c**
		12d
f Employee's address and ZIP code		
15 State Employer's state ID number TX	**16** State wages, tips, etc.	**17** State income tax	**18** Local wages, tips, etc.	**19** Local income tax	**20** Locality name

Form **W-2** Wage and Tax Statement   2020   Department of the Treasury—Internal Revenue Service

Copy B—To Be Filed With Employee's FEDERAL Tax Return.
This information is being furnished to the Internal Revenue Service.

Ray and Maria have interest income as reported on the following 1099-INT:

		☐ CORRECTED (if checked)	

PAYER'S name, street address, city or town, state or province, country, ZIP or foreign postal code, and telephone no. McAllen State Bank 3302 N. 10th Street McAllen, TX 78501	Payer's RTN (optional)	OMB No. 1545-0112 20**20** Form **1099-INT**	**Interest Income**
	1 Interest income $ 147.12		
	2 Early withdrawal penalty $		Copy B
PAYER'S TIN 34-7657651	RECIPIENT'S TIN 444-65-9912	3 Interest on U.S. Savings Bonds and Treas. obligations $	For Recipient
RECIPIENT'S name Maria Gomez	**4 Federal income tax withheld** $	5 Investment expenses $	This is important tax information and is being furnished to the IRS. If you are required to file a return, a negligence penalty or other sanction may be imposed on you if this income is taxable and the IRS determines that it has not been reported.
Street address (including apt. no.) 1610 Quince Ave.	6 Foreign tax paid $	7 Foreign country or U.S. possession	
	8 Tax-exempt interest $	9 Specified private activity bond interest $	
City or town, state or province, country, and ZIP or foreign postal code McAllen, TX 78701	10 Market discount $	11 Bond premium $	
FATCA filing requirement ☐	12 Bond premium on Treasury obligations $	13 Bond premium on tax-exempt bond $	
Account number (see instructions)	14 Tax-exempt and tax credit bond CUSIP no.	15 State 16 State identification no. 17 State tax withheld $ $	

Form **1099-INT**   (keep for your records)   www.irs.gov/Form1099INT   Department of the Treasury - Internal Revenue Service

In addition, they own U.S. Savings bonds (Series EE). The bonds had a value of $10,000 on January 1, 2020, and their value is $10,700 on December 31, 2020. They have not made an election with respect to these bonds.

Ray has an ex-wife named Judy Gomez. Pursuant to their January 27, 2015 divorce decree, Ray pays her $450 per month in alimony. All payments were made on time in 2020. Judy's Social Security number is 566-74-8765.

During 2020, Ray was in the hospital for a successful operation. His health insurance company reimbursed Ray $4,732 for all of his hospital and doctor bills.

In June of 2020, Maria's father died. Under a life insurance policy owned and paid for by her father, Maria was paid death benefits of $25,000. She used $7,800 to cover a portion of the funeral costs for her father.

Maria bought a Texas lottery ticket on impulse during 2020. Her ticket was lucky and she won $4,432. The winning amount was paid to Maria in November 2020, with no income tax withheld.

Palm Oil Corporation provides Ray with a company car to drive while he is working. The Corporation spent $5,000 to maintain this vehicle during 2020. Ray never uses the car for personal purposes.

Ray and Maria received a $2,400 EIP in 2020.

Required: Complete the Gomez's federal tax return for 2020 on Form 1040 and Schedule 1.

2B. Carl Conch and Mary Duval are married and file a joint return. Carl works for the Key Lime Pie Company and Mary is unemployed after losing her job in 2019. Carl's birthdate is June 14, 1975 and Mary's is October 2, 1975. Carl's earnings are reported on the following Form W-2:

a Employee's social security number 835-21-5423	OMB No. 1545-0008	Safe, accurate, FAST! Use	IRS e~file	Visit the IRS website at www.irs.gov/efile

b Employer identification number (EIN) 61-7654321	1 Wages, tips, other compensation 67,894.88	2 Federal income tax withheld 6,232.00

c Employer's name, address, and ZIP code Key Lime Pie Company 223 Key Deer Blvd. Big Pine Key, FL 33043	3 Social security wages 67,894.88	4 Social security tax withheld 4,209.48
	5 Medicare wages and tips 67,894.88	6 Medicare tax withheld 984.48
	7 Social security tips	8 Allocated tips

d Control number	9	10 Dependent care benefits

e Employee's first name and initial Last name Suff. Carl Conch 1234 Mallory Square, Apt. #64 Key West, FL 33040	11 Nonqualified plans	12a See instructions for box 12 C 240.00
	13 Statutory employee ☐ Retirement plan ☐ Third-party sick pay ☐	12b
	14 Other Parking $1,680.00	12c
		12d

f Employee's address and ZIP code		

15 State Employer's state ID number FL	16 State wages, tips, etc.	17 State income tax	18 Local wages, tips, etc.	19 Local income tax	20 Locality name

Form **W-2** Wage and Tax Statement   **2020**   Department of the Treasury—Internal Revenue Service

Copy B—To Be Filed With Employee's FEDERAL Tax Return.
This information is being furnished to the Internal Revenue Service.

Carl and Mary received the following Form 1099:

☐ CORRECTED (if checked)

PAYER'S name, street address, city or town, state or province, country, ZIP or foreign postal code, and telephone no. Coral Reef Bank 3102 Simonton Street Key West, FL 33040	Payer's RTN (optional)	OMB No. 1545-0112 **2020** Form **1099-INT**	**Interest Income**
	1 Interest income $ 426.19		
	2 Early withdrawal penalty $		**Copy B**
PAYER'S TIN 31-1234444	RECIPIENT'S TIN 633-65-7912	3 Interest on U.S. Savings Bonds and Treas. obligations $	**For Recipient**
RECIPIENT'S name Mary Duval and Carl Conch	4 Federal income tax withheld $	5 Investment expenses $	This is important tax information and is being furnished to the IRS. If you are required to file a return, a negligence penalty or other sanction may be imposed on you if this income is taxable and the IRS determines that it has not been reported.
Street address (including apt. no.) 1234 Mallory Sq. #64	6 Foreign tax paid $	7 Foreign country or U.S. possession	
City or town, state or province, country, and ZIP or foreign postal code Key West, FL 33040	8 Tax-exempt interest $	9 Specified private activity bond interest $	
	10 Market discount $	11 Bond premium $	
FATCA filing requirement ☐	12 Bond premium on Treasury obligations $	13 Bond premium on tax-exempt bond $	
Account number (see instructions)	14 Tax-exempt and tax credit bond CUSIP no.	15 State 16 State identification no.	17 State tax withheld $ $

Form **1099-INT**   (keep for your records)   www.irs.gov/Form1099INT   Department of the Treasury - Internal Revenue Service

Mary is divorced and she pays her ex-husband (Tom Tortuga) child support. Pursuant to their January 12, 2017 divorce decree, Mary pays Tom $500 per month in child support. All payments were made on time in 2020.

In June 2020, Mary's father gave her a cash gift of $75,000.

Mary also received unemployment compensation as shown on the following Form 1099-G:

PAYER'S name, street address, city or town, state or province, country, ZIP or foreign postal code, and telephone no. Florida Dept. of Econ. Opportunity 107 E. Jefferson Blvd. Tallahassee, FL 32399		**1** Unemployment compensation $ 3,100.24	OMB No. 1545-0120 20**20** Form **1099-G**	**Certain Government Payments**
		2 State or local income tax refunds, credits, or offsets $		
PAYER'S TIN 21-5556666	RECIPIENT'S TIN 633-65-7912	**3** Box 2 amount is for tax year	**4** Federal income tax withheld $ 180.00	**Copy B** **For Recipient**
RECIPIENT'S name Mary Duval		**5** RTAA payments $	**6** Taxable grants $	This is important tax information and is being furnished to the IRS. If you are required to file a return, a negligence penalty or other sanction may be imposed on you if this income is taxable and the IRS determines that it has not been reported.
Street address (including apt. no.) 1234 Mallory Square Apt 64		**7** Agriculture payments $	**8** If checked, box 2 is trade or business income ▶ ☐	
City or town, state or province, country, and ZIP or foreign postal code Key West, FL 33040		**9** Market gain $		
Account number (see instructions)		**10a** State	**10b** State identification no.	**11** State income tax withheld $ $

Form **1099-G**   (keep for your records)   www.irs.gov/Form1099G   Department of the Treasury - Internal Revenue Service

Mary won a $800 prize in a women's club raffle in 2020. No income tax was withheld from the prize.

The Key Lime Pie Company provides Carl with a company car to drive while he is working. The Company spent $6,475 to maintain this vehicle during 2020. Carl never uses the car for personal purposes. The Key Lime Pie Company also provides a cafeteria for all employees on the factory premises. Other restaurants exist in the area and so Carl is not required to eat in the cafeteria, but he typically does. The value of Carl's meals is $650 in 2020.

Carl and Mary received a $2,400 EIP in 2020.

Required: Complete Carl and Mary's federal tax return for 2020 on Form 1040 and Schedule 1.

GROUP 5:
CUMULATIVE SOFTWARE PROBLEM

1. The following additional information is available for the family of Albert and Allison Gaytor.

In 2020, Albert received a Form W-2 from his employer, Coconut Grove Fishing Charters, Inc. (hint: slightly modified from Chapter 1):

a Employee's social security number 266-51-1966 OMB No. 1545-0008	Safe, accurate, FAST! Use IRS e~file	Visit the IRS website at www.irs.gov/efile

b Employer identification number (EIN) 60-3456789	**1** Wages, tips, other compensation 67,254.70	**2** Federal income tax withheld 5,588.17
c Employer's name, address, and ZIP code Coconut Grove Fishing Charters, Inc. 2432 Bay Blvd. Coconut Grove, FL 33133	**3** Social security wages 67,254.70	**4** Social security tax withheld 4,169.79
	5 Medicare wages and tips 67,254.70	**6** Medicare tax withheld 975.19
	7 Social security tips	**8** Allocated tips
d Control number	**9**	**10** Dependent care benefits
e Employee's first name and initial Last name Suff. Albert T. Gaytor 12340 Cocoshell Road Coral Gables, FL 33134	**11** Nonqualified plans	**12a** See instructions for box 12 DD 8,400.00
	13 Statutory employee ☐ Retirement plan ☐ Third-party sick pay ☐	**12b**
	14 Other Parking $3,240.00	**12c**
		12d
f Employee's address and ZIP code		

15 State Employer's state ID number FL	**16** State wages, tips, etc.	**17** State income tax	**18** Local wages, tips, etc.	**19** Local income tax	**20** Locality name

Form **W-2** Wage and Tax Statement   **2020**   Department of the Treasury—Internal Revenue Service
Copy B—To Be Filed With Employee's FEDERAL Tax Return.
This information is being furnished to the Internal Revenue Service.

In addition to the interest from Chapter 1, Albert and Allison also received three Forms 1099:

☐ CORRECTED (if checked)

PAYER'S name, street address, city or town, state or province, country, ZIP or foreign postal code, and telephone no. Florida Electric Company 100 Palm Boulevard Jupiter, FL 33458	Payer's RTN (optional)	OMB No. 1545-0112 2020 Form **1099-INT**	**Interest Income**
	1 Interest income $ 703.32		
	2 Early withdrawal penalty $		Copy B
PAYER'S TIN 59-0247776	RECIPIENT'S TIN 266-51-1966	**3** Interest on U.S. Savings Bonds and Treas. obligations $	For Recipient
RECIPIENT'S name Albert T. Gaytor		**4** Federal income tax withheld $	**5** Investment expenses $	This is important tax information and is being furnished to the IRS. If you are required to file a return, a negligence penalty or other sanction may be imposed on you if this income is taxable and the IRS determines that it has not been reported.
Street address (including apt. no.) 12340 Cocoshell Rd		**6** Foreign tax paid $	**7** Foreign country or U.S. possession	
City or town, state or province, country, and ZIP or foreign postal code Coral Gables, FL 33134		**8** Tax-exempt interest $	**9** Specified private activity bond interest $	
		10 Market discount $	**11** Bond premium $	
	FATCA filing requirement ☐	**12** Bond premium on Treasury obligations $	**13** Bond premium on tax-exempt bond $	
Account number (see instructions)		**14** Tax-exempt and tax credit bond CUSIP no.	**15** State	**16** State identification no.	**17** State tax withheld $ $

Form **1099-INT**   (keep for your records)   www.irs.gov/Form1099INT   Department of the Treasury - Internal Revenue Service

☐ CORRECTED (if checked)

PAYER'S name, street address, city or town, state or province, country, ZIP or foreign postal code, and telephone no.	1a Total ordinary dividends $ 1,102.32	OMB No. 1545-0110 2020 Form 1099-DIV	Dividends and Distributions
Everglades Bank Corporation 1500 S. Krome Ave. Homestead, FL 33034	1b Qualified dividends $ 1,102.32		
	2a Total capital gain distr. $	2b Unrecap. Sec. 1250 gain $	Copy B For Recipient
PAYER'S TIN 57-4443344	RECIPIENT'S TIN 266-34-1967	2c Section 1202 gain $	2d Collectibles (28%) gain $	
RECIPIENT'S name Allison Gaytor	3 Nondividend distributions $	4 Federal income tax withheld $ 0.00	This is important tax information and is being furnished to the IRS. If you are required to file a return, a negligence penalty or other sanction may be imposed on you if this income is taxable and the IRS determines that it has not been reported.
	5 Section 199A dividends $	6 Investment expenses $	
Street address (including apt. no.) 12340 Cocoshell Road	7 Foreign tax paid $	8 Foreign country or U.S. possession	
City or town, state or province, country, and ZIP or foreign postal code Coral Gables, FL 33134	9 Cash liquidation distributions $	10 Noncash liquidation distributions $	
FATCA filing requirement ☐	11 Exempt-interest dividends $	12 Specified private activity bond interest dividends $	
Account number (see instructions)	13 State	14 State identification no.	15 State tax withheld $ $	

Form **1099-DIV**   (keep for your records)   www.irs.gov/Form1099DIV   Department of the Treasury - Internal Revenue Service

☐ CORRECTED (if checked)

PAYER'S name, street address, city or town, state or province, country, ZIP or foreign postal code, and telephone no.	1a Total ordinary dividends $ 400.00	OMB No. 1545-0110 2020 Form 1099-DIV	Dividends and Distributions
Grapefruit Mutual Fund 1500 S. Orange Blossom Trail Orlando, FL 32809	1b Qualified dividends $ 360.00		
	2a Total capital gain distr. $ 120.00	2b Unrecap. Sec. 1250 gain $	Copy B For Recipient
PAYER'S TIN 51-3334433	RECIPIENT'S TIN 266-34-1967	2c Section 1202 gain $	2d Collectibles (28%) gain $	
RECIPIENT'S name Allison Gaytor	3 Nondividend distributions $	4 Federal income tax withheld $ 0.00	This is important tax information and is being furnished to the IRS. If you are required to file a return, a negligence penalty or other sanction may be imposed on you if this income is taxable and the IRS determines that it has not been reported.
	5 Section 199A dividends $	6 Investment expenses $	
Street address (including apt. no.) 12340 Cocoshell Rd.	7 Foreign tax paid $	8 Foreign country or U.S. possession	
City or town, state or province, country, and ZIP or foreign postal code Coral Gables, FL 33134	9 Cash liquidation distributions $	10 Noncash liquidation distributions $	
FATCA filing requirement ☐	11 Exempt-interest dividends $	12 Specified private activity bond interest dividends $	
Account number (see instructions)	13 State	14 State identification no.	15 State tax withheld $ $	

Form **1099-DIV**   (keep for your records)   www.irs.gov/Form1099DIV   Department of the Treasury - Internal Revenue Service

The Gaytors also received interest of $800 from bonds issued by the Miami-Dade County Airport Authority (Form 1099 not shown).

Albert went to the casino on his birthday and won big, as reflected on the following Form W-2G:

☐ CORRECTED (if checked)		

PAYER'S name, street address, city or town, province or state, country, and ZIP or foreign postal code	1 Reportable winnings $ 6,062.00	2 Date won	OMB No. 1545-0238
Mikkosukee Resort and Gaming 1321 Tamiami Hwy Miami, FL 33194	3 Type of wager	4 Federal income tax withheld $ 1,600.00	20**20** Form **W-2G**
	5 Transaction	6 Race	Certain Gambling Winnings
	7 Winnings from identical wagers $	8 Cashier	
PAYER'S federal identification number 22-7777777	PAYER'S telephone number 305-555-1212	9 Winner's taxpayer identification no. 266-51-1966	10 Window	This information is being furnished to the Internal Revenue Service
WINNER'S name Albert Gaytor	11 First I.D.	12 Second I.D.	
Street address (including apt. no.) 12340 Cocoshell Rd	13 State/Payer's state identification no. DF-124562	14 State winnings $	Copy B Report this income on your federal tax return. If this form shows federal income tax withheld in box 4, attach this copy to your return.
City or town, province or state, country, and ZIP or foreign postal code Coral Gables, FL 33134	15 State income tax withheld $	16 Local winnings $	
	17 Local income tax withheld $	18 Name of locality	

Under penalties of perjury, I declare that, to the best of my knowledge and belief, the name, address, and taxpayer identification number that I have furnished correctly identify me as the recipient of this payment and any payments from identical wagers, and that no other person is entitled to any part of these payments.

Signature ►   Date ►

Form **W-2G**   www.irs.gov/FormW2G   Department of the Treasury - Internal Revenue Service

Albert had no other gambling income or losses for the year.

In February, Allison received $50,000 in life insurance proceeds from the death of her friend, Sharon.

In July, Albert's uncle Ivan died and left him real estate (undeveloped land) worth $72,000.

Five years ago, Albert and Allison divorced. Albert married Iris, but the marriage did not work out and they divorced a year later. Under the July 1, 2016 divorce decree, Albert pays Iris $11,500 per year in alimony. All payments were on time in 2020 and Iris' Social Security number is 667-34-9224. Three years ago, Albert and Allison were remarried.

Coconut Fishing Charters, Inc. pays Albert's captain's license fees and membership dues to the Charter Fisherman's Association. During 2020, Coconut Fishing paid $1,300 for such dues and fees for Albert.

Allison was laid off from her job on January 2, 2020. She received a Form 1099-G for unemployment benefits:

☐ CORRECTED (if checked)		

PAYER'S name, street address, city or town, state or province, country, ZIP or foreign postal code, and telephone no.	1 Unemployment compensation $ 4,074.76	OMB No. 1545-0120	Certain Government Payments
Florida Dept. of Econ. Opportunity 107 E. Jefferson Blvd. Tallahassee, FL 32399	2 State or local income tax refunds, credits, or offsets $	20**20** Form **1099-G**	
PAYER'S TIN 21-5556666	RECIPIENT'S TIN	3 Box 2 amount is for tax year	4 Federal income tax withheld $ 150.00	Copy B For Recipient
RECIPIENT'S name Allison Gaytor		5 RTAA payments $	6 Taxable grants $	This is important tax information and is being furnished to the IRS. If you are required to file a return, a negligence penalty or other sanction may be imposed on you if this income is taxable and the IRS determines that it has not been reported.
Street address (including apt. no.) 12340 Cocoshell Road		7 Agriculture payments $	8 If checked, box 2 is trade or business income ► ☐	
City or town, state or province, country, and ZIP or foreign postal code Coral Gables, FL 33134		9 Market gain $		
Account number (see instructions)		10a State	10b State identification no.	11 State income tax withheld $ $

Form **1099-G**   (keep for your records)   www.irs.gov/Form1099G   Department of the Treasury - Internal Revenue Service

Albert and his family are covered by an employee-sponsored health plan at his work. Coconut Fishing pays $700 per month in premiums for Albert and his family. During the year, Allison was in the hospital for appendix surgery. The bill for the surgery was $10,100 of which the health insurance reimbursed Albert the full $10,100.

Coconut Fishing also pays for Albert's parking at the marina. The monthly cost is $270.

Required: Combine this new information about the Gaytor family with the information from Chapter 1 and complete a revised 2020 tax return for Albert and Allison. Be sure to save your data input files since this case will be expanded with more tax information in later chapters.

Form 1040

Department of the Treasury—Internal Revenue Service (99)

U.S. Individual Income Tax Return | **2020** | OMB No. 1545-0074 | IRS Use Only—Do not write or staple in this space.

Filing Status
Check only one box.

☐ Single ☐ Married filing jointly ☐ Married filing separately (MFS) ☐ Head of household (HOH) ☐ Qualifying widow(er) (QW)

If you checked the MFS box, enter the name of your spouse. If you checked the HOH or QW box, enter the child's name if the qualifying person is a child but not your dependent ▶

Your first name and middle initial	Last name	Your social security number

If joint return, spouse's first name and middle initial	Last name	Spouse's social security number

Home address (number and street). If you have a P.O. box, see instructions.	Apt. no.

City, town, or post office. If you have a foreign address, also complete spaces below.	State	ZIP code

Foreign country name	Foreign province/state/county	Foreign postal code

Presidential Election Campaign
Check here if you, or your spouse if filing jointly, want $3 to go to this fund. Checking a box below will not change your tax or refund. ☐ You ☐ Spouse

At any time during 2020, did you receive, sell, send, exchange, or otherwise acquire any financial interest in any virtual currency? ☐ Yes ☐ No

Standard Deduction

Someone can claim: ☐ You as a dependent ☐ Your spouse as a dependent
☐ Spouse itemizes on a separate return or you were a dual-status alien

Age/Blindness You: ☐ Were born before January 2, 1956 ☐ Are blind **Spouse:** ☐ Was born before January 2, 1956 ☐ Is blind

Dependents (see instructions):
If more than four dependents, see instructions and check here ▶ ☐

(1) First name Last name	(2) Social security number	(3) Relationship to you	(4) ✔ if qualifies for (see instructions):	
			Child tax credit	Credit for other dependents
			☐	☐
			☐	☐
			☐	☐
			☐	☐

Attach Sch. B if required.

1	Wages, salaries, tips, etc. Attach Form(s) W-2		1	
2a	Tax-exempt interest . . .	2a	**b** Taxable interest	2b	
3a	Qualified dividends . . .	3a	**b** Ordinary dividends	3b	
4a	IRA distributions	4a	**b** Taxable amount	4b	
5a	Pensions and annuities . .	5a	**b** Taxable amount	5b	
6a	Social security benefits . .	6a	**b** Taxable amount	6b	

Standard Deduction for—
• Single or Married filing separately, $12,400
• Married filing jointly or Qualifying widow(er), $24,800
• Head of household, $18,650
• If you checked any box under *Standard Deduction,* see instructions.

7	Capital gain or (loss). Attach Schedule D if required. If not required, check here . . . . . ▶ ☐	7	
8	Other income from Schedule 1, line 9	8	
9	Add lines 1, 2b, 3b, 4b, 5b, 6b, 7, and 8. This is your **total income** . . . . ▶	9	
10	Adjustments to income:		
a	From Schedule 1, line 22 . . . . 10a		
b	Charitable contributions if you take the standard deduction. See instructions 10b		
c	Add lines 10a and 10b. These are your **total adjustments to income** . . . . ▶	10c	
11	Subtract line 10c from line 9. This is your **adjusted gross income** . . . . ▶	11	
12	**Standard deduction or itemized deductions** (from Schedule A)	12	
13	Qualified business income deduction. Attach Form 8995 or Form 8995-A	13	
14	Add lines 12 and 13	14	
15	**Taxable income.** Subtract line 14 from line 11. If zero or less, enter -0-	15	

For Disclosure, Privacy Act, and Paperwork Reduction Act Notice, see separate instructions.   Cat. No. 11320B   Form **1040** (2020)

Form 1040 (2020)   Page **2**

16	**Tax** (see instructions). Check if any from Form(s): **1** ☐ 8814 **2** ☐ 4972 **3** ☐ _____ . .		**16**	
17	Amount from Schedule 2, line 3		**17**	
18	Add lines 16 and 17		**18**	
19	Child tax credit or credit for other dependents		**19**	
20	Amount from Schedule 3, line 7		**20**	
21	Add lines 19 and 20		**21**	
22	Subtract line 21 from line 18. If zero or less, enter -0- . . .		**22**	
23	Other taxes, including self-employment tax, from Schedule 2, line 10		**23**	
24	Add lines 22 and 23. This is your **total tax** . . . . . ▶		**24**	

25	Federal income tax withheld from:	
a	Form(s) W-2	**25a**
b	Form(s) 1099	**25b**
c	Other forms (see instructions)	**25c**

• If you have a qualifying child, attach Sch. EIC.
• If you have nontaxable combat pay, see instructions.

d	Add lines 25a through 25c	**25d**	
26	2020 estimated tax payments and amount applied from 2019 return . .	**26**	
27	Earned income credit (EIC)	**27**	
28	Additional child tax credit. Attach Schedule 8812 . .	**28**	
29	American opportunity credit from Form 8863, line 8 . .	**29**	
30	Recovery rebate credit. See instructions	**30**	
31	Amount from Schedule 3, line 13	**31**	
32	Add lines 27 through 31. These are your **total other payments and refundable credits** . . ▶	**32**	
33	Add lines 25d, 26, and 32. These are your **total payments** . . . . ▶	**33**	

Refund

34	If line 33 is more than line 24, subtract line 24 from line 33. This is the amount you **overpaid** . .	**34**
35a	Amount of line 34 you want **refunded to you.** If Form 8888 is attached, check here . . . ▶ ☐	**35a**

Direct deposit? See instructions.

▶ **b** Routing number |_|_|_|_|_|_|_|_|_| ▶ **c** Type: ☐ Checking   ☐ Savings
▶ **d** Account number |_|_|_|_|_|_|_|_|_|_|_|_|_|_|_|_|_|

36	Amount of line 34 you want **applied to your 2021 estimated tax** . . ▶	**36**

Amount You Owe

For details on how to pay, see instructions.

37	Subtract line 33 from line 24. This is the **amount you owe now** . . . . ▶	**37**

Note: Schedule H and Schedule SE filers, line 37 may not represent all of the taxes you owe for 2020. See Schedule 3, line 12e, and its instructions for details.

38	Estimated tax penalty (see instructions) . . . . ▶	**38**

Third Party Designee

Do you want to allow another person to discuss this return with the IRS? See instructions . . . . ▶ ☐ **Yes.** Complete below.   ☐ **No**

Designee's name ▶ _____   Phone no. ▶ _____   Personal identification number (PIN) ▶ |_|_|_|_|_|

Sign Here

Under penalties of perjury, I declare that I have examined this return and accompanying schedules and statements, and to the best of my knowledge and belief, they are true, correct, and complete. Declaration of preparer (other than taxpayer) is based on all information of which preparer has any knowledge.

Joint return? See instructions. Keep a copy for your records.

Your signature	Date	Your occupation	If the IRS sent you an Identity Protection PIN, enter it here (see inst.) ▶ |_|_|_|_|_|_|
▶ Spouse's signature. If a joint return, **both** must sign.	Date	Spouse's occupation	If the IRS sent your spouse an Identity Protection PIN, enter it here (see inst.) ▶ |_|_|_|_|_|_|

Phone no. _____   Email address _____

Paid Preparer Use Only

Preparer's name	Preparer's signature	Date	PTIN	Check if: ☐ Self-employed
Firm's name ▶			Phone no.	
Firm's address ▶			Firm's EIN ▶	

Go to *www.irs.gov/Form1040* for instructions and the latest information.   Form **1040** (2020)

SCHEDULE 1
(Form 1040)

Department of the Treasury
Internal Revenue Service

Additional Income and Adjustments to Income

▶ Attach to Form 1040, 1040-SR, or 1040-NR.
▶ Go to *www.irs.gov/Form1040* for instructions and the latest information.

OMB No. 1545-0074

2020

Attachment
Sequence No. **01**

Name(s) shown on Form 1040, 1040-SR, or 1040-NR

Your social security number

Part I   Additional Income

1	Taxable refunds, credits, or offsets of state and local income taxes	1	
2a	Alimony received	2a	
b	Date of original divorce or separation agreement (see instructions) ▶		
3	Business income or (loss). Attach Schedule C	3	
4	Other gains or (losses). Attach Form 4797	4	
5	Rental real estate, royalties, partnerships, S corporations, trusts, etc. Attach Schedule E	5	
6	Farm income or (loss). Attach Schedule F	6	
7	Unemployment compensation	7	
8	Other income. List type and amount ▶	8	
9	Combine lines 1 through 8. Enter here and on Form 1040, 1040-SR, or 1040-NR, line 8	9	

Part II   Adjustments to Income

10	Educator expenses	10	
11	Certain business expenses of reservists, performing artists, and fee-basis government officials. Attach Form 2106	11	
12	Health savings account deduction. Attach Form 8889	12	
13	Moving expenses for members of the Armed Forces. Attach Form 3903	13	
14	Deductible part of self-employment tax. Attach Schedule SE	14	
15	Self-employed SEP, SIMPLE, and qualified plans	15	
16	Self-employed health insurance deduction	16	
17	Penalty on early withdrawal of savings	17	
18a	Alimony paid	18a	
b	Recipient's SSN ▶		
c	Date of original divorce or separation agreement (see instructions) ▶		
19	IRA deduction	19	
20	Student loan interest deduction	20	
21	Tuition and fees deduction. Attach Form 8917	21	
22	Add lines 10 through 21. These are your **adjustments to income.** Enter here and on Form 1040, 1040-SR, or 1040-NR, line 10a	22	

For Paperwork Reduction Act Notice, see your tax return instructions.   Cat. No. 71479F   **Schedule 1 (Form 1040) 2020**

Qualified Dividends and Capital Gain Tax Worksheet—Line 16

Before you begin:	✓ See the earlier instructions for line 16 to see if you can use this worksheet to figure your tax.
	✓ Before completing this worksheet, complete Form 1040 or 1040-SR through line 15.
	✓ If you don't have to file Schedule D and you received capital gain distributions, be sure you checked the box on Form 1040 or 1040-SR, line 7.

1. Enter the amount from Form 1040 or 1040-SR, line 15. However, if you are filing Form 2555 (relating to foreign earned income), enter the amount from line 3 of the Foreign Earned Income Tax Worksheet .... **1.** _____

2. Enter the amount from Form 1040 or 1040-SR, line 3a* .... **2.** _____

3. Are you filing Schedule D?*
   ☐ **Yes.** Enter the **smaller** of line 15 or 16 of Schedule D. If either line 15 or 16 is blank or a loss, enter -0-.
   ☐ **No.** Enter the amount from Form 1040 or 1040-SR, line 7.   **3.** _____

4. Add lines 2 and 3 .... **4.** _____

5. If filing Form 4952 (used to figure investment interest expense deduction), enter any amount from line 4g of that form. Otherwise, enter -0- .... **5.** _____

6. Subtract line 5 from line 4. If zero or less, enter -0- .... **6.** _____

7. Subtract line 6 from line 1. If zero or less, enter -0- .... **7.** _____

8. Enter:
   $40,000 if single or married filing separately,
   $80,000 if married filing jointly or qualifying widow(er),
   $53,600 if head of household.   .... **8.** _____

9. Enter the smaller of line 1 or line 8 .... **9.** _____

10. Enter the smaller of line 7 or line 9 .... **10.** _____

11. Subtract line 10 from line 9. This amount is taxed at 0% .... **11.** _____

12. Enter the smaller of line 1 or line 6 .... **12.** _____

13. Enter the amount from line 11 .... **13.** _____

14. Subtract line 13 from line 12 .... **14.** _____

15. Enter:
    $441,450 if single,
    $248,300 if married filing separately,
    $496,600 if married filing jointly or qualifying widow(er),
    $469,050 if head of household.   .... **15.** _____

16. Enter the smaller of line 1 or line 15 .... **16.** _____

17. Add lines 7 and 11 .... **17.** _____

18. Subtract line 17 from line 16. If zero or less, enter -0- .... **18.** _____

19. Enter the smaller of line 14 or line 18 .... **19.** _____

20. Multiply line 19 by 15% (0.15) .... **20.** _____

21. Add lines 11 and 19 .... **21.** _____

22. Subtract line 21 from line 12 .... **22.** _____

23. Multiply line 22 by 20% (0.20) .... **23.** _____

24. Figure the tax on the amount on line 7. If the amount on line 7 is less than $100,000, use the Tax Table to figure the tax. If the amount on line 7 is $100,000 or more, use the Tax Computation Worksheet .... **24.** _____

25. Add lines 20, 23, and 24 .... **25.** _____

26. Figure the tax on the amount on line 1. If the amount on line 1 is less than $100,000, use the Tax Table to figure the tax. If the amount on line 1 is $100,000 or more, use the Tax Computation Worksheet .... **26.** _____

27. **Tax on all taxable income.** Enter the **smaller** of line 25 or 26. Also include this amount on the entry space on Form 1040 or 1040-SR, line 16. If you are filing Form 2555, don't enter this amount on the entry space on Form 1040 or 1040-SR, line 16. Instead, enter it on line 4 of the Foreign Earned Income Tax Worksheet .... **27.** _____

* If you are filing Form 2555, see the footnote in the Foreign Earned Income Tax Worksheet before completing this line.

This worksheet adapted from the 2019 worksheet.

Student Name _____

Class/Section _____

Date   _____

KEY NUMBER TAX RETURN SUMMARY

CHAPTER 2

Comprehensive Problem 1

Adjusted Gross Income (Line 11)   _____

Taxable Income (Line 15)   _____

Total Tax (Line 24)   _____

Amount Overpaid (Line 34)   _____

Comprehensive Problem 2A

Adjusted Gross Income (Line 11)   _____

Taxable Income (Line 15)   _____

Total Tax (Line 24)   _____

Amount Overpaid (Line 34)   _____

Comprehensive Problem 2B

Adjusted Gross Income (Line 11)   _____

Taxable Income (Line 15)   _____

Total Tax (Line 24)   _____

Amount Overpaid (Line 34)   _____

Business Income and Expenses

After completing this chapter, you should be able to:

LO 3.1   Complete a basic Schedule C (Profit or Loss from Business).

LO 3.2   Describe the tax treatment of inventories and cost of goods sold.

LO 3.3   Identify the requirements for deducting transportation expenses.

LO 3.4   Identify the requirements for deducting travel expenses.

LO 3.5   Determine the requirements for deducting meals.

LO 3.6   Identify the requirements for claiming business education expenses.

LO 3.7   Identify the tax treatment of dues and subscriptions.

LO 3.8   Determine which clothing and uniforms may be treated as tax deductions.

LO 3.9   Explain the special limits for business gift deductions.

LO 3.10   Explain the tax treatment of bad debt deductions.

LO 3.11   Ascertain when a home office deduction may be claimed and how the deduction is computed.

LO 3.12   Apply the factors used to determine whether an activity is a hobby, and understand the tax treatment of hobby losses.

OVERVIEW

This chapter covers Schedule C, "Profit or Loss from Business (Sole Proprietorship)," and many of the common business expenses allowed as deductions in arriving at net taxable business income. Schedule C is filed by self-employed taxpayers, such as accountants, doctors, lawyers, architects, consultants, small manufacturers, restaurateurs, store owners, gardeners, event planners, bookkeepers, and other small businesses. This form is one of the most commonly used tax forms and, for many taxpayers, the net income reported on Schedule C is the primary component of their adjusted gross income. With the qualified business income (QBI) deduction, the sole proprietorship, along with income from rental properties (Chapter 4), partnerships (Chapter 10), and S corporations (Chapter 11), enjoy a reduction in tax rate in an attempt to match the 21 percent corporate tax rate. The QBI deduction is covered in detail in Chapter 4.

The business expenses discussed in this chapter include travel, transportation, bad debts, inventory, home office, meals and entertainment, business education, dues, subscriptions, publications, special clothing, uniforms, and business gifts. While these expenses are often associated with Schedule C (sole proprietorship income), they may also be reported with rental and royalty income on Schedule E, or farm and ranch income on Schedule F. Employee business expenses are covered in Chapter 5.

<table>
<tr><td>**Learning Objective 3.1**</td><td rowspan="2">

3-1 SCHEDULE C

</td></tr>
<tr><td>

Complete a basic Schedule C (Profit or Loss from Business).

</td></tr>
</table>

A taxpayer who operates a trade or business or practices a profession as a sole proprietorship must file a Schedule C with the Form 1040, reporting his or her taxable income or loss from the activity. Schedule C is similar to the income statement in financial accounting. Taxable income from a business or profession is reported on either Schedule C or Schedule F (a specialized version of Schedule C for farmers and ranchers).

3-1a Trade or Business

The term *trade or business* is not formally defined, although the term is used often in the Internal Revenue Code (the Code). For example, Section 162 of the Code states that a taxpayer is allowed to deduct all the ordinary and necessary expenses in carrying on a trade or business. Generally, a "trade or business" for tax purposes is any activity engaged in for profit. Note that a taxpayer does not have to actually make a profit, but he or she should be seeking to make a profit through regular and continual effort. Intermittent activities (e.g., casual craft sales) or leisure pursuits (e.g., wine making) do not always rise to the level of a trade or business and may require reporting under the hobby loss rules discussed later in this chapter.

3-1b Tests for Deductibility

Expenses must meet several general tests to qualify as a tax deduction. Listed below are three common tests for deductibility. These tests give guidelines for deductibility, but often in practice it is a matter of judgment as to whether an expense is considered a deductible business expense. Taxpayers and IRS agents frequently disagree as to whether specific expenses pass the following tests, and many court cases have been devoted to resolving these disagreements. The tests below overlap and an expense may fail more than one test.

- **The Ordinary and Necessary Test:** Under the tax law, for trade or business expenses to be deductible they must be ordinary and necessary. Generally, this means that the expense is commonly found in the specific business, and is helpful and appropriate in running the business. For example, Rob is a CPA who goes to a "tax boot camp" which offers intensive training on tax return preparation every year. Rob also hires a trainer at his local gym to work out with him to help him maintain the strength and endurance needed to handle the rigors of tax season. The cost of the "tax boot camp" would be deductible. The cost of the personal trainer is not a common or ordinary expense of CPA firms and is not necessary for preparing tax returns and therefore would not be deductible.

- **The Business Purpose Test:** Expenses must have a legitimate business purpose to be considered deductible. Larry is an independent consultant who maintains an office in his home, although he always meets with clients at their place of business. He spent $75,000 upgrading his office to include a large attached glass sunroom and a display area for his orchid collection. This home office upgrade would likely be considered to serve no business purpose, so the expenses related to the improvements would not be allowed.
- **The Reasonableness Test:** The tax law requires that deductions be reasonable to be deducted. For example, Derek owns a small business and takes one of his clients, who is also a friend, to an expensive business dinner every week. They enjoy a variety of restaurants and fine wines, and always spend some time talking about their joint business interests. The yearly cost of the meetings and meals is $20,000, and Derek generates $15,000 of fees from his friend each year. This lavish and extravagant business entertainment would likely not be considered reasonable given the circumstances. If they had met for pizza and a business discussion every week, the expense would likely be considered reasonable and deductible.

The IRS and courts have taken a fairly permissive perspective on the deduction of business expenses; however, the Code does restrict the deduction of certain expenses such as the following:

- Personal, living, and family expenses (although see itemized deductions in Chapter 5)
- Capital expenditures (see Chapter 7)
- Expenses related to tax-exempt income
- Expenditures related to the sale of illegal drugs
- Illegal bribes and kickbacks
- Fines, penalties, and other payments to governments related to the violation of law
- Lobbying and political expenditures
- Settlement or attorney fees related to sexual abuse or harassment if subject to a non-disclosure agreement

Taxes are specifically excepted from the restriction on fines and penalties as are payments made to bring the taxpayer into compliance with the law or as restitution.

EXAMPLE Maria owns and operates a small pizza shop in the city. The City Council is considering new zoning laws that would permit the creation of a large hotel and theme park next to Maria's restaurant which she expects would increase her business significantly. She pays $10,000 to have a study prepared to show the economic benefits of the new zoning to the City Council at a future meeting. Maria also has been a Republican since she was old enough to vote and makes a $1,000 contribution to the Republican National Committee. The $10,000 fee and her contribution to the RNC are lobbying and political expenditures and are not deductible. ◆

3-1c **Schedule C**

Schedule C is used by sole proprietors to report profit or loss from their businesses. The first section (lines A to J) of Schedule C requires disclosure of basic information such as the business name and location, the accounting method (cash, accrual, or other, as covered in Chapter 6), material participation in the business (for passive activity loss classification purposes, see Chapter 4), and whether the business was started or acquired during the year.

Schedule C requires the taxpayer to provide a principal business or professional activity code (see Figure 3.1). These codes are used to classify sole proprietorships by the type of business activity. For example, a full-service restaurant is code 722511, as shown in Figure 3.1.

FIGURE 3.1

PRINCIPAL BUSINESS OR PROFESSIONAL ACTIVITY CODES EXCERPT

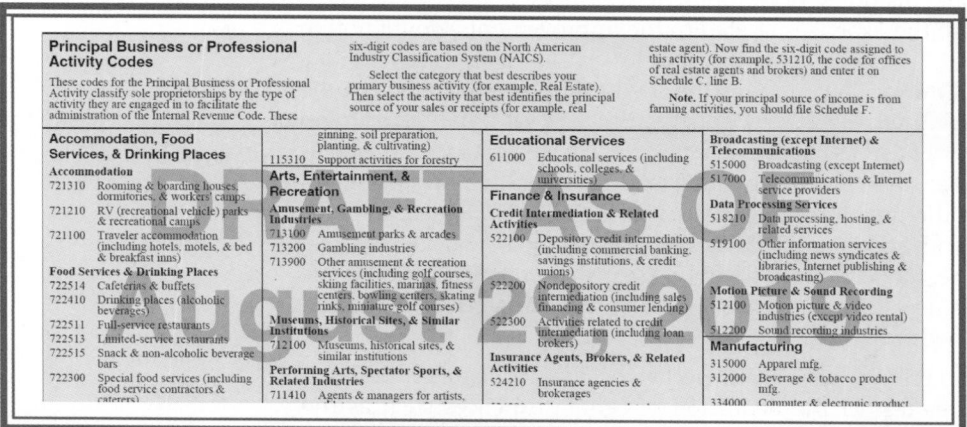

2019 Schedule C instructions presented. 2020 not available as we went to print.

3-1d Schedule C Income (Part I)

Part I of Schedule C (Figure 3.2) contains the calculation of the taxpayer's gross income from the business or profession. The calculation starts with gross receipts or sales (line 1). Returns and allowances (line 2) and cost of goods sold (line 4) are subtracted to arrive at the gross profit from the activity. Other related income from the business (line 6) is added to the gross profit to produce the Schedule C gross income (line 7).

FIGURE 3.2

SCHEDULE C INCOME (PART I)

Part I	Income		
1	Gross receipts or sales. See instructions for line 1 and check the box if this income was reported to you on Form W-2 and the "Statutory employee" box on that form was checked ▶ ☐	1	
2	Returns and allowances	2	
3	Subtract line 2 from line 1	3	
4	Cost of goods sold (from line 42)	4	
5	**Gross profit.** Subtract line 4 from line 3	5	
6	Other income, including federal and state gasoline or fuel tax credit or refund (see instructions)	6	
7	**Gross income.** Add lines 5 and 6 ▶	7	

3-1e Schedule C Expenses (Part II)

The taxpayer reports the expenses from his or her business or profession in Part II of Schedule C (Figure 3.3). Expenses such as advertising, insurance, interest, rent, travel, wages, and utilities are reported on lines 8 through 27. Some expenses such as depreciation may require additional supporting information from another schedule. The expenses are totaled on line 28 and subtracted from gross income (line 7) to arrive at the tentative profit from the activity (line 29). An expense for business use of a taxpayer's home (see LO 3.11) is computed on Form 8829 or using the simplified method. The deductible portion of home office expenses is entered on line 30 and subtracted from tentative profit, resulting in the net profit or loss (line 31) from the activity. Common business expenses are covered in detail later in this chapter.

FIGURE 3.3   SCHEDULE C EXPENSES (PART II)

Part II	**Expenses.** Enter expenses for business use of your home **only** on line 30.					
8	Advertising	8		18	Office expense (see instructions)	18
9	Car and truck expenses (see instructions)	9		19	Pension and profit-sharing plans .	19
10	Commissions and fees .	10		20	Rent or lease (see instructions):	
11	Contract labor (see instructions)	11		a	Vehicles, machinery, and equipment	20a
12	Depletion	12		b	Other business property . . .	20b
13	Depreciation and section 179 expense deduction (not included in Part III) (see instructions)	13		21	Repairs and maintenance . . .	21
				22	Supplies (not included in Part III) .	22
				23	Taxes and licenses	23
				24	Travel and meals:	
14	Employee benefit programs (other than on line 19) . .	14		a	Travel	24a
15	Insurance (other than health)	15		b	Deductible meals (see instructions)	24b
16	Interest (see instructions):			25	Utilities	25
a	Mortgage (paid to banks, etc.)	16a		26	Wages (less employment credits) .	26
b	Other	16b		27a	Other expenses (from line 48) . .	27a
17	Legal and professional services	17		b	Reserved for future use . . .	27b
28	**Total expenses** before expenses for business use of home. Add lines 8 through 27a . . . . . . ▶					28
29	Tentative profit or (loss). Subtract line 28 from line 7					29
30	Expenses for business use of your home. Do not report these expenses elsewhere. Attach Form 8829 unless using the simplified method. See instructions. **Simplified method filers only:** Enter the total square footage of (a) your home: _____ and (b) the part of your home used for business: _____ . Use the Simplified Method Worksheet in the instructions to figure the amount to enter on line 30					30
31	**Net profit or (loss).** Subtract line 30 from line 29. • If a profit, enter on both **Schedule 1 (Form 1040), line 3,** and on **Schedule SE, line 2.** (If you checked the box on line 1, see instructions). Estates and trusts, enter on **Form 1041, line 3.** • If a loss, you **must** go to line 32.					31
32	If you have a loss, check the box that describes your investment in this activity. See instructions. • If you checked 32a, enter the loss on both **Schedule 1 (Form 1040), line 3,** and on **Schedule SE, line 2.** (If you checked the box on line 1, see the line 31 instructions). Estates and trusts, enter on **Form 1041, line 3.** • If you checked 32b, you **must** attach **Form 6198.** Your loss may be limited.			32a ☐ All investment is at risk. 32b ☐ Some investment is not at risk.		

3-1f Schedule C Cost of Goods Sold (Part III)

The calculation of cost of goods sold is reported in Part III (Figure 3.4) of Schedule C. In Part III lines 33 and 34, taxpayers must answer questions about the methods used to calculate inventory. Cost of goods sold (line 42) is equal to the beginning inventory (line 35) plus purchases (line 36), labor (line 37), materials and supplies (line 38), and other costs (line 39) less ending inventory (line 41). Please see LO 3.2 for a more detailed discussion of inventories.

3-1g Schedule C Vehicle Information (Part IV)

If a taxpayer uses a car or truck in his or her sole proprietorship, then Part IV of Schedule C (Figure 3.5) must be completed to provide the IRS with supplemental vehicle information. In Part IV, a taxpayer should provide the date the vehicle was placed in service for business use (line 43), the business miles driven (line 44a), the commuting miles driven (line 44b), and other miles driven (line 44c). On lines 45 to 47 of Part IV, taxpayers must answer questions relevant to obtaining a deduction for business use of a vehicle.

3-1h Schedule C Other Expenses (Part V)

The expenses section of Schedule C (Part II), line 27 contains an entry for other miscellaneous expenses. These other expenses must be itemized in Part V of Schedule C and include deductible items which do not have specific lines already assigned in the expenses section (Part II). Expenses for business gifts, education, professional dues, and consulting fees are commonly listed.

FIGURE 3.4   COST OF GOODS SOLD (PART III)

Part III	Cost of Goods Sold (see instructions)	

33   Method(s) used to value closing inventory: **a** ☐ Cost   **b** ☐ Lower of cost or market   **c** ☐ Other (attach explanation)

34   Was there any change in determining quantities, costs, or valuations between opening and closing inventory? If "Yes," attach explanation . . . . ☐ Yes   ☐ No

35   Inventory at beginning of year. If different from last year's closing inventory, attach explanation . . .   **35**

36   Purchases less cost of items withdrawn for personal use **36**

37   Cost of labor. Do not include any amounts paid to yourself **37**

38   Materials and supplies **38**

39   Other costs **39**

40   Add lines 35 through 39 . . . .   **40**

41   Inventory at end of year **41**

42   **Cost of goods sold.** Subtract line 41 from line 40. Enter the result here and on line 4 . . . .   **42**

FIGURE 3.5   VEHICLE INFORMATION (PART IV)

Part IV	Information on Your Vehicle. Complete this part only if you are claiming car or truck expenses on line 9 and are not required to file Form 4562 for this business. See the instructions for line 13 to find out if you must file Form 4562.

43   When did you place your vehicle in service for business purposes? (month/day/year)   ▶ _____ / _____ / _____

44   Of the total number of miles you drove your vehicle during 2020, enter the number of miles you used your vehicle for:

a Business _____   **b** Commuting (see instructions) _____   **c** Other _____

45   Was your vehicle available for personal use during off-duty hours? . . . . ☐ Yes   ☐ No

46   Do you (or your spouse) have another vehicle available for personal use?. . . . . ☐ Yes   ☐ No

47a Do you have evidence to support your deduction? . . . . ☐ Yes   ☐ No

b If "Yes," is the evidence written? . . . . ☐ Yes   ☐ No

3-1i Self-Employment Tax

Self-employed taxpayers, sole proprietors, and independent contractors with net earnings of $400 or more, many of whom report income on Schedule C, must pay self-employment tax calculated on Schedule SE with their Form 1040. For new business owners, the self-employment tax may come as a particularly unpleasant and costly surprise if they are not aware of its existence.

The self-employment tax is made up of two taxes, the Social Security tax, which is meant to fund old age and disability insurance payments, and the Medicare tax. For 2020, the

Social Security tax rate of 12.4 percent applies to the first $137,700 of net self-employment income, while the Medicare tax rate of 2.9 percent applies to all net self-employment income, with no income ceiling. Half of the self-employment tax is allowed as a deduction on Line 14 of Schedule 1 of Form 1040 in arriving at adjusted gross income. Self-employment taxes are similar to FICA taxes, which are levied on employees partly through payroll withholding and partly through employer contributions. FICA taxes are not paid with Form 1040 as self-employment taxes are. Self-employed Social Security and Medicare taxes, including the 0.9 percent additional Medicare tax, are covered in detail in Chapter 6. Due to the COVID-19 pandemic, a number of temporary provisions designed to provide financial assistance to businesses were implemented. A number of these provisions provide for a credit or deferral of payroll taxes, including in some instances, self-employment taxes. These provisions are covered in Chapter 9.

To report profits from a sole proprietorship in ProConnect, under Income use Business Income (Schedule C) to enter information. Additional businesses can be added using the [+] tab at the top of the main window.

ProConnect™ Tax

TIP

Self-Study Problem 3.1   *See Appendix E for Solutions to Self-Study Problems*

Teri Kataoka is self-employed as a professional golf instructor. She uses the cash method of accounting and her Social Security number is 466-47-8833. Her principal business code is 812990. Teri's business is located at 1234 Pinecrest Dr., Kennesaw, GA 30152. During 2020, Teri had the following income and expenses:

Fees from golf lessons	$40,125
Expenses:	
Car mileage (5,280 business miles)	3,036
Business liability insurance	475
Office expense	660
Rent on office space	2,700
City business license	250
Travel expense	3,000
Meals (deductible portion)	985
Utilities	515
Membership in professional golfers' association	500

Teri bought her car on January 1, 2020. In addition to the business miles listed above, she commuted 1,200 miles and she drove 5,000 miles for nonbusiness purposes.

Complete Schedule C on Pages 3-10 and 3-11 for Teri showing her net income from self-employment. Make realistic assumptions about any missing data.

3-2 INVENTORIES

Inventory is the stock of goods or materials that a business holds for the purpose of resale to generate a profit. The purchase or sale of merchandise is almost always an income-producing factor for manufacturers, retailers, and wholesalers, and cost of goods sold is often the largest expense for these types of businesses.

3.2 Learning Objective

Describe the tax treatment of inventories and cost of goods sold.

EXAMPLE Yashida operates a small business that sells crafts over the Internet. The crafts are manufactured in her small factory. The purchase and sale of merchandise is clearly an income-producing factor for this business. ◆

EXAMPLE Alan is a lawyer that specializes in consumer class-action lawsuits against large corporations. Because his primary product is legal services, inventory is not a significant income-producing factor for Alan's business. ◆

When a business supplies goods in conjunction with providing services to customers, it is not always clear whether providing goods is an income-producing factor that requires the business to keep inventories.

Accounting for inventory can be complex. One of the primary steps in inventory accounting is to measure ending inventory at the end of the accounting period (usually at year end). To do so often requires a physical inventory, which is a process by which the actual count of goods is taken. An additional step is to assign an inventory flow method such as first-in, first-out (FIFO) or last-in, first-out (LIFO). Once ending inventory is established, cost of goods sold can be computed as follows:

Beginning inventory	$ 75,000
Add: purchases	250,000
Costs of goods available for sale	325,000
Less: ending inventory	(100,000)
Cost of goods sold	$ 225,000

Because of the time and effort associated with tracking inventory, the tax law permits small businesses to use the cash method for accounting for inventory. For purposes of this tax provision, a business with three-year average gross receipts of less than $26 million is considered a small business. Under the cash method, the taxpayer has three options:

1. treat inventory as non-incidental materials and supplies,
2. treat inventory the same as on the applicable financial statements of the business, or
3. for taxpayers without applicable financial statements, treat inventory as conforms with the business books and records.

Non-incidental materials and supplies (NIMS) are deducted in the tax year in which they are used or consumed in the taxpayer's operations. Inventory items are used or consumed when the business sells the merchandise. Thus, a taxpayer would deduct the cost of inventory either in the year that the merchandise is sold or the year in which the inventory is paid for, whichever is later.

EXAMPLE Geoff purchases unique goods from a variety of manufacturers and then sells those items over the Internet. Geoff's business is small and he treats inventory as NIMS. He will include the cost of the goods in his cost of goods sold when the items are sold. ◆

The treatment of inventory as NIMS does not differ considerably from typical inventory accounting, which also generally would recover the cost of inventory when the inventory is sold. The tax law contains a safe-harbor provision under which a taxpayer can elect to expense NIMS if the business uses the same policy for its financial statements (if any) or in its books and records. Proposed regulations issued in 2020 disallow the use of the safe-harbor election under NIMS and thus taxpayers must be extremely cautious using this approach.

The second option is to treat inventory the same as that of applicable financial statements (or AFS) of the business. AFS are generally financial statements that have been prepared in accordance with generally accepted accounting principles (GAAP). Since GAAP is going to require proper inventory accounting, this option provides no significant relief from inventory accounting.

The last option is to use the same accounting for inventory as is used on the books and records of the business. Under this option, if a business chooses to expense inventory when purchased, the business would be permitted to deduct the costs in the same year for tax purposes.

EXAMPLE Sue operates a garage that repairs European-made automobiles. As part of the service, the garage purchases and eventually sells a variety of car parts, including oil filters, brake pads, various belts, and motors (such as alternators). Sue expenses any part or supply as it is purchased, in spite of the item not yet being sold. For example, Sue may purchase five oil filters when only one is needed for a current repair with the expectation that the remaining four filters will be sold in the near future. Sue does not prepare applicable financial statements for her business. Sue will be able to conform her tax accounting for inventory with her books and records and thus will deduct inventory when purchased. ♦

However, the regulations proposed in 2020 appear to increase the likelihood that *any* use of typical inventory accounting may preclude deducting the cost of inventory at any time except when sold.

EXAMPLE Sasha is engaged in the retail business of selling beer, wine, and liquor. Sasha has average annual gross receipts for the prior 3-taxable-years of less than $26 million and thus uses the cash method of accounting. Sasha treats all merchandise costs paid during the taxable year as expensed on the bookkeeping software. However, as part of its regular business practice, Sasha takes a physical count of inventory of merchandise on hand at year end. Sasha also makes representations to its creditor of the amount of inventory on hand. Because Sasha's books and records do not accurately reflect the inventory records used for non-tax purposes in its regular business activity, Sasha must use the physical inventory count to determine its ending inventory and thus will deduct only the cost of inventory sold based on that count. ♦

The above examples of the three options for cash-basis inventory accounting show that only a small business that pays very little attention to inventory, can use the cash-basis method of inventory. To the extent that the purchase or sale of merchandise is a significant income-producing activity, recommended business practices would not permit such transactions without some form of tracking and accounting controls. Tax law generally requires the capitalization of certain indirect costs into inventory under Section 263A, sometimes known as the UNICAP rules. Businesses with gross receipts of no more than $26 million are not required to apply the UNICAP rules. The details of the UNICAP rules are beyond the scope of this textbook.

As a result of the current interpretation of inventory tax law, most businesses must calculate cost of goods sold by determining the value of the beginning and ending inventories of the business. This involves determining the cost of the items on hand. This process is not as easy as it seems, since the taxpayer will often have paid different

Self-Study Problem 3.1

SCHEDULE C (Form 1040)	**Profit or Loss From Business** (Sole Proprietorship)	OMB No. 1545-0074 2020
Department of the Treasury Internal Revenue Service (99)	► Go to *www.irs.gov/ScheduleC* for instructions and the latest information. ► **Attach to Form 1040, 1040-SR, 1040-NR, or 1041; partnerships generally must file Form 1065.**	Attachment Sequence No. **09**

Name of proprietor | Social security number (SSN)

A Principal business or profession, including product or service (see instructions)

B Enter code from instructions ►

C Business name. If no separate business name, leave blank.

D Employer ID number (EIN) (see instr.)

E Business address (including suite or room no.) ►

City, town or post office, state, and ZIP code

F Accounting method: **(1)** ☐ Cash **(2)** ☐ Accrual **(3)** ☐ Other (specify) ►

G Did you "materially participate" in the operation of this business during 2020? If "No," see instructions for limit on losses . ☐ Yes ☐ No

H If you started or acquired this business during 2020, check here . . . . ►☐

I Did you make any payments in 2020 that would require you to file Form(s) 1099? See instructions . . . . . ☐ Yes ☐ No

J If "Yes," did you or will you file required Form(s) 1099? . . . . ☐ Yes ☐ No

Part I   Income

1	Gross receipts or sales. See instructions for line 1 and check the box if this income was reported to you on Form W-2 and the "Statutory employee" box on that form was checked . . . . ►☐	**1**	
2	Returns and allowances	**2**	
3	Subtract line 2 from line 1	**3**	
4	Cost of goods sold (from line 42)	**4**	
5	**Gross profit.** Subtract line 4 from line 3	**5**	
6	Other income, including federal and state gasoline or fuel tax credit or refund (see instructions)	**6**	
7	**Gross income.** Add lines 5 and 6 . . . . ►	**7**	

Part II   Expenses. Enter expenses for business use of your home **only** on line 30.

8	Advertising	**8**		**18**	Office expense (see instructions)	**18**	
9	Car and truck expenses (see instructions).	**9**		**19**	Pension and profit-sharing plans .	**19**	
10	Commissions and fees .	**10**		**20**	Rent or lease (see instructions):		
11	Contract labor (see instructions)	**11**		**a**	Vehicles, machinery, and equipment	**20a**	
12	Depletion	**12**		**b**	Other business property . . .	**20b**	
13	Depreciation and section 179 expense deduction (not included in Part III) (see instructions).	**13**		**21**	Repairs and maintenance . . .	**21**	
				22	Supplies (not included in Part III) .	**22**	
				23	Taxes and licenses	**23**	
				24	Travel and meals:		
14	Employee benefit programs (other than on line 19) . .	**14**		**a**	Travel	**24a**	
15	Insurance (other than health)	**15**		**b**	Deductible meals (see instructions)	**24b**	
16	Interest (see instructions):			**25**	Utilities	**25**	
a	Mortgage (paid to banks, etc.)	**16a**		**26**	Wages (less employment credits) .	**26**	
b	Other	**16b**		**27a**	Other expenses (from line 48) . .	**27a**	
17	Legal and professional services	**17**		**b**	**Reserved for future use** . . .	**27b**	

28	**Total expenses** before expenses for business use of home. Add lines 8 through 27a . . . . . . ►	**28**	
29	Tentative profit or (loss). Subtract line 28 from line 7	**29**	
30	Expenses for business use of your home. Do not report these expenses elsewhere. Attach Form 8829 unless using the simplified method. See instructions. **Simplified method filers only:** Enter the total square footage of (a) your home: _____ and (b) the part of your home used for business: _____ . Use the Simplified Method Worksheet in the instructions to figure the amount to enter on line 30	**30**	
31	**Net profit or (loss).** Subtract line 30 from line 29. • If a profit, enter on both **Schedule 1 (Form 1040), line 3,** and on **Schedule SE, line 2.** (If you checked the box on line 1, see instructions). Estates and trusts, enter on **Form 1041, line 3.** • If a loss, you **must** go to line 32.	**31**	
32	If you have a loss, check the box that describes your investment in this activity. See instructions. • If you checked 32a, enter the loss on both **Schedule 1 (Form 1040), line 3,** and on **Schedule SE, line 2.** (If you checked the box on line 1, see the line 31 instructions). Estates and trusts, enter on **Form 1041, line 3.** • If you checked 32b, you **must** attach **Form 6198.** Your loss may be limited.	**32a** ☐ All investment is at risk. **32b** ☐ Some investment is not at risk.	

For Paperwork Reduction Act Notice, see the separate instructions.   Cat. No. 11334P   Schedule C (Form 1040) 2020

DRAFT AS OF JULY 13, 2020 DO NOT FILE

Schedule C (Form 1040) 2020   Page **2**

Part III	**Cost of Goods Sold** (see instructions)

33 Method(s) used to
value closing inventory: **a** ☐ Cost   **b** ☐ Lower of cost or market   **c** ☐ Other (attach explanation)

34 Was there any change in determining quantities, costs, or valuations between opening and closing inventory?
If "Yes," attach explanation . . . .   ☐ **Yes**   ☐ **No**

35	Inventory at beginning of year. If different from last year's closing inventory, attach explanation . .	**35**
36	Purchases less cost of items withdrawn for personal use	**36**
37	Cost of labor. Do not include any amounts paid to yourself	**37**
38	Materials and supplies	**38**
39	Other costs	**39**
40	Add lines 35 through 39	**40**
41	Inventory at end of year	**41**
42	**Cost of goods sold.** Subtract line 41 from line 40. Enter the result here and on line 4	**42**

Part IV	**Information on Your Vehicle.** Complete this part **only** if you are claiming car or truck expenses on line 9 and are not required to file Form 4562 for this business. See the instructions for line 13 to find out if you must file Form 4562.

43 When did you place your vehicle in service for business purposes? (month/day/year)   ▶ ____ / ____ / ____

44 Of the total number of miles you drove your vehicle during 2020, enter the number of miles you used your vehicle for:

a Business _____   **b** Commuting (see instructions) _____   **c** Other _____

45 Was your vehicle available for personal use during off-duty hours? . . . .   ☐ **Yes**   ☐ **No**

46 Do you (or your spouse) have another vehicle available for personal use?. . . . .   ☐ **Yes**   ☐ **No**

47a Do you have evidence to support your deduction? . . . .   ☐ **Yes**   ☐ **No**

b If "Yes," is the evidence written? . . . .   ☐ **Yes**   ☐ **No**

Part V	**Other Expenses.** List below business expenses not included on lines 8–26 or line 30.

_____	_____	
_____	_____	
_____	_____	
_____	_____	
_____	_____	
_____	_____	
_____	_____	
_____	_____	

48	**Total other expenses.** Enter here and on line 27a	**48**

Schedule C (Form 1040) 2020

prices during the year for the same item. There are two common methods of inventory valuation used by taxpayers: first in, first out (FIFO) and last in, first out (LIFO). The FIFO method is based on the assumption that the first merchandise acquired is the first to be sold. Accordingly, the inventory on hand consists of the most recently acquired goods. Alternatively, when the taxpayer uses the LIFO method, it is assumed that the most recently acquired goods are sold first and the inventory on hand consists of the earliest purchases. FIFO and LIFO are simply calculation assumptions; the goods that are actually on hand do not have to correspond to the assumptions of the method selected. In addition to the LIFO and FIFO methods which are commonly used by taxpayers in valuing beginning and ending inventories, taxpayers may specifically identify the goods that are sold and the goods that are in ending inventory. However, the process of specifically identifying items sold and on hand is not a practical alternative for most taxpayers.

EXAMPLE   Paige made the following purchases of a particular inventory item during the current year:

March 1	50 units at $120 per unit	$ 6,000
August 1	40 units at $130 per unit	5,200
December 1	25 units at $140 per unit	3,500
Total		$14,700

If the ending inventory is 60 units, it is valued under the FIFO method as illustrated below:

25 units at $140 each	$3,500
35 units at $130 each	4,550
Ending inventory	$8,050

Assuming that Paige had no beginning inventory of the item, the same ending inventory (60 units) would be valued using the LIFO method as follows:

50 units at $120 each	$6,000
10 units at $130 each	1,300
Ending inventory	$7,300

The cost of goods sold for both the FIFO and LIFO methods are presented below:

	FIFO	LIFO
Beginning inventory	$ 0	$ 0
Add: purchases	14,700	14,700
Cost of goods available for sale	$14,700	$14,700
Less: ending inventory	(8,050)	(7,300)
Cost of goods sold	$ 6,650	$ 7,400

Notice that taxable income will be $750 more when the FIFO method is used instead of the LIFO method. During periods of rising inventory prices, taxpayers have lower taxable income and pay less tax if they use the LIFO inventory valuation method. ♦

A taxpayer may adopt the LIFO method by using it in a tax return and attaching Form 970 to make the election. Once the election is made, the method may be changed only with the consent of the IRS. Also, if the LIFO election is made for reporting taxable income, taxpayers must use the same method for preparing their financial statements. In other words, a taxpayer may not use LIFO for his or her tax return and use FIFO for financial statements presented to a bank. This rule is strictly enforced by the IRS.

Self-Study Problem 3.2   *See Appendix E for Solutions to Self-Study Problems*

Kelly owns a small retail store. During the year, Kelly purchases $178,750 worth of inventory. Her beginning inventory is $62,500 and her ending inventory is $68,400. Use Part III of Schedule C below to calculate Kelly's cost of goods sold for the year.

Part III	**Cost of Goods Sold** (see instructions)		
33	Method(s) used to value closing inventory: **a** ☐ Cost **b** ☐ Lower of cost or market **c** ☐ Other (attach explanation)		
34	Was there any change in determining quantities, costs, or valuations between opening and closing inventory? If "Yes," attach explanation . . . . ☐ **Yes** ☐ **No**		
35	Inventory at beginning of year. If different from last year's closing inventory, attach explanation . .	**35**	
36	Purchases less cost of items withdrawn for personal use	**36**	
37	Cost of labor. Do not include any amounts paid to yourself	**37**	
38	Materials and supplies	**38**	
39	Other costs	**39**	
40	Add lines 35 through 39	**40**	
41	Inventory at end of year	**41**	
42	**Cost of goods sold.** Subtract line 41 from line 40. Enter the result here and on line 4	**42**	

DRAFT AS OF July 13, 2020 DO NOT FILE

3-3   TRANSPORTATION

3.3 Learning Objective

Identify the requirements for deducting transportation expenses.

Certain transportation expenses for business purposes are deductible by self-employed taxpayers and employers. Deductible expenses include travel by airplane, rail, and bus, and the cost of operating and maintaining an automobile. Meals and lodging are *not* included in the transportation expense deduction; those expenses may be deducted as travel expenses (see LO 3.4). Transportation expenses may be deducted even if the taxpayer is not away from his or her tax home.

Deductible transportation costs do not include the normal costs of commuting. Commuting includes the expenses of buses, subways, taxis, and operating a private car between home and the taxpayer's principal place of work, and is generally a nondeductible personal expense. The cost of transportation between the taxpayer's home and a work location is generally not deductible, except in the three sets of circumstances described below:

1. A taxpayer is allowed to deduct daily transportation expenses incurred in going between the taxpayer's residence and work locations outside the metropolitan area where the taxpayer lives and normally works.
2. If the taxpayer has a regular place of business, daily expenses for transportation between the taxpayer's home and temporary work locations are deductible.
3. A taxpayer may deduct daily expenses for transportation between the taxpayer's home and other regular or temporary work locations if the taxpayer's residence is the taxpayer's principal place of business, based on the home office rules, which are discussed later in this chapter.

In all cases, the additional costs of hauling tools and instruments are deductible. For example, the cost of renting a trailer to haul tools to a job site is deductible.

If the taxpayer works at two or more jobs during the same day, he or she may deduct the cost of going from one job to the other or from one business location to another.

The deductible expense is based on the cost of travel by the shortest, most normally traveled route, even if the taxpayer uses another route. If the taxpayer works at a second job on a day that he or she does not work at the first job, the commuting expenses to the second job are not deductible.

EXAMPLE   Walter is a self-employed CPA working full time Monday through Friday. On Tuesday night he teaches an accounting class at a local university. Walter leaves the office at 5:30 p.m. on his class day and, after dinner at a local cafe, teaches his class from 7:00 p.m. to 10:00 p.m. The distance from Walter's home to his office is 12 miles, the distance from his office to the university is 15 miles, and the distance from the university to his home is 18 miles. If Walter teaches the class 32 times a year, his mileage deduction is based on 480 miles (32 × 15 miles). While he is traveling from home to the office (12 miles) and from the university to home (18 miles), he is commuting and the mileage is not deductible. If Walter taught the class in the afternoon and returned to his regular job before going home, he could claim a deduction based on the round-trip mileage from his office to and from the university, 30 miles (2 × 15 miles). Alternatively, if he taught the course on a day (Saturday) when he did not work at his full-time job, Walter would not be entitled to any mileage deduction. ◆

Taxpayers may deduct the actual expenses of transportation, or they may be entitled to use a standard mileage rate to calculate their deduction for transportation costs. The standard mileage rate for 2020 is 57.5 cents per mile. Most costs associated with the operation of an automobile, such as gasoline, oil, insurance, repairs, and maintenance, as well as depreciation, are built into the standard mileage rate. The deduction for parking and toll fees related to business transportation (not commuting) and the deduction for interest on car loans and state and local personal property taxes on the automobile are determined separately. Self-employed taxpayers deduct the business portion of the state and local personal property taxes and interest on automobile loans on Schedule C or F. To use the standard mileage method, the taxpayer must:

1. own or lease the automobile,
2. not operate a fleet of automobiles, using five or more at the same time,
3. not have claimed depreciation on the automobile using any method other than straight-line depreciation, and
4. not have claimed Section 179 (expense election) depreciation or bonus depreciation on the automobile (see Chapter 8 for a complete discussion of depreciation).

If the taxpayer is entitled to use either the actual cost or the standard mileage method, he or she may select the method that results in the largest tax deduction for the first year. If the taxpayer does not use the standard mileage method in the first year, the method is no longer available for any subsequent year. A change to the actual cost method can be made any year. If, after using the standard mileage method, the taxpayer uses actual costs to determine the automobile expense deduction, depreciation on the automobile must be calculated using straight-line depreciation (see Chapter 8). The standard mileage method may be used for a car for hire, such as a taxi, if the automobile meets the other requirements for use of this method.

Taxpayers who use the actual cost method to calculate their transportation deductions must keep adequate cost records. The deductible portion of the total automobile expenses is based on the ratio of the number of business miles driven during the year to the total miles driven during the tax year multiplied by the total automobile expenses for the year. The business-use percentage is applied to the total automobile expenses for the year, including depreciation, but excluding any expenses which are directly attributable to business use of the automobile, such as business parking fees and tolls. The deduction for interest and personal property taxes is also separately computed.

EXAMPLE T.J. is a self-employed salesman who drove his automobile 22,500 total miles during the 2020 tax year. The business use of the automobile was 80 percent of the total miles driven. The actual cost of gasoline, oil, repairs, depreciation, and insurance for the year was $10,000. The automobile expense deduction is calculated as follows:

1. Standard mileage method:
   Business mileage = 18,000 miles (22,500 miles × 80%)
   18,000 miles × 57.5 cents/mile $10,350

2. Actual cost method:
   80% × $10,000 (total actual cost) $8,000

   Since the deduction is larger using the standard mileage method, T.J. should deduct that amount. ♦

Vehicle expenses are reported on Form 2106 and are carried over to Schedule C or other forms. To enter deductions associated with a business vehicle, go to Vehicle/Employee Business Expense (2106) under the general Deductions item in the left margin. The deduction can be connected to the appropriate Schedule C or other business using a dropdown box.

ProConnect™ Tax

TIP

Self-Study Problem 3.3 *See Appendix E for Solutions to Self-Study Problems*

Marc Lusebrink, sole proprietor of Oak Company, bought a used automobile and drove it 13,120 miles for business during 2020 and a total (including business miles) of 16,000 miles. His total expenses for his automobile for the year are:

Gasoline	$2,061
Oil changes	92
Insurance	1,030
Tires	225
Repairs	620
Total	$4,028

The automobile cost $20,000 on January 1, and depreciation expense for the year, including business use, was $4,000. His business parking and toll fees for business amount to $327. Calculate Marc's transportation expense deduction for the year.

3-4 TRAVEL EXPENSES

Learning Objective 3.4

Identify the requirements for deducting travel expenses.

Travel expenses are defined as ordinary and necessary expenses incurred in traveling away from home in pursuit of the taxpayer's trade or business. These expenses are deductible as long as they can be substantiated and are not lavish or extravagant. Transportation expenses incurred while not away from home such as business gifts are not included as travel expenses, although these items may be separately deductible, subject to certain limitations. Expenses included as part of the travel deduction include the cost of such items as meals, lodging, taxis, tips, and laundry. Most travel expenses are fully deductible, but Congress decided that a portion of the cost of meals is a personal expense. Therefore, only 50 percent of the cost of meals is deductible. If an employer reimburses an employee for the cost of meals, then the 50 percent limitation applies to the employer so that the employer can deduct only 50 percent of the expense.

To deduct travel expenses, a taxpayer must be away from home "overnight." Overnight does not literally mean 24 hours; it is a period of time longer than an ordinary work day in which rest or relief from work is required. Also, the taxpayer must be away from his or her "tax home" to be on travel status. A tax home is the taxpayer's principal place of business or employment, and not necessarily the same location as his or her family residence. If the taxpayer has two or more places of business, the taxpayer's tax home is at the principal place of business. Factors that determine the principal place of business include total time spent in each location, the degree of business activity, and the relative amount of income from each location.

Expenses of a temporary assignment are deductible if it is not practical to return home at the end of each day's work or if the employer requires the employee's attendance at a business meeting, training activity, or other overnight business function. If the assignment is for a long period of time or indefinite (generally more than 1 year), the new location may be considered the taxpayer's new tax home and he or she may lose the travel deduction. If the travel costs are not deductible, an employee must include as income any reimbursements of non-deductible travel expenses.

Taxpayers who make a combined business and pleasure trip within the United States may deduct all of the costs incurred in traveling to and from the business destination (for example, airfare) provided the trip is primarily for business. Once at the destination, only the business portion of the travel costs for meals, lodging, local transportation, and incidental expenses may be deducted; any costs which are not associated with the taxpayer's business are not deductible. If a taxpayer makes a trip which is primarily for pleasure, the travel expenses to and from the destination are not deductible even though the taxpayer engages in some business activity while at the destination. Although the traveling expenses to and from the destination are not deductible, any expenses incurred while at the destination that are related to the taxpayer's business are deductible.

Special rules and limitations apply to combined business and pleasure travel outside the United States. Even though a trip is primarily for business, if the trip has any element of pleasure, the cost of traveling to and from the destination must be allocated between the business and personal portions of the trip. The travel expenses for transportation to and from the destination must be allocated based on the number of business days compared to the total number of days outside the United States. The rules for travel costs to and from the destination where the trip is primarily for pleasure are the same as the rules for travel within the United States; none of the travel costs are deductible. Once at the destination, the taxpayer's expenses directly related to the taxpayer's business are deductible. For a complete explanation of travel outside the United States, see IRS Publication 463.

No deduction for travel expenses is allowed unless the taxpayer keeps proper expense records. Taxpayers must substantiate the following:

1. The amount of each separate expenditure, such as airfare and lodging. Expenses such as meals and taxi fares may be accumulated and reported in reasonable categories. As an alternative to reporting actual expenses, a per diem method may be used in certain circumstances.

2. The dates of departure and return for each trip and the number of business days on the trip.
3. The destination or locality of the travel described by the name of the city or town.
4. The business reason for the travel or the business benefit expected to be gained from the travel.

EXAMPLE During 2020, Susan travels from Los Angeles to Hawaii for a 3-day business trip and pays $450 for the airfare. While in Hawaii, Susan spends 3 days on business and an additional 2 days on vacation. The lodging and meal costs are $300 and $120, respectively, for the business portion of the trip. The total cost of meals and lodging for the personal portion of the trip is $260. Susan may deduct $450 for the airfare, $300 for the business lodging, and $60 (50 percent of $120) for the business meals. None of the $260 of personal expenses is deductible. ♦

3-4a Per Diem Substantiation

Instead of requiring actual expense records, employers who reimburse employees for travel expenses can choose a per diem method of substantiation. The primary advantage of using a per diem method to substantiate expenses is that it eliminates much of the record keeping usually associated with travel expenses. The IRS has approved two per diem methods to substantiate travel expenses: (1) the standard per diem method and (2) the high-low per diem method. Employers can use per diem for all travel expenses including lodging, meals, and incidentals or an employer can use per diem for only meals and incidentals. Self-employed taxpayers may only use per diem for meals and incidentals.

1. *The Standard Federal Rate Method.* Under this method, the employee is allowed a per diem amount for travel equal to the current federal per diem rate which varies based on the travel location. A complete list of the regular per diem rates in effect for each area of the United States is available at the U.S. General Services Administration website (**www.gsa.gov**). The GSA also offers a mobile app.
2. *The High-Low Method.* The high-low method provides a simplified way of computing the federal per diem rate for travel within the United States. This method avoids the need to keep a current list of the per diem rates for all localities in the United States. Under this method a small number of locations are designated as high-cost localities and all other locations are deemed to be low-cost areas. In 2020, the high-cost allowance is $297 per day and the low-cost amount is $200 per day. If an employer uses this method to reimburse an employee any time during a calendar year, this method must be used for all travel for that employee in the same calendar year.

Under either the standard method or the high-low method, the employee can use a current per diem amount for meals and incidental expenses (M&IE) only. Actual cost records are required for lodging expenses. The M&IE rate may be taken from the standard per diem rate tables or the high-low method may be used. For 2020, the M&IE allowance using the high-low method is $71 per day for high-cost localities and $60 per day for low-cost localities. Employees and self-employed taxpayers who do not incur meal expenses when traveling are allowed an incidental expense allowance of $5 per day.

Per diem rates are revised on October 1 every year with additional revisions made for specific locations throughout the year. For purposes of illustration and problems, the rates above are assumed to be chosen for the full year. Different rates than those shown above may apply.

Self-Study Problem 3.4   *See Appendix E for Solutions to Self-Study Problems*

Byron is a certified public accountant who is self-employed. He is required to make a 5-day business trip to Salt Lake City for an audit. Since he is going to be in Utah, Byron decides to stay for the weekend and go skiing. His expenses for the trip are as follows:

Airfare to Salt Lake City and return	$ 480
Hotel while on the audit (5 nights at $165 per night)	825
Deductible portion of meals while on the audit	168
Laundry in Salt Lake City	22
Taxi fares in Salt Lake City	72
Transportation from Salt Lake City to and from Park City ski resort	100
Lodging at Park City ski resort	380
Lift tickets	99
Ski rental	89
Meals at Park City	182
Total	$2,417

If Byron has proper records to substantiate the above expenses, how much may he deduct as travel expenses for the 7-day trip?

$ _____

3-5 MEALS AND ENTERTAINMENT

Starting in 2018, there is no deduction for (1) an activity generally considered to be entertainment, amusement, or recreation, (2) membership dues for any club organized for business, pleasure, recreation, or other social purposes, or (3) a facility used in connection with any of the above items. Entertainment costs related to a recreation, social, or similar activities for the benefit of employees remain deductible.

EXAMPLE Dee Skotech operates a small business and hosted two parties at a local night club during 2020. The first was a party for all of her clients to celebrate a great year and to thank them for their loyalty. The second party was a holiday celebration for all the employees in Dee's company. The costs associated with the client party are nondeductible entertainment costs. The costs for the employee holiday party are 100 percent deductible. ♦

Because meals and entertainment are often closely aligned, taxpayers should be cautious in attempting to deduct meals associated with an entertainment event. Client meals in which business is conducted (and the taxpayer or taxpayer's employee is present) and which are not lavish or extravagant remain 50 percent deductible. An entertainment-related meal such as one associated with a cocktail party, theatre, golf outing, or other entertainment event is only deductible if the meal is purchased or invoiced separately.

EXAMPLE Beau Gee is a salesperson for Hamilton Company. Beau has a meeting with an important customer at a local diner. Business is conducted at the meal as Beau and the customer discuss pricing, delivery dates, and other particulars, although no sale is actually closed. After the meal, Beau suggests they play a round of golf at the local golf course. After playing a round of golf, Beau and the customer stop in the golf club's "19th hole" and have a drink or two and some appetizers. Because business was conducted at the diner, the cost of the first meal is 50 percent deductible; however, the golf is entertainment and is not deductible. If the drinks and appetizers are separately purchased, the cost is 50 percent deductible. ◆

In addition to celebratory meals such as holiday parties and company picnics, other meals remain either 50 or 100 percent deductible:

Type of meal	Deductible
Meals for the convenience of the employer	50 percent (see Chapter 2) until after 2025 and thereafter not deductible
Water, coffee, and other office snacks	50 percent deductible
Meals provided for in-office meetings with employees	50 percent deductible
Meals during business travel	50 percent deductible
Meals offered for free to the public (e.g., a free seminar)	100 percent deductible

Although entertainment-related club dues are nondeductible, dues paid to professional organizations, such as bar or medical organizations, are deductible. Dues paid to civic or public organizations, such as Chambers of Commerce, Kiwanis, and Rotary, are also allowed as legitimate business deductions. These clubs do public service work and are not organizations like country clubs which are entertainment or pleasure driven. Many business people belong to clubs such as Kiwanis or Rotary to network, meet potential clients, and increase their visibility in the community, but the club must do significant service work for the members' dues to qualify as deductions.

Self-Study Problem 3.5   *See Appendix E for Solutions to Self-Study Problems*

Milly operates a small business and incurs the following expenses:

Annual dues Tampa Bay Golf Club	$2,000
Meals with clients after golf	500
Meals with clients at the Club's dining room where business was conducted	600
Greens fees (personal and with clients)	700
Meals (personal)	250
Total	$4,050

Calculate the portion of the $4,050 that Milly can deduct.

$ _____

3-6 EDUCATIONAL EXPENSES

3.6 Learning Objective

Identify the requirements for claiming business education expenses.

Please note: Educational incentives such as qualified tuition programs and educational savings accounts are discussed in Chapter 2. The deduction for education loan interest is discussed in Chapter 5. Education tax credits are discussed in Chapter 7. Because there are numerous education incentives, the tax law in this area has become very complex. There may be more than one tax option for treating a particular education

expense. **This section deals primarily with the deduction of continuing education expenses incurred by self-employed taxpayers. The suspension of the deduction for miscellaneous expenses subject to 2 percent of AGI has effectively eliminated the deduction of unreimbursed educational costs for employees.**

There are two tests related to the deduction of educational expenses, at least one of which must be met to deduct the expenses. The tests are:

1. the educational expenses must be paid to meet *the requirements of the taxpayer's employer or the requirements of law or regulation* for keeping the taxpayer's salary, status, or job, or
2. the educational expenses must be paid to *maintain* or *improve existing skills* required in performing the duties of the taxpayer's present work.

Educational expenses meeting one of the above tests, which have a bona fide business purpose, may be deducted even if the education leads to a college degree.

Educational expenses are not deductible, even if one of the above tests is met, if (1) the education is required to meet the minimum requirements for the taxpayer's current job, or (2) the education is part of a program that will lead to a new trade or business even if the taxpayer does not intend to enter that new trade or business.

3-6a Education Required by Employer or Law

Taxpayers who are required to meet educational standards beyond minimum requirements may deduct the expenses of the education. However, the expenses must be paid for education to maintain the taxpayer's current job, not to meet the minimum requirements for that job. If the education qualifies the taxpayer for a new trade or business, the expenses are not deductible.

EXAMPLE   Jenny is a high school teacher working under a temporary teaching certificate. The state in which she teaches requires a master's degree to receive a permanent certificate, and Jenny only has a bachelor's degree. Her expenses to obtain a master's degree are not deductible even though the degree is required by her school district, since she has not yet met the minimum educational requirements to be a permanent teacher.

However, Jenny may qualify for the lifetime learning credit discussed in Chapter 7 ♦

3-6b Maintaining or Improving Existing Skills

Expenses that are paid by a taxpayer for education to maintain or improve existing skills are deductible. Expenses deductible under this category include the costs of continuing education courses and academic work at a college or university. However, the education must not lead to qualification in a new trade or business. The deduction of a review course for the CPA exam and bar exam is consistently disallowed by the IRS.

EXAMPLE   John is a certified public accountant (CPA) in practice with a CPA firm. He decides a law degree would be helpful to him in his present job since he does a lot of income tax planning for clients. He enrolls in a night program at a local law school. John's educational expenses are not deductible since the program leads to a new trade or business, the practice of law. Whether or not John plans to practice law is not relevant. However, John may qualify for the lifetime learning credit discussed in Chapter 7 ♦

EXAMPLE   Kenzie recently completed her degree in accounting and went to work for a local CPA firm. She spends $1,000 for a CPA exam review course to help her pass the exam. The $1,000 is not deductible since passing the CPA exam leads to a new trade or business, that of being a licensed CPA as opposed to an accountant. Depending on whether Kenzie takes this course at a qualified institution of higher education, and other circumstances, she may qualify for the lifetime learning credit discussed in Chapter 7 ◆

3-6c Expenses of Travel for Educational Purposes

Travel expenses incurred while away from home for trips that are primarily to obtain qualifying education are also deductible. For example, a taxpayer may deduct travel expenses for attending a continuing education course in a distant city. Whether a trip is primarily personal or primarily educational depends on the relative amount of time devoted to each activity. If the trip qualifies as primarily for educational purposes, the cost of transportation to and from the destination is fully deductible. The lodging and meal expenses directly connected with the educational activity are also deductible. As is the case with travel expenses, the cost of meals is only 50 percent deductible. Expenses for "travel as a form of education" are not deductible.

EXAMPLE Jay is a doctor who attended a continuing education seminar in New York. His expenses related to attendance at the program are as follows:

Lodging in New York	$ 350
Transportation	700
Meals	150
Fee for the course	250
Total	$1,450

Jay's educational expense deduction for the seminar would be $1,375 including lodging of $350, transportation of $700, meals of $75 (50 percent of the cost of the meals), and the course fee of $250. ◆

EXAMPLE Natalie is an instructor of Japanese at Big State University. She spends the summer traveling in Japan to improve her understanding of the Japanese language and culture. Although Natalie arranges her trip to improve her ability to teach the Japanese language, no education deduction is allowed for the travel expenses. ◆

Self-Study Problem 3.6   *See Appendix E for Solutions to Self-Study Problems*

Nadine is a self-employed attorney. Her expenses for continuing legal education are as follows:

Lodging in Tempe, Arizona	$1,200
Transportation	350
Meals	200
Books	175
Tuition	550
Weekend trip to the Grand Canyon	175
Total	$2,650

Calculate Nadine's educational expense deduction for the current year. Assume Nadine's household income is too high for her to qualify for the lifetime learning credit discussed in Chapter 7

$ _____

3-7 DUES, SUBSCRIPTIONS, AND PUBLICATIONS

Learning Objective 3.7

Identify the tax treatment of dues and subscriptions.

Doctors, lawyers, accountants, engineers, teachers, and other professionals who are self-employed or are employers may deduct certain dues and the cost of certain subscriptions and publications. Included in this category of deductions are items such as membership to the local bar for a lawyer, dues to the American Institute of Certified Public Accountants (AICPA) for an accountant, and the cost of subscriptions to any journal that is directly related to the taxpayer's profession. Due to the suspension of miscellaneous deductions subject to 2 percent of AGI through 2025, only self-employed taxpayers can deduct dues and subscriptions. Employees can no longer deduct these costs; however, if the dues or subscription costs are reimbursed by the employer, the employer can deduct those costs.

EXAMPLE   Hal is a federal law enforcement officer who pays $200 per year for a subscription to the official agency work manual. The agency provides a manual in the office for its employees, but Hal spends a lot of time on the road away from the office. As an employee, Hal may not deduct the cost of the subscription. If Hal's employer reimbursed Hal for the manual, the employer could deduct the cost. If Hal were self-employed, the cost would be deductible. ◆

Self-Study Problem 3.7   *See Appendix E for Solutions to Self-Study Problems*

Indicate which of the following dues, subscriptions, and publications are deductible (D) and which are not deductible (ND) by circling the correct answer.

1. Dues to the American Medical Association paid by a self-employed physician.   D   ND

2. A subscription to a tax journal paid for by an accounting professor.   D   ND

3. Dues to a health spa paid by a lawyer.   D   ND

4. Union dues paid by a carpenter that works for a large construction company.   D   ND

5. Subscription to *Motor Trend* magazine paid for by a registered nurse.   D   ND

3-8 SPECIAL CLOTHING AND UNIFORMS

Learning Objective 3.8

Determine which clothing and uniforms may be treated as tax deductions.

Self-employed individuals and employers are allowed a deduction for the costs of special work clothing or uniforms. The deduction is not allowed for the general cost and upkeep of normal work clothes; the clothing must be specialized. To be deductible, the clothing or uniforms must (1) be required as a condition of employment, and (2) not be suitable for everyday use. Both conditions must be met for the deduction to be allowed. It is not enough that the taxpayer is required to wear special clothing if the clothing can be worn while the taxpayer is not on the job. The costs of protective clothing, such as safety shoes, hard hats, and rubber boots, required for the job are also deductible. If the clothing or uniforms qualify, the costs of purchase, alterations, laundry, and their maintenance are deductible. Any uniforms purchased by an employer for its employees are deductible by the employer.

The suspension of miscellaneous deductions subject to 2 percent of AGI has severely limited the deduction of uniforms and related costs by employees. In the past, uniforms worn by police officers, firefighters, nurses, and letter carriers would have qualified as an unreimbursed employee business expense. Because of the suspension of these miscellaneous deductions, taxpayers that serve in these roles as an employee are no longer permitted to deduct uniform costs. To the extent they serve as an independent contractor or are self-employed, qualifying uniform costs may be deducted. Similar to dues and subscriptions, if the employer reimburses the employee for qualifying uniform costs, the employer may deduct the costs. Self-employed taxpayers deduct special clothing and uniforms on Schedule C.

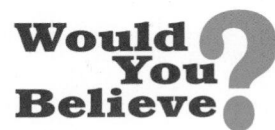

In his book, Bjorn Ulvaeus, one of the founders of 1970s megahit band Abba, states that the costumes that the band wore were intended to be so outrageous that they could not be considered suitable for general attire and thus garner a Swedish tax deduction (the tax laws are very similar to those in the U.S. regarding uniforms). Lady Gaga's "meat dress" worn at the 2010 Video Music Awards qualified for a deduction as well.

Self-Study Problem 3.8 — *See Appendix E for Solutions to Self-Study Problems*

Steve has his own business as an installer for the light company, and he wears regular work clothes that cost $400 during the year. Also, Steve must wear safety shoes and an orange neon vest on the job that cost $650 this year, and he purchased pole-climbing equipment, spikes, and a safety belt that cost $275. What is Steve's deduction on Schedule C for these items?

$ _____

3-9 BUSINESS GIFTS

3.9 Learning Objective

Explain the special limits for business gift deductions.

Within limits, taxpayers are allowed a deduction for business gifts. Salespersons and other taxpayers may deduct up to $25 per year per donee. For purposes of this limitation, a husband and wife count as one donee. Thus, the maximum that a taxpayer could deduct for gifts to a client or potential client and his or her spouse is a total of $25 per year, unless the spouse is also a client, in which case the spouse may receive a separate $25 gift. Incidental expenses such as gift wrapping and shipping may be excluded from the limitation and are fully deductible.

There is no limitation for small business gifts costing up to $4 each that have the taxpayer's name or company name imprinted on them, such as pencils and calendars, and no limitation on promotional materials, such as signs and display racks. Also, the cost of gifts of tangible personal property made to employees for length of service on the job and safety achievement may be deducted up to a limit of $400 per employee per year. If the gift is made in conjunction with a "qualified plan," the limit is raised to $1,600. Gifts made to a taxpayer's supervisor (or individuals at a higher employment level) are not deductible. Those gifts are considered nondeductible personal expenses.

EXAMPLE Marc is a salesperson who gives gifts to his clients. During the year, Marc gives Mr. Alford a gift costing $20 and Mrs. Alford (not a client) a gift costing $15. He also gives Ms. Bland a gift that cost $24 plus $2 for wrapping. Marc may deduct a total of $25 for the two gifts to Mr. and Mrs. Alford, and $26 for the gift to Ms. Bland. The $2 gift-wrapping charge is not included as part of the $25 limitation on the gift to Ms. Bland. ♦

3-9a **Substantiation Requirement**

To deduct meals and business gifts, taxpayers must be able to substantiate the deduction. The four items that must be substantiated to deduct meals expenses and gifts are the:

1. Amount of the expense,
2. Date and description,
3. Business purpose, and
4. Business relationship.

   If any of the above information is not available, the IRS will disallow the deduction for meals expenses or gifts.

Self-Study Problem 3.9   *See Appendix E for Solutions to Self-Study Problems*

Carol makes the following business gifts during the tax year:

Donee	Amount	Deduction
1. Mr. Jones (a client)	$ 20	$_____
2. Mr. Brown (a client)	32	_____
3. Mrs. Green (a client) received a $15 gift while her husband, Mr. Green (a non-client) received an $18 gift	33	_____
4. Ms. Gray (Carol's supervisor)	45	_____
5. Mr. Edwards (a client) receiving a display rack with Carol's company name on it	75	_____
6. Various customers (receiving ball point pens with the company name on them)	140	_____
Total business gift deduction		$_____

Calculate Carol's allowed deduction for each business gift and her total allowed deduction.

Learning Objective 3.10

Explain the tax treatment of bad debt deductions.

3-10 **BAD DEBTS**

When a taxpayer sells goods or services on credit and the accounts receivable subsequently become worthless (uncollectible), a bad debt deduction is allowed to the extent that income arising from the sales was previously included in income. Taxpayers must use the specific charge-off method and are allowed deductions for bad debts only after the debts are determined to be partially or completely worthless.

   A taxpayer who uses the specific charge-off method must be able to satisfy the IRS requirement that the debt is worthless and demonstrate the amount of the worthlessness. For a totally worthless account, a deduction is allowed for the entire amount of the taxpayer's basis in the account in the year the debt becomes worthless. The taxpayer's basis in the debt is the amount of income recognized from the recording of the debt, or the amount paid for the debt if it was purchased.

EXAMPLE Todd owns a small retail store. During the current tax year, Todd has $8,500 worth of uncollectible accounts receivable. Assuming he reported $7,800 in sales income from the accounts, that amount is his basis in the accounts receivable. Therefore, Todd's deduction for bad debts is limited to $7,800 for the year. ◆

Business and Nonbusiness Bad Debts

Bad debts fall into two categories, business bad debts and nonbusiness bad debts. Debts that arise from the taxpayer's trade or business are classified as business bad debts, while all other debts are considered nonbusiness bad debts. The distinction between the two types of debts is important, since business bad debts are ordinary deductions and non-business bad debts are short-term capital losses. Short-term and long-term capital gains may be offset by short-term capital losses. If there are net capital losses, only $3,000 of net capital losses may be deducted against ordinary income in any one tax year. Unused short-term capital losses are carried forward and may be deductible in future years, sub-ject to the $3,000 annual limitation. The treatment of capital gains and losses is discussed in Chapter 4.

EXAMPLE Robert loaned his friend, Calvin, $5,000 to start a business. In the current year, Calvin went bankrupt and the debt became completely worthless. Since the debt is a nonbusiness debt, Robert may claim only a $3,000 short-term capital loss deduction this year (assuming no other capital transactions). The $2,000 unused deduction may be carried forward to the next year. This is not a business bad-debt deduction, because Robert is not in the business of loaning funds. ◆

Nonbusiness bad debts are treated as short-term capital losses. To report these items, use the Schedule D/4797/etc., item under Income. Drill down into the Schedule D entry form and select the Nonbusiness Bad Debt button after entering the other relevant information.

ProConnect™ Tax

TIP

Self-Study Problem 3.10   *See Appendix E for Solutions to Self-Study Problems*

Indicate whether the debt in each of the following cases is a business or nonbusiness debt.

	Business	Nonbusiness
1. Accounts receivable of a doctor from patients	_____	_____
2. A father loans his son $2,000 to buy a car	_____	_____
3. A corporate president personally loans another corporation $100,000	_____	_____
4. Loans by a bank to its customers	_____	_____
5. A taxpayer loans her sister $15,000 to start a business	_____	_____

Sign Here	Under penalties of perjury, I declare that I have examined this return and accompanying schedules and statements, and to the best of my knowledge and belief, they are true, correct, and complete. Declaration of preparer (other than taxpayer) is based on all information of which preparer has any knowledge.				
	Your signature	Date	Your occupation		If the IRS sent you an Identity Protection PIN, enter it here (see inst.) ▶
Joint return? See instructions. Keep a copy for your records.	▶ Spouse's signature. If a joint return, **both** must sign.	Date	Spouse's occupation		If the IRS sent your spouse an Identity Protection PIN, enter it here (see inst.) ▶
	Phone no.		Email address		
Paid Preparer Use Only	Preparer's name	Preparer's signature		Date	PTIN Check if: ☐ Self-employed
	Firm's name ▶			Phone no.	
	Firm's address ▶			Firm's EIN ▶	

Would You Sign This Tax Return?

Your clients, Tom (age 48) and Teri (age 45) Trendy, have a son, Tim (age 27). Tim lives in Hawaii, where he studies the effects of various sunscreens on his ability to surf. Last year, Tim was out of money and wanted to move back home and live with Tom and Teri. To prevent this, Tom lent Tim $20,000 with the understanding that he would stay in Hawaii and not come home. Tom had Tim sign a formal note, including a stated interest rate and due date. Tom has a substantial portfolio of stocks and bonds and has generated a significant amount of capital gains in the current year. He concluded that Tim is a deadbeat and the $20,000 note is worthless. Consequently, Tom wants to report Tim's bad debt on his and Teri's current tax return and net it against his other capital gains and losses. Tom is adamant about this. Would you sign the Paid Preparer's declaration (see example above) on this return? Why or why not?

Learning Objective 3.11

Ascertain when a home office deduction may be claimed and how the deduction is computed.

3-11 OFFICE IN THE HOME

Some taxpayers operate a trade or business in their homes and qualify for home office deductions. The tax law imposes strict limits on the availability of the deduction. In fact, the deduction for an office in the home is allowed by exception. The general rule for a home office deduction states that a taxpayer will not be allowed a deduction for the use of a dwelling unit used by the taxpayer as a residence. The law provides four exceptions to the general rule under which a deduction may be allowed.

Under the first exception, a deduction is allowed if the home office is used on a regular basis and exclusively as the self-employed taxpayer's principal place of business. To meet the exclusive use test, a specific area of the home must be used only for the trade or business. If the area is used for both business and personal purposes, no home office deduction is allowed. With the suspension of miscellaneous deductions subject to 2 percent of AGI, employees may no longer deduct home office expenses.

A second exception states that a deduction is allowed if the home office is used exclusively and on a regular basis by patients, clients, or customers in meetings or dealings with the taxpayer in the normal course of a trade or business. This exception allows doctors and salespeople to deduct home office expenses even though they maintain another office away from their residence, and even though the office is not the self-employed taxpayer's principal place of business.

Under the third exception, the deduction of home office expenses is allowed if the home office is a separate structure not attached to the dwelling unit and is used exclusively and on a regular basis in the taxpayer's trade or business.

The fourth and final exception to the rule allows a deduction of a portion of the cost of a dwelling unit if it is used on a regular basis for the storage of business inventory or product samples held for use in the self-employed taxpayer's trade or business of selling products. Under this fourth exception, the taxpayer's home must be the taxpayer's sole place of business.

3-11a **The Income Limitation**

The home office deduction may not reduce the net income from the business below zero, except for mortgage interest and property taxes allocable to the office, which are generally tax deductible anyway. The other costs of operating a home, which are included in the home office allocation, include rent, home insurance, repairs, cleaning, utilities and other services, homeowners' association dues, and depreciation on the cost of the home. Depreciation expense is considered only after all other expenses have been allowed. These expenses are typically allocated to the home office on the basis of the square footage of the office to the total square footage of the home. Any unused deductions may be carried over to offset income in future years.

EXAMPLE Jane, an accounting professor, maintains an office in her apartment where she conducts a small tax practice. Jane properly allocates $1,500 in rent to the home office, and during the year she collects $1,400 in fees from various clients. Assuming Jane has no other expenses associated with her practice, only $1,400 of the rent may be claimed as a home office deduction, since she may not show a loss from the practice due to the gross income limitation. The unused portion is carried over to the next taxable year. ♦

EXAMPLE Assume the same facts as those in the previous example, except Jane owns her home. She has real estate taxes of $100, mortgage interest of $600, maintenance expenses of $200, and depreciation of $1,000 attributable to the home office. Her deduction for home office expenses is calculated as follows:

Gross income from tax practice	$1,400
Less: mortgage interest and real estate taxes	(700)
Balance	700
Less: maintenance expense	(200)
Balance	500
Depreciation (maximum allowed)	(500)
Net income from tax practice	$ 0

Please note that the only way the home office can generate an overall business loss for Jane is if her home office mortgage interest and taxes exceed her gross business income. The unused portion of depreciation is carried over to the next taxable year. ♦

If a home office is used for both business and personal purposes, no deduction is allowed. For example, Professor Jane in the previous example would not be allowed a deduction for any expenses associated with the office in her home if the office was also used for personal activities, such as watching television.

3-11b **The Home Office Allocation**

The calculation of home office expenses involves the allocation of the total expenses of a self-employed taxpayer's dwelling between business and personal use. This allocation is usually made on the basis of the number of square feet of business space as a percentage of the total number of square feet in the residence, or on the basis of the number of rooms devoted to business use as a percentage of the total number of rooms in the dwelling.

EXAMPLE   Lois operates a hair-styling salon in her rental home. The salon occupies 400 square feet of her residence, which has a total of 1,600 square feet. Her expenses for her residence are presented below and allocated as shown.

Expenses	Total Amount	Business Percentage*	Business Portion
Rent	$10,000	25%	$2,500
Utilities	4,000	25%	1,000
Cleaning	2,000	25%	500

*400 sq. ft./1,600 sq. ft.   ◆

Self-employed taxpayers filing Schedule C and claiming a deduction for home office expenses are required to file Form 8829, Expenses for Business Use of Your Home.

3-11c Optional Safe Harbor Method

In an effort to reduce the complexity of the home office deduction, the IRS has introduced a simplified method. Under the simplified method, the self-employed taxpayer may deduct home office expenses at the applicable rate ($5) multiplied by the number of square feet used in the home office, up to a maximum of 300 square feet, thus limiting the home office deduction under the safe harbor to $1,500. The deduction is still limited to the net profit from the business. Any deduction in excess of the income limit may not be carried forward. The same home office qualifications apply but no allocations are required. A taxpayer that uses the simplified method may deduct mortgage interest and property taxes as itemized deductions (see Chapter 5) without having to allocate a portion to the home office.

ProConnect™ Tax TIP

Similar to auto expenses, the home office deduction is not entered into Schedule C directly, but rather under Deductions and then Business Use of the Home. The interaction between the cap on taxes (Chapter 5) and the allocation of property taxes can create complexity in this area for certain taxpayers.

EXAMPLE   Martha operates a business that generates $6,700 of income before the home office deduction. She has a qualifying home office of 350 square feet in her home. She properly allocates $1,200 of household expenses to her home office. Under the safe harbor method, Martha's home office deduction is $1,500 ($5 per square foot × maximum 300 square feet). Martha probably elects the larger safe harbor home office deduction. ◆

TAX BREAK

The simplified method may hold advantages that extend beyond ease of use. One possible advantage is that no depreciation is deducted from the basis of a taxpayer's home and thus "depreciation recapture" (see LO 8.8) can be avoided and the exclusion of the gain on the sale of a principal residence (see LO 4.6) can still apply. A second advantage is that the property taxes and interest allocated to the small business can still be deducted on Schedule A as an itemized deduction (Chapter 5).

3-11d **Home Office Deduction for an Employee**

Under certain circumstances, an employee was eligible to take a home office deduction. One of the most important requirements was that the use of the home office was for the convenience of the employer. The deduction of unreimbursed employee business expenses is suspended through 2025.

Self-Study Problem 3.11   *See Appendix E for Solutions to Self-Study Problems*

Terry is a self-employed lawyer who maintains an office in her home. The office is used exclusively for client work, and clients regularly visit her home office. The mortgage interest and real estate taxes allocated to the business use of the home amount to $2,100, and maintenance, utilities, and cleaning service allocable to the business use of the home total $1,400. If gross billings of Terry's practice are $2,900 for this year and Terry has no other expenses allocable to the business, calculate the net income or loss she may report from the practice.

$ _____

3-12 **HOBBY LOSSES**

3.12 Learning Objective

Apply the factors used to determine whether an activity is a hobby, and understand the tax treatment of hobby losses.

If a taxpayer enters into an activity without a profit motive, the tax law limits the amount of tax deductions available. Under the hobby loss provisions, a taxpayer may not show a loss from an activity that is not engaged in for profit. For example, the breeding of race horses is an activity which might not be considered a trade or business when carried on by a full-time dentist. The IRS might contend that the activity was for personal enjoyment and disallow any loss for tax purposes. Despite the limitation on losses, any profits from hobbies must be included in taxable income. Hobby income is reported on Line 8, Other Income on Schedule 1 of Form 1040.

3-12a **Operational Rules**

Individual taxpayers (or S corporations) can avoid the hobby loss rules if they can show that the activity was conducted with the intent to earn a profit. To determine whether the activity was engaged in for profit, the IRS will look at the following factors:

1. carrying on the activity in a businesslike manner,
2. the time and effort put into the activity indicate an intent to make it profitable,
3. dependence on the income for the taxpayer's livelihood,
4. whether the losses are due to circumstances beyond the taxpayer's control (or are normal in the startup phase of this type of business),
5. attempts to change methods of operation to improve profitability,
6. the taxpayer or advisors have the knowledge needed to carry on the activity as a successful business,
7. success in making a profit in similar activities in the past,
8. the activity makes a profit in some years, and
9. the activity is expected to make a future profit from the appreciation of the assets used in the activity.

The tax law provides a rebuttable presumption that if an activity shows a profit for 3 of the 5 previous years (2 of the 7 previous years for activities involving horses), the activity is engaged in for profit. For example, if an activity shows a profit for 3 of the previous 5 years, it is presumed to be a trade or business, and the IRS has the burden to prove that it is a hobby.

3-12b Loss Limitations

Historically, the deduction of hobby expenses have been limited. Hobby expenses were deductible to the extent of hobby income (unless otherwise deductible such as mortgage interest and property taxes) and claimed as a miscellaneous itemized deduction subject to the 2 percent of AGI floor. Thus, they were only available to deduct if the taxpayer itemized deductions.

The miscellaneous expense deduction for items subject to the 2 percent of AGI floor is suspended through 2025; thus, no miscellaneous hobby expenses are deductible. Hobby expenses associated with other allowable itemized deductions (e.g., taxes or interest) are deductible subject to the limitations on those items (see Chapter 5). The income, net of cost of goods sold, must still be reported as other income on Schedule 1, Line 8.

EXAMPLE   Fred, the president of a bank, decides that he wants to be a famous wine maker. He has the following expenses related to this activity:

Costs of the wine sold	$2,000
Personal property taxes on equipment	2,500
Advertising costs	4,600

During the year, Fred sells 200 cases of wine for $7,500. If the activity is not a hobby, then Fred may take a loss, against his other income, of $1,600 ($7,500 − $2,000 − $2,500 − $4,600). However, if the activity is deemed to be a hobby, Fred would potentially be allowed to deduct the property taxes of $2,500 as an itemized deduction. The cost of the wine sold can be netted against the revenue. The advertising expenses are not deductible. ◆

ProConnect™ Tax

TIP

Hobby income can be entered under Income and then Alimony and Other Income. Be sure and net the cost of goods sold against gross income when reporting this amount. Hobby expenses are not deductible.

Self-Study Problem 3.12   *See Appendix E for Solutions to Self-Study Problems*

Kana is a CPA who loves chinchillas. She breeds chinchillas as pets (she currently owns thirteen of them) and every so often sells a baby chinchilla to a suitable family to keep as a pet. In the current year, she sells $250 worth of chinchillas and incurs the following expenses:

Chinchilla cages	$ 300
Advertising for chinchilla sales	$2,500

This activity is considered a hobby. Kana has adjusted gross income of $72,000. What is the amount of income and expense Kana recognizes (assume she itemizes deductions) associated with her chinchilla hobby?

Income $ _____

Deduction $ _____

KEY TERMS

Schedule C, 3-2
trade or business, 3-2
cost of goods sold, 3-5
self-employment tax, 3-6
inventory, 3-7
first in, first out (FIFO), 3-8
last in, first out (LIFO), 3-8

non-incidental materials and
  supplies (NIMS), 3-8
standard mileage rate, 3-14
standard mileage method, 3-14
actual cost method, 3-14
tax home, 3-16
per diem substantiation, 3-17

standard federal rate method, 3-17
high-low method, 3-17
business gifts, 3-23
business and nonbusiness bad
  debts, 3-25
home office, 3-26
hobby losses, 3-29

KEY POINTS

Learning Objectives	Key Points
LO 3.1: Complete a basic Schedule C (Profit or Loss from Business).	• Taxpayers who operate a business or practice a profession as a sole proprietorship must file a Schedule C to report the net profit or loss from the sole proprietorship. • Deductions taken on Schedule C must be ordinary and necessary, reasonable, and have a business purpose. • Schedule C filers such as sole proprietors and independent contractors with net earnings of $400 or more must pay a self-employment tax calculated on Schedule SE with their Form 1040.
LO 3.2: Describe the tax treatment of inventories and cost of goods sold.	• Inventory is the stock of goods or materials that a business holds for the purpose of resale to generate a profit. • Cost of goods sold, which is the largest single deduction for many businesses, is calculated as follows: beginning inventory + purchases − ending inventory. • Small businesses are permitted to use the cash method to account for inventory but in many instances, typical inventory accounting is still used. • There are two common methods of inventory valuation used by taxpayers: first in, first out (FIFO) and last in, first out (LIFO).
LO 3.3: Identify the requirements for deducting transportation expenses.	• Deductible transportation expenses include travel by airplane, rail, bus, and automobile. Normal commuting costs to and from the taxpayer's place of regular employment are not deductible. • If the taxpayer works at two or more jobs during the same day, he or she may deduct the cost of going from one job to the other or from one business location to another. • The standard mileage rate for 2020 is 57.5 cents per mile.
LO 3.4: Identify the requirements for deducting travel expenses.	• Travel expenses are defined as ordinary and necessary expenses incurred in traveling away from home in pursuit of the taxpayer's trade or business. • Deductible travel expenses include the cost of such items as meals, lodging, taxis, tips, and laundry. • A taxpayer must be away from home "overnight" in order to deduct travel expenses. Overnight is a period of time longer than an ordinary work day in which rest or relief from work is required. Also, the taxpayer must be away from his or her "tax home" to be on travel status. • Taxpayers must substantiate the following: the amount of each separate expenditure, the dates of departure and return for each trip and the number of business days on the trip, the destination or locality of the travel, and the business reason for the travel. • As an alternative to reporting actual expenses, a per diem method may be used in certain circumstances.

LO 3.5: Determine the requirements for deducting meals.	• Self-employed taxpayers are allowed deductions for 50 percent of the cost of meals at which business is conducted. • Generally, entertainment costs are not deductible. • Certain meals and entertainment costs are deductible in full when celebratory for all employees.
LO 3.6: Identify the requirements for claiming business education expenses.	• To be deductible as a business expense, education expenditures must be paid to meet the requirements of the taxpayer's employer or the requirements of law or regulation for keeping the taxpayer's salary, status, or job, or the expenses must be paid to maintain or improve existing skills required in performing the duties of the taxpayer's present work.
LO 3.7: Identify the tax treatment of dues and subscriptions.	• Self-employed professionals may deduct dues and the cost of subscriptions and publications. Included are items such as membership to the local bar for a lawyer, dues to the AICPA for an accountant, and the cost of subscriptions to any journal that is directly related to the self-employed taxpayer's profession. Employees may no longer deduct these costs due to the suspension of miscellaneous deductions subject to the 2 percent of AGI through 2025.
LO 3.8: Determine which clothing and uniforms may be treated as tax deductions.	• Self-employed individuals are allowed a deduction for the costs of special work clothing or uniforms. • In order to be deductible, clothing or uniforms must (1) be required as a condition of employment, and (2) not be suitable for everyday use.
LO 3.9: Explain the special limits for business gift deductions.	• Taxpayers are allowed a deduction for business gifts up to $25 per year per donee. For purposes of this limitation, a husband and wife count as one donee, unless the husband and wife are both clients. • To deduct meals and business gifts, taxpayers must be able to substantiate the deduction with the expense amounts, the dates and descriptions, the business purposes, and the business relationships.
LO 3.10: Explain the tax treatment of bad debt deductions.	• Bad debts are classified as either business bad debts or nonbusiness bad debts. Debts arising from a taxpayer's trade or business are classified as business bad debts, while all other debts are considered nonbusiness bad debts. • Business bad debts are treated as ordinary deductions and nonbusiness bad debts are treated as short-term capital losses, of which only $3,000 can be deducted against ordinary income each year.
LO 3.11: Ascertain when a home office deduction may be claimed and how the deduction is computed.	• A home office is generally not deductible. However, there are four exceptions to the general rule. • A home office deduction is allowed if the home office is used on a regular basis and exclusively as the self-employed taxpayer's principal place of business. • A home office deduction is allowed if the home office is used exclusively and on a regular basis by patients, clients, or customers in meetings or dealings with the self-employed taxpayer in the normal course of a trade or business. • The deduction of home office expenses is allowed if the home office is a separate structure not attached to the dwelling unit and is used exclusively and on a regular basis in the taxpayer's trade or business. • A home office deduction of a portion of the cost of a dwelling unit is allowed if it is used on a regular basis for the storage of business inventory or product samples. • The home office deduction is limited by the amount of net income from the associated trade or business. • A simplified home office deduction is also available at $5 per square foot up to an annual maximum of $1,500. • Employees may no longer deduct a home office, even when at the convenience of his or her employer, due to the suspension of the miscellaneous business expense deduction.

LO 3.12:

Apply the factors used to determine whether an activity is a hobby, and understand the tax treatment of hobby losses.

- Under the hobby loss provisions, a taxpayer may not show a loss from an activity that is not engaged in for profit.
- To determine whether the activity was engaged in for profit, the IRS will look at numerous factors including whether the activity is conducted like a business.
- Hobby expenses are no longer deductible due to the TCJA suspension of miscellaneous itemized deductions subject to the 2 percent of AGI floor.

QUESTIONS and PROBLEMS

GROUP 1:
MULTIPLE CHOICE QUESTIONS

LO 3.1

1. Which of the following is _not_ a test for the deductibility of a business expense?
   a. Ordinary and necessary test
   b. Expectation of profit test
   c. Reasonableness test
   d. Business purpose test

LO 3.1

2. In the current year, Mary started a profitable housekeeping business as a sole proprietor. She has ten housekeepers working for her and spends her time selling their services and coordinating her employees' time. Mary made $50,000 in her first year of operations. In addition to filing a Schedule C to report her business earnings, Mary *must* also file
   a. Schedule A
   b. Schedule F
   c. Schedule B
   d. Schedule SE
   e. None of the above

LO 3.1
LO 3.3
LO 3.4
LO 3.5

3. Daniel just became a self-employed consultant. Prior to this year he was always an employee. He comes to discuss his new business with you. As his tax accountant, you should:
   a. Discuss setting up a good record-keeping system for his new business
   b. Discuss the substantiation requirements for meals
   c. Discuss the self-employment tax, as well as the income tax, on business earnings in order to help Daniel estimate what he might owe in taxes for the year
   d. Discuss the rules for deducting automobile expenses
   e. Discuss all of the above

LO 3.2

4. Which of the following formulas represents the proper method of calculating cost of goods sold?
   a. Beginning inventory + Ending inventory − Purchases
   b. Ending inventory − Purchases − Beginning inventory
   c. Purchases − Beginning inventory − Ending inventory
   d. Beginning inventory + Purchases − Ending inventory
   e. None of the above

LO 3.2

5. If a taxpayer has beginning inventory of $45,000, purchases of $175,000, and ending inventory of $25,000, what is the amount of the cost of goods sold for the current year?
   a. $155,000
   b. $180,000
   c. $175,000
   d. $195,000
   e. None of the above

LO 3.3   *E*

6. Which of the following taxpayers may use the standard mileage method of calculating transportation costs?
   a. A taxi driver who owns a fleet of six cars for hire
   b. A taxpayer who used accelerated depreciation on his automobile
   c. A business executive who claimed bonus depreciation in the first year she used the car
   d. An attorney who uses his European sports car for calling on clients
   e. None of the above

LO 3.3   *BC*

7. Heather drives her minivan 903 miles for business purposes in 2020. She elects to use the standard mileage rate for her auto expense deduction. Her deduction will be
   a. $510
   b. $515
   c. $519
   d. $553
   e. $953

LO 3.4   *C*

8. In which of the following cases is the employer entitled to a travel expense deduction?
   a. An employee, who worked in the Salt Lake City plant of a company, who is assigned to the Denver plant of the company for 4 years
   b. An employee who travels between several business locations within the same city each day
   c. A manager of a chain of department stores who works in the main store 3 weeks out of every month and visits distant branch locations on overnight trips during the remainder of the month
   d. An employee who resigns from his current job and accepts a new job in a city 500 miles away from his current residence
   e. A bank employee who travels to a branch office for a couple of hours of work and decides to stay overnight to attend a play

LO 3.4   *D*

9. Which of the following expenses incurred while the taxpayer is away from home "overnight" is *not* included as a travel expense?
   a. Laundry expenses
   b. Transportation expenses
   c. Meal expenses
   d. Business gifts
   e. Lodging expenses

LO 3.4   *E*

10. Under the high-low method, the federal per diem amount is
   a. The same in every city in the U.S.
   b. Different for every city in the U.S.
   c. The same for most cities but higher in certain locations
   d. An average of the highest and lowest costs for that city
   e. The boundary for expenses incurred in a city (never higher than the high amount but never lower than the low amount)

LO 3.4   *C*

11. Joe is a self-employed information technology consultant from San Francisco. He takes a week-long trip to Chicago primarily for business. He takes two personal days to go to museums and see the sights of Chicago. How should he treat the expenses related to this trip?
   a. One hundred percent of the trip should be deducted as a business expense since the trip was primarily for business.
   b. Fifty percent of the trip should be deducted as a business expense since the IRS limits such business expenses to 50 percent of the actual cost.

c. The cost of all of the airfare and the business days should be deducted, while the cost of the personal days are not deductible.

d. None of the expenses are deductible since there was an element of personal enjoyment in the trip.

E

LO 3.5   12. Which of the following expenses is deductible as an entertainment expense?
a. The depreciation on an airplane used to entertain customers
b. The cost of a hunting camp used to entertain customers
c. The dues of a racquet club used to keep in shape
d. The cost of a paintball party for clients paid for by a computer salesman at a computer fair
e. None of these are deductible

A

LO 3.5   13. Which of the following is *not* likely to be a deductible expense?
a. The cost of tickets to a stage play for a client and the taxpayer.
b. The cost for Rosa to take a potential customer to lunch to describe a new service Rosa's company is offering. Unfortunately, the customer explains that they are not interested in the service.
c. The cost of a party for all of Dan's employees to celebrate a record-breaking profits year.
d. The dues for Charles Coke to join the City Chamber of Commerce to generally improve the reputation of his business in the community.
e. None of the above are deductible expenses.

E

LO 3.6   14. Which of the following taxpayers may *not* deduct their educational expense?
a. A CPA who attends a course to review for the real estate agents' exam
b. An independent sales representative who attends a customer relations course at a local university
c. A self-employed attorney who attends a course on computing legal damages
d. An independent real estate broker who attends a college course on real estate law
e. All of the above are deductible

A

LO 3.6   15. Which of the following is likely a deductible business educational expense?
a. Leah is a self-employed tax preparer. The State Board of Taxation requires Leah to attend federal and state taxation training each year to maintain her tax preparation licence.
b. Mike is an auto mechanic. He decides he wants to be a high school math teacher but the state Department of Education requires Mike to earn a bachelor's degree in education.
c. John teaches European History at Ridgemont High School. In order to better understand the material he teaches, John takes a summer trip with *American Geographic* magazine to tour Western Europe.
d. Becca is an auto mechanic. She sees that the local community college is offering courses in jet engine repair which would prepare her to work for one of the airlines. Becca would like to work for an airline because they let employees fly for free.

E

LO 3.7   16. Which of the following is *not* deductible by the self-employed taxpayer?
a. A subscription to *The CPA Journal* by a CPA
b. A subscription to *The Yale Medical Journal* by a doctor
c. A subscription to *Financial Management* by a financial planner
d. A subscription to *The Harvard Law Review* by a lawyer
e. All of the above are deductible

LO 3.8

D

17. Which of the following self-employed taxpayers are most likely permitted to deduct the cost of their uniform?
    a. A lawyer who wears a business suit
    b. A furnace repairman who must wear overalls while on the job
    c. A nurse who can wear casual clothes while on duty
    d. A pair of stainless steel safety gloves for a butcher

LO 3.9

E

18. Which of the following business gifts are fully deductible?
    a. A gift to a client that cost $35
    b. A gift to an employee, for 10 years of continued service, costing $250
    c. A gift to a client and her nonclient spouse that cost $45
    d. A gift to an employee paid under a qualified plan, for not having an on-the-job injury for 25 years, that cost $1,650
    e. None of the above are fully deductible

LO 3.10

C

19. Loren loaned a friend $9,000 as financing for a new business venture. In the current year, Loren's friend declares bankruptcy and the debt is considered totally worthless. What amount may Loren deduct on his individual income tax return for the current year as a result of the worthless debt, assuming he has no other capital gains or losses for the year?
    a. $9,000 ordinary loss
    b. $9,000 short-term capital loss
    c. $3,000 short-term capital loss
    d. $3,000 ordinary loss
    e. $6,000 short-term capital loss

LO 3.11

C

20. Kathy is a self-employed taxpayer working exclusively from her home office. Before the home office deduction, Kathy has $3,000 of net income. Her allocable home office expenses are $5,000 in total (includes $2,000 of allocated interest and property taxes). How are the home office expenses treated on her current year tax return?
    a. All home office expenses may be deducted, resulting in a business loss of $2,000.
    b. Only $3,000 of home office expenses may be deducted, resulting in net business income of zero. None of the extra $2,000 of home office expenses may be carried forward or deducted.
    c. Only $3,000 of home office expenses may be deducted, resulting in net business income of zero. The extra $2,000 of home office expenses may be carried forward and deducted in a future year against home office income.
    d. None of the home office expenses may be deducted since Kathy's income is too low.

LO 3.11

C

21. Which of the following taxpayers qualifies for a home office deduction?
    a. An attorney who is employed by a law firm and has a home office in which to read cases
    b. A doctor who has a regular office downtown and a library at home to store medical journals
    c. An accounting student who maintains a home office used exclusively for her business preparing tax returns
    d. A nurse who maintains a home office to pay bills and read nursing journals
    e. A corporate president who uses his home office to entertain friends and customers

E

LO 3.11   22. Carol maintains an office in her home where she conducts a dressmaking business. During the year she collects $4,000 from sales, pays $1,300 for various materials and supplies, and properly allocates $2,500 of rent expense and $500 of her utilities expense to the use of her home office. What amount of the rent and utilities expense may Carol deduct in the current year in computing her net income or loss from the dressmaking business?
   a. $0
   b. $500
   c. $2,500
   d. $2,700
   e. $3,000

E

LO 3.12   23. Which of the following factors is not considered by the IRS in determining whether an activity is a hobby?
   a. Whether the activity is conducted like a business
   b. The time and effort expended by the taxpayer
   c. Whether there have been changes in the methods of operation in an attempt to improve profitability
   d. Income and loss history of the activity
   e. All of the above are considered to determine if an activity is a hobby

A

LO 3.12   24. Stewie, a single taxpayer, operates an activity as a hobby. Brian operates a similar activity as a bona fide business. Stewie's gross income from his activity is $5,000 and his expenses are $6,000. Brian's gross income and expenses are coincidentally the same as Stewie. Neither Stewie nor Brian itemize, but both have other forms of taxable income. What is the impact on taxable income for Stewie and Brian from these activities?
   a. Stewie will report $0 income and Brian will report a $1,000 loss.
   b. Stewie will report $5,000 income and $0 deduction and Brian will report a $1,000 loss.
   c. Stewie and Brian will report $0 taxable income.
   d. Stewie and Brian will report a $1,000 loss.
   e. Stewie will report a $1,000 loss and Brian will report $5,000 income.

LO 3.1
LO 3.3
LO 3.5
LO 3.7

1. Scott Butterfield is self-employed as a CPA. He uses the cash method of accounting, and his Social Security number is 644-47-7833. His principal business code is 541211. Scott's CPA practice is located at 678 Third Street, Riverside, CA 92860. Scott's income statement for the year shows the following:

Income Statement

Scott Butterfield, CPA
Income Statement
12/31/2020

	Current Period 1/1/2020 to 12/31/2020	Prior Period 1/1/2019 to 12/31/2019
REVENUES		
Tax Services	$ 76,123	$ 75,067
Accounting Services	49,001	48,860
Other Consulting Services	10,095	10,115
TOTAL REVENUES	135,219	134,042
COST OF SERVICES		
Salaries	32,000	30,100
Payroll Taxes	2,868	2,387
Supplies	1,391	1,548
TOTAL COST OF SERVICES	36,259	34,035
GROSS PROFIT (LOSS)	98,960	100,007
OPERATING EXPENSES		
Advertising and Promotion	300	350
Business Licenses and Permits	250	250
Charitable Contributions	425	275
Continuing Education	300	300
Dues and Subscriptions	3,500	3,500
Insurance	875	875
Meals and Entertainment	4,400	5,500
Office Expense	150	150
Postage and Delivery	50	50
Printing and Reproduction	100	100
Office Rent	14,000	14,000
Travel	865	865
Utilities	2,978	2,978
TOTAL OPERATING EXPENSES	28,193	29,193
NET INCOME (LOSS)	$ 70,767	$ 70,814

Scott also mentioned the following:

- The expenses for dues and subscriptions were his country club membership dues for the year.
- $425 of the charitable contributions were made to a political action committee.
- Scott does not generate income from the sale of goods and therefore does not record supplies and wages as part of cost of goods sold.
- Scott placed a business auto in service on January 1, 2017 and drove it 3,824 miles for business, 3,250 miles for commuting, and 4,500 miles for nonbusiness purposes. His wife has a car for personal use.

Complete Schedule C on Pages 3-39 and 3-40 for Scott showing Scott's net taxable profit from self-employment.

SCHEDULE C
(Form 1040)

Department of the Treasury
Internal Revenue Service (99)

Profit or Loss From Business
(Sole Proprietorship)

▶ Go to *www.irs.gov/ScheduleC* for instructions and the latest information.

▶ **Attach to Form 1040, 1040-SR, 1040-NR, or 1041; partnerships generally must file Form 1065.**

OMB No. 1545-0074

2020

Attachment
Sequence No. **09**

Name of proprietor

Social security number (SSN)

A	Principal business or profession, including product or service (see instructions)	**B Enter code from instructions** ▶

C	Business name. If no separate business name, leave blank.	**D Employer ID number (EIN)** (see instr.)

E   Business address (including suite or room no.) ▶
City, town or post office, state, and ZIP code

F   Accounting method: **(1)** ☐ Cash   **(2)** ☐ Accrual   **(3)** ☐ Other (specify) ▶

G   Did you "materially participate" in the operation of this business during 2020? If "No," see instructions for limit on losses   ☐ Yes   ☐ No

H   If you started or acquired this business during 2020, check here   ▶ ☐

I   Did you make any payments in 2020 that would require you to file Form(s) 1099? See instructions   ☐ Yes   ☐ No

J   If "Yes," did you or will you file required Form(s) 1099?   ☐ Yes   ☐ No

Part I   Income

1	Gross receipts or sales. See instructions for line 1 and check the box if this income was reported to you on Form W-2 and the "Statutory employee" box on that form was checked ▶ ☐	1	
2	Returns and allowances	2	
3	Subtract line 2 from line 1	3	
4	Cost of goods sold (from line 42)	4	
5	**Gross profit.** Subtract line 4 from line 3	5	
6	Other income, including federal and state gasoline or fuel tax credit or refund (see instructions)	6	
7	**Gross income.** Add lines 5 and 6 ▶	7	

Part II   Expenses. Enter expenses for business use of your home **only** on line 30.

8	Advertising	8		18	Office expense (see instructions)	18	
9	Car and truck expenses (see instructions)	9		19	Pension and profit-sharing plans	19	
10	Commissions and fees	10		20	Rent or lease (see instructions):		
11	Contract labor (see instructions)	11		a	Vehicles, machinery, and equipment	20a	
12	Depletion	12		b	Other business property	20b	
13	Depreciation and section 179 expense deduction (not included in Part III) (see instructions)	13		21	Repairs and maintenance	21	
				22	Supplies (not included in Part III)	22	
				23	Taxes and licenses	23	
14	Employee benefit programs (other than on line 19)	14		24	Travel and meals:		
				a	Travel	24a	
15	Insurance (other than health)	15		b	Deductible meals (see instructions)	24b	
16	Interest (see instructions):			25	Utilities	25	
a	Mortgage (paid to banks, etc.)	16a		26	Wages (less employment credits)	26	
b	Other	16b		27a	Other expenses (from line 48)	27a	
17	Legal and professional services	17		b	**Reserved for future use**	27b	

28	**Total expenses** before expenses for business use of home. Add lines 8 through 27a ▶	28	
29	Tentative profit or (loss). Subtract line 28 from line 7	29	
30	Expenses for business use of your home. Do not report these expenses elsewhere. Attach Form 8829 unless using the simplified method. See instructions. **Simplified method filers only:** Enter the total square footage of (a) your home: _____ and (b) the part of your home used for business: _____ . Use the Simplified Method Worksheet in the instructions to figure the amount to enter on line 30	30	
31	**Net profit or (loss).** Subtract line 30 from line 29. • If a profit, enter on both **Schedule 1 (Form 1040), line 3,** and on **Schedule SE, line 2.** (If you checked the box on line 1, see instructions). Estates and trusts, enter on **Form 1041, line 3.** • If a loss, you **must** go to line 32.	31	
32	If you have a loss, check the box that describes your investment in this activity. See instructions. • If you checked 32a, enter the loss on both **Schedule 1 (Form 1040), line 3**, and on **Schedule SE, line 2.** (If you checked the box on line 1, see the line 31 instructions). Estates and trusts, enter on **Form 1041, line 3.** • If you checked 32b, you **must** attach **Form 6198.** Your loss may be limited.	32a ☐ All investment is at risk. 32b ☐ Some investment is not at risk.

For Paperwork Reduction Act Notice, see the separate instructions.   Cat. No. 11334P   Schedule C (Form 1040) 2020

Schedule C (Form 1040) 2020   Page **2**

Part III   **Cost of Goods Sold** (see instructions)

33   Method(s) used to
value closing inventory: **a** ☐ Cost   **b** ☐ Lower of cost or market   **c** ☐ Other (attach explanation)

34   Was there any change in determining quantities, costs, or valuations between opening and closing inventory?
If "Yes," attach explanation . . . . ☐ **Yes**   ☐ **No**

35   Inventory at beginning of year. If different from last year's closing inventory, attach explanation . . . | **35** |

36   Purchases less cost of items withdrawn for personal use . . . . | **36** |

37   Cost of labor. Do not include any amounts paid to yourself . . . . | **37** |

38   Materials and supplies . . . . | **38** |

39   Other costs . . . . | **39** |

40   Add lines 35 through 39 . . . . | **40** |

41   Inventory at end of year . . . . | **41** |

42   **Cost of goods sold.** Subtract line 41 from line 40. Enter the result here and on line 4 . . . . . . | **42** |

Part IV   **Information on Your Vehicle.** Complete this part **only** if you are claiming car or truck expenses on line 9 and are not required to file Form 4562 for this business. See the instructions for line 13 to find out if you must file Form 4562.

43   When did you place your vehicle in service for business purposes? (month/day/year)   ▶ _____ / _____ / _____

44   Of the total number of miles you drove your vehicle during 2020, enter the number of miles you used your vehicle for:

  a Business _____   **b** Commuting (see instructions) _____   **c** Other _____

45   Was your vehicle available for personal use during off-duty hours? . . . . ☐ **Yes**   ☐ **No**

46   Do you (or your spouse) have another vehicle available for personal use?. . . . . ☐ **Yes**   ☐ **No**

47a   Do you have evidence to support your deduction? . . . . ☐ **Yes**   ☐ **No**

  b If "Yes," is the evidence written? . . . . ☐ **Yes**   ☐ **No**

Part V   **Other Expenses.** List below business expenses not included on lines 8–26 or line 30.

_____ | _____

_____ | _____

_____ | _____

_____ | _____

_____ | _____

_____ | _____

_____ | _____

_____ | _____

48   **Total other expenses.** Enter here and on line 27a . . . . | **48** |

Schedule C (Form 1040) 2020

LO 3.1
LO 3.3
LO 3.4
LO 3.9
LO 3.11

2. Margaret started her own business in the current year and will report a profit for her first year. Her results of operations are as follows:

Gross income	$45,000
Travel	1,000
Contribution to Presidential Election Campaign	100
Transportation 5,426 miles, using standard mileage method	?
Entertainment in total	4,200
Nine gifts at $50 each	450
Rent and utilities for apartment in total (25% is used for a home office)	10,500

What is the net income Margaret should show on her Schedule C? Show the calculation of her taxable business income.

Gross income _____

Expenses (describe each) _____

_____

_____

_____

_____

_____

Taxable business income ══════════

LO 3.2

3. Lawrence owns a small candy store that sells one type of candy. His beginning inventory of candy was made up of 10,000 boxes costing $1.50 per box ($15,000), and he made the following purchases of candy during the year:

March 1	10,000 boxes at $1.60	$16,000
August 15	20,000 boxes at $1.70	34,000
November 20	10,000 boxes at $1.80	18,000

At the end of the year, Lawrence's inventory consisted of 15,000 boxes of candy.

a. Calculate Lawrence's ending inventory and cost of goods sold using the FIFO inventory valuation method.

Ending inventory $ _____
Cost of goods sold $ _____

b. Calculate Lawrence's ending inventory and cost of goods sold using the LIFO inventory valuation method.

Ending inventory $ _____
Cost of goods sold $ _____

LO 3.2

4. Kevin owns a retail store, and during the current year he purchased $610,000 worth of inventory. Kevin's beginning inventory was $67,000, and his ending inventory is $77,200. During the year, Kevin withdrew $1,780 in inventory for his personal use. Use Part III of Schedule C below to calculate Kevin's cost of goods sold for the year.

Part III   Cost of Goods Sold (see instructions)

33 Method(s) used to
    value closing inventory: **a** ☐ Cost   **b** ☐ Lower of cost or market   **c** ☐ Other (attach explanation)

34 Was there any change in determining quantities, costs, or valuations between opening and closing inventory?
    If "Yes," attach explanation . . . . ☐ Yes   ☐ No

35 Inventory at beginning of year. If different from last year's closing inventory, attach explanation . . .   **35**

36 Purchases less cost of items withdrawn for personal use **36**

37 Cost of labor. Do not include any amounts paid to yourself **37**

38 Materials and supplies **38**

39 Other costs **39**

40 Add lines 35 through 39 . . . .   **40**

41 Inventory at end of year **41**

42 **Cost of goods sold.** Subtract line 41 from line 40. Enter the result here and on line 4 . . . . . .   **42**

LO 3.2

5. Frank owns an auto repair shop that serves a particular model of auto and he tends to purchase parts in bulk. Frank is eligible to treat inventory as non-incidental materials and could elect to do so. In December of 2019 he purchases 24 oil filters. He uses one to service an auto in January 2020, and then about 2 per month and ends 2020 with 14 filters. Frank's business has gross receipts of around $1.2 million per year. Frank expenses oil filters when he purchases them on his book and records (Frank does not have financial statements other than for taxes). Explain how Frank could treat his oil filter inventory.

LO 3.3

6. Teresa is a self-employed civil engineer who uses her automobile for business. Teresa drove her automobile a total of 11,965 miles during 2020, of which 80 percent was business mileage. The actual cost of gasoline, oil, depreciation, repairs, and insurance for the year was $6,440. Teresa is eligible to use the actual or standard method.
   a. How much is Teresa's transportation deduction based on the standard mileage method?

   $ _____

   b. How much is Teresa's transportation deduction based on the actual cost method?

   $ _____

   c. Which method should Teresa use to calculate her transportation deduction?

   Why? _____

   _____

LO 3.3

7. Art is a self-employed installer of home entertainment systems, and he drives his car frequently to installation locations. Art drove his car 15,000 miles for business purposes and 20,000 miles in total. His actual expenses, including depreciation, for operating the auto are $10,000 since he had to have the car repaired several times. Art has always used the actual cost method in the past. How much is Art's deductible auto expense for the year?

   _____

   _____

LO 3.3

8. Martha is a self-employed tax accountant who drives her car to visit clients on a regular basis. She drives her car 4,000 miles for business and 10,000 for commuting and other personal use. Assuming Martha uses the standard mileage method, how much is her auto expense for the year? Where in her tax return should Martha claim this deduction? _____

   _____

   _____

LO 3.4

9. Joan is a self-employed attorney in New York City. Joan took a trip to San Diego, CA, primarily for business, to consult with a client and take a short vacation. On the trip, Joan incurred the following expenses:

Airfare to and from San Diego	$ 478
Hotel charges while on business	340
Meals while on business	260
Car rental while on business (she drove 240 miles)	110
Hotel charges while on vacation	460
Meals while on vacation	290
Car rental while on vacation	180
Total	$2,118

Calculate Joan's travel expense deduction for the trip, assuming the trip was made in 2020.

$ _____

LO 3.4

10. Go to the U.S. General Services Administration (GSA) website (**www.gsa.gov**). For the month of September 30, 2020, what is the per diem rate for each of the following towns:
    a. Flagstaff, AZ
    b. Palm Springs, CA
    c. Denver, CO

LO 3.4
LO 3.6

11. Bob is a self-employed lawyer and is required to take a week of continuing legal education every year to maintain his license. This year he paid $1,150 in course fees for his continuing legal education in a different city. He also paid $354 for airfare and a hotel room and paid $234 for meals. What is the total amount he can deduct on his Schedule C related to these expenses?

_____
_____
_____

LO 3.5

12. Grace is a self-employed sales consultant who spends significant time entertaining potential customers. She keeps all the appropriate records to substantiate her entertainment. She has the following expenses in the current year:

Meals where business was conducted	$5,000
Greens fees (all business)	500
Tickets to baseball games (all business)	500
Country Club dues (all business use)	6,000

What are the tax-deductible meals and entertainment expenses Grace may claim in the current year? On which tax form should she claim the deduction?

_____
_____

LO 3.5

13. Marty is a sales consultant. Marty incurs the following expenses related to the entertainment of his clients in the current year:

Dues to a country club	$4,500
(The country club was used for business 25 days of the total 75 days that it was used.)	
Business meals at the country club not associated with golf or tennis	1,200
Dues to a tennis club	1,000
(The club was used 75 percent for directly related business.)	
Tennis fees (personal use)	260
Business meals at various restaurants	1,844

a. How much is Marty's deduction for meals and entertainment expenses for the current year?

$ _____

b. For each item listed above that you believe is not allowed as a deduction, explain the reason it is not allowed.

_____

_____

_____

_____

LO 3.6   14. a. Loren is a secretary in a lawyer's office. Since he often deals with legal matters, Loren feels that a law degree will be beneficial to him. May Loren deduct his educational expenses for law school?

_____

Explain _____

_____

b. Alicia is an employee in the sales department for an international firm. She wishes to learn Spanish to improve her ability to communicate with foreign clients. May Alicia deduct her educational expenses for language school as a miscellaneous itemized deduction?

_____

Explain _____

_____

c. Joan is a practicing lawyer. She enrolls in a local medical school and works toward a medical degree in her spare time. May Joan deduct her educational expenses for the medical classes?

_____

Explain _____

_____

LO 3.7   15. Carey opens a law office in Chicago on January 1, 2020. On January 1, 2020, Carey purchases an annual subscription to a law journal for $170 and a 1-year legal reference service for $1,500. Carey also subscribes to *Chicago Magazine* for $54 so she can find great places to take client's to dinner and review the Best 50 Lawyers in Chicago list published each year. Calculate Carey's deduction for the above items for the 2020 tax year.

$ _____

LO 3.8   16. Cooper and Brandy are married and file a joint income tax return with two separate Schedule Cs. Cooper is an independent security specialist who spent $395 on uniforms during the year. His laundry expenses for the uniforms were $175 for this year, plus $65 for altering them. Brandy works as a drill press operator and wears jeans and a work shirt on the job, which cost $175 this year. Her laundry costs were $50 for the work clothes. Brandy is also required by state regulators to wear safety glasses and safety shoes when working, which cost a total of $115.

a. How much is Cooper's total deduction on his Schedule C for special clothing and uniforms?

$ _____

b. How much is Brandy's total deduction on her Schedule C for special clothing and uniforms?

$ _____

LO 3.9

17. Sam owns an insurance agency and makes the following business gifts during the year. Calculate Sam's deduction for business gifts.

Donee	Amount	Amount Allowed
Ms. Sears (a client)	$35, plus $4 shipping	$ _____
Mr. Williams (a tennis partner, not a business prospect or client)	55	_____
Mr. Sample (a client) received $22 and Mrs. Sample (nonclient spouse of Mr. Sample) received a gift valued at $20	42	_____
Various customers (calendars costing $3 each with the company name on them)	300	_____
Mr. Shiver (an employee gift, a watch, for 25 years of continuous service)	175	_____
Total business gift deduction		$ ═══════════

LO 3.10

18. Steinar loaned a friend $9,500 to buy some stock 3 years ago. In the current year the debt became worthless.
   a. How much is Steinar's deduction for the bad debt for this year? (Assume he has no other capital gains or losses.)

   $ _____

   b. What can Steinar do with the deduction not used this year?

   _____
   _____
   _____
   _____

LO 3.10

19. Sharon is an orthopedic surgeon. She performed a surgery 2 years ago and billed $10,000 to her patient. After 2 years of attempting to collect the money, it is clear that Sharon will not be able to collect anything. Sharon reports income on her tax return on the cash basis, so she only reports the income she actually receives in cash each year. Can she claim a bad debt deduction for the $10,000?

   _____
   _____
   _____
   _____

LO 3.10

20. Carrie loaned her friend $4,500 to buy a used car. She had her friend sign a note with repayment terms and set a reasonable interest rate on the note because the $4,500 was most of her savings. Her friend left town without a forwarding address, and nobody Carrie knows has heard from her in the last year. How should Carrie treat the bad loan for tax purposes?

   _____
   _____
   _____
   _____

LO 3.11   21. Cindy operates a computerized engineering drawing business from her home. Cindy maintains a home office and properly allocates the following expenses to her office:

Depreciation	$1,500
Utilities	500
Real estate taxes	325
Mortgage interest (100 percent deductible)	500

a. Assume that Cindy earns income of $4,400 from her business for the year before deducting home office expenses. She has no other expenses associated with the business. Calculate Cindy's deduction for home office expenses.

$ _____

b. Assume that Cindy earns income of $2,600 from her business during the year before deducting home office expenses. Calculate Cindy's deduction for home office expenses.

$ _____

LO 3.11   22. Pete qualifies for a home office deduction. The amount of space devoted to business use is 300 square feet of the total 1,200 square feet in his apartment. Pete's total rent for the year is $9,600, and he pays utilities (other than telephone) of $2,500 for the year. Calculate Pete's deduction for home office expenses before the gross income limitation.

Rent	$ _____
Utilities other than telephone	_____
Total home office expenses	$ _____

LO 3.11   23. Randi qualifies for a home deduction. The amount of space devoted to business use is 400 square feet of the total 2,000 square feet of her home. Randi's mortgage interest and property taxes in total are $1,600. Other deductions properly allocated to the home office total $300. In addition, Randi purchases and uses business supplies costing $200 during the year. Assume Randi earns income of $3,400 for the year before deducting any home office or supplies deduction. Calculate the largest deduction Randi can take for her home office (ignore self-employment taxes).

$ _____

LO 3.11   24. Ann is a self-employed restaurant critic who does her work exclusively from a home office. Ann's income is $25,000 before the home office deduction this year. Her office takes up 200 square feet of her 1,000-square-foot apartment. The total expenses for her apartment are $6,000 for rent, $1,000 for utilities, $200 for renter's insurance, and $800 for pest control and other maintenance. What is Ann's home office deduction? Please show your calculations.

_____

_____

_____

LO 3.12   25. Lew is a practicing CPA who decides to raise bonsai as a business. Lew engages in the activity and has the following revenue and expenses:

Sales	$ 5,000
Depreciation on greenhouse	10,000
Fertilizer, soil, pots	1,500

a. What are the factors that the IRS will consider when evaluating whether the activity is a business or a hobby?

_____

_____

_____

b. If the activity is deemed to be a regular business, what is the amount of Lew's loss from the activity?

$ _____

c. If the activity is deemed to be a hobby, what is the amount of Lew's expenses (if any) from the activity that may be deducted?

$ _____

GROUP 3:
WRITING ASSIGNMENT

ETHICS   1. Bobby Reynolds, a new client of yours, is a self-employed caterer in Santa Fe, New Mexico. Bobby drives his personal van when delivering catered meals to customers. You have asked him to provide the amount of business miles driven using his vehicle. You are planning on using the standard mileage method to calculate Bobby's deduction for transportation costs. Bobby has responded by saying, "Well, I don't really keep track of my miles. I guess I drove around 3,000 miles last year for the business." What would you say to Bobby?

RESEARCH   2. Your supervisor has asked you to research a potential tax deduction for a client, Randall Stevens. Randall is a self-employed loan agent that lives in Portland, Maine. His specialty is marine loans; in particular, loans for the renovation of classic boats. Over the years, Randall has developed a very unique expertise in valuation of classic boats and is considered a global expert in the field. In 2020, Randall is hoping to attend the North American Classic Marine Boat Show that takes place in Zihuatanejo, Mexico. Randall attends the show more or less every year in order to stay current on classic boat valuations. Interested parties from around the world attend the show in the quaint Mexican coastal town. Randall's costs to attend are $800 for show registration, $1,750 for airfare from Portland to Zihuatanejo, $2,400 for lodging. Meals are estimated at $600. Please prepare a letter for Randall that describes the issues he will face when attempting to deduct the cost of attending the show. Use IRS Publication 463 (available at **www.irs.gov**) to assist you.

(An example of a client letter is available at the website for this textbook located at **www.cengage.com.**)

GROUP 4:
COMPREHENSIVE PROBLEMS

1. Ken (birthdate July 1, 1989) and Amy (birthdate July 4, 1991) Booth have brought you the following information regarding their income, expenses, and withholding for the year. They are unsure which of these items must be used to calculate taxable income.

Income:

Ken's salary (salesman)	$28,700
Amy's wages (part-time nurse)	17,600
Insurance reimbursement for repairs from an auto accident	500
Gift from Uncle George	2,000
Interest income from Lodge State Bank	906

Federal income taxes withheld:

From Ken's salary	2,800
From Amy's wages	650

Amy owns and operates a computer bookstore named "The Disk Drive." The store is located at 2000 Broadway Street, Menomonie, WI 54751. The business EIN is 27-1234567 and the principal business code for bookstores is 451211. During 2020, Amy had the following income and expenses:

Sales of books	$321,450
Expenses	
Store rental	16,000
Office expense	6,067
Advertising	11,711
City business license	1,020
Payroll	83,550
Payroll taxes	8,400
Utilities	8,050
Other	3,000
Beginning inventory	$ 75,000
Purchases	191,000
Ending inventory	80,000

Amy treats inventory as non-incidental materials and supplies.

This year, Amy loaned a friend $10,000 so that he could make an investment. Instead of making the investment, the friend lost all the money gambling and left for parts unknown. Amy has no hope of ever collecting on this bad debt.

Ken, who ordinarily never gambles, won $20,677 at a casino birthday party for one of his friends.

The Booths provide the sole support for Ken's parents, Rod (Social Security number 124-80-9050) and Mary (Social Security number 489-37-6676) Booth, who live in their own home. Ken and Amy live at 2345 Wilson Avenue, Menomonie, WI, 54751, and their Social Security numbers are 343-75-3456 (Ken) and 123-45-7890 (Amy). Ken and Amy can claim a $500 other dependent credit for each parent. Ken and Amy received a $2,400 EIP in 2020.

Required: Complete the Booths' federal income tax return for 2020 on Form 1040, Schedule 1, Schedule C, Schedule D, and Form 8949. A statement is required to be attached to a return for a nonbusiness bad debt, but this requirement may be ignored for this problem. Assume no 1099-B is filed in association with the bad debt when filling out Form 8949.

2A. Russell (birthdate February 2, 1969) and Linda (birthdate August 30, 1974) Long have brought you the following information regarding their income and expenses for the current year. Russell owns and operates a landscaping business called Lawns and Landscapes Unlimited (EIN: 32-1456789). The business is operated out of their home, located at 1234 Cherry Lane, Nampa, ID 83687. The principal business code is 561730. Russell's bookkeeper provided the following income statement from the landscaping business:

Lawns and Landscapes
Income Statement
12/31/2020

	Current Period 1/1/2020 to 12/31/2020	Prior Period 1/1/2019 to 12/31/2019
REVENUES		
Lawn maintenance	$ 82,350	$ 71,998
Lawn and plant installation	34,600	48,576
Other	17,100	8,001
TOTAL REVENUES	**134,050**	**128,575**
COST OF SERVICES		
Salaries	83,433	78,445
Payroll Taxes	6,700	6,432
Equipment Rental	12,600	10,651
Maintenance (Equipment)	8,300	8,435
Special Clothing and Safety Shoes	660	200
Contract Labor	7,780	6,790
TOTAL COST OF SERVICES	**119,473**	**110,953**
GROSS PROFIT (LOSS)	**14,577**	**17,622**
OPERATING EXPENSES		
Advertising and Promotion	1,500	700
Donations	600	500
Insurance	4,000	870
Meals and Entertainment	2,300	2,100
Subscriptions	120	120
Business Gifts	790	600
Telephone	2,015	1,956
Training	1,975	-
Travel	865	750
Other	1,700	2,724
TOTAL OPERATING EXPENSES	**15,865**	**10,320**
NET INCOME (LOSS)	$ **(1,288)**	$ **7,302**

The bookkeeper provided the following additional information:

- Donations expense is a $600 donation to the Campaign to Re-Elect Senator Ami Dahla.
- Training includes $575 for an educational seminar on bug control. It also includes the cost for Russell to attend an online certificate program in landscaping in order to improve his skills and advertise his designation as a certified landscaper. The tuition, fees, and books cost $1,400. He also drove his personal car 57 miles round trip to Boise to take exams three times for a total of 171 miles.
- No business gift exceeded $22 in value.
- The subscription is for a trade magazine titled Plants Unlimited.

The business uses the cash method of accounting and has no accounts receivable or inventory held for resale.

In addition to the above expenses, the Longs have set aside one room of their house as a home office. The room is 160 square feet and their house has a total of 1,600 square feet. They pay $13,200 per year rental on their house, and the utilities amount to $1,800 for the year.

The Longs also have the following interest income for the year:

Qualified dividends from Potato High Yield Dividend Mutual Fund $44,500

The Longs have two dependent children, Bill (Social Security number 123-23-7654) and Martha (Social Security number 345-67-8654). Both Bill and Martha are full-time high school students, ages 17 and 18, respectively, and each can be claimed for the $500 other dependent credit. Russell's Social Security number is 664-98-5678 and Linda's is 554-98-3946. They made an estimated tax payment to the IRS of $300 on December 31, 2020. The Longs received a $2,400 EIP in 2020.

Required: Complete the Longs' federal tax return for 2020 on Form 1040, Schedule 1, Schedule B, Schedule C, Form 8829, and the Qualified Dividends and Capital Gain Tax Worksheet. Do not complete Form 4562 (depreciation).

2B. Christopher Crosphit (birthdate April 28, 1978) owns and operates a health club called "Catawba Fitness." The business is located at 4321 New Cut Road, Spartanburg, SC 29303. The principal business code is 812190 and the EIN is 12-3456789. Chris had the following income and expenses from the health club:

Income	$216,000
Expenses:	
Business insurance	3,600
Office supplies	3,300
Payroll	98,900
Payroll taxes	9,112
Travel	2,420
Equipment & club maintenance	10,720
Cleaning service	8,775
Equipment rent	22,820
Utilities (electric, water, gas)	13,975
Telephone	2,778
Rent	32,600
Advertising	5,200
Special workout clothing and boxing gloves	780
Subscription to *Biceps Monthly* magazine	120
Educational seminar on weight training	770
Other expenses	1,830

The business uses the cash method of accounting and has no accounts receivable or inventory held for resale.

Chris has the following interest income for the year:

Upper Piedmont Savings Bank savings account	$13,000
Morgan Bank bond portfolio interest	12,400

Chris also dabbles as a broker of antique and rare books. He acquires and scavenges for books and then sells them on the Internet. He generated $4,000 of sales in 2020 and the books he sold cost $3,500. He also incurred $7,600 in travel and other expenses related to this activity. Chris has never turned a profit in the book business, but he loves books and book selling and does not mind losing money doing it.

Chris has been a widower for 10 years with a dependent son, Arnold (Social Security number 276-23-3954), and Chris files his tax return as head of household. Arnold (birthdate July 1, 2002) is a high school student; he does not qualify for the child tax credit but does qualify for the $500 other dependent credit. They live next door to the health club at 4323 New Cut Road. Chris does all the administrative work for the health club out of an office in his home. The room is 171 square feet and the house has a total of 1,800 square feet. Chris pays $20,000 per year in rent and $4,000 in utilities.

Chris' Social Security number is 565-12-6789. He made an estimated tax payment to the IRS of $500 on April 15, 2020. Chris received a $1,700 EIP in 2020.

Required: Complete Chris' federal tax return for 2020 on Form 1040, Schedule 1, Schedule B, Schedule C, and Form 8829. Do not complete Form 4562 (depreciation).

GROUP 5:
CUMULATIVE SOFTWARE PROBLEM

1. The following additional information is available for the Albert and Allison Gaytor family from Chapters 1 and 2.

On September 1, Allison opened a retail store that specializes in sports car accessories. The name of the store is "Toge Pass." The store is located at 617 Crandon Boulevard, Key Biscayne, FL 33149. The store uses the cash method of accounting for everything except inventory which is kept on an accrual basis. The store's EIN is 98-7321654. Allison purchased inventory in August and then started her business on September 1 with $40,100 of inventory. The Toge Pass accountant provided the following financial information:

Income Statement

Toge Pass Auto Parts
Calendar Year 2020

Financial Statements in U.S. Dollars

Revenue		
Gross Sales	64,100	
Less: Sales Returns and Allowances	500	
Net Sales		63,600
Cost of Goods Sold		
Beginning Inventory	40,100	
Add: Purchases	37,886	
Inventory Available	77,986	
Less: Ending Inventory	37,917	
Cost of Goods Sold		40,069
Gross Profit (Loss)		23,531
Expenses		
Advertising	2,997	
Dues and Subscriptions	-	
Gifts	180	
Insurance	805	
Interest	1,700	
Legal and Professional Fees	315	
Licenses and Fees	900	
Miscellaneous	82	
Office Expense	1,266	
Payroll Taxes	510	
Postage	-	
Rent	7,500	
Repairs and Maintenance	401	
Supplies	630	
Telephone	781	
Travel	940	
Uniforms	390	
Utilities	975	
Vehicle Expenses	-	
Wages	3,470	
Total Expenses		23,842
Net Operating Income		(311)
Other Income		
Gain (Loss) on Sale of Assets		
Interest Income		
Total Other Income		-
Net Income (Loss)		(311)

A review of the expense account detail reveals the following:

- The travel expense includes the costs Allison incurred to attend a seminar on sports car accessories. She spent $300 on airfare, $400 on lodging, $90 on a rental car, and $150 on meals. Allison has proper receipts for these amounts.
- The gift account details show that Allison gave a $30 gift to each of her six best suppliers.

- The supplies expense account detail reflects the purchase of 250 pens with the "Toge Pass" logo inscribed on each pen. Allison gave the pens away to suppliers, customers, and other business contacts before the end of the year.
- Uniforms expense reflects the cost to purchase polo shirts Allison provided for each employee (but not herself). The shirts have the Toge Pass logo printed on the front and back and are the required apparel while working but otherwise are just like any other polo shirts.
- The license and fee account includes a $600 fine Toge Pass paid to the state of Washington for environmental damage resulting from an oil spill.

Allison drove her 2012 Ford Explorer 1,701 miles for business related to Toge Pass. The Explorer was driven a total of 11,450 miles for the year. Included in the total 11,450 miles is 5,000 miles spent commuting to the store. Allison has the required substantiation for this business mileage. She uses the standard mileage method.

In July, Albert loaned a friend $7,000 so he could buy a car. Albert's friend lost his job in 2020 and stopped making payments on the loan. He plans to start making payments again, however, with additional interest as soon as he has new employment.

In late 2020, Albert started to mount and stuff some of his trophy fish to display in his "man cave" at the Gaytor's home. Some of his friends liked Albert's taxidermy work and asked him to prepare a couple of trophy fish for them as well. Although he doubts he will ever sell any more stuffed fish, he received $150 and had no expenses related to this activity in 2020.

Required: Combine this new information about the Gaytor family with the information from Chapters 1 and 2 and complete a revised 2020 tax return for Albert and Allison. Be sure to save your data input files since this case will be expanded with more tax information in later chapters.

Form **1040**

Department of the Treasury—Internal Revenue Service   (99)

U.S. Individual Income Tax Return   2020   OMB No. 1545-0074   IRS Use Only—Do not write or staple in this space.

Filing Status
Check only one box.

☐ Single ☐ Married filing jointly ☐ Married filing separately (MFS) ☐ Head of household (HOH) ☐ Qualifying widow(er) (QW)

If you checked the MFS box, enter the name of your spouse. If you checked the HOH or QW box, enter the child's name if the qualifying person is a child but not your dependent ▶

Your first name and middle initial	Last name	Your social security number

If joint return, spouse's first name and middle initial	Last name	Spouse's social security number

Home address (number and street). If you have a P.O. box, see instructions.		Apt. no.

Presidential Election Campaign
Check here if you, or your spouse if filing jointly, want $3 to go to this fund. Checking a box below will not change your tax or refund.   ☐ You ☐ Spouse

City, town, or post office. If you have a foreign address, also complete spaces below.	State	ZIP code

Foreign country name	Foreign province/state/county	Foreign postal code

At any time during 2020, did you receive, sell, send, exchange, or otherwise acquire any financial interest in any virtual currency?   ☐ Yes ☐ No

Standard Deduction

Someone can claim: ☐ You as a dependent ☐ Your spouse as a dependent

☐ Spouse itemizes on a separate return or you were a dual-status alien

Age/Blindness You: ☐ Were born before January 2, 1956 ☐ Are blind **Spouse:** ☐ Was born before January 2, 1956 ☐ Is blind

Dependents (see instructions):

If more than four dependents, see instructions and check here ▶ ☐

(1) First name Last name	(2) Social security number	(3) Relationship to you	(4) ✔ if qualifies for (see instructions):	
			Child tax credit	Credit for other dependents
			☐	☐
			☐	☐
			☐	☐
			☐	☐

Attach Sch. B if required.

Standard Deduction for—
- Single or Married filing separately, $12,400
- Married filing jointly or Qualifying widow(er), $24,800
- Head of household, $18,650
- If you checked any box under *Standard Deduction,* see instructions.

1	Wages, salaries, tips, etc. Attach Form(s) W-2		1
2a	Tax-exempt interest . . .	2a	b Taxable interest	2b
3a	Qualified dividends . . .	3a	b Ordinary dividends	3b
4a	IRA distributions	4a	b Taxable amount	4b
5a	Pensions and annuities . .	5a	b Taxable amount	5b
6a	Social security benefits . .	6a	b Taxable amount	6b
7	Capital gain or (loss). Attach Schedule D if required. If not required, check here . . . . . ▶ ☐		7
8	Other income from Schedule 1, line 9		8
9	Add lines 1, 2b, 3b, 4b, 5b, 6b, 7, and 8. This is your **total income** . . . . ▶		9
10	Adjustments to income:		
a	From Schedule 1, line 22	10a	
b	Charitable contributions if you take the standard deduction. See instructions	10b	
c	Add lines 10a and 10b. These are your **total adjustments to income** . . . . . ▶		10c
11	Subtract line 10c from line 9. This is your **adjusted gross income** . . . . ▶		11
12	**Standard deduction or itemized deductions** (from Schedule A)		12
13	Qualified business income deduction. Attach Form 8995 or Form 8995-A		13
14	Add lines 12 and 13		14
15	**Taxable income.** Subtract line 14 from line 11. If zero or less, enter -0-		15

For Disclosure, Privacy Act, and Paperwork Reduction Act Notice, see separate instructions.   Cat. No. 11320B   Form **1040** (2020)

Form 1040 (2020)   Page **2**

16	**Tax** (see instructions). Check if any from Form(s): 1 ☐ 8814 2 ☐ 4972 3 ☐ _____	16	
17	Amount from Schedule 2, line 3	17	
18	Add lines 16 and 17	18	
19	Child tax credit or credit for other dependents	19	
20	Amount from Schedule 3, line 7	20	
21	Add lines 19 and 20	21	
22	Subtract line 21 from line 18. If zero or less, enter -0-	22	
23	Other taxes, including self-employment tax, from Schedule 2, line 10	23	
24	Add lines 22 and 23. This is your **total tax** ▶	24	
25	Federal income tax withheld from:		
a	Form(s) W-2	25a	
b	Form(s) 1099	25b	
c	Other forms (see instructions)	25c	
d	Add lines 25a through 25c	25d	

- If you have a qualifying child, attach Sch. EIC.
- If you have nontaxable combat pay, see instructions.

26	2020 estimated tax payments and amount applied from 2019 return	26	
27	Earned income credit (EIC)	27	
28	Additional child tax credit. Attach Schedule 8812	28	
29	American opportunity credit from Form 8863, line 8	29	
30	Recovery rebate credit. See instructions	30	
31	Amount from Schedule 3, line 13	31	
32	Add lines 27 through 31. These are your **total other payments and refundable credits**	32	
33	Add lines 25d, 26, and 32. These are your **total payments** ▶	33	

Refund

34	If line 33 is more than line 24, subtract line 24 from line 33. This is the amount you **overpaid**	34	
35a	Amount of line 34 you want **refunded to you.** If Form 8888 is attached, check here ▶ ☐	35a	

Direct deposit? See instructions.

▶b Routing number _____   ▶c Type: ☐ Checking ☐ Savings
▶d Account number _____

36	Amount of line 34 you want **applied to your 2021 estimated tax** ▶	36	

Amount You Owe

For details on how to pay, see instructions.

37	Subtract line 33 from line 24. This is the **amount you owe now** ▶	37	

Note: Schedule H and Schedule SE filers, line 37 may not represent all of the taxes you owe for 2020. See Schedule 3, line 12e, and its instructions for details.

38	Estimated tax penalty (see instructions) ▶	38	

Third Party Designee

Do you want to allow another person to discuss this return with the IRS? See instructions ▶ ☐ **Yes.** Complete below. ☐ **No**

Designee's name ▶ _____   Phone no. ▶ _____   Personal identification number (PIN) ▶ _____

Sign Here

Under penalties of perjury, I declare that I have examined this return and accompanying schedules and statements, and to the best of my knowledge and belief, they are true, correct, and complete. Declaration of preparer (other than taxpayer) is based on all information of which preparer has any knowledge.

Joint return? See instructions. Keep a copy for your records.

Your signature	Date	Your occupation	If the IRS sent you an Identity Protection PIN, enter it here (see inst.) ▶
Spouse's signature. If a joint return, **both** must sign.	Date	Spouse's occupation	If the IRS sent your spouse an Identity Protection PIN, enter it here (see inst.) ▶

Phone no. _____   Email address _____

Paid Preparer Use Only

Preparer's name	Preparer's signature	Date	PTIN	Check if: ☐ Self-employed

Firm's name ▶ _____   Phone no. _____

Firm's address ▶ _____   Firm's EIN ▶ _____

Go to *www.irs.gov/Form1040* for instructions and the latest information.   Form **1040** (2020)

SCHEDULE C
(Form 1040)

Department of the Treasury
Internal Revenue Service (99)

Profit or Loss From Business
(Sole Proprietorship)

▶ Go to *www.irs.gov/ScheduleC* for instructions and the latest information.
▶ **Attach to Form 1040, 1040-SR, 1040-NR, or 1041; partnerships generally must file Form 1065.**

OMB No. 1545-0074

20**20**

Attachment
Sequence No. **09**

Name of proprietor | Social security number (SSN)

A	Principal business or profession, including product or service (see instructions)		**B Enter code from instructions** ▶
C	Business name. If no separate business name, leave blank.		**D Employer ID number (EIN)** (see instr.)
E	Business address (including suite or room no.) ▶		
	City, town or post office, state, and ZIP code		

F Accounting method: **(1)** ☐ Cash **(2)** ☐ Accrual **(3)** ☐ Other (specify) ▶
G Did you "materially participate" in the operation of this business during 2020? If "No," see instructions for limit on losses . ☐ Yes ☐ No
H If you started or acquired this business during 2020, check here . . . . ▶ ☐
I Did you make any payments in 2020 that would require you to file Form(s) 1099? See instructions . . . ☐ Yes ☐ No
J If "Yes," did you or will you file required Form(s) 1099? . . . . ☐ Yes ☐ No

(watermark: DRAFT AS OF July 13, 2020 DO NOT FILE)

Part I — Income

1	Gross receipts or sales. See instructions for line 1 and check the box if this income was reported to you on Form W-2 and the "Statutory employee" box on that form was checked . . . . ▶ ☐	**1**	
2	Returns and allowances	**2**	
3	Subtract line 2 from line 1	**3**	
4	Cost of goods sold (from line 42)	**4**	
5	**Gross profit.** Subtract line 4 from line 3	**5**	
6	Other income, including federal and state gasoline or fuel tax credit or refund (see instructions)	**6**	
7	**Gross income.** Add lines 5 and 6 . . . . ▶	**7**	

Part II — Expenses. Enter expenses for business use of your home **only** on line 30.

8	Advertising	**8**		18	Office expense (see instructions)	**18**	
9	Car and truck expenses (see instructions).	**9**		19	Pension and profit-sharing plans .	**19**	
10	Commissions and fees .	**10**		20	Rent or lease (see instructions):		
11	Contract labor (see instructions)	**11**		a	Vehicles, machinery, and equipment	**20a**	
12	Depletion	**12**		b	Other business property . . .	**20b**	
13	Depreciation and section 179 expense deduction (not included in Part III) (see instructions). . . .	**13**		21	Repairs and maintenance . . .	**21**	
				22	Supplies (not included in Part III) .	**22**	
				23	Taxes and licenses	**23**	
				24	Travel and meals:		
14	Employee benefit programs (other than on line 19). .	**14**		a	Travel	**24a**	
15	Insurance (other than health)	**15**		b	Deductible meals (see instructions)	**24b**	
16	Interest (see instructions):			25	Utilities	**25**	
a	Mortgage (paid to banks, etc.)	**16a**		26	Wages (less employment credits) .	**26**	
b	Other	**16b**		27a	Other expenses (from line 48) . .	**27a**	
17	Legal and professional services	**17**		b	**Reserved for future use** . . .	**27b**	

28	**Total expenses** before expenses for business use of home. Add lines 8 through 27a . . . . . . ▶	**28**	
29	Tentative profit or (loss). Subtract line 28 from line 7	**29**	
30	Expenses for business use of your home. Do not report these expenses elsewhere. Attach Form 8829 unless using the simplified method. See instructions. **Simplified method filers only:** Enter the total square footage of (a) your home: _____ and (b) the part of your home used for business: _____. Use the Simplified Method Worksheet in the instructions to figure the amount to enter on line 30	**30**	
31	**Net profit or (loss).** Subtract line 30 from line 29.		
	• If a profit, enter on both **Schedule 1 (Form 1040), line 3,** and on **Schedule SE, line 2.** (If you checked the box on line 1, see instructions). Estates and trusts, enter on **Form 1041, line 3.**	**31**	
	• If a loss, you **must** go to line 32.		
32	If you have a loss, check the box that describes your investment in this activity. See instructions.		
	• If you checked 32a, enter the loss on both **Schedule 1 (Form 1040), line 3,** and on **Schedule SE, line 2.** (If you checked the box on line 1, see the line 31 instructions). Estates and trusts, enter on **Form 1041, line 3.**	**32a** ☐ All investment is at risk. **32b** ☐ Some investment is not at risk.	
	• If you checked 32b, you **must** attach **Form 6198.** Your loss may be limited.		

For Paperwork Reduction Act Notice, see the separate instructions. Cat. No. 11334P Schedule C (Form 1040) 2020

Schedule C (Form 1040) 2020   Page **2**

Part III	**Cost of Goods Sold** (see instructions)

33 Method(s) used to
value closing inventory: **a** ☐ Cost   **b** ☐ Lower of cost or market   **c** ☐ Other (attach explanation)

34 Was there any change in determining quantities, costs, or valuations between opening and closing inventory?
If "Yes," attach explanation . . . . ☐ Yes   ☐ No

35 Inventory at beginning of year. If different from last year's closing inventory, attach explanation . . | **35** | |

36 Purchases less cost of items withdrawn for personal use . . . . | **36** | |

37 Cost of labor. Do not include any amounts paid to yourself . . . . | **37** | |

38 Materials and supplies . . . . | **38** | |

39 Other costs . . . . | **39** | |

40 Add lines 35 through 39 . . . . | **40** | |

41 Inventory at end of year . . . . | **41** | |

42 **Cost of goods sold.** Subtract line 41 from line 40. Enter the result here and on line 4 . . . . . . | **42** | |

Part IV	**Information on Your Vehicle.** Complete this part **only** if you are claiming car or truck expenses on line 9 and are not required to file Form 4562 for this business. See the instructions for line 13 to find out if you must file Form 4562.

43 When did you place your vehicle in service for business purposes? (month/day/year)   ▶ _____ / _____ / _____

44 Of the total number of miles you drove your vehicle during 2020, enter the number of miles you used your vehicle for:

a Business _____   **b** Commuting (see instructions) _____   **c** Other _____

45 Was your vehicle available for personal use during off-duty hours? . . . . ☐ Yes   ☐ No

46 Do you (or your spouse) have another vehicle available for personal use?. . . . . ☐ Yes   ☐ No

47a Do you have evidence to support your deduction? . . . . ☐ Yes   ☐ No

  b If "Yes," is the evidence written? . . . . ☐ Yes   ☐ No

Part V	**Other Expenses.** List below business expenses not included on lines 8–26 or line 30.

_____ | |
_____ | |
_____ | |
_____ | |
_____ | |
_____ | |
_____ | |
_____ | |
_____ | |

48 **Total other expenses.** Enter here and on line 27a . . . . | **48** | |

Schedule C (Form 1040) 2020

SCHEDULE D (Form 1040) Department of the Treasury Internal Revenue Service (99)	**Capital Gains and Losses** ▶ Attach to Form 1040, 1040-SR, or 1040-NR. ▶ Go to *www.irs.gov/ScheduleD* for instructions and the latest information. ▶ Use Form 8949 to list your transactions for lines 1b, 2, 3, 8b, 9, and 10.	OMB No. 1545-0074 20**20** Attachment Sequence No. **12**

Name(s) shown on return	Your social security number

Did you dispose of any investment(s) in a qualified opportunity fund during the tax year? ☐ **Yes** ☐ **No**
If "Yes," attach Form 8949 and see its instructions for additional requirements for reporting your gain or loss.

Part I Short-Term Capital Gains and Losses—Generally Assets Held One Year or Less (see instructions)

See instructions for how to figure the amounts to enter on the lines below. This form may be easier to complete if you round off cents to whole dollars.	**(d)** Proceeds (sales price)	**(e)** Cost (or other basis)	**(g)** Adjustments to gain or loss from Form(s) 8949, Part I, line 2, column (g)	**(h) Gain or (loss)** Subtract column (e) from column (d) and combine the result with column (g)
1a Totals for all short-term transactions reported on Form 1099-B for which basis was reported to the IRS and for which you have no adjustments (see instructions). However, if you choose to report all these transactions on Form 8949, leave this line blank and go to line 1b .				
1b Totals for all transactions reported on Form(s) 8949 with **Box A** checked				
2 Totals for all transactions reported on Form(s) 8949 with **Box B** checked				
3 Totals for all transactions reported on Form(s) 8949 with **Box C** checked				

4 Short-term gain from Form 6252 and short-term gain or (loss) from Forms 4684, 6781, and 8824 . .	**4**	
5 Net short-term gain or (loss) from partnerships, S corporations, estates, and trusts from Schedule(s) K-1	**5**	
6 Short-term capital loss carryover. Enter the amount, if any, from line 8 of your **Capital Loss Carryover Worksheet** in the instructions	**6** ( )
7 **Net short-term capital gain or (loss).** Combine lines 1a through 6 in column (h). If you have any long-term capital gains or losses, go to Part II below. Otherwise, go to Part III on the back	**7**	

Part II Long-Term Capital Gains and Losses—Generally Assets Held More Than One Year (see instructions)

See instructions for how to figure the amounts to enter on the lines below. This form may be easier to complete if you round off cents to whole dollars.	**(d)** Proceeds (sales price)	**(e)** Cost (or other basis)	**(g)** Adjustments to gain or loss from Form(s) 8949, Part II, line 2, column (g)	**(h) Gain or (loss)** Subtract column (e) from column (d) and combine the result with column (g)
8a Totals for all long-term transactions reported on Form 1099-B for which basis was reported to the IRS and for which you have no adjustments (see instructions). However, if you choose to report all these transactions on Form 8949, leave this line blank and go to line 8b .				
8b Totals for all transactions reported on Form(s) 8949 with **Box D** checked				
9 Totals for all transactions reported on Form(s) 8949 with **Box E** checked				
10 Totals for all transactions reported on Form(s) 8949 with **Box F** checked.				

11 Gain from Form 4797, Part I; long-term gain from Forms 2439 and 6252; and long-term gain or (loss) from Forms 4684, 6781, and 8824	**11**	
12 Net long-term gain or (loss) from partnerships, S corporations, estates, and trusts from Schedule(s) K-1	**12**	
13 Capital gain distributions. See the instructions	**13**	
14 Long-term capital loss carryover. Enter the amount, if any, from line 13 of your **Capital Loss Carryover Worksheet** in the instructions	**14** ( )
15 **Net long-term capital gain or (loss).** Combine lines 8a through 14 in column (h). Then, go to Part III on the back	**15**	

For Paperwork Reduction Act Notice, see your tax return instructions.   Cat. No. 11338H   Schedule D (Form 1040) 2020

Schedule D (Form 1040) 2020   Page **2**

Part III	**Summary**

16 Combine lines 7 and 15 and enter the result **16**

- If line 16 is a **gain,** enter the amount from line 16 on Form 1040, 1040-SR, or 1040-NR, line 7. Then, go to line 17 below.
- If line 16 is a **loss,** skip lines 17 through 20 below. Then, go to line 21. Also be sure to complete line 22.
- If line 16 is **zero,** skip lines 17 through 21 below and enter -0- on Form 1040, 1040-SR, or 1040-NR, line 7. Then, go to line 22.

17 Are lines 15 and 16 **both** gains?
☐ **Yes.** Go to line 18.
☐ **No.** Skip lines 18 through 21, and go to line 22.

18 If you are required to complete the **28% Rate Gain Worksheet** (see instructions), enter the amount, if any, from line 7 of that worksheet . . . . ▶   **18**

19 If you are required to complete the **Unrecaptured Section 1250 Gain Worksheet** (see instructions), enter the amount, if any, from line 18 of that worksheet . . . . ▶   **19**

20 Are lines 18 and 19 **both** zero or blank?
☐ **Yes.** Complete the **Qualified Dividends and Capital Gain Tax Worksheet** in the instructions for Forms 1040 and 1040-SR, line 16. **Don't** complete lines 21 and 22 below.

☐ **No.** Complete the **Schedule D Tax Worksheet** in the instructions. **Don't** complete lines 21 and 22 below.

21 If line 16 is a loss, enter here and on Form 1040, 1040-SR, or 1040-NR, line 7, the **smaller** of:

- The loss on line 16; or
- ($3,000), or if married filing separately, ($1,500)   . . . .   **21** ( )

Note: When figuring which amount is smaller, treat both amounts as positive numbers.

22 Do you have qualified dividends on Form 1040, 1040-SR, or 1040-NR, line 3a?

☐ **Yes.** Complete the **Qualified Dividends and Capital Gain Tax Worksheet** in the instructions for Forms 1040 and 1040-SR, line 16.

☐ **No.** Complete the rest of Form 1040, 1040-SR, or 1040-NR.

Schedule D (Form 1040) 2020

Form **8949**

Department of the Treasury
Internal Revenue Service

Sales and Other Dispositions of Capital Assets

▶ Go to *www.irs.gov/Form8949* for instructions and the latest information.
▶ File with your Schedule D to list your transactions for lines 1b, 2, 3, 8b, 9, and 10 of Schedule D.

OMB No. 1545-0074

2020

Attachment
Sequence No. **12A**

Name(s) shown on return

Social security number or taxpayer identification number

Before you check Box A, B, or C below, see whether you received any Form(s) 1099-B or substitute statement(s) from your broker. A substitute statement will have the same information as Form 1099-B. Either will show whether your basis (usually your cost) was reported to the IRS by your broker and may even tell you which box to check.

Part I   **Short-Term.** Transactions involving capital assets you held 1 year or less are generally short-term (see instructions). For long-term transactions, see page 2.

Note: You may aggregate all short-term transactions reported on Form(s) 1099-B showing basis was reported to the IRS and for which no adjustments or codes are required. Enter the totals directly on Schedule D, line 1a; you aren't required to report these transactions on Form 8949 (see instructions).

You *must* **check Box A, B, or C below. Check only one box.** If more than one box applies for your short-term transactions, complete a separate Form 8949, page 1, for each applicable box. If you have more short-term transactions than will fit on this page for one or more of the boxes, complete as many forms with the same box checked as you need.

☐ **(A)** Short-term transactions reported on Form(s) 1099-B showing basis was reported to the IRS (see **Note** above)
☐ **(B)** Short-term transactions reported on Form(s) 1099-B showing basis **wasn't** reported to the IRS
☐ **(C)** Short-term transactions not reported to you on Form 1099-B

1 (a) Description of property (Example: 100 sh. XYZ Co.)	(b) Date acquired (Mo., day, yr.)	(c) Date sold or disposed of (Mo., day, yr.)	(d) Proceeds (sales price) (see instructions)	(e) Cost or other basis. See the **Note** below and see *Column (e)* in the separate instructions	Adjustment, if any, to gain or loss. If you enter an amount in column (g), enter a code in column (f). See the separate instructions.		(h) Gain or (loss). Subtract column (e) from column (d) and combine the result with column (g)
					(f) Code(s) from instructions	(g) Amount of adjustment	
2 Totals. Add the amounts in columns (d), (e), (g), and (h) (subtract negative amounts). Enter each total here and include on your Schedule D, **line 1b** (if **Box A** above is checked), **line 2** (if **Box B** above is checked), or **line 3** (if **Box C** above is checked) ▶							

Note: If you checked Box A above but the basis reported to the IRS was incorrect, enter in column (e) the basis as reported to the IRS, and enter an adjustment in column (g) to correct the basis. See *Column (g)* in the separate instructions for how to figure the amount of the adjustment.

For Paperwork Reduction Act Notice, see your tax return instructions.   Cat. No. 37768Z   Form **8949** (2020)

Form 8949 (2020)   Attachment Sequence No. **12A**   Page **2**

Name(s) shown on return. Name and SSN or taxpayer identification no. not required if shown on other side	Social security number or taxpayer identification number

Before you check Box D, E, or F below, see whether you received any Form(s) 1099-B or substitute statement(s) from your broker. A substitute statement will have the same information as Form 1099-B. Either will show whether your basis (usually your cost) was reported to the IRS by your broker and may even tell you which box to check.

Part II   **Long-Term.** Transactions involving capital assets you held more than 1 year are generally long-term (see instructions). For short-term transactions, see page 1.

Note: You may aggregate all long-term transactions reported on Form(s) 1099-B showing basis was reported to the IRS and for which no adjustments or codes are required. Enter the totals directly on Schedule D, line 8a; you aren't required to report these transactions on Form 8949 (see instructions).

You *must* **check Box D, E,** *or* **F below. Check only one box.** If more than one box applies for your long-term transactions, complete a separate Form 8949, page 2, for each applicable box. If you have more long-term transactions than will fit on this page for one or more of the boxes, complete as many forms with the same box checked as you need.

- ☐ **(D)** Long-term transactions reported on Form(s) 1099-B showing basis was reported to the IRS (see **Note** above)
- ☐ **(E)** Long-term transactions reported on Form(s) 1099-B showing basis **wasn't** reported to the IRS
- ☐ **(F)** Long-term transactions not reported to you on Form 1099-B

(a) Description of property (Example: 100 sh. XYZ Co.)	**(b)** Date acquired (Mo., day, yr.)	**(c)** Date sold or disposed of (Mo., day, yr.)	**(d)** Proceeds (sales price) (see instructions)	**(e)** Cost or other basis. See the **Note** below and see *Column (e)* in the separate instructions	**(f)** Code(s) from instructions	**(g)** Amount of adjustment	**(h)** Gain or (loss). Subtract column (e) from column (d) and combine the result with column (g)

1

Adjustment, if any, to gain or loss. If you enter an amount in column (g), enter a code in column (f). See the separate instructions.

2 Totals. Add the amounts in columns (d), (e), (g), and (h) (subtract negative amounts). Enter each total here and include on your Schedule D, **line 8b** (if **Box D** above is checked), **line 9** (if **Box E** above is checked), or **line 10** (if **Box F** above is checked) ▶

Note: If you checked Box D above but the basis reported to the IRS was incorrect, enter in column (e) the basis as reported to the IRS, and enter an adjustment in column (g) to correct the basis. See *Column (g)* in the separate instructions for how to figure the amount of the adjustment.

Form **8949** (2020)

SCHEDULE B
(Form 1040)

Department of the Treasury
Internal Revenue Service (99)

Interest and Ordinary Dividends

▶ Go to *www.irs.gov/ScheduleB* for instructions and the latest information.
▶ Attach to Form 1040 or 1040-SR.

OMB No. 1545-0074

2020

Attachment
Sequence No. **08**

Name(s) shown on return

Your social security number

Part I				Amount
Interest	**1**	List name of payer. If any interest is from a seller-financed mortgage and the buyer used the property as a personal residence, see the instructions and list this interest first. Also, show that buyer's social security number and address ▶		
(See instructions and the instructions for Forms 1040 and 1040-SR, line 2b.)				
Note: If you received a Form 1099-INT, Form 1099-OID, or substitute statement from a brokerage firm, list the firm's name as the payer and enter the total interest shown on that form.			**1**	
	2	Add the amounts on line 1	**2**	
	3	Excludable interest on series EE and I U.S. savings bonds issued after 1989. Attach Form 8815	**3**	
	4	Subtract line 3 from line 2. Enter the result here and on Form 1040 or 1040-SR, line 2b . . . . ▶	**4**	

Note: If line 4 is over $1,500, you must complete Part III.

Part II				Amount
Ordinary Dividends	**5**	List name of payer ▶		
(See instructions and the instructions for Forms 1040 and 1040-SR, line 3b.)				
Note: If you received a Form 1099-DIV or substitute statement from a brokerage firm, list the firm's name as the payer and enter the ordinary dividends shown on that form.			**5**	
	6	Add the amounts on line 5. Enter the total here and on Form 1040 or 1040-SR, line 3b . . . . ▶	**6**	

Note: If line 6 is over $1,500, you must complete Part III.

Part III	You must complete this part if you **(a)** had over $1,500 of taxable interest or ordinary dividends; **(b)** had a foreign account; or **(c)** received a distribution from, or were a grantor of, or a transferor to, a foreign trust.	Yes	No
Foreign Accounts and Trusts	**7a** At any time during 2020, did you have a financial interest in or signature authority over a financial account (such as a bank account, securities account, or brokerage account) located in a foreign country? See instructions		
Caution: If required, failure to file FinCEN Form 114 may result in substantial penalties. See instructions.	If "Yes," are you required to file FinCEN Form 114, Report of Foreign Bank and Financial Accounts (FBAR), to report that financial interest or signature authority? See FinCEN Form 114 and its instructions for filing requirements and exceptions to those requirements		
	b If you are required to file FinCEN Form 114, enter the name of the foreign country where the financial account is located ▶		
	8 During 2020, did you receive a distribution from, or were you the grantor of, or transferor to, a foreign trust? If "Yes," you may have to file Form 3520. See instructions		

For Paperwork Reduction Act Notice, see your tax return instructions.   Cat. No. 17146N   **Schedule B (Form 1040) 2020**

Form **8829**	**Expenses for Business Use of Your Home**	OMB No. 1545-0074
Department of the Treasury Internal Revenue Service (99)	▶ File only with Schedule C (Form 1040). Use a separate Form 8829 for each home you used for business during the year. ▶ Go to www.irs.gov/Form8829 for instructions and the latest information.	**2020** Attachment Sequence No. **176**

Name(s) of proprietor(s)   Your social security number

Part I — Part of Your Home Used for Business

1	Area used regularly and exclusively for business, regularly for daycare, or for storage of inventory or product samples (see instructions)	1	
2	Total area of home	2	
3	Divide line 1 by line 2. Enter the result as a percentage	3	%
	For daycare facilities not used exclusively for business, go to line 4. All others, go to line 7.		
4	Multiply days used for daycare during year by hours used per day	4	hr.
5	If you started or stopped using your home for daycare during the year, see instructions; otherwise, enter 8,784	5	hr.
6	Divide line 4 by line 5. Enter the result as a decimal amount	6	.
7	Business percentage. For daycare facilities not used exclusively for business, multiply line 6 by line 3 (enter the result as a percentage). All others, enter the amount from line 3 ▶	7	%

Part II — Figure Your Allowable Deduction

8	Enter the amount from Schedule C, line 29, **plus** any gain derived from the business use of your home, **minus** any loss from the trade or business not derived from the business use of your home. See instructions.		8	

See instructions for columns (a) and (b) before completing lines 9–22. | (a) Direct expenses | (b) Indirect expenses

9	Casualty losses (see instructions)	9		
10	Deductible mortgage interest (see instructions)	10		
11	Real estate taxes (see instructions)	11		
12	Add lines 9, 10, and 11	12		
13	Multiply line 12, column (b), by line 7	13		
14	Add line 12, column (a), and line 13	14		
15	Subtract line 14 from line 8. If zero or less, enter -0-	15		
16	Excess mortgage interest (see instructions)	16		
17	Excess real estate taxes (see instructions)	17		
18	Insurance	18		
19	Rent	19		
20	Repairs and maintenance	20		
21	Utilities	21		
22	Other expenses (see instructions)	22		
23	Add lines 16 through 22	23		
24	Multiply line 23, column (b), by line 7	24		
25	Carryover of prior year operating expenses (see instructions)	25		
26	Add line 23, column (a), line 24, and line 25	26		
27	Allowable operating expenses. Enter the **smaller** of line 15 or line 26	27		
28	Limit on excess casualty losses and depreciation. Subtract line 27 from line 15	28		
29	Excess casualty losses (see instructions)	29		
30	Depreciation of your home from line 42 below	30		
31	Carryover of prior year excess casualty losses and depreciation (see instructions)	31		
32	Add lines 29 through 31	32		
33	Allowable excess casualty losses and depreciation. Enter the **smaller** of line 28 or line 32	33		
34	Add lines 14, 27, and 33	34		
35	Casualty loss portion, if any, from lines 14 and 33. Carry amount to **Form 4684**. See instructions	35		
36	**Allowable expenses for business use of your home.** Subtract line 35 from line 34. Enter here and on Schedule C, line 30. If your home was used for more than one business, see instructions. ▶	36		

Part III — Depreciation of Your Home

37	Enter the **smaller** of your home's adjusted basis or its fair market value. See instructions	37	
38	Value of land included on line 37	38	
39	Basis of building. Subtract line 38 from line 37	39	
40	Business basis of building. Multiply line 39 by line 7	40	
41	Depreciation percentage (see instructions)	41	%
42	Depreciation allowable (see instructions). Multiply line 40 by line 41. Enter here and on line 30 above	42	

Part IV — Carryover of Unallowed Expenses to 2021

43	Operating expenses. Subtract line 27 from line 26. If less than zero, enter -0-	43	
44	Excess casualty losses and depreciation. Subtract line 33 from line 32. If less than zero, enter -0-	44	

For Paperwork Reduction Act Notice, see your tax return instructions.   Cat. No. 13232M   Form **8829** (2020)

Qualified Dividends and Capital Gain Tax Worksheet—Line 16

Before you begin:	✓ See the earlier instructions for line 16 to see if you can use this worksheet to figure your tax.
	✓ Before completing this worksheet, complete Form 1040 or 1040-SR through line 15.
	✓ If you don't have to file Schedule D and you received capital gain distributions, be sure you checked the box on Form 1040 or 1040-SR, line 7.

1. Enter the amount from Form 1040 or 1040-SR, line 15. However, if you are filing Form 2555 (relating to foreign earned income), enter the amount from line 3 of the Foreign Earned Income Tax Worksheet . . . . **1.** _____

2. Enter the amount from Form 1040 or 1040-SR, line 3a* . . . . **2.** _____

3. Are you filing Schedule D?*
   ☐ **Yes.** Enter the **smaller** of line 15 or 16 of Schedule D. If either line 15 or 16 is blank or a loss, enter -0-.   **3.** _____
   ☐ **No.** Enter the amount from Form 1040 or 1040-SR, line 7.

4. Add lines 2 and 3 . . . . **4.** _____

5. If filing Form 4952 (used to figure investment interest expense deduction), enter any amount from line 4g of that form. Otherwise, enter -0- . . . . **5.** _____

6. Subtract line 5 from line 4. If zero or less, enter -0- . . . . **6.** _____

7. Subtract line 6 from line 1. If zero or less, enter -0- . . . . **7.** _____

8. Enter:
   $40,000 if single or married filing separately,
   $80,000 if married filing jointly or qualifying widow(er),
   $53,600 if head of household.   . . . . **8.** _____

9. Enter the smaller of line 1 or line 8 . . . . **9.** _____

10. Enter the smaller of line 7 or line 9 . . . . **10.** _____

11. Subtract line 10 from line 9. This amount is taxed at 0% . . . . **11.** _____

12. Enter the smaller of line 1 or line 6 . . . . **12.** _____

13. Enter the amount from line 11 . . . . **13.** _____

14. Subtract line 13 from line 12 . . . . **14.** _____

15. Enter:
    $441,450 if single,
    $248,300 if married filing separately,
    $496,600 if married filing jointly or qualifying widow(er),
    $469,050 if head of household.   . . . . **15.** _____

16. Enter the smaller of line 1 or line 15 . . . . **16.** _____

17. Add lines 7 and 11 . . . . **17.** _____

18. Subtract line 17 from line 16. If zero or less, enter -0- . . . . **18.** _____

19. Enter the smaller of line 14 or line 18 . . . . **19.** _____

20. Multiply line 19 by 15% (0.15) . . . . **20.** _____

21. Add lines 11 and 19 . . . . **21.** _____

22. Subtract line 21 from line 12 . . . . **22.** _____

23. Multiply line 22 by 20% (0.20) . . . . **23.** _____

24. Figure the tax on the amount on line 7. If the amount on line 7 is less than $100,000, use the Tax Table to figure the tax. If the amount on line 7 is $100,000 or more, use the Tax Computation Worksheet . . . . **24.** _____

25. Add lines 20, 23, and 24 . . . . **25.** _____

26. Figure the tax on the amount on line 1. If the amount on line 1 is less than $100,000, use the Tax Table to figure the tax. If the amount on line 1 is $100,000 or more, use the Tax Computation Worksheet . . . . **26.** _____

27. **Tax on all taxable income.** Enter the **smaller** of line 25 or 26. Also include this amount on the entry space on Form 1040 or 1040-SR, line 16. If you are filing Form 2555, don't enter this amount on the entry space on Form 1040 or 1040-SR, line 16. Instead, enter it on line 4 of the Foreign Earned Income Tax Worksheet . . . . **27.** _____

If you are filing Form 2555, see the footnote in the Foreign Earned Income Tax Worksheet before completing this line.

This worksheet adapted from the 2019 worksheet.

Student Name _____

Class/Section _____

Date _____

KEY NUMBER TAX RETURN SUMMARY

CHAPTER 3

Comprehensive Problem 1

Adjusted Gross Income (Line 11) _____

Standard Deduction (Line 12) _____

Taxable Income (Line 15) _____

Total Tax (Line 24) _____

Comprehensive Problem 2A

Adjusted Gross Income (Line 11) _____

Tentative Profit or (Loss), Schedule C (Line 29) _____

Allowable Expenses for Business Use of Your Home,
Form 8829 (Line 36) _____

Total Tax (Line 24) _____

Amount Overpaid (Line 34) _____

Comprehensive Problem 2B

Adjusted Gross Income (Line 11) _____

Tentative Profit or (Loss), Schedule C (Line 29) _____

Allowable Expenses for Business Use of Your Home,
Form 8829 (Line 36) _____

Total Tax (Line 24) _____

Amount Overpaid (Line 34) _____

Additional Income and the Qualified Business Income Deduction

LEARNING OBJECTIVES

After completing this chapter, you should be able to:

LO 4.1   Define the term "capital asset."

LO 4.2   Apply the holding period for long-term and short-term capital gains and losses.

LO 4.3   Calculate the gain or loss on the disposition of an asset.

LO 4.4   Compute the tax on capital gains.

LO 4.5   Describe the treatment of capital losses.

LO 4.6   Apply the exclusion of gain from personal residence sales.

LO 4.7   Apply the tax rules for rental property and vacation homes.

LO 4.8   Explain the treatment of passive income and losses.

LO 4.9   Describe the basic tax treatment of deductions for net operating losses.

LO 4.10 Compute the qualified business income (QBI) deduction.

OVERVIEW

Chapter 4 covers additional important elements of income and expense which enter into the calculation of adjusted gross income (AGI). The first part of this chapter includes capital gains and other items reported through Schedule D. The second part covers the tax rules for rental properties and other business activities including limitations on passive activities reported through Schedule E. This chapter concludes with the qualified business income deduction introduced for use in 2018 by the TCJA. The business income and expenses included in this chapter are all part of the calculation of a taxpayer's AGI.

4-1 WHAT IS A CAPITAL ASSET?

When taxpayers dispose of property, they must calculate any gain or loss on the transaction and report the gain or loss on their tax returns. The gain or loss realized is equal to the difference between the amount realized on the sale or exchange of the property and the taxpayer's adjusted basis in the property. How gains and losses are reported is dependent on the nature of the property and the length of time the property has been owned. Gains and losses on the sale of capital assets are known as capital gains and losses and are classified as either short-term or long-term. For a gain or loss on the sale of a capital asset to be classified as a long-term capital gain or loss, the taxpayer must have held the asset for the required holding period.

The tax law defines a capital asset as any property, whether used in a trade or business or not, other than:

1. Stock in trade, inventory, or property held primarily for sale to customers in the ordinary course of a trade or business;
2. Depreciable property or real property used in a trade or business (Section 1231 assets);
3. A patent, invention, model or design (whether or not patented), a secret formula or process, a copyright, a literary, musical, or artistic composition, a letter or memorandum, or similar property, if the property is created by the taxpayer;
4. Accounts or notes receivable; and
5. Certain U.S. government publications.

The definition of a capital asset is a definition by exception. All property owned by a taxpayer, other than property specifically noted as an exception, is a capital asset. Depreciable property and real estate used in a trade or business are referred to as Section 1231 assets and will be discussed in Chapter 8 because special rules apply to such assets.

Self-Study Problem 4.1   *See Appendix E for Solutions to Self-Study Problems*

Indicate, by circling your answer, whether each of the following properties is or is not a capital asset.

Property	Capital	Asset?
1. Shoes held by a shoe store	Yes	No
2. A taxpayer's personal residence	Yes	No
3. A painting held by the artist	Yes	No
4. Accounts receivable of a dentist	Yes	No
5. A copyright purchased from a company	Yes	No
6. A truck used in the taxpayer's business	Yes	No
7. IBM stock owned by an investor	Yes	No
8. AT&T bonds owned by an investor	Yes	No
9. Land held as an investment	Yes	No
10. A taxpayer's television	Yes	No
11. Automobiles for sale owned by a car dealer	Yes	No
12. A taxpayer's sailboat	Yes	No

4-2 HOLDING PERIOD

Assets must be held for more than 1 year for the gain or loss to be considered long-term. A capital asset sold before it is owned for the required holding period results in a short-term capital gain or loss. A net short-term capital gain is treated as ordinary income for tax purposes. In calculating the holding period, the taxpayer excludes the date of acquisition and includes the date of disposition.

EXAMPLE Glen purchased stock as an investment on March 27, 2019. The first day the stock may be sold for long-term capital gain treatment is March 28, 2020. ◆

To satisfy the long-term holding period requirement, a capital asset acquired on the last day of a month must not be disposed of before the first day of the thirteenth month following the month of purchase.

EXAMPLE If Elwood purchases a painting on March 31, 2019, the first day the painting may be sold for long-term capital gain treatment is April 1, 2020. ◆

Self-Study Problem 4.2 *See Appendix E for Solutions to Self-Study Problems*

Indicate whether a gain or loss realized in each of the following situations would be long-term or short-term by putting an "X" in the appropriate blank.

Date Acquired	Date Sold	Long-Term	Short-Term
1. October 16, 2019	May 30, 2020	_____	_____
2. May 2, 2019	October 12, 2020	_____	_____
3. July 18, 2019	July 18, 2020	_____	_____
4. August 31, 2018	March 1, 2020	_____	_____

4-3 CALCULATION OF GAIN OR LOSS

A taxpayer must calculate the amount realized and the adjusted basis of property sold or exchanged to arrive at the amount of the gain or loss realized on the disposition. The taxpayer's gain or loss is calculated using the following formula:

Amount realized − Adjusted basis = Gain or loss realized

4-3a Sale or Exchange

The realization of a gain or loss requires the "sale or exchange" of an asset. The term "sale or exchange" is not defined in the tax law, but a sale generally requires the receipt of money or the relief from liabilities in exchange for property, and an exchange is the transfer of ownership of one property for another property.

EXAMPLE Maggie sells stock for $8,500 that she purchased 2 years ago for $6,000. Maggie's adjusted basis in the stock is its cost, $6,000; therefore, she realizes a long-term capital gain of $2,500 ($8,500 − $6,000) on the sale. ◆

EXAMPLE Art owns a home which has increased in value during the tax year. If Art does not sell the home, there is no realized gain during the tax year. ◆

4-3b Amount Realized

The amount realized from a sale or other disposition of property is equal to the sum of the money received, plus the fair market value of other property received, less the costs paid to transfer the property. If the taxpayer is relieved of a liability, the amount of the liability is added to the amount realized.

EXAMPLE During the tax year, Ted sells real estate held as an investment for $75,000 in cash, and the buyer assumes the mortgage on the property of $120,000. Ted pays real estate commissions and other transfer costs of $11,000. The amount realized on the sale is calculated as:

Cash received	$ 75,000
Liabilities transferred	120,000
Total sales price	195,000
Less: transfer costs	(11,000)
Amount realized	$ 184,000

◆

4-3c Adjusted Basis

The adjusted basis of property is equal to the original basis adjusted by adding capital (major) improvements and deducting depreciation allowed or allowable, as illustrated by the following formula:

Adjusted basis = Original basis + Capital improvements − Accumulated depreciation

The original basis of property is usually its cost. The cost is the amount paid in cash, debt obligations, other property, or services. The original basis also includes amounts you pay for the sales tax, freight, installation and testing, excise taxes, revenue stamps, recording fees, and real estate taxes if you assume the liability of the seller. If the acquired asset is real property, certain fees and other expenses are part of the cost basis in the property such as the settlement fees and closing costs you paid for buying the property but does not include fees and costs for getting a loan on the property.

The following are some of the settlement fees or closing costs included in the basis of real property:

- Charges for installing utility services
- Legal fees (including fees for the title search and preparation of the sales contract and deed)
- Recording fees
- Survey fees
- Transfer taxes
- Owner's title insurance
- Any amounts the seller owes that you agree to pay, such as back taxes or interest, recording or mortgage fees, charges for improvements or repairs, and sales commissions

The following are some of the settlement fees and closing costs that cannot be included in the basis of property:

- Amounts placed in escrow for the future payment of items such as taxes and insurance
- Casualty insurance premiums
- Rent for occupancy of the property before closing
- Charges for utilities or other services related to occupancy of the property before closing

- Charges connected with getting a loan, such as points (discount points, loan origination fees), mortgage insurance premiums, loan assumption fees, cost of a credit report, and fees for an appraisal required by a lender

Capital improvements are major expenditures for permanent improvements to or restoration of the taxpayer's property. These expenditures include amounts which result in an increase in the value of the taxpayer's property or substantially increase the useful life of the property, as well as amounts which are spent to adapt property to a new use. For example, architect fees paid to plan an addition to a building, as well as the cost of the addition, must be added to the original basis of the asset as capital improvements. Ordinary repairs and maintenance expenditures are not capital expenditures.

EXAMPLE   Alan and his wife purchased a house on September 15, 2020. Their closing statement for the purchase is illustrated on Pages 4-6 and 4-7. Their original tax basis in the house is equal to the purchase price of $130,000 plus the incidental costs of the owner's title insurance (not lender's), government recording fees, and transfer taxes. Therefore, their original basis is $130,740 ($130,000 + $500 + $50 + $190). The loan origination fee represents "points" on the mortgage loan. If the house is their principal residence, the points are deductible as interest in the year of payment. The prorated interest and taxes affect their deductions for interest and taxes, as described in Chapter 5. The homeowners' insurance is a nondeductible personal expense, assuming the house is their personal residence. ♦

EXAMPLE   Paul acquired a rental house 4 years ago for $91,000. Depreciation claimed on the house for the 4 years totals $14,000. Paul installed a new patio at a cost of $2,500. The adjusted basis of the house is $79,500, as calculated below:

Adjusted basis = original basis + capital improvements − accumulated depreciation
$79,500 = $91,000 + $2,500 − $14,000 ♦

If property is received from a decedent (as an inheritance), the original basis is generally equal to the fair market value at the decedent's date of death. For property acquired as a gift, the amount of the donee's basis depends on whether the property is sold for a gain or a loss by the donee. If a gain results from the disposition of the property, the donee's basis is equal to the donor's basis. If the disposition of the property results in a loss, the donee's basis is equal to the lesser of the donor's basis or the fair market value of the property on the date of the gift. When property acquired by gift is disposed of at an amount between the basis for gain and the basis for loss, no gain or loss is recognized. Note that the basis for gain and the basis for loss will be different only where the gifted property has a fair market value, on the date of the gift, that is less than the donor's adjusted basis in the property.

EXAMPLE   Ron received AT&T stock upon the death of his grandfather. The stock cost his grandfather $6,000 forty years ago and was worth $97,000 on the date of his grandfather's death. Ron's basis in the stock is $97,000. ♦

EXAMPLE   Jane received a gift of stock from her mother. The stock cost her mother $9,000 five years ago and was worth $6,500 on the date of the gift. If the stock is sold by Jane for $12,000, her gain would be $3,000 ($12,000 − $9,000). However, if the stock is sold for $5,000, the loss would be only $1,500 ($5,000 − $6,500). If the stock is sold for an amount between $6,500 and $9,000, no gain or loss is recognized on the sale. ♦

OMB Approval No. 2502-0265

 A. **Settlement Statement (HUD-1)**

B. Type of Loan				
1. ☐ FHA 2. ☐ RHS 3. ☒ Conv. Unins.	6. File Number:	7. Loan Number:	8. Mortgage Insurance Case Number:	
4. ☐ VA 5. ☐ Conv. Ins.				

C. Note: This form is furnished to give you a statement of actual settlement costs. Amounts paid to and by the settlement agent are shown. Items marked "(p.o.c.)" were paid outside the closing; they are shown here for informational purposes and are not included in the totals.

D. Name & Address of Borrower:	E. Name & Address of Seller:	F. Name & Address of Lender:
Alan & Julie Young 66 W. 2nd Street, Apt. 3F Peru, IN 46970	Chris and Fiona Everett 89 Payson Street Denver, IN 46926	2nd Farmers Bank 120 N. Broadway Peru, IN 46970

G. Property Location:	H. Settlement Agent:	I. Settlement Date:
68 W. Canal Street Peru, IN 46970		
	Place of Settlement:	

J. Summary of Borrower's Transaction		K. Summary of Seller's Transaction	
100. Gross Amount Due from Borrower		**400. Gross Amount Due to Seller**	
101. Contract sales price	$130,000.00	401. Contract sales price	$130,000.00
102. Personal property		402. Personal property	
103. Settlement charges to borrower (line 1400)	$4,354.40	403.	
104.		404.	
105.		405.	
Adjustment for items paid by seller in advance		**Adjustment for items paid by seller in advance**	
106. City/town taxes to		406. City/town taxes to	
107. County taxes 10/1/2020 to 12/31/2020	$1,000.00	407. County taxes 10/1/2020 to 12/31/2020	$1,000.00
108. Assessments to		408. Assessments to	
109.		409.	
110.		410.	
111.		411.	
112.		412.	
120. Gross Amount Due from Borrower	$135,354.40	**420. Gross Amount Due to Seller**	$131,000.00
200. Amount Paid by or in Behalf of Borrower		**500. Reductions In Amount Due to seller**	
201. Deposit or earnest money	$1,000.00	501. Excess deposit (see instructions)	
202. Principal amount of new loan(s)	$104,000.00	502. Settlement charges to seller (line 1400)	$8,240.00
203. Existing loan(s) taken subject to		503. Existing loan(s) taken subject to	
204.		504. Payoff of first mortgage loan	
205.		505. Payoff of second mortgage loan	
206.		506.	
207.		507.	
208.		508.	
209.		509.	
Adjustments for items unpaid by seller		**Adjustments for items unpaid by seller**	
210. City/town taxes to		510. City/town taxes to	
211. County taxes to		511. County taxes to	
212. Assessments to		512. Assessments to	
213.		513.	
214.		514.	
215.		515.	
216.		516.	
217.		517.	
218.		518.	
219.		519.	
220. Total Paid by/for Borrower	$105,000.00	**520. Total Reduction Amount Due Seller**	$8,240.00
300. Cash at Settlement from/to Borrower		**600. Cash at Settlement to/from Seller**	
301. Gross amount due from borrower (line 120)	$135,354.40	601. Gross amount due to seller (line 420)	$131,000.00
302. Less amounts paid by/for borrower (line 220)	( )	602. Less reductions in amounts due seller (line 520)	($8,240.00)
303. Cash ☒ From ☐ To Borrower	$30,354.40	**603. Cash ☒ To ☐ From Seller**	$122,760.00

The Public Reporting Burden for this collection of information is estimated at 35 minutes per response for collecting, reviewing, and reporting the data. This agency may not collect this information, and you are not required to complete this form, unless it displays a currently valid OMB control number. No confidentiality is assured; this disclosure is mandatory. This is designed to provide the parties to a RESPA covered transaction with information during the settlement process.

L. Settlement Charges

700. Total Real Estate Broker Fees $7,800		Paid From Borrower's Funds at Settlement	Paid From Seller's Funds at Settlement
Division of commission (line 700) as follows :			
701. $ 3,900.00 to ABC Realtor			
702. $ 3,900.00 to XYZ Realtor			
703. Commission paid at settlement			$7,800.00
704.			

800. Items Payable in Connection with Loan			
801. Our origination charge incl. origination points (1% or $1,040.00)	$ 1,040.00 (from GFE #1)		
802. Your credit or charge (points) for the specific interest rate chosen	$ (from GFE #2)		
803. Your adjusted origination charges	(from GFE #A)	$1,040.00	
804. Appraisal fee to Appraisers R Us	(from GFE #3)	$400.00	
805. Credit report to Equifacts	(from GFE #3)	$50.00	
806. Tax service to	(from GFE #3)		
807. Flood certification to	(from GFE #3)		
808.			
809.			
810.			
811.			

900. Items Required by Lender to be Paid in Advance			
901. Daily interest charges from 9/15/20 to 10/31/20 @ $ 11.40 /day	(from GFE #10)	$524.40	
902. Mortgage insurance premium for months to	(from GFE #3)		
903. Homeowner's insurance for 1 years to ($600 P.O.C.)	(from GFE #11)		
904.			

1000. Reserves Deposited with Lender					
1001. Initial deposit for your escrow account			(from GFE #9)	$250.00	
1002. Homeowner's insurance	1	months @ $ 50.00	per month $ 50.00		
1003. Mortgage insurance		months @ $	per month $		
1004. Property Taxes	2	months @ $ 100.00	per month $ 200.00		
1005.		months @ $	per month $		
1006.		months @ $	per month $		
1007. Aggregate Adjustment			-$		

1100. Title Charges			
1101. Title services and lender's title insurance	(from GFE #4)	$1,350.00	
1102. Settlement or closing fee	$ 100.00		$250.00
1103. Owner's title insurance Title Company, Inc.	(from GFE #5)	$500.00	
1104. Lender's title insurance	$ 500.00		
1105. Lender's title policy limit $ 130,000.00			
1106. Owner's title policy limit $ 130,000.00			
1107. Agent's portion of the total title insurance premium to Title Company Inc	$ 300.00		
1108. Underwriter's portion of the total title insurance premium to Underwriter	$ 75.00		
1109.			
1110.			
1111.			

1200. Government Recording and Transfer Charges			
1201. Government recording charges	(from GFE #7)	$50.00	
1202. Deed $ 25.00 Mortgage $ 25.00 Release $ 15.00			$15.00
1203. Transfer taxes	(from GFE #8)	$190.00	
1204. City/County tax/stamps Deed $ 130.00 Mortgage $			
1205. State tax/stamps Deed $ 60.00 Mortgage $			
1206.			

1300. Additional Settlement Charges			
1301. Required services that you can shop for	(from GFE #6)		
1302. Pest Inspection	$ 75.00		$75.00
1303. Home warranty	$ 100.00		$100.00
1304.			
1305.			

1400. Total Settlement Charges (enter on lines 103, Section J and 502, Section K)	$4,354.40	$8,240.00

Self-Study Problem 4.3   *See Appendix E for Solutions to Self-Study Problems*

Supply the missing information in the following blanks:

	Original Cost	Accumulated Depreciation	Capital Improvements	Adjusted Basis
1.	$15,000	$5,000	$1,000	$_____
2.	15,000	8,000		9,000
3.	30,000		2,000	17,000
4.	_____	9,000	4,000	18,000

Learning Objective 4.4

4-4 NET CAPITAL GAINS

Compute the tax on capital gains.

In recent years, the tax rates on long-term and short-term capital gains have become complex. Short-term capital gains are taxed as ordinary income, while there are various different preferential long-term capital gains tax rates. The 2020 capital gains tax rates are as follows:

Type of Gains	Tax Rate*
Short-Term Capital Gains	Taxed at ordinary income rates consistent with filing status
Typical Long-Term Capital Gains	Taxed at 0, 15, or 20 percent depending on level of other taxable income (see Chapter 2)
Long-Term Unrecaptured Section 1250 Gain (see Chapter 8)	Capped at 25 percent
Long-Term Collectibles Gains (Art, Gems, Coins, Stamps, etc.)	Capped at 28 percent

*The 3.8 percent Medicare tax on net investment income, including qualifying dividends, applies to high-income taxpayers with income over certain thresholds. Please see Chapter 6 for further details.

The application of the typical long-term capital gains rates of 0, 15, or 20 percent depends on the taxable income and filing status of the taxpayer. Formerly, the different rates applied to a taxpayer depending on which ordinary tax bracket the taxpayer was in (e.g., a taxpayer in the 12 percent tax bracket would pay tax on long-term gains at 0 percent since 15 percent is not preferential). The current long-term capital gains tax rates do not align perfectly with the existing ordinary income tax rates. For 2020, typical long-term capital gains (and dividends as discussed in Chapter 2) are taxed as follows:

Income level	Long-term capital gains rate*
Married filing jointly	
$0–$80,000	0%
$80,001–$496,600	15%
>$496,600	20%
Single	
$0–$40,000	0%
$40,001–$441,450	15%
>$441,450	20%

Head of household

$0–$53,600	0%
$53,601–$469,050	15%
>$469,050	20%

Married filing separately

$0–$40,000	0%
$40,001–$248,300	15%
>$248,300	20%

*Special higher rates for "high-income" taxpayers are covered in Chapter 6.

The 2020 break points between the ordinary rates and the typical long-term capital gains rates differ by minor amounts. For example, a single taxpayer moves from an ordinary income tax rate of 12 percent to 22 percent at $40,125; whereas the same taxpayer moves from a 0 percent to 15 percent long-term capital gains tax rate at $40,000.

EXAMPLE   Dee is a single taxpayer with wage income of $45,000 and long-term capital gains of $8,000 in 2020. Assume Dee has no other deductions or income except the standard deduction. Dee's taxable income is

Wage income	$45,000
Long-term capital gains	8,000
Standard deduction	(12,400)
Exemption (repealed by the TCJA)	0
Taxable income	$40,600

Dee's income now must be separated into the ordinary and long-term capital gain portions:

Taxable income	$40,600
Long-term capital gains	(8,000)
Ordinary income	$32,600

The 2020 tax on $32,600 of ordinary income is $3,718. Dee's taxable income without the long-term gain is below the 15 percent threshold of $40,000 for a single taxpayer in 2020, but her taxable income with the long-term gain is above the threshold; thus, a portion of the long-term gain will be taxed at 0 percent and a portion at 15 percent. Of her $8,000 long-term capital gain, $7,400 is below the threshold and taxed at 0 percent while $600 is above the threshold and is taxed at 15 percent for an additional capital gains tax of $90 to bring Dee's total tax liability to $3,808. The Qualified Dividends and Capital Gain Tax Worksheet introduced in Chapter 2 can be used to calculate the ordinary and long-term capital gains tax. ♦

4-4a **Ordering Rules for Capital Gains**

Since there are multiple kinds of capital gains on which to calculate tax, an ordering system is necessary to know which capital gains to tax at what rates. The various kinds of gains are included in taxable income in the following order:

1. Short-term capital gains
2. Unrecaptured Section 1250 gains on real estate
3. Gains on collectibles
4. Long-term capital gains

If taxpayers (or tax practitioners) have several different types of capital gains that interact with each other, the calculation may become very complex. A good tax preparation software will provide the calculation along with supporting worksheets for further review. The rules for the taxation of capital gains are exceptionally complex, and a complete discussion of them is beyond the scope of this textbook.

4-4b Calculation of a Net Capital Position

If a taxpayer has a "net long-term capital gain" (net long-term capital gain in excess of net short-term capital loss), the gain is subject to a preferential tax rate as discussed above. Thus, a taxpayer has to net all of the long-term and short-term capital transactions that take place during a year to calculate tax liability. In calculating a taxpayer's net capital gain or net capital loss, the following procedure is followed:

1. Capital gains and losses are classified into two groups, long-term and short-term.
2. Long-term capital gains are offset by long-term capital losses, resulting in either a net long-term capital gain or a net long-term capital loss.
3. Short-term capital gains are offset by short-term capital losses, resulting in a net short-term capital gain or a net short-term capital loss.
4. If Step 2 above results in a net long-term capital gain, it is offset by any net short-term capital loss (Step 3), resulting in either a net long-term capital gain (net long-term capital gain exceeds net short-term capital loss) or a net short-term capital loss (net short-term capital loss exceeds net long-term capital gain). If Step 2 above results in a net long-term capital loss, it is offset against any net short-term capital gain (Step 3), resulting in either a net long-term capital loss (net long-term capital loss exceeds net short-term capital gain) or ordinary income (net short-term capital gain exceeds net long-term capital loss).

EXAMPLE   The net capital gain computation is illustrated in the following table:

Taxpayer	Net LT Capital Gain or (Loss)	Net ST Capital Gain or (Loss)	Net Capital Position	Taxable LT Gain	Taxable ST Gain
A.	$10,000	$ 0	$ 10,000	$10,000	$ 0
B.	10,000	(4,000)	6,000	6,000	0
C.	0	20,000	20,000	0	20,000
D.	0	(20,000)	(20,000)	0	0
E.	10,000	8,000	18,000	10,000	8,000
F.	(8,000)	12,000	4,000	0	4,000
G.	(8,000)	(6,000)	(14,000)	0	0

◆

> ### Self-Study Problem 4.4   *See Appendix E for Solutions to Self-Study Problems*
>
> In October 2020, Jack, a single taxpayer, sold IBM stock for $12,000, which he purchased 4 years ago for $4,000. He also sold GM stock for $14,000, which cost $17,500 3 years ago, and he had a short-term capital loss of $1,800 on the sale of land. If Jack's other taxable income (salary) is $78,000, what is the amount of Jack's tax on these capital transactions?
>
> $ _____

Learning Objective 4.5

4-5 NET CAPITAL LOSSES

Describe the treatment of capital losses.

4-5a Calculation of Net Capital Losses

The computation of an individual taxpayer's net capital loss is accomplished in a manner similar to the computation of a net capital gain. A net capital loss is incurred when the total capital losses for the period exceed the total capital gains for the period.

EXAMPLE   Connie has net long-term capital gains of $6,500 and a short-term capital loss of $8,000. The net short-term capital loss is $1,500 ($6,500 − $8,000). ◆

EXAMPLE   Delvin has net long-term capital losses of $8,000 and a short-term capital gain of $4,500. The net long-term capital loss is $3,500 ($4,500 − $8,000). ◆

4-5b Treatment of Net Capital Losses

Individual taxpayers may deduct net capital losses against ordinary income in amounts up to $3,000 per year. Unused capital losses in a particular year may be carried forward indefinitely. Capital losses and capital loss carryovers first offset capital gains using the ordering rules discussed on the next page. Any remaining net capital loss may be used to offset ordinary income, subject to the $3,000 annual limitation.

EXAMPLE   Carter has a net long-term capital loss of $15,000 and other taxable income for the year of $25,000. He may deduct $3,000 of the loss against the $25,000 of other taxable income. The remaining capital loss of $12,000 ($15,000 − $3,000) is carried forward to future years. ◆

When unused capital losses are carried forward, they maintain their character as either long-term or short-term. If an individual taxpayer has both net long-term losses and net short-term losses in the same year, the net short-term losses are deducted first.

EXAMPLE   Frances has a long-term capital loss of $7,000 and a $2,000 short-term capital loss in Year 1. For that year, Frances may deduct $3,000 in capital losses, the $2,000 short-term capital loss, and $1,000 of the long-term capital loss. Her carryforward would be a $6,000 long-term capital loss. If Frances has no capital gains or losses in Year 2, she would deduct $3,000 in long-term capital losses and carry forward $3,000 ($6,000 − $3,000) to Year 3. Assuming she has no other capital gains and losses, the deduction of losses by year can be summarized as follows:

	Year 1	Year 2	Year 3
Long-term capital loss	$7,000	$6,000	$3,000
Short-term capital loss	2,000	0	0
Deduction	3,000	3,000	3,000
Long-term capital loss used	1,000	3,000	3,000
Carryforward, long-term capital loss	6,000	3,000	0 ◆

TAX BREAK

Taxpayers who have recognized a large capital loss during the year may wish to sell stock or other property to generate enough capital gains prior to year-end to use up all but $3,000 of the capital loss. This way, the capital loss in excess of $3,000 will be used in the current period rather than carried forward, and the capital gains will be fully sheltered from tax.

4-5c Personal Capital Losses

Losses from the sale of personal capital assets are not allowed for tax purposes. For instance, the sale of a personal automobile at a loss or the sale of a personal residence at a loss does not generate a tax-deductible capital loss for individual taxpayers.

EXAMPLE   Rose moved to a nursing home in 2020 and sold both her personal auto and her principal residence. She originally purchased her auto for $20,000 and sold it for $10,000. She originally purchased her residence for $125,000 and sold it for $100,000. The losses on these sales are not tax deductible to Rose because the assets were personal-use assets. ◆

4-5d Ordering Rules for Capital Losses

When a taxpayer ends up with net capital losses, the losses offset capital gains using the following ordering rules:

- Net short-term capital losses first reduce 28 percent gains, then 25 percent gains, then regular long-term capital gains.
- Net long-term capital losses first reduce 28 percent gains, then 25 percent gains, then any short-term capital gains.

As with the ordering rules for capital gains, the ordering calculation may become quite complex when different classes of capital assets are present. A detailed discussion is beyond the scope of this textbook.

Self-Study Problem 4.5 — See Appendix E for Solutions to Self-Study Problems

During 2020, Louis Winthorp, who is single, received the following Form 1099-B:

☐ CORRECTED (if checked)

PAYER'S name, street address, city or town, state or province, country, ZIP or foreign postal code, and telephone no. Duke Brothers Brokerage 135 S. Broad Street Philadelphia, PA 19103	Applicable checkbox on Form 8949 — **Box D** — OMB No. 1545-0715 **2020** Form **1099-B** — **Proceeds From Broker and Barter Exchange Transactions**

1a Description of property (Example: 100 sh. XYZ Co.)
100 shs. Purple Corp.

1b Date acquired	1c Date sold or disposed
6/21/2011	8/15/2020

PAYER'S TIN	RECIPIENT'S TIN	1d Proceeds	1e Cost or other basis	Copy B
34-9876543	123-44-3214	$ 18,000.00	$ 12,500.00	For Recipient

1f Accrued market discount	1g Wash sale loss disallowed
$	$

RECIPIENT'S name
Louis Winthorp

2 Short-term gain or loss ☐
Long-term gain or loss ☒
Ordinary ☐

3 If checked, proceeds from:
Collectibles ☐
QOF ☐

Street address (including apt. no.)
2014 Delancey Street

4 Federal income tax withheld $ 0.00
5 If checked, noncovered security ☐

City or town, state or province, country, and ZIP or foreign postal code
Philadelphia, PA 19103

6 Reported to IRS:
Gross proceeds ☒
Net proceeds ☐

7 If checked, loss is not allowed based on amount in 1d ☐

Account number (see instructions)

8 Profit or (loss) realized in 2020 on closed contracts $
9 Unrealized profit or (loss) on open contracts—12/31/2019 $

CUSIP number | FATCA filing requirement ☐

10 Unrealized profit or (loss) on open contracts—12/31/2020 $
11 Aggregate profit or (loss) on contracts $

14 State name | **15** State identification no. | **16** State tax withheld $ / $

12 If checked, basis reported to IRS ☒
13 Bartering $

This is important tax information and is being furnished to the IRS. If you are required to file a return, a negligence penalty or other sanction may be imposed on you if this income is taxable and the IRS determines that it has not been reported.

Form **1099-B**   (Keep for your records)   www.irs.gov/Form1099B   Department of the Treasury - Internal Revenue Service

He also received the following information (1099-B not shown):

Description	Date Acquired	Date Sold	Selling Price	Cost Basis
100 shs. Rose stock	04/18/20	12/07/20	$12,000	$19,200
50 shs. Blue stock	12/18/12	10/02/20	25,000	21,000

The basis was reported to the IRS for all sales. His taxable income is $59,000 (including gains and losses from above). Calculate Louis' net capital gain or loss and tax liability using Schedule D of Form 1040, Parts I, II, and III; Form 8949, Parts I and II; and the Qualified Dividends and Capital Gain Tax Worksheet on Pages 4-13 to 4-17.

Self-Study Problem 4.5

| SCHEDULE D
(Form 1040)

Department of the Treasury
Internal Revenue Service (99) | **Capital Gains and Losses**

▶ Attach to Form 1040, 1040-SR, or 1040-NR.
▶ Go to *www.irs.gov/ScheduleD* for instructions and the latest information.
▶ Use Form 8949 to list your transactions for lines 1b, 2, 3, 8b, 9, and 10. | OMB No. 1545-0074

2020

Attachment
Sequence No. **12** |

Name(s) shown on return	Your social security number

Did you dispose of any investment(s) in a qualified opportunity fund during the tax year? ☐ **Yes** ☐ **No**
If "Yes," attach Form 8949 and see its instructions for additional requirements for reporting your gain or loss.

Part I **Short-Term Capital Gains and Losses—Generally Assets Held One Year or Less** (see instructions)

See instructions for how to figure the amounts to enter on the lines below. This form may be easier to complete if you round off cents to whole dollars.	**(d)** Proceeds (sales price)	**(e)** Cost (or other basis)	**(g)** Adjustments to gain or loss from Form(s) 8949, Part I, line 2, column (g)	**(h) Gain or (loss)** Subtract column (e) from column (d) and combine the result with column (g)
1a Totals for all short-term transactions reported on Form 1099-B for which basis was reported to the IRS and for which you have no adjustments (see instructions). However, if you choose to report all these transactions on Form 8949, leave this line blank and go to line 1b .				
1b Totals for all transactions reported on Form(s) 8949 with **Box A** checked				
2 Totals for all transactions reported on Form(s) 8949 with **Box B** checked				
3 Totals for all transactions reported on Form(s) 8949 with **Box C** checked				

4 Short-term gain from Form 6252 and short-term gain or (loss) from Forms 4684, 6781, and 8824 . .	**4**	
5 Net short-term gain or (loss) from partnerships, S corporations, estates, and trusts from Schedule(s) K-1	**5**	
6 Short-term capital loss carryover. Enter the amount, if any, from line 8 of your **Capital Loss Carryover Worksheet** in the instructions	**6**	( )
7 **Net short-term capital gain or (loss).** Combine lines 1a through 6 in column (h). If you have any long-term capital gains or losses, go to Part II below. Otherwise, go to Part III on the back	**7**	

Part II **Long-Term Capital Gains and Losses—Generally Assets Held More Than One Year** (see instructions)

See instructions for how to figure the amounts to enter on the lines below. This form may be easier to complete if you round off cents to whole dollars.	**(d)** Proceeds (sales price)	**(e)** Cost (or other basis)	**(g)** Adjustments to gain or loss from Form(s) 8949, Part II, line 2, column (g)	**(h) Gain or (loss)** Subtract column (e) from column (d) and combine the result with column (g)
8a Totals for all long-term transactions reported on Form 1099-B for which basis was reported to the IRS and for which you have no adjustments (see instructions). However, if you choose to report all these transactions on Form 8949, leave this line blank and go to line 8b .				
8b Totals for all transactions reported on Form(s) 8949 with **Box D** checked				
9 Totals for all transactions reported on Form(s) 8949 with **Box E** checked				
10 Totals for all transactions reported on Form(s) 8949 with **Box F** checked.				

11 Gain from Form 4797, Part I; long-term gain from Forms 2439 and 6252; and long-term gain or (loss) from Forms 4684, 6781, and 8824	**11**	
12 Net long-term gain or (loss) from partnerships, S corporations, estates, and trusts from Schedule(s) K-1	**12**	
13 Capital gain distributions. See the instructions	**13**	
14 Long-term capital loss carryover. Enter the amount, if any, from line 13 of your **Capital Loss Carryover Worksheet** in the instructions	**14**	( )
15 **Net long-term capital gain or (loss).** Combine lines 8a through 14 in column (h). Then, go to Part III on the back	**15**	

For Paperwork Reduction Act Notice, see your tax return instructions.	Cat. No. 11338H	Schedule D (Form 1040) 2020

Schedule D (Form 1040) 2020   Page **2**

Part III	**Summary**

16   Combine lines 7 and 15 and enter the result **16**

      • If line 16 is a **gain,** enter the amount from line 16 on Form 1040, 1040-SR, or 1040-NR, line 7. Then, go to line 17 below.

      • If line 16 is a **loss,** skip lines 17 through 20 below. Then, go to line 21. Also be sure to complete line 22.

      • If line 16 is **zero,** skip lines 17 through 21 below and enter -0- on Form 1040, 1040-SR, or 1040-NR, line 7. Then, go to line 22.

17   Are lines 15 and 16 **both** gains?

      ☐ **Yes.** Go to line 18.

      ☐ **No.** Skip lines 18 through 21, and go to line 22.

18   If you are required to complete the **28% Rate Gain Worksheet** (see instructions), enter the amount, if any, from line 7 of that worksheet . . . . ▶   **18**

19   If you are required to complete the **Unrecaptured Section 1250 Gain Worksheet** (see instructions), enter the amount, if any, from line 18 of that worksheet . . . . ▶   **19**

20   Are lines 18 and 19 **both** zero or blank?

      ☐ **Yes.** Complete the **Qualified Dividends and Capital Gain Tax Worksheet** in the instructions for Forms 1040 and 1040-SR, line 16. **Don't** complete lines 21 and 22 below.

      ☐ **No.** Complete the **Schedule D Tax Worksheet** in the instructions. **Don't** complete lines 21 and 22 below.

21   If line 16 is a loss, enter here and on Form 1040, 1040-SR, or 1040-NR, line 7, the **smaller** of:

      • The loss on line 16; or

      • ($3,000), or if married filing separately, ($1,500)   }   . . . .   **21** (   )

      Note: When figuring which amount is smaller, treat both amounts as positive numbers.

22   Do you have qualified dividends on Form 1040, 1040-SR, or 1040-NR, line 3a?

      ☐ **Yes.** Complete the **Qualified Dividends and Capital Gain Tax Worksheet** in the instructions for Forms 1040 and 1040-SR, line 16.

      ☐ **No.** Complete the rest of Form 1040, 1040-SR, or 1040-NR.

Schedule D (Form 1040) 2020

DRAFT AS OF August 24, 2020 DO NOT FILE

Self-Study Problem 4.5

Form **8949**

Department of the Treasury
Internal Revenue Service

Sales and Other Dispositions of Capital Assets

► Go to *www.irs.gov/Form8949* for instructions and the latest information.

► File with your Schedule D to list your transactions for lines 1b, 2, 3, 8b, 9, and 10 of Schedule D.

OMB No. 1545-0074

2020

Attachment
Sequence No. **12A**

Name(s) shown on return

Social security number or taxpayer identification number

Before you check Box A, B, or C below, see whether you received any Form(s) 1099-B or substitute statement(s) from your broker. A substitute statement will have the same information as Form 1099-B. Either will show whether your basis (usually your cost) was reported to the IRS by your broker and may even tell you which box to check.

Part I

Short-Term. Transactions involving capital assets you held 1 year or less are generally short-term (see instructions). For long-term transactions, see page 2.

Note: You may aggregate all short-term transactions reported on Form(s) 1099-B showing basis was reported to the IRS and for which no adjustments or codes are required. Enter the totals directly on Schedule D, line 1a; you aren't required to report these transactions on Form 8949 (see instructions).

You *must* check Box A, B, *or* C below. Check only one box. If more than one box applies for your short-term transactions, complete a separate Form 8949, page 1, for each applicable box. If you have more short-term transactions than will fit on this page for one or more of the boxes, complete as many forms with the same box checked as you need.

- ☐ **(A)** Short-term transactions reported on Form(s) 1099-B showing basis was reported to the IRS (see **Note** above)
- ☐ **(B)** Short-term transactions reported on Form(s) 1099-B showing basis **wasn't** reported to the IRS
- ☐ **(C)** Short-term transactions not reported to you on Form 1099-B

1 **(a)** Description of property (Example: 100 sh. XYZ Co.)	**(b)** Date acquired (Mo., day, yr.)	**(c)** Date sold or disposed of (Mo., day, yr.)	**(d)** Proceeds (sales price) (see instructions)	**(e)** Cost or other basis. See the **Note** below and see *Column (e)* in the separate instructions	**(f)** Code(s) from instructions	**(g)** Amount of adjustment	**(h)** Gain or (loss). Subtract column (e) from column (d) and combine the result with column (g)

Adjustment, if any, to gain or loss. If you enter an amount in column (g), enter a code in column (f). See the separate instructions.

2 Totals. Add the amounts in columns (d), (e), (g), and (h) (subtract negative amounts). Enter each total here and include on your Schedule D, **line 1b** (if **Box A** above is checked), **line 2** (if **Box B** above is checked), or **line 3** (if **Box C** above is checked) ►

Note: If you checked Box A above but the basis reported to the IRS was incorrect, enter in column (e) the basis as reported to the IRS, and enter an adjustment in column (g) to correct the basis. See *Column (g)* in the separate instructions for how to figure the amount of the adjustment.

For Paperwork Reduction Act Notice, see your tax return instructions.   Cat. No. 37768Z   Form **8949** (2020)

Form 8949 (2020)   Attachment Sequence No. **12A**   Page **2**

Name(s) shown on return. Name and SSN or taxpayer identification no. not required if shown on other side	Social security number or taxpayer identification number

Before you check Box D, E, or F below, see whether you received any Form(s) 1099-B or substitute statement(s) from your broker. A substitute statement will have the same information as Form 1099-B. Either will show whether your basis (usually your cost) was reported to the IRS by your broker and may even tell you which box to check.

Part II **Long-Term.** Transactions involving capital assets you held more than 1 year are generally long-term (see instructions). For short-term transactions, see page 1.

Note: You may aggregate all long-term transactions reported on Form(s) 1099-B showing basis was reported to the IRS and for which no adjustments or codes are required. Enter the totals directly on Schedule D, line 8a; you aren't required to report these transactions on Form 8949 (see instructions).

You *must* **check Box D, E, *or* F below. Check only one box.** If more than one box applies for your long-term transactions, complete a separate Form 8949, page 2, for each applicable box. If you have more long-term transactions than will fit on this page for one or more of the boxes, complete as many forms with the same box checked as you need.

☐ **(D)** Long-term transactions reported on Form(s) 1099-B showing basis was reported to the IRS (see **Note** above)

☐ **(E)** Long-term transactions reported on Form(s) 1099-B showing basis **wasn't** reported to the IRS

☐ **(F)** Long-term transactions not reported to you on Form 1099-B

1					Adjustment, if any, to gain or loss. If you enter an amount in column (g), enter a code in column (f). See the separate instructions.		
(a) Description of property (Example: 100 sh. XYZ Co.)	**(b)** Date acquired (Mo., day, yr.)	**(c)** Date sold or disposed of (Mo., day, yr.)	**(d)** Proceeds (sales price) (see instructions)	**(e)** Cost or other basis. See the **Note** below and see *Column (e)* in the separate instructions	**(f)** Code(s) from instructions	**(g)** Amount of adjustment	**(h)** Gain or (loss). Subtract column (e) from column (d) and combine the result with column (g)

2 Totals. Add the amounts in columns (d), (e), (g), and (h) (subtract negative amounts). Enter each total here and include on your Schedule D, **line 8b** (if **Box D** above is checked), **line 9** (if **Box E** above is checked), or **line 10** (if **Box F** above is checked) ▶

Note: If you checked Box D above but the basis reported to the IRS was incorrect, enter in column (e) the basis as reported to the IRS, and enter an adjustment in column (g) to correct the basis. See *Column (g)* in the separate instructions for how to figure the amount of the adjustment.

Form **8949** (2020)

Self-Study Problem 4.5

Qualified Dividends and Capital Gain Tax Worksheet—Line 16

Before you begin:	✓ See the earlier instructions for line 16 to see if you can use this worksheet to figure your tax.
	✓ Before completing this worksheet, complete Form 1040 or 1040-SR through line 15.
	✓ If you don't have to file Schedule D and you received capital gain distributions, be sure you checked the box on Form 1040 or 1040-SR, line 7.

1. Enter the amount from Form 1040 or 1040-SR, line 15. However, if you are filing Form 2555 (relating to foreign earned income), enter the amount from line 3 of the Foreign Earned Income Tax Worksheet .... **1.** _____

2. Enter the amount from Form 1040 or 1040-SR, line 3a* .... **2.** _____

3. Are you filing Schedule D?*
   ☐ **Yes.** Enter the **smaller** of line 15 or 16 of Schedule D. If either line 15 or 16 is blank or a loss, enter -0-.
   ☐ **No.** Enter the amount from Form 1040 or 1040-SR, line 7. **3.** _____

4. Add lines 2 and 3 .... **4.** _____

5. If filing Form 4952 (used to figure investment interest expense deduction), enter any amount from line 4g of that form. Otherwise, enter -0- .... **5.** _____

6. Subtract line 5 from line 4. If zero or less, enter -0- .... **6.** _____

7. Subtract line 6 from line 1. If zero or less, enter -0- .... **7.** _____

8. Enter:
   $40,000 if single or married filing separately,
   $80,000 if married filing jointly or qualifying widow(er),
   $53,600 if head of household. .... **8.** _____

9. Enter the smaller of line 1 or line 8 .... **9.** _____

10. Enter the smaller of line 7 or line 9 .... **10.** _____

11. Subtract line 10 from line 9. This amount is taxed at 0% .... **11.** _____

12. Enter the smaller of line 1 or line 6 .... **12.** _____

13. Enter the amount from line 11 .... **13.** _____

14. Subtract line 13 from line 12 .... **14.** _____

15. Enter:
    $441,450 if single,
    $248,300 if married filing separately,
    $496,600 if married filing jointly or qualifying widow(er),
    $469,050 if head of household. .... **15.** _____

16. Enter the smaller of line 1 or line 15 .... **16.** _____

17. Add lines 7 and 11 .... **17.** _____

18. Subtract line 17 from line 16. If zero or less, enter -0- .... **18.** _____

19. Enter the smaller of line 14 or line 18 .... **19.** _____

20. Multiply line 19 by 15% (0.15) .... **20.** _____

21. Add lines 11 and 19 .... **21.** _____

22. Subtract line 21 from line 12 .... **22.** _____

23. Multiply line 22 by 20% (0.20) .... **23.** _____

24. Figure the tax on the amount on line 7. If the amount on line 7 is less than $100,000, use the Tax Table to figure the tax. If the amount on line 7 is $100,000 or more, use the Tax Computation Worksheet .... **24.** _____

25. Add lines 20, 23, and 24 .... **25.** _____

26. Figure the tax on the amount on line 1. If the amount on line 1 is less than $100,000, use the Tax Table to figure the tax. If the amount on line 1 is $100,000 or more, use the Tax Computation Worksheet .... **26.** _____

27. **Tax on all taxable income.** Enter the **smaller** of line 25 or 26. Also include this amount on the entry space on Form 1040 or 1040-SR, line 16. If you are filing Form 2555, don't enter this amount on the entry space on Form 1040 or 1040-SR, line 16. Instead, enter it on line 4 of the Foreign Earned Income Tax Worksheet .... **27.** _____

* If you are filing Form 2555, see the footnote in the Foreign Earned Income Tax Worksheet before completing this line.

4-6 SALE OF A PERSONAL RESIDENCE

4-6a Sales After May 6, 1997

For gains on the sale of a personal residence after May 6, 1997, a seller who has owned and used a home as a principal residence for at least 2 of the last 5 years before the sale can exclude from income up to $250,000 of gain ($500,000 for joint return filers). In general, this personal residence exclusion can be used only once every 2 years. A personal residence includes single-family homes, mobile homes, houseboats, condominiums, cooperative apartments, duplexes, or row houses.

EXAMPLE Joe, a single taxpayer, bought his home 22 years ago for $25,000. He has lived in the home continuously since he purchased it. In November 2020, he sells his home for $300,000. Therefore, his realized gain on the sale of his personal residence is $275,000 ($300,000 − $25,000). Joe's recognized taxable gain on this sale is $25,000, which is his total gain of $275,000 less the exclusion of $250,000. ♦

A seller otherwise qualified to exclude gain on a principal residence who fails to satisfy the 2-year ownership and use requirements may calculate the amount of excluded gain by prorating the exclusion amount if the residence sale is due to an employment-related move, health, or unforeseen circumstances. Unforeseen circumstances include death, divorce or separation, a change in employment that leaves the taxpayer unable to pay the mortgage, multiple births from the same pregnancy, and becoming eligible for unemployment compensation. The $250,000 or $500,000 exclusion amount is prorated by multiplying the exclusion amount by the length of time the taxpayer owned and used the home divided by 2 years.

EXAMPLE John is a single taxpayer who owns and uses his principal residence for 1 year. He then sells the residence due to an employment-related move at a $100,000 gain. Because he may exclude up to one-half (1 year divided by 2 years) of the $250,000 exclusion amount, or $125,000, none of his gain is taxable. ♦

4-6b Married Taxpayers

Taxpayers who are married and file a joint return for the year of sale may exclude up to $500,000 of gain realized on the sale of a personal residence. The full $500,000 for a married couple can be excluded if:

1. Either spouse owned the home for at least 2 of the 5 years before the sale,
2. Both spouses used the home as a principal residence for at least 2 of the last 5 years, and
3. Neither spouse has used the exclusion during the prior 2 years.

EXAMPLE Don and Dolly have been married for 20 years. At the time they were married, they purchased a home for $200,000 and have lived in the home since their marriage. Don and Dolly sell their home for $800,000 and retire to Arizona. Their realized gain on the sale is $600,000 ($800,000 − $200,000), of which only $100,000 is taxable because of the $500,000 exclusion. ♦

The $500,000 exclusion for married taxpayers has been extended to spouses who sell the residence within 2 years of their spouse's death. If a portion of the sale of a residence is taxable, then it should be reported (e.g., Form 8949 using Code H and Schedule D). If no portion is taxable, then no reporting is generally required.

Beginning in 2009, Congress closed a loophole in the residence gain exclusion laws, which was used effectively by some owners of multiple rental properties. Under the residence gain exclusion laws in operation prior to 2009, taxpayers with multiple rental properties could move into a previously rented property every 2 years, reside in the property for the required 2-year period, and then sell the property using the $250,000 or $500,000 gain exclusion. Over a period of 10 years, a married couple could theoretically exclude $2.5 million of taxable gain on five separate properties. Beginning in 2009, taxpayers who rent their residence prior to their

2 years of personal use are generally limited to an exclusion smaller than the full $250,000 or $500,000 amounts. For details, examples, and exceptions to the law, visit **www.irs.gov.**

4-6c **Sales Before May 7, 1997**

Please note: The law below no longer applies to sales of principal residences. However, because many taxpayers still own residences with "rollover" basis determined under this law, it is important to understand how the law operated.

For sales of a personal residence before May 7, 1997, taxpayers did not have to recognize gain on the sale if they rolled the gain into a new house with a cost as high as the adjusted sales price of the old residence. The adjusted sales price was the amount realized on the sale less any qualified fixing-up expenses. Fixing-up expenses must have been incurred within 90 days prior to the date of sale and paid within 30 days after the date of sale. In addition, the purchase of the new residence had to be within 2 years of the date of sale of the old residence to qualify for nonrecognition of the gain. The adjusted basis of the new residence was reduced by any gain not recognized on the sale of the old residence.

EXAMPLE Mary sold her personal residence for $60,000 in 1994 and paid selling expenses of $3,600. Mary had fixing-up expenses of $1,400, and the basis of her old residence was $40,000. If Mary purchased a new residence within 2 years for $85,000, her recognized gain and the basis of the new residence was calculated as follows:

1. Sales price	$ 60,000
Less: selling expenses	(3,600)
Amount realized	56,400
Adjusted basis of the old residence	(40,000)
Gain realized on the sale	$ 16,400
2. Amount realized	$ 56,400
Less: fixing-up expenses	(1,400)
Adjusted sales price	55,000
Less: cost of the new residence	(85,000)
Gain recognized	$ 0
3. Gain realized	$ 16,400
Less: gain recognized	(0)
Gain not recognized (deferred)	$ 16,400
4. Cost of the new residence	$ 85,000
Less: gain deferred	(16,400)
Basis of the new residence	$ 68,600

◆

EXAMPLE Assume instead that Mary paid only $50,000 for a new residence. The gain and basis of the new residence are calculated as follows:

1. Adjusted sales price (from above)	$ 55,000
Less: cost of new residence	(50,000)
Gain recognized	$ 5,000
2. Gain realized (from above example)	$ 16,400
Less: gain recognized	(5,000)
Gain not recognized (deferred)	$ 11,400
3. Cost of the new residence	$ 50,000
Less: gain deferred	(11,400)
Basis of the new residence	$ 38,600

◆

The calculations on the previous page show that a taxpayer who sold one or more principal residences over a period of years and has a "rollover" basis under the old law may have a principal residence basis that is far lower than the cost of the taxpayer's residence. Because the current law does not require rollover treatment, taxpayers receive a fresh basis in a newly purchased residence which is equal to the purchase price.

Self-Study Problem 4.6 *See Appendix E for Solutions to Self-Study Problems*

Mike, a single taxpayer, purchased a house 20 years ago for $30,000. He sells the house in December 2020 for $350,000. He has always lived in the house.

a. How much taxable gain does Mike have from the sale of his personal residence?

$ _____

b. Assume Mike married Mary 3 years ago and she has lived in the house since their marriage. If they sell the house in December 2020 for $350,000, what is their taxable gain on a joint tax return?

$ _____

c. Assume Mike is not married and purchased the house only 1 year ago for $200,000, and he sells the house for $350,000 due to an employment-related move. What is Mike's taxable gain?

$ _____

Sign Here	Under penalties of perjury, I declare that I have examined this return and accompanying schedules and statements, and to the best of my knowledge and belief, they are true, correct, and complete. Declaration of preparer (other than taxpayer) is based on all information of which preparer has any knowledge.					
	Your signature	Date	Your occupation		If the IRS sent you an Identity Protection PIN, enter it here (see inst.) ▶	
Joint return? See instructions. Keep a copy for your records.	Spouse's signature. If a joint return, **both** must sign.	Date	Spouse's occupation		If the IRS sent your spouse an Identity Protection PIN, enter it here (see inst.) ▶	
	Phone no.		Email address			
Paid Preparer Use Only	Preparer's name	Preparer's signature		Date	PTIN	Check if: ☐ Self-employed
	Firm's name ▶				Phone no.	
	Firm's address ▶				Firm's EIN ▶	

Would You Sign This Tax Return?

Ivy Tower (age 45), a history professor at Coastal State University, recently purchased a house near the beach. In the current year, she accepted an offer from a buyer who wants to make the house into a bed and breakfast. Ivy sold her personal residence for a $100,000 gain. She owned the house 11 months as of the date of sale. After the sale closed, she discovered that the $100,000 is taxable as a short-term taxable gain (i.e., ordinary income) because she had not lived there the 2 years required for exclusion of gain on the sale of a residence. She is upset that she will have to pay substantial tax on the sale. Her best friend's husband is an M.D. who signed a letter that Ivy had to move due to the dampness and humidity at the beach. She is not a regular patient of the doctor and Ivy has no history of respiratory problems. Ivy claims she meets the medical extraordinary circumstances exception and therefore refuses to report the gain on her Form 1040. If Ivy were your tax client, would you sign the Paid Preparer's declaration (see example above) on her return? Why or why not?

| Learning Objective 4.7 | ## 4-7 RENTAL INCOME AND EXPENSES |

Apply the tax rules for rental property and vacation homes.

The net income from rental property is taxable income to the taxpayer. In most cases, rental income is reported with the related expenses on Part I of Schedule E. If services are provided to the tenant beyond those customarily provided, such as cleaning and maid services, the income is reported on Schedule C and is subject to the self-employment tax. Expenditures deductible as rental expenses include real estate taxes, mortgage interest, insurance, commissions, repairs, and depreciation.

EXAMPLE   June Sanchez owns a house that she rents to a tenant for $600 per month. The following are her expenses for the year:

Real estate taxes	$ 800
Mortgage interest	2,000
Insurance	200
Rent collection commissions	432
General repairs	350

June bought the property on July 1, 2004, and her original basis for depreciation of the house is $55,000. She uses straight-line depreciation with a 27.5 year life.

In 2020, June bought a new stove for the rental house that cost $500. The stove has a 5-year life, and 20 percent of the stove's cost is depreciated this year. June's net rental income for the year is calculated as follows:

Rental income ($600 × 12)		$ 7,200
Less expenses:		
Real estate taxes	$ 800	
Mortgage interest	2,000	
Insurance	200	
Commissions	432	
General repairs	350	
Depreciation:		
House ($55,000/27.5)	$2,000	
Stove ($500 × 20%)	100	
Total expenses		(5,882)
Net rental income		$ 1,318

Please note that depreciation is an advanced topic which will be covered in detail in Chapter 8. ◆

4-7a Vacation Homes

Many taxpayers own residences which they use personally as part-year residences and rent during the remainder of the year. Such part-year rental properties are often referred to as "vacation homes." The tax law limits the deduction of expenses associated with the rental of vacation homes.

EXAMPLE   Jean owns a condo in Vail, Colorado. The condo is rented for 3 months during the year and is used by Jean for 1 month. If there were no vacation home limitations, Jean could deduct 11 months' worth of depreciation, maintenance, and other costs associated with the property. The resulting loss could then be deducted against Jean's other taxable income. ◆

To prevent taxpayers from claiming a deduction for expenses effectively personal in nature (associated with a personal residence), the tax law limits the deductions a taxpayer can claim for expenses associated with a vacation home. Deductions attributable to vacation homes used primarily as personal residences are limited to the income generated from the rental of the property. In general, only profit or breakeven (no loss) tax situations are allowed on the rental of vacation homes.

The expenses associated with the rental of a residence used for both personal and rental purposes are subject to three possible tax treatments. The tax treatment depends on the period of time the residence is used for personal versus rental purposes.

1. **Primarily Personal Use**

   If a residence is rented for fewer than 15 days during the year, the rental period is disregarded and it is treated as a personal residence for tax purposes. The rental income is not taxable and the mortgage interest and real estate taxes may be allowed as itemized deductions. Other expenses, such as utilities and maintenance, are considered nondeductible personal expenses.

EXAMPLE Glenn owns a lake home. During the year he rented the home for $1,800 for 2 weeks, lived in the home for 3 months, and left the home vacant during the remainder of the year. The expenses for the lake home included $5,000 in mortgage interest, $700 in property taxes, $2,100 in utilities and maintenance, and $3,000 in depreciation. Since the lake home was rented for fewer than 15 days, Glenn would not report the $1,800 of income and would deduct only the interest and property taxes as itemized deductions on Schedule A. The other expenses are nondeductible personal expenses. ◆

2. **Primarily Rental Use**

   If the residence is rented for 15 days or more and is used for personal purposes for not more than *14 days or 10 percent of the days rented, whichever is greater,* the residence is treated as rental property. The expenses must then be allocated between the personal and rental days. If this is the case, the rental expenses may exceed the rental income, and the resulting loss would be deducted against other income, subject to the passive loss rules. (See LO 4.8 for further details.)

EXAMPLE Assume the same facts as in the preceding example except that the $1,800 rental fee is for 20 days and Glenn uses the lake home for only 10 days during the year. Since the lake home is now rented for 15 days or more and Glenn's use of the home is not more than 14 days (or 10 percent of the days rented, if greater), the property is treated partially as rental property and partially as a personal residence. Allocation of expenses associated with the home is based on the number of days of rental or personal use compared to the total number of days of use. Glenn's personal use percentage is 33.33 percent (10 days/30 days) and the rental portion is 66.67 percent (20 days/30 days). For tax purposes, the rental income or loss is calculated as follows:

	Rental (66.67%)	Personal (33.33%)
Income	$ 1,800	$ 0
Interest and taxes	(3,800)	(1,900)
Utilities and maintenance	(1,400)	(700)
Depreciation	(2,000)	(1,000)
Rental loss	$(5,400)	$ 0

The interest and taxes allocable to Glenn's personal use of the property may be deductible as itemized deductions on Schedule A (see Chapter 5). The personal portion of utilities, maintenance, and depreciation are nondeductible personal expenses. ◆

3. **Rental/Personal Use**

If the residence is rented for 15 days or more and is used for personal purposes for more than *14 days or 10 percent of the days rented, whichever is greater,* allocable rental expenses are allowed only to the extent of rental income. Allocable rental expenses are deducted in three separate steps: first, the interest and taxes are deducted; second, utilities and maintenance expenses are deducted; and third, depreciation expense is deducted. For utilities, maintenance, and depreciation expenses to be deductible, there must be positive income following the deduction of items in the preceding step(s). In addition, the expenses, other than interest and taxes, are only deductible to the extent of that positive income. Expenses are allocated between the rental and personal days before the limits are applied. The IRS requires that the allocation be on the basis of the total days of rental use or personal use divided by the total days of use.

EXAMPLE   Assume Glenn rents the lake home for $2,500 for 20 days and uses it for personal purposes for 60 days. Assume Glenn has the same operating expenses as in the previous examples. Since the lake home is rented for 15 days or more and Glenn uses the home for personal purposes for more than 14 days (or 10 percent of the days rented, if greater), the property is subject to the vacation home limitations. Glenn's personal use percentage is 75 percent (60 days/80 days) and the rental portion is 25 percent (20 days/80 days). The IRS requires that the rental income or loss be calculated as follows:

Gross rental income	$ 2,500
Less: interest and taxes ($5,700 × 25%)	(1,425)
Balance	1,075
Less: utilities and maintenance ($2,100 × 25%)	(525)
Balance	550
Less: depreciation ($3,000 × 25%, limited to $550)	(550)
Net income	$ 0

The interest and taxes allocable to Glenn's personal use of the property may be deductible as itemized deductions on Schedule A (see Chapter 5). The personal portion of utilities, maintenance, and depreciation are nondeductible personal expenses. The nondeductible portion of the depreciation can be carried forward to the next tax year. ♦

It should be noted that the U.S. Tax Court has allowed taxpayers to use 365 days for the allocation of interest and taxes. Under the Tax Court rules, the interest and taxes allocable to the rental use of the property in the above example would be 5.5 percent (20 days/365 days) instead of 25 percent (20 days/80 days). The allocation of utilities and maintenance would remain unchanged, while a full $750 of depreciation (25% of $3,000) would be allowed. The remaining interest and taxes (345 days/365 days) would be included in itemized deductions.

ProConnect™ Tax

TIP

Rental activity is entered under Income and then Rental and Royalty Income (Schedule E). Key fields to consider are the Type of Property (dropdown), the number of days rented, the number of days of personal use (located below the expenses fields), and the number of days owned (if the Tax Court method is to be used).

Nancy Valentino lives in a duplex that she owns at 14 Lancaster Drive, Salem, OR 97305. Nancy rents one-half of her duplex and lives in the other half. Her rental income for the year is $6,000. Nancy's basis for depreciation in the rental portion is $15,000, and she uses straight-line depreciation with a 27.5 year useful life. On the whole duplex, real estate taxes are $1,200, interest on the mortgage is $3,400, utilities are $1,800, and insurance is $450. Use Part I of Schedule E on Page 4-27 to report Nancy's income from rental of part of the duplex.

4-8 PASSIVE LOSS LIMITATIONS

4.8 Learning Objective

Explain the treatment of passive income and losses.

Because of past abuses primarily involving tax shelters and loss deductions from rental real estate, Congress enacted legislation limiting the deduction of certain "passive" losses from other taxable income. A passive activity is a trade or business in which the taxpayer does not materially participate and includes most rental real estate activity. Because the most common passive loss seen on tax returns is from ordinary real estate rental activities, many taxpayers with an investment in a real estate rental property are affected by these rules. In establishing the limitations, the tax law classifies individual income into three categories. These categories are (1) active income (e.g., wages, self-employment income, and salaries), (2) portfolio income (e.g., dividends and interest), and (3) passive income and losses (e.g., rental real estate income and loss, and income and loss passed through from limited partnerships and other ventures in which the taxpayer has minimal or no involvement).

Generally, passive losses cannot be used to offset either active or portfolio income. Also, any tax credits derived from passive activities can only offset income taxes attributable to passive income. Any unused passive losses and credits are carried over and may be used to offset future passive income or taxes attributable to such income, respectively. Generally, losses remaining when the taxpayer disposes of his or her entire interest in the passive activity may be used in full; however, the taxpayer can only use remaining credits to offset the income tax arising from any gain recognized on the disposition of the activity.

EXAMPLE Mike's income and loss items for 2020 are:

Salary	$40,000
Sales commissions	15,000
Dividends on Microsoft stock	2,000
Rental income from real estate	5,000
Loss from limited partnership	(9,000)
Interest on savings account	4,000

Mike's active income for the year is $55,000 ($40,000 + $15,000), his portfolio income is $6,000 ($2,000 + $4,000), and his passive loss is $4,000 ($5,000 − $9,000). Mike must report gross income of $61,000 ($55,000 + $6,000), since the passive loss cannot be used to offset his active or portfolio income. The net passive loss of $4,000 will be carried over to 2021. ♦

Under the passive loss rules, real estate rental activities are specifically defined as passive, even if the taxpayer actively manages the property and even if the activity is not conducted as a partnership. Individual taxpayers, however, may deduct up to $25,000 of rental property losses against other income, if they are actively involved in the management of the property and their income does not exceed certain limits. The $25,000 loss deduction is phased out when the taxpayer's modified adjusted gross income (adjusted gross income before passive losses and Individual Retirement Account deductions) exceeds $100,000. The $25,000 is reduced by 50 cents for each $1.00 the taxpayer's modified adjusted gross income exceeds that amount. Therefore, no deduction is allowed when the taxpayer's modified adjusted gross income reaches $150,000 (this threshold is not adjusted for inflation). Special limitations apply to taxpayers filing as Married, Filing Separately and claiming a deduction for real estate rental losses under this special rule.

EXAMPLE   Mary has modified AGI before passive losses of $120,000. In addition, she has a rental house that she actively manages which shows a loss of $18,000 for the year. She may deduct only $15,000 ($25,000 − 50% of $20,000) of the loss because of the phase-out of the $25,000 allowance for passive rental losses where modified AGI is over $100,000. ♦

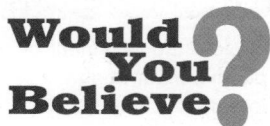

The Tax Reform Act of 1986 (TRA 86) introduced the concept of a passive loss limitation. TRA 86 also introduced the active management exception of $25,000 with a phase-out starting at $100,000 of AGI. These amounts have not been adjusted since. For tax year 1987, about 2 million individual income tax returns (about 2 percent) had adjusted gross income of $100,000 or more. In the 2017 tax year (most recent complete year released by the IRS), 18 percent of individual tax returns reported AGI of $100,000 or more. Clearly, far fewer taxpayers are eligible for the exception today.

ProConnect™ Tax TIP

ProConnect assumes that a rental property is actively managed and will apply the appropriate phase-out based on the modified AGI information entered elsewhere. There is a box on the General Information page of the rental property section to indicate otherwise.

4-8a Real Estate Rental as Trade or Business

Taxpayers heavily involved in real estate rental activities may qualify as having an active business rather than a passive activity. If so, the income and losses from qualified rental activities are not subject to passive loss limitations. For a real estate rental to be considered active, the taxpayer must materially participate in the activity. An individual will satisfy this requirement if both of the following are met:

1. More than 50 percent of the individual's personal service during the tax year is performed in real property trades or businesses, and
2. The individual performs more than 750 hours of service during the tax year in the real property trade or business in which he or she claims material participation.

EXAMPLE   In 2020, Allan owns eighteen rental houses and spends 100 percent of his personal service time (1,800 hours in 2020) managing them. Allan spends his 1,800 hours of management time doing repairs, gardening, collecting rents, cleaning and painting vacant houses, advertising for and interviewing new tenants, doing bookkeeping, and purchasing/installing new appliances, drapes, carpets, and toilets. He keeps a log to prove how many hours he works on his property in case he is audited. Since both the above tests are met, Allan's real estate rental activity is not a passive activity. If Allan has an overall loss of $40,000 on the real estate rentals, he can deduct the entire loss on his tax return as an active business, not a passive loss. ♦

Real estate professionals who report large losses tend to attract the attention of the IRS. The real estate professional exception to the passive loss rules consider a two-step hurdle to deducting losses: (1) the real estate professional exception is used to overcome the presumption that a rental real estate activity is a passive activity but that does not guarantee treatment as non-passive; (2) the taxpayer is still going to have to demonstrate material participation. When multiple properties are owned, electing to treat them as a single activity can be useful for meeting the material participations rules.

Self-Study Problem 4.7

SCHEDULE E
(Form 1040)

Department of the Treasury
Internal Revenue Service (99)

Supplemental Income and Loss

(From rental real estate, royalties, partnerships, S corporations, estates, trusts, REMICs, etc.)

▶ Attach to Form 1040, 1040-SR, 1040-NR, or 1041.
▶ Go to *www.irs.gov/ScheduleE* for instructions and the latest information.

OMB No. 1545-0074

2020

Attachment
Sequence No. **13**

Name(s) shown on return

Your social security number

Part I	**Income or Loss From Rental Real Estate and Royalties** Note: If you are in the business of renting personal property, use **Schedule C.** See instructions. If you are an individual, report farm rental income or loss from **Form 4835** on page 2, line 40.

A Did you make any payments in 2020 that would require you to file Form(s) 1099? See instructions . . . . . ☐ **Yes** ☐ **No**
B If "Yes," did you or will you file required Form(s) 1099? . . . . ☐ **Yes** ☐ **No**

1a Physical address of each property (street, city, state, ZIP code)

A	
B	
C	

1b	Type of Property (from list below)	**2** For each rental real estate property listed above, report the number of fair rental and personal use days. Check the **QJV** box only if you meet the requirements to file as a qualified joint venture. See instructions.		Fair Rental Days	Personal Use Days	QJV
A			**A**			☐
B			**B**			☐
C			**C**			☐

Type of Property:
1 Single Family Residence   3 Vacation/Short-Term Rental   5 Land   7 Self-Rental
2 Multi-Family Residence   4 Commercial   6 Royalties   8 Other (describe)

Income:	**Properties:**		**A**	**B**	**C**
3	Rents received	**3**			
4	Royalties received	**4**			
Expenses:					
5	Advertising	**5**			
6	Auto and travel (see instructions)	**6**			
7	Cleaning and maintenance	**7**			
8	Commissions.	**8**			
9	Insurance	**9**			
10	Legal and other professional fees	**10**			
11	Management fees	**11**			
12	Mortgage interest paid to banks, etc. (see instructions)	**12**			
13	Other interest.	**13**			
14	Repairs.	**14**			
15	Supplies	**15**			
16	Taxes	**16**			
17	Utilities	**17**			
18	Depreciation expense or depletion	**18**			
19	Other (list) ▶ _____	**19**			
20	Total expenses. Add lines 5 through 19	**20**			
21	Subtract line 20 from line 3 (rents) and/or 4 (royalties). If result is a (loss), see instructions to find out if you must file **Form 6198**	**21**			
22	Deductible rental real estate loss after limitation, if any, on **Form 8582** (see instructions)	**22**	( )	( )	( )

23a	Total of all amounts reported on line 3 for all rental properties	**23a**	
b	Total of all amounts reported on line 4 for all royalty properties	**23b**	
c	Total of all amounts reported on line 12 for all properties	**23c**	
d	Total of all amounts reported on line 18 for all properties	**23d**	
e	Total of all amounts reported on line 20 for all properties	**23e**	
24	**Income.** Add positive amounts shown on line 21. **Do not** include any losses	**24**	
25	**Losses.** Add royalty losses from line 21 and rental real estate losses from line 22. Enter total losses here .	**25**	( )
26	**Total rental real estate and royalty income or (loss).** Combine lines 24 and 25. Enter the result here. If Parts II, III, IV, and line 40 on page 2 do not apply to you, also enter this amount on Schedule 1 (Form 1040), line 5. Otherwise, include this amount in the total on line 41 on page 2 .	**26**	

For Paperwork Reduction Act Notice, see the separate instructions.   Cat. No. 11344L   **Schedule E (Form 1040) 2020**

Income from passive activities can be used by taxpayers to absorb passive losses that would otherwise be disallowed. The passive loss limitations are very complex. Certain oil and gas investments are not subject to the passive loss limitations, and special rules apply to investments in qualified low-income housing.

Rental real estate is a common form of passive income and is input through the Rental and Royalty Income (Sch E) window. Another source of passive income is from partnerships, LLCs or S corporations. As discussed in Chapters 10 and 11, these entities report income to individual owners through a Schedule K-1. K-1 income is input under Income in the left margin and the applicable Partnership K-1 or S Corporation K-1 input.	**ProConnect™ Tax** **TIP**

Self-Study Problem 4.8   *See Appendix E for Solutions to Self-Study Problems*

Sherry Lockey has a new limited partnership investment in a commercial rental project in which she has no personal involvement. During 2020, her share of the partnership loss equals $15,000. Sherry also has a new rental house that she actively manages, and this activity generated a $9,000 loss for 2020. Sherry had no passive loss carryover from prior years. If Sherry's modified adjusted gross income before passive losses is $138,000, calculate the deduction amounts for Sherry's 2020 tax return using page 1 of Form 8582 on Page 4-33.

4-9 NET OPERATING LOSSES

> **4.9 Learning Objective**
>
> Describe the basic tax treatment of deductions for net operating losses.

Taxpayers are required to file an annual tax return. The pattern of a taxpayer's income, however, can lead to inequities among taxpayers with the same total amount of taxable income over a number of years. To alleviate this problem, Congress enacted the Net Operating Loss (NOL) provision.

The NOL provision is primarily designed to provide relief for trade or business losses. Generally, only losses from the operation of a trade or business and casualty and theft losses can generate a net operating loss. Thus, individual taxpayers with only wages, itemized deductions (except casualty losses), and personal exemptions (although currently suspended) cannot generate a net operating loss.

The tax law is designed to permit individuals to deduct business NOLs and prevent the deductions of nonbusiness NOLs. Thus, the NOL computation for individual taxpayers requires the categorization of items of income, deductions, gains, and losses as either business or nonbusiness related. The NOL is not simply the total taxable loss shown at the bottom of page 1 of Form 1040. In general, when calculating a current net operating loss, the following tax items should be considered:

- No personal or dependency exemptions (exemptions are suspended after 2017)
- No deduction for an NOL from a different year
- Capital losses in excess of capital gains are not allowed
- "Nonbusiness" capital losses (those arising outside of a trade or business, or employment) can only be used against "nonbusiness" capital gains. Excess capital losses cannot increase the NOL
- "Business" capital losses can only be used against "business" capital gains, except that they can be used to offset a net nonbusiness capital gain if one exists
- "Nonbusiness" deductions (e.g., charitable donations, deductible medical expenses, mortgage interest, alimony, etc.) can only be used against "nonbusiness" income (interest, dividends, etc.). However, if nonbusiness capital gains exceed nonbusiness capital losses (see above), "excess" nonbusiness deductions can be offset against these gains. (Note that casualty losses are treated as "business deductions" for NOL purposes.)

EXAMPLE Yujian, a single taxpayer, has completed her 2020 Schedule C and her net loss is $70,000. She also has wages of $45,000 and interest income from her savings of $500. Her business sold property during the year and generated a $3,000 ordinary gain and a separate $5,000 long-term capital gain. Yujian also had several capital gains and losses from the sale of stock investments. Her net results are a $17,000 short-term capital gain and a $6,000 long-term capital loss from these stock sales. Yujian itemizes her deductions and her Schedule A reports the following:

Taxes paid	$ 8,500
Mortgage interest	6,000
Charitable gifts	500
Casualty loss (federal disaster area loss)	2,500
Total itemized deductions	$ 17,500

Yujian calculates her taxable income as follows:

Wages	$ 45,000
Interest income	500
Business loss	(70,000)
Capital gains[1]	16,000
Other gains	3,000
Total income (loss) and AGI	(5,500)
Itemized deductions	(17,500)
Taxable income (loss)	$(23,000)

To compute Yujian's NOL, we need to categorize business and non-business items:

	Business	Nonbusiness
Wages	$ 45,000	
Interest income		$ 500
Business loss	(70,000)	
Capital gains	5,000	11,000
Other gains	3,000	
Itemized deductions	(2,500)	(15,000)
Total	$(19,500)	$ (3,500)

Using the above information, we can modify taxable income to compute the NOL.

Step 1: Excess nonbusiness capital losses cannot exceed nonbusiness capital gains.

Since the $6,000 nonbusiness capital losses do not exceed $17,000 of nonbusiness capital gains, no adjustment is required. In addition, we can use the $11,000 "excess" nonbusiness capital gain to absorb any nonbusiness deductions in the next step.

Step 2: Nonbusiness deductions cannot exceed nonbusiness income.

Nonbusiness deductions $15,000 − Nonbusiness income $500 = Net nonbusiness deductions $14,500

However, as previously mentioned, net nonbusiness deductions can also offset any net nonbusiness capital gains. Thus $11,000 of the nonbusiness deductions can be used; however, the remaining $3,500 ($14,500 − $11,000) are not deductible and must be added back to the tentative NOL $(23,000) + $3,500 = $(19,500).

---

[1] $1,000 long-term capital loss ($5,000 long-term capital gain from business less $6,000 long-term capital loss from stocks) netted against $17,000 short-term capital gain from stocks.

Step 3: The business capital (casualty) loss of $2,500 can only be offset by business capital gains of $5,000. There is no excess loss and thus no adjustment is needed.

This agrees to the business category total loss of $19,500 above which is consistent with the NOL representing only business losses.

Yujian may carryforward (or temporarily carryback) the NOL of $19,500 to offset future income. ♦

4-9a NOLs Affected by COVID-19 Provisions

The rules related to NOLs have changed three times in recent years and with each change, NOLs are treated slightly differently. The three periods are: (1) the Pre-2018 period, (2) the 2018–2020 period (due to COVID-19 provisions), and (3) the post-2020 period.

In the pre-2018 period, NOLs were eligible to be carried back two years and forward for 20 years. Any NOL carryforward or carryback could be used to offset 100 percent of the income generated in the carryback or forward period. NOLs generated in this period can continue to be utilized in the same manner.

EXAMPLE Henri generated a loss in 2017 of $45,000. His business income was $2,000 and $5,000 in 2015 and 2016, respectively. Henri will first carryback the NOL to offset the income generated in 2015 and 2016. The remaining NOL of $38,000 can be carried forward for 20 years and offset any income generated in those years. ♦

The TCJA of 2017 changed the treatment of NOLs to permit only the indefinite carryforward of NOLs generated after 2017. In addition, the use of an NOL generated after December 31, 2017 is limited to 80 percent of the current year's taxable income (without regard to the NOL deduction) when used.

EXAMPLE Zlatan generated an NOL in 2018 of $10,000. At that time, he is unable to carry the NOL back and must carry it forward only. In 2019, Zlatan generates $11,000 of business income. Zlatan may only offset up to 80 percent or $8,800 of the 2019 income ($11,000 × 80%). The remaining $1,200 NOL can be carried forward indefinitely. ♦

In the COVID-19 pandemic period (2018-2020), a number of retroactive provisions regarding NOLs were put into place to assist taxpayers with remaining financially viable during the economic downturn. NOLs generated in 2018, 2019, and 2020 were given a 5-year carryback period (but keep the indefinite carryforward) and the 80 percent income limitation is suspended on NOLs generated and used in those three years.

EXAMPLE Zlatan (from the previous example) may now carryback his 2018 $10,000 NOL up to five years (to 2013). If no income was available in the carryback years (or Zlatan elects out of the carryback), the NOL can be used to offset any income in the future year. Thus, Zlatan could carry the $10,000 NOL forward to 2019 and reduce 2019 income to $1,000 (no 80 percent limitation). ♦

Pre-COVID but post-2018 NOL rules will become effective again after 2020. NOLs generated in 2021 and after may only be carried forward and any post-2017 NOLs will again be limited to 80 percent.

EXAMPLE Lionel started his sole proprietorship in 2018 and generated an NOL of $5,000 in 2018 and another NOL of $8,000 in 2019. In 2020, Lionel made a very small business profit of $2,000. In 2021, he generated $11,000 of business income. Because he has no pre-2018 business income, Lionel is unable to carryback any of the 2018 NOL and instead carries it forward. He offsets the entire $2,000 of 2020 income (no 80 percent limitation) leaving $3,000 of 2018 NOL and $8,000 of 2019 NOL. In 2021, he is limited to using only $8,800 ($11,000 × 80%) of the NOLs. ♦

4-9b Overall Business Loss Limitation

To reduce the potential for large business losses being claimed in a single year, starting in 2018, the tax law places an annual limitation on noncorporate business losses for taxpayers. After adjusting for inflation, the limits were set to be $518,000 for married filing jointly and $259,000 for all other returns. The CARES Act suspended the excess loss limitation provisions through the end of 2020. Tax returns for the years 2018 and 2019 may be amended to deduct the excess loss.

EXAMPLE Bettina is a single taxpayer with wages of $20,000 and a business with income of $5,000 in 2020. In addition, Bettina disposed of a passive loss activity for which she has accumulated suspended losses of $280,000 (including her share of the current year loss). Bettina's excess business loss is $275,000 ($280,000 − $5,000) less the single threshold for 2020 of $259,000 yielding an excess loss of $16,000. This amount would have become part of Bettina's net operating loss and subject to the NOL limitation and carryforward rules; however, due to the suspension of the limitation, Bettina can now deduct the entire loss in 2020. ♦

ProConnect™ Tax

TIP

When a taxpayer creates a net operating loss (NOL), no specific entry is required by the preparer. Instead, supplemental schedules that track the NOL will be created automatically by the software.

Self-Study Problem 4.8

Form **8582**	**Passive Activity Loss Limitations**	OMB No. 1545-1008
Department of the Treasury Internal Revenue Service (99)	▶ See separate instructions. ▶ Attach to Form 1040, 1040-SR, or 1041. ▶ Go to *www.irs.gov/Form8582* for instructions and the latest information.	**2020** Attachment Sequence No. **858**

Name(s) shown on return | Identifying number

Part I   2020 Passive Activity Loss

Caution: Complete Worksheets 1, 2, and 3 before completing Part I.

Rental Real Estate Activities With Active Participation (For the definition of active participation, see **Special Allowance for Rental Real Estate Activities** in the instructions.)

1a	Activities with net income (enter the amount from Worksheet 1, column (a)) . .	1a	
b	Activities with net loss (enter the amount from Worksheet 1, column (b)) . .	1b (	)
c	Prior years' unallowed losses (enter the amount from Worksheet 1, column (c))	1c (	)
d	Combine lines 1a, 1b, and 1c	1d	

Commercial Revitalization Deductions From Rental Real Estate Activities

2a	Commercial revitalization deductions from Worksheet 2, column (a) . . .	2a	
b	Prior year unallowed commercial revitalization deductions from Worksheet 2, column (b)	2b (	)
c	Add lines 2a and 2b	2c (	)

All Other Passive Activities

3a	Activities with net income (enter the amount from Worksheet 3, column (a)) . .	3a	
b	Activities with net loss (enter the amount from Worksheet 3, column (b)) . .	3b (	)
c	Prior years' unallowed losses (enter the amount from Worksheet 3, column (c))	3c (	)
d	Combine lines 3a, 3b, and 3c	3d	

4   Combine lines 1d, 2c, and 3d. If this line is zero or more, stop here and include this form with your return; all losses are allowed, including any prior year unallowed losses entered on line 1c, 2b, or 3c. Report the losses on the forms and schedules normally used . . . . | **4** |

If line 4 is a loss and: • Line 1d is a loss, go to Part II.
• Line 2c is a loss (and line 1d is zero or more), skip Part II and go to Part III.
• Line 3d is a loss (and lines 1d and 2c are zero or more), skip Parts II and III and go to line 15.

Caution: If your filing status is married filing separately and you lived with your spouse at any time during the year, **do not** complete Part II or Part III. Instead, go to line 15.

Part II   Special Allowance for Rental Real Estate Activities With Active Participation

Note: Enter all numbers in Part II as positive amounts. See instructions for an example.

5	Enter the **smaller** of the loss on line 1d or the loss on line 4		5
6	Enter $150,000. If married filing separately, see instructions	6	
7	Enter modified adjusted gross income, but not less than zero. See instructions	7	
	Note: If line 7 is greater than or equal to line 6, skip lines 8 and 9, enter -0- on line 10. Otherwise, go to line 8.		
8	Subtract line 7 from line 6	8	
9	Multiply line 8 by 50% (0.50). **Do not** enter more than $25,000. If married filing separately, see instructions		9
10	Enter the **smaller** of line 5 or line 9		10
	If line 2c is a loss, go to Part III. Otherwise, go to line 15.		

Part III   Special Allowance for Commercial Revitalization Deductions From Rental Real Estate Activities

Note: Enter all numbers in Part III as positive amounts. See the example for Part II in the instructions.

11	Enter $25,000 reduced by the amount, if any, on line 10. If married filing separately, see instructions .	11
12	Enter the loss from line 4	12
13	Reduce line 12 by the amount on line 10	13
14	Enter the **smallest** of line 2c (treated as a positive amount), line 11, or line 13	14

Part IV   Total Losses Allowed

15	Add the income, if any, on lines 1a and 3a and enter the total	15
16	**Total losses allowed from all passive activities for 2020.** Add lines 10, 14, and 15. See instructions to find out how to report the losses on your tax return	16

For Paperwork Reduction Act Notice, see instructions. | Cat. No. 63704F | Form **8582** (2020)

Self-Study Problem 4.9 *See Appendix E for Solutions to Self-Study Problems*

Indicate whether the following statements are true or false as of December 31, 2020 by circling the appropriate letter.

T F 1. NOL deductions from 2020 are first carried back 2 years and then forward 20 years.

T F 2. The itemized deduction for home mortgage interest can generate an NOL for an individual taxpayer.

T F 3. An individual taxpayer's NOL is equal to the net taxable loss from page 1 of Form 1040.

T F 4. Individual taxpayers' total business losses can be limited.

T F 5. There is no limitation for using a 2020 NOL against the taxable income in 2021.

Sign Here	Under penalties of perjury, I declare that I have examined this return and accompanying schedules and statements, and to the best of my knowledge and belief, they are true, correct, and complete. Declaration of preparer (other than taxpayer) is based on all information of which preparer has any knowledge.			
	Your signature	Date	Your occupation	If the IRS sent you an Identity Protection PIN, enter it here (see inst.) ▶
Joint return? See instructions. Keep a copy for your records.	Spouse's signature. If a joint return, **both** must sign.	Date	Spouse's occupation	If the IRS sent your spouse an Identity Protection PIN, enter it here (see inst.) ▶
	Phone no.	Email address		
Paid Preparer Use Only	Preparer's name	Preparer's signature	Date	PTIN	Check if: ☐ Self-employed
	Firm's name ▶		Phone no.	
	Firm's address ▶		Firm's EIN ▶	

Would You Sign This Tax Return?

Mark (age 44) and Mary (age 41) Mower are your tax clients. They have two children, Matthew (age 20) and Mindy (age 17), who live at home. Mindy is a senior in high school and Matthew commutes to a local college where he is studying soil management. Mark owns and operates a successful lawn maintenance and landscaping business. He has 6 employees and 3 pick-up trucks used for transportation to the job sites. The business has a credit card in its name for use by the employees and Mark, who fills the trucks with gas almost daily. Mark gave a business credit card to Mary, Matthew, and Mindy and told them to use it to buy gas for their automobiles used for shopping, going to school, and short trips. In the current year, his wife and children put $5,210 of gasoline in their automobiles using the business credit card. Mark is adamant that the $5,210 be deducted on his Schedule C. He feels the amount is small compared to the business gas purchases of approximately $28,000. Mark says the amounts charged are spread throughout the credit card statements and would be very difficult for the IRS to detect in an audit. Would you sign the Paid Preparer's declaration (see example above) on this return? Why or why not?

4-10 QUALIFIED BUSINESS INCOME (QBI) DEDUCTION

4.10 Learning Objective

Compute the qualified business income (QBI) deduction.

The Qualified Business Income (QBI) deduction was introduced in 2018 and applies to tax years through 2025. The QBI deduction is a deduction for individual taxpayers reporting business income from a passthrough entity such as a sole proprietorship, partnership, limited liability company, or S corporation. It is also referred to as the Section 199A deduction, the passthrough deduction, or the QBI deduction. The QBI deduction requires no additional outlay or investment of funds but is simply granted as a function of legislative grace. A discussion of the QBI deduction related specifically to partnerships and S corporations is covered in Chapters 10 and 11, respectively.

The QBI deduction is available to individual taxpayers as a "below the line" deduction (after adjusted gross income) and is also available to taxpayers who take the standard deduction. The deduction is generally 20 percent of a taxpayer's qualified business income (QBI) from a partnership (including LLC if so treated), S corporation, or sole proprietorship.

4-10a Definition of Qualified Business Income

Qualified business income for a tax year is the net amount of qualified items of income, gain, deduction, and loss relating to any qualified trade or business of the taxpayer in the United States (foreign income is not considered). QBI excludes the following:

- Short-term capital gain, short-term capital loss, long-term capital gain, or long-term capital loss
- Dividend income
- Interest income
- Commodity transaction income or foreign currency gain or loss
- Any item of income, gain, deduction, or loss relating to certain notional principal contracts
- Amounts received from an annuity that is not received in connection with the trade or business
- Any item of deduction or loss properly allocable to an amount described in any of the preceding items in this list (e.g., interest expense associated with investment income)

Reasonable employee compensation paid to the taxpayer by the qualified trade or business and guaranteed payments to a partner are not QBI and therefore the QBI deduction is not applicable to such income.

EXAMPLE   Princess is a single taxpayer and operates a small business as a sole proprietor. In 2020, her business generates $80,000 of gross business income, $50,000 of business expenses, $3,000 of interest income, and a $2,000 capital gain. Princess' QBI is $30,000 ($80,000 − $50,000). The interest and capital gains are excluded from QBI. ♦

With respect to the QBI deduction, the term *"qualified* trade or business" means any trade or business other than a specified service trade or business, or the trade or business of performing services as an employee. Unfortunately, "trade or business" is not defined in the tax law. The regulations interpret trade or business to be consistent with the same phrase in Internal Revenue Code Section 162 related to the deduction of trade or business expenses. This does not provide an exceptional level of guidance for many businesses but certainly hobby activities (Chapter 3) would not qualify. The tax law provides a safe-harbor under which income from rental real estate (even if treated as passive) can qualify as qualified business income. The requirements are:

1. 250 hours or more are spent by the taxpayer with respect to the rental activity
2. Contemporaneous records of the time are maintained
3. Separate books and records for the rental activity are maintained

Note that 250 hours per year amounts to an average of over 20 hours per month. Time spent related to the rental activity on advertising, negotiating with tenants, verifying applications, daily operation, repair and maintenance, purchase of materials, and supervision of employees all count toward the required 250 hours. Time spent purchasing or financing the acquisition of the property and time spent traveling to and from the property do not generally qualify.

4-10b QBI Deduction Taxable Income Limitation

The QBI deduction is subject to a number of limitations and exceptions. A limitation that applies to all taxpayers is that the QBI deduction cannot exceed 20 percent of the taxpayer's taxable income (excluding net long-term capital gains and qualified dividend income).

EXAMPLE Alice operates a small accounting business that generates $60,000 of qualified business income. She also operates a separate investment advising business that focuses on providing crypto-currency investment advice that lost $20,000. Both of Alice's businesses are sole proprietorships. Her pre-limitation QBI deduction is $8,000 [($60,000 − $20,000) × 20%]. Alice also earned $5,000 in net capital gains but had no other forms of income and elects the standard deduction. In 2020, Alice's taxable income subject to the 20 percent limit is $27,600 ($40,000 of business income less her standard deduction of $12,400; capital gains are excluded from this calculation). Her QBI deduction is limited to $5,520 ($27,600 × 20%). ♦

4-10c **Wage Limitation**

The two additional limitations on the QBI deduction are (1) the wage limitation and (2) the specified service business limitation. These limitations apply to taxpayers that have taxable income (*total* taxable income not just *business* income and including long-term capital gains or qualified dividends) above the threshold amounts, which in 2020 are $326,600 for married filing jointly and $163,300 for all other taxpayers. These threshold amounts are indexed for inflation each year. The limitations are computed before considering the QBI deduction.

For taxpayers with income below the thresholds, the QBI deduction is as described above. For taxpayers with taxable income above the threshold amounts, the two limitations apply and subject to a complex phase-out.

The wage limit is the greater of:

- 50 percent of the allocable share of W-2 wages with respect to the business (the "wage limit") or
- 25 percent of the allocable share of W-2 wages with respect to the business plus 2.5 percent of the unadjusted basis of all qualified business property (the "wage and capital limit")

W-2 wages are defined as wages paid to employees (not independent contractors) including deferrals into Section 401(k) plans and the like. The term allocable share pertains to the allocation of wages similar to that associated with the allocation of partnership income (see further discussion of allocation of wages in Chapter 10). Because the tax law was designed to encourage investment in employees and business capital investment, the wage and capital limit includes a percentage of the unadjusted basis (basis prior to any depreciation) of business property.

EXAMPLE Pat operates a sole proprietorship which generates $200,000 of qualified business income that includes the deduction for wages of $66,000 that Pat pays to employees. Pat's business has invested $20,000 in qualified business property. Pat has no other sources of income and files as a single taxpayer and elects the standard deduction. Pat's initial QBI deduction is $200,000 × 20% or $40,000 which is limited to 20 percent of Pat's taxable income [$187,600 ($200,000 − standard deduction of $12,400) × 20% = $37,520]. Furthermore, since Pat's income exceeds the $163,300 threshold, the wage limit applies. The wage limit is the greater of 50 percent of the wages ($66,000 × 50% = $33,000) or the wage and capital limit of 25 percent of the wages ($66,000 × 25% = $16,500) plus 2.5 percent of the unadjusted basis of qualified business property ($20,000 × 2.5% = $500) which totals $17,000. The greater of the two wage limit amounts applies and thus, Pat's QBI deduction is limited to $33,000. Pat's final taxable income will be $154,600 ($200,000 − $33,000 − $12,400). Recall that the wage limit applies if the taxpayer's taxable income *before* the QBI deduction exceeds the threshold. ◆

Qualified business property for purposes of the wage and capital limit is defined as tangible property subject to depreciation (i.e., not inventory or land) for which the depreciable period has not ended before the close of the taxable year, held by the business at year end, and used at any point during the year in the production of QBI. If the "depreciation period" for a property ended in any prior tax year, that property is not included in the calculation of tangible property. The depreciable period is defined as starting when the property was placed in service and ending on the later of (1) 10 years or (2) the last day in the last year of the property's regular depreciation.

EXAMPLE   Josh, a single taxpayer, operates a sole proprietorship. He qualifies for the QBI deduction and his taxable income subjects him to the wage and capital limitations. Josh has purchased and placed in service the following property (all of which is currently being used in 2020):

Year	5-year recovery period	39-year recovery period
2009	$20,000	$600,000
2010	0	0
2011	4,000	0
2012	0	0
2013	0	0
2014	0	0
2015	25,000	0
2016	0	0
2017	10,000	0
2018	2,000	0
2019	50,000	0
2020	13,000	0
Total	$124,000	$600,000

▢ Qualified business property still within recovery period

In determining qualified business property for purposes of the QBI wage limit in 2020, Josh's property must still be within the depreciable period which ends on the later of the last full year of the recovery period or 10 years. The 2009–2015 five-year property is fully depreciated BUT only the property placed in service before 2011 is no longer qualified; thus Josh has $104,000 of qualified five-year property. In spite of being placed in service more than 10 years ago, all of the building in the 39-year category is qualified as it is still being depreciated. Josh's total qualified property under the wage and capital limit for the QBI deduction is $704,000 ($104,000 + $600,000). ◆

Recall that the wage limitations apply only if the taxpayer's taxable income exceeds the threshold amount ($326,600 or $163,300). As is typical in the tax law, a taxpayer's opportunity to use the QBI deduction does not cease entirely if the threshold is exceeded. Instead, the QBI deduction is subject to a phase-out up to an excess of $100,000 for married filing jointly taxpayers and $50,000 for all others. First, the QBI deduction is computed as if no wage limitation applies. The next step is to compute the QBI deduction including the wage limitation. The excess of the QBI deduction with no limitation over the QBI deduction with limitation is known as the "excess amount." The excess amount is subject to a pro rata phase-out based on the taxpayer's income over the threshold amount.

EXAMPLE   Phil is a single taxpayer with a QBI eligible small business and his taxable income as measured for the QBI deduction is $177,500 and thus exceeds the 163,300 threshold. Phil's QBI is $150,000 and his business paid wages of $42,000 in 2020 and has qualified business property of $660,000.

Phil's QBI deduction with no limitation = $30,000 ($150,000 × 20%)
The wage limitation is $27,000, which is the greater of:

$21,000 ($42,000 wages × 50%) or
$27,000 [($42,000 × 25%) + ($660,000 × 2.5%)]

Phil's QBI deduction is limited to $27,000; however, Phil is not subject to the entire wage limitation as his income is not $50,000 or more over the threshold amount. Thus, the wage limitation is "phased-in."

Phil's taxable income for QBI deduction purposes	$177,500
Phil's threshold amount (single taxpayer)	163,300
Excess	$ 14,200
Excess divided by the phase-out range	$14,200/$50,000 = 28.4%

Thus Phil will lose 28.4 percent of his "excess amount" of $3,000 ($30,000 QBI deduction without limit less $27,000 QBI deduction with limit) or $852. Phil's QBI deduction is $29,148 ($30,000 − $852). ◆

To summarize thus far, the QBI deduction is 20 percent of qualified business income, which is the income of a business held in any form but corporate form. QBI excludes forms of "portfolio" income such as interest, dividends, and gains. For taxpayers below the income thresholds ($326,600 married filing jointly and $163,300 for all other taxpayers), there are no explicit limitations other than the taxable income limit. For those with taxable income above the thresholds, the QBI deduction is limited by the wage limitation and also by the specified service business limitation (which is covered below).

4-10d Specified Service Business Limitation

For taxpayers with income in excess of the threshold, certain types of businesses are not eligible for the QBI deduction:

1. a taxpayer whose business is being an employee, and
2. a specified service trade or business.

A specified service trade or business is defined as any trade or business involving the performance of services in the fields of health, law, accounting, actuarial science, performing arts, consulting, athletics, financial services, brokerage services, or any trade or business where the principal asset of such trade or business is the reputation or skill of one or more of its owners or employees. Also, specified service businesses include those involved in investing and investment management, trading, or dealing in securities, partnership interests, or commodities.

To be clear, recall that a taxpayer in a specified service business is not necessarily prohibited from the QBI deduction but rather is not eligible for the QBI deduction if the taxpayer's taxable income exceeds the aforementioned thresholds. The same phase-out for the wage limitation also applies to a specified service business (i.e., the with and without comparison of the QBI deduction and pro-rata reduction of the excess amount). However, the phase-out applies in a two-step process that is almost certainly better left to tax software.

EXAMPLE   Jenny and Jason file jointly in 2020. Jenny is a physician and works for her pass-through business that has QBI of $310,000 in 2020. The S corporation paid Jenny wages of $80,000 and her employee wages of $40,000 in 2020. Jenny and Jason's taxable income before any QBI deduction is $385,000. Jenny's S corporation has qualified business property of $300,000.

Jenny's QBI without any limits would be $62,000 ($310,000 × 20%). However, Jenny and Jason exceed the threshold income by $58,400 ($385,000 − $326,600). The excess income of $58,400 is 58.4 percent of the phase-out range of $100,000 for married filing jointly taxpayers and thus Jenny is eligible for only 41.6 percent of the benefits from the deduction. This eligible share is applied to each of the limits as follows:

QBI is $310,000 × 41.6% = $128,960

W-2 wages of $120,000 × 41.6% = $49,920

Qualified business property $300,000 × 41.6% = $124,800

Using this information, Jenny's tentative QBI deduction under the general rules is

20% of QBI: $25,792 ($128,960 × 20%)

Or the greater of

Wages limit: $24,960 ($49,920 × 50%) or

Wages and capital limit: $15,600 [($49,920 × 25%) + $124,800 × 2.5%]

Under the first step, the QBI deduction would be $24,960. But now, the phase-out associated with income over the threshold must be applied based on these amounts. Jenny's QBI would be $25,792 with no limitation and $24,960 with limitation or an excess QBI deduction of $832. As previously calculated, Jenny and Jason's income exceeds the threshold by $58,400 or 58.4 percent of the phase-out range of $100,000. Thus, Jenny is going to lose $486 of the QBI deduction (58.4 percent of the excess QBI deduction of $832).

As a result of the above steps, Jenny's QBI deduction for 2020 is $25,306 ($25,792 − $486). ◆

If a taxpayer has net QBI from one or more businesses that is less than zero, no QBI deduction is permitted and the QBI loss is carried over to the following year.

EXAMPLE   Alice operates a small business that generates $20,000 of qualified business income. She also operates a separate business that lost $60,000. Both of Alice's businesses are sole proprietorships. Alice's total net QBI is less than $0 ($40,000 net loss). As a result, Alice is not permitted a QBI deduction in the current year and will carry the QBI loss forward in next year. ◆

The regulations that cover the QBI deduction are complex and the calculation of the QBI deduction can become unwieldy when a taxpayer subject to the limitations has multiple businesses eligible for the QBI deduction and some of these businesses operate at a loss and others generate income. These computations are beyond the scope of this textbook.

4-10e Reporting the QBI Deduction

Forms 8995 and 8995-A are used for reporting the QBI deduction. Form 8995 is for taxpayers whose taxable income before the QBI deduction does not exceed the phase-out thresholds ($326,600 for married filing jointly and $163,300 for all other taxpayers in 2020). Otherwise, taxpayers must use Form 8995-A. As the complexity of the QBI deduction increases, taxpayers may also need to use four accompanying schedules (A–D) that are part of Form 8995-A. These additional schedules are beyond the scope of this textbook.

Self-Study Problem 4.10   *See Appendix E for Solutions to Self-Study Problems*

Determine whether the following taxpayers are eligible for the QBI deduction and the deduction amount, if any.

Taxpayer	Eligible for QBI deduction (Y/N)?	QBI deduction amount
a. Aretha is a married taxpayer filing jointly and a shareholder in Soul Corporation (not an S corporation). She owns 10 percent of the outstanding stock and the corporation generates $700,000 of taxable income from its business operations and distributes a $70,000 dividend to Aretha. Her total taxable income before the QBI deduction is $92,000.	_____	$_____
b. Terri Jones is a single taxpayer and sole proprietor that operates a small chain of hair salons called The Bee Hive that specialize in obscure hair colors. Her business has no employees since all the stylists operate as independent contractors. The taxpayer identification number of the Bee Hive is 317-65-4321. Terri's business generated business income of $120,000 in 2020. Her taxable income before any QBI deduction is $132,500. Use Form 8995 on Page 4–43 to determine her QBI deduction.	_____	$_____
c. Alice Delvecchio is married and files a joint return with her spouse, Chris Delvecchio. Alice operates a small family restaurant called D's Pizza as a sole proprietor (taxpayer identification number 565-22-4321). She pays wages of $36,000, has qualified property with a basis of $67,000, and the QBI from the restaurant is $100,000. Chris has wages of $250,000 and their joint taxable income before the QBI deduction is $364,000 and includes $12,000 of qualified dividends. Use Form 8995-A on Pages 4–44 and 4-45 to determine their QBI deduction amount.	_____	$_____

All of the different entry points for information for a tax return are located on the left-hand margin of ProConnect. At the top of that list are two tabs: All and In Use. The All tab shows all of the possible data entry points and aids in the prevention of overlooking a tax item while preparing the return. For reviewing a return, the In Use tab hides the areas not in use and can be very useful.

ProConnect™ Tax

TIP

Self-Study Problem 4.10b

Form **8995**	Qualified Business Income Deduction Simplified Computation	OMB No. 1545-0123
Department of the Treasury Internal Revenue Service	▶ Attach to your tax return. ▶ Go to *www.irs.gov/Form8995* for instructions and the latest information.	**2020** Attachment Sequence No. **55**

Name(s) shown on return	Your taxpayer identification number

Note. *You can claim the qualified business income deduction* **only** *if you have qualified business income from a qualified trade or business, real estate investment trust dividends, publicly traded partnership income, or a domestic production activities deduction passed through from an agricultural or horticultural cooperative. See instructions.*
Use this form if your taxable income, before your qualified business income deduction, is at or below $163,300 ($326,600 if married filing jointly), and you aren't a patron of an agricultural or horticultural cooperative.

1		(a) Trade, business, or aggregation name	(b) Taxpayer identification number	(c) Qualified business income or (loss)
i				
ii				
iii				
iv				
v				

2	Total qualified business income or (loss). Combine lines 1i through 1v, column (c)	**2**	
3	Qualified business net (loss) carryforward from the prior year	**3** ( )	
4	Total qualified business income. Combine lines 2 and 3. If zero or less, enter -0-	**4**	
5	Qualified business income component. Multiply line 4 by 20% (0.20)		**5**
6	Qualified REIT dividends and publicly traded partnership (PTP) income or (loss) (see instructions)	**6**	
7	Qualified REIT dividends and qualified PTP (loss) carryforward from the prior year	**7** ( )	
8	Total qualified REIT dividends and PTP income. Combine lines 6 and 7. If zero or less, enter -0-	**8**	
9	REIT and PTP component. Multiply line 8 by 20% (0.20)		**9**
10	Qualified business income deduction before the income limitation. Add lines 5 and 9		**10**
11	Taxable income before qualified business income deduction	**11**	
12	Net capital gain (see instructions)	**12**	
13	Subtract line 12 from line 11. If zero or less, enter -0-	**13**	
14	Income limitation. Multiply line 13 by 20% (0.20)		**14**
15	Qualified business income deduction. Enter the lesser of line 10 or line 14. Also enter this amount on the applicable line of your return ▶		**15**
16	Total qualified business (loss) carryforward. Combine lines 2 and 3. If greater than zero, enter -0-		**16** ( )
17	Total qualified REIT dividends and PTP (loss) carryforward. Combine lines 6 and 7. If greater than zero, enter -0-		**17** ( )

For Privacy Act and Paperwork Reduction Act Notice, see instructions.   Cat. No. 37806C   Form **8995** (2020)

Self-Study Problem 4.10c

Form **8995-A**	**Qualified Business Income Deduction**	OMB No. 1545-0123
Department of the Treasury Internal Revenue Service	▶ **Attach to your tax return.** ▶ **Go to** *www.irs.gov/Form8995A* **for instructions and the latest information.**	**2019*** Attachment Sequence No. **55A**

Name(s) shown on return   Your taxpayer identification number

Part I   Trade, Business, or Aggregation Information

Complete Schedules A, B, and/or C (Form 8995-A), as applicable, before starting Part I. Attach additional worksheets when needed. See instructions.

1	**(a)** Trade, business, or aggregation name	**(b)** Check if specified service	**(c)** Check if aggregation	**(d)** Taxpayer identification number	**(e)** Check if patron
A		☐	☐		☐
B		☐	☐		☐
C		☐	☐		☐

Part II   Determine Your Adjusted Qualified Business Income

			A	**B**	**C**
2	Qualified business income from the trade, business, or aggregation. See instructions	2			
3	Multiply line 2 by 20% (0.20). If your taxable income is $160,700 or less ($160,725 if married filing separately; $321,400 if married filing jointly), skip lines 4 through 12 and enter the amount from line 3 on line 13	3		see note below	
4	Allocable share of W-2 wages from the trade, business, or aggregation	4			
5	Multiply line 4 by 50% (0.50)	5			
6	Multiply line 4 by 25% (0.25)	6			
7	Allocable share of the unadjusted basis immediately after acquisition (UBIA) of all qualified property	7			
8	Multiply line 7 by 2.5% (0.025)	8			
9	Add lines 6 and 8	9			
10	Enter the greater of line 5 or line 9	10			
11	W-2 wage and qualified property limitation. Enter the smaller of line 3 or line 10	11			
12	Phased-in reduction. Enter the amount from line 26, if any. See instructions	12			
13	Qualified business income deduction before patron reduction. Enter the greater of line 11 or line 12	13			
14	Patron reduction. Enter the amount from Schedule D (Form 8995-A), line 6, if any. See instructions	14			
15	Qualified business income component. Subtract line 14 from line 13	15			
16	Total qualified business income component. Add all amounts reported on line 15 . . . . ▶	16			

For Privacy Act and Paperwork Reduction Act Notice, see separate instructions.   Cat. No. 71661B   Form **8995-A** (2019)

*Please go to www.irs.gov to download the latest Form 8995-A. The 2020 version of Form 8995-A was not available as we went to print. If using the prior year form included in the textbook, be sure and use updated income limits on Line 3 and Line 21 ($326,600 for married filing jointly and $163,300 for all other).

Form 8995-A (2019) Page **2**

Part III Phased-in Reduction*

Complete Part III only if your taxable income is more than $160,700 but not $210,700 ($160,725 and $210,725 if married filing separately; $321,400 and $421,400 if married filing jointly) and line 10 is less than line 3. Otherwise, skip Part III.

			A	B	C
17	Enter the amounts from line 3	17			
18	Enter the amounts from line 10	18			
19	Subtract line 18 from line 17	19			
20	Taxable income before qualified business income deduction	20			
21	Threshold. Enter $160,700 ($160,725 if married filing separately; $321,400 if married filing jointly)	21 see note below			
22	Subtract line 21 from line 20	22			
23	Phase-in range. Enter $50,000 ($100,000 if married filing jointly)	23			
24	Phase-in percentage. Divide line 22 by line 23	24 %			
25	Total phase-in reduction. Multiply line 19 by line 24	25			
26	Qualified business income after phase-in reduction. Subtract line 25 from line 17. Enter this amount here and on line 12, for the corresponding trade or business	26			

Part IV Determine Your Qualified Business Income Deduction

27	Total qualified business income component from all qualified trades, businesses, or aggregations. Enter the amount from line 16	27	
28	Qualified REIT dividends and publicly traded partnership (PTP) income or (loss). See instructions	28	
29	Qualified REIT dividends and PTP (loss) carryforward from prior years	29 ( )	
30	Total qualified REIT dividends and PTP income. Combine lines 28 and 29. If less than zero, enter -0-	30	
31	REIT and PTP component. Multiply line 30 by 20% (0.20)	31	
32	Qualified business income deduction before the income limitation. Add lines 27 and 31 ▶		32
33	Taxable income before qualified business income deduction	33	
34	Net capital gain. See instructions	34	
35	Subtract line 34 from line 33. If zero or less, enter -0-		35
36	Income limitation. Multiply line 35 by 20% (0.20)		36
37	Qualified business income deduction before the domestic production activities deduction (DPAD) under section 199A(g). Enter the smaller of line 32 or line 36 ▶		37
38	DPAD under section 199A(g) allocated from an agricultural or horticultural cooperative. Don't enter more than line 33 minus line 37		38
39	Total qualified business income deduction. Add lines 37 and 38 ▶		39
40	Total qualified REIT dividends and PTP (loss) carryforward. Combine lines 28 and 29. If zero or greater, enter -0-		40 ( )

Form **8995-A** (2019)

*Please go to www.irs.gov to download the latest Form 8995-A. The 2020 version of Form 8995-A was not available as we went to print. If using the prior year form included in the textbook, be sure and use updated income limits on Line 3 and Line 21 ($326,600 for married filing jointly and $163,300 for all other).

KEY TERMS

capital asset, 4-2
capital gain or loss, 4-2
Section 1231 assets, 4-2
holding period, 4-3
"sale or exchange," 4-3
amount realized, 4-4
adjusted basis, 4-4
capital improvements, 4-5
net capital gains, 4-10

net capital losses, 4-10
capital loss carryovers, 4-11
personal residence exclusion, 4-19
vacation homes, 4-22
primarily personal use, 4-23
primarily rental use, 4-23
passive activity, 4-25
passive income and losses, 4-25
net operating loss (NOL), 4-29

excess loss limitation, 4-32
qualified business income (QBI)
    deduction, 4-35
wage limitation, 4-37
wage and capital limit, 4-37
qualified business property, 4-38
specified service business limitation,
    4-39

KEY POINTS

Learning Objectives	Key Points
LO 4.1: Define the term "capital asset."	• A capital asset is any property, whether or not used in a trade or business, except: (1) inventory, (2) depreciable property or real property used in a trade or business, (3) patents, inventions, models or designs, secret formulas or processes, copyrights, literary, musical, or artistic compositions, letters or memorandums, or similar property if the property is created by the taxpayer, (4) accounts or notes receivable, and (5) certain U.S. government publications.
LO 4.2: Apply the holding period for long-term and short-term capital gains and losses.	• Assets must be held for more than 1 year for the gain or loss to be considered long-term. • A capital asset held 1 year or less results in a short-term capital gain or loss. • A net short-term capital gain is treated as ordinary income. • In calculating the holding period, the taxpayer excludes the date of acquisition and includes the date of disposition.
LO 4.3: Calculate the gain or loss on the disposition of an asset.	• The taxpayer's gain or loss is calculated using the following formula: amount realized − adjusted basis = gain or loss realized. • The amount realized from a sale or other disposition of property is equal to the sum of the money received, plus the fair market value of other property received, plus any liabilities relieved, less the costs paid to transfer the property. • The adjusted basis of property = the original basis + capital improvements − accumulated depreciation. • In most cases, the original basis is the cost of the property at the date of acquisition, plus any costs incidental to the purchase, such as title insurance, escrow fees, and inspection fees. • Capital improvements are major expenditures for permanent improvements to or restoration of the taxpayer's property.
LO 4.4: Compute the tax on capital gains.	• Short-term capital gains are taxed as ordinary income, while there are various different preferential long-term capital gains tax rates. • Net long-term capital gains may be subject to rates ranging from 0 percent to 28 percent (an additional 3.8 percent Medicare tax on net investment income applies to high-income individuals). • Special rates apply to long-term gains on collectibles (e.g., art, stamps, gems, coins, etc.) and depreciation recapture on the disposition of certain Section 1250 assets.

LO 4.5: Describe the treatment of capital losses.	• Individual taxpayers may deduct net capital losses against ordinary income in amounts up to $3,000 per year with any unused capital losses carried forward indefinitely. • When a taxpayer ends up with net capital losses, the losses offset capital gains as follows: (1) net short-term capital losses first reduce 28 percent gains, then 25 percent gains, then regular long-term capital gains, and (2) net long-term capital losses first reduce 28 percent gains, then 25 percent gains, then any short-term capital gains. • Personal capital losses are not deductible for tax purposes.
LO 4.6: Apply the exclusion of gain from personal residence sales.	• Taxpayers who have owned their personal residence and lived in it for at least 2 of the 5 years before the sale can exclude from income up to $250,000 of gain ($500,000 for joint return filers).
LO 4.7: Apply the tax rules for rental property and vacation homes.	• Rental income and related expenses are reported on Schedule E. • Rental expenses include real estate taxes, mortgage interest, insurance, commissions, repairs, and depreciation. • If a residence is rented for fewer than 15 days during the year, the rental income is disregarded and the property is treated as a personal residence for tax purposes. • If the residence is rented for 15 days or more and is used for personal purposes for not more than 14 days or 10 percent of the days rented, whichever is greater, the residence is treated as a rental property. • If the residence is rented for 15 days or more and is used for personal purposes for more than 14 days or 10 percent of the days rented, whichever is greater, allocable rental expenses are allowed only to the extent of rental income.
LO 4.8: Explain the treatment of passive income and losses.	• The tax law defines three categories of income: (1) active income, (2) portfolio income, and (3) passive income and losses. • Normally, passive losses cannot be used to offset either active or portfolio income. Passive losses not used to offset passive income are carried forward indefinitely. • Generally, losses remaining when the taxpayer disposes of his or her entire interest in a passive activity may be used in full. • Under the passive loss rules, real estate rental activities are specifically defined as passive, even if the taxpayer actively manages the property. • Individual taxpayers may deduct up to $25,000 of rental property losses against other income, if they are actively involved in the management of the property and their modified adjusted gross income does not exceed certain limits. • Taxpayers heavily involved in real estate rental activities may qualify as running an active trade or business rather than a passive activity and may fully deduct all rental losses.
LO 4.9: Describe the basic tax treatment of deductions for net operating losses.	• Net operating losses (NOL) allow taxpayers to "smooth out" their income. • Computation of an individual taxpayer NOL requires classification of income and deductions as business and nonbusiness. • An NOL generated between 2018 and 2020 may be carried back 5 years and carried forward indefinitely. The requirement to limit NOLs to 80 percent of income is temporary suspended until 2021. • An NOL generated in 2017 or before may be carried back 2 years and forward 20 years. • Total business losses are limited after 2020.
LO 4.10: Compute the qualified business income (QBI) deduction.	• Flow-through entities are eligible for a deduction of 20 percent of QBI, subject to limitations. • QBI is business income only and generally does not include interest, dividends, or capital gains. • Tax law provides a safe-harbor under which income from rental real estate can qualify as QBI if it meets the necessary requirements. • The QBI deduction may not exceed 20 percent of taxable income. • If taxable income exceeds $326,600 (MFJ) or $163,300 (all other taxpayers), the QBI deduction is limited by the wage limitation or the wage and capital limitation, whichever is greater. • QBI from service-related business may also be subject to limitation if income thresholds are surpassed.

QUESTIONS and PROBLEMS

GROUP 1:
MULTIPLE CHOICE QUESTIONS

LO 4.1

1. All of the following assets are capital assets, *except*:
   a. A personal automobile
   b. IBM stock
   c. A child's bicycle
   d. Personal furniture
   e. Used car inventory held by a car dealer

LO 4.1

2. Which of the following is a capital asset?
   a. Account receivable
   b. Copyright created by the taxpayer
   c. Copyright (held by the writer)
   d. Business inventory
   e. A taxpayer's residence

LO 4.2

3. Yasmeen purchases stock on January 30, 2019. If she wishes to achieve a long-term holding period, what is the first date that she can sell the stock as a long-term gain?
   a. January 20, 2020
   b. January 31, 2020
   c. February 1, 2020
   d. July 31, 2019
   e. July 30, 2019

LO 4.3

4. Vijay sells land and receives $5,000 cash, a motorcycle worth $1,600, and two tickets to the Super Bowl with a total face value (cost) of $800 but worth $1,200. In addition, the buyer assumes the mortgage on the land of $12,000. What is Vijay's amount received in this transaction?
   a. $5,000
   b. $7,800
   c. $8,200
   d. $19,800
   e. $20,200

LO 4.3

5. Bob sells a stock investment for $35,000 cash, and the purchaser assumes Bob's $32,500 debt on the investment. The basis of Bob's stock investment is $55,000. What is the gain or loss realized on the sale?
   a. $10,000 loss
   b. $10,000 gain
   c. $12,500 gain
   d. $22,500 loss
   e. $22,500 gain

LO 4.4

6. In 2020, what is the top tax rate for individual long-term capital gains and the top tax rate for long-term capital gains of collectible items assuming that the Medicare tax does not apply.
   a. 10; 20
   b. 20; 28
   c. 15; 25
   d. 25; 28

LO 4.4

7. In November 2020, Ben and Betty (married, filing jointly) have a long-term capital gain of $54,000 on the sale of stock. They have no other capital gains and losses for the year. Their ordinary income for the year after the standard deduction is $72,500, making their total taxable income for the year $126,500 ($72,500 + $54,000). In 2020, married taxpayers pay 0 percent on long-term gains up to $80,000. What will be their 2020 total tax liability assuming a tax of $8,308 on the $72,500 of ordinary income?
   a. $8,322
   b. $15,283
   c. $15,478
   d. $16,408

LO 4.4

8. Harold, a single taxpayer, has $30,000 of ordinary income after the standard deduction, and $10,000 in long-term capital gains, for total taxable income of $40,000. For 2020, single taxpayers pay 0 percent on long-term gains up to $40,000. Assuming a tax of $3,406 on the $30,000 of ordinary income, what is Harold's tax?
   a. $3,406
   b. $3,503
   c. $3,623
   d. $4,094
   e. $4,906

LO 4.4
LO 4.5

9. In 2020, Tim, a single taxpayer, has ordinary income of $30,000. In addition, he has $2,000 in short-term capital gains, long-term capital losses of $10,000, and long-term capital gains of $4,000. What is Tim's AGI for 2020?
   a. $26,000
   b. $27,000
   c. $30,000
   d. $32,000

LO 4.6

10. Oscar, a single taxpayer, sells his residence of the last 10 years in January of 2020 for $190,000. Oscar's basis in the residence is $45,000, and his selling expenses are $11,000. If Oscar does not buy a new residence, what is the taxable gain on the sale of his residence?
   a. $145,000
   b. $134,000
   c. $45,000
   d. $9,000
   e. $0

LO 4.6

11. Jim, a single taxpayer, bought his home 20 years ago for $25,000. He has lived in the home continuously since he purchased it. In 2020, he sells his home for $300,000. What is Jim's taxable gain on the sale?
   a. $0
   b. $25,000
   c. $125,000
   d. $275,000

LO 4.6

12. Susan, a single taxpayer, bought her home 25 years ago for $30,000. She has lived in the home continuously since she purchased it. In 2020, she sells her home for $200,000. What is Susan's taxable gain on the sale?
   a. $0
   b. $20,000
   c. $250,000
   d. $170,000

LO 4.6

13. Kevin purchased a house 20 years ago for $100,000 and he has always lived in the house. Three years ago Kevin married Karen, and she has lived in the house since their marriage. If they sell Kevin's house in December 2020 for $425,000, what is their taxable gain on a joint tax return?
   a. $0
   b. $75,000
   c. $125,000
   d. $250,000

LO 4.6

14. Gene, a single taxpayer, purchased a house 18 months ago for $350,000. If Gene sells his house due to unforeseen circumstances for $550,000 after living in it for a full 18 months, what is his taxable gain?
   a. $0
   b. $12,500
   c. $50,000
   d. $200,000

LO 4.7

15. Which of the following is true about the rental of real estate?
   a. Depreciation and maintenance expenses for an apartment complex are deductible.
   b. The expenses deductions for a home rented for 100 days and used for personal use for 17 days will be limited to the gross rental income.
   c. If a home is rented for less than 15 days a year, the rent is not taxable.
   d. Repairs on rental property are deductible by the taxpayer.
   e. All of the above.

LO 4.7

16. John owns a second home in Palm Springs, CA. During the year, he rented the house for $5,000 for 56 days and used the house for 14 days during the summer. The house remained vacant during the remainder of the year. The expenses for the home included $5,000 in mortgage interest, $850 in property taxes, $900 for utilities and maintenance, and $3,500 of depreciation. What is John's deductible rental loss, before considering the passive loss limitations?
   a. $200
   b. $875
   c. $2,500
   d. $3,200
   e. $0

LO 4.8

17. Helen, a single taxpayer, has modified adjusted gross income (before passive losses) of $124,000. During the tax year, Helen's rental house generated a loss of $15,000. Assuming Helen is actively involved in the management of the property, what is the amount of Helen's passive loss deduction from the rental house?
   a. $0
   b. $3,000
   c. $10,000
   d. $12,000
   e. $13,000

LO 4.8

18. Which of the following is *not* classified as portfolio income for tax purposes?
   a. Interest income on savings accounts
   b. Dividends paid from a credit union
   c. Net rental income from real estate partnership
   d. Dividend income from stock
   e. All of the above are classified as portfolio income

LO 4.8   19. Which of the following types of income is passive income?
  a. Net rental income from real estate limited partnership investments
  b. Dividends from domestic corporations
  c. Wages
  d. Interest income from certificates of deposit
  e. None of the above

LO 4.8   20. Which of the following is classified as active income?
  a. Self-employment income from a small business
  b. Interest income
  c. Limited partnership income
  d. Bonus paid by an employer to an employee
  e. a. and d.

LO 4.8   21. Nancy has active modified adjusted gross income before passive losses of $75,000. She has a loss of $5,000 on a rental property she actively manages. How much of the loss is she allowed to take against the $75,000 of other income?
  a. None
  b. $2,500
  c. $5,000
  d. $25,000

LO 4.8   22. Ned has active modified adjusted gross income before passive losses of $250,000. He has a loss of $15,000 on rental property he actively manages. How much of the loss is he allowed to take against the $250,000 of other income?
  a. $15,000
  b. $10,000
  c. $5,000
  d. None

LO 4.8   23. Norm is a real estate professional with a real estate trade or business as defined in the tax law. He has $80,000 of business income and $40,000 of losses from actively managed real estate rentals. How much of the $40,000 in losses is he allowed to claim on his tax return?
  a. $40,000
  b. $25,000
  c. $20,000
  d. None

LO 4.9   24. Bonita earns $31,000 from her job, and she has $1,000 of interest income. She has itemized deductions of $35,000. There are no casualty or theft losses in the itemized deductions. What is Bonita's net operating loss for the current year?
  a. $0
  b. $1,000
  c. $3,000
  d. $4,000
  e. Some other amount

LO 4.9   25. Jim has a net operating loss in 2020. If he does not make any special elections, what is the first year to which Jim carries the net operating loss?
  a. 2015
  b. 2016
  c. 2017
  d. 2018
  e. 2020

LO 4.10 26. The qualified business income deduction is unavailable to which of the following businesses:
a. A sole proprietor dental practice that generates about $70,000 in income each year
b. An incorporated small tools manufacturer
c. A partnership operated by a husband and wife that sells wood carvings over the Internet
d. A S corporation that owns and operates a restaurant. The S corporation has six different owners.
e. The QBI deduction is available to all of the above.

LO 4.10 27. Qualified business income does not include which of the following:
a. Income from sales of goods
b. Deductions related to cost of goods sold
c. Deductions for business expenses such as rent
d. Interest income from an investment in bonds

LO 4.10 28. In 2020, Tracy generates a $10,000 loss from an otherwise qualified business activity. Fortunately, she also works as an employee and has taxable wages of $40,000. Tracy's 2020 QBI deduction is
a. $0
b. $2,000
c. $8,000
d. $6,000

GROUP 2:
PROBLEMS

LO 4.1
LO 4.2
LO 4.3
1. Martin sells a stock investment for $26,000 on August 2, 2020. Martin's adjusted basis in the stock is $15,000.
a. If Martin acquired the stock on November 15, 2018, calculate the amount and the nature of the gain or loss.

$_____

b. If Martin had acquired the stock on September 10, 2019, calculate the amount and nature of the gain or loss.

$_____

LO 4.1
LO 4.2
LO 4.3
LO 4.5
2. During 2020, Tom sold GM stock for $10,000. The stock was purchased 4 years ago for $13,000. Tom also sold Ford Motor Company bonds for $35,000. The bonds were purchased 2 months ago for $30,000. Home Depot stock, purchased 2 years ago for $1,000, was sold by Tom for $2,500. Calculate Tom's net gain or loss, and indicate the nature of the gain or loss.

$_____

LO 4.1
LO 4.2
LO 4.3
LO 4.5
3. Charu Khanna received a Form 1099-B showing the following stock transactions and basis during 2020:

Stock	Date Purchased	Date Sold	Sales Price ($)	Cost Basis ($)
4,000 shares Green Co.	06/04/09	08/05/20	12,000	3,000
500 shares Gold Co.	02/12/20	09/05/20	49,000	62,000
5,000 shares Blue Co.	02/04/10	10/08/20	18,000	22,000
100 shares Orange Co.	11/15/19	07/12/20	19,000	18,000

None of the stock is qualified small business stock. The stock basis was reported to the IRS. Calculate Charu's net capital gain or loss using Schedule D and Form 8949 on Pages 4-53 through 4-56.

SCHEDULE D	**Capital Gains and Losses**	OMB No. 1545-0074
(Form 1040)		**2020**
Department of the Treasury	▶ Attach to Form 1040, 1040-SR, or 1040-NR. ▶ Go to *www.irs.gov/ScheduleD* for instructions and the latest information. ▶ Use Form 8949 to list your transactions for lines 1b, 2, 3, 8b, 9, and 10.	Attachment
Internal Revenue Service (99)		Sequence No. **12**

Name(s) shown on return	Your social security number

Did you dispose of any investment(s) in a qualified opportunity fund during the tax year? ☐ **Yes** ☐ **No**

If "Yes," attach Form 8949 and see its instructions for additional requirements for reporting your gain or loss.

Part I **Short-Term Capital Gains and Losses—Generally Assets Held One Year or Less** (see instructions)

See instructions for how to figure the amounts to enter on the lines below. This form may be easier to complete if you round off cents to whole dollars.	**(d)** Proceeds (sales price)	**(e)** Cost (or other basis)	**(g)** Adjustments to gain or loss from Form(s) 8949, Part I, line 2, column (g)	**(h) Gain or (loss)** Subtract column (e) from column (d) and combine the result with column (g)
1a Totals for all short-term transactions reported on Form 1099-B for which basis was reported to the IRS and for which you have no adjustments (see instructions). However, if you choose to report all these transactions on Form 8949, leave this line blank and go to line 1b .				
1b Totals for all transactions reported on Form(s) 8949 with **Box A** checked				
2 Totals for all transactions reported on Form(s) 8949 with **Box B** checked				
3 Totals for all transactions reported on Form(s) 8949 with **Box C** checked				

4 Short-term gain from Form 6252 and short-term gain or (loss) from Forms 4684, 6781, and 8824 . .	**4**	
5 Net short-term gain or (loss) from partnerships, S corporations, estates, and trusts from Schedule(s) K-1	**5**	
6 Short-term capital loss carryover. Enter the amount, if any, from line 8 of your **Capital Loss Carryover Worksheet** in the instructions	**6**	( )
7 **Net short-term capital gain or (loss).** Combine lines 1a through 6 in column (h). If you have any long-term capital gains or losses, go to Part II below. Otherwise, go to Part III on the back	**7**	

Part II **Long-Term Capital Gains and Losses—Generally Assets Held More Than One Year** (see instructions)

See instructions for how to figure the amounts to enter on the lines below. This form may be easier to complete if you round off cents to whole dollars.	**(d)** Proceeds (sales price)	**(e)** Cost (or other basis)	**(g)** Adjustments to gain or loss from Form(s) 8949, Part II, line 2, column (g)	**(h) Gain or (loss)** Subtract column (e) from column (d) and combine the result with column (g)
8a Totals for all long-term transactions reported on Form 1099-B for which basis was reported to the IRS and for which you have no adjustments (see instructions). However, if you choose to report all these transactions on Form 8949, leave this line blank and go to line 8b .				
8b Totals for all transactions reported on Form(s) 8949 with **Box D** checked				
9 Totals for all transactions reported on Form(s) 8949 with **Box E** checked				
10 Totals for all transactions reported on Form(s) 8949 with **Box F** checked.				

11 Gain from Form 4797, Part I; long-term gain from Forms 2439 and 6252; and long-term gain or (loss) from Forms 4684, 6781, and 8824	**11**	
12 Net long-term gain or (loss) from partnerships, S corporations, estates, and trusts from Schedule(s) K-1	**12**	
13 Capital gain distributions. See the instructions	**13**	
14 Long-term capital loss carryover. Enter the amount, if any, from line 13 of your **Capital Loss Carryover Worksheet** in the instructions	**14**	( )
15 **Net long-term capital gain or (loss).** Combine lines 8a through 14 in column (h). Then, go to Part III on the back	**15**	

For Paperwork Reduction Act Notice, see your tax return instructions.   Cat. No. 11338H   Schedule D (Form 1040) 2020

Schedule D (Form 1040) 2020   Page **2**

| **Part III** | **Summary** |

16 Combine lines 7 and 15 and enter the result . . . . | **16** |

- If line 16 is a **gain,** enter the amount from line 16 on Form 1040, 1040-SR, or 1040-NR, line 7. Then, go to line 17 below.
- If line 16 is a **loss,** skip lines 17 through 20 below. Then, go to line 21. Also be sure to complete line 22.
- If line 16 is **zero,** skip lines 17 through 21 below and enter -0- on Form 1040, 1040-SR, or 1040-NR, line 7. Then, go to line 22.

17 Are lines 15 and 16 **both** gains?
☐ **Yes.** Go to line 18.
☐ **No.** Skip lines 18 through 21, and go to line 22.

18 If you are required to complete the **28% Rate Gain Worksheet** (see instructions), enter the amount, if any, from line 7 of that worksheet . . . . ▶ | **18** |

19 If you are required to complete the **Unrecaptured Section 1250 Gain Worksheet** (see instructions), enter the amount, if any, from line 18 of that worksheet . . . . ▶ | **19** |

20 Are lines 18 and 19 **both** zero or blank?
☐ **Yes.** Complete the **Qualified Dividends and Capital Gain Tax Worksheet** in the instructions for Forms 1040 and 1040-SR, line 16. **Don't** complete lines 21 and 22 below.

☐ **No.** Complete the **Schedule D Tax Worksheet** in the instructions. **Don't** complete lines 21 and 22 below.

21 If line 16 is a loss, enter here and on Form 1040, 1040-SR, or 1040-NR, line 7, the **smaller** of:

- The loss on line 16; or
- ($3,000), or if married filing separately, ($1,500)   } . . . . | **21** | ( ) |

Note: When figuring which amount is smaller, treat both amounts as positive numbers.

22 Do you have qualified dividends on Form 1040, 1040-SR, or 1040-NR, line 3a?

☐ **Yes.** Complete the **Qualified Dividends and Capital Gain Tax Worksheet** in the instructions for Forms 1040 and 1040-SR, line 16.

☐ **No.** Complete the rest of Form 1040, 1040-SR, or 1040-NR.

Schedule D (Form 1040) 2020

Form **8949**

Department of the Treasury
Internal Revenue Service

Sales and Other Dispositions of Capital Assets

▶ Go to *www.irs.gov/Form8949* for instructions and the latest information.
▶ File with your Schedule D to list your transactions for lines 1b, 2, 3, 8b, 9, and 10 of Schedule D.

OMB No. 1545-0074

2020

Attachment
Sequence No. **12A**

Name(s) shown on return

Social security number or taxpayer identification number

Before you check Box A, B, or C below, see whether you received any Form(s) 1099-B or substitute statement(s) from your broker. A substitute statement will have the same information as Form 1099-B. Either will show whether your basis (usually your cost) was reported to the IRS by your broker and may even tell you which box to check.

Part I   **Short-Term.** Transactions involving capital assets you held 1 year or less are generally short-term (see instructions). For long-term transactions, see page 2.

Note: You may aggregate all short-term transactions reported on Form(s) 1099-B showing basis was reported to the IRS and for which no adjustments or codes are required. Enter the totals directly on Schedule D, line 1a; you aren't required to report these transactions on Form 8949 (see instructions).

You *must* check Box A, B, *or* C below. Check only one box. If more than one box applies for your short-term transactions, complete a separate Form 8949, page 1, for each applicable box. If you have more short-term transactions than will fit on this page for one or more of the boxes, complete as many forms with the same box checked as you need.

- ☐ **(A)** Short-term transactions reported on Form(s) 1099-B showing basis was reported to the IRS (see **Note** above)
- ☐ **(B)** Short-term transactions reported on Form(s) 1099-B showing basis **wasn't** reported to the IRS
- ☐ **(C)** Short-term transactions not reported to you on Form 1099-B

1 (a) Description of property (Example: 100 sh. XYZ Co.)	(b) Date acquired (Mo., day, yr.)	(c) Date sold or disposed of (Mo., day, yr.)	(d) Proceeds (sales price) (see instructions)	(e) Cost or other basis. See the **Note** below and see *Column (e)* in the separate instructions	Adjustment, if any, to gain or loss. If you enter an amount in column (g), enter a code in column (f). See the separate instructions.		(h) Gain or (loss). Subtract column (e) from column (d) and combine the result with column (g)
					(f) Code(s) from instructions	(g) Amount of adjustment	
2 Totals. Add the amounts in columns (d), (e), (g), and (h) (subtract negative amounts). Enter each total here and include on your Schedule D, **line 1b** (if **Box A** above is checked), **line 2** (if **Box B** above is checked), or **line 3** (if **Box C** above is checked) ▶							

Note: If you checked Box A above but the basis reported to the IRS was incorrect, enter in column (e) the basis as reported to the IRS, and enter an adjustment in column (g) to correct the basis. See *Column (g)* in the separate instructions for how to figure the amount of the adjustment.

For Paperwork Reduction Act Notice, see your tax return instructions.   Cat. No. 37768Z   Form **8949** (2020)

Form 8949 (2020)   Attachment Sequence No. **12A**   Page **2**

Name(s) shown on return. Name and SSN or taxpayer identification no. not required if shown on other side	Social security number or taxpayer identification number

Before you check Box D, E, or F below, see whether you received any Form(s) 1099-B or substitute statement(s) from your broker. A substitute statement will have the same information as Form 1099-B. Either will show whether your basis (usually your cost) was reported to the IRS by your broker and may even tell you which box to check.

Part II **Long-Term.** Transactions involving capital assets you held more than 1 year are generally long-term (see instructions). For short-term transactions, see page 1.

Note: You may aggregate all long-term transactions reported on Form(s) 1099-B showing basis was reported to the IRS and for which no adjustments or codes are required. Enter the totals directly on Schedule D, line 8a; you aren't required to report these transactions on Form 8949 (see instructions).

You *must* **check Box D, E,** *or* **F below. Check only one box.** If more than one box applies for your long-term transactions, complete a separate Form 8949, page 2, for each applicable box. If you have more long-term transactions than will fit on this page for one or more of the boxes, complete as many forms with the same box checked as you need.

- ☐ **(D)** Long-term transactions reported on Form(s) 1099-B showing basis was reported to the IRS (see **Note** above)
- ☐ **(E)** Long-term transactions reported on Form(s) 1099-B showing basis **wasn't** reported to the IRS
- ☐ **(F)** Long-term transactions not reported to you on Form 1099-B

1 (a) Description of property (Example: 100 sh. XYZ Co.)	(b) Date acquired (Mo., day, yr.)	(c) Date sold or disposed of (Mo., day, yr.)	(d) Proceeds (sales price) (see instructions)	(e) Cost or other basis. See the **Note** below and see *Column (e)* in the separate instructions	Adjustment, if any, to gain or loss. If you enter an amount in column (g), enter a code in column (f). See the separate instructions.		(h) Gain or (loss). Subtract column (e) from column (d) and combine the result with column (g)
					(f) Code(s) from instructions	(g) Amount of adjustment	
2 Totals. Add the amounts in columns (d), (e), (g), and (h) (subtract negative amounts). Enter each total here and include on your Schedule D, **line 8b** (if **Box D** above is checked), **line 9** (if **Box E** above is checked), or **line 10** (if **Box F** above is checked) ▶							

Note: If you checked Box D above but the basis reported to the IRS was incorrect, enter in column (e) the basis as reported to the IRS, and enter an adjustment in column (g) to correct the basis. See *Column (g)* in the separate instructions for how to figure the amount of the adjustment.

Form **8949** (2020)

LO 4.3

4. Jocasta owns an apartment complex that she purchased 6 years ago for $700,000. Jocasta has made $75,000 of capital improvements on the complex, and her depreciation claimed on the building to date is $130,000. Calculate Jocasta's adjusted basis in the building.

$_____

LO 4.3

5. Chrissy receives 200 shares of Chevron stock as a gift from her father. The stock cost her father $9,000 10 years ago and is worth $10,500 at the date of the gift.
   a. If Chrissy sells the stock for $12,500, calculate the amount of the gain or loss on the sale.

$_____

   b. If Chrissy sells the stock for $4,600, calculate the amount of the gain or loss on the sale.

$_____

LO 4.4
LO 4.5

6. In 2020, Michael has net short-term capital losses of $1,500, a net long-term capital loss of $27,000, and other ordinary taxable income of $45,000.
   a. Calculate the amount of Michael's deduction for capital losses for 2020.

$_____

   b. Calculate the amount and nature of his capital loss carryforward.

$_____

   c. For how long may Michael carry forward the unused loss?

_____

LO 4.6

7. Larry Gaines, a single taxpayer, age 42, sells his personal residence on November 12, 2020, for $160,000. He lived in the house for 7 years. The expenses of the sale are $9,100, and he has made capital improvements of $11,000. Larry's cost basis in his residence is $85,000. On November 30, 2020, Larry purchases and occupies a new residence at a cost of $150,000. Calculate Larry's realized gain, recognized gain, and the adjusted basis of his new residence.
   a. Realized gain $_____
   b. Recognized gain $_____
   c. Adjusted basis of new residence $_____

LO 4.6

8. On July 1, 2020, Ted, age 73 and single, sells his personal residence of the last 30 years for $368,000. Ted's basis in his residence is $49,000. The expenses associated with the sale of his home total $22,000. On December 15, 2020, Ted purchases and occupies a new residence at a cost of $175,000. Calculate Ted's realized gain, recognized gain, and the adjusted basis of his new residence.
   a. Realized gain $_____
   b. Recognized gain $_____
   c. Adjusted basis of the new residence $_____

LO 4.7

9. Dick owns a house that he rents to college students. Dick receives $800 per month rent and incurs the following expenses during the year:

Real estate taxes	$1,250
Mortgage interest	1,500
Insurance	425
Repairs	562
Association dues	1,500

Dick purchased the house in 1980 for $48,000. The house is fully depreciated. Calculate Dick's net rental income for the year, assuming the house was rented for a full 12 months.

Rental income	$_____
Expenses:	
_____	_____
_____	_____
_____	_____
_____	_____
Net rental income	$_____

LO 4.7

10. Sherry rents her vacation home for 6 months and lives in it for 6 months during the year. Her gross rental income during the year is $6,000. Total real estate taxes for the home are $950, and interest on the home mortgage is $3,000. Annual utilities and maintenance expenses total $1,800, and depreciation expense is $4,500. Calculate Sherry's net income or loss from the vacation home for this tax year.

$_____

LO 4.8

11. Walter, a single taxpayer, purchased a limited partnership interest in a tax shelter in 1994. He also acquired a rental house in 2020, which he actively manages. During 2020, Walter's share of the partnership's losses was $30,000, and his rental house generated $20,000 in losses. Walter's modified adjusted gross income before passive losses is $130,000.

a. Calculate the amount of Walter's allowable loss for rental house activities for 2020.

$_____

b. Calculate the amount of Walter's allowable loss for the partnership activities for 2020.

$_____

c. What may be done with the unused losses, if anything?

_____

_____

_____

_____

LO 4.8

12. Clifford Johnson has a limited partnership investment and a rental condominium. Clifford actively manages the rental condominium. During 2020, his share of the loss from the limited partnership was $12,000, and his loss from the rental condo was $16,000. Assuming Clifford's modified adjusted gross income is $130,000 for 2020, and he has no prior year unallowed losses from either activity, complete Form 8582 on Page 4-60.

LO 4.9

13. Tyler, a single taxpayer, generates business income of $3,000 in 2016. In 2017, he generates an NOL of $2,000. In 2018, he incurs another NOL of $5,000. In 2019, he generates a modest business income of $6,000 and then in 2020, the COVID-19 pandemic results in an NOL of $13,000. Assume that in all years, Tyler adopts the NOL treatment that results in the earliest and greatest refund. Provide a chronological analysis of Tyler's treatment of NOLs through 2020.

LO 4.9

14. Julie, a single taxpayer, has completed her 2020 Schedule C and her net loss is $40,000. Her only other income is wages of $30,000. Julie takes the standard deduction of $12,400 in 2020.

a. Calculate Julie's taxable income or loss.

$_____

b. Calculate the business and nonbusiness portions of her taxable income or loss.

Business $_____

Nonbusiness $_____

c. Determine Julie's 2020 NOL.

$_____

LO 4.10   15. Sanjay is a single taxpayer that operates a curry cart on the streets of Baltimore. The business is operated as a sole proprietorship with no employees (Sanjay does everything). Sanjay's Schedule C reports income of $87,000. His taxable income is $80,000 and includes no capital gains. Compute Sanjay's QBI deduction.

$\underline{\hspace{3cm}}

LO 4.10   16. Rob Wriggle operates a small plumbing supplies business as a sole proprietor. In 2020, the plumbing business has gross business income of $421,000 and business expenses of $267,000, including wages paid of $58,000. The business sold some land that had been held for investment generating a long-term capital gain of $15,000. The business has $300,000 of qualified business property in 2020. Rob's wife, Marie, has wage income of $250,000. They jointly sold stocks in 2020 and generated a long-term capital gain of $13,000. Rob and Marie have no dependents and in 2020, they take the standard deduction of $24,800.
   a. What is Rob and Marie's taxable income before the QBI deduction?
   b. What is Rob and Marie's QBI?
   c. What is Rob and Marie's QBI deduction?
   d. Complete Form 8995-A on Pages 4-61 and 4-62 to report Rob's QBI deduction.

GROUP 3:
WRITING ASSIGNMENT

RESEARCH   You recently received the following e-mail from a client and friend:

Hey Great Student,

I cannot believe it is almost year end! Only a few days before it's 2021.

As you recall, I was lucky enough to win big at the casino back on New Year's Day earlier this year (thanks for celebrating with me). I took the $3,000 I won and bought 100 shares of stock in that cool new smartphone app company, TriviaAddiction. I just love playing that game. Anyway, the stock has done well, and I am thinking of selling before year end now that the price has reached $240 per share. Since you are my tax adviser, I thought I'd ask a couple of questions:

   1. Is there any reason to wait and sell later?
   2. If I don't sell, the price might go down (TriviaMaster seems to be replacing TriviaAddiction as the "hot" new game). I'm thinking the price might be as low as $220 by early next year.

My taxable income this year and next year is expected to be $40,000 (not including the stock sale). I think that puts me in the 12 percent tax bracket? Any suggestions on what I should do?

Thanks!

Sue

Prepare an e-mail to your friend Sue addressing her questions. Be certain to include estimates of the different after-tax outcomes she is suggesting. Sue is a single taxpayer and not a tax expert and so your language should reflect her limited understanding of tax law and avoid technical jargon. Although Sue is your friend, she is also a client and your e-mail should maintain a professional style.

Form **8582**

Department of the Treasury
Internal Revenue Service (99)

Passive Activity Loss Limitations

▶ See separate instructions.
▶ **Attach to Form 1040, 1040-SR, or 1041.**
▶ Go to *www.irs.gov/Form8582* for instructions and the latest information.

OMB No. 1545-1008

2020

Attachment
Sequence No. **858**

Name(s) shown on return

Identifying number

Part I   2020 Passive Activity Loss

Caution: Complete Worksheets 1, 2, and 3 before completing Part I.

Rental Real Estate Activities With Active Participation (For the definition of active participation, see **Special Allowance for Rental Real Estate Activities** in the instructions.)

1a	Activities with net income (enter the amount from Worksheet 1, column (a)) .	**1a**	
b	Activities with net loss (enter the amount from Worksheet 1, column (b)) . .	**1b** (	)
c	Prior years' unallowed losses (enter the amount from Worksheet 1, column (c))	**1c** (	)
d	Combine lines 1a, 1b, and 1c	**1d**	

Commercial Revitalization Deductions From Rental Real Estate Activities

2a	Commercial revitalization deductions from Worksheet 2, column (a) . . .	**2a** (	)
b	Prior year unallowed commercial revitalization deductions from Worksheet 2, column (b)	**2b** (	)
c	Add lines 2a and 2b	**2c** (	)

All Other Passive Activities

3a	Activities with net income (enter the amount from Worksheet 3, column (a)) .	**3a**	
b	Activities with net loss (enter the amount from Worksheet 3, column (b)) . .	**3b** (	)
c	Prior years' unallowed losses (enter the amount from Worksheet 3, column (c))	**3c** (	)
d	Combine lines 3a, 3b, and 3c	**3d**	

4	Combine lines 1d, 2c, and 3d. If this line is zero or more, stop here and include this form with your return; all losses are allowed, including any prior year unallowed losses entered on line 1c, 2b, or 3c. Report the losses on the forms and schedules normally used	**4**	

If line 4 is a loss and: • Line 1d is a loss, go to Part II.
                             • Line 2c is a loss (and line 1d is zero or more), skip Part II and go to Part III.
                             • Line 3d is a loss (and lines 1d and 2c are zero or more), skip Parts II and III and go to line 15.

Caution: If your filing status is married filing separately and you lived with your spouse at any time during the year, **do not** complete Part II or Part III. Instead, go to line 15.

Part II   Special Allowance for Rental Real Estate Activities With Active Participation

Note: Enter all numbers in Part II as positive amounts. See instructions for an example.

5	Enter the **smaller** of the loss on line 1d or the loss on line 4		**5**	
6	Enter $150,000. If married filing separately, see instructions	**6**		
7	Enter modified adjusted gross income, but not less than zero. See instructions	**7**		
	Note: If line 7 is greater than or equal to line 6, skip lines 8 and 9, enter -0- on line 10. Otherwise, go to line 8.			
8	Subtract line 7 from line 6	**8**		
9	Multiply line 8 by 50% (0.50). **Do not** enter more than $25,000. If married filing separately, see instructions		**9**	
10	Enter the **smaller** of line 5 or line 9		**10**	

If line 2c is a loss, go to Part III. Otherwise, go to line 15.

Part III   Special Allowance for Commercial Revitalization Deductions From Rental Real Estate Activities

Note: Enter all numbers in Part III as positive amounts. See the example for Part II in the instructions.

11	Enter $25,000 reduced by the amount, if any, on line 10. If married filing separately, see instructions .	**11**	
12	Enter the loss from line 4	**12**	
13	Reduce line 12 by the amount on line 10	**13**	
14	Enter the **smallest** of line 2c (treated as a positive amount), line 11, or line 13	**14**	

Part IV   Total Losses Allowed

15	Add the income, if any, on lines 1a and 3a and enter the total	**15**	
16	**Total losses allowed from all passive activities for 2020.** Add lines 10, 14, and 15. See instructions to find out how to report the losses on your tax return	**16**	

For Paperwork Reduction Act Notice, see instructions.   Cat. No. 63704F   Form **8582** (2020)

Form **8995-A**	**Qualified Business Income Deduction**	OMB No. 1545-0123
Department of the Treasury Internal Revenue Service	▶ Attach to your tax return. ▶ Go to *www.irs.gov/Form8995A* for instructions and the latest information.	**2019*** Attachment Sequence No. **55A**

Name(s) shown on return	Your taxpayer identification number

Part I   Trade, Business, or Aggregation Information

Complete Schedules A, B, and/or C (Form 8995-A), as applicable, before starting Part I. Attach additional worksheets when needed. See instructions.

1	(a) Trade, business, or aggregation name	(b) Check if specified service	(c) Check if aggregation	(d) Taxpayer identification number	(e) Check if patron
A		☐	☐		☐
B		☐	☐		☐
C		☐	☐		☐

Part II   Determine Your Adjusted Qualified Business Income

			A	B	C
2	Qualified business income from the trade, business, or aggregation. See instructions	2			
3	Multiply line 2 by 20% (0.20). If your taxable income is $160,700 or less ($160,725 if married filing separately; $321,400 if married filing jointly), skip lines 4 through 12 and enter the amount from line 3 on line 13	3	see note below		
4	Allocable share of W-2 wages from the trade, business, or aggregation	4			
5	Multiply line 4 by 50% (0.50)	5			
6	Multiply line 4 by 25% (0.25)	6			
7	Allocable share of the unadjusted basis immediately after acquisition (UBIA) of all qualified property	7			
8	Multiply line 7 by 2.5% (0.025)	8			
9	Add lines 6 and 8	9			
10	Enter the greater of line 5 or line 9	10			
11	W-2 wage and qualified property limitation. Enter the smaller of line 3 or line 10	11			
12	Phased-in reduction. Enter the amount from line 26, if any. See instructions	12			
13	Qualified business income deduction before patron reduction. Enter the greater of line 11 or line 12	13			
14	Patron reduction. Enter the amount from Schedule D (Form 8995-A), line 6, if any. See instructions	14			
15	Qualified business income component. Subtract line 14 from line 13	15			
16	Total qualified business income component. Add all amounts reported on line 15 . . . . ▶	16			

For Privacy Act and Paperwork Reduction Act Notice, see separate instructions.   Cat. No. 71661B   Form **8995-A** (2019)

*Please go to www.irs.gov to download the latest Form 8995-A. The 2020 version of Form 8995-A was not available as we went to print. If using the prior year form included in the textbook, be sure and use updated income limits on Line 3 and Line 21 ($326,600 for married filing jointly and $163,300 for all other).

Form 8995-A (2019)   Page **2**

Part III   Phased-in Reduction*

Complete Part III only if your taxable income is more than $160,700 but not $210,700 ($160,725 and $210,725 if married filing separately; $321,400 and $421,400 if married filing jointly) and line 10 is less than line 3. Otherwise, skip Part III.

			A	B	C
17	Enter the amounts from line 3	**17**			
18	Enter the amounts from line 10	**18**			
19	Subtract line 18 from line 17	**19**			
20	Taxable income before qualified business income deduction	**20**			
21	Threshold. Enter $160,700 ($160,725 if married filing separately; $321,400 if married filing jointly)	**21**	see note below		
22	Subtract line 21 from line 20	**22**			
23	Phase-in range. Enter $50,000 ($100,000 if married filing jointly)	**23**			
24	Phase-in percentage. Divide line 22 by line 23	**24**	%		
25	Total phase-in reduction. Multiply line 19 by line 24	**25**			
26	Qualified business income after phase-in reduction. Subtract line 25 from line 17. Enter this amount here and on line 12, for the corresponding trade or business	**26**			

Part IV   Determine Your Qualified Business Income Deduction

27	Total qualified business income component from all qualified trades, businesses, or aggregations. Enter the amount from line 16	**27**	
28	Qualified REIT dividends and publicly traded partnership (PTP) income or (loss). See instructions	**28**	
29	Qualified REIT dividends and PTP (loss) carryforward from prior years . . .	**29**	( )
30	Total qualified REIT dividends and PTP income. Combine lines 28 and 29. If less than zero, enter -0-	**30**	
31	REIT and PTP component. Multiply line 30 by 20% (0.20)	**31**	
32	Qualified business income deduction before the income limitation. Add lines 27 and 31 . . . . ▶	**32**	
33	Taxable income before qualified business income deduction	**33**	
34	Net capital gain. See instructions	**34**	
35	Subtract line 34 from line 33. If zero or less, enter -0-	**35**	
36	Income limitation. Multiply line 35 by 20% (0.20)	**36**	
37	Qualified business income deduction before the domestic production activities deduction (DPAD) under section 199A(g). Enter the smaller of line 32 or line 36 . . . . ▶	**37**	
38	DPAD under section 199A(g) allocated from an agricultural or horticultural cooperative. Don't enter more than line 33 minus line 37	**38**	
39	Total qualified business income deduction. Add lines 37 and 38 . . . . ▶	**39**	
40	Total qualified REIT dividends and PTP (loss) carryforward. Combine lines 28 and 29. If zero or greater, enter -0-	**40**	( )

Form **8995-A** (2019)

*Please go to www.irs.gov to download the latest Form 8995-A. The 2020 version of Form 8995-A was not available as we went to print. If using the prior year form included in the textbook, be sure and use updated income limits on Line 3 and Line 21 ($326,600 for married filing jointly and $163,300 for all other).

COMPREHENSIVE PROBLEMS

1. Skylar and Walter Black have been married for 25 years. They live at 883 Scrub Brush Street, Apt. 52B, Las Vegas, NV 89125. Skylar is a stay-at-home parent and Walt is a high school teacher. Skylar's Social Security number is 222-43-7690 and Walt's is 700-01-0002. Neither are age 65 or older. The Blacks provide all the support for Skylar's mother, Rebecca Backin (Social Security number 411-66-2121), who lives in a nursing home in Reno, NV and has no income. Walter's father, Alton Black (Social Security number 343-22-8899), lives with the Blacks in Las Vegas. Although Alton received Social Security benefits of $7,600 in 2020, the Blacks provide over half of Alton's support. Skylar and Walt claim a $500 other dependent credit each for Rebecca and Alton. Walt's earnings from teaching are:

a Employee's social security number 700-01-0002	OMB No. 1545-0008	Safe, accurate, FAST! Use *IRS e~file*	Visit the IRS website at www.irs.gov/efile

b Employer identification number (EIN) 31-1239867	1 Wages, tips, other compensation 54,300.00	2 Federal income tax withheld 4,100.00

c Employer's name, address, and ZIP code Las Vegas School District 2234 Vegas Valley Drive Las Vegas, NV 89169	3 Social security wages 54,300.00	4 Social security tax withheld 3,366.60
	5 Medicare wages and tips 54,300.00	6 Medicare tax withheld 787.35
	7 Social security tips	8 Allocated tips

d Control number	9	10 Dependent care benefits

e Employee's first name and initial Last name Suff. Walter Black 883 Scrub Brush Street, Apt. 52B Las Vegas, NV 89125	11 Nonqualified plans	12a See instructions for box 12 DD 7,900.00
	13 Statutory employee ☐ Retirement plan ☒ Third-party sick pay ☐	12b
	14 Other	12c
		12d

f Employee's address and ZIP code						
15 State Employer's state ID number NV	16 State wages, tips, etc.	17 State income tax	18 Local wages, tips, etc.	19 Local income tax	20 Locality name

Form **W-2** Wage and Tax Statement   2020   Department of the Treasury—Internal Revenue Service

Copy B—To Be Filed With Employee's **FEDERAL** Tax Return.
This information is being furnished to the Internal Revenue Service.

    The Blacks moved from Maine to Nevada. As a result, they sold their house in Maine on January 4, 2020. They originally paid $75,000 for the home on July 3, 1995, but managed to sell it for $604,000. They spent $14,000 on improvements over the years. They are currently renting in Las Vegas while they look for a new home.

The Blacks received the following 1099-DIV from their mutual fund investments:

☐ CORRECTED (if checked)

PAYER'S name, street address, city or town, state or province, country, ZIP or foreign postal code, and telephone no. Cyber Equities Fund 41 Wall Street New York, NY 10005	1a Total ordinary dividends $ 1,500.00	OMB No. 1545-0110 2020 Form 1099-DIV	Dividends and Distributions
	1b Qualified dividends $ 1,050.00		
	2a Total capital gain distr. $ 6,700.23	2b Unrecap. Sec. 1250 gain $	Copy B For Recipient
PAYER'S TIN 17-1234326 RECIPIENT'S TIN 222-43-7690	2c Section 1202 gain $	2d Collectibles (28%) gain $	
RECIPIENT'S name Skylar B. Black	3 Nondividend distributions $	4 Federal income tax withheld $	This is important tax information and is being furnished to the IRS. If you are required to file a return, a negligence penalty or other sanction may be imposed on you if this income is taxable and the IRS determines that it has not been reported.
Street address (including apt. no.) 883 Scrub Brush Street, #52B	5 Section 199A dividends $	6 Investment expenses $	
City or town, state or province, country, and ZIP or foreign postal code Las Vegas, NV 89125	7 Foreign tax paid $	8 Foreign country or U.S. possession	
	9 Cash liquidation distributions $	10 Noncash liquidation distributions $	
FATCA filing requirement ☐	11 Exempt-interest dividends $	12 Specified private activity bond interest dividends $	
Account number (see instructions)	13 State 14 State identification no. - - - - - - - -	15 State tax withheld $ $	

Form **1099-DIV**   (keep for your records)   www.irs.gov/Form1099DIV   Department of the Treasury - Internal Revenue Service

The Blacks own a ski condo located at 123 Buncombe Lane, Brian Head, UT 84719. The condo was rented for 185 days during 2020 and used by the Blacks for 15 days. The rental activity does not rise to the level to qualify for the QBI deduction. Pertinent information about the condo rental is as follows:

Rental income	$23,700
Mortgage interest reported on Form 1098	16,000
Homeowners' association dues	5,200
Utilities	3,400
Maintenance	6,600
Depreciation (assume fully depreciated)	0

The above amounts do not reflect any allocation between rental and personal use of the condo. The Blacks are active managers of the condo.

The Blacks received a $2,400 EIP in 2020.

Required: Complete the Black's federal tax return for 2020. Use Form 1040, Schedule 1, Schedule D, Form 8949, Schedule E (page 1 only), Form 8582 (page 1 only) and the Qualified Dividends and Capital Gain Tax Worksheet to complete their tax return.

2A. Dr. George E. Beeper is a single taxpayer born on September 22, 1972. He lives at 45 Mountain View Dr., Apt. 321, Spokane, WA 99210. Dr. Beeper's Social Security number is 775-88-9531. Dr. Beeper works for the Pine Medical Group, and his earnings and income tax withholding for 2020 are:

a Employee's social security number 775-88-9531	OMB No. 1545-0008	Safe, accurate, FAST! Use	IRS e-file	Visit the IRS website at www.irs.gov/efile
b Employer identification number (EIN) 36-1389676		**1** Wages, tips, other compensation 134,100.00		**2** Federal income tax withheld 21,000.00
c Employer's name, address, and ZIP code Pine Medical Group 800 W. 7th Ave. Spokane, WA 92204		**3** Social security wages 134,100.00		**4** Social security tax withheld 8,314.20
		5 Medicare wages and tips 134,100.00		**6** Medicare tax withheld 1,944.45
		7 Social security tips		**8** Allocated tips
d Control number		**9**		**10** Dependent care benefits
e Employee's first name and initial Last name Suff. George Beeper 45 Mountain View Drive Apt 321 Spokane, WA 99210		**11** Nonqualified plans		**12a** See instructions for box 12 DD 5,800.00
		13 Statutory employee ☐ Retirement plan ☒ Third-party sick pay ☐		**12b**
		14 Other		**12c**
				12d
f Employee's address and ZIP code				

15 State Employer's state ID number	**16** State wages, tips, etc.	**17** State income tax	**18** Local wages, tips, etc.	**19** Local income tax	**20** Locality name
WA					

Form **W-2** Wage and Tax Statement   **2020**   Department of the Treasury—Internal Revenue Service
Copy B—To Be Filed With Employee's **FEDERAL** Tax Return.
This information is being furnished to the Internal Revenue Service.

Dr. Beeper owns a rental house located at 672 Lake Street, Spokane, WA 99212. The house rents for $1,000 per month and was rented for the entire year. The following are the related expenses for the rental house:

Real estate taxes	$ 6,000
Mortgage interest	14,500
Insurance	2,200
Depreciation (assume fully depreciated)	0
Repairs	600
Maintenance	2,000

The house was purchased on July 5, 1985. Dr. Beeper handles all rental activities (e.g., rent collection, finding tenants, etc.) himself. He spends about 10 hours per month on the rental.

In 2020, Dr. Beeper sold his primary residence as he wished to move to an apartment to avoid the maintenance and upkeep of a single-family home. Dr. Beeper's home sold on February 12, 2020 for $345,000 net after commissions. He acquired the home on June 3, 2002 for $260,000 and had made improvements of $10,000.

Dr. Beeper was divorced on January 1, 2014. The divorce decree requires Dr. Beeper to pay his ex-wife, Meredith Gray (Social Security number 333-45-1234), $800 per month. Dr. Beeper made all his monthly alimony payments in 2020.

Dr. Beeper did not receive an EIP in 2020.

Required: Complete Dr. Beeper's federal tax return for 2020. Determine if Form 8949 and Schedule D are required. If so, use those forms and Form 1040, Schedule E (page 1 only), and Form 8582 (page 1 only) to complete this tax return. Do not complete Form 4562 for reporting depreciation.

2B. In 2020, Professor Patricia (Patty) Pâté retired from the Palm Springs Culinary Arts Academy (PSCAA). She is a single taxpayer and is 62 years old. Patty lives at 98 Colander Street, Apt. 206D, Henderson, NV 89052. Professor Pâté's Social Security number is 565-66-9378. In 2020, Patty had just a few months of salary from her previous job:

Wages	$9,900
Federal tax withheld	450
State tax withheld	0

Patty owns a rental condo located at 392 Spatula Way, Mount Charleston, NV 89124. The condo rented for two months of 2020 for $850 a month but a mold problem was discovered in the condo, her renters moved out, and she was unable to rent the apartment after the repairs (despite Patty vigorously pursuing new tenants). Patty actively manages the property herself. The following are the related expenses for the rental house:

Real estate taxes	$4,000
Mortgage interest	9,000
Insurance	550
Depreciation (assume fully depreciated)	0
Homeowners' Association dues	1,250
Repairs	1,200
Gardening	575
Advertising	1,200

The condo was purchased on August 31, 1981. Patty handles all rental activities (e.g., rent collection, finding tenants, etc.) herself.

In 2020, Patty sold her beloved home of almost 30 years for $380,000 on February 27, 2020. Her basis in the home was $120,000 and she acquired the home sometime in July of 1990 (she could not remember the day).

Patty received a $1,200 EIP in 2020.

Required: Complete Professor Pâté's federal tax return for 2020. Use Form 1040, Schedule D, Form 8949, Schedule E, and Form 8582 (page 1 only) to complete this tax return. Also, to compute Patty's net operating loss carryforward, prepare only Schedule A of Form 1045.

GROUP 5:
CUMULATIVE SOFTWARE PROBLEM

1. The following additional information is available for the Albert and Allison Gaytor family.

The Gaytors own a rental beach house in Hawaii. The beach house was rented for the full year during 2020 and was not used by the Gaytors during the year. The Gaytors were active participants in the management of the rental house but the activity is not eligible for a QBI deduction. Pertinent information about the rental house is as follows:

Address: 1237 Pineapple St., Lihue, HI 96766

Gross rental income	$20,000
Mortgage interest	8,000
Real estate taxes	2,200
Utilities	1,400
Cleaning	2,400
Repairs	650

The house is fully depreciated so there is no depreciation expense.

Albert and Allison received the following combined statements 1099-DIV and 1099-B from their investment manager:

IMPORTANT TAX DOCUMENT
2020 Form 1099-DIV
Dividends and Distributions

RECIPIENT'S TIN: 266-51-1966

Albert T. Gaytor
Allison A Gaytor
JT TEN WROS
12340 Cocoshell Rd
Coral Gables, FL 33134

Fortress Securities

PO Box 1300
Gaithersburg, MD 20877
Copy B for Recipient

Fund Name	Total Ordinary Dividends	Qualified Dividends	Capital Gain Distrib	Unrecap 1250 Gain	Nondividend Distrib	Fed Tax Withheld	Exempt-Interest Dividends	State Tax Withheld
Peach Fund	0.00	0.00	475.00			0.00		

2020 Form 1099-B
Proceeds from Broker and Barter Exchange Transactions

Descript.	Date Acq	Date Sold	Proceeds	Cost	Fed Tax Withheld	Proceeds Reported to IRS	Basis Reported to IRS
100 shs. Orange Co	02/11/2020	04/16/2020	$3,000.00	$2,350.00	$0.00	Net	Yes
100 shs. Banana Co.	07/17/2019	07/31/2020	2,100.00	4,200.00	0.00	Net	Yes
100 shs Grape Corp	12/18/2019	09/25/2020	9,050.00	10,400.00	0.00	Net	Yes
5 $1,000 Par Value Bonds due 4/2020	12/30/2010	01/02/2020	5,100.00	5,415.00	0.00	Net	Yes
5,011.23 shs. Peach Mutual Fund	05/30/2011	10/22/2020	59,750.00	56,000.00	0.00	Net	Yes

On January 12, 2020, Albert and Allison sold their personal residence for $716,000 and purchased a new house for $725,000. This was their personal residence before and after the divorce (they have lived in it together for three years since remarrying). The old house cost $120,000 back in January of 2008 and they added on a new bedroom and bathroom a few years ago for a cost of $20,000. They also built a pool for a cost of $61,500. They moved into the new house on January 19, 2020.

Required: Combine this new information about the Gaytor family with the information from Chapters 1–3 and complete a revised 2020 tax return for Albert and Allison. Be sure to save your data input files since this case will be expanded with more tax information in later chapters.

Form 1040

Department of the Treasury—Internal Revenue Service (99)

U.S. Individual Income Tax Return 2020 OMB No. 1545-0074 | IRS Use Only—Do not write or staple in this space.

Filing Status
Check only one box.

☐ Single ☐ Married filing jointly ☐ Married filing separately (MFS) ☐ Head of household (HOH) ☐ Qualifying widow(er) (QW)

If you checked the MFS box, enter the name of your spouse. If you checked the HOH or QW box, enter the child's name if the qualifying person is a child but not your dependent ▶

Your first name and middle initial	Last name		Your social security number

If joint return, spouse's first name and middle initial	Last name		Spouse's social security number

Home address (number and street). If you have a P.O. box, see instructions.		Apt. no.	**Presidential Election Campaign**

City, town, or post office. If you have a foreign address, also complete spaces below.	State	ZIP code	Check here if you, or your spouse if filing jointly, want $3 to go to this fund. Checking a box below will not change your tax or refund.

Foreign country name	Foreign province/state/county	Foreign postal code	☐ You ☐ Spouse

At any time during 2020, did you receive, sell, send, exchange, or otherwise acquire any financial interest in any virtual currency? ☐ Yes ☐ No

Standard Deduction

Someone can claim: ☐ You as a dependent ☐ Your spouse as a dependent
☐ Spouse itemizes on a separate return or you were a dual-status alien

Age/Blindness You: ☐ Were born before January 2, 1956 ☐ Are blind **Spouse:** ☐ Was born before January 2, 1956 ☐ Is blind

Dependents (see instructions):

If more than four dependents, see instructions and check here ▶ ☐

(1) First name Last name	(2) Social security number	(3) Relationship to you	(4) ✔ if qualifies for (see instructions):	
			Child tax credit	Credit for other dependents
			☐	☐
			☐	☐
			☐	☐
			☐	☐

Attach Sch. B if required.

1	Wages, salaries, tips, etc. Attach Form(s) W-2		**1**	
2a	Tax-exempt interest	2a	**b** Taxable interest	**2b**
3a	Qualified dividends	3a	**b** Ordinary dividends	**3b**
4a	IRA distributions	4a	**b** Taxable amount	**4b**
5a	Pensions and annuities	5a	**b** Taxable amount	**5b**
6a	Social security benefits	6a	**b** Taxable amount	**6b**
7	Capital gain or (loss). Attach Schedule D if required. If not required, check here ▶ ☐			**7**
8	Other income from Schedule 1, line 9			**8**
9	Add lines 1, 2b, 3b, 4b, 5b, 6b, 7, and 8. This is your **total income** ▶			**9**
10	Adjustments to income:			
a	From Schedule 1, line 22		10a	
b	Charitable contributions if you take the standard deduction. See instructions		10b	
c	Add lines 10a and 10b. These are your **total adjustments to income** ▶			**10c**
11	Subtract line 10c from line 9. This is your **adjusted gross income** ▶			**11**
12	**Standard deduction or itemized deductions** (from Schedule A)			**12**
13	Qualified business income deduction. Attach Form 8995 or Form 8995-A			**13**
14	Add lines 12 and 13			**14**
15	**Taxable income.** Subtract line 14 from line 11. If zero or less, enter -0-			**15**

Standard Deduction for—
- Single or Married filing separately, $12,400
- Married filing jointly or Qualifying widow(er), $24,800
- Head of household, $18,650
- If you checked any box under Standard Deduction, see instructions.

For Disclosure, Privacy Act, and Paperwork Reduction Act Notice, see separate instructions.   Cat. No. 11320B   Form **1040** (2020)

Form 1040 (2020)   Page **2**

16	**Tax** (see instructions). Check if any from Form(s): **1** ☐ 8814 **2** ☐ 4972 **3** ☐ _____	16	
17	Amount from Schedule 2, line 3	17	
18	Add lines 16 and 17	18	
19	Child tax credit or credit for other dependents	19	
20	Amount from Schedule 3, line 7	20	
21	Add lines 19 and 20	21	
22	Subtract line 21 from line 18. If zero or less, enter -0-	22	
23	Other taxes, including self-employment tax, from Schedule 2, line 10	23	
24	Add lines 22 and 23. This is your **total tax** ▶	24	
25	Federal income tax withheld from:		
a	Form(s) W-2	25a	
b	Form(s) 1099	25b	
c	Other forms (see instructions)	25c	
d	Add lines 25a through 25c	25d	
26	2020 estimated tax payments and amount applied from 2019 return	26	
27	Earned income credit (EIC)	27	
28	Additional child tax credit. Attach Schedule 8812	28	
29	American opportunity credit from Form 8863, line 8	29	
30	Recovery rebate credit. See instructions	30	
31	Amount from Schedule 3, line 13	31	
32	Add lines 27 through 31. These are your **total other payments and refundable credits** ▶	32	
33	Add lines 25d, 26, and 32. These are your **total payments**	33	

• If you have a qualifying child, attach Sch. EIC.
• If you have nontaxable combat pay, see instructions.

Refund

Direct deposit?
See instructions.

34	If line 33 is more than line 24, subtract line 24 from line 33. This is the amount you **overpaid**	34	
35a	Amount of line 34 you want **refunded to you**. If Form 8888 is attached, check here ▶ ☐	35a	
▶ b	Routing number _____ ▶ c Type: ☐ Checking ☐ Savings		
▶ d	Account number _____		
36	Amount of line 34 you want **applied to your 2021 estimated tax** ▶	36	

Amount You Owe

For details on how to pay, see instructions.

37	Subtract line 33 from line 24. This is the **amount you owe now** ▶	37	
	Note: Schedule H and Schedule SE filers, line 37 may not represent all of the taxes you owe for 2020. See Schedule 3, line 12e, and its instructions for details.		
38	Estimated tax penalty (see instructions) ▶	38	

Third Party Designee

Do you want to allow another person to discuss this return with the IRS? See instructions ▶ ☐ **Yes.** Complete below. ☐ **No**

Designee's name ▶ _____ Phone no. ▶ _____ Personal identification number (PIN) ▶ _____

Sign Here

Joint return?
See instructions.
Keep a copy for your records.

Under penalties of perjury, I declare that I have examined this return and accompanying schedules and statements, and to the best of my knowledge and belief, they are true, correct, and complete. Declaration of preparer (other than taxpayer) is based on all information of which preparer has any knowledge.

Your signature	Date	Your occupation	If the IRS sent you an Identity Protection PIN, enter it here (see inst.) ▶
Spouse's signature. If a joint return, **both** must sign.	Date	Spouse's occupation	If the IRS sent your spouse an Identity Protection PIN, enter it here (see inst.) ▶
Phone no.		Email address	

Paid Preparer Use Only

Preparer's name	Preparer's signature	Date	PTIN	Check if: ☐ Self-employed
Firm's name ▶			Phone no. ▶	
Firm's address ▶			Firm's EIN ▶	

Go to *www.irs.gov/Form1040* for instructions and the latest information.   Form **1040** (2020)

SCHEDULE 1
(Form 1040)

Department of the Treasury
Internal Revenue Service

Additional Income and Adjustments to Income

▶ Attach to Form 1040, 1040-SR, or 1040-NR.
▶ Go to *www.irs.gov/Form1040* for instructions and the latest information.

OMB No. 1545-0074

2020

Attachment
Sequence No. **01**

Name(s) shown on Form 1040, 1040-SR, or 1040-NR

Your social security number

Part I Additional Income

1	Taxable refunds, credits, or offsets of state and local income taxes	**1**	
2a	Alimony received	**2a**	
b	Date of original divorce or separation agreement (see instructions) ▶ _____		
3	Business income or (loss). Attach Schedule C	**3**	
4	Other gains or (losses). Attach Form 4797	**4**	
5	Rental real estate, royalties, partnerships, S corporations, trusts, etc. Attach Schedule E	**5**	
6	Farm income or (loss). Attach Schedule F	**6**	
7	Unemployment compensation	**7**	
8	Other income. List type and amount ▶ _____		
		8	
9	Combine lines 1 through 8. Enter here and on Form 1040, 1040-SR, or 1040-NR, line 8	**9**	

Part II Adjustments to Income

10	Educator expenses	**10**	
11	Certain business expenses of reservists, performing artists, and fee-basis government officials. Attach Form 2106	**11**	
12	Health savings account deduction. Attach Form 8889	**12**	
13	Moving expenses for members of the Armed Forces. Attach Form 3903	**13**	
14	Deductible part of self-employment tax. Attach Schedule SE	**14**	
15	Self-employed SEP, SIMPLE, and qualified plans	**15**	
16	Self-employed health insurance deduction	**16**	
17	Penalty on early withdrawal of savings	**17**	
18a	Alimony paid	**18a**	
b	Recipient's SSN . . . . ▶		
c	Date of original divorce or separation agreement (see instructions) ▶ _____		
19	IRA deduction	**19**	
20	Student loan interest deduction	**20**	
21	Tuition and fees deduction. Attach Form 8917	**21**	
22	Add lines 10 through 21. These are your **adjustments to income.** Enter here and on Form 1040, 1040-SR, or 1040-NR, line 10a	**22**	

For Paperwork Reduction Act Notice, see your tax return instructions. Cat. No. 71479F **Schedule 1 (Form 1040) 2020**

SCHEDULE D
(Form 1040)

Department of the Treasury
Internal Revenue Service (99)

Capital Gains and Losses

▶ Attach to Form 1040, 1040-SR, or 1040-NR.
▶ Go to *www.irs.gov/ScheduleD* for instructions and the latest information.
▶ Use Form 8949 to list your transactions for lines 1b, 2, 3, 8b, 9, and 10.

OMB No. 1545-0074

2020

Attachment
Sequence No. **12**

Name(s) shown on return

Your social security number

Did you dispose of any investment(s) in a qualified opportunity fund during the tax year? ☐ **Yes** ☐ **No**
If "Yes," attach Form 8949 and see its instructions for additional requirements for reporting your gain or loss.

Part I   **Short-Term Capital Gains and Losses—Generally Assets Held One Year or Less** (see instructions)

See instructions for how to figure the amounts to enter on the lines below. This form may be easier to complete if you round off cents to whole dollars.	**(d)** Proceeds (sales price)	**(e)** Cost (or other basis)	**(g)** Adjustments to gain or loss from Form(s) 8949, Part I, line 2, column (g)	**(h) Gain or (loss)** Subtract column (e) from column (d) and combine the result with column (g)
1a Totals for all short-term transactions reported on Form 1099-B for which basis was reported to the IRS and for which you have no adjustments (see instructions). However, if you choose to report all these transactions on Form 8949, leave this line blank and go to line 1b .				
1b Totals for all transactions reported on Form(s) 8949 with **Box A** checked				
2 Totals for all transactions reported on Form(s) 8949 with **Box B** checked				
3 Totals for all transactions reported on Form(s) 8949 with **Box C** checked				

4 Short-term gain from Form 6252 and short-term gain or (loss) from Forms 4684, 6781, and 8824 . .	**4**	
5 Net short-term gain or (loss) from partnerships, S corporations, estates, and trusts from Schedule(s) K-1	**5**	
6 Short-term capital loss carryover. Enter the amount, if any, from line 8 of your **Capital Loss Carryover Worksheet** in the instructions	**6** ( )
7 **Net short-term capital gain or (loss).** Combine lines 1a through 6 in column (h). If you have any long-term capital gains or losses, go to Part II below. Otherwise, go to Part III on the back	**7**	

Part II   **Long-Term Capital Gains and Losses—Generally Assets Held More Than One Year** (see instructions)

See instructions for how to figure the amounts to enter on the lines below. This form may be easier to complete if you round off cents to whole dollars.	**(d)** Proceeds (sales price)	**(e)** Cost (or other basis)	**(g)** Adjustments to gain or loss from Form(s) 8949, Part II, line 2, column (g)	**(h) Gain or (loss)** Subtract column (e) from column (d) and combine the result with column (g)
8a Totals for all long-term transactions reported on Form 1099-B for which basis was reported to the IRS and for which you have no adjustments (see instructions). However, if you choose to report all these transactions on Form 8949, leave this line blank and go to line 8b .				
8b Totals for all transactions reported on Form(s) 8949 with **Box D** checked				
9 Totals for all transactions reported on Form(s) 8949 with **Box E** checked				
10 Totals for all transactions reported on Form(s) 8949 with **Box F** checked.				

11 Gain from Form 4797, Part I; long-term gain from Forms 2439 and 6252; and long-term gain or (loss) from Forms 4684, 6781, and 8824	**11**	
12 Net long-term gain or (loss) from partnerships, S corporations, estates, and trusts from Schedule(s) K-1	**12**	
13 Capital gain distributions. See the instructions	**13**	
14 Long-term capital loss carryover. Enter the amount, if any, from line 13 of your **Capital Loss Carryover Worksheet** in the instructions	**14** ( )
15 **Net long-term capital gain or (loss).** Combine lines 8a through 14 in column (h). Then, go to Part III on the back	**15**	

For Paperwork Reduction Act Notice, see your tax return instructions.   Cat. No. 11338H   Schedule D (Form 1040) 2020

Schedule D (Form 1040) 2020   Page **2**

| **Part III** | **Summary** |

16   Combine lines 7 and 15 and enter the result **16**

- If line 16 is a **gain,** enter the amount from line 16 on Form 1040, 1040-SR, or 1040-NR, line 7. Then, go to line 17 below.
- If line 16 is a **loss,** skip lines 17 through 20 below. Then, go to line 21. Also be sure to complete line 22.
- If line 16 is **zero,** skip lines 17 through 21 below and enter -0- on Form 1040, 1040-SR, or 1040-NR, line 7. Then, go to line 22.

17   Are lines 15 and 16 **both** gains?
   ☐ **Yes.** Go to line 18.
   ☐ **No.** Skip lines 18 through 21, and go to line 22.

18   If you are required to complete the **28% Rate Gain Worksheet** (see instructions), enter the amount, if any, from line 7 of that worksheet   . . . . ▶   **18**

19   If you are required to complete the **Unrecaptured Section 1250 Gain Worksheet** (see instructions), enter the amount, if any, from line 18 of that worksheet   . . . . ▶   **19**

20   Are lines 18 and 19 **both** zero or blank?
   ☐ **Yes.** Complete the **Qualified Dividends and Capital Gain Tax Worksheet** in the instructions for Forms 1040 and 1040-SR, line 16. **Don't** complete lines 21 and 22 below.

   ☐ **No.** Complete the **Schedule D Tax Worksheet** in the instructions. **Don't** complete lines 21 and 22 below.

21   If line 16 is a loss, enter here and on Form 1040, 1040-SR, or 1040-NR, line 7, the **smaller** of:

   - The loss on line 16; or
   - ($3,000), or if married filing separately, ($1,500)   } . . . .   **21** (   )

   Note: When figuring which amount is smaller, treat both amounts as positive numbers.

22   Do you have qualified dividends on Form 1040, 1040-SR, or 1040-NR, line 3a?

   ☐ **Yes.** Complete the **Qualified Dividends and Capital Gain Tax Worksheet** in the instructions for Forms 1040 and 1040-SR, line 16.

   ☐ **No.** Complete the rest of Form 1040, 1040-SR, or 1040-NR.

Schedule D (Form 1040) 2020

Form **8949**

Department of the Treasury
Internal Revenue Service

Sales and Other Dispositions of Capital Assets

▶ Go to *www.irs.gov/Form8949* for instructions and the latest information.

▶ File with your Schedule D to list your transactions for lines 1b, 2, 3, 8b, 9, and 10 of Schedule D.

OMB No. 1545-0074

2020

Attachment
Sequence No. **12A**

Name(s) shown on return

Social security number or taxpayer identification number

Before you check Box A, B, or C below, see whether you received any Form(s) 1099-B or substitute statement(s) from your broker. A substitute statement will have the same information as Form 1099-B. Either will show whether your basis (usually your cost) was reported to the IRS by your broker and may even tell you which box to check.

Part I **Short-Term.** Transactions involving capital assets you held 1 year or less are generally short-term (see instructions). For long-term transactions, see page 2.

Note: You may aggregate all short-term transactions reported on Form(s) 1099-B showing basis was reported to the IRS and for which no adjustments or codes are required. Enter the totals directly on Schedule D, line 1a; you aren't required to report these transactions on Form 8949 (see instructions).

You *must* check Box A, B, *or* C below. Check only one box. If more than one box applies for your short-term transactions, complete a separate Form 8949, page 1, for each applicable box. If you have more short-term transactions than will fit on this page for one or more of the boxes, complete as many forms with the same box checked as you need.

☐ **(A)** Short-term transactions reported on Form(s) 1099-B showing basis was reported to the IRS (see **Note** above)

☐ **(B)** Short-term transactions reported on Form(s) 1099-B showing basis **wasn't** reported to the IRS

☐ **(C)** Short-term transactions not reported to you on Form 1099-B

1	(a) Description of property (Example: 100 sh. XYZ Co.)	(b) Date acquired (Mo., day, yr.)	(c) Date sold or disposed of (Mo., day, yr.)	(d) Proceeds (sales price) (see instructions)	(e) Cost or other basis. See the **Note** below and see *Column (e)* in the separate instructions	Adjustment, if any, to gain or loss. If you enter an amount in column (g), enter a code in column (f). See the separate instructions.		(h) Gain or (loss). Subtract column (e) from column (d) and combine the result with column (g)
						(f) Code(s) from instructions	(g) Amount of adjustment	

2 Totals. Add the amounts in columns (d), (e), (g), and (h) (subtract negative amounts). Enter each total here and include on your Schedule D, **line 1b** (if **Box A** above is checked), **line 2** (if **Box B** above is checked), or **line 3** (if **Box C** above is checked) ▶

Note: If you checked Box A above but the basis reported to the IRS was incorrect, enter in column (e) the basis as reported to the IRS, and enter an adjustment in column (g) to correct the basis. See *Column (g)* in the separate instructions for how to figure the amount of the adjustment.

For Paperwork Reduction Act Notice, see your tax return instructions.   Cat. No. 37768Z   Form **8949** (2020)

Form 8949 (2020)   Attachment Sequence No. **12A**   Page **2**

Name(s) shown on return. Name and SSN or taxpayer identification no. not required if shown on other side	Social security number or taxpayer identification number

Before you check Box D, E, or F below, see whether you received any Form(s) 1099-B or substitute statement(s) from your broker. A substitute statement will have the same information as Form 1099-B. Either will show whether your basis (usually your cost) was reported to the IRS by your broker and may even tell you which box to check.

Part II **Long-Term.** Transactions involving capital assets you held more than 1 year are generally long-term (see instructions). For short-term transactions, see page 1.

Note: You may aggregate all long-term transactions reported on Form(s) 1099-B showing basis was reported to the IRS and for which no adjustments or codes are required. Enter the totals directly on Schedule D, line 8a; you aren't required to report these transactions on Form 8949 (see instructions).

You *must* check Box D, E, *or* F below. Check only one box. If more than one box applies for your long-term transactions, complete a separate Form 8949, page 2, for each applicable box. If you have more long-term transactions than will fit on this page for one or more of the boxes, complete as many forms with the same box checked as you need.

☐ **(D)** Long-term transactions reported on Form(s) 1099-B showing basis was reported to the IRS (see **Note** above)

☐ **(E)** Long-term transactions reported on Form(s) 1099-B showing basis **wasn't** reported to the IRS

☐ **(F)** Long-term transactions not reported to you on Form 1099-B

1 **(a)** Description of property (Example: 100 sh. XYZ Co.)	**(b)** Date acquired (Mo., day, yr.)	**(c)** Date sold or disposed of (Mo., day, yr.)	**(d)** Proceeds (sales price) (see instructions)	**(e)** Cost or other basis. See the **Note** below and see *Column (e)* in the separate instructions	Adjustment, if any, to gain or loss. If you enter an amount in column (g), enter a code in column (f). See the separate instructions. **(f)** Code(s) from instructions	**(g)** Amount of adjustment	**(h)** Gain or (loss). Subtract column (e) from column (d) and combine the result with column (g)
2 Totals. Add the amounts in columns (d), (e), (g), and (h) (subtract negative amounts). Enter each total here and include on your Schedule D, **line 8b** (if **Box D** above is checked), **line 9** (if **Box E** above is checked), or **line 10** (if **Box F** above is checked) ▶							

Note: If you checked Box D above but the basis reported to the IRS was incorrect, enter in column (e) the basis as reported to the IRS, and enter an adjustment in column (g) to correct the basis. See *Column (g)* in the separate instructions for how to figure the amount of the adjustment.

Form **8949** (2020)

SCHEDULE E (Form 1040) Department of the Treasury Internal Revenue Service (99)	**Supplemental Income and Loss** (From rental real estate, royalties, partnerships, S corporations, estates, trusts, REMICs, etc.) ▶ Attach to Form 1040, 1040-SR, 1040-NR, or 1041. ▶ Go to *www.irs.gov/ScheduleE* for instructions and the latest information.	OMB No. 1545-0074 2020 Attachment Sequence No. **13**
Name(s) shown on return		Your social security number

Part I — Income or Loss From Rental Real Estate and Royalties

Note: If you are in the business of renting personal property, use **Schedule C.** See instructions. If you are an individual, report farm rental income or loss from **Form 4835** on page 2, line 40.

A Did you make any payments in 2020 that would require you to file Form(s) 1099? See instructions . . . . ☐ Yes ☐ No

B If "Yes," did you or will you file required Form(s) 1099? . . . . ☐ Yes ☐ No

1a Physical address of each property (street, city, state, ZIP code)

A

B

C

1b	Type of Property (from list below)	2 For each rental real estate property listed above, report the number of fair rental and personal use days. Check the **QJV** box only if you meet the requirements to file as a qualified joint venture. See instructions.	Fair Rental Days	Personal Use Days	QJV
A		A			☐
B		B			☐
C		C			☐

Type of Property:

1 Single Family Residence   3 Vacation/Short-Term Rental   5 Land   7 Self-Rental

2 Multi-Family Residence   4 Commercial   6 Royalties   8 Other (describe)

Income:	Properties:		A	B	C
3 Rents received	3				
4 Royalties received	4				
Expenses:					
5 Advertising	5				
6 Auto and travel (see instructions)	6				
7 Cleaning and maintenance	7				
8 Commissions.	8				
9 Insurance	9				
10 Legal and other professional fees	10				
11 Management fees	11				
12 Mortgage interest paid to banks, etc. (see instructions)	12				
13 Other interest.	13				
14 Repairs.	14				
15 Supplies	15				
16 Taxes	16				
17 Utilities	17				
18 Depreciation expense or depletion	18				
19 Other (list) ▶ _____	19				
20 Total expenses. Add lines 5 through 19	20				
21 Subtract line 20 from line 3 (rents) and/or 4 (royalties). If result is a (loss), see instructions to find out if you must file **Form 6198**	21				
22 Deductible rental real estate loss after limitation, if any, on **Form 8582** (see instructions)	22	(	)(	)(	)

23a Total of all amounts reported on line 3 for all rental properties	23a		
b Total of all amounts reported on line 4 for all royalty properties	23b		
c Total of all amounts reported on line 12 for all properties	23c		
d Total of all amounts reported on line 18 for all properties	23d		
e Total of all amounts reported on line 20 for all properties	23e		
24 **Income.** Add positive amounts shown on line 21. **Do not** include any losses	24		
25 **Losses.** Add royalty losses from line 21 and rental real estate losses from line 22. Enter total losses here .	25	(	)
26 **Total rental real estate and royalty income or (loss).** Combine lines 24 and 25. Enter the result here. If Parts II, III, IV, and line 40 on page 2 do not apply to you, also enter this amount on Schedule 1 (Form 1040), line 5. Otherwise, include this amount in the total on line 41 on page 2 .	26		

For Paperwork Reduction Act Notice, see the separate instructions.   Cat. No. 11344L   **Schedule E (Form 1040) 2020**

Form **8582**	**Passive Activity Loss Limitations**	OMB No. 1545-1008

Department of the Treasury
Internal Revenue Service (99)

► See separate instructions.
► Attach to Form 1040, 1040-SR, or 1041.
► Go to *www.irs.gov/Form8582* for instructions and the latest information.

2020

Attachment
Sequence No. **858**

Name(s) shown on return

Identifying number

Part I   2020 Passive Activity Loss

Caution: Complete Worksheets 1, 2, and 3 before completing Part I.

Rental Real Estate Activities With Active Participation (For the definition of active participation, see **Special Allowance for Rental Real Estate Activities** in the instructions.)

1a	Activities with net income (enter the amount from Worksheet 1, column (a)) .	**1a**	
b	Activities with net loss (enter the amount from Worksheet 1, column (b)) . .	**1b** (	)
c	Prior years' unallowed losses (enter the amount from Worksheet 1, column (c))	**1c** (	)
d	Combine lines 1a, 1b, and 1c	**1d**	

Commercial Revitalization Deductions From Rental Real Estate Activities

2a	Commercial revitalization deductions from Worksheet 2, column (a) . .	**2a** (	)
b	Prior year unallowed commercial revitalization deductions from Worksheet 2, column (b)	**2b** (	)
c	Add lines 2a and 2b	**2c** (	)

All Other Passive Activities

3a	Activities with net income (enter the amount from Worksheet 3, column (a)) .	**3a**	
b	Activities with net loss (enter the amount from Worksheet 3, column (b)) . .	**3b** (	)
c	Prior years' unallowed losses (enter the amount from Worksheet 3, column (c))	**3c** (	)
d	Combine lines 3a, 3b, and 3c	**3d**	

4 Combine lines 1d, 2c, and 3d. If this line is zero or more, stop here and include this form with your return; all losses are allowed, including any prior year unallowed losses entered on line 1c, 2b, or 3c. Report the losses on the forms and schedules normally used **4**

If line 4 is a loss and: • Line 1d is a loss, go to Part II.

• Line 2c is a loss (and line 1d is zero or more), skip Part II and go to Part III.

• Line 3d is a loss (and lines 1d and 2c are zero or more), skip Parts II and III and go to line 15.

Caution: If your filing status is married filing separately and you lived with your spouse at any time during the year, **do not** complete Part II or Part III. Instead, go to line 15.

Part II   Special Allowance for Rental Real Estate Activities With Active Participation

Note: Enter all numbers in Part II as positive amounts. See instructions for an example.

5	Enter the **smaller** of the loss on line 1d or the loss on line 4	**5**	
6	Enter $150,000. If married filing separately, see instructions	**6**	
7	Enter modified adjusted gross income, but not less than zero. See instructions	**7**	
	Note: If line 7 is greater than or equal to line 6, skip lines 8 and 9, enter -0- on line 10. Otherwise, go to line 8.		
8	Subtract line 7 from line 6	**8**	
9	Multiply line 8 by 50% (0.50). **Do not** enter more than $25,000. If married filing separately, see instructions	**9**	
10	Enter the **smaller** of line 5 or line 9	**10**	

If line 2c is a loss, go to Part III. Otherwise, go to line 15.

Part III   Special Allowance for Commercial Revitalization Deductions From Rental Real Estate Activities

Note: Enter all numbers in Part III as positive amounts. See the example for Part II in the instructions.

11	Enter $25,000 reduced by the amount, if any, on line 10. If married filing separately, see instructions .	**11**	
12	Enter the loss from line 4	**12**	
13	Reduce line 12 by the amount on line 10	**13**	
14	Enter the **smallest** of line 2c (treated as a positive amount), line 11, or line 13	**14**	

Part IV   Total Losses Allowed

15	Add the income, if any, on lines 1a and 3a and enter the total	**15**	
16	**Total losses allowed from all passive activities for 2020.** Add lines 10, 14, and 15. See instructions to find out how to report the losses on your tax return	**16**	

For Paperwork Reduction Act Notice, see instructions.   Cat. No. 63704F   Form **8582** (2020)

Form 1045 (2020)   Page **3**

Schedule A—NOL (see instructions)

1	For individuals, subtract your standard deduction or itemized deductions from your adjusted gross income and enter it here. For estates and trusts, enter taxable income increased by the total of the charitable deduction, income distribution deduction, and exemption amount (see instructions)		**1**
2	Nonbusiness capital losses before limitation. Enter as a positive number (see instructions)	**2**	
3	Nonbusiness capital gains (without regard to any section 1202 exclusion)	**3**	
4	If line 2 is more than line 3, enter the difference. Otherwise, enter -0-	**4**	
5	If line 3 is more than line 2, enter the difference. Otherwise, enter -0-	**5**	
6	Nonbusiness deductions (see instructions)	**6**	
7	Nonbusiness income other than capital gains (see instructions)	**7**	
8	Add lines 5 and 7	**8**	
9	If line 6 is more than line 8, enter the difference. Otherwise, enter -0-		**9**
10	If line 8 is more than line 6, enter the difference. Otherwise, enter -0-. **But don't enter more than line 5**	**10**	
11	Business capital losses before limitation. Enter as a positive number	**11**	
12	Business capital gains (without regard to any section 1202 exclusion)	**12**	
13	Add lines 10 and 12	**13**	
14	Subtract line 13 from line 11. If zero or less, enter -0-	**14**	
15	Add lines 4 and 14	**15**	
16	Enter the loss, if any, from line 16 of your 2020 Schedule D (Form 1040). (For estates and trusts, enter the loss, if any, from line 19, column (3), of Schedule D (Form 1041).) Enter as a positive number. If you don't have a loss on that line (and don't have a section 1202 exclusion), skip lines 16 through 21 and enter on line 22 the amount from line 15	**16**	
17	Section 1202 exclusion. Enter as a positive number (see instructions)		**17**
18	Subtract line 17 from line 16. If zero or less, enter -0-	**18**	
19	Enter the loss, if any, from line 21 of your 2020 Schedule D (Form 1040). (For estates and trusts, enter the loss, if any, from line 20 of Schedule D (Form 1041).) Enter as a positive number	**19**	
20	If line 18 is more than line 19, enter the difference. Otherwise, enter -0-	**20**	
21	If line 19 is more than line 18, enter the difference. Otherwise, enter -0-		**21**
22	Subtract line 20 from line 15. If zero or less, enter -0-		**22**
23	NOL deduction for losses from other years. Enter as a positive number		**23**
24	**NOL.** Combine lines 1, 9, 17, and 21 through 23. If the result is less than zero, enter it here and on page 1, line 1a. If the result is zero or more, you **don't** have an NOL		**24**

Form **1045** (2020)

Qualified Dividends and Capital Gain Tax Worksheet—Line 16

Before you begin:	✓ See the earlier instructions for line 16 to see if you can use this worksheet to figure your tax.	
	✓ Before completing this worksheet, complete Form 1040 or 1040-SR through line 15.	
	✓ If you don't have to file Schedule D and you received capital gain distributions, be sure you checked the box on Form 1040 or 1040-SR, line 7.	

1. Enter the amount from Form 1040 or 1040-SR, line 15. However, if you are filing Form 2555 (relating to foreign earned income), enter the amount from line 3 of the Foreign Earned Income Tax Worksheet . . . . **1.** _____

2. Enter the amount from Form 1040 or 1040-SR, line 3a* . . . . **2.** _____

3. Are you filing Schedule D?*
   - ☐ **Yes.** Enter the **smaller** of line 15 or 16 of Schedule D. If either line 15 or 16 is blank or a loss, enter -0-.
   - ☐ **No.** Enter the amount from Form 1040 or 1040-SR, line 7.

   3. _____

4. Add lines 2 and 3 . . . . **4.** _____

5. If filing Form 4952 (used to figure investment interest expense deduction), enter any amount from line 4g of that form. Otherwise, enter -0- . . . . **5.** _____

6. Subtract line 5 from line 4. If zero or less, enter -0- . . . . **6.** _____

7. Subtract line 6 from line 1. If zero or less, enter -0- . . . . **7.** _____

8. Enter:
   $40,000 if single or married filing separately,
   $80,000 if married filing jointly or qualifying widow(er),
   $53,600 if head of household. } . . . . **8.** _____

9. Enter the smaller of line 1 or line 8 . . . . **9.** _____

10. Enter the smaller of line 7 or line 9 . . . . **10.** _____

11. Subtract line 10 from line 9. This amount is taxed at 0% . . . . **11.** _____

12. Enter the smaller of line 1 or line 6 . . . . **12.** _____

13. Enter the amount from line 11 . . . . **13.** _____

14. Subtract line 13 from line 12 . . . . **14.** _____

15. Enter:
    $441,450 if single,
    $248,300 if married filing separately,
    $496,600 if married filing jointly or qualifying widow(er),
    $469,050 if head of household. } . . . . **15.** _____

16. Enter the smaller of line 1 or line 15 . . . . **16.** _____

17. Add lines 7 and 11 . . . . **17.** _____

18. Subtract line 17 from line 16. If zero or less, enter -0- . . . . **18.** _____

19. Enter the smaller of line 14 or line 18 . . . . **19.** _____

20. Multiply line 19 by 15% (0.15) . . . . **20.** _____

21. Add lines 11 and 19 . . . . **21.** _____

22. Subtract line 21 from line 12 . . . . **22.** _____

23. Multiply line 22 by 20% (0.20) . . . . **23.** _____

24. Figure the tax on the amount on line 7. If the amount on line 7 is less than $100,000, use the Tax Table to figure the tax. If the amount on line 7 is $100,000 or more, use the Tax Computation Worksheet . . . . **24.** _____

25. Add lines 20, 23, and 24 . . . . **25.** _____

26. Figure the tax on the amount on line 1. If the amount on line 1 is less than $100,000, use the Tax Table to figure the tax. If the amount on line 1 is $100,000 or more, use the Tax Computation Worksheet . . . . **26.** _____

27. **Tax on all taxable income.** Enter the **smaller** of line 25 or 26. Also include this amount on the entry space on Form 1040 or 1040-SR, line 16. If you are filing Form 2555, don't enter this amount on the entry space on Form 1040 or 1040-SR, line 16. Instead, enter it on line 4 of the Foreign Earned Income Tax Worksheet . . . . **27.** _____

* If you are filing Form 2555, see the footnote in the Foreign Earned Income Tax Worksheet before completing this line.

Student Name _____

Class/Section _____

Date _____

KEY NUMBER TAX RETURN SUMMARY

CHAPTER 4

Comprehensive Problem 1

Capital Gain or (Loss) (Line 7) _____

Rental Real Estate (Schedule 1, Line 5) _____

Adjusted Gross Income (Line 11) _____

Total Tax (Line 24) _____

Amount Overpaid (Line 34) _____

Comprehensive Problem 2A

Rental Real Estate (Schedule 1, Line 5) _____

Adjusted Gross Income (Line 11) _____

Total Tax (Line 24) _____

Amount Overpaid (Line 34) _____

Comprehensive Problem 2B

Capital Gain or (Loss) (Line 7) _____

Rental Real Estate (Schedule 1, Line 5) _____

Adjusted Gross Income (Line 11) _____

Total Tax (Line 24) _____

Net Operating Loss (Form 1045, Schedule A, Line 24) _____

Deductions For and From AGI

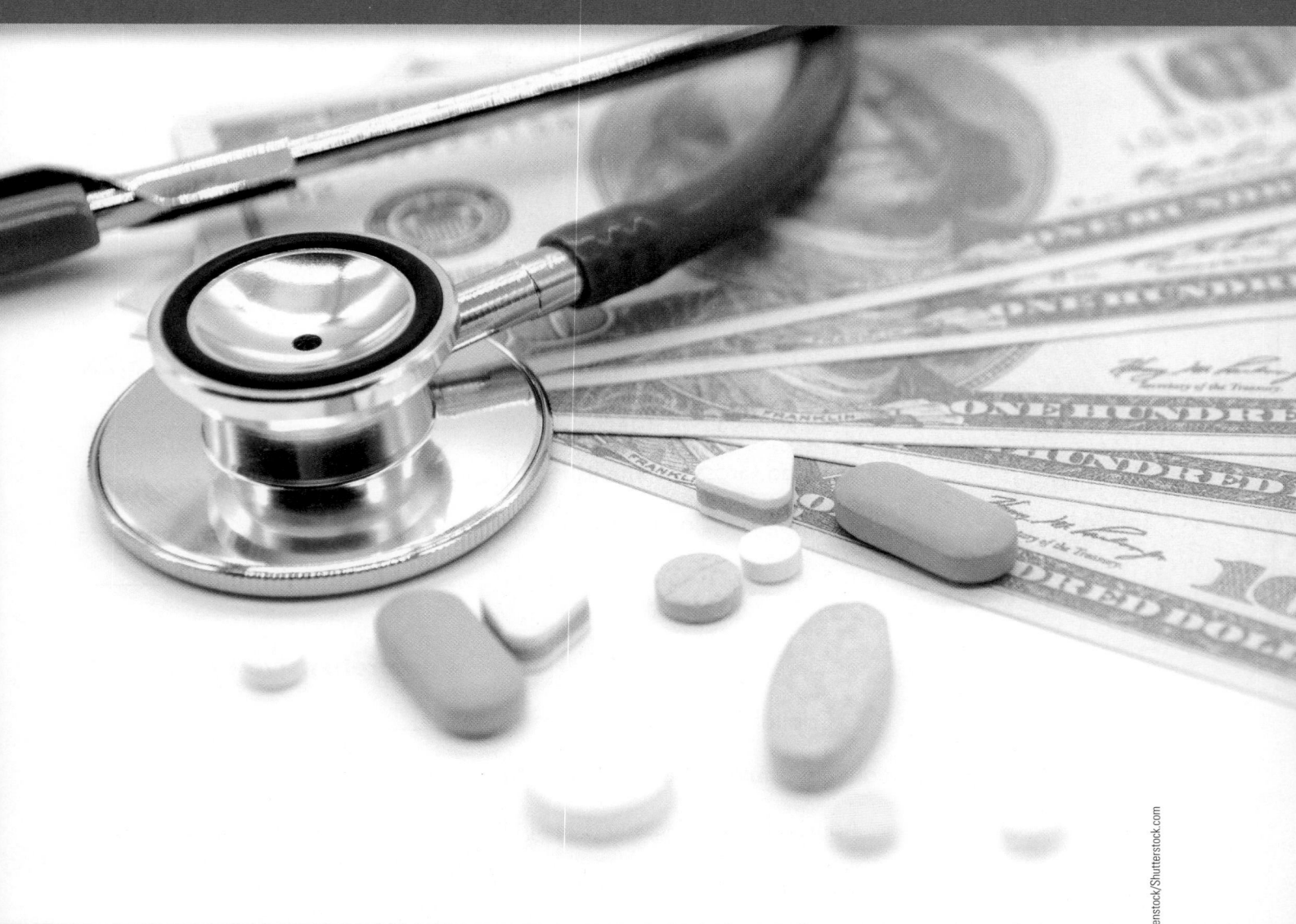

LEARNING OBJECTIVES

After completing this chapter, you should be able to:

LO 5.1   Explain how Health Savings Accounts (HSAs) can be used for tax-advantaged medical care.

LO 5.2   Describe the self-employed health insurance deduction.

LO 5.3   Explain the treatment of Individual Retirement Accounts (IRAs), including Roth IRAs.

LO 5.4   Explain the general contribution rules for small business and self-employed retirement plans.

LO 5.5   Describe other adjustments for adjusted gross income.

LO 5.6   Calculate the itemized deduction for medical expenses.

LO 5.7   Calculate the itemized deduction for taxes.

LO 5.8   Apply the rules for an individual taxpayer's interest deduction.

LO 5.9   Determine the charitable contributions deduction.

LO 5.10 Describe other itemized deductions.

OVERVIEW

Deductions related to a business (for example, Schedule C in Chapter 3) or the production of income or investment (for example, Schedules D and E in Chapter 4) represent deductions that are for AGI (above-the-line). The business deductions are generally reported on the separate schedules. However, the tax law permits additional for AGI deductions that may be associated with business activity or, in some instances unrelated to business activity, such as the student loan interest deduction, as simply a matter of legislative grace for individual taxpayers. These additional deductions are reported on the bottom half of Schedule 1 of Form 1040 and include one-half of self-employment taxes, deductible contributions to an individual retirement account, and others.

Deductions that occur after AGI (from AGI deductions, or below-the-line) include the standard deduction discussed in Chapter 1 and Schedule A itemized deductions, introduced here in Chapter 5. Itemized deductions fall into six categories: medical and dental expenses, state and local taxes, interest expenses, charitable contributions, casualty and theft losses, and miscellaneous deductions.

Recall from Chapter 1, that when calculating taxable income, individuals determine their standard deduction and their allowable itemized deductions and use the larger of the two. For example, if a taxpayer's standard deduction is $12,400 and her itemized deductions are $18,100, she would use her itemized deductions in calculating taxable income. On the other hand, if her itemized deductions were $9,500, she would use the larger standard deduction of $12,400 in computing taxable income.

Starting in 2018, a number of limitations were placed on itemized deductions. One example is the $10,000 limit on state and local taxes. For federal budget reasons, many of these limitations only suspend, rather than repeal the deduction. The suspensions are largely scheduled to end after 2025. As a result, brief explanations of the pre-limitation deductions are provided.

5-1 HEALTH SAVINGS ACCOUNTS

Learning Objective 5.1

Explain how Health Savings Accounts (HSAs) can be used for tax-advantaged medical care.

There are four types of tax-favored medical spending plans available to taxpayers:

1. Health care flexible spending arrangements or FSAs (covered in Chapter 2) in which employees can set aside money to cover medical expenses and exclude the funds from gross income.
2. Health Reimbursements Arrangements (HRAs) in which the employer funds an account that may be used by employees for medical expenses (these do not generally affect an individual taxpayer's taxable income and thus are not covered in detail in this textbook).
3. Medical Savings Accounts (MSAs or Archer MSAs) which permit (limited) deductions for amounts contributed to an account established to cover medical expenses for small business and self-employed individuals. Effective January 1, 2008, no new MSA accounts may be established and thus these are not covered in detail in this textbook. Note that an Archer MSA can be rolled over into an HSA.
4. Health Savings Accounts (HSAs) are a type of savings account which may be established for the purpose of paying unreimbursed medical expenses by taxpayers who carry qualifying high-deductible medical insurance.

Contributions to HSAs are a deduction for AGI and are limited to certain dollar amounts depending on age and whether the high-deductible insurance covers an individual or a family. Earnings and unused contributions accumulated in an HSA are not taxed, and distributions to cover medical expenses are not taxed or penalized.

Health insurance with a high deductible is less expensive than standard health insurance since the issuing insurance company does not have to pay any of the taxpayer's medical expenses until a certain threshold (the deductible plus any other required out-of-pocket medical costs) is reached. The funds contributed to the HSA may then be used by the taxpayer to pay medical expenses not covered by health insurance. This popular combination of tax benefits and less expensive insurance is designed to encourage taxpayers to carry health insurance.

5-1a Deductions for Contributions to HSAs

The following table shows the contribution limits for HSA deductions for 2020. The table also shows the additional "catch-up" contributions allowed for individuals beginning at age 55 and ending at age 65, the age for Medicare eligibility. Individuals are not allowed to make contributions to HSAs once they attain the age of 65 and qualify for Medicare coverage. Finally, the table shows the lower and upper deductible and out-of-pocket medical expense limits (excluding the actual cost of insurance) required for insurance to qualify as a high-deductible health plan.

2020 Limits for HSAs		
	Family	*Self-Only*
Contribution limit	$ 7,100	$ 3,550
Additional catch-up contribution for taxpayer age 55 or older	1,000 per qualifying spouse	1,000
Minimum health insurance deductible	2,800	1,400
Maximum health insurance out-of-pocket	13,800	6,900

Although the out-of-pocket limits under the Affordable Care Act (ACA) are slightly higher than those listed above, the IRS limits determine tax compliance for HSAs. Contributions to HSAs must generally be made by April 15 of the year following the year for which the contribution is made. IRS Form 8889 is used to provide information to the IRS regarding HSA deductions claimed on Line 12 of Schedule 1 of Form 1040 and to compute the deduction amount.

EXAMPLE Gary is 35 years old and carries self-only coverage in a qualifying high-deductible health insurance plan during 2020. Gary may contribute up to $3,550 to his HSA account and deduct this amount for AGI. Gary may use some or all of the contributions to pay medical expenses he has incurred. Any amount he leaves in the HSA account will accumulate earnings tax free and carry forward to be available for payment of qualifying medical expenses in the future. ◆

5-1b Distributions

Distributions from HSAs are free of tax when used to pay for qualified medical expenses. Distributions which are not used to pay for qualified medical expenses are subject to both income tax and a 20 percent penalty. Once a taxpayer is 65 years old, distributions may be taken for nonmedical expenses and will be subject to income tax, but not the 20 percent penalty. Distributions from an HSA are reported on Form 1099-SA (see Self-Study Problem 5.1). The amount of the distribution is reported in Box 1 and codes indicating the proper treatment are provided in Box 3. A normal distribution is coded 1. HSA distributions are reported by the taxpayer on Form 8889.

ProConnect™ Tax

TIP

To report HSA information and complete a Form 8889, the input area can be found in the left-hand margin under Deductions/Adjustments to Income. The input area is conveniently called Health Savings Account (Form 8889).

EXAMPLE   Debbie is 66 years old and has $30,000 in her HSA. She can withdraw the $30,000 to purchase a new car, but will have to pay income tax on the distribution. If she takes the distribution to pay medical expenses, no income tax will be due. If Debbie were 55 years old and took a distribution from her HSA to buy a car, she would owe both income tax and a 20 percent penalty on the distribution. ◆

5-1c Guidance

The rules governing HSAs are more detailed and lengthy than the summaries above. IRS Publication 969 is a good source of information on a range of additional issues related to HSAs and their operation.

Self-Study Problem 5.1   *See Appendix E for Solutions to Self-Study Problems*

a. Give the deductible HSA amount for each of the following taxpayers for 2020:

1. Amy is 40 years old, has a qualifying high-deductible health plan, carries family coverage, and contributes the maximum amount to her family HSA. Deductible HSA amount: $_____

2. Cary is 60 years old, has self-only health insurance with no deductible, and contributes $1,200 to an HSA. Deductible HSA amount: $_____

3. Annabelle is 52 years old and contributes $2,000 to her HSA. She has qualifying self-only coverage in a high-deductible health plan. Deductible HSA amount: $_____

4. Lucille is 70 years old and is covered by Medicare. She contributes $3,050 to her HSA. Deductible HSA amount: $_____

b. Alex Morton is a single taxpayer, age 34. She is part of a qualifying high-deductible health plan. In 2020, Alex made contributions of $2,750 to her HSA. Alex's employer reported making $300 of contributions to her HSA in Box 12 of her Form W-2 (code W). Alex spent $2,500 on qualified medical expenses. Alex received the following Form 1099-SA from her HSA administrator:

☐ CORRECTED (if checked)		
TRUSTEE'S/PAYER'S name, street address, city or town, state or province, country, ZIP or foreign postal code, and telephone number Heritage Health Partners PO Box 12345 Dallas, TX 75621	OMB No. 1545-1517 Form **1099-SA** (Rev. November 2019) For calendar year 20 20	**Distributions From an HSA, Archer MSA, or Medicare Advantage MSA**
PAYER'S TIN **13-0080072** RECIPIENT'S TIN **213-21-3121**	1 Gross distribution $ 1,783.00	2 Earnings on excess cont. $	Copy B
RECIPIENT'S name Alex Morton	3 Distribution code 1	4 FMV on date of death $	For Recipient
Street address (including apt. no.) 1921 S. Orange Ave. City or town, state or province, country, and ZIP or foreign postal code Orlando, FL 32806	5 HSA ☒ Archer MSA ☐ MA MSA ☐		This information is being furnished to the IRS.
Account number (see instructions)		

Form **1099-SA** (Rev. 11-2019)   (keep for your records)   www.irs.gov/Form1099SA   Department of the Treasury - Internal Revenue Service

Prepare Form 8889 (page 1 only) on Page 5-5 to determine Alex's HSA deduction and taxable HSA distribution.

Self-Study Problem 5.1

Form 8889

Department of the Treasury
Internal Revenue Service

Health Savings Accounts (HSAs)

▶ Attach to Form 1040, 1040-SR, or 1040-NR.
▶ Go to *www.irs.gov/Form8889* for instructions and the latest information.

OMB No. 1545-0074

2020

Attachment
Sequence No. **52**

Name(s) shown on Form 1040, 1040-SR, or 1040-NR

Social security number of HSA beneficiary. If both spouses have HSAs, see instructions ▶

Before you begin: Complete Form 8853, Archer MSAs and Long-Term Care Insurance Contracts, if required.

Part I | **HSA Contributions and Deduction.** See the instructions before completing this part. If you are filing jointly and both you and your spouse each have separate HSAs, complete a separate Part I for each spouse.

1	Check the box to indicate your coverage under a high-deductible health plan (HDHP) during 2020. See instructions . . . . ▶		☐ Self-only ☐ Family
2	HSA contributions you made for 2020 (or those made on your behalf), including those made from January 1, 2021, through April 15, 2021, that were for 2020. **Do not** include employer contributions, contributions through a cafeteria plan, or rollovers. See instructions	**2**	
3	If you were under age 55 at the end of 2020 and, on the first day of **every** month during 2020, you were, or were considered, an eligible individual with the **same** coverage, enter $3,550 ($7,100 for family coverage). **All others,** see the instructions for the amount to enter	**3**	
4	Enter the amount you and your employer contributed to your Archer MSAs for 2020 from Form 8853, lines 1 and 2. If you or your spouse had family coverage under an HDHP at any time during 2020, also include any amount contributed to your spouse's Archer MSAs	**4**	
5	Subtract line 4 from line 3. If zero or less, enter -0-	**5**	
6	Enter the amount from line 5. But if you and your spouse each have separate HSAs and had family coverage under an HDHP at any time during 2020, see the instructions for the amount to enter . .	**6**	
7	If you were age 55 or older at the end of 2020, married, and you or your spouse had family coverage under an HDHP at any time during 2020, enter your additional contribution amount. See instructions	**7**	
8	Add lines 6 and 7	**8**	
9	Employer contributions made to your HSAs for 2020	**9**	
10	Qualified HSA funding distributions	**10**	
11	Add lines 9 and 10	**11**	
12	Subtract line 11 from line 8. If zero or less, enter -0-	**12**	
13	**HSA deduction.** Enter the **smaller** of line 2 or line 12 here and on Schedule 1 (Form 1040), Part II, line 12	**13**	
	Caution: If line 2 is more than line 13, you may have to pay an additional tax. See instructions.		

Part II | **HSA Distributions.** If you are filing jointly and both you and your spouse each have separate HSAs, complete a separate Part II for each spouse.

14a	Total distributions you received in 2020 from all HSAs (see instructions)	**14a**	
b	Distributions included on line 14a that you rolled over to another HSA. Also include any excess contributions (and the earnings on those excess contributions) included on line 14a that were withdrawn by the due date of your return. See instructions	**14b**	
c	Subtract line 14b from line 14a	**14c**	
15	Qualified medical expenses paid using HSA distributions (see instructions)	**15**	
16	**Taxable HSA distributions.** Subtract line 15 from line 14c. If zero or less, enter -0-. Also, include this amount in the total on Schedule 1 (Form 1040), Part I, line 8, and enter "HSA" and the amount on the dotted line	**16**	
17a	If any of the distributions included on line 16 meet any of the **Exceptions to the Additional 20% Tax** (see instructions), check here . . . . ▶ ☐		
b	**Additional 20% tax** (see instructions). Enter 20% (0.20) of the distributions included on line 16 that are subject to the additional 20% tax. Also, include this amount in the total on Schedule 2 (Form 1040), Part II, line 8; check box c and enter "HSA" and the amount on the line next to the box . . .	**17b**	

Part III | **Income and Additional Tax for Failure To Maintain HDHP Coverage.** See the instructions before completing this part. If you are filing jointly and both you and your spouse each have separate HSAs, complete a separate Part III for each spouse.

18	Last-month rule	**18**	
19	Qualified HSA funding distribution	**19**	
20	**Total income.** Add lines 18 and 19. Include this amount on Schedule 1 (Form 1040), Part I, line 8, and enter "HSA" and the amount on the dotted line	**20**	
21	**Additional tax.** Multiply line 20 by 10% (0.10). Include this amount in the total on Schedule 2 (Form 1040), Part II, line 8; check box c and enter "HDHP" and the amount on the line next to the box . .	**21**	

For Paperwork Reduction Act Notice, see your tax return instructions. Cat. No. 37621P Form **8889** (2020)

5-2 SELF-EMPLOYED HEALTH INSURANCE DEDUCTION

Self-employed taxpayers are allowed an above-the-line deduction for the cost of providing health insurance for themselves and their families. This deduction is meant to give self-employed taxpayers the same tax treatment available to employees who are offered health insurance as a tax-free benefit of employment. Deductible insurance includes the following:

- Medical and dental insurance paid to cover the self-employed taxpayer, spouse, and dependents;
- Medical and dental insurance paid for children under the age of 27 who are not dependents;
- Medicare premiums;
- Long-term care insurance paid for the taxpayer and the family of the taxpayer, within certain dollar limitations shown below.

EXAMPLE Joe has a barbershop and earns $60,000 in 2020 which he reports on Schedule C. Joe pays $10,000 in health and dental insurance costs for himself, his unemployed wife, and his 10-year-old daughter. The full $10,000 is a deduction for Joe's AGI. ♦

5-2a Special Rules

The following special rules limit the treatment of health insurance as a deduction for AGI:

- Other Health Care Plan Available: The self-employed health insurance deduction is not allowed for any months in which the taxpayer is eligible to participate in a subsidized health care plan offered by an employer of either the taxpayer or the spouse of the taxpayer.
- Earned Income Limitation: The deduction for self-employed health insurance is only allowed to the extent of the taxpayer's net self-employed earned income. For example, a taxpayer with a Schedule C business loss would not be allowed to claim a self-employed health insurance deduction even though he or she paid for health insurance. The deduction would instead be allowed as an itemized medical deduction subject to the limits discussed in LO 5.6.
- Long-Term Care Premium Limitation: The individual limitations on the deduction of long-term care premiums are as follows:

Attained Age Before the Close of the Taxable Year	2020 Limitation on Premiums
40 or less	$ 430
More than 40 but not more than 50	810
More than 50 but not more than 60	1,630
More than 60 but not more than 70	4,350
More than 70	5,430

- Definition of Self-Employment: Taxpayers with income reportable on Schedule C are generally considered self-employed. However, taxpayers with earnings from certain partnerships, S corporations, LLCs, and farm businesses may also be considered self-employed and may be allowed the above-the-line deduction for self-employed health insurance. Taxpayers with income from these sources sometimes present more complex health insurance deduction issues which should be researched as they appear.
- Deductible Portion: Self-employed taxpayers that receive advance premium tax credits under the ACA may deduct only the portion paid out of pocket, not the portion covered by the premium tax credit.

ProConnect™ Tax TIP

To enter self-employed health insurance and many of the other for-AGI deductions, go to Deductions/Adjustments to Income. There is a long input page, and a number of subheadings are available in the left-hand margin.

EXAMPLE   Candace is a 55-year-old massage therapist who earns $40,000 of net self-employment income in 2020. She pays $6,000 for medical insurance and $1,650 for long-term care insurance. Candace can take $7,630 ($6,000 + $1,630) as a deduction for AGI. ◆

Self-Study Problem 5.2   *See Appendix E for Solutions to Self-Study Problems*

During the 2020 tax year, Gwen supports her family as a physical therapist. She reports $90,000 of earned income on her Schedule C and paid the following insurance premiums:

- Family health insurance: $15,000
- Family dental insurance: $2,000
- Health insurance for her 24-year-old son who is not a dependent: $3,000
- Long-term care insurance for her 49-year-old husband: $900

What is Gwen's self-employed health insurance deduction for 2020? $_____

Learning Objective 5.3

Explain the treatment of Individual Retirement Accounts (IRAs), including Roth IRAs.

5-3 INDIVIDUAL RETIREMENT ACCOUNTS

The two principal types of individual retirement accounts (IRAs) are the *traditional IRA* and the *Roth IRA*. Generally, annual contributions to a traditional IRA are deductible, and retirement distributions are taxable. Annual contributions to a Roth IRA are not deductible, but retirement distributions are nontaxable. Earnings in both types of IRAs are not taxable in the current year.

EXAMPLE   Gene has $30,000 in his IRA in 2020. The earnings for the year on this IRA are $1,600. These earnings are not taxed to Gene in the current year. ◆

5-3a IRA Annual Contributions and Deductions

There are annual contribution limits for both traditional and Roth IRAs. In 2020, the maximum annual contribution that may be made to either type of IRA is equal to the lesser of (1) 100 percent of the taxpayer's compensation or self-employment income (earned income) or (2) $6,000 (or $12,000 if an additional $6,000 is contributed to a spouse's IRA, and the spouse has no earned income). The limits apply to the total contribution made to both types of IRAs combined. It is possible for a taxpayer to contribute $4,000 to a traditional IRA and up to $2,000 to a Roth IRA. The maximum contribution to a spouse's IRA may not exceed $6,000. In 2020, an additional $1,000 annual "catch-up" contribution is allowed for taxpayers and spouses age 50 and over, increasing the maximum contribution to $7,000.

EXAMPLE   Quincy, age 31, works for Big Corporation and has a salary of $40,000 for 2020. Quincy is eligible to contribute the maximum $6,000 to his traditional or Roth IRA for 2020. If Quincy has a spouse who does not work, he could also contribute $6,000 into her IRA or Roth IRA. If Quincy is 55 years old instead of 31 years old, he could contribute $7,000 to his traditional or Roth IRA, and $6,000 or $7,000 for his spouse, depending on whether she is old enough to qualify for the $1,000 "catch-up" contribution. ◆

The IRA limitation calculations discussed below are quite complex and change every year. Most taxpayers and tax preparers use tax software to assist them in calculating allowable IRA deductions. It is a standard belief in the tax community that computer software has paved the way for the enormous complexity we see in today's tax law. Although it is important to understand the rules for calculating IRA contributions, please take solace in the fact that these calculations, as well as many others shown in this textbook, are not often done by hand in practice.

The annual deduction maximums on the previous page may be reduced for traditional IRAs if the taxpayer is an active participant in another qualified retirement plan. The annual contribution allowed for a Roth IRA is reduced for all taxpayers over certain income levels, but is not affected by whether the taxpayer or spouse is an active participant in another retirement plan. In each case, the maximum annual contribution is phased out proportionately between certain adjusted gross income ranges, as shown below.

2020 AGI Phase-Out Ranges for Roth IRA Contributions	
Filing Status	*AGI Phase-Out Range*
Single or HOH	$124,000–$139,000
Married filing jointly	$196,000–$206,000
Note: Active plan participation status is not relevant to the Roth IRA phase-out calculation. Special rules apply to married filing separate taxpayers.	

2020 AGI Phase-Out Ranges for Deductible Traditional IRA Contributions	
Type of Taxpayer	*AGI Phase-Out Range*
Single or HOH, not a plan participant	No phase-out
Single or HOH, active plan participant	$65,000–$75,000
Married filing jointly, both active participants	$104,000–$124,000
Married filing jointly, neither active plan participants	No phase-out
Married filing jointly, one an active participant:	(See Note 1 below)
Active participant spouse	$104,000–$124,000 (Joint AGI)
Nonactive participant spouse	$196,000–$206,000 (Joint AGI)
Note 1: When one spouse is an active participant in a retirement plan and the other is not, two separate income limitations apply. The active participant spouse may make a full deductible IRA contribution unless the $104,000–$124,000 phase-out range applies to the couple's joint income. The spouse who is not an active participant may make a full deductible IRA contribution unless the higher $196,000–$206,000 phase-out range applies to the couple's joint income.	

A nondeductible traditional IRA contribution may be made by taxpayers with income over the phase-out ranges shown above. Although the taxpayer cannot deduct the contribution, all income earned in the IRA account is sheltered from tax until the earnings are withdrawn. When there have been nondeductible IRA contributions, the taxable portion of the withdrawn IRA money is calculated similar to the treatment of annuities discussed in Chapter 2. Many high-income taxpayers make nondeductible traditional IRA contributions each year because of the deferral of tax on the earnings of the IRA.

EXAMPLE   Ed, age 31, is single and is covered by a retirement plan. If his modified adjusted gross income is $68,000, Ed's maximum deductible traditional IRA contribution is $4,200. With income of $68,000, his $6,000 contribution is proportionately phased out by dividing the amount remaining in his phase-out range, $75,000 − $68,000, or $7,000, by the $10,000 phase-out range (the difference between the bottom and top of the $65,000 and $75,000 phase-out range) and multiplying this by the $6,000 maximum IRA deduction as follows:

$$\frac{(\$75,000 - \$68,000)}{\$10,000} \times \$6,000 = \$4,200 \text{ allowed IRA deduction}$$

Ed may choose to contribute the $6,000 maximum to a traditional IRA, but the remaining $1,800 will not be deductible. Alternatively, he may contribute the remaining $1,800 to a Roth IRA since his income is below the phase-out range for Roth IRA contributions. He could also choose to ignore the allowed traditional IRA contribution and contribute the full nondeductible $6,000 to a Roth IRA. In any event, he cannot contribute more than $6,000 in total to IRAs, and his maximum allowed tax deduction for a traditional IRA contribution will be $4,200. ♦

EXAMPLE   Ann, who is 36 and single, would like to contribute $6,000 to her Roth IRA. However, her AGI is $125,000, so her contribution is limited to $5,600 calculated as follows:

$$\frac{(\$139,000 - \$125,000)}{\$15,000} \times \$6,000 = \$5,600 \text{ allowed Roth IRA}$$

The $15,000 denominator in the calculation above is the amount of the phase-out range between $124,000 and $139,000. If she were 50 or older and wanted to contribute $7,000, her contribution would be limited to $6,533. ♦

EXAMPLE   Paul and Lucy are married and are both 36 years old. Lucy is covered by a retirement plan and earns $64,000. Paul is not covered by a retirement plan and earns $60,000. Lucy cannot make a deductible contribution to a traditional IRA since the income on their joint tax return is greater than the $124,000 maximum phase-out range for married couples. Paul, however, can make a fully deductible IRA contribution of $6,000 since Paul and Lucy's AGI is below the $196,000–$206,000 phase-out range used when one spouse is an active participant in a plan and the other is not. Lucy could still choose to make a $6,000 contribution to a Roth IRA since their joint income is below the Roth IRA phase-out range for married couples. Paul would have a choice between making a $6,000 deductible contribution to a traditional IRA or a contribution of $6,000 to a Roth IRA or some combination thereof, not greater than $6,000. ♦

An IRA contribution may be made at any time before the original due date of the tax return for the year in which the deduction is to be claimed. This means, for example, that an individual can contribute to an IRA as late as the filing deadline of April 15, 2021, and still deduct the amount on the 2020 tax return. Due to the extension of the individual tax filing deadline in 2020, contributions for the 2019 tax year could be made up to July 15, 2020.

5-3b **Roth IRA Conversions**

Taxpayers may benefit from a rule allowing conversions of traditional IRAs into Roth IRAs. Although the income generated by the conversion is subject to current income tax, tax-payers with certain factors in their favor such as number of years to retirement, a low current tax bracket, or a high expected tax bracket in retirement may wish to convert. Also, taxpayers with negative taxable income due to large personal deductions may wish to convert enough of their regular IRAs to Roth IRAs to bring taxable income to zero. This way the conversion can be done with no tax cost since deductions which would otherwise be lost are used to offset the taxable IRA income.

For tax years 2010 and beyond, a rule that required taxpayers to have $100,000 or less in AGI to convert regular IRA accounts to Roth IRA accounts was eliminated. Congress expects that many high-income taxpayers will take advantage of this opportunity and pay income tax due up-front on conversions.

5-3c **Traditional IRA Distributions**

Money removed from a traditional IRA is taxable as ordinary income and may be subject to a 10 percent penalty for early withdrawal.

EXAMPLE Tomas is 48 years old and has a midlife crisis and decides he must have a red sports car. He withdraws $35,000 from his traditional IRA to purchase the car. Tomas does not qualify for any of the penalty-free withdrawals listed below. The $35,000 is taxable to Tomas as ordinary income and he is subject to a $3,500 (10% × $35,000) penalty for removing the funds before age 59½. ◆

To avoid the 10 percent penalty, distributions from an IRA generally cannot begin before age 59½. However, penalty-free withdrawals from IRAs may be made by taxpayers under age 59½ who are:

1. Disabled
2. Using a special level payment option
3. Using the withdrawals for unreimbursed medical expenses in excess of 7.5 percent of their AGI
4. The recipients of at least 12 weeks of unemployment compensation and to the extent they are paying medical insurance premiums for their dependents
5. Paying the costs of higher education, including tuition, fees, books, and room and board for the taxpayers or their spouses, children, or grandchildren
6. Withdrawing up to $10,000 for first-time home-buying expenses
7. Beneficiaries due to the death of the IRA owner
8. Withdrawing funds due to an IRS levy
9. A qualified reservist
10. Withdrawals of up to $5,000 in the year of a qualified birth or adoption

Due to COVID-related financial distress, the CARES Act extends the 10 percent penalty tax exemption to distributions of up to $100,000 made on or after March 27, 2020 and before December 31, 2020 to a taxpayer (or spouse or dependent) diagnosed with COVID-19 (using a CDC-approved test) or to a taxpayer that experiences adverse financial consequences as a result of quarantine, business closure, layoff, or reduced hours due to the virus. As with other exempted withdrawals, this exception does not apply to the normal income tax on the income; however, two special rules do apply. The first is that the taxpayer may include the income ratably over a three-year period starting in 2020. The second exception is that amounts recontributed to the qualified retirement plan within three years can be treated as a rollover and thus the original distribution would not be subject to tax.

EXAMPLE Juanita's spouse is stricken with COVID and she and her spouse are unable to work for three months in 2020. To cover expenses, Juanita takes a $30,000 COVID-related distribution from her IRA. The income is recognized ratably over

2020, 2021 and 2022. In 2022, Juanita contributes $30,000 to her IRA and may amend her 2020 and 2021 tax returns to exclude the income from the distribution. She is not required to report any distribution income on her 2022 tax return. ♦

Before 2020, taxpayers were required to take minimum annual distributions from their IRA starting no later than April 1 of the year following the year the taxpayer reaches age 70½. However, due to COVID-19-related provisions, no required minimum distributions (RMDs) are required in 2020. For taxpayers that have not turned age 70½ by the start of 2020, RMDs now begin by April in the year following the year the taxpayer reaches age 72.

EXAMPLE Wade turns 70 in February 2018. Normally, Wade would be required to take RMDs by April 2020 since he turned 70½ in 2018. Due to the COVID-19 relief provisions he will not be required to take a RMD in 2020. ♦

EXAMPLE Dalton turns 70 in February 2020. Because Dalton was not 70½ by the start of 2020, he is not required to take RMDs in 2020, irrespective of the COVID-19 relief provisions. When he turns 72 in 2022, he will start RMDs by April of 2023. ♦

Once the first year of RMDs begin, all future RMDs must be paid by December 31. Plan sponsors or financial institutions generally take on the burden of calculating RMDs for taxpayers.

5-3d Roth IRA Distributions

A taxpayer can make tax-free withdrawals from a Roth IRA after a 5-year holding period if any of the following requirements are satisfied:

1. The distribution is made on or after the date on which the participant attains age 59½.
2. The distribution is made to a beneficiary (or the participant's estate) on or after the participant's death.
3. The participant becomes disabled.
4. The distribution is used to pay for qualified first-time home-buyer's expenses.

EXAMPLE Bob establishes a Roth IRA at age 50 and contributes to the Roth each year for 10 years. The account is now worth $61,000, consisting of $35,000 of nondeductible contributions and $26,000 in earnings that have not been taxed. Bob may withdraw the $61,000 tax-free from the Roth IRA because he is over age 59½ and has met the 5-year holding period requirement. ♦

The distributions may be taxable if the taxpayer receives distributions from a Roth IRA and does not satisfy the above requirements. The part of the distributions that represents a return of capital is tax-free, and the part that represents a payout of earnings is taxable. Under the ordering rules for Roth IRA distributions, distributions are treated as first made from contributions (return of capital) and then from earnings.

EXAMPLE Assume the same facts in the previous example, except that Bob is only age 56 and receives distributions of $10,000. Assume his adjusted basis for the Roth IRA is $12,000 (contributions made of $2,000 × 6 years). The distribution is tax-free and his adjusted basis is reduced to $2,000 ($12,000 − $10,000). ♦

TAX BREAK A gift of a contribution to a Roth IRA for a child or grandchild with a summer job can grow into a very large gift over time. The amount that may be contributed to a child's Roth IRA is the lesser of $6,000 or the child's earnings. A child with $6,000 in a Roth IRA at age 16 will have well over $100,000 at age 65 if the Roth IRA investment earns 7 percent annually.

Self-Study Problem 5.3   *See Appendix E for Solutions to Self-Study Problems*

a. During 2020, George (a 24-year-old single taxpayer) has a salary of $48,000, dividend income of $14,000, and interest income of $4,000. In addition, he has rental income of $1,000. George is covered by a qualified retirement plan. Calculate the maximum regular IRA deduction that George is allowed.

$_____

b. During 2020, Irene (a single taxpayer, under age 50) has a salary of $115,500 and dividend income of $10,000. Calculate Irene's maximum contribution to a Roth IRA.

$_____

5-4 SMALL BUSINESS AND SELF-EMPLOYED RETIREMENT PLANS

> **5.4 Learning Objective**
>
> Explain the general contribution rules for small business and self-employed retirement plans.

The tax law provides employees, employers, and the self-employed with an incentive to plan for retirement through qualified retirement plans. Under the tax law, favorable tax treatment is granted to contributions, by or for employees, to qualified retirement plans. Employers may claim a deduction in the current year for contributions to qualified retirement plans on the employees' behalf, while the employees do not include the employer contributions in income until the contributed amounts are distributed (generally during their retirement years). Tax on earnings on the amounts contributed to the plan is also deferred. This deferral of income taxation is a significant benefit to most taxpayers.

EXAMPLE In the current year, Polly's employer makes a $2,000 contribution to a qualified plan for Polly's retirement. The $2,000 is deductible to the employer in the current year and is not taxable to Polly until she withdraws the money from the plan. Any earnings on the money contributed to the plan are also taxable only upon withdrawal from the plan (usually many years later). ♦

The tax code provides for a number of different types of plans for taxpayers to save for retirement. Most retirement plans have a number of requirements in order to be classified as "qualified," thereby extending the tax benefits described previously:

- Funding requirements: Most plans require that the benefit be extended to all employees and not favor only the highly compensated (nondiscriminatory).
- Fiduciary responsibility: Most plans require a separate account to hold the retirement assets, typically handled by a bank or financial institution.
- Early withdrawals: Most plans penalize or prohibit early distributions from the plan with limited hardship exceptions.
- Vesting requirement: Some plans require immediate "vesting" of contributions (i.e., the contributions are immediately set aside for an employee and will not be returned to the employer even if the employee leaves the company).

The retirement plan area has become one of the most complex areas of the tax law. Many tax accountants refer taxpayers to a specialist for help in choosing a plan and for guidance with the ongoing employee coverage, tax reporting, and contribution requirements. The coverage in this textbook is meant to give a simple overview of several common options available to taxpayers for tax-deferred retirement plans, which remain some of the best completely legal tax shelters available. Retirement plans for small businesses are covered here while large retirement plans, which are generally operated by larger employers, are covered in Chapter 9.

5-4a Self-Employed and Small Business Retirement Plan Options

Although available to small businesses, complex retirement plans such as defined-benefit plans or employee stock ownership plans are generally used by only large companies due to their complexity and cost to operate (see Chapter 9). However, over time, the tax law has created a number of retirement plans directed at the small business owner or even a self-employed sole proprietor.

5-4b IRA-Based Plans

IRA-based plans include the Payroll Deduction IRA, the Simplified Employee Pension (SEP or SEP IRA), and the SIMPLE IRA. All are quite easy to establish and require no annual reporting by the employer.

A Payroll Deduction IRA is probably the easiest type of plan to offer. Contributions are withheld from an employee's pay and directed into a traditional IRA account. No plan setup is necessary other than having the employee direct the payroll withholding to the IRA custodian. Contribution limits are the same as the traditional IRA limits ($6,000 or $7,000, if a catch-up contribution). There are no requirements for minimum employee coverage and employees can elect how much they want directed to the IRA at any time.

A SEP is an IRA-based retirement plan available to any employer (including a self-employed individual). These plans are simple to establish; the IRS even provides a one-page Form 5305-SEP that can be used to set up the plan. SEPs have flexible funding requirements in case funding the plan with consistent contribution amounts might be an issue for the underlying business. The amount of contributions can change from year-to-year and can be zero. Employees that meet the SEP requirements for minimum age (21) and years of service (employed by the employer for at least 3 of the last 5 years), and make at least $600 in annual compensation, *must* be offered an opportunity to participate in the SEP.

SEP contributions and deductions are limited under different rules for employees versus a self-employed business owner. The maximum contribution made for an employee and the related deduction cannot exceed the lesser of 25 percent of the employee's compensation or $57,000 in 2020. For the self-employed business owner, the contribution maximum is the same 25 percent as for employees; however, the deduction limit considers the net self-employment income after consideration of the deduction for the contribution to the SEP. As a result, the deduction available for the self-employed will be slightly lower than that of an employee and is derived by taking the plan contribution rate and dividing by one plus the contribution rate; thus, effectively lowering the maximum contribution rate to 20 percent (0.25 ÷ 1.25).

EXAMPLE   Dan is a self-employed doctor. His net earned income (Schedule C net income less one-half of self-employment tax) from his practice is $125,000. Under the terms of his SEP plan, Dan contributes 20 percent of compensation (up to the maximum allowable) to the plan for his employees. Dan's maximum deduction is calculated as follows: Dan's self-employed rate is 0.20 ÷ 1.20 = 0.1666 or 16.667 percent. His maximum deduction is $20,834, which is the lesser of 16.667% × $125,000 ($20,834) or $57,000. ♦

In the past, a plan similar to a current SEP, known as a SARSEP, was available. SARSEPs could not be created after January 31, 1996 and although some plans were grandfathered in, many are no longer in operation.

A SIMPLE IRA is available to any employer with 100 or fewer employees (including a self-employed individual). SIMPLE IRAs are also easy to establish (Form 5304-SIMPLE or 5305-SIMPLE) and administer. Both the employee and the employer are eligible to contribute with an annual limit of $13,500 ($16,500 for taxpayers age 50 or older) in 2020. The SIMPLE IRA must be offered to employees with compensation of at least $5,000 in any prior 2 years and are expected to have compensation of $5,000 in the current year. Unlike a SEP, a SIMPLE IRA requires certain contributions *must* be made by the employer. Employees decide how much they would like to contribute and the employer must match employees for the first 3 percent of compensation (with some flexibility) or 2 percent of each eligible employee's compensation regardless of the employee's contributions.

5-4c **401(k)-Based Plans**

One of the more popular qualified retirement plans is the Section 401(k) plan, which permits an employee to choose to receive a direct payment of compensation in cash or to defer the amount through an employer contribution on behalf of the employee to plan. Such a plan may be structured as a salary reduction agreement. The agreement may allow the employee to reduce his or her compensation or forgo an increase in compensation, with the amount contributed to the qualified retirement plan, thereby deferring tax on the compensation. Employees choose the percentage of their pay which will be withheld and contributed to the plan. Some employers match employee contributions up to a certain percentage in order to encourage participation.

EXAMPLE   In 2019, Margo elects to defer 5 percent of her next year's salary into her company's 401k plan. Margo's 2020 salary is $50,000 and thus $2,500 ($50,000 × 5 percent) will be contributed to the 401k plan. Her taxable wages for 2020 will be $47,500. ♦

Any matching amount contributed to the plan by the employer on behalf of the employee is also excluded from the employee's gross income. The contributions and the earnings on the amounts invested in the plan are taxable only when withdrawn.

EXAMPLE   In the previous example, Margo's employer matches contributions up to 4 percent and thus contributes an additional $2,000 ($50,000 × 4 percent) to Margo's 401k plan. The $2,000 is also excluded from Margo's taxable wages. ♦

Employment taxes (covered in Chapter 9) apply to the employee's contribution but do not apply to the employer's match.

In all 401(k) plans, contributions are limited in two ways: (1) for 2020, an employee may elect to make an annual contribution up to $19,500 ($26,000 for taxpayers age 50 or older) to a Section 401(k) plan, and (2) the amount of total contributions (employee plus employer) made to the Section 401(k) plan are also subject to the limitations applicable to all qualified plans (25 percent of compensation subject to a limit of $57,000, $63,000 if over age 50). The annual maximum ($19,500, or $26,000 if age 50 or over, in 2020) is reduced dollar for dollar by amounts contributed as a result of the employee's participation in other salary reduction plans of any employer. Contributions in excess of the maximum allowed may be subject to a 10 percent excise tax imposed on the employer.

EXAMPLE   Carol, age 48, participates in a Section 401(k) plan. Carol's salary is $30,000 per year and she chooses to contribute 15 percent to the 401(k) plan. The maximum amount she may contribute on a tax-deferred basis to the Section 401(k) plan under a salary reduction agreement is $4,500 (15% × $30,000, not to exceed $19,500, in 2020). ♦

Finally, Section 401(k) plans must meet certain requirements in addition to the general qualification requirements for all qualified plans. Generally, any employee with at least 1,000 hours of work in a previous year that is at least 21 years old must be permitted to participate. Starting in 2020, an employee with over 500 hours in each of three consecutive years must also be permitted to participate. The amount deferred must be 100 percent vested and may be distributed only upon retirement, death, disability, or other separation from service, attainment of age 59½, or hardship.

A traditional 401(k) plan can be used by any type of company but is generally thought to be more appropriate for business with at least 20 employees due to the cost to establish and administer the plan. An annual reporting of the plan assets is required (Form 5500) and special annual IRS testing is required to ensure that the plan does not favor highly-compensated employees. One of the newest types of traditional 401k plans is the automatic enrollment 401k. As the name describes, in this type of plan, employees are automatically enrolled in the plan unless they opt out. Not only does auto-enroll plans nudge employees into saving for retirement, the typically higher participation rates decrease the chances of the plan favoring highly-compensated employees. To provide incentive to employers to create auto-enroll plans, starting in 2019 there is an annual $500 Small Employer Automatic Enrollment credit which can be claimed for up to three years.

For small businesses with employees, a safe harbor 401(k) plan operates like other 401(k) plans with one important distinction: it must provide for employer contributions that are fully vested when made. These contributions may be employer-matching contributions, limited to employees who defer, or employer contributions made on behalf of all eligible employees, regardless of whether they make elective deferrals. The safe harbor 401(k) plan is not subject to the complex annual nondiscrimination tests that apply to traditional 401(k) plans.

Beginning in 2006, employers were allowed to set up Roth 401(k)s for their employees. The amounts allowed to be set aside are the same as for regular 401(k)s, but the dollars paid in do not reduce the employees' taxable income, which is similar to the tax treatment of Roth IRAs. Withdrawals, including earnings, are generally tax-free based on rules similar to those for Roth IRA withdrawals. Roth 401(k)s are popular because they allow a significantly higher Roth contribution than a Roth IRA and because there is no AGI limitation, they may be used by high-income taxpayers.

A self-employed 401(k) or solo 401(k) is designed for self-employed individuals with no employees (spouse is permitted). Setup and maintenance of the plan are relatively inexpensive and easy.

Self-Study Problem 5.4   *See Appendix E for Solutions to Self-Study Problems*

a. Lewis, a self-employed individual, has net earned income of $50,000 in 2020. If Lewis has no employees, calculate the maximum contribution to a SEP plan that he may deduct from his adjusted gross income.

$_____

b. During 2020, Linda, age 32, has a salary of $40,000. She participates in a Section 401(k) plan and chooses to defer 25 percent of her compensation.

   i. What is the maximum amount Linda can contribute to the Section 401(k) plan on a tax-deferred basis?

$_____

   ii. If Linda's salary was $125,000, instead of $40,000, what is the maximum amount that she could contribute to the Section 401(k) plan on a tax-deferred basis?

$_____

Learning Objective 5.5

Describe other adjustments for adjusted gross income.

5-5 OTHER FOR AGI DEDUCTIONS

There are a number of other deductions for AGI available under the tax law. Because of the limited nature of these deductions, a less detailed description is provided. The deduction for one-half of self-employment tax, which affects almost all self-employed taxpayers, is described in Chapter 6. The for AGI deduction related to charitable contributions in 2020 resulting from COVID-relief provisions is discussed later in this chapter.

5-5a Educator Expenses

Eligible educators may deduct up to $250 for the unreimbursed cost of classroom materials such as books, supplies, computer equipment, and supplementary materials as a deduction in arriving at AGI. An eligible educator is a kindergarten through grade 12 teacher, instructor, counselor, principal or aide who works at least 900 hours a school year in a school that provides elementary or secondary education. If a married filing jointly couple are both eligible educators, the total deduction is up to $500 but not more than $250 for either spouse.

EXAMPLE Glen and Iris Holland are a married couple that files jointly and both are high school teachers. In 2020, Glen and Iris spent $270 and $120 on various school supplies, respectively. The Hollands are eligible for a $370 ($250 + $120) educator expense for AGI deduction. ♦

5-5b Unreimbursed Business Expenses for Performing Artists and Others

As discussed later in this chapter, employees that incur business expenses are no longer permitted to deduct those costs as an itemized deduction subject to a 2 percent of AGI floor. Certain employee taxpayers, however, are eligible to take a for AGI deduction for unreimbursed employee costs and thus, are not required to itemize to deduct these costs.

There are three different types of taxpayers eligible for this deduction (and the rules are different for each one):

1. Performing artists who worked for two or more employers during the year
2. National Guard or Reserve member
3. Fee-based government officials

Performing artists may deduct employee business expenses as a for AGI deduction if they meet the following qualifications:

1. The taxpayer was paid for providing performing arts as an employee for at least two employers.
2. The taxpayer received at least $200 each from any two of these employers.
3. The related performing-arts business expenses are more than 10 percent of gross income from the performance of those services, and
4. AGI is not more than $16,000 before deducting these business expenses.

Members of a reserve component of the Armed Forces of the United States that travel more than 100 miles away from home in connection with services in the reserves can deduct travel expenses. The travel expense deduction is limited to the regular federal per diem rate (for lodging, meals, and incidental expenses) and the standard mileage rate (for car expenses) plus any parking fees, ferry fees, and tolls. Per diems are discussed in Chapter 3.

Certain fee-basis officials can claim their employee business expenses. Fee-basis officials are persons who are employed by a state or local government and who are paid in whole or in part on a fee basis.

EXAMPLE Sally is a building inspector for the city of Hickory, Indiana. Sally is compensated solely from fees paid directly to her by clients and is not considered an employee of Hickory. Sally's travel and other business expenses can be deducted as a for AGI deduction. ♦

Unreimbursed business expenses that are deductible are claimed on Form 2106.

5-5c Moving Expenses

In the past, the tax law provided a deduction for moving expenses to help relieve taxpayers of a portion of the financial burden of moving from one job location to another. The TCJA suspended the deduction for moving expenses (through 2025) for all taxpayers except members of the Armed Forces of the United States on active duty whose move is pursuant to a military order and incident to a permanent change of station.

Starting in 2018, reimbursements to an employee from an employer for qualified moving costs are no longer excluded from the employee's income.

Under the former law, taxpayers (except for those in the Armed Forces) had to meet three tests in order to deduct moving costs:

1. The taxpayer must change job sites.
2. The taxpayer must move so that the distance from the taxpayer's former residence to the new job location must be at least 50 miles more than the distance from the former residence to the former job location.
3. The taxpayer must remain at the new job location for a certain period of time, generally, 39 weeks. Taxpayers who were self-employed had to work at least 78 weeks at the new location.

Taxpayers in the Armed Forces are not required to meet the time or distance tests. For the members of the military that qualify, moving expenses are reported on Form 3903.

Self-Study Problem 5.5   *See Appendix E for Solutions to Self-Study Problems*

For each of the following situations, determine whether a deduction for AGI is permitted for the taxpayer.

a. Professor Hill teaches at Bunker Hall Community College. In 2020, he spent $267 on supplies for his classroom and was not reimbursed.

b. Jackie Rights played the lead role in two different plays in 2020 in the local community theatre. Two different production companies sponsored the plays and so she was an employee of both in 2020 and was paid the same by both employers: $4,000 per play. Jackie spent $1,100 in business expenses such as new business cards, personal management fees, and new head-shots for her portfolio. Her 2020 AGI was $15,200 (she also generated income as a shared-ride vehicle driver).

c. Lieutenant Dan of the U.S. Army was stationed in Fort Bragg, NC. In 2020, his permanent post was moved from Bragg to Fort Jackson. The unreimbursed moving costs for he and his wife are $4,500.

Learning Objective 5.6

Calculate the itemized deduction for medical expenses.

5-6 MEDICAL EXPENSES

Medical expenses are the first itemized deduction listed on Schedule A. Taxpayers are allowed a deduction for the medical expenses paid for themselves, their spouse, and dependents. Unreimbursed medical expenses can only be deducted to the extent that they exceed 7.5 percent of the taxpayer's AGI. The formula for calculating a taxpayer's medical expense deduction is as follows:

Prescription medicines and drugs, insulin, doctors, dentists, hospitals, medical insurance premiums	$ xxx
Other medical and dental expenses, such as lodging, transportation, eyeglasses, contact lenses, etc.	xxx
Less: insurance reimbursements	(xxx)
Subtotal	xxx
Less: 7.5 percent of adjusted gross income	(xxx)
Excess expenses qualifying for the medical deduction	$ xxx

5-6a What Qualifies as a Medical Expense?

Expenses that are deductible as medical expenses include the cost of items for the diagnosis, cure, mitigation, treatment, and prevention of disease. Also included are expenditures incurred that affect any structure or function of the body. Therefore, amounts for all of the following categories of expenditures qualify as medical expenses:

- Prescription medicines and drugs and insulin
- Fees for doctors, dentists, nurses, and other medical professionals

- Hospital fees
- Hearing aids, dentures, prescription eyeglasses, and contact lenses
- Medical transportation and lodging
- Medical aids, such as crutches, wheelchairs, and guide dogs
- Birth control prescriptions
- Acupuncture
- Psychiatric care
- Medical insurance premiums, including Medicare premiums
- Certain capital expenditures deemed medically necessary by a doctor
- Nursing home care for the chronically ill (e.g., Alzheimer's disease care)

The IRS has allowed a deduction for the following unusual medical expenses:
- Long-distance phone calls made to a psychological counselor
- Hair transplants for premature baldness
- A wig prescribed by a psychiatrist for a taxpayer upset by hair loss
- A mobile phone for a taxpayer who may need instantaneous medical help
- Treatments provided by a Native American medicine man

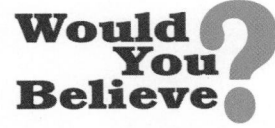

Certain medical expenses are not deductible. For example, the cost of travel for the general improvement of the taxpayer's health is not deductible. The expense of a swimming pool is not deductible unless the pool is designed specially for the hydrotherapeutic treatment of the taxpayer's illness. No deduction is allowed for the cost of weight-loss programs (unless prescribed by a doctor; diet foods do not qualify) or marriage counseling. Medical expenses for unnecessary cosmetic surgery or similar procedures are not deductible. Cosmetic surgery is considered unnecessary unless it corrects (1) a congenital abnormality, (2) a personal injury resulting from an accident or trauma, or (3) a disfiguring disease. In general, unnecessary cosmetic surgery is any procedure which is directed at improving the patient's appearance and does not meaningfully promote the proper function of the body or prevent or treat illness or disease.

Taxpayers that do not spend medical expenses greater than 7.5 percent of AGI can still enjoy the tax benefit associated with the deduction by using the medical flexible spending account discussed in Chapter 2. By excluding up to $2,750 from gross income, the after-tax savings is basically identical to taking the medical expense deduction for the same amount.

5-6b Medical Insurance

Medical insurance includes standard health policies, whether the benefits are paid to the taxpayer or to the provider of the services directly. In addition, the premiums paid for membership in health maintenance plans are deductible as medical insurance, as are supplemental payments for optional Medicare coverage. Insurance policies that pay a specific amount each day or week the taxpayer is hospitalized are not considered medical insurance and the premiums are not deductible. Premiums paid for qualified long-term care insurance policies are also deductible medical expenses up to specified limits which change each year and are based on the age of the taxpayer.

Self-employed taxpayers are allowed, subject to certain limitations, a deduction for adjusted gross income for the medical insurance premiums paid for themselves and their families. Long-term care insurance premiums, up to a specified amount based on the taxpayer's age, are considered health insurance for this purpose. These deductions are covered earlier in this chapter. If a deduction is taken for these items in arriving at AGI, then these same expenses are excluded from the medical expense deduction on Schedule A. However, if the self-employed insurance deduction is limited by net self-employment income, the excess medical insurance expenses can be included on Schedule A.

5-6c **Medicines and Drugs**

Prescription medicines and drugs and insulin are the only drugs deductible as medical expenses. No deduction is allowed for drugs purchased illegally from abroad, including Canada and Mexico. Nonprescription medicines such as over-the-counter antacids, allergy medications, and pain relievers, even if recommended by a physician, are not deductible as a medical expense.

5-6d **Capital Expenditures**

Payments for capital improvements purchased and installed in the taxpayer's home for medical reasons may also be deductible. Examples include support railings, lowering kitchen cabinets, and medically necessary swimming pools. Unlike other capital expenditures, allowable amounts are deducted fully in the year the item is purchased. If the expenditure is for an improvement that increases the value of the taxpayer's property, the deduction is limited to the amount by which the expenditure exceeds the increase in the value of the property. If the value of the property does not increase as a result of the expenditure, the entire cost is deductible. The cost of upkeep and operation of an item, the cost of which qualified as a medical expense, is also deductible, provided the medical reason for the improvement or special equipment still exists. To take advantage of this deduction, the taxpayer must show the improvement is used primarily for and directly related to medical care. A doctor's recommendation is an important factor in supporting the deduction.

EXAMPLE   A taxpayer has a heart condition and installs an elevator in his home at a cost of $6,000. The value of the home is increased by $4,000 as a result of the improvement. The taxpayer is allowed a deduction of $2,000 ($6,000 − $4,000), the excess of the cost of the equipment over the increase in the value of the taxpayer's home. ♦

5-6e **Transportation**

Transportation expenses primarily and necessary for medical care are deductible, including amounts paid for taxis, trains, buses, airplanes, and ambulances. Taxpayers may also claim a deduction for the use of their personal automobile for medical transportation. However, only out-of-pocket expenses such as the cost of gas and oil are deductible. Maintenance, insurance, general repair, and depreciation expenses are not deductible. If the taxpayer does not wish to deduct actual costs of transportation by personal automobile, the standard mileage rate for medical care purposes is 17 cents per mile for 2020. In addition to the deduction for actual automobile costs or the standard mileage amount, parking and toll fees for medical transportation are deductible medical expenses. If the transportation expenses are for the medical care of a dependent child, the amounts are deductible by the parent.

5-6f **Lodging for Medical Care**

Taxpayers may deduct the cost of lodging up to $50 per night, per person, on a trip primarily for and essential to medical care provided by a physician or a licensed hospital. The deduction is allowed for the patient and an individual accompanying the patient, such as the parent of a child. However, no deduction is allowed if the trip involves a significant element of recreation or vacation. No deduction is allowed for meal costs.

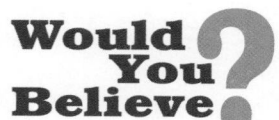

A Las Vegas dentist admitted he provided free dental work to an IRS revenue officer in exchange for reductions of his $100,000 tax debt. Both men were indicted on conspiracy and bribery charges.

Itemized deductions are located under Deductions/Itemized Deductions (Schedule A). Subheadings for each of the itemized deductions will be found in the left-hand margin.

Self-Study Problem 5.6   *See Appendix E for Solutions to Self-Study Problems*

During the 2020 tax year, Frank (age 65) and Betty (age 63) paid the following medical expenses:

Medical insurance	$ 425
Prescription medicines and drugs	364
Hospital bills	2,424
Doctor bills	725
Prescription Eyeglasses for Frank's dependent mother	75
Doctor bills for Betty's sister, who is claimed as a dependent by Frank and Betty	220

In addition, during 2020, they drove 700 miles for medical transportation in their personal automobile. Their insurance company reimbursed Frank and Betty $1,420 during the year for the medical expenses. If their adjusted gross income for the year is $25,400, calculate their medical expense deduction. Use Schedule A of Form 1040 on Page 5-23.

5-7 TAXES

Taxpayers are allowed to deduct certain state, local, and foreign taxes paid during the year. The purpose of the deduction for taxes is to relieve the burden of multiple taxation of the same income. However, the tax law distinguishes between a "tax" and a "fee." A tax is imposed by a government to raise revenue for general public purposes, and a fee is a charge with a direct benefit to the person paying the fee. Taxes are generally deductible; fees are not deductible. For example, postage, fishing licenses, and dog tags are considered fees that are not deductible as taxes.

Prior to the enactment of the TCJA, tax law provided for an itemized deduction for the following taxes:

- State, local, and foreign income taxes
- Sales taxes (in lieu of state and local income taxes)
- State, local, and foreign real property taxes
- State, local, and foreign personal property taxes

After the TCJA, these taxes largely remain deductible; however, foreign property taxes are only deductible if incurred in carrying on a business or for the production of income (e.g., rental activity). In addition, the aggregate amount of the deduction for state and local real property taxes, state and local personal property taxes, state and local, and foreign, income taxes, and general sales taxes (if elected) for any tax year is limited to $10,000 ($5,000 for married filing separately). But, the $10,000 aggregate limitation rule does not apply to (i) foreign income taxes; (ii) state and local, and foreign real property taxes; and (iii) state and local personal property taxes, if these taxes are paid or accrued in carrying on a business or for the production of income. In other words, taxes deductible on an individual's Schedule C, Schedule E, or Schedule F remain fully deductible and are not subject to the limitation. Note that state and local *income* taxes are not included in the business-related exclusion from the limitation as these taxes have always been deductible as an itemized deduction on an individual's Schedule A. These provisions (the loss of the foreign property tax deduction and $10,000 deduction limitation) apply through 2025.

EXAMPLE   Britney and Brad are married taxpayers filing jointly. In 2020, Britney has $7,800 in state income taxes withheld by her employer from her wages. Brad operates a sole proprietorship that owns a building and pays property taxes of $2,300. Brad also pays estimated state income tax payments on his business of $4,000. Lastly, in 2020 Brad and Britney pay property taxes on their home of $1,600. The $2,300 of property taxes associated with the business building are deductible on Schedule C as a business deduction. The $13,400 of itemized deduction for taxes includes Britney's state income taxes ($7,800), Brad's estimated tax payments ($4,000), and the property taxes on their home ($1,600). However, the itemized deduction for taxes is limited to $10,000 in 2020. ◆

The following taxes are not deductible:

- Federal income taxes
- Employee portion of Social Security taxes
- Estate, inheritance, and gift taxes (except in unusual situations not discussed here)
- Excise taxes and gasoline taxes (except when business-related)
- Foreign income taxes if the taxpayer elects a foreign tax credit

5-7a Income Taxes and Sales Taxes

Taxpayers may elect to deduct either state and local sales and use taxes or state and local income taxes as itemized deductions. The election to deduct state and local sales tax instead of income tax primarily benefits taxpayers in states with no income taxes or low income tax rates.

For taxpayers electing to deduct state and local income taxes paid during 2020, the amount of the deduction is the total amount of state and local taxes withheld from wages plus any amounts actually paid during the year, even if the tax payments are for a prior year's tax liability. If the taxpayer receives a refund of taxes deducted in a previous year, the refund must generally be included in gross income (e.g., Line 1 on Schedule 1 of the Form 1040) in the year the refund is received. Taxes which did not provide any tax benefit (reduction in taxes) in the year paid are not required to be included in income in the year received as a refund. For example, a taxpayer claiming the standard deduction in the year taxes are paid does not receive a tax benefit for the payment and is not required to include in income a tax refund received the following year.

EXAMPLE   For 2020, Mary's total itemized deductions are $4,500, including state income tax withheld of $1,800. As a result, Mary uses the standard deduction of $12,400. When Mary prepares her 2020 state income taxes, she realizes that she overpaid state income tax through withholding by $200 and receives a refund in 2021. In early 2022, she receives a Form 1099-G reporting her $200 state income tax refund. Because Mary did not benefit from the state tax deduction since she used the standard deduction, she is not required to include the $200 refund in income. ◆

EXAMPLE   Damone paid state income and property taxes of $10,250 in 2020. Damone claimed total itemized deductions of $12,500, including the $10,000 limit on state and local taxes. In 2021, Damone received a state income tax refund of $1,000. If Damone had deducted the actual amount of state taxes in 2020, he would have deducted on $9,250 ($10,250 paid in 2020 less $1,000 refund). His adjusted total itemized deductions would have been $11,750. As a result, Damone would have elected the standard deduction of $12,400 in 2020. The difference between his 2020 claimed itemized deductions ($12,500) and his properly adjusted standard deduction ($12,400) is $100. Thus, he received a $100 benefit from the overpayment of taxes, and Damone must include $100 in his 2021 income. ◆

Self-Study Problems 5.6, 5.7, 5.8, 5.9, and 5.10

SCHEDULE A
(Form 1040)

Department of the Treasury
Internal Revenue Service (99)

Itemized Deductions

▶ Go to *www.irs.gov/ScheduleA* for instructions and the latest information.
▶ Attach to Form 1040 or 1040-SR.

Caution: If you are claiming a net qualified disaster loss on Form 4684, see the instructions for line 16.

OMB No. 1545-0074

2020

Attachment
Sequence No. **07**

Name(s) shown on Form 1040 or 1040-SR

Your social security number

Medical and Dental Expenses		
Caution: Do not include expenses reimbursed or paid by others.		
1 Medical and dental expenses (see instructions)	**1**	
2 Enter amount from Form 1040 or 1040-SR, line 11	**2**	
3 Multiply line 2 by 7.5% (0.075)	**3**	
4 Subtract line 3 from line 1. If line 3 is more than line 1, enter -0-		**4**

Taxes You Paid

5 State and local taxes.

a State and local income taxes or general sales taxes. You may include either income taxes or general sales taxes on line 5a, but not both. If you elect to include general sales taxes instead of income taxes, check this box ▶ ☐ — **5a**

b State and local real estate taxes (see instructions) — **5b**

c State and local personal property taxes — **5c**

d Add lines 5a through 5c — **5d**

e Enter the smaller of line 5d or $10,000 ($5,000 if married filing separately) — **5e**

6 Other taxes. List type and amount ▶ _____ — **6**

7 Add lines 5e and 6 — **7**

Interest You Paid

Caution: Your mortgage interest deduction may be limited (see instructions).

8 Home mortgage interest and points. If you didn't use all of your home mortgage loan(s) to buy, build, or improve your home, see instructions and check this box ▶ ☐

a Home mortgage interest and points reported to you on Form 1098. See instructions if limited — **8a**

b Home mortgage interest not reported to you on Form 1098. See instructions if limited. If paid to the person from whom you bought the home, see instructions and show that person's name, identifying no., and address

▶ _____ — **8b**

c Points not reported to you on Form 1098. See instructions for special rules — **8c**

d Mortgage insurance premiums (see instructions) — **8d**

e Add lines 8a through 8d — **8e**

9 Investment interest. Attach Form 4952 if required. See instructions — **9**

10 Add lines 8e and 9 — **10**

Gifts to Charity

Caution: If you made a gift and got a benefit for it, see instructions.

11 Gifts by cash or check. If you made any gift of $250 or more, see instructions — **11**

12 Other than by cash or check. If you made any gift of $250 or more, see instructions. You **must** attach Form 8283 if over $500. — **12**

13 Carryover from prior year — **13**

14 Add lines 11 through 13 — **14**

Casualty and Theft Losses

15 Casualty and theft loss(es) from a federally declared disaster (other than net qualified disaster losses). Attach Form 4684 and enter the amount from line 18 of that form. See instructions — **15**

Other Itemized Deductions

16 Other—from list in instructions. List type and amount ▶ _____
_____ — **16**

Total Itemized Deductions

17 Add the amounts in the far right column for lines 4 through 16. Also, enter this amount on Form 1040 or 1040-SR, line 12 — **17**

18 If you elect to itemize deductions even though they are less than your standard deduction, check this box ▶ ☐

For Paperwork Reduction Act Notice, see the Instructions for Forms 1040 and 1040-SR.

Cat. No. 17145C

Schedule A (Form 1040) 2020

DRAFT AS OF July 13, 2020 DO NOT FILE

For taxpayers electing to deduct sales taxes in 2020, the deduction is calculated by using either (a) actual sales taxes paid or (b) estimated sales taxes from IRS tables. Actual sales and use tax expenses are based on a "general sales tax," which is a tax imposed at one rate with respect to the retail sale of a broad range of classes of items. To the extent a higher sales tax rate than the general rate applies to motor vehicles, that excess amount is specifically excluded from the deduction amount.

The actual sales taxes paid method requires a taxpayer to maintain extensive records to substantiate the sales and use taxes paid during the year. To ease the burden on taxpayers, the tax law also permits taxpayers to use estimated state sales tax tables to calculate the deduction. Taxpayers using the estimation tables may add the sales taxes paid on items that include motor vehicles (car, truck, van, motor home, recreational vehicle), aircraft, boats, a home or a substantial addition or renovation to a home. The estimated state sales tax tables are based on the taxpayer's adjusted gross income modified by adding back certain tax-exempt sources of income such as tax-exempt interest, workers compensation, and the nontaxable parts of Social Security or qualified retirement plan distributions. The estimated sales tax also differs by the number of dependents a taxpayer has. The following is a portion of the sales tax estimation table:

2019 Optional State Sales Tax Tables*

Income At least	But less than	Family Size 1	2	3	4	5	Over 5	Family Size 1	2	3	4	5	Over 5	Family Size 1	2	3	4	5	Over 5
		Alabama			**1**		**4.0000%**	**Arizona**			**2**		**5.6000%**	**Arkansas**			**2**		**6.5000%**
$0	$20,000	261	301	327	348	366	390	261	285	301	312	322	336	327	353	370	382	392	406
$20,000	$30,000	378	433	471	500	524	558	403	438	461	478	493	512	511	551	576	596	611	632
$30,000	$40,000	439	501	544	577	605	644	478	519	545	566	583	606	610	657	687	709	728	753
$40,000	$50,000	490	559	606	643	673	716	543	589	619	642	661	687	696	749	783	809	829	858
$50,000	$60,000	536	610	661	700	733	780	602	652	685	710	731	759	774	833	870	898	921	952
$60,000	$70,000	577	656	710	752	787	837	656	709	745	772	794	825	845	908	949	980	1004	1038
$70,000	$80,000	614	698	755	800	837	889	705	762	800	829	853	886	911	979	1022	1055	1082	1118
$80,000	$90,000	649	737	797	844	883	937	751	812	852	882	908	942	972	1044	1091	1126	1154	1193
$90,000	$100,000	682	773	836	885	925	982	795	858	900	933	959	996	1030	1107	1156	1192	1222	1263
$100,000	$120,000	725	822	888	939	982	1042	853	921	965	1000	1028	1067	1108	1190	1242	1282	1313	1357
$120,000	$140,000	782	884	955	1009	1055	1119	929	1002	1050	1087	1118	1160	1210	1299	1356	1398	1433	1480
$140,000	$160,000	834	943	1017	1075	1123	1191	1001	1078	1130	1169	1202	1247	1306	1401	1462	1508	1545	1596
$160,000	$180,000	882	996	1074	1134	1185	1256	1067	1149	1203	1245	1279	1327	1395	1496	1560	1609	1649	1703
$180,000	$200,000	928	1046	1127	1191	1243	1318	1130	1216	1273	1317	1353	1403	1479	1586	1654	1705	1747	1804
$200,000	$225,000	975	1098	1183	1249	1304	1382	1195	1286	1346	1392	1430	1482	1567	1680	1752	1806	1850	1910
$225,000	$250,000	1026	1154	1242	1311	1369	1450	1266	1361	1424	1473	1513	1568	1662	1781	1857	1915	1961	2025
$250,000	$275,000	1074	1207	1298	1370	1429	1513	1333	1432	1498	1549	1591	1648	1753	1877	1957	2018	2066	2133
$275,000	$300,000	1119	1257	1351	1425	1487	1574	1397	1500	1569	1622	1665	1726	1839	1969	2053	2116	2167	2237
$300,000	or more	1388	1551	1664	1752	1826	1930	1781	1908	1993	2058	2111	2186	2359	2522	2627	2707	2771	2858
Income		**California**			**3**		**7.2500%**	**Colorado**			**2**		**2.9000%**	**Connecticut**			**4**		**6.3500%**
$0	$20,000	328	352	367	379	389	402	135	148	156	162	167	174	299	323	338	349	358	370
$20,000	$30,000	504	538	561	578	592	611	206	225	236	246	253	263	466	503	527	544	558	577
$30,000	$40,000	597	637	663	683	699	721	244	265	279	289	298	310	556	600	627	648	665	687
$40,000	$50,000	678	722	751	773	791	816	277	300	316	327	337	350	633	683	715	738	757	783
$50,000	$60,000	750	799	831	855	875	902	306	332	348	361	372	386	703	759	794	820	841	869
$60,000	$70,000	816	869	903	929	950	979	333	360	378	392	403	419	767	827	865	894	917	948
$70,000	$80,000	877	933	969	997	1019	1050	357	386	406	420	432	449	826	891	932	962	987	1021
$80,000	$90,000	935	993	1031	1061	1084	1117	380	411	431	447	460	477	881	950	994	1027	1053	1088
$90,000	$100,000	988	1050	1090	1120	1145	1180	402	434	455	472	485	504	932	1006	1052	1087	1115	1152
$100,000	$120,000	1060	1125	1168	1200	1227	1263	431	465	488	505	519	539	1002	1081	1131	1168	1198	1238

*The 2020 version of the Optional State Sales Tax Tables was not available as we went to print. Please check the IRS website (**www.irs.gov**) for updates to the instructions for Form 1040 Schedule A.

Because a number of states permit localities to also charge a general sale tax, a local sales tax table for some of the states is provided to assist with that calculation. Because the estimation method is fairly complex, the IRS provides a worksheet to assist with the deduction calculation and most tax preparation software will compute the amounts as well.

When it comes to entering state tax deduction information, much of the work will be done elsewhere. For example, income taxes withheld are generally input as part of the W-2 input. Estimated payments are input under the primary heading Payments, Penalties, and Extensions. Lastly, Intuit ProConnect has the state sales tax calculator built in and does not require the manual completion of the state and local sales tax worksheet.

ProConnect™ Tax

TIP

State and Local General Sales Tax Deduction
Worksheet—Line 5a

Keep for Your Records

 Instead of using this worksheet, you can find your deduction by using the Sales Tax Deduction Calculator at IRS.gov/SalesTax.

Before you begin: See the instructions for line 1 of the worksheet if you:

  ✓ Lived in more than one state during 2020, or
  ✓ Had any **nontaxable** income in 2020.

---

1. Enter your **state** general sales taxes from the 2020 Optional State Sales Tax Table . . . .   **1.** $ _____

   Next. If, for all of 2020, you lived only in Connecticut, the District of Columbia, Indiana, Kentucky, Maine, Maryland, Massachusetts, Michigan, New Jersey, or Rhode Island, skip lines 2 through 5, enter -0- on line 6, and go to line 7. Otherwise, go to line 2.

2. Did you live in Alaska, Arizona, Arkansas, Colorado, Georgia, Illinois, Louisiana, Mississippi, Missouri, New York, North Carolina, South Carolina, Tennessee, Utah, or Virginia in 2020?

   ☐ **No.** Enter -0-.

   ☐ **Yes.** Enter your base **local** general sales taxes from the 2020 Optional Local Sales Tax Tables.

   } . . . .   **2.** $ _____

3. Did your locality impose a **local** general sales tax in 2020? Residents of California and Nevada, see the instructions for line 3 of the worksheet.

   ☐ **No.** Skip lines 3 through 5, enter -0- on line 6, and go to line 7.

   ☐ **Yes.** Enter your **local** general sales tax rate, but omit the percentage sign. For example, if your local general sales tax rate was 2.5%, enter 2.5. If your local general sales tax rate changed or you lived in more than one locality in the same state during 2020, see the instructions for line 3 of the worksheet . . . .   **3.** _____ ._____

4. Did you enter -0- on line 2?

   ☐ **No.** Skip lines 4 and 5 and go to line 6.

   ☐ **Yes.** Enter your **state** general sales tax rate (shown in the table heading for your state), but omit the percentage sign. For example, if your state general sales tax rate is 6%, enter 6.0 . . . .   **4.** _____ ._____

5. Divide line 3 by line 4. Enter the result as a decimal (rounded to at least three places) . . . .   **5.** _____ ._____

6. Did you enter -0- on line 2?

   ☐ **No.** Multiply line 2 by line 3.

   ☐ **Yes.** Multiply line 1 by line 5. If you lived in more than one locality in the same state during 2020, see the instructions for line 6 of the worksheet.

   } . . . .   **6.** $ _____

7. Enter your state and local general sales taxes paid on specified items, if any. See the instructions for line 7 of the worksheet . . . .   **7.** $ _____

8. **Deduction for general sales taxes.** Add lines 1, 6, and 7. Enter the result here and the total from all your state and local general sales tax deduction worksheets, if you completed more than one, on Schedule A, line 5a. Be sure to check the **box** on that line . . . .   **8.** $ _____

The IRS also provides an online sales tax deduction calculator at **www.irs.gov**.

EXAMPLE Jason and Tina Sterling are married filing jointly taxpayers and residents of Rock Hill, South Carolina (York County, zip code 29732). They have no dependents and their AGI for 2020 is $85,000. Rock Hill has a 7 percent sales tax that includes 6 percent for the state portion and 1 percent for the local portion. The Sterlings paid no sales tax on specified items during the year.

The state sales tax table for South Carolina provides a general sales tax amount for income between $80,000 and $90,000 for married filing jointly as $872. South Carolina permits a local general sales tax, and thus the Sterlings use the Local Sales Tax Table for income between $80,000 and $90,000 with two family members to derive a local sales tax estimate of $135. Using the sales tax deduction worksheet, the local amount of $135 is multiplied by 1 to yield a total local sales tax amount of $135. Thus the total sales tax deduction is $1,007. ♦

This example uses 2019 state and local general sales tax estimates as the 2020 amounts were not available as we went to print.

When a married couple files separately, if one spouse uses the optional sales tax tables, the other spouse must use the optional sales tax tables as well.

5-7b **Property Taxes**

Taxes that are levied on state and local real property for the general public welfare are deductible. However, special assessments charged to provide local benefit to property owners are not deductible; these amounts increase the basis of the taxpayer's property. Also, service fees, such as garbage fees and homeowner association fees, are not deductible as property taxes.

If real estate is sold during the year, the taxes must be allocated between the buyer and the seller, and the division must be made according to the number of days in the year that each taxpayer held the property. The seller is generally responsible for the property taxes up to, but not including, the date the house was sold.

EXAMPLE Sally sells her home to Patty on March 3, 2020. The taxes for 2020 are paid by Patty and they total $1,830, or $5.00 per day ($1,830/366 days). The purchaser is treated as the owner on the day of sale. Sally is entitled to deduct 62 days of real property taxes or $310 (62 days × $5.00 per day). Patty deducts $1,520 (304 days × $5.00 per day). ♦

Generally, the escrow company or closing agent handling the sale of the property will make the allocation of taxes between the buyer and the seller and the result will be reflected in the settlement charges on the transfer of the title. These amounts are itemized on closing statements for the sale, which are provided to the buyer and the seller.

EXAMPLE William purchased a new residence from John in 2020. William's closing statement shows that he receives a credit for $299.80 in taxes that he will pay later in the year on behalf of the seller. Assuming that William pays $525.00 in total taxes on the property later in 2020, his property tax deduction for 2020 would be $225.20 ($525.00 − $299.80). John, the seller, would be allowed a deduction for $299.80 plus any other taxes he paid during the year prior to selling the property. ♦

5-7c **Personal Property Taxes**

To be deductible as an itemized deduction, personal property taxes must be levied based on the value of the property. Taxes of a fixed amount, or those calculated on a basis other than value, are not deductible. For example, automobile fees that are calculated on the basis of the automobile's weight are not deductible.

EXAMPLE   Rich lives in a state that charges $20 per year plus 2 percent of the value of the automobile for vehicle registration. If Rich pays $160 [$20 + (2% × $7,000)] for his automobile registration, he may deduct only $140, the amount that is based on the value of the automobile. ♦

Self-Study Problem 5.7   *See Appendix E for Solutions to Self-Study Problems*

Sharon is single, lives in Idaho, and has adjusted gross income of $81,000 for 2020. Sharon deducts state income tax rather than state sales tax. The tax withheld from her salary for state income taxes in 2020 is $1,050, and in May of 2020 she received a $225 refund on her state income tax return for the prior year. Sharon paid real estate taxes on her house of $825 for the year and an automobile registration fee of $110, of which $25 is based on the weight of the automobile and the balance on the value of the property. Use the Taxes You Paid section of Schedule A on Page 5-23 to report Sharon's deduction for state and local taxes.

Learning Objective 5.8

Apply the rules for an individual taxpayer's interest deduction.

5-8 INTEREST

Taxpayers are allowed a deduction for certain interest paid or accrued during the tax year. Interest is defined as an amount paid for the use of borrowed funds. The type and amount of the deduction depend on the purpose for which the money is borrowed. Interest on loans for business, rent, and royalty activities is deducted for adjusted gross income. Certain interest on personal loans is deductible as an itemized deduction. The following types of personal interest are deductible:

- Qualified residence interest (mortgage interest)
- Mortgage interest prepayment penalties
- Investment interest
- Certain interest associated with a passive activity

Interest on other loans for personal purposes which do not fall into one of the above categories is generally referred to as consumer interest and is not deductible. Consumer interest includes interest on any loan, the proceeds of which are used for personal purposes, such as credit card interest, finance charges, and automobile loan interest. Interest on loans used to acquire assets generating tax-exempt income is also not deductible.

The following items are not considered "interest" and, therefore, are not deductible as an itemized deduction for interest:

- Service charges
- Credit investigation fees
- Loan fees other than "points" discussed later under Prepaid Interest
- Interest paid to carry single premium life insurance
- Premium on convertible bonds

Many lenders require that home mortgage borrowers purchase private mortgage insurance (PMI) to protect the lender. The deduction for PMI had been allowed to expire at the end of 2017; however, in 2019, the PMI deduction was retroactively reinstated back to 2018 and is scheduled to expire at the end of 2020. The deduction for PMI phases out for taxpayers with AGI between $100,000 and $109,000.

EXAMPLE Fred and Betty Pebblestone, married filing jointly taxpayers, acquired their principal residence in 2014. The Pebblestone's AGI has never exceeded $100,000. At the time of the mortgage, the lender required that the Pebblestones acquire private mortgage insurance. In 2020, the Pebblestones paid PMI premiums of $1,700. The Pebblestones may include the PMI premiums as an itemized deduction for interest in 2020. The Pebblstones may also amend their 2019 and 2018 returns to claim a deduction for PMI. ◆

As we go to print, it is unknown whether Congress will extend the PMI deduction after 2020.

5-8a Taxpayer's Obligation

To deduct interest on a debt, the taxpayer must be legally liable for the debt. No deduction is allowed for payments made for another's obligation, where the taxpayer is not liable for payment. Also, both the lender and the borrower must intend for the loan to be repaid.

EXAMPLE Bill makes a payment on his son's home mortgage since his son is unable to make the current payment. The interest included in the mortgage payment is not deductible by Bill since the mortgage is not his obligation. Bill's son cannot deduct the interest since he did not make the payment. ◆

EXAMPLE Mary loans her daughter $50,000 to start a business. The daughter is 19 years old and unsophisticated in business. No note is signed and no repayment date is mentioned. Mary would be surprised if the daughter's business venture is a success. In all likelihood, a true debtor-creditor relationship is not created. ◆

A taxpayer who assumes the benefits and burdens of ownership, and is considered to essentially be an owner under state law, may be allowed to deduct mortgage interest on a residence even if not directly liable on the mortgage. This situation is not typical and the deduction is allowed only on a case-by-case basis.

5-8b Prepaid Interest

Cash basis taxpayers are required to use the accrual basis for deducting prepaid interest. Prepaid interest must be capitalized and the deduction spread over the life of the loan. This requirement does not apply to points paid on a mortgage loan for purchasing or improving a taxpayer's principal residence, provided points are customarily charged and they do not exceed the normal rate. Such points paid on a mortgage for the purchase or improvement of a personal residence may be deducted in the year they are paid. Points paid to refinance a home mortgage are not deductible when paid, but must be capitalized and the deduction spread over the life of the loan. Points charged for specific loan services, such as the lender's appraisal fee and other settlement fees, are not deductible.

EXAMPLE On November 1, 2020, Allen, a cash-basis taxpayer, obtains a 6-month loan of $500,000 on a new apartment building. On November 1, Allen prepays $36,000 interest on the loan. He must capitalize the prepaid interest and deduct it over the 6-month loan period. Therefore, his interest deduction for 2020 is $12,000 ($36,000/6 months × 2 months). ◆

5-8c Qualified Residence, Home Equity, and Consumer Interest

No deduction is available for consumer (personal) interest, such as interest on credit cards and loans for personal automobiles. Qualified residence interest, however, is a type of personal interest specifically allowed as a deduction. The term "qualified residence interest" is the interest paid on "qualified residence acquisition debt." The term "qualified residence acquisition debt" is defined as debt secured by the taxpayer's principal or second residence in acquiring, constructing, or substantially improving that residence. Qualified residence acquisition debt can include the original mortgage, home equity debt, or refinanced debt. Refinanced debt is treated as acquisition debt only to the extent it does not exceed the principal amount of acquisition debt immediately before the refinancing.

The limit on the amount of interest has changed under the TCJA. The interest deduction pre-TCJA has been available to qualified mortgage debt up to $1 million ($500,000 married filing separately). Through 2025, the TCJA has lowered the amount of qualified mortgage debt to $750,000. For qualified mortgage debt incurred on or before December 15, 2017, the $1 million limit remains in place.

After 2025, the qualified mortgage debt limit returns to $1 million, regardless of the date of the mortgage. Refinancing of pre-TCJA qualified mortgage debt retains the $1 million limit as long as the refinanced debt does not exceed the debt balance at the time of the refinancing.

TAX BREAK

In order to take a home mortgage interest deduction, debt must be secured by a qualified home (primary residence or second home). A "home" includes a house, condominium, cooperative, and mobile home. A home also includes house trailer, recreational vehicle, boat, or similar property that has sleeping, cooking, and toilet facilities.

EXAMPLE Klaus and Len file jointly in 2020. They purchased their primary residence in New Jersey in January 2016 using a 30-year mortgage of $1,000,000. In 2020, Klaus and Len decide to refinance the full amount of their $950,000 mortgage balance. Because the refinanced amount is the same or less than the mortgage balance at the time of the refinancing, the interest on the entire $950,000 balance will remain deductible. ♦

EXAMPLE Meredith and Scott file jointly in 2020. They purchase their primary residence in Palo Alto, CA in January 2020 using a 30-year mortgage of $1,000,000. In 2020, Meredith and Scott pay interest of $38,000 and make no payments toward loan principle and thus the average loan balance is $1,000,000. Because Meredith and Scott's 2020 mortgage exceeds $750,000, the interest deduction will be limited to $28,500 ($38,000 × $750,000/$1,000,000). ♦

The previously permitted deduction of interest on up to $100,000 of home equity debt has been suspended through 2025 (unless the home equity debt is qualified acquisition debt). Unlike the qualified mortgage debt, interest on home equity loans incurred prior to the enactment of the TCJA are not deductible.

EXAMPLE Michael and Jeanette Stern file jointly in 2020. In 2004, the Sterns purchased a home using a mortgage of $400,000. In 2016, when the mortgage balance was $50,000, the Sterns used a $300,000 home equity loan to build a substantial addition to their home. The home equity loan is treated as acquisition financing and thus is treated as qualified mortgage debt and the interest remains deductible. The Sterns could also have used the home equity to refinance the original mortgage debt and retained the deduction of interest. ♦

EXAMPLE Barb is a single taxpayer. In 2020, she uses a home equity loan of $46,000 to pay for a new car and part of her nephew's college tuition. Barb may not deduct any of the interest on the home equity loan. ♦

If the sum of mortgage interest and other itemized deductions is less than the standard deduction, no tax benefit is received from the mortgage interest payments. In this case, a taxpayer may wish to pay the mortgage off as quickly as possible if the taxpayer believes its investments will generate an after-tax rate of return less than the interest rate on the home mortgage.

TAX BREAK

5-8d Education Loan Interest

Taxpayers are allowed a deduction for adjusted gross income (above-the-line) for certain interest paid on qualified education loans. The deduction is limited to $2,500 for 2020, and is phased out for single taxpayers with modified AGI of $70,000 to $85,000 and for married taxpayers with modified AGI of $140,000 to $170,000. Qualified higher education expenses include tuition, room and board, and related expenses.

EXAMPLE Sam graduated from college in 2019, taking a job with a salary of $55,000 per year. During 2020, he pays $2,500 interest on qualified education loans. Because his income is below the $70,000 phase-out amount for individual taxpayers, he can deduct the full $2,500 of the interest in arriving at adjusted gross income on his 2020 tax return. If he had paid more than $2,500 in interest, the excess would be considered nondeductible consumer interest. ♦

If the interest is paid through the use of funds from a Section 529 program or through an employer's education assistance program, the interest may not also be deducted as an itemized deduction.

5-8e Investment Interest

To prevent abuses by taxpayers, the Internal Revenue Code includes a provision limiting the deduction of investment interest expense. This provision limits the amount of deductible interest on loans to finance investments. The investment interest deduction is limited to the taxpayer's net investment income. Net investment income is income such as dividends and interest, less investment expenses other than interest. Special rules apply to dividends and capital gains included as investment income due to their preferential tax rates. The general rule is that they may only be included as investment income if the taxpayer chooses to calculate tax on them at ordinary income rates. Any disallowed interest expense is carried over and may be deducted in succeeding years, but only to the extent that the taxpayer's net investment income exceeds investment interest expense for the year. The investment interest deduction is reported on Form 4952.

EXAMPLE Karen borrows $150,000 at 12 percent interest on January 1, 2020. The proceeds are used to purchase $100,000 worth of raw land and a $50,000 Certificate of Deposit (CD). During 2020, the CD pays interest of $1,500. Karen incurs expenses attributable to the investment property of $500. Of the $18,000 (12% of $150,000) interest expense incurred in 2020, $1,000 is deductible due to being limited by the total net investment income in 2020. The deduction is computed as follows:

Investment income	$1,500
Less: investment expenses	(500)
Net investment income	$1,000
Interest deductible in 2020	$1,000

The unused deduction of $17,000 ($18,000 − $1,000) is carried forward and may be used as an interest deduction in future years, subject to the net investment income limitation. ♦

Self-Study Problem 5.8   *See Appendix E for Solutions to Self-Study Problems*

Dorothie paid the following amounts during the current year:

Interest on her home mortgage (pre-12/16/17)	$9,250
Service charges on her checking account	48
Credit card interest	168
Auto loan interest	675
Interest from a home equity line of credit (HELOC)	2,300
Interest from a loan used to purchase stock	1,600
Credit investigation fee for loan	75

Dorothie's residence has a fair market value of $250,000. The mortgage is secured by the home at the time of purchase and has a balance of $180,000. Dorothie used the same home to secure her HELOC with a balance of $50,000. Dorothie used the proceeds of her HELOC to pay for college and to buy a new car. Dorothie has $1,000 of net investment income. Compute Dorothie's interest deduction in the following scenarios:

a. Use the Interest You Paid section of Schedule A on Page 5-23 to calculate Dorothie's interest deduction for 2020. $_____

b. Same as part a, and Dorothie used the HELOC proceeds to add a new bedroom to her home. $_____

c. Same as part a, but Dorothie's home is valued at $1.2 million and her mortgage balance is $900,000. $_____

Learning Objective 5.9

Determine the charitable contributions deduction.

5-9 CHARITABLE CONTRIBUTIONS

As part of the temporary COVID-related provisions, a few small but important changes were made to charitable deductions. This includes a temporary increase in the limitation to 100 percent for cash donations and the advent of a for AGI (above-the-line) deduction for charitable contributions made in 2020. These changes are both discussed in this section.

To encourage individuals to be socially responsible, the Internal Revenue Code allows a deduction for charitable contributions. To be deductible, the donation must be made in cash or property; the value of free use of the taxpayer's property by the charitable organization does not qualify. In addition, out-of-pocket expenses related to qualified charitable activities are deductible as charitable contributions. For example, a taxpayer who drives his car 200 miles during 2020 to take a church group to a meeting out of town would be allowed a charitable deduction of $28 (200 miles × 14 cents per mile).

EXAMPLE   Lucille allows the Red Cross to use her building rent-free for 8 months. The building normally rents for $600 per month. There is no deduction allowed for the free use of the building. ◆

To be deductible, the donation must be made to a qualified recipient as listed in the tax law, including:

1. the United States, a state, or political subdivision thereof, if the donation is made for exclusively public purposes (such as a contribution to pay down the federal debt);
2. domestic organizations formed and operated exclusively for charitable, religious, educational, scientific, or literary purposes, or for the prevention of cruelty to children or animals;
3. church, synagogue, or other religious organizations;
4. war veterans' organizations;

5. civil defense organizations;
6. fraternal societies operating under the lodge system, but only if the contribution is used for one or more of the charitable purposes listed in (2) above; and
7. certain nonprofit cemetery companies.

The following contributions are *not* deductible:

1. Gifts to nonqualified recipients, for example, needy individuals, social clubs, labor unions, international organizations, and political parties;
2. Contributions of time, service, the use of property, or blood;
3. Contributions where benefit is received from the contribution, for example, tuition at a parochial school; and
4. Wagering losses, such as church bingo and raffle tickets.

If a taxpayer has doubt as to the deductibility of a payment to a specific organization, he or she should review the IRS's online search tool called "Tax Exempt Organization Search."

If cash is donated, the deduction is equal to the amount of the cash. For donated property other than cash, the general rule is that the deduction is equal to the fair market value of the property at the time of the donation. The fair market value is the price at which the property would be sold between a willing buyer and seller. There is an exception to this general rule for property that would have resulted in ordinary income or short-term capital gain had it been sold on the date of the contribution. In that situation, the deduction for the contribution is equal to the property's fair market value less the amount of the ordinary income or short-term capital gain that would have resulted from sale of the property. If the sale of the property would have produced a long-term capital gain, the deduction is generally equal to the fair market value of the property. However, the fair market value is reduced by the amount of the potential long-term capital gain, if the donation is made to certain private nonoperating foundations or the donation is a contribution of tangible personal property to an organization that uses the property for a purpose unrelated to the organization's primary purpose.

EXAMPLE Jeano B. donates a painting acquired 5 years ago at a cost of $4,000 to a museum for exhibition. The painting's fair market value is $12,000. If Jeano had sold the painting, the difference between the sales price ($12,000) and its cost ($4,000) would have been a long-term capital gain. The deduction is $12,000, and it is not reduced by the amount of the appreciation, since the painting was put to a use related to the museum's primary purpose. If the painting had been donated to a hospital, the deduction would be $4,000, which is $12,000 less $8,000 ($12,000 − $4,000), the amount of the long-term capital gain that would have resulted if the painting had been sold. ◆

5-9a **Above-The-Line Deduction for Charitable Contributions**

For the 2020 tax year only, an up to $300 above-the-line deduction (adjusted for AGI) will be available for cash charitable contributions made in 2020 to a church, nonprofit educational institution, nonprofit medical institution, or public charity. This deduction is *not* available if the taxpayer itemizes deductions. The $300 maximum applies to all filing statuses. The deduction is reported on Line 10b of the 2020 Form 1040.

EXAMPLE Edward makes a series of cash donations that total $500 to his church during 2020. Edward's itemized deductions are less than his standard deduction; however Edward can still take a $300 for AGI deduction due to the COVID-relief provisions. ◆

5-9b **Percentage Limitations**

Generally, a taxpayer may not deduct total contributions in excess of 50 percent of the taxpayer's adjusted gross income. This 50 percent limitation applies to donations to all public charities, all private operating foundations, and private nonoperating foundations if they distribute their contributions to public charities within a specified time period. The TCJA increased the 50 percent limit to a 60 percent limit for contributions of *cash* to public charities and other 50 percent organizations. For 2020, the limitation for cash donations was temporarily raised to 100 percent. Contributions of other than cash remain subject to the 50 percent limit.

Gifts to other qualified organizations, such as certain private nonoperating foundations, fraternal societies, and veterans' organizations, as well as gifts for the use of an organization, are limited to 30 percent of adjusted gross income. Special rules apply to contributions of long-term capital gain property. If the full fair market value of a gift of long-term capital gain property is deducted, and the contribution is to a 50 percent organization, the contribution is subject to the 30 percent limit. Taxpayers may avoid the 30 percent limit on contributions of long-term capital gain property by electing to reduce the value of the property by the appreciation that would otherwise be a long-term capital gain, in which case the 50 percent limitation applies. Long-term capital gain property donated to other than a 50 percent organization is subject to a 20 percent of adjusted gross income limitation.

EXAMPLE   In 2020, Tim gave $13,000 to his church. Tim's adjusted gross income is $21,000. In 2020, Tim's donation is limited to his AGI and thus the entire donation is deductible. If the gift were made in 2021 and thereafter, the deduction would be limited to $12,600 (60 percent of $21,000) ◆

EXAMPLE   Carol donates publicly traded stock worth $15,000 to a qualified 50 percent organization. The original purchase price of the stock, 10 years ago, was $10,000. Because the stock is a gift of long-term capital gain property, Carol's deduction is limited to 30 percent of her adjusted gross income. Given that Carol's AGI is $20,000, she may take a deduction for $6,000 (30% of $20,000) and may carry the remaining $9,000 ($15,000 − $6,000) forward to the following year. Alternatively, Carol may deduct the original $10,000 cost of the stock using the 50 percent of AGI rule, which would give her a $10,000 deduction in the current year. Even though she would have a larger deduction in the current year, she would lose $5,000 of her potential charitable contributions deduction by choosing this alternative. ◆

Generally, contributions to 50 percent organizations are deducted first, followed by contributions subject to the 30 percent and 20 percent limitations, respectively. Contributions subject to the 30 percent and 20 percent of adjusted gross income limitations are allowed only to the extent that they do not exceed 50 percent of adjusted gross income reduced by the amount of contributions subject to the 50 percent limitation.

In general, any contributions not allowed due to the adjusted gross income limitations may be carried forward for 5 years. The contributions may be deducted in the carryover years subject to the same percentage of income limitations which were applicable to the contributions in the year they originated. Contribution carryovers are allowed only after taking into account the current year contributions in the same category.

EXAMPLE   In March of 2021, Grace contributes $15,000 in cash to a public university. In addition, at the same time she donates $7,000 in cash to an organization subject to the 30 percent of adjusted gross income limitation. Grace has adjusted gross income in 2021 of $35,000. Her contribution deduction is determined as follows:

Adjusted gross income	$35,000
	×50%
50% limitation	17,500
Allowable 50% limitation contributions	(15,000)
Excess 50% limitation	$ 2,500

Maximum 30% contributions:
    Lesser of $2,500 or 30% of adjusted
        gross income, $10,500 $ 2,500
Total deductible contributions:
    50% contributions   15,000
    30% contributions   2,500
    Total $17,500

$4,500 of the $7,000 subject to the 30 percent limitation can be carried forward to 2022. ♦

Another change made by the TCJA is that no charitable contribution deduction is permitted for a payment to a college or university in exchange for the right to purchase tickets or seating at an athletic event. Pre-TCJA law permitted an 80 percent deduction for such amounts.

EXAMPLE   In 2020, Marco donates $5,000 to Big State University in exchange for the right to purchase 2020 season tickets to Big State football games. Marco may not deduct any of the $5,000 payment. ♦

A tax lawyer pleaded guilty to tax evasion in Federal District Court for substantially overstating his charitable contributions. He told an IRS agent that he put $500 in cash into the church collection basket each week. His pastor, however, said that the church never received more than $500 in currency at all of its weekly church services combined.

5-9c Substantiation Rules

Taxpayers should keep records, receipts, cancelled checks, and other proof of charitable contributions. For gifts of property, such as clothes and household goods given to the Salvation Army, totaling over $500, the taxpayer must attach a Form 8283 to his or her return giving the name and address of the donee, the date of the contribution, a description of the property, the approximate date of acquisition of the property, and certain other required information. For large gifts of property worth $5,000 or more, the donor must also obtain and submit an appraisal.

No charitable deduction is allowed for contributions of $250 or more unless the taxpayer substantiates the contributions with written acknowledgments from the recipient charitable organizations. The acknowledgments must contain this information:

- The amount of cash and a description (but not the value) of property other than cash contributed.
- Whether the charitable organization provided any goods or services in consideration, in whole or in part, for any property contributed. (If a payment is partly a gift and partly in consideration for goods or services provided to the donor, it is a "quid pro quo contribution" and special rules apply.)
- A description and good-faith estimate of the value of any goods or services provided by the donor, or, if the goods and services consist solely of intangible religious benefits, a statement to that effect. Intangible religious benefits are any benefits provided by organizations formed exclusively for religious purposes and not generally sold in a commercial setting. For example, attendance at church is considered an intangible religious benefit while attendance at a private religious school is not. Therefore, a donation made at a church service is generally considered a charitable contribution while tuition paid to a private religious school is not considered a charitable contribution.

Taxpayers donating amounts of cash smaller than the $250 limit are required to keep a bank record (cancelled check) or a written communication from the charity. Taxpayers who itemize deductions should use checks instead of cash for church and similar cash donations.

Gifts of clothing and household items (including furnishings, electronics, appliances, and linens) must be in "good" condition or better to qualify for a deduction. Also, charitable deductions may be denied for contributions of items with minimal value, such as used socks and undergarments. The rules for noncash contributions were enacted because some taxpayers significantly overstated the value of noncash contributions deducted.

No particular form is prescribed for the written acknowledgment, nor does the donor's tax identification number have to be contained on the acknowledgment. It may be a receipt, letter, postcard, or computer form. The acknowledgment must be obtained on or before the date on which the tax return for the tax year of the contribution is filed, or by the due date (plus extensions) if it is earlier than the actual filing date.

Taxpayers donating used vehicles to charity cannot claim a deduction greater than the amount for which the charity actually sells the vehicle. The charity is required to provide the resale information on Form 1098-C to taxpayers donating vehicles. The same rule also applies to boats and planes donated to charity. Taxpayers must attach Form 1098-C to their tax return to substantiate the deduction. Taxpayers may claim an estimated value for the automobile if the charity does not sell it but rather uses it or gives it to a needy individual. The charity must certify that an exception applies if no resale amount is provided on Form 1098-C.

For quid pro quo contributions (donations involving the receipt of goods or services by the donee), written statements (disclosures) are required from the charitable organization to donors making contributions of more than $75. The disclosures need not be individual letters to donors; they simply provide the donors with good-faith estimates of the value of the goods or services and inform the donors that only the amounts of the contributions in excess of the value of the goods or services are deductible for federal income tax purposes.

A charitable organization knowingly providing false written acknowledgments is subject to penalty (generally $1,000) for aiding and abetting in the understatement of tax liability. A penalty of $10 per contribution per event, capped at $5,000, may be imposed on charities failing to make the required disclosures for quid pro quo contributions.

TAX BREAK A cash basis taxpayer may charge year-end expenses on a credit card and still deduct the expenses even when payment on the credit card is not made until the next year. Instead of paying medical bills, charitable contributions, or even property taxes by check at year-end, the taxpayer may prefer to charge the expense. Note, however, that the credit card may not be one issued by the company supplying the deductible goods or services, but must be a card issued by a third party.

Self-Study Problem 5.9   *See Appendix E for Solutions to Self-Study Problems*

In 2020, Eric gave $11,000 to his church. He donated $75 to Boy Scouts of America and $125 to the Mexican Red Cross. Eric gave the Salvation Army used clothes in good condition worth $150 (original cost $1,700). Eric donated $500 to Rhode Island State University (his alma mater) for the right to buy season tickets to the Fightin' Nutmeggers basketball games. Eric's adjusted gross income is $21,000. Use the Gifts to Charity section of Schedule A on Page 5-23 to report Eric's deduction for the current year.

5-10 **OTHER ITEMIZED DEDUCTIONS**

The final portion of this chapter discusses casualty and theft losses, other miscellaneous deductions, and the phase-out of itemized deductions for high income taxpayers (the "Pease" phase-out).

5-10a **Casualty and Theft Losses**

Taxpayers are allowed deductions for certain casualty and theft losses. The deductions may be itemized deductions or, if related to a business, deductions for adjusted gross income. A casualty is a complete or partial destruction of property resulting from an identifiable event of a sudden, unexpected, or unusual nature. Examples of casualties include property damage from storms, floods, shipwrecks, fires, automobile accidents, and vandalism. For damage from weather conditions to be deductible, the condition must be unusual for the particular region. To qualify as a casualty, an automobile accident must not be caused by the taxpayer's willful act or willful negligence.

EXAMPLE A taxpayer has an automobile that he decides is a lemon, and he wants to get rid of it. He drives the automobile to the top of a cliff and pushes it off. There is no casualty loss deduction since the act is willful. ♦

Many events do not qualify as casualties. For example, progressive deterioration from rust or corrosion and disease or insect damage are usually not "sudden" enough to qualify as casualties. The IRS has held that termite damage is not deductible as a casualty; however, several courts have in the past allowed the deduction. Indirect losses, such as losses in property value due to damage to neighboring property, also are not deductible.

If the taxpayer can establish that theft occurred, theft losses are deductible. It is important to show that the item was not simply misplaced. Theft losses are deductible in the year the theft is discovered, not in the year the theft took place. This is important in cases of embezzlement, where the theft has gone on for many years and the statute of limitations has run out on earlier years, otherwise preventing the taxpayer from amending returns for those years.

As a general rule, casualty losses are deductible in the year of occurrence, but there is an exception for federally declared disaster area losses. Taxpayers may elect to treat the losses in a disaster area as a deduction in the year prior to the year the casualty occurred. If a return has already been filed for the prior year, an amended return may be filed and a refund claimed for the prior year's taxes paid. This provision is designed to provide taxpayers with cash on a more timely basis when they have suffered severe casualties.

EXAMPLE In May of 2020, Amy's house is damaged by flooding. Shortly thereafter, the president of the United States declared the region a disaster area. The damage to the house is $6,000 and the loss may be deducted in 2019 or 2020, even if the 2019 return has already been filed. If Amy elects to take the deduction in 2019, she may immediately file an amended tax return for that year and collect a refund of previously paid taxes. ♦

5-10b **Measuring the Loss**

The amount of the casualty or theft loss is measured by one of the following two rules:

Rule A—The deduction is based on the decrease in fair market value of the property, not to exceed the adjusted basis of the property.

Rule B—The deduction is based on the adjusted basis of the property.

Rule A applies to the partial destruction of business or investment property and the partial or complete destruction of personal property, while Rule B applies to the complete destruction of business and investment property. The cost of repairs is usually used for the measurement of loss from automobile damage. Repair costs may also be used to measure losses involving other types of property, but it is not controlling. Indirect costs, such as cleanup costs, are part of the loss, provided the payments do not restore the property to better than its previous condition.

EXAMPLE   A taxpayer purchased his house 15 years ago for $25,000. Today it is worth $160,000, and heavy rains cause the house to slide into a canyon and be completely destroyed. The taxpayer's casualty loss deduction under Rule A is the decrease in fair market value ($160,000 − $0) not to exceed the taxpayer's basis ($25,000). Thus, the deduction is limited to $25,000. ♦

5-10c **Deduction Limitations**

The TCJA suspended the allowable loss for personal casualty losses except when the loss is attributable to a federally declared disaster. Such losses are subject to a $100 floor per casualty and must exceed 10 percent of AGI to be deducted. The restriction to a federally declared disaster applies to tax years 2018 to 2025. If a taxpayer has a net casualty gain, the declared disaster restriction does not apply to the extent of the gain. If related to business property, there is no adjusted gross income limitation or dollar reduction applicable to casualty and theft losses; such losses are deductions for adjusted gross income.

EXAMPLE   In 2020, Wanda incurs a loss due to a complete destruction of her personal use car due to a casualty event not attributable to a federally declared disaster. Her adjusted basis in the car was $19,000 and the fair market value at the time of the loss was $8,000. Wanda's AGI is $55,000. Wanda was not insured for this type of loss and received no reimbursement. Wanda will not be able to deduct any of her loss as it was not attributable to a federally declared disaster.

If instead Wanda's loss was attributable to a federally declared disaster, she can deduct $8,000 less the $100 floor and also less 10 percent of her AGI:

$$\$2,400 = \$8,000 - \$100 - \$5,500 \blacklozenge$$

EXAMPLE   Cosmo incurs two personal losses during 2020. His car was stolen and destroyed by the thieves. His basis in the car was $22,000 and the fair market value at the time of the theft was $16,000. Cosmo also lost a family heirloom watch with a basis of $4,000 in a different theft. Neither of these losses is attributable to a federally declared disaster. Cosmo's insurance covered the auto and reimbursed him $22,000 but the loss of the watch was not covered. Cosmo's casualty gain on the auto is $6,000 ($22,000 − $16,000) and his loss on the watch is $3,900 ($4,000 − $100 floor). Because Cosmo experienced a net casualty gain of $2,100, he may deduct the casualty loss against the gain despite the loss not being attributable to a federally declared disaster. ♦

Certain disasters can be deemed "qualified" federal disasters and were eligible for additional relief. For example, certain areas affected by Hurricanes Harvey, Irma, and Maria as well as the California wildfires, were declared qualified federal disaster areas. The rules for qualified federal disasters require the taxpayer to use a $500 floor (instead of $100) but do not subject the casualty loss to the 10 percent AGI limitation. In addition, taxpayers that do not itemize were permitted to add the qualified federal disaster area loss to the standard deduction. At the time we go to print, areas affected by Hurricane Laura were declared a federal disaster area and eligible for personal casualty losses, but were not declared *qualified* federal disaster areas extending additional loss benefits.

A casualty or theft loss is reported on Form 4684 and then the deductible amount is generally taken as an itemized deduction on Schedule A.

Entering the loss from a casualty is input on the left navigation menu. Select Income and then Schedule D/4797/etc. Scroll down to Casualties and Thefts (4868).

ProConnect™ Tax
TIP

5-10d Miscellaneous Expenses

Miscellaneous itemized deductions are categorized into two types: (1) those subject to the 2 percent of AGI floor and (2) those not subject to the 2 percent of AGI floor.

The TCJA suspended the deduction of all miscellaneous itemized deductions subject to the 2 percent of AGI rule; thus, these items will no longer be deductible for tax years 2018 to 2025. The most common deductions subject to the 2 percent of AGI rule are:

- Unreimbursed employee business expenses and employee expenses reimbursed under a nonaccountable plan
- Investment expenses
- Other miscellaneous expenses including the all-important tax preparation fees

The most common unreimbursed employee expenses are included in the following list:

- Business bad debt of an employee. - Business liability insurance premiums. - Damages paid to a former employer for breach of an employment contract. - Depreciation on a computer your employer requires you to use in your work. - Dues to a chamber of commerce if membership helps you do your job. - Dues to professional societies. - Educator expenses. - Home office or part of your home used regularly and exclusively in your work. - Job search expenses in your present occupation. - Laboratory breakage fees. - Legal fees related to your job. - Licenses and regulatory fees.	- Malpractice insurance premiums. - Medical examinations required by an employer. - Occupational taxes. - Passport for a business trip. - Repayment of an income aid payment received under an employer's plan. - Research expenses of a college professor. - Rural mail carriers' vehicle expenses. - Subscriptions to professional journals and trade magazines related to your work. - Tools and supplies used in your work. - Travel, transportation, meals, entertainment, gifts, and local lodging related to your work. - Union dues and expenses. - Work clothes and uniforms if required and not suitable for everyday use. - Work-related education.

The repeal of miscellaneous deductions subject to the 2 percent floor could result in an employee being subject to additional tax liability when receiving reimbursement from an employer without an accountable plan. Since changing from an employee to an independent contractor is generally not possible without a significant change in the relationship between the individual and the business (this is a matter of law, not a choice by either the employee or employer), taxpayers that are employees in this situation may want to inquire if an accountable plan can be implemented by their employer going forward.

Miscellaneous itemized deductions not subject to the 2 percent floor were not affected by the TCJA. This category of expenses includes the following items:

- Amortizable premium on taxable bonds.
- Casualty and theft losses from income-producing property.
- Federal estate tax on income in respect of a decedent.
- Gambling losses up to the amount of gambling winnings.
- Impairment-related work expenses of persons with disabilities.
- Loss from other activities from Schedule K-1 (Form 1065-B), Box 2.
- Losses from Ponzi-type investment schemes.
- Repayments of more than $3,000 under a claim of right.
- Unrecovered investment in an annuity.

Gambling losses are not subject to the 2 percent limitation and are not directly limited. Because gambling losses are only deductible for taxpayers that itemize deductions and the TCJA increased the standard deduction and limited itemized deductions for many taxpayers, fewer taxpayers may itemize and therefore be eligible to deduct gambling losses. Gambling winnings must be reported as other income on Schedule 1 and losses may be deducted on Schedule A only to the extent of winnings.

5-10e Phase-out of Itemized Deductions

Prior to 2018, certain high-income taxpayers were subject to limits on the amount of itemized deductions. Certain AGI limits for different filing status triggered a reduction in itemized deductions by the lesser of 3 percent of the excess of the taxpayer's AGI over the threshold amount or 80 percent of itemized deductions excluding the deductions for medical expenses, investment interest expense, casualty and theft losses, and gambling losses to the extent of gambling income. The TCJA suspended the phase-out.

Self-Study Problem 5.10   *See Appendix E for Solutions to Self-Study Problems*

During 2020, Robert (a single taxpayer) is an employee and has AGI of $35,000. He lives in Jupiter, FL 33477.

a. Robert's community was struck by a hurricane. During the storm a tree blew over and destroyed his car. The storm was declared a federal disaster (FEMA Code EM-5566). The market value of the car on the date of destruction was $14,000. Robert purchased the car in July 2017 at a cost of $18,500. Robert's car was only partially covered for this type of loss and his insurance paid him $5,000. Calculate Robert's casualty or theft loss on Form 4684 on Page 5-41 and carry any deductible amount to the Casualty and Theft Losses section of the Schedule A on Page 5-23.

b. Robert also incurs the following expenses:

Safe-deposit box rental (for investments)	$ 25
Tax return preparation fees	450
Professional dues	175
Trade journals	125
Bank trust fees	1,055
Qualifying job hunting expenses	1,400
Total	$3,230

Robert also had a big day at the casinos and won $1,400. Over the year, he had substantiation for $1,700 in gambling losses. Assuming Robert is not self-employed, calculate any miscellaneous deductions and enter them in the Other Itemized Deductions section of Schedule A on Page 5-23.

Self-Study Problem 5.10

Form 4684

Department of the Treasury
Internal Revenue Service

Casualties and Thefts

▶ Go to *www.irs.gov/Form4684* for instructions and the latest information.
▶ **Attach to your tax return.**
▶ **Use a separate Form 4684 for each casualty or theft.**

OMB No. 1545-0177

2020

Attachment
Sequence No. **26**

Name(s) shown on tax return

Identifying number

SECTION A—Personal Use Property (Use this section to report casualties and thefts of property **not** used in a trade or business or for income-producing purposes. You must use a separate Form 4684 (through line 12) for each casualty or theft event involving personal use property. **If reporting a qualified disaster loss, see the instructions for special rules that apply before completing this section.**)

If the casualty or theft loss is attributable to a federally declared disaster, check here ☐ and enter the DR-_____ or EM-_____ declaration number assigned by FEMA. (See instructions.)

1 Description of properties (show type, location (city, state, and ZIP code), and date acquired for each property). Use a separate line for each property lost or damaged from the same casualty or theft. If you checked the box and entered the FEMA disaster declaration number above, enter the ZIP code for the property most affected on the line for Property **A**.

	Type of Property	City and State	ZIP Code	Date Acquired
Property **A**				
Property **B**				
Property **C**				
Property **D**				

		Properties			
		A	**B**	**C**	**D**
2	Cost or other basis of each property				
3	Insurance or other reimbursement (whether or not you filed a claim) (see instructions) . . . . **Note:** If line 2 is **more** than line 3, skip line 4.				
4	Gain from casualty or theft. If line 3 is **more** than line 2, enter the difference here and skip lines 5 through 9 for that column. See instructions if line 3 includes insurance or other reimbursement you did not claim, or you received payment for your loss in a later tax year . .				
5	Fair market value **before** casualty or theft . . .				
6	Fair market value **after** casualty or theft				
7	Subtract line 6 from line 5				
8	Enter the **smaller** of line 2 or line 7				
9	Subtract line 3 from line 8. If zero or less, enter -0- .				

10 Casualty or theft loss. Add the amounts on line 9 in columns A through D . . . . | **10** |

11 Enter $100 ($500 if qualified disaster loss rules apply; see instructions) . . . . | **11** |

12 Subtract line 11 from line 10. If zero or less, enter -0- . . . . | **12** |

Caution: Use only one Form 4684 for lines 13 through 18.

13 Add the amounts on line 4 of all Forms 4684 . . . . | **13** |

14 Add the amounts on line 12 of all Forms 4684. If you have losses not attributable to a federally declared disaster, see the instructions . . . . | **14** |

Caution: See instructions before completing line 15.

15 • If line 13 is **more** than line 14, enter the difference here and on Schedule D. **Do not** complete the rest of this section.

• If line 13 is **equal** to line 14, enter -0- here. **Do not** complete the rest of this section.

• If line 13 is **less** than line 14, and you have no qualified disaster losses subject to the $500 reduction on line 11 on any Form(s) 4684, enter -0- here and go to line 16. If you have qualified disaster losses subject to the $500 reduction, subtract line 13 from line 14 and enter the smaller of this difference or the amount on line 12 of the Form(s) 4684 reporting those losses. Enter that result here and on Schedule A (Form 1040), line 16, or Form 1040-NR, Schedule A, line 7. If you claim the standard deduction, also include on Schedule A (Form 1040), line 16, the amount of your standard deduction (see the Instructions for Forms 1040 and 1040-SR). Do not complete the rest of this section if all of your casualty or theft losses are subject to the $500 reduction. | **15** |

16 Add lines 13 and 15. Subtract the result from line 14 . . . . | **16** |

17 Enter 10% of your adjusted gross income from Form 1040, 1040-SR, or 1040-NR, line 11. Estates and trusts, see instructions . . . . | **17** |

18 Subtract line 17 from line 16. If zero or less, enter -0-. Also, enter the result on Schedule A (Form 1040), line 15, or Form 1040-NR, Schedule A, line 6. Estates and trusts, enter the result on the "Other deductions" line of your tax return . . . . | **18** |

For Paperwork Reduction Act Notice, see instructions. Cat. No. 12997O Form **4684** (2020)

KEY TERMS

Health Savings Accounts (HSAs), 5-2
traditional IRA, 5-8
Roth IRA, 5-8
annual contribution limits, 5-8
"catch-up" contribution, 5-8
nondeductible traditional IRA, 5-10
Roth IRA conversions, 5-11
early withdrawal, 5-11
distributions, 5-11
required minimum distributions
    (RMDs), 5-12
Payroll Deduction IRA, 5-14
SEP IRA, 5-14
SIMPLE IRA, 5-14

Section 401(k) plan, 5-15
safe harbor 401(k), 5-16
Roth 401(k), 5-16
self-employed or solo 401(k), 5-16
tax, 5-21
fee, 5-21
estimated sales taxes from IRS
    tables, 5-25
consumer interest, 5-28
prepaid interest, 5-29
qualified residence interest
    (mortgage interest), 5-29
qualified residence acquisition
    debt, 5-30

home equity debt, 5-30
investment interest, 5-31
charitable contributions, 5-32
qualified recipient, 5-32
nonqualified recipients, 5-33
Tax Exempt Organization Search,
    5-33
50 percent limitation, 5-33
30 percent limitation, 5-34
20 percent limitation, 5-34
substantiation rules, 5-35
casualty, 5-37
"qualified" federal disasters, 5-38

KEY POINTS

Learning Objectives	Key Points
LO 5.1: Explain how Health Savings Accounts (HSAs) can be used for tax-advantaged medical care.	• Health Savings Accounts (HSAs) are used for the purpose of paying unreimbursed medical expenses. • HSAs have an annual age-based contribution dollar limitation for deductions for individuals ($3,550) and families ($7,100). There is an additional $1,000 "catch-up" contribution allowed for individuals beginning at age 55 and ending at age 65, the age for Medicare eligibility. • Distributions from HSAs are tax-exempt when used to pay for qualified medical expenses. Distributions which are not used to pay for qualified medical expenses may be subject to income tax and a 20 percent penalty. • Once a taxpayer is 65 years old, distributions may be taken for nonmedical expenses and will be subject to income tax, but not the 20 percent penalty.
LO 5.2: Describe the self-employed health insurance deduction.	• Deductible health insurance includes: (1) medical and dental insurance paid to cover the self-employed taxpayer, spouse, and dependents; (2) medical and dental insurance paid for children under the age of 27 who are not dependents; (3) Medicare premiums; and (4) long-term care insurance paid for the taxpayer and the family of the taxpayer. • Taxpayers with income reportable on Schedule C are generally considered self-employed. • Taxpayers with earnings from certain partnerships, S corporations, LLCs, and farm businesses may also be considered self-employed and may be allowed the deduction for self-employed health insurance. • The deduction for self-employed health insurance is only allowed to the extent of the taxpayer's net self-employed income.

LO 5.3: Explain the treatment of Individual Retirement Accounts (IRAs), including Roth IRAs.	• Generally, annual contributions to a traditional IRA are deductible and retirement distributions are taxable; whereas, annual contributions to a Roth IRA are not deductible and retirement distributions are nontaxable. • Earnings in both types of IRAs are not taxable in the current year. • In 2020, the maximum annual contribution that may be made to either type of IRA is equal to the lesser of (1) 100 percent of the taxpayer's compensation or self-employment income (earned income) or (2) $6,000 (plus an additional $6,000 which may be contributed on behalf of a spouse with no earned income). An additional catch-up $1,000 annual contribution is allowed for taxpayers age 50 and over. • The tax deduction for contributions to traditional IRAs is limited for taxpayers who are active participants in qualified retirement plans and have income over certain limits. Contributions to Roth IRAs are limited for taxpayers with income over certain limits; however, they are not affected by taxpayer participation in other retirement plans. • Taxpayers may benefit from a rule allowing conversions of traditional IRAs into Roth IRAs. • Generally, money distributed from a traditional IRA is taxable as ordinary income and may be subject to a 10 percent penalty for early withdrawal (before age 59½). Some types of early withdrawals may be made without penalty. • A taxpayer can make tax-free withdrawals from a Roth IRA after a 5-year holding period if the distribution is made on or after the date on which the participant attains age 59½. Other tax-free withdrawals may also apply.
LO 5.4: Explain the general contribution rules for small business and self-employed retirement plans.	• Employers may claim a deduction in the current year for contributions to qualified retirement plans on employees' behalf. The employees do not include the employer contributions in income until the contributed amounts are distributed. • For 2020, contributions to retirement plans by self-employed taxpayers are generally limited to the lesser of 20 percent of their net earned income before the contribution deduction or $57,000. • For 2020, the maximum employee contribution to a SEP is the lesser of 25 percent of compensation or $57,000. • For 2020, an employee may elect to make an annual contribution up to $19,500 ($26,000 for taxpayers age 50 or older) to a Section 401(k) plan. In addition, any matching amount contributed to the plan by the employer on behalf of the employee is excluded from the employee's gross income.
LO 5.5: Describe other adjustments for adjusted gross income.	• Eligible educators may deduct up to $250 for the unreimbursed cost of classroom materials as a for AGI deduction. • Certain performing artists, reservists, and fee-based government officials can deduct unreimbursed employee expenses as a for AGI deduction. • Starting in 2018, moving expenses are only deductible for members of the Armed Forces pursuant to a military order and permanent change of station.
LO 5.6: Calculate the itemized deduction for medical expenses.	• Taxpayers are allowed an itemized deduction on Schedule A for medical expenses paid for themselves, their spouse, and their dependents. • Qualified medical expenses are deductible only to the extent they exceed 7.5 percent of a taxpayer's adjusted gross income. • Qualified medical expenses include such items as prescription medicines and drugs, insulin, fees for doctors, dentists, nurses, and other medical professionals, hospital fees, hearing aids, dentures, prescription eyeglasses, contact lenses, medical transportation and lodging, crutches, wheelchairs, guide dogs, birth control prescriptions, acupuncture, psychiatric care, medical and Medicare insurance premiums, and various other listed medical expenses.

LO 5.7: Calculate the itemized deduction for taxes.	• The following taxes are deductible on Schedule A: state and local income taxes or state and local sales taxes, real property taxes (state and local), and personal property taxes (state and local). • The itemized deduction for taxes is limited to $10,000. • Nondeductible taxes include the following: federal income taxes, employee portion of Social Security taxes, estate, inheritance, and gift taxes (except in unusual situations), gasoline taxes, excise taxes, and foreign taxes if the taxpayer elects a foreign tax credit. • If real estate is sold during the year, the taxes must be allocated between the buyer and seller based on the number of days in the year that each taxpayer held the property to determine each party's deductible amount. • To be deductible, personal property taxes must be levied based on the value of the property. Personal property taxes of a fixed amount, or those calculated on a basis other than value, are not deductible.
LO 5.8: Apply the rules for an individual taxpayer's interest deduction.	• Deductible personal interest includes qualified residence interest (mortgage interest), mortgage interest prepayment penalties, investment interest, and certain interest associated with a passive activity. • Nondeductible consumer interest includes interest on any loan, the proceeds of which are used for personal purposes, such as credit card interest, finance charges, and automobile loan interest. • "Qualified residence interest" is the sum of the interest paid on "qualified residence acquisition debt." • Taxpayers are allowed a deduction for AGI for certain interest paid on qualified education loans. • Deductible investment interest is limited to the taxpayer's net investment income, which is investment income such as dividends and interest, less investment expenses other than interest.
LO 5.9: Determine the charitable contributions deduction.	• To be deductible, the donation must be made in cash or property. • Donations must be made to a qualified recipient. • The following contributions are not deductible: gifts to needy individuals, social clubs, labor unions, international organizations, and political parties; contributions of time, service, the use of property, or blood; contributions where benefit is received from the contribution, for example, tuition at a parochial school; and wagering losses, such as church bingo and raffle tickets. • For donated property other than cash, the general rule is that the deduction is equal to the fair market value of the property at the time of the donation. • A for AGI deduction for up to $300 of cash contributions is available to taxpayers that do not itemize in 2020. • For 2020, the AGI limitation for cash donations was temporarily raised to 100 percent. • Donations are limited to 60, 50, 30, or 20 percent of AGI in certain cases.
LO 5.10: Describe other itemized deductions.	• Starting in 2018, a loss from a personal casualty such as property damage from storms, floods, shipwrecks, fires, automobile accidents, and vandalism is only deductible if associated with a federally declared disaster. • For the partial destruction of business or investment property and the partial or complete destruction of personal property, the deduction is based on the decrease in fair market value of the property, not to exceed the adjusted basis of the property. • For the complete destruction of business and investment property, the deduction is based on the adjusted basis of the property. • The amount of each personal casualty loss attributable to a federally declared disaster, is reduced by $100 and only the excess over 10 percent of the taxpayer's AGI is deductible. • Starting in 2018, the deduction for miscellaneous expenses subject to the 2 percent of AGI limit is suspended until 2025. • Miscellaneous expenses not subject to the 2 percent of AGI limit such as gambling losses to the extent of gambling winnings, handicapped "impairment-related work expenses," certain estate taxes, amortizable bond premiums, and unrecovered annuity costs at death remain deductible. • The phase-out of itemized deductions for high-income taxpayers has been suspended.

QUESTIONS and PROBLEMS

GROUP 1:
MULTIPLE CHOICE QUESTIONS

LO 5.1

1. Which of the following is a *false* statement about Health Savings Accounts (HSAs)?
   a. Taxpayers who contribute to an HSA must carry qualifying high-deductible health insurance.
   b. HSAs are available to any taxpayer using a health plan purchased through the state or federal exchange under the Affordable Care Act.
   c. Distributions from HSAs are not taxable when used to pay qualifying medical expenses.
   d. Taxpayers must contribute to the HSA by April 15 of the year following the tax year for which they want the deduction.
   e. Distributions from HSAs which are not used to pay qualifying medical expenses are generally subject to a 20 percent penalty as well as income taxes.

LO 5.1

2. Charlene has family coverage in a qualifying high-deductible health insurance plan. She is 47 years old and wishes to contribute the maximum amount to her HSA. How much is she allowed to contribute and deduct in 2020?
   a. $1,000
   b. $1,300
   c. $3,500
   d. $3,550
   e. $7,100

LO 5.2

3. Which type of insurance is *not* deductible as self-employed health insurance?
   a. Medical insurance
   b. Disability insurance
   c. Dental insurance
   d. Long-term care insurance
   e. Spousal medical insurance

LO 5.2

4. Which of the following is *true* about the self-employed health insurance deduction?
   a. The deduction can be claimed when a subsidized employer health insurance plan is also available.
   b. The deduction can be claimed if the taxpayer has an overall business loss from self-employment.
   c. Long-term care premiums may not be deducted within specified dollar limitations based on age.
   d. The self-employed health insurance deduction is a for AGI deduction.
   e. Dental insurance is not included as deductible self-employed health insurance.

LO 5.3

5. Lyndon, age 24, has a nonworking spouse and earns wages of $36,000 for 2020. He also received rental income of $5,000 and dividend income of $900 for the year. What is the maximum amount Lyndon can deduct for contributions to his and his wife's individual retirement accounts for the 2020 tax year?
   a. $11,000
   b. $5,500
   c. $6,000
   d. $12,000
   e. None of the above

LO 5.3

6. Martha and Rob, a married couple, under 50 years of age, have adjusted gross income on their 2020 joint income tax return of $45,000, before considering any IRA deduction. Martha and Rob have no earned income. What is the amount of Martha's maximum deductible IRA contribution?
   a. $2,700
   b. $3,500
   c. $6,000
   d. $12,000
   e. $0

LO 5.3

7. Donna, age 42 and a single taxpayer, has a salary of $104,500 and interest income of $20,000. What is the maximum amount Donna can contribute to a Roth IRA for 2020?
   a. $5,000
   b. $3,850
   c. $5,800
   d. $6,000
   e. Some other amount

LO 5.3

8. Mary has a Roth IRA held more than 5 years to which she has contributed $30,000. The IRA has a current value of $62,000. Mary is 55 years old and she takes a distribution of $40,000. How much of the distribution will be taxable to Mary?
   a. $0
   b. $8,000
   c. $10,000
   d. $40,000
   e. Some other amount

LO 5.3

9. Marge has a Roth IRA held more than 5 years to which she has contributed $38,000. The IRA has a current value of $62,000. Marge is 65 years old and she takes a distribution of $40,000. How much of the distribution will be taxable to Marge?
   a. $0
   b. $8,000
   c. $30,000
   d. $40,000
   e. Some other amount

LO 5.3

10. Mindy has a Roth IRA held longer than 5 years to which she has contributed $30,000. The IRA has a current value of $62,000. Mindy is 55 years old and she takes a distribution of $40,000 after retiring on disability. How much of the distribution will be taxable to Mindy?
    a. $0
    b. $8,000
    c. $30,000
    d. $40,000
    e. Some other amount

LO 5.3

11. What is the deadline for making a contribution to a traditional IRA or a Roth IRA for 2020?
    a. April 15, 2021
    b. July 15, 2020
    c. December 31, 2020
    d. October 15, 2021

LO 5.4

12. Which of the following statements with respect to a qualified retirement plan is accurate?
    a. Self-employed individuals are not eligible to be members of a SEP.
    b. Contributions to SIMPLE IRAs are limited to 15 percent of the taxpayer's net earned income or $100,000, whichever is greater.
    c. Employer matching of employee contributions to a 401(k) plan is taxable in the year contributed.
    d. Taxpayers must begin receiving distributions from a qualified plan by the age of 65.
    e. None of these statements are accurate.

LO 5.4   13. What is the maximum tax-deferred contribution that can be made to a Section 401(k) plan by an employee under age 50 in 2020?
  a. $19,000
  b. $20,000
  c. $19,500
  d. $26,000
  e. $56,000

LO 5.4   14. Paul, age 37, participates in a Section 401(k) plan which allows employees to contribute up to 15 percent of their salary. His annual salary is $125,000 in 2020. What is the maximum he can contribute, on a tax-deferred basis under a salary reduction agreement, to this plan?
  a. $24,000
  b. $20,500
  c. $18,500
  d. $18,750
  e. None of the above

LO 5.5
LO 5.10   15. Eliza is a kindergarten teacher for Alexander Hamilton Elementary School. Eliza decorates her classroom with new artwork, posters, bulletin boards, etc. In 2020, she spends $470 on materials and supplies for her classroom. The school reimburses her $100 (the annual reimbursement limit). Eliza can deduct _____ for AGI and _____ from AGI.
  a. $0 for and $0 from AGI
  b. $370 for and $0 from AGI
  c. $250 for and $120 from AGI
  d. $250 for and $0 from AGI
  e. $0 for and $370 from AGI

LO 5.5   16. Jessica is a U.S. Army Reservist and in 2020 traveled 130 miles each way to serve duty at a local military installation. She was required to report four times in 2020. Her normal route from home to the base included a $1.75 toll each way. Jessica's for AGI deduction for these costs is:
  a. $0
  b. $617.20
  c. $122.00
  d. $612.00
  e. $580.80

LO 5.6   17. The cost of which of the following expenses is *not* deductible as a medical expense on Schedule A, before the 7.5 percent of adjusted gross income limitation?
  a. A psychiatrist
  b. Botox treatment to reduce wrinkles around eyes
  c. Acupuncture
  d. Expense to hire and train a guide dog for a visually-impaired taxpayer

LO 5.6   18. The cost of which of the following is deductible as a medical expense?
  a. Travel to a warm climate
  b. Birth control pills
  c. A disability insurance policy that pays $200 for each day the taxpayer is in the hospital
  d. Liposuction to reduce waist size

LO 5.6   19. Which of the following is not considered a deductible medical expense?
  a. Once daily multivitamin
  b. Prescription eyeglasses
  c. Acupuncture
  d. Filling a tooth cavity

LO 5.7

20. Which of the following taxes may be deducted as itemized deduction?
    a. State gasoline taxes
    b. Local property taxes
    c. Federal income taxes
    d. Social Security taxes
    e. Medicare taxes

LO 5.7

21. In April 2020, Fred paid $40 of state income tax that was due when he filed his 2019 income tax return. During 2020, Fred's employer withheld $1,200 of state income tax from his pay. In April 2021, Fred determined that his 2020 state tax liability was $1,100 and received his state income tax refund of $100 in May 2021. Assuming Fred itemizes, how much state income tax deduction should he report on his 2020 federal income tax return?
    a. $1,200
    b. $1,240
    c. $1,100
    d. $1,140
    e. $1,000

LO 5.7

22. Antonio is a small business owner and files jointly with his spouse. In 2020, he generates $100,000 of net profits from his business. His spouse, Maria, has $4,000 of state income tax withheld from her wages in 2020. They also pay $4,500 in property taxes on their home. Antonio determines that their state income taxes associated with his business are about $5,600 and makes estimated state income tax payments of that amount in 2020. How much should Antonio and Maria deduct for state taxes?
    a. Itemized deductions of $9,500 and deduct $5,600 for taxes on Antonio's Schedule C for his business
    b. Itemized deductions of $10,000 and deduct $5,100 for taxes on Antonio's Schedule C for his business
    c. Itemized deductions of $10,000
    d. Itemized deductions of $4,000 and deduct $5,600 for taxes on Antonio's Schedule C for his business

LO 5.7

23. The itemized deduction for state and local taxes in 2020 is
    a. Total taxes less 10 percent of AGI
    b. Limited to no more than $10,000
    c. Unlimited
    d. Only deductible if the taxes are business related
    e. Deductible if your home value is less than $750,000

LO 5.8

24. Which of the following is deductible as interest on Schedule A?
    a. Fees for having the home's value assessed by the bank for purposes of getting a mortgage
    b. Purchase mortgage insurance paid in 2020
    c. Interest on a credit card balance from the purchase of home furnishings.
    d. Interest on loans to finance tax-exempt bonds
    e. None of the above are deductible as interest

LO 5.8

25. Carrie, a single taxpayer, finished her undergraduate degree using money from a student loan. She earned $56,000 her first year and paid $2,600 in interest in 2020. She can take a deduction for student loan interest in the amount of:
    a. $2,600
    b. $2,500
    c. $1,500
    d. $0
    e. None of the above

LO 5.8
26. Which of the following interest expense amounts is *not* deductible in the current year?
    a. Education loan interest of $2,000, assuming the taxpayer has income of $30,000.
    b. Home equity loan interest of $6,000, on a loan of $90,000, the proceeds of which were used to add a new bedroom and bathroom to an existing primary residence.
    c. Investment interest expense of $10,000, assuming the taxpayer has no investment income.
    d. Qualified residence interest of $70,000 on a $730,000 loan used to purchase a luxury apartment in downtown San Diego.

LO 5.9
27. Which of the following donations are *not* deductible as a charitable contribution?
    a. A donation of clothing to Goodwill Industries
    b. A cash contribution to a church
    c. A contribution of stock to a public university
    d. A contribution of a taxpayer's time picking up trash on the beach
    e. A painting contributed to a museum

LO 5.9
28. Stanley donates a hotel to a university for use as a conference center. The building was purchased 3 years ago for $1,500,000 and has a fair market value of $1,900,000 on the date the contribution is made. If Stanley had sold the building, the $400,000 difference between the sales price and cost would have been a long-term capital gain. What is the amount of Stanley's deduction for this contribution, before considering any limitation based on adjusted gross income?
    a. $2,300,000
    b. $1,500,000
    c. $1,900,000
    d. $0
    e. The amount cannot be determined from the information given

LO 5.9
29. Rico makes $5,000 of cash donations in 2020. His itemized deductions exceed his standard deduction. What amount will Rico deduct as a for AGI deduction for charitable contributions? His AGI in 2020 is $48,000.
    a. $300
    b. $5,000
    c. $4,800
    d. $0
    e. $48,000

LO 5.9
30. Which of the following gifts is a deductible contribution?
    a. A gift of $100 to a homeless person
    b. A $500 gift to the Democratic National Committee
    c. $1,000 spent on church bingo games
    d. A $200 contribution to your child's public elementary school

LO 5.10
31. Which of the following would typically be deductible as a casualty loss in 2020?
    a. Long-term damage to a home from termites
    b. An automobile accident during the daily commute
    c. A theft of a big screen television
    d. Dropping your smartphone in the pool
    e. None of the above

LO 5.10
32. Which of the following is *not* a possible limitation on the deduction of a personal casualty loss?
    a. The lesser of the fair market value of the property or the adjusted basis at the time of the loss
    b. A $100 floor for each casualty event
    c. A 10 percent of AGI floor for all casualty losses during the year
    d. A personal casualty not associated with a federally declared disaster
    e. All of the above are possible limitations on a personal casualty loss

LO 5.10   33. Which of the following is deductible as a miscellaneous itemized deduction in 2020?
   a. Tax preparation fees
   b. Gambling losses in excess of gambling winnings
   c. Losses from Ponzi-type schemes
   d. Job-hunting expenses subject to the 2 percent of AGI floor
   e. None of the above are deductible as a miscellaneous itemized deduction.

LO 5.10   34. Which of the following items is deductible as a miscellaneous deduction on Schedule A?
   a. Investment expenses
   b. Gambling losses to the extent of gambling winnings
   c. Unreimbursed business expenses
   d. Subscriptions to professional publications
   e. Charitable contributions

GROUP 2:
PROBLEMS

LO 5.1   1. Evan participates in an HSA carrying family coverage for himself, his spouse, and two children. In 2020, Evan has $200 per month deducted from his paycheck and contributed to the HSA. In addition, Evan makes a one-time contribution of $2,000 on April 15, 2021 when he files his tax return. Evan also receives a 2020 Form 1099-SA that reports distributions to Evan of $3,200 which Evan used for medical expenses. Compute the effect of the HSA transactions on Evan's adjusted gross income.

LO 5.2   2. Serena is a 38-year-old single taxpayer. She operates a small business on the side as a sole proprietor. Her 2020 Schedule C reports net profits of $15,000. Her employer does not offer health insurance. Serena pays health insurance premiums of $7,800 in 2020. Serena also pays long-term care insurance premiums of $600 in 2020. Calculate Serena's self-employed health care deduction.

LO 5.3   3. Karen, 28 years old and a single taxpayer, has a salary of $33,000 and rental income of $33,000 for the 2020 calendar tax year. Karen is covered by a pension through her employer.
   a. What is the maximum amount that Karen may deduct for contributions to her IRA for 2020?

   $_____

   b. If Karen is a calendar year taxpayer and files her tax return on August 15, what is the last date on which she can make her contribution to the IRA and deduct it for 2020?

   $_____

LO 5.3   4. Phil and Linda are 25-year-old newlyweds and file a joint tax return. Linda is covered by a retirement plan at work, but Phil is not.
   a. Assuming Phil's wages were $27,000 and Linda's wages were $18,500 for 2020 and they had no other income, what is the maximum amount of their deduction for contributions to a traditional IRA for 2020?

   Phil $_____
   Linda $_____

   b. Assuming Phil's wages were $55,000 and Linda's wages were $70,000 for 2020 and they had no other income, what is the maximum amount of their deduction for contributions to a traditional IRA for 2020?

   Phil $_____
   Linda $_____

LO 5.3   5. What is the maximum amount a 45-year-old taxpayer and 45-year-old spouse can put into a Traditional or Roth IRA for 2020 (assuming they have sufficient earned income, but do not have an income limitation and are not covered by another pension plan)? _____

LO 5.3   6. What is the maximum amount a 55-year-old taxpayer and 52-year-old spouse can put into a Traditional or Roth IRA for 2020, assuming they earn $70,000 in total and are not participants in pension plans? _____

LO 5.3   7. Barry is a single, 40-year-old software engineer earning $190,000 a year and is not covered by a pension plan at work. How much can he put into a Roth IRA in 2020? _____

LO 5.3   8. Bob is a single, 40-year-old doctor earning $190,000 a year and is not covered by a pension plan at work. What is the maximum deductible contribution into a Traditional IRA in 2020? _____

LO 5.3   9. Dori is 58 years old and retired in 2020. She receives a pension of $25,000 a year and no other income. She wishes to put the maximum allowed into an IRA. How much can she contribute to her IRA? _____

LO 5.4   10. During 2020, Jerry is a self-employed therapist, and his net earned income is $160,000 from his practice. Jerry's SEP Plan, a defined contribution plan, states that he will contribute the maximum amount allowable. Calculate Jerry's contribution.

$_____

LO 5.4   11. Tony is a 45-year-old psychiatrist who has net earned income of $300,000 in 2020. What is the maximum amount he can contribute to his SEP for the year? _____

LO 5.4   12. Mario, a self-employed plumber, makes a maximum contribution to a SEP for his employee, Peach. Peach's compensation is $50,000 for the year. How much is he allowed to contribute to the plan for Peach?

$_____

LO 5.4   13. During 2020, Jill, age 39, participated in a Section 401(k) plan which provides for maximum employee contributions of 12 percent. Jill's salary was $80,000 for the year. Jill elects to make the maximum contribution. What is Jill's maximum tax-deferred contribution to the plan for the year?

$_____

LO 5.6   14. Linda installed a special pool for the hydrotherapeutic treatment of severe arthritis, as prescribed by her doctor. The cost of installing the pool was $20,000, and her insurance company paid $5,000 toward its cost. The pool increased the value of Linda's house by $7,000, and it has a useful life of 10 years. How much of a deduction is Linda entitled to in the year of installation of the pool?

$ _____

Explain _____

_____

_____

LO 5.6

15. In 2020, Margaret and John Murphy (both over age 65) are married taxpayers who file a joint tax return with AGI of $28,108. During the year they incurred the following expenses:

Medical insurance premiums	$1,200
Premiums on an insurance policy that pays $100 per day for each day Margaret is hospitalized	400
Medical care lodging (two people, one night)	80
Hospital bills	2,200
Doctor bills	750
Dentist bills	240
Prescription drugs and medicines	360
Marriage counseling	400

In addition, they drove 90 miles for medical transportation, and their insurance company reimbursed them $850 for the above expenses. On the following segment of Schedule A of Form 1040, calculate the Murphy's medical expense deduction.

Medical and Dental Expenses	**Caution:** Do not include expenses reimbursed or paid by others.		
	1 Medical and dental expenses (see instructions)	1	
	2 Enter amount from Form 1040 or 1040-SR, line 11 2		
	3 Multiply line 2 by 7.5% (0.075)	3	
	4 Subtract line 3 from line 1. If line 3 is more than line 1, enter -0-		4

LO 5.6

16. Janet needs an elevator seat attached to her stairs since she has a medical condition that makes her unable to climb the stairs in her house. The $10,000 spent on the elevator seat does not increase the value of her house according to a local appraiser. How much of the capital asset is deductible in Janet's tax return as a medical expense?

_____

_____

_____

_____

LO 5.7

17. Lyndon's employer withheld $9,300 in state income taxes from Lyndon's wages in 2020. Lyndon obtained a refund of $1,700 this year for overpayment of state income taxes for 2019. State income taxes were an itemized deduction on his 2019 return. His 2020 liability for state income tax is $8,700. Indicate the amount of Lyndon's deduction for state income taxes on his federal tax return assuming he elects to deduct state income taxes for 2020.

$ _____

LO 5.7

18. Mike sells his home to Jane on April 2, 2020. Jane pays the property taxes covering the full calendar year in October, which amount to $2,500. How much may Mike and Jane each deduct for property taxes in 2020?

Mike's deduction $ _____

Jane's deduction $ _____

LO 5.7

19. Laura is a single taxpayer living in New Jersey with adjusted gross income for the 2020 tax year of $36,000. Laura's employer withheld $3,400 in state income tax from her salary. In April of 2020, she pays $600 in additional state taxes for her prior year's tax return. The real estate taxes on her home are $2,100 for 2020, and her personal property taxes, based on the value of the property, amount to $130. Also, she paid $80 for state gasoline taxes for the year. Complete the taxes section of Schedule A below to report Laura's 2020 deduction for taxes assuming she chooses to deduct state and local income taxes.

Taxes You Paid	**5** State and local taxes.		
	a State and local income taxes or general sales taxes. You may include either income taxes or general sales taxes on line 5a, but not both. If you elect to include general sales taxes instead of income taxes, check this box . . . . ▶ ☐	**5a**	
	b State and local real estate taxes (see instructions)	**5b**	
	c State and local personal property taxes	**5c**	
	d Add lines 5a through 5c	**5d**	
	e Enter the smaller of line 5d or $10,000 ($5,000 if married filing separately)	**5e**	
	6 Other taxes. List type and amount ▶ _____		
	_____	**6**	
	7 Add lines 5e and 6		**7**

LO 5.7

20. Mary paid $2,000 of state income taxes in 2020. She paid $1,500 of state sales tax on the purchase of goods and she also purchased a car in 2020 and paid sales tax of $3,000. How should Mary treat the taxes paid on her 2020 tax return?

_____

_____

_____

_____

LO 5.8

21. Mary's mother defaults on a home loan and Mary pays $600 in loan payments, including $175 in interest. Mary is not legally obligated on the loan and has no ownership interest in her mother's home.

a. What amount, if any, may Mary claim as an itemized deduction for the current tax year?

$ _____

b. Why? _____

_____

LO 5.8

22. Matthew borrows $250,000 to invest in bonds. During the current year, his interest on the loan is $30,000. Matthew's taxable interest income from the bonds is $10,000. This is Matthew's only investment income and he has no other investment expenses other than the interest on the loan.

a. Calculate Matthew's itemized deduction for investment interest expense for this year.

$ _____

b. Is Matthew entitled to a deduction in future years?

Explain _____

_____

LO 5.8

23. Ken paid the following amounts for interest during 2020:

Qualified interest on home mortgage	$6,023
Auto loan interest	850
"Points" on the mortgage for acquisition of his personal residence	360
Home equity loan interest (proceeds used to pay for college)	500
Mastercard interest	300

Calculate Ken's itemized deduction for interest on the following portion of Schedule A.

Interest You Paid	8 Home mortgage interest and points. If you didn't use all of your home mortgage loan(s) to buy, build, or improve your home, see instructions and check this box . . . . ▶ ☐		
Caution: Your mortgage interest deduction may be limited (see instructions).	a Home mortgage interest and points reported to you on Form 1098. See instructions if limited	**8a**	
	b Home mortgage interest not reported to you on Form 1098. See instructions if limited. If paid to the person from whom you bought the home, see instructions and show that person's name, identifying no., and address . . . . ▶ _____	**8b**	
	c Points not reported to you on Form 1098. See instructions for special rules	**8c**	
	d Mortgage insurance premiums (see instructions)	**8d**	
	e Add lines 8a through 8d	**8e**	
	9 Investment interest. Attach Form 4952 if required. See instructions .	**9**	
	10 Add lines 8e and 9	**10**	

LO 5.8

24. Janet and James purchased their personal residence 15 years ago for $300,000. For the current year, they have an $80,000 first mortgage on their home, on which they paid $5,750 in interest. They also have a home equity loan to pay for the children's college tuition secured by their home with a balance throughout the year of $150,000. They paid interest on the home equity loan of $9,000 for the year. Calculate the amount of their deduction for interest paid on qualified residence acquisition debt and qualified home equity debt for the current year.

Qualified residence acquisition debt interest $ _____

Qualified home equity debt interest $ _____

LO 5.8

25. Helen paid the following amounts of interest during the 2020 tax year:

Mortgage interest on Dallas residence (loan balance $50,000)	$1,600
Automobile loan interest (personal use only)	440
Mortgage interest on Vail residence (loan balance $50,000)	3,100
Student loan interest	775

Calculate the amount of Helen's itemized deduction for interest (after limitations, if any) for 2020.

$ _____

LO 5.8

26. At the end of 2020, Mark owes $250,000 on the mortgage related to the 2016 purchase of his residence. When his daughter went to college in the fall of 2020, he borrowed $20,000 through a home equity loan on his house to help pay for her education. The interest expense on the main mortgage is $15,000, and the interest expense on the home equity loan is $1,500. How much of the interest is deductible as an itemized deduction and why?

_____

_____

_____

_____

LO 5.9

27. Barbara donates a painting that she purchased three years ago for $8,000, to a university for display in the president's office. The fair market value of the painting on the date of the gift is $14,000. If Barbara had sold the painting, the difference between the sales price and her cost would have been a long-term capital gain.

a. How much is Barbara's charitable contribution deduction for this donation?

$ _____

b. Explain_____

_____

_____

LO 5.9

28. Jerry made the following contributions during 2020:

His synagogue (by check)	$1,100
The Republican Party (by check)	180
The American Red Cross (by check)	200
His fraternal organization for tickets to a holiday party	100

In addition, Jerry donated used furniture to the Salvation Army that he purchased years ago for $400 with a fair market value of $200. Assuming Jerry has adjusted gross income of $45,000, has the necessary written acknowledgments, and itemizes deductions, complete the Gifts to Charity section of Schedule A below to show Jerry's deduction for 2020.

Gifts to Charity	11	Gifts by cash or check. If you made any gift of $250 or more, see instructions	11	
Caution: If you made a gift and got a benefit for it, see instructions.	12	Other than by cash or check. If you made any gift of $250 or more, see instructions. You **must** attach Form 8283 if over $500.	12	
	13	Carryover from prior year	13	
	14	Add lines 11 through 13		14

LO 5.9

29. Richard donates publicly traded Gold Company stock with a basis of $1,000 and a fair market value of $15,000 to the college he attended, which is considered a public charity. Richard has owned the shares for 10 years. How is this contribution treated on Richard's tax return?

_____

_____

_____

_____

LO 5.9

30. Kathy donates cash of $600 and also provides some gently-used clothing worth $150 to a local church. Kathy does not itemize deductions. What is the nature of any deduction for these items for Kathy in 2020?

_____

_____

_____

LO 5.10

31. On January 3, 2020, Carey discovers his diamond bracelet has been stolen. The bracelet had a fair market value and adjusted basis of $7,500. Assuming Carey had no insurance coverage on the bracelet and his adjusted gross income for 2020 is $45,000, calculate the amount of his theft loss deduction.

$ _____

LO 5.10

32. Kerry's car is totaled in an auto accident. The car originally cost $18,000, but is worth $7,500 at the time of the accident. Kerry's insurance company gives her a check for $7,500. Kerry has $30,000 of adjusted gross income. How much can Kerry claim as a casualty loss on her tax return? Please explain.

_____

_____

_____

_____

LO 5.10

33. During the 2020 tax year, Irma incurred the following expenses:

Union dues	$244
Tax return preparation fee	150
Brokerage fees for the purchase of stocks	35
Uniform expenses not reimbursed by her employer	315

If Irma's adjusted gross income is $23,000, calculate her miscellaneous deductions.

GROUP 3:
WRITING ASSIGNMENT

ETHICS

1. While preparing Massie Miller's 2020 Schedule A, you review the following list of possible charitable deductions provided by Massie:

Cash contribution to a family whose house burned down	$1,000
Time while working as a volunteer at Food Bank	
(5 hours @ $50/hour)	250
Cash contribution to United Methodist Church (receipt provided)	800
Cash contribution to Salvation Army (note from Massie: "I can't remember exactly the amount that I gave and I can't find the receipt. I think it was around $500.")	500
Total	$2,550

What would you say to Massie regarding her listed deductions? How much of the deduction is allowed for charitable contributions?

RESEARCH

2. In 2020, Gale and Cathy Alexander hosted an exchange student, Axel Muller, for 9 months. Axel was part of International Student Exchange Programs (a qualified organization). Axel attended tenth grade at the local high school. Gale and Cathy did not claim Axel as a dependent but paid the following items for Axel's well-being:

Food and clothing	$1,500
Medical care	200
Fair market value of lodging	2,700
Entertainment	100
Total	$4,500

Gale and Cathy have asked for your help in determining if any of the $4,500 can be deducted as a charitable contribution.

Required: Go to the IRS website (**www.irs.gov**) and locate Publication 526. Write a letter to Gale and Cathy answering their question. If they can claim a deduction, be sure to include in your letter the amount that can be deducted and any substantiation requirements. (An example of a client letter is available at the website for this textbook located at **www.cengage.com.**)

1. James Dangell (birthdate August 2, 1976) is a single taxpayer. Jim's earnings and with-holdings as the manager of a local casino for 2020 are reported on his Form W-2:

a Employee's social security number			
555-94-9358	OMB No. 1545-0008	Safe, accurate, FAST! Use	Visit the IRS website at www.irs.gov/efile

b Employer identification number (EIN) 31-1459656	1 Wages, tips, other compensation 192,000.00	2 Federal income tax withheld 24,500.00
c Employer's name, address, and ZIP code Lucky Ace Casino 700 N. Sierra Street Reno, NV 89503	3 Social security wages 137,700.00	4 Social security tax withheld 8,537.40
	5 Medicare wages and tips 200,000.00	6 Medicare tax withheld 2,900.00
	7 Social security tips	8 Allocated tips
d Control number	9	10 Dependent care benefits
e Employee's first name and initial Last name Suff. James Dangell 911 Parr Blvd. Reno, NV 89512	11 Nonqualified plans	12a See instructions for box 12 D 8,000.00
	13 Statutory employee ☐ Retirement plan ☒ Third-party sick pay ☐	12b W 1,200.00
	14 Other	12c
		12d

15 State Employer's state ID number NV	16 State wages, tips, etc.	17 State income tax	18 Local wages, tips, etc.	19 Local income tax	20 Locality name

Form **W-2** Wage and Tax Statement **2020** Department of the Treasury—Internal Revenue Service

Copy B—To Be Filed With Employee's FEDERAL Tax Return.
This information is being furnished to the Internal Revenue Service.

Jim's other income includes interest on a savings account at Nevada National Bank of $13,700.

Jim pays his ex-spouse, Sarah McLoughlin, $3,900 per month in accordance with their February 12, 2019 divorce decree. When their 12-year-old child (in the ex-wife's custody) reaches the age of 18, the payments are reduced to $2,800 per month. His ex-wife's Social Security number is 554-44-5555.

In 2020, Jim purchased a new car and so he kept track of his sales tax receipts during the year. His actual sales tax paid is $3,650, which exceeds the estimated amount per the IRS tables.

Jim participates in a high-deductible health plan and is eligible to contribute to a health savings account. His HSA earned $75 in 2020.

During the year, Jim paid the following amounts (all of which can be substantiated):

Credit card interest	$1,760
Auto loan interest	4,300
Auto insurance	900
Property taxes on personal residence	2,988
Contributions to HSA	2,000
Income tax preparation fee	900
Charitable contributions (all cash):	
Boy Scouts	1,350
St. Matthews Church	3,100
Nevada Democratic Party	250
Fund-raising dinner for the Reno Auto Museum	100
(value of dinner is $25)	

In 2020, Jim inherited over $500,000 from his Uncle Travis that died in 2020. Although Jim invested a large portion, he also contributed $125,000 cash to the newly named Travis School of Criminal Justice at the University of Reno.

Jim also received the following Form 1098:

	☐ CORRECTED (if checked)	

RECIPIENT'S/LENDER'S name, street address, city or town, state or province, country, ZIP or foreign postal code, and telephone no. Reno Savings & Loan 49 Commerce Street Reno, NV 89501	*Caution: The amount shown may not be fully deductible by you. Limits based on the loan amount and the cost and value of the secured property may apply. Also, you may only deduct interest to the extent it was incurred by you, actually paid by you, and not reimbursed by another person.	OMB No. 1545-1380 20**20** Form **1098**	Mortgage Interest Statement
	1 Mortgage interest received from payer(s)/borrower(s)* $ 18,888.78		**Copy B** **For Payer/Borrower**
RECIPIENT'S/LENDER'S TIN 33-1234569	PAYER'S/BORROWER'S TIN 555-94-9358	**2** Outstanding mortgage principal $ 592,355.15	**3** Mortgage origination date Mar 3, 2004	The information in boxes 1 through 9 and 11 is important tax information and is being furnished to the IRS. If you are required to file a return, a negligence penalty or other sanction may be imposed on you if the IRS determines that an underpayment of tax results because you overstated a deduction for this mortgage interest or for these points, reported in boxes 1 and 6; or because you didn't report the refund of interest (box 4); or because you claimed a nondeductible item.

(Form 1098 layout)

4 Refund of overpaid interest $	**5** Mortgage insurance premiums $
PAYER'S/BORROWER'S name James Dangell	**6** Points paid on purchase of principal residence $
Street address (including apt. no.) 911 Parr Boulevard	**7** ☐ If address of property securing mortgage is the same as PAYER'S/BORROWER'S address, the box is checked, or the address or description is entered in box 8.
City or town, state or province, country, and ZIP or foreign postal code Reno, NV 89512	**8** Address or description of property securing mortgage (see instructions)
9 Number of properties securing the mortgage 1	**10** Other
Account number (see instructions)	**11** Mortgage acquisition date

Form **1098**   (Keep for your records)   www.irs.gov/Form1098   Department of the Treasury - Internal Revenue Service

Required: Complete Jim's federal tax return for 2020. Use Form 1040, Schedule 1, Schedule A, Schedule B, and Form 8889 to complete this tax return. Make realistic assumptions about any missing data.

2A. Bea Jones (birthdate March 27, 1985) moved from Texas to Florida in January 2020 after divorcing her spouse in 2019. She and her daughter, Dee Jones (birthdate 5/30/2010, Social Security number 121-44-6666) live at 654 Ocean Way, Gulfport, FL 33707. Bea provides all of Dee's support. Bea can claim a child tax credit for Dee. Bea's Social Security number is 466-78-7359 and she is single. Her earnings and income tax withholding for 2020 for her job as a manager at a Florida shrimp-processing plant are:

a Employee's social security number 466-78-7359	OMB No. 1545-0008 Safe, accurate, FAST! Use IRS e~file	Visit the IRS website at www.irs.gov/efile
b Employer identification number (EIN) 22-3134145	**1** Wages, tips, other compensation 51,200.00	**2** Federal income tax withheld 3,600.00
c Employer's name, address, and ZIP code Gulf Shrimp Co. 101 Bay Shore Dr. Unit Q10 St. Petersburg, FL 33701	**3** Social security wages 51,200.00	**4** Social security tax withheld 3,174.40
	5 Medicare wages and tips 51,200.00	**6** Medicare tax withheld 742.40
	7 Social security tips	**8** Allocated tips
d Control number	**9**	**10** Dependent care benefits
e Employee's first name and initial Last name Suff. Bea Jones 654 Ocean Way Gulfport, FL 33707	**11** Nonqualified plans	**12a** See instructions for box 12
	13 Statutory employee ☐ Retirement plan ☒ Third-party sick pay ☐	**12b**
	14 Other	**12c**
		12d
f Employee's address and ZIP code		
15 State Employer's state ID number FL	**16** State wages, tips, etc. **17** State income tax	**18** Local wages, tips, etc. **19** Local income tax **20** Locality name

Form **W-2**   Wage and Tax Statement   2020   Department of the Treasury—Internal Revenue Service

Copy B—To Be Filed With Employee's FEDERAL Tax Return.
This information is being furnished to the Internal Revenue Service.

Bea's other income includes interest on a savings account at Beach National Bank of $1,200 and $600 per month alimony from her ex-husband in accordance with their August 2019 divorce decree. In 2020, during the COVID pandemic, Bea's employer agreed to pay $5,250 of her student loans under the employee educational assistance plan. $4,500 went to the loan principal and the rest was interest. Unfortunately, that did not cover all of Bea's student loan payment and she was required to pay another $450 of student loan interest herself.

Bea received a $1,700 EIP in 2020.

In order to move herself and Dee after the divorce, Bea spent $800 moving her household goods (trailer rental), $200 on meals and $300 on lodging while traveling between Texas and Florida. The drive was 1,005 miles.

After moving to Gulfport, Bea sent Dee to a local private school for the remainder of 5th grade. Bea used $4,000 from Dee's Section 529 plan to pay for private school tuition as reported on the Form 1099-Q below. Dee had always attended public schools in Texas.

☐ CORRECTED (if checked)		
PAYER'S/TRUSTEE'S name, street address, city or town, state or province, country, ZIP or foreign postal code, and telephone no. Texas College Savings Plan PO Box 13400 Austin, TX 78711	**1 Gross distribution** $ 4,000.00 **2 Earnings** $ 254.00	OMB No. 1545-1760 Form **1099-Q** (Rev. November 2019) For calendar year 20 _20_	**Payments From Qualified Education Programs (Under Sections 529 and 530)**
PAYER'S/TRUSTEE'S TIN 22-1456712 **RECIPIENT'S TIN** 121-44-6666	**3 Basis** $ 3,746.00	**4 Trustee-to-trustee transfer** ☐	**Copy B** **For Recipient**
RECIPIENT'S name Dee Jones **Street address (including apt. no.)** 654 Ocean Way City or town, state or province, country, and ZIP or foreign postal code Gulfport, FL 33707	**5 Distribution is from:** • Qualified tuition program— Private ☐ or State ☒ • Coverdell ESA ☐ If the fair market value (FMV) is shown below, see **Pub. 970**, Tax Benefits for Education, for how to figure earnings. Dist Code = 1	**6 If this box is checked, the recipient is not the designated beneficiary** ☐	This is important tax information and is being furnished to the IRS. If you are required to file a return, a negligence penalty or other sanction may be imposed on you if this income is taxable and the IRS determines that it has not been reported.
Account number (see instructions)			

Form **1099-Q** (Rev. 11-2019)   (keep for your records)   www.irs.gov/Form1099Q   Department of the Treasury - Internal Revenue Service

Bea's employer operates a 401(k) plan, and although she is eligible, Bea does not participate.

During 2020, Bea paid the following amounts (all of which can be substantiated):

Home mortgage interest (1098 not shown)	$8,921
Auto loan interest	2,300
Property taxes on personal residence	3,200
Unreimbursed hospital bills	3,300
Doctor bills	2,612
Other deductible medical expenses	800
Income tax preparation fee	600
Job-hunting expenses	925
Contribution to IRA	3,300

After the divorce, Bea had to purchase a car for herself and all the furnishings for her home. She kept her receipts and has total sales taxes of $2,730, which exceeds the sales tax estimate from the IRS tables.

In September 2020, Tropical Storm Yuri struck Gulfport and a tree fell on Bea's home. Bea acquired the home in January 2020 for $112,000. The estimated loss in market value from damage was equal to her repair charge of $12,000. The damage caused by TS Yuri was declared a federal disaster (code EM-1212). Bea's deductible was quite high and her insurance company only reimbursed her $2,000.

Required: Complete Bea's federal tax return for 2020. Use Form 1040, Schedule 1, Schedule A, and Form 4684 (if needed) to complete this tax return. Make realistic assumptions about any missing data.

2B. John Fuji (birthdate June 6, 1981) received the following Form W-2 from his employer related to his job as a manager at a Washington apple-processing plant:

a Employee's social security number 571-78-5974		OMB No. 1545-0008	Safe, accurate, FAST! Use	IRS e-file	Visit the IRS website at www.irs.gov/efile
b Employer identification number (EIN) 34-7654321			**1** Wages, tips, other compensation 75,000.00		**2** Federal income tax withheld 9,700.00
c Employer's name, address, and ZIP code Granny Smith Apple Co. 200 Ahtanum Road Yakima, WA 98903			**3** Social security wages 75,000.00		**4** Social security tax withheld 4,650.00
			5 Medicare wages and tips 75,000.00		**6** Medicare tax withheld 1,087.50
			7 Social security tips		**8** Allocated tips
d Control number			**9**		**10** Dependent care benefits
e Employee's first name and initial Last name Suff. John Fuji 468 Bonnie Doon Avenue Yakima, WA 98902			**11** Nonqualified plans		**12a** See instructions for box 12
			13 Statutory employee ☐ Retirement plan ☒ Third-party sick pay ☐		**12b**
			14 Other		**12c**
					12d
f Employee's address and ZIP code					

15 State Employer's state ID number	**16** State wages, tips, etc.	**17** State income tax	**18** Local wages, tips, etc.	**19** Local income tax	**20** Locality name
WA					

Form **W-2** Wage and Tax Statement   **2020**   Department of the Treasury—Internal Revenue Service

Copy B—To Be Filed With Employee's FEDERAL Tax Return.
This information is being furnished to the Internal Revenue Service.

John's other income includes interest on a Certificate of Deposit reported on a Form 1099-INT:

☐ CORRECTED (if checked)

PAYER'S name, street address, city or town, state or province, country, ZIP or foreign postal code, and telephone no. Braeburn National Bank 1600 W. Nob Hill Rd. Yakima, WA 98902	Payer's RTN (optional)	OMB No. 1545-0112	**Interest Income**
	1 Interest income $ 984.55	2020 Form **1099-INT**	
	2 Early withdrawal penalty $		**Copy B**
PAYER'S TIN 54-9019016	RECIPIENT'S TIN 571-78-5974	**3** Interest on U.S. Savings Bonds and Treas. obligations $	**For Recipient**
RECIPIENT'S name John Fuji		**4** Federal income tax withheld $ 0.00	**5** Investment expenses $	This is important tax information and is being furnished to the IRS. If you are required to file a return, a negligence penalty or other sanction may be imposed on you if this income is taxable and the IRS determines that it has not been reported.
Street address (including apt. no.) 468 Bonnie Doon Ave.		**6** Foreign tax paid $	**7** Foreign country or U.S. possession	
		8 Tax-exempt interest $	**9** Specified private activity bond interest $	
City or town, state or province, country, and ZIP or foreign postal code Yakima, WA 98902		**10** Market discount $	**11** Bond premium $	
	FATCA filing requirement ☐	**12** Bond premium on Treasury obligations $	**13** Bond premium on tax-exempt bond $	
Account number (see instructions)		**14** Tax-exempt and tax credit bond CUSIP no.	**15** State **16** State identification no. **17** State tax withheld $ $	

Form **1099-INT**   (keep for your records)   www.irs.gov/Form1099INT   Department of the Treasury - Internal Revenue Service

Also, in accordance with the January 2016 divorce decree he paid $500 per month alimony to his ex-wife (Dora Fuji, Social Security number 573-79-6075) in 2020.

John received the following Form 1098 reporting mortgage interest and property taxes:

☐ CORRECTED (if checked)

| RECIPIENT'S/LENDER'S name, street address, city or town, state or province, country, ZIP or foreign postal code, and telephone no.

Braeburn National Bank
1600 W. Nob Hill Blvd.
Yakima, WA 98902 | *Caution: The amount shown may not be fully deductible by you. Limits based on the loan amount and the cost and value of the secured property may apply. Also, you may only deduct interest to the extent it was incurred by you, actually paid by you, and not reimbursed by another person. | OMB No. 1545-1380

2020

Form **1098** | **Mortgage Interest Statement** |

| | **1** Mortgage interest received from payer(s)/borrower(s)*
$ 7,803.22 | | **Copy B**
For Payer/ Borrower |
| RECIPIENT'S/LENDER'S TIN   54-9019016 | PAYER'S/BORROWER'S TIN   571-78-5974 | **2** Outstanding mortgage principal
$ 256,341.99 | **3** Mortgage origination date   10/1/2017 | The information in boxes 1 through 9 and 11 is important tax information and is being furnished to the IRS. If you are required to file a return, a negligence penalty or other sanction may be imposed on you if the IRS determines that an underpayment of tax results because you overstated a deduction for this mortgage interest or for these points, reported in boxes 1 and 6; or because you didn't report the refund of interest (box 4); or because you claimed a nondeductible item. |
| | | **4** Refund of overpaid interest
$ | **5** Mortgage insurance premiums
$ | |
| PAYER'S/BORROWER'S name   John Fuji | | **6** Points paid on purchase of principal residence
$ | | |
Street address (including apt. no.) 468 Bonnie Doon Avenue		**7** [X] If address of property securing mortgage is the same as PAYER'S/BORROWER'S address, the box is checked, or the address or description is entered in box 8.		
City or town, state or province, country, and ZIP or foreign postal code Yakima, WA 98902		**8** Address or description of property securing mortgage (see instructions)		
9 Number of properties securing the mortgage 1	**10** Other Prop. Taxes $2,000.00			
Account number (see instructions)				**11** Mortgage acquisition date

Form **1098**   (Keep for your records)   www.irs.gov/Form1098   Department of the Treasury - Internal Revenue Service

John tried his hand at day trading for one week in February 2020. He received a substitute Form 1099-B from his broker. Because the IRS was provided the acquisition date and basis for all trades and none required any adjustments or codes, these can be entered as a summary entry into Schedule D and no Form 8949 needs to be prepared.

Little John Brokerage Statement
100 Nottingham Street
Sherwood Forest, MA 01233
Substitute Form 1099-B
Tax Year 2020

John Fuji
468 Bonnie Doon Ave.
Yakima, WA 98902
XXX-XX-5974

1a		1b	1c	1d	1e	Net Gain	2
Descrip	**Shares**	**Purchase**	**Sale**	**Proceeds**	**Cost Basis**	**or Loss**	**ST/LT**
Moderni Pharm	44	2/3/2020	2/3/2020	890.00	888.00	2.00	ST
Moderni Pharm	37	2/3/2020	2/3/2020	740.00	738.00	2.00	ST
Moderni Pharm	31	2/3/2020	2/3/2020	623.00	473.00	150.00	ST
Moderni Pharm	28	2/3/2020	2/3/2020	569.00	593.00	(24.00)	ST
Moderni Pharm	34	2/3/2020	2/3/2020	683.00	443.00	240.00	ST
Moderni Pharm	21	2/4/2020	2/4/2020	422.00	172.00	250.00	ST
Moderni Pharm	40	2/4/2020	2/4/2020	786.00	767.00	19.00	ST
Moderni Pharm	32	2/4/2020	2/4/2020	646.00	464.00	182.00	ST
Moderni Pharm	35	2/4/2020	2/4/2020	692.00	495.00	197.00	ST
Moderni Pharm	30	2/4/2020	2/4/2020	595.00	478.00	117.00	ST
Moderni Pharm	42	2/5/2020	2/5/2020	847.00	579.00	268.00	ST
Moderni Pharm	28	2/5/2020	2/5/2020	565.00	433.00	132.00	ST
Moderni Pharm	33	2/5/2020	2/5/2020	664.00	421.00	243.00	ST
Moderni Pharm	21	2/5/2020	2/5/2020	422.00	277.00	145.00	ST
Moderni Pharm	32	2/5/2020	2/5/2020	630.00	478.00	152.00	ST
Moderni Pharm	39	2/6/2020	2/6/2020	780.00	509.00	271.00	ST
Moderni Pharm	40	2/6/2020	2/6/2020	796.00	711.00	85.00	ST
Moderni Pharm	38	2/6/2020	2/6/2020	754.00	484.00	270.00	ST
Moderni Pharm	34	2/6/2020	2/6/2020	674.00	424.00	250.00	ST
				12,778.00	9,827.00	2,951.00	

During 2020, John paid the following amounts (all of which can be substantiated):

Auto loan interest	1,575
Credit card interest	655
State sales tax (actual exceeds estimated)	1,780
Doctor bills	4,000
Other deductible medical expenses	1,800
Income tax preparation fee	500
Job-hunting expenses	925
Cash charitable donation to the Jonagold Research Center	400

John's employer offers a retirement plan, but John does not participate. Instead, he made a $4,000 contribution to a Roth IRA.

John received a $1,200 EIP in 2020.

Required: Complete John's federal tax return for 2020. Use Form 1040, Schedule 1, Schedule A, and Schedule D as needed to complete this tax return. Make realistic assumptions about any missing data.

GROUP 5:
CUMULATIVE SOFTWARE PROBLEM

1. The following information is available for the Albert and Allison Gaytor family in addition to that provided in Chapters 1–4.

Albert and Allison received the following form:

☐ CORRECTED (if checked)

RECIPIENT'S/LENDER'S name, street address, city or town, state or province, country, ZIP or foreign postal code, and telephone no. Vizcaya National Bank 9871 Coral Way Miami, FL 33134	*Caution: The amount shown may not be fully deductible by you. Limits based on the loan amount and the cost and value of the secured property may apply. Also, you may only deduct interest to the extent it was incurred by you, actually paid by you, and not reimbursed by another person. — OMB No. 1545-1380 — 2020 — Form 1098 — **Mortgage Interest Statement**

	1 Mortgage interest received from payer(s)/borrower(s)* $ 11,428.19

Copy B
For Payer/Borrower

RECIPIENT'S/LENDER'S TIN	PAYER'S/BORROWER'S TIN	**2** Outstanding mortgage principal $ 317,034.44	**3** Mortgage origination date 03/01/2006
60-7654321	266-51-1966	**4** Refund of overpaid interest $	**5** Mortgage insurance premiums $

The information in boxes 1 through 9 and 11 is important tax information and is being furnished to the IRS. If you are required to file a return, a negligence penalty or other sanction may be imposed on you if the IRS determines that an underpayment of tax results because you overstated a deduction for this mortgage interest or for these points, reported in boxes 1 and 6; or because you didn't report the refund of interest (box 4); or because you claimed a nondeductible item.

PAYER'S/BORROWER'S name Albert and Allison Gaytor	**6** Points paid on purchase of principal residence $

Street address (including apt. no.) 12340 Cocoshell Road	**7** ☒ If address of property securing mortgage is the same as PAYER'S/BORROWER'S address, the box is checked, or the address or description is entered in box 8.

City or town, state or province, country, and ZIP or foreign postal code Coral Gables, FL 33134	**8** Address or description of property securing mortgage (see instructions)

9 Number of properties securing the mortgage	**10** Other

11 Mortgage acquisition date

Account number (see instructions)

Form **1098**   (Keep for your records)   www.irs.gov/Form1098   Department of the Treasury - Internal Revenue Service

Albert and Allison paid the following in 2020 (all by check or can otherwise be substantiated):

Contributions to St. Anne's Catholic Church	$ 600
Tuition to St. Anne's Catholic School for Crocker (spring 2020)	6,000
Clothes to Salvation Army (10 bags in good condition)	240
Contributions to Marcus Rubius Congressional campaign	250
Psychotherapy for Allison	2,300
Prescription eyeglasses for Crocker	413
Prescription medication and drugs	1,903
Credit card interest	1,345
Interest on Albert's college loans	3,125
Actual state sales tax (including sales tax on new auto of $2,000)	3,421
Investment interest expense on stock margin account	345
Auto loan interest reported on Form 1098 (not shown here; auto was paid for by a home equity loan on residence)	860
Auto insurance	1,600
Cosmetic surgery for Albert	4,500
Dave Deduction, CPA, for preparation of last year's tax return	765
Safe-deposit box for storage of stocks and tax data	100
Contribution to an educational savings account for Crocker	1,000
Home property taxes	4,677
Unreimbursed business expense (seminar on dealing with hijacking at sea)	700

In August 2020, Crocker was on an out-of-town field trip with the university band and his appendix burst. He required immediate surgery which was considered "out of network" for the Gaytor's health plan resulting in hospital and doctor's fees of $3,150 not covered by insurance. In addition, Allison drove 310 miles round trip to be with Crocker after the surgery and drove him home after he recovered. She spent two nights in a hotel at a cost of $170 per night.

In June, Albert purchased a new professional digital SLR camera for $7,950. While the Gaytors were on vacation in August, someone broke into their residence and stole the camera. Albert's homeowners' insurance did not reimburse him for any part of the loss since he declined the special premium add-on for high value items required by his policy.

For the 2020 tax year, on April 15, 2021, Albert contributes $6,000 to his traditional IRA and Allison contributes $6,000 to her traditional IRA. Albert is not covered by a qualified retirement plan at work.

Albert managed to gather his gambling loss documentation and can substantiate gambling losses of $4,561 in 2020 (refer back to Chapter 2 for gambling winnings).

Required: Combine this new information about the Gaytor family with the information from Chapters 1–4 and complete a revised 2020 tax return for Albert and Allison. Be sure to save your data input files since this case will be expanded with more tax information in later chapters.

Form **1040**	Department of the Treasury—Internal Revenue Service (99)									

U.S. Individual Income Tax Return | **2020** | OMB No. 1545-0074 | IRS Use Only—Do not write or staple in this space.

Filing Status
Check only one box.

☐ Single ☐ Married filing jointly ☐ Married filing separately (MFS) ☐ Head of household (HOH) ☐ Qualifying widow(er) (QW)

If you checked the MFS box, enter the name of your spouse. If you checked the HOH or QW box, enter the child's name if the qualifying person is a child but not your dependent ▶

Your first name and middle initial	Last name		Your social security number

If joint return, spouse's first name and middle initial	Last name		Spouse's social security number

Home address (number and street). If you have a P.O. box, see instructions. | Apt. no.

City, town, or post office. If you have a foreign address, also complete spaces below. | State | ZIP code

Foreign country name | Foreign province/state/county | Foreign postal code

Presidential Election Campaign
Check here if you, or your spouse if filing jointly, want $3 to go to this fund. Checking a box below will not change your tax or refund. ☐ You ☐ Spouse

At any time during 2020, did you receive, sell, send, exchange, or otherwise acquire any financial interest in any virtual currency? ☐ Yes ☐ No

Standard Deduction

Someone can claim: ☐ You as a dependent ☐ Your spouse as a dependent

☐ Spouse itemizes on a separate return or you were a dual-status alien

Age/Blindness You: ☐ Were born before January 2, 1956 ☐ Are blind **Spouse:** ☐ Was born before January 2, 1956 ☐ Is blind

Dependents (see instructions):

(1) First name Last name	(2) Social security number	(3) Relationship to you	(4) ✔ if qualifies for (see instructions):	
			Child tax credit	Credit for other dependents
			☐	☐
			☐	☐
			☐	☐
			☐	☐

If more than four dependents, see instructions and check here ▶ ☐

Attach Sch. B if required.

1	Wages, salaries, tips, etc. Attach Form(s) W-2		**1**	
2a	Tax-exempt interest . . .	2a	**b** Taxable interest	**2b**
3a	Qualified dividends . . .	3a	**b** Ordinary dividends	**3b**
4a	IRA distributions . . .	4a	**b** Taxable amount	**4b**
5a	Pensions and annuities .	5a	**b** Taxable amount	**5b**
6a	Social security benefits .	6a	**b** Taxable amount	**6b**
7	Capital gain or (loss). Attach Schedule D if required. If not required, check here . . . . . ▶ ☐		**7**	
8	Other income from Schedule 1, line 9		**8**	
9	Add lines 1, 2b, 3b, 4b, 5b, 6b, 7, and 8. This is your **total income** . . . . . ▶		**9**	
10	Adjustments to income:			
a	From Schedule 1, line 22	10a		
b	Charitable contributions if you take the standard deduction. See instructions	10b		
c	Add lines 10a and 10b. These are your **total adjustments to income** . . . . . ▶		**10c**	
11	Subtract line 10c from line 9. This is your **adjusted gross income** . . . . . . ▶		**11**	
12	**Standard deduction or itemized deductions** (from Schedule A)		**12**	
13	Qualified business income deduction. Attach Form 8995 or Form 8995-A		**13**	
14	Add lines 12 and 13		**14**	
15	**Taxable income.** Subtract line 14 from line 11. If zero or less, enter -0-		**15**	

Standard Deduction for—

• Single or Married filing separately, $12,400

• Married filing jointly or Qualifying widow(er), $24,800

• Head of household, $18,650

• If you checked any box under *Standard Deduction,* see instructions.

For Disclosure, Privacy Act, and Paperwork Reduction Act Notice, see separate instructions. | Cat. No. 11320B | Form **1040** (2020)

Form 1040 (2020)

16	**Tax** (see instructions). Check if any from Form(s): **1** ☐ 8814 **2** ☐ 4972 **3** ☐ _____		16	
17	Amount from Schedule 2, line 3		17	
18	Add lines 16 and 17		18	
19	Child tax credit or credit for other dependents		19	
20	Amount from Schedule 3, line 7		20	
21	Add lines 19 and 20		21	
22	Subtract line 21 from line 18. If zero or less, enter -0-		22	
23	Other taxes, including self-employment tax, from Schedule 2, line 10		23	
24	Add lines 22 and 23. This is your **total tax** ▶		24	
25	Federal income tax withheld from:			
a	Form(s) W-2	25a		
b	Form(s) 1099	25b		
c	Other forms (see instructions)	25c		
d	Add lines 25a through 25c		25d	
26	2020 estimated tax payments and amount applied from 2019 return		26	
27	Earned income credit (EIC)	27		
28	Additional child tax credit. Attach Schedule 8812	28		
29	American opportunity credit from Form 8863, line 8	29		
30	Recovery rebate credit. See instructions	30		
31	Amount from Schedule 3, line 13	31		
32	Add lines 27 through 31. These are your **total other payments and refundable credits** ▶		32	
33	Add lines 25d, 26, and 32. These are your **total payments** ▶		33	

• If you have a qualifying child, attach Sch. EIC.
• If you have nontaxable combat pay, see instructions.

Refund

Direct deposit? See instructions.

34	If line 33 is more than line 24, subtract line 24 from line 33. This is the amount you **overpaid**		34	
35a	Amount of line 34 you want **refunded to you.** If Form 8888 is attached, check here ▶ ☐		35a	
▶ b	Routing number _____ ▶ c Type: ☐ Checking ☐ Savings			
▶ d	Account number _____			
36	Amount of line 34 you want **applied to your 2021 estimated tax** ▶	36		

Amount You Owe

For details on how to pay, see instructions.

37	Subtract line 33 from line 24. This is the **amount you owe now** ▶		37	

Note: Schedule H and Schedule SE filers, line 37 may not represent all of the taxes you owe for 2020. See Schedule 3, line 12e, and its instructions for details.

38	Estimated tax penalty (see instructions) ▶	38

Third Party Designee

Do you want to allow another person to discuss this return with the IRS? See instructions ▶ ☐ **Yes. Complete below.** ☐ **No**

Designee's name ▶	Phone no. ▶	Personal identification number (PIN) ▶

Sign Here

Under penalties of perjury, I declare that I have examined this return and accompanying schedules and statements, and to the best of my knowledge and belief, they are true, correct, and complete. Declaration of preparer (other than taxpayer) is based on all information of which preparer has any knowledge.

Joint return? See instructions. Keep a copy for your records.

Your signature	Date	Your occupation	If the IRS sent you an Identity Protection PIN, enter it here (see inst.) ▶
Spouse's signature. If a joint return, **both** must sign.	Date	Spouse's occupation	If the IRS sent your spouse an Identity Protection PIN, enter it here (see inst.) ▶

Phone no.	Email address

Paid Preparer Use Only

Preparer's name	Preparer's signature	Date	PTIN	Check if: ☐ Self-employed
Firm's name ▶			Phone no.	
Firm's address ▶			Firm's EIN ▶	

Go to *www.irs.gov/Form1040* for instructions and the latest information.   Form **1040** (2020)

SCHEDULE 1
(Form 1040)

Department of the Treasury
Internal Revenue Service

Additional Income and Adjustments to Income

▶ **Attach to Form 1040, 1040-SR, or 1040-NR.**
▶ **Go to** *www.irs.gov/Form1040* **for instructions and the latest information.**

OMB No. 1545-0074

2020

Attachment
Sequence No. **01**

Name(s) shown on Form 1040, 1040-SR, or 1040-NR

Your social security number

Part I   Additional Income

1	Taxable refunds, credits, or offsets of state and local income taxes	1	
2a	Alimony received	2a	
b	Date of original divorce or separation agreement (see instructions) ▶		
3	Business income or (loss). Attach Schedule C	3	
4	Other gains or (losses). Attach Form 4797	4	
5	Rental real estate, royalties, partnerships, S corporations, trusts, etc. Attach Schedule E	5	
6	Farm income or (loss). Attach Schedule F	6	
7	Unemployment compensation	7	
8	Other income. List type and amount ▶	8	
9	Combine lines 1 through 8. Enter here and on Form 1040, 1040-SR, or 1040-NR, line 8	9	

Part II   Adjustments to Income

10	Educator expenses	10	
11	Certain business expenses of reservists, performing artists, and fee-basis government officials. Attach Form 2106	11	
12	Health savings account deduction. Attach Form 8889	12	
13	Moving expenses for members of the Armed Forces. Attach Form 3903	13	
14	Deductible part of self-employment tax. Attach Schedule SE	14	
15	Self-employed SEP, SIMPLE, and qualified plans	15	
16	Self-employed health insurance deduction	16	
17	Penalty on early withdrawal of savings	17	
18a	Alimony paid	18a	
b	Recipient's SSN ▶		
c	Date of original divorce or separation agreement (see instructions) ▶		
19	IRA deduction	19	
20	Student loan interest deduction	20	
21	Tuition and fees deduction. Attach Form 8917	21	
22	Add lines 10 through 21. These are your **adjustments to income.** Enter here and on Form 1040, 1040-SR, or 1040-NR, line 10a	22	

For Paperwork Reduction Act Notice, see your tax return instructions.   Cat. No. 71479F   Schedule 1 (Form 1040) 2020

SCHEDULE A
(Form 1040)

Department of the Treasury
Internal Revenue Service (99)

Itemized Deductions

▶ Go to *www.irs.gov/ScheduleA* for instructions and the latest information.
▶ Attach to Form 1040 or 1040-SR.

Caution: If you are claiming a net qualified disaster loss on Form 4684, see the instructions for line 16.

OMB No. 1545-0074

20 20

Attachment
Sequence No. **07**

Name(s) shown on Form 1040 or 1040-SR

Your social security number

Medical and Dental Expenses		**Caution:** Do not include expenses reimbursed or paid by others.		
	1	Medical and dental expenses (see instructions)	**1**	
	2	Enter amount from Form 1040 or 1040-SR, line 11 **2**		
	3	Multiply line 2 by 7.5% (0.075)	**3**	
	4	Subtract line 3 from line 1. If line 3 is more than line 1, enter -0-		**4**
Taxes You Paid	**5**	State and local taxes.		
	a	State and local income taxes or general sales taxes. You may include either income taxes or general sales taxes on line 5a, but not both. If you elect to include general sales taxes instead of income taxes, check this box . . . . ▶ ☐	**5a**	
	b	State and local real estate taxes (see instructions)	**5b**	
	c	State and local personal property taxes	**5c**	
	d	Add lines 5a through 5c	**5d**	
	e	Enter the smaller of line 5d or $10,000 ($5,000 if married filing separately)	**5e**	
	6	Other taxes. List type and amount ▶ _____ _____	**6**	
	7	Add lines 5e and 6		**7**
Interest You Paid **Caution:** Your mortgage interest deduction may be limited (see instructions).	**8**	Home mortgage interest and points. If you didn't use all of your home mortgage loan(s) to buy, build, or improve your home, see instructions and check this box . . . . ▶ ☐		
	a	Home mortgage interest and points reported to you on Form 1098. See instructions if limited	**8a**	
	b	Home mortgage interest not reported to you on Form 1098. See instructions if limited. If paid to the person from whom you bought the home, see instructions and show that person's name, identifying no., and address . . . . ▶ _____ _____	**8b**	
	c	Points not reported to you on Form 1098. See instructions for special rules	**8c**	
	d	Mortgage insurance premiums (see instructions)	**8d**	
	e	Add lines 8a through 8d	**8e**	
	9	Investment interest. Attach Form 4952 if required. See instructions .	**9**	
	10	Add lines 8e and 9		**10**
Gifts to Charity **Caution:** If you made a gift and got a benefit for it, see instructions.	**11**	Gifts by cash or check. If you made any gift of $250 or more, see instructions	**11**	
	12	Other than by cash or check. If you made any gift of $250 or more, see instructions. You **must** attach Form 8283 if over $500	**12**	
	13	Carryover from prior year	**13**	
	14	Add lines 11 through 13		**14**
Casualty and Theft Losses	**15**	Casualty and theft loss(es) from a federally declared disaster (other than net qualified disaster losses). Attach Form 4684 and enter the amount from line 18 of that form. See instructions		**15**
Other Itemized Deductions	**16**	Other—from list in instructions. List type and amount ▶ _____ _____		**16**
Total Itemized Deductions	**17**	Add the amounts in the far right column for lines 4 through 16. Also, enter this amount on Form 1040 or 1040-SR, line 12		**17**
	18	If you elect to itemize deductions even though they are less than your standard deduction, check this box . . . . ▶ ☐		

For Paperwork Reduction Act Notice, see the Instructions for Forms 1040 and 1040-SR.   Cat. No. 17145C   **Schedule A (Form 1040) 2020**

SCHEDULE B (Form 1040)	Interest and Ordinary Dividends	OMB No. 1545-0074

SCHEDULE B
(Form 1040)

Department of the Treasury
Internal Revenue Service (99)

Interest and Ordinary Dividends

▶ Go to *www.irs.gov/ScheduleB* for instructions and the latest information.
▶ Attach to Form 1040 or 1040-SR.

OMB No. 1545-0074

2020

Attachment
Sequence No. **08**

Name(s) shown on return

Your social security number

DRAFT AS OF
July 8, 2020
DO NOT FILE

Part I

Interest

(See instructions
and the
instructions for
Forms 1040 and
1040-SR, line 2b.)

Note: If you
received a Form
1099-INT, Form
1099-OID, or
substitute
statement from
a brokerage firm,
list the firm's
name as the
payer and enter
the total interest
shown on that
form.

1 List name of payer. If any interest is from a seller-financed mortgage and the buyer used the property as a personal residence, see the instructions and list this interest first. Also, show that buyer's social security number and address ▶

	Amount

1

2 Add the amounts on line 1 . . . . **2**

3 Excludable interest on series EE and I U.S. savings bonds issued after 1989. Attach Form 8815 . . . . **3**

4 Subtract line 3 from line 2. Enter the result here and on Form 1040 or 1040-SR, line 2b . . . . ▶ **4**

Note: If line 4 is over $1,500, you must complete Part III.

Part II

Ordinary Dividends

(See instructions
and the
instructions for
Forms 1040 and
1040-SR, line 3b.)

Note: If you
received a Form
1099-DIV or
substitute
statement from
a brokerage firm,
list the firm's
name as the
payer and enter
the ordinary
dividends shown
on that form.

5 List name of payer ▶

	Amount

5

6 Add the amounts on line 5. Enter the total here and on Form 1040 or 1040-SR, line 3b . . . . ▶ **6**

Note: If line 6 is over $1,500, you must complete Part III.

Part III

Foreign Accounts and Trusts

Caution: If
required, failure
to file FinCEN
Form 114 may
result in
substantial
penalties. See
instructions.

You must complete this part if you **(a)** had over $1,500 of taxable interest or ordinary dividends; **(b)** had a foreign account; or **(c)** received a distribution from, or were a grantor of, or a transferor to, a foreign trust.

		Yes	No

7a At any time during 2020, did you have a financial interest in or signature authority over a financial account (such as a bank account, securities account, or brokerage account) located in a foreign country? See instructions . . . .

If "Yes," are you required to file FinCEN Form 114, Report of Foreign Bank and Financial Accounts (FBAR), to report that financial interest or signature authority? See FinCEN Form 114 and its instructions for filing requirements and exceptions to those requirements . . . .

b If you are required to file FinCEN Form 114, enter the name of the foreign country where the financial account is located ▶

8 During 2020, did you receive a distribution from, or were you the grantor of, or transferor to, a foreign trust? If "Yes," you may have to file Form 3520. See instructions . . . .

For Paperwork Reduction Act Notice, see your tax return instructions.   Cat. No. 17146N   **Schedule B (Form 1040) 2020**

SCHEDULE D
(Form 1040)

Department of the Treasury
Internal Revenue Service (99)

Capital Gains and Losses

▶ Attach to Form 1040, 1040-SR, or 1040-NR.
▶ Go to *www.irs.gov/ScheduleD* for instructions and the latest information.
▶ Use Form 8949 to list your transactions for lines 1b, 2, 3, 8b, 9, and 10.

OMB No. 1545-0074

2020

Attachment
Sequence No. **12**

Name(s) shown on return

Your social security number

Did you dispose of any investment(s) in a qualified opportunity fund during the tax year? ☐ **Yes** ☐ **No**
If "Yes," attach Form 8949 and see its instructions for additional requirements for reporting your gain or loss.

| Part I | **Short-Term Capital Gains and Losses—Generally Assets Held One Year or Less** (see instructions) |

See instructions for how to figure the amounts to enter on the lines below. This form may be easier to complete if you round off cents to whole dollars.	(d) Proceeds (sales price)	(e) Cost (or other basis)	(g) Adjustments to gain or loss from Form(s) 8949, Part I, line 2, column (g)	(h) Gain or (loss) Subtract column (e) from column (d) and combine the result with column (g)
1a Totals for all short-term transactions reported on Form 1099-B for which basis was reported to the IRS and for which you have no adjustments (see instructions). However, if you choose to report all these transactions on Form 8949, leave this line blank and go to line 1b .				
1b Totals for all transactions reported on Form(s) 8949 with **Box A** checked				
2 Totals for all transactions reported on Form(s) 8949 with **Box B** checked				
3 Totals for all transactions reported on Form(s) 8949 with **Box C** checked				
4 Short-term gain from Form 6252 and short-term gain or (loss) from Forms 4684, 6781, and 8824 . .	**4**			
5 Net short-term gain or (loss) from partnerships, S corporations, estates, and trusts from Schedule(s) K-1	**5**			
6 Short-term capital loss carryover. Enter the amount, if any, from line 8 of your **Capital Loss Carryover Worksheet** in the instructions	**6** (			)
7 **Net short-term capital gain or (loss).** Combine lines 1a through 6 in column (h). If you have any long-term capital gains or losses, go to Part II below. Otherwise, go to Part III on the back	**7**			

| Part II | **Long-Term Capital Gains and Losses—Generally Assets Held More Than One Year** (see instructions) |

See instructions for how to figure the amounts to enter on the lines below. This form may be easier to complete if you round off cents to whole dollars.	(d) Proceeds (sales price)	(e) Cost (or other basis)	(g) Adjustments to gain or loss from Form(s) 8949, Part II, line 2, column (g)	(h) Gain or (loss) Subtract column (e) from column (d) and combine the result with column (g)
8a Totals for all long-term transactions reported on Form 1099-B for which basis was reported to the IRS and for which you have no adjustments (see instructions). However, if you choose to report all these transactions on Form 8949, leave this line blank and go to line 8b .				
8b Totals for all transactions reported on Form(s) 8949 with **Box D** checked				
9 Totals for all transactions reported on Form(s) 8949 with **Box E** checked				
10 Totals for all transactions reported on Form(s) 8949 with **Box F** checked.				
11 Gain from Form 4797, Part I; long-term gain from Forms 2439 and 6252; and long-term gain or (loss) from Forms 4684, 6781, and 8824	**11**			
12 Net long-term gain or (loss) from partnerships, S corporations, estates, and trusts from Schedule(s) K-1	**12**			
13 Capital gain distributions. See the instructions	**13**			
14 Long-term capital loss carryover. Enter the amount, if any, from line 13 of your **Capital Loss Carryover Worksheet** in the instructions	**14** (			)
15 **Net long-term capital gain or (loss).** Combine lines 8a through 14 in column (h). Then, go to Part III on the back	**15**			

For Paperwork Reduction Act Notice, see your tax return instructions. Cat. No. 11338H Schedule D (Form 1040) 2020

Schedule D (Form 1040) 2020   Page **2**

Part III	**Summary**	

16 Combine lines 7 and 15 and enter the result **16**

    • If line 16 is a **gain,** enter the amount from line 16 on Form 1040, 1040-SR, or 1040-NR, line 7. Then, go to line 17 below.

    • If line 16 is a **loss,** skip lines 17 through 20 below. Then, go to line 21. Also be sure to complete line 22.

    • If line 16 is **zero,** skip lines 17 through 21 below and enter -0- on Form 1040, 1040-SR, or 1040-NR, line 7. Then, go to line 22.

17 Are lines 15 and 16 **both** gains?

    ☐ **Yes.** Go to line 18.

    ☐ **No.** Skip lines 18 through 21, and go to line 22.

18 If you are required to complete the **28% Rate Gain Worksheet** (see instructions), enter the amount, if any, from line 7 of that worksheet . . . . ▶ **18**

19 If you are required to complete the **Unrecaptured Section 1250 Gain Worksheet** (see instructions), enter the amount, if any, from line 18 of that worksheet . . . . ▶ **19**

20 Are lines 18 and 19 **both** zero or blank?

    ☐ **Yes.** Complete the **Qualified Dividends and Capital Gain Tax Worksheet** in the instructions for Forms 1040 and 1040-SR, line 16. **Don't** complete lines 21 and 22 below.

    ☐ **No.** Complete the **Schedule D Tax Worksheet** in the instructions. **Don't** complete lines 21 and 22 below.

21 If line 16 is a loss, enter here and on Form 1040, 1040-SR, or 1040-NR, line 7, the **smaller** of:

    • The loss on line 16; or

    • ($3,000), or if married filing separately, ($1,500)   }   . . . . **21** (   )

    Note: When figuring which amount is smaller, treat both amounts as positive numbers.

22 Do you have qualified dividends on Form 1040, 1040-SR, or 1040-NR, line 3a?

    ☐ **Yes.** Complete the **Qualified Dividends and Capital Gain Tax Worksheet** in the instructions for Forms 1040 and 1040-SR, line 16.

    ☐ **No.** Complete the rest of Form 1040, 1040-SR, or 1040-NR.

Schedule D (Form 1040) 2020

DRAFT AS OF August 24, 2020 DO NOT FILE

Form **4684**

Department of the Treasury
Internal Revenue Service

Casualties and Thefts

▶ Go to *www.irs.gov/Form4684* for instructions and the latest information.
▶ **Attach to your tax return.**
▶ **Use a separate Form 4684 for each casualty or theft.**

OMB No. 1545-0177

2020

Attachment
Sequence No. **26**

Name(s) shown on tax return

Identifying number

SECTION A—Personal Use Property (Use this section to report casualties and thefts of property **not** used in a trade or business or for income-producing purposes. You must use a separate Form 4684 (through line 12) for each casualty or theft event involving personal use property. **If reporting a qualified disaster loss, see the instructions for special rules that apply before completing this section.**)

If the casualty or theft loss is attributable to a federally declared disaster, check here ☐ and enter the DR-_____
or EM- _____ declaration number assigned by FEMA. (See instructions.)

1 Description of properties (show type, location (city, state, and ZIP code), and date acquired for each property). Use a separate line for each property lost or damaged from the same casualty or theft. If you checked the box and entered the FEMA disaster declaration number above, enter the ZIP code for the property most affected on the line for Property **A**.

	Type of Property	City and State	ZIP Code	Date Acquired
Property **A**				
Property **B**				
Property **C**				
Property **D**				

		Properties			
		A	**B**	**C**	**D**
2	Cost or other basis of each property	**2**				
3	Insurance or other reimbursement (whether or not you filed a claim) (see instructions) . . . . **Note:** If line 2 is **more** than line 3, skip line 4.	**3**				
4	Gain from casualty or theft. If line 3 is **more** than line 2, enter the difference here and skip lines 5 through 9 for that column. See instructions if line 3 includes insurance or other reimbursement you did not claim, or you received payment for your loss in a later tax year . .	**4**				
5	Fair market value **before** casualty or theft	**5**				
6	Fair market value **after** casualty or theft	**6**				
7	Subtract line 6 from line 5	**7**				
8	Enter the **smaller** of line 2 or line 7	**8**				
9	Subtract line 3 from line 8. If zero or less, enter -0- . .	**9**				

10	Casualty or theft loss. Add the amounts on line 9 in columns A through D	**10**	
11	Enter $100 ($500 if qualified disaster loss rules apply; see instructions)	**11**	
12	Subtract line 11 from line 10. If zero or less, enter -0- . . . . **Caution:** Use only one Form 4684 for lines 13 through 18.	**12**	
13	Add the amounts on line 4 of all Forms 4684	**13**	
14	Add the amounts on line 12 of all Forms 4684. If you have losses not attributable to a federally declared disaster, see the instructions . . . . **Caution:** See instructions before completing line 15.	**14**	
15	• If line 13 is **more** than line 14, enter the difference here and on Schedule D. **Do not** complete the rest of this section. • If line 13 is **equal** to line 14, enter -0- here. **Do not** complete the rest of this section. • If line 13 is **less** than line 14, and you have no qualified disaster losses subject to the $500 reduction on line 11 on any Form(s) 4684, enter -0- here and go to line 16. If you have qualified disaster losses subject to the $500 reduction, subtract line 13 from line 14 and enter the smaller of this difference or the amount on line 12 of the Form(s) 4684 reporting those losses. Enter that result here and on Schedule A (Form 1040), line 16, or Form 1040-NR, Schedule A, line 7. If you claim the standard deduction, also include on Schedule A (Form 1040), line 16, the amount of your standard deduction (see the Instructions for Forms 1040 and 1040-SR). Do not complete the rest of this section if all of your casualty or theft losses are subject to the $500 reduction.	**15**	
16	Add lines 13 and 15. Subtract the result from line 14	**16**	
17	Enter 10% of your adjusted gross income from Form 1040, 1040-SR, or 1040-NR, line 11. Estates and trusts, see instructions	**17**	
18	Subtract line 17 from line 16. If zero or less, enter -0-. Also, enter the result on Schedule A (Form 1040), line 15, or Form 1040-NR, Schedule A, line 6. Estates and trusts, enter the result on the "Other deductions" line of your tax return	**18**	

For Paperwork Reduction Act Notice, see instructions.   Cat. No. 12997O   Form **4684** (2020)

Form **8889**	**Health Savings Accounts (HSAs)**	OMB No. 1545-0074
Department of the Treasury Internal Revenue Service	▶ Attach to Form 1040, 1040-SR, or 1040-NR. ▶ Go to *www.irs.gov/Form8889* for instructions and the latest information.	**20**20 Attachment Sequence No. **52**

Name(s) shown on Form 1040, 1040-SR, or 1040-NR	Social security number of HSA beneficiary. If both spouses have HSAs, see instructions ▶

Before you begin: Complete Form 8853, Archer MSAs and Long-Term Care Insurance Contracts, if required.

Part I   **HSA Contributions and Deduction.** See the instructions before completing this part. If you are filing jointly and both you and your spouse each have separate HSAs, complete a separate Part I for each spouse.

1	Check the box to indicate your coverage under a high-deductible health plan (HDHP) during 2020. See instructions . . . . ▶	☐ Self-only ☐ Family	
2	HSA contributions you made for 2020 (or those made on your behalf), including those made from January 1, 2021, through April 15, 2021, that were for 2020. **Do not** include employer contributions, contributions through a cafeteria plan, or rollovers. See instructions	**2**	
3	If you were under age 55 at the end of 2020 and, on the first day of **every** month during 2020, you were, or were considered, an eligible individual with the **same** coverage, enter $3,550 ($7,100 for family coverage). **All others,** see the instructions for the amount to enter	**3**	
4	Enter the amount you and your employer contributed to your Archer MSAs for 2020 from Form 8853, lines 1 and 2. If you or your spouse had family coverage under an HDHP at any time during 2020, also include any amount contributed to your spouse's Archer MSAs	**4**	
5	Subtract line 4 from line 3. If zero or less, enter -0-	**5**	
6	Enter the amount from line 5. But if you and your spouse each have separate HSAs and had family coverage under an HDHP at any time during 2020, see the instructions for the amount to enter . .	**6**	
7	If you were age 55 or older at the end of 2020, married, and you or your spouse had family coverage under an HDHP at any time during 2020, enter your additional contribution amount. See instructions	**7**	
8	Add lines 6 and 7	**8**	
9	Employer contributions made to your HSAs for 2020	**9**	
10	Qualified HSA funding distributions	**10**	
11	Add lines 9 and 10	**11**	
12	Subtract line 11 from line 8. If zero or less, enter -0-	**12**	
13	**HSA deduction.** Enter the **smaller** of line 2 or line 12 here and on Schedule 1 (Form 1040), Part II, line 12	**13**	
	Caution: If line 2 is more than line 13, you may have to pay an additional tax. See instructions.		

Part II   **HSA Distributions.** If you are filing jointly and both you and your spouse each have separate HSAs, complete a separate Part II for each spouse.

14a	Total distributions you received in 2020 from all HSAs (see instructions)	**14a**	
b	Distributions included on line 14a that you rolled over to another HSA. Also include any excess contributions (and the earnings on those excess contributions) included on line 14a that were withdrawn by the due date of your return. See instructions	**14b**	
c	Subtract line 14b from line 14a	**14c**	
15	Qualified medical expenses paid using HSA distributions (see instructions)	**15**	
16	**Taxable HSA distributions.** Subtract line 15 from line 14c. If zero or less, enter -0-. Also, include this amount in the total on Schedule 1 (Form 1040), Part I, line 8, and enter "HSA" and the amount on the dotted line	**16**	
17a	If any of the distributions included on line 16 meet any of the **Exceptions to the Additional 20% Tax** (see instructions), check here . . . . ▶ ☐		
b	**Additional 20% tax** (see instructions). Enter 20% (0.20) of the distributions included on line 16 that are subject to the additional 20% tax. Also, include this amount in the total on Schedule 2 (Form 1040), Part II, line 8; check box c and enter "HSA" and the amount on the line next to the box . .	**17b**	

Part III   **Income and Additional Tax for Failure To Maintain HDHP Coverage.** See the instructions before completing this part. If you are filing jointly and both you and your spouse each have separate HSAs, complete a separate Part III for each spouse.

18	Last-month rule	**18**	
19	Qualified HSA funding distribution	**19**	
20	**Total income.** Add lines 18 and 19. Include this amount on Schedule 1 (Form 1040), Part I, line 8, and enter "HSA" and the amount on the dotted line	**20**	
21	**Additional tax.** Multiply line 20 by 10% (0.10). Include this amount in the total on Schedule 2 (Form 1040), Part II, line 8; check box c and enter "HDHP" and the amount on the line next to the box . .	**21**	

For Paperwork Reduction Act Notice, see your tax return instructions.   Cat. No. 37621P   Form **8889** (2020)

Student Name _____

Class/Section _____

Date _____

KEY NUMBER TAX RETURN SUMMARY

CHAPTER 5

Comprehensive Problem 1

Adjusted Gross Income (Line 11) _____

Standard or Itemized Deductions (Line 12) _____

Taxable Income (Line 15) _____

Total Tax (Line 24) _____

Amount Overpaid (Line 34) _____

Comprehensive Problem 2A

Adjusted Gross Income (Line 11) _____

Standard or Itemized Deductions (Line 12) _____

Casualties and Thefts (Form 4684, Line 18) _____

Total Tax (Line 24) _____

Amount Overpaid (Line 34) _____

Comprehensive Problem 2B

Adjusted Gross Income (Line 11) _____

Standard or Itemized Deductions (Line 12) _____

Total Tax (Line 24) _____

Amount Overpaid (Line 34) _____

Accounting Periods and Other Taxes

After completing this chapter, you should be able to:

LO 6.1   Determine the different accounting periods allowed for tax purposes.

LO 6.2   Determine the different accounting methods allowed for tax purposes.

LO 6.3   Determine whether parties are considered related for tax purposes, and classify the tax treatment of certain related-party transactions.

LO 6.4   Apply the rules for computing tax on the unearned income of minor children and certain students (the "kiddie tax").

LO 6.5   Calculate a basic alternative minimum tax.

LO 6.6   Calculate and report the self-employment tax (both Social Security and Medicare portions) for self-employed taxpayers.

LO 6.7   Apply the special tax and reporting requirements for household employees (the "nanny tax").

LO 6.8   Compute the special taxes for high-income taxpayers.

OVERVIEW

Taxpayers operating a business, whether professional, rental, manufacturing, or another activity, should have an understanding of the accounting periods (calendar, fiscal, or short-period tax years) and accounting methods (cash, accrual, or hybrid methods) allowed. Transactions involving related parties often have different rules for inclusion or exclusion of income and deductions. This chapter begins by addressing how and when individual, partnership, and corporate taxpayers should report taxable income.

In addition to the typical income tax, a number of other taxes are also reported through the individual income tax return. On the 2020 Form 1040, Schedule 2 is the primary reporting mechanism for additional taxes. This chapter covers the computation of taxes such as the "kiddie tax," the "nanny tax," the alternative minimum tax, the self-employment tax, the net investment income tax, and the additional Medicare tax.

Learning Objective 6.1

Determine the different accounting periods allowed for tax purposes.

6-1 ACCOUNTING PERIODS

6-1a Individual Tax Years

Almost all individuals file tax returns using a calendar-year accounting period. Individuals reporting for tax purposes on a fiscal year other than a calendar year are extremely rare since the tax system is set up to accommodate calendar-year taxpayers. However, there are no restrictions on an individual taking a tax year other than a calendar year. The choice to file on a fiscal year basis must be made with an initial tax return, and books and records must be kept on that basis. An individual may also request IRS approval to change to a fiscal year if certain conditions are met.

6-1b Partnership and Corporation Tax Years

Many individual tax returns include the pass-through of income from partnerships, limited liability companies, S corporations, and personal service corporations. The income or loss from partnerships and S corporations is passed through on Schedule K-1 to the owners and taxed on the owners' personal tax returns. Partnerships and S corporations are not taxable entities, only reporting entities. Similarly, wages are passed through to doctors, lawyers, accountants, actuaries, and other professionals from personal service corporations owned by them. Many individuals carry on businesses in partnerships which comprise a large part of the income shown on their tax returns. Other individuals make investments, including the operation of real estate rental activities, in these pass-through entities. Because the pass-through of income and loss from partnerships and S corporations plays a large role in the taxation of many individuals, it is important to understand the rules governing the allowed accounting periods for these entities.

Partnerships and corporations had a great deal of freedom in selecting a tax year in the past. However, Congress decided that this freedom often resulted in an inappropriate deferral of taxable income. For example, if an individual taxpayer has a calendar tax year and receives income from a partnership with a tax year ending September 30, the taxpayer is able to defer 3 months of partnership income for an indefinite period of time. Therefore, the tax law was changed to include provisions that specify the required tax year for many partnerships and certain corporations, reducing the opportunities for deferring income.

Corporations have much more flexibility and can generally choose any fiscal year-end for tax purposes. The primary restriction on choosing a fiscal year-end for a corporation is that its books and records must also be maintained on the same fiscal year-end. Fiscal year-ends must always occur on the last day of a month unless the taxpayer adopts a 52-53-week year, which permits the year-end to always fall on the same day of the week. That day of the week must be the one closest to the last day of the month.

Most partnerships, S corporations, and personal service corporations owned by individual taxpayers now conform to the same calendar-year reporting used by almost all individuals. These entities are allowed a September, October, or November year-end if the owners make an annual cash deposit on behalf of the entity or perform other required calculations to assure the IRS that they are not using the fiscal year to defer the payment of federal taxes. The details of the complex requirements which must be met by entities filing non-calendar tax years are beyond the scope of this textbook.

6-1c Short-Period Taxable Income

If taxpayers have a short year other than their first or last year of operations, they are required to annualize their taxable income to calculate the tax for the short period. The tax liability is calculated for the annualized period and allocated back to the short period. With the flat 21 percent corporate tax rate, the annualization method is somewhat simplified.

EXAMPLE Omoto Corporation obtains permission to change from a calendar year to a tax year ending August 31. For the short period, January 1 through August 31, 2020, the corporation's taxable income was $40,000. Omoto Corporation's tax for the short period is calculated as follows:

Step 1: Annualize the income $40,000 \times 12/8 = \underline{\$60,000}$

Step 2: Tax on annualized income $21\% \times \$60,000 = \underline{\$12,600}$

Step 3: Short period tax $\$12,600 \times 8/12 = \underline{\$\ 8,400}$

With a flat tax rate, this is equivalent to $\$40,000 \times 21$ percent. ♦

Self-Study Problem 6.1   *See Appendix E for Solutions to Self-Study Problems*

For the following taxpayers, determine the choice of year-end and place an X in the correct column.

Taxpayer	Calendar year-end	Fiscal year-end	Fiscal year-end but some restrictions
1. Individual with no separate books and records	_____	_____	_____
2. Partnership for which all the partners are calendar year-end individuals	_____	_____	_____
3. A corporation that keeps in book and records on a fiscal year ending June 30	_____	_____	_____
4. An S corporation for which all shareholders are calendar year-end individuals	_____	_____	_____

6-2 ACCOUNTING METHODS

6.2 Learning Objective

Determine the different accounting methods allowed for tax purposes.

The tax law requires taxpayers to report taxable income using the method of accounting regularly used by the taxpayer in keeping his or her books, provided the method clearly reflects the taxpayer's income. The cash receipts and disbursements method, the accrual method, and the hybrid method are accounting methods specifically recognized in the tax law.

The cash receipts and disbursements method of accounting (commonly referred to as the cash method or cash basis) is used by most individuals for their overall method of accounting. Generally, wages, interest and dividend income, capital gains, and personal deductions are accounted for on the cash basis for individuals. Individuals may choose to account for a particular business, such as a sole proprietorship reported on Schedule C, using the accrual or hybrid method of accounting. If a taxpayer has two businesses, a different method of accounting may be used for each. The choice of a tax accounting method is a general rule which will be overridden by tax laws for some items of income and expense. For example, individuals reporting on a cash basis may deduct IRAs or pension contributions which are paid in cash in the year following the deduction, the income from savings bonds may be included in taxable income even though it is not received in cash, and prepaid interest may not be allowed as a deduction in the year paid.

The cash method generally results in the recognition of income when it is actually or constructively received; deductions are recognized in the year of payment. Taxpayers on the accrual basis generally recognize income when it is earned, regardless of when it is received, and generally recognize deductions when they are incurred, regardless of when they are paid. Cash-basis taxpayers may not use the cash method for all expenses. Tax rules require cash-basis taxpayers to always use the accrual basis for prepayments of interest. Other business expenses such as rent must also follow the accrual method if the prepayment extends substantially (generally 12 months) beyond the end of the tax year. Conversely, accrual-basis taxpayers who receive certain types of prepaid income, such as rent in advance, must generally recognize the income on the cash basis.

EXAMPLE   On December 1, 2020, Carol entered into a lease on a building for use in her business for $2,000 per month. Under the lease terms, Carol pays 18 months' rent ($36,000) in advance on December 1. Carol may deduct only 1 month's rent ($2,000) for the calendar year ended December 31, 2020 because the prepayment extends substantially beyond the end of the tax year, even though she is a cash-basis taxpayer. The remainder of the prepaid rent is deducted at $2,000 per month in 2021 and 2022. The taxpayer receiving the rent must report all $36,000 as income even if he or she is an accrual-basis taxpayer. ◆

EXAMPLE   If in the previous example, the lease was for only 12 months, then as a cash-basis taxpayer, Carol could deduct the entire $36,000 in 2020 at the time of payment. ◆

The accrual method of accounting requires that income be recognized when (1) all events have occurred which fix the right to receive the income, and (2) the amount of income can be estimated with reasonable accuracy. An expense is deductible in the year in which all events have occurred that determine a liability exists and the amount can be estimated with reasonable accuracy. Also, "economic performance" must occur before an accrual-basis deduction can be claimed. Economic performance means that all activities related to the incurrence of the liability have been performed. For example, economic performance occurs for the purchase of services when the taxpayer uses the services.

A hybrid method of accounting involves the use of both the cash and accrual methods of accounting. The tax law permits the use of a hybrid method, provided the taxpayer's income is clearly reflected by the method. An example of a hybrid method is the use of the accrual method for cost of products sold by the business and the use of the cash method for income and other expenses.

Taxpayers make an election to use an accounting method when they file an initial tax return and use that method. To change methods, taxpayers must obtain permission from the IRS.

TAX BREAK   The cash method allows a certain amount of flexibility in tax planning. Payment of business expenses may be accelerated before year-end to generate additional deductions, if desired. In addition, billings for services may be postponed at year-end so payment will not be received and included in income until the following year. Some itemized deductions such as property taxes, state income taxes, and charitable contributions may also be paid before year-end for an immediate deduction.

Self-Study Problem 6.2A   *See Appendix E for Solutions to Self-Study Problems*

Melaleuca, Inc., is an accrual-basis taxpayer with the following transactions during the calendar tax year:

Accrual business income (except rent and interest)	$63,000
Accrual business expenses (except rent)	42,000
Three months' rent received on a leased building on November 1 of this year	9,000
Prepaid interest for 1 year received on a note on July 1 of the current year	12,000
Six months' rent paid on December 1 for business property	7,200
Calculate Melaleuca, Inc.'s, net income for this year.	$_____

6-2a **Restrictions on the Use of the Cash Method**

The tax law contains certain restrictions on the use of the cash method of accounting. Regular corporations, partnerships that have a regular corporation as a partner, and tax-exempt trusts with unrelated business income are generally prohibited from using the cash method. However, this requirement does not apply to farming businesses, qualified personal service corporations, and entities with average annual gross receipts of $26 million or less in 2020.

EXAMPLE   Orange Associates is a manufacturer of light bulbs with average gross receipts of $27 million. Orange would not be allowed to use the cash method of accounting for tax purposes. ◆

The IRS will pay informants cash rewards based on the value of the information they furnish and the amount recovered from the target of the investigation. In 2014, 2015, and 2016 the IRS paid 101, 99, and 418 whistleblowers $52 million, $103 million, and $61 million, respectively. Over the last three years, the amount of tax collected by the IRS as a result of whistleblowers was almost $1.2 billion.

Self-Study Problem 6.2B   *See Appendix E for Solutions to Self-Study Problems*

Indicate whether or not each of the following entities may use the cash method for tax purposes during 2020.

	Yes or No
1. A corporation engaged in orange farming.	_____
2. A dentist with a personal service corporation.	_____
3. A corporate car dealer with sales of $28 million per year.	_____
4. A corporation engaged in certified public accounting.	_____

6-3 **RELATED PARTIES (SECTION 267)**

> **6.3 Learning Objective**
>
> Determine whether parties are considered related for tax purposes, and classify the tax treatment of certain related-party transactions.

When taxpayers who are related to each other engage in transactions, there is potential for abuse of the tax system. To prevent this abuse, the tax law contains provisions that govern related-party transactions. Under these rules, related parties who undertake certain types of transactions may find the timing of income or deduction recognition differs from typical rules.

There are two types of transactions between related parties restricted by Section 267 of the tax law. These transactions are:

1. Sales of property at a loss
2. Unpaid expenses and interest

6-3a **Losses**

Under the tax law "losses from sale or exchange of property . . . directly or indirectly" are disallowed between related parties. When the property is later sold to an unrelated party, any disallowed loss may be used to offset gain on that transaction.

EXAMPLE Mary sells IBM stock with a basis of $10,000 to her son, Steve, for $8,000, resulting in a disallowed loss of $2,000. Three years later, Steve sells the stock to an unrelated party for $13,000. Steve has a gain on the sale of $5,000 ($13,000 − $8,000). However, only $3,000 ($5,000 − $2,000) of the gain is taxable to Steve since the previously disallowed loss can reduce his gain. ◆

EXAMPLE Assume the same facts as in the example above, except the IBM stock is sold for $9,500 (instead of $13,000). None of the gain of $1,500 ($9,500 − $8,000) would be taxable, because the disallowed loss would absorb it. $500 of Mary's disallowed loss is not available to her son. ◆

EXAMPLE Assume the same facts as in the example above, except Steve sells the IBM stock 3 years later for $7,000 (instead of $9,500). Steve now has a $1,000 realized loss, which can be deducted subject to any capital loss limitations. Because there is no gain on this transaction, the tax benefit of Mary's $2,000 disallowed loss is not available to her son. ◆

6-3b Unpaid Expenses and Interest

Under Section 267, related taxpayers are prevented from engaging in tax avoidance schemes in which one taxpayer uses the cash method of accounting and the other taxpayer uses the accrual method.

EXAMPLE Ficus Corporation, an accrual-basis taxpayer, is owned by Bill, an individual who uses the cash method of accounting for tax purposes. On December 31, Ficus Corporation accrues interest expense of $10,000 on a loan from Bill, but the interest is not paid to him. Ficus Corporation may not deduct the $10,000 until the tax year in which it is actually paid to Bill. This rule also applies to other expenses such as salaries and bonuses. ◆

6-3c Relationships

Section 267 has a complex set of rules to define who is a related party for disallowance purposes. The common related parties under Section 267 include the following:

1. Family members. A taxpayer's family includes brothers and sisters (whole or half), a spouse, ancestors (parents, grandparents, etc.), and lineal descendants (children, grandchildren, etc.).
2. A corporation or an individual who directly or indirectly owns more than 50 percent of the corporation.
3. Two corporations that are members of the same controlled group.
4. Trusts, corporations, and certain charitable organizations. They are subject to a complex set of relationship rules.

EXAMPLE Kalmia Corporation is owned 70 percent by Jim and 30 percent by Kathy. Jim and Kathy are unrelated to each other. Since Jim owns over 50 percent of the corporation, he is deemed to be a related party to the corporation. As a result, if Jim sells property to the corporation at a loss, the loss will be disallowed. Since Kathy is not related to the corporation, the rules of Section 267 do not apply to Kathy. ◆

Related-party rules also consider constructive ownership in determining whether parties are related to each other. Under these rules, taxpayers are deemed to own stock owned by certain relatives and related entities. The common constructive ownership rules are as follows:

1. A taxpayer is deemed to own all the stock owned by his or her spouse, brothers and sisters (whole or half), ancestors, and lineal descendants.
2. A taxpayer is deemed to own his or her proportionate share of stock owned by any partnership, corporation, trust, or estate in which he or she is a partner, shareholder, or beneficiary.
3. A taxpayer is deemed to own any stock owned directly or indirectly by a partner.

EXAMPLE ABC Corporation is owned 40 percent by Andy, 30 percent by Betty, and 30 percent by Chee. Betty and Chee are married to each other. For purposes of related-party rules, Andy is not a related party to the corporation since he does not own more than 50 percent of the corporation. Betty is a related party because she is a 60 percent shareholder (30 percent directly and 30 percent from her husband, Chee). Using the same rule, Chee is also a related party since he also owns 60 percent (30 percent directly and 30 percent from his wife, Betty). ♦

EXAMPLE Robert owns 40 percent of R Corporation and 40 percent of T Corporation. T Corporation owns 60 percent of R Corporation. Robert is deemed to own 64 percent of R Corporation; therefore, he is a related party to R Corp. The 64 percent is calculated as 40 percent direct ownership and 24 percent (40% × 60%) constructive ownership. ♦

There are other sets of related-party and constructive ownership rules in the tax law, which differ from the related-party rules discussed in this section and should not be confused with the Section 267 related-party provisions.

Tax cuts and tax reform do not always represent the same change. Tax cuts often involve temporary provisions designed to stimulate the economy. The cuts are often paid for with the expiration of many of the favorable tax provisions toward the end of the budget window. Tax reform represents a long-term change in the method by which taxes are applied or calculated. Parts of the TCJA passed in 2017 are consistent with reform (permanent cut in corporate tax rates to 21 percent) while other parts more closely resemble a temporary cut (the bevy of provisions expiring after 2025).

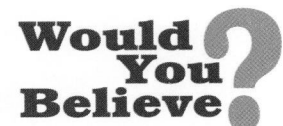

Self-Study Problem 6.3   *See Appendix E for Solutions to Self-Study Problems*

EFG Corporation is owned 40 percent by Ed, 20 percent by Frank, 20 percent by Gene, and 20 percent by X Corporation. X Corporation is owned 80 percent by Ed and 20 percent by an unrelated party. Frank and Gene are brothers. Answer each of the following questions about EFG under the constructive ownership rules of Section 267.

1. What is Ed's percentage ownership? _____%
2. What is Frank's percentage ownership? _____%
3. What is Gene's percentage ownership? _____%
4. If EFG sells property to Ed for a $15,000 loss, what amount of that loss can be recognized for tax purposes?

$_____

Learning Objective 6.4

Apply the rules for computing tax on the unearned income of minor children and certain students (the "kiddie tax").

6-4 UNEARNED INCOME OF MINOR CHILDREN AND CERTAIN STUDENTS

A child generally computes their income tax liability the same as any other taxpayer except for the decreased standard deduction is claimed as a dependent. However, many parents have found it beneficial from a tax-planning standpoint to give income-earning assets, such as stocks, bonds, bank certificates of deposit, and mutual funds, to their minor children. Since]the children are generally in a lower income tax bracket, the unearned income from assets such as interest, dividends, and capital gains on stock sales would have been taxed at a lower rate than the parents' rate. However, one of the provisions of the tax law is that certain unearned income can be taxed at their parent's rate, if higher. This is commonly referred to as the "kiddie tax."

A child is subject to the kiddie tax if:

- the child is required to file a tax return
- the child's unearned income is more than $2,200 (in 2020)
- either parent is alive
- the child
    - Is under 18, or
    - Is age 18 and does not provide more than one-half of their own support, or
    - Is age 19-24, a full-time student, and does provide more than one-half of their own support

Although there is no statutory definition for a parent, the term is generally considered to mean a parent or step-parent of the child. For purposes of determining the child's (or young adult's) income subject to the parental tax rate, net unearned income is never considered to include wages or salary of a minor child and is computed as follows:

Unearned income	$xxxx.xx
Less the greater of:	
1. $1,100 (child's standard deduction), or	
2. The allowable itemized deductions	(xxx.xx)
directly connected with the production	
of the unearned income	xxxx.xx
Less the 2020 statutory deduction	(1,100.00)
Net unearned income	$xxxx.xx

If the net unearned income is zero or less, the child's tax is calculated using the child's tax rate. However, if the net earned income amount is positive, the child's tax is calculated by applying the parents' tax rate, if higher, to that amount.

EXAMPLE Don and Melanie are a high-income married couple in the 37 percent tax bracket. Their 11-year-old son, Boris, generates $5,000 of interest income from investments. The tax on Boris' income will be computed at his parents' tax rate as follows:

Unearned income	$5,000
Standard deduction	(1,100)
Statutory standard deduction for 2020	(1,100)
Net unearned income	2,800
Taxed at parent's rate	37%
Tax	1,036
Statutory deduction	1,100
Taxed at child's rate	10%
Tax	110
Total tax	$1,146

♦

The more precise method of describing the computation of the kiddie tax is to compute the parent's tax without the child's unearned income and the recompute the parent's tax with the child's unearned income. If more than one child is subject to the kiddie tax, then a complex allocation of the tax to each child is required. The kiddie tax is reported on Form 8615.

The taxation of a child's unearned income is made even more complex in situations where the child's earned income is unusually high (over approximately $70,000) or where the unearned income is subject to preferential rates such as qualified dividends or long-term capital gains. These situations are beyond the scope of this textbook.

Although the computation of the kiddie tax is complex, having ProConnect compute the kiddie tax requires no extra input on the part of the preparer. If the taxpayer is noted as being claimed as a dependent, fits the age requirements, and unearned income that exceeds the threshold is input (for example, form Forms 1099-INT or 1099-DIV), the software will automatically generate and populate the Form 8615 and calculate the kiddie tax.

ProConnect™ Tax

TIP

6-4a Election to Include a Child's Unearned Income on Parents' Return

If certain conditions are met, parents may elect to include a child's gross income on the parents' tax return. The election eliminates the child's return filing requirements and saves the parents from the trouble of filing the special calculation on Form 8615 for the "kiddie tax." To qualify for this election, the following conditions must be met:

1. The child's gross income is from interest and dividends only.
2. The gross income is more than $1,100 and less than $11,000 (or 10 times the lower amount).
3. No estimated tax has been paid in the name of the child and the child is not subject to backup withholding.

EXAMPLE Sam Jackson is 12 years old and has $2,300 of interest from a savings account established for him by his grandparents. This is Sam's only income for the year. Instead of completing Form 8615 and paying the kiddie tax on his $2,300 in income, Sam's parents, Michael and Janet, may elect to include the $2,300 on their tax return, thereby eliminating Sam's filing requirement. ♦

The election to include the income of a minor child on the parents' return is made on Form 8814, as illustrated on Page 6-13.

Self-Study Problem 6.4   *See Appendix E for Solutions to Self-Study Problems*

Bill and Janet are a married couple filing jointly in 2020. They have one 12-year old child, Robert, whose only income in 2020 is $3,000 of interest income. Bill and Janet's AGI in 2020 is $70,800 and is all taxed at ordinary rates. Their only other deduction is the $24,800 standard deduction. Bill and Janet are eligible for a $2,000 child tax credit

a. Complete Form 8615 (Page 6-11) assuming Bill and Janet do not make the election to include Robert's income on their tax return.

b. Complete Form 8814 (Page 6-13) assuming Bill and Janet make the election to include Robert's income on their tax return.

Form **8615**

Department of the Treasury
Internal Revenue Service (99)

Tax for Certain Children Who Have Unearned Income

▶ Attach only to the child's Form 1040 or Form 1040-NR.
▶ Go to *www.irs.gov/Form8615* for instructions and the latest information.

OMB No. 1545-0074

2020

Attachment
Sequence No. **33**

Child's name shown on return | Child's social security number

Before you begin: If the child, the parent, or any of the parent's other children for whom Form 8615 must be filed must use the Schedule D Tax Worksheet or has income from farming or fishing, see **Pub. 929**, Tax Rules for Children and Dependents. It explains how to figure the child's tax using the **Schedule D Tax Worksheet** or **Schedule J** (Form 1040).

A Parent's name (first, initial, and last). **Caution:** See instructions before completing. | **B** Parent's social security number

C Parent's filing status (check one):
☐ Single   ☐ Married filing jointly   ☐ Married filing separately   ☐ Head of household   ☐ Qualifying widow(er)

Part I Child's Net Unearned Income

1	Enter the child's unearned income. See Instructions	1	
2	If the child **did not** itemize deductions on **Schedule A** (Form 1040 or Form 1040-NR), enter $2,200. Otherwise, see instructions	2	
3	Subtract line 2 from line 1. If zero or less, **stop;** do not complete the rest of this form but **do** attach it to the child's return	3	
4	Enter the child's **taxable income** from Form 1040 or 1040-NR, line 15. If the child files Form 2555, see the instructions	4	
5	Enter the **smaller** of line 3 or line 4. If zero, **stop;** do not complete the rest of this form but **do** attach it to the child's return	5	

Part II Tentative Tax Based on the Tax Rate of the Parent

6	Enter the parent's **taxable income** from Form 1040 or 1040-NR, line 15. If zero or less, enter -0-. If the parent files Form 2555, see the instructions	6	
7	Enter the total, if any, from Forms 8615, line 5, of **all other** children of the parent named above. **Do not** include the amount from line 5 above	7	
8	Add lines 5, 6, and 7. See instructions	8	
9	Enter the tax on the amount on line 8 based on the **parent's** filing status above. See instructions. If the Qualified Dividends and Capital Gain Tax Worksheet, Schedule D Tax Worksheet, or Schedule J (Form 1040) is used to figure the tax, check here ▶ ☐	9	
10	Enter the parent's tax from Form 1040 or 1040-NR, line 16, minus any alternative minimum tax. **Do not** include any tax from **Form 4972, 8814,** or **8885** or any tax from recapture of an education credit. If the parent files Form 2555, see the instructions. If the Qualified Dividends and Capital Gain Tax Worksheet, Schedule D Tax Worksheet, or Schedule J (Form 1040) was used to figure the tax, check here ▶ ☐	10	
11	Subtract line 10 from line 9 and enter the result. If line 7 is blank, also enter this amount on line 13 and go to **Part III**	11	
12a	Add lines 5 and 7	12a	
b	Divide line 5 by line 12a. Enter the result as a decimal (rounded to at least three places)	12b	× .
13	Multiply line 11 by line 12b	13	

Part III Child's Tax—If lines 4 and 5 above are the same, enter -0- on line 15 and go to line 16.

14	Subtract line 5 from line 4	14	
15	Enter the tax on the amount on line 14 based on the **child's** filing status. See instructions. If the Qualified Dividends and Capital Gain Tax Worksheet, Schedule D Tax Worksheet, or Schedule J (Form 1040) is used to figure the tax, check here ▶ ☐	15	
16	Add lines 13 and 15	16	
17	Enter the tax on the amount on line 4 based on the **child's** filing status. See instructions. If the Qualified Dividends and Capital Gain Tax Worksheet, Schedule D Tax Worksheet, or Schedule J (Form 1040) is used to figure the tax, check here ▶ ☐	17	
18	Enter the **larger** of line 16 or line 17 here and on the **child's** Form 1040 or 1040-NR, line 16. If the child files Form 2555, see the instructions	18	

For Paperwork Reduction Act Notice, see your tax return instructions.   Cat. No. 64113U   Form **8615** (2020)

DRAFT AS OF July 27, 2020 DO NOT FILE

Form **8814**	**Parents' Election To Report Child's Interest and Dividends**	OMB No. 1545-0074
Department of the Treasury Internal Revenue Service (99)	▶ Go to *www.irs.gov/Form8814* for the latest information. ▶ **Attach to parents' Form 1040, 1040-SR, or 1040-NR.**	**2020** Attachment Sequence No. **40**

Name(s) shown on your return	Your social security number
Michael and Janet Jackson	

Caution: The federal income tax on your child's income, including qualified dividends and capital gain distributions, may be less if you file a separate tax return for the child instead of making this election. This is because you cannot take certain tax benefits that your child could take on his or her own return. For details, see *Tax benefits you cannot take* in the instructions.

A Child's name (first, initial, and last)	**B** Child's social security number
Sam Jackson	

C If more than one Form 8814 is attached, check here . . . . ▶ ☐

Part I Child's Interest and Dividends To Report on Your Return

1a	Enter your child's **taxable** interest. If this amount is different from the amounts shown on the child's Forms 1099-INT and 1099-OID, see the instructions	**1a**	2,300
b	Enter your child's **tax-exempt** interest. **Do not** include this amount on line 1a **1b**		
2a	Enter your child's ordinary dividends, including any Alaska Permanent Fund dividends. If your child received any ordinary dividends as a nominee, see the instructions	**2a**	
b	Enter your child's qualified dividends included on line 2a. See the instructions **2b**		
3	Enter your child's capital gain distributions. If your child received any capital gain distributions as a nominee, see the instructions	**3**	
4	Add lines 1a, 2a, and 3. If the total is $2,200 or less, skip lines 5 through 12 and go to line 13. If the total is $11,000 or more, **do not** file this form. Your child **must** file his or her own return to report the income	**4**	2,300
5	Base amount. Enter 2,200	**5**	*2,200*
6	Subtract line 5 from line 4	**6**	100
	If both lines 2b and 3 are zero or blank, skip lines 7 through 10, enter -0- on line 11, and go to line 12. Otherwise, go to line 7.		
7	Divide line 2b by line 4. Enter the result as a decimal (rounded to at least three places) . . . . **7** ⎢ .		
8	Divide line 3 by line 4. Enter the result as a decimal (rounded to at least three places) . . . . **8** ⎢ .		
9	Multiply line 6 by line 7. Enter the result here. See the instructions for where to report this amount on your return **9**		
10	Multiply line 6 by line 8. Enter the result here. See the instructions for where to report this amount on your return **10**		
11	Add lines 9 and 10	**11**	0
12	Subtract line 11 from line 6. Include this amount in the total on Schedule 1 (Form 1040), line 8. In the space next to that line, enter "Form 8814" and show the amount. If you checked the box on line C above, see the instructions. Go to line 13 below	**12**	100

Part II Tax on the First $2,200 of Child's Interest and Dividends

13	Amount not taxed. Enter 1,100	**13**	*1,100*
14	Subtract line 13 from line 4. If the result is zero or less, enter -0-	**14**	1,200
15	**Tax.** Is the amount on line 14 less than $1,100? ☑ **No.** Enter $110 here and see the **Note** below. ☐ **Yes.** Multiply line 14 by 10% (0.10). Enter the result here and see the **Note** below.	**15**	110

Note: If you checked the box on line C above, see the instructions. Otherwise, include the amount from line 15 in the tax you enter on Form 1040,1040-SR, or 1040-NR, line 16. Be sure to check box 1 on Form 1040, 1040-SR, or 1040-NR, line 16.

For Paperwork Reduction Act Notice, see your tax return instructions.	Cat. No. 10750J	Form **8814** (2020)

6-5 THE INDIVIDUAL ALTERNATIVE MINIMUM TAX (AMT)

A small number of individual taxpayers are subject to two parallel tax calculations, the regular tax and the alternative minimum tax (AMT). The AMT was designed in the 1960s to ensure that wealthy taxpayers could not take advantage of special tax write-offs (tax preferences and other adjustments) to avoid paying tax. In general, taxpayers must pay the alternative minimum tax if their AMT tax liability is larger than their regular tax liability.

The AMT is calculated on Form 6251, using the following formula simplified for purposes of this textbook:

> Regular taxable income (before exemptions (suspended in 2018) and standard deduction)
> ± Plus or minus AMT preferences and adjustments
> = Equals alternative minimum taxable income (AMTI)
> − Less AMT exemption (phased out to zero as AMTI increases)
> = Equals amount subject to AMT
> × Multiplied by the AMT tax rate(s)
> = Equals tentative minimum tax
> − Less regular tax
> = Equals amount of AMT due with tax return, if a positive amount

6-5a Common AMT Adjustments and Preferences

The terms "AMT adjustments" and "AMT preferences" are often used interchangeably, though they have slightly different meanings. In general, adjustments are *timing* differences that arise because of differences in the regular and AMT tax calculations (e.g., depreciation timing differences), while preferences are special provisions for the regular tax that are not allowed for the AMT (e.g., state income taxes). Both terms refer to items which adjust regular taxable income to arrive at income which is subject to alternative minimum tax. There are over twenty different types of adjustments and preferences used in the calculation of AMT on Form 6251. Some of the common adjustments and preferences are as follows:

- The standard deduction allowed for regular tax is not allowed for AMT.
- The deductions for property tax, state income tax, and other taxes allowed as itemized deductions for regular tax are not allowed for AMT.
- Depreciation is generally calculated over a longer life for AMT, sometimes using a different method.
- Net operating losses are calculated differently for AMT and often result in an adjustment when they are present.
- State income tax refunds are not considered income for AMT since the state income tax deduction is not allowed for AMT.
- Interest from specified private activity bonds is not taxed for regular tax purposes, but is taxable for AMT.
- Other less commonly seen AMT differences include such items as the calculations related to incentive stock options, oil and gas depletion, research and development expenses, gains on asset sales such as rental real estate, passive losses, and the gain exclusion for small business stock and other items.

The actual details of the calculation of several of the AMT tax preferences and adjustments are complex and infrequently seen in practice. For further information, please consult the IRS website, a tax service, or an advanced tax textbook.

6-5b AMT Exemption

To reduce the chances of subjecting a greater number of taxpayers to the AMT, an exemption amount is permitted as a deduction against AMT income. The 2020 AMT exemptions and thresholds are:

	Married filing jointly	Single and H of H	Married filing separately
Exemption amount	$ 113,400	$ 72,900	$ 56,700
Threshold	1,036,800	518,400	518,400

The exemption amount is phased out (reduced) 25 cents for each dollar by which the taxpayer's alternative minimum taxable income exceeds the threshold amounts.

EXAMPLE Abby, a single taxpayer, has AMTI of $126,000 in 2020. Her AMT exemption is $72,900 as she has not reached the threshold for phase-out. ◆

EXAMPLE Damon and Tiffany are married and file jointly. They have AMTI of $1,234,000 in 2020. Their AMT exemption is $64,100 [$113,400 − (($1,234,000 − $1,036,800) × 25%)]. ◆

The exemption amounts and phase-out thresholds are both indexed for inflation, but the amounts are scheduled to be reduced significantly after 2025.

6-5c Alternative Minimum Tax Rates

For 2020, the alternative minimum tax rates for calculating the tentative minimum tax are 26 percent of the first $197,900 ($98,950 for married taxpayers filing separately), plus 28 percent on amounts above $197,900 (amounts above $98,950 for married filing separately). These rates are applied to the taxpayer's alternative minimum tax base from the formula above. The alternative minimum tax rate for capital gains and dividends is limited to the rate paid for regular tax purposes (e.g., capital gain or qualified dividends taxed at 15 percent for regular tax purposes will also be taxed at a 15 percent alternative minimum tax rate).

EXAMPLE Teddy has alternative minimum taxable income after the exemption deduction of $270,000, none of which is from capital gains. His tentative minimum tax is $71,642, which is calculated as (26% × $197,900) + (28% × [$270,000 − $197,900]). ◆

The increase in the AMT exemption amount and exemption phase-out threshold in conjunction with the limitation on the itemized deduction for state and local taxes and the suspension of miscellaneous itemized deduction subject to the 2 percent floor, results in many fewer taxpayers being subject to the AMT than prior to the enactment of the TCJA.

EXAMPLE Gram and Sally are married taxpayers who file a joint tax return. Their taxable income and regular tax liability can be calculated as follows:

2020

Adjusted gross income	$200,000
Itemized deductions:	
State income tax	10,000
Home mortgage interest	20,000
Contributions	1,906
Total itemized deductions	(31,906)
Taxable income	$168,094
Tax from rate schedule	$ 28,561

Gram and Sally have $30,000 of private activity bond interest which is taxable for AMT but not for regular tax. The AMT is calculated as follows (same format as the Form 6251 presented on Page 6-17):

2020

Taxable income	$168,094
Interest on private activity bonds	30,000
Add back:	
Taxes	10,000
Alternative minimum	
taxable income	208,094
AMT exemption	(113,400)
AMT Base	$ 94,694
Tentative minimum tax	$ 24,620
AMT	$ 0

Because the regular tax of $28,561 exceeds the tentative minimum tax of $24,620 in 2020, no AMT is due. ◆

Self-Study Problem 6.5   *See Appendix E for Solutions to Self-Study Problems*

Harold Brown, a single taxpayer, has adjusted gross income of $600,000. He has a deduction for home mortgage interest of $23,000, cash contributions of $11,000, state income taxes of $10,000, and private activity bond interest income of $100,000. Assuming Harold's regular tax liability is $170,147, use Form 6251 on Page 6-17 to calculate the amount of Harold's net alternative minimum tax.

Self-Study Problem 6.5

Form **6251**	Alternative Minimum Tax—Individuals	OMB No. 1545-0074

Department of the Treasury
Internal Revenue Service (99)

► Go to *www.irs.gov/Form6251* for instructions and the latest information.
► **Attach to Form 1040, 1040-SR, or 1040-NR.**

2020

Attachment
Sequence No. **32**

Name(s) shown on Form 1040, 1040-SR, or 1040-NR | **Your social security number**

Part I — Alternative Minimum Taxable Income (See instructions for how to complete each line.)

1	Enter the amount from Form 1040 or 1040-SR, line 15, if more than zero. If Form 1040 or 1040-SR, line 15, is zero, subtract lines 12 and 13 of Form 1040 or 1040-SR from line 11 of Form 1040 or 1040-SR and enter the result here. (If less than zero, enter as a negative amount.)	**1**
2a	If filing Schedule A (Form 1040), enter the taxes from Schedule A, line 7; otherwise, enter the amount from Form 1040 or 1040-SR, line 12	**2a**
b	Tax refund from Schedule 1 (Form 1040), line 1 or line 8	**2b** ( )
c	Investment interest expense (difference between regular tax and AMT)	**2c**
d	Depletion (difference between regular tax and AMT)	**2d**
e	Net operating loss deduction from Schedule 1 (Form 1040), line 8. Enter as a positive amount	**2e**
f	Alternative tax net operating loss deduction	**2f** ( )
g	Interest from specified private activity bonds exempt from the regular tax	**2g**
h	Qualified small business stock, see instructions	**2h**
i	Exercise of incentive stock options (excess of AMT income over regular tax income)	**2i**
j	Estates and trusts (amount from Schedule K-1 (Form 1041), box 12, code A)	**2j**
k	Disposition of property (difference between AMT and regular tax gain or loss)	**2k**
l	Depreciation on assets placed in service after 1986 (difference between regular tax and AMT)	**2l**
m	Passive activities (difference between AMT and regular tax income or loss)	**2m**
n	Loss limitations (difference between AMT and regular tax income or loss)	**2n**
o	Circulation costs (difference between regular tax and AMT)	**2o**
p	Long-term contracts (difference between AMT and regular tax income)	**2p**
q	Mining costs (difference between regular tax and AMT)	**2q**
r	Research and experimental costs (difference between regular tax and AMT)	**2r**
s	Income from certain installment sales before January 1, 1987	**2s** ( )
t	Intangible drilling costs preference	**2t**
3	Other adjustments, including income-based related adjustments	**3**
4	**Alternative minimum taxable income.** Combine lines 1 through 3. (If married filing separately and line 4 is more than $745,200, see instructions.)	**4**

Part II — Alternative Minimum Tax (AMT)

5	Exemption.	

IF your filing status is . . .	AND line 4 is not over . . .	THEN enter on line 5 . . .
Single or head of household	$ 518,400	$ 72,900
Married filing jointly or qualifying widow(er)	1,036,800	113,400
Married filing separately	518,400	56,700

If line 4 is **over** the amount shown above for your filing status, see instructions.

5

6	Subtract line 5 from line 4. If more than zero, go to line 7. If zero or less, enter -0- here and on lines 7, 9, and 11, and go to line 10 .	**6**
7	• If you are filing Form 2555, see instructions for the amount to enter. • If you reported capital gain distributions directly on Form 1040 or 1040-SR, line 7; you reported qualified dividends on Form 1040 or 1040-SR, line 3a; **or** you had a gain on both lines 15 and 16 of Schedule D (Form 1040) (as refigured for the AMT, if necessary), complete Part III on the back and enter the amount from line 40 here. • **All others:** If line 6 is $197,900 or less ($98,950 or less if married filing separately), multiply line 6 by 26% (0.26). Otherwise, multiply line 6 by 28% (0.28) and subtract $3,958 ($1,979 if married filing separately) from the result.	**7**
8	Alternative minimum tax foreign tax credit (see instructions)	**8**
9	Tentative minimum tax. Subtract line 8 from line 7	**9**
10	Add Form 1040 or 1040-SR, line 16 (minus any tax from Form 4972), and Schedule 2 (Form 1040), line 2. Subtract from the result any foreign tax credit from Schedule 3 (Form 1040), line 1. If you used Schedule J to figure your tax on Form 1040 or 1040-SR, line 16, refigure that tax without using Schedule J before completing this line (see instructions)	**10**
11	**AMT.** Subtract line 10 from line 9. If zero or less, enter -0-. Enter here and on Schedule 2 (Form 1040), line 1	**11**

For Paperwork Reduction Act Notice, see your tax return instructions. | Cat. No. 13600G | Form **6251** (2020)

Sign Here	Under penalties of perjury, I declare that I have examined this return and accompanying schedules and statements, and to the best of my knowledge and belief, they are true, correct, and complete. Declaration of preparer (other than taxpayer) is based on all information of which preparer has any knowledge.			
Joint return? See instructions. Keep a copy for your records.	Your signature	Date	Your occupation	If the IRS sent you an Identity Protection PIN, enter it here (see inst.) ▶
	Spouse's signature. If a joint return, **both** must sign.	Date	Spouse's occupation	If the IRS sent your spouse an Identity Protection PIN, enter it here (see inst.) ▶
	Phone no.		Email address	
Paid Preparer Use Only	Preparer's name	Preparer's signature	Date	PTIN / Check if: ☐ Self-employed
	Firm's name ▶			Phone no.
	Firm's address ▶			Firm's EIN ▶

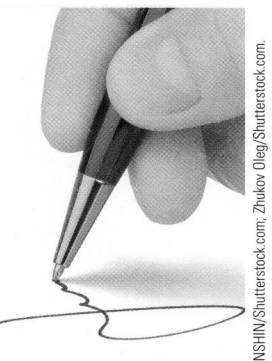

Would You Sign This Tax Return?

Your client, William Warrant, was hired for a management position at an Internet company planning to start a website called "indulgedanimals.com" for dogs, cats, and other pets. When he was hired, William was given an incentive stock option (ISO) worth $500,000, which he exercised during the year. Exercise of the ISO creates a tax preference item for alternative minimum tax (AMT) and causes him to have to pay substantial additional tax when combined with his other tax items for the year. He is livid about the extra tax and refuses to file the AMT Form 6251 with his tax return because the AMT tax is "unfair" and "un-American" according to him. Would you sign this tax return?

6-6 SELF-EMPLOYMENT TAX

6.6 Learning Objective

Calculate and report the self-employment tax (both Social Security and Medicare portions) for self-employed taxpayers.

The Federal Insurance Contributions Act (FICA) imposes Social Security (Old Age, Survivors, and Disability Insurance (OASDI)) and Medicare taxes. As discussed in Chapter 9, employees and their employers are both required to pay FICA taxes. Employers withhold a specified percentage of each employee's wages up to a maximum base amount, match the amount withheld with an equal amount, and pay the total to the Social Security Administration.

Self-employed individuals pay self-employment taxes instead of FICA taxes. Since these individuals have no employers, the entire tax is paid by self-employed individuals. Like the FICA taxes to which employees and their employers are subject, the self-employment tax also consists of two parts, Social Security and Medicare. The maximum base amount of earnings subject to the Social Security portion of the self-employment tax is $137,700 in 2020. All earnings are subject to the Medicare portion of the self-employment tax. The Social Security tax rate is 12.4 percent and the Medicare tax rate is 2.9 percent. The self-employment tax rates and the maximum base amounts for 5 years are illustrated in the following table:

Year	Maximum $ Base for 12.4%	Maximum $ Base for 2.90%*
2016	118,500	Unlimited
2017	127,200	Unlimited
2018	128,400	Unlimited
2019	132,900	Unlimited
2020	137,700	Unlimited

*A 0.9 percent additional Medicare tax on self-employment income over $200,000 single and head of household ($250,000 married filing jointly). See LO 6.8 for more information.

If a self-employed individual also receives wages subject to FICA taxes during a tax year, the Social Security tax maximum base amount for self-employment taxes is reduced by the amount of wages. Therefore, the total amount of earnings subject to the Social Security tax portion of both FICA and self-employment tax for 2020 cannot exceed $137,700.

The self-employment tax is imposed on net earnings of $400 or more from self-employment. Net earnings from self-employment include gross income from a trade or business less trade or business deductions, the distributive share of partnership income from a trade or business, and net income earned as an independent contractor. Gains and losses from property transactions, except inventory transactions, and other unearned income are not considered self-employment income. In arriving at net earnings for purposes of computing the self-employment tax, self-employed taxpayers are allowed a deduction for AGI of one-half of the otherwise applicable self-employment tax. A shortcut to arriving at the self-employment income subject to self-employment tax is to multiply the net earnings from self-employment by 92.35 percent. This shortcut is used on Schedule SE as illustrated below.

EXAMPLE Norman is a self-employed accountant in 2020. From his practice, Norman earns $140,000, and has wages subject to FICA from a part-time job of $9,100. Norman's self-employment tax is calculated as follows:

Step 1:

Net earnings from self-employment, before the self-employment tax deduction	$140,000
	× 92.35%
Tentative net earnings from self-employment after deduction for self-employment tax	$129,290

Step 2:

	Social Security	Medicare
Maximum base for 2020	$137,700	Unlimited
Less: FICA wages	(9,100)	Not Applicable
Maximum self-employment tax base	$128,600	Unlimited
Lesser of net earnings from self-employment after deduction for self-employment tax or maximum base	$128,600	$129,290
Self-employment tax rate	12.4%	2.9%
Self-employment tax for 2020	$ 15,946	$ 3,749

Norman's total self-employment tax for 2020 is $19,695 ($15,946 + $3,749). On his 2020 income tax return, Norman will report net earnings from self-employment of $140,000, a deduction for adjusted gross income of $9,848 (50% × $19,695), and a self-employment tax liability of $19,695. ◆

The calculation in this example is reported on page 1 of Schedule SE, Part I, and must be included with a taxpayer's Form 1040. See Page 6-23 which shows the same calculation on Schedule SE.

6-6a COVID-Related Provisions for Self-Employed

A series of tax provisions were enacted in 2020 due to the economic crisis brought on by the COVID-19 pandemic. Some of the more significant provisions related to employment taxes are covered on detail in Chapter 9; however, some of these same provisions are available to self-employed taxpayers.

Self-Employment Tax Deferral

Just as an employer is entitled to a payroll tax deferral, so too is a self-employed taxpayer on their own self-employment income (a sole proprietorship that has employees would apply the provisions covered in Chapter 9 for employee-related payroll tax deferrals). The deferral is available for one-half of the Social Security portion (12.4 percent) of self-employment tax for net business profits from March 27 through December 31, 2020. The payroll taxes deferred are due one-half by the end of 2021 and the remaining half by the end of 2022.

The IRS has stated that self-employed individuals may use any reasonable method to allocate net earnings from self-employment earned during March 27, 2020, through December 31, 2020. For example, an individual may allocate 22.5 percent of the individual's annual earnings from self-employment to the period from January 1, 2020, through March 26, 2020, and 77.5 percent of the individual's annual earnings to the period from March 27, 2020, through December 31, 2020.

EXAMPLE Using the information from the previous example, Norman determines that 77.5 percent of his $140,000 of net profits are allocable to the period March 27 through December 31, 2020. He can calculate the portion eligible for deferral as:

$$\$140,000 \times 77.5\% = \$108,500$$
$$\$108,500 \times 0.9235 = \$100,200$$
$$\$100,200 \times 6.2\% = \$6,212$$

Norman will report a payroll tax credit due to the deferral on Schedule 3 of Form 1040. The reporting of the deferral is presented on page 2 of Schedule SE shown on Page 6-24. ♦

The deferral portion of one-half of the Social Security portion of self-employment taxes remains deductible as a for AGI deduction.

Sick and Family Leave Credits

Consistent with the treatment for employers, the self-employed are also eligible for sick and family leave credits (see Chapter 9 for a detailed discussion). A self-employed individual may claim a refundable credit for a qualified sick leave equivalent amount if the individual is unable to work or telework due to:

1. The self-employed individual is subject to a quarantine ordered by a governmental authority.
2. The self-employed individual has been advised to self-quarantine by a health care provider.
3. The self-employed individual has COVID-19 symptoms.
4. The self-employed individual is caring for someone subject to quarantine as per items 1 and 2 above.
5. The self-employed individual is caring for a child because the school or normal place of care is closed due to COVID-19.

To compute the qualified sick leave equivalent amount, the first step is to determine the number of days the self-employed individual was unable to work. That number of days is multiplied by either:

- The lesser of $511 or 100 percent of the individual's average daily self-employment income (if sick time was due to reasons 1-3 above), or
- The lesser of $200 or 67 percent of the individual's average daily self-employment income (if sick time was due to reasons 4-5 above),

The number of days for sick time is limited to 10. An individual's average daily self-employment income is net earnings from self-employment income divided by 260.

EXAMPLE Greta runs a shoe repair shop as a sole proprietor. She has no employees. In April 2020, she was stricken by COVID-19 and spend 26 days quarantined and recovering. Her Schedule C profits are $68,000 and her net earnings from self-employment are $62,798 ($68,000 × 0.9235). Her average daily self-employment income is $242 ($62,798 ÷ 260 rounded to the nearest whole number). Her sick leave credit is $242 × 10 days or $2,420. ◆

The family leave credit works in much the same way as the sick leave credit. In the case of the family leave credit, the self-employed individual was unable to work because they needed to care for a child under the age of 18, due to school or the place of care being closed or unavailable due to COVID-19.

The family leave equivalent amount is the number of days the self-employed individual was unable to work up to a maximum of 50, multiplied by the lesser of:

- 67 percent of the individual's average daily self-employment income, or
- $200

EXAMPLE Greta, from the previous example, is unable to work for another 73 days as her daughter also catches COVID and is quarantined and unable to go to day care for over two months. Greta's average daily self-employment income x 67 percent is $162; therefore her family leave equivalent amount is $8,100 ($162 × 50). ◆

Both the sick and family leave credits for self-employed individuals are reported on Form 7202. The above two examples are presented on Form 7202 on Page 6-25.

Self-Study Problem 6.6   *See Appendix E for Solutions to Self-Study Problems*

1. (no COVID provisions) Joanne Plummer is self-employed in 2020. Her Schedule C net income is $36,600 for the year, and Joanne also had a part-time job and earned $4,400 that was subject to FICA tax. Joanne received taxable dividends of $1,110 during the year, and she had a capital gain on the sale of stock of $9,100. Joanne did not elect to defer her payroll taxes or claim any sick and family leave credits. Calculate Joanne's self-employment tax using Schedule SE (page 1 only) of Form 1040 on Page 6-27.

2. Assume that Joanne from part 1 elects to defer her payroll tax to 2021 and that she also has 10 days of qualified sick leave and 21 days of qualified family leave and elects to take both of those credits. Joanne allocates 77.5 percent of her self-employment income to March 27–December 31, 2020. Complete page 2 of Form SE on Page 6-28 and Form 7202 on Page 6-29.

SCHEDULE SE
(Form 1040)

Department of the Treasury
Internal Revenue Service (99)

Self-Employment Tax

▶ Go to *www.irs.gov/ScheduleSE* for instructions and the latest information.
▶ Attach to Form 1040, 1040-SR, or 1040-NR.

OMB No. 1545-0074

2020

Attachment
Sequence No. **17**

Name of person with self-employment income (as shown on Form 1040, 1040-SR, or 1040-NR)
Norman

Social security number of person
with **self-employment** income ▶

DRAFT AS OF August 10, 2020 DO NOT FILE

Part I   Self-Employment Tax

Note: If your only income subject to self-employment tax is **church employee income,** see instructions for how to report your income and the definition of church employee income.

A   If you are a minister, member of a religious order, or Christian Science practitioner **and** you filed Form 4361, but you had $400 or more of **other** net earnings from self-employment, check here and continue with Part I . . . . ▶ ☐

Skip lines 1a and 1b if you use the farm optional method in Part II. See instructions.

1a   Net farm profit or (loss) from Schedule F, line 34, and farm partnerships, Schedule K-1 (Form 1065), box 14, code A . . . | **1a** |

b   If you received social security retirement or disability benefits, enter the amount of Conservation Reserve Program payments included on Schedule F, line 4b, or listed on Schedule K-1 (Form 1065), box 20, code AH | **1b** | ( )

Skip line 2 if you use the nonfarm optional method in Part II. See instructions.

2   Net profit or (loss) from Schedule C, line 31; and Schedule K-1 (Form 1065), box 14, code A (other than farming). See instructions for other income to report or if you are a minister or member of a religious order | **2** | 140,000 *143,750*

3   Combine lines 1a, 1b, and 2 . . . | **3** | 140,000 ✓

4a   If line 3 is more than zero, multiply line 3 by (92.35%) (0.9235). Otherwise, enter amount from line 3 | **4a** | 129,290
Note: If line 4a is less than $400 due to Conservation Reserve Program payments on line 1b, see instructions.

b   If you elect one or both of the optional methods, enter the total of lines 15 and 17 here . . . . | **4b** |

c   Combine lines 4a and 4b. If less than $400, **stop;** you don't owe self-employment tax. **Exception:** If less than $400 and you had **church employee income,** enter -0- and continue . . . . . . ▶ | **4c** | 129,290 ✓

5a   Enter your **church employee income** from Form W-2. See instructions for definition of church employee income . . . | **5a** |

b   Multiply line 5a by 92.35% (0.9235). If less than $100, enter -0- . . | **5b** | ✓

6   Add lines 4c and 5b . . . | **6** | 129,290 ✓

7   Maximum amount of combined wages and self-employment earnings subject to social security tax or the 6.2% portion of the 7.65% railroad retirement (tier 1) tax for 2020 | **7** | 137,700 ✓

8a   Total social security wages and tips (total of boxes 3 and 7 on Form(s) W-2) and railroad retirement (tier 1) compensation. If $137,700 or more, skip lines 8b through 10, and go to line 11 | **8a** | 9,100

b   Unreported tips subject to social security tax from Form 4137, line 10 . . . | **8b** |

c   Wages subject to social security tax from Form 8919, line 10 . . . . . | **8c** |

0 - 137,700

d   Add lines 8a, 8b, and 8c . . . | **8d** | 9,100
9   Subtract line 8d from line 7. If zero or less, enter -0- here and on line 10 and go to line 11 . . . ▶ | **9** | 128,600
10   Multiply the **smaller** of line 6 or line 9 by 12.4% (0.124) . . . | **10** | 15,946
11   Multiply line 6 by 2.9% (0.029) . . . | **11** | 3,749
12   **Self-employment tax.** Add lines 10 and 11. Enter here and on **Schedule 2 (Form 1040), line 4** . . | **12** | 19,695
13   **Deduction for one-half of self-employment tax.**
Multiply line 12 by 50% (0.50). Enter here and on **Schedule 1 (Form 1040), line 14** . . . | **13** | 9,848

Part II   Optional Methods To Figure Net Earnings (see instructions)

Farm Optional Method. You may use this method **only** if **(a)** your gross farm income[1] wasn't more than $8,460, **or (b)** your net farm profits[2] were less than $6,107.

14   Maximum income for optional methods . . . | **14** | 5,640
15   Enter the **smaller** of: two-thirds (2/3) of gross farm income[1] (not less than zero) **or** $5,640. Also, include this amount on line 4b above . . . | **15** |

Nonfarm Optional Method. You may use this method **only** if **(a)** your net nonfarm profits[3] were less than $6,107 and also less than 72.189% of your gross nonfarm income,[4] **and (b)** you had net earnings from self-employment of at least $400 in 2 of the prior 3 years. **Caution:** You may use this method no more than five times.

16   Subtract line 15 from line 14 . . . | **16** |
17   Enter the **smaller** of: two-thirds (2/3) of gross nonfarm income[4] (not less than zero) **or** the amount on line 16. Also, include this amount on line 4b above . . . | **17** |

[1] From Sch. F, line 9; and Sch. K-1 (Form 1065), box 14, code B.
[2] From Sch. F, line 34; and Sch. K-1 (Form 1065), box 14, code A—minus the amount you would have entered on line 1b had you not used the optional method.
[3] From Sch. C, line 31; and Sch. K-1 (Form 1065), box 14, code A.
[4] From Sch. C, line 7; and Sch. K-1 (Form 1065), box 14, code C.

For Paperwork Reduction Act Notice, see your tax return instructions.   Cat. No. 11358Z   Schedule SE (Form 1040) 2020

Schedule SE (Form 1040) 2020   Attachment Sequence No. **17**   Page **2**

Part III	Maximum Deferral of Self-Employment Tax Payments		

If line 4c is zero, skip lines 18 through 20, and enter -0- on line 21.

18	Enter the portion of line 3 that can be attributed to March 27, 2020, through December 31, 2020 . .	**18**	108,500
19	If line 18 is more than zero, multiply line 18 by 92.35% (0.9235); otherwise, enter the amount from line 18	**19**	100,200
20	Enter the portion of lines 15 and 17 that can be attributed to March 27, 2020, through December 31, 2020	**20**	
21	Combine lines 19 and 20	**21**	100,200

If line 5b is zero, skip line 22 and enter -0- on line 23.

22	Enter the portion of line 5a that can be attributed to March 27, 2020, through December 31, 2020 . .	**22**	
23	Multiply line 22 by 92.35% (0.9235)	**23**	
24	Add lines 21 and 23	**24**	100,200
25	Enter the smaller of line 9 or line 24	**25**	100,200
26	Multiply line 25 by 6.2% (0.062). Enter here and see the instructions for line 12e of Schedule 3 (Form 1040)	**26**	6,212

Schedule SE (Form 1040) 2020

Form **7202**

Department of the Treasury
Internal Revenue Service

**Credits for Sick Leave and Family Leave
for Certain Self-Employed Individuals**

▶ Attach to Form 1040 or 1040-SR.
▶ Go to *www.irs.gov/Form7202* for instructions and the latest information.

OMB No. 1545-0074

2020

Attachment
Sequence No. **202**

Name of person with self-employment income (as shown on Form 1040 or 1040-SR)

Greta

Social security number of person with
self-employment income

Part I — Credit for Sick Leave for Certain Self-Employed Individuals

1	Number of days you were unable to perform services as a self-employed individual because of certain coronavirus-related care you required. See instructions	1	26
2	Number of days you were unable to perform services as a self-employed individual because of certain coronavirus-related care you provided to another. (Do not include days you included in line 1.) See instructions	2	
3	If you are filing a fiscal year return, see instructions; otherwise enter 10	3	10
4	Enter the smaller of line 1 or line 3	4	10
5	Subtract line 4 from line 3	5	0
6	Enter the smaller of line 2 or line 5	6	0
7	Net earnings from self-employment (see instructions)	7	62,798
8	Divide line 7 by 260 (round to nearest whole number)	8	242
9	Enter the smaller of line 8 or $511	9	242
10	Multiply line 4 by line 9	10	2,420
11	Multiply line 8 by 67% (0.67)	11	162
12	Enter the smaller of line 11 or $200	12	162
13	Multiply line 6 by line 12	13	0
14	Add lines 10 and 13	14	2,420
15	Amount of emergency paid sick leave subject to the $511 per day limit you received from an employer (see instructions)	15	0
16	Amount of emergency paid sick leave subject to the $200 per day limit you received from an employer (see instructions)	16	0
	If line 15 and line 16 are both zero, skip to line 24 and enter the amount from line 14.		
17	Add line 13 and line 16	17	
18	Enter the smaller of line 17 or $2,000	18	
19	Subtract line 18 from line 17	19	
20	Add lines 10, 15, and 18	20	
21	Enter the smaller of line 20 or $5,110	21	
22	Subtract line 21 from line 20	22	
23	Add line 19 and line 22	23	
24	Subtract line 23 from line 14. If zero or less, enter -0-. Enter here and include on Schedule 3 (Form 1040), line 12b	24	2,420

Part II — Credit for Family Leave for Certain Self-Employed Individuals

25	Number of days you were unable to perform services as a self-employed individual because of certain coronavirus-related care you provided to a son or daughter under the age of 18. (Do not enter more than 50 days.) See instructions	25	50
26	Net earnings from self-employment (see instructions)	26	62,798
27	Divide line 26 by 260 (round to nearest whole number)	27	242
28	Multiply line 27 by 67% (0.67)	28	162
29	Enter the smaller of line 28 or $200	29	162
30	Multiply line 25 by line 29	30	8,100
31	Amount of emergency family leave wages you received from an employer (see instructions)	31	0
	If line 31 is zero, skip to line 35 and enter the amount from line 30.		
32	Add line 30 and line 31	32	
33	Enter the smaller of line 32 or $10,000	33	
34	Subtract line 33 from line 32	34	
35	Subtract line 34 from line 30. If zero or less, enter -0-. Enter here and include on Schedule 3 (Form 1040), line 12b	35	8,100

For Privacy Act and Paperwork Reduction Act Notice, see your tax return instructions.   Cat. No. 56395K   Form **7202** (2020)

Self-Study Problem 6.6

SCHEDULE SE
(Form 1040)

Department of the Treasury
Internal Revenue Service (99)

Self-Employment Tax

▶ Go to *www.irs.gov/ScheduleSE* for instructions and the latest information.
▶ Attach to Form 1040, 1040-SR, or 1040-NR.

OMB No. 1545-0074

2020

Attachment
Sequence No. **17**

Name of person with self-employment income (as shown on Form 1040, 1040-SR, or 1040-NR)

Social security number of person
with **self-employment** income ▶

Part I Self-Employment Tax

Note: If your only income subject to self-employment tax is **church employee income,** see instructions for how to report your income and the definition of church employee income.

A If you are a minister, member of a religious order, or Christian Science practitioner **and** you filed Form 4361, but you had $400 or more of **other** net earnings from self-employment, check here and continue with Part I . . . . ▶ ☐

Skip lines 1a and 1b if you use the farm optional method in Part II. See instructions.

1a	Net farm profit or (loss) from Schedule F, line 34, and farm partnerships, Schedule K-1 (Form 1065), box 14, code A	**1a**	
b	If you received social security retirement or disability benefits, enter the amount of Conservation Reserve Program payments included on Schedule F, line 4b, or listed on Schedule K-1 (Form 1065), box 20, code AH	**1b**	( )

Skip line 2 if you use the nonfarm optional method in Part II. See instructions.

2	Net profit or (loss) from Schedule C, line 31; and Schedule K-1 (Form 1065), box 14, code A (other than farming). See instructions for other income to report or if you are a minister or member of a religious order	**2**	
3	Combine lines 1a, 1b, and 2	**3**	
4a	If line 3 is more than zero, multiply line 3 by 92.35% (0.9235). Otherwise, enter amount from line 3 .	**4a**	
	Note: If line 4a is less than $400 due to Conservation Reserve Program payments on line 1b, see instructions.		
b	If you elect one or both of the optional methods, enter the total of lines 15 and 17 here	**4b**	
c	Combine lines 4a and 4b. If less than $400, **stop;** you don't owe self-employment tax. **Exception:** If less than $400 and you had **church employee income,** enter -0- and continue . . . . ▶	**4c**	
5a	Enter your **church employee income** from Form W-2. See instructions for definition of church employee income . . . . | **5a** |		
b	Multiply line 5a by 92.35% (0.9235). If less than $100, enter -0-	**5b**	
6	Add lines 4c and 5b	**6**	
7	Maximum amount of combined wages and self-employment earnings subject to social security tax or the 6.2% portion of the 7.65% railroad retirement (tier 1) tax for 2020	**7**	137,700
8a	Total social security wages and tips (total of boxes 3 and 7 on Form(s) W-2) and railroad retirement (tier 1) compensation. If $137,700 or more, skip lines 8b through 10, and go to line 11 . . . . | **8a** |		
b	Unreported tips subject to social security tax from Form 4137, line 10 . . . | **8b** |		
c	Wages subject to social security tax from Form 8919, line 10 . . . . . . | **8c** |		
d	Add lines 8a, 8b, and 8c	**8d**	
9	Subtract line 8d from line 7. If zero or less, enter -0- here and on line 10 and go to line 11 . . . ▶	**9**	
10	Multiply the **smaller** of line 6 or line 9 by 12.4% (0.124)	**10**	
11	Multiply line 6 by 2.9% (0.029)	**11**	
12	**Self-employment tax.** Add lines 10 and 11. Enter here and on **Schedule 2 (Form 1040), line 4** . .	**12**	
13	**Deduction for one-half of self-employment tax.** Multiply line 12 by 50% (0.50). Enter here and on **Schedule 1 (Form 1040), line 14** . . . . | **13** |		

Part II Optional Methods To Figure Net Earnings (see instructions)

Farm Optional Method. You may use this method **only** if **(a)** your gross farm income[1] wasn't more than $8,460, **or (b)** your net farm profits[2] were less than $6,107.

14	Maximum income for optional methods	**14**	5,640
15	Enter the **smaller** of: two-thirds (2/3) of gross farm income[1] (not less than zero) or $5,640. Also, include this amount on line 4b above	**15**	

Nonfarm Optional Method. You may use this method **only** if **(a)** your net nonfarm profits[3] were less than $6,107 and also less than 72.189% of your gross nonfarm income,[4] **and (b)** you had net earnings from self-employment of at least $400 in 2 of the prior 3 years. **Caution:** You may use this method no more than five times.

16	Subtract line 15 from line 14	**16**	
17	Enter the **smaller** of: two-thirds (2/3) of gross nonfarm income[4] (not less than zero) **or** the amount on line 16. Also, include this amount on line 4b above	**17**	

[1] From Sch. F, line 9; and Sch. K-1 (Form 1065), box 14, code B.
[2] From Sch. F, line 34; and Sch. K-1 (Form 1065), box 14, code A—minus the amount you would have entered on line 1b had you not used the optional method.
[3] From Sch. C, line 31; and Sch. K-1 (Form 1065), box 14, code A.
[4] From Sch. C, line 7; and Sch. K-1 (Form 1065), box 14, code C.

For Paperwork Reduction Act Notice, see your tax return instructions.   Cat. No. 11358Z   **Schedule SE (Form 1040) 2020**

Schedule SE (Form 1040) 2020　　　　　　　　　　　　　　　　　Attachment Sequence No. **17**　　　　　　Page **2**

Part III	**Maximum Deferral of Self-Employment Tax Payments**	

If line 4c is zero, skip lines 18 through 20, and enter -0- on line 21.

18	Enter the portion of line 3 that can be attributed to March 27, 2020, through December 31, 2020 . .	**18**	
19	If line 18 is more than zero, multiply line 18 by 92.35% (0.9235); otherwise, enter the amount from line 18	**19**	
20	Enter the portion of lines 15 and 17 that can be attributed to March 27, 2020, through December 31, 2020	**20**	
21	Combine lines 19 and 20	**21**	

If line 5b is zero, skip line 22 and enter -0- on line 23.

22	Enter the portion of line 5a that can be attributed to March 27, 2020, through December 31, 2020	**22**	
23	Multiply line 22 by 92.35% (0.9235)	**23**	
24	Add lines 21 and 23	**24**	
25	Enter the smaller of line 9 or line 24	**25**	
26	Multiply line 25 by 6.2% (0.062). Enter here and see the instructions for line 12e of Schedule 3 (Form 1040)	**26**	

Schedule SE (Form 1040) 2020

Self-Study Problem 6.6

Form **7202**	Credits for Sick Leave and Family Leave for Certain Self-Employed Individuals	OMB No. 1545-0074
Department of the Treasury Internal Revenue Service	▶ Attach to Form 1040 or 1040-SR. ▶ Go to *www.irs.gov/Form7202* for instructions and the latest information.	20**20** Attachment Sequence No. **202**

Name of person with self-employment income (as shown on Form 1040 or 1040-SR) | Social security number of person with self-employment income

Part I — Credit for Sick Leave for Certain Self-Employed Individuals

1	Number of days you were unable to perform services as a self-employed individual because of certain coronavirus-related care you required. See instructions	1
2	Number of days you were unable to perform services as a self-employed individual because of certain coronavirus-related care you provided to another. (Do not include days you included in line 1.) See instructions	2
3	If you are filing a fiscal year return, see instructions; otherwise enter 10	3
4	Enter the smaller of line 1 or line 3	4
5	Subtract line 4 from line 3	5
6	Enter the smaller of line 2 or line 5	6
7	Net earnings from self-employment (see instructions)	7
8	Divide line 7 by 260 (round to nearest whole number)	8
9	Enter the smaller of line 8 or $511	9
10	Multiply line 4 by line 9	10
11	Multiply line 8 by 67% (0.67)	11
12	Enter the smaller of line 11 or $200	12
13	Multiply line 6 by line 12	13
14	Add lines 10 and 13	14
15	Amount of emergency paid sick leave subject to the $511 per day limit you received from an employer (see instructions)	15
16	Amount of emergency paid sick leave subject to the $200 per day limit you received from an employer (see instructions)	16
	If line 15 and line 16 are both zero, skip to line 24 and enter the amount from line 14.	
17	Add line 13 and line 16	17
18	Enter the smaller of line 17 or $2,000	18
19	Subtract line 18 from line 17	19
20	Add lines 10, 15, and 18	20
21	Enter the smaller of line 20 or $5,110	21
22	Subtract line 21 from line 20	22
23	Add line 19 and line 22	23
24	Subtract line 23 from line 14. If zero or less, enter -0-. Enter here and include on Schedule 3 (Form 1040), line 12b	24

Part II — Credit for Family Leave for Certain Self-Employed Individuals

25	Number of days you were unable to perform services as a self-employed individual because of certain coronavirus-related care you provided to a son or daughter under the age of 18. (Do not enter more than 50 days.) See instructions	25
26	Net earnings from self-employment (see instructions)	26
27	Divide line 26 by 260 (round to nearest whole number)	27
28	Multiply line 27 by 67% (0.67)	28
29	Enter the smaller of line 28 or $200	29
30	Multiply line 25 by line 29	30
31	Amount of emergency family leave wages you received from an employer (see instructions)	31
	If line 31 is zero, skip to line 35 and enter the amount from line 30.	
32	Add line 30 and line 31	32
33	Enter the smaller of line 32 or $10,000	33
34	Subtract line 33 from line 32	34
35	Subtract line 34 from line 30. If zero or less, enter -0-. Enter here and include on Schedule 3 (Form 1040), line 12b	35

For Privacy Act and Paperwork Reduction Act Notice, see your tax return instructions. Cat. No. 56395K Form **7202** (2020)

6-7 THE NANNY TAX

6.7 Learning Objective

Apply the special tax and reporting requirements for household employees (the "nanny tax").

Over the years, the taxation and reporting of household employees' wages has caused many problems for taxpayers and the IRS. The threshold for filing was low ($50 per quarter of wages), and the tax forms to be completed were complex. As a result, many taxpayers ignored the reporting of household workers' wages and taxes. Congress addressed this problem by enacting what are commonly referred to as the "nanny tax" provisions. These provisions simplified the reporting process for employers of domestic household workers.

Household employers are not required to pay FICA taxes on cash payments of less than $2,200 paid to any household employee in a calendar year. If the cash payment to any household employee is $2,200 or more in a calendar year, all the cash payments (including the first $2,200) are subject to FICA taxes (see LO 9.3). The $2,200 threshold is adjusted for inflation each year. Household employers must also withhold income taxes if requested by the employee and are required to pay FUTA (Federal Unemployment Tax Act) tax (see LO 9.6) if more than $1,000 in cash wages are paid to household employees during any calendar quarter. The federal unemployment tax rate is 6 percent of an employee's wages up to $7,000.

A taxpayer is a household employer if he or she hires workers to perform household services, in or around the taxpayer's home, that are subject to the "will and control" of the taxpayer. Examples of household workers include:

- Babysitters
- Caretakers
- Cooks
- Drivers
- Gardeners
- Housekeepers
- Maids

If the household worker has an employee-employer relationship with the taxpayer, it does not matter if the worker is called something else, such as "independent contractor." Also, it does not matter if the worker is full-time or part-time. The household employer is responsible for the proper reporting, withholding, and payment of any taxes due.

The following workers are not subject to FICA taxes on wages paid for *work in the home*:

- The taxpayer's spouse
- The taxpayer's father or mother
- The taxpayer's children under 21 years of age
- Anyone who is under age 18 during the year, unless providing household services is his or her principal occupation (being a student is considered an occupation for purposes of this requirement)

EXAMPLE Allison is a 17-year-old high school student. During the year, she earns $2,300 by babysitting for a neighbor with four children. Any amount she earns is exempt from FICA requirements. However, if Allison is not a student and works full-time as a nanny, she will be subject to the general FICA withholding requirements under the nanny tax rules. ♦

Under the nanny tax provisions, household employers only have to report FICA, federal income tax withholding, and FUTA tax once a year. The taxpayer completes Schedule H and files it with his or her individual Form 1040. Taxpayers who have nonhousehold worker(s) in addition to household worker(s) can elect to report any FICA taxes and withholding on Forms 941 and 940 with their regular employees. Also, at the close of a tax year, taxpayers must file Form W-2 (Copy A) and Form W-3 with the Social Security Administration for each household employee who earned $2,200 or more in cash wages subject to FICA tax or had federal income taxes withheld from wages. For complete details on reporting the wages of household employees, see IRS Publication 926.

ProConnect™ Tax
TIP

Taxes for household employees are input in ProConnect under Taxes. There is a separate subheading for Household Employment Taxes (Schedule H).

Would You Believe?

In 1993, shortly after he was elected, President Bill Clinton nominated Zoë Baird as U.S. Attorney General. Her nomination was derailed in what would become known as "Nannygate" when it was discovered that Baird had hired household employees and not paid taxes. During that time, the level of scrutiny on this type of arrangement increased significantly and some Americans were being asked if they had a "Zoë Baird problem." Based on a 2006 study, some of the fear of Nannygate has subsided as filing rates for Schedule H have dropped on average across the United States. Interestingly, the filing rate for Schedule H was more than three times greater if you lived in or around Washington, DC.

Self-Study Problem 6.7   *See Appendix E for Solutions to Self-Study Problems*

Susan Green lives in Virginia and hires Helen in February 2020 to clean her house for $80 per week. Susan does not withhold income taxes from Helen's wages. Helen's quarterly wages are as follows:

1st quarter	$ 480	($80 × 6 weeks)
2nd quarter	1,040	($80 × 13 weeks)
3rd quarter	1,040	($80 × 13 weeks)
4th quarter	1,040	($80 × 13 weeks)
Total	$3,600	

Assume Susan pays her state unemployment of $194 to the state of Virginia during the year. Complete her 2020 Schedule H (Form 1040) on Pages 6-33 and 6-34, using the above information.

Learning Objective 6.8

Compute the special taxes for high-income taxpayers.

6-8 SPECIAL TAXES FOR HIGH-INCOME TAXPAYERS

There are two separate Medicare taxes for certain high-income taxpayers to help cover the cost of the Affordable Care Act (ACA). The first is the 3.8 percent net investment income tax. The second is a 0.9 percent additional Medicare tax on wages and self-employment income.

6-8a The 3.8 Percent Medicare Tax on Net Investment Income

The ACA imposes a 3.8 percent Medicare tax on the net investment income of individuals with modified AGI over $250,000 for joint filers ($125,000 if married filing separate), and $200,000 for single filers (note that these amounts are not adjusted for inflation). Modified AGI is adjusted gross income increased by certain foreign earned income amounts not covered in this textbook. Investment income subject to the additional 3.8 percent tax includes the following:

- Interest and dividends
- Royalties
- Annuities
- Net rental income, with some exceptions
- Passive activities
- Most gains on the sale of capital and other assets

Self-Study Problem 6.7

SCHEDULE H
(Form 1040)

Department of the Treasury
Internal Revenue Service (99)

Household Employment Taxes

(For Social Security, Medicare, Withheld Income, and Federal Unemployment (FUTA) Taxes)

▶ **Attach to Form 1040, 1040-SR, 1040-NR, 1040-SS, or 1041.**
▶ **Go to www.irs.gov/ScheduleH for instructions and the latest information.**

OMB No. 1545-1971

2020

Attachment
Sequence No. **44**

Name of employer

Social security number

Employer identification number

Calendar year taxpayers having no household employees in 2020 don't have to complete this form for 2020.

A   Did you pay **any one** household employee cash wages of $2,200 or more in 2020? (If any household employee was your spouse, your child under age 21, your parent, or anyone under age 18, see the line A instructions before you answer this question.)

☐ **Yes.** Skip lines B and C and go to line 1a.
☐ **No.** Go to line B.

B   Did you withhold federal income tax during 2020 for any household employee?

☐ **Yes.** Skip line C and go to line 7.
☐ **No.** Go to line C.

C   Did you pay **total** cash wages of $1,000 or more in **any** calendar **quarter** of 2019 or 2020 to **all** household employees? (**Don't** count cash wages paid in 2019 or 2020 to your spouse, your child under age 21, or your parent.)

☐ **No.** **Stop.** Don't file this schedule.
☐ **Yes.** Skip lines 1a–9 and go to line 10.

Part I	Social Security, Medicare, and Federal Income Taxes	

1a	Total cash wages subject to social security tax	1a	
b	Qualified sick and family wages included on line 1a	1b	
2a	Social security tax. Multiply line 1a by 12.4% (0.124)	2a	
b	Employer share of social security tax on qualified sick and family leave wages. Multiply line 1b by 6.2% (0.062)	2b	
c	Total social security tax. Subtract line 2b from line 2a	2c	
3	Total cash wages subject to Medicare tax	3	
4	Medicare tax. Multiply line 3 by 2.9% (0.029)	4	
5	Total cash wages subject to Additional Medicare Tax withholding	5	
6	Additional Medicare Tax withholding. Multiply line 5 by 0.9% (0.009)	6	
7	Federal income tax withheld, if any	7	
8a	Total social security, Medicare, and federal income taxes. Add lines 2c, 4, 6, and 7.	8a	
b	Nonrefundable portion of credit for qualified sick and family leave wages from Worksheet 3	8b	
c	Total social security, Medicare, and federal income taxes after nonrefundable credit. Subtract line 8b from line 8a	8c	
d	Maximum amount of the employer share of social security tax that can be deferred; see instructions	8d	
e	Refundable portion of credit for qualified sick and family leave wages from Worksheet 3	8e	
f	Qualified sick leave wages	8f	
g	Qualified health plan expenses allocable to qualified sick leave wages	8g	
h	Qualified family leave wages	8h	
i	Qualified health plan expenses allocable to qualified family leave wages	8i	

9   Did you pay **total** cash wages of $1,000 or more in **any** calendar **quarter** of 2019 or 2020 to **all** household employees? (**Don't** count cash wages paid in 2019 or 2020 to your spouse, your child under age 21, or your parent.)

☐ **No.** **Stop.** Include the amount from line 8c above on Schedule 2 (Form 1040), line 7a. Include the amount, if any, from line 8e, on Schedule 3 (Form 1040), line 12b. If you're not required to file Form 1040, see the line 9 instructions.
☐ **Yes.** Go to line 10.

For Privacy Act and Paperwork Reduction Act Notice, see the instructions.   Cat. No. 12187K   Schedule H (Form 1040) 2020

Schedule H (Form 1040) 2020   Page **2**

Part II   Federal Unemployment (FUTA) Tax

		Yes	No
10	Did you pay unemployment contributions to only one state? If you paid contributions to a credit reduction state, see instructions and check **"No"** **10**		
11	Did you pay all state unemployment contributions for 2020 by April 15, 2021? Fiscal year filers, see instructions **11**		
12	Were all wages that are taxable for FUTA tax also taxable for your state's unemployment tax? . **12**		

Next: If you checked the **"Yes"** box on **all** the lines above, complete Section A.
If you checked the **"No"** box on **any** of the lines above, skip Section A and complete Section B.

Section A

13	Name of the state where you paid unemployment contributions ▶ _____	
14	Contributions paid to your state unemployment fund **14**	
15	Total cash wages subject to FUTA tax **15**	
16	**FUTA tax.** Multiply line 15 by 0.6% (0.006). Enter the result here, skip Section B, and go to line 25 . **16**	

Section B

17 Complete all columns below that apply (if you need more space, see instructions):

(a) Name of state	(b) Taxable wages (as defined in state act)	(c) State experience rate period		(d) State experience rate	(e) Multiply col. (b) by 0.054	(f) Multiply col. (b) by col. (d)	(g) Subtract col. (f) from col. (e). If zero or less, enter -0-.	(h) Contributions paid to state unemployment fund
		From	To					

18	Totals **18**	
19	Add columns (g) and (h) of line 18 . . . . **19**	
20	Total cash wages subject to FUTA tax (see the line 15 instructions) **20**	
21	Multiply line 20 by 6.0% (0.06) **21**	
22	Multiply line 20 by 5.4% (0.054) **22**	
23	Enter the **smaller** of line 19 or line 22	
	(If you paid state unemployment contributions late or you're in a credit reduction state, see instructions and check here) . . . . ☐ **23**	
24	**FUTA tax.** Subtract line 23 from line 21. Enter the result here and go to line 25 . . . . . **24**	

Part III   Total Household Employment Taxes

25	Enter the amount from line 8c. If you checked the **"Yes"** box on line C of page 1, enter -0- **25**	
26	Add line 16 (or line 24) and line 25 . . . . **26**	

27 Are you required to file Form 1040?

☐ **Yes. Stop.** Include the amount from line 26 above on Schedule 2 (Form 1040), line 7a. Include the amount, if any, from line 8e, on Schedule 3 (Form 1040), line 12b. **Don't** complete Part IV below.

☐ **No.** You may have to complete Part IV. See instructions for details.

Part IV   Address and Signature — Complete this part **only** if required. See the line 27 instructions.

Address (number and street) or P.O. box if mail isn't delivered to street address	Apt., room, or suite no.
City, town or post office, state, and ZIP code	

Under penalties of perjury, I declare that I have examined this schedule, including accompanying statements, and to the best of my knowledge and belief, it is true, correct, and complete. No part of any payment made to a state unemployment fund claimed as a credit was, or is to be, deducted from the payments to employees. Declaration of preparer (other than taxpayer) is based on all information of which preparer has any knowledge.

▶

Employer's signature	Date

Paid Preparer Use Only	Print/Type preparer's name	Preparer's signature	Date	Check ☐ if self-employed	PTIN
	Firm's name ▶			Firm's EIN ▶	
	Firm's address ▶			Phone no.	

Schedule H (Form 1040) 2020

Income not subject to the 3.8 percent tax includes the following:

- Tax-exempt interest
- Excluded gain on the sale of a principal residence
- Distributions from retirement plans and individual retirement accounts
- Wages and self-employment income (earned income); however, this income may be subject to a 0.9 percent Medicare tax

Deductions allowed in arriving at net investment income subject to tax include:

- State income taxes reasonably allocated to the investment income
- Investment interest expense

The $3,000 net deduction allowed for capital losses in excess of capital gains for regular tax purposes and net operating losses are not allowed to reduce net investment income. Additional rules govern which income and deductions are included in calculating net investment income. The net investment income tax is reported on Form 8960 shown on Page 6-39.

EXAMPLE Consider each of the following single taxpayers:

Taxpayer	A	B	C
Investment Income	$ 50,000	$ 80,000	$ 80,000
Modified AGI	190,000	220,000	340,000

The 3.8 percent net investment income tax would be calculated in each case as follows:

Taxpayer	A	B	C
Modified AGI	$190,000	$220,000	$340,000
Threshold	200,000	200,000	200,000
Excess over Threshold	n/a	20,000	140,000
Investment Income	50,000	80,000	80,000
Lesser of Excess or Investment Income	n/a	20,000	80,000
Tax Rate	3.8%	3.8%	3.8%
Net Investment Income Tax	$ 0	$ 760	$ 3,040

6-8b The 0.9 Percent Additional Medicare Tax on Earned Income

In addition to the 3.8 percent Medicare tax on net investment income, the ACA imposed a 0.9 percent Medicare tax on high-income taxpayers' earned income such as salaries, wages, and self-employment income. The 0.9 percent tax applies to high-income taxpayers defined as taxpayers with earned income from wages, compensation, and self-employment income over the following thresholds (which are not adjusted for inflation each year):

a. $250,000 for joint filers
b. $125,000 if married filing separately
c. $200,000 for single filers (including head of household and qualifying widow(er)s)

The ordinary Medicare tax is 2.9 percent of earned income with no upper limitation. Employees split the cost of this tax with employers, with the employee paying 1.45 percent through withholding, and the employer paying 1.45 percent directly. Self-employed individuals pay the full 2.9 percent as calculated on Schedule SE with their Form 1040 income tax return. There is no employer match for the 0.9 percent tax. The 0.9 percent Medicare tax is reported on Form 8959 (see Page 6-41).

6-8c Employees

The 0.9 percent Medicare tax must be withheld from each employee with a salary in excess of $200,000, whether single or married. Married couples must combine their earned income and compare the total with the $250,000 threshold for married taxpayers to determine if they owe the 0.9 percent Medicare tax. Depending on the income of each spouse, the couple may owe more 0.9 percent Medicare tax when computing the 0.9 percent Medicare tax on their Form 1040 to make up for amounts not fully withheld, or they may treat the excess amount withheld as an additional tax payment. The withholding is reported on each individual's Form W-2 along with other Medicare withholding.

> **EXAMPLE** Will and Karen are married. Will earns $225,000 in 2020 and Karen does not work. They have no other income in 2020. Will's employer must withhold $225 [0.9% × ($225,000 − $200,000)], from his wages. Because Will and Karen do not have earned income in their joint return in excess of the $250,000 threshold for joint filers, the $225 withholding will be treated as an additional payment when they file their Form 1040 income tax return for 2020. ◆

> **EXAMPLE** Fran and Steve are married and each has wages of $150,000. Because they each earn less than $200,000, their employers are not required to withhold the 0.9 percent Medicare tax. However, when they file their 2020 Form 1040, they will be required to pay $450 (0.9% × $50,000) with their tax return since their $300,000 in joint earnings exceeds the $250,000 threshold for married taxpayers filing jointly. ◆

> **EXAMPLE** Johnny is single and changes jobs during 2020. His wages are $175,000 from each job for a total of $350,000 of wage income. Johnny's employers are not required to withhold any 0.9 percent Medicare tax from his wages since he does not reach the $200,000 threshold in either job. Johnny must pay $1,350 (0.9% × $150,000, the excess of $350,000 over the $200,000 single threshold amount) with his tax return for 2020. ◆

6-8d Self-Employed Taxpayers

Self-employed taxpayers generally report earnings on Schedule C, Schedule F, and Schedule E in the case of earned royalty income and partnership income passed through on Schedule K-l. The 0.9 percent Medicare tax for self-employed taxpayers must be paid with Form 1040. The following additional rules apply to high-income, self-employed taxpayers:

a. The 0.9 percent Medicare tax is not allowed as part of the computation of the deductible self-employment tax adjustment for AGI shown on the front page of Form 1040.

b. A loss from self-employment may offset gains from another self-employment enterprise by the same individual. In the case of married individuals, a loss incurred by one spouse may offset the income earned by the other self-employed spouse for purposes of the 0.9 percent Medicare tax. This is not true for the 2.9 percent Medicare tax on self-employment income because the 2.9 percent Medicare tax of each spouse is required to be computed separately.

c. Losses from self-employment are not allowed to offset salary or wages for purposes of the 0.9 percent Medicare tax.

EXAMPLE In 2020, Barry is single and earns $500,000 from his construction business, and has a loss of $100,000 from his commercial nursery business. Both businesses are reported on Schedule C in his income tax return. His net self-employment earnings of $400,000 exceed the single individual threshold by $200,000. He must pay $1,800 with his 2020 Form 1040 (0.9% × $200,000) to cover his 0.9 percent Medicare tax. None of the $1,800 is allowed as part of the computation of the self-employment tax adjustment included with his deductions for AGI. ♦

Self-Study Problem 6.8   *See Appendix E for Solutions to Self-Study Problems*

A. Ronald Trunk is single and independently wealthy. In 2020, Ronald's investment income is $110,000 (all interest) and his adjusted gross income is $380,000. He has no investment expenses associated with this income, no foreign earnings exclusion, and lives where there is no state income tax. Complete Form 8960 on Page 6-39 to calculate Ronald's 2020 net investment income tax.

B. Meng and Eang Ung are married. Meng is self-employed and generates self-employment income of $130,000. Eang is a physician at a local hospital and earns Social Security (Box 5) wages of $265,000. Her Medicare withholding (Box 6) is $4,427.50. Eang and Meng have no other earned or unearned income. Complete Form 8959 on Page 6-41 to determine how much 0.9 percent additional Medicare tax on earned income Meng and Eang must pay with their joint tax return in 2020 and what 0.9 percent additional Medicare tax withholding will they report?

The IRS recommends considering the following when getting married:

- Social Security numbers on the tax return need to match the Social Security Administration's (SSA) records. Be sure and report any name changes to the SSA.
- Taxpayers may want to consider changing their withholding, especially if both spouses work.
- Marriage is likely to trigger a "change in circumstance" if a taxpayer is receiving advance payments on the premium tax credit. The appropriate health insurance marketplace should be notified.
- Change of address with the U.S. Postal Service (online) and with the IRS (Form 8822).
- Change in filing status to married filing jointly or separately should be considered.

TAX BREAK

Self-Study Problem 6.8A

Form **8960**	Net Investment Income Tax— Individuals, Estates, and Trusts	OMB No. 1545-2227

Department of the Treasury
Internal Revenue Service (99)

▶ **Attach to your tax return.**
▶ **Go to** *www.irs.gov/Form8960* **for instructions and the latest information.**

2020
Attachment Sequence No. **72**

Name(s) shown on your tax return

Your social security number or EIN

Part I   Investment Income
☐ Section 6013(g) election (see instructions)
☐ Section 6013(h) election (see instructions)
☐ Regulations section 1.1411-10(g) election (see instructions)

1	Taxable interest (see instructions)	**1**	
2	Ordinary dividends (see instructions)	**2**	
3	Annuities (see instructions)	**3**	
4a	Rental real estate, royalties, partnerships, S corporations, trusts, etc. (see instructions)	**4a**	
b	Adjustment for net income or loss derived in the ordinary course of a non-section 1411 trade or business (see instructions)	**4b**	
c	Combine lines 4a and 4b	**4c**	
5a	Net gain or loss from disposition of property (see instructions)	**5a**	
b	Net gain or loss from disposition of property that is not subject to net investment income tax (see instructions)	**5b**	
c	Adjustment from disposition of partnership interest or S corporation stock (see instructions)	**5c**	
d	Combine lines 5a through 5c	**5d**	
6	Adjustments to investment income for certain CFCs and PFICs (see instructions)	**6**	
7	Other modifications to investment income (see instructions)	**7**	
8	Total investment income. Combine lines 1, 2, 3, 4c, 5d, 6, and 7	**8**	

Part II   Investment Expenses Allocable to Investment Income and Modifications

9a	Investment interest expenses (see instructions)	**9a**	
b	State, local, and foreign income tax (see instructions)	**9b**	
c	Miscellaneous investment expenses (see instructions)	**9c**	
d	Add lines 9a, 9b, and 9c	**9d**	
10	Additional modifications (see instructions)	**10**	
11	Total deductions and modifications. Add lines 9d and 10	**11**	

Part III   Tax Computation

12	Net investment income. Subtract Part II, line 11, from Part I, line 8. Individuals, complete lines 13–17. Estates and trusts, complete lines 18a–21. If zero or less, enter -0-	**12**	
	Individuals:		
13	Modified adjusted gross income (see instructions)	**13**	
14	Threshold based on filing status (see instructions)	**14**	
15	Subtract line 14 from line 13. If zero or less, enter -0-	**15**	
16	Enter the smaller of line 12 or line 15	**16**	
17	Net investment income tax for individuals. Multiply line 16 by 3.8% (0.038). **Enter here and include on your tax return** (see instructions)	**17**	
	Estates and Trusts:		
18a	Net investment income (line 12 above)	**18a**	
b	Deductions for distributions of net investment income and deductions under section 642(c) (see instructions)	**18b**	
c	Undistributed net investment income. Subtract line 18b from 18a (see instructions). If zero or less, enter -0-	**18c**	
19a	Adjusted gross income (see instructions)	**19a**	
b	Highest tax bracket for estates and trusts for the year (see instructions)	**19b**	
c	Subtract line 19b from line 19a. If zero or less, enter -0-	**19c**	
20	Enter the smaller of line 18c or line 19c	**20**	
21	Net investment income tax for estates and trusts. Multiply line 20 by 3.8% (0.038). **Enter here and include on your tax return** (see instructions)	**21**	

For Paperwork Reduction Act Notice, see your tax return instructions.   Cat. No. 59474M   Form **8960** (2020)

DRAFT AS OF October 13, 2020 DO NOT FILE

Self-Study Problem 6.8B

Form 8959

Department of the Treasury
Internal Revenue Service

Additional Medicare Tax

► If any line does not apply to you, leave it blank. See separate instructions.

► Attach to Form 1040, 1040-SR, 1040-NR, 1040-PR, or 1040-SS.

► Go to *www.irs.gov/Form8959* for instructions and the latest information.

OMB No. 1545-0074

2020

Attachment
Sequence No. **71**

Name(s) shown on return

Your social security number

	Part I	Additional Medicare Tax on Medicare Wages		
1	Medicare wages and tips from Form W-2, box 5. If you have more than one Form W-2, enter the total of the amounts from box 5	**1**		
2	Unreported tips from Form 4137, line 6	**2**		
3	Wages from Form 8919, line 6	**3**		
4	Add lines 1 through 3	**4**		
5	Enter the following amount for your filing status:			
	Married filing jointly	$250,000		
	Married filing separately	$125,000		
	Single, Head of household, or Qualifying widow(er)	$200,000	**5**	
6	Subtract line 5 from line 4. If zero or less, enter -0-			**6**
7	Additional Medicare Tax on Medicare wages. Multiply line 6 by 0.9% (0.009). Enter here and go to Part II			**7**

	Part II	Additional Medicare Tax on Self-Employment Income		
8	Self-employment income from Schedule SE (Form 1040), Part I, line 6. If you had a loss, enter -0- (Form 1040-PR or 1040-SS filers, see instructions.)	**8**		
9	Enter the following amount for your filing status:			
	Married filing jointly	$250,000		
	Married filing separately	$125,000		
	Single, Head of household, or Qualifying widow(er)	$200,000	**9**	
10	Enter the amount from line 4	**10**		
11	Subtract line 10 from line 9. If zero or less, enter -0-	**11**		
12	Subtract line 11 from line 8. If zero or less, enter -0-			**12**
13	Additional Medicare Tax on self-employment income. Multiply line 12 by 0.9% (0.009). Enter here and go to Part III			**13**

	Part III	Additional Medicare Tax on Railroad Retirement Tax Act (RRTA) Compensation		
14	Railroad retirement (RRTA) compensation and tips from Form(s) W-2, box 14 (see instructions)	**14**		
15	Enter the following amount for your filing status:			
	Married filing jointly	$250,000		
	Married filing separately	$125,000		
	Single, Head of household, or Qualifying widow(er)	$200,000	**15**	
16	Subtract line 15 from line 14. If zero or less, enter -0-			**16**
17	Additional Medicare Tax on railroad retirement (RRTA) compensation. Multiply line 16 by 0.9% (0.009). Enter here and go to Part IV			**17**

	Part IV	Total Additional Medicare Tax	
18	Add lines 7, 13, and 17. Also include this amount on Schedule 2 (Form 1040), line 8 (check box a) (Form 1040-PR or 1040-SS filers, see instructions), and go to Part V		**18**

	Part V	Withholding Reconciliation		
19	Medicare tax withheld from Form W-2, box 6. If you have more than one Form W-2, enter the total of the amounts from box 6	**19**		
20	Enter the amount from line 1	**20**		
21	Multiply line 20 by 1.45% (0.0145). This is your regular Medicare tax withholding on Medicare wages	**21**		
22	Subtract line 21 from line 19. If zero or less, enter -0-. This is your Additional Medicare Tax withholding on Medicare wages			**22**
23	Additional Medicare Tax withholding on railroad retirement (RRTA) compensation from Form W-2, box 14 (see instructions)			**23**
24	**Total Additional Medicare Tax withholding.** Add lines 22 and 23. Also include this amount with federal income tax withholding on Form 1040, 1040-SR, or 1040-NR, line 25c (Form 1040-PR or 1040-SS filers, see instructions)			**24**

For Paperwork Reduction Act Notice, see your tax return instructions.   Cat. No. 59475X   Form **8959** (2020)

KEY TERMS

accounting periods, 6-2
fiscal year, 6-2
short-period taxable income, 6-2
annualized period, 6-2
accounting methods, 6-3
cash method, 6-3
accrual method, 6-4
economic performance, 6-4
hybrid method, 6-4
Section 267, 6-5
related parties, 6-6

constructive ownership, 6-6
"kiddie tax," 6-8
alternative minimum tax (AMT), 6-14
AMT adjustments, 6-14
AMT preferences, 6-14
AMT exemption, 6-15
alternative minimum tax rates, 6-15
self-employment tax, 6-19
self-employment tax deferral,
  6-21

sick leave equivalent amount, 6-21
average daily self-employment
  income, 6-21
family leave equivalent amount,
  6-22
nanny tax, 6-31
household workers, 6-31
net investment income tax, 6-32
0.9 percent additional Medicare
  tax, 6-35

KEY POINTS

Learning Objectives	Key Points
LO 6.1: Determine the different accounting periods allowed for tax purposes.	• Almost all individuals file tax returns using a calendar-year accounting period. • Partnerships and corporations had a great deal of freedom in selecting a tax year in the past. However, Congress set limits on this freedom when it resulted in an inappropriate deferral of taxable income. • A personal service corporation is a corporation whose shareholder-employees provide personal services (e.g., medical, legal, accounting, actuarial, or consulting services) for the corporation's patients or clients. Personal service corporations generally must adopt a calendar year-end. • If taxpayers have a short year other than their first or last year of operations, they are required to annualize their taxable income to calculate the tax for the short period.
LO 6.2: Determine the different accounting methods allowed for tax purposes.	• The tax law requires taxpayers to report taxable income using the method of accounting regularly used by the taxpayer in keeping his or her books, provided the method clearly reflects the taxpayer's income. • The cash receipts and disbursements (cash) method, the accrual method, and the hybrid method are accounting methods specifically recognized in the tax law.
LO 6.3: Determine whether parties are considered related for tax purposes, and classify the tax treatment of certain related-party transactions.	• The two types of disallowed related-party transactions are (1) sales of property at a loss and (2) unpaid expenses and interest. • Any loss or deduction arising from transactions between related parties are disallowed by Section 267. • The common related parties under Section 267 include brothers and sisters (whole or half), a spouse, ancestors (parents, grandparents, etc.), lineal descendants (children, grandchildren, etc.), and a corporation or an individual shareholder who directly or constructively owns more than 50 percent of the corporation. • Related-party rules also consider constructive ownership in determining whether parties are related to each other (e.g., taxpayers are deemed to own stock owned by certain relatives and related entities).

LO 6.4: Apply the rules for computing tax on the unearned income of minor children and certain students (the "kiddie tax").	• The tax law contains provisions that limit the benefit of shifting income to certain dependent children. • The net unearned income of dependent children ("kiddie tax") may be taxed at the parent's rate, if higher. • The kiddie tax applies to dependent children who are required to file a tax return, are ages 18 or younger, or are students ages 19 through 24, who have at least one living parent, and who have "net unearned income" of more than $2,200 for 2020. • If certain conditions are met, parents may elect to include a child's gross income on the parents' tax return. The election eliminates the child's return filing requirements including the special calculation on Form 8615 for the kiddie tax.
LO 6.5: Calculate a basic alternative minimum tax.	• The AMT was designed in the 1960s to ensure that wealthy taxpayers could not take advantage of special tax write-offs (tax preferences and other adjustments) to avoid paying tax. In general, taxpayers must pay the AMT if their AMT liability is greater than their regular tax liability. • Adjustments are timing differences that arise because of differences in the regular and AMT tax calculations (e.g., depreciation timing differences), while preferences are special provisions for the regular tax that are not allowed for the AMT (e.g., state income taxes). • For 2020, the AMT exemption allowance is $113,400 for married taxpayers filing joint returns, $72,900 for single and head of household taxpayers, and $56,700 for married taxpayers filing separate returns. The AMT exemption allowance amount is phased out for high-income taxpayers. • For 2020, the alternative minimum tax rates for calculating the tentative minimum tax are 26 percent of the first $197,900 ($98,950 for married taxpayers filing separately), plus 28 percent on amounts above $197,900 applied to the taxpayer's alternative minimum tax base. • The increases in the AMT exemptions and thresholds coupled with the limitations or suspension of certain itemized deduction are expected to reduce the number of taxpayers subject to the AMT.
LO 6.6: Calculate and report the self-employment tax (both Social Security and Medicare portions) for self-employed taxpayers.	• Self-employed individuals pay self-employment (SE) taxes instead of FICA taxes and, since these individuals have no employers, the entire tax is paid by the self-employed individuals. • For 2020, the Social Security (OASDI) tax rate is 12.4 percent, with a maximum base amount of earnings subject to the Social Security portion of $137,700. The Medicare tax rate is 2.9 percent with all earnings subject to the Medicare portion, without limitation. • If an individual, subject to self-employment taxes, also receives wages subject to FICA taxes during a tax year, the individual's maximum base amount for SE taxes is reduced by the amount of the wages when calculating the SE taxes. • Net earnings from self-employment include gross income from a trade or business, less trade or business deductions, the distributive share of partnership income from a trade or business, and net income earned as an independent contractor. • Self-employed taxpayers are allowed a deduction for AGI of one-half of the self-employment tax. • Self-employed taxpayers are eligible for a temporary payroll tax deferral in 2020 due to COVID-relief provisions. • Self-employed taxpayers are eligible for sick and family leave credits in 2020 related to the COVID-19 pandemic.

LO 6.7: Apply the special tax and reporting requirements for household employees (the "nanny tax").	• The "nanny tax" provisions provide a simplified reporting process for employers of household workers. • Household employers are not required to pay FICA taxes on cash payments of less than $2,200 paid to any household employee in a calendar year. • If the cash payment to any household employee is $2,200 or more in a calendar year, all the cash payments (including the first $2,200) are subject to Social Security and Medicare taxes. • If more than $1,000 in cash wages are paid to household employees during any calendar quarter, employers are required to pay FUTA taxes. • A taxpayer is a household employer if he or she hires workers to perform household services, in or around the taxpayer's home, that are subject to the "will and control" of the taxpayer (e.g., babysitters, caretakers, cooks, drivers, gardeners, housekeepers, and maids). • Certain workers are not subject to Social Security and Medicare taxes on wages paid for work in the home. These workers include the taxpayer's spouse, the taxpayer's father or mother, the taxpayer's children under 21 years of age, and anyone who is under age 18 during the year, unless providing household services is his or her principal occupation. • Under the nanny tax provisions, a household employer must report Social Security and Medicare taxes, federal income tax withholding, and FUTA tax once a year by filing Schedule H with his or her individual Form 1040. • At the close of the tax year, household employers must also file Form W-2 (copy A) and Form W-3 for each household employee whose income is reflected on Schedule H or had federal income tax withheld from wages.
LO 6.8 Compute the special taxes for high-income taxpayers.	• The Affordable Care Act (ACA) added a 3.8 percent Medicare tax on net investment income and a 0.9 percent additional Medicare tax on earned income for certain high-income taxpayers. • The 3.8 percent net investment income tax applies to the net investment income of individuals with modified AGI over $250,000 for joint filers ($125,000 if married filing separate), and $200,000 for single filers. • The 0.9 percent Medicare tax is imposed on earned income from salaries, wages, and self-employment income of joint filers with earned income over $250,000 ($125,000 if married filing separate) and single taxpayers with earned income over $200,000. • Employers are required to withhold the 0.9 percent Medicare tax when a taxpayer's salary exceeds $200,000. • Self-employed taxpayers must pay the tax with their individual income tax returns.

QUESTIONS and PROBLEMS

GROUP 1:
MULTIPLE CHOICE QUESTIONS

LO 6.1

1. E Corporation is a subchapter S corporation owned by three individuals with calendar year-ends. The corporation sells a sports drink as its principal product and has similar sales each month. What options does E Corporation have in choosing a tax year?

   a. E Corporation may choose any month end as its tax year.

   b. Because the owners of E Corporation have tax years ending in December, E Corporation must also choose a December year-end.

   c. E Corporation may choose an October, November, or December tax year-end.

   d. E Corporation may choose a tax year ending in September, October, or November, but only if the corporation also makes an annual cash deposit and adjusts the amount every year depending on the income deferred.

LO 6.1   2. Income and loss from which of the following entities is passed through and taxed on the individual's personal tax returns?
   a. S corporation
   b. Partnership
   c. Sole proprietor
   d. All of the above

LO 6.1   3. Which of the following entities is likely to have the greatest flexibility in choosing a year-end other than a calendar year-end?
   a. Sole proprietor
   b. General partnership
   c. Corporation
   d. S corporation

LO 6.2   4. Which of the following is an acceptable method of accounting under the tax law?
   a. The accrual method
   b. The hybrid method
   c. The cash method
   d. All of the above are acceptable
   e. None of the above

LO 6.2   5. Which of the following entities is required to report on the accrual basis?
   a. An accounting firm operating as a Personal Service Corporation.
   b. A manufacturing business with $30 million of gross receipts operating as a regular C corporation.
   c. A corporation engaged in tropical fruit farming in Southern California.
   d. A partnership with gross receipts of $13 million and all of the partners are individuals with a December year-end.

LO 6.3   6. Pekoe sold stock to his sister Rose for $12,000, its fair market value. Pekoe bought the stock 5 years ago for $16,000. Also, Pekoe sold Earl (an unrelated party) stock for $6,500 that he bought 3 years ago for $8,500. What is Pekoe's recognized gain or loss?
   a. $6,500 loss
   b. $6,000 loss
   c. $3,000 loss
   d. $2,000 loss
   e. $1,000 gain

LO 6.3   7. B Corporation, a calendar year-end, accrual basis taxpayer, is owned 75 percent by Bonnie, a cash basis taxpayer. On December 31, 2020, the corporation accrues interest of $4,000 on a loan from Bonnie and also accrues a $15,000 bonus to Bonnie. The bonus is paid to Bonnie on February 1, 2021; the interest is not paid until 2022. How much can B Corporation deduct on its 2020 tax return for these two expenses?
   a. $0
   b. $4,000
   c. $15,000
   d. $19,000
   e. $12,000

LO 6.3   8. Using the same facts as in Question 7, how much can B Corporation deduct on its 2021 tax return?
   a. $0
   b. $4,000
   c. $15,000
   d. $19,000
   e. $12,000

LO 6.3

9. BJT Corporation is owned 40 percent by Bill, 30 percent by Jack, and 30 percent by the Trumpet Partnership. Bill and Jack are father and son. Jack has a 10 percent interest in Trumpet Partnership. What is Jack's total direct and constructive ownership of BJT Corporation under Section 267?
   a. 30 percent
   b. 70 percent
   c. 100 percent
   d. 73 percent
   e. 33 percent

LO 6.4

10. Which of the following is required for a taxpayer to be subject to the tax on unearned income of minors (kiddie tax) in 2020?
    a. Must have no earned income
    b. 21 years of age or younger
    c. Both parents must be living
    d. Net unearned income must exceed $2,200
    e. All of the above are required

LO 6.4

11. Generally, the tax rate that applies to the unearned income of a minor under the kiddie tax in 2020 is:
    a. The same as the parents' tax rate
    b. The same as the single taxpayer rate
    c. The same as the head of household rate
    d. The same as the trust and estate rate
    e. The unearned income of a minor is not taxed

LO 6.5

12. The alternative minimum tax exemption:
    a. Is a direct reduction of the tentative minimum tax
    b. Is a reduction of alternative minimum taxable income for certain taxpayers
    c. Permits certain taxpayers to elect to treat AMT as a reduction of tax
    d. Is subject to carryback and carryforward provisions
    e. Increases the effects of tax preference items

LO 6.6

13. For 2020, Roberta is a self-employed truck driver with earnings of $48,728 from her business. During the year, Roberta received $2,500 in interest income and dividends of $500. She also sold investment property and recognized a $1,500 gain. What is the amount of Roberta's self-employment tax (Social Security and Medicare taxes) liability for 2020?
    a. $7,304
    b. $6,641
    c. $6,358
    d. $6,885
    e. $7,455

LO 6.6

14. Which of the following is *not* subject to self-employment tax?
    a. Gain on the sale of real estate held for investment
    b. Net earnings of a self-employed lawyer
    c. Distributive share of earnings of a partnership
    d. Net earnings of the owner of a shoe store
    e. Net earnings of the owner of a dry cleaner

LO 6.6

15. Which of the following is not a COVID-19 tax relief provision available to a self-employed taxpayer?
    a. Payroll tax deferral
    b. Sick leave credit
    c. Family leave credit
    d. Self-employment tax rate reduction
    e. All of the above

LO 6.7

16. Bob employs a maid to clean his house. He pays her $1,040 during the current year. What is the proper tax treatment of the Social Security and Medicare tax for the maid?
    a. Bob is not required to pay or withhold Social Security and Medicare taxes on the $1,040.
    b. The $1,040 is subject to the Medicare tax, but not the Social Security tax.
    c. $500 is subject to the Social Security and Medicare tax.
    d. Bob is required to withhold Social Security and Medicare taxes on the entire $1,040.

LO 6.7

17. Which of the following employees would *not* be exempt from Social Security and Medicare taxes on wages paid for household work?
    a. The taxpayer's 16-year-old daughter
    b. The taxpayer's wife
    c. The taxpayer's 20-year-old sister
    d. The 14-year-old babysitter from down the street

LO 6.7

18. Individual taxpayers may pay withholding taxes due with their individual income tax returns using Schedule H for each of the following workers *except*:
    a. A nanny hired to watch their children
    b. A maid hired to clean house and cook every day
    c. An attorney with her own business, hired to handle a legal dispute with the taxpayers' neighbor
    d. An unlicensed caregiver for a disabled spouse

LO 6.8

19. The 3.8 percent Medicare tax on net investment income applies to:
    a. Tax-exempt interest income
    b. Interest and dividends
    c. IRA distributions
    d. Wages

LO 6.8

20. Skylar is single and earns $410,000 in salary during 2020. What is the amount of 0.9 percent Medicare tax for high-income taxpayers that his employer must withhold from his wages?
    a. $1,890
    b. $1,800
    c. $1,440
    d. $900

LO 6.8

21. Christine and Doug are married. In 2020, Christine earns a salary of $250,000 and Doug earns a salary of $50,000. They have no other income and work for the same employers for all of 2020. How much 0.9 percent Medicare tax for high-income taxpayers will Christine and Doug have to pay with their 2020 income tax return?
    a. $450
    b. $900
    c. $2,700
    d. None

GROUP 2:
PROBLEMS

LO 6.1

1. Explain why the tax law prefers flowthrough entities like partnerships and S corporations to have a year-end that matches the year-end of its owners.

_____

_____

_____

LO 6.2

2. Yolanda is a cash-basis taxpayer with the following transactions during the year:

Cash received from sales of products	$70,000
Cash paid for expenses (except rent and interest)	40,000
Rent prepaid on a leased building for 18 months beginning December 1	48,600
Prepaid interest on a bank loan, paid on December 31 for the next 3 months	5,000

Calculate Yolanda's income from her business for this calendar year.

Sales income	$_____
Expenses:	
Other than rent and interest	$_____
Rent	$_____
Interest	$_____
Net income	$_____

LO 6.2

3. Geraldine is an accrual-basis taxpayer who has the following transactions during the current calendar tax year:

Accrued business income (except rent)	$220,000
Accrued business expenses (except rent)	170,000
Rental income on a building lease for the next 6 months, received on December 1	21,000
Prepaid rent expense for 6 months, paid on December 1	9,000

Calculate Geraldine's net income from her business for the current year.

Income:	
Other than rental	$_____
Rental	$_____
Expenses:	
Other than rental	$_____
Rental	$_____
Net income	$_____

LO 6.2

4. Amy is a calendar-year taxpayer reporting on the cash basis. Please indicate how she should treat the following items for 2020:

a. She makes a deductible contribution to an IRA on April 15, 2021.

_____

b. She has made an election to accrue the increase in value of savings bonds even though the increase is not received in cash.

_____

c. She prepays half a year of interest in advance on her mortgage on the last day of 2020. _____

d. She pays all of her outstanding invoices for standard business expenses in the last week of December. _____

e. She sends out a big bill to a customer on January 1, 2021, even though she did all of the work in December of 2020. _____

LO 6.3

5. JBC Corporation is owned 20 percent by John, 30 percent by Brian, 30 percent by Charlie, and 20 percent by Z Corporation. Z Corporation is owned 80 percent by John and 20 percent by an unrelated party. Brian and Charlie are brothers. Answer each of the following questions about JBC under the constructive ownership rules of Section 267:

a. What is John's percentage ownership? _____%

b. What is Brian's percentage ownership? _____%

c. What is Charlie's percentage ownership?   _____%

d. If Brian sells property to JBC for a $6,000 loss,
    what amount of that loss can be recognized for tax
    purposes (before any annual limitations)?

                                                                    $_____

LO 6.3   6. You have a problem and need a full-text copy of the Related Party Code Section 267.
              Go to the Office of the Law Revision Counsel of the United States House of Rep-
              resentatives website (**uscode.house.gov**) and enter Title 26 (the Internal Revenue
              Code) and Section 267 in the Jump To boxes. Print out a copy of Section 267(a).

LO 6.4   7. Explain the purpose of the provision in the tax law that taxes unearned income of
              certain minor children at their parents' tax rates.

              _____

              _____

              _____

LO 6.4   8. Brian and Kim have a 12-year-old child, Stan. For 2020, Brian and Kim have taxable
              income of $52,000, and Stan has interest income of $4,500. No election is made to
              include Stan's income on Brian and Kim's return.

              a. For purposes of the tax on a child's unearned income, calculate Stan's
                  taxable income. $_____
              b. Calculate Stan's net unearned income. $_____
              c. Calculate Stan's tax for 2020. $_____

LO 6.4   9. Refer to the previous problem 8. If there was no kiddie tax and Stan were taxed at his
              own rate, what would the tax on Stan's income be?

LO 6.4   10. Explain the two different ways that the tax on unearned income of minor children, or
              "kiddie tax," can be reported.

              _____

              _____

              _____

LO 6.4   11. Does the tax on unearned income of minor children, or "kiddie tax," apply to wages
              earned by minors in summer and other jobs?

              _____

              _____

              _____

LO 6.5   12. Otto and Monica are married taxpayers who file a joint tax return. For the current
              tax year, they have AGI of $80,300. They have excess depreciation on real estate
              of $67,500, which must be added back to AGI to arrive at AMTI. The amount of
              their mortgage interest expense for the year was $25,000, and they made charitable
              contributions of $7,500. If Otto and Monica's taxable income for the current year
              is $47,800 determine the amount of their AMTI.

              _____

LO 6.5   13. List two common deductions which are allowed for regular tax purposes but are not
              deductible for AMT purposes.

              _____

              _____

LO 6.5   14. What are the two tax rates which are used to calculate AMT, ignoring the special
              treatment of dividends and capital gains?

              _____

LO 6.5

15. Show the simplified formula for calculating AMT. Do not show tax rates or an exemption amount.

_____

_____

_____

_____

_____

_____

_____

_____

_____

LO 6.6

16. James Felon is a self-employed surfboard maker in 2020. His Schedule C net income is $126,503 for the year. He also has a part-time job and earns $20,900 in wages subject to FICA taxes. Calculate James' self-employment tax for 2020 using page 1 of Schedule SE on Page 6-51.

LO 6.7

17. Sally hires a maid to work in her home for $250 per month. The maid is 25 years old and not related to Sally. During 2020, the maid worked 9 months for Sally.
    a. What is the amount of Social Security tax Sally must pay as the maid's employer?

    $ _____

    b. What is the amount of Medicare tax Sally must pay as the maid's employer?

    $ _____

    c. What is the amount of Social Security and Medicare tax which must be withheld from the maid's wages?

    $ _____

LO 6.7

18. Ann hires a nanny to watch her two children while she works at a local hospital. She pays the 19-year-old nanny $180 per week for 42 weeks during the current year.
    a. What is the employer's portion of Social Security and Medicare tax for the nanny that Ann should pay when she files her Form 1040 for 2020?

    $ _____

    b. What is the nanny's portion of the Social Security and Medicare tax?

    $ _____

LO 6.8

19. Rachel is single and has wages of $150,000 and dividend income of $90,000. She has no investment expenses. Calculate the amount of the 3.8 percent net investment income tax she must pay.

_____

LO 6.8

20. Married taxpayers Otto and Ruth are both self-employed. Otto earns $352,000 of self-employment income and Ruth has a self-employment loss of $13,500. How much 0.9 percent Medicare tax for high-income taxpayers will Otto and Ruth have to pay with their 2020 income tax return?

    $ _____

GROUP 3:
WRITING ASSIGNMENT

ETHICS

Charlie's Green Lawn Care is a cash-basis taxpayer. Charlie Adame, the sole proprietor, is considering delaying some of his December 2020 customer billings for lawn care into the next year. In addition, he is thinking about paying some of the bills in late December 2020, which he would ordinarily pay in January 2021. This way, Charlie claims, he will have "less income and more expenses, thereby paying less tax!" Is Charlie's way of thinking acceptable?

SCHEDULE SE
(Form 1040)

Department of the Treasury
Internal Revenue Service (99)

Self-Employment Tax

▶ Go to *www.irs.gov/ScheduleSE* for instructions and the latest information.
▶ Attach to Form 1040, 1040-SR, or 1040-NR.

OMB No. 1545-0074

2020

Attachment
Sequence No. **17**

Name of person with self-employment income (as shown on Form 1040, 1040-SR, or 1040-NR)

Social security number of person
with **self-employment** income ▶

Part I   Self-Employment Tax

Note: If your only income subject to self-employment tax is **church employee income,** see instructions for how to report your income and the definition of church employee income.

A   If you are a minister, member of a religious order, or Christian Science practitioner **and** you filed Form 4361, but you had $400 or more of **other** net earnings from self-employment, check here and continue with Part I . . . . ▶ ☐

Skip lines 1a and 1b if you use the farm optional method in Part II. See instructions.

1a	Net farm profit or (loss) from Schedule F, line 34, and farm partnerships, Schedule K-1 (Form 1065), box 14, code A	**1a**	
b	If you received social security retirement or disability benefits, enter the amount of Conservation Reserve Program payments included on Schedule F, line 4b, or listed on Schedule K-1 (Form 1065), box 20, code AH	**1b**	( )

Skip line 2 if you use the nonfarm optional method in Part II. See instructions.

2	Net profit or (loss) from Schedule C, line 31; and Schedule K-1 (Form 1065), box 14, code A (other than farming). See instructions for other income to report or if you are a minister or member of a religious order	**2**	
3	Combine lines 1a, 1b, and 2	**3**	
4a	If line 3 is more than zero, multiply line 3 by 92.35% (0.9235). Otherwise, enter amount from line 3	**4a**	
	Note: If line 4a is less than $400 due to Conservation Reserve Program payments on line 1b, see instructions.		
b	If you elect one or both of the optional methods, enter the total of lines 15 and 17 here	**4b**	
c	Combine lines 4a and 4b. If less than $400, **stop;** you don't owe self-employment tax. **Exception:** If less than $400 and you had **church employee income,** enter -0- and continue . . . . ▶	**4c**	
5a	Enter your **church employee income** from Form W-2. See instructions for definition of church employee income	**5a**	
b	Multiply line 5a by 92.35% (0.9235). If less than $100, enter -0-	**5b**	
6	Add lines 4c and 5b	**6**	
7	Maximum amount of combined wages and self-employment earnings subject to social security tax or the 6.2% portion of the 7.65% railroad retirement (tier 1) tax for 2020	**7**	137,700
8a	Total social security wages and tips (total of boxes 3 and 7 on Form(s) W-2) and railroad retirement (tier 1) compensation. If $137,700 or more, skip lines 8b through 10, and go to line 11	**8a**	
b	Unreported tips subject to social security tax from Form 4137, line 10 . . .	**8b**	
c	Wages subject to social security tax from Form 8919, line 10	**8c**	
d	Add lines 8a, 8b, and 8c	**8d**	
9	Subtract line 8d from line 7. If zero or less, enter -0- here and on line 10 and go to line 11 . . . ▶	**9**	
10	Multiply the **smaller** of line 6 or line 9 by 12.4% (0.124)	**10**	
11	Multiply line 6 by 2.9% (0.029)	**11**	
12	**Self-employment tax.** Add lines 10 and 11. Enter here and on **Schedule 2 (Form 1040), line 4** . .	**12**	
13	**Deduction for one-half of self-employment tax.** Multiply line 12 by 50% (0.50). Enter here and on **Schedule 1 (Form 1040), line 14**	**13**	

Part II   Optional Methods To Figure Net Earnings (see instructions)

Farm Optional Method. You may use this method **only** if **(a)** your gross farm income[1] wasn't more than $8,460, **or (b)** your net farm profits[2] were less than $6,107.

14	Maximum income for optional methods	**14**	5,640
15	Enter the **smaller** of: two-thirds (2/3) of gross farm income[1] (not less than zero) or $5,640. Also, include this amount on line 4b above	**15**	

Nonfarm Optional Method. You may use this method **only** if **(a)** your net nonfarm profits[3] were less than $6,107 and also less than 72.189% of your gross nonfarm income,[4] **and (b)** you had net earnings from self-employment of at least $400 in 2 of the prior 3 years. **Caution:** You may use this method no more than five times.

16	Subtract line 15 from line 14	**16**	
17	Enter the **smaller** of: two-thirds (2/3) of gross nonfarm income[4] (not less than zero) **or** the amount on line 16. Also, include this amount on line 4b above	**17**	

[1] From Sch. F, line 9; and Sch. K-1 (Form 1065), box 14, code B.
[2] From Sch. F, line 34; and Sch. K-1 (Form 1065), box 14, code A—minus the amount you would have entered on line 1b had you not used the optional method.
[3] From Sch. C, line 31; and Sch. K-1 (Form 1065), box 14, code A.
[4] From Sch. C, line 7; and Sch. K-1 (Form 1065), box 14, code C.

For Paperwork Reduction Act Notice, see your tax return instructions.   Cat. No. 11358Z   Schedule SE (Form 1040) 2020

Schedule SE (Form 1040) 2020   Attachment Sequence No. **17**   Page **2**

Part III	Maximum Deferral of Self-Employment Tax Payments		

If line 4c is zero, skip lines 18 through 20, and enter -0- on line 21.

18	Enter the portion of line 3 that can be attributed to March 27, 2020, through December 31, 2020 . .	**18**	
19	If line 18 is more than zero, multiply line 18 by 92.35% (0.9235); otherwise, enter the amount from line 18	**19**	
20	Enter the portion of lines 15 and 17 that can be attributed to March 27, 2020, through December 31, 2020	**20**	
21	Combine lines 19 and 20	**21**	

If line 5b is zero, skip line 22 and enter -0- on line 23.

22	Enter the portion of line 5a that can be attributed to March 27, 2020, through December 31, 2020 . .	**22**	
23	Multiply line 22 by 92.35% (0.9235)	**23**	
24	Add lines 21 and 23	**24**	
25	Enter the smaller of line 9 or line 24	**25**	
26	Multiply line 25 by 6.2% (0.062). Enter here and see the instructions for line 12e of Schedule 3 (Form 1040)	**26**	

Schedule SE (Form 1040) 2020

GROUP 4:
COMPREHENSIVE PROBLEMS

1A. Richard McCarthy (born 2/14/1966; Social Security number 100-10-9090) and Christine McCarthy (born 6/1/1968; Social Security number 101-21-3434) have a 19-year-old son Jack, (born 10/2/2001; Social Security number 555-55-1212), who is a full-time student at the University of Key West. The McCarthys also have a 12-year-old daughter Justine, (Social Security number 444-23-1212), who lives with them. The McCarthys can claim a $2,000 child tax credit for Justine and a $500 other dependent credit for Jack. The McCarthys did not receive an EIP in 2020. Richard is the CEO at a paper company. His 2020 Form W-2:

a Employee's social security number 100-10-9090	OMB No. 1545-0008	Safe, accurate, FAST! Use IRS e-file	Visit the IRS website at www.irs.gov/efile
b Employer identification number (EIN) 32-5656567		**1** Wages, tips, other compensation 230,800.00	**2** Federal income tax withheld 55,800.00
c Employer's name, address, and ZIP code Mufflin-Dunder Paper 302 Lackawanna Ave. Scranton, PA 18503		**3** Social security wages 137,700.00	**4** Social security tax withheld 8,537.40
		5 Medicare wages and tips 235,800.00	**6** Medicare tax withheld 3,741.30
		7 Social security tips	**8** Allocated tips
d Control number		**9**	**10** Dependent care benefits
e Employee's first name and initial Last name Suff. Richard McCarthy 32 Sleep Hollow Road Clarks Summit, PA 18411		**11** Nonqualified plans	**12a** See instructions for box 12 D | 5,000.00
		13 Statutory employee ☐ Retirement plan ☒ Third-party sick pay ☐	**12b** DD | 10,328.12
		14 Other	**12c**
			12d
f Employee's address and ZIP code			

15 State Employer's state ID number PA | 1234824	**16** State wages, tips, etc. 230,800.00	**17** State income tax 13,800.00	**18** Local wages, tips, etc.	**19** Local income tax	**20** Locality name

Form **W-2** Wage and Tax Statement   **2020**   Department of the Treasury—Internal Revenue Service

Copy B—To Be Filed With Employee's **FEDERAL** Tax Return.
This information is being furnished to the Internal Revenue Service.

Christine is an optometrist and operates her own practice ("The Eyes of March") in town as a sole proprietor. The shop address is 1030 Morgan Highway, Clarks Summit, PA 18411 and the business code is 621320. Christine keeps her books on the accrual basis and her bookkeeper provided the following information:

Gross sales		$270,500
Returns		9,000
Inventory:		
Beginning inventory	$ 25,000	
Purchases	120,000	
Ending inventory	29,000	
Rent		24,000
Insurance		11,000
Professional fees		3,000
Payroll		35,000
Payroll taxes		2,877
Utilities		3,975
Office expenses		1,995
Depreciation		5,000

Christine came into contact with a client that had COVID and was unable to work for 14 days under orders of state health officials. Her employees were unaffected. She also elected to defer self-employment taxes (but not household taxes) under the COVID provisions. She allocates 77.5 percent of her income to the March 27 to December 31, 2020 COVID period.

The McCarthys have a nanny/housekeeper whom they paid $12,700 during 2020. They did not withhold income or FICA taxes. The McCarthys paid Pennsylvania state unemployment tax of $378 in 2020.

Christine received a 2020 Form 1099-INT from the National Bank of Scranton that listed interest income of $23,500. Note that McCarthys reasonably allocate $751 to state income tax expense for purposes of the net investment income tax.

The McCarthys received a Form 1099-G from Pennsylvania that reported a $477 state income tax refund from 2019. The McCarthys filed a Schedule A in 2019 and had $14,223 of state income tax expense that was limited to a $10,000 deduction.

The McCarthys paid the following in 2020:

Home mortgage interest	$15,600
Property taxes	5,450
Estimated state income tax payments	2,400
Estimated Federal income tax payments	4,500
Charitable contributions (all cash)	7,600
Student loan interest	2,690

Required: Complete the McCarthys' federal tax return for 2020. Use Form 1040, Schedule 1, Schedule 2, Schedule 3, Schedule A, Schedule B, Schedule C, Schedule H, Schedule SE, Form 7202, Form 8995, Form 8959, and Form 8960 to complete this tax return. Make realistic assumptions about any missing data and ignore any alternative minimum tax. Do not complete Form 4952, which is used for depreciation.

1B. Complete Problem 1A above before completing Problem 1B. Richard and Christine McCarthy have a 19-year-old son Jack, (born 10/2/2001; Social Security number 555-55-1212), who is a full-time student at the University of Key West. Years ago, the McCarthys shifted a significant amount of investments into Jack's name. In 2020, Jack received Forms 1099-INT and 1099-DIV that reported the following:

Tandy Corporation Bonds interest	$11,300
Tandy Corporation ordinary dividends	3,400

The dividends are not qualified dividends. In addition, Jack works part-time as a waiter in an upscale seafood restaurant in Miami, FL. His 2020 Form W-2 reported:

Wages	$12,800
Federal withholding	1,080

In spite of his fairly large income, the McCarthys provide over 50 percent of his support and claim Jack as a dependent in 2020. Jack's mailing address is 100 Duval Street, Apt. #B12, Key West, FL 33040. Use the parent's information from Problem 1A, Form 1040, Schedule B, and Form 8615, to compute Jack's 2020 income tax.

2. Warner and Augustine Robins, both 35 years old, have been married for 9 years and have no dependents. Warner is the president of Jaystar Corporation located in Macon, Georgia. The Jaystar stock is owned 40 percent by Warner, 40 percent by Augustine, and 20 percent by Warner's father. Warner and Augustine received the following tax documents:

Form W-2 (2020)

a	Employee's social security number	798-09-8526
b	Employer identification number (EIN)	43-4321567
c	Employer's name, address, and ZIP code	Jaystar Corp., 1670 Eisenhower Pkwy., Macon, GA 31206
e	Employee's name	Warner Robins, 638 Russell Parkway, Macon, GA 31207
1	Wages, tips, other compensation	153,000.00
2	Federal income tax withheld	7,100.00
3	Social security wages	137,700.00
4	Social security tax withheld	8,537.40
5	Medicare wages and tips	153,000.00
6	Medicare tax withheld	2,218.50
15	State / Employer's state ID number	GA 5643E25
16	State wages, tips, etc.	153,000.00
17	State income tax	4,500.00

Form **W-2** Wage and Tax Statement — Copy B—To Be Filed With Employee's FEDERAL Tax Return.

Form 1099-INT (2020) — Interest Income

CORRECTED (if checked)

PAYER'S name: Georgia National Bank, 520 Walnut Street, Macon, GA 31201

OMB No. 1545-0112

PAYER'S TIN: 23-8787878   RECIPIENT'S TIN: 445-81-1423

RECIPIENT'S name: Augustine and Warner Robins
638 Russell Parkway
Macon, GA 31207

Box	Description	Amount
1	Interest income	503.87
2	Early withdrawal penalty	300.00

Form **1099-INT** (keep for your records)   www.irs.gov/Form1099INT   Department of the Treasury - Internal Revenue Service

☐ CORRECTED (if checked)

RECIPIENT'S/LENDER'S name, street address, city or town, state or province, country, ZIP or foreign postal code, and telephone no. Georgia National Bank 520 Walnut Street Macon, GA 31201	*Caution: The amount shown may not be fully deductible by you. Limits based on the loan amount and the cost and value of the secured property may apply. Also, you may only deduct interest to the extent it was incurred by you, actually paid by you, and not reimbursed by another person.	OMB No. 1545-1380 20**20** Form **1098**	Mortgage Interest Statement
	1 Mortgage interest received from payer(s)/borrower(s)* $ 35,402.12		Copy B For Payer/ Borrower
RECIPIENT'S/LENDER'S TIN PAYER'S/BORROWER'S TIN 23-8787878 798-09-8526	**2** Outstanding mortgage principal $ 870,000.00	**3** Mortgage origination date 10/13/2012	The information in boxes 1 through 9 and 11 is important tax information and is being furnished to the IRS. If you are required to file a return, a
	4 Refund of overpaid interest $	**5** Mortgage insurance premiums $	negligence penalty or other sanction may be imposed on you if the IRS determines
PAYER'S/BORROWER'S name Warner & Augustine Robins	**6** Points paid on purchase of principal residence $		that an underpayment of tax results because you overstated a deduction for
Street address (including apt. no.) 638 Russell Pkwy.	**7** ☒ If address of property securing mortgage is the same as PAYER'S/BORROWER'S address, the box is checked, or the address or description is entered in box 8.		this mortgage interest or for these points, reported in boxes 1 and 6; or because you didn't report the refund
City or town, state or province, country, and ZIP or foreign postal code Macon, GA 31207	**8** Address or description of property securing mortgage (see instructions)		of interest (box 4); or because you claimed a nondeductible item.
9 Number of properties securing the mortgage 1	**10** Other Prop Tax = $6,602.00		
Account number (see instructions)			**11** Mortgage acquisition date

Form **1098**   (Keep for your records)   www.irs.gov/Form1098   Department of the Treasury - Internal Revenue Service

☐ CORRECTED (if checked)

PAYER'S name, street address, city or town, state or province, country, ZIP or foreign postal code, and telephone no. State of Georgia Treasurer 200 Piedmont Avenue SE, Suite 1204 Atlanta, GA 30334	**1** Unemployment compensation $	OMB No. 1545-0120 20**20** Form **1099-G**	Certain Government Payments
	2 State or local income tax refunds, credits, or offsets $ 690.10		Copy B For Recipient
PAYER'S TIN RECIPIENT'S TIN 21-4315123 798-09-8526	**3** Box 2 amount is for tax year	**4** Federal income tax withheld $	This is important tax information and is
RECIPIENT'S name Warner and Augustine Robins	**5** RTAA payments $	**6** Taxable grants $	being furnished to the IRS. If you are required to file a return, a negligence penalty or
Street address (including apt. no.) 638 Russell Parkway	**7** Agriculture payments $	**8** If checked, box 2 is trade or business income ► ☐	other sanction may be imposed on you if this income is taxable and
City or town, state or province, country, and ZIP or foreign postal code Macon, GA 31207	**9** Market gain $		the IRS determines that it has not been reported.
Account number (see instructions)	**10a** State **10b** State identification no. ------------ ------------------	**11** State income tax withheld $ -------------- $ --------------	

Form **1099-G**   (keep for your records)   www.irs.gov/Form1099G   Department of the Treasury - Internal Revenue Service

Macon Museum of Arts
3231 Vineville Ave.
Macon, GA 31204

November 23, 2020

Mr. and Mrs. Warner and Augustine Robins
638 Russell Parkway
Macon, GA 31207

Dear Mr. and Mrs. Robins:

Thank you for your contribution of the original album cover art for the Almond Sisters Band to the Macon Museum of Arts.

This gift supports the Macon Museum's efforts to bring original and locally-sourced art work to Macon. This continuing support will guarantee our ability to display Almond Sister art work for many years to come.

We have attached a copy of the appraiser's market valuation. Her analysis estimates the value of the painting at $34,200.

Please keep this written acknowledgement of your donation for your tax records. As a token of our appreciation for your support, we have mailed you the Macon Museum tote bag. We estimate the value of the tote bag to be $5. We are required to inform you that your federal income tax deduction for your contribution is the amount of your contribution less the value of the tote bag. Thank you for your continuing support for our important work in this field!

Please retain this letter as proof of your charitable contribution.

Sincerely,

Jack T. Mann

Jack T. Mann
Art Development Officer

Employer Identification Number **22-1234567**
Macon Museum of Arts is a registered 501(c)(3) corporation

The Robins paid the following amounts (all can be substantiated):

General state sales tax	2,120
Auto loan interest	4,800
Medical insurance	11,400
Income tax preparation fee	750
Charitable contributions in cash:	
Church	2,665
Tree Huggers Foundation (a qualified charity)	3,000
Central Georgia Technical University	5,000
Safe-deposit box	200

The Robins had total itemized deductions of $33,567 in 2019 which included a $9,600 state tax deduction.

The tax basis for the donated painting is $25,000 and the painting has been owned by Warner and Augustine for 5 years.

Jaystar does not cover health insurance for its employees. In addition to Warner and Augustine's health insurance premiums shown above, Augustine required surgery which cost $6,663 for which only $3,021 was covered by insurance. Warner had to drive Augustine 125 miles each way to a surgical center.

On January 1, 2020, Warner sold land to Jaystar Corporation for $75,000. He acquired the land 5 years ago for $160,000. No Form 1099-B was filed for this transaction.

Jaystar Corporation does not have a qualified pension plan or Section 401(k) plan for its employees. Therefore, Warner deposited $12,000 ($6,000 each) into traditional IRA accounts for Augustine and himself (neither are covered by a qualified plan at work).

The Robins received a $2,400 EIP in 2020.

Required: Complete the Robins' federal tax return for 2020. Use Form 1040, Schedule 1, Schedule A, Schedule D, and Form 8949 to complete this tax return. Make realistic assumptions about any missing data and ignore any alternative minimum tax. Do not complete Form 8283, which is used when large noncash donations are made to charity.

GROUP 5:
CUMULATIVE SOFTWARE PROBLEM

1. The following information is available for the Albert and Allison Gaytor family in addition to that provided in Chapters 1–5.

   Allison discovered a bookkeeping error in her business records. The revenues from Toge Pass should have been $85,100 (not the $64,100 originally recorded). Allison elected to defer her self-employment taxes under the COVID provisions. She allocated 77.5 percent of her income to the March 27 to December 31, 2020 COVID period.

   Albert owned 1,000 shares of Behemoth Airline stock with a basis of $25 per share. The stock was purchased 6 years ago on June 10. Albert sells 500 shares of Behemoth stock to his uncle Seth and 500 of the shares to his sister Sara for $5 per share on December 31, 2020.

Required: Combine this new information about the Gaytor family with the information from Chapters 1–5 and complete a revised 2020 tax return for Albert and Allison. Be sure to save your data input files since this case will be expanded with more tax information in the next chapter.

Form **1040**   Department of the Treasury—Internal Revenue Service   (99)
U.S. Individual Income Tax Return   **2020**   OMB No. 1545-0074   IRS Use Only—Do not write or staple in this space.

Filing Status
Check only one box.
☐ Single ☐ Married filing jointly ☐ Married filing separately (MFS) ☐ Head of household (HOH) ☐ Qualifying widow(er) (QW)

If you checked the MFS box, enter the name of your spouse. If you checked the HOH or QW box, enter the child's name if the qualifying person is a child but not your dependent ▶

Your first name and middle initial	Last name	Your social security number

If joint return, spouse's first name and middle initial	Last name	Spouse's social security number

Home address (number and street). If you have a P.O. box, see instructions.   Apt. no.

City, town, or post office. If you have a foreign address, also complete spaces below.   State   ZIP code

Foreign country name   Foreign province/state/county   Foreign postal code

Presidential Election Campaign
Check here if you, or your spouse if filing jointly, want $3 to go to this fund. Checking a box below will not change your tax or refund.
☐ You   ☐ Spouse

At any time during 2020, did you receive, sell, send, exchange, or otherwise acquire any financial interest in any virtual currency?   ☐ Yes   ☐ No

Standard Deduction
Someone can claim: ☐ You as a dependent   ☐ Your spouse as a dependent
☐ Spouse itemizes on a separate return or you were a dual-status alien

Age/Blindness **You:** ☐ Were born before January 2, 1956 ☐ Are blind **Spouse:** ☐ Was born before January 2, 1956 ☐ Is blind

Dependents (see instructions):
If more than four dependents, see instructions and check here ▶ ☐

(1) First name Last name	(2) Social security number	(3) Relationship to you	(4) ✔ if qualifies for (see instructions):	
			Child tax credit	Credit for other dependents
			☐	☐
			☐	☐
			☐	☐
			☐	☐

Attach Sch. B if required.

1	Wages, salaries, tips, etc. Attach Form(s) W-2		**1**	
2a	Tax-exempt interest	**2a**	**b** Taxable interest	**2b**
3a	Qualified dividends	**3a**	**b** Ordinary dividends	**3b**
4a	IRA distributions	**4a**	**b** Taxable amount	**4b**
5a	Pensions and annuities	**5a**	**b** Taxable amount	**5b**
6a	Social security benefits	**6a**	**b** Taxable amount	**6b**
7	Capital gain or (loss). Attach Schedule D if required. If not required, check here ▶ ☐		**7**	
8	Other income from Schedule 1, line 9		**8**	
9	Add lines 1, 2b, 3b, 4b, 5b, 6b, 7, and 8. This is your **total income** ▶		**9**	

Standard Deduction for—
- Single or Married filing separately, $12,400
- Married filing jointly or Qualifying widow(er), $24,800
- Head of household, $18,650
- If you checked any box under *Standard Deduction,* see instructions.

10	Adjustments to income:		
a	From Schedule 1, line 22	**10a**	
b	Charitable contributions if you take the standard deduction. See instructions	**10b**	
c	Add lines 10a and 10b. These are your **total adjustments to income** ▶	**10c**	
11	Subtract line 10c from line 9. This is your **adjusted gross income** ▶	**11**	
12	**Standard deduction or itemized deductions** (from Schedule A)	**12**	
13	Qualified business income deduction. Attach Form 8995 or Form 8995-A	**13**	
14	Add lines 12 and 13	**14**	
15	**Taxable income.** Subtract line 14 from line 11. If zero or less, enter -0-	**15**	

For Disclosure, Privacy Act, and Paperwork Reduction Act Notice, see separate instructions.   Cat. No. 11320B   Form **1040** (2020)

Form 1040 (2020)   Page **2**

16	**Tax** (see instructions). Check if any from Form(s): 1 ☐ 8814 2 ☐ 4972 3 ☐ _____		**16**	
17	Amount from Schedule 2, line 3		**17**	
18	Add lines 16 and 17		**18**	
19	Child tax credit or credit for other dependents		**19**	
20	Amount from Schedule 3, line 7		**20**	
21	Add lines 19 and 20		**21**	
22	Subtract line 21 from line 18. If zero or less, enter -0-		**22**	
23	Other taxes, including self-employment tax, from Schedule 2, line 10		**23**	
24	Add lines 22 and 23. This is your **total tax** ▶		**24**	
25	Federal income tax withheld from:			
a	Form(s) W-2	**25a**		
b	Form(s) 1099	**25b**		
c	Other forms (see instructions)	**25c**		
d	Add lines 25a through 25c		**25d**	
26	2020 estimated tax payments and amount applied from 2019 return		**26**	
27	Earned income credit (EIC)	**27**		
28	Additional child tax credit. Attach Schedule 8812	**28**		
29	American opportunity credit from Form 8863, line 8	**29**		
30	Recovery rebate credit. See instructions	**30**		
31	Amount from Schedule 3, line 13	**31**		
32	Add lines 27 through 31. These are your **total other payments and refundable credits** ▶		**32**	
33	Add lines 25d, 26, and 32. These are your **total payments** ▶		**33**	

• If you have a qualifying child, attach Sch. EIC.
• If you have nontaxable combat pay, see instructions.

Refund

Direct deposit? See instructions.

34	If line 33 is more than line 24, subtract line 24 from line 33. This is the amount you **overpaid**	**34**	
35a	Amount of line 34 you want **refunded to you.** If Form 8888 is attached, check here ▶ ☐	**35a**	
▶**b**	Routing number |_|_|_|_|_|_|_|_|_| ▶**c** Type: ☐ Checking ☐ Savings		
▶**d**	Account number |_|_|_|_|_|_|_|_|_|		
36	Amount of line 34 you want **applied to your 2021 estimated tax** ▶	**36**	

Amount You Owe

For details on how to pay, see instructions.

37	Subtract line 33 from line 24. This is the **amount you owe now** ▶	**37**	
	Note: Schedule H and Schedule SE filers, line 37 may not represent all of the taxes you owe for 2020. See Schedule 3, line 12e, and its instructions for details.		
38	Estimated tax penalty (see instructions) ▶	**38**	

Third Party Designee

Do you want to allow another person to discuss this return with the IRS? See instructions ▶ ☐ **Yes.** Complete below. ☐ **No**

Designee's name ▶	Phone no. ▶	Personal identification number (PIN) ▶

Sign Here

Under penalties of perjury, I declare that I have examined this return and accompanying schedules and statements, and to the best of my knowledge and belief, they are true, correct, and complete. Declaration of preparer (other than taxpayer) is based on all information of which preparer has any knowledge.

Joint return? See instructions. Keep a copy for your records.

Your signature	Date	Your occupation	If the IRS sent you an Identity Protection PIN, enter it here (see inst.) ▶
Spouse's signature. If a joint return, **both** must sign.	Date	Spouse's occupation	If the IRS sent your spouse an Identity Protection PIN, enter it here (see inst.) ▶
Phone no.		Email address	

Paid Preparer Use Only

Preparer's name	Preparer's signature	Date	PTIN	Check if: ☐ Self-employed
Firm's name ▶			Phone no. ▶	
Firm's address ▶			Firm's EIN ▶	

Go to *www.irs.gov/Form1040* for instructions and the latest information.   Form **1040** (2020)

SCHEDULE 1 (Form 1040) Department of the Treasury Internal Revenue Service	**Additional Income and Adjustments to Income** ▶ Attach to Form 1040, 1040-SR, or 1040-NR. ▶ Go to *www.irs.gov/Form1040* for instructions and the latest information.	OMB No. 1545-0074 20**20** Attachment Sequence No. **01**

Name(s) shown on Form 1040, 1040-SR, or 1040-NR	**Your social security number**

Part I Additional Income

1	Taxable refunds, credits, or offsets of state and local income taxes	**1**	
2a	Alimony received	**2a**	
b	Date of original divorce or separation agreement (see instructions) ▶		
3	Business income or (loss). Attach Schedule C	**3**	
4	Other gains or (losses). Attach Form 4797	**4**	
5	Rental real estate, royalties, partnerships, S corporations, trusts, etc. Attach Schedule E	**5**	
6	Farm income or (loss). Attach Schedule F	**6**	
7	Unemployment compensation	**7**	
8	Other income. List type and amount ▶	**8**	
9	Combine lines 1 through 8. Enter here and on Form 1040, 1040-SR, or 1040-NR, line 8	**9**	

Part II Adjustments to Income

10	Educator expenses	**10**	
11	Certain business expenses of reservists, performing artists, and fee-basis government officials. Attach Form 2106	**11**	
12	Health savings account deduction. Attach Form 8889	**12**	
13	Moving expenses for members of the Armed Forces. Attach Form 3903	**13**	
14	Deductible part of self-employment tax. Attach Schedule SE	**14**	
15	Self-employed SEP, SIMPLE, and qualified plans	**15**	
16	Self-employed health insurance deduction	**16**	
17	Penalty on early withdrawal of savings	**17**	
18a	Alimony paid	**18a**	
b	Recipient's SSN ▶		
c	Date of original divorce or separation agreement (see instructions) ▶		
19	IRA deduction	**19**	
20	Student loan interest deduction	**20**	
21	Tuition and fees deduction. Attach Form 8917	**21**	
22	Add lines 10 through 21. These are your **adjustments to income.** Enter here and on Form 1040, 1040-SR, or 1040-NR, line 10a	**22**	

For Paperwork Reduction Act Notice, see your tax return instructions.   Cat. No. 71479F   Schedule 1 (Form 1040) 2020

DRAFT AS OF August 18, 2020 DO NOT FILE

SCHEDULE 2
(Form 1040)

Department of the Treasury
Internal Revenue Service

Additional Taxes

▶ **Attach to Form 1040, 1040-SR, or 1040-NR.**
▶ **Go to** *www.irs.gov/Form1040* **for instructions and the latest information.**

OMB No. 1545-0074

20**20**

Attachment
Sequence No. **02**

Name(s) shown on Form 1040, 1040-SR, or 1040-NR

Your social security number

Part I	**Tax**	
1	Alternative minimum tax. Attach Form 6251	**1**
2	Excess advance premium tax credit repayment. Attach Form 8962	**2**
3	Add lines 1 and 2. Enter here and on Form 1040, 1040-SR, or 1040-NR, line 17 . .	**3**

Part II	**Other Taxes**	
4	Self-employment tax. Attach Schedule SE	**4**
5	Unreported social security and Medicare tax from Form: **a** ☐ 4137 **b** ☐ 8919 .	**5**
6	Additional tax on IRAs, other qualified retirement plans, and other tax-favored accounts. Attach Form 5329 if required	**6**
7a	Household employment taxes. Attach Schedule H	**7a**
b	Repayment of first-time homebuyer credit from Form 5405. Attach Form 5405 if required	**7b**
8	Taxes from: **a** ☐ Form 8959 **b** ☐ Form 8960	
	c ☐ Instructions; enter code(s)_____	**8**
9	Section 965 net tax liability installment from Form 965-A . . . **9**	
10	Add lines 4 through 8. These are your **total other taxes.** Enter here and on Form 1040 or 1040-SR, line 23, or Form 1040-NR, line 23b	**10**

For Paperwork Reduction Act Notice, see your tax return instructions.   Cat. No. 71478U   **Schedule 2 (Form 1040) 2020**

SCHEDULE 3
(Form 1040)

Department of the Treasury
Internal Revenue Service

Additional Credits and Payments

▶ Attach to Form 1040, 1040-SR, or 1040-NR.
▶ Go to *www.irs.gov/Form1040* for instructions and the latest information.

OMB No. 1545-0074

2020

Attachment
Sequence No. **03**

Name(s) shown on Form 1040, 1040-SR, or 1040-NR

Your social security number

Part I	Nonrefundable Credits	
1	Foreign tax credit. Attach Form 1116 if required	**1**
2	Credit for child and dependent care expenses. Attach Form 2441	**2**
3	Education credits from Form 8863, line 19	**3**
4	Retirement savings contributions credit. Attach Form 8880	**4**
5	Residential energy credits. Attach Form 5695	**5**
6	Other credits from Form: **a** ☐ 3800 **b** ☐ 8801 **c** ☐ _____	**6**
7	Add lines 1 through 6. Enter here and on Form 1040, 1040-SR, or 1040-NR, line 20	**7**

Part II	Other Payments and Refundable Credits		
8	Net premium tax credit. Attach Form 8962		**8**
9	Amount paid with request for extension to file (see instructions)		**9**
10	Excess social security and tier 1 RRTA tax withheld		**10**
11	Credit for federal tax on fuels. Attach Form 4136		**11**
12	Other payments or refundable credits:		
a	Form 2439	**12a**	
b	Qualified sick and family leave credits from Schedule(s) H and Form(s) 7202	**12b**	
c	Health coverage tax credit from Form 8885	**12c**	
d	Other: _____	**12d**	
e	Deferral for certain Schedule H or SE filers (see instructions) .	**12e**	
f	Add lines 12a through 12e		**12f**
13	Add lines 8 through 12f. Enter here and on Form 1040, 1040-SR, or 1040-NR, line 31	**13**	

For Paperwork Reduction Act Notice, see your tax return instructions.   Cat. No. 71480G   Schedule 3 (Form 1040) 2020

DRAFT AS OF August 18, 2020 DO NOT FILE

SCHEDULE A
(Form 1040)

Department of the Treasury
Internal Revenue Service (99)

Itemized Deductions

▶ Go to *www.irs.gov/ScheduleA* for instructions and the latest information.
▶ Attach to Form 1040 or 1040-SR.

Caution: If you are claiming a net qualified disaster loss on Form 4684, see the instructions for line 16.

OMB No. 1545-0074

2020

Attachment
Sequence No. **07**

Name(s) shown on Form 1040 or 1040-SR

Your social security number

Medical and Dental Expenses		
Caution: Do not include expenses reimbursed or paid by others.		
1	Medical and dental expenses (see instructions)	**1**
2	Enter amount from Form 1040 or 1040-SR, line 11 **2**	
3	Multiply line 2 by 7.5% (0.075)	**3**
4	Subtract line 3 from line 1. If line 3 is more than line 1, enter -0-	**4**

Taxes You Paid

5 State and local taxes.

   a State and local income taxes or general sales taxes. You may include either income taxes or general sales taxes on line 5a, but not both. If you elect to include general sales taxes instead of income taxes, check this box ▶ ☐   **5a**

   b State and local real estate taxes (see instructions)   **5b**

   c State and local personal property taxes   **5c**

   d Add lines 5a through 5c   **5d**

   e Enter the smaller of line 5d or $10,000 ($5,000 if married filing separately)   **5e**

6 Other taxes. List type and amount ▶ _____   **6**

7 Add lines 5e and 6   **7**

Interest You Paid

Caution: Your mortgage interest deduction may be limited (see instructions).

8 Home mortgage interest and points. If you didn't use all of your home mortgage loan(s) to buy, build, or improve your home, see instructions and check this box ▶ ☐

   a Home mortgage interest and points reported to you on Form 1098. See instructions if limited   **8a**

   b Home mortgage interest not reported to you on Form 1098. See instructions if limited. If paid to the person from whom you bought the home, see instructions and show that person's name, identifying no., and address

   ▶ _____   **8b**

   c Points not reported to you on Form 1098. See instructions for special rules   **8c**

   d Mortgage insurance premiums (see instructions)   **8d**

   e Add lines 8a through 8d   **8e**

9 Investment interest. Attach Form 4952 if required. See instructions .   **9**

10 Add lines 8e and 9   **10**

Gifts to Charity

Caution: If you made a gift and got a benefit for it, see instructions.

11 Gifts by cash or check. If you made any gift of $250 or more, see instructions   **11**

12 Other than by cash or check. If you made any gift of $250 or more, see instructions. You **must** attach Form 8283 if over $500.   **12**

13 Carryover from prior year   **13**

14 Add lines 11 through 13   **14**

Casualty and Theft Losses

15 Casualty and theft loss(es) from a federally declared disaster (other than net qualified disaster losses). Attach Form 4684 and enter the amount from line 18 of that form. See instructions   **15**

Other Itemized Deductions

16 Other—from list in instructions. List type and amount ▶ _____   **16**

Total Itemized Deductions

17 Add the amounts in the far right column for lines 4 through 16. Also, enter this amount on Form 1040 or 1040-SR, line 12   **17**

18 If you elect to itemize deductions even though they are less than your standard deduction, check this box ▶ ☐

For Paperwork Reduction Act Notice, see the Instructions for Forms 1040 and 1040-SR.   Cat. No. 17145C   **Schedule A (Form 1040) 2020**

SCHEDULE B
(Form 1040)

Department of the Treasury
Internal Revenue Service (99)

Interest and Ordinary Dividends

▶ Go to *www.irs.gov/ScheduleB* for instructions and the latest information.
▶ Attach to Form 1040 or 1040-SR.

OMB No. 1545-0074

2020

Attachment
Sequence No. **08**

Name(s) shown on return

Your social security number

Part I

Interest

(See instructions and the instructions for Forms 1040 and 1040-SR, line 2b.)

Note: If you received a Form 1099-INT, Form 1099-OID, or substitute statement from a brokerage firm, list the firm's name as the payer and enter the total interest shown on that form.

1 List name of payer. If any interest is from a seller-financed mortgage and the buyer used the property as a personal residence, see the instructions and list this interest first. Also, show that buyer's social security number and address ▶

	Amount
1	

2 Add the amounts on line 1 . . . . | **2** | |

3 Excludable interest on series EE and I U.S. savings bonds issued after 1989. Attach Form 8815 . . . . | **3** | |

4 Subtract line 3 from line 2. Enter the result here and on Form 1040 or 1040-SR, line 2b . . . . ▶ | **4** | |

Note: If line 4 is over $1,500, you must complete Part III.

Part II

Ordinary Dividends

(See instructions and the instructions for Forms 1040 and 1040-SR, line 3b.)

Note: If you received a Form 1099-DIV or substitute statement from a brokerage firm, list the firm's name as the payer and enter the ordinary dividends shown on that form.

5 List name of payer ▶

	Amount
5	

6 Add the amounts on line 5. Enter the total here and on Form 1040 or 1040-SR, line 3b . . . . ▶ | **6** | |

Note: If line 6 is over $1,500, you must complete Part III.

Part III

Foreign Accounts and Trusts

Caution: If required, failure to file FinCEN Form 114 may result in substantial penalties. See instructions.

You must complete this part if you **(a)** had over $1,500 of taxable interest or ordinary dividends; **(b)** had a foreign account; or **(c)** received a distribution from, or were a grantor of, or a transferor to, a foreign trust.

	Yes	No
7a At any time during 2020, did you have a financial interest in or signature authority over a financial account (such as a bank account, securities account, or brokerage account) located in a foreign country? See instructions		
If "Yes," are you required to file FinCEN Form 114, Report of Foreign Bank and Financial Accounts (FBAR), to report that financial interest or signature authority? See FinCEN Form 114 and its instructions for filing requirements and exceptions to those requirements		
b If you are required to file FinCEN Form 114, enter the name of the foreign country where the financial account is located ▶		
8 During 2020, did you receive a distribution from, or were you the grantor of, or transferor to, a foreign trust? If "Yes," you may have to file Form 3520. See instructions		

For Paperwork Reduction Act Notice, see your tax return instructions.   Cat. No. 17146N   **Schedule B (Form 1040) 2020**

**SCHEDULE C
(Form 1040)**

Department of the Treasury
Internal Revenue Service (99)

Profit or Loss From Business
(Sole Proprietorship)

▶ Go to *www.irs.gov/ScheduleC* for instructions and the latest information.
▶ **Attach to Form 1040, 1040-SR, 1040-NR, or 1041; partnerships generally must file Form 1065.**

OMB No. 1545-0074

2020

Attachment
Sequence No. **09**

Name of proprietor | Social security number (SSN)

A Principal business or profession, including product or service (see instructions)

B Enter code from instructions ▶

C Business name. If no separate business name, leave blank.

D Employer ID number (EIN) (see instr.)

E Business address (including suite or room no.) ▶
City, town or post office, state, and ZIP code

F Accounting method: **(1)** ☐ Cash **(2)** ☐ Accrual **(3)** ☐ Other (specify) ▶

G Did you "materially participate" in the operation of this business during 2020? If "No," see instructions for limit on losses . ☐ Yes ☐ No

H If you started or acquired this business during 2020, check here . . . . ▶ ☐

I Did you make any payments in 2020 that would require you to file Form(s) 1099? See instructions . . . . . ☐ Yes ☐ No

J If "Yes," did you or will you file required Form(s) 1099? . . . . ☐ Yes ☐ No

Part I Income

1	Gross receipts or sales. See instructions for line 1 and check the box if this income was reported to you on Form W-2 and the "Statutory employee" box on that form was checked . . . . ▶ ☐	**1**
2	Returns and allowances	**2**
3	Subtract line 2 from line 1	**3**
4	Cost of goods sold (from line 42)	**4**
5	**Gross profit.** Subtract line 4 from line 3	**5**
6	Other income, including federal and state gasoline or fuel tax credit or refund (see instructions)	**6**
7	**Gross income.** Add lines 5 and 6 . . . . ▶	**7**

Part II Expenses. Enter expenses for business use of your home **only** on line 30.

8	Advertising	**8**	18	Office expense (see instructions)	**18**
9	Car and truck expenses (see instructions)	**9**	19	Pension and profit-sharing plans .	**19**
10	Commissions and fees .	**10**	20	Rent or lease (see instructions):	
11	Contract labor (see instructions)	**11**	a	Vehicles, machinery, and equipment	**20a**
12	Depletion	**12**	b	Other business property . . .	**20b**
13	Depreciation and section 179 expense deduction (not included in Part III) (see instructions)	**13**	21	Repairs and maintenance . . .	**21**
			22	Supplies (not included in Part III)	**22**
			23	Taxes and licenses	**23**
			24	Travel and meals:	
14	Employee benefit programs (other than on line 19) . .	**14**	a	Travel	**24a**
15	Insurance (other than health)	**15**	b	Deductible meals (see instructions)	**24b**
16	Interest (see instructions):		25	Utilities	**25**
a	Mortgage (paid to banks, etc.)	**16a**	26	Wages (less employment credits) .	**26**
b	Other	**16b**	27a	Other expenses (from line 48) . .	**27a**
17	Legal and professional services	**17**	b	**Reserved for future use** . . .	**27b**

28	**Total expenses** before expenses for business use of home. Add lines 8 through 27a . . . . . ▶	**28**
29	Tentative profit or (loss). Subtract line 28 from line 7	**29**
30	Expenses for business use of your home. Do not report these expenses elsewhere. Attach Form 8829 unless using the simplified method. See instructions.
Simplified method filers only: Enter the total square footage of (a) your home: _____
and (b) the part of your home used for business: _____. Use the Simplified Method Worksheet in the instructions to figure the amount to enter on line 30	**30**
31	**Net profit or (loss).** Subtract line 30 from line 29.
• If a profit, enter on both **Schedule 1 (Form 1040), line 3,** and on **Schedule SE, line 2.** (If you checked the box on line 1, see instructions). Estates and trusts, enter on **Form 1041, line 3.**
• If a loss, you **must** go to line 32.	**31**
32	If you have a loss, check the box that describes your investment in this activity. See instructions.
• If you checked 32a, enter the loss on both **Schedule 1 (Form 1040), line 3,** and on **Schedule SE, line 2.** (If you checked the box on line 1, see the line 31 instructions). Estates and trusts, enter on **Form 1041, line 3.**
• If you checked 32b, you **must** attach **Form 6198.** Your loss may be limited.	**32a** ☐ All investment is at risk.
32b ☐ Some investment is not at risk.

For Paperwork Reduction Act Notice, see the separate instructions. Cat. No. 11334P **Schedule C (Form 1040) 2020**

Schedule C (Form 1040) 2020   Page **2**

Part III	**Cost of Goods Sold** (see instructions)

33 Method(s) used to
value closing inventory: **a** ☐ Cost   **b** ☐ Lower of cost or market   **c** ☐ Other (attach explanation)

34 Was there any change in determining quantities, costs, or valuations between opening and closing inventory?
If "Yes," attach explanation . . . . ☐ Yes   ☐ No

35	Inventory at beginning of year. If different from last year's closing inventory, attach explanation . . .	**35**
36	Purchases less cost of items withdrawn for personal use	**36**
37	Cost of labor. Do not include any amounts paid to yourself	**37**
38	Materials and supplies	**38**
39	Other costs	**39**
40	Add lines 35 through 39	**40**
41	Inventory at end of year	**41**
42	**Cost of goods sold.** Subtract line 41 from line 40. Enter the result here and on line 4	**42**

Part IV	**Information on Your Vehicle.** Complete this part **only** if you are claiming car or truck expenses on line 9 and are not required to file Form 4562 for this business. See the instructions for line 13 to find out if you must file Form 4562.

43 When did you place your vehicle in service for business purposes? (month/day/year)   ▶ ____ / ____ / ____

44 Of the total number of miles you drove your vehicle during 2020, enter the number of miles you used your vehicle for:

a Business _____   **b** Commuting (see instructions) _____   **c** Other _____

45 Was your vehicle available for personal use during off-duty hours? . . . . ☐ Yes   ☐ No

46 Do you (or your spouse) have another vehicle available for personal use? . . . . ☐ Yes   ☐ No

47a Do you have evidence to support your deduction? . . . . ☐ Yes   ☐ No

b If "Yes," is the evidence written? . . . . ☐ Yes   ☐ No

Part V	**Other Expenses.** List below business expenses not included on lines 8–26 or line 30.

_____	
_____	
_____	
_____	
_____	
_____	
_____	

48	**Total other expenses.** Enter here and on line 27a	**48**

Schedule C (Form 1040) 2020

SCHEDULE D		OMB No. 1545-0074
(Form 1040)	**Capital Gains and Losses**	**20**20

SCHEDULE D
(Form 1040)

Department of the Treasury
Internal Revenue Service (99)

Capital Gains and Losses

▶ **Attach to Form 1040, 1040-SR, or 1040-NR.**
▶ **Go to *www.irs.gov/ScheduleD* for instructions and the latest information.**
▶ **Use Form 8949 to list your transactions for lines 1b, 2, 3, 8b, 9, and 10.**

OMB No. 1545-0074

20**20**

Attachment
Sequence No. **12**

Name(s) shown on return

Your social security number

Did you dispose of any investment(s) in a qualified opportunity fund during the tax year? ☐ **Yes** ☐ **No**
If "Yes," attach Form 8949 and see its instructions for additional requirements for reporting your gain or loss.

Part I	Short-Term Capital Gains and Losses—Generally Assets Held One Year or Less (see instructions)

See instructions for how to figure the amounts to enter on the lines below. This form may be easier to complete if you round off cents to whole dollars.	**(d)** Proceeds (sales price)	**(e)** Cost (or other basis)	**(g)** Adjustments to gain or loss from Form(s) 8949, Part I, line 2, column (g)	**(h) Gain or (loss)** Subtract column (e) from column (d) and combine the result with column (g)
1a Totals for all short-term transactions reported on Form 1099-B for which basis was reported to the IRS and for which you have no adjustments (see instructions). However, if you choose to report all these transactions on Form 8949, leave this line blank and go to line 1b .				
1b Totals for all transactions reported on Form(s) 8949 with **Box A** checked				
2 Totals for all transactions reported on Form(s) 8949 with **Box B** checked				
3 Totals for all transactions reported on Form(s) 8949 with **Box C** checked				

4 Short-term gain from Form 6252 and short-term gain or (loss) from Forms 4684, 6781, and 8824 . .	**4**	
5 Net short-term gain or (loss) from partnerships, S corporations, estates, and trusts from Schedule(s) K-1	**5**	
6 Short-term capital loss carryover. Enter the amount, if any, from line 8 of your **Capital Loss Carryover Worksheet** in the instructions	**6** ( )
7 **Net short-term capital gain or (loss).** Combine lines 1a through 6 in column (h). If you have any long-term capital gains or losses, go to Part II below. Otherwise, go to Part III on the back	**7**	

Part II	Long-Term Capital Gains and Losses—Generally Assets Held More Than One Year (see instructions)

See instructions for how to figure the amounts to enter on the lines below. This form may be easier to complete if you round off cents to whole dollars.	**(d)** Proceeds (sales price)	**(e)** Cost (or other basis)	**(g)** Adjustments to gain or loss from Form(s) 8949, Part II, line 2, column (g)	**(h) Gain or (loss)** Subtract column (e) from column (d) and combine the result with column (g)
8a Totals for all long-term transactions reported on Form 1099-B for which basis was reported to the IRS and for which you have no adjustments (see instructions). However, if you choose to report all these transactions on Form 8949, leave this line blank and go to line 8b .				
8b Totals for all transactions reported on Form(s) 8949 with **Box D** checked				
9 Totals for all transactions reported on Form(s) 8949 with **Box E** checked				
10 Totals for all transactions reported on Form(s) 8949 with **Box F** checked				

11 Gain from Form 4797, Part I; long-term gain from Forms 2439 and 6252; and long-term gain or (loss) from Forms 4684, 6781, and 8824	**11**	
12 Net long-term gain or (loss) from partnerships, S corporations, estates, and trusts from Schedule(s) K-1	**12**	
13 Capital gain distributions. See the instructions	**13**	
14 Long-term capital loss carryover. Enter the amount, if any, from line 13 of your **Capital Loss Carryover Worksheet** in the instructions	**14** ( )
15 **Net long-term capital gain or (loss).** Combine lines 8a through 14 in column (h). Then, go to Part III on the back	**15**	

For Paperwork Reduction Act Notice, see your tax return instructions.   Cat. No. 11338H   Schedule D (Form 1040) 2020

Schedule D (Form 1040) 2020   Page **2**

Part III	**Summary**

16 Combine lines 7 and 15 and enter the result **16**

  • If line 16 is a **gain,** enter the amount from line 16 on Form 1040, 1040-SR, or 1040-NR, line 7. Then, go to line 17 below.

  • If line 16 is a **loss,** skip lines 17 through 20 below. Then, go to line 21. Also be sure to complete line 22.

  • If line 16 is zero, skip lines 17 through 21 below and enter -0- on Form 1040, 1040-SR, or 1040-NR, line 7. Then, go to line 22.

17 Are lines 15 and 16 **both** gains?
  ☐ **Yes.** Go to line 18.
  ☐ **No.** Skip lines 18 through 21, and go to line 22.

18 If you are required to complete the **28% Rate Gain Worksheet** (see instructions), enter the amount, if any, from line 7 of that worksheet . . . . ▶   **18**

19 If you are required to complete the **Unrecaptured Section 1250 Gain Worksheet** (see instructions), enter the amount, if any, from line 18 of that worksheet . . . . ▶   **19**

20 Are lines 18 and 19 **both** zero or blank?
  ☐ **Yes.** Complete the **Qualified Dividends and Capital Gain Tax Worksheet** in the instructions for Forms 1040 and 1040-SR, line 16. **Don't** complete lines 21 and 22 below.

  ☐ **No.** Complete the **Schedule D Tax Worksheet** in the instructions. **Don't** complete lines 21 and 22 below.

21 If line 16 is a loss, enter here and on Form 1040, 1040-SR, or 1040-NR, line 7, the **smaller** of:

  • The loss on line 16; or
  • ($3,000), or if married filing separately, ($1,500)   } . . . .   **21** (   )

  Note: When figuring which amount is smaller, treat both amounts as positive numbers.

22 Do you have qualified dividends on Form 1040, 1040-SR, or 1040-NR, line 3a?

  ☐ **Yes.** Complete the **Qualified Dividends and Capital Gain Tax Worksheet** in the instructions for Forms 1040 and 1040-SR, line 16.

  ☐ **No.** Complete the rest of Form 1040, 1040-SR, or 1040-NR.

Schedule D (Form 1040) 2020

SCHEDULE H
(Form 1040)

Department of the Treasury
Internal Revenue Service (99)

Household Employment Taxes

(For Social Security, Medicare, Withheld Income, and Federal Unemployment (FUTA) Taxes)

▶ **Attach to Form 1040, 1040-SR, 1040-NR, 1040-SS, or 1041.**
▶ **Go to** *www.irs.gov/ScheduleH* **for instructions and the latest information.**

OMB No. 1545-1971

2020

Attachment
Sequence No. **44**

Name of employer

Social security number

Employer identification number

Calendar year taxpayers having no household employees in 2020 don't have to complete this form for 2020.

A Did you pay **any one** household employee cash wages of $2,200 or more in 2020? (If any household employee was your spouse, your child under age 21, your parent, or anyone under age 18, see the line A instructions before you answer this question.)

☐ **Yes.** Skip lines B and C and go to line 1a.
☐ **No.** Go to line B.

B Did you withhold federal income tax during 2020 for any household employee?

☐ **Yes.** Skip line C and go to line 7.
☐ **No.** Go to line C.

C Did you pay **total** cash wages of $1,000 or more in **any** calendar **quarter** of 2019 or 2020 to **all** household employees? (**Don't** count cash wages paid in 2019 or 2020 to your spouse, your child under age 21, or your parent.)

☐ **No.** **Stop.** Don't file this schedule.
☐ **Yes.** Skip lines 1a–9 and go to line 10.

Part I   Social Security, Medicare, and Federal Income Taxes

1a	Total cash wages subject to social security tax	**1a**	
b	Qualified sick and family wages included on line 1a	**1b**	
2a	Social security tax. Multiply line 1a by 12.4% (0.124)	**2a**	
b	Employer share of social security tax on qualified sick and family leave wages. Multiply line 1b by 6.2% (0.062)	**2b**	
c	Total social security tax. Subtract line 2b from line 2a	**2c**	
3	Total cash wages subject to Medicare tax	**3**	
4	Medicare tax. Multiply line 3 by 2.9% (0.029)	**4**	
5	Total cash wages subject to Additional Medicare Tax withholding	**5**	
6	Additional Medicare Tax withholding. Multiply line 5 by 0.9% (0.009)	**6**	
7	Federal income tax withheld, if any	**7**	
8a	Total social security, Medicare, and federal income taxes. Add lines 2c, 4, 6, and 7.	**8a**	
b	Nonrefundable portion of credit for qualified sick and family leave wages from Worksheet 3	**8b**	
c	Total social security, Medicare, and federal income taxes after nonrefundable credit. Subtract line 8b from line 8a	**8c**	
d	Maximum amount of the employer share of social security tax that can be deferred; see instructions .	**8d**	
e	Refundable portion of credit for qualified sick and family leave wages from Worksheet 3	**8e**	
f	Qualified sick leave wages	**8f**	
g	Qualified health plan expenses allocable to qualified sick leave wages	**8g**	
h	Qualified family leave wages	**8h**	
i	Qualified health plan expenses allocable to qualified family leave wages	**8i**	

9 Did you pay **total** cash wages of $1,000 or more in **any** calendar **quarter** of 2019 or 2020 to **all** household employees? (**Don't** count cash wages paid in 2019 or 2020 to your spouse, your child under age 21, or your parent.)

☐ **No.** **Stop.** Include the amount from line 8c above on Schedule 2 (Form 1040), line 7a. Include the amount, if any, from line 8e, on Schedule 3 (Form 1040), line 12b. If you're not required to file Form 1040, see the line 9 instructions.
☐ **Yes.** Go to line 10.

For Privacy Act and Paperwork Reduction Act Notice, see the instructions.   Cat. No. 12187K   **Schedule H (Form 1040) 2020**

Schedule H (Form 1040) 2020   Page **2**

Part II   Federal Unemployment (FUTA) Tax

		Yes	No
10	Did you pay unemployment contributions to only one state? If you paid contributions to a credit reduction state, see instructions and check **"No"** **10**		
11	Did you pay all state unemployment contributions for 2020 by April 15, 2021? Fiscal year filers, see instructions **11**		
12	Were all wages that are taxable for FUTA tax also taxable for your state's unemployment tax? **12**		

Next: If you checked the **"Yes"** box on **all** the lines above, complete Section A.
If you checked the **"No"** box on **any** of the lines above, skip Section A and complete Section B.

Section A

13	Name of the state where you paid unemployment contributions ▶ _____	
14	Contributions paid to your state unemployment fund . . . **14**	
15	Total cash wages subject to FUTA tax **15**	
16	**FUTA tax.** Multiply line 15 by 0.6% (0.006). Enter the result here, skip Section B, and go to line 25 . **16**	

Section B

17 Complete all columns below that apply (if you need more space, see instructions):

(a) Name of state	(b) Taxable wages (as defined in state act)	(c) State experience rate period		(d) State experience rate	(e) Multiply col. (b) by 0.054	(f) Multiply col. (b) by col. (d)	(g) Subtract col. (f) from col. (e). If zero or less, enter -0-.	(h) Contributions paid to state unemployment fund
		From	To					

18	Totals **18**	
19	Add columns (g) and (h) of line 18 . . . . **19**	
20	Total cash wages subject to FUTA tax (see the line 15 instructions) **20**	
21	Multiply line 20 by 6.0% (0.06) **21**	
22	Multiply line 20 by 5.4% (0.054) **22**	
23	Enter the **smaller** of line 19 or line 22	
	(If you paid state unemployment contributions late or you're in a credit reduction state, see instructions and check here). . . . . ☐ **23**	
24	**FUTA tax.** Subtract line 23 from line 21. Enter the result here and go to line 25 . . . . **24**	

Part III   Total Household Employment Taxes

25	Enter the amount from line 8c. If you checked the **"Yes"** box on line C of page 1, enter -0- **25**	
26	Add line 16 (or line 24) and line 25 . . . . **26**	
27	Are you required to file Form 1040?	

    ☐ **Yes. Stop.** Include the amount from line 26 above on Schedule 2 (Form 1040), line 7a. Include the amount, if any, from line 8e, on Schedule 3 (Form 1040), line 12b. **Don't** complete Part IV below.

    ☐ **No.** You may have to complete Part IV. See instructions for details.

Part IV   Address and Signature — Complete this part **only** if required. See the line 27 instructions.

Address (number and street) or P.O. box if mail isn't delivered to street address	Apt., room, or suite no.
City, town or post office, state, and ZIP code	

Under penalties of perjury, I declare that I have examined this schedule, including accompanying statements, and to the best of my knowledge and belief, it is true, correct, and complete. No part of any payment made to a state unemployment fund claimed as a credit was, or is to be, deducted from the payments to employees. Declaration of preparer (other than taxpayer) is based on all information of which preparer has any knowledge.

▶ Employer's signature   ▶ Date

Paid Preparer Use Only	Print/Type preparer's name	Preparer's signature	Date	Check ☐ if self-employed	PTIN
	Firm's name ▶			Firm's EIN ▶	
	Firm's address ▶			Phone no.	

Schedule H (Form 1040) 2020

SCHEDULE SE
(Form 1040)

Department of the Treasury
Internal Revenue Service (99)

Self-Employment Tax

▶ Go to *www.irs.gov/ScheduleSE* for instructions and the latest information.
▶ Attach to Form 1040, 1040-SR, or 1040-NR.

OMB No. 1545-0074

2020

Attachment
Sequence No. **17**

Name of person with self-employment income (as shown on Form 1040, 1040-SR, or 1040-NR)

Social security number of person
with **self-employment** income ▶

Part I   Self-Employment Tax

Note: If your only income subject to self-employment tax is **church employee income,** see instructions for how to report your income and the definition of church employee income.

A   If you are a minister, member of a religious order, or Christian Science practitioner **and** you filed Form 4361, but you had $400 or more of **other** net earnings from self-employment, check here and continue with Part I . . . . ▶ ☐

Skip lines 1a and 1b if you use the farm optional method in Part II. See instructions.

1a	Net farm profit or (loss) from Schedule F, line 34, and farm partnerships, Schedule K-1 (Form 1065), box 14, code A	**1a**	
b	If you received social security retirement or disability benefits, enter the amount of Conservation Reserve Program payments included on Schedule F, line 4b, or listed on Schedule K-1 (Form 1065), box 20, code AH	**1b**	( )

Skip line 2 if you use the nonfarm optional method in Part II. See instructions.

2	Net profit or (loss) from Schedule C, line 31; and Schedule K-1 (Form 1065), box 14, code A (other than farming). See instructions for other income to report or if you are a minister or member of a religious order	**2**	
3	Combine lines 1a, 1b, and 2	**3**	
4a	If line 3 is more than zero, multiply line 3 by 92.35% (0.9235). Otherwise, enter amount from line 3	**4a**	
	Note: If line 4a is less than $400 due to Conservation Reserve Program payments on line 1b, see instructions.		
b	If you elect one or both of the optional methods, enter the total of lines 15 and 17 here	**4b**	
c	Combine lines 4a and 4b. If less than $400, **stop;** you don't owe self-employment tax. **Exception:** If less than $400 and you had **church employee income,** enter -0- and continue . . . . ▶	**4c**	
5a	Enter your **church employee income** from Form W-2. See instructions for definition of church employee income	**5a**		
b	Multiply line 5a by 92.35% (0.9235). If less than $100, enter -0-	**5b**	
6	Add lines 4c and 5b	**6**	
7	Maximum amount of combined wages and self-employment earnings subject to social security tax or the 6.2% portion of the 7.65% railroad retirement (tier 1) tax for 2020	**7**	137,700
8a	Total social security wages and tips (total of boxes 3 and 7 on Form(s) W-2) and railroad retirement (tier 1) compensation. If $137,700 or more, skip lines 8b through 10, and go to line 11	**8a**		
b	Unreported tips subject to social security tax from Form 4137, line 10 . . .	**8b**		
c	Wages subject to social security tax from Form 8919, line 10	**8c**		
d	Add lines 8a, 8b, and 8c	**8d**	
9	Subtract line 8d from line 7. If zero or less, enter -0- here and on line 10 and go to line 11 . . . ▶	**9**	
10	Multiply the **smaller** of line 6 or line 9 by 12.4% (0.124)	**10**	
11	Multiply line 6 by 2.9% (0.029)	**11**	
12	**Self-employment tax.** Add lines 10 and 11. Enter here and on **Schedule 2 (Form 1040), line 4** . .	**12**	
13	**Deduction for one-half of self-employment tax.** Multiply line 12 by 50% (0.50). Enter here and on **Schedule 1 (Form 1040), line 14**	**13**		

Part II   Optional Methods To Figure Net Earnings (see instructions)

Farm Optional Method. You may use this method **only** if **(a)** your gross farm income[1] wasn't more than $8,460, **or (b)** your net farm profits[2] were less than $6,107.

14	Maximum income for optional methods	**14**	5,640
15	Enter the **smaller** of: two-thirds (⅔) of gross farm income[1] (not less than zero) or **$5,640.** Also, include this amount on line 4b above	**15**	

Nonfarm Optional Method. You may use this method **only** if **(a)** your net nonfarm profits[3] were less than $6,107 and also less than 72.189% of your gross nonfarm income,[4] **and (b)** you had net earnings from self-employment of at least $400 in 2 of the prior 3 years. **Caution:** You may use this method no more than five times.

16	Subtract line 15 from line 14	**16**	
17	Enter the **smaller** of: two-thirds (⅔) of gross nonfarm income[4] (not less than zero) **or** the amount on line 16. Also, include this amount on line 4b above	**17**	

[1] From Sch. F, line 9; and Sch. K-1 (Form 1065), box 14, code B.
[2] From Sch. F, line 34; and Sch. K-1 (Form 1065), box 14, code A—minus the amount you would have entered on line 1b had you not used the optional method.

[3] From Sch. C, line 31; and Sch. K-1 (Form 1065), box 14, code A.
[4] From Sch. C, line 7; and Sch. K-1 (Form 1065), box 14, code C.

For Paperwork Reduction Act Notice, see your tax return instructions.   Cat. No. 11358Z   Schedule SE (Form 1040) 2020

Attachment Sequence No. **17**   Page **2**

Part III	Maximum Deferral of Self-Employment Tax Payments		
If line 4c is zero, skip lines 18 through 20, and enter -0- on line 21.			
18	Enter the portion of line 3 that can be attributed to March 27, 2020, through December 31, 2020 . .	**18**	
19	If line 18 is more than zero, multiply line 18 by 92.35% (0.9235); otherwise, enter the amount from line 18	**19**	
20	Enter the portion of lines 15 and 17 that can be attributed to March 27, 2020, through December 31, 2020	**20**	
21	Combine lines 19 and 20	**21**	
If line 5b is zero, skip line 22 and enter -0- on line 23.			
22	Enter the portion of line 5a that can be attributed to March 27, 2020, through December 31, 2020 . .	**22**	
23	Multiply line 22 by 92.35% (0.9235)	**23**	
24	Add lines 21 and 23	**24**	
25	Enter the smaller of line 9 or line 24	**25**	
26	Multiply line 25 by 6.2% (0.062). Enter here and see the instructions for line 12e of Schedule 3 (Form 1040)	**26**	

Schedule SE (Form 1040) 2020

Form **7202**	**Credits for Sick Leave and Family Leave for Certain Self-Employed Individuals**	OMB No. 1545-0074

Department of the Treasury
Internal Revenue Service

▶ **Attach to Form 1040 or 1040-SR.**
▶ **Go to** *www.irs.gov/Form7202* **for instructions and the latest information.**

2020

Attachment
Sequence No. **202**

Name of person with self-employment income (as shown on Form 1040 or 1040-SR)

Social security number of person with self-employment income

Part I	**Credit for Sick Leave for Certain Self-Employed Individuals**		
1	Number of days you were unable to perform services as a self-employed individual because of certain coronavirus-related care you required. See instructions	1	
2	Number of days you were unable to perform services as a self-employed individual because of certain coronavirus-related care you provided to another. (Do not include days you included in line 1.) See instructions	2	
3	If you are filing a fiscal year return, see instructions; otherwise enter 10	3	
4	Enter the smaller of line 1 or line 3	4	
5	Subtract line 4 from line 3	5	
6	Enter the smaller of line 2 or line 5	6	
7	Net earnings from self-employment (see instructions)	7	
8	Divide line 7 by 260 (round to nearest whole number)	8	
9	Enter the smaller of line 8 or $511	9	
10	Multiply line 4 by line 9	10	
11	Multiply line 8 by 67% (0.67)	11	
12	Enter the smaller of line 11 or $200	12	
13	Multiply line 6 by line 12	13	
14	Add lines 10 and 13	14	
15	Amount of emergency paid sick leave subject to the $511 per day limit you received from an employer (see instructions)	15	
16	Amount of emergency paid sick leave subject to the $200 per day limit you received from an employer (see instructions)	16	
	If line 15 and line 16 are both zero, skip to line 24 and enter the amount from line 14.		
17	Add line 13 and line 16	17	
18	Enter the smaller of line 17 or $2,000	18	
19	Subtract line 18 from line 17	19	
20	Add lines 10, 15, and 18	20	
21	Enter the smaller of line 20 or $5,110	21	
22	Subtract line 21 from line 20	22	
23	Add line 19 and line 22	23	
24	Subtract line 23 from line 14. If zero or less, enter -0-. Enter here and include on Schedule 3 (Form 1040), line 12b	24	

Part II	**Credit for Family Leave for Certain Self-Employed Individuals**		
25	Number of days you were unable to perform services as a self-employed individual because of certain coronavirus-related care you provided to a son or daughter under the age of 18. (Do not enter more than 50 days.) See instructions	25	
26	Net earnings from self-employment (see instructions)	26	
27	Divide line 26 by 260 (round to nearest whole number)	27	
28	Multiply line 27 by 67% (0.67)	28	
29	Enter the smaller of line 28 or $200	29	
30	Multiply line 25 by line 29	30	
31	Amount of emergency family leave wages you received from an employer (see instructions)	31	
	If line 31 is zero, skip to line 35 and enter the amount from line 30.		
32	Add line 30 and line 31	32	
33	Enter the smaller of line 32 or $10,000	33	
34	Subtract line 33 from line 32	34	
35	Subtract line 34 from line 30. If zero or less, enter -0-. Enter here and include on Schedule 3 (Form 1040), line 12b	35	

For Privacy Act and Paperwork Reduction Act Notice, see your tax return instructions.   Cat. No. 56395K   Form **7202** (2020)

DRAFT AS OF September 2, 2020 DO NOT FILE

Form **8949**

Department of the Treasury
Internal Revenue Service

Sales and Other Dispositions of Capital Assets

▶ Go to *www.irs.gov/Form8949* for instructions and the latest information.
▶ File with your Schedule D to list your transactions for lines 1b, 2, 3, 8b, 9, and 10 of Schedule D.

OMB No. 1545-0074

2020

Attachment
Sequence No. **12A**

Name(s) shown on return

Social security number or taxpayer identification number

Before you check Box A, B, or C below, see whether you received any Form(s) 1099-B or substitute statement(s) from your broker. A substitute statement will have the same information as Form 1099-B. Either will show whether your basis (usually your cost) was reported to the IRS by your broker and may even tell you which box to check.

Part I   **Short-Term.** Transactions involving capital assets you held 1 year or less are generally short-term (see instructions). For long-term transactions, see page 2.

Note: You may aggregate all short-term transactions reported on Form(s) 1099-B showing basis was reported to the IRS and for which no adjustments or codes are required. Enter the totals directly on Schedule D, line 1a; you aren't required to report these transactions on Form 8949 (see instructions).

You *must* check Box A, B, *or* C below. Check only one box. If more than one box applies for your short-term transactions, complete a separate Form 8949, page 1, for each applicable box. If you have more short-term transactions than will fit on this page for one or more of the boxes, complete as many forms with the same box checked as you need.

☐ **(A)** Short-term transactions reported on Form(s) 1099-B showing basis was reported to the IRS (see **Note** above)
☐ **(B)** Short-term transactions reported on Form(s) 1099-B showing basis **wasn't** reported to the IRS
☐ **(C)** Short-term transactions not reported to you on Form 1099-B

1 **(a)** Description of property (Example: 100 sh. XYZ Co.)	**(b)** Date acquired (Mo., day, yr.)	**(c)** Date sold or disposed of (Mo., day, yr.)	**(d)** Proceeds (sales price) (see instructions)	**(e)** Cost or other basis. See the **Note** below and see *Column (e)* in the separate instructions	Adjustment, if any, to gain or loss. If you enter an amount in column (g), enter a code in column (f). See the separate instructions. **(f)** Code(s) from instructions	**(g)** Amount of adjustment	**(h)** Gain or (loss). Subtract column (e) from column (d) and combine the result with column (g)

2 Totals. Add the amounts in columns (d), (e), (g), and (h) (subtract negative amounts). Enter each total here and include on your Schedule D, **line 1b** (if **Box A** above is checked), **line 2** (if **Box B** above is checked), or **line 3** (if **Box C** above is checked) ▶

Note: If you checked Box A above but the basis reported to the IRS was incorrect, enter in column (e) the basis as reported to the IRS, and enter an adjustment in column (g) to correct the basis. See *Column (g)* in the separate instructions for how to figure the amount of the adjustment.

For Paperwork Reduction Act Notice, see your tax return instructions.   Cat. No. 37768Z   Form **8949** (2020)

Form 8949 (2020)   Attachment Sequence No. **12A**   Page **2**

Name(s) shown on return. Name and SSN or taxpayer identification no. not required if shown on other side	Social security number or taxpayer identification number

Before you check Box D, E, or F below, see whether you received any Form(s) 1099-B or substitute statement(s) from your broker. A substitute statement will have the same information as Form 1099-B. Either will show whether your basis (usually your cost) was reported to the IRS by your broker and may even tell you which box to check.

Part II **Long-Term.** Transactions involving capital assets you held more than 1 year are generally long-term (see instructions). For short-term transactions, see page 1.

Note: You may aggregate all long-term transactions reported on Form(s) 1099-B showing basis was reported to the IRS and for which no adjustments or codes are required. Enter the totals directly on Schedule D, line 8a; you aren't required to report these transactions on Form 8949 (see instructions).

You *must* **check Box D, E,** *or* **F below. Check only one box.** If more than one box applies for your long-term transactions, complete a separate Form 8949, page 2, for each applicable box. If you have more long-term transactions than will fit on this page for one or more of the boxes, complete as many forms with the same box checked as you need.

☐ **(D)** Long-term transactions reported on Form(s) 1099-B showing basis was reported to the IRS (see **Note** above)

☐ **(E)** Long-term transactions reported on Form(s) 1099-B showing basis **wasn't** reported to the IRS

☐ **(F)** Long-term transactions not reported to you on Form 1099-B

1 (a) Description of property (Example: 100 sh. XYZ Co.)	(b) Date acquired (Mo., day, yr.)	(c) Date sold or disposed of (Mo., day, yr.)	(d) Proceeds (sales price) (see instructions)	(e) Cost or other basis. See the **Note** below and see *Column (e)* in the separate instructions	Adjustment, if any, to gain or loss. If you enter an amount in column (g), enter a code in column (f). See the separate instructions. (f) Code(s) from instructions	(g) Amount of adjustment	(h) Gain or (loss). Subtract column (e) from column (d) and combine the result with column (g)
2 **Totals.** Add the amounts in columns (d), (e), (g), and (h) (subtract negative amounts). Enter each total here and include on your Schedule D, **line 8b** (if **Box D** above is checked), **line 9** (if **Box E** above is checked), or **line 10** (if **Box F** above is checked) ▶							

Note: If you checked Box D above but the basis reported to the IRS was incorrect, enter in column (e) the basis as reported to the IRS, and enter an adjustment in column (g) to correct the basis. See *Column (g)* in the separate instructions for how to figure the amount of the adjustment.

Form **8949** (2020)

Form **8995**

Department of the Treasury
Internal Revenue Service

**Qualified Business Income Deduction
Simplified Computation**

▶ **Attach to your tax return.**
▶ **Go to** *www.irs.gov/Form8995* **for instructions and the latest information.**

OMB No. 1545-0123

20**20**

Attachment
Sequence No. **55**

Name(s) shown on return

Your taxpayer identification number

Note. *You can claim the qualified business income deduction* **only** *if you have qualified business income from a qualified trade or business, real estate investment trust dividends, publicly traded partnership income, or a domestic production activities deduction passed through from an agricultural or horticultural cooperative. See instructions.*

Use this form if your taxable income, before your qualified business income deduction, is at or below $163,300 ($326,600 if married filing jointly), and you aren't a patron of an agricultural or horticultural cooperative.

1	(a) Trade, business, or aggregation name	(b) Taxpayer identification number	(c) Qualified business income or (loss)
i			
ii			
iii			
iv			
v			

2	Total qualified business income or (loss). Combine lines 1i through 1v, column (c)	2	
3	Qualified business net (loss) carryforward from the prior year	3 ( )	
4	Total qualified business income. Combine lines 2 and 3. If zero or less, enter -0-	4	
5	Qualified business income component. Multiply line 4 by 20% (0.20)		5
6	Qualified REIT dividends and publicly traded partnership (PTP) income or (loss) (see instructions)	6	
7	Qualified REIT dividends and qualified PTP (loss) carryforward from the prior year	7 ( )	
8	Total qualified REIT dividends and PTP income. Combine lines 6 and 7. If zero or less, enter -0-	8	
9	REIT and PTP component. Multiply line 8 by 20% (0.20)		9
10	Qualified business income deduction before the income limitation. Add lines 5 and 9		10
11	Taxable income before qualified business income deduction	11	
12	Net capital gain (see instructions)	12	
13	Subtract line 12 from line 11. If zero or less, enter -0-	13	
14	Income limitation. Multiply line 13 by 20% (0.20)		14
15	Qualified business income deduction. Enter the lesser of line 10 or line 14. Also enter this amount on the applicable line of your return . . . . ▶		15
16	Total qualified business (loss) carryforward. Combine lines 2 and 3. If greater than zero, enter -0- . .		16 ( )
17	Total qualified REIT dividends and PTP (loss) carryforward. Combine lines 6 and 7. If greater than zero, enter -0-		17 ( )

For Privacy Act and Paperwork Reduction Act Notice, see instructions.   Cat. No. 37806C   Form **8995** (2020)

Form **8959**

Department of the Treasury
Internal Revenue Service

Additional Medicare Tax

► If any line does not apply to you, leave it blank. See separate instructions.

► Attach to Form 1040, 1040-SR, 1040-NR, 1040-PR, or 1040-SS.

► Go to *www.irs.gov/Form8959* for instructions and the latest information.

OMB No. 1545-0074

2020

Attachment
Sequence No. **71**

Name(s) shown on return

Your social security number

Part I   Additional Medicare Tax on Medicare Wages

1	Medicare wages and tips from Form W-2, box 5. If you have more than one Form W-2, enter the total of the amounts from box 5	**1**	
2	Unreported tips from Form 4137, line 6	**2**	
3	Wages from Form 8919, line 6	**3**	
4	Add lines 1 through 3	**4**	
5	Enter the following amount for your filing status:		
	Married filing jointly $250,000		
	Married filing separately $125,000		
	Single, Head of household, or Qualifying widow(er) $200,000	**5**	
6	Subtract line 5 from line 4. If zero or less, enter -0-		**6**
7	Additional Medicare Tax on Medicare wages. Multiply line 6 by 0.9% (0.009). Enter here and go to Part II		**7**

Part II   Additional Medicare Tax on Self-Employment Income

8	Self-employment income from Schedule SE (Form 1040), Part I, line 6. If you had a loss, enter -0- (Form 1040-PR or 1040-SS filers, see instructions.)	**8**	
9	Enter the following amount for your filing status:		
	Married filing jointly. $250,000		
	Married filing separately $125,000		
	Single, Head of household, or Qualifying widow(er) $200,000	**9**	
10	Enter the amount from line 4	**10**	
11	Subtract line 10 from line 9. If zero or less, enter -0-	**11**	
12	Subtract line 11 from line 8. If zero or less, enter -0-		**12**
13	Additional Medicare Tax on self-employment income. Multiply line 12 by 0.9% (0.009). Enter here and go to Part III		**13**

Part III   Additional Medicare Tax on Railroad Retirement Tax Act (RRTA) Compensation

14	Railroad retirement (RRTA) compensation and tips from Form(s) W-2, box 14 (see instructions)	**14**	
15	Enter the following amount for your filing status:		
	Married filing jointly $250,000		
	Married filing separately $125,000		
	Single, Head of household, or Qualifying widow(er) $200,000	**15**	
16	Subtract line 15 from line 14. If zero or less, enter -0-		**16**
17	Additional Medicare Tax on railroad retirement (RRTA) compensation. Multiply line 16 by 0.9% (0.009). Enter here and go to Part IV		**17**

Part IV   Total Additional Medicare Tax

18	Add lines 7, 13, and 17. Also include this amount on Schedule 2 (Form 1040), line 8 (check box a) (Form 1040-PR or 1040-SS filers, see instructions), and go to Part V		**18**

Part V   Withholding Reconciliation

19	Medicare tax withheld from Form W-2, box 6. If you have more than one Form W-2, enter the total of the amounts from box 6	**19**	
20	Enter the amount from line 1	**20**	
21	Multiply line 20 by 1.45% (0.0145). This is your regular Medicare tax withholding on Medicare wages	**21**	
22	Subtract line 21 from line 19. If zero or less, enter -0-. This is your Additional Medicare Tax withholding on Medicare wages		**22**
23	Additional Medicare Tax withholding on railroad retirement (RRTA) compensation from Form W-2, box 14 (see instructions)		**23**
24	**Total Additional Medicare Tax withholding.** Add lines 22 and 23. Also include this amount with federal income tax withholding on Form 1040, 1040-SR, or 1040-NR, line 25c (Form 1040-PR or 1040-SS filers, see instructions)		**24**

For Paperwork Reduction Act Notice, see your tax return instructions.   Cat. No. 59475X   Form **8959** (2020)

DRAFT AS OF August 28, 2020 DO NOT FILE

Form **8960**

Department of the Treasury
Internal Revenue Service (99)

**Net Investment Income Tax—
Individuals, Estates, and Trusts**

▶ Attach to your tax return.
▶ Go to *www.irs.gov/Form8960* for instructions and the latest information.

OMB No. 1545-2227

20**20**

Attachment
Sequence No. **72**

Name(s) shown on your tax return

Your social security number or EIN

Part I Investment Income

☐ Section 6013(g) election (see instructions)
☐ Section 6013(h) election (see instructions)
☐ Regulations section 1.1411-10(g) election (see instructions)

1	Taxable interest (see instructions)	**1**
2	Ordinary dividends (see instructions)	**2**
3	Annuities (see instructions)	**3**
4a	Rental real estate, royalties, partnerships, S corporations, trusts, etc. (see instructions)	**4a**
b	Adjustment for net income or loss derived in the ordinary course of a non-section 1411 trade or business (see instructions)	**4b**
c	Combine lines 4a and 4b	**4c**
5a	Net gain or loss from disposition of property (see instructions)	**5a**
b	Net gain or loss from disposition of property that is not subject to net investment income tax (see instructions)	**5b**
c	Adjustment from disposition of partnership interest or S corporation stock (see instructions)	**5c**
d	Combine lines 5a through 5c	**5d**
6	Adjustments to investment income for certain CFCs and PFICs (see instructions)	**6**
7	Other modifications to investment income (see instructions)	**7**
8	Total investment income. Combine lines 1, 2, 3, 4c, 5d, 6, and 7	**8**

Part II Investment Expenses Allocable to Investment Income and Modifications

9a	Investment interest expenses (see instructions)	**9a**
b	State, local, and foreign income tax (see instructions)	**9b**
c	Miscellaneous investment expenses (see instructions)	**9c**
d	Add lines 9a, 9b, and 9c	**9d**
10	Additional modifications (see instructions)	**10**
11	Total deductions and modifications. Add lines 9d and 10	**11**

Part III Tax Computation

12	Net investment income. Subtract Part II, line 11, from Part I, line 8. Individuals, complete lines 13–17. Estates and trusts, complete lines 18a–21. If zero or less, enter -0-	**12**
	Individuals:	
13	Modified adjusted gross income (see instructions)	**13**
14	Threshold based on filing status (see instructions)	**14**
15	Subtract line 14 from line 13. If zero or less, enter -0-	**15**
16	Enter the smaller of line 12 or line 15	**16**
17	Net investment income tax for individuals. Multiply line 16 by 3.8% (0.038). **Enter here and include on your tax return** (see instructions)	**17**
	Estates and Trusts:	
18a	Net investment income (line 12 above)	**18a**
b	Deductions for distributions of net investment income and deductions under section 642(c) (see instructions)	**18b**
c	Undistributed net investment income. Subtract line 18b from 18a (see instructions). If zero or less, enter -0-	**18c**
19a	Adjusted gross income (see instructions)	**19a**
b	Highest tax bracket for estates and trusts for the year (see instructions)	**19b**
c	Subtract line 19b from line 19a. If zero or less, enter -0-	**19c**
20	Enter the smaller of line 18c or line 19c	**20**
21	Net investment income tax for estates and trusts. Multiply line 20 by 3.8% (0.038). **Enter here and include on your tax return** (see instructions)	**21**

For Paperwork Reduction Act Notice, see your tax return instructions.   Cat. No. 59474M   Form **8960** (2020)

Form **8615**

Department of the Treasury
Internal Revenue Service (99)

**Tax for Certain Children Who
Have Unearned Income**

▶ Attach only to the child's Form 1040 or Form 1040-NR.
▶ Go to *www.irs.gov/Form8615* for instructions and the latest information.

OMB No. 1545-0074

2020

Attachment
Sequence No. **33**

Child's name shown on return

Child's social security number

Before you begin: If the child, the parent, or any of the parent's other children for whom Form 8615 must be filed must use the Schedule D Tax Worksheet or has income from farming or fishing, see **Pub. 929,** Tax Rules for Children and Dependents. It explains how to figure the child's tax using the **Schedule D Tax Worksheet** or **Schedule J** (Form 1040).

A Parent's name (first, initial, and last). **Caution:** See instructions before completing.

B Parent's social security number

C Parent's filing status (check one):

☐ Single   ☐ Married filing jointly   ☐ Married filing separately   ☐ Head of household   ☐ Qualifying widow(er)

Part I	Child's Net Unearned Income		
1	Enter the child's unearned income. See Instructions	**1**	
2	If the child **did not** itemize deductions on **Schedule A** (Form 1040 or Form 1040-NR), enter $2,200. Otherwise, see instructions	**2**	
3	Subtract line 2 from line 1. If zero or less, **stop;** do not complete the rest of this form but **do** attach it to the child's return	**3**	
4	Enter the child's **taxable income** from Form 1040 or 1040-NR, line 15. If the child files Form 2555, see the instructions	**4**	
5	Enter the **smaller** of line 3 or line 4. If zero, **stop;** do not complete the rest of this form but **do** attach it to the child's return	**5**	

Part II	Tentative Tax Based on the Tax Rate of the Parent		
6	Enter the parent's **taxable income** from Form 1040 or 1040-NR, line 15. If zero or less, enter -0-. If the parent files Form 2555, see the instructions	**6**	
7	Enter the total, if any, from Forms 8615, line 5, of **all other** children of the parent named above. **Do not** include the amount from line 5 above	**7**	
8	Add lines 5, 6, and 7. See instructions	**8**	
9	Enter the tax on the amount on line 8 based on the **parent's** filing status above. See instructions. If the Qualified Dividends and Capital Gain Tax Worksheet, Schedule D Tax Worksheet, or Schedule J (Form 1040) is used to figure the tax, check here . . . . . ▶ ☐	**9**	
10	Enter the parent's tax from Form 1040 or 1040-NR, line 16, minus any alternative minimum tax. **Do not** include any tax from **Form 4972, 8814,** or **8885** or any tax from recapture of an education credit. If the parent files Form 2555, see the instructions. If the Qualified Dividends and Capital Gain Tax Worksheet, Schedule D Tax Worksheet, or Schedule J (Form 1040) was used to figure the tax, check here . . . . . ▶ ☐	**10**	
11	Subtract line 10 from line 9 and enter the result. If line 7 is blank, also enter this amount on line 13 and go to **Part III**	**11**	
12a	Add lines 5 and 7 . . . . **12a**		
b	Divide line 5 by line 12a. Enter the result as a decimal (rounded to at least three places)	**12b**	× .
13	Multiply line 11 by line 12b	**13**	

Part III	Child's Tax—If lines 4 and 5 above are the same, enter -0- on line 15 and go to line 16.		
14	Subtract line 5 from line 4 . . . . **14**		
15	Enter the tax on the amount on line 14 based on the **child's** filing status. See instructions. If the Qualified Dividends and Capital Gain Tax Worksheet, Schedule D Tax Worksheet, or Schedule J (Form 1040) is used to figure the tax, check here . . . . ▶ ☐	**15**	
16	Add lines 13 and 15	**16**	
17	Enter the tax on the amount on line 4 based on the **child's** filing status. See instructions. If the Qualified Dividends and Capital Gain Tax Worksheet, Schedule D Tax Worksheet, or Schedule J (Form 1040) is used to figure the tax, check here . . . . ▶ ☐	**17**	
18	Enter the **larger** of line 16 or line 17 here and on the **child's** Form 1040 or 1040-NR, line 16. If the child files Form 2555, see the instructions	**18**	

For Paperwork Reduction Act Notice, see your tax return instructions.   Cat. No. 64113U   Form **8615** (2020)

Student Name _____

Class/Section _____

Date _____

KEY NUMBER TAX RETURN SUMMARY

CHAPTER 6

Comprehensive Problem 1A

Schedule C, Net Profit or (Loss) (Line 31) _____

Schedule SE, Self-Employment Tax (Line 12) _____

Schedule H, Total Household Employment Taxes (Line 26) _____

Form 1040, Taxable Income (Line 15) _____

Form 1040, Total Tax (Line 24) _____

Comprehensive Problem 1B

Form 8615, Child's Net Unearned Income (Line 3) _____

Form 8615, Tentative Tax Based on Parent Tax Rate (Line 11) _____

Form 8615, Child's Tax (Line 18) _____

Form 1040, Taxable Income (Line 15) _____

Form 1040, Amount You Owe (line 37) _____

Comprehensive Problem 2

Total Income (Line 9) _____

Adjusted Gross Income (Line 11) _____

Standard Deduction or Itemized Deductions (Line 12) _____

Total Tax (Line 24) _____

Amount Overpaid (Line 34)

Tax Credits

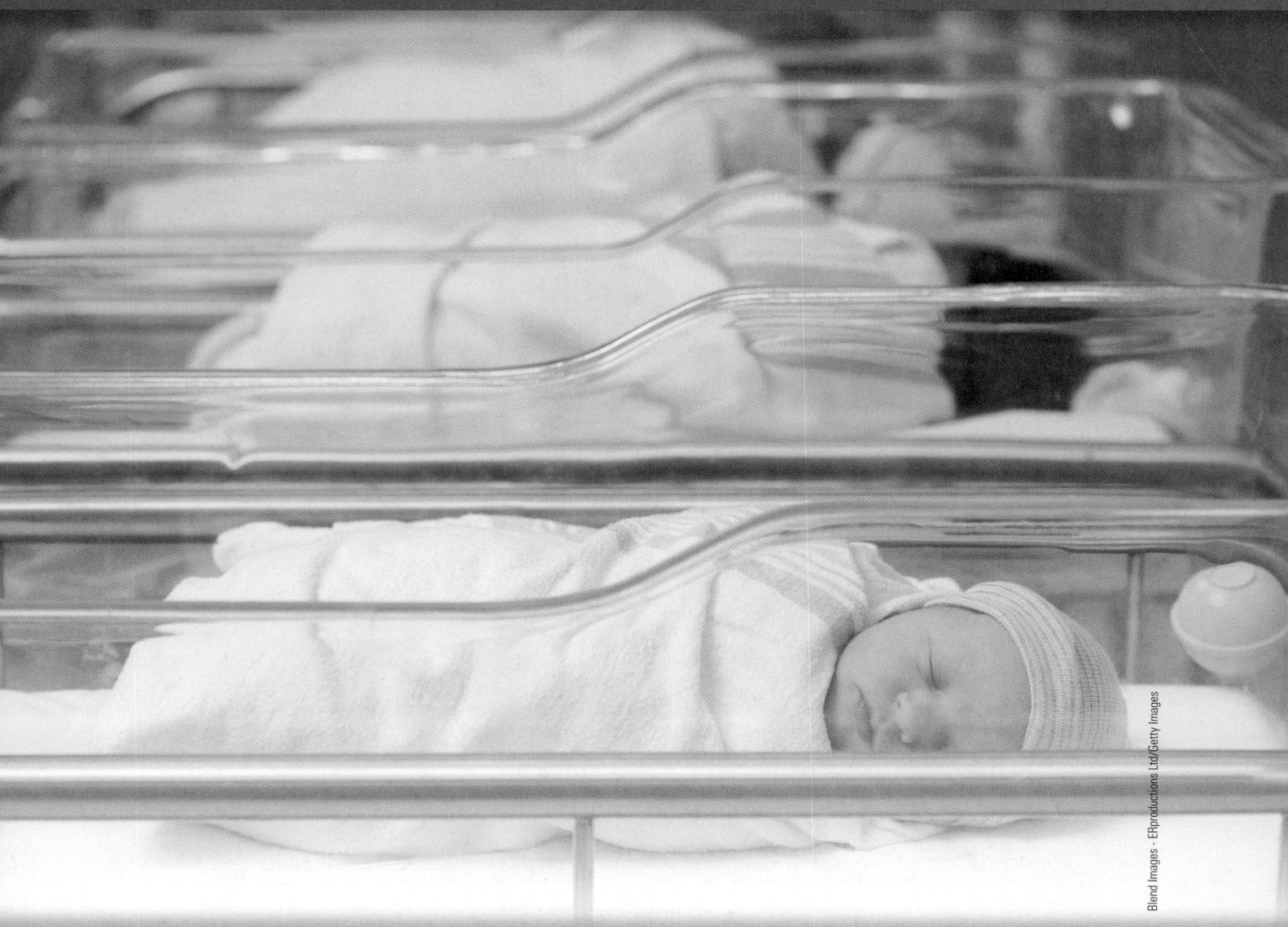

After completing this chapter, you should be able to:

LO 7.1   Calculate the child tax credit.

LO 7.2   Determine the earned income credit (EIC).

LO 7.3   Compute the child and dependent care credit for an individual taxpayer.

LO 7.4   Calculate the premium tax credit available under the Affordable Care Act.

LO 7.5   Apply the special rules applicable to the American Opportunity tax credit and lifetime learning credit.

LO 7.6   Compute the foreign income exclusion and tax credit.

LO 7.7   Determine the proper use and calculation of the adoption credit.

LO 7.8   Recognize the basic individual credits for energy efficiency.

LO 7.9   Calculate the low-income Retirement Plan Contribution Credit.

OVERVIEW

This chapter covers the most common tax credits. Credits differ from deductions. A credit is a direct reduction in tax liability while a deduction decreases taxable income. Credits are used because they target tax relief to certain groups of taxpayers. Because of the progressive rate structure of the income tax, a deduction provides greater benefit to higher-income taxpayers, while a tax credit provides equal benefit, regardless of the taxpayer's income level.

A deduction reduces taxable income by the amount of the deduction and thus results in a tax savings equal to the deduction multiplied by the tax rate. A credit is a dollar-for-dollar reduction of the taxpayer's tax liability. If a taxpayer has a choice between a credit or a deduction of equal amounts, generally the credit will result in greater tax savings.

Many credits exist in the tax law that are not covered here, such as the credit for research and development, the Work Opportunity Tax Credit, and the credit for the elderly and disabled.

A new temporary rebate recovery credit was introduced in 2020. This credit is covered in Chapter 1, as it applies to almost all taxpayers.

EXAMPLE   Gordon is a single taxpayer. His 2020 taxable income is $60,000 placing him in the 22 percent tax bracket for ordinary income. His income tax liability is $8,996. Not included in the $60,000 of taxable income is a choice between a $1,000 deduction or a $1,000 credit.

	Deduction	Credit
Taxable income	$60,000	$60,000
Deduction	(1,000)	n/a
Revised taxable income	59,000	60,000
Tax on revised income	8,776	8,996
Tax credit	n/a	(1,000)
Tax after credits	8,776	7,996
Original tax	8,996	8,996
Tax savings	$ 220	$ 1,000

Gordon saves $1,000 (a dollar-for-dollar reduction in tax liability) with the credit. He saves on $220 ($1,000 × 22% tax rate) for the deduction. ♦

Most tax credits are limited to the amount of total tax liability that a taxpayer has and thus are "nonrefundable." Certain credits allow taxpayers to claim the credit even when the amount of the credit exceeds their tax liability – these are known as refundable credits since they result in a "refund" of taxes that were never actually paid by the taxpayer.

EXAMPLE   Sandy is a taxpayer who files as head of household, with taxable income of $16,125 and a tax liability of $1,653 before any tax credits. Sandy has total tax payments (including withholding) of $2,200. Sandy is eligible for a tax credit of $2,000. Sandy's refund is calculated as follows if the credit is refundable versus nonrefundable:

	Nonrefundable	Refundable
Total tax before credits	$1,653	$1,653
Tax credit	1,653	(2,000)
Tax after credits	0	(347)
Tax payments	(2,200)	(2,200)
Total refund	$(2,200)	$(2,547)

The refundable credit increases Sandy's refund to an amount in excess of her taxes paid. ♦

Learning Objective 7.1

Calculate the child tax credit.

7-1 CHILD TAX CREDIT

The child tax credit permits individual taxpayers to take a tax credit based on the number of their dependent children. The child tax credit comes in two parts, the nonrefundable child tax credit and the refundable additional child tax credit. The TCJA made three significant, but temporary, changes to the child tax credit that apply in 2020: (1) increased the credit per child to $2,000, (2) increased the threshold for which the phase-out starts, and (3) increased the refundable amount of the credit for taxpayers whose credit is limited by their pre-credit tax liability. In addition, the TCJA added a new qualifying dependent credit of $500 for certain dependents.

To qualify for the child tax credit, the child must be under age 17, a U.S. citizen or U.S. resident alien, claimed as a dependent on the taxpayer's return, and meet the definition of "qualifying child" as discussed in Chapter 1. Thus the child must meet the six tests outlined in LO 1.6: (1) relationship test, (2) domicile test, (3) age test (except in the case of the child tax credit, the child must be under age 17), (4) joint return test, (5) citizenship test, and (6) self-support test. All qualifying children must have a Social Security number at the time of filing.

The maximum credit is $2,000 per qualifying child; however, the available credit begins phasing out when AGI reaches $400,000 for joint filers and $200,000 for all other taxpayers. The credit is phased out by $50 for each $1,000 (or part thereof) of AGI above the threshold amounts. Since the maximum credit available depends on the number of qualifying children, the income level at which the credit is fully phased out also depends on the number of children qualifying for the credit. The phase-out thresholds for the child tax credit are currently not adjusted for cost-of-living increases.

EXAMPLE Donna and Chris Howser are married and file a joint tax return. They have two children, ages 5 and 7, that are qualifying children under the dependency rules. All members of the family are U.S. citizens with Social Security numbers. In 2020, their AGI was $120,006. In 2020, both children qualify for the child tax credit of $2,000; thus, the maximum credit is $4,000. Because the phase-out for married filing jointly taxpayers in 2020 starts at $400,000, the Howsers are eligible for the maximum credit of $4,000. ◆

EXAMPLE Fiona and Kris Everest are married and file a joint return. They have one child aged 13. Each member of the Everest family has a Social Security number and their 2020 AGI is $409,800. The maximum child tax credit in 2020 is $2,000 per child; however, the Everest's AGI exceeds the $400,000 threshold. The phase-out amount is $500.

$409,100 − $400,000 = $9,100
$9,100/$1,000 = 9.1 rounded to 10
10 × $50 = $500

The Everest's child tax credit is $1,500 ($2,000 − $500). ◆

Since a portion of the child tax credit is nonrefundable, that portion is limited to the amount of tax liability before taking the child tax credit. Because taxpayers may be eligible for other tax credits that also reduce tax liability, the tax law prescribes a "pecking order" to prevent taxpayers from claiming more than one nonrefundable tax credit and creating a refundable credit.

EXAMPLE Eugene has a tax liability of $2,200 before any tax credits. Eugene has determined he is eligible for an education credit of $400 and a child tax credit of $2,000. Because his two nonrefundable credits exceed his tax liability, Eugene will take a $400 education credit and his nonrefundable child tax credit will be limited to $1,800 ($2,200 − $400). ◆

The refundable portion of the child tax credit is the amount of child tax credit that was limited by the taxpayer's tax liability.

EXAMPLE Eugene in the previous example, was eligible for a total child tax credit of $2,000; however, he could only take a credit of $1,800 due to the tax liability limitation. The $200 unclaimed child tax credit *may* be refundable. ◆

If the taxpayer has fewer than three children that are eligible for the child tax credit, the refundable portion of the child tax credit is subject to two additional limitations. The first limitation is that the additional child tax credit cannot exceed $1,400 per child. The second limitation is that the refundable child tax credit cannot exceed 15 percent of the taxpayer's earned income over $2,500. The lower of these two amounts will apply.

EXAMPLE In 2020, Mike and Laura, married filing jointly taxpayers, have two qualifying children, AGI of $72,000 (all earned income) and tax liability before any credits of $1,043. As a result, their child tax credit of $4,000 is limited to $1,043. Mike and Laura can claim the refundable portion of child tax credit of $2,800; the lesser of the unclaimed child tax credit $2,957 ($4,000 − $1,043) or 15 percent of earned income over $2,500 [($72,000 − $2,500) × 15% = $10,425], limited to $2,800 ($1,400 per qualifying child). ◆

For taxpayers with three or more qualifying children, the child tax credit amount in excess of tax liability is subject to limitations. The same overall $1,400 limit per child applies. The refundable child tax credit is also limited by the greater of (1) 15 percent of earned income over $2,500 or (2) the amount of Social Security and Medicare taxes paid up to the unclaimed child tax credit. For purposes of the refundable child tax credit, Social Security and Medicare taxes are the amounts withheld for the employee and 50 percent of self-employment taxes.

EXAMPLE   Molly and Sam are married, file a joint tax return, have five qualifying children and earned income of $6,000. The children are qualifying children for purposes of the child tax credit, but do not qualify under the earned income tax credit. Molly and Sam had $459 of Social Security and Medicare taxes withheld by their employers. Their pre-credit tax liability is $0. Because their pre-credit tax liability is $0, Molly and Sam are not eligible for the $10,000 ($2,000 × 5 children) child tax credit. The refundable portion of the child tax credit is $525 which starts at $10,000 but is first limited to $7,000 ($1,400 × 5) and then further limited to the greater of $459 or $525 [($6,000 − $2,500) × 15%]. ◆

No form is required for the nonrefundable child tax credit. It is simply claimed on Line 19 of Form 1040. The child tax credit can be computed using the Child Tax Credit Worksheet included as part of Form 1040 Instructions and included on Pages 7-7 and 7-8. Fortunately, tax software is proficient at calculating the child tax credit. The refundable child tax credit is available to taxpayers whose child tax credit was limited by their tax liability and requires completion of Form 8812 (see Page 7-9). The amount from Form 8812 is carried over to Form 1040 Line 28.

The $400,000 and $200,000 income thresholds are not adjusted for inflation while the $1,400 limit on the refundable portion is adjusted for inflation. Both of these provisions are scheduled to expire after 2025.

The child tax credit also includes a $500 "other dependent credit" for each qualifying dependent other than qualifying children under the child tax credit. For example, a dependent parent or dependent child age 17 or older can still be eligible dependents for the other dependent credit. The qualifying relative test for purposes of the other dependent credit requires the individual must be a U.S. citizen, a U.S. national, or a U.S. resident in order to be eligible for the credit. A Social Security number is not required for the other dependent credit and the credit is nonrefundable. The other dependent credit is reported in combination with the child tax credit on Line 19 of Form 1040.

EXAMPLE   Alex is a single taxpayer with a 15-year-old child. Alex also takes care of her elderly mother who qualifies as a dependent. Alex is eligible for a $2,000 child tax credit and a $500 other dependent credit for her mother. ◆

EXAMPLE   Marty is a single taxpayer with a dependent 21-year-old child who is a full-time student. Marty also takes care of his elderly mother who qualifies as a dependent. Marty is eligible for a $1,000 other dependent tax credit for his child and his mother. ◆

A taxpayer who erroneously claims the child tax credit due to reckless or intentional disregard of rules or regulations is ineligible to claim the credit for a period of two tax years. If the IRS determines the claim for the credit was fraudulent, the ineligibility window is extended to ten years.

If the IRS rejects a child tax credit for any reason other than a math or clerical error, the taxpayer must complete a Form 8862 in a year after a rejection. Form 8862 is also used for claiming an earned income credit or American Opportunities credit after rejection. Tax preparers that prepare returns on which the child tax credit is claimed are required to complete Form 8867, a due diligence checklist that was previously used for only the earned income credit.

The IRS will not issue refunds for any tax returns that claim a child tax credit (or earned income credit) until February 15 of the year following the tax year. This tax provision is intended to provide the IRS with additional time to review refund claims that stem from refundable child tax credit claims.

ProConnect™ Tax

TIP

The child tax credit is handled by ProConnect in an almost seamless fashion. By entering the dependent birthdate and status (e.g., full-time student) the software will automatically compute the child tax credit, other dependent credit, and additional child credit. A number of dropdown boxes are available under the Dependent entry screen that permit overrides and other options for these credits. For this reason, child tax credits or related information will not be found under the Credits input.

Self-Study Problem 7.1   See Appendix E for Solutions to Self-Study Problems

a. Jose and Jane are married and file a joint tax return claiming their three children, ages 4, 5, and 18, as dependents. Their AGI for 2020 is $125,400 and their pre-credit tax liability is $13,712. They are not claiming any other tax credits in 2020. Complete the Child Tax Credit Worksheet Parts 1 and 2 on Pages 7-7 and 7-8 to determine Jose and Jane's child tax credit for 2020.

$_____

b. Herb and Carol are married and file a joint tax return claiming their three children, ages 4, 5, and 18, as dependents. Their AGI for 2020 is $405,600 and their pre-credit tax liability is about $84,000. What is Herb and Carol's child tax credit for 2020?

$_____

c. Marie and Pierre Curry are married and file a joint tax return claiming their three children, ages 4, 5, and 16, as dependents. Their AGI for 2020 is $36,400 (all wage income) and their pre-credit tax liability is $383. Marie and Pierre's employers withheld $2,785 in Social Security and Medicare taxes in 2020. They are not claiming any other tax credits. Complete the Child Tax Credit Worksheet Parts 1 and 2 on Pages 7-7 and 7-8 and Form 8812 on Page 7-9 to determine Marie and Pierre's child tax credit and additional child tax credit, if any, for 2020.

7-2 EARNED INCOME CREDIT

7.2 Learning Objective

Determine the earned income credit (EIC).

The earned income credit (EIC or sometimes EITC) is available to qualifying individuals with earned income and AGI below certain levels. The earned income credit is meant to assist the working poor by reducing their tax burden and to supplement wage income through a refundable credit when earnings are less than the taxpayer's maximum income for their filing status. Qualifying taxpayers can receive a refundable EIC even in situations when they have no filing requirement, owe no tax, and had no income tax withheld. Similar to the additional child tax credit, the refundable EIC can in effect produce a "negative" income tax.

Proper calculation of the EIC requires a taxpayer to answer three important questions:
 (1) Does the taxpayer qualify for the EIC?
 (2) Does the taxpayer have a qualifying child?
 (3) What is the amount of the EIC?

7-2a **Does the Taxpayer Qualify?**

There are seven rules that all taxpayers must meet in order to claim the EIC and the taxpayer must meet *all seven* rules. Failure to meet just one precludes the taxpayer from claiming the EIC. The seven rules fall into the following categories:

1. AGI limit–AGI limits are indexed for inflation and can change each year. In addition, the AGI limits vary based on filing status and number of qualifying children. The EIC phases out for taxpayers with income over the limits. For 2020, the limits are:

Qualifying Children	Other Than Joint Filers		Joint Filers	
	Phase-out Begins	Phase-out Ends	Phase-out Begins	Phase-out Ends
None	$ 8,790	$15,820	$14,860	$21,710
1	19,330	41,756	25,220	47,646
2	19,330	47,440	25,220	53,330
3 or more	19,330	50,594	25,220	56,844

The phase-out percentages vary; however, only the IRS EIC Tables (Appendix B) may be used to calculate the EIC amount.

2. Social Security numbers – The taxpayer (and spouse, if filing jointly) plus any qualifying children, must all have valid Social Security numbers.
3. Married filing separate not allowed.
4. U.S. citizenship or resident alien status is required for the entire tax year.
5. Foreign income exclusion not allowed – tax law provides for certain taxpayers to exclude income earned overseas (reported on Form 2555 or Form 2555-EZ). The foreign income exclusion is beyond the scope of this textbook.
6. Investment income limit – generating a certain amount of "disqualified" income ($3,650 in 2020) precludes claiming the EIC. Disqualified income includes most typical forms of investment income such as interest, dividends, net income from rents and royalties and most forms of capital gains.
7. Earned income requirement – Since the design of the EIC is to assist the working poor, an obvious requirement is that the taxpayer (or spouse, if filing jointly) have earned income. For self-employed taxpayers, earned income includes income reported on Schedule SE. The earned income limits for 2020 are:

Qualifying Children	Other Than Joint Filers		Joint Filers	
	Minimum Earned Income	Maximum Earned Income	Minimum Earned Income	Maximum Earned Income
None	$1	$15,820	$1	$21,710
1	1	41,756	1	47,646
2	1	47,440	1	53,330
3 or more	1	50,954	1	56,844

EXAMPLE   Doug is married but files separately in 2020. Married filing separately taxpayers do not qualify for the EIC. ◆

EXAMPLE   In 2020, Jane has income of $7,000, is single, has a valid Social Security number, and is not a qualifying child of another taxpayer. Her income includes $4,500 of interest on a corporate bond. Jane is not eligible for the EIC because her investment income exceeds $3,650. ◆

Self-Study Problem 7.1a and 7.1c

2020 Child Tax Credit and Credit for Other Dependents
Worksheet—Line 19 *

Keep for Your Records

1. To be a qualifying child for the child tax credit, the child must be your dependent, **under age 17** at the end of 2020, and meet all the conditions in Steps 1 through 3 under *Who Qualifies as Your Dependent*. Make sure you checked the "child tax credit" box in column (4) of the *Dependents* section on Form 1040 or 1040-SR for each qualifying child.

2. If you don't have a qualifying child, you can't claim the child tax credit; but you may be able to claim the credit for other dependents for that child. See Step 3 under *Who Qualifies as Your Dependent*.

3. To see if your qualifying relative qualifies you to take the credit for other dependents, see Step 5 under *Who Qualifies as Your Dependent*.

4. Be sure to see *Social security number* under *Who Qualifies as Your Dependent*.

5. Do **not** use this worksheet, but use Pub. 972 instead, if:

    a. You are claiming the adoption credit, mortgage interest credit, District of Columbia first-time homebuyer credit, or residential energy efficient property credit*;

    b. You are excluding income from Puerto Rico; or

    c. You are filing Form 2555 or 4563.

    * If applicable.

Part 1

1. Number of qualifying children under age 17 with the required social security number: _____ × $2,000. Enter the result.   **1** [ ]

2. Number of other dependents, including qualifying children without the required social security number: _____ × $500. Enter the result.   **2** [ ]

    Caution. Don't include yourself, your spouse, or anyone who is not a U.S. citizen, U.S. national, or U.S. resident alien. Also, don't include anyone you included on line 1.

3. Add lines 1 and 2.   **3** [ ]

4. Enter the amount from Form 1040 or 1040-SR, line 11.   **4** [ ]

5. Enter the amount shown below for your filing status.

    • Married filing jointly — $400,000

    • All other filing statuses — $200,000   **5** [ ]

6. Is the amount on line 4 more than the amount on line 5?

    [ ] **No.** Leave line 6 blank. Enter -0- on line 7, and go to line 8.

    [ ] **Yes.** Subtract line 5 from line 4.   **6** [ ]

    If the result isn't a multiple of $1,000, increase it to the next multiple of $1,000. For example, increase $425 to $1,000, increase $1,025 to $2,000, etc.

7. Multiply the amount on line 6 by 5% (0.05). Enter the result.   **7** [ ]

8. Is the amount on line 3 more than the amount on line 7?

    [ ] **No.** (STOP)

    You can't take the child tax credit on Form 1040 or 1040-SR, line 19. You also can't take the additional child tax credit on Form 1040 or 1040-SR, line 28. Complete the rest of your Form 1040 or 1040-SR.

    [ ] **Yes.** Subtract line 7 from line 3. Enter the result.   **8** [ ]
    Go to Part 2.

---

* Download the latest version of this worksheet from the Form 1040 Instructions available at www.irs.gov. The 2020 worksheet was not available as we went to print. This worksheet is adapted from the 2019 version.

Self-Study Problem 7.1a and 7.1c

2020 Child Tax Credit and Credit for Other Dependents
Worksheet—*Continued* *

Keep for Your Records

Before you begin Part 2: ✓ Figure the amount of any credits you are claiming on Schedule 3; Form 5695, Part II*;
Form 8910; Form 8936; or Schedule R.

Part 2

9. Enter the amount from Form 1040 or 1040-SR, line 16. ..... **9** [   ]

10. Add any amounts from:

Schedule 3, line 1 _____

Schedule 3, line 2 + _____

Schedule 3, line 3 + _____

Schedule 3, line 4 + _____

Form 5695, line 30* + _____

Form 8910, line 15* + _____

Form 8936, line 23 + _____

Schedule R, line 22 + _____

Enter the total. **10** [   ]

11. Are the amounts on lines 9 and 10 the same?

☐ **Yes.** (STOP)
You can't take this credit because there is no tax to reduce.
However, you may be able to take the **additional child tax
credit** if line 1 is more than zero. See the **TIP** below.

☐ **No.** Subtract line 10 from line 9. ..... **11** [   ]

12. Is the amount on line 8 more than the amount on line 11?

☐ **Yes.** Enter the amount from line 11.
Also, you may be able to take the
additional child tax credit if line 1
is more than zero. See the **TIP** below.

☐ **No.** Enter the amount from line 8.

} **This is your child tax
credit and credit for
other dependents.**

12 [   ]

Enter this amount on
Form 1040 or 1040-SR,
line 19.

**1040
or
1040-SR** ◄ · · · ·

TIP *You may be able to take the **additional child tax credit**
on Form 1040 or 1040-SR, line 28, if you answered "Yes" on
line 11 **or** line 12 above.*

● *First, complete your Form 1040 or 1040-SR through line
27 (also complete Schedule 3, line 10).*

● *Then, use Schedule 8812 to figure any additional child tax
credit.*

⚠ **CAUTION** *If your child tax credit or additional child tax credit for a year after
2015 was reduced or disallowed, see Form 8862, who must file to
find out if you must file Form 8862 to take the credit for 2020.*

*If applicable.

* Download the latest version of this worksheet from the Form 1040 Instructions available at www.irs.gov. The 2020 worksheet was not
available as we went to print. This worksheet is adapted from the 2019 version.

Self-Study Problem 7.1c

| SCHEDULE 8812
(Form 1040)

Department of the Treasury
Internal Revenue Service (99) | **Additional Child Tax Credit**

▶ Attach to Form 1040, 1040-SR, or 1040-NR.
▶ Go to *www.irs.gov/Schedule8812* for instructions and the latest information. | 
OMB No. 1545-0074

2020

Attachment
Sequence No. **47** |

Name(s) shown on return | Your social security number

Part I   All Filers

Caution: If you file Form 2555, **stop here;** you cannot claim the additional child tax credit.

1	If you are required to use the worksheet in Pub. 972, enter the amount from line 10 of the Child Tax Credit and Credit for Other Dependents Worksheet in the publication. Otherwise, enter the amount from line 8 of your Child Tax Credit and Credit for Other Dependents Worksheet. (See the instructions for Forms 1040 and 1040-SR, line 19, or the instructions for Form 1040-NR, line 19.)	1
2	Enter the amount from line 19 of your Form 1040, Form 1040-SR, or 1040-NR	2
3	Subtract line 2 from line 1. If zero, **stop here;** you cannot claim this credit.	3
4	Number of qualifying children under 17 with the required social security number: _____ x $1,400. Enter the result. If zero, **stop here;** you cannot claim this credit. **TIP:** The number of children you use for this line is the same as the number of children you used for line 1 of the Child Tax Credit and Credit for Other Dependents Worksheet.	4
5	Enter the **smaller** of line 3 or line 4	5
6a	Earned income (see instructions)	6a
b	Nontaxable combat pay (see instructions) 6b	
7	Is the amount on line 6a more than $2,500? ☐ **No.** Leave line 7 blank and enter -0- on line 8. ☐ **Yes.** Subtract $2,500 from the amount on line 6a. Enter the result	7
8	Multiply the amount on line 7 by 15% (0.15) and enter the result . . . . **Next.** On line 4, is the amount $4,200 or more? ☐ **No.** If line 8 is zero, **stop here;** you cannot claim this credit. Otherwise, skip Part II and enter the **smaller** of line 5 or line 8 on line 15. ☐ **Yes.** If line 8 is equal to or more than line 5, skip Part II and enter the amount from line 5 on line 15. Otherwise, go to line 9.	8

Part II   Certain Filers Who Have Three or More Qualifying Children

9	Withheld social security, Medicare, and Additional Medicare taxes from Form(s) W-2, boxes 4 and 6. If married filing jointly, include your spouse's amounts with yours. If your employer withheld or you paid Additional Medicare Tax or tier 1 RRTA taxes, see instructions .	9
10	Enter the total of the amounts from Schedule 1 (Form 1040), line 14, and Schedule 2 (Form 1040), line 5, plus any taxes that you identified using code "UT" and entered on Schedule 2 (Form 1040), line 8	10
11	Add lines 9 and 10	11
12	**1040 and** **1040-SR filers:** Enter the total of the amounts from Form 1040 or 1040-SR, line 27, and Schedule 3 (Form 1040), line 10. **1040-NR filers:** Enter the amount from Schedule 3 (Form 1040), line 10.	12
13	Subtract line 12 from line 11. If zero or less, enter -0-	13
14	Enter the **larger** of line 8 or line 13 . . . . **Next,** enter the **smaller** of line 5 or line 14 on line 15.	14

Part III   Additional Child Tax Credit

15	**This is your additional child tax credit**	15

Enter this amount on
Form 1040, line 28;
Form 1040-SR, line 28; or
Form 1040-NR, line 28.

For Paperwork Reduction Act Notice, see your tax return instructions.   Cat. No. 59761M   **Schedule 8812 (Form 1040) 2020**

EXAMPLE   In 2020, Eddie and Lindsey had a new baby. Their earned income and AGI in 2020 was $12,500, they filed jointly, lived in the United States, and had no investment income. Eddie and Lindsey have Social Security numbers but have not had the time to get a Social Security number for the baby yet. Eddie and Lindsey may claim an EIC in 2020 but only with no qualifying child since the baby does not have a valid Social Security number. They should consider applying for a Social Security number by the filing deadline. ♦

EXAMPLE   In 2020, Jerry earns wages of $16,000 from his job and has no adjustments or other forms of income. He has no qualifying children and no investment income. Even if Jerry meets all the other requirements (Social Security number, U.S. residence, etc.), he will not be eligible for the EIC as his AGI exceeds the threshold amount for an unmarried taxpayer with no qualifying children ($15,820 in 2020). ♦

7-2b Does the Taxpayer Have a Qualifying Child?

Determining whether the taxpayer has a qualifying child is important because the eligibility rules differ based on whether a qualifying child is claimed or not. Because the rules defining a qualifying child for the EIC are similar to the rules for claiming a dependent, a review of the rules in Chapter 1 is suggested.

7-2c Taxpayer with No Qualifying Child

If the taxpayer does not have a qualifying child, the previous seven rules *must* be met along with four additional rules:

1. Taxpayer's age – the taxpayer or the spouse (but not both) must be at least 25 years of age by the end of the tax year but less than 65 years of age. For 2020, the taxpayer (or spouse) must have been born after December 31, 1955 but before January 2, 1996.
2. Dependency status – the taxpayer (or spouse, if filing jointly) must not be eligible to be claimed as a dependent on another taxpayer's return, whether they are claimed or not.
3. Cannot be a qualifying child – the taxpayer claiming the EIC may not be the qualifying child of another taxpayer. Note the qualifying child definition discussed in Chapter 1 applies here with two notable exceptions: (1) the child need not meet the support test, and (2) the child must live in a U.S. home for more than one-half of the year (a slight extension of the domicile test).
4. U.S. home – the taxpayer must have lived in the United States for more than one-half of the tax year.

EXAMPLE   Marco and Llewelyn are married and file jointly with no qualifying children in 2020 and meet the general rules to claim the EIC. Marco turns 65 on December 14, 2020 and Llewelyn turns 64 on April 3, 2020. Marco and Llewelyn qualify to claim the EIC because Llewelyn is under age 65 at the end of the tax year. ♦

EXAMPLE   Monica is a 23-year-old single taxpayer with no qualifying children in 2020. She is a full-time student at State College and generates enough income to live on from her nontaxable scholarships and a job on campus; however, she lets her father claim her as a dependent as the scholarship money is not included in her support test. Even if Monica meets the seven general rules, because she is claimed as a dependent by another taxpayer, she is not eligible to claim the EIC. ♦

7-2d Taxpayer with a Qualifying Child

To claim an EIC with a qualifying child, three additional rules must be considered:

1. Qualifying child tests – the child must meet the qualifying child tests. These are the same tests as discussed in Chapter 1 with two notable exceptions: (1) the child need not meet the support test, and (2) the child must live in a U.S. home for more than one-half of the year (a slight extension of the domicile test).
2. Qualifying child cannot be claimed by more than one person–only one taxpayer may claim a qualifying child for the EIC. If the child meets the definition of a qualifying child for more than one taxpayer, tiebreaker rules similar to those discussed in Chapter 1 must be applied.
3. Taxpayer cannot be a qualifying child of another taxpayer–see rule 3 under taxpayer with no qualifying child at Section 7-2c.

With so many qualification rules, it is no wonder that taxpayers and tax preparers have been known to make numerous errors when determining the EIC. Numerous checklists and aids have been prepared to assist taxpayers with preparing the EIC calculation. IRS Publication 596 contains an EIC Eligibility Checklist as shown on Page 7-15.

In addition to checklists, the IRS has implemented some additional procedural steps to ensure the EIC is not being abused by taxpayers. Similar to the child tax credit rules, taxpayers claiming an earned income credit must have a Social Security number for the taxpayer, spouse (if married), and each qualifying child by the due date (including extensions) of the return.

If the IRS rejects an earned income credit for any reason other than a math or clerical error, the taxpayer must complete a Form 8862 in order to claim the earned income credit in a future year.

In addition, a taxpayer who erroneously claims the earned income credit due to reckless or intentional disregard of rules or regulations is ineligible to claim the credit for a period of two tax years. If the IRS determines the claim for the credit was fraudulent, the ineligibility window is extended to ten years.

The IRS will not issue refunds for any tax returns that claim an earned income credit until February 15th of the following year to provide the IRS with additional time to review refund claims that stem from refundable earned income credit claims.

To assist tax preparers with the accurate completion of the EIC (and the child tax credit and American Opportunities tax credit), Form 8867 (see Pages 7-13 and 7-14) must be prepared and filed with the tax return and a copy retained by the tax preparer. If a taxpayer is claiming more than one of the credits covered by Form 8867, only one form is required to be filed. Failure to file Form 8867 could result in a $540 penalty.

7-2e What Is the Amount of the EIC?

Taxpayers are required to have some earned income to qualify for the EIC; however, too much earned income renders the taxpayer ineligible for the EIC (see Rule 7 under the general rules on Page 7-6). As stated previously, the EIC amount must be derived from the EIC Tables in Appendix B and should not be calculated using the statutory credit percentages to avoid rounding issues. To find the correct amount of EIC in the EIC Tables, the taxpayer must compare the EIC Table amount based on the taxpayer's earned income with the EIC Table amount associated with the taxpayer's AGI. The taxpayer is required to claim the smaller of the two EIC amounts.

Part of the complexity of the EIC is that a number of the thresholds, amounts, and limits change each year. As a result, new EIC tables must be used each year. The EIC is reported on Line 27 of Form 1040. Similar to the child tax credit, a specific form to support the EIC computation is not always required to be prepared and filed. Instead, a series of supporting worksheets found within the instructions to the Form 1040 are available to assist with preparation. Worksheet A is used for taxpayers with wage income only and Worksheet B is used by taxpayers with self-employment income. For taxpayers claiming a qualifying child for the EIC, Schedule EIC must also be filed.

Form **8867**

Department of the Treasury
Internal Revenue Service

Paid Preparer's Due Diligence Checklist

Earned Income Credit (EIC), American Opportunity Tax Credit (AOTC),
Child Tax Credit (CTC) (including the Additional Child Tax Credit (ACTC) and
Credit for Other Dependents (ODC)), and Head of Household (HOH) Filing Status

▶ To be completed by preparer and filed with Form 1040, 1040-SR, 1040-NR, 1040-PR, or 1040-SS.
▶ Go to *www.irs.gov/Form8867* for instructions and the latest information.

OMB No. 1545-0074

2020

Attachment
Sequence No. **70**

Taxpayer name(s) shown on return	Taxpayer identification number

Enter preparer's name and PTIN

DRAFT AS OF
August 11, 2020
DO NOT FILE

Part I	**Due Diligence Requirements**

Please check the appropriate box for the credit(s) and/or HOH filing status claimed on the return and complete the related Parts I–V for the benefit(s) claimed (check all that apply). ☐ EIC ☐ CTC/ACTC/ODC ☐ AOTC ☐ HOH

		Yes	No	N/A
1	Did you complete the return based on information for tax year 2020 provided by the taxpayer or reasonably obtained by you?	☐	☐	
2	If credits are claimed on the return, did you complete the applicable EIC and/or CTC/ACTC/ODC worksheets found in the Form 1040, 1040-SR, 1040-NR, 1040-PR, or 1040-SS instructions, and/or the AOTC worksheet found in the Form 8863 instructions, or your own worksheet(s) that provides the same information, and all related forms and schedules for each credit claimed?	☐	☐	☐
3	Did you satisfy the knowledge requirement? To meet the knowledge requirement, you must do both of the following.			
	• Interview the taxpayer, ask questions, and contemporaneously document the taxpayer's responses to determine that the taxpayer is eligible to claim the credit(s) and/or HOH filing status.			
	• Review information to determine that the taxpayer is eligible to claim the credit(s) and/or HOH filing status and to figure the amount(s) of any credit(s)	☐	☐	
4	Did any information provided by the taxpayer or a third party for use in preparing the return, or information reasonably known to you, appear to be incorrect, incomplete, or inconsistent? (If "Yes," answer questions 4a and 4b. If "No," go to question 5.)	☐	☐	
a	Did you make reasonable inquiries to determine the correct, complete, and consistent information?	☐	☐	
b	Did you contemporaneously document your inquiries? (Documentation should include the questions you asked, whom you asked, when you asked, the information that was provided, and the impact the information had on your preparation of the return.)	☐	☐	
5	Did you satisfy the record retention requirement? To meet the record retention requirement, you must keep a copy of your documentation referenced in 4b, a copy of this Form 8867, a copy of any applicable worksheet(s), a record of how, when, and from whom the information used to prepare Form 8867 and any applicable worksheet(s) was obtained, and a copy of any document(s) provided by the taxpayer that you relied on to determine eligibility for the credit(s) and/or HOH filing status or to figure the amount(s) of the credit(s)	☐	☐	
	List those documents provided by the taxpayer, if any, that you relied on: _____ _____ _____ _____			
6	Did you ask the taxpayer whether he/she could provide documentation to substantiate eligibility for the credit(s) and/or HOH filing status and the amount(s) of any credit(s) claimed on the return if his/her return is selected for audit?	☐	☐	
7	Did you ask the taxpayer if any of these credits were disallowed or reduced in a previous year?	☐	☐	☐
	(If credits were disallowed or reduced, go to question 7a; if not, go to question 8.)			
a	Did you complete the required recertification Form 8862?	☐	☐	☐
8	If the taxpayer is reporting self-employment income, did you ask questions to prepare a complete and correct Schedule C (Form 1040)?	☐	☐	☐

For Paperwork Reduction Act Notice, see separate instructions.   Cat. No. 26142H   Form **8867** (2020)

Form 8867 (2020)   Page **2**

Part II	**Due Diligence Questions for Returns Claiming EIC** (If the return does not claim EIC, go to Part III.)	Yes	No	N/A
9a	Have you determined that the taxpayer is eligible to claim the EIC for the number of qualifying children claimed, or is eligible to claim the EIC without a qualifying child? **(If the taxpayer is claiming the EIC and does not have a qualifying child, go to question 10.)**	☐	☐	
b	Did you ask the taxpayer if the child lived with the taxpayer for over half of the year, even if the taxpayer has supported the child the entire year?	☐	☐	
c	Did you explain to the taxpayer the rules about claiming the EIC when a child is the qualifying child of more than one person (tiebreaker rules)?	☐	☐	☐

Part III	**Due Diligence Questions for Returns Claiming CTC/ACTC/ODC** (If the return does not claim CTC, ACTC, or ODC, go to Part IV.)	Yes	No	N/A
10	Have you determined that each qualifying person for the CTC/ACTC/ODC is the taxpayer's dependent who is a citizen, national, or resident of the United States?	☐	☐	
11	Did you explain to the taxpayer that he/she may not claim the CTC/ACTC if the taxpayer has not lived with the child for over half of the year, even if the taxpayer has supported the child, unless the child's custodial parent has released a claim to exemption for the child?	☐	☐	☐
12	Did you explain to the taxpayer the rules about claiming the CTC/ACTC/ODC for a child of divorced or separated parents (or parents who live apart), including any requirement to attach a Form 8332 or similar statement to the return?	☐	☐	☐

Part IV	**Due Diligence Questions for Returns Claiming AOTC** (If the return does not claim AOTC, go to Part V.)	Yes	No
13	Did the taxpayer provide substantiation for the credit, such as a Form 1098-T and/or receipts for the qualified tuition and related expenses for the claimed AOTC?	☐	☐

Part V	**Due Diligence Questions for Claiming HOH** (If the return does not claim HOH filing status, go to Part VI.)	Yes	No
14	Have you determined that the taxpayer was unmarried or considered unmarried on the last day of the tax year and provided more than half of the cost of keeping up a home for the year for a qualifying person?	☐	☐

Part VI	**Eligibility Certification**

▶ **You will have complied with all due diligence requirements for claiming the applicable credit(s) and/or HOH filing status on the return of the taxpayer identified above if you:**

    A. Interview the taxpayer, ask adequate questions, contemporaneously document the taxpayer's responses on the return or in your notes, review adequate information to determine if the taxpayer is eligible to claim the credit(s) and/or HOH filing status and to figure the amount(s) of the credit(s);

    B. Complete this Form 8867 truthfully and accurately and complete the actions described in this checklist for any applicable credit(s) claimed and HOH filing status, if claimed;

    C. Submit Form 8867 in the manner required; **and**

    D. Keep all five of the following records for 3 years from the latest of the dates specified in the Form 8867 instructions under *Document Retention.*

        1. A copy of this Form 8867.

        2. The applicable worksheet(s) or your own worksheet(s) for any credit(s) claimed.

        3. Copies of any documents provided by the taxpayer on which you relied to determine the taxpayer's eligibility for the credit(s) and/or HOH filing status and to figure the amount(s) of the credit(s).

        4. A record of how, when, and from whom the information used to prepare this form and the applicable worksheet(s) was obtained.

        5. A record of any additional information you relied upon, including questions you asked and the taxpayer's responses, to determine the taxpayer's eligibility for the credit(s) and/or HOH filing status and to figure the amount(s) of the credit(s).

▶ **If you have not complied with all due diligence requirements, you may have to pay a $540 penalty for each failure to comply related to a claim of an applicable credit or HOH filing status.**

15	Do you certify that all of the answers on this Form 8867 are, to the best of your knowledge, true, correct, and complete?	Yes	No
		☐	☐

Form **8867** (2020)

EIC Eligibility Checklist

1. Is your AGI less than: ☐ Yes ☐ No
   - $15,820 ($21,710 for married filing jointly) if you do not have a qualifying child,
   - $41,756 ($47,646 for married filing jointly) if you have one qualifying child,
   - $47,440 ($53,330 for married filing jointly) if you have two qualifying children, or
   - $50,594 ($56,844 for married filing jointly) if you have more than two qualifying children?

2. Do you and your spouse each have a valid SSN (by the due date of your return including extensions)?   ☐ Yes ☐ No

3. Is your filing status married filing jointly, head of household, qualifying widow(er), or single?   ☐ Yes ☐ No

4. Answer "**Yes**" if you are not filing Form 2555 or Form 2555-EZ. Otherwise, answer "**No**."   ☐ Yes ☐ No

5. Is your investment income $3,650 or less?   ☐ Yes ☐ No

6. Is your total earned income at least $1 but less than: ☐ Yes ☐ No
   - $15,820 ($21,710 for married filing jointly) if you do not have a qualifying child,
   - $41,756 ($47,646 for married filing jointly) if you have one qualifying child,
   - $47,440 ($53,330 for married filing jointly) if you have two qualifying children, or
   - $50,954 ($56,844 for married filing jointly) if you have more than two qualifying children?

7. Answer "**Yes**" if (a) you are not a qualifying child of another taxpayer or (b) you are filing a joint return. Otherwise, answer "NO."   ☐ Yes ☐ No

8. Does your child meet the relationship, age, residency, and joint return tests for a qualifying child and have a Social Security number received by the due date of the tax return (including extensions)?   ☐ Yes ☐ No

9. Is your child a qualifying child only for you? Answer "**Yes**" if (a) your qualifying child does not meet the tests to be a qualifying child of any other person or (b) your qualifying child meets the tests to be a qualifying child of another person but you are the person entitled to treat the child as a qualifying child under the tiebreaker rules. Answer "**No**" if the other person is the one entitled to treat the child as a qualifying child under the tiebreaker rules.   ☐ Yes ☐ No

10. Were you (or your spouse if filing a joint return) at least age 25 but under age 65 at the end of 2020?   ☐ Yes ☐ No

11. Answer "**Yes**" if (a) you cannot be claimed as a dependent on anyone else's return or (b) you are filing a joint return. Otherwise, answer "**No**."   ☐ Yes ☐ No

12. Was your main home (and your spouse's if filing a joint return) in the United States for more than half the year?   ☐ Yes ☐ No

PERSONS WITH A QUALIFYING CHILD: If you answered "**Yes**" to questions 1 through 9, you can claim the EIC. Remember to fill out Schedule EIC and attach it to your Form 1040. If you answered "**Yes**" to questions 1 through 7 and "**No**" to question 8, answer questions 10 through 12 to see if you can claim the EIC without a qualifying child.

PERSONS WITHOUT A QUALIFYING CHILD: If you answered "**Yes**" to questions 1 through 7, and 10 through 12, you can claim the EIC.

If you answered "No" to any questions that applies to you: You cannot claim the EIC.

EXAMPLE Ying and Michael are married filing jointly taxpayers with earned income and AGI of $23,200 in 2020. They have two children ages 3 and 5. All members of the family have Social Security numbers, are U.S. citizens, and lived together in the United States all year. Ying had $820 of tax withheld from her wages during the year. Michael did not work. Ying and Michael can claim the EIC as they meet all the tests for taxpayers with a qualifying child. Based on earned income of $23,200, filing jointly with two qualifying children, their EIC per the 2020 table (Appendix B) is $5,920. ♦

Self-Study Problem 7.2   *See Appendix E for Solutions to Self-Study Problems*

Dennis and Lynne have a 5-year-old child. Dennis has a salary of $16,200. Lynne is self-employed with a loss of $400 from her business. Dennis and Lynne receive $100 of taxable interest income during the year. Their earned income for the year is $15,800 and their adjusted gross income is $15,900 ($16,200 − $400 + $100).

Use the worksheet below and calculate their earned income credit from the EIC table in Appendix B.

$ _____

Worksheet A—2020 EIC—Line 27*   *Keep for Your Records*

Before you begin: √ Be sure you are using the correct worksheet. Use this worksheet only if you answered "No" to Step 5, question 2. Otherwise, use Worksheet B.

Part 1	**1.** Enter your earned income from Step 5.	**1**
All Filers Using Worksheet A	Wages, salaries	
	2. Look up the amount on line 1 above in the EIC Table (right after Worksheet B) to find the credit. Be sure you use the correct column for your filing status and the number of children you have. Enter the credit here.	**2**
	If line 2 is zero, (STOP) You can't take the credit. Enter "No" on the dotted line next to Form 1040 or 1040-SR, line 27.	
	3. Enter the amount from Form 1040 or 1040-SR, line 11. **3**	
	Adjusted gross income	
	4. Are the amounts on lines 3 and 1 the same?	
	☐ **Yes.** Skip line 5; enter the amount from line 2 on line 6.	
	☐ **No.** Go to line 5.	

Part 2	**5.** If you have:	
Filers Who Answered "No" on Line 4	● No qualifying children, is the amount on line 3 less than $8,800 ($14,700 if married filing jointly)?	
	● 1 or more qualifying children, is the amount on line 3 less than $19,350 ($25,250 if married filing jointly)?	
	☐ **Yes.** Leave line 5 blank; enter the amount from line 2 on line 6.	
	☐ **No.** Look up the amount on line 3 in the EIC Table to find the credit. Be sure you use the correct column for your filing status and the number of children you have. Enter the credit here. Look at the amounts on lines 5 and 2. Then, enter the **smaller** amount on line 6.	**5**

Part 3	**6.** **This is your earned income credit.**	**6**
Your Earned Income Credit		Enter this amount on Form 1040 or 1040-SR, line 27.
	Reminder—	
	√ If you have a qualifying child, complete and attach Schedule EIC.	

⚠ CAUTION *If your EIC for a year after 1996 was reduced or disallowed, see Form 8862, who must file, earlier, to find out if you must file Form 8862 to take the credit for 2020.*

---

*Download the latest version of this worksheet from the Form 1040 Instructions available at www.irs.gov. The 2020 worksheet was not available as we went to print. This worksheet is adapted from the 2019 version.

ProConnect™ Tax TIP

ProConnect determines whether the earned income credit applies based on the information that the preparer inputs (most importantly income and dependent information). However, if the earned income credit is not computing and the preparer believes the taxpayer is eligible, the earned income credit worksheets can be produced by ProConnect to allow for review of the calculation. To produce the EIC worksheets, click on the Credits section and on the EIC, Residential Energy, Other Credits screen, expand the Earned Income Credit section and scroll down to the bottom to select the box Force Earned Income Credit Worksheets.

7-3 CHILD AND DEPENDENT CARE CREDIT

7.3 Learning Objective

Compute the child and dependent care credit for an individual taxpayer.

Congress enacted tax laws to provide benefits to taxpayers with dependents who must be provided with care and supervision while the taxpayers work. Taxpayers are allowed a credit for expenses for the care of their children and certain other dependents. To be eligible for the child and dependent care credit, the dependent must either be under the age of 13 or be a dependent or spouse of any age who is incapable of self-care. If a child's parents are divorced, the child need not be the dependent of the taxpayer claiming the credit, but the child must live with that parent more than he or she lives with the other parent. For example, a divorced mother with custody of a child may be entitled to the credit even though the child is a dependent of the father.

7-3a Qualified Expenses

The expenses that qualify for the credit include amounts paid to enable both the taxpayer and his or her spouse to be employed. Qualified expenses include amounts paid for in-home care, such as a nanny, as well as out-of-home care, such as a day care center. Overnight camps do not qualify for the credit, nor do activities providing standard education such as kindergarten. Day camps such as soccer camps, music camps, math camps, and dinosaur camps do qualify for the credit since they are not considered standard education. Payments to relatives are eligible for the credit, unless the payments are to a dependent of the taxpayer or to the taxpayer's child who is under the age of 19 at the end of the tax year. To claim the credit, the taxpayer must include on his or her tax return, the name, address, and taxpayer identification number of the person or organization providing the care.

7-3b Allowable Credit

For taxpayers with AGI of less than $15,000, the child and dependent care credit is equal to 35 percent of the qualified expenses. For taxpayers with AGI of $15,000 or more, the amount of the percentage of qualified expenses is reduced as income increases. See Line 8 on Form 2441 on Page 7-19 for the applicable credit percentage (these amounts are not adjusted for inflation). In determining the credit, the maximum amount of qualified expenses to which the applicable percentage is applied is $3,000 for one dependent and $6,000 for two or more dependents. Form 2441 is used to calculate and report the credit for child and dependent care expenses.

Married taxpayers must file a joint return to claim the child and dependent care credit, and the qualifying dependent care expenses are limited to the lesser of either spouse's earned income. For example, if a taxpayer makes $22,000 and the spouse earns $1,500, and they spend $1,900 on child care, the maximum qualifying expenses are $1,500. A special rule applies when a taxpayer or spouse is a full-time student or disabled. Full-time students or disabled taxpayers with little or no income are deemed to have earned income of $250 per month for one dependent and $500 per month for two or more dependents for purposes of calculating this limitation. For example, if a taxpayer's spouse is a full-time student for 9 months of the year and has no income, the maximum amount of the qualifying expenses for the care of one dependent is $2,250 ($250 per month × 9 months).

EXAMPLE   Harry and Molly Grant are married and file a joint return. They have one child and pay $4,000 for child care expenses during the year. Harry earns $16,000 and Molly earns $8,500 during the year, resulting in adjusted gross income of $24,500. The Grant's child care credit is calculated as follows:

Qualified expenses	$4,000
Maximum for one dependent	3,000
Credit percentage from Form 2441	× 30%
Credit allowed	$ 900

♦

EXAMPLE   Assume the same facts as in the example above, except the qualified expenses are $2,100 (instead of $4,000). The credit is 30 percent of $2,100, or $630. ♦

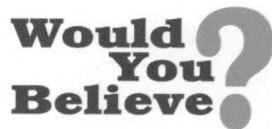

Congress' choice to not adjust certain thresholds or amounts for inflation has over time, slowly reduced the advantage of a deduction or tax benefit. The last update to the deemed value placed on the earned income of a spouse that is a full-time student was in 2002 (for tax year 2003) and increased from $200 to $250 ($400 to $500 for two qualified dependents). Using inflation from the consumer price index, the value of $250 in 2003 would be $353 today. According to National Center for Education Statistics, the average cost of a university education in 2003 was $12,953 per year. In 2018 (the most current data available), the cost had increased to $23,835.

Self-Study Problem 7.3   *See Appendix E for Solutions to Self-Study Problems*

Julie Brown (Social Security number 456-23-6543) has been widowed for 5 years and has one dependent child, Chuck Brown (Social Security number 123-33-4444). Julie's adjusted gross income and her earned income are $90,000. Julie's employer withheld $2,000 in the dependent care flexible spending account (see Chapter 2). This amount was excluded from her wage income. Assume her taxable income is $45,500, and her regular tax is $5,181 (line 10 on Form 2441). Julie paid child care expenses of $1,500 to Ivy Childcare (1 Sunflower Street, Terre Haute, IN 47803, EIN 56-7654321) and expenses for the care of her disabled dependent mother, Devona Neuporte (Social Security number 214-55-6666), of $2,400 paid to De Anza Adult Care (13 Fort Harrison Rd., Dewey, IN 47805, EIN 43-1234567). Calculate Julie's child and dependent care credit for 2020 using Form 2441 on Pages 7-19 and 7-20. Make realistic assumptions about any missing data.

ProConnect™ Tax

TIP

The child and dependent care credit is a function of two entry points in ProConnect. The first is the input in Dependents as discussed in Chapter 1 and in the other credits mentioned earlier in this chapter. The second important input occurs under Credits/Ind Qualifying for Dependant Care Cr. This screen and the Persons and Expenses Qualifying for the Dependant Care Credit are where you identify the dependant for which the expenses were incurred. The provider of the care is entered in the Provider of Dependent Care screen.

Self-Study Problem 7.3

Form **2441**	**Child and Dependent Care Expenses**		OMB No. 1545-0074

Form 2441

Department of the Treasury
Internal Revenue Service (99)

Child and Dependent Care Expenses

▶ Attach to Form 1040, 1040-SR, or 1040-NR.

▶ Go to *www.irs.gov/Form2441* for instructions and the latest information.

1040
1040-SR
1040-NR
2441

OMB No. 1545-0074

20**20**

Attachment
Sequence No. **21**

Name(s) shown on return

Your social security number

You cannot claim a credit for child and dependent care expenses if your filing status is married filing separately unless you meet the requirements listed in the instructions under "Married Persons Filing Separately." If you meet these requirements, check this box. ☐

Part I   **Persons or Organizations Who Provided the Care**—You **must** complete this part.
(If you have more than two care providers, see the instructions.)

1	**(a)** Care provider's name	**(b)** Address (number, street, apt. no., city, state, and ZIP code)	**(c)** Identifying number (SSN or EIN)	**(d)** Amount paid (see instructions)

Did you receive **dependent care benefits?**	**No** ▶ Complete only Part II below.
	Yes ▶ Complete Part III on the back next.

Caution: If the care was provided in your home, you may owe employment taxes. For details, see the instructions for Schedule 2 (Form 1040), line 7a.

Part II   **Credit for Child and Dependent Care Expenses**

2   Information about your **qualifying person(s)**. If you have more than two qualifying persons, see the instructions.

(a) Qualifying person's name		**(b)** Qualifying person's social security number	**(c) Qualified expenses** you incurred and paid in 2020 for the person listed in column (a)
First	Last		

3	Add the amounts in column (c) of line 2. **Don't** enter more than $3,000 for one qualifying person or $6,000 for two or more persons. If you completed Part III, enter the amount from line 31 . .	**3**	
4	Enter your **earned income.** See instructions	**4**	
5	If married filing jointly, enter your spouse's earned income (if you or your spouse was a student or was disabled, see the instructions); **all others**, enter the amount from line 4	**5**	
6	Enter the **smallest** of line 3, 4, or 5	**6**	
7	Enter the amount from Form 1040, 1040-SR, or 1040-NR, line 11 . **7**		
8	Enter on line 8 the decimal amount shown below that applies to the amount on line 7.		

If line 7 is:			If line 7 is:		
Over	**But not over**	**Decimal amount is**	**Over**	**But not over**	**Decimal amount is**
$0—15,000		.35	$29,000—31,000		.27
15,000—17,000		.34	31,000—33,000		.26
17,000—19,000		.33	33,000—35,000		.25
19,000—21,000		.32	35,000—37,000		.24
21,000—23,000		.31	37,000—39,000		.23
23,000—25,000		.30	39,000—41,000		.22
25,000—27,000		.29	41,000—43,000		.21
27,000—29,000		.28	43,000—No limit		.20

8   X .

9	Multiply line 6 by the decimal amount on line 8. If you paid 2019 expenses in 2020, see the instructions	**9**	
10	Tax liability limit. Enter the amount from the Credit Limit Worksheet in the instructions **10**		
11	**Credit for child and dependent care expenses.** Enter the **smaller** of line 9 or line 10 here and on Schedule 3 (Form 1040), line 2	**11**	

For Paperwork Reduction Act Notice, see your tax return instructions.   Cat. No. 11862M   Form **2441** (2020)

Form 2441 (2020)   Page **2**

Part III	Dependent Care Benefits

12 Enter the total amount of **dependent care benefits** you received in 2020. Amounts you received as an employee should be shown in box 10 of your Form(s) W-2. **Don't** include amounts reported as wages in box 1 of Form(s) W-2. If you were self-employed or a partner, include amounts you received under a dependent care assistance program from your sole proprietorship or partnership . | **12** |

13 Enter the amount, if any, you carried over from 2019 and used in 2020 during the grace period. See instructions . . . . | **13** |

14 Enter the amount, if any, you forfeited or carried forward to 2021. See instructions . . . . | **14** ( ) |

15 Combine lines 12 through 14. See instructions . . . . | **15** |

16 Enter the total amount of **qualified expenses** incurred in 2020 for the care of the **qualifying person(s)** . . . . | **16** |

17 Enter the **smaller** of line 15 or 16 . . . . | **17** |

18 Enter your **earned income**. See instructions . . . . . . | **18** |

19 Enter the amount shown below that applies to you.
- If married filing jointly, enter your spouse's earned income (if you or your spouse was a student or was disabled, see the instructions for line 5).
- If married filing separately, see instructions.
- All others, enter the amount from line 18. | **19** |

20 Enter the **smallest** of line 17, 18, or 19 . . . . | **20** |

21 Enter $5,000 ($2,500 if married filing separately **and** you were required to enter your spouse's earned income on line 19) . . . | **21** |

22 Is any amount on line 12 from your sole proprietorship or partnership?
☐ **No.** Enter -0-.
☐ **Yes.** Enter the amount here . . . . | **22** |

23 Subtract line 22 from line 15 . . . . | **23** |

24 **Deductible benefits.** Enter the **smallest** of line 20, 21, or 22. Also, include this amount on the appropriate line(s) of your return. See instructions . . . . | **24** |

25 **Excluded benefits.** If you checked "No" on line 22, enter the smaller of line 20 or 21. Otherwise, subtract line 24 from the smaller of line 20 or line 21. If zero or less, enter -0- . . . . | **25** |

26 **Taxable benefits.** Subtract line 25 from line 23. If zero or less, enter -0-. Also, include this amount on Form 1040 or 1040-SR, line 1; or Form 1040-NR, line 1a. On the dotted line next to Form 1040 or 1040-SR, line 1; or Form 1040-NR, line 1a, enter "DCB" . . . . | **26** |

To claim the child and dependent care
credit, complete lines 27 through 31 below.

27 Enter $3,000 ($6,000 if two or more qualifying persons) . . . . | **27** |

28 Add lines 24 and 25 . . . . | **28** |

29 Subtract line 28 from line 27. If zero or less, **stop.** You can't take the credit. **Exception.** If you paid 2019 expenses in 2020, see the instructions for line 9 . . . . | **29** |

30 Complete line 2 on the front of this form. **Don't** include in column (c) any benefits shown on line 28 above. Then, add the amounts in column (c) and enter the total here . . . . | **30** |

31 Enter the **smaller** of line 29 or 30. Also, enter this amount on line 3 on the front of this form and complete lines 4 through 11 . . . . | **31** |

Form **2441** (2020)

7-4 THE AFFORDABLE CARE ACT

7.4 Learning Objective

Calculate the premium tax credit available under the Affordable Care Act.

The Affordable Care Act (also called the "ACA" or "Obamacare") contains a number of different provisions that affect a taxpayer's income tax liability and reporting. The net investment income tax of 3.8 percent and 0.9 percent Medicare tax (both discussed in Chapter 6) are additional taxes for certain high-income taxpayers.

Changes to the tax law now leave only one significant tax provision that relates to individuals from the ACA: health insurance premium tax credits. The other previous provision, the individual shared responsibility, was repealed starting in 2019.

7-4a Premium Tax Credit

Under the ACA, eligible taxpayers may receive a tax credit intended to lower the cost of health care. To be eligible, a taxpayer must meet all of the following requirements:

- Health insurance is purchased through one of the state exchanges or the federal exchange
- The taxpayer is not eligible for coverage through an employer or government plan
- The taxpayer's income falls below certain limits
- The taxpayer does not file Married Filing Separately except under very limited conditions
- The taxpayer cannot be claimed as a dependent by another

The income eligibility is based on household income, where modified AGI requires the add-back of tax-exempt interest and any nontaxable Social Security benefits. The maximum household income is 400 percent of the federal poverty line for the taxpayer's family size. Taxpayers below the federal poverty line are eligible for Medicaid and thus not eligible for the credit.

Calculating the premium tax credit is similar to the EIC in that specific tables are required to compute the allowable credit. The credit is intended to take the form of the lesser of (1) actual health care premiums paid or (2) silver plan premiums, less the amount the taxpayer is expected to contribute to health care. To calculate the premium tax credit, the following steps are required:

Step 1. Calculate modified AGI for all members of the household. This is AGI for all individuals claimed as a dependent (dependent's income is includable if they are required to file a tax return) adjusted for a number of items including tax-exempt interest and nontaxable Social Security benefits.

Step 2. Compare the household income to the previous year's federal poverty line (FPL). Under the ACA, the FPL is set in the *previous* year during open enrollment (around October). The FPL is defined in three ways: (a) the 48 contiguous states and the District of Columbia, (b) Alaska, or (c) Hawaii. The FPL selected is based on the household's state of residence (see FPL amounts below).

Persons in Family/Household	2020 FPL for 48 States and DC
1	$12,490
2	16,910
3	21,330
4	25,750
5	30,170
6	34,590
7	39,010
8	43,340
Each additional person	+ 4,420

The household income is then expressed as a percentage of the FPL.

Step 3. The amount of income deemed appropriately spent on health care premiums is then identified on the 2020 Applicable Figure Table shown on Page 7-23. The applicable figure is designed to represent the maximum percentage of income a household will spend on health care premiums.

EXAMPLE Ed and Milly are married with two children under the age of 21. Household income is $51,500. Ed and Milly's household income is at 200 percent of the FPL ($51,500 ÷ $25,750 = 2.0 or 200%). For household income of 200 percent of the FPL, the applicable figure is 0.0649; thus the intended or deemed to be paid for annual health care premiums is $51,500 × 6.49% or $3,342.35. ♦

Step 4. The amount of the credit is based on comparing the cost of premiums for a designated silver plan in the taxpayer's state with the deemed premium cost calculated above. For example, if the deemed annual premium to be paid by the taxpayer is $3,342 and the annual cost of a silver plan for that household is $10,000 then the premium tax credit is $6,658 ($10,000 − $3,342). For households that did not have coverage for the entire year, the credit is prorated based on the number of months coverage was maintained.

Step 5. Lastly, the amount calculated in steps 1–4 is compared to the actual premiums paid and the lesser of the two is the premium tax credit (i.e., the credit cannot exceed the actual premiums paid).

EXAMPLE Thus, to continue with the example above, if Ed and Milly paid annual health care premiums of $4,500, their premium tax credit calculated of $6,658 is limited to $4,500. ♦

The premium tax credit can be obtained at two different times: (1) in advance (i.e., as a direct reduction in the monthly health care premiums) or (2) at the end of the year when the tax return is filed. If the taxpayer elects to have the credit paid in advance, the exchange will automatically adjust the premiums to reflect an estimated credit based on estimated household income. Since the actual premium tax credit is not known until household income can be computed after the end of the tax year, Form 8962, shown on Page 7-25, provides a reconciliation of the estimated credit and the actual credit. If the actual credit is greater than the estimated credit, the difference between the two amounts is a refundable credit on the taxpayer's tax return. If the estimated credit taken throughout the year is greater than the actual credit, the difference is treated as additional tax due on the taxpayer's tax return. However, as long as the household income remains below 400 percent of the FPL, the repayment amount of the credit is limited:

	Single	Taxpayers Other Than Single
Less than 200%	$ 325	$ 650
At least 200% but less than 300%	800	1,600
At least 300% but less than 400%	1,350	2,700
At least 400%	No limit	No limit

2020 Applicable Figure Table

 If the amount on line 5 is less than 133, your applicable figure is 0.0206. If the amount on line 5 is between 300 through 400, your applicable figure is 0.0978.

IF Form 8962, line 5, is . . .	ENTER on Form 8962, line 7 . . .	IF Form 8962, line 5, is . . .	ENTER on Form 8962, line 7 . . .	IF Form 8962, line 5, is . . .	ENTER on Form 8962, line 7 . . .	IF Form 8962, line 5, is . . .	ENTER on Form 8962, line 7 . . .
less than 133	0.0206	175	0.0531	218	0.0714	261	0.0862
133	0.0309	176	0.0535	219	0.0717	262	0.0865
134	0.0315	177	0.0540	220	0.0721	263	0.0868
135	0.0321	178	0.0545	221	0.0725	264	0.0871
136	0.0327	179	0.0549	222	0.0728	265	0.0874
137	0.0333	180	0.0554	223	0.0732	266	0.0877
138	0.0339	181	0.0559	224	0.0735	267	0.0880
139	0.0345	182	0.0564	225	0.0739	268	0.0883
140	0.0351	183	0.0568	226	0.0743	269	0.0886
141	0.0357	184	0.0573	227	0.0746	270	0.0889
142	0.0364	185	0.0578	228	0.0750	271	0.0892
143	0.0370	186	0.0583	229	0.0753	272	0.0895
144	0.0376	187	0.0587	230	0.0757	273	0.0898
145	0.0382	188	0.0592	231	0.0761	274	0.0901
146	0.0388	189	0.0597	232	0.0764	275	0.0904
147	0.0394	190	0.0602	233	0.0768	276	0.0906
148	0.0400	191	0.0606	234	0.0771	277	0.0909
149	0.0406	192	0.0611	235	0.0775	278	0.0912
150	0.0412	193	0.0616	236	0.0779	279	0.0915
151	0.0417	194	0.0621	237	0.0782	280	0.0918
152	0.0421	195	0.0625	238	0.0786	281	0.0921
153	0.0426	196	0.0630	239	0.0789	282	0.0924
154	0.0431	197	0.0635	240	0.0793	283	0.0927
155	0.0436	198	0.0640	241	0.0797	284	0.0930
156	0.0440	199	0.0644	242	0.0800	285	0.0933
157	0.0445	200	0.0649	243	0.0804	286	0.0936
158	0.0450	201	0.0653	244	0.0807	287	0.0939
159	0.0455	202	0.0656	245	0.0811	288	0.0942
160	0.0459	203	0.0660	246	0.0815	289	0.0945
161	0.0464	204	0.0663	247	0.0818	290	0.0948
162	0.0469	205	0.0667	248	0.0822	291	0.0951
163	0.0474	206	0.0671	249	0.0825	292	0.0954
164	0.0478	207	0.0674	250	0.0829	293	0.0957
165	0.0483	208	0.0678	251	0.0832	294	0.0960
166	0.0488	209	0.0681	252	0.0835	295	0.0963
167	0.0493	210	0.0685	253	0.0838	296	0.0966
168	0.0497	211	0.0689	254	0.0841	297	0.0969
169	0.0502	212	0.0692	255	0.0844	298	0.0972
170	0.0507	213	0.0696	256	0.0847	299	0.0975
171	0.0512	214	0.0699	257	0.0850	300 thru 400	0.0978
172	0.0516	215	0.0703	258	0.0853		
173	0.0521	216	0.0707	259	0.0856		
174	0.0526	217	0.0710	260	0.0859		

Self-Study Problem 7.4

Form **1095-A**	**Health Insurance Marketplace Statement**	☐ VOID	OMB No. 1545-2232
Department of the Treasury Internal Revenue Service	► Do not attach to your tax return. Keep for your records. ► Go to *www.irs.gov/Form1095A* for instructions and the latest information.	☐ CORRECTED	2020

Part I   Recipient Information

1 Marketplace identifier	2 Marketplace-assigned policy number	3 Policy issuer's name
12-3456999	XXX	Covered California

4 Recipient's name	5 Recipient's SSN	6 Recipient's date of birth
Tracy Brigantine	123-44-5555	07/01/1968

7 Recipient's spouse's name	8 Recipient's spouse's SSN	9 Recipient's spouse's date of birth
Marco Brigantine	124-55-6666	09/22/1972

10 Policy start date	11 Policy termination date	12 Street address (including apartment no.)
01/01/2020	12/31/2020	3167 Kendra Lane

13 City or town	14 State or province	15 Country and ZIP or foreign postal code
Poway	CA	92064

Part II   Covered Individuals

	A. Covered individual name	B. Covered individual SSN	C. Covered individual date of birth	D. Coverage start date	E. Coverage termination date
16	Tracy Brigantine	123-44-5555	07/01/1968	01/01/2020	12/31/2020
17	Marco Brigantine	124-55-6666	09/22/1972	01/01/2020	12/31/2020
18	Alex Brigantine	503-11-2222	04/28/2006	01/01/2020	12/31/2020
19	Bryan Brigantine	867-53-0922	01/28/2004	01/01/2020	12/31/2020
20					

Part III   Coverage Information

	Month	A. Monthly enrollment premiums	B. Monthly second lowest cost silver plan (SLCSP) premium	C. Monthly advance payment of premium tax credit
21	January	957.00	825.00	487.00
22	February	957.00	825.00	487.00
23	March	957.00	825.00	487.00
24	April	957.00	825.00	487.00
25	May	957.00	825.00	487.00
26	June	957.00	825.00	487.00
27	July	957.00	825.00	487.00
28	August	957.00	825.00	487.00
29	September	957.00	825.00	487.00
30	October	957.00	825.00	487.00
31	November	957.00	825.00	487.00
32	December	957.00	825.00	487.00
33	**Annual Totals**	11,484.00	9,900.00	5,844.00

For Privacy Act and Paperwork Reduction Act Notice, see separate instructions.   Cat. No. 60703Q   Form **1095-A** (2020)

Self-Study Problem 7.4

Form **8962**

Department of the Treasury
Internal Revenue Service

Premium Tax Credit (PTC)

▶ Attach to Form 1040, 1040-SR, or 1040-NR.
▶ Go to *www.irs.gov/Form8962* for instructions and the latest information.

OMB No. 1545-0074

20**20**

Attachment
Sequence No. **73**

Name shown on your return

Your social security number

You cannot take the PTC if your filing status is married filing separately unless you qualify for an exception. See instructions. If you qualify, check the box . . ▶ ☐

Part I   Annual and Monthly Contribution Amount

1	Tax family size. Enter your tax family size. See instructions	**1**
2a	Modified AGI. Enter your modified AGI. See instructions	**2a**
b	Enter the total of your dependents' modified AGI. See instructions	**2b**
3	Household income. Add the amounts on lines 2a and 2b. See instructions	**3**
4	Federal poverty line. Enter the federal poverty line amount from Table 1-1, 1-2, or 1-3. See instructions. Check the appropriate box for the federal poverty table used. **a** ☐ Alaska **b** ☐ Hawaii **c** ☐ Other 48 states and DC	**4**
5	Household income as a percentage of federal poverty line (see instructions)	**5** %
6	Did you enter 401% on line 5? (See instructions if you entered less than 100%.)	

☐ **No.** Continue to line 7.

☐ **Yes.** You are not eligible to take the PTC. If advance payment of the PTC was made, see the instructions for how to report your excess advance PTC repayment amount.

7	Applicable figure. Using your line 5 percentage, locate your "applicable figure" on the table in the instructions . .	**7**
8a	Annual contribution amount. Multiply line 3 by line 7. Round to nearest whole dollar amount **8a**	**b** Monthly contribution amount. Divide line 8a by 12. Round to nearest whole dollar amount **8b**

Part II   Premium Tax Credit Claim and Reconciliation of Advance Payment of Premium Tax Credit

9   Are you allocating policy amounts with another taxpayer or do you want to use the alternative calculation for year of marriage? See instructions.

☐ **Yes.** Skip to Part IV, Allocation of Policy Amounts, or Part V, Alternative Calculation for Year of Marriage.   ☐ **No.** Continue to line 10.

10   See the instructions to determine if you can use line 11 or must complete lines 12 through 23.

☐ **Yes.** Continue to line 11. Compute your annual PTC. Then skip lines 12–23 and continue to line 24.   ☐ **No.** Continue to lines 12–23. Compute your monthly PTC and continue to line 24.

Annual Calculation	(a) Annual enrollment premiums (Form(s) 1095-A, line 33A)	(b) Annual applicable SLCSP premium (Form(s) 1095-A, line 33B)	(c) Annual contribution amount (line 8a)	(d) Annual maximum premium assistance (subtract (c) from (b); if zero or less, enter -0-)	(e) Annual premium tax credit allowed (smaller of (a) or (d))	(f) Annual advance payment of PTC (Form(s) 1095-A, line 33C)
11 Annual Totals						

Monthly Calculation	(a) Monthly enrollment premiums (Form(s) 1095-A, lines 21–32, column A)	(b) Monthly applicable SLCSP premium (Form(s) 1095-A, lines 21–32, column B)	(c) Monthly contribution amount (amount from line 8b or alternative marriage monthly calculation)	(d) Monthly maximum premium assistance (subtract (c) from (b); if zero or less, enter -0-)	(e) Monthly premium tax credit allowed (smaller of (a) or (d))	(f) Monthly advance payment of PTC (Form(s) 1095-A, lines 21–32, column C)
12 January						
13 February						
14 March						
15 April						
16 May						
17 June						
18 July						
19 August						
20 September						
21 October						
22 November						
23 December						

24	Total premium tax credit. Enter the amount from line 11(e) or add lines 12(e) through 23(e) and enter the total here	**24**
25	Advance payment of PTC. Enter the amount from line 11(f) or add lines 12(f) through 23(f) and enter the total here	**25**
26	Net premium tax credit. If line 24 is greater than line 25, subtract line 25 from line 24. Enter the difference here and on Schedule 3 (Form 1040), line 8. If line 24 equals line 25, enter -0-. Stop here. If line 25 is greater than line 24, leave this line blank and continue to line 27	**26**

Part III   Repayment of Excess Advance Payment of the Premium Tax Credit

27	Excess advance payment of PTC. If line 25 is greater than line 24, subtract line 24 from line 25. Enter the difference here	**27**
28	Repayment limitation (see instructions)	**28**
29	Excess advance premium tax credit repayment. Enter the smaller of line 27 or line 28 here and on Schedule 2 (Form 1040), line 2	**29**

For Paperwork Reduction Act Notice, see your tax return instructions.   Cat. No. 37784Z   Form **8962** (2020)

DRAFT AS OF August 19, 2020 DO NOT FILE

Form 1095-A reports the taxpayer's actual premiums paid, the cost of the silver plan, and any advance credits received during the year from the exchange on which they purchased the insurance.

Self-Study Problem 7.4   *See Appendix E for Solutions to Self-Study Problems*

Marco and Tracy Brigantine live in California, are married filing jointly, under age 65, and have three children ages 14, 16, and 26. However, the oldest child is not claimed as a dependent and does not live at home. Tracy's adjusted gross income is $44,040 and Marco's is $22,000 and both are self-employed. They also have $2,000 in interest income from tax-exempt bonds. The Brigantines are enrolled in health insurance for all of 2020 through their state exchange and elected to have the credit paid in advance. Using the Brigantine's 2020 Form 1095-A on Page 7-24, complete the Form 8962 on Page 7-25 to determine the following:

1. The actual premium tax credit (Line 24).

2. The net premium tax credit to be claimed on the return, if any (Line 26) or the excess advance payment, if any (Line 27).

3. The repayment amount required, if any (line 29).

7-5 EDUCATION TAX CREDITS

7.5 Learning Objective

Apply the special rules applicable to the American Opportunity tax credit and lifetime learning credit.

The tax law contains a number of provisions that are intended to reduce the cost of education for taxpayers. Educational credits represent the last of these provisions covered in this textbook:

Educational Tax Benefit	Learning Objective
Exclusion from gross income for scholarships	2.12
Employer-provided education assistance plans	2.5
Tuition reduction for school employees	2.5
Deduction of business educational expenses	3.6
Student loan interest deduction	5.8
Qualified tuition programs (529 plans)	2.14
Coverdell educational savings accounts	2.14
Tuition deduction	2.14
American Opportunity tax credit	7.5
Lifetime learning credit	7.5

7-5a American Opportunity Tax Credit

The American Opportunity tax credit (AOTC) is an education credit available to help qualifying low-income and middle-income individuals defray the cost of higher education.

The AOTC is a credit for students in their first 4 years of postsecondary education. The AOTC may be claimed for the expenses of students pursuing bachelor's or associate's degrees or vocational training. To be eligible, the student must meet all of the following:

- Pursuing a degree or recognized credential,
- Enrolled at least half-time for one semester, quarter, trimester, etc. starting during the tax year,
- Received a Form 1098-T from the eligible education institution,
- Not have completed the first four years of higher education at the start of the tax year,
- The AOTC has not been claimed for more than four years, and
- Has not been convicted of a felony drug conviction.

Meeting either of the following criteria precludes claiming the AOTC:

- Married filing separate status, or
- Taxpayer is listed as a dependent on another's return.

EXAMPLE Alice is a single parent filing as head of household. Alice has been taking nursing classes at night to help her improve her job performance at the hospital. Alice has a 19-year-old daughter, Melanie, who is a second year full-time student at Wake Tech Community College pursing her associate degree in accounting. She might go on to pursue a four-year degree at some later date. Alice claims Melanie as a dependent but Melanie files her own tax return to report the income she earns from her part-time job. Alice claimed the AOTC for Melanie last year. As Melanie is enrolled in school at least half-time, is pursuing a degree, and has not claimed the AOTC for more than 4 years, she is an eligible student for the AOTC. Although Alice's school expense does not qualify for the AOTC, since she is not pursuing a degree or certification, she may qualify for the lifetime learning credit (LLC) discussed below. ♦

Like many other education tax benefits, the AOTC depends on an accurate computation of "qualified higher education expenses." The table below shows how qualified educational expenses can differ across some of the common education benefits:

Qualifying expenses for the AOTC can be paid on behalf of the taxpayer, his or her spouse, or dependents. As noted previously, expenses paid for room and board, nonacademic fees or for expenses that are not related to the student's course of instruction, do not qualify. Also, expenses for courses that involve sports, games, and hobbies do not qualify for the credit unless the course is part of a degree program. Expenses paid from a gift or inheritance (which is tax-free) do qualify for credits.

Qualified Educational Expenses

Cost	Scholarship	AOTC	LLC	Student Loan Interest	Coverdell	QTP (529 Plan)	Employer Provided Education Assistance Plan	Business Deduction for Work-related Education
Tuition and enrollment fees	X	X	X	X	X	X	X	X
Course-related Books	X	X	X[a]	X	X	X	X	X
Course-related supplies and equipment	X	X	X[a]	X	X	X	X	X
Room and board				X	X	X		
Transportation				X				X
Certain K-12 education costs					X	X		
Student loan payments (2020 only)						X	X	
Other necessary expenses including special needs services				X	X	X		X

[a] Only if required to be paid to educational institution

EXAMPLE Trinity's grandmother paid her $4,000 tuition directly to the university. Assuming Trinity meets the qualifying requirements for the AOTC otherwise, Trinity's parents may include the $4,000 as a qualifying expense when calculating the AOTC. ♦

Qualifying expenses must be reduced by any tax-free scholarships, grants or other education assistance. Taxpayers claiming the AOTC must have received a Form 1098-T (shown below) and must report the employer identification number of the educational institution on Form 8863.

☐ CORRECTED		
FILER'S name, street address, city or town, state or province, country, ZIP or foreign postal code, and telephone number	**1** Payments received for qualified tuition and related expenses $	OMB No. 1545-1574 **2020** Form **1098-T**
	2	**Tuition Statement**
FILER'S employer identification no.	STUDENT'S TIN	**3**
STUDENT'S name	**4** Adjustments made for a prior year $	**5** Scholarships or grants $
Street address (including apt. no.)	**6** Adjustments to scholarships or grants for a prior year $	**7** Checked if the amount in box 1 includes amounts for an academic period beginning January–March 2021 ☐
City or town, state or province, country, and ZIP or foreign postal code		
Service Provider/Acct. No. (see instr.)	**8** Check if at least half-time student ☐	**9** Checked if a graduate student ☐ **10** Ins. contract reimb./refund $

Copy B
For Student

This is important tax information and is being furnished to the IRS. This form must be used to complete Form 8863 to claim education credits. Give it to the tax preparer or use it to prepare the tax return.

Form **1098-T**   (keep for your records)   www.irs.gov/Form1098T   Department of the Treasury - Internal Revenue Service

EXAMPLE Alice's daughter Melanie is an eligible student for the AOTC. Melanie received a 2020 Form 1098-T from Wake Tech that reported $4,000 in Box 1 and $1,000 in Box 5. Additionally, Alice paid $400 for course-related books and materials related to Melanie's school in 2020. Qualified education expenses for the AOTC are $3,400 ($4,000 of tuition and fees less $1,000 of tax-free scholarships plus $400 for books). ♦

The AOTC is calculated as 100 percent of the first $2,000 of qualified expenses paid, and 25 percent of the next $2,000, for a maximum annual credit of $2,500 per student. For 2020, the AOTC is phased out ratably for joint return filers with income between $160,000 and $180,000 and for single, head of household, or qualifying widow(er) filers with income between $80,000 and $90,000 (these amounts are not adjusted for inflation). The AOTC is 40 percent refundable, so up to $1,000 (40 percent of $2,500) may be refunded to the taxpayer if the credit exceeds the taxpayer's tax liability.

Many college students earn income and provide some of their own support. As a result, many parents of college-age students start to consider the consequences of claiming a child as a dependent versus allowing the child to claim themselves as a dependent on the student's own tax return (of course, the support test and others discussed in Chapter 1 generally dictate whether a full-time college student can be claimed by their parents). In order to prevent abuse of the AOTC by students attempting to maximize the credit by filing their own tax return, there are special rules related to the refundable portion of the AOTC. If a student under the age of 24, with at least one parent still living, is filing his or her own tax return (is not a joint return), and any of the following apply, they may not claim the refundable portion of the AOTC:

- Under age 18 at end of 2020, or
- At age 18 and earned income is less than one-half of support, or
- Over age 18 and a full-time student and earned income is less than one-half of support

EXAMPLE Vance Wilder is a single, 20-year-old full-time student at Harrison College. Vance earned $11,000 from his part-time accounting job and in 2020, provided over one-half of his own support. As a result, his parents no longer claim him as a dependent. Although Vance has a living parent and is not filing a joint return, because he is over age 18 and a full-time student whose earned income is over one-half of his support, he is eligible for the refundable portion of the AOTC. ♦

EXAMPLE   Jenny graduates from high school in June 2020. In the fall, she enrolls for twelve units at Gwinett University. Gwinett University considers students who take twelve or more units to be full-time students. Jenny's father pays her tuition and fees of $2,300. The American Opportunity tax credit for Jenny is $2,075 [(100% × $2,000) + (25% × $300)]. ♦

EXAMPLE   Jason, a single father, has AGI of $85,000 in 2020. In 2020, he pays $5,000 in qualified tuition for his son, who just started at Alamance University. Without any limitations, Jason would be entitled to a maximum American Opportunity tax credit of $2,500. However, after applying the AGI limitations, Jason's American Opportunity tax credit is reduced by $1,250 ($2,500 × ($90,000 − $85,000)/$10,000), resulting in a credit of $1,250. ♦

Qualifying expenses must be paid during the tax year for education during an academic year beginning within that tax year. If tuition expenses are paid during the tax year for an academic period beginning during the first 3 months of the following tax year, the expenses may be claimed during the payment year.

Similar to the child tax credit rules, a taxpayer identification number (Social Security number or individual tax identification number) is required for each AOTC qualifying student by the due date of the return (including extensions).

If the IRS rejects an AOTC for any reason other than a math or clerical error, the taxpayer must complete Form 8862 used for claiming an earned income credit in a year after a rejection.

In addition, a taxpayer who erroneously claims the AOTC due to reckless or intentional disregard of rules or regulations is ineligible to claim the credit for a period of two tax years. If the IRS determines the claim for the credit was fraudulent, the ineligibility window is extended to ten years.

Unlike the child tax credit and EIC, no time restriction was placed on the IRS issuing refunds for any tax returns that claim an AOTC.

Form 8867, a due diligence checklist for tax preparers previously required for only the earned income credit, has been expanded to include steps to be taken for returns that include a child tax credit or the AOTC. Failure to file Form 8867 could result in a $540 penalty.

7-5b Lifetime Learning Credit

Taxpayers can elect a nonrefundable tax credit of 20 percent of qualified expenses of up to $10,000 in 2020, for a maximum credit of $2,000. The lifetime learning credit is available for qualified expenses paid for education of the taxpayer, his or her spouse, and dependents. The credit is available for undergraduate, graduate, or professional courses at eligible educational institutions. The student can be enrolled in just one course and still get the credit. There is no limit on the number of years a taxpayer can claim the credit. The credit is not subject to felony drug offense restrictions. The purpose of this credit is to encourage taxpayers to take courses at eligible institutions to acquire or improve job skills.

EXAMPLE   In September 2020, Scott pays $1,200 to take a course to improve his job skills to qualify for a new position at work. His lifetime learning credit for 2020 is $240 (20% × $1,200). ♦

The lifetime learning credit is phased out at different levels than the American Opportunity tax credit. Married taxpayers with income between $118,000 and $138,000, and single, head of household, or qualifying widow(er) taxpayers with income between $59,000 and $69,000, must phase the credit out evenly over the phase-out range for 2020.

EXAMPLE   During 2020, Jason, a single father with AGI of $85,000, paid $2,500 of tuition for a master's degree program in fine arts which he has been attending with the hope of eventually becoming a writer. Without any limitations, Jason would be entitled to a maximum lifetime learning credit of

$500 (20% × $2,500). However, due to the income phase-out ranges for the lifetime learning credit, none of the credit may be claimed on his tax return. ◆

7-5c Using Both Credits

Taxpayers cannot take both the American Opportunity tax credit and the lifetime learning credit for the same student in the same tax year. An American Opportunity tax credit can be claimed for one or more students, and the lifetime learning credit can be claimed for other students in the same tax year. Also, the choice in one year does not bind the taxpayer for future years. For example, a taxpayer can claim the American Opportunity tax credit for a student in one tax year and take the lifetime learning credit for the same student the following year. Taxpayers should claim the credit or combination of credits that provides the best tax benefit. Both the AOTC and the lifetime learning credit are claimed using Form 8863 (see Pages 7-32 and 7-33).

Education credits are input under Credits/Education Tuition (1098-T). The typical starting point would be to enter the information from the student's 1098-T.

ProConnect™ Tax

TIP

Self-Study Problem 7.5   *See Appendix E for Solutions to Self-Study Problems*

a. Judy Estudiante graduates from high school in June 2020. In the fall, she enrolls for twelve units in Southwest University and receives the following Form 1098-T.

☐ CORRECTED		
FILER'S name, street address, city or town, state or province, country, ZIP or foreign postal code, and telephone number Southwest University 1234 Cleveland Avenue El Paso, TX 79925	**1** Payments received for qualified tuition and related expenses $ 5,923.00 **2**	OMB No. 1545-1574 20**20** Form **1098-T**	Tuition Statement
FILER'S employer identification no. 12-7652311	STUDENT'S TIN 434-11-7812	**3**	Copy B For Student
STUDENT'S name Judy Estudiante		**4** Adjustments made for a prior year $	**5** Scholarships or grants $	This is important tax information and is being furnished to the IRS. This form must be used to complete Form 8863 to claim education credits. Give it to the tax preparer or use it to prepare the tax return.
Street address (including apt. no.) 12 Fannin Street		**6** Adjustments to scholarships or grants for a prior year $	**7** Checked if the amount in box 1 includes amounts for an academic period beginning January–March 2021 ☐
City or town, state or province, country, and ZIP or foreign postal code Van Horn, TX 79855			
Service Provider/Acct. No. (see instr.)	**8** Check if at least half-time student ☐	**9** Checked if a graduate student ☐	**10** Ins. contract reimb./refund $
Form **1098-T**	(keep for your records)	www.irs.gov/Form1098T	Department of the Treasury - Internal Revenue Service

Judy's parents, Santiago and Sophia Estudiante, pay her tuition and fees, have AGI of $170,000, have pre-credit tax liability of over $20,000, are claiming no other tax credits, and claim Judy as a dependent. Judy has never been arrested or convicted of any crimes. Complete Form 8863 on Pages 7-32 and 7-33 to determine what is the refundable and nonrefundable American Opportunity tax credit Judy's parents can claim for Judy if they file a joint return.

Refundable American Opportunity tax credit $_____

Nonrefundable American Opportunity tax credit $_____

b. In September 2020, Gene pays $5,200 to take a course to improve his job skills at work. Gene's AGI is $35,000 for 2020. What is Gene's lifetime learning credit for 2020?

$_____

Self-Study Problem 7.5a

Form 8863

Department of the Treasury
Internal Revenue Service (99)

Education Credits
(American Opportunity and Lifetime Learning Credits)
▶ Attach to Form 1040 or 1040-SR.
▶ Go to *www.irs.gov/Form8863* for instructions and the latest information.

OMB No. 1545-0074

2020

Attachment
Sequence No. **50**

Name(s) shown on return

Your social security number

⚠ **CAUTION**

Complete a separate Part III on page 2 for each student for whom you're claiming either credit before you complete Parts I and II.

Part I	**Refundable American Opportunity Credit**		
1	After completing Part III for each student, enter the total of all amounts from all Parts III, line 30	1	
2	Enter: $180,000 if married filing jointly; $90,000 if single, head of household, or qualifying widow(er)	2	
3	Enter the amount from Form 1040 or 1040-SR, line 11. If you're filing Form 2555 or 4563, or you're excluding income from Puerto Rico, see Pub. 970 for the amount to enter	3	
4	Subtract line 3 from line 2. If zero or less, **stop**; you can't take any education credit	4	
5	Enter: $20,000 if married filing jointly; $10,000 if single, head of household, or qualifying widow(er)	5	
6	If line 4 is: • Equal to or more than line 5, enter 1.000 on line 6 • Less than line 5, divide line 4 by line 5. Enter the result as a decimal (rounded to at least three places)	6	.
7	Multiply line 1 by line 6. **Caution:** If you were under age 24 at the end of the year **and** meet the conditions described in the instructions, you **can't** take the refundable American opportunity credit; skip line 8, enter the amount from line 7 on line 9, and check this box ▶ ☐	7	
8	**Refundable American opportunity credit.** Multiply line 7 by 40% (0.40). Enter the amount here and on Form 1040 or 1040-SR, line 29. Then go to line 9 below.	8	

Part II	**Nonrefundable Education Credits**		
9	Subtract line 8 from line 7. Enter here and on line 2 of the Credit Limit Worksheet (see instructions)	9	
10	After completing Part III for each student, enter the total of all amounts from all Parts III, line 31. If zero, skip lines 11 through 17, enter -0- on line 18, and go to line 19	10	
11	Enter the smaller of line 10 or $10,000	11	
12	Multiply line 11 by 20% (0.20)	12	
13	Enter: $138,000 if married filing jointly; $69,000 if single, head of household, or qualifying widow(er)	13	
14	Enter the amount from Form 1040, line 11. If you're filing Form 2555 or 4563, or you're excluding income from Puerto Rico, see Pub. 970 for the amount to enter	14	
15	Subtract line 14 from line 13. If zero or less, skip lines 16 and 17, enter -0- on line 18, and go to line 19	15	
16	Enter: $20,000 if married filing jointly; $10,000 if single, head of household, or qualifying widow(er)	16	
17	If line 15 is: • Equal to or more than line 16, enter 1.000 on line 17 and go to line 18 • Less than line 16, divide line 15 by line 16. Enter the result as a decimal (rounded to at least three places)	17	.
18	Multiply line 12 by line 17. Enter here and on line 1 of the Credit Limit Worksheet (see instructions) ▶	18	
19	**Nonrefundable education credits.** Enter the amount from line 7 of the Credit Limit Worksheet (see instructions) here and on Schedule 3 (Form 1040), line 3	19	

For Paperwork Reduction Act Notice, see your tax return instructions.   Cat. No. 25379M   Form **8863** (2020)

DRAFT AS OF September 16, 2020 DO NOT FILE

Self-Study Problem 7.5a

Form 8863 (2020)

Page **2**

Name(s) shown on return

Your social security number

> ⚠️ **CAUTION** *Complete Part III for each student for whom you're claiming either the American opportunity credit or lifetime learning credit. Use additional copies of page 2 as needed for each student.*

Part III   Student and Educational Institution Information. See instructions.

20 Student name (as shown on page 1 of your tax return)

21 Student social security number (as shown on page 1 of your tax return)

22 Educational institution information (see instructions)

a. Name of first educational institution

b. Name of second educational institution (if any)

(1) Address. Number and street (or P.O. box). City, town or post office, state, and ZIP code. If a foreign address, see instructions.

(1) Address. Number and street (or P.O. box). City, town or post office, state, and ZIP code. If a foreign address, see instructions.

(2) Did the student receive Form 1098-T from this institution for 2020? ☐ Yes ☐ No

(2) Did the student receive Form 1098-T from this institution for 2020? ☐ Yes ☐ No

(3) Did the student receive Form 1098-T from this institution for 2019 with box 7 checked? ☐ Yes ☐ No

(3) Did the student receive Form 1098-T from this institution for 2019 with box 7 checked? ☐ Yes ☐ No

(4) Enter the institution's employer identification number (EIN) if you're claiming the American opportunity credit or if you checked "Yes" in **(2)** or **(3)**. You can get the EIN from Form 1098-T or from the institution.

—— —— - —— —— —— —— —— —— ——

(4) Enter the institution's employer identification number (EIN) if you're claiming the American opportunity credit or if you checked "Yes" in **(2)** or **(3)**. You can get the EIN from Form 1098-T or from the institution.

—— —— - —— —— —— —— —— —— ——

23 Has the Hope Scholarship Credit or American opportunity credit been claimed for this student for any 4 tax years before 2020?

☐ Yes — **Stop!** Go to line 31 for this student.   ☐ No — Go to line 24.

24 Was the student enrolled at least half-time for at least one academic period that began or is treated as having begun in 2020 at an eligible educational institution in a program leading towards a postsecondary degree, certificate, or other recognized postsecondary educational credential? See instructions.

☐ Yes — Go to line 25.   ☐ No — **Stop!** Go to line 31 for this student.

25 Did the student complete the first 4 years of postsecondary education before 2020? See instructions.

☐ Yes — **Stop!** Go to line 31 for this student.   ☐ No — Go to line 26.

26 Was the student convicted, before the end of 2020, of a felony for possession or distribution of a controlled substance?

☐ Yes — **Stop!** Go to line 31 for this student.   ☐ No — Complete lines 27 through 30 for this student.

> ⚠️ **CAUTION** *You **can't** take the American opportunity credit and the lifetime learning credit for the **same student** in the same year. If you complete lines 27 through 30 for this student, don't complete line 31.*

American Opportunity Credit

27 Adjusted qualified education expenses (see instructions). **Don't enter more than $4,000**	**27**	
28 Subtract $2,000 from line 27. If zero or less, enter -0-	**28**	
29 Multiply line 28 by 25% (0.25)	**29**	
30 If line 28 is zero, enter the amount from line 27. Otherwise, add $2,000 to the amount on line 29 and enter the result. Skip line 31. Include the total of all amounts from all Parts III, line 30, on Part I, line 1 .	**30**	

Lifetime Learning Credit

31 Adjusted qualified education expenses (see instructions). Include the total of all amounts from all Parts III, line 31, on Part II, line 10	**31**	

Form **8863** (2020)

7-6 FOREIGN EXCLUSION AND TAX CREDIT

Some of the most sweeping changes to the tax law under the TCJA are related to the taxation of international income but virtually all of these changes were directed at U.S. corporations; with little applying specifically to individuals. However, there are two main provisions related to U.S. taxation of international income that apply to individuals: (1) the foreign income exclusion and (2) the foreign tax credit.

7-6a Foreign Income Exclusion

Certain taxpayers working and living outside the U.S. are eligible to exclude a certain portion of their foreign income from taxable income under the foreign income exclusion. In addition, certain foreign housing can also be excluded or deducted. To qualify, the taxpayer must have a bona fide tax home outside the U.S. for a certain number of days. The exclusion limit in 2020 is $107,600.

EXAMPLE   John Adams, a single U.S. citizen, is an employee of a large multinational corporation and works at the company's Mexican subsidiary. He has established a bona fide tax home in Mexico. During the year, John spent 355 days in Mexico and 10 days vacationing in Hawaii. His employer paid him wages of $109,000 in 2020. John excludes $107,600 of his wages from U.S. taxable income. John will not be eligible to claim a foreign tax credit (see below) on the wages excluded. ♦

The foreign income exclusion is claimed on Form 2555. Use of the foreign income exclusion precludes the use of certain credits or deductions (for example, the EITC). In addition, a number of provisions that require the computation of modified taxable income require the foreign income exclusion to be added back (for example, the limits for a deduction for contributions to an IRA).

Employees and self-employed taxpayers that qualify for the foreign income exclusion are also eligible for a housing exclusion or deduction. The foreign housing exclusion is an additional exclusion designed to represent the incremental cost of housing in a foreign country above a base amount. The details are beyond the scope of this textbook.

7-6b Foreign Tax Credit

An individual will typically incur foreign taxes under two possible scenarios: (1) they have engaged in work outside the United States as either an employee or as self-employed individual (expats) or (2) as a result of foreign investments either directly or through an investment portfolio such as a mutual fund or exchange-traded fund. Although the tax treatment of expats is beyond the scope of this textbook, aside from the benefit available for many expats under the foreign income exclusions described above, an expat may use a foreign tax credit for foreign taxes paid to reduce their U.S. income tax liability. The same is true of an investor whose income is subject to foreign taxes. In both cases, the amount of the credit is limited to the U.S. tax that applies to that income.

EXAMPLE   Thomas Jefferson, a single U.S. citizen, works for his employer in France and he is not eligible to use the foreign income exclusion. In 2020, Thomas paid income taxes in France of $3,500 on his income of $50,000. This was his only income during the year (U.S. or otherwise). Thomas claims the standard deduction. Thomas' foreign-sourced income is $37,600 ($50,000 less standard deduction of $12,400). His U.S. income for purposes of the foreign tax credit limitation is also $37,600. Thomas calculates his U.S.

income tax liability before any credits as $4,318. His foreign tax credit limit in this case is:

$$\frac{\text{Net foreign income } \$37,600}{\text{Total taxable income } \$37,600} \times \text{U.S. tax liability } \$4,318 = \$4,318$$

Thomas' actual foreign taxes paid are $3,500; thus, his foreign tax credit is not limited and he is eligible for a $3,500 foreign tax credit. ◆

EXAMPLE   Alexander Hamilton held shares in the Federalist International Stock Fund, a mutual fund with extensive foreign holdings. Alexander's earnings of $2,300 from the fund and foreign taxes paid of $632 were reported to him on a Form 1099-DIV. This was Alexander's only portfolio income during the year. Alexander's taxable income was $75,950 and his tax liability before the credit was $12,505 including Alexander's U.S. tax liability associated with dividend income of $345. Alexander's limitation is calculated as

$$\frac{\text{Net foreign income } \$2,300}{\text{Total taxable income } \$75,950} \times \text{U.S. tax liability } \$12,505 = \$379$$

As a result, Alexander's foreign tax credit is limited to $379. The unused credit of $253 ($632 foreign taxes paid less $379 limitation) can be carried back one year or forward for up to 10 years. ◆

A number of simplifications were used in the above examples and the actual computation of the limit can be considerably more complex. Different rules apply to income earned in a U.S. possession. The foreign tax credit is typically claimed on Form 1116 and the rules are explained in the instructions to Form 1116.

A simplified foreign tax credit that does not require the completion of Form 1116 is available if you meet all of the following requirements:

1. All of the foreign-sourced gross income was "passive category income" (which includes most interest and dividends).
2. All the income and any foreign taxes paid on it were reported on a qualified payee statement such as a Form 1099-DIV, Form 1099-INT, Schedule K-1, or similar substitute statements.
3. Total creditable foreign taxes aren't more than $300 ($600, if married filing a joint return).

If the Form 1116 is not used, the foreign tax credit is entered directly on Schedule 3 of Form 1040, Line 1. The foreign tax credit is nonrefundable, and thus, limited to the pre-credit tax amount. Use of the simplified method precludes a carryback of any limited foreign tax credit but the unused credit can be carried forward up to 10 years.

As a reminder, this is just an overview of these areas which are, in most instances, extremely complex. Useful publications are IRS Publication 54, Form 1116 and instructions, and Form 2555 and instructions.

ProConnect™ Tax
TIP

One of the most common ways to pay foreign taxes is through an investment in a mutual fund that happens to hold some international investments and pays foreign taxes at the fund level. The foreign tax payments are generally reported on the taxpayer's Form 1099-DIV and are entered into ProConnect as part of recording the dividend income.

Self-Study Problem 7.6 *See Appendix E for Solutions to Self-Study Problems*

Benny Franklin receives a Form 1099-DIV from his investment manager that lists foreign taxes paid of $432 and Benny's foreign investment earnings of $1,500. Benny had no other investment earnings and his total taxable income for the year is $58,000. Benny's tax liability before any foreign taxes is $8,556. Calculate the amount of the foreign tax credit.

$_____

Learning Objective 7.7

Determine the proper use and calculation of the adoption credit.

7-7 ADOPTION EXPENSES

Taxpayers are allowed two tax breaks for adoption expenses. A tax credit is allowed for qualified adoption expenses paid by taxpayers, and an exclusion from W-2 income is allowed for qualified adoption expenses paid by taxpayers' employers.

7-7a Adoption Credit

Individuals are allowed a nonrefundable income tax credit for qualified adoption expenses (defined below). Form 8839 is used to calculate and report the adoption credit. The total expense that can be taken as a credit for all tax years with respect to an adoption of a child is $14,300 for 2020. The credit is the total amount for each adoption and is not an annual amount (i.e., there is only one $14,300 credit per adopted child). The amount of the credit allowable for any tax year is reduced for taxpayers with AGI over $214,520 and is fully phased out when AGI reaches $254,520. The amount of the credit is reduced (but not below zero) by a factor equal to the excess of the taxpayer's AGI over $214,520 divided by $40,000. In some cases, beyond the scope of this textbook, AGI must be modified prior to calculating the adoption credit phase-out. For additional information on calculating modified adjusted gross income (MAGI) with respect to the adoption credit, see the IRS website at **www.irs.gov**.

EXAMPLE   Ben and Beverly pay $5,000 of qualified adoption expenses in 2020 to adopt a qualified child. Their AGI is $217,520 for 2020, which causes an adoption credit reduction for 2020 of $375 [$5,000 × ($217,520 − $214,520)/$40,000)]. Thus, Ben and Beverly's allowable adoption credit for 2020 is $4,625 ($5,000 − $375). ♦

The credit is not refundable; however, the unused portion may be carried forward for 5 years. To claim the credit, married individuals must file jointly, and the taxpayer must include (if known) the name, age, and taxpayer identification number (TIN) of the child on the return.

7-7b Domestic Multiyear Adoptions

In the case of the adoption of an eligible child who is a U.S. citizen or resident of the United States at the time the adoption commenced, the credit for qualified adoption expenses is allowed for the tax year that follows the year during which the expenses are paid or incurred, unless the expenses are paid or incurred in the tax year the adoption becomes final. If the expenses are paid or incurred during the tax year in which the adoption becomes final, the credit is allowed for that year. The full $14,300 credit is allowed in special-needs adoptions regardless of the amount of qualified adoption expenses paid.

EXAMPLE   In connection with the adoption of an eligible child who is a U.S. citizen and is not a child with special needs, a taxpayer pays $6,000 of qualified adoption expenses in 2019 and $8,600 of qualified adoption expenses in 2020. The adoption is not finalized until 2021. The $6,000 of expenses paid or incurred in 2019 would be allowed in 2020, and $8,300 of the $8,600 paid or incurred in 2020 would be allowed in 2021. On the other hand, if the adoption were finalized in 2020, then $14,300 of qualified expenses would be allowed in 2020 (the maximum credit permitted as of 2020). ◆

7-7c Foreign Multiyear Adoptions

In the case of the adoption of a child who is *not* a U.S. citizen or resident of the United States, the credit for qualified adoption expenses is not available unless the adoption becomes final. Qualified adoption expenses paid or incurred before the tax year in which the adoption becomes final are taken into account for the credit as if the expenses were paid or incurred in the tax year in which the adoption becomes final. Therefore, the credit for qualified adoption expenses paid or incurred in the tax year in which the adoption becomes final, or in any earlier tax year, is allowed only in the tax year the adoption becomes final.

EXAMPLE   In 2018 and 2019, a taxpayer pays $3,000 and $6,000, respectively, of qualified adoption expenses in connection with the adoption of an eligible child who is not a U.S. citizen or resident of the United States. In 2020, the year the adoption becomes final, the taxpayer pays an additional $3,000 of qualified expenses. The taxpayer may claim a credit of $12,000 on his or her income tax return for 2020 (the year the adoption becomes final). Note: If a foreign adoption does not become final, no credit is allowed. ◆

7-7d Employer-Provided Adoption Assistance

An employee may exclude from W-2 earnings amounts paid or expenses incurred by his or her employer for qualified adoption expenses connected with the adoption of a child by the employee, if the amounts are furnished under an adoption assistance program. The total amount excludable per child is the same as the adoption credit amount ($14,300). The phase-out is calculated in the same manner as the phase-out for the adoption credit. An individual may claim both a credit and an exclusion in connection with the adoption of an eligible child, but may not claim both a credit and an exclusion for the same expense.

The following quotation is often attributed to Albert Einstein: "The hardest thing in the world to understand is the income tax."

Self-Study Problem 7.7   *See Appendix E for Solutions to Self-Study Problems*

James and Michael Bass finalized the adoption of their daughter Allison in October 2020, one month after her birth. Allison is a U.S. citizen and is not a child with special needs. Her Social Security number is 466-47-3311. In 2020, James and Michael paid $17,000 in qualified adoption expenses. In addition, Michael's employer paid $4,000 directly to an adoption agency as an employer-provided adoption benefit. The Bass' AGI for 2020 is $222,520 (assume adjusted gross income and modified adjusted gross income are the same for purposes of this problem). The Bass' tax liability is $27,343 and they are not using tax credits except the adoption credit. Use Form 8839 on Pages 7-39 and 7-40 to calculate the Bass' adoption credit and the amount of any employee adoption exclusion.

Learning Objective 7.8

Recognize the basic individual credits for energy efficiency.

7-8 ENERGY CREDITS

Over the past decade, the tax law has included a number of personal tax credits associated with energy-efficient products. These credits have been slowly expiring. By design, many tax credits are temporary additions to the tax law and are designed to create short-term or limited changes in taxpayer behavior as mentioned in Chapter 1. The current status of many of these credits is presented below:

Credit	IRC Section	Status
Electric vehicle credit	30D	Active
Nonbusiness energy property credit	25C	Expired 2017
Residential energy efficient property (REEP) credit	25D	Active
Qualified fuel cell motor vehicle credit	30B	Expires at end of 2020
Qualified alternative fuel vehicle refueling property	30C	Expires at end of 2020

Because credits are often retroactively extended, be sure and check **www.irs.gov** for any changes that may have occurred after we went to print.

Two of the remaining credits are discussed here.

7-8a Electric Vehicle Credits

Taxpayers are allowed a credit for the purchase of plug-in electric drive vehicles used for either business or personal purposes. The credit, which ranges between $2,500 and $7,500 for light-duty vehicles, varies depending on the weight of the vehicle and the kilowatt hour of battery capacity. The Hyundai Kona, Nissan Leaf, Honda Clarity, and numerous other new electric vehicles qualify for the full $7,500 credit. The credit phases out for each car manufacturer when they reach a total of 200,000 electric cars sold for use in the United States (e.g., Tesla and GM). More information on federal and state electric vehicle tax incentives may be found at **www.fueleconomy.gov.**

7-8b Credits for Residential Energy-Efficient Property (REEP Credit)

Taxpayers may claim a credit of 26 percent of the amount paid for qualified solar electric property (property which uses solar power to generate electricity in a home), qualified solar water-heating property, qualified fuel cell property, qualified small wind energy property, and qualified geothermal heat pump property. The REEP credit for all property types

Self-Study Problem 7.7

Form **8839**	**Qualified Adoption Expenses**	OMB No. 1545-0074
Department of the Treasury Internal Revenue Service (99)	▶ **Attach to Form 1040, 1040-SR, or 1040-NR.** ▶ **Go to *www.irs.gov/Form8839* for instructions and the latest information.**	**2020** Attachment Sequence No. **38**

Name(s) shown on return | Your social security number

Part I Information About Your Eligible Child or Children—You **must** complete this part. See instructions for details, including what to do if you need more space.

DRAFT AS OF July 27, 2020 DO NOT FILE

1	(a) Child's name First / Last	(b) Child's year of birth	Check if child was— (c) born **before 2003** and disabled	(d) a child with special needs	(e) a foreign child	(f) Child's identifying number	(g) Check if adoption became final in 2020 or earlier
Child 1			☐	☐	☐		☐
Child 2			☐	☐	☐		☐
Child 3			☐	☐	☐		☐

Caution: If the child was a foreign child, see **Special rules** in the instructions for line 1, column (e), before you complete Part II or Part III. If you received **employer-provided adoption benefits,** complete Part III on the back next.

Part II Adoption Credit

			Child 1	Child 2	Child 3	
2	Maximum adoption credit per child. Enter $14,300 (see instructions)	2				
3	Did you file Form 8839 for a prior year for the same child? ☐ **No.** Enter -0-. ☐ **Yes.** See instructions for the amount to enter.	3				
4	Subtract line 3 from line 2	4				
5	**Qualified adoption expenses** (see instructions) . . **Caution:** Your qualified adoption expenses may not be equal to the adoption expenses you paid in 2020.	5				
6	Enter the **smaller** of line 4 or line 5	6				
7	Enter modified adjusted gross income (see instructions)	7				
8	Is line 7 more than $214,520? ☐ **No.** Skip lines 8 and 9, and enter -0- on line 10. ☐ **Yes.** Subtract $214,520 from line 7	8				
9	Divide line 8 by $40,000. Enter the result as a decimal (rounded to at least three places). Do not enter more than 1.000	9	×	.		
10	Multiply each amount on line 6 by line 9	10				
11	Subtract line 10 from line 6	11				
12	Add the amounts on line 11					12
13	Credit carryforward, if any, from prior years. See your Adoption Credit Carryforward Worksheet in the 2019 Form 8839 instructions					13
14	Add lines 12 and 13					14
15	Enter the amount from line 5 of the Credit Limit Worksheet in the instructions					15
16	**Adoption Credit.** Enter the smaller of line 14 or line 15 here and on Schedule 3 (Form 1040), line 6. Check box **c** on that line and enter "**8839**" in the space next to box **c**. If line 15 is smaller than line 14, you may have a credit carryforward (see instructions)					16

For Paperwork Reduction Act Notice, see your tax return instructions.   Cat. No. 22843L   Form **8839** (2020)

Form 8839 (2020)   Page **2**

Part III	Employer-Provided Adoption Benefits		Child 1	Child 2	Child 3		

17 Maximum exclusion per child. Enter $14,300 (see instructions) **17**

18 Did you receive employer-provided adoption benefits for a prior year for the same child?
☐ **No.** Enter -0-.
☐ **Yes.** See instructions for the amount to enter. } **18**

19 Subtract line 18 from line 17 . . . . **19**

20 Employer-provided adoption benefits you received in 2020. This amount should be shown in box 12 of your 2020 Form(s) W-2 with code **T** **20**

21 Add the amounts on line 20 . . . . **21**

22 Enter the **smaller** of line 19 or line 20. But if the child was a child with special needs and the adoption became final in 2020, enter the amount from line 19 . **22**

23 Enter modified adjusted gross income (from the worksheet in the instructions) **23**

24 Is line 23 more than $214,520?
☐ **No.** Skip lines 24 and 25, and enter -0- on line 26.
☐ **Yes.** Subtract $214,520 from line 23 . . . . **24**

25 Divide line 24 by $40,000. Enter the result as a decimal (rounded to at least three places). Do not enter more than 1.000 . . . . **25** × .

26 Multiply each amount on line 22 by line 25 . . . . . **26**

27 **Excluded benefits.** Subtract line 26 from line 22 . . **27**

28 Add the amounts on line 27 . . . . **28**

29 **Taxable benefits.** Is line 28 more than line 21?
☐ **No.** Subtract line 28 from line 21. Also, include this amount, if more than zero, on line 1 of Form 1040 or 1040-SR or line 1a of Form 1040-NR. On the dotted line next to line 1 of Form 1040 or 1040-SR or line 1a of Form 1040-NR, enter "AB."
☐ **Yes.** Subtract line 21 from line 28. Enter the result as a negative number. Reduce the total you would enter on line 1 of Form 1040 or 1040-SR or line 1a of Form 1040-NR by the amount on Form 8839, line 29. Enter the result on line 1 of Form 1040 or 1040-SR or line 1a of Form 1040-NR. Enter "SNE" on the dotted line next to the entry line. } **29**

You may be able to claim the adoption credit in Part II on the front of this form if any of the following apply.

- You paid adoption expenses in 2019, those expenses were not fully reimbursed by your employer or otherwise, and the adoption was not final by the end of 2019.
- The total adoption expenses you paid in 2020 were not fully reimbursed by your employer or otherwise, and the adoption became final in 2020 or earlier.
- You adopted a child with special needs and the adoption became final in 2020.

Form **8839** (2020)

except for qualified solar electric and water heating had expired at the end of 2017 but was extended through 2022. The credit percentage is reduced to 22 percent for property placed in service starting in 2021.

The REEP credits described in the paragraph above may be claimed for both principal residences and vacation homes. No credit is allowed for installations used to heat swimming pools or hot tubs. The REEP credit is reported on Form 5695.

EXAMPLE In 2020, Mary buys $30,000 of solar electric property for her second (vacation) home. The equipment is not used to heat her swimming pool or hot tub. She may claim a credit of $7,800 ($30,000 × 26%) for 2020. ◆

Self-Study Problem 7.8 *See Appendix E for Solutions to Self-Study Problems*

Calculate the energy credit allowed for the following purchases:

a. Geoffrey purchases a Nissan Leaf in May of 2020.

Credit Allowed $_____

b. Betty purchases a solar system to heat her hot tub for $2,000 and a second, certified, energy-efficient solar system to heat her home for $10,000 in 2020.

Credit Allowed $_____

7-9 LOW-INCOME RETIREMENT PLAN CONTRIBUTION CREDIT

7.9 Learning Objective

Calculate the low-income Retirement Plan Contribution Credit.

Certain low-income taxpayers may claim a nonrefundable "Low-Income Retirement Plan Contribution Credit," also called the "Saver's Credit," to encourage them to participate in tax-saving retirement plans, including IRAs. The credit rate is 50 percent, 20 percent, or 10 percent depending on the taxpayer's filing status and adjusted gross income. The credit is a direct deduction from income taxes otherwise payable, and the cash saved may be used to make part of the contribution to the plan. Taxpayers receive up to a 50 percent credit for contribution amounts up to $2,000 ($4,000 married filing jointly) or a maximum credit of $1,000 ($2,000 for married filing jointly). The credit phases out for adjusted gross income over certain income limits, as shown below.

Filing Status/Adjusted Gross Income for 2020—Saver's Credit			
Amount of Credit	*Joint*	*Head of Household*	*Single/Others*
50% of first $2,000 ($4,000) deferred	$0 to $39,000	$0 to $29,250	$0 to $19,500
20% of first $2,000 ($4,000) deferred	$39,001 to $42,500	$29,251 to $31,875	$19,501 to $21,250
10% of first $2,000 ($4,000) deferred	$42,501 to $65,000	$31,876 to $48,750	$21,251 to $32,500

EXAMPLE In 2020, Teddy and Abby file a joint tax return with AGI of $29,000. Teddy contributes $1,500 to a Section 401(k) plan at work. Teddy and Abby are entitled to a $750 (50% × $1,500) Retirement Plan Contribution Credit. The credit is in addition to any deduction or exclusion allowed for the contribution. ◆

The Saver's Credit is claimed on Form 8880. Because the Saver's Credit is nonrefundable, the amount of the credit is limited to the income tax liability after reflecting any foreign tax credit, child and dependent care expense credit, educations credits, or credit for the elderly and disabled.

EXAMPLE   In 2020, Whitney and Melissa file a joint tax return that reflects AGI of $37,100, income tax liability before any credits of $1,233, and a lifetime learning credit of $240. If Whitney and Melissa contribute $2,100 to an IRA, their Saver's Credit is $993 calculated as the credit amount of $1,050 ($2,100 × 50%) limited to tax liability before the credit of $993 ($1,233 − $240). ♦

Self-Study Problem 7.9   *See Appendix E for Solutions to Self-Study Problems*

Steve and Robin Harrington are married filing jointly taxpayers, both 61 years of age and semi-retired. Robin earns wages of $32,000 as a part-time school librarian and Steve sharpens knives as a hobby and their 2020 AGI is $39,500. Their tax liability before any credit is $1,473. The Harringtons are not eligible for any other tax credits. Neither Harrington is active in any other income deferral plans. Because the Harringtons have limited financial needs, they also made an IRA contribution of $12,000 ($6,000 each) trying to get ready for retirement. Use the Form 8880 on Pages 7-43 and 7-44 to determine the Harrington's Saver's Credit.

TAX BREAK

Numerous tax credits may be claimed by taxpayers in addition to the tax credits discussed in this textbook. Several of the more common credits not covered here include:

- **The Elderly or Disabled Credit** provides relief for low-income taxpayers who are not receiving substantial tax-free retirement benefits.
- **The Disabled Access Credit** is 50 percent of eligible access expenditures up to a maximum credit of $5,000, and is meant to encourage small businesses to become more accessible to disabled individuals.
- **The General Business Credit** is made up of a number of credits which are bundled into one credit for carryback and carryforward purposes, including the credit for **rehabilitation expenditures**, the **low-income housing credit**, and the credit for **employer-provided child care.**
- **The Small Employer Health Insurance Credit** provides small employers a credit for health insurance paid on behalf of workers who are not owners and who meet certain criteria.
- **The Research Activities Credit** is an incremental credit of 20 percent of expenditures in excess of a base amount, and is intended to encourage high-tech and energy research.
- **The Work Opportunity Credit** is limited to 40 percent of the first $6,000 of wages paid to each eligible employee. The purpose is to encourage employment of individuals in certain specified disadvantaged groups and has been extended through December 31, 2020.

Credits have a greater tendency to expire after a few years than do other tax code provisions. Be sure and check on the latest status of available individual and business credits at **www.irs.gov/credits-deductions**.

Self-Study Problem 7.9

Form **8880**

Department of the Treasury
Internal Revenue Service

Credit for Qualified Retirement Savings Contributions

► Attach to Form 1040, 1040-SR, or 1040-NR.
► Go to *www.irs.gov/Form8880* for the latest information.

OMB No. 1545-0074

2020

Attachment
Sequence No. **54**

Name(s) shown on return

Your social security number

CAUTION

You **cannot** take this credit if **either** of the following applies.

• The amount on Form 1040, 1040-SR, or 1040-NR, line 11, is more than $32,500 ($48,750 if head of household; $65,000 if married filing jointly).

• The person(s) who made the qualified contribution or elective deferral **(a)** was born after January 1, 2003; **(b)** is claimed as a dependent on someone else's 2020 tax return; or **(c)** was a **student** (see instructions).

		(a) You	(b) Your spouse
1	Traditional and Roth IRA contributions, and ABLE account contributions by the designated beneficiary for 2020. **Do not** include rollover contributions **1**		
2	Elective deferrals to a 401(k) or other qualified employer plan, voluntary employee contributions, and 501(c)(18)(D) plan contributions for 2020 (see instructions) **2**		
3	Add lines 1 and 2 . . . . . . **3**		
4	Certain distributions received **after** 2017 and **before** the due date (including extensions) of your 2020 tax return (see instructions). If married filing jointly, include **both** spouses' amounts in **both** columns. See instructions for an exception . . . **4**		
5	Subtract line 4 from line 3. If zero or less, enter -0- **5**		
6	In each column, enter the **smaller** of line 5 or $2,000 . . . . **6**		
7	Add the amounts on line 6. If zero, **stop;** you can't take this credit **7**		
8	Enter the amount from Form 1040, 1040-SR, or 1040-NR, line 11* **8**		
9	Enter the applicable decimal amount from the table below.	**9** x 0.	

If line 8 is—		And your filing status is—		
Over—	But not over—	Married filing jointly	Head of household	Single, Married filing separately, or Qualifying widow(er)
		Enter on line 9—		
---	$19,500	0.5	0.5	0.5
$19,500	$21,250	0.5	0.5	0.2
$21,250	$29,250	0.5	0.5	0.1
$29,250	$31,875	0.5	0.2	0.1
$31,875	$32,500	0.5	0.1	0.1
$32,500	$39,000	0.5	0.1	0.0
$39,000	$42,500	0.2	0.1	0.0
$42,500	$48,750	0.1	0.1	0.0
$48,750	$65,000	0.1	0.0	0.0
$65,000	---	0.0	0.0	0.0

Note: If line 9 is zero, **stop;** you can't take this credit.

10	Multiply line 7 by line 9	**10**
11	Limitation based on tax liability. Enter the amount from the Credit Limit Worksheet in the instructions	**11**
12	**Credit for qualified retirement savings contributions.** Enter the **smaller** of line 10 or line 11 here and on Schedule 3 (Form 1040), line 4	**12**

* See Pub. 590-A for the amount to enter if you claim any exclusion or deduction for foreign earned income, foreign housing, or income from Puerto Rico or for bona fide residents of American Samoa.

For Paperwork Reduction Act Notice, see your tax return instructions. Cat. No. 33394D Form **8880** (2020)

Form 8880 (2020)

Page **2**

General Instructions

Section references are to the Internal Revenue Code.

Reminder

Contributions by a designated beneficiary to an Achieving a Better Life Experience (ABLE) account. A retirement savings contribution credit may be claimed for the amount of contributions you, as the designated beneficiary of an ABLE account, make before January 1, 2026, to the ABLE account. See Pub. 907, Tax Highlights for Persons With Disabilities, for more information.

Future Developments

For the latest information about developments related to Form 8880 and its instructions, such as legislation enacted after they were published, go to *www.irs.gov/Form8880*.

Purpose of Form

Use Form 8880 to figure the amount, if any, of your retirement savings contributions credit (also known as the saver's credit).

 This credit can be claimed in addition to any IRA deduction claimed on Schedule 1 (Form 1040), line 19.

Who Can Take This Credit

You may be able to take this credit if you, or your spouse if filing jointly, made (a) contributions (other than rollover contributions) to a traditional or Roth IRA; (b) elective deferrals to a 401(k), 403(b), governmental 457(b), SEP, SIMPLE, or to the federal Thrift Savings Plan (TSP); (c) voluntary employee contributions to a qualified retirement plan, as defined in section 4974(c) (including the federal TSP); (d) contributions to a 501(c)(18)(D) plan; or (e) contributions, as a designated beneficiary of an ABLE account, to the ABLE account, as defined in section 529A.

However, you can't take the credit if either of the following applies.

• The amount on Form 1040, 1040-SR, or 1040-NR, line 11, is more than $32,500 ($48,750 if head of household; $65,000 if married filing jointly).

• The person(s) who made the qualified contribution or elective deferral (a) was born after January 1, 2003; (b) is claimed as a dependent on someone else's 2020 tax return; or (c) was a student.

 You'll need to refigure the amount on Form 1040 or 1040-SR, line 11, if you're filing Form 2555 or Form 4563 or you're excluding income from Puerto Rico. See Pub. 590-A at www.irs.gov/Pub590A for details.

You were a student if during any part of 5 calendar months of 2020 you:

• Were enrolled as a full-time student at a school; or

• Took a full-time, on-farm training course given by a school or a state, county, or local government agency.

A school includes technical, trade, and mechanical schools. It doesn't include on-the-job training courses, correspondence schools, or schools offering courses only through the Internet.

Specific Instructions

Column (b)

Complete column (b) only if you're filing a joint return.

Line 2

Include on line 2 any of the following amounts.

• Elective deferrals (including designated Roth contributions under section 402A, if applicable) to a 401(k), 403(b), governmental 457(b), SEP, SIMPLE, or to the federal TSP.

• Voluntary employee contributions to a qualified retirement plan, as defined in section 4974(c) (including the federal TSP).

• Contributions to a 501(c)(18)(D) plan.

These amounts may be shown in box 12 of your Form(s) W-2 for 2020.

Note: Contributions designated under section 414(h)(2) are treated as employer contributions and, as such, they aren't voluntary contributions made by the employee. They don't qualify for the credit and shouldn't be included on line 2.

Line 4

Enter the total amount of distributions you, and your spouse if filing jointly, received after 2017 and before the due date of your 2020 return (including extensions) from any of the following types of plans.

• Traditional or Roth IRAs (including *my*RAs), or ABLE accounts.

• 401(k), 403(b), governmental 457(b), 501(c)(18)(D), SEP, SIMPLE, or to the federal TSP.

• Qualified retirement plans, as defined in section 4974(c).

Don't include any of the following.

• Distributions not taxable as the result of a rollover or a trustee-to-trustee transfer.

• Distributions that are taxable as the result of an in-plan rollover to your designated Roth account.

• Distributions from your eligible retirement plan (other than a Roth IRA) rolled over or converted to your Roth IRA.

• Loans from a qualified employer plan treated as a distribution.

• Distributions of excess contributions or deferrals (and income allocable to such contributions or deferrals).

• Distributions of contributions made to an IRA during a tax year and returned (with any income allocable to such contributions) on or before the due date (including extensions) for that tax year.

• Distributions of dividends paid on stock held by an employee stock ownership plan under section 404(k).

• Distributions from a military retirement plan (other than the federal TSP).

• Distributions from an inherited IRA by a nonspousal beneficiary.

If you're filing a joint return, include both spouses' amounts in both columns.

Exception. Don't include your spouse's distributions with yours when entering an amount on line 4 if you and your spouse didn't file a joint return for the year the distribution was received.

Example. You received a distribution of $5,000 from a qualified retirement plan in 2020. Your spouse received a distribution of $2,000 from a Roth IRA in 2018. You and your spouse file a joint return in 2020, but didn't file a joint return in 2018. You would include $5,000 in column (a) and $7,000 in column (b).

Line 7

Add the amounts from line 6, columns (a) and (b), and enter the total.

Line 11

Before you complete the following worksheet, figure the amount of any credit for the elderly or the disabled you're claiming on Schedule 3 (Form 1040), line 6. See Schedule R (Form 1040) to figure the credit.

Credit Limit Worksheet

Complete this worksheet to figure the amount to enter on line 11.

1. Enter the amount from Form 1040, 1040-SR, or 1040-NR, line 17 . . . . **1.** _____

2. Form 1040 or 1040-SR filers: Enter the total of your credits from Schedule 3, lines 1 through 3, and Schedule R, line 22.

   Form 1040-NR filers: Enter the total of your credits from Schedule 3, lines 1 through 3 . . **2.** _____

3. Subtract line 2 from line 1. Also enter this amount on Form 8880, line 11. But if zero or less, **stop; you can't take the credit—don't file this form** . **3.** _____

KEY TERMS

child tax credit, 7-2
nonrefundable child tax credit, 7-2
refundable additional child tax
    credit, 7-2
qualifying dependent credit, 7-2
earned income credit (EIC), 7-5
"negative" income tax, 7-5
child and dependent care credit, 7-17

Affordable Care Act (ACA), 7-21
premium tax credit, 7-21
federal poverty line (FPL), 7-21
American Opportunity tax
    credit, 7-27
qualified higher education
    expenses, 7-28
lifetime learning credit, 7-30

foreign income exclusion, 7-34
foreign tax credit, 7-34
adoption credit, 7-36
energy credit, 7-38
low-income Retirement Plan
    Contribution Credit, 7-41
Saver's Credit, 7-41

KEY POINTS

Learning Objectives	Key Points
LO 7.1: Calculate the child tax credit.	• Credits are a direct reduction in tax liability instead of a deduction from income. • The child tax credit is $2,000 per qualifying child. • All qualifying children must have a Social Security number at the time of filing. • The child tax credit begins phasing out when AGI reaches $400,000 for joint filers and $200,000 for all others. • The additional child tax credit is available to certain taxpayers whose child tax credit was limited by their tax liability. • The child tax credit also includes an "other dependent credit" of $500 for taxpayers with dependents that do not qualify for the child tax credit.
LO 7.2: Determine the earned income credit (EIC).	• The earned income credit (EIC) is available to qualifying individuals with earned income and AGI below certain levels and is meant to assist the working poor. • The EIC formula for calculating the credit is based on the AGI of the taxpayer and the number of qualifying children of the taxpayer. • To compute the credit, the taxpayer must fill out a worksheet calculating the credit from the tables based on earned income from wages, salaries, and self-employment income. • To be eligible for the credit with no qualifying children, a worker must be over 25 and under 65 years old and not be claimed as a dependent by another taxpayer.
LO 7.3: Compute the child and dependent care credit for an individual taxpayer.	• To be eligible for the child and dependent care credit, the dependent must either be under the age of 13 or be a dependent or spouse of any age who is incapable of self-care. • If a child's parents are divorced, the child need not be the dependent of the taxpayer claiming the credit, but the child must live with that parent more than he or she lives with the other parent. • The expenses that qualify for the credit include amounts paid to enable both the taxpayer and his or her spouse to be employed. • For taxpayers with AGI of less than $15,000, the child and dependent care credit is equal to 35 percent of qualified expenses. For taxpayers with AGI of $15,000 or more, the credit gradually decreases from 35 percent to 20 percent. • In determining the credit, the maximum amount of qualified expenses to which the applicable percentage is applied is $3,000 for one dependent and $6,000 for two or more dependents. • Full-time students with little or no income are deemed to have earned income of $250 per month for one dependent and $500 per month for two or more dependents for purposes of calculating this limitation.

LO 7.4: Calculate the premium tax credit available under the Affordable Care Act.	• Certain lower income taxpayers may be eligible for a premium tax credit to offset some or all of the cost of health care purchased through an exchange. • The premium tax credit can be received in advance or at the time the tax return is filed. • The advanced premium tax credit and the actual premium tax credit are reconciled at the time the tax return is prepared. Repayments may be limited.
LO 7.5: Apply the special rules applicable to the American Opportunity tax credit and lifetime learning credit.	• The partially refundable American Opportunity tax credit is 100 percent of the first $2,000 of tuition, fees, books, and course materials paid and 25 percent of the next $2,000, for a total maximum annual credit of $2,500 per student. • The American Opportunity tax credit is available for the first 4 years of postsecondary education. • Taxpayers can elect a nonrefundable lifetime learning credit of 20 percent of the first $10,000 in qualified expenses for education. • The American Opportunity tax credit is phased out for joint filers with income between $160,000 and $180,000 and for single and head of household filers with income between $80,000 and $90,000. The lifetime learning credit is phased out between $118,000 and $138,000 for joint filers, and between $59,000 and $69,000 for those single or head of household taxpayers. • Taxpayers cannot take both the American Opportunity tax credit and the lifetime learning credit for the same student in the same tax year.
LO 7.6: Compute the foreign income exclusion and tax credit.	• The foreign income exclusion amount for 2020 is $107,600. • U.S. taxpayers are allowed to claim a foreign tax credit on income earned in a foreign country and subject to income taxes in that country. • Generally, the foreign tax credit is equal to the amount of the taxes paid to foreign governments; however, there is an "overall" limitation on the amount of the credit, which is calculated as the ratio of net foreign income to U.S. taxable income multiplied by the U.S. tax liability. • Unused foreign tax credits may be carried back 1 year and forward 10 years to reduce any tax liability in those years.
LO 7.7: Determine the proper use and calculation of the adoption credit.	• Individuals are allowed an income tax credit for qualified adoption expenses. The maximum total expense that can be taken as a credit for all tax years with respect to an adoption of a child is $14,300 for 2020. • The maximum exclusion from income for benefits under an employer's adoption assistance program is $14,300. • These amounts are phased out if modified AGI is between $214,520 and $254,520.
LO 7.8: Recognize the basic individual credits for energy efficiency.	• A tax credit of up to $7,500 for the purchase of new plug-in electric drive vehicles is available. • Taxpayers may claim a 26 percent credit of the amount paid for qualified property such as solar electric property and solar water-heating property.
LO 7.9: Calculate the low-income Retirement Plan Contribution Credit.	• Certain low-income taxpayers may claim a nonrefundable low-income Retirement Plan Contribution. • Credit, also called the "Saver's Credit," to encourage them to participate in tax-saving retirement plans.

QUESTIONS and PROBLEMS

GROUP 1:
MULTIPLE CHOICE QUESTIONS

LO 7.1

1. Russ and Linda are married and file a joint tax return claiming their three children, ages 4, 7, and 18, as dependents. Their adjusted gross income for 2020 is $421,400. What is Russ and Linda's total child and other dependent tax credit for 2020?
   a. $2,000
   b. $3,400
   c. $3,700
   d. $4,500
   e. $6,000

LO 7.1

2. Jennifer is divorced and files a head of household tax return claiming her children, ages 4, 7, and 11, as dependents. Her adjusted gross income for 2020 is $81,200. What is Jennifer's total child tax credit for 2020?
   a. $500
   b. $2,500
   c. $3,700
   d. $4,500
   e. $6,000

LO 7.2

3. Assuming they all meet the income requirements, which of the following taxpayers qualify for the earned income credit in 2020?
   a. A married taxpayer who files a separate tax return and has a dependent child
   b. A single taxpayer who waited on tables for 3 months of the tax year and is claimed as a dependent by her mother
   c. A single taxpayer who is self-employed and has a dependent child
   d. a and c above
   e. None of the above qualify for the earned income credit

LO 7.3

4. Which of the following payments does *not* qualify as a child care expense for purposes of the child and dependent care credit?
   a. Payments to a day care center
   b. Payments to the taxpayer's sister (21 years old) for daytime babysitting
   c. Payments to a housekeeper who also babysits the child
   d. Payments to the taxpayer's dependent brother (16 years old) for daytime babysitting
   e. All of the above qualify for the child and dependent care credit

LO 7.4

5. Which of the following is *not* a requirement to receive the premium tax credit for health care?
   a. Health care through the employer is not available
   b. Health insurance is purchased through the state or federal exchange
   c. Income must be no greater than 200 percent of the federal poverty line
   d. The taxpayer cannot be claimed as a dependent

LO 7.4

6. For purposes of determining income eligibility for the premium tax credit, household AGI is
   a. AGI for the taxpayer and spouse
   b. AGI for the taxpayer, spouse, and any other household members required to file a tax return
   c. AGI for the taxpayer, spouse, and any other household members required to file a tax return plus any tax-exempt income
   d. AGI for the taxpayer, spouse, and any other household members required to file a tax return plus any tax-exempt income and untaxed Social Security benefits

LO 7.5

7. The American Opportunity tax credit is 100 percent of the first _____ of tuition and fees paid and 25 percent of the next _____.
   a. $600; $1,200
   b. $1,100; $550
   c. $2,000; $2,000
   d. $1,100; $5,500
   e. None of the above

LO 7.5

8. Jane graduates from high school in June 2020. In the fall, she enrolls for twelve units at Big State University. Big State University considers students who take twelve or more units to be full-time. Jane's father pays her tuition and fees of $2,500 for the fall semester and in December 2020 prepays $2,500 for the spring semester. In 2020, the American Opportunity tax credit for Jane's tuition and fees before any AGI limitation is:
   a. $5,000
   b. $2,500
   c. $2,200
   d. $2,000
   e. Some other amount

LO 7.5

9. Which of the following costs is *not* a qualified education expense for the American Opportunity tax credit?
   a. tuition
   b. student loan payments
   c. course-related books
   d. lab supplies required by the course

LO 7.5

10. In September 2020, Sam pays $1,100 to take a course to improve his job skills to qualify for a new position at work. Assuming there is no phase-out of the credit, his lifetime learning credit for 2020 is:
    a. $220
    b. $1,100
    c. $275
    d. $1,000
    e. None of the above

LO 7.5

11. In November 2020, Simon pays $1,000 to take a course to improve his job skills to qualify for a new position at work. Simon's employer reimbursed him for the cost of the course. For 2020, Simon's lifetime learning credit is:
    a. $200
    b. $500
    c. $1,000
    d. $2,500
    e. None of the above

LO 7.5

12. John, a single father, has AGI of $83,000 in 2020. During the year, he pays $4,000 in qualified tuition for his dependent son, who just started attending Small University. What is John's American Opportunity tax credit for 2020?
    a. $0
    b. $1,750
    c. $2,250
    d. $2,500
    e. $4,000

LO 7.5

13. Joan, a single mother, has AGI of $72,000 in 2020. In September 2020, she pays $5,000 in qualified tuition for her dependent son who just started at Big University. What is Joan's American Opportunity credit for 2020?
    a. $0
    b. $1,250
    c. $2,125
    d. $2,500
    e. Some other amount

LO 7.5

14. Becky, a college freshman, works part-time and pays $1,650 of her college tuition expenses. Although Becky files her own tax return, her parents claim her as a dependent on their tax return. Becky's parents file jointly and have AGI of $50,000. What is the amount of American Opportunity tax credit her parents can claim on their tax return for the tuition Becky paid?
    a. $0
    b. $413
    c. $1,600
    d. $1,650
    e. Some other amount

LO 7.6

15. Lucas, a single U.S. citizen, works in Denmark for MNC Corp during all of 2020. His MNC salary is $187,000. Lucas may exclude from his gross income wages of:
    a. $0
    b. $40,000
    c. $107,600
    d. $187,000

LO 7.6

16. Taxpayer L has income of $55,000 from Norway, which imposes a 40 percent income tax, and income of $45,000 from France, which imposes a 30 percent income tax. L has additional taxable income from U.S. sources of $200,000 and U.S. tax liability before credits of $105,000. What is the amount of the foreign tax credit?
    a. $16,500
    b. $35,000
    c. $35,500
    d. $100,000
    e. $45,000

LO 7.7

17. John and Joan pay $16,500 of qualified adoption expenses in 2020 to finalize the adoption of a qualified child. Their AGI is $197,000 for 2020. What is their adoption credit for 2020?
    a. $0
    b. $16,500
    c. $14,080
    d. $14,300

LO 7.7

18. In connection with the adoption of an eligible child who is a U.S. citizen and who is not a child with special needs, Sean pays $4,000 of qualified adoption expenses in 2019 and $3,000 of qualified adoption expenses in 2020. The adoption is finalized in 2020. There is no phase-out of the adoption credit. What are the adoption credits for both 2019 and 2020, respectively?
    a. $0; $7,000
    b. $4,000; $1,000
    c. $4,000; $3,000
    d. $7,000; $0

LO 7.7   19. If a taxpayer does not have enough tax liability to use all the available adoption credit, the unused portion may be carried forward for how many years?
   a. Two
   b. Three
   c. Five
   d. There is no carryforward

LO 7.8   20. Barbara purchased a new Honda Clarity electric vehicle in 2020 for $36,000. Her federal tax credit will be:
   a. $0
   b. $2,500
   c. $5,000
   d. $7,500
   e. $10,000

LO 7.9   21. Virginia and Richard are married taxpayers with adjusted gross income of $28,000 in 2020. If Virginia is able to make a $1,500 contribution to her IRA and Richard makes a $1,500 contribution to his IRA, what is the Saver's Credit Virginia and Richard will be eligible for?
   a. $0
   b. $1,500
   c. $2,000
   d. $3,000
   e. $4,000

GROUP 2: PROBLEMS

LO 7.1   1. Calculate the total child and other dependent credit for the following taxpayers. Please show your work.
   a. Jeremy is a single (head of household) father with $80,100 of AGI and has a dependent 8-year-old son:

   _____

   b. Jerry and Ann have $100,000 of AGI, file jointly, and claim two dependent preschool children:

   _____

   c. James and Apple have AGI of $430,300, file jointly, and claim three dependent children (ages 7, 10, and 19):

   _____

LO 7.2   2. How does the earned income credit (EIC) produce a "negative" income tax?

   _____
   _____
   _____

LO 7.2   3. List the 7 rules that all taxpayers must meet in order to claim the EIC.

   _____
   _____
   _____

LO 7.2   4. List the 4 rules that apply to taxpayers without a qualifying child in order to claim the EIC.

   _____
   _____

LO 7.2   5. List the 3 rules that apply to taxpayers with a qualifying child in order to claim the EIC.

   _____
   _____

LO 7.2

6. Diane is a single taxpayer who qualifies for the earned income credit. Diane has two qualifying children who are 3 and 5 years old. During 2020, Diane's wages are $18,900 and she receives dividend income of $900. Calculate Diane's earned income credit using the EIC table in Appendix B.

$_____

LO 7.2

7. Margaret and David Simmons are married and file a joint income tax return. They have two dependent children, Margo, 5 years old (Social Security number 316-31-4890), and Daniel, who was born during the year (Social Security number 316-31-7894). Margaret's wages are $3,000, and David has wages of $14,000. In addition, they receive interest income of $200 during the year. Margaret and David do not have any other items of income and do not have any deductions for adjusted gross income. Assuming the Simmons file Form 1040 for 2020, complete Schedule EIC and the Earned Income Credit Worksheet A, on Pages 7-55 and 7-56. (The EIC table is in Appendix B.)

LO 7.2

8. What is the maximum investment income a taxpayer is allowed to have and still be allowed to claim the earned income credit? Please speculate as to why there is an investment income limit in the tax law.

_____

_____

_____

LO 7.3

9. Calculate the amount of the child and dependent care credit allowed before any tax liability limitations or other credits for 2020 in each of the following cases, assuming the taxpayers had no income other than the stated amounts.
   a. William and Carla file a joint tax return. Carla earned $27,500 during the year, while William attended law school full-time for 9 months and earned no income. They paid $3,500 for the care of their 3-year-old child, Carl.

   $_____

   b. Raymond and Michele file a joint tax return. Raymond earned $13,000 during the year, while Michele earned $9,000 for the year from a part-time job. They paid $7,000 for the care of their two children under age 13.

   $_____

   c. Beth is a single taxpayer who has two dependent children under age 5. Beth earned $25,500 in wages during the year and paid $6,700 for the care of her children.

   $_____

LO 7.2
LO 7.3

10. Clarita is a single taxpayer with two dependent children, ages 10 and 12. Clarita pays $3,000 in qualified child care expenses during the year. If her adjusted gross income (all from wages) for the year is $20,200 and she takes the standard deduction, calculate Clarita's earned income credit and child and dependent care credit for 2020.

$_____

LO 7.3

11. Go to the IRS website (**www.irs.gov**) and redo Problem 10 above using the most recent Form 2441, Child and Dependent Care Expenses. Print out the *completed Form 2441*. Do not calculate the earned income credit here.

LO 7.3

12. Mary and John are married and have AGI of $100,000 and two young children. John doesn't work, and they pay $6,000 a year to day care providers so he can shop, clean, and read a little bit in peace. How much child and dependent care credit can Mary and John claim? Why?

LO 7.3

13. Martha has a 3-year-old child and pays $10,000 a year in day care costs. Her salary is $45,000. How much is her child and dependent care credit?

LO 7.3   14. Marty and Jean are married and have 4-year-old twins. Jean is going to school full-time for 9 months of the year, and Marty earns $45,000. The twins are in day care so Jean can go to school while Marty is at work. The cost of day care is $10,000. What is their child and dependent care credit? Please explain your calculation.

_____

_____

_____

LO 7.4   15. Susan and Stan Collins live in Iowa, are married and have two children ages 6 and 10. In 2020, Susan's income is $43,120 and Stan's is $12,000 and both are self-employed. They also have $500 in interest income from tax-exempt bonds. The Collins enrolled in health insurance for all of 2020 through their state exchange but did not elect to have the credit paid in advance. The 2020 Form 1095-A that the Collins received from the exchange lists the following information:

Annual premiums	$9,800
Annual premium for the designated silver plan in the state	$10,800

Compute the Collins' premium tax credit for 2020.

LO 7.4   16. Using the information in the previous question, assume that the Collins' Form 1095-A also indicated that the total advance payment of the premium tax credit was $9,200. Calculate the excess advance premium tax credit and the repayment amount for 2020.

LO 7.5   17. What is the reason there are education tax credits in the tax law?

_____

_____

_____

LO 7.5   18. Please explain the difference between the types of education covered by the American Opportunity tax credit and the lifetime learning credit.

_____

_____

_____

LO 7.5   19. Janie graduates from high school in 2020 and enrolls in college in the fall. Her parents pay $4,000 for her tuition and fees.
   a. Assuming Janie's parents have AGI of $172,000, what is the American Opportunity tax credit they can claim for Janie?

_____

_____

   b. Assuming Janie's parents have AGI of $75,000, what is the American Opportunity tax credit they can claim for Janie?

LO 7.5

20. Jasper is single and is a computer software consultant with a college degree. He feels that one of the reasons for his success is that he continually updates his knowledge by taking classes at the local college in various areas related to software design and information technology. This year he spent $2,000 on course tuition and fees.
    a. Assuming Jasper has AGI of $92,000, how much lifetime learning credit can Jasper claim on his tax return? Would the answer be different if Jasper were married and supporting a wife who was not working?

    _____

    _____

    _____

    b. Assuming Jasper has AGI of $45,000, how much lifetime learning credit can Jasper claim on his tax return?

    _____

    _____

    _____

LO 7.6

21. Martha and Lew are married taxpayers with $400 of foreign tax withholding from dividends in a mutual fund. They have enough foreign income from the mutual fund to claim the full $400 as a foreign tax credit. Their tax bracket is 24 percent and they itemize deductions. Should they claim the foreign tax credit or a deduction for foreign taxes on their Schedule A? Why?

    _____

    _____

    _____

LO 7.7

22. Carl and Jenny adopt a Korean orphan. The adoption takes 2 years and two trips to Korea and is finalized in 2020. They pay $7,000 in 2019 and $7,500 in 2020 for qualified adoption expenses. In 2020, Carl and Jenny have AGI of $150,000.
    a. What is the adoption credit Carl and Jenny can claim in 2020?
    $_____
    b. How much credit could they claim if the adoption falls through and is never finalized?

    _____

    c. How much credit could they claim if their AGI was $219,520?

    _____

LO 7.8

23. Mike bought a solar electric pump to heat his pool at a cost of $2,500 in 2020. What is Mike's credit?
    $_____

LO 7.8

24. In 2020, Jeff spends $6,000 on solar panels to heat water for his main home. What is Jeff's credit for his 2020 purchases?
    $_____

LO 7.9

25. George and Amal file a joint return in 2020 and have AGI of $38,200. They each make a $1,600 contribution to their respective IRAs. Assuming that they are not eligible for any other credits, what is the amount of their Saver's Credit?
    $_____

SCHEDULE EIC
(Form 1040)

Department of the Treasury
Internal Revenue Service (99)

Earned Income Credit
Qualifying Child Information

▶ **Complete and attach to Form 1040 or 1040-SR only if you have a qualifying child.**
▶ Go to *www.irs.gov/ScheduleEIC* for the latest information.

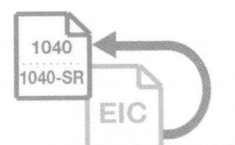

OMB No. 1545-0074

2020

Attachment
Sequence No. **43**

Name(s) shown on return | Your social security number

Before you begin:
- See the instructions for Form 1040 or 1040-SR, line 27, to make sure that **(a)** you can take the EIC, and **(b)** you have a qualifying child.
- Be sure the child's name on line 1 and social security number (SSN) on line 2 agree with the child's social security card. Otherwise, at the time we process your return, we may reduce or disallow your EIC. If the name or SSN on the child's social security card is not correct, call the Social Security Administration at 1-800-772-1213.

 CAUTION
- *You can't claim the EIC for a child who didn't live with you for more than half of the year.*
- *If you take the EIC even though you are not eligible, you may not be allowed to take the credit for up to 10 years. See the instructions for details.*
- *It will take us longer to process your return and issue your refund if you do not fill in all lines that apply for each qualifying child.*

Qualifying Child Information

	Child 1	Child 2	Child 3
1 Child's name If you have more than three qualifying children, you have to list only three to get the maximum credit.	First name Last name	First name Last name	First name Last name
2 Child's SSN The child must have an SSN as defined in the instructions for Form 1040 or 1040-SR, line 27, unless the child was born and died in 2020. If your child was born and died in 2020 and did not have an SSN, enter "Died" on this line and attach a copy of the child's birth certificate, death certificate, or hospital medical records showing a live birth.			
3 Child's year of birth	Year _____ *If born after 2001 **and** the child is younger than you (or your spouse, if filing jointly), skip lines 4a and 4b; go to line 5.*	Year _____ *If born after 2001 **and** the child is younger than you (or your spouse, if filing jointly), skip lines 4a and 4b; go to line 5.*	Year _____ *If born after 2001 **and** the child is younger than you (or your spouse, if filing jointly), skip lines 4a and 4b; go to line 5.*
4 a Was the child under age 24 at the end of 2020, a student, and younger than you (or your spouse, if filing jointly)?	☐ **Yes.** *Go to line 5.* ☐ **No.** *Go to line 4b.*	☐ **Yes.** *Go to line 5.* ☐ **No.** *Go to line 4b.*	☐ **Yes.** *Go to line 5.* ☐ **No.** *Go to line 4b.*
b Was the child permanently and totally disabled during any part of 2020?	☐ **Yes.** *Go to line 5.* ☐ **No.** The child is not a qualifying child.	☐ **Yes.** *Go to line 5.* ☐ **No.** The child is not a qualifying child.	☐ **Yes.** *Go to line 5.* ☐ **No.** The child is not a qualifying child.
5 Child's relationship to you (for example, son, daughter, grandchild, niece, nephew, eligible foster child, etc.)			
6 Number of months child lived with you in the United States during 2020 • If the child lived with you for more than half of 2020 but less than 7 months, enter "7." • If the child was born or died in 2020 and your home was the child's home for more than half the time he or she was alive during 2020, enter "12."	_____ months *Do not enter more than 12 months.*	_____ months *Do not enter more than 12 months.*	_____ months *Do not enter more than 12 months.*

For Paperwork Reduction Act Notice, see your tax return instructions.   Cat. No. 13339M   **Schedule EIC (Form 1040) 2020**

Worksheet **A**—2020 EIC—Line 27*

Keep for Your Records

Before you begin: √ Be sure you are using the correct worksheet. Use this worksheet only if you answered "No" to Step 5, question 2. Otherwise, use Worksheet B.

Part 1

All Filers Using Worksheet A

1. Enter your earned income from Step 5.   **1** ☐
   Wages, salaries

2. Look up the amount on line 1 above in the EIC Table (right after Worksheet B) to find the credit. Be sure you use the correct column for your filing status and the number of children you have. Enter the credit here.   **2** ☐

   If line 2 is zero, (STOP) You can't take the credit.
   Enter "No" on the dotted line next to Form 1040 or 1040-SR, line 27.

3. Enter the amount from Form 1040 or 1040-SR, line 11.   **3** ☐
   Adjusted gross income

4. Are the amounts on lines 3 and 1 the same?

   ☐ **Yes.** Skip line 5; enter the amount from line 2 on line 6.

   ☐ **No.** Go to line 5.

Part 2

Filers Who Answered "No" on Line 4

5. If you have:
   - No qualifying children, is the amount on line 3 less than $8,800 ($14,700 if married filing jointly)?
   - 1 or more qualifying children, is the amount on line 3 less than $19,350 ($25,250 if married filing jointly)?

   ☐ **Yes.** Leave line 5 blank; enter the amount from line 2 on line 6.

   ☐ **No.** Look up the amount on line 3 in the EIC Table to find the credit. Be sure you use the correct column for your filing status and the number of children you have. Enter the credit here.   **5** ☐
   Look at the amounts on lines 5 and 2.
   Then, enter the **smaller** amount on line 6.

Part 3

Your Earned Income Credit

6. **This is your earned income credit.**   **6** ☐

   Enter this amount on Form 1040 or 1040-SR, line 27.

   Reminder—

   √ If you have a qualifying child, complete and attach Schedule EIC.   [1040 or 1040-SR] [EIC] → [1040 or 1040-SR]

   ⚠ CAUTION *If your EIC for a year after 1996 was reduced or disallowed, see Form 8862, who must file, earlier, to find out if you must file Form 8862 to take the credit for 2020.*

---

*Download the latest version of this worksheet from the Form 1040 Instructions available at www.irs.gov. The 2020 worksheet was not available as we went to print. This worksheet is adapted from the 2019 version.

GROUP 3:
WRITING ASSIGNMENT

RESEARCH   Your supervisor has asked you to research the following situation concerning Scott and Heather Moore. Scott and Heather are married and file a joint return. Scott works full-time as a wildlife biologist, and Heather is a full-time student enrolled at Online University. Scott's earned income for the year is $36,000. Heather does not have a job and concentrates solely on her schoolwork. The university she is enrolled in offers courses only through the Internet. Scott and Heather have one child, Elizabeth (age 8), and pay $3,000 for child care expenses during the year.

Required: Go to the IRS website **(www.irs.gov)**. Locate and review Publication 503. Write a file memorandum stating the amount of child and dependent care credit that Scott and Heather Moore can claim. (An example of a file memorandum is available at the website for this textbook located at **www.cengage.com.)**

GROUP 4:
COMPREHENSIVE PROBLEMS

1. David and Darlene Jasper have one child, Sam, who is 6 years old (birthdate July 1, 2014). The Jaspers reside at 4639 Honeysuckle Lane, Los Angeles, CA 90248. David's Social Security number is 577-11-3311, Darlene's is 477-98-4731, and Sam's is 589-22-1142. David's birthdate is May 29, 1987 and Darlene's birthday is January 31, 1989. David and Darlene's earnings and withholdings for 2020 are:

David:	Earnings from Apple Company (office manager)	$26,750
	Federal income tax withheld	800
	State income tax withheld	1,050
Darlene:	Earnings from Rose Company (perfume tester)	$26,200
	Federal income tax withheld	1,050
	State income tax withheld	1,000

Their other income includes interest from Pine Tree Savings and Loan of $950. Other information and expenditures for 2020 are as follows:

Interest:	On home acquisition mortgage	$11,300
	Credit card	925
Taxes:	Property taxes on personal residence	1,300
	State income taxes paid in 2020 (for 2019)	300
Contribution (with written acknowledgement) to church		1,045
Medical insurance		675
Medical and dental expenses		6,175
Income tax return preparation fee paid in 2020		200
Actual general state sales tax for 2020		1,016
Payment of union dues		225
Contribution to David's IRA (no retirement plan at his work)		500

The Jaspers received a $2,900 EIP in 2020.

David and Darlene received the following letter from Sam's daycare provider:

KIDDIECARE INC.

10250 Santa Monica Blvd.
Los Angeles, CA 90067
EIN: 13-3345678

January 14, 2021

David and Darlene Jasper
4639 Honeysuckle Lane
Los Angeles, CA 90248

Dear David and Darlene,

Thank you for your patronage of our day care center with your child, Sam Jasper, in 2020. This statement serves as a record of the cost of daycare services we provided during calendar year 2020:

Child	Amount	Dates of Service
Sam Jasper	$3,680.00	1/1/2020 – 08/25/2020

Sincerely,

/s/ Marcia Clarke

Marcia Clarke
Director, KiddieCare Inc.

Required: Complete the Jaspers' federal tax return for 2020. Use Form 1040, Schedule 1, Schedule 3, Schedule A, Form 2441, and Form 8880, as needed. Make realistic assumptions about any missing data.

2A. Steve Jackson (birthdate December 13, 1967) is a single taxpayer living at 3215 Pacific Dr., Apt. B, Pacific Beach, CA 92109. His Social Security number is 465-88-9415. In 2020, Steve's earnings and income tax withholding as laundry attendant of a local hotel are:

Earnings from the Ocean View Hotel	$22,250
Federal income tax withheld	219
State income tax withheld	100

Steve has a daughter, Janet, from a previous marriage. Janet is 11 years old (Social Security number 654-12-6543). Steve provides all Janet's support. Also living with Steve is his younger brother, Reggie (Social Security number 667-21-8998). Reggie, age 47, is unable to care for himself due to a disability. On a reasonably regular basis, Steve has a care giver come to the house to help with Reggie. He uses a company called HomeAid, 456 La Jolla Dr., San Diego, CA 92182 (EIN 17-9876543). Steve made payments of $1,000 to HomeAid in 2020. Janet receives free after-school care provided by the local school district.

Steve made a modest cash donation to local charity in the amount of $50. Steve received a $1,700 EIP in 2020.

Required: Complete Steve's federal tax return for 2020. Use Form 1040, Schedule 3, Form 2441, Child Tax Credit Worksheet, Form 8812, EITC Worksheet A, and Schedule EIC.

2B. David Fleming is a single taxpayer living at 169 Trendie Street, Apartment 6B, La Jolla, CA 92037. His Social Security number is 865-68-9635 and his birthdate is September 18, 1975.

David was employed as a delivery person for a local pizza restaurant. David's W-2 showed the following:

a Employee's social security number 865-68-9635	OMB No. 1545-0008	Safe, accurate, FAST! Use IRS e~file	Visit the IRS website at www.irs.gov/efile
b Employer identification number (EIN) 23-4567321		**1** Wages, tips, other compensation 23,700.00	**2** Federal income tax withheld 1,280.00
c Employer's name, address, and ZIP code California Pizza Cafe 231 Foodie Street La Jolla, CA 92037		**3** Social security wages 23,700.00	**4** Social security tax withheld 1,469.40
		5 Medicare wages and tips 23,700.00	**6** Medicare tax withheld 343.65
		7 Social security tips	**8** Allocated tips
d Control number		**9**	**10** Dependent care benefits
e Employee's first name and initial Last name Suff. David Fleming 169 Trendie Street, Apt 6B La Jolla, CA 92037		**11** Nonqualified plans	**12a** See instructions for box 12
		13 Statutory employee ☐ Retirement plan ☐ Third-party sick pay ☐	**12b**
		14 Other	**12c**
			12d
f Employee's address and ZIP code			
15 State Employer's state ID number CA D4567221	**16** State wages, tips, etc. 23,700.00	**17** State income tax 370.00	**18** Local wages, tips, etc. **19** Local income tax **20** Locality name

Form **W-2** Wage and Tax Statement   **2020**   Department of the Treasury—Internal Revenue Service

Copy B—To Be Filed With Employee's FEDERAL Tax Return.
This information is being furnished to the Internal Revenue Service.

David's only other source of income during the year was a prize he won appearing on a game show. The game show sent David home with a Form 1099-MISC:

☐ CORRECTED (if checked)

PAYER'S name, street address, city or town, state or province, country, ZIP or foreign postal code, and telephone no. Price is Accurate Studios, Inc. Studio 44 Studio City, CA 91604	**1** Rents $	OMB No. 1545-0115 **2020** Form **1099-MISC** **Miscellaneous Income**
	2 Royalties $	
	3 Other income $ 10,000.00	**4** Federal income tax withheld $ 2,400.00 **Copy B For Recipient**
PAYER'S TIN 21-8675309	RECIPIENT'S TIN 865-68-9635	**5** Fishing boat proceeds $	**6** Medical and health care payments $
RECIPIENT'S name David Fleming	**7** Payer made direct sales of $5,000 or more of consumer products to a buyer (recipient) for resale ☐	**8** Substitute payments in lieu of dividends or interest $	This is important tax information and is being furnished to the IRS. If you are required to file a return, a negligence penalty or other sanction may be imposed on you if this income is taxable and the IRS determines that it has not been reported.
Street address (including apt. no.) 169 Trendie Street, #6B	**9** Crop insurance proceeds $	**10** Gross proceeds paid to an attorney $	
City or town, state or province, country, and ZIP or foreign postal code La Jolla, CA 92037	**11**	**12** Section 409A deferrals $	
Account number (see instructions) FATCA filing requirement ☐	**13** Excess golden parachute payments $	**14** Nonqualified deferred compensation $	
	15 State tax withheld $ 200.00 $	**16** State/Payer's state no.	**17** State income $ $

Form **1099-MISC**   (keep for your records)   www.irs.gov/Form1099MISC   Department of the Treasury - Internal Revenue Service

He has no other adjustments to income or deductible expenses except for a single cash payment of $500 to a charity after winning big at the game show and a $1,200 EIP received in 2020. Unfortunately, David's employer did not provide health care to its employees but David signed up for coverage through his state's health care exchange. The exchange sent him a Form 1095-A as shown on Page 7-61.

Required: Complete David's federal tax return for 2020. Use Form 1040, Schedule 1, Schedule 2, and Form 8962. Make realistic assumptions about any missing data.

GROUP 5:
CUMULATIVE SOFTWARE PROBLEM

1. The following information is available for the Albert and Allison Gaytor family in addition to that provided in Chapters 1–6.

The Gaytors paid tuition and fees for both Crocker and Cayman to attend college. Recall that Crocker is a freshman at Brickell State and Cayman is a part-time student in community college. Crocker received a $1,000 scholarship from Brickell State. Crocker's Form 1098-T is shown below. The Gaytors paid tuition and fees of $1,400 for Cayman in 2020.

☐ CORRECTED		

FILER'S name, street address, city or town, state or province, country, ZIP or foreign postal code, and telephone number Brickell State University 605 Crandon Blvd. Key Biscayne, FL 33149	**1** Payments received for qualified tuition and related expenses $ 4,800.00 **2**	OMB No. 1545-1574 20**20** Form **1098-T**	**Tuition Statement**
FILER'S employer identification no. 44-3421456	STUDENT'S TIN 261-55-1212	**3**	**Copy B** **For Student**
STUDENT'S name Crocker Gaytor		**4** Adjustments made for a prior year $	**5** Scholarships or grants $ 1,000.00	This is important tax information and is being furnished to the IRS. This form must be used to complete Form 8863 to claim education credits. Give it to the tax preparer or use it to prepare the tax return.
Street address (including apt. no.) 12340 Cocoshell Rd.		**6** Adjustments to scholarships or grants for a prior year	**7** Checked if the amount in box 1 includes amounts for an academic period beginning January–March 2021 ☐	
City or town, state or province, country, and ZIP or foreign postal code Coral Gables, FL 33134		$		
Service Provider/Acct. No. (see instr.)	**8** Check if at least half-time student ☒	**9** Checked if a graduate student ☐	**10** Ins. contract reimb./refund $	

Form **1098-T**   (keep for your records)   www.irs.gov/Form1098T   Department of the Treasury - Internal Revenue Service

In December 2019, Albert's 82 year-old aunt, Virginia Everglades (Social Security number 699-19-9000), was unable to support herself and moved in with the Gaytors. She lived with them for all of 2020. The Gaytors provided more than one-half of Aunt Virginia's support. Virginia's only source of income is a small annuity that paid her $3,100 in 2020. While Albert and Allison were working, the Gaytors hired a nanny service from time to time to take care of Aunt Virginia. The Gaytors paid $3,400 to Nannys R Us in 2020. Nannys R Us (EIN 34-1234123) is located at 80 SW 22nd Avenue, Miami, FL 33133.

Required: Combine this new information about the Gaytor family with the information from Chapters 1–6 and complete a revised 2020 tax return for Albert and Allison. Be sure to save your data input files since this case will be expanded and completed with more tax information in Chapter 8.

Form **1095-A**

Department of the Treasury
Internal Revenue Service

Health Insurance Marketplace Statement

▶ Do not attach to your tax return. Keep for your records.
▶ Go to *www.irs.gov/Form1095A* for instructions and the latest information.

☐ VOID

☐ CORRECTED

OMB No. 1545-2232

2020

Part I   **Recipient Information**

1 Marketplace identifier 31-9876543	**2** Marketplace-assigned policy number B1234TH	**3** Policy issuer's name Covered California

4 Recipient's name David Fleming	**5** Recipient's SSN 865-68-9635	**6** Recipient's date of birth 09/18/1975
7 Recipient's spouse's name	**8** Recipient's spouse's SSN	**9** Recipient's spouse's date of birth

10 Policy start date Jan 1, 2020	**11** Policy termination date Dec 31, 2020	**12** Street address (including apartment no.) 169 Trendie Street, Apt 6B
13 City or town La Jolla	**14** State or province CA	**15** Country and ZIP or foreign postal code 92037

Part II   **Covered Individuals**

	A. Covered individual name	**B.** Covered individual SSN	**C.** Covered individual date of birth	**D.** Coverage start date	**E.** Coverage termination date
16	David Fleming	865-68-9635	09/18/1975	01/01/2020	12/31/2020
17					
18					
19					
20					

Part III   **Coverage Information**

Month	**A.** Monthly enrollment premiums	**B.** Monthly second lowest cost silver plan (SLCSP) premium	**C.** Monthly advance payment of premium tax credit
21 January	311.00	341.00	147.00
22 February	311.00	341.00	147.00
23 March	311.00	341.00	147.00
24 April	311.00	341.00	147.00
25 May	311.00	341.00	147.00
26 June	311.00	341.00	147.00
27 July	311.00	341.00	147.00
28 August	311.00	341.00	147.00
29 September	311.00	341.00	147.00
30 October	311.00	341.00	147.00
31 November	311.00	341.00	147.00
32 December	311.00	341.00	147.00
33 Annual Totals	3,732.00	4,092.00	1,764.00

For Privacy Act and Paperwork Reduction Act Notice, see separate instructions.   Cat. No. 60703Q   Form **1095-A** (2020)

Form **1040** Department of the Treasury—Internal Revenue Service (99)
U.S. Individual Income Tax Return **2020** OMB No. 1545-0074 IRS Use Only—Do not write or staple in this space.

Filing Status
Check only one box.

☐ Single ☐ Married filing jointly ☐ Married filing separately (MFS) ☐ Head of household (HOH) ☐ Qualifying widow(er) (QW)

If you checked the MFS box, enter the name of your spouse. If you checked the HOH or QW box, enter the child's name if the qualifying person is a child but not your dependent ▶

Your first name and middle initial	Last name		Your social security number
If joint return, spouse's first name and middle initial	Last name		Spouse's social security number

Home address (number and street). If you have a P.O. box, see instructions.		Apt. no.	**Presidential Election Campaign**
City, town, or post office. If you have a foreign address, also complete spaces below.	State	ZIP code	Check here if you, or your spouse if filing jointly, want $3 to go to this fund. Checking a box below will not change your tax or refund.
Foreign country name	Foreign province/state/county	Foreign postal code	☐ You ☐ Spouse

At any time during 2020, did you receive, sell, send, exchange, or otherwise acquire any financial interest in any virtual currency? ☐ Yes ☐ No

Standard Deduction

Someone can claim: ☐ You as a dependent ☐ Your spouse as a dependent
☐ Spouse itemizes on a separate return or you were a dual-status alien

Age/Blindness **You:** ☐ Were born before January 2, 1956 ☐ Are blind **Spouse:** ☐ Was born before January 2, 1956 ☐ Is blind

Dependents (see instructions):

If more than four dependents, see instructions and check here ▶ ☐

(1) First name Last name	(2) Social security number	(3) Relationship to you	(4) ✔ if qualifies for (see instructions):	
			Child tax credit	Credit for other dependents
			☐	☐
			☐	☐
			☐	☐
			☐	☐

Attach Sch. B if required.

1	Wages, salaries, tips, etc. Attach Form(s) W-2		**1**	
2a	Tax-exempt interest . . .	**2a**	**b** Taxable interest	**2b**
3a	Qualified dividends . . .	**3a**	**b** Ordinary dividends	**3b**
4a	IRA distributions . . .	**4a**	**b** Taxable amount	**4b**
5a	Pensions and annuities . . .	**5a**	**b** Taxable amount	**5b**
6a	Social security benefits . .	**6a**	**b** Taxable amount	**6b**
7	Capital gain or (loss). Attach Schedule D if required. If not required, check here . . . ▶ ☐		**7**	
8	Other income from Schedule 1, line 9 . . .		**8**	
9	Add lines 1, 2b, 3b, 4b, 5b, 6b, 7, and 8. This is your **total income** . . . ▶		**9**	

Standard Deduction for—
- Single or Married filing separately, $12,400
- Married filing jointly or Qualifying widow(er), $24,800
- Head of household, $18,650
- If you checked any box under *Standard Deduction,* see instructions.

10	Adjustments to income:			
a	From Schedule 1, line 22 . . .	**10a**		
b	Charitable contributions if you take the standard deduction. See instructions	**10b**		
c	Add lines 10a and 10b. These are your **total adjustments to income** . . . ▶		**10c**	
11	Subtract line 10c from line 9. This is your **adjusted gross income** . . . ▶		**11**	
12	**Standard deduction or itemized deductions** (from Schedule A) . . .		**12**	
13	Qualified business income deduction. Attach Form 8995 or Form 8995-A . . .		**13**	
14	Add lines 12 and 13 . . .		**14**	
15	**Taxable income.** Subtract line 14 from line 11. If zero or less, enter -0- . . .		**15**	

For Disclosure, Privacy Act, and Paperwork Reduction Act Notice, see separate instructions.   Cat. No. 11320B   Form **1040** (2020)

Form 1040 (2020)   Page **2**

16	**Tax** (see instructions). Check if any from Form(s): **1** ☐ 8814 **2** ☐ 4972 **3** ☐ _____	**16**	
17	Amount from Schedule 2, line 3	**17**	
18	Add lines 16 and 17	**18**	
19	Child tax credit or credit for other dependents	**19**	
20	Amount from Schedule 3, line 7	**20**	
21	Add lines 19 and 20	**21**	
22	Subtract line 21 from line 18. If zero or less, enter -0-	**22**	
23	Other taxes, including self-employment tax, from Schedule 2, line 10	**23**	
24	Add lines 22 and 23. This is your **total tax** ▶	**24**	
25	Federal income tax withheld from:		
a	Form(s) W-2	**25a**	
b	Form(s) 1099	**25b**	
c	Other forms (see instructions)	**25c**	
d	Add lines 25a through 25c	**25d**	
26	2020 estimated tax payments and amount applied from 2019 return	**26**	

• If you have a qualifying child, attach Sch. EIC.
• If you have nontaxable combat pay, see instructions.

27	Earned income credit (EIC)	**27**	
28	Additional child tax credit. Attach Schedule 8812	**28**	
29	American opportunity credit from Form 8863, line 8	**29**	
30	Recovery rebate credit. See instructions	**30**	
31	Amount from Schedule 3, line 13	**31**	
32	Add lines 27 through 31. These are your **total other payments and refundable credits** ▶	**32**	
33	Add lines 25d, 26, and 32. These are your **total payments** ▶	**33**	

Refund

34	If line 33 is more than line 24, subtract line 24 from line 33. This is the amount you **overpaid**	**34**	
35a	Amount of line 34 you want **refunded to you.** If Form 8888 is attached, check here ▶ ☐	**35a**	

Direct deposit?
See instructions.

▶ **b** Routing number ☐☐☐☐☐☐☐☐☐   ▶ **c** Type: ☐ Checking ☐ Savings
▶ **d** Account number ☐☐☐☐☐☐☐☐☐☐☐☐☐☐☐☐☐

36	Amount of line 34 you want **applied to your 2021 estimated tax** ▶	**36**	

Amount You Owe

For details on how to pay, see instructions.

37	Subtract line 33 from line 24. This is the **amount you owe now** ▶	**37**	

Note: Schedule H and Schedule SE filers, line 37 may not represent all of the taxes you owe for 2020. See Schedule 3, line 12e, and its instructions for details.

38	Estimated tax penalty (see instructions) ▶	**38**	

Third Party Designee

Do you want to allow another person to discuss this return with the IRS? See instructions ▶   ☐ **Yes.** Complete below.   ☐ **No**

Designee's name ▶ _____   Phone no. ▶ _____   Personal identification number (PIN) ▶ ☐☐☐☐☐

Sign Here

Under penalties of perjury, I declare that I have examined this return and accompanying schedules and statements, and to the best of my knowledge and belief, they are true, correct, and complete. Declaration of preparer (other than taxpayer) is based on all information of which preparer has any knowledge.

Joint return?
See instructions.
Keep a copy for your records.

Your signature	Date	Your occupation	If the IRS sent you an Identity Protection PIN, enter it here (see inst.) ▶
Spouse's signature. If a joint return, **both** must sign.	Date	Spouse's occupation	If the IRS sent your spouse an Identity Protection PIN, enter it here (see inst.) ▶

Phone no. _____   Email address _____

Paid Preparer Use Only

Preparer's name	Preparer's signature	Date	PTIN	Check if: ☐ Self-employed
Firm's name ▶			Phone no.	
Firm's address ▶			Firm's EIN ▶	

Go to *www.irs.gov/Form1040* for instructions and the latest information.   Form **1040** (2020)

SCHEDULE 1
(Form 1040)

Department of the Treasury
Internal Revenue Service

Additional Income and Adjustments to Income

▶ **Attach to Form 1040, 1040-SR, or 1040-NR.**
▶ **Go to www.irs.gov/Form1040 for instructions and the latest information.**

OMB No. 1545-0074

20**20**

Attachment
Sequence No. **01**

Name(s) shown on Form 1040, 1040-SR, or 1040-NR

Your social security number

Part I Additional Income

1	Taxable refunds, credits, or offsets of state and local income taxes	**1**	
2a	Alimony received	**2a**	
b	Date of original divorce or separation agreement (see instructions) ▶		
3	Business income or (loss). Attach Schedule C	**3**	
4	Other gains or (losses). Attach Form 4797	**4**	
5	Rental real estate, royalties, partnerships, S corporations, trusts, etc. Attach Schedule E	**5**	
6	Farm income or (loss). Attach Schedule F	**6**	
7	Unemployment compensation	**7**	
8	Other income. List type and amount ▶	**8**	
9	Combine lines 1 through 8. Enter here and on Form 1040, 1040-SR, or 1040-NR, line 8	**9**	

Part II Adjustments to Income

10	Educator expenses	**10**	
11	Certain business expenses of reservists, performing artists, and fee-basis government officials. Attach Form 2106	**11**	
12	Health savings account deduction. Attach Form 8889	**12**	
13	Moving expenses for members of the Armed Forces. Attach Form 3903	**13**	
14	Deductible part of self-employment tax. Attach Schedule SE	**14**	
15	Self-employed SEP, SIMPLE, and qualified plans	**15**	
16	Self-employed health insurance deduction	**16**	
17	Penalty on early withdrawal of savings	**17**	
18a	Alimony paid	**18a**	
b	Recipient's SSN . . . . ▶		
c	Date of original divorce or separation agreement (see instructions) ▶		
19	IRA deduction	**19**	
20	Student loan interest deduction	**20**	
21	Tuition and fees deduction. Attach Form 8917	**21**	
22	Add lines 10 through 21. These are your **adjustments to income.** Enter here and on Form 1040, 1040-SR, or 1040-NR, line 10a	**22**	

For Paperwork Reduction Act Notice, see your tax return instructions.   Cat. No. 71479F   Schedule 1 (Form 1040) 2020

DRAFT AS OF August 18, 2020 DO NOT FILE

SCHEDULE 2
(Form 1040)

Department of the Treasury
Internal Revenue Service

Additional Taxes

▶ Attach to Form 1040, 1040-SR, or 1040-NR.
▶ Go to *www.irs.gov/Form1040* for instructions and the latest information.

OMB No. 1545-0074

2020

Attachment
Sequence No. **02**

Name(s) shown on Form 1040, 1040-SR, or 1040-NR | Your social security number

Part I   Tax

1	Alternative minimum tax. Attach Form 6251	**1**	
2	Excess advance premium tax credit repayment. Attach Form 8962	**2**	
3	Add lines 1 and 2. Enter here and on Form 1040, 1040-SR, or 1040-NR, line 17 . .	**3**	

Part II   Other Taxes

4	Self-employment tax. Attach Schedule SE	**4**	
5	Unreported social security and Medicare tax from Form: **a** ☐ 4137 **b** ☐ 8919 .	**5**	
6	Additional tax on IRAs, other qualified retirement plans, and other tax-favored accounts. Attach Form 5329 if required	**6**	
7a	Household employment taxes. Attach Schedule H	**7a**	
b	Repayment of first-time homebuyer credit from Form 5405. Attach Form 5405 if required	**7b**	
8	Taxes from: **a** ☐ Form 8959 **b** ☐ Form 8960		
	c ☐ Instructions; enter code(s) _____	**8**	
9	Section 965 net tax liability installment from Form 965-A . . .	**9**		
10	Add lines 4 through 8. These are your **total other taxes.** Enter here and on Form 1040 or 1040-SR, line 23, or Form 1040-NR, line 23b	**10**	

For Paperwork Reduction Act Notice, see your tax return instructions.   Cat. No. 71478U   **Schedule 2 (Form 1040) 2020**

SCHEDULE 3
(Form 1040)

Department of the Treasury
Internal Revenue Service

Additional Credits and Payments

▶ Attach to Form 1040, 1040-SR, or 1040-NR.
▶ Go to *www.irs.gov/Form1040* for instructions and the latest information.

OMB No. 1545-0074

2020

Attachment
Sequence No. **03**

Name(s) shown on Form 1040, 1040-SR, or 1040-NR

Your social security number

Part I Nonrefundable Credits

1	Foreign tax credit. Attach Form 1116 if required	1
2	Credit for child and dependent care expenses. Attach Form 2441	2
3	Education credits from Form 8863, line 19	3
4	Retirement savings contributions credit. Attach Form 8880	4
5	Residential energy credits. Attach Form 5695	5
6	Other credits from Form: a ☐ 3800 b ☐ 8801 c ☐ _____	6
7	Add lines 1 through 6. Enter here and on Form 1040, 1040-SR, or 1040-NR, line 20	7

Part II Other Payments and Refundable Credits

8	Net premium tax credit. Attach Form 8962	8
9	Amount paid with request for extension to file (see instructions)	9
10	Excess social security and tier 1 RRTA tax withheld	10
11	Credit for federal tax on fuels. Attach Form 4136	11
12	Other payments or refundable credits:	
a	Form 2439	12a
b	Qualified sick and family leave credits from Schedule(s) H and Form(s) 7202	12b
c	Health coverage tax credit from Form 8885	12c
d	Other: _____	12d
e	Deferral for certain Schedule H or SE filers (see instructions) .	12e
f	Add lines 12a through 12e	12f
13	Add lines 8 through 12f. Enter here and on Form 1040, 1040-SR, or 1040-NR, line 31	13

For Paperwork Reduction Act Notice, see your tax return instructions. Cat. No. 71480G **Schedule 3 (Form 1040) 2020**

SCHEDULE A
(Form 1040)

Department of the Treasury
Internal Revenue Service (99)

Itemized Deductions

► Go to *www.irs.gov/ScheduleA* for instructions and the latest information.
► Attach to Form 1040 or 1040-SR.

Caution: If you are claiming a net qualified disaster loss on Form 4684, see the instructions for line 16.

OMB No. 1545-0074

2020

Attachment
Sequence No. **07**

Name(s) shown on Form 1040 or 1040-SR

Your social security number

Medical and Dental Expenses	**Caution:** Do not include expenses reimbursed or paid by others.	
	1 Medical and dental expenses (see instructions)	**1**
	2 Enter amount from Form 1040 or 1040-SR, line 11 **2**	
	3 Multiply line 2 by 7.5% (0.075)	**3**
	4 Subtract line 3 from line 1. If line 3 is more than line 1, enter -0-	**4**
Taxes You Paid	**5** State and local taxes.	
	a State and local income taxes or general sales taxes. You may include either income taxes or general sales taxes on line 5a, but not both. If you elect to include general sales taxes instead of income taxes, check this box . . . . ► ☐	**5a**
	b State and local real estate taxes (see instructions)	**5b**
	c State and local personal property taxes	**5c**
	d Add lines 5a through 5c	**5d**
	e Enter the smaller of line 5d or $10,000 ($5,000 if married filing separately)	**5e**
	6 Other taxes. List type and amount ► _____	**6**
	7 Add lines 5e and 6	**7**
Interest You Paid	**8** Home mortgage interest and points. If you didn't use all of your home mortgage loan(s) to buy, build, or improve your home, see instructions and check this box . . . . ► ☐	
Caution: Your mortgage interest deduction may be limited (see instructions).	**a** Home mortgage interest and points reported to you on Form 1098. See instructions if limited	**8a**
	b Home mortgage interest not reported to you on Form 1098. See instructions if limited. If paid to the person from whom you bought the home, see instructions and show that person's name, identifying no., and address . . . . ► _____	**8b**
	c Points not reported to you on Form 1098. See instructions for special rules	**8c**
	d Mortgage insurance premiums (see instructions)	**8d**
	e Add lines 8a through 8d	**8e**
	9 Investment interest. Attach Form 4952 if required. See instructions .	**9**
	10 Add lines 8e and 9	**10**
Gifts to Charity	**11** Gifts by cash or check. If you made any gift of $250 or more, see instructions	**11**
Caution: If you made a gift and got a benefit for it, see instructions.	**12** Other than by cash or check. If you made any gift of $250 or more, see instructions. You **must** attach Form 8283 if over $500. . . .	**12**
	13 Carryover from prior year	**13**
	14 Add lines 11 through 13	**14**
Casualty and Theft Losses	**15** Casualty and theft loss(es) from a federally declared disaster (other than net qualified disaster losses). Attach Form 4684 and enter the amount from line 18 of that form. See instructions	**15**
Other Itemized Deductions	**16** Other—from list in instructions. List type and amount ► _____	**16**
Total Itemized Deductions	**17** Add the amounts in the far right column for lines 4 through 16. Also, enter this amount on Form 1040 or 1040-SR, line 12	**17**
	18 If you elect to itemize deductions even though they are less than your standard deduction, check this box . . . . ► ☐	

For Paperwork Reduction Act Notice, see the Instructions for Forms 1040 and 1040-SR.   Cat. No. 17145C   **Schedule A (Form 1040) 2020**

Form **2441**

Department of the Treasury
Internal Revenue Service (99)

Child and Dependent Care Expenses

▶ Attach to Form 1040, 1040-SR, or 1040-NR.

▶ Go to *www.irs.gov/Form2441* for instructions and the latest information.

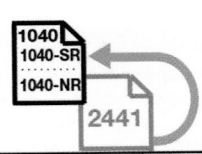

OMB No. 1545-0074

2020

Attachment
Sequence No. **21**

Name(s) shown on return

Your social security number

You cannot claim a credit for child and dependent care expenses if your filing status is married filing separately unless you meet the requirements listed in the instructions under "Married Persons Filing Separately." If you meet these requirements, check this box. ☐

Part I **Persons or Organizations Who Provided the Care**—You **must** complete this part.
(If you have more than two care providers, see the instructions.)

1	(a) Care provider's name	(b) Address (number, street, apt. no., city, state, and ZIP code)	(c) Identifying number (SSN or EIN)	(d) Amount paid (see instructions)

Did you receive dependent care benefits?
→ **No** → Complete only Part II below.
→ **Yes** → Complete Part III on the back next.

Caution: If the care was provided in your home, you may owe employment taxes. For details, see the instructions for Schedule 2 (Form 1040), line 7a.

Part II **Credit for Child and Dependent Care Expenses**

2   Information about your **qualifying person(s).** If you have more than two qualifying persons, see the instructions.

(a) Qualifying person's name		(b) Qualifying person's social security number	(c) **Qualified expenses** you incurred and paid in 2020 for the person listed in column (a)
First	Last		

3	Add the amounts in column (c) of line 2. **Don't** enter more than $3,000 for one qualifying person or $6,000 for two or more persons. If you completed Part III, enter the amount from line 31 . .	**3**	
4	Enter your **earned income.** See instructions	**4**	
5	If married filing jointly, enter your spouse's earned income (if you or your spouse was a student or was disabled, see the instructions); **all others**, enter the amount from line 4	**5**	
6	Enter the **smallest** of line 3, 4, or 5	**6**	
7	Enter the amount from Form 1040, 1040-SR, or 1040-NR, line 11 .	**7**	
8	Enter on line 8 the decimal amount shown below that applies to the amount on line 7.		

If line 7 is:

Over	But not over	Decimal amount is
$0 — 15,000		.35
15,000 — 17,000		.34
17,000 — 19,000		.33
19,000 — 21,000		.32
21,000 — 23,000		.31
23,000 — 25,000		.30
25,000 — 27,000		.29
27,000 — 29,000		.28

If line 7 is:

Over	But not over	Decimal amount is
$29,000 — 31,000		.27
31,000 — 33,000		.26
33,000 — 35,000		.25
35,000 — 37,000		.24
37,000 — 39,000		.23
39,000 — 41,000		.22
41,000 — 43,000		.21
43,000 — No limit		.20

8   X.

9	Multiply line 6 by the decimal amount on line 8. If you paid 2019 expenses in 2020, see the instructions	**9**	
10	Tax liability limit. Enter the amount from the Credit Limit Worksheet in the instructions	**10**	
11	**Credit for child and dependent care expenses.** Enter the **smaller** of line 9 or line 10 here and on Schedule 3 (Form 1040), line 2	**11**	

For Paperwork Reduction Act Notice, see your tax return instructions.   Cat. No. 11862M   Form **2441** (2020)

DRAFT AS OF August 20, 2020 DO NOT FILE

Form 2441 (2020)   Page **2**

Part III	**Dependent Care Benefits**

12 Enter the total amount of **dependent care benefits** you received in 2020. Amounts you received as an employee should be shown in box 10 of your Form(s) W-2. **Don't** include amounts reported as wages in box 1 of Form(s) W-2. If you were self-employed or a partner, include amounts you received under a dependent care assistance program from your sole proprietorship or partnership. **12**

13 Enter the amount, if any, you carried over from 2019 and used in 2020 during the grace period. See instructions **13**

14 Enter the amount, if any, you forfeited or carried forward to 2021. See instructions . . . . **14** ( )

15 Combine lines 12 through 14. See instructions **15**

16 Enter the total amount of **qualified expenses** incurred in 2020 for the care of the **qualifying person(s)** **16**

17 Enter the **smaller** of line 15 or 16 . . . . **17**

18 Enter your **earned income.** See instructions **18**

19 Enter the amount shown below that applies to you.
- If married filing jointly, enter your spouse's earned income (if you or your spouse was a student or was disabled, see the instructions for line 5).
- If married filing separately, see instructions.
- All others, enter the amount from line 18. **19**

20 Enter the **smallest** of line 17, 18, or 19 . . . . **20**

21 Enter $5,000 ($2,500 if married filing separately **and** you were required to enter your spouse's earned income on line 19) . . . **21**

22 Is any amount on line 12 from your sole proprietorship or partnership?
☐ **No.** Enter -0-.
☐ **Yes.** Enter the amount here **22**

23 Subtract line 22 from line 15 . . . . **23**

24 **Deductible benefits.** Enter the **smallest** of line 20, 21, or 22. Also, include this amount on the appropriate line(s) of your return. See instructions **24**

25 **Excluded benefits.** If you checked "No" on line 22, enter the smaller of line 20 or 21. Otherwise, subtract line 24 from the smaller of line 20 or line 21. If zero or less, enter -0- **25**

26 **Taxable benefits.** Subtract line 25 from line 23. If zero or less, enter -0-. Also, include this amount on Form 1040 or 1040-SR, line 1; or Form 1040-NR, line 1a. On the dotted line next to Form 1040 or 1040-SR, line 1; or Form 1040-NR, line 1a, enter "DCB" **26**

To claim the child and dependent care
credit, complete lines 27 through 31 below.

27 Enter $3,000 ($6,000 if two or more qualifying persons) **27**

28 Add lines 24 and 25 . . . . **28**

29 Subtract line 28 from line 27. If zero or less, **stop.** You can't take the credit. **Exception.** If you paid 2019 expenses in 2020, see the instructions for line 9 . . . . **29**

30 Complete line 2 on the front of this form. **Don't** include in column (c) any benefits shown on line 28 above. Then, add the amounts in column (c) and enter the total here **30**

31 Enter the **smaller** of line 29 or 30. Also, enter this amount on line 3 on the front of this form and complete lines 4 through 11 . . . . **31**

Form **2441** (2020)

Form **8880**

Department of the Treasury
Internal Revenue Service

Credit for Qualified Retirement Savings Contributions

► Attach to Form 1040, 1040-SR, or 1040-NR.
► Go to *www.irs.gov/Form8880* for the latest information.

OMB No. 1545-0074

2020

Attachment
Sequence No. **54**

Name(s) shown on return

Your social security number

*You **cannot** take this credit if **either** of the following applies.*

- *The amount on Form 1040, 1040-SR, or 1040-NR, line 11, is more than $32,500 ($48,750 if head of household; $65,000 if married filing jointly).*
- *The person(s) who made the qualified contribution or elective deferral **(a)** was born after January 1, 2003; **(b)** is claimed as a dependent on someone else's 2020 tax return; or **(c)** was a **student** (see instructions).*

		(a) You	(b) Your spouse
1	Traditional and Roth IRA contributions, and ABLE account contributions by the designated beneficiary for 2020. **Do not** include rollover contributions **1**		
2	Elective deferrals to a 401(k) or other qualified employer plan, voluntary employee contributions, and 501(c)(18)(D) plan contributions for 2020 (see instructions) **2**		
3	Add lines 1 and 2 . . . . **3**		
4	Certain distributions received **after** 2017 and **before** the due date (including extensions) of your 2020 tax return (see instructions). If married filing jointly, include **both** spouses' amounts in **both** columns. See instructions for an exception . . . **4**		
5	Subtract line 4 from line 3. If zero or less, enter -0- **5**		
6	In each column, enter the **smaller** of line 5 or $2,000 . . . . . . **6**		

7	Add the amounts on line 6. If zero, **stop;** you can't take this credit	**7**	
8	Enter the amount from Form 1040, 1040-SR, or 1040-NR, line 11*	**8**	
9	Enter the applicable decimal amount from the table below.		

If line 8 is—		And your filing status is—		
Over—	But not over—	Married filing jointly	Head of household	Single, Married filing separately, or Qualifying widow(er)
		Enter on line 9—		
---	$19,500	0.5	0.5	0.5
$19,500	$21,250	0.5	0.5	0.2
$21,250	$29,250	0.5	0.5	0.1
$29,250	$31,875	0.5	0.2	0.1
$31,875	$32,500	0.5	0.1	0.1
$32,500	$39,000	0.5	0.1	0.0
$39,000	$42,500	0.2	0.1	0.0
$42,500	$48,750	0.1	0.1	0.0
$48,750	$65,000	0.1	0.0	0.0
$65,000	---	0.0	0.0	0.0

9   x 0.

Note: If line 9 is zero, **stop;** you can't take this credit.

10	Multiply line 7 by line 9	**10**	
11	Limitation based on tax liability. Enter the amount from the Credit Limit Worksheet in the instructions	**11**	
12	**Credit for qualified retirement savings contributions.** Enter the **smaller** of line 10 or line 11 here and on Schedule 3 (Form 1040), line 4	**12**	

* See Pub. 590-A for the amount to enter if you claim any exclusion or deduction for foreign earned income, foreign housing, or income from Puerto Rico or for bona fide residents of American Samoa.

For Paperwork Reduction Act Notice, see your tax return instructions.   Cat. No. 33394D   Form **8880** (2020)

Form 8880 (2020)

Page **2**

General Instructions

Section references are to the Internal Revenue Code.

Reminder

Contributions by a designated beneficiary to an Achieving a Better Life Experience (ABLE) account. A retirement savings contribution credit may be claimed for the amount of contributions you, as the designated beneficiary of an ABLE account, make before January 1, 2026, to the ABLE account. See Pub. 907, Tax Highlights for Persons With Disabilities, for more information.

Future Developments

For the latest information about developments related to Form 8880 and its instructions, such as legislation enacted after they were published, go to www.irs.gov/Form8880.

Purpose of Form

Use Form 8880 to figure the amount, if any, of your retirement savings contributions credit (also known as the saver's credit).

 This credit can be claimed in addition to any IRA deduction claimed on Schedule 1 (Form 1040), line 19.

Who Can Take This Credit

You may be able to take this credit if you, or your spouse if filing jointly, made (a) contributions (other than rollover contributions) to a traditional or Roth IRA; (b) elective deferrals to a 401(k), 403(b), governmental 457(b), SEP, SIMPLE, or to the federal Thrift Savings Plan (TSP); (c) voluntary employee contributions to a qualified retirement plan, as defined in section 4974(c) (including the federal TSP); (d) contributions to a 501(c)(18)(D) plan; or (e) contributions, as a designated beneficiary of an ABLE account, to the ABLE account, as defined in section 529A.

However, you can't take the credit if either of the following applies.

• The amount on Form 1040, 1040-SR, or 1040-NR, line 11, is more than $32,500 ($48,750 if head of household; $65,000 if married filing jointly).

• The person(s) who made the qualified contribution or elective deferral (a) was born after January 1, 2003; (b) is claimed as a dependent on someone else's 2020 tax return; or (c) was a student.

 You'll need to refigure the amount on Form 1040 or 1040-SR, line 11, if you're filing Form 2555 or Form 4563 or you're excluding income from Puerto Rico. See Pub. 590-A at www.irs.gov/Pub590A for details.

You were a student if during any part of 5 calendar months of 2020 you:

• Were enrolled as a full-time student at a school; or

• Took a full-time, on-farm training course given by a school or a state, county, or local government agency.

A school includes technical, trade, and mechanical schools. It doesn't include on-the-job training courses, correspondence schools, or schools offering courses only through the Internet.

Specific Instructions

Column (b)

Complete column (b) only if you're filing a joint return.

Line 2

Include on line 2 any of the following amounts.

• Elective deferrals (including designated Roth contributions under section 402A, if applicable) to a 401(k), 403(b), governmental 457(b), SEP, SIMPLE, or to the federal TSP.

• Voluntary employee contributions to a qualified retirement plan, as defined in section 4974(c) (including the federal TSP).

• Contributions to a 501(c)(18)(D) plan.

These amounts may be shown in box 12 of your Form(s) W-2 for 2020.

Note: Contributions designated under section 414(h)(2) are treated as employer contributions and, as such, they aren't voluntary contributions made by the employee. They don't qualify for the credit and shouldn't be included on line 2.

Line 4

Enter the total amount of distributions you, and your spouse if filing jointly, received after 2017 and before the due date of your 2020 return (including extensions) from any of the following types of plans.

• Traditional or Roth IRAs (including *my*RAs), or ABLE accounts.

• 401(k), 403(b), governmental 457(b), 501(c)(18)(D), SEP, SIMPLE, or to the federal TSP.

• Qualified retirement plans, as defined in section 4974(c).

Don't include any of the following.

• Distributions not taxable as the result of a rollover or a trustee-to-trustee transfer.

• Distributions that are taxable as the result of an in-plan rollover to your designated Roth account.

• Distributions from your eligible retirement plan (other than a Roth IRA) rolled over or converted to your Roth IRA.

• Loans from a qualified employer plan treated as a distribution.

• Distributions of excess contributions or deferrals (and income allocable to such contributions or deferrals).

• Distributions of contributions made to an IRA during a tax year and returned (with any income allocable to such contributions) on or before the due date (including extensions) for that tax year.

• Distributions of dividends paid on stock held by an employee stock ownership plan under section 404(k).

• Distributions from a military retirement plan (other than the federal TSP).

• Distributions from an inherited IRA by a nonspousal beneficiary.

If you're filing a joint return, include both spouses' amounts in both columns.

Exception. Don't include your spouse's distributions with yours when entering an amount on line 4 if you and your spouse didn't file a joint return for the year the distribution was received.

Example. You received a distribution of $5,000 from a qualified retirement plan in 2020. Your spouse received a distribution of $2,000 from a Roth IRA in 2018. You and your spouse file a joint return in 2020, but didn't file a joint return in 2018. You would include $5,000 in column (a) and $7,000 in column (b).

Line 7

Add the amounts from line 6, columns (a) and (b), and enter the total.

Line 11

Before you complete the following worksheet, figure the amount of any credit for the elderly or the disabled you're claiming on Schedule 3 (Form 1040), line 6. See Schedule R (Form 1040) to figure the credit.

Credit Limit Worksheet

Complete this worksheet to figure the amount to enter on line 11.

1. Enter the amount from Form 1040, 1040-SR, or 1040-NR, line 17 . . . .   1._____

2. **Form 1040 or 1040-SR filers:** Enter the total of your credits from Schedule 3, lines 1 through 3, and Schedule R, line 22.

   Form 1040-NR filers: Enter the total of your credits from Schedule 3, lines 1 through 3 . .   2._____

3. Subtract line 2 from line 1. Also enter this amount on Form 8880, line 11. But if zero or less, **stop;** you can't take the credit—don't file this form .   3._____

2020 Child Tax Credit and Credit for Other Dependents
Worksheet—Line 19 *

Keep for Your Records

1. To be a qualifying child for the child tax credit, the child must be your dependent, **under age 17** at the end of 2020, and meet all the conditions in Steps 1 through 3 under *Who Qualifies as Your Dependent*. Make sure you checked the "child tax credit" box in column (4) of the *Dependents* section on Form 1040 or 1040-SR for each qualifying child.

2. If you don't have a qualifying child, you can't claim the child tax credit; but you may be able to claim the credit for other dependents for that child. See Step 3 under *Who Qualifies as Your Dependent*.

3. To see if your qualifying relative qualifies you to take the credit for other dependents, see Step 5 under *Who Qualifies as Your Dependent*.

4. Be sure to see *Social security number* under *Who Qualifies as Your Dependent*.

5. Do **not** use this worksheet, but use Pub. 972 instead, if:

   a. You are claiming the adoption credit, mortgage interest credit, District of Columbia first-time homebuyer credit, or residential energy efficient property credit*;

   b. You are excluding income from Puerto Rico; or

   c. You are filing Form 2555 or 4563.

   * If applicable.

Part 1

1. Number of qualifying children under age 17 with the required social security number: _____ × $2,000. Enter the result. **1** _____

2. Number of other dependents, including qualifying children without the required social security number: _____ × $500. Enter the result. **2** _____

   Caution. Don't include yourself, your spouse, or anyone who is not a U.S. citizen, U.S. national, or U.S. resident alien. Also, don't include anyone you included on line 1.

3. Add lines 1 and 2. **3** _____

4. Enter the amount from Form 1040 or 1040-SR, line 11. **4** _____

5. Enter the amount shown below for your filing status.

   ● Married filing jointly — $400,000

   ● All other filing statuses — $200,000 **5** _____

6. Is the amount on line 4 more than the amount on line 5?

   ☐ **No.** Leave line 6 blank. Enter -0- on line 7, and go to line 8.

   ☐ **Yes.** Subtract line 5 from line 4.

      If the result isn't a multiple of $1,000, increase it to the next multiple of $1,000. For example, increase $425 to $1,000, increase $1,025 to $2,000, etc. **6** _____

7. Multiply the amount on line 6 by 5% (0.05). Enter the result. **7** _____

8. Is the amount on line 3 more than the amount on line 7?

   ☐ **No.** (STOP)

      You can't take the child tax credit on Form 1040 or 1040-SR, line 19. You also can't take the additional child tax credit on Form 1040 or 1040-SR, line 28. Complete the rest of your Form 1040 or 1040-SR.

   ☐ **Yes.** Subtract line 7 from line 3. Enter the result. *Go to Part 2.* **8** _____

* Download the latest version of this worksheet from the Form 1040 Instructions available at www.irs.gov. The 2020 worksheet was not available as we went to print. This worksheet is adapted from the 2019 version.

2020 Child Tax Credit and Credit for Other Dependents
Worksheet—Continued *

Keep for Your Records

Before you begin Part 2: √ Figure the amount of any credits you are claiming on Schedule 3; Form 5695, Part II*; Form 8910; Form 8936; or Schedule R.

Part 2

9. Enter the amount from Form 1040 or 1040-SR, line 16.

9 _____

10. Add any amounts from:

Schedule 3, line 1   _____

Schedule 3, line 2 + _____

Schedule 3, line 3 + _____

Schedule 3, line 4 + _____

Form 5695, line 30* + _____

Form 8910, line 15* + _____

Form 8936, line 23 + _____

Schedule R, line 22 + _____

Enter the total.   **10** _____

11. Are the amounts on lines 9 and 10 the same?

☐ **Yes.** (STOP)
You can't take this credit because there is no tax to reduce. However, you may be able to take the **additional child tax credit** if line 1 is more than zero. See the **TIP** below.

☐ **No.** Subtract line 10 from line 9.   **11** _____

12. Is the amount on line 8 more than the amount on line 11?

☐ **Yes.** Enter the amount from line 11.
Also, you may be able to take the **additional child tax credit** if line 1 is more than zero. See the **TIP** below.

☐ **No.** Enter the amount from line 8.

} **This is your child tax credit and credit for other dependents.**

12 _____

Enter this amount on Form 1040 or 1040-SR, line 19.

1040 or 1040-SR ◄ · · ·

TIP *You may be able to take the **additional child tax credit** on Form 1040 or 1040-SR, line 28, if you answered "Yes" on line 11 **or** line 12 above.*

- *First, complete your Form 1040 or 1040-SR through line 27 (also complete Schedule 3, line 10).*
- *Then, use Schedule 8812 to figure any additional child tax credit.*

⚠ CAUTION *If your child tax credit or additional child tax credit for a year after 2015 was reduced or disallowed, see Form 8862, who must file to find out if you must file Form 8862 to take the credit for 2020.*

* If applicable.

* Download the latest version of this worksheet from the Form 1040 Instructions available at www.irs.gov. The 2020 worksheet was not available as we went to print. This worksheet is adapted from the 2019 version.

SCHEDULE 8812
(Form 1040)

Department of the Treasury
Internal Revenue Service (99)

Additional Child Tax Credit

▶ **Attach to Form 1040, 1040-SR, or 1040-NR.**

▶ **Go to** *www.irs.gov/Schedule8812* **for instructions and the latest information.**

OMB No. 1545-0074

2020

Attachment
Sequence No. **47**

Name(s) shown on return

Your social security number

Part I	**All Filers**	

Caution: If you file Form 2555, **stop here; you cannot claim the additional child tax credit.**

1	If you are required to use the worksheet in Pub. 972, enter the amount from line 10 of the Child Tax Credit and Credit for Other Dependents Worksheet in the publication. Otherwise, enter the amount from line 8 of your Child Tax Credit and Credit for Other Dependents Worksheet. (See the instructions for Forms 1040 and 1040-SR, line 19, or the instructions for Form 1040-NR, line 19.)	**1**
2	Enter the amount from line 19 of your Form 1040, Form 1040-SR, or Form 1040-NR	**2**
3	Subtract line 2 from line 1. If zero, **stop here;** you cannot claim this credit	**3**
4	Number of qualifying children under 17 with the required social security number: _____ x $1,400. Enter the result. If zero, **stop here;** you cannot claim this credit	**4**
	TIP: The number of children you use for this line is the same as the number of children you used for line 1 of the Child Tax Credit and Credit for Other Dependents Worksheet.	
5	Enter the **smaller** of line 3 or line 4	**5**
6a	Earned income (see instructions)	**6a**
b	Nontaxable combat pay (see instructions) **6b**	
7	Is the amount on line 6a more than $2,500?	
	☐ **No.** Leave line 7 blank and enter -0- on line 8.	
	☐ **Yes.** Subtract $2,500 from the amount on line 6a. Enter the result	**7**
8	Multiply the amount on line 7 by 15% (0.15) and enter the result	**8**
	Next. On line 4, is the amount $4,200 or more?	
	☐ **No.** If line 8 is zero, **stop here;** you cannot claim this credit. Otherwise, skip Part II and enter the **smaller** of line 5 or line 8 on line 15.	
	☐ **Yes.** If line 8 is equal to or more than line 5, skip Part II and enter the amount from line 5 on line 15. Otherwise, go to line 9.	

Part II	**Certain Filers Who Have Three or More Qualifying Children**	

9	Withheld social security, Medicare, and Additional Medicare taxes from Form(s) W-2, boxes 4 and 6. If married filing jointly, include your spouse's amounts with yours. If your employer withheld or you paid Additional Medicare Tax or tier 1 RRTA taxes, see instructions	**9**
10	Enter the total of the amounts from Schedule 1 (Form 1040), line 14, and Schedule 2 (Form 1040), line 5, plus any taxes that you identified using code "UT" and entered on Schedule 2 (Form 1040), line 8	**10**
11	Add lines 9 and 10	**11**
12	**1040 and** Enter the total of the amounts from Form 1040 or 1040-SR, line 27, **1040-SR filers:** and Schedule 3 (Form 1040), line 10. **1040-NR filers:** Enter the amount from Schedule 3 (Form 1040), line 10.	**12**
13	Subtract line 12 from line 11. If zero or less, enter -0-	**13**
14	Enter the **larger** of line 8 or line 13	**14**
	Next, enter the **smaller** of line 5 or line 14 on line 15.	

Part III	**Additional Child Tax Credit**	

15	**This is your additional child tax credit**	**15**

Enter this amount on
Form 1040, line 28;
Form 1040-SR, line 28; or
Form 1040-NR, line 28.

For Paperwork Reduction Act Notice, see your tax return instructions.   Cat. No. 59761M   **Schedule 8812 (Form 1040) 2020**

Worksheet **A**—2020 EIC—Line 27*

Keep for Your Records

Before you begin: √ Be sure you are using the correct worksheet. Use this worksheet only if you answered "No" to Step 5, question 2. Otherwise, use Worksheet B.

Part 1

All Filers Using Worksheet A

1. Enter your earned income from Step 5.

   Wages, salaries

   `1` _____

2. Look up the amount on line 1 above in the EIC Table (right after Worksheet B) to find the credit. Be sure you use the correct column for your filing status and the number of children you have. Enter the credit here.

   If line 2 is zero, (STOP) You can't take the credit.
   Enter "No" on the dotted line next to Form 1040 or 1040-SR, line 27.

   `2` _____

3. Enter the amount from Form 1040 or 1040-SR, line 11.

   Adjusted gross income

   `3` _____

4. Are the amounts on lines 3 and 1 the same?

   ☐ **Yes.** Skip line 5; enter the amount from line 2 on line 6.

   ☐ **No.** Go to line 5.

Part 2

Filers Who Answered "No" on Line 4

5. If you have:
   - No qualifying children, is the amount on line 3 less than $8,800 ($14,700 if married filing jointly)?
   - 1 or more qualifying children, is the amount on line 3 less than $19,350 ($25,250 if married filing jointly)?

   ☐ **Yes.** Leave line 5 blank; enter the amount from line 2 on line 6.

   ☐ **No.** Look up the amount on line 3 in the EIC Table to find the credit. Be sure you use the correct column for your filing status and the number of children you have. Enter the credit here.
   Look at the amounts on lines 5 and 2.
   Then, enter the **smaller** amount on line 6.

   `5` _____

Part 3

Your Earned Income Credit

6. **This is your earned income credit.**

   `6` _____

   Enter this amount on Form 1040 or 1040-SR, line 27.

   Reminder—

   √ If you have a qualifying child, complete and attach Schedule EIC.

   1040 or 1040-SR EIC → 1040 or 1040-SR

   ⚠ **CAUTION** *If your EIC for a year after 1996 was reduced or disallowed, see Form 8862, who must file, earlier, to find out if you must file Form 8862 to take the credit for 2020.*

---

*Download the latest version of this worksheet from the Form 1040 Instructions available at www.irs.gov. The 2020 worksheet was not available as we went to print. This worksheet is adapted from the 2019 version.

SCHEDULE EIC
(Form 1040)

Department of the Treasury
Internal Revenue Service (99)

Earned Income Credit
Qualifying Child Information

► **Complete and attach to Form 1040 or 1040-SR only if you have a qualifying child.**
► **Go to** *www.irs.gov/ScheduleEIC* **for the latest information.**

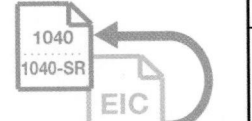

OMB No. 1545-0074

2020

Attachment
Sequence No. **43**

Name(s) shown on return

Your social security number

Before you begin:
- See the instructions for Form 1040 or 1040-SR, line 27, to make sure that **(a)** you can take the EIC, and **(b)** you have a qualifying child.
- Be sure the child's name on line 1 and social security number (SSN) on line 2 agree with the child's social security card. Otherwise, at the time we process your return, we may reduce or disallow your EIC. If the name or SSN on the child's social security card is not correct, call the Social Security Administration at 1-800-772-1213.

- *You can't claim the EIC for a child who didn't live with you for more than half of the year.*
- *If you take the EIC even though you are not eligible, you may not be allowed to take the credit for up to 10 years. See the instructions for details.*
- *It will take us longer to process your return and issue your refund if you do not fill in all lines that apply for each qualifying child.*

Qualifying Child Information

		Child 1		Child 2		Child 3	
1	**Child's name** If you have more than three qualifying children, you have to list only three to get the maximum credit.	First name	Last name	First name	Last name	First name	Last name
2	**Child's SSN** The child must have an SSN as defined in the instructions for Form 1040 or 1040-SR, line 27, unless the child was born and died in 2020. If your child was born and died in 2020 and did not have an SSN, enter "Died" on this line and attach a copy of the child's birth certificate, death certificate, or hospital medical records showing a live birth.						
3	**Child's year of birth**	Year _ _ _ _ *If born after 2001 and the child is younger than you (or your spouse, if filing jointly), skip lines 4a and 4b; go to line 5.*		Year _ _ _ _ *If born after 2001 and the child is younger than you (or your spouse, if filing jointly), skip lines 4a and 4b; go to line 5.*		Year _ _ _ _ *If born after 2001 and the child is younger than you (or your spouse, if filing jointly), skip lines 4a and 4b; go to line 5.*	
4 a	Was the child under age 24 at the end of 2020, a student, and younger than you (or your spouse, if filing jointly)?	☐ **Yes.** *Go to line 5.*	☐ **No.** *Go to line 4b.*	☐ **Yes.** *Go to line 5.*	☐ **No.** *Go to line 4b.*	☐ **Yes.** *Go to line 5.*	☐ **No.** *Go to line 4b.*
b	Was the child permanently and totally disabled during any part of 2020?	☐ **Yes.** *Go to line 5.*	☐ **No.** The child is not a qualifying child.	☐ **Yes.** *Go to line 5.*	☐ **No.** The child is not a qualifying child.	☐ **Yes.** *Go to line 5.*	☐ **No.** The child is not a qualifying child.
5	**Child's relationship to you** (for example, son, daughter, grandchild, niece, nephew, eligible foster child, etc.)						
6	**Number of months child lived with you in the United States during 2020** • If the child lived with you for more than half of 2020 but less than 7 months, enter "7." • If the child was born or died in 2020 and your home was the child's home for more than half the time he or she was alive during 2020, enter "12."	_ _ _ months *Do not enter more than 12 months.*		_ _ _ months *Do not enter more than 12 months.*		_ _ _ months *Do not enter more than 12 months.*	

For Paperwork Reduction Act Notice, see your tax return instructions.   Cat. No. 13339M   **Schedule EIC (Form 1040) 2020**

Form **8962**

Department of the Treasury
Internal Revenue Service

Premium Tax Credit (PTC)

▶ Attach to Form 1040, 1040-SR, or 1040-NR.
▶ Go to *www.irs.gov/Form8962* for instructions and the latest information.

OMB No. 1545-0074

20**20**

Attachment
Sequence No. **73**

Name shown on your return

Your social security number

You cannot take the PTC if your filing status is married filing separately unless you qualify for an exception. See instructions. If you qualify, check the box . . ▶ ☐

Part I Annual and Monthly Contribution Amount

1	Tax family size. Enter your tax family size. See instructions		**1**	
2a	Modified AGI. Enter your modified AGI. See instructions	**2a**		
b	Enter the total of your dependents' modified AGI. See instructions	**2b**		
3	Household income. Add the amounts on lines 2a and 2b. See instructions		**3**	
4	Federal poverty line. Enter the federal poverty line amount from Table 1-1, 1-2, or 1-3. See instructions. Check the appropriate box for the federal poverty table used. **a** ☐ Alaska **b** ☐ Hawaii **c** ☐ Other 48 states and DC		**4**	
5	Household income as a percentage of federal poverty line (see instructions)		**5**	%
6	Did you enter 401% on line 5? (See instructions if you entered less than 100%.)			

☐ **No.** Continue to line 7.

☐ **Yes.** You are not eligible to take the PTC. If advance payment of the PTC was made, see the instructions for how to report your excess advance PTC repayment amount.

7	Applicable figure. Using your line 5 percentage, locate your "applicable figure" on the table in the instructions		**7**	
8a	Annual contribution amount. Multiply line 3 by line 7. Round to nearest whole dollar amount	**8a**	**b** Monthly contribution amount. Divide line 8a by 12. Round to nearest whole dollar amount	**8b**

Part II Premium Tax Credit Claim and Reconciliation of Advance Payment of Premium Tax Credit

9 Are you allocating policy amounts with another taxpayer or do you want to use the alternative calculation for year of marriage? See instructions.

☐ **Yes.** Skip to Part IV, Allocation of Policy Amounts, or Part V, Alternative Calculation for Year of Marriage. ☐ **No.** Continue to line 10.

10 See the instructions to determine if you can use line 11 or must complete lines 12 through 23.

☐ **Yes.** Continue to line 11. Compute your annual PTC. Then skip lines 12–23 and continue to line 24.

☐ **No.** Continue to lines 12–23. Compute your monthly PTC and continue to line 24.

Annual Calculation	**(a)** Annual enrollment premiums (Form(s) 1095-A, line 33A)	**(b)** Annual applicable SLCSP premium (Form(s) 1095-A, line 33B)	**(c)** Annual contribution amount (line 8a)	**(d)** Annual maximum premium assistance (subtract (c) from (b); if zero or less, enter -0-)	**(e)** Annual premium tax credit allowed (smaller of (a) or (d))	**(f)** Annual advance payment of PTC (Form(s) 1095-A, line 33C)
11 Annual Totals						
Monthly Calculation	**(a)** Monthly enrollment premiums (Form(s) 1095-A, lines 21–32, column A)	**(b)** Monthly applicable SLCSP premium (Form(s) 1095-A, lines 21–32, column B)	**(c)** Monthly contribution amount (amount from line 8b or alternative marriage monthly calculation)	**(d)** Monthly maximum premium assistance (subtract (c) from (b); if zero or less, enter -0-)	**(e)** Monthly premium tax credit allowed (smaller of (a) or (d))	**(f)** Monthly advance payment of PTC (Form(s) 1095-A, lines 21–32, column C)
12 January						
13 February						
14 March						
15 April						
16 May						
17 June						
18 July						
19 August						
20 September						
21 October						
22 November						
23 December						

24	Total premium tax credit. Enter the amount from line 11(e) or add lines 12(e) through 23(e) and enter the total here	**24**	
25	Advance payment of PTC. Enter the amount from line 11(f) or add lines 12(f) through 23(f) and enter the total here	**25**	
26	Net premium tax credit. If line 24 is greater than line 25, subtract line 25 from line 24. Enter the difference here and on Schedule 3 (Form 1040), line 8. If line 24 equals line 25, enter -0-. Stop here. If line 25 is greater than line 24, leave this line blank and continue to line 27	**26**	

Part III Repayment of Excess Advance Payment of the Premium Tax Credit

27	Excess advance payment of PTC. If line 25 is greater than line 24, subtract line 24 from line 25. Enter the difference here	**27**	
28	Repayment limitation (see instructions)	**28**	
29	Excess advance premium tax credit repayment. Enter the smaller of line 27 or line 28 here and on Schedule 2 (Form 1040), line 2	**29**	

For Paperwork Reduction Act Notice, see your tax return instructions.   Cat. No. 37784Z   Form **8962** (2020)

DRAFT AS OF August 19, 2020 DO NOT FILE

Student Name _____

Class/Section _____

Date _____

KEY NUMBER TAX RETURN SUMMARY

CHAPTER 7

Comprehensive Problem 1

Adjusted Gross Income (Line 11)   _____

Taxable Income (Line 15)   _____

Total Nonrefundable Credits (Schedule 3, Line 7)   _____

Child Tax Credit (Line 19)   _____

Amount Overpaid (Line 34)   _____

Comprehensive Problem 2A

Adjusted Gross Income (Line 11)   _____

Taxable Income (Line 15)   _____

Credit for Child and Dependent Care Expenses (Schedule 3, Line 2)   _____

Earned Income Credit (line 27)   _____

Amount Overpaid (Line 34)   _____

Comprehensive Problem 2B

Adjusted Gross Income (Line 11)   _____

Taxable Income (Line 15)   _____

Excess Advance Premium Tax Credit Repayment (Schedule 2, Line 2)   _____

Total Tax (Line 24)   _____

Amount Overpaid (Line 34)   _____

CHAPTER 8

Depreciation and Sale of Business Property

Andy Dean Photography/Shutterstock.com

LEARNING OBJECTIVES

After completing this chapter, you should be able to:

LO 8.1   Explain the concept of depreciation.

LO 8.2   Calculate depreciation expense using the MACRS tables.

LO 8.3   Identify when a Section 179 election to expense the cost of property may be used.

LO 8.4   Apply the limitations placed on depreciation of "listed property."

LO 8.5   Apply the limitations on depreciation of "luxury automobiles."

LO 8.6   Calculate the amortization of goodwill and certain other intangibles.

LO 8.7   Classify gains and losses from Section 1231 assets.

LO 8.8   Apply the depreciation recapture rules.

LO 8.9   Apply the general treatment of casualty gains and losses for business purposes.

LO 8.10   Compute the gain on installment sales.

LO 8.11   Calculate recognized and deferred gains on like-kind exchanges.

LO 8.12   Calculate recognized and deferred gains on involuntary conversions.

OVERVIEW

The calculation of depreciation of business assets is an important issue for most businesses. The Modified Accelerated Cost Recovery System (MACRS) is the tax depreciation method currently in use under U.S. tax law. Many special depreciation provisions which are discussed in this chapter, including bonus depreciation and the election to expense (Section 179), allow businesses to immediately deduct the cost of many capital expenditures.

The chapter covers the tax treatment of goodwill, going-concern value, covenants not to compete, franchises, trademarks, and other intangibles.

As discussed in Chapter 4, realized gains and losses are generally recognized for tax purposes unless there is a tax provision that specifically allows for a different treatment. This chapter focuses on business-related gains and losses. Transactions covered in this chapter include:

- Section 1231 (business) gains and losses
- Depreciation recapture on business assets
- Installment sales
- Like-kind exchanges
- Involuntary conversions

Unlike capital gains and losses which are generally reported on Schedule D, many business asset sale transactions are reported on Form 4797, and installment sales are reported on Form 6252.

Learning Objective 8.1

Explain the concept of depreciation.

8-1 DEPRECIATION

Since many assets are used in the production of income over a number of years, accrual-based income is not properly measured if the entire cost of these assets is deducted in the year the assets are purchased. Depreciation is the accounting process of allocating and deducting the cost of an asset over a period of years. The term *depreciation* does not necessarily mean physical deterioration or loss of value of the asset. In fact, in some cases the value of the asset may increase while it is being depreciated. Certain assets, such as land, cannot be depreciated for tax purposes. Under U.S. tax law, land is considered an asset that is not subject to obsolescence. These assets remain on the taxpayer's records at original cost.

It is important to distinguish maintenance expenses from depreciation. Depreciation expense is the deduction of a portion of the original cost of the asset, whereas maintenance expenses are those expenditures incurred to keep the asset in good operating condition. For example, a taxpayer who purchases a truck for use in his business depreciates the cost of the truck over a period of years. Maintenance costs such as tires and repairs are deducted in the year they are incurred.

The simplest method of depreciation is the straight-line method. Use of the straight-line method results in an equal portion of the cost being deducted in each period of the asset's life. Straight-line depreciation expense is calculated by dividing the cost by the asset's estimated useful life. The formula is:

$$\frac{\text{Cost}}{\text{Estimated useful life}} = \text{Depreciation for the period}$$

EXAMPLE   Wilson purchases an asset for use in his business. The asset cost $14,400 on October 1, 20X1, and has a 3-year (36-month) useful life. Depreciation is calculated as follows:

$$\frac{\$14,400}{36 \text{ months}} = \$400 \text{ per month}$$

The depreciation for each year is displayed in the following table:

Year	Months	Rate	Depreciation Deduction
20X1	3	$400	$ 1,200
20X2	12	400	4,800
20X3	12	400	4,800
20X4	9	400	3,600
Total depreciation deduction			$14,400

At the end of 36 months, the asset has a basis of $0. ◆

The calculation of depreciation expense for tax purposes involves certain conventions and limitations which are not reflected in the previous example. The example is intended to illustrate the *concept* of depreciation expense as an allocation of the cost of an asset over the asset's estimated useful life. If more information is needed about depreciation, see any standard financial accounting textbook.

The regular straight-line depreciation method described above may be used for financial accounting purposes and for calculating tax depreciation expense on assets acquired before 1981. The tax depreciation rules for assets acquired after 1980 are described in the following sections of this chapter.

Self-Study Problem 8.1   See Appendix E for Solutions to Self-Study Problems

On March 1, 20X1, Jack purchases office equipment for use in his business. The equipment cost $3,500 and has a 5-year (60-month) estimated useful life. Calculate the depreciation expense for the following years, assuming the regular straight-line depreciation method (used for financial accounting purposes or for pre-1981 assets) is used.

Year	Depreciation Deduction
20X1	$_____
20X2	$_____
20X3	$_____
20X4	$_____
20X5	$_____
20X6	$_____
Total	$_____

8-2 MODIFIED ACCELERATED COST RECOVERY SYSTEM (MACRS) AND BONUS DEPRECIATION

8.2 Learning Objective

Calculate depreciation expense using the MACRS tables.

For tax years after 1980, modifications in the tax law were made to encourage capital investment. As a major part of this tax law change, the Accelerated Cost Recovery System (ACRS) was enacted and later modified in 1986 to become the current tax depreciation system referred to as the Modified Accelerated Cost Recovery System (MACRS). The current MACRS allows taxpayers who invest in capital assets to write off an asset's cost over a period designated in the tax law and to use an accelerated method for depreciation of assets other than real estate. The minimum number of years over which the cost of an asset may be deducted (the recovery period) depends on the type of the property and the year in which the property was acquired. The recovery periods are based on asset depreciation ranges (ADRs) as published by the IRS. A schedule of the recovery periods for assets acquired after 1986 is presented in Table 8.1.

TABLE 8.1   RECOVERY PERIODS FOR ASSETS PLACED IN SERVICE AFTER 1986

Recovery Period	Recovery Method	Assets
3-year	200% declining balance	ADR midpoint life of 4 years or less, excluding cars and light trucks.
5-year	200% declining balance	ADR midpoint life of more than 4 years but less than 10 years, cars and light trucks, office machinery, certain energy property, R&D property, computers, and certain equipment.
7-year	200% declining balance	ADR midpoint life of 10 years or more but less than 16 years and property without an ADR life (e.g., most business furniture and certain equipment).
10-year	200% declining balance	ADR midpoint life of 16 years or more but less than 20 years, including trees and vines.
15-year	150% declining balance	ADR midpoint life of 20 years or more but less than 25 years, including treatment plants and land improvements (sidewalks, roads, fences, and landscaping).
20-year	150% declining balance	ADR midpoint life of 25 years or more, other than real property with an ADR life of 27.5 years or longer and municipal sewers.
27.5-year	Straight-line	Residential rental real estate, elevators, and escalators.
39-year	Straight-line	Other real property purchased generally on or after May 13, 1993 (previously 31.5-year straight-line).

The recovery period classification for assets acquired after 1980, but before 1987, differs from the recovery period classification presented in Table 8.1.

Under MACRS, taxpayers calculate the depreciation of an asset using a table which contains a percentage rate for each year of the property's recovery period. The yearly rate is applied to the cost of the asset. The cost of the property to which the rate is applied is not reduced for prior years' depreciation. For personal property (all property except real estate) the percentages in Table 8.2 apply.

EXAMPLE   Assume a taxpayer acquires an asset (5-year class property) in 2020 with a cost basis of $15,000 and uses accelerated depreciation under MACRS. The depreciation expense deduction for each year of the asset's life is calculated (using the percentages in Table 8.2) as follows:

Year	Percent		Cost		Deduction
2020	20.00	×	$15,000	=	$ 3,000
2021	32.00	×	15,000	=	4,800
2022	19.20	×	15,000	=	2,880
2023	11.52	×	15,000	=	1,728
2024	11.52	×	15,000	=	1,728
2025	5.76	×	15,000	=	864
Total	100.00%				$15,000

In the above example, note that even though the asset is a 5-year class property, the cost is written off over a period of 6 tax years. This is due to the convention under MACRS which provides for 6 months of depreciation during the year the asset is first placed in service and 6 months of depreciation during the year the asset is fully depreciated, sold, or disposed. This convention is referred to as the *half-year convention* since only one-half of the year of depreciation is allowed in both the year of acquisition and the year of disposition, regardless of the actual acquisition and disposition dates. The half-year convention is built into the rates in Table 8.2.

TABLE 8.2

Accelerated Depreciation for Personal Property Assuming Half-Year Convention (For Property Placed in Service after December 31, 1986)

Recovery Year	3-Year (200% DB)	5-Year (200% DB)	7-Year (200% DB)	10-Year (200% DB)	15-Year (150% DB)	20-Year (150% DB)
1	33.33	20.00	14.29	10.00	5.00	3.750
2	44.45	32.00	24.49	18.00	9.50	7.219
3	14.81*	19.20	17.49	14.40	8.55	6.677
4	7.41	11.52*	12.49	11.52	7.70	6.177
5		11.52	8.93*	9.22	6.93	5.713
6		5.76	8.92	7.37	6.23	5.285
7			8.93	6.55*	5.90*	4.888
8			4.46	6.55	5.90	4.522
9				6.56	5.91	4.462*
10				6.55	5.90	4.461
11				3.28	5.91	4.462
12					5.90	4.461
13					5.91	4.462
14					5.90	4.461
15					5.91	4.462
16					2.95	4.461
17						4.462
18						4.461
19						4.462
20						4.461
21						2.231

*Switch to straight-line depreciation.

For property (other than real estate), a taxpayer may elect to use straight-line depreciation instead of the accelerated depreciation rates under MACRS. The taxpayer must use the straight-line MACRS tables for assets for which a straight-line election has been made. The annual percentage rates to be applied to the cost of an asset for which a straight-line election under MACRS has been made are presented in Table 8.3.

TABLE 8.3

Straight-Line Depreciation for Personal Property, Assuming Half-Year Convention* (For Property Placed in Service after December 31, 1986)

Recovery Period	% First Recovery Year	Other Recovery Years		Last Recovery Years	
		Years	%	Year	%
3-year	16.67	2–3	33.33	4	16.67
5-year	10.00	2–5	20.00	6	10.00
7-year	7.14	2–7	14.29	8	7.14
10-year	5.00	2–10	10.00	11	5.00
15-year	3.33	2–15	6.67	16	3.33
20-year	2.50	2–20	5.00	21	2.50

*The official table contains a separate row for each year. For ease of presentation, certain years are grouped together in this table. In some instances, this will cause a difference of 0.01 percent for the last digit when compared with the official table.

EXAMPLE On April 1, 2020, Lori purchased and placed in service a specialized computer for use in her business. The computer cost $18,000 and Lori elects to use straight-line depreciation over 5 years instead of accelerated depreciation under MACRS. The annual deduction for depreciation over the life of the computer is calculated below (the percentages are taken from Table 8.3).

Year	Percent		Cost		Deduction
2020	10.00	×	$18,000	=	$ 1,800
2021	20.00	×	18,000	=	3,600
2022	20.00	×	18,000	=	3,600
2023	20.00	×	18,000	=	3,600
2024	20.00	×	18,000	=	3,600
2025	10.00	×	18,000	=	1,800
Total	100.00%				$18,000

Note that Lori receives a deduction based on 6 months in the year of purchase (half-year convention), even though the asset was put into service on April 1. If the asset had been placed into service on September 1, Lori still would have received a deduction for 6 months of depreciation. ◆

Under MACRS, the same method of depreciation (accelerated or straight-line) must be used for all property in a given class placed in service during that year.

8-2a Mid-Quarter Convention

When a taxpayer acquires a significant amount of assets during the last quarter of the tax year, the half-year convention, referred to in the above examples, is replaced by the *mid-quarter convention*. The mid-quarter convention must be applied if more than 40 percent of the total cost of a taxpayer's property acquired during the year, other than real property, is placed in service during the last 3 months of the tax year. The mid-quarter convention treats all property placed in service during any quarter of the tax year as being

TABLE 8.4

Accelerated Depreciation for Personal Property Assuming Mid-Quarter Convention* (For Property Placed in Service after December 31, 1986)

Recovery Year	3-Year (200% DB)	5-Year (200% DB)	7-Year (200% DB)
First Quarter			
1	58.33	35.00	25.00
2	27.78	26.00	21.43
3	12.35	15.60	15.31
4	1.54	11.01	10.93
5		11.01	8.75
Second Quarter			
1	41.67	25.00	17.85
2	38.89	30.00	23.47
3	14.14	18.00	16.76
4	5.30	11.37	11.97
5		11.37	8.87
Third Quarter			
1	25.00	15.00	10.71
2	50.00	34.00	25.51
3	16.67	20.40	18.22
4	8.33	12.24	13.02
5		11.30	9.30
Fourth Quarter			
1	8.33	5.00	3.57
2	61.11	38.00	27.55
3	20.37	22.80	19.68
4	10.19	13.68	14.06
5		10.94	10.04

*For ease of presentation, only 3-year, 5-year, and 7-year property and only depreciation rates for the first 5 years are provided. The official table also includes 10-, 15-, and 20-year property. See IRS Publication 946 for the complete table.

placed in service on the midpoint of the quarter. The mid-quarter convention, if applied in the year the asset is acquired, also applies upon the disposition of the asset. Assets placed in service and disposed of during the same tax year are not considered in determining whether the taxpayer meets the 40-percent test. An excerpt from the mid-quarter tables can be found in Table 8.4. Complete mid-quarter tables may be found in IRS Publication 946.

EXAMPLE   Jane, a calendar-year taxpayer, purchases the following property during 2020 for use in her business:

Placed in Service	Property	Original Cost	Recovery Period
March 2	Office furniture	$ 3,000	7 years
July 31	Apartment building	200,000	27.5 years
November 1	Automobile	18,000	5 years

Jane does not elect Section 179 and elects out of bonus depreciation. The cost of the automobile acquired during the last 3 months of the year represents 86 percent of the total cost of assets, other than real property, acquired during the tax year. Since more than 40 percent of Jane's purchases, other than real property, were made during the last 3 months of the tax year, the mid-quarter convention would apply. Depreciation for 2020 on the furniture is $750 ($3,000 × 25%) and on the auto is $900 ($18,000 × 5%). ◆

8-2b Bonus Depreciation

Because the cost recovery of long-lived assets occurs over many years, one way to lower the after-tax cost of capital expenditures is through accelerated depreciation. At times, the tax law has provided for "bonus depreciation," which is the immediate deduction of all or some of the cost of otherwise slowly depreciated property. The TCJA increased the bonus depreciation percentage to 100 percent for qualified property acquired and placed in service after September 27, 2017 and through December 31, 2022 (certain long-lived assets have an additional year), but the 100 percent bonus depreciation phases out starting in 2023 as follows:

Year	Bonus Percentage
2023	80
2024	60
2025	40
2026	20
2027	0

The bonus depreciation rules allow taxpayers purchasing property with a MACRS recovery period of 20 years or less (see Table 8.1), computer software, and certain leasehold improvements to directly write off up to 100 percent of the cost of the assets in the year placed in service. Bonus depreciation is presumed to apply unless the taxpayer elects out of the provision. The taxable income limits and thresholds associated with Section 179 (see LO 8.3) do not apply to bonus depreciation.

Both new and used property are generally eligible for bonus depreciation.

EXAMPLE Mary places a new 5-year MACRS-class machine costing $20,000 into service on March 1, 2020. She does not elect out of bonus depreciation on the machine. The bonus depreciation on the machine for 2020 is $20,000. The basis is reduced to $0 and no additional MACRS depreciation on the machine is deducted. ◆

Between bonus depreciation and the expanded immediate expensing under Section 179, small businesses are not likely to capitalize the cost of any non-real property unless they have a net operating loss or anticipate using larger depreciation deductions during higher tax bracket years in the future.

The TCJA of 2017 contained an oversight related to a classification of real property called "qualified improvement property." Qualified improvement property (QIP) is defined as an internal improvement to nonresidential property *excluding* escalators, elevators, internal structural framework, and enlargements to the building. When TCJA was passed, Congress intended to assign a 15-year life to QIP but inadvertently failed to do so. An amendment to classify QIP retroactively to 2018 as 15-year property was included in the CARES Act in 2020. This effectively classifies QIP as property eligible for bonus depreciation and thus can be recovered immediately in the year placed in service.

EXAMPLE In 2020, Bordeaux decided to upgrade the office building that it owns. The lobby area was completely redesigned to reflect the current standards for security and aesthetics. Also, additional space was added to the rear of the building to provide for storage for some high-value goods that need additional security not available in the existing building. The redesign of the lobby (unless changes were made to the structure of the building) is likely to qualify for bonus depreciation, whereas the expansion for additional space will not. ◆

8-2c **Real Estate**

For real estate acquired after 1986, MACRS requires the property to be depreciated using the straight-line method. The straight-line MACRS realty tables for residential realty (e.g., an apartment building) provide for depreciation over 27.5 years. Nonresidential realty (e.g., an office building) is depreciated over 39 years (31.5 years for realty acquired generally before May 13, 1993). The annual depreciation percentages for real estate under MACRS are shown in Table 8.5.

TABLE 8.5

Straight-Line Depreciation for Real Property Assuming Mid-Month Convention*

27.5-Year Residential Real Property

The applicable annual percentage is (use the column for the month in the first year the property is placed in service):

Recovery Year(s)	1	2	3	4	5	6	7	8	9	10	11	12
1	3.485	3.182	2.879	2.576	2.273	1.970	1.667	1.364	1.061	0.758	0.455	0.152
2–18	3.636	3.636	3.636	3.636	3.636	3.636	3.636	3.636	3.636	3.636	3.636	3.636
19–27	3.637	3.637	3.637	3.637	3.637	3.637	3.637	3.637	3.637	3.637	3.637	3.637
28	1.970	2.273	2.576	2.879	3.182	3.485	3.636	3.636	3.636	3.636	3.636	3.636
29	0.000	0.000	0.000	0.000	0.000	0.000	0.152	0.455	0.758	1.061	1.364	1.667

39-Year Nonresidential Real Property

The applicable annual percentage is (use the column for the month in the first year the property is placed in service):

Recovery Year(s)	1	2	3	4	5	6	7	8	9	10	11	12
1	2.461	2.247	2.033	1.819	1.605	1.391	1.177	0.963	0.749	0.535	0.321	0.107
2–39	2.564	2.564	2.564	2.564	2.564	2.564	2.564	2.564	2.564	2.564	2.564	2.564
40	0.107	0.321	0.535	0.749	0.963	1.177	1.391	1.605	1.819	2.033	2.247	2.461

*The official tables contain a separate row for each year. For ease of presentation, certain years are grouped together in these two tables. In some instances, this will produce a difference of 0.001 percent when compared with the official tables.

EXAMPLE Carlos purchases a rental house on September 3, 2020, for $90,000 (the land is accounted for separately). The house is already rented to a tenant. The annual depreciation expense deduction under MACRS for each of the first 4 years is illustrated below (the percentages are taken from Table 8.5, 27.5-Year Residential Real Property).

Year	Percent		Cost		Deduction
2020	1.061	×	$90,000	=	$ 955
2021	3.636	×	90,000	=	3,272
2022	3.636	×	90,000	=	3,272
2023	3.636	×	90,000	=	3,272

Note that the percentages are taken from Table 8.5 under column 9, because the month of acquisition (September) is the ninth month of the year. ◆

Most real property (except QIP) is not eligible for bonus depreciation or Section 179 immediate expensing (LO 8.3).

8-2d Mid-Month Convention

For the depreciation of real property under MACRS, a *mid-month convention* replaces the half-year convention. Real estate is treated as placed in service in the middle of the month the property is placed in service. Likewise, a disposition during a month is treated as occurring on the midpoint of such month. For example, under the mid-month convention, an asset purchased and placed in service on April 2 is treated as being placed in service on April 15. The mid-month convention is built into the first year's rates in Table 8.5.

8-2e Reporting Depreciation Expense

Depreciation expense is reported on Form 4562, Depreciation and Amortization. Individual taxpayers who have no current year asset additions and who are not reporting depreciation on listed property (see LO 8.4) are not required to file Form 4562 with their return.

Intuit ProConnect includes a powerful depreciation calculator included as part of the software. There are two ways to report depreciation. The first method is to enter the property details into the software. Property can be entered through either a quick entry or detailed input screen. Both are located under Deductions. The first subheading in the left-hand margin is depreciation. The property is linked to a business (for example, Schedule C or Schedule E). Based on the type and cost of property placed in service, the software will automatically apply bonus depreciation ("SDA") unless overridden in the detail screen. Section 179 immediate expensing can be input directly. The second method is to compute depreciation outside the ProConnect software and input the deduction as an override. The screens for direct input are located under the normal depreciation screens in the left-hand margin.

ProConnect™ Tax
TIP

Self-Study Problem 8.2   *See Appendix E for Solutions to Self-Study Problems*

During 2020, Mary Moser purchases the following items for use in her business:

Manufacturing equipment	$ 12,000
(7-year property, placed in service August 1)	
Office furniture	4,000
(7-year property, placed in service December 15)	
Office building, land is accounted for separately	175,000
(placed in service March 30)	

Assume that Mary uses the accelerated depreciation method under MACRS.

a. Use Form 4562 on Pages 8-11 and 8-12 to report Mary's depreciation deduction for 2020 including bonus depreciation.

b. Calculate Mary's depreciation (but do not complete Form 4562) assuming she elects out of bonus depreciation.

7-year property $_____

Office building $_____

c. Calculate Mary's depreciation deduction on the assets for 2021 (Year 2). Compute amounts assuming bonus depreciation was taken in 2020.

Year 2 Depreciation Deduction

7-year property $_____

Office building $_____

8-3 ELECTION TO EXPENSE (SECTION 179)

As part of the landmark Tax Reform Act of 1986, Internal Revenue Code Section 179 was implemented to decrease the cost of investments in business property by permitting small businesses to expense the costs of certain property that would otherwise be capitalized and depreciated over time.

Under Section 179, taxpayers may elect to expense the acquisition cost of certain property, subject to certain limitations. This cost would otherwise have been deducted over a period of time using the regular cost recovery depreciation rules. Similar to bonus depreciation, the Section 179 deduction applies to both new and used property. To qualify for this limited expensing election, the property must be personal property (property other than real estate or assets used in residential real estate rental activities except for certain qualified improvement property) placed in service during the year and used in a trade or business.

Section 179 places three limitations on the expensing election: (1) a maximum on the annual amount expensed, (2) a phase-out of the annual amount limit, and (3) the taxable income limit.

Originally, the maximum annual expensing amount was a modest $10,000. Over the years the amount was adjusted for inflation and also increased with economic stimulus in mind. As a result of the financial crisis, the annual maximum was increased to $250,000 in 2008 and then increased again to $500,000 in 2010. Although subject to repeated expiration and extension, the limit had remained at $500,000 until 2015 when it was made permanent and subject to inflation adjustment each year. The maximum annual amount that can be expensed under Section 179 is $1,040,000 in 2020.

The annual maximum expense amount is reduced dollar-for-dollar by the amount of Section 179 property acquired during the year in excess of a threshold amount. Similar to the annual limit, the Section 179 phase-out threshold amount has fluctuated over time. In 2020, the threshold is $2,590,000. As a result, a taxpayer that acquires $3,630,000 or more of Section 179 property during 2020 may not immediately expense under Section 179.

Lastly, the amount of acquired qualified property that may be expensed annually is limited to the taxpayer's taxable income, before considering any amount expensed under the Section 179 election, from any trade or business of the taxpayer. Any amount which is limited due to the taxable income limitation may be carried over to succeeding tax years.

EXAMPLE During 2020, Bob buys used equipment that cost $1,520,000 for his factory. Bob's business generates taxable income of well over $3,000,000 and he elects out of bonus depreciation. Bob's Section 179 property placed in service is below $2,590,000 and thus is not subject to phase-out. With $3 million in taxable income, Bob's Section 179 deduction is not subject to the income limitation. Bob may immediately expense $1,040,000 of his equipment. The remaining $480,000 of equipment cost will be depreciated over the recovery period under MACRS. ◆

EXAMPLE During 2020, Shuri places in service used manufacturing equipment for use in her business. The machinery cost $1,050,000. Shuri has taxable income (after considering any MACRS depreciation) from her business of $200,000. Under the annual maximum limitation, Shuri can immediately expense up to $1,040,000 and would depreciate the remaining $10,000 under MACRS. However, the maximum amount allowed under the taxable income limitation is only $200,000. The remaining $840,000 ($1,040,000 annual maximum less $200,000 permitted under the income limit) is carried forward to succeeding tax years. ◆

Self-Study Problem 8.2

Form **4562**

Department of the Treasury
Internal Revenue Service (99)

Depreciation and Amortization
(Including Information on Listed Property)
▶ Attach to your tax return.
▶ Go to *www.irs.gov/Form4562* for instructions and the latest information.

OMB No. 1545-0172

2020

Attachment
Sequence No. **179**

Name(s) shown on return | Business or activity to which this form relates | Identifying number

Part I	**Election To Expense Certain Property Under Section 179**	

Note: If you have any listed property, complete Part V before you complete Part I.

1	Maximum amount (see instructions)	**1**
2	Total cost of section 179 property placed in service (see instructions)	**2**
3	Threshold cost of section 179 property before reduction in limitation (see instructions)	**3**
4	Reduction in limitation. Subtract line 3 from line 2. If zero or less, enter -0-	**4**
5	Dollar limitation for tax year. Subtract line 4 from line 1. If zero or less, enter -0-. If married filing separately, see instructions	**5**

6	**(a)** Description of property	**(b)** Cost (business use only)	**(c)** Elected cost

7	Listed property. Enter the amount from line 29 . . . . **7**	
8	Total elected cost of section 179 property. Add amounts in column (c), lines 6 and 7	**8**
9	Tentative deduction. Enter the **smaller** of line 5 or line 8	**9**
10	Carryover of disallowed deduction from line 13 of your 2019 Form 4562	**10**
11	Business income limitation. Enter the smaller of business income (not less than zero) or line 5. See instructions	**11**
12	Section 179 expense deduction. Add lines 9 and 10, but don't enter more than line 11	**12**
13	Carryover of disallowed deduction to 2021. Add lines 9 and 10, less line 12 ▶ **13**	

Note: Don't use Part II or Part III below for listed property. Instead, use Part V.

Part II	**Special Depreciation Allowance and Other Depreciation (Don't** include listed property. See instructions.)	

14	Special depreciation allowance for qualified property (other than listed property) placed in service during the tax year. See instructions	**14**
15	Property subject to section 168(f)(1) election	**15**
16	Other depreciation (including ACRS)	**16**

Part III	**MACRS Depreciation (Don't** include listed property. See instructions.)	

Section A

17	MACRS deductions for assets placed in service in tax years beginning before 2020	**17**
18	If you are electing to group any assets placed in service during the tax year into one or more general asset accounts, check here . . . . ▶ ☐	

Section B—Assets Placed in Service During 2020 Tax Year Using the General Depreciation System

(a) Classification of property	**(b)** Month and year placed in service	**(c)** Basis for depreciation (business/investment use only—see instructions)	**(d)** Recovery period	**(e)** Convention	**(f)** Method	**(g)** Depreciation deduction
19a 3-year property						
b 5-year property						
c 7-year property						
d 10-year property						
e 15-year property						
f 20-year property						
g 25-year property			25 yrs.		S/L	
h Residential rental property			27.5 yrs.	MM	S/L	
			27.5 yrs.	MM	S/L	
i Nonresidential real property			39 yrs.	MM	S/L	
				MM	S/L	

Section C—Assets Placed in Service During 2020 Tax Year Using the Alternative Depreciation System

20a Class life					S/L	
b 12-year			12 yrs.		S/L	
c 30-year			30 yrs.	MM	S/L	
d 40-year			40 yrs.	MM	S/L	

Part IV	**Summary** (See instructions.)	

21	Listed property. Enter amount from line 28	**21**
22	**Total.** Add amounts from line 12, lines 14 through 17, lines 19 and 20 in column (g), and line 21. Enter here and on the appropriate lines of your return. Partnerships and S corporations—see instructions .	**22**
23	For assets shown above and placed in service during the current year, enter the portion of the basis attributable to section 263A costs **23**	

For Paperwork Reduction Act Notice, see separate instructions. Cat. No. 12906N Form **4562** (2020)

Form 4562 (2020)   Page **2**

| **Part V** | **Listed Property** (Include automobiles, certain other vehicles, certain aircraft, and property used for entertainment, recreation, or amusement.) |

Note: For any vehicle for which you are using the standard mileage rate or deducting lease expense, complete **only** 24a, 24b, columns (a) through (c) of Section A, all of Section B, and Section C if applicable.

Section A—Depreciation and Other Information (Caution: See the instructions for limits for passenger automobiles.)

24a Do you have evidence to support the business/investment use claimed? ☐ Yes ☐ No | 24b If "Yes," is the evidence written? ☐ Yes ☐ No

(a) Type of property (list vehicles first)	(b) Date placed in service	(c) Business/ investment use percentage	(d) Cost or other basis	(e) Basis for depreciation (business/investment use only)	(f) Recovery period	(g) Method/ Convention	(h) Depreciation deduction	(i) Elected section 179 cost
25 Special depreciation allowance for qualified listed property placed in service during the tax year and used more than 50% in a qualified business use. See instructions .				25				
26 Property used more than 50% in a qualified business use:								
		%						
		%						
		%						
27 Property used 50% or less in a qualified business use:								
		%				S/L –		
		%				S/L –		
		%				S/L –		
28 Add amounts in column (h), lines 25 through 27. Enter here and on line 21, page 1 .					28			
29 Add amounts in column (i), line 26. Enter here and on line 7, page 1							29	

Section B—Information on Use of Vehicles

Complete this section for vehicles used by a sole proprietor, partner, or other "more than 5% owner," or related person. If you provided vehicles to your employees, first answer the questions in Section C to see if you meet an exception to completing this section for those vehicles.

		(a) Vehicle 1		(b) Vehicle 2		(c) Vehicle 3		(d) Vehicle 4		(e) Vehicle 5		(f) Vehicle 6	
30	Total business/investment miles driven during the year (**don't** include commuting miles) .												
31	Total commuting miles driven during the year												
32	Total other personal (noncommuting) miles driven												
33	Total miles driven during the year. Add lines 30 through 32												
34	Was the vehicle available for personal use during off-duty hours?	Yes	No	Yes	No	Yes	No	Yes	No	Yes	No	Yes	No
35	Was the vehicle used primarily by a more than 5% owner or related person? . .												
36	Is another vehicle available for personal use?												

Section C—Questions for Employers Who Provide Vehicles for Use by Their Employees

Answer these questions to determine if you meet an exception to completing Section B for vehicles used by employees who **aren't** more than 5% owners or related persons. See instructions.

		Yes	No
37	Do you maintain a written policy statement that prohibits all personal use of vehicles, including commuting, by your employees?		
38	Do you maintain a written policy statement that prohibits personal use of vehicles, except commuting, by your employees? See the instructions for vehicles used by corporate officers, directors, or 1% or more owners . .		
39	Do you treat all use of vehicles by employees as personal use?		
40	Do you provide more than five vehicles to your employees, obtain information from your employees about the use of the vehicles, and retain the information received?		
41	Do you meet the requirements concerning qualified automobile demonstration use? See instructions.		

Note: If your answer to 37, 38, 39, 40, or 41 is "Yes," don't complete Section B for the covered vehicles.

| **Part VI** | **Amortization** |

(a) Description of costs	(b) Date amortization begins	(c) Amortizable amount	(d) Code section	(e) Amortization period or percentage	(f) Amortization for this year
42 Amortization of costs that begins during your 2020 tax year (see instructions):					
43 Amortization of costs that began before your 2020 tax year				43	
44 **Total.** Add amounts in column (f). See the instructions for where to report				44	

Form **4562** (2020)

EXAMPLE During 2020, Portia purchased $2,760,000 of new equipment for use in her business. Portia's taxable income before considering immediate expensing is over $4 million. Because the amount of Section 179 property placed in service during the year exceeds the phase-out threshold of $2,590,000, Portia's annual Section 179 expensing limit of $1,040,000 is reduced by the $170,000 phase-out ($2,760,000 − $2,590,000) resulting in a maximum allowable expensing amount of only $870,000. ♦

A taxpayer who has made the Section 179 election to expense must reduce the basis of the asset by the amount expensed before calculating regular MACRS depreciation on the remaining cost of the asset. Even if the taxpayer is not able to deduct the full amount expensed in the current year due to the *taxable income limitation*, the basis must be reduced by the full amount of the Section 179 expense election.

When calculating depreciation on an asset, if an election to expense only part of the asset has been made, the amount of the Section 179 election to expense must be decided first. When a taxpayer decides to take only a portion of the cost of the asset as a Section 179 deduction, the rest of the cost of the asset must be depreciated. The depreciation must be deducted from taxable income to determine the income limitation for the Section 179 deduction.

EXAMPLE On August 1, 2020, Joan purchases a machine for use in her business. It is her only purchase of business property in 2020. The machine cost $1,070,000 and qualifies as 5-year MACRS property. Her business income before any cost recovery is $1,018,000. Joan elects to immediately expense the entire $1,040,000. She elects out of bonus depreciation, thus $30,000 of remaining basis is subject to MACRS depreciation of $6,000 ($30,000 × 0.20 depreciation factor). As a result of deducting MACRS depreciation of $6,000, Joan's taxable income before Section 179 is reduced to $1,012,000. Joan may only immediately expense $1,012,000 due to the income limit. The excess $28,000 of Section 179 deduction will be carried forward to 2021. ♦

The effects of bonus depreciation, Section 179 and MACRS depreciation can combine to create substantially accelerated cost recovery. If a taxpayer elects Section 179 immediate expensing and uses bonus depreciation, the cost basis of the property is first reduced by the Section 179 deduction, then by bonus depreciation then lastly, by typical MACRS depreciation. With 100 percent bonus depreciation, the need to deduct Section 179 and then bonus depreciation is an unlikely occurrence since the entire cost of many types of property can be recovered under bonus depreciation without annual or income limits.

Self-Study Problem 8.3   *See Appendix E for Solutions to Self-Study Problems*

On June 15, 2020, Chang purchases $2,837,000 of equipment (7-year property) for use in her business. It is her only purchase of business property in 2020. Chang has taxable income from her business of $2.5 million before any cost recovery.

a. Assuming Chang does not elect Section 179 and elects out of bonus depreciation, what is her total 2020 cost recovery?

b. Assuming Chang elects the maximum Section 179 deduction allowable and elects out of bonus depreciation, what is her total 2020 cost recovery?

c. Assuming Chang does not elect Section 179 deduction allowable and does not elect out of bonus depreciation, what is her total cost recovery?

8-4 LISTED PROPERTY

Congress felt some taxpayers were using the favorable tax incentives of the accelerated cost recovery system and the limited expensing election to claim depreciation deductions on assets used for personal purposes. To curtail this perceived abuse of the tax system, Congress enacted special rules which apply to the depreciation of "listed property." Listed property includes those types of assets which lend themselves to personal use, including the following:

1. Passenger automobiles, defined to include any four-wheeled vehicle manufactured primarily for use on public streets, roads, and highways, rated at 6,000 pounds or less unloaded gross vehicle weight. Specifically excluded from the definition of passenger automobiles are vehicles used directly in the trade or business of transporting persons or property, ambulances and hearses used in a trade or business, and certain trucks and vans not likely to be used more than a de minimis amount for personal purposes, including vehicles which display the company name or advertising.

2. Other property used as a means of transportation (trucks, buses, boats, airplanes, and motorcycles), except vehicles which are not likely to be used for personal purposes, such as marked police cars, school buses, and tractors, or vehicles used for transporting persons or cargo for compensation.

3. Property generally used for entertainment, recreation, or amusement (video recording equipment, communication equipment, etc.).

If listed property is used 50 percent or less in a qualified business use, any depreciation deduction must be calculated using the straight-line method of depreciation over an alternate recovery period, and the special election to expense under Section 179 and bonus depreciation are not allowed.

Qualified business use does not include investment use or the use of property owned by an employee in performing services as an employee, unless the use meets the convenience-of-employer and condition-of-employment tests. In addition, the excess depreciation allowed by reason of the property meeting the more-than-50-percent-use test must be included in income if property which meets the test in one year subsequently fails to meet the more-than-50-percent-use test in a succeeding year.

EXAMPLE Oscar has an automobile he uses 45 percent of the time for personal use and 55 percent of the time in his accounting business. Since Oscar's business-use percentage of 55 percent exceeds 50 percent, Oscar is not required to use the straight-line method in calculating depreciation. The accelerated depreciation method and the election to expense may be used by Oscar. ◆

Self-Study Problem 8.4   *See Appendix E for Solutions to Self-Study Problems*

For each of the following independent situations, indicate with a Y (yes) or an N (no) whether or not the taxpayer is required to depreciate the property using the straight-line method over the alternate recovery period:

	Straight Line Required?
1. Alvarez uses an automobile 20 percent for his business and 80 percent for personal reasons.	_____
2. Laura has a truck she uses in her business 55 percent of the time, 15 percent for her real estate investment, and 30 percent for personal use.	_____

8-5 LIMITATION ON DEPRECIATION OF LUXURY AUTOMOBILES

In addition to the limitations on the depreciation of passenger automobiles imposed by the listed property rules discussed in the preceding section, the depreciation of passenger automobiles is subject to an additional limitation, commonly referred to as the "luxury automobile" limitation. Regardless of the method of depreciation used by the taxpayer, accelerated or straight-line, the election to expense, or bonus depreciation, the amount of depreciation expense that may be claimed on a passenger automobile is subject to an annual dollar limitation. The annual dollar limitations that apply to passenger automobiles acquired in 2020 are listed below. Any automobile which would have actual MACRS depreciation exceeding the limits is considered a "luxury automobile" by the IRS for purposes of the depreciation limitation rules.

Apply the limitations on depreciation of "luxury automobiles."

ANNUAL AUTOMOBILE DEPRECIATION LIMITATIONS

Year of Use	2019 and 2020 Limits
Year 1	$18,100*
Year 2	16,100
Year 3	9,700
Year 4 (and subsequent years until fully depreciated)	5,760

*Additional bonus depreciation of $8,000 is included in this amount.

Separate higher depreciation limits apply for certain trucks and vans and also for electric automobiles.

Some sport utility vehicles fall outside of the definition of passenger automobiles and can be depreciated or expensed under Section 179 or the bonus depreciation rules without regard to the automobile depreciation limits. To qualify for the exception, the sport utility vehicle must have a gross vehicle weight rating above 6,000 pounds. Vehicles that meet the large sport utility vehicle exception are limited to $25,900 in Section 179 expensing but may depreciate using the 5-year MACRS percentages without the typical auto depreciation limitations.

The annual limitations must be reduced to reflect the actual business-use percentage where business use is less than 100 percent.

EXAMPLE Sally purchased a new car for $60,000 in September 2020 which she uses 75 percent for business. Sally elects out of bonus depreciation. Depreciation on the automobile is calculated as follows:

Total cost	$60,000
	× 0.75
Limited to business use	$45,000
MACRS depreciation (half-year convention)	$45,000 × 20% = $ 9,000
Compared to:	
Maximum luxury automobile depreciation allowed	$10,100 × 75% = $ 7,575

Because the luxury automobile limitation is less than the actual depreciation calculated, Sally's depreciation deduction is limited to $7,575. ◆

EXAMPLE In September 2020, Joan purchased a passenger automobile which cost $60,000. The automobile is used 100 percent for business purposes and

Joan elects out of bonus depreciation. A comparison of MACRS, with and without the limitation, is as follows:

	Five-Year MACRS	Annual Limit
Year 1	$12,000	$10,100
Year 2	19,200	16,100
Year 3	11,520	9,700
Year 4	6,912	5,760
Year 5	6,912	5,760
Year 6	3,456	5,760
Year 7		5,760
Year 8		1,060

Note that, although the automobile is a 5-year property, it will take 8 years to recover the entire cost of the asset because of the annual dollar limits, assuming no election to expense under Section 179 or bonus depreciation. ◆

TAX BREAK

Taxpayers hoping to get around the luxury auto depreciation limits by leasing an auto should be aware that there is a rule designed to put them in the same economic position as if they had purchased the auto. The IRS issued tables for computation of an "income inclusion" which must be used to reduce the lease expense deduction for leased autos.

Bonus depreciation on autos is subject to annual depreciation limits also. For years after the first year, the unrecovered basis of the auto is subject to MACRS depreciation but remains limited by the auto limits.

EXAMPLE   Sally purchased a new automobile for $60,000 in September 2020 which she uses 100 percent for business during the life of the auto. Assuming half-year convention, bonus depreciation and no Section 179 depreciation, Sally's 2020 cost recovery is computed as follows:

Cost basis	$60,000
Depreciation limit for autos, Year 1	18,100
Basis unrecovered at end of 2020	$41,900

In 2021, MACRS depreciation is $13,408 (unrecovered basis of $41,900 × 32%, which is the depreciation factor for the second year of 5-year property). The second year limit of $16,100 exceeds the deduction and thus, does not apply. ◆

Self-Study Problem 8.5   *See Appendix E for Solutions to Self-Study Problems*

On June 17, 2020, Travis purchased a passenger automobile at a cost of $56,000. The automobile is used 90 percent for qualified business use and 10 percent for personal purposes. Calculate the depreciation expense (without bonus depreciation) for the automobile for 2020, 2021, and 2022, assuming half-year convention and no Section 179 immediate expensing.

$ _____

$ _____

$ _____

Sign Here	Under penalties of perjury, I declare that I have examined this return and accompanying schedules and statements, and to the best of my knowledge and belief, they are true, correct, and complete. Declaration of preparer (other than taxpayer) is based on all information of which preparer has any knowledge.			
	Your signature	Date	Your occupation	If the IRS sent you an Identity Protection PIN, enter it here (see inst.) ▶
Joint return? See instructions. Keep a copy for your records.	Spouse's signature. If a joint return, **both** must sign.	Date	Spouse's occupation	If the IRS sent your spouse an Identity Protection PIN, enter it here (see inst.) ▶
	Phone no.		Email address	
Paid Preparer Use Only	Preparer's name	Preparer's signature	Date	PTIN / Check if: ☐ Self-employed
	Firm's name ▶			Phone no.
	Firm's address ▶			Firm's EIN ▶

Duncan Devious (age 52) is a self-employed attorney. Duncan loves to be noticed in public and, therefore, he drives a 7,000-pound, military-type, SUV, the only vehicle he owns. When you are preparing his tax return, you notice that he claims 90 percent of his total auto expenses as a business deduction on his Schedule C and 10 percent as personal use, with total miles driven in 2020 as 10,000. You note from his home and office addresses on his tax return that he lives approximately 15 miles from his office. The total of the expenses (i.e., gas, oil, maintenance, depreciation) he claims is $31,200. He does not have a mileage log to substantiate the business use of the SUV. Would you sign the Paid Preparer's declaration (see example above) on this return? Why or why not?

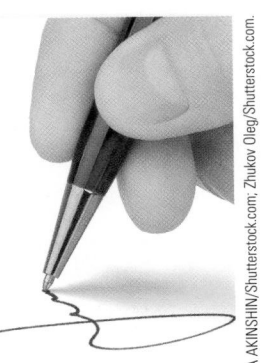

Would You Sign This Tax Return?

8-6 INTANGIBLES

8.6 Learning Objective

Calculate the amortization of goodwill and certain other intangibles.

The current tax guidance provides for two main categories of intangibles: (1) Section 197 intangibles and (2) non-Section 197 intangibles. Section 197 intangibles are those acquired by a taxpayer as part of the acquisition of a trade or business. Section 197 intangibles are amortized over a 15-year period, beginning with the month of acquisition. Amortization is a cost recovery method similar to depreciation in that it spreads the cost recovery over a fixed period of years. It differs from depreciation in that it is applied to intangible assets rather than tangible personal or real property and does not include the half-year or mid-quarter conventions. The 15-year life applies regardless of the actual useful life of the intangible asset. No other amortization or depreciation method may be claimed on Section 197 assets. When acquired as part of a trade or business, the following are defined as qualified Section 197 intangibles:

- Goodwill
- Going-concern value
- Workforce in place
- Information bases, including business books and records and operating systems
- Know-how
- Customer-based intangibles
- License, permit, or right granted by a governmental unit
- Covenant not to compete
- Franchise, trademark, or trade name

EXAMPLE In March 2020, Mary purchases a business from Bill for $250,000. Section 197 goodwill of $36,000 is included in the $250,000 purchase price. Mary amortizes the goodwill over a 15-year period at the rate of $200 per month, starting with the month of purchase. ◆

8-6a Exclusions

Many intangible assets are specifically excluded from the definition of Section 197 intangibles. Examples of these Section 197 exclusions include items which are not generally amortizable:

- Interests in a corporation, partnership, trust, or estate
- Interests in land

Section 197 exclusions that are generally amortizable:

- Computer software readily available for purchase by the general public
- Interests in films, sound recordings, video recordings, and similar property
- Self-created intangible assets

Non-Section 197 intangibles that are separately acquired are generally amortized over their remaining useful life using the straight-line method. For example, a patent could be acquired as part of the purchase of a business (Section 197 intangible) or a patent could be acquired separately (non-Section 197 intangible). A franchise, trademark, or tradename is treated as a Section 197 intangible whether acquired as part of a business or not.

EXAMPLE   Sam purchases computer software sold to the general public for $20,000. The $20,000 is not a Section 197 intangible and therefore the amount would be amortized under regular amortization rules (typically 3 years). ♦

Amortization expense is reported on the bottom of page 2 in Part VI of Form 4562.

ProConnect™ Tax TIP

Amortization is entered into the software in the Depreciation section. Select Non-recovery/Straight-line as the depreciation method. The recovery period (e.g., 15 years for Section 197 intangibles) must be input. An amortization code is available in the detailed input screen.

Self-Study Problem 8.6   *See Appendix E for Solutions to Self-Study Problems*

Indicate by check marks whether the following items are generally amortizable over 15 years, amortized over their useful life, or not amortized.

	15-Year Amortization	*Useful Life*	*Not Amortizable*
1. Patent acquired as part of a business	_____	_____	_____
2. Separately acquired film rights	_____	_____	_____
3. Computer software sold at an office supply store	_____	_____	_____
4. Goodwill	_____	_____	_____
5. Franchise	_____	_____	_____
6. Land	_____	_____	_____
7. Trademark	_____	_____	_____
8. Interest in a corporation	_____	_____	_____

Learning Objective 8.7

Classify gains and losses from Section 1231 assets.

8-7 SECTION 1231 GAINS AND LOSSES

The first part of this chapter has dealt with the acquisition and cost recovery of business property. The remaining sections deal with the sale, exchange, or disposal of business property. The tax rules on capital gains and losses covered in Chapter 4 continue to apply here, but the tax law has been crafted in a way to provide capital treatment for certain business gains and losses and ordinary treatment for others. Unlike much of the tax law covered elsewhere in this textbook, these tax concepts often refer to the Internal Revenue Code section number as the identifying name. For example, Section 1231 is used to describe property used in a trade or business and held for more than one year. Depreciation recapture is commonly referred to as Section 1245 or Section 1250 recapture.

Section 1231 assets are not capital assets (see Chapter 4), but they are given special tax treatment. Gains on Section 1231 assets may be treated as long-term capital gains, while losses in some cases may be deducted as ordinary losses. Section 1231 assets include:

1. Depreciable or real property used in a trade or business;
2. Timber, coal, or domestic iron ore;
3. Livestock (not including poultry) held for draft, breeding, dairy, or sporting purposes; and
4. Unharvested crops on land used in a trade or business.

Any property held 1 year or less, inventory and property held for sale to customers, and copyrights, paintings, government publications, etc., are not Section 1231 property.

The calculation of net Section 1231 gains and losses is summarized as follows:

Combine *all* Section 1231 gains and losses to compute *net* Section 1231 gains or losses. If the gains exceed the losses, the excess is a long-term capital gain. When the losses exceed the gains, all gains are treated as ordinary income, and all losses are fully deductible as ordinary losses.

EXAMPLE Frank Harper had the following business gains and (losses) on the sale of business property during August of 2020:

Sale of land held for 4 years	$ 9,500
Sale of truck held for 3 years	(2,100)
Sale of inventory	6,000

Frank's Section 1231 gains and losses would be calculated as follows:

Gain on land	$ 9,500
Loss on truck	(2,100)
Net Section 1231 gain	$ 7,400

The $7,400 net Section 1231 gain would be treated as a long-term capital gain and would be reported on Form 4797 and transferred to Line 11 of Schedule D of Form 1040. Inventory is not Section 1231 property and thus, results in an ordinary gain. ◆

Self-Study Problem 8.7 *See Appendix E for Solutions to Self-Study Problems*

Serena had the following sales of business property during the 2020 tax year:

1. Sold land acquired on December 3, 2009, at a cost of $24,000, for $37,000 on January 5, 2020. The cost of selling the land was $500, and there was no depreciation allowable or capital improvements made to the asset over the life of the asset.

2. Sold a business computer with an adjusted basis of $20,700 that was acquired on April 5, 2017. The original cost was $25,875, and accumulated depreciation was $5,175. The computer was sold on May 2, 2020, for $14,000, resulting in a $6,700 loss.

3. Sold equipment on July 22, 2020 for gross proceeds of $16,000. The equipment was acquired on October 21, 2019 at a cost of $25,000 and accumulated depreciation was $4,300 at the time of the sale. Serena used an equipment broker on this sale and paid a sales commission of $1,600.

Calculate Serena's net gain or loss and determine the character as either capital or ordinary (ignore any depreciation recapture).

8-8 DEPRECIATION RECAPTURE

Apply the depreciation recapture rules.

Since long-term capital gains traditionally have been taxed at a lower tax rate than ordinary income, taxpayers have attempted to maximize the amount of income treated as capital gain. Congress enacted depreciation recapture provisions to prevent taxpayers from converting ordinary income into capital gains by claiming maximum depreciation deductions over the life of the asset and then selling the asset and receiving capital gain treatment on the resulting gain at the time of the sale. There are three major depreciation recapture provisions: (1) Section 1245, which generally applies to personal property, (2) Section 1250, which applies to real estate, and (3) "unrecaptured depreciation" previously taken on real estate. The depreciation recapture provisions are extremely complex. Only a brief overview of the general provisions contained in the tax law is presented here.

8-8a Section 1245 Recapture

Under the provisions of Section 1245, any gain recognized on the disposition of a Section 1245 asset will be classified as ordinary income up to an amount equal to the depreciation claimed. Any gain in excess of depreciation taken is classified as a Section 1231 gain. Section 1245 property is:

- Depreciable tangible personal property such as furniture, machines, computers, and automobiles
- Amortizable intangible personal property such as patents, copyrights, leaseholds, and professional sports contracts
- Other tangible property (except buildings) used as an integral part of manufacturing, production or extraction
- Single purpose agricultural or horticultural structures

Section 1245 recapture potential is defined as the total depreciation claimed on Section 1245 property. The amount of ordinary income recognized upon the sale of an asset under Section 1245 is equal to the lesser of (1) total depreciation claimed on the asset, or (2) the amount of the realized gain on the sale. Any gain recognized in excess of the amount of ordinary income is a Section 1231 gain.

EXAMPLE On March 1 of the current year, Melvin sells Section 1245 property, which was purchased four years ago for $6,000. Melvin had claimed depreciation on the property of $2,500, and sold the property for $5,000. The recapture under Section 1245 is calculated below:

Amount realized	$5,000
Adjusted basis ($6,000–$2,500)	3,500
Realized gain	$1,500
Total depreciation taken	$2,500

The amount of Section 1245 recapture (the gain characterized as ordinary) is $1,500, which is the lesser of the realized gain ($1,500) or the total depreciation taken ($2,500). ♦

EXAMPLE   Assume the same facts as in the previous example, except that the property is sold for $7,800. The recapture under Section 1245 is calculated below:

Amount realized	$7,800
Adjusted basis ($6,000 − $2,500)	3,500
Realized gain	$4,300
Total depreciation taken	$2,500

The amount of Section 1245 recapture (the gain characterized as ordinary) is $2,500, which is the lesser of the realized gain ($4,300) or the total depreciation taken ($2,500). The residual gain of $1,800 ($4,300 − $2,500) is a Section 1231 gain. ◆

EXAMPLE   Assume the same facts as in the previous example, except that the property is sold for $2,800. Because the property is sold at a loss of $700 ($2,800 − $3,500), Section 1245 recapture does not apply and the loss is treated as a Section 1231 loss. ◆

8-8b Section 1250 Recapture

Section 1250 applies to the gain on the sale of depreciable real property, other than real property included in the definition of Section 1245 property. The amount of Section 1250 recapture potential is equal to the excess of depreciation expense claimed over the life of the asset under an *accelerated* method of depreciation over the amount of depreciation that would have been allowed if the straight-line method of depreciation had been used. If property is depreciated using the straight-line method, there is no Section 1250 recapture potential. Since the use of the straight-line method is required for real property acquired after 1986, there will be no Section 1250 recapture on the disposition of such property. In practice, Section 1250 recapture is rarely seen.

8-8c "Unrecaptured Depreciation" on Real Estate—25 Percent Rate

A special 25 percent tax rate applies to real property gains attributable to depreciation previously taken and not already recaptured under the Section 1245 or Section 1250 rules discussed above. Any remaining gain attributable to "unrecaptured depreciation" previously taken, including straight-line depreciation, is taxed at 25 percent rather than the long-term capital gain rate of 15 percent. When the taxpayer's ordinary tax rate is below 25 percent, the depreciation recapture will be taxed at the lower ordinary tax rate to the extent of the remaining amount in the less than 25 percent bracket and then at 25 percent. The application of the 25 percent rate for "unrecaptured depreciation" is frequently seen in practice because it applies to every rental property which is depreciated and then sold at a gain. If the 3.8 percent net investment income tax discussed in Chapter 6 applies, the 25 percent rate will be increased to 28.8 percent and the 15 percent rate will be increased to 18.8 percent.

EXAMPLE   Lew, an individual taxpayer, acquires an apartment building in 2010 for $300,000, and he sells it in October 2020 for $500,000. The accumulated straight-line depreciation on the building at the time of the sale is $45,000. Lew is in the 35 percent tax bracket for ordinary income. Lew's gain on the sale of the property is $245,000 ($500,000 less adjusted basis of $255,000). $45,000 of the gain is attributable to unrecaptured depreciation and is taxed at 25 percent, while the remaining $200,000 gain is taxed at the 15 percent long-term capital gains rate. Lew may also be subject to the 3.8 percent net investment income tax which is discussed in Chapter 6. If this is the case, his tax rates will increase to 28.8 percent and 18.8 percent, respectively. ◆

The reporting of unrecaptured depreciation on 1250 property gains subject to the 25 percent rate is considerably complex. The amounts from the Form 4797 are reported on Schedule D and the use of the Unrecaptured Section 1250 Gain Worksheet from the Schedule D instructions is also suggested. Amounts from this worksheet are transferred to the Schedule D Tax worksheet (also part of the Schedule D instructions) which is similar to the Qualified Dividends and Capital Gain Tax Worksheet used in earlier chapters of this textbook.

Self-Study Problem 8.8   *See Appendix E for Solutions to Self-Study Problems*

The following information is from Self-Study Problem 8.7:

Serena, an individual taxpayer, had the following sales of business property during the 2020 tax year:

1. Sold land acquired on December 3, 2009, at a cost of $24,000, for $37,000 on January 5, 2020. The cost of selling the land was $500, and there was no depreciation allowable or capital improvements made to the asset over the life of the asset.

2. Sold a business computer with an adjusted basis of $20,700 that was acquired on April 5, 2017. The original cost was $25,875, and accumulated depreciation was $5,175. The computer was sold on May 2, 2020, for $14,000, resulting in a $6,700 loss.

3. Sold equipment on July 22, 2020 for gross proceeds of $16,000. The equipment was acquired on October 21, 2019 at a cost of $25,000 and accumulated depreciation was $4,300 at the time of the sale. Serena used an equipment broker on this sale and paid a sales commission of $1,600.

Add this new information:

4. Sold a building on October 7, 2020 for $340,000, net of sales commissions of $15,000. Serena acquired the building on December 3, 2009 at a cost of $320,000. Accumulated depreciation has been computed using the straight-line method since acquisition and totaled $126,050 at the time of the sale.

5. Sold furniture on October 7, 2020 for $7,600. The furniture was acquired on December 3, 2009 for $15,000 and accumulated depreciation was $15,000 at the time of the sale.

Serena's employer identification number is 74-8976432. Use Form 4797 on Pages 8-23 and 8-24 to report the above gains and losses (hint: do **not** ignore depreciation recapture and complete Part III first).

ProConnect™ Tax TIP

The sale of business property is entered on the Sale of Asset 4797/6252 screens under deductions.

Self-Study Problem 8.8

Form **4797**	**Sales of Business Property** (Also Involuntary Conversions and Recapture Amounts Under Sections 179 and 280F(b)(2)) ▶ Attach to your tax return. ▶ Go to *www.irs.gov/Form4797* for instructions and the latest information.	OMB No. 1545-0184 **2020** Attachment Sequence No. **27**
Department of the Treasury Internal Revenue Service		

Name(s) shown on return | Identifying number

1 Enter the gross proceeds from sales or exchanges reported to you for 2020 on Form(s) 1099-B or 1099-S (or substitute statement) that you are including on line 2, 10, or 20. See instructions . . . . | **1**

Part I — Sales or Exchanges of Property Used in a Trade or Business and Involuntary Conversions From Other Than Casualty or Theft—Most Property Held More Than 1 Year (see instructions)

2	**(a)** Description of property	**(b)** Date acquired (mo., day, yr.)	**(c)** Date sold (mo., day, yr.)	**(d)** Gross sales price	**(e)** Depreciation allowed or allowable since acquisition	**(f)** Cost or other basis, plus improvements and expense of sale	**(g)** Gain or (loss) Subtract (f) from the sum of (d) and (e)

3 Gain, if any, from Form 4684, line 39 . . . . | **3**

4 Section 1231 gain from installment sales from Form 6252, line 26 or 37 . . . | **4**

5 Section 1231 gain or (loss) from like-kind exchanges from Form 8824 . . . | **5**

6 Gain, if any, from line 32, from other than casualty or theft . . . . . . | **6**

7 Combine lines 2 through 6. Enter the gain or (loss) here and on the appropriate line as follows . . . . . . | **7**

Partnerships and S corporations. Report the gain or (loss) following the instructions for Form 1065, Schedule K, line 10, or Form 1120-S, Schedule K, line 9. Skip lines 8, 9, 11, and 12 below.

Individuals, partners, S corporation shareholders, and all others. If line 7 is zero or a loss, enter the amount from line 7 on line 11 below and skip lines 8 and 9. If line 7 is a gain and you didn't have any prior year section 1231 losses, or they were recaptured in an earlier year, enter the gain from line 7 as a long-term capital gain on the Schedule D filed with your return and skip lines 8, 9, 11, and 12 below.

8 Nonrecaptured net section 1231 losses from prior years. See instructions . . . . | **8**

9 Subtract line 8 from line 7. If zero or less, enter -0-. If line 9 is zero, enter the gain from line 7 on line 12 below. If line 9 is more than zero, enter the amount from line 8 on line 12 below and enter the gain from line 9 as a long-term capital gain on the Schedule D filed with your return. See instructions . . . . | **9**

Part II — Ordinary Gains and Losses (see instructions)

10 Ordinary gains and losses not included on lines 11 through 16 (include property held 1 year or less):

11 Loss, if any, from line 7 . . . . | **11** ( )

12 Gain, if any, from line 7 or amount from line 8, if applicable . . . . | **12**

13 Gain, if any, from line 31 . . . . | **13**

14 Net gain or (loss) from Form 4684, lines 31 and 38a . . . . | **14**

15 Ordinary gain from installment sales from Form 6252, line 25 or 36 . . . . | **15**

16 Ordinary gain or (loss) from like-kind exchanges from Form 8824 . . . . . | **16**

17 Combine lines 10 through 16 . . . . | **17**

18 For all except individual returns, enter the amount from line 17 on the appropriate line of your return and skip lines a and b below. For individual returns, complete lines a and b below.

a If the loss on line 11 includes a loss from Form 4684, line 35, column (b)(ii), enter that part of the loss here. Enter the loss from income-producing property on Schedule A (Form 1040), line 16. (Do not include any loss on property used as an employee.) Identify as from "Form 4797, line 18a." See instructions . . . . | **18a**

b Redetermine the gain or (loss) on line 17 excluding the loss, if any, on line 18a. Enter here and on Schedule 1 (Form 1040), Part I, line 4 . . . . | **18b**

For Paperwork Reduction Act Notice, see separate instructions. | Cat. No. 13086I | Form **4797** (2020)

Form 4797 (2020)   Page **2**

| Part III | Gain From Disposition of Property Under Sections 1245, 1250, 1252, 1254, and 1255 (see instructions) |

19	(a) Description of section 1245, 1250, 1252, 1254, or 1255 property:		**(b)** Date acquired (mo., day, yr.)	**(c)** Date sold (mo., day, yr.)
A				
B				
C				
D				

	These columns relate to the properties on lines 19A through 19D. ▶		Property A	Property B	Property C	Property D
20	Gross sales price (**Note:** *See line 1 before completing.*)	**20**				
21	Cost or other basis plus expense of sale	**21**				
22	Depreciation (or depletion) allowed or allowable	**22**				
23	Adjusted basis. Subtract line 22 from line 21	**23**				
24	Total gain. Subtract line 23 from line 20	**24**				
25	**If section 1245 property:**					
a	Depreciation allowed or allowable from line 22	**25a**				
b	Enter the **smaller** of line 24 or 25a	**25b**				
26	**If section 1250 property:** If straight line depreciation was used, enter -0- on line 26g, except for a corporation subject to section 291.					
a	Additional depreciation after 1975. See instructions	**26a**				
b	Applicable percentage multiplied by the **smaller** of line 24 or line 26a. See instructions	**26b**				
c	Subtract line 26a from line 24. If residential rental property **or** line 24 isn't more than line 26a, skip lines 26d and 26e	**26c**				
d	Additional depreciation after 1969 and before 1976	**26d**				
e	Enter the **smaller** of line 26c or 26d	**26e**				
f	Section 291 amount (corporations only)	**26f**				
g	Add lines 26b, 26e, and 26f	**26g**				
27	**If section 1252 property:** Skip this section if you didn't dispose of farmland or if this form is being completed for a partnership.					
a	Soil, water, and land clearing expenses	**27a**				
b	Line 27a multiplied by applicable percentage. See instructions	**27b**				
c	Enter the **smaller** of line 24 or 27b	**27c**				
28	**If section 1254 property:**					
a	Intangible drilling and development costs, expenditures for development of mines and other natural deposits, mining exploration costs, and depletion. See instructions	**28a**				
b	Enter the **smaller** of line 24 or 28a	**28b**				
29	**If section 1255 property:**					
a	Applicable percentage of payments excluded from income under section 126. See instructions	**29a**				
b	Enter the **smaller** of line 24 or 29a. See instructions	**29b**				

Summary of Part III Gains. Complete property columns A through D through line 29b before going to line 30.

30	Total gains for all properties. Add property columns A through D, line 24	**30**	
31	Add property columns A through D, lines 25b, 26g, 27c, 28b, and 29b. Enter here and on line 13	**31**	
32	Subtract line 31 from line 30. Enter the portion from casualty or theft on Form 4684, line 33. Enter the portion from other than casualty or theft on Form 4797, line 6	**32**	

| Part IV | Recapture Amounts Under Sections 179 and 280F(b)(2) When Business Use Drops to 50% or Less (see instructions) |

			(a) Section 179	**(b)** Section 280F(b)(2)
33	Section 179 expense deduction or depreciation allowable in prior years	**33**		
34	Recomputed depreciation. See instructions	**34**		
35	Recapture amount. Subtract line 34 from line 33. See the instructions for where to report	**35**		

Form **4797** (2020)

8-9 BUSINESS CASUALTY GAINS AND LOSSES

The treatment of casualty gains and losses differs depending on whether the property involved is held for personal use or held for business or investment purposes. Therefore, a taxpayer's business and investment casualty gains and losses are computed separately from personal casualty gains and losses. Deductions for personal casualty losses are restricted to those associated with a federally-declared disaster area. Since the casualty loss is an itemized deduction, the rules for personal casualties are discussed in Chapter 5.

Apply the general treatment of casualty gains and losses for business purposes.

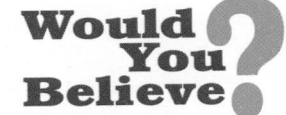
Would You Believe?

> The Ninth Circuit Court decided that a man's payment to a woman to keep her from revealing their extramarital affair was not a deductible casualty loss.

The amount of a business casualty or loss depends on whether the property was completely or partially destroyed. If business property is completely destroyed, the loss is the adjusted basis of the property less any insurance reimbursement. If business property is partially destroyed, the loss is insurance proceeds less the lesser of the adjusted basis at the time of the casualty or the decrease in the property's fair market value associated with the casualty.

EXAMPLE Joan's business suffered two casualties in the current year. Theft 1: One of Joan's employees stole a business vehicle and ended up abandoning the vehicle. The car was vandalized and damaged. The adjusted basis of the car was $14,000 at the time of the theft and the car was repairable but decreased in value $7,000 because of the damage. Theft 2: A car owned by Joan's business was stolen. The thief was involved in a traffic accident and the car was totally destroyed. The basis of the car was $7,600 at the time of the theft and had fair market value of $5,000 before the crash. Joan's insurance company reimbursed her $6,000 for the first theft and $4,000 for the second. Theft 1 is a partial destruction and the lesser of the decrease in market value or the adjusted basis is used to compute the loss. Theft 2 is a complete destruction and so the adjusted basis is used to compute the loss.

	Theft 1 Partial Destruction	Theft 2 Complete Destruction
Insurance proceeds	$ 6,000	$ 4,000
Adjusted basis	14,000	**7,600**
Decrease in FMV	**7,000**	n/a
Loss	$(1,000)	$(3,600)

Business and investment property must be identified as a capital asset, trade or business property subject to an allowance for depreciation, or ordinary income property. The following rules apply to the treatment of business or investment property:

1. Property held for 1 year or less—gains from trade or business property (including property used in the production of rental or royalty income) and gains from investment property are netted against losses from trade or business property, and the resulting net gain or loss is treated as ordinary income or loss. Losses from investment property are considered separately.

2. Property held over 1 year—gains and losses from trade or business property and investment property are netted.

   a. Net gain—if the result is a net gain, the net gain is included in the calculation of the net Section 1231 gain or loss (the gains and losses are treated as Section 1231 gains and losses).

   b. Net loss—if the result is a net loss, the gains and losses from business and investment property are excluded from Section 1231 treatment.

The tax treatment of the gains and losses depends on whether the property was used in the taxpayer's trade or business or held for investment. Gains and losses from business-use assets are treated as ordinary income and ordinary losses, respectively.

If the taxpayer recognizes a gain as a result of a casualty, and the property involved is depreciable property, the depreciation recapture provisions may cause all or a part of the gain to be treated as ordinary income. A casualty involving business property is included in the definition of an involuntary conversion, so that gain realized may be eligible for deferral under the special involuntary conversion provisions discussed in LO 8.12 of this chapter. The interaction of Section 1231 and casualty gains and losses from business or investment property is complex. Taxpayers should follow the instructions included with Form 4684 and Form 4797. See the IRS website (**www.irs.gov**) for samples of these forms and instructions.

EXAMPLE Two pieces of manufacturing equipment used by Robert in his business are completely destroyed by fire. One of the pieces of equipment had an adjusted basis of $5,000 ($11,000 original basis less $6,000 accumulated depreciation) and a fair market value of $3,000 on the date of the fire. The other piece of equipment had an adjusted basis of $7,000 ($18,000 original basis less $11,000 of accumulated depreciation) and a fair market value of $10,000. Robert receives $3,000 from his insurance company to compensate him for the loss of the first piece of equipment, and he receives $8,000 for the second piece of equipment. As a result of the casualty, Robert's casualty gain or loss is calculated as follows:

	Item 1	Item 2
Insurance proceeds	$ 3,000	$ 8,000
Adjusted basis of property	(5,000)	(7,000)
(Loss) gain	$(2,000)	$ 1,000

The netting of the business casualty gains and losses results in a net loss of $1,000; thus, the gains and losses are excluded from Section 1231 treatment. Since the loss on Item 1 represents a loss arising from an asset used in the taxpayer's business (not an asset held for investment), the loss is considered an ordinary loss. The $1,000 gain from Item 2 is treated as ordinary income under Section 1245 recapture. ◆

Self-Study Problem 8.9   *See Appendix E for Solutions to Self-Study Problems*

Jonathan has the following separate casualties during the year:

	Decrease in Fair Market Value	Adjusted Basis	Insurance Reimbursement	Holding Period
Business furniture	$ 4,000	$ 5,000	$ 0	3 years
Business machinery	15,000	14,000	10,000	3 years

The furniture was completely destroyed while the machinery was partially destroyed. Jonathan also sold business land for a Section 1231 gain of $10,000. Calculate the amount and nature of Jonathan's gains and losses as a result of these casualties.

8-10 INSTALLMENT SALES

Some taxpayers sell property and do not receive payment immediately. Instead, they take a note from the purchaser and receive payments over an extended period of time. It would be a financial hardship to require those taxpayers to pay tax on all of the gain on the sale of the property in the year of sale when they may not have received enough cash to cover the taxes. To provide equity in such situations, Congress passed the installment sale provision. The installment sale provision allows taxpayers to spread the gain (but not a loss) over the tax years in which payments are received. On an installment sale, the taxable gain reported each year is determined as follows:

$$\text{Taxable gain} = \frac{\text{Total gain realized on the sale}}{\text{Contract price}} \times \text{Cash collections during the year}$$

Taxpayers who receive payments over a period of time automatically report gain on the installment method, unless they elect to report all the gain in the year of the sale. An election to report all the gain in the year of sale is made by including all the gain in income for the year of the sale. Taxpayers use Form 6252, Installment Sale Income, to report the installment sale gain on their income tax returns.

EXAMPLE Howard Scripp sells land with an adjusted basis of $20,000 for $50,000. He receives $10,000 in the year of sale, and the balance is payable at $8,000 per year for 5 years, plus a reasonable amount of interest. If Howard elects not to report under the installment method, the gain in the year of sale would be calculated in the following manner:

Cash	$ 10,000
Note at fair market value	40,000
Amount realized	50,000
Less: the land's basis	(20,000)
Taxable gain	$ 30,000

◆

EXAMPLE If, instead, Howard reports the gain on the installment method, the amount of the taxable gain in the year of sale is $6,000, which is calculated below.

$$\text{Taxable gain} = \frac{\text{Total gain}}{\text{Contract price}} \times \text{Cash collections}$$

$$\text{Taxable gain} = \frac{\$30,000}{\$50,000} \times \$10,000 = \$6,000$$

Howard must complete Form 6252 as illustrated on Page 8-29.

If $8,000 is collected in the first year after the year of sale, the gain in that year would be $4,800, as illustrated below.

$$\text{Taxable gain} = \frac{\$30,000}{\$50,000} \times \$8,000 = \$4,800$$

Of course, any interest income received on the note is also included in income as portfolio income. ◆

Complex installment sale rules apply to taxpayers who regularly sell real or personal property and to taxpayers who sell certain business or rental real property. For example, any recapture under Section 1245 or Section 1250 must be reported in full in the year of sale, regardless of the taxpayer's use of the installment method. Any remaining gain may be reported under the installment method. In addition, certain limitations apply where there is an installment sale between related parties.

8-10a The Contract Price

The contract price used in calculating the taxable gain is the amount the seller will ultimately collect from the purchaser (other than interest). This amount is usually the sale price of the property. However, the purchaser will occasionally assume the seller's liability on the property, in which case the contract price is computed by subtracting from the selling price any mortgage or notes assumed by the buyer. If the mortgage or notes assumed by the buyer exceed the adjusted basis of the property, the excess is treated as a cash payment received in the year of sale and must be included in the contract price.

EXAMPLE Roger receives the following for an installment sale of real estate:

Cash	$ 3,000
Roger's mortgage assumed by the purchaser	9,000
Note payable to Roger from the purchaser	39,000
Selling price	$ 51,000

Roger's total gain is computed as follows:

Selling price	$ 51,000
Less: selling expenses	(1,500)
Amount realized	49,500
Less: Roger's basis in the property	(30,000)
Total gain	$ 19,500

The contract price is $42,000 ($51,000 − $9,000), and assuming the $3,000 is the only cash received in the year of sale, the taxable gain in the year of sale is $1,393 as shown below:

$$\text{Taxable gain} = \frac{\$19,500}{\$42,000} \times \$3,000 = \$1,393 \blacklozenge$$

Self-Study Problem 8.10   *See Appendix E for Solutions to Self-Study Problems*

Brian acquired a rental house in 2004 for a cost of $80,000. Straight-line depreciation on the property of $26,000 has been claimed by Brian. In January 2020, he sells the property for $120,000, receiving $20,000 cash on March 1 and the buyer's note for $100,000 at 10 percent interest. The note is payable at $10,000 per year for 10 years, with the first payment to be received 1 year after the date of sale. Calculate his taxable gain under the installment method for the year of sale of the rental house.

Gain reportable in 2020 $ _____

Taxpayers may wish to elect out of the installment treatment for a sale which could qualify, and instead recognize all of the gain in the year of sale when they have low income and expect that the gain would be taxed at a higher rate if deferred to later years.

Form **6252**	**Installment Sale Income**	OMB No. 1545-0228
Department of the Treasury Internal Revenue Service	▶ **Attach to your tax return.** ▶ **Use a separate form for each sale or other disposition of property on the installment method.** ▶ **Go to** *www.irs.gov/Form6252* **for the latest information.**	**2020** Attachment Sequence No. **625**

Name(s) shown on return: Howard Scripp   Identifying number

1	Description of property ▶ Land

2a Date acquired (mm/dd/yyyy) ▶ _____ **b** Date sold (mm/dd/yyyy) ▶ _____

3 Was the property sold to a related party (see instructions) after May 14, 1980? If "No," skip line 4 . . . . . ☐ Yes ☐ No

4 Was the property you sold to a related party a marketable security? If "Yes," complete Part III. If "No," complete Part III for the year of sale and the 2 years after the year of sale . . . . ☐ Yes ☐ No

Part I Gross Profit and Contract Price. Complete this part for all years of the installment agreement.

5	Selling price including mortgages and other debts. **Don't** include interest, whether stated or unstated	**5**	50,000
6	Mortgages, debts, and other liabilities the buyer assumed or took the property subject to (see instructions)	**6**	0	
7	Subtract line 6 from line 5	**7**	50,000	
8	Cost or other basis of property sold	**8**	20,000	
9	Depreciation allowed or allowable	**9**	0	
10	Adjusted basis. Subtract line 9 from line 8	**10**	20,000	
11	Commissions and other expenses of sale	**11**		
12	Income recapture from Form 4797, Part III (see instructions)	**12**		
13	Add lines 10, 11, and 12	**13**	20,000
14	Subtract line 13 from line 5. If zero or less, **don't** complete the rest of this form. See instructions . .	**14**	30,000
15	If the property described on line 1 above was your main home, enter the amount of your excluded gain. See instructions. Otherwise, enter -0-	**15**	
16	**Gross profit.** Subtract line 15 from line 14	**16**	30,000
17	Subtract line 13 from line 6. If zero or less, enter -0-	**17**	0
18	**Contract price.** Add line 7 and line 17	**18**	50,000

Part II Installment Sale Income. Complete this part for all years of the installment agreement.

19	Gross profit percentage (expressed as a decimal amount). Divide line 16 by line 18. (For years after the year of sale, see instructions.)	**19**	.60
20	If this is the year of sale, enter the amount from line 17. Otherwise, enter -0-	**20**	0
21	Payments received during year (see instructions). **Don't** include interest, whether stated or unstated .	**21**	10,000
22	Add lines 20 and 21	**22**	10,000
23	Payments received in prior years (see instructions). **Don't** include interest, whether stated or unstated	**23**		
24	**Installment sale income.** Multiply line 22 by line 19	**24**	6,000
25	Enter the part of line 24 that is ordinary income under the recapture rules. See instructions	**25**	
26	Subtract line 25 from line 24. Enter here and on Schedule D or Form 4797. See instructions . . .	**26**	6,000

Part III Related Party Installment Sale Income. **Don't** complete if you received the final payment this tax year.

27 Name, address, and taxpayer identifying number of related party ▶ _____

28 Did the related party resell or dispose of the property ("second disposition") during this tax year? . . . . . ☐ Yes ☐ No

29 **If the answer to question 28 is "Yes," complete lines 30 through 37 below unless one of the following conditions is met. Check the box that applies.**

a ☐ The second disposition was more than 2 years after the first disposition (other than dispositions of marketable securities). If this box is checked, enter the date of disposition (mm/dd/yyyy) . . . . ▶ _____

b ☐ The first disposition was a sale or exchange of stock to the issuing corporation.

c ☐ The second disposition was an involuntary conversion and the threat of conversion occurred after the first disposition.

d ☐ The second disposition occurred after the death of the original seller or buyer.

e ☐ It can be established to the satisfaction of the IRS that tax avoidance wasn't a principal purpose for either of the dispositions. If this box is checked, attach an explanation. See instructions.

30	Selling price of property sold by related party (see instructions)	**30**	
31	Enter contract price from line 18 for year of first sale	**31**	
32	Enter the **smaller** of line 30 or line 31	**32**	
33	Total payments received by the end of your 2020 tax year (see instructions)	**33**	
34	Subtract line 33 from line 32. If zero or less, enter -0-	**34**	
35	Multiply line 34 by the gross profit percentage on line 19 for year of first sale	**35**	
36	Enter the part of line 35 that is ordinary income under the recapture rules. See instructions	**36**	
37	Subtract line 36 from line 35. Enter here and on Schedule D or Form 4797. See instructions . . .	**37**	

For Paperwork Reduction Act Notice, see page 4.   Cat. No. 13601R   Form **6252** (2020)

8-11 LIKE-KIND EXCHANGES

Although a taxpayer realizes a gain or loss on the sale or exchange of property, the recognition of the gain or loss may be deferred for tax purposes. One example of such a situation arises when a taxpayer exchanges real property for other real property of a like kind. Under certain circumstances, the transaction may be nontaxable. To qualify as a nontaxable exchange, the property exchanged must be real property, held for productive use in a trade or business, or held for investment. Exchanges of personal or intangible property used in a business or for investment such as machines, cars, trucks, patents, furniture, etc. do not qualify as like-kind. Property held for personal purposes, such as a taxpayer's residence, also does not qualify for a like-kind exchange.

When the exchange involves only qualified like-kind property, no gain or loss is recognized. However, some exchanges include cash or other property in addition to the like-kind property. Even when the exchange is not solely for like-kind assets, the nontaxable treatment usually is not completely lost. Gain is recognized in an amount equal to the lesser of (1) the gain realized or (2) the "boot" received. Boot is money or the fair market value of other property received in addition to the like-kind property. Relief from a liability is the same as receiving cash and is treated as boot.

The basis of other property received as boot in an exchange is its fair market value on the date of the exchange. The basis of the like-kind property received is:

> The basis of the like-kind property given up
> + Any boot paid
> − Any boot received
> + Any gain recognized
> Basis of property received

The holding period for property acquired in a like-kind exchange includes the holding period of the property exchanged. For example, if long-term capital gain property is exchanged today, the new property may be sold immediately, and the gain recognized would be long-term capital gain.

Taxpayers must file Form 8824, Like-Kind Exchanges, to report the exchange of property. This form must be completed even if no gain is recognized.

EXAMPLE Janis and Kevin exchange real estate held as an investment. Janis gives up property with an adjusted basis of $350,000 and a fair market value of $560,000. The property is subject to a mortgage of $105,000 which is assumed by Kevin. In return for this property, Janis receives from Kevin land with a fair market value of $420,000 and cash of $35,000. Kevin's adjusted basis in the property he exchanges is $280,000.

1. Janis recognizes a gain of $140,000, equal to the lesser of the gain realized or the boot received as calculated below.

Calculation of gain realized:	
Fair market value of property received	$ 420,000
Cash received	35,000
Liability assumed by Kevin	105,000
Total amount realized	$ 560,000
Less: the adjusted basis of the property given up	(350,000)
Gain realized	$ 210,000
Calculation of boot received:	
Cash received	$ 35,000
Liability assumed by Kevin	105,000
Total boot received	$ 140,000
Gain recognized: Lesser of gain realized or boot received	$ 140,000

2. The basis of Janis's property is calculated below.

Basis of the property given up	$ 350,000
+ Boot paid	0
− Boot received	(140,000)
+ Gain recognized	140,000
Basis of the like-kind property received	$ 350,000

3. Kevin's recognized gain is equal to the lesser of the gain realized or the boot received. Since he received no boot, the recognized gain is zero.

Calculation of gain realized:

Fair market value of the property received	$ 560,000
Less: boot paid ($105,000 + $35,000)	(140,000)
Less: adjusted basis of property given up	(280,000)
Gain realized	$ 140,000
Boot received	$ 0

4. The basis of Kevin's new property is calculated below.

Basis of the property given up	$ 280,000
+ Boot paid	140,000
− Boot received	0
+ Gain recognized	0
Basis of the property received	$ 420,000

◆

8-11a Like-Kind Property

The term "like-kind property" does not include inventory, stocks, bonds, or other securities or any personal property such as equipment, cars, trucks, machines, and furniture. Real property is more or less considered to be like-kind with any other real property so long as the original property and the new property are both used in a trade or business or held for investment.

Although the repeal of like-kind treatment for personal property does not permit the deferral of gains on that type of property, this may result in some favorable outcomes as well. The deferral on a like-kind exchange is not elective, it is required. One of the most common forms of exchange for a small business is the trade-in of a business auto. Because the market value of a used auto is almost always below its adjusted basis, the losses were not deductible under the previous like-kind exchange rules. Now that personal property is not eligible for like-kind treatment, these losses may be deductible.

TAX BREAK

Self-Study Problem 8.11   *See Appendix E for Solutions to Self-Study Problems*

During the current year, Daniel James exchanges land used in his business for a new parcel of land. Daniel's basis in the land is $18,000, and the land is subject to a mortgage of $8,000, which is assumed by the other party to the exchange. Daniel receives new land worth $22,000. Calculate Daniel's recognized gain on the exchange and his basis in the new land.

Recognized gain $_____
Basis in the new land $_____

Learning Objective 8.12	# 8-12 **INVOLUNTARY CONVERSIONS**

Calculate recognized and deferred gains on involuntary conversions.

Occasionally, taxpayers are forced to dispose of property as a result of circumstances beyond their control. At the election of the taxpayer, and provided certain conditions are met, the gain on an involuntary conversion of property may be deferred. The provisions require that the property must be replaced and the basis of the replacement property reduced by the amount of the gain deferred. An involuntary conversion is defined as the destruction of the taxpayer's property in whole or in part, or loss of the property by theft, seizure, requisition, or condemnation. Also, property sold pursuant to reclamation laws, and livestock destroyed by disease or drought, are subject to the involuntary conversion rules. To qualify for nonrecognition of gain, the taxpayer must obtain qualified replacement property. The replacement property must be "similar or related in service or use." This definition is narrower than the like-kind rule; the property must be very similar to the property converted. Generally, a taxpayer has 2 years after the close of the tax year in which a gain was realized to obtain replacement property.

A realized gain on the involuntary conversion of property occurs when the taxpayer receives insurance proceeds or other payments in excess of his or her adjusted basis in the converted property. Taxpayers need not recognize any gain if they completely reinvest the proceeds or payments in qualified replacement property within the required time period. If they do not reinvest the total amount of the payments received, they must recognize a gain equal to the amount of the payment not reinvested (but limited to the gain realized). The basis of the replacement property is equal to the cost of the replacement property reduced by any gain not recognized on the transaction. The holding period of the replacement property includes the period the original property was held.

EXAMPLE Tammy's office building, which has an adjusted basis of $600,000, is destroyed by fire in 2020. In the same year, Tammy receives $700,000 of insurance proceeds for the loss. She has until December 31, 2022 (2 years after the end of the taxable year in which the gain is realized), to acquire a replacement building. In 2021, Tammy replaces the building with a new building costing $680,000. Her realized gain on the involuntary conversion is $100,000 ($700,000 − $600,000), and the gain recognized is $20,000, which is the $700,000 of cash received less the amount reinvested ($680,000). The basis of the new building is $600,000 ($680,000 − $80,000), the cost of the new building less the portion of the gain not recognized. ♦

The involuntary conversion provision applies only to gains, not to losses. The provision must be elected by the taxpayer. In contrast, the like-kind exchange provision discussed previously applies to both gains and losses and is not elective.

Self-Study Problem 8.12	*See Appendix E for Solutions to Self-Study Problems*

Sam's store is destroyed in 2020 as a result of a flood. The store has an adjusted basis of $70,000, and Sam receives insurance proceeds of $150,000 on the loss. Sam invests $135,000 in a replacement store in 2021.

1. Calculate Sam's recognized gain, assuming an election under the involuntary conversion provision is made. $_____

2. Calculate Sam's basis in the replacement store. $_____

KEY TERMS

depreciation, 8-2
straight-line depreciation, 8-2
Modified Accelerated Cost Recovery
  System (MACRS), 8-3
recovery period, 8-3
asset depreciation ranges
  (ADRs), 8-3
accelerated depreciation, 8-4
half-year convention, 8-4
mid-quarter convention, 8-5
bonus depreciation, 8-7

qualified improvement property
  (QIP), 8-7
mid-month convention, 8-9
Section 179, 8-10
election to expense, 8-10
listed property, 8-14
intangibles, 8-17
Section 197 intangibles, 8-17
amortization, 8-17
goodwill and going-concern
  value, 8-17

Section 1231 assets, 8-19
depreciation recapture, 8-20
Section 1245 recapture, 8-20
Section 1250 recapture, 8-21
installment sales, 8-27
like-kind exchange, 8-30
boot, 8-30
like-kind property, 8-31
involuntary conversion, 8-32
qualified replacement property, 8-32

KEY POINTS

Learning Objectives	Key Points
LO 8.1: Explain the concept of depreciation.	• Depreciation is the accounting process of allocating and deducting the cost of an asset over a period of years and does not necessarily mean physical deterioration or loss of value of the asset. • The simplest method of depreciation is the straight-line method, which results in an equal portion of the cost of an asset being deducted in each period of the asset's life.
LO 8.2: Calculate depreciation expense using the MACRS tables.	• The Modified Accelerated Cost Recovery System (MACRS) allows taxpayers who invest in capital assets to write off an asset's cost over a period designated in the tax law and to use an accelerated method of depreciation for assets other than real estate. • The minimum number of years over which the cost of an asset may be deducted (the recovery period) depends on the type of property and the year in which the property was acquired. • Under MACRS, taxpayers calculate the depreciation of an asset using a table, which contains a percentage rate for each year of the property's recovery period and includes the half-year convention for personal property and mid-month convention for real property. • The mid-quarter convention must be applied if more than 40 percent of the total cost of a taxpayer's tangible property acquired during the year, other than real property, is placed in service during the last quarter of the tax year. • The bonus depreciation rules allow taxpayers purchasing property with a MACRS recovery period of 20 years or less (see Table 8.1), computer software, and certain leasehold improvements to directly write off 100 percent of the cost of the assets in the year placed in service. • There are no taxable income limits or thresholds associated with bonus depreciation. • For post-1986 acquired real estate, MACRS uses the straight-line method over 27.5 years for residential realty and 39 years for nonresidential realty (31.5 years for realty acquired generally before May 13, 1993).

LO 8.3: Identify when a Section 179 election to expense the cost of property may be used.	• Qualified Section 179 property is personal property (property other than real estate or assets used in residential real estate rental activities) placed in service during the year and used in a trade or business. • The maximum cost that may be expensed in the year of acquisition under Section 179 is $1,040,000 for 2020. The property may be new or used. • The $1,040,000 maximum is reduced dollar for dollar by the cost of qualifying property placed in service during the year in excess of $2,590,000. • The amount that may be expensed is limited to the taxpayer's taxable income, before considering any amount expensed under this election, from any trade or business of the taxpayer. • Section 179 expensed amounts reduce the basis of the asset before calculating any regular MACRS depreciation on the remaining cost of the asset.
LO 8.4: Apply the limitations placed on depreciation of "listed property."	• Special rules apply to the depreciation of listed property. • Listed property includes those types of assets which lend themselves to personal use. • Listed property includes automobiles, certain other vehicles, and property used for entertainment, recreation, or amusement. • If listed property is used 50 percent or less in a qualified business use, any depreciation deduction must be calculated using the straight-line method of depreciation over an alternate recovery period, and the special election to expense under Section 179 and bonus depreciation are not allowed.
LO 8.5: Apply the limitations on depreciation of "luxury automobiles."	• The depreciation of passenger automobiles is subject to a limitation, commonly referred to as the luxury automobile limitation. • For automobiles acquired in 2020, the maximum depreciation is $18,100 (Year 1), $16,100 (Year 2), $9,700 (Year 3), and $5,760 (Year 4 and subsequent years until fully depreciated). Bonus depreciation of $8,000 is included in the first year limit of $18,100.
LO 8.6: Calculate the amortization of goodwill and certain other intangibles.	• Section 197 intangibles are amortized over a 15-year period, beginning with the month of acquisition. • Qualified Section 197 intangibles include goodwill, going-concern value, workforce in place, information bases, know-how, customer-based intangibles, licenses, permits, rights granted by a governmental unit, covenants not to compete, franchises, trademarks, and trade names. • Examples of Section 197 exclusions are interests in a corporation, partnership, trust, or estate; interests in land; computer software readily available for purchase by the general public; interests in films, sound recordings, and video recordings; and self-created intangible assets.
LO 8.7: Classify gains and losses from Section 1231 assets.	• Section 1231 assets include (1) depreciable or real property used in a trade or business, (2) timber, coal, or domestic iron ore, (3) livestock (not including poultry) held for draft, breeding, dairy, or sporting purposes, and (4) unharvested crops on land used in a trade or business. • If net Section 1231 gains exceed the losses, the excess is a long-term capital gain. When the net Section 1231 losses exceed the gains, all gains are treated as ordinary income, and all losses are fully deductible as ordinary losses.

LO 8.8: Apply the depreciation recapture rules.	• Depreciation recapture provisions are meant to prevent taxpayers from converting ordinary income into capital gain by claiming maximum depreciation deductions over the life of the asset and then selling the asset and receiving capital gain treatment on the resulting gain at sale. • Under Section 1245, any gain recognized on the disposition of a Section 1245 asset (generally personal property) will be classified as ordinary income up to an amount equal to the accumulated depreciation. Any gain in excess of depreciation taken is classified as a Section 1231 gain. • Section 1250 real property recapture is the excess of depreciation expense claimed, using an accelerated method of depreciation, over what would have been allowed if the straight-line method were used. • Since the straight-line method is required for real property acquired after 1986, there will be no Section 1250 recapture on the disposition of real property. • A special 25 or 28.8 percent tax rate applies to real property gains attributable to depreciation previously taken and not already recaptured under Section 1245 or Section 1250.
LO 8.9: Apply the general treatment of casualty gains and losses for business purposes.	• The amount of a partial casualty loss from business property is insurance proceeds less the decrease in the value of the property or the adjusted basis, whichever is smaller. • The amount of a casualty loss from a complete destruction of business property is the insurance proceeds less the adjusted basis of the property.
LO 8.10: Compute the gain on installment sales.	• On an installment sale, the taxable gain reported each year is determined as follows: taxable gain equals total gain realized on the sale, divided by the contract price, and multiplied by the payment received during the year.
LO 8.11: Calculate recognized and deferred gains on like-kind exchanges.	• To qualify as a nontaxable like-kind exchange, the property exchanged must be real property, held for use in a trade or business or held for investment, and exchanged for property of a like kind. • Personal property no longer qualifies for like-kind exchange treatment. • Like-kind gain is recognized in an amount equal to the lesser of (1) the gain realized or (2) the "boot" received. Boot is money or the fair market value of other property received in addition to the like-kind property. • If a transaction qualifies as a like-kind exchange, the like-kind exchange provisions must be followed.
LO 8.12: Calculate recognized and deferred gains on involuntary conversions.	• A realized gain on the involuntary conversion of property occurs when the taxpayer receives proceeds in excess of his or her adjusted basis. • Involuntary conversion gain is not recognized if the proceeds or payments are reinvested in qualified replacement property within the required time period and the taxpayer makes the proper election.

QUESTIONS and PROBLEMS

GROUP 1:
MULTIPLE CHOICE QUESTIONS

LO 8.2

1. Alice purchases a rental house on June 22, 2020, for a cost of $174,000. Of this amount, $100,000 is considered to be allocable to the cost of the home, with the remaining $74,000 allocable to the cost of the land. What is Alice's maximum depreciation deduction for 2020 using MACRS?
   a. $2,373
   b. $1,970
   c. $1,364
   d. $1,061
   e. $1,009

LO 8.2

2. An asset (not an automobile) put in service in June 2020 has a depreciable basis of $25,000 and a recovery period of 5 years. Assuming half-year convention, no bonus depreciation, and no election to expense is made, what is the maximum amount of cost that can be deducted in 2020?
   a. $2,500
   b. $5,000
   c. $6,000
   d. $30,000
   e. None of the above

LO 8.2

3. An asset (not an automobile) put in service in June 2020 has a depreciable basis of $28,000 and a recovery period of 5 years. Assuming bonus depreciation is used, half-year convention and no election to expense is made, what is the maximum amount of cost that can be deducted in 2020?
   a. $5,600
   b. $14,000
   c. $24,000
   d. $28,000
   e. $40,000

LO 8.2

4. James purchased office equipment for his business. The equipment has a depreciable basis of $14,000 and was put in service on June 1, 2020. James decides to elect straight-line depreciation under MACRS for the asset over the minimum number of years (7 years), and does not use bonus depreciation or make the election to expense. What is the amount of his depreciation deduction for the equipment for the 2020 tax year?
   a. $2,000
   b. $1,000
   c. $500
   d. $0
   e. None of the above

LO 8.2

5. Which of the following statements with respect to the depreciation of property under MACRS is *incorrect*?
   a. Under the half-year convention, one-half year of depreciation is allowed in the year the property is placed in service.
   b. If a taxpayer elects to use the straight-line method of depreciation for property in the 5-year class, all other 5-year class property acquired during the year must also be depreciated using the straight-line method.

c. In some cases, when a taxpayer places a significant amount of property in service during the last quarter of the year, real property must be depreciated using a mid-quarter convention.

d. Real property acquired after 1986 must be depreciated using the straight-line method.

e. The cost of property to which the MACRS rate is applied is not reduced for estimated salvage value.

LO 8.2

6. Which of the following is true about the MACRS depreciation system:

a. A salvage value must be determined before depreciation percentages are applied to depreciable real estate.

b. Residential rental buildings are depreciated over 39 years straight-line.

c. Commercial real estate buildings are depreciated over 27.5 years straight-line.

d. No matter when during the month depreciable real estate is purchased, it is considered to have been placed in service at mid-month for MACRS depreciation purposes.

LO 8.3

7. On July 20, 2020, Kelli purchases office equipment at a cost of $24,000. Kelli elects out of bonus depreciation but makes the election to expense for 2020. She is self-employed as an attorney, and, in 2020, her business has a net income of $12,000 before considering this election to expense. Kelli has no other income or expenses for the year. What is the maximum amount that Kelli may deduct for 2020 under the election to expense, assuming she elects to expense the entire $24,000 purchase?

a. $24,000
b. $12,000
c. $6,000
d. $3,000
e. $1,000

LO 8.3

8. Which of the following is *not* considered a limit on the immediate expensing election of Section 179?

a. Fifty percent of qualified improvement property

b. Total Section 179-eligible property acquired in excess of $3,630,000

c. The taxable income of the taxpayer considering all income and deductions except for Section 179 immediate expensing

d. An annual limit of $1,040,000

e. None of the above

LO 8.5

9. In 2020, Ben purchases and places in service a new auto for his business. The auto costs $57,000 and will be used 60 percent for business. Assuming the half-year convention applies and Ben elects out of bonus depreciation and Section 179, what will depreciation on the auto be in 2020?

a. $11,400
b. $6,840
c. $6,060
d. $6,000
e. None of the above

LO 8.5

10. In 2020, Ben purchases and places in service a new auto for his business. The auto costs $57,000 and will be used 100 percent for business. Assuming the half-year convention applies and Ben does not elect out of bonus depreciation, what will depreciation on the auto be in 2020?

a. $57,000
b. $18,000
c. $18,100
d. $10,000
e. None of the above

LO 8.6

11. The amortization period for Section 197 intangibles is:
    a. 5 years
    b. 7 years
    c. 10 years
    d. 15 years
    e. 40 years

LO 8.6

12. Which of the following intangibles is defined as a Section 197 intangible asset?
    a. An interest in land
    b. A partnership interest
    c. An interest in a corporation
    d. A covenant not to compete acquired as part of a business
    e. A separately acquired sound recording

LO 8.7

13. Which of the following is Section 1231 property?
    a. Land held for investment purposes
    b. A machine used in a business
    c. Accounts receivable
    d. Inventory
    e. Paintings owned by the artist

LO 8.7
LO 8.8

14. In 2020, Mary sells for $24,000 a machine used in her business. The machine was purchased on May 1, 2018, at a cost of $22,000. Mary has deducted depreciation on the machine of $6,000. What is the amount and nature of Mary's gain as a result of the sale of the machine?
    a. $2,000 Section 1231 gain
    b. $8,000 ordinary income under Section 1245
    c. $6,000 ordinary income and $2,000 Section 1231 gain
    d. $6,000 Section 1231 gain and $2,000 ordinary income under Section 1245
    e. None of the above

LO 8.7
LO 8.8

15. During 2020, Paul sells residential rental property for $240,000, which he acquired in 1999 for $160,000. Paul has claimed straight-line depreciation on the building of $60,000. What is the amount and nature of Paul's gain on the sale of the rental property?
    a. $140,000 ordinary income
    b. $80,000 "unrecaptured depreciation" and $60,000 ordinary gain
    c. $140,000 Section 1231 gain
    d. $80,000 Section 1231 gain, $60,000 "unrecaptured depreciation"
    e. None of the above

LO 8.8

16. Jeanie acquires an apartment building in 2009 for $280,000 and sells it for $480,000 in 2020. At the time of sale there is $60,000 of accumulated straight-line depreciation on the apartment building. Assuming Jeanie is in the highest tax bracket for ordinary income and the Medicare tax on net investment income applies, how much of her gain is taxed at 28.8 percent?
    a. None
    b. $60,000
    c. $200,000
    d. $280,000
    e. $260,000

LO 8.9

17. Virginia has business property that is stolen and partially destroyed by the time it was recovered. She receives an insurance reimbursement of $6,000 on property that had a $14,000 basis and a decrease in market value of $10,000 due to damage caused by the theft. What is the amount of Virginia's casualty loss?
    a. $14,000
    b. $8,000
    c. $10,000
    d. $4,000
    e. None of the above

LO 8.10 18. Pat sells land for $25,000 cash and a $75,000 5-year note. If her basis in the property is $30,000 and she receives only the $25,000 down payment in the year of sale, how much is Pat's taxable gain in the year of sale using the installment sales method?

    a. $0
    b. $5,000
    c. $17,500
    d. $25,000
    e. $75,000

LO 8.11 19. Fred and Sarajane exchanged land in a qualifying like-kind exchange. Fred gives up land with an adjusted basis of $11,000 (fair market value of $16,000) in exchange for Sarajane's land with a fair market value of $12,000 plus $4,000 cash. How much gain should Fred recognize on the exchange?

    a. $5,000
    b. $4,000
    c. $1,000
    d. $0
    e. None of the above

LO 8.11 20. What is Sarajane's basis in the land received in the exchange described in Question 19, assuming her basis in the land given up was $12,000?

    a. $0
    b. $12,000
    c. $14,000
    d. $16,000
    e. None of the above

LO 8.12 21. Oscar owns a building that is destroyed in a hurricane. His adjusted basis in the building before the hurricane is $130,000. His insurance company pays him $140,000 and he immediately invests in a new building at a cost of $142,000. What is the amount of recognized gain or loss on the destruction of Oscar's building?

    a. $0
    b. $10,000 gain
    c. $8,000 gain
    d. $12,000 gain
    e. $2,000 loss

LO 8.12 22. Using the information from Question 21, what is Oscar's basis on his new building?

    a. $130,000
    b. $132,000
    c. $140,000
    d. $142,000

GROUP 2:
PROBLEMS

LO 8.2 1. Is land allowed to be depreciated? Why or why not?

_____

_____

_____

LO 8.2 2. Is it possible to depreciate a residential rental building when it is actually increasing in value? Why?

_____

_____

LO 8.2
LO 8.3

3. Mike purchases a new heavy-duty truck (5-year class recovery property) for his delivery service on March 30, 2020. No other assets were purchased during the year. The truck is not considered a passenger automobile for purposes of the listed property and luxury automobile limitations. The truck has a depreciable basis of $46,000 and an estimated useful life of 5 years. Assume half-year convention for tax.

   a. Calculate the amount of depreciation for 2020 using financial accounting straight-line depreciation (not the straight-line MACRS election) over the truck's estimated useful life.

   $_____

   b. Calculate the amount of depreciation for 2020 using the straight-line depreciation election, using MACRS tables over the minimum number of years with no bonus depreciation or election to expense.

   $_____

   c. Calculate the amount of depreciation for 2020, including bonus depreciation but no election to expense, that Mike could deduct using the MACRS tables.

   $_____

   d. Calculate the amount of depreciation for 2020 including the election to expense but no bonus depreciation that Mike could deduct. Assume no income limit on the expense election.

   $_____

LO 8.2

4. On July 8, 2020, Holly purchased a residential apartment building. The cost basis assigned to the building is $750,000. Holly also owns another residential apartment building that she purchased on November 15, 2020, with a cost basis of $410,000.

   a. Calculate Holly's total depreciation deduction for the apartments for 2020 using MACRS.

   $_____

   b. Calculate Holly's total depreciation deduction for the apartments for 2021 using MACRS.

   $_____

LO 8.2

5. Give the MACRS depreciation life of the following assets:
   a. An automobile   _____
   b. Business furniture   _____
   c. A computer   _____
   d. Residential real estate _____
   e. Commercial real estate   _____
   f. Land   _____

LO 8.2

6. Explain the use of the mid-quarter convention for MACRS depreciation:

   _____

   _____

   _____

   _____

LO 8.2

7. Calculate the following:
   a. The first year of depreciation on a residential rental building that cost $250,000 purchased June 2, 2020.

   $_____

   b. The second year (2021) of depreciation on a computer that cost $5,000 purchased in May 2020, using the half-year convention and accelerated depreciation considering any bonus depreciation taken.

   $_____

c. The first year of depreciation on a computer costing $2,800 purchased in May 2020, using the half-year convention and straight-line depreciation with no bonus depreciation.

$_____

d. The third year of depreciation on business furniture costing $10,000 purchased in March 2018, using the half-year convention and accelerated depreciation but no bonus depreciation.

$_____

LO 8.2
LO 8.3
LO 8.4
LO 8.5

8. During 2020, William purchases the following capital assets for use in his catering business:

New passenger automobile (September 30)	$54,000
Baking equipment (June 30)	7,000

Assume that William decides to use the election to expense on the baking equipment (and has adequate taxable income to cover the deduction) but not on the automobile, and he also uses the MACRS accelerated method to calculate depreciation but elects out of bonus depreciation. Calculate William's maximum depreciation deduction for 2020, assuming he uses the automobile 100 percent in his business.

$_____

LO 8.2
LO 8.4

9. On February 2, 2020, Alexandra purchases a personal computer. The computer cost $2,200. Alexandra uses the computer 75 percent of the time in her accounting business, and the remaining 25 percent of the time for various personal uses. Calculate Alexandra's maximum depreciation deduction for 2020 for the computer, assuming half-year convention and she does not use bonus depreciation or make the election to expense.

$_____

LO 8.2
LO 8.4
LO 8.5

10. On September 14, 2020, Jay purchased a passenger automobile that is used 75 percent in his business. The automobile has a basis for depreciation purposes of $45,000, and Jay uses the accelerated method under MACRS. Jay does not elect to expense. Calculate Jay's depreciation deduction for 2020 assuming bonus depreciation.

$_____

LO 8.2
LO 8.4
LO 8.5

11. During 2020, Pepe Guardio purchases the following property for use in his calendar year-end manufacturing business:

Item	Date Acquired	Cost
Manufacturing equipment (7 year)	June 2	$ 50,000
Office furniture	September 15	8,000
Office computer	November 18	2,000
Passenger automobile (used 85 percent for business)	May 31	55,000
Warehouse	July 23	
Building		170,000
Land		135,000

Pepe uses the accelerated depreciation method under MACRS, if available, and does not make the election to expense and elects out of bonus depreciation. Use Form 4562 on Pages 8-43 and 8-44 to report Pepe's depreciation expense for 2020.

LO 8.2
LO 8.4
LO 8.5

12. Go to the IRS website (**www.irs.gov**) and assuming bonus depreciation is used, redo Problem 11, using the most recent interactive Form 4562, Depreciation and Amortization. Print out the *completed Form 4562*.

LO 8.2
LO 8.3

13. Tom has a successful business with $100,000 of taxable income before the election to expense in 2020. He purchases one new asset in 2020, a new machine which is 7-year MACRS property and costs $25,000. If you are Tom's tax advisor, how would you advise Tom to treat the purchase for tax purposes in 2020? Why?

_____

_____

LO 8.6

14. Derek purchases a small business from Art on June 30, 2020. He paid the following amounts for the business:

Fixed assets	$180,000
Goodwill	40,000
Covenant not to compete	30,000
Total	$250,000

a. How much of the $250,000 purchase price is for Section 197 intangible assets?

$_____

b. What amount can Derek deduct on his 2020 tax return as Section 197 intangible amortization?

$_____

LO 8.6

15. Annie develops a successful tax practice. She sells the practice to her friend Carol for $54,000 and moves to Florida to retire. The tax practice has no assets except intangible benefits such as the goodwill and going-concern value Annie has developed over the years. How should Carol treat the $54,000 cost of the tax practice she has purchased?

LO 8.7
LO 8.8

16. Nadia Shalom has the following transactions during the year:
   Sale of office equipment on March 15 that cost $21,500 when purchased on July 1, 2018. Nadia has claimed $21,500 in depreciation and sells the asset for $13,500 with no selling costs.
   Sale of land on April 19 for $125,000. The land cost $132,500 when purchased on February 1, 2009. Nadia's selling costs are $6,500.
   Assume there were no capital improvements on either business asset sold. Nadia's Social Security number is 924-56-5783. Complete Form 4797 on Pages 8-45 and 8-46 to report the above gains or losses.

LO 8.8
LO 8.10

17. Steve Drake sells a rental house on January 1, 2020, and receives $90,000 cash and a note for $55,000 at 7 percent interest. The purchaser also assumes the mortgage on the property of $30,000. Steve's original cost for the house was $172,000 on January 1, 2012 and accumulated depreciation was $32,000 on the date of sale. He collects only the $90,000 down payment in the year of sale.

a. If Steve elects to recognize the total gain on the property in the year of sale, calculate the taxable gain.

$_____

b. Assuming Steve uses the installment sale method, complete Form 6252 on Page 8-47 for the year of the sale.

c. Assuming Steve collects $5,000 (not including interest) of the note principal in the year following the year of sale, calculate the amount of income recognized in that year under the installment sale method.

$_____

GROUP 2:
PROBLEM 11

Form **4562**	**Depreciation and Amortization**	OMB No. 1545-0172
	(Including Information on Listed Property)	**2020**
Department of the Treasury Internal Revenue Service (99)	▶ Attach to your tax return. ▶ Go to *www.irs.gov/Form4562* for instructions and the latest information.	Attachment Sequence No. **179**

Name(s) shown on return	Business or activity to which this form relates	Identifying number

Part I   **Election To Expense Certain Property Under Section 179**
Note: If you have any listed property, complete Part V before you complete Part I.

1	Maximum amount (see instructions)	**1**
2	Total cost of section 179 property placed in service (see instructions)	**2**
3	Threshold cost of section 179 property before reduction in limitation (see instructions)	**3**
4	Reduction in limitation. Subtract line 3 from line 2. If zero or less, enter -0-	**4**
5	Dollar limitation for tax year. Subtract line 4 from line 1. If zero or less, enter -0-. If married filing separately, see instructions	**5**

6	**(a)** Description of property	**(b)** Cost (business use only)	**(c)** Elected cost

7	Listed property. Enter the amount from line 29 . . . . **7**	
8	Total elected cost of section 179 property. Add amounts in column (c), lines 6 and 7	**8**
9	Tentative deduction. Enter the **smaller** of line 5 or line 8	**9**
10	Carryover of disallowed deduction from line 13 of your 2019 Form 4562	**10**
11	Business income limitation. Enter the smaller of business income (not less than zero) or line 5. See instructions	**11**
12	Section 179 expense deduction. Add lines 9 and 10, but don't enter more than line 11	**12**
13	Carryover of disallowed deduction to 2021. Add lines 9 and 10, less line 12 ▶ **13**	

Note: Don't use Part II or Part III below for listed property. Instead, use Part V.

Part II   **Special Depreciation Allowance and Other Depreciation (Don't** include listed property. See instructions.**)**

14	Special depreciation allowance for qualified property (other than listed property) placed in service during the tax year. See instructions	**14**
15	Property subject to section 168(f)(1) election	**15**
16	Other depreciation (including ACRS)	**16**

Part III   **MACRS Depreciation (Don't** include listed property. See instructions.**)**

Section A

17	MACRS deductions for assets placed in service in tax years beginning before 2020	**17**
18	If you are electing to group any assets placed in service during the tax year into one or more general asset accounts, check here . . . . ▶ ☐	

Section B—Assets Placed in Service During 2020 Tax Year Using the General Depreciation System

(a) Classification of property	(b) Month and year placed in service	(c) Basis for depreciation (business/investment use only—see instructions)	(d) Recovery period	(e) Convention	(f) Method	(g) Depreciation deduction
19a 3-year property						
b 5-year property						
c 7-year property						
d 10-year property						
e 15-year property						
f 20-year property						
g 25-year property			25 yrs.		S/L	
h Residential rental property			27.5 yrs.	MM	S/L	
			27.5 yrs.	MM	S/L	
i Nonresidential real property			39 yrs.	MM	S/L	
				MM	S/L	

Section C—Assets Placed in Service During 2020 Tax Year Using the Alternative Depreciation System

20a Class life					S/L	
b 12-year			12 yrs.		S/L	
c 30-year			30 yrs.	MM	S/L	
d 40-year			40 yrs.	MM	S/L	

Part IV   **Summary** (See instructions.)

21	Listed property. Enter amount from line 28	**21**
22	**Total.** Add amounts from line 12, lines 14 through 17, lines 19 and 20 in column (g), and line 21. Enter here and on the appropriate lines of your return. Partnerships and S corporations—see instructions .	**22**
23	For assets shown above and placed in service during the current year, enter the portion of the basis attributable to section 263A costs **23**	

For Paperwork Reduction Act Notice, see separate instructions.   Cat. No. 12906N   Form **4562** (2020)

Form 4562 (2020)   Page **2**

Part V   Listed Property (Include automobiles, certain other vehicles, certain aircraft, and property used for entertainment, recreation, or amusement.)

Note: For any vehicle for which you are using the standard mileage rate or deducting lease expense, complete **only** 24a, 24b, columns (a) through (c) of Section A, all of Section B, and Section C if applicable.

Section A—Depreciation and Other Information (Caution: See the instructions for limits for passenger automobiles.)

24a Do you have evidence to support the business/investment use claimed? ☐ Yes ☐ No | 24b If "Yes," is the evidence written? ☐ Yes ☐ No

(a) Type of property (list vehicles first)	(b) Date placed in service	(c) Business/investment use percentage	(d) Cost or other basis	(e) Basis for depreciation (business/investment use only)	(f) Recovery period	(g) Method/ Convention	(h) Depreciation deduction	(i) Elected section 179 cost
25 Special depreciation allowance for qualified listed property placed in service during the tax year and used more than 50% in a qualified business use. See instructions .					25			
26 Property used more than 50% in a qualified business use:								
		%						
		%						
		%						
27 Property used 50% or less in a qualified business use:								
		%				S/L –		
		%				S/L –		
		%				S/L –		

28 Add amounts in column (h), lines 25 through 27. Enter here and on line 21, page 1 . | 28 |
29 Add amounts in column (i), line 26. Enter here and on line 7, page 1 . . . . | 29 |

Section B—Information on Use of Vehicles

Complete this section for vehicles used by a sole proprietor, partner, or other "more than 5% owner," or related person. If you provided vehicles to your employees, first answer the questions in Section C to see if you meet an exception to completing this section for those vehicles.

		(a) Vehicle 1		(b) Vehicle 2		(c) Vehicle 3		(d) Vehicle 4		(e) Vehicle 5		(f) Vehicle 6	
30	Total business/investment miles driven during the year (**don't** include commuting miles) .												
31	Total commuting miles driven during the year												
32	Total other personal (noncommuting) miles driven												
33	Total miles driven during the year. Add lines 30 through 32												
34	Was the vehicle available for personal use during off-duty hours?	Yes	No	Yes	No	Yes	No	Yes	No	Yes	No	Yes	No
35	Was the vehicle used primarily by a more than 5% owner or related person? . .												
36	Is another vehicle available for personal use?												

Section C—Questions for Employers Who Provide Vehicles for Use by Their Employees

Answer these questions to determine if you meet an exception to completing Section B for vehicles used by employees who **aren't** more than 5% owners or related persons. See instructions.

	Yes	No
37 Do you maintain a written policy statement that prohibits all personal use of vehicles, including commuting, by your employees?		
38 Do you maintain a written policy statement that prohibits personal use of vehicles, except commuting, by your employees? See the instructions for vehicles used by corporate officers, directors, or 1% or more owners . .		
39 Do you treat all use of vehicles by employees as personal use?		
40 Do you provide more than five vehicles to your employees, obtain information from your employees about the use of the vehicles, and retain the information received?		
41 Do you meet the requirements concerning qualified automobile demonstration use? See instructions.		

Note: If your answer to 37, 38, 39, 40, or 41 is "Yes," don't complete Section B for the covered vehicles.

Part VI   Amortization

(a) Description of costs	(b) Date amortization begins	(c) Amortizable amount	(d) Code section	(e) Amortization period or percentage	(f) Amortization for this year
42 Amortization of costs that begins during your 2020 tax year (see instructions):					

43 Amortization of costs that began before your 2020 tax year . . . . | 43 |
44 **Total.** Add amounts in column (f). See the instructions for where to report . . . . | 44 |

Form **4562** (2020)

Form **4797**		**Sales of Business Property**				OMB No. 1545-0184	
		(Also Involuntary Conversions and Recapture Amounts Under Sections 179 and 280F(b)(2))				**2020**	
Department of the Treasury Internal Revenue Service		▶ **Attach to your tax return.** ▶ **Go to** *www.irs.gov/Form4797* **for instructions and the latest information.**				Attachment Sequence No. **27**	

Name(s) shown on return   Identifying number

| 1 | Enter the gross proceeds from sales or exchanges reported to you for 2020 on Form(s) 1099-B or 1099-S (or substitute statement) that you are including on line 2, 10, or 20. See instructions . . . . | 1 | |

Part I **Sales or Exchanges of Property Used in a Trade or Business and Involuntary Conversions From Other Than Casualty or Theft—Most Property Held More Than 1 Year** (see instructions)

2	(a) Description of property	(b) Date acquired (mo., day, yr.)	(c) Date sold (mo., day, yr.)	(d) Gross sales price	(e) Depreciation allowed or allowable since acquisition	(f) Cost or other basis, plus improvements and expense of sale	(g) Gain or (loss) Subtract (f) from the sum of (d) and (e)

3	Gain, if any, from Form 4684, line 39	3	
4	Section 1231 gain from installment sales from Form 6252, line 26 or 37	4	
5	Section 1231 gain or (loss) from like-kind exchanges from Form 8824	5	
6	Gain, if any, from line 32, from other than casualty or theft	6	
7	Combine lines 2 through 6. Enter the gain or (loss) here and on the appropriate line as follows . .	7	

Partnerships and S corporations. Report the gain or (loss) following the instructions for Form 1065, Schedule K, line 10, or Form 1120-S, Schedule K, line 9. Skip lines 8, 9, 11, and 12 below.

Individuals, partners, S corporation shareholders, and all others. If line 7 is zero or a loss, enter the amount from line 7 on line 11 below and skip lines 8 and 9. If line 7 is a gain and you didn't have any prior year section 1231 losses, or they were recaptured in an earlier year, enter the gain from line 7 as a long-term capital gain on the Schedule D filed with your return and skip lines 8, 9, 11, and 12 below.

| 8 | Nonrecaptured net section 1231 losses from prior years. See instructions . . . . | 8 | |
| 9 | Subtract line 8 from line 7. If zero or less, enter -0-. If line 9 is zero, enter the gain from line 7 on line 12 below. If line 9 is more than zero, enter the amount from line 8 on line 12 below and enter the gain from line 9 as a long-term capital gain on the Schedule D filed with your return. See instructions . . . . | 9 | |

Part II **Ordinary Gains and Losses** (see instructions)

10	Ordinary gains and losses not included on lines 11 through 16 (include property held 1 year or less):						

11	Loss, if any, from line 7	11	( )
12	Gain, if any, from line 7 or amount from line 8, if applicable	12	
13	Gain, if any, from line 31	13	
14	Net gain or (loss) from Form 4684, lines 31 and 38a	14	
15	Ordinary gain from installment sales from Form 6252, line 25 or 36	15	
16	Ordinary gain or (loss) from like-kind exchanges from Form 8824	16	
17	Combine lines 10 through 16	17	

18	For all except individual returns, enter the amount from line 17 on the appropriate line of your return and skip lines a and b below. For individual returns, complete lines a and b below.		
a	If the loss on line 11 includes a loss from Form 4684, line 35, column (b)(ii), enter that part of the loss here. Enter the loss from income-producing property on Schedule A (Form 1040), line 16. (Do not include any loss on property used as an employee.) Identify as from "Form 4797, line 18a." See instructions	18a	
b	Redetermine the gain or (loss) on line 17 excluding the loss, if any, on line 18a. Enter here and on Schedule 1 (Form 1040), Part I, line 4	18b	

For Paperwork Reduction Act Notice, see separate instructions.   Cat. No. 13086I   Form **4797** (2020)

Form 4797 (2020)   Page **2**

| **Part III** | **Gain From Disposition of Property Under Sections 1245, 1250, 1252, 1254, and 1255** (see instructions) |

19	**(a)** Description of section 1245, 1250, 1252, 1254, or 1255 property:	**(b)** Date acquired (mo., day, yr.)	**(c)** Date sold (mo., day, yr.)
A			
B			
C			
D			

These columns relate to the properties on lines 19A through 19D. ▶		**Property A**	**Property B**	**Property C**	**Property D**
20	Gross sales price (**Note:** See line 1 before completing.)	**20**				
21	Cost or other basis plus expense of sale	**21**				
22	Depreciation (or depletion) allowed or allowable	**22**				
23	Adjusted basis. Subtract line 22 from line 21	**23**				
24	Total gain. Subtract line 23 from line 20	**24**				
25	**If section 1245 property:**					
a	Depreciation allowed or allowable from line 22	**25a**				
b	Enter the **smaller** of line 24 or 25a	**25b**				
26	**If section 1250 property:** If straight line depreciation was used, enter -0- on line 26g, except for a corporation subject to section 291.					
a	Additional depreciation after 1975. See instructions	**26a**				
b	Applicable percentage multiplied by the **smaller** of line 24 or line 26a. See instructions.	**26b**				
c	Subtract line 26a from line 24. If residential rental property **or** line 24 isn't more than line 26a, skip lines 26d and 26e	**26c**				
d	Additional depreciation after 1969 and before 1976.	**26d**				
e	Enter the **smaller** of line 26c or 26d	**26e**				
f	Section 291 amount (corporations only)	**26f**				
g	Add lines 26b, 26e, and 26f	**26g**				
27	**If section 1252 property:** Skip this section if you didn't dispose of farmland or if this form is being completed for a partnership.					
a	Soil, water, and land clearing expenses	**27a**				
b	Line 27a multiplied by applicable percentage. See instructions	**27b**				
c	Enter the **smaller** of line 24 or 27b	**27c**				
28	**If section 1254 property:**					
a	Intangible drilling and development costs, expenditures for development of mines and other natural deposits, mining exploration costs, and depletion. See instructions	**28a**				
b	Enter the **smaller** of line 24 or 28a	**28b**				
29	**If section 1255 property:**					
a	Applicable percentage of payments excluded from income under section 126. See instructions	**29a**				
b	Enter the **smaller** of line 24 or 29a. See instructions	**29b**				

Summary of Part III Gains. Complete property columns A through D through line 29b before going to line 30.

30	Total gains for all properties. Add property columns A through D, line 24	**30**	
31	Add property columns A through D, lines 25b, 26g, 27c, 28b, and 29b. Enter here and on line 13	**31**	
32	Subtract line 31 from line 30. Enter the portion from casualty or theft on Form 4684, line 33. Enter the portion from other than casualty or theft on Form 4797, line 6	**32**	

| **Part IV** | **Recapture Amounts Under Sections 179 and 280F(b)(2) When Business Use Drops to 50% or Less** (see instructions) |

			(a) Section 179	**(b)** Section 280F(b)(2)
33	Section 179 expense deduction or depreciation allowable in prior years	**33**		
34	Recomputed depreciation. See instructions	**34**		
35	Recapture amount. Subtract line 34 from line 33. See the instructions for where to report	**35**		

Form **4797** (2020)

GROUP 2:
PROBLEM 17

Form **6252**	**Installment Sale Income**	OMB No. 1545-0228
	▶ **Attach to your tax return.**	20**20**
Department of the Treasury Internal Revenue Service	▶ **Use a separate form for each sale or other disposition of property on the installment method.** ▶ Go to *www.irs.gov/Form6252* for the latest information.	Attachment Sequence No. **625**

Name(s) shown on return	Identifying number

1 Description of property ▶ _____

2a Date acquired (mm/dd/yyyy) ▶ _____   **b** Date sold (mm/dd/yyyy) ▶ _____

3 Was the property sold to a related party (see instructions) after May 14, 1980? If "No," skip line 4 . . . . . ☐ Yes ☐ No

4 Was the property you sold to a related party a marketable security? If "Yes," complete Part III. If "No," complete Part III for the year of sale and the 2 years after the year of sale . . . . ☐ Yes ☐ No

Part I	**Gross Profit and Contract Price.** Complete this part for all years of the installment agreement.		
5	Selling price including mortgages and other debts. **Don't** include interest, whether stated or unstated		**5**
6	Mortgages, debts, and other liabilities the buyer assumed or took the property subject to (see instructions)	**6**	
7	Subtract line 6 from line 5	**7**	
8	Cost or other basis of property sold	**8**	
9	Depreciation allowed or allowable	**9**	
10	Adjusted basis. Subtract line 9 from line 8	**10**	
11	Commissions and other expenses of sale	**11**	
12	Income recapture from Form 4797, Part III (see instructions)	**12**	
13	Add lines 10, 11, and 12		**13**
14	Subtract line 13 from line 5. If zero or less, **don't** complete the rest of this form. See instructions . .		**14**
15	If the property described on line 1 above was your main home, enter the amount of your excluded gain. See instructions. Otherwise, enter -0-		**15**
16	**Gross profit.** Subtract line 15 from line 14		**16**
17	Subtract line 13 from line 6. If zero or less, enter -0-		**17**
18	**Contract price.** Add line 7 and line 17		**18**

Part II	**Installment Sale Income.** Complete this part for all years of the installment agreement.		
19	Gross profit percentage (expressed as a decimal amount). Divide line 16 by line 18. (For years after the year of sale, see instructions.)		**19**
20	If this is the year of sale, enter the amount from line 17. Otherwise, enter -0-		**20**
21	Payments received during year (see instructions). **Don't** include interest, whether stated or unstated .		**21**
22	Add lines 20 and 21		**22**
23	Payments received in prior years (see instructions). **Don't** include interest, whether stated or unstated . .	**23**	
24	**Installment sale income.** Multiply line 22 by line 19		**24**
25	Enter the part of line 24 that is ordinary income under the recapture rules. See instructions		**25**
26	Subtract line 25 from line 24. Enter here and on Schedule D or Form 4797. See instructions . . .		**26**

Part III	**Related Party Installment Sale Income. Don't** complete if you received the final payment this tax year.		
27	Name, address, and taxpayer identifying number of related party ▶ _____		

28 Did the related party resell or dispose of the property ("second disposition") during this tax year? . . . . . ☐ Yes ☐ No

29 If the answer to question 28 is "Yes," complete lines 30 through 37 below unless one of the following conditions is met. Check the box that applies.

   a ☐ The second disposition was more than 2 years after the first disposition (other than dispositions of marketable securities). If this box is checked, enter the date of disposition (mm/dd/yyyy) . . . . ▶ _____

   b ☐ The first disposition was a sale or exchange of stock to the issuing corporation.

   c ☐ The second disposition was an involuntary conversion and the threat of conversion occurred after the first disposition.

   d ☐ The second disposition occurred after the death of the original seller or buyer.

   e ☐ It can be established to the satisfaction of the IRS that tax avoidance wasn't a principal purpose for either of the dispositions. If this box is checked, attach an explanation. See instructions.

30	Selling price of property sold by related party (see instructions)	**30**	
31	Enter contract price from line 18 for year of first sale	**31**	
32	Enter the **smaller** of line 30 or line 31	**32**	
33	Total payments received by the end of your 2020 tax year (see instructions)	**33**	
34	Subtract line 33 from line 32. If zero or less, enter -0-	**34**	
35	Multiply line 34 by the gross profit percentage on line 19 for year of first sale	**35**	
36	Enter the part of line 35 that is ordinary income under the recapture rules. See instructions	**36**	
37	Subtract line 36 from line 35. Enter here and on Schedule D or Form 4797. See instructions	**37**	

For Paperwork Reduction Act Notice, see page 4.   Cat. No. 13601R   Form **6252** (2020)

LO 8.7
LO 8.8

18. William sold Section 1245 property for $25,000 in 2020. The property cost $40,000 when it was purchased 5 years ago. The depreciation claimed on the property was $21,000.
    a. Calculate the adjusted basis of the property. $_____
    b. Calculate the realized gain on the sale. $_____
    c. Calculate the amount of ordinary income under Section 1245. $_____
    d. Calculate the Section 1231 gain. $_____

LO 8.9

19. An office machine used by Josie in her accounting business was completely destroyed by fire. The adjusted basis of the machine was $8,000 (original basis of $14,000 less accumulated depreciation of $6,000). The machine was not insured. Calculate the amount and nature of Josie's gain or loss as a result of this casualty.

    Amount of gain or loss $_____
    Nature   _____

LO 8.11

20. Carey exchanges land for other land in a qualifying like-kind exchange. Carey's basis in the land given up is $115,000, and the property has a fair market value of $150,000. In exchange for her property, Carey receives land with a fair market value of $100,000 and cash of $10,000. In addition, the other party to the exchange assumes a mortgage loan on Carey's property of $40,000.
    a. Calculate Carey's recognized gain, if any, on the exchange. $_____
    b. Calculate Carey's basis in the property received. $_____

LO 8.12

21. Teresa's manufacturing plant is destroyed by fire. The plant has an adjusted basis of $270,000, and Teresa receives insurance proceeds of $410,000 for the loss. Teresa reinvests $420,000 in a replacement plant within 2 years of receiving the insurance proceeds.
    a. Calculate Teresa's recognized gain if she elects to utilize the involuntary conversion provision. $_____
    b. Calculate Teresa's basis in the new plant. $_____

GROUP 3:
WRITING ASSIGNMENT

RESEARCH

1. Your supervisor has asked you to research the following situation concerning Owen and Lisa Cordoncillo. Owen and Lisa are brother and sister. In May 2020, Owen and Lisa exchange land they both held separately for investment. Lisa gives up a 2 acre property in Texas with an adjusted basis of $2,000 and a fair market value of $6,000. In return for this property, Lisa receives from Owen a 1 acre property in Arkansas with a fair market value of $5,500 and cash of $500. Owen's adjusted basis in the land he exchanges is $2,500. In March 2021, Owen sells the Texas land to a third party for $5,800.

    Required: Go to the IRS website (**www.irs.gov**). Locate and review Publication 544, Chapter 1, Nontaxable Exchanges. Write a file memorandum stating the amount of Owen and Lisa's gain recognition for 2020. Also determine the effect, if any, of the subsequent sale in 2021. (An example of a file memorandum is available at the website for this textbook located at **www.cengage.com.**)

GROUP 4:
COMPREHENSIVE PROBLEMS

1. Trish Himple owns a retail family clothing store. Her store is located at 4321 Heather Drive, Henderson, NV 89002. Her employer identification number is 95-1234321 and her Social Security number is 123-45-6789. Trish keeps her books on an accrual basis. The income and expenses for the year are:

Gross sales		$340,000
Returns and allowances		14,000
Expenses:		
Beginning inventory (at cost)	$ 85,000	
Add: purchases	101,000	
Cost of goods available for sale	186,000	
Less: ending inventory (at cost)	71,000	
Cost of goods sold		$115,000
Rent		24,400
Insurance		2,000
Legal and accounting fees		5,000
Payroll		56,400
Payroll taxes		4,400
Utilities		2,200
Office supplies		750
Advertising		6,200

Trish's bookkeeper has provided the following *book-basis* fixed asset rollforward:

Himple Retail
Fixed Asset Rollforward
12/31/2020
(book basis)

ASSET	IN SERVICE	DEPR METHOD	LIFE	COST BASIS	2018 DEPR	2019 DEPR	2020 DEPR	ACCUM DEPR	NET BOOK VALUE
CASH REGISTER	12/15/2018	SL	5	9,900.00	165.00	1,980.00	1,980.00	4,125.00	5,775.00
2018 TOTAL ADDITIONS				9,900.00	165.00	1,980.00	1,980.00	4,125.00	5,775.00
RETAIL FIXTURES	9/12/2019	SL	7	4,750.00		226.19	678.57	904.76	3,845.24
FURNITURE	9/12/2019	SL	7	3,900.00		185.71	557.14	742.85	3,157.15
2019 TOTAL ADDITIONS				8,650.00	-	411.90	1,235.71	1,647.61	7,002.39
TOTAL				18,550.00	165.00	2,391.90	3,215.71	5,772.61	12,777.39
DELIVERY TRUCK	6/1/2020	SL	5	37,500.00			4,375.00	4,375.00	33,125.00
DESK AND CABINETRY	6/1/2020	SL	7	11,900.00			991.67	991.67	10,908.33
COMPUTER	6/1/2020	SL	5	2,800.00			326.67	326.67	2,473.33
2020 TOTAL ADDITIONS				52,200.00	-	-	5,693.34	5,693.34	46,506.66
TOTAL				70,750.00	165.00	2,391.90	8,909.05	11,465.95	59,284.05

The truck is not considered a passenger automobile for purposes of the luxury automobile limitations.

Trish also has a qualified home office of 250 sq. ft. Her home is 2,000 sq. ft. Her 2015 purchase price and basis in the home, not including land, is $100,000 (the home's market value is $150,000). She incurred the following costs in 2020 related to the entire home:

Utilities	$3,000
Cleaning	1,000
Insurance	1,100
Property taxes	2,000

Required: For tax purposes, Trish elected out of bonus depreciation in all years except 2020. She did not elect immediate expensing in any year. The tax lives of the assets are the same as the book lives shown in the fixed asset schedule above. Complete Trish's Schedule C, Form 8829, and Form 4562 (as necessary). Make realistic assumptions about any missing data.

2. Tsate Kongia (birthdate 02/14/1954) is an unmarried high school principal. Tsate received the following tax documents:

a Employee's social security number 467-98-9784	OMB No. 1545-0008	Safe, accurate, FAST! Use	IRS e-file	Visit the IRS website at www.irs.gov/efile

b Employer identification number (EIN) 56-1357924	1 Wages, tips, other compensation 57,000.00	2 Federal income tax withheld 6,100.00

c Employer's name, address, and ZIP code	3 Social security wages 60,000.00	4 Social security tax withheld 3,720.00
Shawnee Mission School District 8200 W. 71st Street Shawnee Mission, KS 66204	5 Medicare wages and tips 60,000.00	6 Medicare tax withheld 870.00
	7 Social security tips	8 Allocated tips

d Control number	9	10 Dependent care benefits

e Employee's first name and initial Last name Suff.	11 Nonqualified plans	12a See instructions for box 12 D	3,000.00
Tsate Kongia 212 Quivera Road Overland Park, KS 66210	13 Statutory employee ☐ Retirement plan ☒ Third-party sick pay ☐	12b
	14 Other	12c
		12d

f Employee's address and ZIP code					

15 State Employer's state ID number	16 State wages, tips, etc.	17 State income tax	18 Local wages, tips, etc.	19 Local income tax	20 Locality name
KS 34511DF	57,000.00	1,200.00			

Form **W-2** Wage and Tax Statement   **2020**   Department of the Treasury—Internal Revenue Service

Copy B—To Be Filed With Employee's FEDERAL Tax Return.
This information is being furnished to the Internal Revenue Service.

☐ CORRECTED (if checked)

PAYER'S name, street address, city or town, state or province, country, ZIP or foreign postal code, and telephone no.	Payer's RTN (optional)	OMB No. 1545-0112	**Interest Income**
Olanthe National Bank 1240 E. Sante Fe Street Olanthe, KS 66061	1 Interest income $ 205.61	20**20** Form **1099-INT**	
	2 Early withdrawal penalty $		**Copy B**
PAYER'S TIN 44-1352469	RECIPIENT'S TIN 467-98-9784	3 Interest on U.S. Savings Bonds and Treas. obligations $	**For Recipient**
RECIPIENT'S name Tsate Kongia		4 Federal income tax withheld $	5 Investment expenses $	This is important tax information and is being furnished to the IRS. If you are required to file a return, a negligence penalty or other sanction may be imposed on you if this income is taxable and the IRS determines that it has not been reported.
Street address (including apt. no.) 212 Quivera Road		6 Foreign tax paid $	7 Foreign country or U.S. possession
City or town, state or province, country, and ZIP or foreign postal code Overland Park, KS 66210		8 Tax-exempt interest $	9 Specified private activity bond interest $
		10 Market discount $	11 Bond premium $
	FATCA filing requirement ☐	12 Bond premium on Treasury obligations $	13 Bond premium on tax-exempt bond $
Account number (see instructions)		14 Tax-exempt and tax credit bond CUSIP no.	15 State	16 State identification no.	17 State tax withheld $ $

Form **1099-INT**   (keep for your records)   www.irs.gov/Form1099INT   Department of the Treasury - Internal Revenue Service

☐ CORRECTED (if checked)

PAYER'S name, street address, city or town, state or province, country, ZIP or foreign postal code, and telephone no. Johnson Corporation 100 E. 49th Street New York, NY 10017	**1a** Total ordinary dividends $ 4,117.00	OMB No. 1545-0110 20**20** Form **1099-DIV**	**Dividends and Distributions**
	1b Qualified dividends $ 4,117.00		

PAYER'S TIN 17-2468135	RECIPIENT'S TIN 467-98-9784	**2a** Total capital gain distr. $	**2b** Unrecap. Sec. 1250 gain $	**Copy B** **For Recipient**
		2c Section 1202 gain $	**2d** Collectibles (28%) gain $	
RECIPIENT'S name Tsate Kongai		**3** Nondividend distributions $	**4** Federal income tax withheld $ 0.00	This is important tax information and is being furnished to the IRS. If you are required to file a return, a negligence penalty or other sanction may be imposed on you if this income is taxable and the IRS determines that it has not been reported.
		5 Section 199A dividends $	**6** Investment expenses $	
Street address (including apt. no.) 212 Quivera Road		**7** Foreign tax paid $	**8** Foreign country or U.S. possession	
City or town, state or province, country, and ZIP or foreign postal code Overland Park, KS 66210		**9** Cash liquidation distributions $	**10** Noncash liquidation distributions $	
	FATCA filing requirement ☐	**11** Exempt-interest dividends $	**12** Specified private activity bond interest dividends $	
Account number (see instructions)		**13** State	**14** State identification no.	**15** State tax withheld $ $

Form **1099-DIV**   (keep for your records)   www.irs.gov/Form1099DIV   Department of the Treasury - Internal Revenue Service

During the year, Tsate paid the following amounts (all of which can be substantiated):

Home mortgage interest reported on Form 1098 (not shown)	$9,600
KS state income tax payment for 2019	$500
MasterCard interest	550
Life insurance (whole life policy)	750
Property taxes on personal residence	1,500
Blue Cross medical insurance premiums	250
Other medical expenses	800
Income tax preparation fee	300
Charitable contributions (in cash)	750

Tsate's sole stock transaction was reported on a Form 1099-B:

☐ CORRECTED (if checked)

PAYER'S name, street address, city or town, state or province, country, ZIP or foreign postal code, and telephone no. Little John Trading 123 Wall Street New York, NY 10014	Applicable checkbox on Form 8949	OMB No. 1545-0715 20**20** Form **1099-B**	**Proceeds From Broker and Barter Exchange Transactions**
	1a Description of property (Example: 100 sh. XYZ Co.) 100 shs. Johnson Corp		

PAYER'S TIN 11-0010011	RECIPIENT'S TIN 467-98-9784	**1b** Date acquired 12/13/2019	**1c** Date sold or disposed 11/05/2020	**Copy B** **For Recipient**
		1d Proceeds $ 14,500.00	**1e** Cost or other basis $ 35,600.00	
		1f Accrued market discount $	**1g** Wash sale loss disallowed $	
RECIPIENT'S name Tsate Kongai		**2** Short-term gain or loss ☐ Long-term gain or loss ☐ Ordinary ☐	**3** If checked, proceeds from: Collectibles ☐ QOF ☐	This is important tax information and is being furnished to the IRS. If you are required to file a return, a negligence penalty or other sanction may be imposed on you if this income is taxable and the IRS determines that it has not been reported.
Street address (including apt. no.) 212 Quivera Road		**4** Federal income tax withheld $	**5** If checked, noncovered security ☐	
		6 Reported to IRS: Gross proceeds ☐ Net proceeds ☒	**7** If checked, loss is not allowed based on amount in 1d ☐	
City or town, state or province, country, and ZIP or foreign postal code Overland Park, KS 66210		**8** Profit or (loss) realized in 2020 on closed contracts $	**9** Unrealized profit or (loss) on open contracts—12/31/2019 $	
Account number (see instructions)				
CUSIP number	FATCA filing requirement ☐	**10** Unrealized profit or (loss) on open contracts—12/31/2020 $	**11** Aggregate profit or (loss) on contracts $	
14 State name	**15** State identification no.	**16** State tax withheld $ $	**12** If checked, basis reported to IRS ☒	**13** Bartering $

Form **1099-B**   (Keep for your records)   www.irs.gov/Form1099B   Department of the Treasury - Internal Revenue Service

On January 28, 2020, Tsate sold land for $180,000 (basis to Tsate of $130,000). The land was purchased 6 years ago as an investment. Tsate received $50,000 as a down payment and the buyer's 10-year note for $130,000. The note is payable at the rate of $13,000 per year plus 8 percent interest. On December 31, 2020, the first of the ten principal and interest payments was received by Tsate.

Tsate also helps support his father, Jay Hawke, who lives in a nearby senior facility. Jay's Social Security number is 433-33-2121. Tsate provides over one-half of Jay's support but Jay also has a pension that paid him income of $14,000 in 2020. His Social Security benefits were $3,200 in 2020. Tsate received a $1,200 EIP in 2020.

Required: Complete Tsate's federal tax return for 2020. Use Form 1040-SR, Schedule A, Schedule B, Schedule D, Form 8949, the Qualified Dividends and Capital Gain Tax Worksheet, and Form 6252, as needed, to complete this tax return. Make realistic assumptions about any missing data.

GROUP 5:
CUMULATIVE SOFTWARE PROBLEM

1. The following information is available for the Albert and Allison Gaytor family in addition to that provided in Chapters 1–7.

On September 14, 2020, Allison purchased the building where her store is located. She paid $375,000 for the building (which includes $100,000 for the land it is located on). Allison's store is the only business in the building. The depreciation on the store needs to be reflected on Schedule C of the business.

Required: Combine this new information about the Gaytor family with the information from Chapters 1 to 7 and complete a revised 2020 tax return for Albert and Allison. This completes the Group 5 multichapter case.

SCHEDULE C
(Form 1040)

Department of the Treasury
Internal Revenue Service (99)

Profit or Loss From Business
(Sole Proprietorship)

▶ Go to *www.irs.gov/ScheduleC* for instructions and the latest information.
▶ Attach to Form 1040, 1040-SR, 1040-NR, or 1041; partnerships generally must file Form 1065.

OMB No. 1545-0074

2020

Attachment
Sequence No. **09**

Name of proprietor

Social security number (SSN)

A	Principal business or profession, including product or service (see instructions)	**B Enter code from instructions** ▶
C	Business name. If no separate business name, leave blank.	**D Employer ID number (EIN)** (see instr.)

E Business address (including suite or room no.) ▶
City, town or post office, state, and ZIP code

F Accounting method: **(1)** ☐ Cash **(2)** ☐ Accrual **(3)** ☐ Other (specify) ▶

G Did you "materially participate" in the operation of this business during 2020? If "No," see instructions for limit on losses . ☐ Yes ☐ No

H If you started or acquired this business during 2020, check here . . . . ▶ ☐

I Did you make any payments in 2020 that would require you to file Form(s) 1099? See instructions . . . . . . ☐ Yes ☐ No

J If "Yes," did you or will you file required Form(s) 1099? . . . . ☐ Yes ☐ No

Part I Income

1	Gross receipts or sales. See instructions for line 1 and check the box if this income was reported to you on Form W-2 and the "Statutory employee" box on that form was checked . . . . . ▶ ☐	**1**	
2	Returns and allowances	**2**	
3	Subtract line 2 from line 1	**3**	
4	Cost of goods sold (from line 42)	**4**	
5	**Gross profit.** Subtract line 4 from line 3	**5**	
6	Other income, including federal and state gasoline or fuel tax credit or refund (see instructions) . . . ▶	**6**	
7	**Gross income.** Add lines 5 and 6 . . . . ▶	**7**	

Part II Expenses. Enter expenses for business use of your home **only** on line 30.

8	Advertising	**8**		18	Office expense (see instructions)	**18**	
9	Car and truck expenses (see instructions).	**9**		19	Pension and profit-sharing plans	**19**	
				20	Rent or lease (see instructions):		
10	Commissions and fees .	**10**		a	Vehicles, machinery, and equipment	**20a**	
11	Contract labor (see instructions)	**11**		b	Other business property . . .	**20b**	
12	Depletion	**12**		21	Repairs and maintenance . .	**21**	
13	Depreciation and section 179 expense deduction (not included in Part III) (see instructions).	**13**		22	Supplies (not included in Part III) .	**22**	
				23	Taxes and licenses	**23**	
				24	Travel and meals:		
14	Employee benefit programs (other than on line 19) . .	**14**		a	Travel	**24a**	
15	Insurance (other than health)	**15**		b	Deductible meals (see instructions)	**24b**	
16	Interest (see instructions):			25	Utilities	**25**	
a	Mortgage (paid to banks, etc.)	**16a**		26	Wages (less employment credits) .	**26**	
b	Other	**16b**		27a	Other expenses (from line 48) . .	**27a**	
17	Legal and professional services	**17**		b	**Reserved for future use** . . .	**27b**	

28	**Total expenses** before expenses for business use of home. Add lines 8 through 27a . . . . . . ▶	**28**	
29	Tentative profit or (loss). Subtract line 28 from line 7	**29**	
30	Expenses for business use of your home. Do not report these expenses elsewhere. Attach Form 8829 unless using the simplified method. See instructions. **Simplified method filers only:** Enter the total square footage of (a) your home: _____ and (b) the part of your home used for business: _____ . Use the Simplified Method Worksheet in the instructions to figure the amount to enter on line 30	**30**	
31	**Net profit or (loss).** Subtract line 30 from line 29. • If a profit, enter on both **Schedule 1 (Form 1040), line 3,** and on **Schedule SE, line 2.** (If you checked the box on line 1, see instructions). Estates and trusts, enter on **Form 1041, line 3.** • If a loss, you **must** go to line 32.	**31**	
32	If you have a loss, check the box that describes your investment in this activity. See instructions. • If you checked 32a, enter the loss on both **Schedule 1 (Form 1040), line 3,** and on **Schedule SE, line 2.** (If you checked the box on line 1, see the line 31 instructions). Estates and trusts, enter on **Form 1041, line 3.** • If you checked 32b, you **must** attach **Form 6198.** Your loss may be limited.	**32a** ☐ All investment is at risk. **32b** ☐ Some investment is not at risk.	

For Paperwork Reduction Act Notice, see the separate instructions.   Cat. No. 11334P   Schedule C (Form 1040) 2020

Schedule C (Form 1040) 2020

Page **2**

Part III   Cost of Goods Sold (see instructions)

33   Method(s) used to
     value closing inventory: **a** ☐ Cost   **b** ☐ Lower of cost or market   **c** ☐ Other (attach explanation)

34   Was there any change in determining quantities, costs, or valuations between opening and closing inventory?
     If "Yes," attach explanation . . . .   ☐ **Yes**   ☐ **No**

35 Inventory at beginning of year. If different from last year's closing inventory, attach explanation . . .	**35**	
36 Purchases less cost of items withdrawn for personal use	**36**	
37 Cost of labor. Do not include any amounts paid to yourself	**37**	
38 Materials and supplies	**38**	
39 Other costs	**39**	
40 Add lines 35 through 39	**40**	
41 Inventory at end of year	**41**	
42 **Cost of goods sold.** Subtract line 41 from line 40. Enter the result here and on line 4	**42**	

Part IV   Information on Your Vehicle.   Complete this part **only** if you are claiming car or truck expenses on line 9 and are not required to file Form 4562 for this business. See the instructions for line 13 to find out if you must file Form 4562.

43   When did you place your vehicle in service for business purposes? (month/day/year)   ▶ ____ / ____ / ____

44   Of the total number of miles you drove your vehicle during 2020, enter the number of miles you used your vehicle for:

a Business _____   **b** Commuting (see instructions) _____   **c** Other _____

45   Was your vehicle available for personal use during off-duty hours? . . . .   ☐ **Yes**   ☐ **No**

46   Do you (or your spouse) have another vehicle available for personal use?. . . . .   ☐ **Yes**   ☐ **No**

47a Do you have evidence to support your deduction? . . . .   ☐ **Yes**   ☐ **No**

b If "Yes," is the evidence written? . . . .   ☐ **Yes**   ☐ **No**

Part V   Other Expenses.   List below business expenses not included on lines 8–26 or line 30.

_____	
_____	
_____	
_____	
_____	
_____	
_____	
_____	
_____	
48 **Total other expenses.** Enter here and on line 27a	**48**

Schedule C (Form 1040) 2020

Form **4562**

Department of the Treasury
Internal Revenue Service (99)

Depreciation and Amortization
(Including Information on Listed Property)
▶ Attach to your tax return.
▶ Go to *www.irs.gov/Form4562* for instructions and the latest information.

OMB No. 1545-0172

2020

Attachment
Sequence No. **179**

Name(s) shown on return | Business or activity to which this form relates | Identifying number

Part I	**Election To Expense Certain Property Under Section 179**

Note: If you have any listed property, complete Part V before you complete Part I.

1	Maximum amount (see instructions)	1	
2	Total cost of section 179 property placed in service (see instructions)	2	
3	Threshold cost of section 179 property before reduction in limitation (see instructions)	3	
4	Reduction in limitation. Subtract line 3 from line 2. If zero or less, enter -0-	4	
5	Dollar limitation for tax year. Subtract line 4 from line 1. If zero or less, enter -0-. If married filing separately, see instructions	5	

6	**(a)** Description of property	**(b)** Cost (business use only)	**(c)** Elected cost

7	Listed property. Enter the amount from line 29	7		
8	Total elected cost of section 179 property. Add amounts in column (c), lines 6 and 7	8	
9	Tentative deduction. Enter the **smaller** of line 5 or line 8	9	
10	Carryover of disallowed deduction from line 13 of your 2019 Form 4562	10	
11	Business income limitation. Enter the smaller of business income (not less than zero) or line 5. See instructions	11	
12	Section 179 expense deduction. Add lines 9 and 10, but don't enter more than line 11	12	
13	Carryover of disallowed deduction to 2021. Add lines 9 and 10, less line 12 ▶	13	

Note: Don't use Part II or Part III below for listed property. Instead, use Part V.

Part II	**Special Depreciation Allowance and Other Depreciation (Don't** include listed property. See instructions.)

14	Special depreciation allowance for qualified property (other than listed property) placed in service during the tax year. See instructions	14	
15	Property subject to section 168(f)(1) election	15	
16	Other depreciation (including ACRS)	16	

Part III	**MACRS Depreciation (Don't** include listed property. See instructions.)

Section A

| 17 | MACRS deductions for assets placed in service in tax years beginning before 2020 | 17 | |
| 18 | If you are electing to group any assets placed in service during the tax year into one or more general asset accounts, check here ▶ ☐ | | |

Section B—Assets Placed in Service During 2020 Tax Year Using the General Depreciation System

(a) Classification of property	**(b)** Month and year placed in service	**(c)** Basis for depreciation (business/investment use only—see instructions)	**(d)** Recovery period	**(e)** Convention	**(f)** Method	**(g)** Depreciation deduction
19a 3-year property						
b 5-year property						
c 7-year property						
d 10-year property						
e 15-year property						
f 20-year property						
g 25-year property			25 yrs.		S/L	
h Residential rental property			27.5 yrs.	MM	S/L	
			27.5 yrs.	MM	S/L	
i Nonresidential real property			39 yrs.	MM	S/L	
				MM	S/L	

Section C—Assets Placed in Service During 2020 Tax Year Using the Alternative Depreciation System

20a Class life					S/L	
b 12-year			12 yrs.		S/L	
c 30-year			30 yrs.	MM	S/L	
d 40-year			40 yrs.	MM	S/L	

Part IV	**Summary** (See instructions.)

21	Listed property. Enter amount from line 28	21	
22	**Total.** Add amounts from line 12, lines 14 through 17, lines 19 and 20 in column (g), and line 21. Enter here and on the appropriate lines of your return. Partnerships and S corporations—see instructions	22	
23	For assets shown above and placed in service during the current year, enter the portion of the basis attributable to section 263A costs	23	

For Paperwork Reduction Act Notice, see separate instructions.   Cat. No. 12906N   Form **4562** (2020)

Form 4562 (2020)
Page **2**

Part V Listed Property (Include automobiles, certain other vehicles, certain aircraft, and property used for entertainment, recreation, or amusement.)

Note: For any vehicle for which you are using the standard mileage rate or deducting lease expense, complete **only** 24a, 24b, columns (a) through (c) of Section A, all of Section B, and Section C if applicable.

Section A—Depreciation and Other Information (Caution: See the instructions for limits for passenger automobiles.)

24a Do you have evidence to support the business/investment use claimed? ☐ Yes ☐ No   **24b** If "Yes," is the evidence written? ☐ Yes ☐ No

(a) Type of property (list vehicles first)	(b) Date placed in service	(c) Business/ investment use percentage	(d) Cost or other basis	(e) Basis for depreciation (business/investment use only)	(f) Recovery period	(g) Method/ Convention	(h) Depreciation deduction	(i) Elected section 179 cost
25 Special depreciation allowance for qualified listed property placed in service during the tax year and used more than 50% in a qualified business use. See instructions .					**25**			
26 Property used more than 50% in a qualified business use:								
		%						
		%						
		%						
27 Property used 50% or less in a qualified business use:								
		%				S/L –		
		%				S/L –		
		%				S/L –		
28 Add amounts in column (h), lines 25 through 27. Enter here and on line 21, page 1 .					**28**			
29 Add amounts in column (i), line 26. Enter here and on line 7, page 1							**29**	

Section B—Information on Use of Vehicles

Complete this section for vehicles used by a sole proprietor, partner, or other "more than 5% owner," or related person. If you provided vehicles to your employees, first answer the questions in Section C to see if you meet an exception to completing this section for those vehicles.

	(a) Vehicle 1		(b) Vehicle 2		(c) Vehicle 3		(d) Vehicle 4		(e) Vehicle 5		(f) Vehicle 6	
30 Total business/investment miles driven during the year (**don't** include commuting miles) .												
31 Total commuting miles driven during the year												
32 Total other personal (noncommuting) miles driven												
33 Total miles driven during the year. Add lines 30 through 32												
	Yes	No	Yes	No	Yes	No	Yes	No	Yes	No	Yes	No
34 Was the vehicle available for personal use during off-duty hours?												
35 Was the vehicle used primarily by a more than 5% owner or related person? . .												
36 Is another vehicle available for personal use?												

Section C—Questions for Employers Who Provide Vehicles for Use by Their Employees

Answer these questions to determine if you meet an exception to completing Section B for vehicles used by employees who **aren't** more than 5% owners or related persons. See instructions.

		Yes	No
37	Do you maintain a written policy statement that prohibits all personal use of vehicles, including commuting, by your employees?		
38	Do you maintain a written policy statement that prohibits personal use of vehicles, except commuting, by your employees? See the instructions for vehicles used by corporate officers, directors, or 1% or more owners . .		
39	Do you treat all use of vehicles by employees as personal use?		
40	Do you provide more than five vehicles to your employees, obtain information from your employees about the use of the vehicles, and retain the information received?		
41	Do you meet the requirements concerning qualified automobile demonstration use? See instructions.		

Note: If your answer to 37, 38, 39, 40, or 41 is "Yes," don't complete Section B for the covered vehicles.

Part VI Amortization

(a) Description of costs	(b) Date amortization begins	(c) Amortizable amount	(d) Code section	(e) Amortization period or percentage	(f) Amortization for this year
42 Amortization of costs that begins during your 2020 tax year (see instructions):					
43 Amortization of costs that began before your 2020 tax year				**43**	
44 **Total.** Add amounts in column (f). See the instructions for where to report				**44**	

Form **4562** (2020)

Form **8829**

Department of the Treasury
Internal Revenue Service (99)

Expenses for Business Use of Your Home

▶ File only with Schedule C (Form 1040). Use a separate Form 8829 for each home you used for business during the year.
▶ Go to *www.irs.gov/Form8829* for instructions and the latest information.

OMB No. 1545-0074

2020

Attachment
Sequence No. **176**

Name(s) of proprietor(s)

Your social security number

Part I	**Part of Your Home Used for Business**			
1	Area used regularly and exclusively for business, regularly for daycare, or for storage of inventory or product samples (see instructions)		1	
2	Total area of home		2	
3	Divide line 1 by line 2. Enter the result as a percentage		3	%
	For daycare facilities not used exclusively for business, go to line 4. All others, go to line 7.			
4	Multiply days used for daycare during year by hours used per day	4	hr.	
5	If you started or stopped using your home for daycare during the year, see instructions; otherwise, enter 8,784	5	hr.	
6	Divide line 4 by line 5. Enter the result as a decimal amount	6		
7	Business percentage. For daycare facilities not used exclusively for business, multiply line 6 by line 3 (enter the result as a percentage). All others, enter the amount from line 3 ▶		7	%

Part II	**Figure Your Allowable Deduction**			
8	Enter the amount from Schedule C, line 29, **plus** any gain derived from the business use of your home, **minus** any loss from the trade or business not derived from the business use of your home. See instructions.		8	
	See instructions for columns (a) and (b) before completing lines 9–22.	(a) Direct expenses	(b) Indirect expenses	
9	Casualty losses (see instructions)	9		
10	Deductible mortgage interest (see instructions)	10		
11	Real estate taxes (see instructions)	11		
12	Add lines 9, 10, and 11	12		
13	Multiply line 12, column (b), by line 7	13		
14	Add line 12, column (a), and line 13		14	
15	Subtract line 14 from line 8. If zero or less, enter -0-		15	
16	Excess mortgage interest (see instructions)	16		
17	Excess real estate taxes (see instructions)	17		
18	Insurance	18		
19	Rent	19		
20	Repairs and maintenance	20		
21	Utilities	21		
22	Other expenses (see instructions)	22		
23	Add lines 16 through 22	23		
24	Multiply line 23, column (b), by line 7	24		
25	Carryover of prior year operating expenses (see instructions)	25		
26	Add line 23, column (a), line 24, and line 25		26	
27	Allowable operating expenses. Enter the **smaller** of line 15 or line 26		27	
28	Limit on excess casualty losses and depreciation. Subtract line 27 from line 15		28	
29	Excess casualty losses (see instructions)	29		
30	Depreciation of your home from line 42 below	30		
31	Carryover of prior year excess casualty losses and depreciation (see instructions)	31		
32	Add lines 29 through 31		32	
33	Allowable excess casualty losses and depreciation. Enter the **smaller** of line 28 or line 32		33	
34	Add lines 14, 27, and 33		34	
35	Casualty loss portion, if any, from lines 14 and 33. Carry amount to **Form 4684.** See instructions		35	
36	**Allowable expenses for business use of your home.** Subtract line 35 from line 34. Enter here and on Schedule C, line 30. If your home was used for more than one business, see instructions. ▶		36	

Part III	**Depreciation of Your Home**			
37	Enter the **smaller** of your home's adjusted basis or its fair market value. See instructions		37	
38	Value of land included on line 37		38	
39	Basis of building. Subtract line 38 from line 37		39	
40	Business basis of building. Multiply line 39 by line 7		40	
41	Depreciation percentage (see instructions)		41	%
42	Depreciation allowable (see instructions). Multiply line 40 by line 41. Enter here and on line 30 above		42	

Part IV	**Carryover of Unallowed Expenses to 2021**			
43	Operating expenses. Subtract line 27 from line 26. If less than zero, enter -0-		43	
44	Excess casualty losses and depreciation. Subtract line 33 from line 32. If less than zero, enter -0-		44	

For Paperwork Reduction Act Notice, see your tax return instructions.   Cat. No. 13232M   Form **8829** (2020)

Form **1040-SR** Department of the Treasury—Internal Revenue Service (99) **2020** OMB No. 1545-0074 | IRS Use Only—Do not write or staple in this space.

U.S. Tax Return for Seniors

Filing Status
Check only one box.

☐ Single ☐ Married filing jointly ☐ Married filing separately (MFS)
☐ Head of household (HOH) ☐ Qualifying widow(er) (QW)

If you checked the MFS box, enter the name of your spouse. If you checked the HOH or QW box, enter the child's name if the qualifying person is a child but not your dependent ▶

Your first name and middle initial	Last name	Your social security number

If joint return, spouse's first name and middle initial	Last name	Spouse's social security number

Home address (number and street). If you have a P.O. box, see instructions.		Apt. no.	**Presidential Election Campaign**
City, town, or post office. If you have a foreign address, also complete spaces below.	State	ZIP code	Check here if you, or your spouse if filing jointly, want $3 to go to this fund. Checking a box below will not change your tax or refund. ☐ **You** ☐ **Spouse**
Foreign country name	Foreign province/state/county	Foreign postal code	

At any time during 2020, did you receive, sell, send, exchange, or otherwise acquire any financial interest in any virtual currency? . . . . ▶ ☐ Yes ☐ No

Standard Deduction

Someone can claim: ☐ You as a dependent ☐ Your spouse as a dependent
☐ Spouse itemizes on a separate return or you were a dual-status alien

Age/Blindness {
You: ☐ Were born before January 2, 1956 ☐ Are blind
Spouse: ☐ Was born before January 2, 1956 ☐ Is blind

Dependents (see instructions):

(1) First name Last name	(2) Social security number	(3) Relationship to you	(4) ✔ if qualifies for (see instructions):	
			Child tax credit	Credit for other dependents
			☐	☐
			☐	☐
			☐	☐
			☐	☐

If more than four dependents, see instructions and check here ▶ ☐

Attach Schedule B if required.

1	Wages, salaries, tips, etc. Attach Form(s) W-2	**1**	
2a	Tax-exempt interest .	**2a**	**b** Taxable interest . .	**2b**	
3a	Qualified dividends . .	**3a**	**b** Ordinary dividends .	**3b**	
4a	IRA distributions . . .	**4a**	**b** Taxable amount . .	**4b**	
5a	Pensions and annuities	**5a**	**b** Taxable amount . .	**5b**	
6a	Social security benefits .	**6a**	**b** Taxable amount . .	**6b**	
7	Capital gain or (loss). Attach Schedule D if required. If not required, check here . . . . ▶ ☐	**7**	
8	Other income from Schedule 1, line 9	**8**	
9	Add lines 1, 2b, 3b, 4b, 5b, 6b, 7, and 8. This is your **total income** . . ▶	**9**	
10	Adjustments to income:		
a	From Schedule 1, line 22	**10a**	
b	Charitable contributions if you take the standard deduction. See instructions	**10b**	
c	Add lines 10a and 10b. These are your **total adjustments to income** ▶	**10c**	
11	Subtract line 10c from line 9. This is your **adjusted gross income** . . ▶	**11**	

For Disclosure, Privacy Act, and Paperwork Reduction Act Notice, see separate instructions. Cat. No. 71930F Form **1040-SR** (2020)

Form 1040-SR (2020)   Page **2**

Standard Deduction	12	**Standard deduction or itemized deductions** (from Schedule A) . . .	12	
See *Standard Deduction Chart* on the last page of this form.	13	Qualified business income deduction. Attach Form 8995 or Form 8995-A	13	
	14	Add lines 12 and 13	14	
	15	**Taxable income.** Subtract line 14 from line 11. If zero or less, enter -0- .	15	
	16	**Tax** (see instructions). Check if any from:		
		1 ☐ Form(s) 8814 **2** ☐ Form 4972 **3** ☐	16	
	17	Amount from Schedule 2, line 3	17	
	18	Add lines 16 and 17	18	
	19	Child tax credit or credit for other dependents	19	
	20	Amount from Schedule 3, line 7	20	
	21	Add lines 19 and 20	21	
	22	Subtract line 21 from line 18. If zero or less, enter -0-	22	
	23	Other taxes, including self-employment tax, from Schedule 2, line 10 . .	23	
	24	Add lines 22 and 23. This is your **total tax** . . . . ▶	24	

	25	Federal income tax withheld from:		
	a	Form(s) W-2	25a	
	b	Form(s) 1099	25b	
	c	Other forms (see instructions)	25c	
	d	Add lines 25a through 25c	25d	
	26	2020 estimated tax payments and amount applied from 2019 return . .	26	
• If you have a qualifying child, attach Sch. EIC.	27	Earned income credit (EIC)	27	
	28	Additional child tax credit. Attach Schedule 8812 . .	28	
	29	American opportunity credit from Form 8863, line 8 .	29	
• If you have nontaxable combat pay, see instructions.	30	Recovery rebate credit. See instructions	30	
	31	Amount from Schedule 3, line 13	31	
	32	Add lines 27 through 31. These are your **total other payments and refundable credits** . . . . ▶	32	
	33	Add lines 25d, 26, and 32. These are your **total payments** . . . . . ▶	33	

Go to *www.irs.gov/Form1040SR* for instructions and the latest information.   Form **1040-SR** (2020)

Form 1040-SR (2020)   Page **3**

Refund	**34**	If line 33 is more than line 24, subtract line 24 from line 33. This is the amount you **overpaid**	**34**
	35a	Amount of line 34 you want **refunded to you.** If Form 8888 is attached, check here . . . . ▶ ☐	**35a**

Direct deposit?
See
instructions.

▶ **b** Routing number [ ] ▶ **c** Type: ☐ Checking ☐ Savings

▶ **d** Account number [ ]

	36	Amount of line 34 you want **applied to your 2021 estimated tax** . . . . ▶ **36**

Amount You Owe	**37**	Subtract line 33 from line 24. This is the **amount you owe now** . . ▶	**37**

For details on
how to pay,
see
instructions.

Note: Schedule H and Schedule SE filers, line 37 may not represent all of the taxes you owe for 2020. See Schedule 3, line 12e, and its instructions for details.

	38	Estimated tax penalty (see instructions) . . . . . ▶ **38**

Third Party Designee	Do you want to allow another person to discuss this return with the IRS? See instructions . . . . ▶	☐ **Yes. Complete below.** ☐ **No**

Designee's name ▶   Phone no. ▶   Personal identification number (PIN) ▶ [ ]

Sign Here	Under penalties of perjury, I declare that I have examined this return and accompanying schedules and statements, and to the best of my knowledge and belief, they are true, correct, and complete. Declaration of preparer (other than taxpayer) is based on all information of which preparer has any knowledge.

	Your signature	Date	Your occupation	If the IRS sent you an Identity Protection PIN, enter it here (see inst.) [ ]

Joint return?
See instructions.
Keep a copy for
your records.

	Spouse's signature. If a joint return, **both** must sign.	Date	Spouse's occupation	If the IRS sent your spouse an Identity Protection PIN, enter it here (see inst.) [ ]

	Phone no.	Email address		

Paid Preparer Use Only	Preparer's name	Preparer's signature	Date	PTIN	Check if: ☐ Self-employed

Firm's name ▶   Phone no.

Firm's address ▶   Firm's EIN ▶

Go to *www.irs.gov/Form1040SR* for instructions and the latest information.   Form **1040-SR** (2020)

Form 1040-SR (2020)   Page **4**

Standard Deduction Chart*

Add the number of boxes checked in the "Age/Blindness" section of *Standard Deduction* on page 1 . . . . . ▶

IF your filing status is. . .	AND the number of boxes checked is. . .	THEN your standard deduction is. . .
Single	1	$14,050
	2	15,700
Married filing jointly	1	$26,100
	2	27,400
	3	28,700
	4	30,000
Qualifying widow(er)	1	$26,100
	2	27,400
Head of household	1	$20,300
	2	21,950
Married filing separately**	1	$13,700
	2	15,000
	3	16,300
	4	17,600

*Don't use this chart if someone can claim you (or your spouse if filing jointly) as a dependent, your spouse itemizes on a separate return, or you were a dual-status alien. Instead, see instructions.

**You can check the boxes for your spouse if your filing status is married filing separately and your spouse had no income, isn't filing a return, and can't be claimed as a dependent on another person's return.

Go to *www.irs.gov/Form1040SR* for instructions and the latest information.   Form **1040-SR** (2020)

SCHEDULE A (Form 1040) Department of the Treasury Internal Revenue Service (99)	**Itemized Deductions** ▶ Go to *www.irs.gov/ScheduleA* for instructions and the latest information. ▶ Attach to Form 1040 or 1040-SR. **Caution:** If you are claiming a net qualified disaster loss on Form 4684, see the instructions for line 16.	OMB No. 1545-0074 20**20** Attachment Sequence No. **07**

Name(s) shown on Form 1040 or 1040-SR | Your social security number

Medical and Dental Expenses		**Caution:** Do not include expenses reimbursed or paid by others.		
	1	Medical and dental expenses (see instructions)	1	
	2	Enter amount from Form 1040 or 1040-SR, line 11 ⎢ 2 ⎢		
	3	Multiply line 2 by 7.5% (0.075)	3	
	4	Subtract line 3 from line 1. If line 3 is more than line 1, enter -0-		4
Taxes You Paid	5	State and local taxes.		
	a	State and local income taxes or general sales taxes. You may include either income taxes or general sales taxes on line 5a, but not both. If you elect to include general sales taxes instead of income taxes, check this box . . . . ▶ ☐	5a	
	b	State and local real estate taxes (see instructions)	5b	
	c	State and local personal property taxes	5c	
	d	Add lines 5a through 5c	5d	
	e	Enter the smaller of line 5d or $10,000 ($5,000 if married filing separately)	5e	
	6	Other taxes. List type and amount ▶ _____	6	
	7	Add lines 5e and 6		7
Interest You Paid **Caution:** Your mortgage interest deduction may be limited (see instructions).	8	Home mortgage interest and points. If you didn't use all of your home mortgage loan(s) to buy, build, or improve your home, see instructions and check this box . . . . ▶ ☐		
	a	Home mortgage interest and points reported to you on Form 1098. See instructions if limited	8a	
	b	Home mortgage interest not reported to you on Form 1098. See instructions if limited. If paid to the person from whom you bought the home, see instructions and show that person's name, identifying no., and address . . . . ▶ _____	8b	
	c	Points not reported to you on Form 1098. See instructions for special rules	8c	
	d	Mortgage insurance premiums (see instructions)	8d	
	e	Add lines 8a through 8d	8e	
	9	Investment interest. Attach Form 4952 if required. See instructions .	9	
	10	Add lines 8e and 9		10
Gifts to Charity **Caution:** If you made a gift and got a benefit for it, see instructions.	11	Gifts by cash or check. If you made any gift of $250 or more, see instructions	11	
	12	Other than by cash or check. If you made any gift of $250 or more, see instructions. You **must** attach Form 8283 if over $500. . . .	12	
	13	Carryover from prior year	13	
	14	Add lines 11 through 13		14
Casualty and Theft Losses	15	Casualty and theft loss(es) from a federally declared disaster (other than net qualified disaster losses). Attach Form 4684 and enter the amount from line 18 of that form. See instructions		15
Other Itemized Deductions	16	Other—from list in instructions. List type and amount ▶ _____		16
Total Itemized Deductions	17	Add the amounts in the far right column for lines 4 through 16. Also, enter this amount on Form 1040 or 1040-SR, line 12		17
	18	If you elect to itemize deductions even though they are less than your standard deduction, check this box . . . . ▶ ☐		

For Paperwork Reduction Act Notice, see the Instructions for Forms 1040 and 1040-SR.   Cat. No. 17145C   **Schedule A (Form 1040) 2020**

SCHEDULE B
(Form 1040)

Department of the Treasury
Internal Revenue Service (99)

Interest and Ordinary Dividends

▶ **Go to** *www.irs.gov/ScheduleB* **for instructions and the latest information.**
▶ **Attach to Form 1040 or 1040-SR.**

OMB No. 1545-0074

2020

Attachment
Sequence No. **08**

Name(s) shown on return

Your social security number

DRAFT AS OF
July 8, 2020
DO NOT FILE

Part I Interest	1	List name of payer. If any interest is from a seller-financed mortgage and the buyer used the property as a personal residence, see the instructions and list this interest first. Also, show that buyer's social security number and address ▶	**Amount**

(See instructions and the instructions for Forms 1040 and 1040-SR, line 2b.)

Note: If you received a Form 1099-INT, Form 1099-OID, or substitute statement from a brokerage firm, list the firm's name as the payer and enter the total interest shown on that form.

	1		
	2	Add the amounts on line 1	2
	3	Excludable interest on series EE and I U.S. savings bonds issued after 1989. Attach Form 8815	3
	4	Subtract line 3 from line 2. Enter the result here and on Form 1040 or 1040-SR, line 2b . . . . ▶	4

Note: If line 4 is over $1,500, you must complete Part III.

Part II Ordinary Dividends	5	List name of payer ▶	**Amount**

(See instructions and the instructions for Forms 1040 and 1040-SR, line 3b.)

Note: If you received a Form 1099-DIV or substitute statement from a brokerage firm, list the firm's name as the payer and enter the ordinary dividends shown on that form.

	5		
	6	Add the amounts on line 5. Enter the total here and on Form 1040 or 1040-SR, line 3b . . . . ▶	6

Note: If line 6 is over $1,500, you must complete Part III.

Part III Foreign Accounts and Trusts	You must complete this part if you **(a)** had over $1,500 of taxable interest or ordinary dividends; **(b)** had a foreign account; or **(c)** received a distribution from, or were a grantor of, or a transferor to, a foreign trust.	Yes	No

Caution: If required, failure to file FinCEN Form 114 may result in substantial penalties. See instructions.

7a At any time during 2020, did you have a financial interest in or signature authority over a financial account (such as a bank account, securities account, or brokerage account) located in a foreign country? See instructions . . . .

If "Yes," are you required to file FinCEN Form 114, Report of Foreign Bank and Financial Accounts (FBAR), to report that financial interest or signature authority? See FinCEN Form 114 and its instructions for filing requirements and exceptions to those requirements . . . . . .

b If you are required to file FinCEN Form 114, enter the name of the foreign country where the financial account is located ▶

8 During 2020, did you receive a distribution from, or were you the grantor of, or transferor to, a foreign trust? If "Yes," you may have to file Form 3520. See instructions . . . .

For Paperwork Reduction Act Notice, see your tax return instructions.   Cat. No. 17146N   **Schedule B (Form 1040) 2020**

SCHEDULE D
(Form 1040)

Department of the Treasury
Internal Revenue Service (99)

Capital Gains and Losses

▶ Attach to Form 1040, 1040-SR, or 1040-NR.
▶ Go to *www.irs.gov/ScheduleD* for instructions and the latest information.
▶ Use Form 8949 to list your transactions for lines 1b, 2, 3, 8b, 9, and 10.

OMB No. 1545-0074

2020

Attachment
Sequence No. **12**

Name(s) shown on return

Your social security number

Did you dispose of any investment(s) in a qualified opportunity fund during the tax year? ☐ **Yes** ☐ **No**
If "Yes," attach Form 8949 and see its instructions for additional requirements for reporting your gain or loss.

Part I   Short-Term Capital Gains and Losses—Generally Assets Held One Year or Less (see instructions)

See instructions for how to figure the amounts to enter on the lines below. This form may be easier to complete if you round off cents to whole dollars.	(d) Proceeds (sales price)	(e) Cost (or other basis)	(g) Adjustments to gain or loss from Form(s) 8949, Part I, line 2, column (g)	(h) Gain or (loss) Subtract column (e) from column (d) and combine the result with column (g)
1a Totals for all short-term transactions reported on Form 1099-B for which basis was reported to the IRS and for which you have no adjustments (see instructions). However, if you choose to report all these transactions on Form 8949, leave this line blank and go to line 1b .				
1b Totals for all transactions reported on Form(s) 8949 with **Box A** checked				
2 Totals for all transactions reported on Form(s) 8949 with **Box B** checked				
3 Totals for all transactions reported on Form(s) 8949 with **Box C** checked				

4 Short-term gain from Form 6252 and short-term gain or (loss) from Forms 4684, 6781, and 8824 . .	**4**	
5 Net short-term gain or (loss) from partnerships, S corporations, estates, and trusts from Schedule(s) K-1	**5**	
6 Short-term capital loss carryover. Enter the amount, if any, from line 8 of your **Capital Loss Carryover Worksheet** in the instructions	**6** ( )
7 **Net short-term capital gain or (loss).** Combine lines 1a through 6 in column (h). If you have any long-term capital gains or losses, go to Part II below. Otherwise, go to Part III on the back	**7**	

Part II   Long-Term Capital Gains and Losses—Generally Assets Held More Than One Year (see instructions)

See instructions for how to figure the amounts to enter on the lines below. This form may be easier to complete if you round off cents to whole dollars.	(d) Proceeds (sales price)	(e) Cost (or other basis)	(g) Adjustments to gain or loss from Form(s) 8949, Part II, line 2, column (g)	(h) Gain or (loss) Subtract column (e) from column (d) and combine the result with column (g)
8a Totals for all long-term transactions reported on Form 1099-B for which basis was reported to the IRS and for which you have no adjustments (see instructions). However, if you choose to report all these transactions on Form 8949, leave this line blank and go to line 8b .				
8b Totals for all transactions reported on Form(s) 8949 with **Box D** checked				
9 Totals for all transactions reported on Form(s) 8949 with **Box E** checked				
10 Totals for all transactions reported on Form(s) 8949 with **Box F** checked.				

11 Gain from Form 4797, Part I; long-term gain from Forms 2439 and 6252; and long-term gain or (loss) from Forms 4684, 6781, and 8824	**11**	
12 Net long-term gain or (loss) from partnerships, S corporations, estates, and trusts from Schedule(s) K-1	**12**	
13 Capital gain distributions. See the instructions	**13**	
14 Long-term capital loss carryover. Enter the amount, if any, from line 13 of your **Capital Loss Carryover Worksheet** in the instructions	**14** ( )
15 **Net long-term capital gain or (loss).** Combine lines 8a through 14 in column (h). Then, go to Part III on the back	**15**	

For Paperwork Reduction Act Notice, see your tax return instructions.   Cat. No. 11338H   Schedule D (Form 1040) 2020

Schedule D (Form 1040) 2020

Page **2**

| **Part III** | **Summary** |

16 Combine lines 7 and 15 and enter the result . . . . | **16** |

- If line 16 is a **gain,** enter the amount from line 16 on Form 1040, 1040-SR, or 1040-NR, line 7. Then, go to line 17 below.
- If line 16 is a **loss,** skip lines 17 through 20 below. Then, go to line 21. Also be sure to complete line 22.
- If line 16 is **zero,** skip lines 17 through 21 below and enter -0- on Form 1040, 1040-SR, or 1040-NR, line 7. Then, go to line 22.

17 Are lines 15 and 16 **both** gains?

☐ **Yes.** Go to line 18.

☐ **No.** Skip lines 18 through 21, and go to line 22.

18 If you are required to complete the **28% Rate Gain Worksheet** (see instructions), enter the amount, if any, from line 7 of that worksheet . . . . ▶ | **18** |

19 If you are required to complete the **Unrecaptured Section 1250 Gain Worksheet** (see instructions), enter the amount, if any, from line 18 of that worksheet . . . . ▶ | **19** |

20 Are lines 18 and 19 **both** zero or blank?

☐ **Yes.** Complete the **Qualified Dividends and Capital Gain Tax Worksheet** in the instructions for Forms 1040 and 1040-SR, line 16. **Don't** complete lines 21 and 22 below.

☐ **No.** Complete the **Schedule D Tax Worksheet** in the instructions. **Don't** complete lines 21 and 22 below.

21 If line 16 is a loss, enter here and on Form 1040, 1040-SR, or 1040-NR, line 7, the **smaller** of:

- The loss on line 16; or
- ($3,000), or if married filing separately, ($1,500)   } . . . . | **21** (|) |

Note: When figuring which amount is smaller, treat both amounts as positive numbers.

22 Do you have qualified dividends on Form 1040, 1040-SR, or 1040-NR, line 3a?

☐ **Yes.** Complete the **Qualified Dividends and Capital Gain Tax Worksheet** in the instructions for Forms 1040 and 1040-SR, line 16.

☐ **No.** Complete the rest of Form 1040, 1040-SR, or 1040-NR.

Schedule D (Form 1040) 2020

Form **6252**

Department of the Treasury
Internal Revenue Service

Installment Sale Income

▶ Attach to your tax return.
▶ Use a separate form for each sale or other disposition of property on the installment method.
▶ Go to *www.irs.gov/Form6252* for the latest information.

OMB No. 1545-0228

20**20**

Attachment
Sequence No. **625**

Name(s) shown on return

Identifying number

1	Description of property ▶			
2a	Date acquired (mm/dd/yyyy) ▶	**b** Date sold (mm/dd/yyyy) ▶		
3	Was the property sold to a related party (see instructions) after May 14, 1980? If "No," skip line 4		☐ Yes	☐ No
4	Was the property you sold to a related party a marketable security? If "Yes," complete Part III. If "No," complete Part III for the year of sale and the 2 years after the year of sale		☐ Yes	☐ No

Part I   **Gross Profit and Contract Price.** Complete this part for all years of the installment agreement.

5	Selling price including mortgages and other debts. **Don't** include interest, whether stated or unstated	**5**	
6	Mortgages, debts, and other liabilities the buyer assumed or took the property subject to (see instructions)	**6**	
7	Subtract line 6 from line 5	**7**	
8	Cost or other basis of property sold	**8**	
9	Depreciation allowed or allowable	**9**	
10	Adjusted basis. Subtract line 9 from line 8	**10**	
11	Commissions and other expenses of sale	**11**	
12	Income recapture from Form 4797, Part III (see instructions)	**12**	
13	Add lines 10, 11, and 12	**13**	
14	Subtract line 13 from line 5. If zero or less, **don't** complete the rest of this form. See instructions	**14**	
15	If the property described on line 1 above was your main home, enter the amount of your excluded gain. See instructions. Otherwise, enter -0-	**15**	
16	**Gross profit.** Subtract line 15 from line 14	**16**	
17	Subtract line 13 from line 6. If zero or less, enter -0-	**17**	
18	**Contract price.** Add line 7 and line 17	**18**	

Part II   **Installment Sale Income.** Complete this part for all years of the installment agreement.

19	Gross profit percentage (expressed as a decimal amount). Divide line 16 by line 18. (For years after the year of sale, see instructions.)	**19**	
20	If this is the year of sale, enter the amount from line 17. Otherwise, enter -0-	**20**	
21	Payments received during year (see instructions). **Don't** include interest, whether stated or unstated	**21**	
22	Add lines 20 and 21	**22**	
23	Payments received in prior years (see instructions). **Don't** include interest, whether stated or unstated	**23**	
24	**Installment sale income.** Multiply line 22 by line 19	**24**	
25	Enter the part of line 24 that is ordinary income under the recapture rules. See instructions	**25**	
26	Subtract line 25 from line 24. Enter here and on Schedule D or Form 4797. See instructions	**26**	

Part III   **Related Party Installment Sale Income. Don't** complete if you received the final payment this tax year.

27	Name, address, and taxpayer identifying number of related party ▶		
28	Did the related party resell or dispose of the property ("second disposition") during this tax year?	☐ Yes	☐ No
29	**If the answer to question 28 is "Yes," complete lines 30 through 37 below unless one of the following conditions is met. Check the box that applies.**		
a	☐ The second disposition was more than 2 years after the first disposition (other than dispositions of marketable securities). If this box is checked, enter the date of disposition (mm/dd/yyyy) ▶ _____		
b	☐ The first disposition was a sale or exchange of stock to the issuing corporation.		
c	☐ The second disposition was an involuntary conversion and the threat of conversion occurred after the first disposition.		
d	☐ The second disposition occurred after the death of the original seller or buyer.		
e	☐ It can be established to the satisfaction of the IRS that tax avoidance wasn't a principal purpose for either of the dispositions. If this box is checked, attach an explanation. See instructions.		
30	Selling price of property sold by related party (see instructions)	**30**	
31	Enter contract price from line 18 for year of first sale	**31**	
32	Enter the **smaller** of line 30 or line 31	**32**	
33	Total payments received by the end of your 2020 tax year (see instructions)	**33**	
34	Subtract line 33 from line 32. If zero or less, enter -0-	**34**	
35	Multiply line 34 by the gross profit percentage on line 19 for year of first sale	**35**	
36	Enter the part of line 35 that is ordinary income under the recapture rules. See instructions	**36**	
37	Subtract line 36 from line 35. Enter here and on Schedule D or Form 4797. See instructions	**37**	

For Paperwork Reduction Act Notice, see page 4.   Cat. No. 13601R   Form **6252** (2020)

Form **8949**

Department of the Treasury
Internal Revenue Service

Sales and Other Dispositions of Capital Assets

▶ Go to *www.irs.gov/Form8949* for instructions and the latest information.
▶ File with your Schedule D to list your transactions for lines 1b, 2, 3, 8b, 9, and 10 of Schedule D.

OMB No. 1545-0074

2020

Attachment
Sequence No. **12A**

Name(s) shown on return

Social security number or taxpayer identification number

Before you check Box A, B, or C below, see whether you received any Form(s) 1099-B or substitute statement(s) from your broker. A substitute statement will have the same information as Form 1099-B. Either will show whether your basis (usually your cost) was reported to the IRS by your broker and may even tell you which box to check.

Part I   **Short-Term.** Transactions involving capital assets you held 1 year or less are generally short-term (see instructions). For long-term transactions, see page 2.

Note: You may aggregate all short-term transactions reported on Form(s) 1099-B showing basis was reported to the IRS and for which no adjustments or codes are required. Enter the totals directly on Schedule D, line 1a; you aren't required to report these transactions on Form 8949 (see instructions).

You *must* check Box A, B, or C below. Check only one box. If more than one box applies for your short-term transactions, complete a separate Form 8949, page 1, for each applicable box. If you have more short-term transactions than will fit on this page for one or more of the boxes, complete as many forms with the same box checked as you need.

- ☐ **(A)** Short-term transactions reported on Form(s) 1099-B showing basis was reported to the IRS (see **Note** above)
- ☐ **(B)** Short-term transactions reported on Form(s) 1099-B showing basis **wasn't** reported to the IRS
- ☐ **(C)** Short-term transactions not reported to you on Form 1099-B

1 **(a)** Description of property (Example: 100 sh. XYZ Co.)	**(b)** Date acquired (Mo., day, yr.)	**(c)** Date sold or disposed of (Mo., day, yr.)	**(d)** Proceeds (sales price) (see instructions)	**(e)** Cost or other basis. See the **Note** below and see *Column (e)* in the separate instructions	Adjustment, if any, to gain or loss. If you enter an amount in column (g), enter a code in column (f). See the separate instructions. **(f)** Code(s) from instructions	**(g)** Amount of adjustment	**(h)** Gain or (loss). Subtract column (e) from column (d) and combine the result with column (g)

2 Totals. Add the amounts in columns (d), (e), (g), and (h) (subtract negative amounts). Enter each total here and include on your Schedule D, **line 1b** (if **Box A** above is checked), **line 2** (if **Box B** above is checked), or **line 3** (if **Box C** above is checked) ▶

Note: If you checked Box A above but the basis reported to the IRS was incorrect, enter in column (e) the basis as reported to the IRS, and enter an adjustment in column (g) to correct the basis. See *Column (g)* in the separate instructions for how to figure the amount of the adjustment.

For Paperwork Reduction Act Notice, see your tax return instructions.   Cat. No. 37768Z   Form **8949** (2020)

Form 8949 (2020)

Attachment Sequence No. **12A**   Page **2**

Name(s) shown on return. Name and SSN or taxpayer identification no. not required if shown on other side	Social security number or taxpayer identification number

Before you check Box D, E, or F below, see whether you received any Form(s) 1099-B or substitute statement(s) from your broker. A substitute statement will have the same information as Form 1099-B. Either will show whether your basis (usually your cost) was reported to the IRS by your broker and may even tell you which box to check.

Part II   **Long-Term.** Transactions involving capital assets you held more than 1 year are generally long-term (see instructions). For short-term transactions, see page 1.

Note: You may aggregate all long-term transactions reported on Form(s) 1099-B showing basis was reported to the IRS and for which no adjustments or codes are required. Enter the totals directly on Schedule D, line 8a; you aren't required to report these transactions on Form 8949 (see instructions).

You _must_ check Box D, E, _or_ F below. Check only one box. If more than one box applies for your long-term transactions, complete a separate Form 8949, page 2, for each applicable box. If you have more long-term transactions than will fit on this page for one or more of the boxes, complete as many forms with the same box checked as you need.

- ☐ **(D)** Long-term transactions reported on Form(s) 1099-B showing basis was reported to the IRS (see **Note** above)
- ☐ **(E)** Long-term transactions reported on Form(s) 1099-B showing basis **wasn't** reported to the IRS
- ☐ **(F)** Long-term transactions not reported to you on Form 1099-B

1	(a) Description of property (Example: 100 sh. XYZ Co.)	(b) Date acquired (Mo., day, yr.)	(c) Date sold or disposed of (Mo., day, yr.)	(d) Proceeds (sales price) (see instructions)	(e) Cost or other basis. See the **Note** below and see *Column (e)* in the separate instructions	Adjustment, if any, to gain or loss. If you enter an amount in column (g), enter a code in column (f). See the separate instructions.		(h) Gain or (loss). Subtract column (e) from column (d) and combine the result with column (g)
						(f) Code(s) from instructions	(g) Amount of adjustment	
2 **Totals.** Add the amounts in columns (d), (e), (g), and (h) (subtract negative amounts). Enter each total here and include on your Schedule D, **line 8b** (if **Box D** above is checked), **line 9** (if **Box E** above is checked), or **line 10** (if **Box F** above is checked) ▶								

Note: If you checked Box D above but the basis reported to the IRS was incorrect, enter in column (e) the basis as reported to the IRS, and enter an adjustment in column (g) to correct the basis. See *Column (g)* in the separate instructions for how to figure the amount of the adjustment.

Form **8949** (2020)

Qualified Dividends and Capital Gain Tax Worksheet—Line 16

Before you begin: ✓ See the earlier instructions for line 16 to see if you can use this worksheet to figure your tax.
✓ Before completing this worksheet, complete Form 1040 or 1040-SR through line 15.
✓ If you don't have to file Schedule D and you received capital gain distributions, be sure you checked the box on Form 1040 or 1040-SR, line 7.

1. Enter the amount from Form 1040 or 1040-SR, line 15. However, if you are filing Form 2555 (relating to foreign earned income), enter the amount from line 3 of the Foreign Earned Income Tax Worksheet .... **1.** _____

2. Enter the amount from Form 1040 or 1040-SR, line 3a* .... **2.** _____

3. Are you filing Schedule D?*
   ☐ **Yes.** Enter the **smaller** of line 15 or 16 of Schedule D. If either line 15 or 16 is blank or a loss, enter -0-.
   ☐ **No.** Enter the amount from Form 1040 or 1040-SR, line 7. } **3.** _____

4. Add lines 2 and 3 .... **4.** _____

5. If filing Form 4952 (used to figure investment interest expense deduction), enter any amount from line 4g of that form. Otherwise, enter -0- .... **5.** _____

6. Subtract line 5 from line 4. If zero or less, enter -0- .... **6.** _____

7. Subtract line 6 from line 1. If zero or less, enter -0- .... **7.** _____

8. Enter:
   $40,000 if single or married filing separately,
   $80,000 if married filing jointly or qualifying widow(er),
   $53,600 if head of household. } .... **8.** _____

9. Enter the smaller of line 1 or line 8 .... **9.** _____

10. Enter the smaller of line 7 or line 9 .... **10.** _____

11. Subtract line 10 from line 9. This amount is taxed at 0% .... **11.** _____

12. Enter the smaller of line 1 or line 6 .... **12.** _____

13. Enter the amount from line 11 .... **13.** _____

14. Subtract line 13 from line 12 .... **14.** _____

15. Enter:
    $441,450 if single,
    $248,300 if married filing separately,
    $496,600 if married filing jointly or qualifying widow(er),
    $469,050 if head of household. } .... **15.** _____

16. Enter the smaller of line 1 or line 15 .... **16.** _____

17. Add lines 7 and 11 .... **17.** _____

18. Subtract line 17 from line 16. If zero or less, enter -0- .... **18.** _____

19. Enter the smaller of line 14 or line 18 .... **19.** _____

20. Multiply line 19 by 15% (0.15) .... **20.** _____

21. Add lines 11 and 19 .... **21.** _____

22. Subtract line 21 from line 12 .... **22.** _____

23. Multiply line 22 by 20% (0.20) .... **23.** _____

24. Figure the tax on the amount on line 7. If the amount on line 7 is less than $100,000, use the Tax Table to figure the tax. If the amount on line 7 is $100,000 or more, use the Tax Computation Worksheet .... **24.** _____

25. Add lines 20, 23, and 24 .... **25.** _____

26. Figure the tax on the amount on line 1. If the amount on line 1 is less than $100,000, use the Tax Table to figure the tax. If the amount on line 1 is $100,000 or more, use the Tax Computation Worksheet .... **26.** _____

27. **Tax on all taxable income.** Enter the **smaller** of line 25 or 26. Also include this amount on the entry space on Form 1040 or 1040-SR, line 16. If you are filing Form 2555, don't enter this amount on the entry space on Form 1040 or 1040-SR, line 16. Instead, enter it on line 4 of the Foreign Earned Income Tax Worksheet .... **27.** _____

If you are filing Form 2555, see the footnote in the Foreign Earned Income Tax Worksheet before completing this line.

Student Name _____

Class/Section _____

Date   _____

KEY NUMBER TAX RETURN SUMMARY

CHAPTER 8

Comprehensive Problem 1

Form 4562, Special Depreciation Allowance (Line 14) _____

Form 4562, MACRS Deduction for Assets Placed in
Service Before 2020 (Line 17) _____

Schedule C, Depreciation (Line 13) _____

Schedule C, Total Expenses (Line 28) _____

Schedule C, Net Profit or (Loss) (Line 31) _____

Comprehensive Problem 2

Capital Gain or (Loss) (Line 7) _____

Adjusted Gross Income (Line 11) _____

Standard Deduction or Itemized Deductions (Line 12) _____

Total Tax (Line 24) _____

Amount Overpaid (Line 34) _____

CHAPTER 9

Payroll, Estimated Payments, and Retirement Plans

After completing this chapter, you should be able to:

LO 9.1　Compute the income tax withholding from employee wages.

LO 9.2　Determine taxpayers' quarterly estimated payments.

LO 9.3　Compute the FICA tax.

LO 9.4　Apply the federal deposit system to payroll withholding.

LO 9.5　Prepare employer payroll reporting.

LO 9.6　Compute the amount of FUTA tax for an employer.

LO 9.7　Describe the general rules for qualified retirement plans.

LO 9.8　Explain the pension plan rollover rules.

OVERVIEW

This chapter focuses on the payment and reporting of income and other taxes by employers, employees, and self-employed taxpayers. Payroll and other tax topics covered include withholding methods for employees, estimated payments, the FICA tax (Social Security and Medicare taxes), the federal tax deposit system, and employer reporting requirements. In addition, other payroll-related topics such as retirement plans and pensions are covered.

The FICA tax is a combined Social Security (6.2 percent up to the annual wage limit, $137,700 in 2020) and Medicare tax (1.45 percent with no limit) that is paid by both employees and employers. The FICA tax is withheld from each employee's paycheck, the tax is then matched by the employer, and the total amount is remitted to the IRS.

The Federal Unemployment Tax Act (FUTA) tax is unemployment insurance with a joint state and federal payment plan to provide benefits for taxpayers when they become unemployed. The FUTA tax is paid only by employers, not employees.

Learning Objective 9.1

Compute the income tax withholding from employee wages.

9-1 WITHHOLDING METHODS

Employers are required to withhold taxes from amounts paid to employees for wages, including salaries, fees, bonuses, commissions, vacation and retirement pay. Employees complete Form W-4 to provide the information necessary for the employer to withhold income taxes at the prescribed amount. Although most taxpayers' withholding should be adequate to result in an income tax refund at filing time, calculating withholding is more of an art than a science and is subject to the accurate estimation of income and deductions that are ultimately reported for the tax year.

The Form W-4 was redesigned again in 2020. In previous years, withholding allowances were tied to the amount of the personal exemptions expected to be claimed by a taxpayer. Since exemptions were suspended starting in 2018 (through 2025), the 2020 Form W-4 has been adapted and no longer asks an employee to report the number of withholding allowances that they expect to claim.

The revised Form W-4 is divided into five steps. Steps 1 and 5 are completed by all taxpayers. Step 1 asks for personal information such as name, address, and filing status. Step 5 is the taxpayer's signature. By design, Steps 1 and 5 are all that most taxpayers would have to complete, and withholding will be based on that taxpayer's wages and filing status only.

For taxpayers with more complex income tax situations—such as those with a working spouse, dependents, or having additional forms of income such as self-employment, investment income—or for taxpayers that itemize, two options for computing additional withholding are provided. The first option is for the taxpayer to use the IRS online withholding estimator (**www.irs.gov/individuals/tax-withholding-estimator**). The online estimator uses information from recent paystubs of the taxpayer and spouse, details from other sources of income, and a previous tax return to estimate any additional withholding needs. Using the online estimator can be a complex process that contemplates a wide variety of taxpayer situations and effectively estimates the current year's income tax liability. As a result, it requires the greatest amount of preparation and likely provides the most accurate result.

The second option is to use Steps 2-4 on the Form W-4:

- Step 2 is for taxpayers with a working spouse or multiple jobs.
- Step 3 is for taxpayers with dependents.
- Step 4 is for taxpayers that have other forms of income or itemized or other deductions.

Under Step 2, if the taxpayer and the spouse have similar income, the taxpayer can simply check a box (the spouse should do the same on their Form W-4) and withholding will be adjusted to reflect a two-income household by halving the standard deduction and tax brackets. Alternatively, the Form W-4 instructions include a multiple jobs worksheet that uses a series of tables to estimate the required additional withholding in situations where the taxpayer has multiple job or the spouse's wages differ from the taxpayer.

EXAMPLE Dot and Peg expect to file joint tax return in 2020. Dot and Peg expect to be paid wages of $37,000 and $62,000, respectively. Dot is paid monthly and Peg is paid every two weeks (26 times a year). Because Dot and Peg's wages are not similar in amount, they should use the Multiple Jobs Worksheet included on page 3 of Form W-4 (see Page 9–7). Using the Married Filing Jointly table from page 4 of the Form W-4 (see Page 9–8), Line 1 of the Multiple Jobs Worksheet is $3,440 where the higher paying job of $62,000 and the lower paying job of $37,000 intersect in the table. Because Peg has the higher-paying job, 26 is entered on Line 3 to match the number of payroll periods during the year and Line 4 of the Multiple Jobs Worksheet is $132.31 ($3,440 ÷ 26). Peg will carry that amount forward to Line 4(c) of page 1 of the Form W-4 as additional withholding for each pay period. ♦

Under Step 3, taxpayers report the impact of the child tax credit or the other dependents credit on tax liability. This amount will be used by the employer to compute withholding.

EXAMPLE   Shirin and Hamed are married filing jointly and have two dependent children ages 13 and 17. Hamed expects his 2020 wages to be $78,000 and Shirin works part-time and expects to earn $45,000. Both are paid monthly. As the higher paid spouse, Hamed completes a Form W-4 that reflects the additional withholding and dependents. Shirin would not need to reflect this information on her W-4. Using the Multiple Jobs Worksheet, Hamed reports $464.17 ($5,570 ÷ 12) on Line 4(c) of Form W-4. Hamed also reports $2,500 (one child under 17 at $2,000 and one other dependent at $500) on Line 3. ♦

Step 4 is associated with the complexities of other sources of income (e.g., interest, dividends, retirement) or other deductions such as itemized deductions, deductible IRA contributions, or student loan interest. Line 4(a) of Form W-4 is where the expected amount of any additional income is reported and Line 4(b) is where any additional deductions are reported. Step 4(b) refers the taxpayer to a simple deduction worksheet included with Form W-4 that ensures the taxpayer compares the total itemized deductions with the standard deduction to capture only the excess amount as an adjustment. A taxpayer that has a two-income household, non-wage income, dependents, and itemizes deductions is effectively estimating their current year taxes in preparing the W-4. Generally, only more sophisticated taxpayers would be required to estimate withholding using this degree of complexity.

EXAMPLE   Fei and Zhi Han are married filing jointly and have three dependent children aged 13, 14, and 18. Zhi's elderly mother is also a dependent. Wage estimates for 2020 are $26,000 and $94,000 for Fei and Zhi, respectively. Both are paid twice per month (24 times a year). They have an investment portfolio expected to pay $1,200 in interest and $2,300 in qualified dividends. They are not certain if they will have capital gains in 2020 since it depends on the stock market. The Hans own a home and estimate 2020 itemized deductions at $27,000. The Hans expect to make a $6,000 deductible IRA contribution and pay $3,200 in student loan interest. Zhi, as the higher income spouse, will have a fairly complex Form W-4. Zhi should use the multiple jobs worksheet and will report $212.08 ($5,090 ÷ 24) on Line 4 of the worksheet. In Step 3, Zhi will report two qualifying children under 17 and two other dependents for a total of $5,000 ($2,000 × 2 plus $500 × 2). In Step 4, Zhi will include $3,500 of investment income on Line 4(a) of Form W-4. Zhi will complete the Deductions Worksheet and report $2,200 ($27,000 − $24,800) on Line 3 and $8,500 ($6,000 IRA deduction and the limit of $2,500 of deductible student loan interest) on Line 4 giving a total of $10,700 in Line 5 of the Deductions Worksheet. As a result, the first page of Zhi's W-4 will report $5,000 on Line 3, $3,500 on Line 4(a), $10,700 on Line 4(b) and $212.08 on Line 4(c). Note that the possible taxation of qualified dividends at a lower 15 percent rate and the possibility that the student loan interest or the IRA contribution may not be deductible due to income would need to be considered by Zhi if she wanted to estimate withholding accurately. In this example, Zhi may want to consider using the IRS online withholding estimator. ♦

The process is considerably more complex if for some reason a Form W-4 is completed during the middle of a year since the withholding amounts are often associated with annual figures.

The amounts reported on the Form W-4 will be used by the employer to make adjustments to the employee's withholding based on tables provided by the IRS. A taxpayer that is exempt from withholding should complete Steps 1 (do not check the box in 1(c)) and 5 and write "Exempt" in the space underneath Line 4(c). A Form W-4 claiming exemption from withholding is effective only for that calendar year.

The IRS revised Form W-4 again for 2020. The previous use of "allowances" was abandoned in lieu of a new approach. However, most states also have an income tax and require withholding. Although some states still rely on the Form W-4 for state income tax withholding, many states were required to develop their own state-specific form.

The guidance on how an employer handles an unusual Form W-4 is somewhat contradictory. If an employer receives a W-4 from an employee that is known to be false based on oral or written statements made by the employee, the employer should notify the employee to file a corrected W-4. If the employee does not file a corrected W-4, the employer should withhold based on single with no entries on Lines 3–4. However, employees do not have to provide proof to their employers that they are entitled to the number of allowances claimed on their Forms W-4. An employee should only claim "exempt" if (1) that the employee was entitled to a full refund of all income taxes withheld because there was no income tax liability for the prior year, and (2) that the taxpayer expects a full refund during the current year because the taxpayer expects to have no tax liability. The employer is not required to verify this information and should withhold based on the Form W-4. The employer may want to advise the employee that the IRS may review the withholding and direct the employer to withhold at a certain rate if the review indicates the employee's withholding is inadequate. Employers are also instructed to carefully consider a large increase in withholding allowances, especially if the employee has otherwise had regular withholdings during the rest of the year.

Form **W-4**	**Employee's Withholding Certificate**	OMB No. 1545-0074
Department of the Treasury Internal Revenue Service	▶ Complete Form W-4 so that your employer can withhold the correct federal income tax from your pay. ▶ Give Form W-4 to your employer. ▶ Your withholding is subject to review by the IRS.	20**20**

Step 1:

Enter Personal Information

(a) First name and middle initial	Last name	(b) Social security number
Address		▶ **Does your name match the name on your social security card?** If not, to ensure you get credit for your earnings, contact SSA at 800-772-1213 or go to *www.ssa.gov.*
City or town, state, and ZIP code		

(c) ☐ **Single or Married filing separately**

☐ **Married filing jointly** (or Qualifying widow(er))

☐ **Head of household** (Check only if you're unmarried and pay more than half the costs of keeping up a home for yourself and a qualifying individual.)

Complete Steps 2–4 ONLY if they apply to you; otherwise, skip to Step 5. See page 2 for more information on each step, who can claim exemption from withholding, when to use the online estimator, and privacy.

Step 2:

Multiple Jobs or Spouse Works

Complete this step if you (1) hold more than one job at a time, or (2) are married filing jointly and your spouse also works. The correct amount of withholding depends on income earned from all of these jobs.

Do **only one** of the following.

(a) Use the estimator at *www.irs.gov/W4App* for most accurate withholding for this step (and Steps 3–4); **or**

(b) Use the Multiple Jobs Worksheet on page 3 and enter the result in Step 4(c) below for roughly accurate withholding; **or**

(c) If there are only two jobs total, you may check this box. Do the same on Form W-4 for the other job. This option is accurate for jobs with similar pay; otherwise, more tax than necessary may be withheld . . . . . ▶ ☐

TIP: To be accurate, submit a 2020 Form W-4 for all other jobs. If you (or your spouse) have self-employment income, including as an independent contractor, use the estimator.

Complete Steps 3–4(b) on Form W-4 for only ONE of these jobs. Leave those steps blank for the other jobs. (Your withholding will be most accurate if you complete Steps 3–4(b) on the Form W-4 for the highest paying job.)

Step 3:

Claim Dependents

If your income will be $200,000 or less ($400,000 or less if married filing jointly):

Multiply the number of qualifying children under age 17 by $2,000 ▶ $ _____

Multiply the number of other dependents by $500 . . . . ▶ $ _____

Add the amounts above and enter the total here . . . . | **3** | $ |

Step 4 (optional):

Other Adjustments

(a) Other income (not from jobs). If you want tax withheld for other income you expect this year that won't have withholding, enter the amount of other income here. This may include interest, dividends, and retirement income . . . . | **4(a)** | $ |

(b) Deductions. If you expect to claim deductions other than the standard deduction and want to reduce your withholding, use the Deductions Worksheet on page 3 and enter the result here . . . . | **4(b)** | $ |

(c) Extra withholding. Enter any additional tax you want withheld each **pay period** . | **4(c)** | $ |

Step 5:

Sign Here

Under penalties of perjury, I declare that this certificate, to the best of my knowledge and belief, is true, correct, and complete.

▶ _____ ▶ _____

Employee's signature (This form is not valid unless you sign it.) **Date**

Employers Only	Employer's name and address	First date of employment	Employer identification number (EIN)

For Privacy Act and Paperwork Reduction Act Notice, see page 3. Cat. No. 10220Q Form **W-4** (2020)

General Instructions

Future Developments

For the latest information about developments related to Form W-4, such as legislation enacted after it was published, go to *www.irs.gov/FormW4*.

Purpose of Form

Complete Form W-4 so that your employer can withhold the correct federal income tax from your pay. If too little is withheld, you will generally owe tax when you file your tax return and may owe a penalty. If too much is withheld, you will generally be due a refund. Complete a new Form W-4 when changes to your personal or financial situation would change the entries on the form. For more information on withholding and when you must furnish a new Form W-4, see Pub. 505.

Exemption from withholding. You may claim exemption from withholding for 2020 if you meet both of the following conditions: you had no federal income tax liability in 2019 **and** you expect to have no federal income tax liability in 2020. You had no federal income tax liability in 2019 if (1) your total tax on line 16 on your 2019 Form 1040 or 1040-SR is zero (or less than the sum of lines 18a, 18b, and 18c), or (2) you were not required to file a return because your income was below the filing threshold for your correct filing status. If you claim exemption, you will have no income tax withheld from your paycheck and may owe taxes and penalties when you file your 2020 tax return. To claim exemption from withholding, certify that you meet both of the conditions above by writing "Exempt" on Form W-4 in the space below Step 4(c). Then, complete Steps 1(a), 1(b), and 5. Do not complete any other steps. You will need to submit a new Form W-4 by February 16, 2021.

Your privacy. If you prefer to limit information provided in Steps 2 through 4, use the online estimator, which will also increase accuracy.

As an alternative to the estimator: if you have concerns with Step 2(c), you may choose Step 2(b); if you have concerns with Step 4(a), you may enter an additional amount you want withheld per pay period in Step 4(c). If this is the only job in your household, you may instead check the box in Step 2(c), which will increase your withholding and significantly reduce your paycheck (often by thousands of dollars over the year).

When to use the estimator. Consider using the estimator at *www.irs.gov/W4App* if you:

1. Expect to work only part of the year;

2. Have dividend or capital gain income, or are subject to additional taxes, such as the additional Medicare tax;

3. Have self-employment income (see below); or

4. Prefer the most accurate withholding for multiple job situations.

Self-employment. Generally, you will owe both income and self-employment taxes on any self-employment income you receive separate from the wages you receive as an employee. If you want to pay these taxes through withholding from your wages, use the estimator at *www.irs.gov/W4App* to figure the amount to have withheld.

Nonresident alien. If you're a nonresident alien, see Notice 1392, Supplemental Form W-4 Instructions for Nonresident Aliens, before completing this form.

Specific Instructions

Step 1(c). Check your anticipated filing status. This will determine the standard deduction and tax rates used to compute your withholding.

Step 2. Use this step if you (1) have more than one job at the same time, or (2) are married filing jointly and you and your spouse both work.

Option **(a)** most accurately calculates the additional tax you need to have withheld, while option **(b)** does so with a little less accuracy.

If you (and your spouse) have a total of only two jobs, you may instead check the box in option **(c)**. The box must also be checked on the Form W-4 for the other job. If the box is checked, the standard deduction and tax brackets will be cut in half for each job to calculate withholding. This option is roughly accurate for jobs with similar pay; otherwise, more tax than necessary may be withheld, and this extra amount will be larger the greater the difference in pay is between the two jobs.

 Multiple jobs. Complete Steps 3 through 4(b) on only one Form W-4. Withholding will be most accurate if you do this on the Form W-4 for the highest paying job.

Step 3. Step 3 of Form W-4 provides instructions for determining the amount of the child tax credit and the credit for other dependents that you may be able to claim when you file your tax return. To qualify for the child tax credit, the child must be under age 17 as of December 31, must be your dependent who generally lives with you for more than half the year, and must have the required social security number. You may be able to claim a credit for other dependents for whom a child tax credit can't be claimed, such as an older child or a qualifying relative. For additional eligibility requirements for these credits, see Pub. 972, Child Tax Credit and Credit for Other Dependents. You can also include **other tax credits** in this step, such as education tax credits and the foreign tax credit. To do so, add an estimate of the amount for the year to your credits for dependents and enter the total amount in Step 3. Including these credits will increase your paycheck and reduce the amount of any refund you may receive when you file your tax return.

Step 4 (optional).

Step 4(a). Enter in this step the total of your other estimated income for the year, if any. You shouldn't include income from any jobs or self-employment. If you complete Step 4(a), you likely won't have to make estimated tax payments for that income. If you prefer to pay estimated tax rather than having tax on other income withheld from your paycheck, see Form 1040-ES, Estimated Tax for Individuals.

Step 4(b). Enter in this step the amount from the Deductions Worksheet, line 5, if you expect to claim deductions other than the basic standard deduction on your 2020 tax return and want to reduce your withholding to account for these deductions. This includes both itemized deductions and other deductions such as for student loan interest and IRAs.

Step 4(c). Enter in this step any additional tax you want withheld from your pay **each pay period**, including any amounts from the Multiple Jobs Worksheet, line 4. Entering an amount here will reduce your paycheck and will either increase your refund or reduce any amount of tax that you owe.

Step 2(b)—Multiple Jobs Worksheet *(Keep for your records.)*

If you choose the option in Step 2(b) on Form W-4, complete this worksheet (which calculates the total extra tax for all jobs) on **only ONE** Form W-4. Withholding will be most accurate if you complete the worksheet and enter the result on the Form W-4 for the highest paying job.

Note: If more than one job has annual wages of more than $120,000 or there are more than three jobs, see Pub. 505 for additional tables; or, you can use the online withholding estimator at *www.irs.gov/W4App.*

1   Two jobs. If you have two jobs or you're married filing jointly and you and your spouse each have one job, find the amount from the appropriate table on page 4. Using the "Higher Paying Job" row and the "Lower Paying Job" column, find the value at the intersection of the two household salaries and enter that value on line 1. Then, **skip** to line 3 . . . .   **1** $ _____

2   Three jobs. If you and/or your spouse have three jobs at the same time, complete lines 2a, 2b, and 2c below. Otherwise, skip to line 3.

    a Find the amount from the appropriate table on page 4 using the annual wages from the highest paying job in the "Higher Paying Job" row and the annual wages for your next highest paying job in the "Lower Paying Job" column. Find the value at the intersection of the two household salaries and enter that value on line 2a . . . .   **2a** $ _____

    b Add the annual wages of the two highest paying jobs from line 2a together and use the total as the wages in the "Higher Paying Job" row and use the annual wages for your third job in the "Lower Paying Job" column to find the amount from the appropriate table on page 4 and enter this amount on line 2b . . . .   **2b** $ _____

    c Add the amounts from lines 2a and 2b and enter the result on line 2c . . . .   **2c** $ _____

3   Enter the number of pay periods per year for the highest paying job. For example, if that job pays weekly, enter 52; if it pays every other week, enter 26; if it pays monthly, enter 12, etc. . . . . .   **3** _____

4   Divide the annual amount on line 1 or line 2c by the number of pay periods on line 3. Enter this amount here and in **Step 4(c)** of Form W-4 for the highest paying job (along with any other additional amount you want withheld) . . . .   **4** $ _____

Step 4(b)—Deductions Worksheet *(Keep for your records.)*

1   Enter an estimate of your 2020 itemized deductions (from Schedule A (Form 1040 or 1040-SR)). Such deductions may include qualifying home mortgage interest, charitable contributions, state and local taxes (up to $10,000), and medical expenses in excess of 7.5% of your income . . . .   **1** $ _____

2   Enter: { • $24,800 if you're married filing jointly or qualifying widow(er)
              • $18,650 if you're head of household . . . .   **2** $ _____
              • $12,400 if you're single or married filing separately }

3   If line 1 is greater than line 2, subtract line 2 from line 1. If line 2 is greater than line 1, enter "-0-" . .   **3** $ _____

4   Enter an estimate of your student loan interest, deductible IRA contributions, and certain other adjustments (from Part II of Schedule 1 (Form 1040 or 1040-SR). See Pub. 505 for more information . . . .   **4** $ _____

5   Add lines 3 and 4. Enter the result here and in **Step 4(b)** of Form W-4 . . . .   **5** $ _____

Form W-4 (2020)

Married Filing Jointly or Qualifying Widow(er)

Higher Paying Job Annual Taxable Wage & Salary	Lower Paying Job Annual Taxable Wage & Salary											
	$0 - 9,999	$10,000 - 19,999	$20,000 - 29,999	$30,000 - 39,999	$40,000 - 49,999	$50,000 - 59,999	$60,000 - 69,999	$70,000 - 79,999	$80,000 - 89,999	$90,000 - 99,999	$100,000 - 109,999	$110,000 - 120,000
$0 - 9,999	$0	$220	$850	$900	$1,020	$1,020	$1,020	$1,020	$1,020	$1,210	$1,870	$1,870
$10,000 - 19,999	220	1,220	1,900	2,100	2,220	2,220	2,220	2,220	2,410	3,410	4,070	4,070
$20,000 - 29,999	850	1,900	2,730	2,930	3,050	3,050	3,050	3,240	4,240	5,240	5,900	5,900
$30,000 - 39,999	900	2,100	2,930	3,130	3,250	3,250	3,440	4,440	5,440	6,440	7,100	7,100
$40,000 - 49,999	1,020	2,220	3,050	3,250	3,370	3,570	4,570	5,570	6,570	7,570	8,220	8,220
$50,000 - 59,999	1,020	2,220	3,050	3,250	3,570	4,570	5,570	6,570	7,570	8,570	9,220	9,220
$60,000 - 69,999	1,020	2,220	3,050	3,440	4,570	5,570	6,570	7,570	8,570	9,570	10,220	10,220
$70,000 - 79,999	1,020	2,220	3,240	4,440	5,570	6,570	7,570	8,570	9,570	10,570	11,220	11,240
$80,000 - 99,999	1,060	3,260	5,090	6,290	7,420	8,420	9,420	10,420	11,420	12,420	13,260	13,460
$100,000 - 149,999	1,870	4,070	5,900	7,100	8,220	9,320	10,520	11,720	12,920	14,120	14,980	15,180
$150,000 - 239,999	2,040	4,440	6,470	7,870	9,190	10,390	11,590	12,790	13,990	15,190	16,050	16,250
$240,000 - 259,999	2,040	4,440	6,470	7,870	9,190	10,390	11,590	12,790	13,990	15,520	17,170	18,170
$260,000 - 279,999	2,040	4,440	6,470	7,870	9,190	10,390	11,590	13,120	15,120	17,120	18,770	19,770
$280,000 - 299,999	2,040	4,440	6,470	7,870	9,190	10,720	12,720	14,720	16,720	18,720	20,370	21,370
$300,000 - 319,999	2,040	4,440	6,470	8,200	10,320	12,320	14,320	16,320	18,320	20,320	21,970	22,970
$320,000 - 364,999	2,720	5,920	8,750	10,950	13,070	15,070	17,070	19,070	21,290	23,590	25,540	26,840
$365,000 - 524,999	2,970	6,470	9,600	12,100	14,530	16,830	19,130	21,430	23,730	26,030	27,980	29,280
$525,000 and over	3,140	6,840	10,170	12,870	15,500	18,000	20,500	23,000	25,500	28,000	30,150	31,650

Single or Married Filing Separately

Higher Paying Job Annual Taxable Wage & Salary	Lower Paying Job Annual Taxable Wage & Salary											
	$0 - 9,999	$10,000 - 19,999	$20,000 - 29,999	$30,000 - 39,999	$40,000 - 49,999	$50,000 - 59,999	$60,000 - 69,999	$70,000 - 79,999	$80,000 - 89,999	$90,000 - 99,999	$100,000 - 109,999	$110,000 - 120,000
$0 - 9,999	$460	$940	$1,020	$1,020	$1,470	$1,870	$1,870	$1,870	$1,870	$2,040	$2,040	$2,040
$10,000 - 19,999	940	1,530	1,610	2,060	3,060	3,460	3,460	3,460	3,640	3,830	3,830	3,830
$20,000 - 29,999	1,020	1,610	2,130	3,130	4,130	4,540	4,540	4,720	4,920	5,110	5,110	5,110
$30,000 - 39,999	1,020	2,060	3,130	4,130	5,130	5,540	5,720	5,920	6,120	6,310	6,310	6,310
$40,000 - 59,999	1,870	3,460	4,540	5,540	6,690	7,290	7,490	7,690	7,890	8,080	8,080	8,080
$60,000 - 79,999	1,870	3,460	4,690	5,890	7,090	7,690	7,890	8,090	8,290	8,480	9,260	10,060
$80,000 - 99,999	2,020	3,810	5,090	6,290	7,490	8,090	8,290	8,490	9,470	10,460	11,260	12,060
$100,000 - 124,999	2,040	3,830	5,110	6,310	7,510	8,430	9,430	10,430	11,430	12,420	13,520	14,620
$125,000 - 149,999	2,040	3,830	5,110	7,030	9,030	10,430	11,430	12,580	13,880	15,170	16,270	17,370
$150,000 - 174,999	2,360	4,950	7,030	9,030	11,030	12,730	14,030	15,330	16,630	17,920	19,020	20,120
$175,000 - 199,999	2,720	5,310	7,540	9,840	12,140	13,840	15,140	16,440	17,740	19,030	20,130	21,230
$200,000 - 249,999	2,970	5,860	8,240	10,540	12,840	14,540	15,840	17,140	18,440	19,730	20,830	21,930
$250,000 - 399,999	2,970	5,860	8,240	10,540	12,840	14,540	15,840	17,140	18,440	19,730	20,830	21,930
$400,000 - 449,999	2,970	5,860	8,240	10,540	12,840	14,540	15,840	17,140	18,450	19,940	21,240	22,540
$450,000 and over	3,140	6,230	8,810	11,310	13,810	15,710	17,210	18,710	20,210	21,700	23,000	24,300

Head of Household

Higher Paying Job Annual Taxable Wage & Salary	Lower Paying Job Annual Taxable Wage & Salary											
	$0 - 9,999	$10,000 - 19,999	$20,000 - 29,999	$30,000 - 39,999	$40,000 - 49,999	$50,000 - 59,999	$60,000 - 69,999	$70,000 - 79,999	$80,000 - 89,999	$90,000 - 99,999	$100,000 - 109,999	$110,000 - 120,000
$0 - 9,999	$0	$830	$930	$1,020	$1,020	$1,020	$1,480	$1,870	$1,870	$1,930	$2,040	$2,040
$10,000 - 19,999	830	1,920	2,130	2,220	2,220	2,680	3,680	4,070	4,130	4,330	4,440	4,440
$20,000 - 29,999	930	2,130	2,350	2,430	2,900	3,900	4,900	5,340	5,540	5,740	5,850	5,850
$30,000 - 39,999	1,020	2,220	2,430	2,980	3,980	4,980	6,040	6,630	6,830	7,030	7,140	7,140
$40,000 - 59,999	1,020	2,530	3,750	4,830	5,860	7,060	8,260	8,850	9,050	9,250	9,360	9,360
$60,000 - 79,999	1,870	4,070	5,310	6,600	7,800	9,000	10,200	10,780	10,980	11,180	11,580	12,380
$80,000 - 99,999	1,900	4,300	5,710	7,000	8,200	9,400	10,600	11,180	11,670	12,670	13,580	14,380
$100,000 - 124,999	2,040	4,440	5,850	7,140	8,340	9,540	11,360	12,750	13,750	14,750	15,770	16,870
$125,000 - 149,999	2,040	4,440	5,850	7,360	9,360	11,360	13,360	14,750	16,010	17,310	18,520	19,620
$150,000 - 174,999	2,040	5,060	7,280	9,360	11,360	13,480	15,780	17,460	18,760	20,060	21,270	22,370
$175,000 - 199,999	2,720	5,920	8,130	10,480	12,780	15,080	17,380	19,070	20,370	21,670	22,880	23,980
$200,000 - 249,999	2,970	6,470	8,990	11,370	13,670	15,970	18,270	19,960	21,260	22,560	23,770	24,870
$250,000 - 349,999	2,970	6,470	8,990	11,370	13,670	15,970	18,270	19,960	21,260	22,560	23,770	24,870
$350,000 - 449,999	2,970	6,470	8,990	11,370	13,670	15,970	18,270	19,960	21,260	22,560	23,900	25,200
$450,000 and over	3,140	6,840	9,560	12,140	14,640	17,140	19,640	21,530	23,030	24,530	25,940	27,240

An employee who submits a false Form W-4 may be subject to a $500 penalty. Willfully filing a fraudulent Form W-4 or failing to supply information that would increase the amount withheld can result in a fine of up to $1,000 or imprisonment for up to 1 year, or both. Employers must submit copies of Forms W-4 to the IRS only when directed to do so by written notice. Where there is significant underwithholding for a particular employee, the IRS may require the employer to withhold income tax at a higher rate and will notify the employer in writing (known as a "lock-in" letter). Employees are given the right to contest the IRS determination.

EXAMPLE Brianne is the payroll manager at her company and receives a Form W-4 from her employee, On his Form W-4, Mike. Mike has indicated that he is a married employee with five children under 17. Brianne also noted that Mike did not list his "spouse" or children on his application or retirement plan paperwork and earlier mentioned that he was single. Based on both written and oral statements made by Mike, Brianne should ask Mike to prepare a corrected W-4. If he is unwilling to do so, she should withhold as if Mike is a single taxpayer. ♦

EXAMPLE George works in the payroll department and receives a Form W-4 from a new employee, Beatrice. Beatrice indicates married status and claims $4,000 on Step 3 for dependents on her Form W-4. George notes that her married status is consistent with her other paperwork and Beatrice has provided no oral or written statements that would indicate she is not married and has two children. George is not required to verify the existence of Beatrice's spouse and children. ♦

Although employers are not required to submit Forms W-4 to the Internal Revenue Service, that does not mean that new hires are not reported. In large part designed to assist with the enforcement of child support payments, the Personal Responsibility and Work Opportunity Reconciliation Act of 1996 (PRWORA) was passed requiring states to maintain a database of all new hires. Although many states use a specific form for reporting new hires, they will often also accept a completed Form W-4.

9-1a Computing Income Tax Withholding

The amount of income tax to be withheld by the employer is based on gross taxable wages before deducting FICA taxes, pension payments, union dues, insurance, and other deductions. An employer may elect to use any of several methods to determine the amount of the income tax withholding for each individual employee. Most commonly, withholding amounts are determined by use of the percentage method or by use of wage bracket tables.

Employees who submitted a Form W-4 in any year before 2020 are not required to submit a new 2020 Form W-4. Employers will continue to compute withholding based on the information from the employee's old Form W-4. The withholding tables published by the IRS allow employers to determine withholding based on old and new Forms W-4 under both the percentage and wage bracket methods. All new employees and any existing employees that wish to adjust withholding must use the new 2020 Form W-4.

To compute the withholding amount under the percentage method using an old Form W-4, the employer should:

1. Multiply the number of allowances claimed by the employee (from Form W-4) by the allowance amount;
2. Subtract that amount from the employee's gross taxable wages for the pay period; and
3. Apply the result in Step 2 to the applicable withholding table in Appendix C for the appropriate marital status.

The allowance amounts used in Step 1 for 2020 for various pay periods are from IRS Publication 15-T, "Federal Income Tax Withholding Methods." Although exemptions were repealed by the TCJA, allowance amounts are based on an exemption amount of $4,300.

Pay Period	2020 Allowance Amount
Weekly	$ 83
Biweekly	165
Semimonthly	179
Monthly	358
Quarterly	1,075
Semiannually	2,150
Annually	4,300

EXAMPLE Sharon is married, and her pay is $2,300 per month. On her Form W-4, Sharon claims married with a total of two allowances. Using the percentage method, the amount of withholding for Sharon is calculated as follows:

1. Allowances amount (monthly)	$ 358.00
Number of allowances claimed	× 2
Total	$ 716.00
2. Gross wages	$2,300.00
Less: amount from above	(716.00)
Adjusted wage amount	$1,584.00

3. Withholding from percentage tables in Appendix C:
($1,584.00 − $992.00) × 10% = $59.20 ◆

To compute the withholding amount under the percentage method using a 2020 Form W-4, the employer should use information from the Form W-4 to prepare the adjusted wage amount, the tentative withholding amount, the adjustment for tax credits, and the final withholding. Publication 15-T includes Worksheet 4 for employers to follow in completing the following steps:

1. Adjust the employee's wages for other forms of income (Line 4(a) from the employee's Form W-4) and excess deductions (Line 4(b) from the employee's Form W-4).

2. Determine the tentative withholding amount using the percentage method tables in much the same way as for an employee with a pre-2020 Form W-4 but using the 2020 tables.
3. Account for tax credits.
4. Add any additional withholding requested to determine the final withholding amount.

EXAMPLE Amy is married and her pay is $4,300 per month. Amy's 2020 Form W-4 lists the following:

- Line 3: $2,000 (associated with 1 dependent child)
- Line 4(a): $2,700 (from an investment portfolio)
- Line 4(b): $1,800 (student loan interest)
- Line 4(c): $271 (from the multiple jobs worksheet due to a working spouse)

Using Worksheet 4 from Publication 15-T, Amy's withholding is calculated as follows:

Step 1: The estimated monthly additional income of $225 ($2,700 ÷ 12) is added to Amy's $4,300 monthly wage. The monthly deduction of $150 ($1,800 ÷ 12) is deducted, thus bringing her adjusted monthly wage to $4,375.

Step 2: Using the monthly percentage withholding tables located in Appendix C for a married filing jointly taxpayer that did not check box 2c on the Form W-4, her tentative withholding is $164.60 + ($4,375 − $3,713) × 12% = $244.04.

Step 3: Adjust the result ($244.04) from Step 2 down (but never less than $0) by $166.67 ($2,000 ÷ 12) to equal $77.37.

Step 4: Add the additional withholding of $271 to the result of Step 3 to calculate final withholding of $348.37 ($77.37 + $271.00). ◆

Under the wage bracket method of determining withholding, wage bracket tables are provided for weekly, biweekly, semimonthly, monthly, and daily payroll periods for both married, single, and head of household taxpayers. The amount of withholding is obtained from the table for the appropriate payroll period and marital status, and is based on the total wages and the number of withholding allowances claimed. Similar to the percentage method, the process and tables differ slightly depending on whether the taxpayer uses a pre-2020 Form W-4 or a 2020 Form W-4. The monthly tables for single and married taxpayers are reproduced in Appendix C.

EXAMPLE Sharon's withholding from the previous percentage method example for a married taxpayer with two allowances using the old wage bracket method tables for a married person would be $61. ◆

The wage bracket method for an employee using the 2020 Form W-4 follows the same steps as the percentage method; however the tentative withholding is determined using the wage bracket tables.

EXAMPLE Amy's withholding from the previous percentage method example would follow the following steps:

Step 1: The estimated monthly additional income of $225 ($2,700 ÷ 12) is added to Amy's $4,300 monthly wage. The monthly deduction of $150 ($1,800 ÷ 12) is deducted thus bringing her adjusted monthly wage to $4,375.

Step 2: Using the wage bracket method withholding tables located in Appendix C for a married filing jointly taxpayer that did not check box 2c on the Form W-4, her tentative withholding amount is $243.00.

Step 3: Adjust the result ($243.00) from Step 2 down (but never less than $0) by $166.67 ($2,000 ÷ 12) to equal $76.33.

Step 4: Add the additional withholding of $271 to the result of Step 3 to calculate final withholding of $347.33 ($76.33 + $271.00). ◆

When using the new wage bracket method tables, care should be taken to select the proper tentative withholding amount from the table. There are two tentative withholding amount columns to choose from. The first column is for standard withholding and the second column is for when the taxpayer has checked the box on 2(c) of Form W-4, indicating that the taxpayer's spouse has wages similar to the taxpayer.

TAX BREAK The income tax withholding tables are constructed so that taxpayers that have completed their Form W-4 properly, will receive an income tax refund during tax filing season. Many taxpayers are satisfied with the resulting refund even though a tax refund represents an interest-free loan to the government. The overpayment of taxes serves as a "forced" savings account which provides the opportunity to purchase a big ticket item in late spring when the refund is received. Taxpayers should also be aware that interest is not charged symmetrically: underpayments of tax may result in penalties and interest (see LO 9.2), while overpayments are not usually credited with interest. Given the changes to the 2020 Form W-4, taxpayers should consider using the online estimator at **www.irs.gov/W4App**, complete an accurate Form W-4, and consider a mid-year review to ensure that the withholding amounts are proper given current income and other circumstances.

9-1b Pension and Deferred Income

Income tax withholding is also required on pension and other deferred income payments based on Form W-4P, Withholding Certificate for Pension or Annuity Payments, as completed and signed by the taxpayer. Financial institutions and corporations must withhold on the taxable part of pension, profit sharing, stock bonus, and individual retirement account payments. The rates used for withholding vary depending on the nature of the payment, as described below:

1. Periodic payments (such as annuities): Rates are based on the taxpayer's Form W-4P or if no W-4P is filed, tax will be withheld as if the taxpayer were married and claiming three withholding allowances.
2. Nonperiodic payments: Withholding is deducted at a flat 10 percent rate, except for certain distributions from qualified retirement plans, which have a required 20 percent withholding tax rate. See LO 9.8 for a discussion of withholding on rollover distributions.

EXAMPLE Adam is a retired college professor and receives a pension of $775 per month. The payor should withhold on the pension, based on Adam's signed W-4P, in the same manner as if it were Adam's salary. ◆

9-1c Tip Reporting

Tips are a significant part of the compensation received by employees in many types of jobs such as the following:

- Barber
- Hairdresser
- Parking attendant
- Porter
- Food and beverage servers

- Busser and others who share restaurant tip pools
- Delivery driver
- Airport skycap
- Bartenders

- Hotel housekeepers
- Manicurists
- Taxi, Uber and Lyft drivers

Tips are generally not paid directly by the employer to the employee and as a result, create a unique challenge for tax reporting for both the employee and employer. Additionally, tips are often paid in cash and thus capturing tips as income is difficult for the IRS.

To reduce the underreporting of tip income, the IRS requires employees to report tip income to their employers on Form 4070.

Form **4070** (Rev. August 2005) Department of the Treasury Internal Revenue Service	**Employee's Report of Tips to Employer**	OMB No. 1545-0074
Employee's name and address		Social security number
Employer's name and address (include establishment name, if different)		1 Cash tips received
		2 Credit and debit card tips received
		3 Tips paid out
Month or shorter period in which tips were received from ____ , ____ , to ____ ,		4 Net tips (lines **1 + 2 - 3**)
Signature		Date

For Paperwork Reduction Act Notice, see the instructions on the back of this form.	Cat. No. 41320P	Form **4070** (Rev. 8-2005)

The employer uses the information from Form 4070 to properly withhold employment and income taxes on tip income. To provide some assurance that accurate tip income is being reported by employees in large food or beverage establishments, the employer must compare employee-reported tips to 8 percent of the employer's sales. If the reported tips are less than 8 percent of sales, the employer must allocate the difference to each employee and report this amount on each employee's Form W-2 in Box 8 (Allocated Tips). The allocation of tip income can be accomplished in one of three ways. The employer may allocate the amount based on (1) gross receipts per employee, (2) hours worked by each employee (available only to employers having fewer than the equivalent of twenty-five full-time employees), or (3) a good faith agreement as explained on Form 8027, Employer's Annual Information Return of Tip Income and Allocated Tips. For a detailed explanation of the allocation process, see the instructions for Form 8027. With the diversity of businesses and tipping customs, the IRS also permits employers to enter into the Tip Rate Determination Education Program, in which the employer and the IRS work out a tip rate and reporting system. For more information on tip reporting in general, see the IRS website (**www.irs.gov**) or a tax research service.

The IRS has created two programs to help employers in businesses in which employees are compensated with tips: Tip Rate Determination Agreement (TRDA) and Tip Reporting Alternative Commitment (TRAC). These two programs are designed to help employers and employees more accurately report tip income and simplify the process for reporting tips by employees and employers.

TAX BREAK

9-1d Backup Withholding

In some situations, individuals may be subject to backup withholding on payments such as interest and dividends. The purpose of backup withholding is to ensure that income tax is paid on income reported on Form 1099. If backup withholding applies, the payor (e.g., bank or insurance company) must withhold 24 percent of the amount paid to the taxpayer. Payors are required to use backup withholding in the following cases:

1. The taxpayer does not give the payor his or her taxpayer identification number (e.g., Social Security number),
2. The taxpayer fails to certify that he or she is not subject to backup withholding,
3. The IRS informs the payor that the taxpayer gave an incorrect identification number, or
4. The IRS informs the payor to start withholding because the taxpayer has not reported the income on his or her tax return.

EXAMPLE   Kamili earned $2,000 in interest income from Cactus Savings Bank. Kamili failed to certify that she was not subject to backup withholding. As a result, the bank must withhold taxes of $480 (24 percent of $2,000) from the interest payments to Kamili. ♦

Taxpayers who give false information to avoid backup withholding are subject to a $500 civil penalty and criminal penalties, including fines and/or imprisonment.

Self-Study Problem 9.1   *See Appendix E for Solutions to Self-Study Problems*

1. John and Lillian Miles intend to file jointly in 2020. The Miles' address is 456 Peachtree Court, Atlanta, GA 30310. John expects to earn wages of $39,000 in 2020 and Lillian's wages are expected to be very similar at $39,480. They have two dependent children aged 13 and 17. Lillian also has a small business that she expects to generate income of $6,500 in 2020. She would prefer to increase her withholding rather than make estimated tax payments. They expect to make a $4,000 deductible IRA contribution in 2020 and use the standard deduction. Assuming she is the higher income earner and is paid monthly, prepare a Form W-4 for Lillian Miles including worksheets for steps 2(b) and 4(b), if needed.

2. Assuming that Lillian is paid monthly ($3,290 per month) and using the Form W-4 prepared in part a, compute Lillian's withholding using the percentage method and the wage bracket method.

   Percentage method $_____
   Wage bracket method $_____

Learning Objective 9.2

Determine taxpayers' quarterly estimated payments.

9-2 ESTIMATED PAYMENTS

Self-employed taxpayers are not subject to withholding; however, they must make quarterly estimated tax payments. Taxpayers with large amounts of interest, dividends, and other income not subject to withholding are also generally required to make estimated payments. Payments are made in four installments on April 15, June 15, and

September 15 of the tax year, and January 15 of the following year (or the first business day after if the dates fall on a weekend or holiday), based on the taxpayer's estimate of the amount of the tax liability for the year. A taxpayer with self-employment income must begin making the payments when he or she first meets the filing requirements. Due to the COVID-19 pandemic, the 2020 first and second quarter estimated tax payment due dates were both changed to July 15th. Thus, the first two installments of the year were due on the same date.

Never write out a check to the "IRS." The IRS issues this warning every year, because "IRS" may be easily changed to "MRS" plus an individual's name if the check falls into the wrong hands. Checks must be made payable to the U.S. Treasury, as a reminder that the IRS is merely the collector of revenue for the federal government. Alternatively, individual taxpayers can draft their bank account using Direct Pay or, for a fee, pay using a debit or credit card. Information regarding payment methods is available on the IRS website.

Any individual taxpayer who has estimated tax for the year of $1,000 or more, after subtracting withholding, and whose withholding does not equal or exceed the "required annual payment," must make quarterly estimated payments. The required annual payment is the smallest of the following amounts:

1. Ninety percent of the tax shown on the current year's return,
2. One hundred percent of the tax shown on the preceding year's return (such return must cover a full 12 months), or
3. Ninety percent of the current-year tax determined by placing taxable income, alternative minimum taxable income, and adjusted self-employment income on an annualized basis for each quarter.

A special rule applies to individuals with adjusted gross income in excess of $150,000 for the previous year. These high-income taxpayers must pay 110 percent of the amount of tax shown on the prior year tax return for the current year estimated payments, instead of 100 percent, to meet the requirements in the second option.

Estimated payments need not be paid if the estimated tax, after subtracting withholding, can reasonably be expected to be less than $1,000. Therefore, employees who also have self-employment income may avoid making estimated payments by filing a new Form W-4 and increasing the amount of their withholding on their regular salary.

The IRS imposes a nondeductible penalty on the amounts of any underpayments of estimated tax. The penalty applies when any installment is less than the required annual payment divided by the number of installments that should have been made, which is usually four. Form 2210, Underpayment of Estimated Tax by Individuals, Estates, and Trusts, is used for the calculation of the penalty associated with the underpayment of estimated tax.

Good tax planning dictates that a taxpayer postpone payment of taxes as long as no penalty is imposed. Unpaid taxes are equivalent to an interest-free loan from the government. Therefore, taxpayers should base their estimated payments on the method which results in the lowest amount of required quarterly or annual payment. For example, a taxpayer who expects his tax liability to increase might base his or her estimated payments this year on the amount of the tax liability for the prior year.

Self-Study Problem 9.2   *See Appendix E for Solutions to Self-Study Problems*

Ray Adams (Social Security number 466-47-1131) estimates his required annual payment for 2020 to be $7,600. He has a $255 overpayment of last year's taxes that he wishes to apply to the first quarter estimated tax payment for 2020. Complete the first quarter voucher below for Ray for 2020 by assuming any additional information, such as Ray's address. Assume that Ray's second quarter payment for 2020, although due on the same date due to the COVID-19 pandemic, is paid using a separate voucher.

Form **1040-ES** Department of the Treasury Internal Revenue Service	**2020 Estimated Tax**	**Payment Voucher 1** OMB No. 1545-0074

File only if you are making a payment of estimated tax by check or money order. Mail this voucher with your check or money order payable to **"United States Treasury."** Write your social security number and "2020 Form 1040-ES" on your check or money order. Do not send cash. Enclose, but do not staple or attach, your payment with this voucher.

Calendar year—Due April 15, 2020

Amount of estimated tax you are paying by check or money order.   Dollars | Cents

Pay online at www.irs.gov/etpay

Simple. Fast. Secure.

Print or type

Your first name and middle initial	Your last name	Your social security number
If joint payment, complete for spouse		
Spouse's first name and middle initial	Spouse's last name	Spouse's social security number
Address (number, street, and apt. no.)		
City, state, and ZIP code. (If a foreign address, enter city, also complete spaces below.)		
Foreign country name	Foreign province/county	Foreign postal code

For Privacy Act and Paperwork Reduction Act Notice, see instructions.   Form 1040-ES (2020)

Learning Objective 9.3

Compute the FICA tax.

9-3 THE FICA TAX

Note: As a result of the COVID-19 pandemic, complex but temporary changes were made to employment taxes, including credits for sick pay, family leave pay and employee retention pay. In addition, a deferral of payroll tax deposits was put into service. Because these provisions are expected to be temporary and largely terminate at the end of 2020, the typical employment tax and the temporary provisions have been presented separately.

9-3a Typical FICA Taxes (No COVID Provisions)

The Federal Insurance Contributions Act (FICA) imposes Social Security and Medicare taxes. It was passed by Congress in 1935 to provide benefits for qualified retired and disabled workers. If a worker should die, it would also provide the family of the worker with benefits. The Medicare program for the elderly is also funded by FICA taxes.

FICA taxes have two parts, Social Security (Old Age, Survivors, and Disability Insurance [OASDI]) and Medicare. Employees and their employers are both required to pay FICA taxes. Employers withhold a specified percentage of each employee's wages up to a maximum base amount, match the amount withheld with an equal amount, and pay the total to the Social Security Administration.

The Social Security (OASDI) tax rate is 6.2 percent and the Medicare tax rate is 1.45 percent each for employees and employers in 2020. The original FICA tax in 1935 was 1 percent of the first $3,000 in earnings. The maximum wage subject to the Social Security portion of the FICA tax is $137,700 in 2020, and all wages are subject to the Medicare portion of the FICA tax. The maximum wages to which the rates apply have increased over the years as presented in the following table.

Year	Maximum $ Base for 6.2% (employee and employer)	Maximum $ Base for 1.45% (employee and employer)*
2016	118,500	Unlimited
2017	127,200	Unlimited
2018	128,400	Unlimited
2019	132,900	Unlimited
2020	137,700	Unlimited

*Employees pay a 0.9 percent Medicare tax on wages over $200,000 if single and head of household ($250,000 if married filing jointly). See Chapter 6 for more information.

TAX BREAK

Taxpayers age 18 and older may request an online statement of Social Security benefits including estimates of projected retirement, survivors', and disability benefits. The statement also shows the taxpayer's Social Security earnings history, giving the taxpayer an opportunity to correct any errors or omissions. The personalized online statement is available at **www.ssa.gov/myaccount**. In some cases, the Social Security Administration will provide a paper version of this statement by mail.

EXAMPLE Katherine earns $21,500 for 2020. The FICA tax on her wages is calculated as follows:

Katherine:	Soc. Sec. − 6.2% × $21,500	$1,333.00
	Medicare − 1.45% × $21,500	311.75
	Total employee FICA tax	$1,644.75
Katherine's employer:	Soc. Sec. − 6.2% × $21,500	$1,333.00
	Medicare − 1.45% × $21,500	311.75
	Total employer FICA tax	$1,644.75
Total FICA tax		$3,289.50

◆

EXAMPLE Nora is an employee of Serissa Company. Her salary for 2020 is $140,000. Nora's portion of the FICA tax is calculated as follows:

Soc. Sec. − 6.2% × $137,700	$8,537.40
Medicare − 1.45% × $140,000	2,030.00
Total employee FICA tax	$10,567.40

The total combined FICA tax (employee's and employer's share) is $21,134.80. ◆

FICA taxes are paid one-half by employees through withholding and one-half by employers. Since the employer portion of the tax increases the cost of employees, many economists believe that even the employer's share of FICA tax is passed on to employees in the form of lower compensation. Thus, employees, like self-employed individuals, effectively bear both halves of FICA taxes.

Would You Believe?

9-3b Overpayment of Social Security Taxes

Taxpayers who work for more than one employer during the same tax year may pay more than the maximum amount of Social Security taxes. This occurs when the taxpayer's total wages are more than the maximum base amount for the year. When this happens, the taxpayer should compute the excess taxes paid, and report the excess on Line 10 of Schedule 3 of Form 1040 as an additional payment against his or her tax liability. This way, the taxpayer is refunded the excess Social Security tax. Note that the employer is not entitled to a similar refund for the overpaid matching Social Security tax.

EXAMPLE   Jerry worked for two employers during 2020. The first employer withheld and paid Social Security taxes on $80,000 of salary paid to Jerry, and the second employer withheld and paid Social Security taxes on $61,000 of salary paid to Jerry. The amount of Jerry's excess Social Security taxes paid for 2020 is computed as follows: 6.2% (Social Security rate) × [$80,000 + $61,000 − $137,700 (maximum for Social Security portion of FICA tax)] = $204.60. Jerry receives credit against his 2020 income tax liability equal to the excess Social Security taxes of $205. No excess Medicare tax has been paid, as there is no upper limit on Medicare wages. ♦

9-3c FICA Taxes (Temporary COVID Provisions)

During early 2020, many businesses were forced to close or reduce commercial activity as a result of the COVID-19 pandemic. In order to provide financial support for businesses, a series of temporary changes to payroll taxes were implemented. Most of these measures are currently scheduled to end on December 31, 2020, and are not expected to affect payroll taxes in 2021 and after (except where indicated).

Employee Retention Credit

The employee retention credit (ERC) is not a new credit and has been available to limited business under special provisions that have applied to natural disasters (e.g., California wildfires and east coast hurricanes). The 2020 expanded version of the credit grants eligible employers a credit against employment taxes equal to 50 percent of qualified wages paid to employees.

An employer eligible for the ERC:

- carried on a trade or business in 2020, and
- had operations that were fully or partially suspended during any calendar quarter in 2020 due to orders from a governmental authority limiting commerce, travel, or group meetings due to COVID-19 or
- experienced a significant decline in gross receipts during a 2020 quarter.

A "significant decline" starts when a quarter in which the gross receipts of the business are less than 50 percent of the gross receipts for the business in the same quarter in 2019. A significant decline ends when the gross receipts are greater than 80 percent of the gross receipts in the same quarter of 2020.

EXAMPLE   Mario operates a small plumbing business. His quarterly gross receipts were as follows:

	Q1	Q2	Q3	Q4
2019	$23,000	$25,000	$16,000	$18,000
2020	21,000	6,000	9,000	20,000

Mario's business suffered a significant decline in the second quarter of 2020 when gross receipts in 2020 ($6,000) were less than 50 percent of gross receipts in 2019 ($12,500 = 50% × $25,000). The third quarter of 2020's gross receipts were greater than 50 percent but less than 80 percent of the third quarter of 2019's gross receipts and thus the third quarter of 2020 was also a "significant decline." However, the fourth quarter of 2020's gross receipts exceeded 80 percent of the same quarter's gross receipts in 2019, and thus Mario's business may not be eligible for the ERC in the fourth quarter. The business might still qualify if Mario can establish that the business is suffering hardship due to a governmental order. ♦

The ERC is *not* available to government employers or to small businesses that receive loans under the Paycheck Protection Program.

The amount of the ERC is 50 percent of qualified wages. The amount that constitutes qualified wages depends on the underlying size of the business. If the employer has 100 or fewer employees, then the credit will be based on all wages paid, whether the employee worked or not. If the employer exceeds 100 employees, the qualified wages includes only wages paid to employees for time that they did *not* work.

In both instances, an allocation of the cost of employee-provided health care is included in qualified wages. The credit is claimed on a quarterly basis, but the amount of wages, *including health benefits,* for which the credit can be claimed, is limited to $10,000 in aggregate per employee for all quarters in 2020.

EXAMPLE Mayan Corporation has fewer than 100 employees. Wages paid (including an allocation of health care costs) to any employee in an ERC eligible quarter will be considered qualified wages up to an aggregate limit of $10,000 per employee regardless of whether these employees provided services or not. ♦

EXAMPLE Sioux Incorporated has more than 100 employees and is ERC eligible. Sioux was required to close several of its facilities under governmental order and Sioux continued to pay the employees at these facilities while other facilities continued to operate at normal operating levels. Sioux's qualified wages will include only the wages paid (including an allocation of health care costs) to the employees at the closed facilities (up to an aggregate limit of $10,000 per employee). ♦

EXAMPLE Cherokee Kitchens has more than 100 employees and operates a chain of restaurants in various locations. Under governmental order, four of these locations were required to limit services to carry-out and take-out. Cherokee elected to continue to pay kitchen and delivery personnel at the same hourly rate but was required to reduce these employee's hours to only 30 hours per week. The wages paid to the kitchen and delivery employees are not qualified wages since these employees were providing services. If Cherokee had continued to pay the employees for a normal 40-hour work week even though they were only working for 30 hours, the wages and an allocation of health care costs for the 10 hours of wages for *not* providing services would be qualified wages for the ERC. ♦

EXAMPLE Aztec Foods is an ERC eligible employer in the second quarter of 2020 and during the quarter paid qualified wages of $4,500 to its only four employees plus paid health care costs of $500 per employee ($20,000 total). Aztec did not elect an ERC in the first quarter of 2020. Since Aztec has fewer than

100 employees, Aztec is eligible for a $10,000 ERC (50% of $20,000). Aztec would normally owe payroll taxes as follows:

Wages Paid	6.2% Employee Share	6.2% Employer Share	1.45% Employee Share	1.45% Employer Share	Total
$18,000	$1,116	$1,116	$261	$261	$2,754

Aztec can use the ERC to reduce the $1,377 employer's share of payroll taxes down to $0. The excess credit of $8,623 ($10,000 − $1,377) can be recovered through an advance payment by filing Form 7200. Unlike the payroll tax deferral discussed later in LO 9-4 b, the ERC is not required to be repaid in a future year. Note that if Aztec was eligible for the ERC in the third quarter of 2020 and paid the employees the same $5,000 (including health care costs) each, Aztec would reach the maximum $10,000 of qualified wages for all 4 employees and would not be eligible for an ERC for these employees in the fourth quarter, even if Aztec otherwise remained eligible for the ERC. ◆

EXAMPLE   Inca Optics has over 100 employees and is eligible for the ERC in the second quarter of 2020. In the second quarter, Inca had to close its retail shops under governmental order and fourteen employees were unable to work, telework, or participate in other aspects of the business. Inca continued to pay the fourteen employees at 60 percent of their normal wages including health care. Total wages and health care costs would have been $175,000 or $12,500 per employee, thus Inca paid $7,500 (60 percent of $12,500) of qualified wages to each employee or total qualified wages of $105,000 ($7,500 × 14 employees). Inca's ERC is $52,500 ($105,000 × 50%). Inca may apply that credit against any non-deferred payroll taxes due for the second quarter and claim any excess as a refund. ◆

The ERC applies only to qualified wages paid after March 12, 2020 and before January 1, 2021. The IRS instructed taxpayers to claim the ERC starting on the second quarter's Form 941 and include any first quarter credit at that time, not in the first quarter. Self-employed individuals cannot claim the ERC on their own wages but to the extent they have paid employees that otherwise qualify, the ERC is available. In addition, an employer that received a covered loan under the Paycheck Protecton Program or paid wages under the family and medical leave act, is not eligible for an ERC.

Paid Leave Credits

Another significant COVID-19 provision that affects payroll taxes is the paid leave credits for sick pay and family leave pay. The credits apply to the employer's portion of Social Security tax. Although the two credits function similarly, they are applied differently.

Sick Leave Credit

One of the requirements of the Emergency Paid Sick Leave Act is that an employer with fewer than 500 employees must provide employees with up to two weeks (up to 80 hours) paid sick time if the employee cannot work or telework for the following reasons:

1. The employee is subject to a quarantine ordered by a governmental authority.
2. The employee has been advised to self-quarantine by a health care provider.
3. The employee has COVID-19 symptoms.
4. The employee is caring for someone subject to quarantine as per items 1 and 2 above.
5. The employee is caring for a child because the school or normal place of care is closed due to COVID-19.

Very small businesses (those with fewer than 50 employees) can be exempted from the leave requirements under reasons 4 and 5 on the previous page when the requirements would "jeopardize the ability of the business to continue."

The minimum rate of sick time is the highest of the regular rate of pay, the Federal minimum wage, or the local minimum wage. If, however, the employee is out due to reasons 4 or 5 on the previous page, the rate can be reduced to 2/3 of the rate that would apply. There are also maximums on the amount an employer is required to pay. For employees using sick leave under reasons 1-3, the maximum is $511 per day and $5,110 total. For employees using sick leave under reasons 4 and 5, the maximum is $200 per day and $2,000 in total.

In order to deflect the cost of the sick leave program, a sick leave credit of 100 percent of qualified sick leave wages paid in the quarters between April 1, 2020 and December 31, 2020, is available subject to the exact same limits as the sick pay ($511 or $200 per day with the same total per employee maximums of $5,110 and $2,000).

The credit is reflected as a reduction of the employer's portion of Social Security tax and, like the ERC, is refundable.

EXAMPLE   Antwon operates a business and after March 31, 2020 has 3 employees unable to work because they contracted the COVID-19 virus, 1 additional employee that was ordered to self-quarantine due to exposure to the first 3 employees, and 2 employees that are unable to work because the schools that the employees' children attend has been closed under governmental order. Antwon decided that any employee that contracted COVID-19 would be paid normal wages for the entirety of the sick leave, even though he is not required to do so. Other employees would receive normal wages as sick pay but only for up to 10 days as required by law (note that Antwon could have paid the two school-related employees at only 2/3 of the normal rate). The table below computes Antwon's sick leave credit.

Employee	Work Missed	"Normal" Pay	Actual Sick Leave Paid	Credit	Sick Leave Credit Calculation
#1 (has COVID-19)	65 days	$25 per hour	$13,000	$2,000	Actual pay of $200 per day × 10 days
#2 (has COVID-19)	25 days	$25 per hour	5,000	2,000	Actual pay of $200 per day × 10 days
#3 (has COVID-19)	14 days	$27 per hour	3,024	2,160	Actual pay of $216 per day × 10 days
#4 (self-quarantine)	3 weeks (but only 2 weeks of paid sick)	$3,000 per week ($600 per day)	6,000	5,110	Limit of $511 per day × 10 days
#5 (school closed)	6 weeks (but only 2 weeks of paid sick)	$650 per week ($130 per day)	1,300	1,300	Actual pay of $130 per day × 10 days
#6 (school closed)	1 week	$4,000 per week ($800 per day)	4,000	1,000	Limit of $200 per day × 5 days

As discussed below under Both Credits, an additional credit is available for allocated health care costs associated with qualified sick wages. ◆

Family Leave Credit

The Emergency Family Medical Leave Expansion Act passed in March 2020 expanded the existing Family Medical Leave Act. The expansion took effect on April 1, 2020 and runs through December 31, 2020. Under this plan, eligible employees can take up to 12 weeks of paid leave if they are unable to work because they need to care for a child under the age of 18 due to school or the place of care being closed or unavailable due to COVID-19. The first 10 days of leave can be unpaid. The rate of pay must be no less than 2/3 the normal pay for that employee. Required compensation under this program is capped at $200 per day and $10,000 in the aggregate for each employee and for no more than 10 weeks per employee. These provisions apply to employers with fewer than 500 employees. In addition, the employee is not eligible until they have worked for at least 30 days.

Similar to the sick leave provisions, the credit for family leave matches the amount that is required to be paid: normal wages up to $200 per day and $10,000 in aggregate total.

EXAMPLE   Curtis Company has less than 500 employees and had 24 employees that had to take leave due to children being unable to attend school because of COVID-19 closures. For the first 10 days, these employees would be eligible for sick leave as described in the previous section. After the 10-day period ends, they would become eligible for family leave. ◆

Both Credits

In addition to a credit for qualified sick or family leave wages, an additional credit is permitted for the pro-rata allocated health care costs associated with those employees for those days. This differs from the ERC in that qualified wages under the ERC *included* an allocation of health care costs whereas, under the sick and family leave provisions, the credit for allocated health care costs is an *additional* credit.

An *additional* credit is permitted for the employer's share of Medicare taxes (1.45 percent) on family leave and sick leave wages.

EXAMPLE   Jackson Inc. paid an employee for 12 weeks of family leave. The employee's normal wage rate would have been $600 per week. Jackson paid the employee at 2/3 of the normal rate or $400 per week or $80 per day. The health care costs allocated to the employee are $100 per week. The employer's share of Medicare taxes for this employee are $5.80 per week. Jackson is eligible for a family leave credit against the employer share of Social Security tax in the amount of the sum of a qualified family leave wages credit of $4,000 ($400 per week × 10 weeks) plus a health care costs credit of $1,000 ($100 per week × 10 weeks) plus a Medicare tax credit of $58 ($5.80 × 10 weeks). Note that although Jackson paid the employee for 12 weeks, the family leave credit is limited to only 10 weeks. It is possible for Jackson to have paid sick leave for the first two weeks if the purpose of the employee's leave qualified. Thus, Jackson would be eligible for 2 weeks of sick leave credits and 10 weeks of family leave credits. ◆

On the employer's income tax return, the effects of the credits are neutral. The wages and health care costs included in the credit remain deductible; however, the same amounts are treated as an income inclusion.

EXAMPLE Gamma Corp takes a $5,110 credit on employee sick leave. Gamma also incurred allocated health care costs of $400. Gamma will take a total credit of $5,510. Gamma will deduct the payroll and taxes as per usual but will also report an equal and offsetting income inclusion amount. The result on taxable income is a net zero effect for the items credited. ♦

At the time we go to print, Congress continues to wrangle with the concept of providing a double-benefit (allowing both the credit and the deduction). Be sure and confirm current tax treatment.

Both sick leave and family leave credits are claimed against the employer's share of Social Security taxes and will be claimed on the quarterly Form 941 starting in the second quarter of 2020, as discussed further in LO 9.4. Both credits can be refunded in a process that matches that of the ERC.

Paycheck Protection Program

The Paycheck Protection Program (PPP) does not result in a tax credit against employment taxes or income taxes, for that matter. However, PPP relates to the other COVID-19-related measures and as such has been grouped into this section for discussion purposes.

The PPP is a loan program designed to assist small businesses during the early stages of the COVID-19 pandemic. Loans were made available to provide funds for small businesses to pay payroll, employee benefits, interest on mortgages, rent, and utilities for a period of 8 weeks. When used for these purposes, the loans were intended to be forgiven. The details of the PPP loan programs are beyond the scope of the *Income Tax Fundamentals* textbook; however, attention must be paid to the tax consequences of these loans, specifically, the interaction with other COVID-19-related tax provisions, the deduction of covered business expenses, and the loan forgiveness provisions.

A taxpayer that takes a PPP loan may not also claim a tax credit for employee retention (ERC) or paid leave. A taxpayer with a PPP loan may defer the payment of payroll taxes under those provisions. If the loan is forgiven, the taxpayer is not required to include the amount forgiven as cancellation of debt income.

EXAMPLE Hughes took a $67,000 PPP loan in 2020. All the funds were used to cover payroll and utilities and thus Hughes requested and was granted loan forgiveness on the entire $67,000 balance and any related interest. Hughes will not be required to include the cancellation of debt as taxable income. ♦

The IRS has issued guidance indicating that if the PPP loan is forgiven, then the underlying payroll, benefits, rent, interest, and utilities will not be deductible for income tax purposes. At the time of this update, the IRS's interpretation of the deductibility of these costs is being challenged as not necessarily representing Congressional intent. Be sure and confirm the most current tax treatment.

Employee Payroll Tax Deferral

On August 8, 2020, the White House issued a memorandum giving permission to the Treasury Department to allow certain employees to defer payment of the employee share of Social Security tax (6.2 percent) for wages paid between September 1, 2020 and December 31, 2020. The deferral applies to employees whose bi-weekly wages are less than $4,000. No interest or penalties will apply to any deferred amounts. As we go to print, the process by which this deferral can be made is not clear and employers are seeking additional guidance from the IRS.

Self-Study Problem 9.3   *See Appendix E for Solutions to Self-Study Problems*

Hills Scientific Corp. (EIN 33-4434432) has 6 employees including founder, Juliette Hills. Payroll records indicate the following wages paid to the employees during the first and second quarters of 2020 were as follows:

Employee	Title	Total Q1 Wages	Total Q2 Wages	Sick Pay	Family Leave Pay	ERC Eligible Pay	Unclassified Wages	Income Tax Withheld
Juliette	CEO	$ 91,000	$ 50,000	$ 0	$ 0	$ 8,000	$42,000	$14,000
Yan	Head Scientist	40,000	40,000	0	0	8,000	32,000	10,000
Sai	Laboratory Manager	20,000	20,000	0	0	8,000	12,000	4,400
Yvette	Sr. Lab Analyst	15,000	15,000	2,500	10,000	2,500	0	3,150
Juan	Jr. Lab Analyst	9,000	9,000	2,000	0	7,000	0	1,350
Joe	Maintenance & Custodial	6,000	6,000	0	0	6,000	0	730
Total		$ 181,000	$ 140,000	$ 4,500	$10,000	$39,500	$86,000	$33,630

Hills' business was significantly affected by the COVID pandemic and suffered a significant decline in gross receipts for the second, third, and fourth quarters of 2020 (not the first quarter). Assume Hills did not file a PPP loan and did not defer any payroll taxes. In addition, assume a reasonable allocation of health care costs is $2,000 per quarter per employee and can be allocated to the type of pay pro-rata with the amount of pay. Details for certain employees are as follows:

Yvette started sick leave on April 1, 2020, as her spouse was diagnosed with COVID and she was ordered to quarantine at home for 15 days. On April 15, Yvette started family leave, as her child's school was closed and she was required to stay at home through the end of the second quarter.

Juan was also considered an essential employee but tested positive for COVID on May 15, 2020. Hills paid him $2,000 sick pay and then continued to pay his full salary for the rest of the second quarter while he recovered.

1. (No COVID provisions) Compute Hills' portion of second quarter employment taxes as if no credits were available and all second quarter wages are typical wages:

   a) Employee's portion Social Security tax $_____
   b) Employer's portion Social Security tax $_____
   c) Employee's portion Medicare tax $_____
   d) Employer's portion Medicare tax $_____

2. (COVID provisions) Assume Hills will be taking sick, family leave, and employee retention credits.

   a) Compute the allocation of heath care costs to each type of pay:

       i.   Sick pay $_____
       ii. Family leave pay $_____
       iii. Employee retention credit $_____

   b) Compute Hills' sick pay credit $_____
   c) Compute Hills' family leave credit $_____
   c) Compute Hills' employee retention credit $_____

9-4 FEDERAL TAX DEPOSIT SYSTEM

Employers must make periodic deposits of the taxes that are withheld from employees' wages. The frequency of the deposits depends on the total income tax withheld and the total FICA taxes for all employees. Employers are either monthly depositors or semi-weekly depositors. Prior to the beginning of each calendar year, taxpayers are required to determine which of the two deposit schedules they are required to use. If income tax withholding and FICA taxes of $100,000 or more are accumulated at any time during the year, the depositor is subject to a special one-day deposit rule. Significant temporary changes were made to payroll tax deposit rules as a result of the COVID-19 pandemic. Payroll tax credits are discussed previously in LO 9-3b and payroll tax deferrals are discussed in this section.

9-4a Typical Tax Deposits (No COVID Provisions)

Monthly or semiweekly deposit status is determined by using a lookback period, consisting of the four quarters beginning July 1 of the second preceding year and ending June 30 of the prior year. If the total income tax withheld from wages and FICA taxes attributable to wages for the four quarters in the lookback period is $50,000 or less, employers are monthly depositors for the current year. Monthly depositors must make deposits of employment taxes and taxes withheld by the fifteenth day of the month following the month of withholding. New employers are automatically monthly depositors.

If the total income tax withheld from wages and FICA attributable to wages for the four quarters in the lookback period is more than $50,000, the employer is a semiweekly depositor for the current year. Taxes on payments made on Wednesday, Thursday, or Friday must be deposited by the following Wednesday; taxes on payments made on the other days of the week must be deposited by the following Friday. If a deposit is scheduled for a day that is not a banking day, the deposit is considered to be made timely if it is made by the close of the next banking day.

EXAMPLE Tom runs a small business with ten employees. During the lookback period for the current year, the total withholding and FICA taxes amounted to $40,000. Since this is less than $50,000, Tom is a monthly depositor. His payroll tax deposits must be made by the fifteenth day of the month following the month of withholding. ◆

Tax payments (monthly, semiweekly, or daily for large depositors) must be made by Electronic Federal Tax Payment System (EFTPS), or by another electronic transfer method. Generally, employers must file Form 941, Employer's Quarterly Federal Tax Return, which reports the federal income taxes withheld from wages and the total FICA taxes attributable to wages paid during each quarter. Form 941 must be accompanied by any payroll taxes not yet deposited for the quarter. A special deposit rule allows small employers who accumulate less than $2,500 tax liability during a quarter to skip monthly payments and pay the entire amount of their payroll taxes with their quarterly Form 941. Form 941 must be filed by the last day of the month following the end of the quarter. For example, the first quarter Form 941, covering the months of January through March, must be filed by April 30. The Form 941 e-file program allows a taxpayer to electronically file Form 941 or Form 944.

Nearly a million very small employers with employment tax liability of $1,000 or less per year are allowed to file employment tax returns just once a year, instead of quarterly; for example, by January 31 of 2020 for 2019 employment taxes. Qualifying small employers receive written notification from the IRS that they should file using a Form 944 instead of the standard Form 941 used by most employers. The Form 944 is due annually, at the end of the month, following the taxpayer's year end.

IRS Publication 15-T, "Federal Income Tax Withholding Methods," covers the rules regarding the calculation and deposit of payroll taxes in detail and is an indispensable resource for those working in this complex area.

9-4b Employer Payroll Tax Deferral (COVID Provisions)

Under temporary provisions brought about by the COVID-19 pandemic, employers are eligible to defer the payment of the employer's portion of the Social Security portion of payroll tax for the period March 27 through December 31, 2020. Self-employed individuals can defer one-half of the 12.4 percent self-employment tax. One-half of the payment of these taxes can be deferred until December 31, 2021 and the other half can be deferred until December 31, 2022. The deferral applies to wages of any employee, not just those receiving benefits under some other COVID-19-related provisions. Note however that in cases where loans have been forgiven under the Paycheck Protection Program (PPP), deferral is not available after the decision is made that the loan can be forgiven.

EXAMPLE Jonas Corp is a monthly depositor for payroll taxes. For each of the months of 2020 beginning in March, Jonas paid the following taxable wages (no employee earns over the 2020 FICA cap):

Month	Wages	6.2% Employee Share	6.2% Employer Share	1.45% Employee Share	1.45% Employer Share
March	$ 14,000	$ 868	$ 868	$ 203	$ 203
April	10,000	620	620	145	145
May	6,000	372	372	87	87
June	6,000	372	372	87	87
July	8,000	496	496	116	116
August	10,000	620	620	145	145
September	12,000	744	744	174	174
October	14,000	868	868	203	203
November	14,000	868	868	203	203
December	14,000	868	868	203	203
Total	$108,000	$6,696	$6,696	$1,566	$1,566

Jonas will be eligible to defer the employer's portion of the 6.2 percent Social Security tax of $6,696. One half ($3,348) will be due by December 31, 2021 and the balance will be due December 31, 2022. Note that Jonas' March deposit would normally have been due by April 15 and thus is deferrable since the deposit was due after March 27. ◆

Form 941 has been temporarily revised to report the deferral.

For self-employed individuals, the timing guidance is not as clear; however, the IRS has stated that self-employed individuals may use any reasonable method to allocate 50 percent of the Social Security portion of self-employment tax attributable to net earnings from self-employment earned during March 27, 2020, through December 31, 2020. For example, an individual may allocate 22.5 percent of the individual's annual earnings from self-employment to the period from January 1, 2020, through March 26, 2020, and 77.5 percent of the individual's annual earnings to the period from March 27, 2020, through December 31, 2020.

EXAMPLE Eddie is a self-employed carpenter. In 2020, Eddie generated $48,000 of self-employment income. Normally, his self-employment tax would be calculated as:

- Wage base of $48,000 × 92.35% = $44,328
- The Social Security portion is $44,328 × 12.4% = $5,497
- The Medicare portion is $44,328 × 2.9% = $1,286

His total employment taxes due for 2020 would have been $6,783. Under the deferral, he can reduce the Social Security portion by 77.5 percent of one-half:

- The Social Security portion is $5,497 × 77.5% × 50% = $2,130

Eddie's total employment taxes due for the year are $4,653 ($5,497 + 1,286 − $2,130). ◆

The deferral portion of one-half of the Social Security portion of self-employment taxes remains deductible as a for AGI deduction and is reported on a new section of Schedule SE.

Self-Study Problem 9.4   *See Appendix E for Solutions to Self-Study Problems*

1. Using the information from Self-Study Problem 9.3, Part 1, complete Hills Corporation's second quarter Form 941 (Part 1 only) on Pages 9-29 to 9-30. Assume that Hills made deposits of $40,000 for the second quarter and elects to defer the employer's share of Social Security tax.

2. Using the information from Self-Study Problem 9.3, Part 2, complete the Hills Corporation's second quarter Form 941 (Parts 1 and 3 only) and Worksheet 1 from the Form 941 instructions located on Pages 9-29 to 9-32. Assume that Hills made deposits of $40,000 for the second quarter but does not elect to defer the employer's share of Social Security tax.

Self-Study Problem 9.4

Form **941 for 2020:** Employer's QUARTERLY Federal Tax Return	950120

Form **941 for 2020:** **Employer's QUARTERLY Federal Tax Return**
(Rev. April 2020)
Department of the Treasury — Internal Revenue Service

950120
OMB No. 1545-0029

Employer identification number (EIN) ☐☐ – ☐☐☐☐☐☐☐

Name (not your trade name)

Trade name (if any)

Address
Number   Street   Suite or room number

City   State   ZIP code

Foreign country name   Foreign province/county   Foreign postal code

Report for this Quarter of 2020
(Check one.)

☐ **1:** January, February, March

☐ **2:** April, May, June

☐ **3:** July, August, September

☐ **4:** October, November, December

Go to *www.irs.gov/Form941* for instructions and the latest information.

Read the separate instructions before you complete Form 941. Type or print within the boxes.

Part 1: **Answer these questions for this quarter.**

1 Number of employees who received wages, tips, or other compensation for the pay period including: *June 12* (Quarter 2), *Sept. 12* (Quarter 3), or *Dec. 12* (Quarter 4) . . .   **1** ☐

2 Wages, tips, and other compensation   **2** ☐

3 Federal income tax withheld from wages, tips, and other compensation . . . .   **3** ☐

4 If no wages, tips, and other compensation are subject to social security or Medicare tax   ☐ Check and go to line 6.

		Column 1		Column 2
5a	Taxable social security wages . .	☐	× 0.124 =	☐
5a	(i) Qualified sick leave wages . .	☐	× 0.062 =	☐
5a	(ii) Qualified family leave wages .	☐	× 0.062 =	☐
5b	Taxable social security tips . . .	☐	× 0.124 =	☐
5c	Taxable Medicare wages & tips. . .	☐	× 0.029 =	☐
5d	Taxable wages & tips subject to Additional Medicare Tax withholding	☐	× 0.009 =	☐

5e Total social security and Medicare taxes. Add Column 2 from lines 5a, 5a(i), 5a(ii), 5b, 5c, and 5d   **5e** ☐

5f Section 3121(q) Notice and Demand—Tax due on unreported tips (see instructions) . .   **5f** ☐

6 Total taxes before adjustments. Add lines 3, 5e, and 5f . . . .   **6** ☐

7 Current quarter's adjustment for fractions of cents . . . .   **7** ☐

8 Current quarter's adjustment for sick pay . . . .   **8** ☐

9 Current quarter's adjustments for tips and group-term life insurance . . . . .   **9** ☐

10 Total taxes after adjustments. Combine lines 6 through 9 . . . .   **10** ☐

11a Qualified small business payroll tax credit for increasing research activities. Attach Form 8974   **11a** ☐

11b Nonrefundable portion of credit for qualified sick and family leave wages from Worksheet 1   **11b** ☐

11c Nonrefundable portion of employee retention credit from Worksheet 1 . . . . . .   **11c** ☐

▶ **You MUST complete all three pages of Form 941 and SIGN it.**

Next ▶

For Privacy Act and Paperwork Reduction Act Notice, see the back of the Payment Voucher.   Cat. No. 17001Z   Form **941** (Rev. 4-2020)

950220

Name *(not your trade name)*	**Employer identification number (EIN)**

Part 1:	**Answer these questions for this quarter.** *(continued)*

11d Total nonrefundable credits. Add lines 11a, 11b, and 11c . . . .   **11d** [.   ]

12 Total taxes after adjustments and nonrefundable credits. Subtract line 11d from line 10   .   **12** [.   ]

13a Total deposits for this quarter, including overpayment applied from a prior quarter and overpayments applied from Form 941-X, 941-X (PR), 944-X, or 944-X (SP) filed in the current quarter   **13a** [.   ]

13b Deferred amount of the employer share of social security tax   . . . .   **13b** [.   ]

13c Refundable portion of credit for qualified sick and family leave wages from Worksheet 1   **13c** [.   ]

13d Refundable portion of employee retention credit from Worksheet 1 . . . .   **13d** [.   ]

13e Total deposits, deferrals, and refundable credits. Add lines 13a, 13b, 13c, and 13d . . .   **13e** [.   ]

13f Total advances received from filing Form(s) 7200 for the quarter . . . .   **13f** [.   ]

13g Total deposits, deferrals, and refundable credits less advances. Subtract line 13f from line 13e   **13g** [.   ]

14 Balance due. If line 12 is more than line 13g, enter the difference and see instructions . . .   **14** [.   ]

15 Overpayment. If line 13g is more than line 12, enter the difference [.   ] **Check one:** ☐ Apply to next return.   ☐ Send a refund.

Part 2:	**Tell us about your deposit schedule and tax liability for this quarter.**

If you're unsure about whether you're a monthly schedule depositor or a semiweekly schedule depositor, see section 11 of Pub. 15.

16 Check one: ☐   Line 12 on this return is less than $2,500 or line 12 on the return for the prior quarter was less than $2,500, and you didn't incur a $100,000 next-day deposit obligation during the current quarter. If line 12 for the prior quarter was less than $2,500 but line 12 on this return is $100,000 or more, you must provide a record of your federal tax liability. If you're a monthly schedule depositor, complete the deposit schedule below; if you're a semiweekly schedule depositor, attach Schedule B (Form 941). Go to Part 3.

☐   **You were a monthly schedule depositor for the entire quarter.** Enter your tax liability for each month and total liability for the quarter, then go to Part 3.

Tax liability: **Month 1** [.   ]

Month 2 [.   ]

Month 3 [.   ]

Total liability for quarter [.   ]   **Total must equal line 12.**

☐   **You were a semiweekly schedule depositor for any part of this quarter.** Complete Schedule B (Form 941), Report of Tax Liability for Semiweekly Schedule Depositors, and attach it to Form 941. Go to Part 3.

▶ **You MUST complete all three pages of Form 941 and SIGN it.**   **Next ■▶**

Page **2**

Form **941** (Rev. 4-2020)

950920

Name *(not your trade name)*	Employer identification number (EIN)

Part 3: Tell us about your business. If a question does NOT apply to your business, leave it blank.

17 If your business has closed or you stopped paying wages . . . . ☐ Check here, and

enter the final date you paid wages [/ /] ; also attach a statement to your return. See instructions.

18 If you're a seasonal employer and you don't have to file a return for every quarter of the year . . . ☐ Check here.

19 Qualified health plan expenses allocable to qualified sick leave wages . . . . **19** [.]

20 Qualified health plan expenses allocable to qualified family leave wages . . . . **20** [.]

21 Qualified wages for the employee retention credit . . . . **21** [.]

22 Qualified health plan expenses allocable to wages reported on line 21 . . . . **22** [.]

23 Credit from Form 5884-C, line 11, for this quarter . . . . **23** [.]

24 Qualified wages paid March 13 through March 31, 2020, for the employee retention credit (use this line only for the second quarter filing of Form 941) . . . . **24** [.]

25 Qualified health plan expenses allocable to wages reported on line 24 (use this line only for the second quarter filing of Form 941) . . . . **25** [.]

Part 4: May we speak with your third-party designee?

Do you want to allow an employee, a paid tax preparer, or another person to discuss this return with the IRS? See the instructions for details.

☐ Yes. Designee's name and phone number [ ] [ ]

Select a 5-digit personal identification number (PIN) to use when talking to the IRS. ☐ ☐ ☐ ☐ ☐

☐ No.

Part 5: Sign here. You MUST complete all three pages of Form 941 and SIGN it.

Under penalties of perjury, I declare that I have examined this return, including accompanying schedules and statements, and to the best of my knowledge and belief, it is true, correct, and complete. Declaration of preparer (other than taxpayer) is based on all information of which preparer has any knowledge.

X Sign your name here [ ]

Print your name here [ ]
Print your title here [ ]

Date [/ /]

Best daytime phone [ ]

Paid Preparer Use Only	Check if you're self-employed . . . ☐
Preparer's name [ ]	PTIN [ ]
Preparer's signature [ ]	Date [/ /]
Firm's name (or yours if self-employed) [ ]	EIN [ ]
Address [ ]	Phone [ ]
City [ ] State [ ]	ZIP code [ ]

Form **941** (Rev. 4-2020)

Worksheet 1. Credit for Qualified Sick and Family Leave Wages and the Employee Retention Credit

Keep for Your Records

Determine how you will complete this worksheet

If you paid both qualified sick and family leave wages and qualified wages for purposes of the employee retention credit this quarter, complete Step 1, Step 2, and Step 3. If you paid qualified sick and family leave wages this quarter but you didn't pay any qualified wages for purposes of the employee retention credit this quarter, complete Step 1 and Step 2. If you paid qualified wages for purposes of the employee retention credit this quarter but you didn't pay any qualified sick and family leave wages this quarter, complete Step 1 and Step 3.

Step 1.   **Determine the employer share of social security tax this quarter after it is reduced by any credit claimed on Form 8974 and any credit to be claimed on Form 5884-C**

1a	Enter the amount of social security tax from Form 941, Part 1, line 5a, column 2	1a _____
1b	Enter the amount of social security tax from Form 941, Part 1, line 5b, column 2	1b _____
1c	Add lines 1a and 1b	1c _____
1d	Multiply line 1c by 50% (0.50)	1d _____
1e	If you're a third-party payer of sick pay that isn't an agent and you're claiming credits for amounts paid to your employees, enter the employer share of social security tax included on Form 941, Part 1, line 8 (enter as a positive number)	1e _____
1f	Subtract line 1e from line 1d	1f _____
1g	If you received a Section 3121(q) Notice and Demand during the quarter, enter the amount of the employer share of social security tax from the notice	1g _____
1h	**Employer share of social security tax.** Add lines 1f and 1g	1h _____
1i	Enter the amount from Form 941, Part 1, line 11a (credit from Form 8974)	1i _____
1j	Enter the amount to be claimed on Form 5884-C, line 11, for this quarter	1j _____
1k	**Total nonrefundable credits already used against the employer share of social security tax.** Add lines 1i and 1j	1k _____
1l	**Employer share of social security tax remaining.** Subtract line 1k from line 1h	1l _____

Step 2.   **Figure the sick and family leave credit**

2a	Qualified sick leave wages reported on Form 941, Part 1, line 5a(i), column 1	2a _____
2a(i)	Qualified sick leave wages included on Form 941, Part 1, line 5c, but not included on Form 941, Part 1, line 5a(i), column 1, because the wages reported on that line were limited by the social security wage base	2a(i) _____
2a(ii)	Total qualified sick leave wages. Add lines 2a and 2a(i)	2a(ii) _____
2b	Qualified health plan expenses allocable to qualified sick leave wages (Form 941, Part 3, line 19)	2b _____
2c	Employer share of Medicare tax on qualified sick leave wages. Multiply line 2a(ii) by 1.45% (0.0145)	2c _____
2d	**Credit for qualified sick leave wages.** Add lines 2a(ii), 2b, and 2c	2d _____
2e	Qualified family leave wages reported on Form 941, Part 1, line 5a(ii), column 1	2e _____
2e(i)	Qualified family leave wages included on Form 941, Part 1, line 5c, but not included on Form 941, Part 1, line 5a(ii), column 1, because the wages reported on that line were limited by the social security wage base	2e(i) _____
2e(ii)	Total qualified family leave wages. Add lines 2e and 2e(i)	2e(ii) _____
2f	Qualified health plan expenses allocable to qualified family leave wages (Form 941, Part 3, line 20)	2f _____
2g	Employer share of Medicare tax on qualified family leave wages. Multiply line 2e(ii) by 1.45% (0.0145)	2g _____
2h	**Credit for qualified family leave wages.** Add lines 2e(ii), 2f, and 2g	2h _____
2i	**Credit for qualified sick and family leave wages.** Add lines 2d and 2h	2i _____
2j	**Nonrefundable portion of credit for qualified sick and family leave wages.** Enter the smaller of line 1l or line 2i. Enter this amount on Form 941, Part 1, line 11b	2j _____
2k	**Refundable portion of credit for qualified sick and family leave wages.** Subtract line 2j from line 2i and enter this amount on Form 941, Part 1, line 13c	2k _____

Step 3.   **Figure the employee retention credit**

3a	Qualified wages (excluding qualified health plan expenses) for the employee retention credit (Form 941, Part 3, line 21)	3a _____
3b	Qualified health plan expenses allocable to qualified wages for the employee retention credit (Form 941, Part 3, line 22)	3b _____
3c	Qualified wages (excluding qualified health plan expenses) paid March 13, 2020, through March 31, 2020, for the employee retention credit (Form 941, Part 3, line 24). Enter an amount here only for the second quarter Form 941	3c _____
3d	Qualified health plan expenses allocable to qualified wages paid March 13, 2020, through March 31, 2020, for the employee retention credit (Form 941, Part 3, line 25). Enter an amount here only for the second quarter Form 941	3d _____
3e	Add lines 3a, 3b, 3c, and 3d	3e _____
3f	**Retention credit.** Multiply line 3e by 50% (0.50)	3f _____
3g	Enter the amount of the employer share of social security tax from Step 1, line 1l	3g _____
3h	Enter the amount of the nonrefundable portion of the credit for qualified sick and family leave wages from Step 2, line 2j	3h _____
3i	Subtract line 3h from line 3g	3i _____
3j	**Nonrefundable portion of employee retention credit.** Enter the smaller of line 3f or line 3i. Enter this amount on Form 941, Part 1, line 11c	3j _____
3k	**Refundable portion of employee retention credit.** Subtract line 3j from line 3f and enter this amount on Form 941, Part 1, line 13d	3k _____

Caution: Only complete lines 3c and 3d for your second quarter 2020 Form 941.

9-5 **EMPLOYER REPORTING REQUIREMENTS**

On or before January 31 of the year following the calendar year of payment, an employer must furnish to each employee two copies of the employee's Wage and Tax Statement, Form W-2, for the previous calendar year. If employment is terminated before the end of the year and the employee requests a Form W-2, the employer must furnish the Form W-2 within 30 days after the last wage payment is made or after the employee request, whichever is later. Otherwise, the general rule requiring the W-2 to be furnished to the employee by January 31 applies. The original copy (Copy A) of all Forms W-2 and Form W-3 (Transmittal of Wage and Tax Statements) must be filed by the employer with the Social Security Administration by January 31 of the year following the calendar year of payment. Copy B of Form W-2 is filed with the employee's federal tax return. Employers retain Copy D of Form W-2 for their records. Extra copies of Form W-2 are prepared for the employee to use when filing state and local tax returns.

Form W-2 is used to report wages, tips, and other compensation paid to an employee. Form W-2 also provides the employee with additional supplemental information. Among the items which must be reported on the employee's Form W-2 are the cost of employer-sponsored health coverage, employer contributions to a health savings account (HSA), excess group-term life insurance premiums, Roth contributions to an employer plan, and certain reimbursements of travel and other ordinary and necessary expenses.

Special rules apply to the reimbursement of travel and other ordinary and necessary employee business expenses. If an employee is reimbursed for travel and other ordinary and necessary business expenses, income and employment tax withholding may be required. If a reimbursement payment is considered to have been made under an accountable plan, the amount is excluded from the employee's gross income and consequently is not required to be included on Form W-2, and no withholding is required. Alternatively, reimbursements of travel and other employee business expenses made under a nonaccountable plan must be included as wages on Form W-2, and the amounts are subject to withholding. Payments are considered made under a nonaccountable plan in the following circumstances: (1) the employee receives a reimbursement for expenses under an arrangement which does not require the employee to account adequately to the employer, or the employee receives advances under an arrangement which does not require the employee to return amounts in excess of substantiated expenses; or (2) the employee receives amounts under an arrangement that requires the employee to substantiate reimbursed expenses, but the amounts are not substantiated within a reasonable period of time, or the employee receives amounts under a plan which requires excess reimbursements to be returned to the employer, but the employee does not return such excess amounts within a reasonable period of time. In the first case, the entire amount paid under the expense account plan is considered wages subject to withholding, whereas under the circumstances described in the second situation, only the amounts in excess of the substantiated expenses are subject to withholding.

The Social Security Administration permits employers to prepare and file up to 50 Forms W-2 using their online business services. Employers should go to **www.ssa.gov** to register for the service.

TAX BREAK

9-5a **Form W-2G**

Gambling winnings are reported by gambling establishments on Form W-2G. Amounts that must be reported include certain winnings from horse and dog racing, jai alai, lotteries, state-conducted lotteries, sweepstakes, wagering pools, bingo, keno, and slot machines. In certain cases, withholding of income taxes is required. Forms W-2G must be transmitted to the taxpayer no later than January 31 of the year following the calendar year of payment, and to the IRS along with Form 1096 by March 1 following the calendar year of payment. Requirements to file Form W-2G can differ between the type of wagering or gaming. The due date is March 31 if transmitting electronically to the IRS. More information can be found in the instructions for Form W-2G.

9-5b Information Returns

Taxpayers engaged in a trade or business are required to file Form 1099 for each recipient of certain payments made in the course of their trade or business. Where applicable, federal income tax withheld with respect to the payment is also reported on Form 1099. The common types of payments and the related Form 1099 are summarized in Table 9.1.

TABLE 9.1	1099 FORMS
Form	**Used For**
1099-B	Payments of proceeds from brokers
1099-DIV	Dividend payments
1099-G	Certain government payments (state income tax refund)
1099-INT	Interest payments
1099-K	Merchant card and third-party network transactions
1099-MISC	Miscellaneous payments
1099-NEC	Payments to non-employees
1099-R	Payments of pension, annuity, profit sharing, retirement plan, IRA, insurance contracts, etc.
1099-S	Payments from real estate transactions

Forms 1099 must be mailed to the recipients by January 31 of the year following the calendar year of payment. However, payors are allowed until February 15 of the year following the calendar year of payment to provide Forms 1099-B, 1099-S, and certain 1099-MISC forms. A separate Form 1096 must be used to transmit each type of 1099 to the appropriate IRS Campus Processing Site. Different Forms 1099 have different due dates. The IRS publishes a guide titled General Instructions for Certain Information Returns each year which has a convenient table of due dates.

Typically, nonemployee compensation has been reported in Box 7 on Form 1099-MISC. Nonemployee compensation is generally when an individual who does not qualify as an employee is paid for services provided. Taxpayers should now use Form 1099-NEC to report nonemployee compensation of $600 or more starting in 2020.

9-5c Form 1099-K Reporting Merchant Card and Third-Party Payments

Banks and online payment networks ("payment settlement entities"), such as PayPal, Venmo, VISA, and MasterCard, are required to use Form 1099-K to report credit card sales and other reportable sales transactions to the IRS and to the businesses making reportable sales. The reporting requirement is triggered for an entity when the total dollar amount of transactions for a particular merchant exceeds $20,000 and the total number of transactions exceeds 200.

 **TAX BREAK** If a taxpayer receives a Form 1099, the income reported on that form should be included on the tax return. The IRS is going to match the identification number on the Form 1099 to the taxpayer's tax return and will likely notice if that income is missing. A Form 1099 is not usually required to be attached to the taxpayer's return; however, if tax was withheld on the payment reported, the Form 1099 should be attached as necessary, if paper filing.

Self-Study Problem 9.5   *See Appendix E for Solutions to Self-Study Problems*

Big Bank (P.O. Box 12344, San Diego, CA 92101; E.I.N. 95-1234567; California ID 800 4039250 092; and telephone number 800-555-1212) paid an employee, Mary Jones (6431 Gary Street, San Diego, CA 92115), wages of $16,150 for 2020. The federal income tax withholding for the year amounted to $2,422, and FICA withheld was $1,235.48 ($1,001.30 for Social Security tax and $234.18 for Medicare tax). State income tax withheld was $969.00. Mary's FICA wages were the same as her total wages, and her Social Security number is 464-74-1132.

a. Complete the following Form W-2 for Mary Jones from Big Bank.

a Employee's social security number		OMB No. 1545-0008	Safe, accurate, FAST! Use	IRS e-file	Visit the IRS website at www.irs.gov/efile
b Employer identification number (EIN)		**1** Wages, tips, other compensation		**2** Federal income tax withheld	
c Employer's name, address, and ZIP code		**3** Social security wages		**4** Social security tax withheld	
		5 Medicare wages and tips		**6** Medicare tax withheld	
		7 Social security tips		**8** Allocated tips	
d Control number		**9**		**10** Dependent care benefits	
e Employee's first name and initial Last name Suff.		**11** Nonqualified plans		**12a** See instructions for box 12	
		13 Statutory employee ☐ Retirement plan ☐ Third-party sick pay ☐		**12b**	
		14 Other		**12c**	
				12d	
f Employee's address and ZIP code					

15 State Employer's state ID number	16 State wages, tips, etc.	17 State income tax	18 Local wages, tips, etc.	19 Local income tax	20 Locality name

Form **W-2** Wage and Tax Statement   **2020**   Department of the Treasury—Internal Revenue Service
Copy B—To Be Filed With Employee's **FEDERAL** Tax Return.
This information is being furnished to the Internal Revenue Service.

b. Mary also has a savings account at Big Bank, which paid her interest for 2020 of $461. Complete the following Form 1099-INT for Mary's interest income.

☐ CORRECTED (if checked)

PAYER'S name, street address, city or town, state or province, country, ZIP or foreign postal code, and telephone no.	Payer's RTN (optional)	OMB No. 1545-0112	**Interest Income**
	1 Interest income $	2020 Form **1099-INT**	
	2 Early withdrawal penalty $		**Copy B**
PAYER'S TIN RECIPIENT'S TIN	**3** Interest on U.S. Savings Bonds and Treas. obligations $		**For Recipient**
RECIPIENT'S name	**4** Federal income tax withheld $	**5** Investment expenses $	This is important tax information and is being furnished to the IRS. If you are required to file a return, a negligence penalty or other sanction may be imposed on you if this income is taxable and the IRS determines that it has not been reported.
	6 Foreign tax paid $	**7** Foreign country or U.S. possession	
Street address (including apt. no.)	**8** Tax-exempt interest $	**9** Specified private activity bond interest $	
City or town, state or province, country, and ZIP or foreign postal code	**10** Market discount $	**11** Bond premium $	
FATCA filing requirement ☐	**12** Bond premium on Treasury obligations $	**13** Bond premium on tax-exempt bond $	
Account number (see instructions)	**14** Tax-exempt and tax credit bond CUSIP no.	**15** State **16** State identification no.	**17** State tax withheld $

Form **1099-INT**   (keep for your records)   www.irs.gov/Form1099INT   Department of the Treasury - Internal Revenue Service

Compute the amount of FUTA tax for an employer.

9-6 THE FUTA TAX

Please note: Employers in jurisdictions that have not repaid money borrowed from the federal government for unemployment benefits will have a higher FUTA tax than the 0.6 percent illustrated below. At the time we go to print, only the U.S. Virgin Islands may have a credit reduction in 2020. For purposes of the problems and examples in this textbook, assume that the employer does not reside in one of the jurisdictions where a higher FUTA tax applies.

The Federal Unemployment Tax Act (FUTA) instituted a tax that is not withheld from employees' wages, but instead is paid in full by employers. The federal unemployment tax rate is 6 percent of an employee's wages up to $7,000. A credit is allowed for state unemployment taxes of 5.4 percent. Therefore, the effective federal unemployment tax rate is only 0.6 percent if the state also assesses an unemployment tax.

EXAMPLE Karen has two employees in 2020, John, who earned $12,500 this year, and Sue, who earned $15,000. The FUTA tax is calculated as follows:

John's wages, $12,500 (maximum $7,000)	$ 7,000
Sue's wages, $15,000 (maximum $7,000)	7,000
Total FUTA wages	14,000
FUTA tax at 0.6%	$ 84

♦

Employers report their FUTA liability for the year on Form 940, Employer's Annual Federal Unemployment (FUTA) Tax Return. Like federal income tax withholding and FICA taxes, federal unemployment taxes must be deposited by electronic funds transfer (EFTPS). A deposit is required when the FUTA taxes for the quarter, plus any amount not yet deposited for the prior quarter(s), exceed $500. If required, the deposit must be made by the last day of the month after the end of each quarter.

New Tax Law

Due to the significant increase in unemployment claims during the COVID-19 pandemic, a number of states will have borrowed from the federal government. However, a credit reduction is not enacted until two consecutive years of loans to the state exist.

EXAMPLE Ti Corporation's federal unemployment tax liability after reduction by the credit for state unemployment taxes, is $255 for the first quarter of 2020, $200 for the second quarter, $75 for the third quarter, and $25 for the fourth quarter. Ti Corporation must deposit $530, the sum of the first, second, and third quarters' liability, by October 31, 2020. The remaining $25 may be either deposited or paid with Form 940. ♦

Because states administer federal-state unemployment programs, most of the unemployment tax is paid to the state. Employers must pay all state unemployment taxes for the year by the due date of the federal Form 940 to get full credit for the state taxes against FUTA.

Self-Study Problem 9.6   *See Appendix E for Solutions to Self-Study Problems*

The Anatolian Corporation's payroll information for 2020 is summarized as follows:

	Quarter 1	Quarter 2	Quarter 3	Quarter 4
Gross earnings of employees	$25,000	$30,000	$26,000	$32,000
Individual employee earnings in excess of $7,000	None	$ 4,000	$10,000	$ 8,000

Anatolian Corporation (E.I.N. 94-0001112), located at 400 8th Street N., La Crosse, WI 54601, pays Wisconsin state unemployment tax. The company makes the *required* deposits of both federal and state unemployment taxes on a timely basis and had no overpayment in 2019. Complete Parts 1–5 of the Anatolian Corporation's 2020 Form 940 on Pages 9-38 and 9-39, using the above information.

9-7 QUALIFIED RETIREMENT PLANS

9.7 Learning Objective

Describe the general rules for qualified retirement plans.

9-7a Qualified Plans

For a retirement plan to be a qualified plan for income tax purposes, it must meet the following general requirements:

1. A plan must be created by an employer for the *exclusive benefit* of employees or their beneficiaries.
2. The contributions and benefits under a plan must *not discriminate in* favor of highly compensated employees.
3. A plan must meet certain *participation and coverage requirements*. The plan must provide that all employees who are 21 years old and who have completed at least 1 year of service with the employer are eligible to participate. If the plan provides for 100 percent vesting of accrued benefits upon commencement of participation in the plan, the 1 year of service requirement may be replaced with a requirement that the employee has completed at least 2 years of service.
4. *Minimum vesting* requirements must be met with respect to both employee and employer contributions.
5. *Uniform minimum distribution* rules must be met.

9-7b Types of Qualified Plans

The tax law provides for several types of qualified plans: pension plans, profit-sharing plans, stock bonus plans, and Employee Stock Ownership Plans (ESOPs). The pension plan can take one of two forms: the defined contribution plan or the defined benefit plan. Under a defined contribution plan, the amount of contribution for the employee is determined by reference to a formula based on the employee's current compensation. The employee's retirement benefits will be dependent upon the accumulated contributions and earnings in the account at the time of retirement. Under a defined benefit plan, the future retirement benefits of the employee are specified, and a formula is used to determine the contributions necessary to provide for the defined benefit. Defined benefit plans are being used more sparingly by employers over the last three decades. Profit-sharing plans are structured to allow the employee to share in company profits through employer contributions from such profits. Under a stock bonus plan, employer contributions on behalf of the employee consist of stock of the employer company.

EXAMPLE   Heather is an employee who earned $30,000 during the current year. Her employer contributed $1,200 (4 percent of Heather's salary) to a qualified retirement plan. This plan is a defined contribution plan. ♦

Self-Study Problem 9.6

Form **940** for 2020: **Employer's Annual Federal Unemployment (FUTA) Tax Return**

Department of the Treasury — Internal Revenue Service

850113

OMB No. 1545-0028

Employer identification number (EIN) ☐☐ – ☐☐☐☐☐☐☐

Name *(not your trade name)*

Trade name *(if any)*

Address

Number   Street   Suite or room number

City   State   ZIP code

Foreign country name   Foreign province/county   Foreign postal code

Type of Return
(Check all that apply.)

☐ **a.** Amended

☐ **b.** Successor employer

☐ **c.** No payments to employees in 2020

☐ **d.** Final: Business closed or stopped paying wages

Go to *www.irs.gov/Form940* for instructions and the latest information.

Read the separate instructions before you complete this form. Please type or print within the boxes.

Part 1:   Tell us about your return. If any line does NOT apply, leave it blank. See instructions before completing Part 1.

1a If you had to pay state unemployment tax in one state only, enter the state abbreviation . **1a** ☐☐

1b If you had to pay state unemployment tax in more than one state, you are a multi-state employer . . . . **1b** ☐ Check here. Complete Schedule A (Form 940).

2   If you paid wages in a state that is subject to **CREDIT REDUCTION** . . . . **2** ☐ Check here. Complete Schedule A (Form 940).

Part 2:   Determine your FUTA tax before adjustments. If any line does NOT apply, leave it blank.

3   Total payments to all employees . . . . **3** ☐

4   Payments exempt from FUTA tax . . . . **4** ☐

Check all that apply: **4a** ☐ Fringe benefits   **4c** ☐ Retirement/Pension   **4e** ☐ Other
4b ☐ Group-term life insurance   **4d** ☐ Dependent care

5   Total of payments made to each employee in excess of $7,000 . . . . **5** ☐

6   Subtotal (line 4 + line 5 = line 6) . . . . **6** ☐

7   Total taxable FUTA wages (line 3 – line 6 = line 7). See instructions . . . . **7** ☐

8   FUTA tax before adjustments (line 7 × 0.006 = line 8) . . . . **8** ☐

Part 3:   Determine your adjustments. If any line does NOT apply, leave it blank.

9   If ALL of the taxable FUTA wages you paid were excluded from state unemployment tax, multiply line 7 by 0.054 (line 7 × 0.054 = line 9). Go to line 12 . . . . **9** ☐

10 If SOME of the taxable FUTA wages you paid were excluded from state unemployment tax, OR you paid ANY state unemployment tax late (after the due date for filing Form 940), complete the worksheet in the instructions. Enter the amount from line 7 of the worksheet . . **10** ☐

11 If credit reduction applies, enter the total from Schedule A (Form 940) . . . . **11** ☐

Part 4:   Determine your FUTA tax and balance due or overpayment. If any line does NOT apply, leave it blank.

12 Total FUTA tax after adjustments (lines 8 + 9 + 10 + 11 = line 12) . . . . **12** ☐

13 FUTA tax deposited for the year, including any overpayment applied from a prior year . **13** ☐

14 Balance due. If line 12 is more than line 13, enter the excess on line 14.
• If line 14 is more than $500, you must deposit your tax.
• If line 14 is $500 or less, you may pay with this return. See instructions . . . . **14** ☐

15 Overpayment. If line 13 is more than line 12, enter the excess on line 15 and check a box below **15** ☐

▶ You **MUST** complete both pages of this form and **SIGN** it.   Check one: ☐ Apply to next return. ☐ Send a refund.

Next ▶

For Privacy Act and Paperwork Reduction Act Notice, see the back of the Payment Voucher.   Cat. No. 11234O   Form **940** (2020)

850212

Name *(not your trade name)*	Employer identification number (EIN)

Part 5:   Report your FUTA tax liability by quarter only if line 12 is more than $500. If not, go to Part 6.

16   Report the amount of your FUTA tax liability for each quarter; do NOT enter the amount you deposited. If you had no liability for a quarter, leave the line blank.

16a   **1st quarter** (January 1 – March 31) . . . .   **16a**   [.   ]

16b   **2nd quarter** (April 1 – June 30) . . . .   **16b**   [.   ]

16c   **3rd quarter** (July 1 – September 30) . . . .   **16c**   [.   ]

16d   **4th quarter** (October 1 – December 31) . . . . .   **16d**   [.   ]

17   Total tax liability for the year (lines 16a + 16b + 16c + 16d = line 17) **17**   [.   ]   **Total must equal line 12.**

Part 6:   May we speak with your third-party designee?

Do you want to allow an employee, a paid tax preparer, or another person to discuss this return with the IRS? See the instructions for details.

☐ **Yes.**   Designee's name and phone number   [   ]   [   ]

Select a 5-digit personal identification number (PIN) to use when talking to the IRS.   [   ] [   ] [   ] [   ] [   ]

☐ **No.**

Part 7:   Sign here. You MUST complete both pages of this form and SIGN it.

Under penalties of perjury, I declare that I have examined this return, including accompanying schedules and statements, and to the best of my knowledge and belief, it is true, correct, and complete, and that no part of any payment made to a state unemployment fund claimed as a credit was, or is to be, deducted from the payments made to employees. Declaration of preparer (other than taxpayer) is based on all information of which preparer has any knowledge.

✗ **Sign your name here**   [   ]

Print your name here   [   ]

Print your title here   [   ]

Date   [/   /   ]

Best daytime phone   [   ]

Paid Preparer Use Only   Check if you are self-employed ☐

Preparer's name	[ ]	PTIN	[ ]
Preparer's signature	[ ]	Date	[/ /]
Firm's name (or yours if self-employed)	[ ]	EIN	[ ]
Address	[ ]	Phone	[ ]
City	[ ] State [ ]	ZIP code	[ ]

EXAMPLE Alan works for an employer whose qualified retirement plan states that Alan will receive a retirement benefit at age 65 equal to 40 percent of his last year's salary. The employer must make adequate contributions to the plan to enable the stated retirement benefit to be paid (a sufficient amount of money must be in the plan upon Alan's retirement to pay for Alan's defined retirement benefit). This plan is a defined benefit plan. ♦

9-7c Limitations on Contributions to and Benefits from Qualified Plans

Employee and employer contributions to qualified plans are subject to certain dollar or percentage limitations. Under a defined contribution plan (including profit sharing plans), the annual addition to an employee's account is generally not allowed to exceed the lesser of $57,000 (in 2020) or 25 percent of the employee's compensation. Under a defined benefit plan, the annual benefit payable to an employee upon retirement is limited to the lesser of $230,000 (for 2020) or 100 percent of the employee's average compensation for the highest three consecutive years of employment. The operational rules for qualified pension plans and the other types of qualified plans are complex.

Self-Study Problem 9.7 *See Appendix E for Solutions to Self-Study Problems*

Jeannie is employed by a business that operates a qualified profit-sharing plan.

a. In 2020, when her compensation is $50,000, what is the maximum contribution the business can make for her?

$_____

b. If Jeannie's salary was $250,000, what is the maximum contribution?

$_____

Learning Objective 9.8

Explain the pension plan rollover rules.

9-8 ROLLOVERS

In many situations, taxpayers need to transfer assets from one retirement plan to another plan of the same or different type. For example, the taxpayer may change jobs, take early retirement, or simply seek a better retirement fund manager. There are two ways this transfer can be accomplished: (1) direct transfer, also known as a trustee-to-trustee transfer, and (2) rollover of the distribution, in whole or in part, to an IRA or other qualified plan. There are potentially different tax treatments for the two types of transfers.

9-8a Direct Transfers

In direct transfers, the taxpayer instructs the trustee of the retirement plan to transfer assets to the trustee of another plan. There are no current-year tax consequences for this transaction. Also, there is no limit to the dollar amount of the transfer or the number of times a taxpayer can do this in a single tax year.

EXAMPLE Juan has $90,000 in a Section 401(k) plan with his employer. He also has two IRAs, one with ABC Bank ($20,000) and one with XYZ Mutual Fund ($30,000). In March of 20XX, Juan instructs ABC Bank to make a direct transfer to XYZ Mutual Fund of all of his funds ($20,000). In August of 20XX, Juan quits his job and instructs the trustee of the Section 401(k) plan to transfer his $90,000 directly to XYZ Mutual Fund. On December 31, 20XX, Juan has $140,000 in his XYZ Mutual Fund IRA. Since the two transactions were direct transfers, there are no tax consequences to Juan in the current year. ♦

9-8b Distribution Rollovers

In a distribution rollover, the taxpayer receives a distribution of funds from a retirement plan and then transfers part or all of the funds to the new retirement plan trustee. The taxpayer has a maximum of 60 days in which to transfer funds to the new plan and avoid taxes and penalties. The 60-day rollover period may be waived in cases of casualty, disaster, and other events beyond the reasonable control of the taxpayer such as death, disability, incarceration, and postal error. The 60-day time limit is extended to 120 days for first-time home buyers.

The major drawback to distribution rollovers is that the trustee must withhold 20 percent of the amount distributed for federal income taxes, giving the taxpayer only 80 percent of the amount in his or her plan. However, the taxpayer must contribute 100 percent of the amount in the old plan to the new trustee within the required 60-day period to avoid tax on the distribution. Amounts that are not placed in a new plan within the required period are taxable as ordinary income in the current year. Also, if the taxpayer is under 59½ years old, the portion of the retirement plan distribution not transferred will be subject to a 10 percent penalty tax.

The exception to mandatory withholding is a distribution from an IRA; such distributions are not subject to the 20 percent withholding tax. Also, taxpayers are allowed only one distribution rollover each year for transfers from one IRA to another IRA. There are many other complex rules concerning retirement plan rollovers.

EXAMPLE   Bea is 50 years old, has worked for Gold Company for 25 years, and has $200,000 in her retirement plan. This year, Gold Company is purchased by Green Company. As a result of the takeover, Bea was laid off. Bea requests a distribution of her $200,000 from Gold Company's retirement plan. The trustee of Gold's retirement plan must withhold $40,000 (20 percent of $200,000) from the distribution. Bea only receives $160,000 from her retirement plan distribution. If Bea wants to roll her funds into an IRA and avoid taxes, she must contribute $200,000, even though she only received $160,000. If Bea has no other resources and cannot make up the $40,000, the amount not contributed to the IRA will be taxable income to her and subject to a 10 percent penalty. If Bea makes the total rollover contribution of $200,000 within the 60-day timeframe, then the distribution will be nontaxable. The $40,000 will be reported as taxes withheld on her tax return. ◆

Self-Study Problem 9.8   *See Appendix E for Solutions to Self-Study Problems*

Carol, age 40, has an IRA with Blue Mutual Fund. Her balance in the fund is $150,000. She has heard good things about the management of Red Mutual Fund, so she opens a Red Fund IRA. Carol requests her balance from the Blue Fund be distributed to her on July 1, 20XX. She opted to have no withholding on the distribution.

a. How much will Carol receive from the Blue Fund IRA?

$_____

b. If the funds were distributed from a qualified retirement plan (not an IRA), how much would Carol receive?

$_____

c. When is the last day Carol can roll over the amount received into the Red Fund IRA and avoid taxation in the current year?

$_____

d. Assuming the funds were distributed from a qualified retirement plan, not from an IRA, how much will Carol have to contribute to the Red Fund IRA to avoid taxable income and any penalties?

$_____

KEY TERMS

Form W-4, 9-2
IRS online withholding estimator, 9-2
exempt, 9-4
percentage method, 9-9
IRS Publication 15-T, "Federal Income Tax Withholding Methods," 9-10
wage bracket method, 9-11
backup withholding, 9-14
estimated payments, 9-14
required annual payment, 9-15
FICA, 9-16
Social Security, 9-16
Medicare, 9-16

OASDI, 9-16
Employee retention credit, 9-18
Sick leave credit, 9-20
Family leave credit, 9-22
Paycheck Protection Program, 9-23
Employee payroll tax deferral, 9-23
monthly or semiweekly depositors, 9-25
special one-day deposit rule, 9-25
EFTPS, 9-25
Form 941, 9-25
Form W-2, 9-33
Form W-3, 9-33

Form 1099, 9-34
FUTA, 9-36
Form 940, 9-36
qualified plan, 9-37
pension plans, 9-37
profit-sharing plans, 9-37
stock bonus plans, 9-37
Employee Stock Ownership Plans (ESOPs), 9-37
defined contribution plan, 9-37
defined benefit plan, 9-37
trustee-to-trustee transfer, 9-40
rollover, 9-41

KEY POINTS

Learning Objectives	Key Points
LO 9.1: Compute the income tax withholding from employee wages.	• Employers are required to withhold taxes from amounts paid to employees for wages, including salaries, fees, bonuses, commissions, vacation and retirement pay. • Form W-4, showing the filing status and possible adjustments to withholding is furnished to the employer by the employee. • The percentage method and the wage bracket method of withholding are prescribed for the pre-2020 Form W-4 and the new 2020 Forms W-4. • Tip income must be reported using one of several methods.
LO 9.2: Determine taxpayers' quarterly estimated payments.	• Self-employed taxpayers are not subject to withholding; however, they must make quarterly estimated tax payments. • Estimated payments are made in four installments on April 15, June 15, and September 15 of the tax year, and January 15 of the following year. • Any individual taxpayer who has estimated tax for the year of $1,000 or more, after subtracting withholding, and whose withholding does not equal or exceed the "required annual payment," must make quarterly estimated payments. • The required annual payment is the smallest of three amounts: (1) 90 percent of the tax shown on the current year's return, (2) 100 percent (or 110 percent at higher income levels) of the tax shown on the preceding year's return, or (3) 90 percent of the current-year tax determined each quarter on an annualized basis.
LO 9.3: Compute the FICA tax.	• For 2020, the Social Security (OASDI) tax rate is 6.2 percent and the Medicare tax rate is 1.45 percent for employers and employees. The maximum wage subject to the Social Security portion of the FICA tax is $137,700 for 2020, and all wages are subject to the Medicare portion of the FICA tax. • Taxpayers working for more than one employer during the same tax year may pay more than the maximum amount of Social Security taxes. If this happens, the taxpayer should compute the excess taxes paid, and report the excess on as a payment against his or her income tax liability. • Due to the COVID-19 pandemic, a series of temporary payroll tax incentives were put in place in 2020 including the employee retention credit, sick and family leave credits, the Paycheck Protection Program, and a possible employee payroll tax deferral.

LO 9.4: Apply the federal deposit system to payroll withholding.	• Employers must make periodic deposits of the taxes that are withheld from employees' wages. Deposits must be made electronically. • Employers are either monthly or semiweekly depositors, depending on the total amount of income taxes withheld from wages and FICA taxes attributable to wages. However, if withholding and FICA taxes of $100,000 or more are accumulated at any time during the year, the depositor is subject to a special one-day deposit rule. • Due to the COVID-19 pandemic, payroll tax deferral was implemented for the employer's share of Social Security tax, of which one-half can be deferred until December 31, 2021 and the remaining half can be deferred until December 31, 2022.
LO 9.5: Prepare employer payroll reporting.	• On or before January 31 of the year following the calendar year of payment, an employer must furnish to each employee two copies of the employee's Wage and Tax Statement, Form W-2, for the previous calendar year. • The original copy (Copy A) of all Forms W-2 and Form W-3 (Transmittal of Wage and Tax Statements) must be filed with the Social Security Administration by January 31 of the year following the calendar year of payment. • Forms 1099 must be mailed to the recipients by January 31 of the year following the calendar year of payment.
LO 9.6: Compute the amount of FUTA tax for an employer.	• The FUTA (Federal Unemployment Tax Act) tax is not withheld from employees' wages, but instead is paid in full by employers. • The federal unemployment tax rate is 6.0 percent of an employee's wages up to $7,000. A credit of up to 5.4 percent is allowed if state unemployment taxes are paid, resulting in an effective federal unemployment tax rate of 0.6 percent.
LO 9.7: Describe the general rules for qualified retirement plans.	• In order to be qualified, retirement plans must meet certain requirements related to non-discrimination of lower compensated employees, participation eligibility, vesting requirements, and distribution rules.
LO 9.8: Explain the pension plan rollover rules.	• There are two ways to transfer assets from one retirement plan to another of the same or different type: (1) a direct transfer, also known as a trustee-to-trustee transfer, and (2) a rollover of an actual cash distribution, in whole or in part, to an IRA or other qualified plan. • There are no current-year tax consequences for a direct trustee-to-trustee transfer. • Distribution rollovers are subject to a 60-day time limit for completion and may also be subject to income tax withholding and tax penalties.

QUESTIONS and PROBLEMS

GROUP 1:
MULTIPLE CHOICE QUESTIONS

LO 9.1

1. Which of the following amounts paid by an employer to an employee is *not* subject to withholding?
   a. Salary
   b. Bonus
   c. Commissions
   d. Reimbursement of expenses under a non-accountable plan
   e. All of the above are subject to withholding

LO 9.1 2. Abbe, age 56, started a new job in 2020. At Abbe's previous employer she had filed a Form W-4 with 5 allowances. Abbe's new employer will:

    a. use a copy of Abbe's previous Form W-4 to calculate income tax withholding.

    b. permit Abbe to file a new W-4 using either the old allowances method or the new method.

    c. require Abbe to complete a new 2020 version of Form W-4.

    d. require Abbe to withhold as a single taxpayers with no dependents.

    e. require Abbe to use the IRS on-line withholding estimator.

LO 9.1 3. Michele is single with no dependents and earns $32,000 this year. Michele claims exempt on her Form W-4. Which of the following is correct concerning her Form W-4?

    a. Michele may not under any circumstances claim exempt.

    b. Michele's employer will require her to verify that she had no tax liability and expects to have none this year.

    c. Michele's employer must require her to prepare a corrected Form W-4 under any circumstances. If Michele is unwilling to update her Form W-4, then her employer should disregard her Form W-4 and withhold at the single taxpayer rate with no allowances.

    d. Michele's employer will submit a copy of her W-4 to the IRS if directed to do so by written notice.

    e. None of the above is correct.

LO 9.1 4. Flo is a server at a diner in Phoenix and earns a significant portion of her pay through tips from customers. Some of these tips are paid via credit card and others are paid in cash. Flo's employer will:

    a. withhold employment taxes but no income taxes on the tips

    b. withhold both employment and income taxes on the cash tips but only employment taxes on the tips paid by credit card

    c. withhold both employment and income taxes on all tips

    d. not withhold any taxes on cash tips but will withhold both employment and income taxes on credit card tips

LO 9.1 5. The process for employee withholding involves:

    a. using only a 2020 Form W-4 for all employees to calculate income tax withholding.

    b. using a 2020 Form W-4 for new employees (all existing employees must use a pre-2020 Form W-4) to calculate income tax withholding.

    c. the employee provides filing status and the employer completes the Form W-4 and submits to the IRS for proper withholding.

    d. Existing employees may use either their previous Form W-4 or may complete a new 2020 Form W-4 and new employees must complete a 2020 Form W-4 and the employer uses those forms to calculate income tax withholding.

LO 9.2 6. Typically, estimated payments for individual taxpayers are due on the following dates:

    a. Twice a year on April 15 and September 15

    b. Four installments on April 15, June 15, September 15, and January 15 of the next year

    c. Four times a year on April 15, July 15, September 15, and December 15

    d. Twice a year on June 15 and December 15

LO 9.2 7. Amy is a single taxpayer. Her income tax liability in the prior year was $3,803. Amy earns $50,000 of income ratably during the current year and her tax liability is $4,315. In order to avoid penalty, Amy's smallest amount of required annual withholding and estimated payments is:

    a. $3,423

    b. $3,803

    c. $3,884

    d. $4,315

    e. $4,747

LO 9.2

8. Jane is a single taxpayer with a current year AGI of $181,000 and current year income tax liability of $34,968. Her AGI in the prior year was $150,400 and prior year tax liability was $27,247. Jane earns her income ratably during the year. In order to avoid penalty, the smallest amount of required annual withholding and estimated payments is:
   a. $27,247
   b. $29,972
   c. $31,471
   d. $34,968
   e. $35,400

LO 9.3

9. Which of the following is *not* true about FICA taxes?
   a. The FICA tax has two parts, Social Security (Old Age, Survivors, and Disability Insurance) and Medicare.
   b. In 2020, the maximum wage base for Social Security tax withholding is $132,900.
   c. In 2020, there is no maximum wage base for Medicare tax withholding.
   d. When employees work for more than one employer and exceed the maximum wage base for Social Security tax withholding in total, they are allowed a refund of excess tax withheld.

LO 9.3

10. Terry worked for two employers during 2020. The amount of wages paid to Terry by both employers totaled $168,400 and the employers properly withheld both income and employment taxes. As a result of Terry's two jobs:
    a. Terry will receive a credit against his employment taxes in 2020 from his second employer.
    b. Terry will complete a new Form W-4 for his second employer that will direct the employer to withhold no employment taxes.
    c. Terry will claim a credit for excess Social Security taxes paid on his 2020 income tax return.
    d. Terry will claim an employee retention credit in 2020.
    e. Terry will file a Form 843 with the Social Security Administration to claim back excess withheld employment taxes.

LO 9.3

11. (COVID provisions) Yeet Inc. has 14 employees in 2020. Yeet's 2020 second quarter business was 70 percent lower than 2019 due to COVID-related impacts. Yeet was able to stay in business and kept ten of the fourteen employees working and paid each of them $8,000 in the quarter. In a effort to show solidarity, Yeet paid the four nonworking employees the same amount also. Yeet did not take a PPP loan. Yeet will take an employee retention credit for:
    a. 100 percent of the wages paid to the four nonworking employees.
    b. 50 percent of the wages paid to the four nonworking employees.
    c. 70 percent of the wages paid to all fourteen employees.
    d. 50 percent of the wages paid to all fourteen employees, whether working or not.
    e. 70 percent of the ten working employees.

LO 9.4

12. Employers generally must file a quarterly tax return showing the amount of wages paid and the amount of income tax and FICA tax withholding due. This tax return is filed on:
    a. Form 944 or Form 945
    b. Schedule H
    c. Schedule SE
    d. Form 941

LO 9.4

13. Yamin operates a small business with a few part-time employees. Her annual employment tax withholding in 2020 is $467.80. Yamin should file which employment tax reporting form?
    a. Form 944
    b. Form 940
    c. Form 941
    d. Form 9000
    e. Form 409

LO 9.4   14. (COVID provisions) In 2020, Tyck Tock Corp. paid wages of $105,000 to employees, none of which make more than the 2020 FICA cap. The Social Security tax (employer and employee share) is $13,020. No employee elected to defer payroll taxes. What best describes Tyck Tock's payroll tax payments if they elect to defer?
   a. All $13,020 is due by December 31, 2020.
   b. $6,510 is due as normal while $6,510 can be paid no later than December 31, 2020.
   c. $6,510 is due as normal while $3,255 is due by December 31, 2021 and the remainder is due by December 31, 2022.
   d. $6,510 is due by December 31, 2020 and the remainder is due by December 31, 2021.
   e. All $13,020 is due no later than December 31, 2022.

LO 9.5   15. Which of the following forms is used to report wages, tips and other compensation paid to employees?
   a. Form W-4
   b. Form W-2G
   c. Form W-2
   d. Form 1099-R
   e. Form 1099-MISC

LO 9.5   16. Which of the following forms is used to report non-employee compensation?
   a. Form W-2G
   b. Form 1099-MISC
   c. Form 1099-G
   d. Form 1099-NEC
   e. Form 1099-Comp

LO 9.6   17. The FUTA tax is:
   a. An unemployment tax with a rate of 2.9 percent up to $137,700 of salary per employee.
   b. A disability tax with a rate of 2.9 percent up to $7,000 of salary per employee.
   c. An unemployment tax with a rate as low as 0.6 percent up to $7,000 of salary per employee.
   d. A disability tax with a rate of 0.6 percent up to $100,000 of salary per employee.

LO 9.6   18. Wei has four employees: Anna, Kenny, Stan, and Seth, who were paid $12,000, $5,000, $8,000, and $3,000, respectively. Assuming a full state credit, Wei's FUTA taxable wages for the year are:
   a. $28,000
   b. $21,000
   c. $22,000
   d. $186

LO 9.7   19. Gail's employer contributes $2,000 (5 percent of her $40,000 salary) to a qualified retirement plan for Gail. This pension plan is what kind of plan?
   a. Defined benefit plan
   b. Defined contribution plan
   c. Employee Stock Ownership Plan
   d. Profit-sharing plan
   e. None of the above

LO 9.8   20. When taxpayers receive distributions from qualified retirement plans, how much time is allowed to roll over the amount received into a new plan to avoid paying taxes on the distribution in the current year, assuming there are no unusual events?
   a. 180 days
   b. 90 days
   c. 60 days
   d. 1 year
   e. There is no time limit

LO 9.8

21. Tom quits his job with $150,000 in his employer's qualified retirement plan. Since he is broke, Tom instructs the plan trustee to pay him the balance in his retirement account. How much will Tom receive when he gets his check from the retirement plan?
    a. $120,000
    b. $100,000
    c. $96,000
    d. $24,000
    e. Some other amount

LO 9.8

22. Betty owns three separate IRA accounts with different banks. She wishes to consolidate her three IRAs into one IRA in 2020. How many distribution rollovers may Betty make in 2020?
    a. One
    b. Two
    c. Four
    d. Ten
    e. There is no limit

LO 9.8

23. Bonnie is getting close to retirement and realizes she has three different IRA accounts at three different financial institutions. To make life simpler, Bonnie wishes to consolidate her three IRAs into a single account in 2020 using trustee-to-trustee direct rollovers. How many rollovers of this type can Bonnie make in 2020?
    a. One
    b. Two
    c. Four
    d. Ten
    e. There is no limit

GROUP 2: PROBLEMS

LO 9.1

1. Phan Mai is single with two dependent children under age 17. Phan estimates her wages for the year will be $42,000 and her itemized deductions will be $14,000. In the previous year, Phan had a small tax liability. Assuming Phan files as head of household, use page 1 of Form W-4 on Page 9-49 to determine what Phan should report on lines 3, 4(a), 4(b), and 4(c).

LO 9.1

2. Ralph and Kathy Gump are married with one 20-year-old dependent child. Ralph expects to earn $98,000 (paid monthly) and estimates their itemized deductions to be $29,500 for the year. Kathy expects to earn wages of $54,000. The Gumps expect to have for AGI deductions of $3,600. Use Form W-4 and worksheet on Pages 9-49 to 9-52 to determine what Ralph should report on lines 3, 4(a), 4(b), and 4(c) of Form W-4.

LO 9.1

3. Sophie is a single taxpayer. For the first payroll period in July 2020, she is paid wages of $2,200 monthly. Sophie claims one allowance on her pre-2020 Form W-4.
    a. Use the percentage method to calculate the amount of Sophie's withholding for a monthly pay period.

    $ _____

    b. Use the wage bracket method to determine the amount of Sophie's withholding for the same period.

    $ _____

    c. Use the percentage method assuming Sophie completed a 2020 Form W-4 and checked only the single box in Step 1(c).

    d. Use the wage bracket method using the same assumptions in part c of this question.

LO 9.1

4. Cassie works at Capital Bank and is in charge of issuing Forms 1099 to bank customers. Please describe for Cassie the 4 possible situations that require the bank to implement backup withholding on a customer.

_____

_____

_____

_____

_____

_____

_____

LO 9.2

5. Sherina Smith (Social Security number 785-23-9873) lives at 536 West Lapham Street, Milwaukee, WI 53204, and is self-employed for 2020. She estimates her required annual estimated income tax payment for 2020 to be $8,468. She was required to pay $254 when she timely filed her prior year tax return. Complete the first quarter voucher below for Sherina for 2020.

Form **1040-ES** Department of the Treasury Internal Revenue Service	20**20 Estimated Tax**	Payment Voucher **1** OMB No. 1545-0074

File only if you are making a payment of estimated tax by check or money order. Mail this voucher with your check or money order payable to **"United States Treasury."** Write your social security number and "2020 Form 1040-ES" on your check or money order. Do not send cash. Enclose, but do not staple or attach, your payment with this voucher.

Calendar year—Due April 15, 2020

Amount of estimated tax you are paying by check or money order.

	Dollars	Cents

Pay online at www.irs.gov/etpay

**Simple.
Fast.
Secure.**

Print or type

Your first name and middle initial	Your last name	Your social security number
If joint payment, complete for spouse		
Spouse's first name and middle initial	Spouse's last name	Spouse's social security number
Address (number, street, and apt. no.)		
City, state, and ZIP code. (If a foreign address, enter city, also complete spaces below.)		
Foreign country name	Foreign province/county	Foreign postal code

For Privacy Act and Paperwork Reduction Act Notice, see instructions.   **Form 1040-ES (2020)**

Form **W-4**	**Employee's Withholding Certificate**	OMB No. 1545-0074
Department of the Treasury Internal Revenue Service	▶ Complete Form W-4 so that your employer can withhold the correct federal income tax from your pay. ▶ Give Form W-4 to your employer. ▶ Your withholding is subject to review by the IRS.	20**20**

Step 1:
Enter Personal Information

(a) First name and middle initial	Last name	(b) Social security number
Address		▶ **Does your name match the name on your social security card?** If not, to ensure you get credit for your earnings, contact SSA at 800-772-1213 or go to *www.ssa.gov.*
City or town, state, and ZIP code		

(c) ☐ **Single or Married filing separately**

☐ **Married filing jointly** (or Qualifying widow(er))

☐ **Head of household** (Check only if you're unmarried and pay more than half the costs of keeping up a home for yourself and a qualifying individual.)

Complete Steps 2–4 ONLY if they apply to you; otherwise, skip to Step 5. See page 2 for more information on each step, who can claim exemption from withholding, when to use the online estimator, and privacy.

Step 2:
Multiple Jobs or Spouse Works

Complete this step if you (1) hold more than one job at a time, or (2) are married filing jointly and your spouse also works. The correct amount of withholding depends on income earned from all of these jobs.

Do **only one** of the following.

(a) Use the estimator at *www.irs.gov/W4App* for most accurate withholding for this step (and Steps 3–4); **or**

(b) Use the Multiple Jobs Worksheet on page 3 and enter the result in Step 4(c) below for roughly accurate withholding; **or**

(c) If there are only two jobs total, you may check this box. Do the same on Form W-4 for the other job. This option is accurate for jobs with similar pay; otherwise, more tax than necessary may be withheld . . . . . ▶ ☐

TIP: To be accurate, submit a 2020 Form W-4 for all other jobs. If you (or your spouse) have self-employment income, including as an independent contractor, use the estimator.

Complete Steps 3–4(b) on Form W-4 for only ONE of these jobs. Leave those steps blank for the other jobs. (Your withholding will be most accurate if you complete Steps 3–4(b) on the Form W-4 for the highest paying job.)

Step 3:
Claim Dependents

If your income will be $200,000 or less ($400,000 or less if married filing jointly):

Multiply the number of qualifying children under age 17 by $2,000 ▶ $ _____

Multiply the number of other dependents by $500 . . . . ▶ $ _____

Add the amounts above and enter the total here . . . . | **3** | $ |

Step 4 (optional):
Other Adjustments

(a) **Other income (not from jobs).** If you want tax withheld for other income you expect this year that won't have withholding, enter the amount of other income here. This may include interest, dividends, and retirement income . . . . | **4(a)** | $ |

(b) **Deductions.** If you expect to claim deductions other than the standard deduction and want to reduce your withholding, use the Deductions Worksheet on page 3 and enter the result here . . . . | **4(b)** | $ |

(c) **Extra withholding.** Enter any additional tax you want withheld each **pay period** . | **4(c)** | $ |

Step 5:
Sign Here

Under penalties of perjury, I declare that this certificate, to the best of my knowledge and belief, is true, correct, and complete.

▶ _____
Employee's signature (This form is not valid unless you sign it.)

▶ _____
Date

Employers Only	Employer's name and address	First date of employment	Employer identification number (EIN)

For Privacy Act and Paperwork Reduction Act Notice, see page 3.   Cat. No. 10220Q   Form **W-4** (2020)

Form W-4 (2020)   Page **2**

General Instructions

Future Developments

For the latest information about developments related to Form W-4, such as legislation enacted after it was published, go to *www.irs.gov/FormW4*.

Purpose of Form

Complete Form W-4 so that your employer can withhold the correct federal income tax from your pay. If too little is withheld, you will generally owe tax when you file your tax return and may owe a penalty. If too much is withheld, you will generally be due a refund. Complete a new Form W-4 when changes to your personal or financial situation would change the entries on the form. For more information on withholding and when you must furnish a new Form W-4, see Pub. 505.

Exemption from withholding. You may claim exemption from withholding for 2020 if you meet both of the following conditions: you had no federal income tax liability in 2019 **and** you expect to have no federal income tax liability in 2020. You had no federal income tax liability in 2019 if (1) your total tax on line 16 on your 2019 Form 1040 or 1040-SR is zero (or less than the sum of lines 18a, 18b, and 18c), or (2) you were not required to file a return because your income was below the filing threshold for your correct filing status. If you claim exemption, you will have no income tax withheld from your paycheck and may owe taxes and penalties when you file your 2020 tax return. To claim exemption from withholding, certify that you meet both of the conditions above by writing "Exempt" on Form W-4 in the space below Step 4(c). Then, complete Steps 1(a), 1(b), and 5. Do not complete any other steps. You will need to submit a new Form W-4 by February 16, 2021.

Your privacy. If you prefer to limit information provided in Steps 2 through 4, use the online estimator, which will also increase accuracy.

As an alternative to the estimator: if you have concerns with Step 2(c), you may choose Step 2(b); if you have concerns with Step 4(a), you may enter an additional amount you want withheld per pay period in Step 4(c). If this is the only job in your household, you may instead check the box in Step 2(c), which will increase your withholding and significantly reduce your paycheck (often by thousands of dollars over the year).

When to use the estimator. Consider using the estimator at *www.irs.gov/W4App* if you:

1. Expect to work only part of the year;

2. Have dividend or capital gain income, or are subject to additional taxes, such as the additional Medicare tax;

3. Have self-employment income (see below); or

4. Prefer the most accurate withholding for multiple job situations.

Self-employment. Generally, you will owe both income and self-employment taxes on any self-employment income you receive separate from the wages you receive as an employee. If you want to pay these taxes through withholding from your wages, use the estimator at *www.irs.gov/W4App* to figure the amount to have withheld.

Specific Instructions

Step 1(c). Check your anticipated filing status. This will determine the standard deduction and tax rates used to compute your withholding.

Step 2. Use this step if you (1) have more than one job at the same time, or (2) are married filing jointly and you and your spouse both work.

Option **(a)** most accurately calculates the additional tax you need to have withheld, while option **(b)** does so with a little less accuracy.

If you (and your spouse) have a total of only two jobs, you may instead check the box in option **(c)**. The box must also be checked on the Form W-4 for the other job. If the box is checked, the standard deduction and tax brackets will be cut in half for each job to calculate withholding. This option is roughly accurate for jobs with similar pay; otherwise, more tax than necessary may be withheld, and this extra amount will be larger the greater the difference in pay is between the two jobs.

 Multiple jobs. *Complete Steps 3 through 4(b) on only one Form W-4. Withholding will be most accurate if you do this on the Form W-4 for the highest paying job.*

Step 3. Step 3 of Form W-4 provides instructions for determining the amount of the child tax credit and the credit for other dependents that you may be able to claim when you file your tax return. To qualify for the child tax credit, the child must be under age 17 as of December 31, must be your dependent who generally lives with you for more than half the year, and must have the required social security number. You may be able to claim a credit for other dependents for whom a child tax credit can't be claimed, such as an older child or a qualifying relative. For additional eligibility requirements for these credits, see Pub. 972, Child Tax Credit and Credit for Other Dependents. You can also include **other tax credits** in this step, such as education tax credits and the foreign tax credit. To do so, add an estimate of the amount for the year to your credits for dependents and enter the total amount in Step 3. Including these credits will increase your paycheck and reduce the amount of any refund you may receive when you file your tax return.

Step 4 (optional).

Step 4(a). Enter in this step the total of your other estimated income for the year, if any. You shouldn't include income from any jobs or self-employment. If you complete Step 4(a), you likely won't have to make estimated tax payments for that income. If you prefer to pay estimated tax rather than having tax on other income withheld from your paycheck, see Form 1040-ES, Estimated Tax for Individuals.

Step 4(b). Enter in this step the amount from the Deductions Worksheet, line 5, if you expect to claim deductions other than the basic standard deduction on your 2020 tax return and want to reduce your withholding to account for these deductions. This includes both itemized deductions and other deductions such as for student loan interest and IRAs.

Step 4(c). Enter in this step any additional tax you want withheld from your pay **each pay period**, including any amounts from the Multiple Jobs Worksheet, line 4. Entering an amount here will reduce your paycheck and will either increase

Form W-4 (2020)   Page **3**

Step 2(b)—Multiple Jobs Worksheet *(Keep for your records.)*

If you choose the option in Step 2(b) on Form W-4, complete this worksheet (which calculates the total extra tax for all jobs) on **only ONE** Form W-4. Withholding will be most accurate if you complete the worksheet and enter the result on the Form W-4 for the highest paying job.

Note: If more than one job has annual wages of more than $120,000 or there are more than three jobs, see Pub. 505 for additional tables; or, you can use the online withholding estimator at *www.irs.gov/W4App.*

1   **Two jobs.** If you have two jobs or you're married filing jointly and you and your spouse each have one job, find the amount from the appropriate table on page 4. Using the "Higher Paying Job" row and the "Lower Paying Job" column, find the value at the intersection of the two household salaries and enter that value on line 1. Then, **skip** to line 3 . . . .   **1** $ _____

2   **Three jobs.** If you and/or your spouse have three jobs at the same time, complete lines 2a, 2b, and 2c below. Otherwise, skip to line 3.

    a   Find the amount from the appropriate table on page 4 using the annual wages from the highest paying job in the "Higher Paying Job" row and the annual wages for your next highest paying job in the "Lower Paying Job" column. Find the value at the intersection of the two household salaries and enter that value on line 2a . . . .   **2a** $ _____

    b   Add the annual wages of the two highest paying jobs from line 2a together and use the total as the wages in the "Higher Paying Job" row and use the annual wages for your third job in the "Lower Paying Job" column to find the amount from the appropriate table on page 4 and enter this amount on line 2b . . . .   **2b** $ _____

    c   Add the amounts from lines 2a and 2b and enter the result on line 2c . . . .   **2c** $ _____

3   Enter the number of pay periods per year for the highest paying job. For example, if that job pays weekly, enter 52; if it pays every other week, enter 26; if it pays monthly, enter 12, etc. . . . . .   **3** _____

4   **Divide** the annual amount on line 1 or line 2c by the number of pay periods on line 3. Enter this amount here and in **Step 4(c)** of Form W-4 for the highest paying job (along with any other additional amount you want withheld) . . . .   **4** $ _____

Step 4(b)—Deductions Worksheet *(Keep for your records.)*

1   Enter an estimate of your 2020 itemized deductions (from Schedule A (Form 1040 or 1040-SR)). Such deductions may include qualifying home mortgage interest, charitable contributions, state and local taxes (up to $10,000), and medical expenses in excess of 7.5% of your income . . . .   **1** $ _____

2   Enter: { • $24,800 if you're married filing jointly or qualifying widow(er)

             • $18,650 if you're head of household   }   . . . .   **2** $ _____

             • $12,400 if you're single or married filing separately

3   If line 1 is greater than line 2, subtract line 2 from line 1. If line 2 is greater than line 1, enter "-0-" . .   **3** $ _____

4   Enter an estimate of your student loan interest, deductible IRA contributions, and certain other adjustments (from Part II of Schedule 1 (Form 1040 or 1040-SR)). See Pub. 505 for more information . . . .   **4** $ _____

5   **Add** lines 3 and 4. Enter the result here and in **Step 4(b)** of Form W-4 . . . .   **5** $ _____

Married Filing Jointly or Qualifying Widow(er)

Higher Paying Job Annual Taxable Wage & Salary	Lower Paying Job Annual Taxable Wage & Salary											
	$0 - 9,999	$10,000 - 19,999	$20,000 - 29,999	$30,000 - 39,999	$40,000 - 49,999	$50,000 - 59,999	$60,000 - 69,999	$70,000 - 79,999	$80,000 - 89,999	$90,000 - 99,999	$100,000 - 109,999	$110,000 - 120,000
$0 - 9,999	$0	$220	$850	$900	$1,020	$1,020	$1,020	$1,020	$1,020	$1,210	$1,870	$1,870
$10,000 - 19,999	220	1,220	1,900	2,100	2,220	2,220	2,220	2,220	2,410	3,410	4,070	4,070
$20,000 - 29,999	850	1,900	2,730	2,930	3,050	3,050	3,050	3,240	4,240	5,240	5,900	5,900
$30,000 - 39,999	900	2,100	2,930	3,130	3,250	3,250	3,440	4,440	5,440	6,440	7,100	7,100
$40,000 - 49,999	1,020	2,220	3,050	3,250	3,370	3,570	4,570	5,570	6,570	7,570	8,220	8,220
$50,000 - 59,999	1,020	2,220	3,050	3,250	3,570	4,570	5,570	6,570	7,570	8,570	9,220	9,220
$60,000 - 69,999	1,020	2,220	3,050	3,440	4,570	5,570	6,570	7,570	8,570	9,570	10,220	10,220
$70,000 - 79,999	1,020	2,220	3,240	4,440	5,570	6,570	7,570	8,570	9,570	10,570	11,220	11,240
$80,000 - 99,999	1,060	3,260	5,090	6,290	7,420	8,420	9,420	10,420	11,420	12,420	13,260	13,460
$100,000 - 149,999	1,870	4,070	5,900	7,100	8,220	9,320	10,520	11,720	12,920	14,120	14,980	15,180
$150,000 - 239,999	2,040	4,440	6,470	7,870	9,190	10,390	11,590	12,790	13,990	15,190	16,050	16,250
$240,000 - 259,999	2,040	4,440	6,470	7,870	9,190	10,390	11,590	12,790	13,990	15,520	17,170	18,170
$260,000 - 279,999	2,040	4,440	6,470	7,870	9,190	10,390	11,590	13,120	15,120	17,120	18,770	19,770
$280,000 - 299,999	2,040	4,440	6,470	7,870	9,190	10,720	12,720	14,720	16,720	18,720	20,370	21,370
$300,000 - 319,999	2,040	4,440	6,470	8,200	10,320	12,320	14,320	16,320	18,320	20,320	21,970	22,970
$320,000 - 364,999	2,720	5,920	8,750	10,950	13,070	15,070	17,070	19,070	21,290	23,590	25,540	26,840
$365,000 - 524,999	2,970	6,470	9,600	12,100	14,530	16,830	19,130	21,430	23,730	26,030	27,980	29,280
$525,000 and over	3,140	6,840	10,170	12,870	15,500	18,000	20,500	23,000	25,500	28,000	30,150	31,650

Single or Married Filing Separately

Higher Paying Job Annual Taxable Wage & Salary	Lower Paying Job Annual Taxable Wage & Salary											
	$0 - 9,999	$10,000 - 19,999	$20,000 - 29,999	$30,000 - 39,999	$40,000 - 49,999	$50,000 - 59,999	$60,000 - 69,999	$70,000 - 79,999	$80,000 - 89,999	$90,000 - 99,999	$100,000 - 109,999	$110,000 - 120,000
$0 - 9,999	$460	$940	$1,020	$1,020	$1,470	$1,870	$1,870	$1,870	$1,870	$2,040	$2,040	$2,040
$10,000 - 19,999	940	1,530	1,610	2,060	3,060	3,460	3,460	3,460	3,640	3,830	3,830	3,830
$20,000 - 29,999	1,020	1,610	2,130	3,130	4,130	4,540	4,540	4,720	4,920	5,110	5,110	5,110
$30,000 - 39,999	1,020	2,060	3,130	4,130	5,130	5,540	5,720	5,920	6,120	6,310	6,310	6,310
$40,000 - 59,999	1,870	3,460	4,540	5,540	6,690	7,290	7,490	7,690	7,890	8,080	8,080	8,080
$60,000 - 79,999	1,870	3,460	4,690	5,890	7,090	7,690	7,890	8,090	8,290	8,480	9,260	10,060
$80,000 - 99,999	2,020	3,810	5,090	6,290	7,490	8,090	8,290	8,490	9,470	10,460	11,260	12,060
$100,000 - 124,999	2,040	3,830	5,110	6,310	7,510	8,430	9,430	10,430	11,430	12,420	13,520	14,620
$125,000 - 149,999	2,040	3,830	5,110	7,030	9,030	10,430	11,430	12,580	13,880	15,170	16,270	17,370
$150,000 - 174,999	2,360	4,950	7,030	9,030	11,030	12,730	14,030	15,330	16,630	17,920	19,020	20,120
$175,000 - 199,999	2,720	5,310	7,540	9,840	12,140	13,840	15,140	16,440	17,740	19,030	20,130	21,230
$200,000 - 249,999	2,970	5,860	8,240	10,540	12,840	14,540	15,840	17,140	18,440	19,730	20,830	21,930
$250,000 - 399,999	2,970	5,860	8,240	10,540	12,840	14,540	15,840	17,140	18,440	19,730	20,830	21,930
$400,000 - 449,999	2,970	5,860	8,240	10,540	12,840	14,540	15,840	17,140	18,450	19,940	21,240	22,540
$450,000 and over	3,140	6,230	8,810	11,310	13,810	15,710	17,210	18,710	20,210	21,700	23,000	24,300

Head of Household

Higher Paying Job Annual Taxable Wage & Salary	Lower Paying Job Annual Taxable Wage & Salary											
	$0 - 9,999	$10,000 - 19,999	$20,000 - 29,999	$30,000 - 39,999	$40,000 - 49,999	$50,000 - 59,999	$60,000 - 69,999	$70,000 - 79,999	$80,000 - 89,999	$90,000 - 99,999	$100,000 - 109,999	$110,000 - 120,000
$0 - 9,999	$0	$830	$930	$1,020	$1,020	$1,020	$1,480	$1,870	$1,870	$1,930	$2,040	$2,040
$10,000 - 19,999	830	1,920	2,130	2,220	2,220	2,680	3,680	4,070	4,130	4,330	4,440	4,440
$20,000 - 29,999	930	2,130	2,350	2,430	2,900	3,900	4,900	5,340	5,540	5,740	5,850	5,850
$30,000 - 39,999	1,020	2,220	2,430	2,980	3,980	4,980	6,040	6,630	6,830	7,030	7,140	7,140
$40,000 - 59,999	1,020	2,530	3,750	4,830	5,860	7,060	8,260	8,850	9,050	9,250	9,360	9,360
$60,000 - 79,999	1,870	4,070	5,310	6,600	7,800	9,000	10,200	10,780	10,980	11,180	11,580	12,380
$80,000 - 99,999	1,900	4,300	5,710	7,000	8,200	9,400	10,600	11,180	11,670	12,670	13,580	14,380
$100,000 - 124,999	2,040	4,440	5,850	7,140	8,340	9,540	11,360	12,750	13,750	14,750	15,770	16,870
$125,000 - 149,999	2,040	4,440	5,850	7,360	9,360	11,360	13,360	14,750	16,010	17,310	18,520	19,620
$150,000 - 174,999	2,040	5,060	7,280	9,360	11,360	13,480	15,780	17,460	18,760	20,060	21,270	22,370
$175,000 - 199,999	2,720	5,920	8,130	10,480	12,780	15,080	17,380	19,070	20,370	21,670	22,880	23,980
$200,000 - 249,999	2,970	6,470	8,990	11,370	13,670	15,970	18,270	19,960	21,260	22,560	23,770	24,870
$250,000 - 349,999	2,970	6,470	8,990	11,370	13,670	15,970	18,270	19,960	21,260	22,560	23,770	24,870
$350,000 - 449,999	2,970	6,470	8,990	11,370	13,670	15,970	18,270	19,960	21,260	22,560	23,900	25,200
$450,000 and over	3,140	6,840	9,560	12,140	14,640	17,140	19,640	21,530	23,030	24,530	25,940	27,240

LO 9.2

6. Kana is a single wage earner with no dependents and taxable income of $168,700 in 2020. Her 2019 taxable income was $155,000 and tax liability was $31,375. Calculate the following (note: this question requires the use of the tax tables in Appendix A):

Kana's 2020 income tax liability $_____

Kana's minimum required 2020 annual payment necessary to avoid penalty $_____

LO 9.3

7. (No COVID provisions) Lamden Company paid its employee, Trudy, wages of $61,500 in 2020. Calculate the FICA tax:

Withheld from		
Trudy's wages:	Social Security	$_____
	Medicare	$_____
Paid by Lamden:	Social Security	$_____
	Medicare	$_____
Total FICA Tax		$_____

LO 9.3

8. (COVID provisions) Lamden Company paid its employee Trudy, wages of $61,500 in 2020. Of this amount, $2,400 was allocated to sick pay for two weeks due to Trudy's spouse contracting COVID and Trudy being quarantined. Trudy spent another 10 weeks at home caring for their children that were unable to attend school. Lamden allocated $10,000 in wages to family leave. Lamden allocated $6,000 of Trudy's wages to the employee retention credit (5 weeks). The allocation of health care costs is $200 per week. Compute Lamden's:

Credit for sick pay $_____

Credit for family leave $_____

Employee retention credit $_____

LO 9.3

9. (No COVID provisions) Fiduciary Investments paid its employee, Yolanda, wages of $139,000 in 2020. Calculate the FICA tax:

Withheld from		
Yolanda's wages:	Social Security	$_____
	Medicare	$_____
Paid by Fiduciary:	Social Security	$_____
	Medicare	$_____
Total FICA Tax		$_____

LO 9.3

10. Thuy worked as the assistant manager at Burger Crown through August 2020 and received wages of $81,000. Thuy then worked at Up and Down Burger starting in September of 2020 and received wages of $61,500. Calculate the amount of Thuy's overpayment of Social Security taxes that she should report on her 2020 Form 1040.

$ _____

LO 9.4

11. (No COVID provisions) Drew Fogelman operates a small business and his payroll records for the second quarter of 2020 reflect the following:

Employee	Matt D.	Jack F.	Avery F.	Tiffany Y.
Gross wages	$3,000.00	$1,400.00	$1,800.00	$4,200.00
Federal income tax withheld	45.00	18.00	25.00	191.00
FICA taxes	459.00	214.20	275.40	642.60

Drew's employee identification number is 34-4321321 and his business is located at 732 Nob Hill Blvd. in Yakima, WA 98902. Drew is eligible to pay his withholding at the time he files his quarterly Form 941. Complete pages 1 and 2 of Form 941 located on Pages 9-55 and 9-56 for Drew for the second quarter of 2020.

LO 9.4

12. (COVID provisions) Using the information from Problem 11, complete Form 941 and Worksheet 1 located on Pages 9-55 to 9-58 for Drew for the second quarter of 2020. Assume the following additional information:

   - Drew was eligible for the employee retention credit.
   - All of Jack's wages are for two weeks of sick pay. He was not paid for any other time in the second quarter.
   - All of Avery's wages cover 10 weeks of family leave. She was paid for no other time in the second quarter.
   - The allocation of health care costs is $600 for the quarter for each employee.

LO 9.5

13. For each of the following payments, indicate the form that should be used to report the payment:
   a. Interest of $400 paid by a bank   _____
   b. Payment of $400 in dividends by a corporation to a shareholder

                                                                          _____
   c. Periodic payments from a retirement plan   _____
   d. Salary as president of the company   _____
   e. Las Vegas keno winnings of $25,000   _____
   f. Payments made to a non-employee

Form **941 for 2020:** **Employer's QUARTERLY Federal Tax Return**
(Rev. April 2020)   Department of the Treasury — Internal Revenue Service

950120

OMB No. 1545-0029

Employer identification number (EIN) ☐☐ – ☐☐☐☐☐☐☐

Name *(not your trade name)* ☐

Trade name *(if any)* ☐

Address ☐
Number   Street   Suite or room number

☐ ☐
City   State   ZIP code

☐ ☐ ☐
Foreign country name   Foreign province/county   Foreign postal code

Report for this Quarter of 2020
(Check one.)

☑ **1:** January, February, March

☐ **2:** April, May, June

☐ **3:** July, August, September

☐ **4:** October, November, December

Go to *www.irs.gov/Form941* for instructions and the latest information.

Read the separate instructions before you complete Form 941. Type or print within the boxes.

Part 1: **Answer these questions for this quarter.**

1 Number of employees who received wages, tips, or other compensation for the pay period including: *June 12* (Quarter 2), *Sept. 12* (Quarter 3), or *Dec. 12* (Quarter 4) . . .   **1** ☐

2 Wages, tips, and other compensation . . . .   **2** ☐ .

3 Federal income tax withheld from wages, tips, and other compensation . . . . . .   **3** ☐ .

4 If no wages, tips, and other compensation are subject to social security or Medicare tax   ☐ Check and go to line 6.

	Column 1		Column 2
5a Taxable social security wages . .	☐ .	× 0.124 =	☐ .
5a (i) Qualified sick leave wages . .	☐ .	× 0.062 =	☐ .
5a (ii) Qualified family leave wages .	☐ .	× 0.062 =	☐ .
5b Taxable social security tips . . .	☐ .	× 0.124 =	☐ .
5c Taxable Medicare wages & tips . .	☐ .	× 0.029 =	☐ .
5d Taxable wages & tips subject to Additional Medicare Tax withholding	☐ .	× 0.009 =	☐ .

5e Total social security and Medicare taxes. Add Column 2 from lines 5a, 5a(i), 5a(ii), 5b, 5c, and 5d   **5e** ☐ .

5f Section 3121(q) Notice and Demand—Tax due on unreported tips (see instructions) . .   **5f** ☐ .

6 Total taxes before adjustments. Add lines 3, 5e, and 5f . . . .   **6** ☐ .

7 Current quarter's adjustment for fractions of cents . . . .   **7** ☐ .

8 Current quarter's adjustment for sick pay . . . .   **8** ☐ .

9 Current quarter's adjustments for tips and group-term life insurance . . . . . .   **9** ☐ .

10 Total taxes after adjustments. Combine lines 6 through 9 . . . .   **10** ☐ .

11a Qualified small business payroll tax credit for increasing research activities. Attach Form 8974   **11a** ☐ .

11b Nonrefundable portion of credit for qualified sick and family leave wages from Worksheet 1   **11b** ☐ .

11c Nonrefundable portion of employee retention credit from Worksheet 1 . . . . . .   **11c** ☐ .

▶ **You MUST complete all three pages of Form 941 and SIGN it.**   Next ▶

For Privacy Act and Paperwork Reduction Act Notice, see the back of the Payment Voucher.   Cat. No. 17001Z   Form **941** (Rev. 4-2020)

950220

Name *(not your trade name)*   **Employer identification number (EIN)**

Part 1:	Answer these questions for this quarter. *(continued)*

11d Total nonrefundable credits. Add lines 11a, 11b, and 11c . . . . **11d** [▪   ]

12 Total taxes after adjustments and nonrefundable credits. Subtract line 11d from line 10 . **12** [▪   ]

13a Total deposits for this quarter, including overpayment applied from a prior quarter and overpayments applied from Form 941-X, 941-X (PR), 944-X, or 944-X (SP) filed in the current quarter **13a** [▪   ]

13b Deferred amount of the employer share of social security tax . . . . **13b** [▪   ]

13c Refundable portion of credit for qualified sick and family leave wages from Worksheet 1 **13c** [▪   ]

13d Refundable portion of employee retention credit from Worksheet 1 . . . . **13d** [▪   ]

13e Total deposits, deferrals, and refundable credits. Add lines 13a, 13b, 13c, and 13d . . . **13e** [▪   ]

13f Total advances received from filing Form(s) 7200 for the quarter . . . . **13f** [▪   ]

13g Total deposits, deferrals, and refundable credits less advances. Subtract line 13f from line 13e . **13g** [▪   ]

14 Balance due. If line 12 is more than line 13g, enter the difference and see instructions . . . **14** [▪   ]

15 Overpayment. If line 13g is more than line 12, enter the difference [▪   ] Check one: ☐ Apply to next return. ☐ Send a refund.

Part 2:	Tell us about your deposit schedule and tax liability for this quarter.

If you're unsure about whether you're a monthly schedule depositor or a semiweekly schedule depositor, see section 11 of Pub. 15.

16 Check one: ☐ Line 12 on this return is less than $2,500 or line 12 on the return for the prior quarter was less than $2,500, and you didn't incur a $100,000 next-day deposit obligation during the current quarter. If line 12 for the prior quarter was less than $2,500 but line 12 on this return is $100,000 or more, you must provide a record of your federal tax liability. If you're a monthly schedule depositor, complete the deposit schedule below; if you're a semiweekly schedule depositor, attach Schedule B (Form 941). Go to Part 3.

☐ **You were a monthly schedule depositor for the entire quarter.** Enter your tax liability for each month and total liability for the quarter, then go to Part 3.

   Tax liability: **Month 1** [▪   ]

   Month 2 [▪   ]

   Month 3 [▪   ]

   Total liability for quarter [▪   ]   **Total must equal line 12.**

☐ **You were a semiweekly schedule depositor for any part of this quarter.** Complete Schedule B (Form 941), Report of Tax Liability for Semiweekly Schedule Depositors, and attach it to Form 941. Go to Part 3.

▶ **You MUST complete all three pages of Form 941 and SIGN it.**   Next ▶

Page **2**   Form **941** (Rev. 4-2020)

950920

Name *(not your trade name)*   **Employer identification number (EIN)**

Part 3:	**Tell us about your business. If a question does NOT apply to your business, leave it blank.**

17 If your business has closed or you stopped paying wages . . . . ☐ Check here, and

      enter the final date you paid wages   ⬚ / / ⬚   ; also attach a statement to your return. See instructions.

18 If you're a seasonal employer and you don't have to file a return for every quarter of the year . . . ☐ Check here.

19 Qualified health plan expenses allocable to qualified sick leave wages . . . . . . **19** ⬚   . ⬚

20 Qualified health plan expenses allocable to qualified family leave wages . . . . . . **20** ⬚   . ⬚

21 Qualified wages for the employee retention credit . . . . **21** ⬚   . ⬚

22 Qualified health plan expenses allocable to wages reported on line 21 . . . . **22** ⬚   . ⬚

23 Credit from Form 5884-C, line 11, for this quarter . . . . **23** ⬚   . ⬚

24 Qualified wages paid March 13 through March 31, 2020, for the employee retention credit (use this line only for the second quarter filing of Form 941) . . . . **24** ⬚   . ⬚

25 Qualified health plan expenses allocable to wages reported on line 24 (use this line only for the second quarter filing of Form 941) . . . . **25** ⬚   . ⬚

Part 4:	**May we speak with your third-party designee?**

Do you want to allow an employee, a paid tax preparer, or another person to discuss this return with the IRS? See the instructions for details.

☐ Yes. Designee's name and phone number   ⬚   ⬚

        Select a 5-digit personal identification number (PIN) to use when talking to the IRS. ☐ ☐ ☐ ☐ ☐

☐ No.

Part 5:	**Sign here. You MUST complete all three pages of Form 941 and SIGN it.**

Under penalties of perjury, I declare that I have examined this return, including accompanying schedules and statements, and to the best of my knowledge and belief, it is true, correct, and complete. Declaration of preparer (other than taxpayer) is based on all information of which preparer has any knowledge.

X   **Sign your name here**   ⬚   Print your name here ⬚

                                        Print your title here ⬚

              Date ⬚ / / ⬚   Best daytime phone ⬚

Paid Preparer Use Only   Check if you're self-employed . . . ☐

Preparer's name ⬚   PTIN ⬚

Preparer's signature ⬚   Date ⬚ / / ⬚

Firm's name (or yours if self-employed) ⬚   EIN ⬚

Address ⬚   Phone ⬚

City ⬚   State ⬚   ZIP code ⬚

                                                 Form **941** (Rev. 4-2020)

Worksheet 1. Credit for Qualified Sick and Family Leave Wages and the Employee Retention Credit

Keep for Your Records

Determine how you will complete this worksheet

If you paid both qualified sick and family leave wages and qualified wages for purposes of the employee retention credit this quarter, complete Step 1, Step 2, and Step 3. If you paid qualified sick and family leave wages this quarter but you didn't pay any qualified wages for purposes of the employee retention credit this quarter, complete Step 1 and Step 2. If you paid qualified wages for purposes of the employee retention credit this quarter but you didn't pay any qualified sick and family leave wages this quarter, complete Step 1 and Step 3.

Step 1.   **Determine the employer share of social security tax this quarter after it is reduced by any credit claimed on Form 8974 and any credit to be claimed on Form 5884-C**

1a	Enter the amount of social security tax from Form 941, Part 1, line 5a, column 2 . . . . 1a	_____
1b	Enter the amount of social security tax from Form 941, Part 1, line 5b, column 2 . . . . 1b	_____
1c	Add lines 1a and 1b 1c	_____
1d	Multiply line 1c by 50% (0.50) 1d	_____
1e	If you're a third-party payer of sick pay that isn't an agent and you're claiming credits for amounts paid to your employees, enter the employer share of social security tax included on Form 941, Part 1, line 8 (enter as a positive number) 1e	_____
1f	Subtract line 1e from line 1d 1f	_____
1g	If you received a Section 3121(q) Notice and Demand during the quarter, enter the amount of the employer share of social security tax from the notice 1g	_____
1h	**Employer share of social security tax.** Add lines 1f and 1g	1h _____
1i	Enter the amount from Form 941, Part 1, line 11a (credit from Form 8974) 1i	_____
1j	Enter the amount to be claimed on Form 5884-C, line 11, for this quarter 1j	_____
1k	**Total nonrefundable credits already used against the employer share of social security tax.** Add lines 1i and 1j	1k _____
1l	**Employer share of social security tax remaining.** Subtract line 1k from line 1h	1l _____

Step 2.   **Figure the sick and family leave credit**

2a	Qualified sick leave wages reported on Form 941, Part 1, line 5a(i), column 1 . . . . 2a	_____
2a(i)	Qualified sick leave wages included on Form 941, Part 1, line 5c, but not included on Form 941, Part 1, line 5a(i), column 1, because the wages reported on that line were limited by the social security wage base . . . . 2a(i)	_____
2a(ii)	Total qualified sick leave wages. Add lines 2a and 2a(i) . . . . 2a(ii)	_____
2b	Qualified health plan expenses allocable to qualified sick leave wages (Form 941, Part 3, line 19) 2b	_____
2c	Employer share of Medicare tax on qualified sick leave wages. Multiply line 2a(ii) by 1.45% (0.0145) 2c	_____
2d	**Credit for qualified sick leave wages.** Add lines 2a(ii), 2b, and 2c	2d _____
2e	Qualified family leave wages reported on Form 941, Part 1, line 5a(ii), column 1 . . . . 2e	_____
2e(i)	Qualified family leave wages included on Form 941, Part 1, line 5c, but not included on Form 941, Part 1, line 5a(ii), column 1, because the wages reported on that line were limited by the social security wage base . . . . 2e(i)	_____
2e(ii)	Total qualified family leave wages. Add lines 2e and 2e(i) . . . . 2e(ii)	_____
2f	Qualified health plan expenses allocable to qualified family leave wages (Form 941, Part 3, line 20) 2f	_____
2g	Employer share of Medicare tax on qualified family leave wages. Multiply line 2e(ii) by 1.45% (0.0145) 2g	_____
2h	**Credit for qualified family leave wages.** Add lines 2e(ii), 2f, and 2g	2h _____
2i	**Credit for qualified sick and family leave wages.** Add lines 2d and 2h	2i _____
2j	**Nonrefundable portion of credit for qualified sick and family leave wages.** Enter the smaller of line 1l or line 2i. Enter this amount on Form 941, Part 1, line 11b	2j _____
2k	**Refundable portion of credit for qualified sick and family leave wages.** Subtract line 2j from line 2i and enter this amount on Form 941, Part 1, line 13c	2k _____

Step 3.   **Figure the employee retention credit**

3a	Qualified wages (excluding qualified health plan expenses) for the employee retention credit (Form 941, Part 3, line 21) 3a	_____
3b	Qualified health plan expenses allocable to qualified wages for the employee retention credit (Form 941, Part 3, line 22) 3b	_____
3c	Qualified wages (excluding qualified health plan expenses) paid March 13, 2020, through March 31, 2020, for the employee retention credit (Form 941, Part 3, line 24). Enter an amount here only for the second quarter Form 941 . . . . 3c	_____
3d	Qualified health plan expenses allocable to qualified wages paid March 13, 2020, through March 31, 2020, for the employee retention credit (Form 941, Part 3, line 25). Enter an amount here only for the second quarter Form 941 . . . . 3d	_____
3e	Add lines 3a, 3b, 3c, and 3d 3e	_____
3f	**Retention credit.** Multiply line 3e by 50% (0.50)	3f _____
3g	Enter the amount of the employer share of social security tax from Step 1, line 1l 3g	_____
3h	Enter the amount of the nonrefundable portion of the credit for qualified sick and family leave wages from Step 2, line 2j 3h	_____
3i	Subtract line 3h from line 3g 3i	_____
3j	**Nonrefundable portion of employee retention credit.** Enter the smaller of line 3f or line 3i. Enter this amount on Form 941, Part 1, line 11c	3j _____
3k	**Refundable portion of employee retention credit.** Subtract line 3j from line 3f and enter this amount on Form 941, Part 1, line 13d	3k _____

Caution:
Only complete lines 3c and 3d for your second quarter 2020 Form 941.

LO 9.5   14. Philcon Corporation created the following 2020 employee payroll report for one of its employees.

Philcon Corporation

EIN: 12-3456789

PO Box 4563
Anchorage, AK 99508

Employee Payroll Report
2020

Emp ID	Name	Wage Type	Date	Period Gross Pay	YTD Gross Pay	FIT w/h	SS Tax w/h	Med Tax w/h	Net Pay
A1246G	Louise Chugach	Monthly	1/31/2020	12,100.00	12,100.00	1,990.94	750.20	175.45	9,183.41
A1246G	Louise Chugach	Monthly	2/28/2020	12,100.00	24,200.00	1,990.94	750.20	175.45	9,183.41
A1246G	Louise Chugach	Bonus	3/15/2020	6,400.00	30,600.00	1,408.00	396.80	92.80	4,502.40
A1246G	Louise Chugach	Monthly	3/31/2020	12,100.00	42,700.00	1,990.94	750.20	175.45	9,183.41
A1246G	Louise Chugach	Monthly	4/30/2020	12,100.00	54,800.00	1,990.94	750.20	175.45	9,183.41
A1246G	Louise Chugach	Monthly	5/31/2020	12,100.00	66,900.00	1,990.94	750.20	175.45	9,183.41
A1246G	Louise Chugach	Monthly	6/30/2020	12,100.00	79,000.00	1,990.94	750.20	175.45	9,183.41
A1246G	Louise Chugach	Monthly	7/31/2020	12,100.00	91,100.00	1,990.94	750.20	175.45	9,183.41
A1246G	Louise Chugach	Monthly	8/31/2020	12,100.00	103,200.00	1,990.94	750.20	175.45	9,183.41
A1246G	Louise Chugach	Monthly	9/30/2020	12,100.00	115,300.00	1,990.94	750.20	175.45	9,183.41
A1246G	Louise Chugach	Monthly	10/31/2020	12,100.00	127,400.00	1,990.94	750.20	175.45	9,183.41
A1246G	Louise Chugach	Monthly	11/30/2020	12,100.00	139,500.00	1,990.94	638.60	175.45	9,295.01
A1246G	Louise Chugach	Monthly	12/31/2020	12,100.00	151,600.00	1,990.94	-	175.45	9,933.61
A1246G	Louise Chugach	YTD Total		151,600.00		25,299.28	8,537.40	2,198.20	115,565.12

Employee Mailing Address:

Louise Chugach
5471 East Tudor Road
Anchorage, AK 99508
SSN: 545-64-7745

a. Complete the following Form W-2 for Louise Chugach from Philcon Corporation.

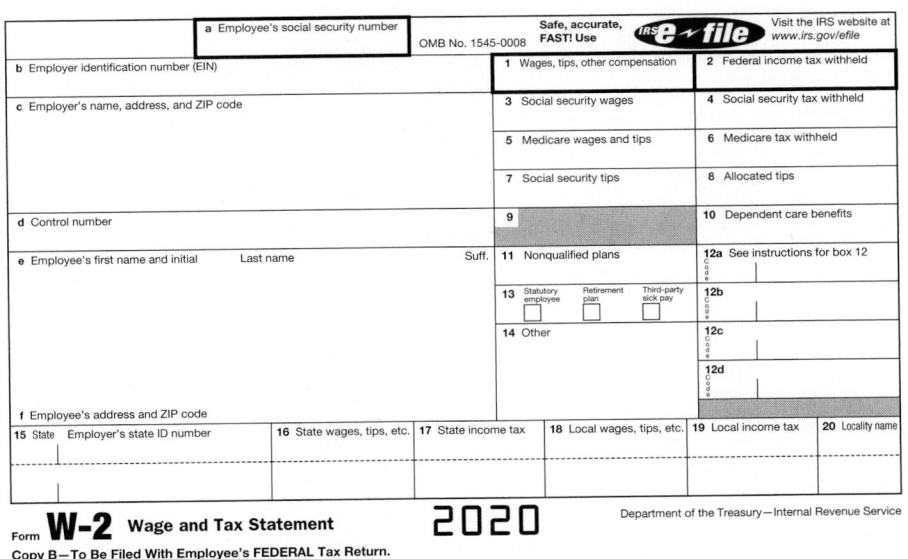

b. Philcon Corporation also paid $1,100 to Ralph Kincaid for presenting a management seminar. Ralph is not a Philcon employee and lives at 1455 Raspberry Road, Anchorage, AK 99508, and his Social Security number is 475-45-3226. Complete the Form 1099-NEC located on Page 9-60 for the payment to Ralph from Philcon Corporation.

☐ CORRECTED (if checked)

PAYER'S name, street address, city or town, state or province, country, ZIP or foreign postal code, and telephone no.			OMB No. 1545-0116
		20**20**	**Nonemployee Compensation**
		Form **1099-NEC**	
	1 Nonemployee compensation $		**Copy B** **For Recipient**
PAYER'S TIN	RECIPIENT'S TIN	**2**	
RECIPIENT'S name	**3**		This is important tax information and is being furnished to the IRS. If you are required to file a return, a negligence penalty or other sanction may be imposed on you if this income is taxable and the IRS determines that it has not been reported.
Street address (including apt. no.)	**4 Federal income tax withheld** $		
City or town, state or province, country, and ZIP or foreign postal code			
	FATCA filing requirement ☐		
Account number (see instructions)	**5** State tax withheld $ - - - - - - - - - - - $	**6** State/Payer's state no. - - - - - - - - - - -	**7** State income $ - - - - - - - $

Form **1099-NEC**   (keep for your records)   www.irs.gov/Form1099NEC   Department of the Treasury - Internal Revenue Service

LO 9.6   15. Thomas is an employer with two employees, Patty and Selma. Patty's wages are $12,450 and Selma's wages are $1,310. The state unemployment tax rate is 5.4 percent. Calculate the following amounts for Thomas:

a. FUTA tax before the state tax credit $_____

b. State unemployment tax $_____

c. FUTA tax after the state tax credit $_____

LO 9.8   16. Telly, age 38, has a $140,000 IRA with Blue Mutual Fund. He has read good things about the management of Green Mutual Fund, so he opens a Green Fund IRA. Telly asked for a distribution rollover and received his balance from the Blue Fund on May 1, 2020. Telly opted to have no withholding on the distribution.

a. What amount will Telly receive from the Blue Fund IRA?

$_____

b. What amount must Telly contribute to the Green Fund IRA to avoid having taxable income and penalties for early withdrawal?

$_____

c. When is the last day Telly can roll over the amount received into the Green Fund IRA and avoid taxation in the current year, assuming no unusual circumstances?

$_____

d. What amount would Telly receive if the distribution were from his employer's qualified retirement plan?

$_____

LO 9.8   17. Allen (age 32) takes a distribution of $20,000 from his traditional IRA account which he plans to deposit into an IRA with a different bank. During the 60-day rollover period, he gambles and loses the entire IRA balance. What income and/or penalties must he show on his tax return related to the failed rollover?

_____

_____

_____

_____

GROUP 3:
WRITING ASSIGNMENT

ETHICS

Eric, your friend, received his Form W-2 from his employer (below) and has asked for your help. Eric's 2020 salary was $146,000 and he does not understand why the amounts in Boxes 1, 3, and 5 are not $146,000? His final paycheck for the year included the following information:

– Eric contributed 5 percent of his salary to the company 401(k) plan on a pre-tax basis.
– Eric is married with two children. He had $5,000 deducted from his wages for a Dependent Care Flexible Spending Account.
– Eric is enrolled in the company-sponsored life insurance program. He has a policy that provides a benefit of $146,000.
– Eric contributed the 2020 maximum amount to the Health Care Flexible Spending Account.

Using the information and Eric's Form W-2, prepare an email to Eric reconciling his salary of $146,000 to the amounts in Boxes 1, 3, and 5.

a Employee's social security number 791-51-4335		OMB No. 1545-0008	Safe, accurate, FAST! Use	IRS e-file	Visit the IRS website at www.irs.gov/efile	

		1 Wages, tips, other compensation 131,080.00	2 Federal income tax withheld 15,190.00
b Employer identification number (EIN) 12-3456789			
c Employer's name, address, and ZIP code Ivy Technologies, Inc. 436 E. 35 Avenue Gary, IN 46409	3 Social security wages 137,700.00	4 Social security tax withheld 8,537.40
	5 Medicare wages and tips 138,380.00	6 Medicare tax withheld 2,006.51
	7 Social security tips	8 Allocated tips
d Control number	9	10 Dependent care benefits 5,000.00
e Employee's first name and initial Last name Suff. Eric Hayes 555 E. 81st Street Merrillville, IN 46410	11 Nonqualified plans	12a See instructions for box 12 DD 11,567.00
	13 Statutory employee ☐ Retirement plan ☒ Third-party sick pay ☐	12b C 130.00
	14 Other	12c D 7,300.00
		12d

15 State Employer's state ID number IN 00122231001	16 State wages, tips, etc. 131,080.00	17 State income tax 4,900.00	18 Local wages, tips, etc. 131,080.00	19 Local income tax 927.00	20 Locality name LAKE

f Employee's address and ZIP code

Form **W-2** **Wage and Tax Statement**   **2020**   Department of the Treasury—Internal Revenue Service

Copy B—To Be Filed With Employee's FEDERAL Tax Return.
This information is being furnished to the Internal Revenue Service.

Partnership Taxation

After completing this chapter, you should be able to:

LO 10.1 Define a partnership for tax purposes.

LO 10.2 Describe the basic tax rules for partnership formation and operation.

LO 10.3 Summarize the rules for partnership income reporting.

LO 10.4 Describe the tax treatment of partnership distributions.

LO 10.5 Determine partnership tax years.

LO 10.6 Describe the tax treatment of transactions between partners and their partnerships.

LO 10.7 Apply the qualified business income deduction to partners.

LO 10.8 Apply the at-risk rule to partnerships.

LO 10.9 Describe the tax treatment of limited liability companies (LLCs).

OVERVIEW

The partnership form allows taxpayers considerable flexibility in terms of contributions, income and loss allocations, and distributions. One of the primary benefits of the partnership is that partnership income is only taxed at the partner level. Corporate taxpayers (other than S corporations) pay tax at the corporate level and often again at the shareholder level (see Chapter 11), which results in corporate double taxation. Since a partnership's income passes through to the partners, there is no federal income tax at the entity level, only at the partner level. Currently, the tax law permits an additional qualified business income deduction for pass-through entities like partnerships.

One of the disadvantages of partnerships compared to corporations is the lack of limited liability for partners whereas corporate shareholders enjoy protection from liability to third parties (e.g., creditors of the corporation). The advent of the limited liability company (LLC) and the limited liability partnership (LLP) has provided partners this important liability protection. Because LLCs and LLPs are taxed like partnerships, they are included in this chapter on partnership taxation.

This chapter will provide an understanding of the tax treatment of partnerships and the tax forms (Form 1065 and Schedule K-1) related to reporting partnership income or loss.

Learning Objective 10.1

Define a partnership for tax purposes.

10-1 NATURE OF PARTNERSHIP TAXATION

Partnership federal income tax returns are information returns only. Returns show the amount of income by type and the allocation of the income to the partners. Partnership income and other items are passed through to the partners, and each partner is taxed on the individual's distributive share of partnership income. Partnership income is taxable to the partner even if he or she does not actually receive the income in cash.

Even though the partnership tax return is only informational, partnerships do have to make various elections and select accounting methods and periods. For example, partnerships must select depreciation and inventory methods. In addition, partnerships are legal entities under civil law, and in most states have rights under the Uniform Partnership Act.

10-1a What Is a Partnership?

The tax law defines a partnership as a syndicate, group, pool, joint venture, or other unincorporated organization through or by means of which any business, financial operation, or venture is carried on, and which is not classified as a corporation, trust, or estate. The mere co-ownership of property does not constitute a partnership; the partners must engage in some type of business or financial activity.

Ordinary partnerships, or general partnerships as they are often called, may be formed by a simple verbal agreement or "handshake" between partners. In contrast, the formation of corporations, limited partnerships, limited liability companies (LLCs), and limited liability partnerships (LLPs) must be documented in writing and the entity must be legally registered in the state in which it is formed. Even though general partnerships may be formed by verbal agreement between partners, partners usually document their agreement in writing with the help of attorneys in the event disagreements arise during the course of operations.

General partners usually take on the risk of legal liability for certain actions of the partnership or debts of the partnership, as specified under state law. To limit some of the liability exposure of operating a joint business, many partnerships are created formally as limited partnerships, LLCs, or LLPs. LLPs are used for licensed professionals such as attorneys and accountants.

Entities generally treated as partnerships for tax law purposes include limited partnerships, LLCs, and LLPs. Limited partnerships have one or more general partners and one or more limited partners. General partners participate in management and have unlimited liability for partnership obligations. Limited partners may not participate in management and have no liability for partnership obligations beyond their capital contributions. Many partnerships are formed as limited partnerships because the limited liability helps to attract passive investors. LLCs and LLPs are legal entities which combine the limited liability of corporations with the tax treatment of partnerships. LLCs and LLPs are discussed later in this chapter.

EXAMPLE Avery and Roberta buy a rental house which they hold jointly. The house is rented and they share the income and expenses for the year. Avery and Roberta have not formed a partnership. However, if they had bought and operated a store together, a partnership would have been formed. Although the ownership of real estate may not rise to the level of a business requiring a partnership return, co-owners of real estate frequently do choose to operate in a partnership, limited partnership, LLP, or LLC form. ♦

For federal tax purposes, an unincorporated business operated by spouses is considered a partnership. As a result, a business co-run by spouses is generally required to comply with filing and record-keeping requirements for partnerships and partners. Married co-owners wishing to avoid the burden of partnership documentation can form a qualified joint venture. The election to do so is made by simply reporting each spouse's share of income, losses, gains, and deductions on a Schedule C (along with other related forms) in respect of each spouse's interest in the joint venture.

TAX BREAK

Self-Study Problem 10.1 — *See Appendix E for Solutions to Self-Study Problems*

Indicate, by placing a check in the appropriate blank, whether each of the following is or is not required to file a partnership return.

	Yes	No
1. Duncan and Clyde, unrelated taxpayers, purchase and operate a plumbing business together.	_____	_____
2. Ellen and Walter form a corporation to operate a plumbing business.	_____	_____
3. George and Marty buy a duplex to hold as rental property, which is not considered an active business.	_____	_____
4. Howard and Sally (both single taxpayers) form a joint venture to drill for and sell oil.	_____	_____
5. Ted and Joyce, a married couple, purchase and operate a candy store.	_____	_____

10-2 PARTNERSHIP FORMATION

10.2 Learning Objective

Describe the basic tax rules for partnership formation and operation.

Generally, there is no gain or loss recognized by a partnership or any of its partners when property is contributed to a partnership in exchange for an interest in the partnership. This rule applies to the formation of a partnership as well as any subsequent contributions to the partnership. However, there are exceptions to the nonrecognition rule. Income may be recognized when a partnership interest is received in exchange for services performed by the partner for the partnership or when a partner transfers to a partnership, property subject to a liability exceeding that partner's basis in the property transferred. In this situation, gain is recognized to the extent that the portion of the liability allocable to the other partners exceeds the basis of the property contributed. If a partner receives money or other property from the partnership, in addition to an interest in the partnership, the transaction may be considered in part a sale or exchange, and a gain or loss may be recognized.

EXAMPLE Dunn and Church form the Dunn & Church Partnership. Dunn contributes a building with a fair market value of $90,000 and an adjusted basis of $55,000 for a 50 percent interest in the partnership. Dunn does not recognize a gain on the transfer of the building to the partnership. Church performs services for the partnership for his 50 percent interest which is worth $90,000. Church must report $90,000 in ordinary income for the receipt of an interest in the partnership in exchange for services provided to the partnership. ♦

EXAMPLE   Ann and Keith form the A&K Partnership. Ann contributes a building with a fair market value of $200,000 and an adjusted basis of $45,000 for a 50 percent interest in the partnership. The building is subject to a liability of $130,000. Keith contributes cash of $70,000 for a 50 percent interest in the partnership. Ann must recognize a gain on the transfer of the building to the partnership equal to $20,000, the amount by which the liability allocable to Keith, $65,000 (50% × $130,000), exceeds the basis of the building, $45,000. Keith does not recognize a gain on the contribution of cash to the partnership. ◆

A partner's initial basis in a partnership interest is equal to the basis of the property transferred plus cash contributed to the partnership. If gain is recognized on the transfer, the partner's basis in the partnership interest is increased by the gain recognized. The basis is reduced by any liabilities of the contributing partner assumed by the other partners through the partnership. For example, if a one-third partner is relieved of a $90,000 liability by the partnership, they would reduce by $60,000 ($\frac{2}{3}$ of $90,000) their partnership interest basis. After the initial basis in the partnership interest is established, the basis is adjusted for future earnings, losses, contributions to the partnership, and distributions from the partnership.

EXAMPLE   Prentice contributes cash of $50,000 and property with a fair market value of $110,000 (adjusted basis of $30,000) to the P&H Partnership. Prentice's basis in the partnership interest is $80,000 ($50,000 + $30,000). ◆

EXAMPLE   Assume that Prentice, in the example above, also received a partnership interest worth $15,000 for services provided to the partnership. She must recognize $15,000 as ordinary income, and her basis in the partnership interest is $95,000 ($80,000 + $15,000). ◆

EXAMPLE   Darnell contributes property with a fair market value of $110,000 and an adjusted basis of $30,000, subject to a liability of $20,000, to a partnership in exchange for a 25 percent interest in the partnership. Darnell's basis in his partnership interest is $15,000 [$30,000 − ($20,000 × 75%)]. ◆

The basis of a partner's interest in a partnership changes due to partnership activities. A partner's basis in their partnership interest is increased by the partner's share of (1) additional contributions to the partnership, (2) net ordinary taxable income of the partnership, and (3) capital gains and other income (including tax-exempt income such as municipal bond income) of the partnership. Alternatively, a partner's basis is reduced (but not below zero) by the partner's share of (1) distributions of partnership property, (2) losses from operations of the partnership, and (3) capital losses and other deductions (including disallowed tax deductions such as entertainment expenses) of the partnership. In addition, changes in the partner's share of partnership liabilities affects the basis of a partner's partnership interest.

EXAMPLE   Reid has a 50 percent interest in the Reid Partnership. Her basis in her partnership interest at the beginning of the tax year is $12,000. For the current tax year, the partnership reports ordinary income of $15,000, a capital gain of $3,000, and charitable contributions of $700. The basis of Reid's partnership interest, after considering the above items, would be $20,650 ($12,000 beginning basis + $7,500 share of partnership ordinary income + $1,500 share of partnership capital gain − $350 share of partnership charitable contributions). ◆

The partnership's basis in property contributed by a partner is equal to the partner's adjusted basis in the property at the time of the contribution plus any gain recognized by the partner. The transfer of liabilities to the partnership by the partner does not impact the basis of the property to the partnership. The partnership's holding period for the property contributed to the partnership includes the partner's holding period. For example, long-term capital gain property may be transferred to a partnership by a partner and sold immediately, and any gain would be long-term, assuming the property is a capital asset to the partnership.

EXAMPLE   Clark contributes property to the Rose Partnership in exchange for a partnership interest. The property contributed has an adjusted basis to Clark of $45,000 and a fair market value of $75,000 on the date of the contribution. The partnership's basis in the property is $45,000. ♦

Self-Study Problem 10.2   *See Appendix E for Solutions to Self-Study Problems*

John and Linda form the J&L Partnership. John contributes cash of $36,000 for a 40 percent interest in the partnership. Linda contributes equipment worth $54,000 with an adjusted basis of $17,500 for a 60 percent partnership interest.

1. What is John's recognized gain or loss on the contribution? $_____

2. What is John's basis in his partnership interest? $_____

3. What is Linda's recognized gain or loss on the contribution? $_____

4. What is Linda's basis in her partnership interest? $_____

5. What is J&L Partnership's basis in the equipment received from Linda? $_____

10-3 PARTNERSHIP INCOME REPORTING

10.3 Learning Objective

Summarize the rules for partnership income reporting.

A partnership is required to report its income and other items on Form 1065, U.S. Return of Partnership Income, even though the partnership entity does not pay federal income tax. The tax return is due on the fifteenth day of the third month following the close of the partnership's tax year. When reporting partnership taxable income, certain transactions must be separated rather than being reported as part of ordinary income. The primary items that must be reported separately are net rental income, interest income, dividend income, capital gains and losses, Section 1231 gains and losses, Section 179 deductions, charitable deductions, tax-exempt income, non-deductible expenses, and most credits. These items are listed as separate income or expenses, since they are often subject to special calculations or limitations on the tax returns of the partners.

After the special items are separated, the partnership reports the remainder of its ordinary income or loss. The ordinary income or loss of a partnership is calculated in the same manner as that of an individual, except the partnership is not allowed to deduct the standard deduction, foreign taxes paid, charitable contributions, net operating losses, or personal itemized deductions. Schedule K-1 of Form 1065 presents the allocation of ordinary income or loss, special income and deductions, and gains and losses to each partner. The partners report the amounts from their Schedules K-1 on their own individual tax returns.

A partner's deductible loss from a partnership is limited to the basis of the partner's partnership interest at the end of the year in which the loss was incurred. The partner's basis is not affected by the qualified business income deduction. The partner's partnership basis cannot be reduced below zero. Any unused losses may be carried forward and reported in a future year when there is partnership basis available to be reduced by the loss.

New Tax Law !

The IRS has proposed changes to partnership tax reporting for tax year 2021. Among the considerations are a new Schedule K-2 and a new Schedule K-3 to provide additional detail of what was reported on Line 16 (foreign transactions) of Schedule K (at the partnership level) and Schedule K-1 (at the partner level).

Self-Study Problem 10.3   *See Appendix E for Solutions to Self-Study Problems*

Wita Caddoan and Sapat Illiniwek (SSN 444-14-1414) are equal partners in the newly formed Cahokia Partnership. Cahokia is located at 40 Rainy Street, Collinsville, IL 62234. Cahokia's employee identification number is 44-4444444. During 2020, the partnership began operations and had the following income and expenses:

Gross income from operations	$255,600
Deductions:	
Salaries to employees	$168,000
Rent	12,000
Payroll taxes	6,100
Depreciation	9,250
Charitable contributions (to 50 percent organizations)	1,500
Cash withdrawals ($25,000 for each partner)	50,000

The partnership's balance sheet is as follows:

Cahokia Partnership Balance Sheet as of December 31, 2020

Assets:		
Cash		$ 27,000
Accounts receivable		10,000
Land		115,000
Building	$115,000	
Less: accumulated depreciation	(9,250)	105,750
Total Assets		$257,750
Liabilities and Partners' Capital:		
Accounts payable		$ 29,750
Mortgage payable		187,750
Partners' capital (includes $31,500 originally contributed, $15,750 by each partner)		40,250
Total Liabilities and Partners' Capital		$257,750

Complete Form 1065, page 1, and Schedules K, L, M-1, and M-2 on Pages 10-7 to 10-11 for Cahokia. Also, complete Schedule K-1 on Pages 10-13 and 10-14 for Sapat.

Self-Study Problem 10.3

Form **1065**	**U.S. Return of Partnership Income**	OMB No. 1545-0123

Department of the Treasury
Internal Revenue Service

For calendar year 2020, or tax year beginning _____ , 2020, ending _____ , 20 _____ .

▶ Go to *www.irs.gov/Form1065* for instructions and the latest information.

2020

		Type or Print		D **Employer identification number**
A **Principal business activity**	Name of partnership			
B **Principal product or service**	Number, street, and room or suite no. If a P.O. box, see instructions.			E **Date business started**
C **Business code number**	City or town, state or province, country, and ZIP or foreign postal code			F **Total assets** (see instructions) $

G   Check applicable boxes: **(1)** ☐ Initial return   **(2)** ☐ Final return   **(3)** ☐ Name change   **(4)** ☐ Address change   **(5)** ☐ Amended return

H   Check accounting method: **(1)** ☐ Cash   **(2)** ☐ Accrual   **(3)** ☐ Other (specify) ▶ _____

I   Number of Schedules K-1. Attach one for each person who was a partner at any time during the tax year ▶ _____ ▶ ☐

J   Check if Schedules C and M-3 are attached

K   Check if partnership: **(1)** ☐ Aggregated activities for section 465 at-risk purposes   **(2)** ☐ Grouped activities for section 469 passive activity purposes

Caution: Include **only** trade or business income and expenses on lines 1a through 22 below. See instructions for more information.

Income	**1a**	Gross receipts or sales	1a	
	b	Returns and allowances	1b	
	c	Balance. Subtract line 1b from line 1a		1c
	2	Cost of goods sold (attach Form 1125-A)		2
	3	Gross profit. Subtract line 2 from line 1c		3
	4	Ordinary income (loss) from other partnerships, estates, and trusts (attach statement)		4
	5	Net farm profit (loss) (attach Schedule F (Form 1040))		5
	6	Net gain (loss) from Form 4797, Part II, line 17 (attach Form 4797)		6
	7	Other income (loss) (attach statement)		7
	8	**Total income (loss).** Combine lines 3 through 7		8
Deductions (see instructions for limitations)	**9**	Salaries and wages (other than to partners) (less employment credits)		9
	10	Guaranteed payments to partners		10
	11	Repairs and maintenance		11
	12	Bad debts		12
	13	Rent		13
	14	Taxes and licenses		14
	15	Interest (see instructions)		15
	16a	Depreciation (if required, attach Form 4562)	16a	
	b	Less depreciation reported on Form 1125-A and elsewhere on return	16b	16c
	17	Depletion **(Do not deduct oil and gas depletion.)**		17
	18	Retirement plans, etc.		18
	19	Employee benefit programs		19
	20	Other deductions (attach statement)		20
	21	**Total deductions.** Add the amounts shown in the far right column for lines 9 through 20		21
	22	**Ordinary business income (loss).** Subtract line 21 from line 8		22
Tax and Payment	**23**	Interest due under the look-back method—completed long-term contracts (attach Form 8697)		23
	24	Interest due under the look-back method—income forecast method (attach Form 8866)		24
	25	BBA AAR imputed underpayment (see instructions)		25
	26	Other taxes (see instructions)		26
	27	**Total balance due.** Add lines 23 through 26		27
	28	Payment (see instructions)		28
	29	**Amount owed.** If line 28 is smaller than line 27, enter amount owed		29
	30	**Overpayment.** If line 28 is larger than line 27, enter overpayment		30

Sign Here

Under penalties of perjury, I declare that I have examined this return, including accompanying schedules and statements, and to the best of my knowledge and belief, it is true, correct, and complete. Declaration of preparer (other than partner or limited liability company member) is based on all information of which preparer has any knowledge.

		May the IRS discuss this return with the preparer shown below? See instructions. ☐ Yes ☐ No
▶ Signature of partner or limited liability company member	Date	

Paid Preparer Use Only

Print/Type preparer's name	Preparer's signature	Date	Check ☐ if self-employed	PTIN
Firm's name ▶			Firm's EIN ▶	
Firm's address ▶			Phone no.	

For Paperwork Reduction Act Notice, see separate instructions.   Cat. No. 11390Z   Form **1065** (2020)

Form 1065 (2020)   Page **2**

Schedule B	**Other Information**		

1 What type of entity is filing this return? Check the applicable box:

					Yes	No
a ☐ Domestic general partnership		**b** ☐ Domestic limited partnership				
c ☐ Domestic limited liability company		**d** ☐ Domestic limited liability partnership				
e ☐ Foreign partnership		**f** ☐ Other ▶				

2 At the end of the tax year:

a Did any foreign or domestic corporation, partnership (including any entity treated as a partnership), trust, or tax-exempt organization, or any foreign government own, directly or indirectly, an interest of 50% or more in the profit, loss, or capital of the partnership? For rules of constructive ownership, see instructions. If "Yes," attach Schedule B-1, Information on Partners Owning 50% or More of the Partnership   . . . .

b Did any individual or estate own, directly or indirectly, an interest of 50% or more in the profit, loss, or capital of the partnership? For rules of constructive ownership, see instructions. If "Yes," attach Schedule B-1, Information on Partners Owning 50% or More of the Partnership   . . . .

3 At the end of the tax year, did the partnership:

a Own directly 20% or more, or own, directly or indirectly, 50% or more of the total voting power of all classes of stock entitled to vote of any foreign or domestic corporation? For rules of constructive ownership, see instructions. If "Yes," complete (i) through (iv) below   . . . .

(i) Name of Corporation	**(ii)** Employer Identification Number (if any)	**(iii)** Country of Incorporation	**(iv)** Percentage Owned in Voting Stock

b Own directly an interest of 20% or more, or own, directly or indirectly, an interest of 50% or more in the profit, loss, or capital in any foreign or domestic partnership (including an entity treated as a partnership) or in the beneficial interest of a trust? For rules of constructive ownership, see instructions. If "Yes," complete (i) through (v) below   . .

(i) Name of Entity	**(ii)** Employer Identification Number (if any)	**(iii)** Type of Entity	**(iv)** Country of Organization	**(v)** Maximum Percentage Owned in Profit, Loss, or Capital

		Yes	No
4	Does the partnership satisfy **all four** of the following conditions?		
a	The partnership's total receipts for the tax year were less than $250,000.		
b	The partnership's total assets at the end of the tax year were less than $1 million.		
c	Schedules K-1 are filed with the return and furnished to the partners on or before the due date (including extensions) for the partnership return.		
d	The partnership is not filing and is not required to file Schedule M-3		
	If "Yes," the partnership is not required to complete Schedules L, M-1, and M-2; item F on page 1 of Form 1065; or item L on Schedule K-1.		
5	Is this partnership a publicly traded partnership, as defined in section 469(k)(2)?		
6	During the tax year, did the partnership have any debt that was canceled, was forgiven, or had the terms modified so as to reduce the principal amount of the debt?		
7	Has this partnership filed, or is it required to file, Form 8918, Material Advisor Disclosure Statement, to provide information on any reportable transaction?		
8	At any time during calendar year 2020, did the partnership have an interest in or a signature or other authority over a financial account in a foreign country (such as a bank account, securities account, or other financial account)? See instructions for exceptions and filing requirements for FinCEN Form 114, Report of Foreign Bank and Financial Accounts (FBAR). If "Yes," enter the name of the foreign country ▶		
9	At any time during the tax year, did the partnership receive a distribution from, or was it the grantor of, or transferor to, a foreign trust? If "Yes," the partnership may have to file Form 3520, Annual Return To Report Transactions With Foreign Trusts and Receipt of Certain Foreign Gifts. See instructions		
10a	Is the partnership making, or had it previously made (and not revoked), a section 754 election? . . . . . . See instructions for details regarding a section 754 election.		
b	Did the partnership make for this tax year an optional basis adjustment under section 743(b) or 734(b)? If "Yes," attach a statement showing the computation and allocation of the basis adjustment. See instructions		

Form **1065** (2020)

Form 1065 (2020) Page **3**

Schedule B	**Other Information** *(continued)*	Yes	No
c	Is the partnership required to adjust the basis of partnership assets under section 743(b) or 734(b) because of a substantial built-in loss (as defined under section 743(d)) or substantial basis reduction (as defined under section 734(d))? If "Yes," attach a statement showing the computation and allocation of the basis adjustment. See instructions		
11	Check this box if, during the current or prior tax year, the partnership distributed any property received in a like-kind exchange or contributed such property to another entity (other than disregarded entities wholly owned by the partnership throughout the tax year) . . . . ▶ ☐		
12	At any time during the tax year, did the partnership distribute to any partner a tenancy-in-common or other undivided interest in partnership property?		
13	If the partnership is required to file Form 8858, Information Return of U.S. Persons With Respect To Foreign Disregarded Entities (FDEs) and Foreign Branches (FBs), enter the number of Forms 8858 attached. See instructions . . . . ▶		
14	Does the partnership have any foreign partners? If "Yes," enter the number of Forms 8805, Foreign Partner's Information Statement of Section 1446 Withholding Tax, filed for this partnership . . . ▶		
15	Enter the number of Forms 8865, Return of U.S. Persons With Respect to Certain Foreign Partnerships, attached to this return . . . . ▶		
16a	Did you make any payments in 2020 that would require you to file Form(s) 1099? See instructions		
b	If "Yes," did you or will you file required Form(s) 1099?		
17	Enter the number of Forms 5471, Information Return of U.S. Persons With Respect To Certain Foreign Corporations, attached to this return . . . . ▶		
18	Enter the number of partners that are foreign governments under section 892 . . . . ▶		
19	During the partnership's tax year, did the partnership make any payments that would require it to file Form 1042 and 1042-S under chapter 3 (sections 1441 through 1464) or chapter 4 (sections 1471 through 1474)?		
20	Was the partnership a specified domestic entity required to file Form 8938 for the tax year? See the Instructions for Form 8938		
21	Is the partnership a section 721(c) partnership, as defined in Regulations section 1.721(c)-1(b)(14)?		
22	During the tax year, did the partnership pay or accrue any interest or royalty for which one or more partners are not allowed a deduction under section 267A? See instructions		
	If "Yes," enter the total amount of the disallowed deductions . . . . ▶ $		
23	Did the partnership have an election under section 163(j) for any real property trade or business or any farming business in effect during the tax year? See instructions		
24	Does the partnership satisfy one or more of the following? See instructions		
a	The partnership owns a pass-through entity with current, or prior year carryover, excess business interest expense.		
b	The partnership's aggregate average annual gross receipts (determined under section 448(c)) for the 3 tax years preceding the current tax year are more than $26 million and the partnership has business interest.		
c	The partnership is a tax shelter (see instructions) and the partnership has business interest expense.		
	If "Yes" to any, complete and attach Form 8990.		
25	Is the partnership electing out of the centralized partnership audit regime under section 6221(b)? See instructions . .		
	If "Yes," the partnership must complete Schedule B-2 (Form 1065). Enter the total from Schedule B-2, Part III, line 3 . . . . ▶ _____		
	If "No," complete Designation of Partnership Representative below.		

Designation of Partnership Representative (see instructions)

Enter below the information for the partnership representative (PR) for the tax year covered by this return.

Name of PR ▶

U.S. address of PR ▶ ———————————————————— 　U.S. phone number of PR ▶

If the PR is an entity, name of the designated individual for the PR ▶

U.S. address of designated individual ▶ ———————————————————— 　U.S. phone number of designated individual ▶

26	Is the partnership attaching Form 8996 to certify as a Qualified Opportunity Fund?		
	If "Yes," enter the amount from Form 8996, line 16 . . . . ▶ $		
27	Enter the number of foreign partners subject to section 864(c)(8) as a result of transferring all or a portion of an interest in the partnership or of receiving a distribution from the partnership . . . . . ▶		
28	At any time during the tax year, were there any transfers between the partnership and its partners subject to the disclosure requirements of Regulations section 1.707-8?		
29	Since December 22, 2017, did a foreign corporation directly or indirectly acquire substantially all of the properties constituting a trade or business of your partnership, and was the ownership percentage (by vote or value) for purposes of section 7874 greater than 50% (for example, the partners held more than 50% of the stock of the foreign corporation)? If "Yes," list the ownership percentage by vote and by value. See instructions. Percentage: By Vote By Value		

Form **1065** (2020)

Form 1065 (2020)   Page **4**

Schedule K	Partners' Distributive Share Items		Total amount

Income (Loss)

1	Ordinary business income (loss) (page 1, line 22)	**1**	
2	Net rental real estate income (loss) (attach Form 8825)	**2**	
3a	Other gross rental income (loss) . . . **3a**		
b	Expenses from other rental activities (attach statement) . . . **3b**		
c	Other net rental income (loss). Subtract line 3b from line 3a	**3c**	
4	Guaranteed payments: **a** Services **4a** **b** Capital **4b**		
	c Total. Add lines 4a and 4b	**4c**	
5	Interest income	**5**	
6	Dividends and dividend equivalents: **a** Ordinary dividends	**6a**	
	b Qualified dividends **6b** **c** Dividend equivalents **6c**		
7	Royalties	**7**	
8	Net short-term capital gain (loss) (attach Schedule D (Form 1065))	**8**	
9a	Net long-term capital gain (loss) (attach Schedule D (Form 1065))	**9a**	
b	Collectibles (28%) gain (loss) . . . **9b**		
c	Unrecaptured section 1250 gain (attach statement) . . . **9c**		
10	Net section 1231 gain (loss) (attach Form 4797)	**10**	
11	Other income (loss) (see instructions) Type ▶	**11**	

Deductions

12	Section 179 deduction (attach Form 4562)	**12**	
13a	Contributions	**13a**	
b	Investment interest expense	**13b**	
c	Section 59(e)(2) expenditures: **(1)** Type ▶ **(2)** Amount ▶	**13c(2)**	
d	Other deductions (see instructions) Type ▶	**13d**	

Self-Employment

14a	Net earnings (loss) from self-employment	**14a**	
b	Gross farming or fishing income	**14b**	
c	Gross nonfarm income	**14c**	

Credits

15a	Low-income housing credit (section 42(j)(5))	**15a**	
b	Low-income housing credit (other)	**15b**	
c	Qualified rehabilitation expenditures (rental real estate) (attach Form 3468, if applicable)	**15c**	
d	Other rental real estate credits (see instructions) Type ▶	**15d**	
e	Other rental credits (see instructions) Type ▶	**15e**	
f	Other credits (see instructions) Type ▶	**15f**	

Foreign Transactions

16a	Name of country or U.S. possession ▶		
b	Gross income from all sources	**16b**	
c	Gross income sourced at partner level	**16c**	
	Foreign gross income sourced at partnership level		
d	Reserved for future use ▶ **e** Foreign branch category ▶	**16e**	
f	Passive category ▶ **g** General category ▶ **h** Other (attach statement) ▶	**16h**	
	Deductions allocated and apportioned at partner level		
i	Interest expense ▶ **j** Other ▶	**16j**	
	Deductions allocated and apportioned at partnership level to foreign source income		
k	Reserved for future use ▶ **l** Foreign branch category ▶	**16l**	
m	Passive category ▶ **n** General category ▶ **o** Other (attach statement) ▶	**16o**	
p	Total foreign taxes (check one): ▶ Paid ☐ Accrued ☐	**16p**	
q	Reduction in taxes available for credit (attach statement)	**16q**	
r	Other foreign tax information (attach statement)		

Alternative Minimum Tax (AMT) Items

17a	Post-1986 depreciation adjustment	**17a**	
b	Adjusted gain or loss	**17b**	
c	Depletion (other than oil and gas)	**17c**	
d	Oil, gas, and geothermal properties—gross income	**17d**	
e	Oil, gas, and geothermal properties—deductions	**17e**	
f	Other AMT items (attach statement)	**17f**	

Other Information

18a	Tax-exempt interest income	**18a**	
b	Other tax-exempt income	**18b**	
c	Nondeductible expenses	**18c**	
19a	Distributions of cash and marketable securities	**19a**	
b	Distributions of other property	**19b**	
20a	Investment income	**20a**	
b	Investment expenses	**20b**	
c	Other items and amounts (attach statement)		

Form **1065** (2020)

Form 1065 (2020)

Analysis of Net Income (Loss)

1	Net income (loss). Combine Schedule K, lines 1 through 11. From the result, subtract the sum of Schedule K, lines 12 through 13d, and 16p					**1**		

		(i) Corporate	(ii) Individual (active)	(iii) Individual (passive)	(iv) Partnership	(v) Exempt Organization	(vi) Nominee/Other
2	Analysis by partner type:						
a	General partners						
b	Limited partners						

Schedule L   Balance Sheets per Books

		Beginning of tax year		End of tax year	
	Assets	(a)	(b)	(c)	(d)
1	Cash				
2a	Trade notes and accounts receivable				
b	Less allowance for bad debts				
3	Inventories				
4	U.S. government obligations				
5	Tax-exempt securities				
6	Other current assets (attach statement)				
7a	Loans to partners (or persons related to partners) .				
b	Mortgage and real estate loans				
8	Other investments (attach statement)				
9a	Buildings and other depreciable assets				
b	Less accumulated depreciation				
10a	Depletable assets				
b	Less accumulated depletion				
11	Land (net of any amortization)				
12a	Intangible assets (amortizable only)				
b	Less accumulated amortization				
13	Other assets (attach statement)				
14	Total assets				
	Liabilities and Capital				
15	Accounts payable				
16	Mortgages, notes, bonds payable in less than 1 year				
17	Other current liabilities (attach statement)				
18	All nonrecourse loans				
19a	Loans from partners (or persons related to partners) .				
b	Mortgages, notes, bonds payable in 1 year or more .				
20	Other liabilities (attach statement)				
21	Partners' capital accounts				
22	Total liabilities and capital				

Schedule M-1   Reconciliation of Income (Loss) per Books With Income (Loss) per Return

Note: The partnership may be required to file Schedule M-3. See instructions.

1	Net income (loss) per books		6	Income recorded on books this year not included on Schedule K, lines 1 through 11 (itemize):	
2	Income included on Schedule K, lines 1, 2, 3c, 5, 6a, 7, 8, 9a, 10, and 11, not recorded on books this year (itemize): _____		a	Tax-exempt interest $_____	
3	Guaranteed payments (other than health insurance)		7	Deductions included on Schedule K, lines 1 through 13d, and 16p, not charged against book income this year (itemize):	
4	Expenses recorded on books this year not included on Schedule K, lines 1 through 13d, and 16p (itemize):		a	Depreciation $_____	
a	Depreciation $_____		8	Add lines 6 and 7	
b	Travel and entertainment $_____		9	Income (loss) (Analysis of Net Income (Loss), line 1). Subtract line 8 from line 5	
5	Add lines 1 through 4				

Schedule M-2   Analysis of Partners' Capital Accounts

1	Balance at beginning of year . . .		6	Distributions: a Cash	
2	Capital contributed: a Cash . . .			b Property	
	b Property . .		7	Other decreases (itemize): _____	
3	Net income (loss) per books				
4	Other increases (itemize): _____		8	Add lines 6 and 7	
5	Add lines 1 through 4		9	Balance at end of year. Subtract line 8 from line 5	

Form **1065** (2020)

Self-Study Problem 10.3

651119

☐ Final K-1   ☐ Amended K-1   OMB No. 1545-0123

Schedule K-1
(Form 1065)
Department of the Treasury
Internal Revenue Service

20**20**

For calendar year 2020, or tax year

beginning ___/___/2020 ending ___/___/___

Partner's Share of Income, Deductions, Credits, etc.
▶ See separate instructions.

Part I	Information About the Partnership

A   Partnership's employer identification number

B   Partnership's name, address, city, state, and ZIP code

C   IRS Center where partnership filed return ▶

D   ☐ Check if this is a publicly traded partnership (PTP)

Part II	Information About the Partner

E   Partner's SSN or TIN (Do not use TIN of a disregarded entity. See instructions.)

F   Name, address, city, state, and ZIP code for partner entered in E. See instructions.

G   ☐ General partner or LLC member-manager ☐ Limited partner or other LLC member

H1 ☐ Domestic partner   ☐ Foreign partner

H2 ☐ If the partner is a disregarded entity (DE), enter the partner's:
    TIN _____ Name _____

I1 What type of entity is this partner? _____

I2 If this partner is a retirement plan (IRA/SEP/Keogh/etc.), check here ☐

J   Partner's share of profit, loss, and capital (see instructions):

	Beginning	Ending
Profit	%	%
Loss	%	%
Capital	%	%

Check if decrease is due to sale or exchange of partnership interest . . ☐

K   Partner's share of liabilities:

	Beginning	Ending
Nonrecourse . . $		$
Qualified nonrecourse financing . . . $		$
Recourse . . . $		$

☐ Check this box if Item K includes liability amounts from lower tier partnerships.

L   **Partner's Capital Account Analysis**

Beginning capital account . . . $ _____
Capital contributed during the year . $ _____
Current year net income (loss) . . . $ _____
Other increase (decrease) (attach explanation) $ _____
Withdrawals & distributions . . . $ (_____)
Ending capital account . . . . $ _____

M   Did the partner contribute property with a built-in gain or loss?
    ☐ Yes ☐ No   If "Yes," attach statement. See instructions.

N   **Partner's Share of Net Unrecognized Section 704(c) Gain or (Loss)**
    Beginning . . . . $ _____
    Ending . . . . $ _____

Part III	Partner's Share of Current Year Income, Deductions, Credits, and Other Items

1	Ordinary business income (loss)	15	Credits
2	Net rental real estate income (loss)		
3	Other net rental income (loss)	16	Foreign transactions
4a	Guaranteed payments for services		
4b	Guaranteed payments for capital		
4c	Total guaranteed payments		
5	Interest income		
6a	Ordinary dividends		
6b	Qualified dividends		
6c	Dividend equivalents	17	Alternative minimum tax (AMT) items
7	Royalties		
8	Net short-term capital gain (loss)		
9a	Net long-term capital gain (loss)	18	Tax-exempt income and nondeductible expenses
9b	Collectibles (28%) gain (loss)		
9c	Unrecaptured section 1250 gain		
10	Net section 1231 gain (loss)		
11	Other income (loss)	19	Distributions
12	Section 179 deduction	20	Other information
13	Other deductions		
14	Self-employment earnings (loss)		

21 ☐ More than one activity for at-risk purposes*
22 ☐ More than one activity for passive activity purposes*
*See attached statement for additional information.

For IRS Use Only

Schedule K-1 (Form 1065) 2019 — Page **2**

This list identifies the codes used on Schedule K-1 for all partners and provides summarized reporting information for partners who file Form 1040 or 1040-SR. For detailed reporting and filing information, see the separate Partner's Instructions for Schedule K-1 and the instructions for your income tax return.

1. Ordinary business income (loss). Determine whether the income (loss) is passive or nonpassive and enter on your return as follows.

	Report on
Passive loss	See the Partner's Instructions
Passive income	Schedule E, line 28, column (h)
Nonpassive loss	See the Partner's Instructions
Nonpassive income	Schedule E, line 28, column (k)

2. Net rental real estate income (loss) — See the Partner's Instructions
3. Other net rental income (loss)
- Net income — Schedule E, line 28, column (h)
- Net loss — See the Partner's Instructions

4a. Guaranteed payment Services — See the Partner's Instructions
4b. Guaranteed payment Capital — See the Partner's Instructions
4c. Guaranteed payment Total — See the Partner's Instructions
5. Interest income — Form 1040 or 1040-SR, line 2b
6a. Ordinary dividends — Form 1040 or 1040-SR, line 3b
6b. Qualified dividends — Form 1040 or 1040-SR, line 3a
6c. Dividend equivalents — See the Partner's Instructions
7. Royalties — Schedule E, line 4
8. Net short-term capital gain (loss) — Schedule D, line 5
9a. Net long-term capital gain (loss) — Schedule D, line 12
9b. Collectibles (28%) gain (loss) — 28% Rate Gain Worksheet, line 4 (Schedule D instructions)
9c. Unrecaptured section 1250 gain — See the Partner's Instructions
10. Net section 1231 gain (loss) — See the Partner's Instructions

11. Other income (loss)
Code		Report on
A	Other portfolio income (loss)	See the Partner's Instructions
B	Involuntary conversions	See the Partner's Instructions
C	Sec. 1256 contracts & straddles	Form 6781, line 1
D	Mining exploration costs recapture	See Pub. 535
E	Cancellation of debt	
F	Section 743(b) positive adjustments	
G	Section 965(a) inclusion	
H	Income under subpart F (other than inclusions under sections 951A and 965)	See the Partner's Instructions
I	Other income (loss)	

12. Section 179 deduction — See the Partner's Instructions

13. Other deductions
Code		Report on
A	Cash contributions (60%)	
B	Cash contributions (30%)	
C	Noncash contributions (50%)	
D	Noncash contributions (30%)	
E	Capital gain property to a 50% organization (30%)	See the Partner's Instructions
F	Capital gain property (20%)	
G	Contributions (100%)	
H	Investment interest expense	Form 4952, line 1
I	Deductions—royalty income	Schedule E, line 19
J	Section 59(e)(2) expenditures	See the Partner's Instructions
K	Excess business interest expense	See the Partner's Instructions
L	Deductions—portfolio (other)	Schedule A, line 16
M	Amounts paid for medical insurance	Schedule A, line 1, or Schedule 1 (Form 1040 or 1040-SR), line 16
N	Educational assistance benefits	See the Partner's Instructions
O	Dependent care benefits	Form 2441, line 12
P	Preproductive period expenses	See the Partner's Instructions
Q	Commercial revitalization deduction from rental real estate activities	See Form 8582 instructions
R	Pensions and IRAs	See the Partner's Instructions
S	Reforestation expense deduction	See the Partner's Instructions
T	through U	Reserved for future use
V	Section 743(b) negative adjustments	
W	Other deductions	See the Partner's Instructions
X	Section 965(c) deduction	

14. Self-employment earnings (loss)
Note: If you have a section 179 deduction or any partner-level deductions, see the Partner's Instructions before completing Schedule SE.
Code		Report on
A	Net earnings (loss) from self-employment	Schedule SE, Section A or B
B	Gross farming or fishing income	See the Partner's Instructions
C	Gross non-farm income	See the Partner's Instructions

15. Credits
Code		Report on
A	Low-income housing credit (section 42(j)(5)) from pre-2008 buildings	
B	Low-income housing credit (other) from pre-2008 buildings	
C	Low-income housing credit (section 42(j)(5)) from post-2007 buildings	See the Partner's Instructions
D	Low-income housing credit (other) from post-2007 buildings	
E	Qualified rehabilitation expenditures (rental real estate)	
F	Other rental real estate credits	
G	Other rental credits	

Code		Report on
H	Undistributed capital gains credit	Schedule 3 (Form 1040 or 1040-SR), line 13, box a
I	Biofuel producer credit	See the Partner's Instructions
J	Work opportunity credit	
K	Disabled access credit	
L	Empowerment zone employment credit	
M	Credit for increasing research activities	See the Partner's Instructions
N	Credit for employer social security and Medicare taxes	
O	Backup withholding	
P	Other credits	

16. Foreign transactions
Code		Report on
A	Name of country or U.S. possession	
B	Gross income from all sources	Form 1116, Part I
C	Gross income sourced at partner level	

Foreign gross income sourced at partnership level
D	Reserved for future use	
E	Foreign branch category	
F	Passive category	
G	General category	Form 1116, Part I
H	Other	

Deductions allocated and apportioned at partner level
| I | Interest expense | Form 1116, Part I |
| J | Other | Form 1116, Part I |

Deductions allocated and apportioned at partnership level to foreign source income
K	Reserved for future use	
L	Foreign branch category	
M	Passive category	
N	General category	Form 1116, Part I
O	Other	

Other information
P	Total foreign taxes paid	Form 1116, Part II
Q	Total foreign taxes accrued	Form 1116, Part II
R	Reduction in taxes available for credit	Form 1116, line 12
S	Foreign trading gross receipts	Form 8873
T	Extraterritorial income exclusion	Form 8873
U	through V	Reserved for future use
W	Section 965 information	See the Partner's Instructions
X	Other foreign transactions	

17. Alternative minimum tax (AMT) items
A	Post-1986 depreciation adjustment	
B	Adjusted gain or loss	See the Partner's Instructions and the Instructions for Form 6251
C	Depletion (other than oil & gas)	
D	Oil, gas, & geothermal—gross income	
E	Oil, gas, & geothermal—deductions	
F	Other AMT items	

18. Tax-exempt income and nondeductible expenses
A	Tax-exempt interest income	Form 1040 or 1040-SR, line 2a
B	Other tax-exempt income	See the Partner's Instructions
C	Nondeductible expenses	See the Partner's Instructions

19. Distributions
A	Cash and marketable securities	
B	Distribution subject to section 737	See the Partner's Instructions
C	Other property	

20. Other information
A	Investment income	Form 4952, line 4a
B	Investment expenses	Form 4952, line 5
C	Fuel tax credit information	Form 4136
D	Qualified rehabilitation expenditures (other than rental real estate)	
E	Basis of energy property	See the Partner's Instructions
F	through G	
H	Recapture of investment credit	See Form 4255
I	Recapture of other credits	See the Partner's Instructions
J	Look-back interest—completed long-term contracts	See Form 8697
K	Look-back interest—income forecast method	See Form 8866
L	Dispositions of property with section 179 deductions	
M	Recapture of section 179 deduction	
N	Interest expense for corporate partners	
O	through Y	
Z	Section 199A information	
AA	Section 704(c) information	
AB	Section 751 gain (loss)	See the Partner's Instructions
AC	Section 1(h)(5) gain (loss)	
AD	Deemed section 1250 unrecaptured gain	
AE	Excess taxable income	
AF	Excess business interest income	
AG	Gross receipts for section 59A(e)	
AH	Other information	

Page 2 of Schedule K-1 is from 2019. 2020 not available when we went to print.

10-4 CURRENT DISTRIBUTIONS AND GUARANTEED PAYMENTS

A partnership may make distributions of money or other property to the partners. A current distribution is defined as one which does not result in the complete termination of the partner's interest in the partnership.

In a current distribution, no gain is recognized by the partner receiving the distribution unless the partner's basis in the partnership has reached zero. In such a case, gain is recognized only to the extent that a distribution of money exceeds the partner's basis in their partnership interest.

The distribution of money or other property reduces the partner's basis in their partnership interest, but not below zero.

EXAMPLE Calvin is a partner in K&G Interests, and his basis in his partnership interest is $75,000. In the current tax year, Calvin receives a $45,000 cash distribution from the partnership. He does not recognize a gain or loss on the distribution, but his basis in his partnership interest is reduced to $30,000 ($75,000 − $45,000). If the distribution of cash were $80,000 instead of $45,000, Calvin would have a taxable gain of $5,000 ($80,000 − $75,000), and his basis in the partnership interest would be reduced to zero ($75,000 − $80,000 + $5,000). ◆

The basis of property received by a partner in a current distribution will generally be the same as the basis of the property to the partnership immediately prior to the distribution. An overall limitation is imposed which states that the basis of the assets distributed cannot exceed the partner's basis in his partnership interest, reduced by any money distributed. In some cases, this overall limitation may require that the partner's basis in the partnership interest be allocated among the assets received in the distribution.

10-4a Guaranteed Payments

Payments made to a partner for services rendered or for the use of the partner's capital that are made without regard to the income of the partnership are termed *guaranteed payments*. Such payments are treated by the partnership in the same manner as payments made to a person who is not a partner. The payments are ordinary income to the partner and deductible by the partnership. Guaranteed payments are separately reported on Line 4 of Schedule K-1.

EXAMPLE Alexander and Bryant operate the A&B Partnership. Alexander, a 50 percent partner, receives guaranteed payments of $15,000 for the year. If A&B has net ordinary income (after guaranteed payments) of $53,000, Alexander's total income from A&B is $41,500 ($15,000 + 50% of $53,000). Alexander's Schedule K-1 would report $26,500 on Line 1 (ordinary business income) and $15,000 on Line 4 (guaranteed payments). ◆

A partnership may show a loss after deducting guaranteed payments. In that case, the partner reports the guaranteed payments as income and reports their share of the partnership loss.

Self-Study Problem 10.4   *See Appendix E for Solutions to Self-Study Problems*

Jim and Jack are equal partners in J&J Interests, which has ordinary income for the year of $32,000 before guaranteed payments. Jim receives guaranteed payments of $36,000 during the year. Calculate the total amount of income or loss from the partnership that should be reported by Jim and by Jack.

1. Jim should report total income (loss) of $_____

2. Jack should report total income (loss) of $_____

Determine partnership tax years.

10-5 TAX YEARS

The tax law requires that each partner include in gross income for a particular tax year the individual's distributive share of income, including guaranteed payments, from a partnership whose tax year ends with or within that partner's tax year. For example, a calendar-year individual partner should report their income from a partnership with a tax year ending June 30, 2020, on his or her 2020 tax return. Since a partner reports only income reported by a partnership whose year ends with or within their tax year, it is possible to delay the reporting of partnership income and guaranteed payments for almost an entire year. This would happen, for example, if the partnership's year-end is January 31, and the partner's tax year is a calendar year. To prevent this deferral of income, rigid rules have been established regarding partnership tax years. Under these rules, unless a partnership can establish a business purpose for a fiscal year-end or meet certain tests, it must adopt the same taxable year as that of the majority partners. If such partners do not have the same tax year, then the partnership is required to adopt the tax year of all its principal partners. If neither of these rules can be met, the partnership must adopt a tax year based on the least aggregate deferral method (see IRS Publication 538 for more information).

Once established, a partnership will not close its tax year early unless the partnership is terminated. The tax year does not generally close upon the entry of a new partner, or the liquidation, sale, or exchange of an existing partnership interest. A partnership is terminated, and will close its tax year, if business activity by the partnership ceases.

Self-Study Problem 10.5 *See Appendix E for Solutions to Self-Study Problems*

R&S Associates is a partnership with a tax year that ends on August 31, 2020. During the partnership's tax year, Robert, a partner, received $1,000 per month as a guaranteed payment, and his share of partnership income after guaranteed payments was $21,000. For September through December of 2020, Robert's guaranteed payment was increased to $1,500 per month. Calculate the amount of income from the partnership that Robert should report for his 2020 calendar tax year.

$_____

Describe the tax treatment of transactions between partners and their partnerships.

10-6 TRANSACTIONS BETWEEN PARTNERS AND THE PARTNERSHIP

When engaging in a transaction with a partnership, a partner is generally regarded as an outside party, and the transaction is reported as it would be if the two parties were unrelated. However, it is recognized that occasionally transactions may lack substance because one party to the transaction exercises significant influence over the other party. Therefore, losses are disallowed for (1) transactions between a partnership and a partner who has a direct or indirect capital or profit interest in the partnership of more than 50 percent, and (2) transactions between two partnerships owned more than 50 percent by the same partners. When a loss is disallowed, the purchaser may reduce a future gain on the disposition of the property by the amount of the disallowed loss.

EXAMPLE Kyle owns 55 percent of Willow Interests, a partnership. During the current year, Kyle sells property to the partnership for $60,000. Kyle's adjusted basis in the property is $75,000. The $15,000 loss is disallowed, since

Kyle is a more than 50 percent partner. If later the partnership sells the property for $80,000, realizing a $20,000 gain ($80,000 − $60,000), only $5,000 of the gain is recognized, since the partnership can use Kyle's disallowed loss to offset $15,000 of the gain. ♦

In a transaction between a partner and a partnership, a gain will be taxed as ordinary income if the partner has more than a 50 percent interest in the partnership and the property sold or transferred is not a capital asset to the transferee. The interest may be owned directly or indirectly. For example, a taxpayer indirectly owns the interests owned by their spouse, brothers, sisters, ancestors, and lineal descendants.

EXAMPLE   Amy is a 50 percent partner in the A&B Partnership, and her brother, Ben, is the other 50 percent partner. Amy sells for $65,000 a building (with a basis of $50,000) to the partnership for use in its business. The property qualifies as a long-term capital asset to Amy. The gain of $15,000 ($65,000 − $50,000), however, is ordinary income, since Amy is considered a 100 percent partner (50 percent directly and 50 percent indirectly) and the building is a Section 1231 asset to the partnership. ♦

Self-Study Problem 10.6   *See Appendix E for Solutions to Self-Study Problems*

Maxwell is a 50 percent partner in M&P Associates. Pam, Maxwell's daughter, owns the other 50 percent interest in the partnership. During the current tax year, Maxwell sells ordinary income property to M&P Associates for $70,000. The property's basis to Maxwell is $75,000. Also, Pam sells her personal Mercedes-Benz, with a basis of $25,000, for $40,000 to M&P Associates for use in the partnership's business.

1. What is the amount of Maxwell's recognized gain or loss on his transaction, and what is the nature of the gain or loss?

    $_____

2. What is the amount and nature of Pam's gain or loss on her transaction with the partnership?

    $_____

10-7 QUALIFIED BUSINESS INCOME DEDUCTION FOR PARTNERS

10.7 Learning Objective

Apply the qualified business income deduction to partners.

The qualified business income deduction is available to individual owners of pass-through businesses such as partnerships and LLCs. The deduction in general is covered in Chapter 4. This section covers some of the items applicable specifically to partnerships.

Qualified business income (QBI) generally includes all items of ordinary business income; however, the tax law specifically excludes certain items including guaranteed payments to partners and payments made to partners by the partnership in situations in which the partner is not acting in their capacity as a partner.

EXAMPLE   Rigby is a 30 percent partner in Regular Partnership. In 2020, Regular has $50,000 of ordinary business income and no other separately stated items. In 2020, Rigby receives guaranteed payments of $10,000. Rigby also enters into a loan between himself and Regular and receives interest income from the partnership of $1,000. Regular makes a cash distribution to Rigby of $5,000 and Rigby maintains a positive basis at year-end. The loan is treated as a transaction in which Rigby is not acting in his capacity as a partner and thus the guaranteed payment and the interest are both excluded from Rigby's QBI. Rigby's QBI is $15,000 ($50,000 × 30%). ◆

Although guaranteed payments and payments to partners not acting as partners are not included in QBI, they are deductible by the partnership in computing ordinary business income (to the extent the items would be deductible otherwise).

TAX BREAK   Partners may want to reconsider a characterization away from guaranteed payments as part of a revision to the partnership agreement. Guaranteed payments and the allocation of business income to an individual partner are both generally subject to self-employment taxes; however, guaranteed payments are a deduction from ordinary business income while cash distributions from basis are not. In addition, guaranteed payments are not part of QBI. By treating former guaranteed payments instead as cash distributions, the partnership (and thus the partner) will have greater QBI eligible for the 20 percent QBI deduction. Of course, the "guarantee" of guaranteed payments will also be eliminated by the recharacterization.

For high income taxpayers, the QBI deduction is limited by W-2 wages or a combination of W-2 wages and qualified property. A partner must be allocated their share of these items in order to properly apply the limitations when applicable.

EXAMPLE   Mordecai is a 50 percent partner in Park Partnership. In 2020, Mordecai's taxable income is high enough to subject his QBI deduction to the wage limitation. Park pays W-2 wages of $70,000 and has qualified property of $300,000 in 2020. If these items are allocated in accordance with the partnership interest, Mordecai will be allocated $35,000 of W-2 wages ($70,000 × 50%) and $150,000 of qualified property ($300,000 × 50%) to compute his wage limitation. ◆

Self-Study Problem 10.7   *See Appendix E for Solutions to Self-Study Problems*

a. Dr. Marla Cratchitt is a single taxpayer and works as cardiologist. Marla is an investor in Salem Healthcare LLC, a business that manufactures stents for a variety of cardiovascular issues. Marla's member's interest in Salem is 20 percent and the LLC agreement calls for guaranteed payments to Marla of $75,000 per year. In 2020, Marla's ordinary business income allocation from Salem is $200,000. Salem also allocated $5,000 of long-term capital gains to Marla. Salem paid wages to employees of $230,000 and has qualified property of $1,200,000. Marla has taxable income of $776,000 for purposes of the QBI limit. Compute Marla's QBI deduction.

$_____

b. Assume that same facts as part a. except that Salem is a service business. Compute Marla's QBI deduction.

$_____

10-8 THE AT-RISK RULE

The at-risk rule is designed to prevent taxpayers from deducting losses from activities in excess of their investment in those activities. Although the at-risk rule applies to most taxpayers, it is discussed here because the rule is a common problem related to investments in partnerships. In general, the at-risk rule limits the losses from a taxpayer's business activities to "amounts at risk" (AAR) in the activity.

To understand the at-risk rule, it is necessary to understand two related terms, "nonrecourse liabilities" and "encumbered property." A nonrecourse liability is a debt for which the borrower is not personally liable. If the debt is not paid, the lender generally can only repossess the property pledged as collateral on the loan. Encumbered property (also referred to as "collateral") is property pledged for the liability. The property is said to be encumbered in the amount of the liability. Taxpayers are at risk in amounts equal to their cash and property contributions to the activities, borrowed amounts to the extent of the property pledged, liabilities for which the taxpayers are personally liable, and retained profits of the activity. For contributions of unencumbered property, the amount considered at risk is the adjusted basis of the property contributed to the activity. For encumbered property, the amount at risk is also the adjusted basis of the property to the taxpayer if he or she is personally liable for repayment of the debt. If there is no personal liability for the debt, the amount at risk is the difference between the adjusted basis of the property and the amount of the nonrecourse debt on the property.

EXAMPLE   A taxpayer contributes property with an adjusted basis of $100,000, subject to a recourse liability of $25,000 and a nonrecourse liability of $40,000. The taxpayer's AAR is the basis of the property less the amount of the nonrecourse liability, or $60,000 ($100,000 − $40,000). ◆

Under the at-risk rule, taxpayers are allowed a deduction for losses allocable to a business activity to the extent of (1) income received or accrued from the activity without regard to the amount at risk, or (2) the taxpayer's amount at risk at the end of the tax year. Any losses not allowed in the current year may be treated as deductions in succeeding years, with no limit on the number of years the losses may be carried forward. Remember that passive loss rules (discussed in Chapter 4) may also limit the taxpayer's ability to deduct certain losses.

EXAMPLE   A taxpayer contributes $100,000 to an activity. Her amount at risk is $100,000. In the current year, the activity incurs losses of $250,000. For the current year, the taxpayer is allowed a loss of $100,000, the amount at risk. ◆

While real estate acquired before 1987 is not subject to the at-risk rules, the at-risk rules do apply to real estate acquired after 1986. For real estate acquired after 1986, "qualified nonrecourse financing" on real estate is considered to be an amount at risk. Qualified nonrecourse financing is debt that is secured by the real estate and loaned or guaranteed by a governmental agency or borrowed from any person who actively and regularly engages in the lending of money, such as a bank, savings and loan, or insurance company. A taxpayer is not considered at risk for financing obtained from sellers or promoters, including loans from parties related to the sellers or promoters.

EXAMPLE   In the current tax year, Donna buys a real estate investment with a $20,000 cash down payment and $80,000 borrowed from a savings and loan company secured by a mortgage on the property. Donna has $100,000 at risk in this investment. If the mortgage were obtained from the seller, her amount at risk would be limited to her down payment of $20,000. ◆

Self-Study Problem 10.8 *See Appendix E for Solutions to Self-Study Problems*

During the current tax year, Joe is a partner in a plumbing business. His amount at risk at the beginning of the year is $45,000. During the year, Joe's share of loss is $60,000.

1. What is the amount of the loss that Joe may deduct for the current tax year? $_____

2. If Joe has a profit of $31,000 in the following tax year, how much is taxable? $_____

Learning Objective 10.9

Describe the tax treatment of limited liability companies (LLCs).

10-9 LIMITED LIABILITY COMPANIES

A limited liability company (LLC) is a hybrid form of business organization having some attributes of a partnership and other attributes of a corporation. Each owner, referred to as a member, of an LLC has limited liability, which may be similar to a stockholder in a corporation. However, an LLC is generally treated as a partnership for tax purposes. Because of this tax treatment, members of LLCs can have the tax advantages of a partnership and still have limited liability similar to a corporation. The benefits of LLCs have made them very popular as an entity choice for small business. LLCs are recognized legal entities in all 50 states and the District of Columbia. Many states prohibit certain licensed professionals such as attorneys, architects, and accountants from operating as an LLC but allow the formation of limited liability partnerships (LLPs) if these businesses wish to operate in a partnership form with legal liability protection similar to LLCs.

For the most part, LLCs follow partnership taxation rules. For example, taxable income and losses pass through to members, thereby either avoiding the corporate tax or allowing the member to use the losses. An LLC may elect to be taxed like a corporation rather than a partnership, but very few do. Like partnerships, LLCs' items of income and expense retain their tax attributes (e.g., capital gains and charitable contributions). However, LLCs are not required to have a general partner, unlike a limited partnership in which there has to be at least one general partner who does not have limited liability. Also, LLC members can participate in the management of the business. Because of the limited liability associated with LLCs, the debt of the LLC is generally treated as non-recourse. Lastly, LLCs may have a single member, whereas a partnership must have at least two partners. A single-member LLC is treated as a disregarded entity for tax purposes (i.e., the taxable income of the single-member LLC is reported directly on the tax return of its member, not on a separate Form 1065).

Self-Study Problem 10.9 *See Appendix E for Solutions to Self-Study Problems*

Indicate whether the following statements are true or false by circling the appropriate letter.

T F 1. A limited liability company is generally treated like a corporation for federal income tax purposes.

T F 2. A general partner is required for a limited liability company.

T F 3. Tax attributes of an LLC transaction pass through to the owners of an LLC.

T F 4. Owners of an LLC can participate in the management of the LLC business.

T F 5. Debt of an LLC is generally treated as recourse debt and thus included in a member's basis computations.

KEY TERMS

partnership, 10-2
general (ordinary) partnerships, 10-2
general partners, 10-2
limited partnerships, 10-2
limited partners, 10-2
initial basis, 10-4
basis, 10-4

Form 1065, 10-5
Schedule K-1, 10-5
current distribution, 10-15
guaranteed payments, 10-15
qualified business income deduction, 10-17
qualified business income, 10-17
at-risk rule, 10-19

nonrecourse liabilities, 10-19
encumbered property ("collateral"), 10-19
qualified nonrecourse financing, 10-19
limited liability companies ("LLCs"), 10-20
limited liability partnerships ("LLPs"), 10-20

KEY POINTS

Learning Objectives	Key Points
LO 10.1: Define a partnership for tax purposes.	• A partnership is a syndicate, group, pool, joint venture, or other unincorporated organization through or by means of which any business, financial operation, or venture is carried on, and which is not classified as a corporation, trust, or estate. • Partnership federal tax returns are information returns only, which show the amount of income by type and the allocation of the income to the partners. • Partnership income is taxable to the partner even if that individual does not actually receive it in cash. • Co-ownership of property does not constitute a partnership (e.g., owning investment property); the partners must engage in some type of business or financial activity. • Limited partnerships, limited liability partnerships (LLPs), and limited liability companies (LLCs) are generally treated as partnerships for tax law purposes.
LO 10.2: Describe the basic tax rules for partnership formation and operation.	• Generally, there is no gain or loss recognized by a partnership or any of its partners when property is contributed to a partnership in exchange for an interest in the partnership. • When a partner receives a partnership interest in exchange for providing services to the partnership, income is recognized by the partner. • When a partner transfers property to a partnership in exchange for a partnership interest and that property is subject to a liability exceeding the partner's basis, income may be recognized by the partner. • A partner's basis is increased by the partner's contributions to the partnership, income and gains of the partnership, and increases in the partner's share of partnership liabilities. • A partner's basis is decreased by distributions by the partnership, losses of the partnership, and decreases in the partner's share of partnership liabilities.
LO 10.3: Summarize the rules for partnership income reporting.	• A partnership is required to report its income and other items on Form 1065, U.S. Return of Partnership Income, even though the partnership does not pay federal income tax. • When reporting partnership taxable income, certain transactions must be separated rather than being reported as part of ordinary income. Separately reported items include net rental income, interest income, dividend income, capital gains and losses, Section 1231 gains and losses, Section 179 deductions, charitable deductions, tax-exempt income, non-deductible expenses, and most credits. • Schedule K-1 of Form 1065 presents the allocation of ordinary income or loss, special income and deductions, and gains and losses to each partner. The partners report the K-1 amounts on their own individual tax returns.

LO 10.4: Describe the tax treatment of partnership distributions.	• No gain is recognized by the partner receiving a current distribution unless the partner's basis in the partnership has reached zero. In such a case, gain is recognized only to the extent that a distribution of money exceeds the partner's basis in their partnership interest. • Payments made to a partner for services rendered or for the use of the partner's capital that are made without regard to the income of the partnership are termed *guaranteed payments*. • Guaranteed payments are treated by the partnership in the same manner as payments made to a person who is not a partner. • Guaranteed payments are ordinary income to the partner and deductible by the partnership. • A partnership may show a loss after deducting guaranteed payments, in which case, the partner reports the guaranteed payments as income and reports their share of the partnership loss.
LO 10.5: Determine partnership tax years.	• Each partner includes in gross income for a particular tax year their individual distributive share of income, including guaranteed payments, from a partnership whose tax year ends with or within that tax year. • Unless a partnership can establish a business purpose for a fiscal year-end or meet certain tests, it must adopt the same taxable year as that of the majority partners. • If the majority partners do not have the same tax year, then the partnership is required to adopt the tax year of all its principal partners; otherwise, the partnership must adopt a tax year based on the least aggregate deferral method. • The tax year does not generally close upon the entry of a new partner, or upon the liquidation, sale, or exchange of an existing partnership interest. • A partnership will not close its tax year early unless the partnership is terminated, which occurs when business activity by the partnership ceases.
LO 10.6: Describe the tax treatment of transactions between partners and their partnerships.	• Generally, in a transaction with a partnership, a partner is regarded as an outside party, and the transaction is reported as it would be if the two parties were unrelated. • Losses, however, are disallowed for (1) transactions between a partnership and a partner who has a direct or indirect capital or profit interest in the partnership of more than 50 percent, and (2) transactions between two partnerships owned more than 50 percent by the same partners. • When a loss is disallowed, the purchaser may reduce a future gain on the disposition of the property by the amount of the disallowed loss. • A gain in a transaction between a partner and a partnership will be taxed as ordinary income if the partner has more than a 50 percent interest in the partnership and the property sold or transferred is not a capital asset to the transferee.
LO 10.7: Apply the qualified business income deduction to partners.	• Qualified business income does not include guaranteed payments or payments made to partners by the partnership in situations in which the partner is not acting in their capacity as a partner. • Partners are allocated their share of W-2 wages paid and qualified property of the partnership when computing the QBI deduction.

| **LO 10.8:**
Apply the at-risk rule to partnerships. | • In general, the at-risk rule limits the losses from a taxpayer's business activities to "amounts at risk" in the activity.
• Taxpayers are at risk in amounts equal to their cash and property contributions to the activities, borrowed amounts to the extent of the property pledged, liabilities for which the taxpayers are personally liable, and retained profits of the activity.
• Under the at-risk rule, taxpayers are allowed a deduction for losses allocable to a business activity to the extent of (1) income received or accrued from the activity without regard to the amount at risk, or (2) the taxpayer's amount at risk at the end of the tax year.
• Any losses not allowed in the current year may be treated as deductions in succeeding years, with no limit on the number of years the losses may be carried forward. |
| **LO 10.9:**
Describe the tax treatment of limited liability companies (LLCs). | • A limited liability company (LLC) is a hybrid form of business organization having some attributes of a partnership and other attributes of a corporation.
• Each member of an LLC has limited liability similar to that of a stockholder in a corporation and at the same time has the tax advantages of a partnership (e.g., no tax at the entity level, loss pass-through, etc.).
• Licensed professionals, such as attorneys, architects, and accountants, most often use a limited liability partnership (LLP) organizational structure, which is similar in many respects to an LLC. |

QUESTIONS and PROBLEMS

GROUP 1:
MULTIPLE CHOICE QUESTIONS

LO 10.1

1. Which of the following may *not* be treated as a partnership for tax purposes?
   a. Arnold and Willis operate a restaurant.
   b. Thelma and Louise establish an LLP to operate an accounting practice.
   c. Lucy and Desi purchase real estate together as a business.
   d. Jennifer and Ben form a corporation to purchase and operate a hardware store.
   e. All of the above are partnerships.

LO 10.1

2. Which of the following is a partnership for tax purposes?
   a. Monica and Chandler form a corporation to acquire a trucking business.
   b. Jimmy and Stephen both purchase a small stock interest in a manufacturing corporation as an investment.
   c. Emeril and Rachel purchase a food truck and sell prepared food dishes at various spots around the city.
   d. Melissa purchases a shoe store and hires her sister, Whitney, to manage the store.
   e. None of the above.

LO 10.2

3. A partner's interest in a partnership is increased by:
   a. Capital losses of the partnership
   b. Tax-exempt interest earned by the partnership
   c. Losses of the partnership
   d. Distributions by the partnership
   e. None of the above

LO 10.2

4. A partner's interest in a partnership is decreased by:
   a. Increases in the partner's share of the partnership liabilities
   b. Debt relief that a partner experiences when contributing to the partnership property subject to a liability
   c. The partner's share of tax-exempt income earned by the partnership
   d. Contributions of cash from the partnership to the partner
   e. None of the above

LO 10.2

5. Abigail contributes land with an adjusted basis of $50,000 and a fair market value of $60,000 to Blair and Partners, a partnership. Abigail receives a 50 percent interest in Blair. What is Blair's basis in the land?
   a. $25,000
   b. $30,000
   c. $50,000
   d. $58,000
   e. $60,000

LO 10.2

6. Abigail contributes land with an adjusted basis of $50,000 and a fair market value of $60,000 to Blair and Partners, a partnership. Abigail receives a 50 percent interest in Blair. What is Abigail's basis in her partnership interest?
   a. $25,000
   b. $30,000
   c. $50,000
   d. $56,000
   e. $60,000

LO 10.2

7. Abigail contributes land with an adjusted basis of $50,000 and a fair market value of $60,000 to Blair and Partners, a partnership. Abigail receives a 50 percent interest in Blair. What is Abigail's recognized gain or loss on the contribution?
   a. $0
   b. $10,000 loss
   c. $10,000 gain
   d. $5,000 loss
   e. $5,000 gain

LO 10.2

8. Abigail contributes land with an adjusted basis of $50,000 and a fair market value of $60,000 to Blair and Partners, a partnership. Abigail receives a 50 percent interest in Blair. What is Blair's recognized gain or loss on the contribution?
   a. $0
   b. $10,000 loss
   c. $10,000 gain
   d. $5,000 loss
   e. $5,000 gain

LO 10.2

9. Blake and Ryan form the Poole Partnership. Blake contributes cash of $15,000. Ryan contributes land with an adjusted basis of $1,000 and a fair market value of $21,000. The land is subject to a $6,000 mortgage that Poole assumes. Blake and Ryan both receive a 50 percent interest in Poole. What is Ryan's recognized gain or loss on the contribution?
   a. $2,000
   b. $3,000
   c. $5,000
   d. $20,000
   e. None of the above

LO 10.3

10. Which of the following items do *not* have to be reported separately on a partnership return?
   a. Tax-exempt income
   b. Dividend income
   c. Typical MACRS depreciation expense
   d. Capital gains and losses
   e. Charitable contributions

LO 10.3 11. Which of the following items is generally reported separately on a partnership return?
  a. Ordinary income from the operations of the partnership business
  b. Bonus depreciation
  c. Interest expense on business debts
  d. Net rental income
  e. Factory rent expense

LO 10.3 12. When calculating ordinary income, partnerships are *not* allowed which of the following deductions?
  a. Miscellaneous expenses
  b. Qualified business income deduction
  c. Depreciation
  d. Cost of goods sold
  e. Employee wages

LO 10.4 13. Feela is a one-third owner of Alchemy LLC, which is taxed as a partnership. Her basis prior to Alchemy paying Feela an $11,000 cash distribution is $6,000. How much income does Feela recognize from the distribution and what is her basis in her interest in Alchemy after the distribution?
  a. $11,000 income and $6,000 basis
  b. $6,000 income and $5,000 basis
  c. $5,000 income and $0 basis
  d. $0 income and negative $5,000 basis
  e. None of these choices

LO 10.4 14. Which of the following items is generally reported separately on a partnership return?
  a. Gross ordinary income from the operations of the partnership business
  b. Typical MACRS depreciation
  c. Employee salaries expense
  d. Insurance expense
  e. Guaranteed payments to a partner

LO 10.4 15. Khushboo's basis in her 25 percent interest in the Rishi Partnership is $40,000 at the start of the current year. During the current year, Rishi reports ordinary business income of $80,000. Rishi also makes a $10,000 guaranteed payment and $16,000 cash distribution, both to Khushboo. What will Khushboo's basis be at the end of the current year and how much income will Khushboo recognize from these transactions?
  a. Basis of $44,000 and income of $30,000
  b. Basis of $34,000 and income of $80,000
  c. Basis of $34,000 and income of $20,000
  d. Basis of $60,000 and income of $20,000
  e. Basis of $50,000 and income of $16,000

LO 10.5 16. Which of the following circumstances will *not* cause a partnership to close its tax year early?
  a. The partnership terminates by agreement of the partners.
  b. The business activity of the partnership permanently ceases.
  c. All the partners decide to retire, permanently close their stores and stop conducting business.
  d. A new partner enters the partnership.

LO 10.5 17. Joe, Ben, and Melissa are partners in Collins Partnership. All three use a calendar year-end for their individual taxes. Collins Partnership's year-end is likely to be:
  a. October 31 since that is only three months prior to calendar year-end
  b. The end of any month during the year
  c. January 31 but only if Collins Partnership's accounting year-end is January 31
  d. December 31
  e. None of the above

LO 10.6

18. Kendra is an attorney and owns 60 percent of a law partnership. Kendra sells land to the partnership for $50,000 in the current tax year. She bought the land for $100,000 eight years ago when real estate prices were at their peak. How much gain or loss must Kendra recognize on the land sale to the partnership?
    a. No gain or loss
    b. $30,000 loss
    c. $50,000 loss
    d. $50,000 short-term capital loss, limited to $3,000 allowed per year

LO 10.6

19. A loss from the sale or exchange of property will be disallowed in which of the following situations?
    a. A transaction between a partnership and a partner who owns 40 percent of the partnership capital
    b. A transaction between a partnership and a partner who has a 40 percent profit interest in the partnership
    c. A transaction between two partnerships owned 80 percent by the same partners
    d. A transaction between two partners with investments in the same partnership
    e. None of the above

LO 10.7

20. In 2020, Gloria, a single taxpayer, receives a Schedule K-1 from a partnership she is invested in. The K-1 reports ordinary business income of $30,000, dividend income of $500, tax-exempt interest of $300, and a guaranteed payment to Gloria of $10,000. Gloria's taxable income before the QBI deduction is $87,000. What is Gloria's QBI deduction?
    a. $16,000
    b. $6,000
    c. $4,100
    d. $17,400
    e. $8,000

LO 10.7

21. Jay is a 30 percent partner in the Closet Partnership. In 2020, Closet paid W-2 wages of $24,000 and held qualified property of $600,000. In 2020, Jay's QBI deduction is subject to the wage limitation due to his income. If Closet allocates wages and qualified property in the same manner as income (based on percentage ownership), what is Jay's wage and qualified property limit on the QBI deduction?
    a. $12,000
    b. $3,600
    c. $6,300
    d. $4,500

LO 10.8

22. Mike purchases a rental property for $200,000 and takes out a loan from a lending institution to finance half of the purchase, or $100,000. The loan is considered to be qualified nonrecourse financing. What is Mike's at-risk amount?
    a. $300,000
    b. $200,000
    c. $100,000
    d. $0

LO 10.8

23. Gloria is a 30 percent general partner in the VH Partnership. During the year, VH borrows $40,000 from a bank to fund operations and is able to pay back $10,000 before year-end. VH also borrows $100,000 from Gloria's wealthy retired uncle on a non-recourse basis using land held by the partnership as the collateral. How much does Gloria's at-risk amount increase or decrease as a result of these transactions?
    a. $9,000 increase
    b. $30,000 decrease
    c. $12,000 increase
    d. $42,000 increase
    e. $42,000 decrease

LO 10.9

24. Which of the following properly describes a difference between a partnership and an LLC?
    a. Partnerships pass income and losses through to the partners while LLCs generally pay an entity level tax and owners pay tax on distributions.
    b. Partners are often personally responsible for the debts of the partnership while LLC members are not liable for LLC debt.
    c. Partnerships may have only one partner but LLCs must have more than one member.
    d. The tax attributes of income in a partnership are retained when included in the partner's income but LLC income is treated as capital income in all cases.

GROUP 2:
PROBLEMS

LO 10.1

1. Debbie and Alan open a web-based bookstore together. They have been friends for so long that they start their business on a handshake after discussing how they will share both work and profits or losses from the business. Explain whether Debbie and Alan formed a partnership given that they have signed no written partnership agreement?

   _____

   _____

LO 10.2

2. Mitchell, Max, and Romeo form a partnership to operate a grocery store. For each of the following contributions by the partners, indicate (1) the amount of income or gain recognized, if any, by the partner, and (2) the partner's basis in the partnership interest immediately after the contribution including the allocation of liabilities.
    a. Mitchell contributes property with a basis of $45,000 and subject to a $75,000 liability to the partnership for a one-third partnership interest worth $105,000. The partnership assumes the liability.

       Income or gain recognized $ _____
       Mitchell's basis in the partnership interest $ _____

    b. Max contributes property with a basis of $25,000 and a fair market value of $105,000 to the partnership for a one-third partnership interest.

       Income or gain recognized $ _____
       Max's basis in the partnership interest $ _____

    c. Romeo performs services valued at $105,000 for the partnership for a one-third interest in the partnership.

       Income or gain recognized $ _____
       Romeo's basis in the partnership interest $ _____

LO 10.2

3. Nan contributes property with an adjusted basis of $50,000 to a partnership. The property has a fair market value of $60,000 on the date of the contribution. What is the partnership's basis in the property contributed by Nan?

   $ _____

LO 10.2

4. Elaine's original basis in the Hornbeam Partnership was $40,000. Her share of the taxable income from the partnership since she purchased the interest has been $70,000, and Elaine has received $80,000 in cash distributions from the partnership. Elaine did not recognize any gains as a result of the distributions. In the current year, Hornbeam also allocated $1,000 of tax-exempt interest to Elaine. Calculate Elaine's current basis in her partnership interest.

   $ _____

LO 10.2

5. Kele and Nova wish to form the Sioux Partnership. Kele contributes property with an adjusted basis of $70,000, a fair market value of $200,000 that is subject to an $80,000 liability in exchange for 40 percent of Sioux. Nova receives a 60 percent interest in Sioux in exchange for providing services worth $10,000 and $170,000 cash.

a. What amount of gain or loss must Kele recognize as a result of transferring property to the partnership?

$ _____

b. What is Kele's basis in the partnership interest immediately after the formation of the partnership including allocation of partnership liabilities?

$ _____

c. What is the partnership's basis in the property contributed by Kele?

$ _____

d. What is Nova's basis in the partnership interest immediately after the formation of the partnership including allocation of partnership liabilities?

$ _____

e. How much income does Nova recognize on the exchange?

$ _____

LO 10.2

6. Juanita contributes property with a fair market value of $30,000 and an adjusted basis of $16,000 to a partnership in exchange for an 10 percent partnership interest.

a. Calculate the amount of gain recognized by Juanita as a result of the transfer of the property to the partnership.

$ _____

b. Calculate Juanita's basis in his partnership interest immediately following the contribution to the partnership.

$ _____

LO 10.2
LO 10.4

7. Meredith has a 40 percent interest in the assets and income of the Gantt Partnership, and the basis in her partnership interest is $60,000 at the beginning of 2020. During 2020, the partnership's net loss is $45,000 and Meredith's share of the loss is $18,000. Also, Meredith receives a cash distribution from the partnership of $8,000 on June 30, 2020.

a. Indicate the amount of income or loss from the partnership that should be reported by Meredith on her 2020 individual income tax return.

$ _____

b. Calculate Meredith's basis in her partnership interest at the end of 2020.

$ _____

LO 10.3

8. Go to the IRS website (**www.irs.gov**) and print pages 1 and 2 of Schedule K-1 (Form 1065), Partner's Share of Income, Deductions, Credits, etc. Review the different elements of income which must be passed through to each partner and be reported as separately stated items. Review the numerous codes on page 2 of Schedule K-1 which identify additional items that are required to be separately stated.

LO 10.4

9. K&T Company is a partnership with two equal partners, Kai and Taonga. The partnership has income of $60,000 for the year *before guaranteed payments*. Guaranteed payments of $25,000 are paid to Kai during the year. Calculate the amount of income that should be reported by Kai and Taonga from the partnership for the year.

Kai should report income of $ _____
Taonga should report income of $ _____

LO 10.4

10. Walter receives cash of $18,000 and land with a fair market value of $75,000 (adjusted basis of $50,000) in a current distribution. His basis in his partnership interest is $16,000 before the distribution.
   a. What amount of gain must Walter recognize as a result of the current distribution?
   $ _____

   b. What amount of gain must the partnership recognize as a result of the distribution?
   $ _____

   c. What is Walter's basis in his partnership interest immediately after the distribution?
   $ _____

LO 10.5

11. Kiwi Interests is a partnership with a tax year that ends on September 30, 2020. During that year, Kereru, a partner, received $2,000 per month as a guaranteed payment, and his share of partnership income after guaranteed payments was $14,000. For October through December of 2020, Kereru received guaranteed payments of $3,000 per month. Calculate the amount of income from the partnership that Kereru should report for the tax year ending December 31, 2020.
   $ _____

LO 10.6

12. Louise owns 45 percent of a partnership, and her brother owns the remaining 55 percent interest. During the current tax year, Louise sold a building to the partnership for $160,000 to be used for the partnership's office. She had held the building for 3 years, and it had an adjusted basis of $120,000 at the time of the sale. What is the amount and nature of Louise's gain on this transaction?
   $ _____

LO 10.7

13. Janie owns a 30 percent interest in Chang Partnership. Chang has W-2 wages of $20,000 and qualified property of $900,000 in 2020.
   a. When computing the W-2 wages limitation, what is the amount of wages that will be allocated to Janie?
   $ _____

   b. What is the amount of qualified property that will be allocated to Janie?
   $ _____

LO 10.8

14. Van makes an investment in a partnership in the current year. Van's capital contributions to the partnership consist of $30,000 cash and a building with an adjusted basis of $70,000, subject to a nonrecourse liability (seller financing) of $20,000.
   a. Calculate the amount that Van has at risk in the partnership immediately after making the capital contributions.
   $ _____

   b. If Van's share of the loss from the partnership is $100,000 in the current year, and assuming that Van has sufficient amounts of passive income, how much of the loss may he deduct in the current year?
   $ _____

   c. What may be done with the nondeductible part of the loss in Part b?
   _____
   _____

LO 10.9

15. Van makes an investment in an LLC in the current year. Van's capital contributions to the LLC consist of $30,000 cash and a building with an adjusted basis of $70,000, subject to a nonrecourse liability (seller financing) of $20,000. Calculate the amount that Van has at risk in the LLC immediately after making the capital contributions.
   $ _____

LO 10.9

16. Describe ways in which LLCs might differ from partnerships.

GROUP 3:
COMPREHENSIVE PROBLEM

Emily Jackson (Social Security number 765-12-4326) and James Stewart (Social Security number 466-74-9932) are partners in a partnership that owns and operates a barber shop. The partnership's first year of operation is 2020. Emily and James divide income and expenses equally. The partnership name is J&S Barbers, it is located at 1023 Lexington Avenue, New York, NY 10128, and its Federal ID number is 95-6767676. The 2020 financial statements for the partnership are presented below.

J&S Barbers Income Statement
for the Year Ending December 31, 2020

Gross income from operations	$349,000
Interest income	1,000
Deductions:	
Salaries to employees	100,000
Payroll taxes	11,000
Supplies	8,000
Rent	90,000
Depreciation	32,000
Short-term capital loss	2,000
Non-deductible entertainment	3,000
Charitable contributions	1,000
Net income	$103,000
Partners' withdrawals (each partner)	$ 50,000

J&S Barbers Balance Sheet
as of December 31, 2020

Assets:		
Cash		$82,000
Accounts receivable		10,000
Land	$ 3,000	
Equipment	32,000	
Accumulated depreciation	(32,000)	3,000
		$95,000
Liabilities and Capital:		
Accounts payable		$30,000
Notes payable		22,000
Partners' capital ($20,000		
contributed by each partner)		43,000
		$95,000

Emily lives at 456 E. 70th Street, New York, NY 10006, and James lives at 436 E. 63rd Street, New York, NY 10012.

Required: Complete J&S Barbers' Form 1065 and Emily and James' Schedule K-1s. Do not fill in Schedule D for the capital loss, Form 4562 for depreciation, or Schedule B-1 related to ownership of the partnership. Make realistic assumptions about any missing data.

Form **1065**		**U.S. Return of Partnership Income**		OMB No. 1545-0123

Department of the Treasury
Internal Revenue Service

For calendar year 2020, or tax year beginning _____, 2020, ending _____, 20 ____.

▶ Go to *www.irs.gov/Form1065* for instructions and the latest information.

2020

A Principal business activity	**Type or Print**	Name of partnership	**D** Employer identification number
B Principal product or service		Number, street, and room or suite no. If a P.O. box, see instructions.	**E** Date business started
C Business code number		City or town, state or province, country, and ZIP or foreign postal code	**F** Total assets (see instructions) $

G Check applicable boxes: **(1)** ☐ Initial return **(2)** ☐ Final return **(3)** ☐ Name change **(4)** ☐ Address change **(5)** ☐ Amended return

H Check accounting method: **(1)** ☐ Cash **(2)** ☐ Accrual **(3)** ☐ Other (specify) ▶ _____

I Number of Schedules K-1. Attach one for each person who was a partner at any time during the tax year ▶ _____

J Check if Schedules C and M-3 are attached . . . . ▶ ☐

K Check if partnership: **(1)** ☐ Aggregated activities for section 465 at-risk purposes **(2)** ☐ Grouped activities for section 469 passive activity purposes

Caution: Include **only** trade or business income and expenses on lines 1a through 22 below. See instructions for more information.

Income	**1a**	Gross receipts or sales	**1a**	
	b	Returns and allowances	**1b**	
	c	Balance. Subtract line 1b from line 1a		**1c**
	2	Cost of goods sold (attach Form 1125-A)		**2**
	3	Gross profit. Subtract line 2 from line 1c		**3**
	4	Ordinary income (loss) from other partnerships, estates, and trusts (attach statement) .		**4**
	5	Net farm profit (loss) (attach Schedule F (Form 1040))		**5**
	6	Net gain (loss) from Form 4797, Part II, line 17 (attach Form 4797) . . .		**6**
	7	Other income (loss) (attach statement)		**7**
	8	**Total income (loss).** Combine lines 3 through 7		**8**
Deductions (see instructions for limitations)	**9**	Salaries and wages (other than to partners) (less employment credits) . . .		**9**
	10	Guaranteed payments to partners		**10**
	11	Repairs and maintenance		**11**
	12	Bad debts		**12**
	13	Rent		**13**
	14	Taxes and licenses		**14**
	15	Interest (see instructions)		**15**
	16a	Depreciation (if required, attach Form 4562)	**16a**	
	b	Less depreciation reported on Form 1125-A and elsewhere on return .	**16b**	**16c**
	17	Depletion **(Do not deduct oil and gas depletion.)**		**17**
	18	Retirement plans, etc.		**18**
	19	Employee benefit programs		**19**
	20	Other deductions (attach statement)		**20**
	21	**Total deductions.** Add the amounts shown in the far right column for lines 9 through 20 . . .		**21**
	22	**Ordinary business income (loss).** Subtract line 21 from line 8		**22**
Tax and Payment	**23**	Interest due under the look-back method—completed long-term contracts (attach Form 8697) .		**23**
	24	Interest due under the look-back method—income forecast method (attach Form 8866) .		**24**
	25	BBA AAR imputed underpayment (see instructions)		**25**
	26	Other taxes (see instructions)		**26**
	27	**Total balance due.** Add lines 23 through 26		**27**
	28	Payment (see instructions)		**28**
	29	**Amount owed.** If line 28 is smaller than line 27, enter amount owed		**29**
	30	**Overpayment.** If line 28 is larger than line 27, enter overpayment		**30**

Sign Here

Under penalties of perjury, I declare that I have examined this return, including accompanying schedules and statements, and to the best of my knowledge and belief, it is true, correct, and complete. Declaration of preparer (other than partner or limited liability company member) is based on all information of which preparer has any knowledge.

▶ _____ ▶ _____
Signature of partner or limited liability company member   Date

May the IRS discuss this return with the preparer shown below? See instructions. ☐ Yes ☐ No

Paid Preparer Use Only	Print/Type preparer's name	Preparer's signature	Date	Check ☐ if self-employed	PTIN
	Firm's name ▶			Firm's EIN ▶	
	Firm's address ▶			Phone no.	

For Paperwork Reduction Act Notice, see separate instructions.   Cat. No. 11390Z   Form **1065** (2020)

Form 1065 (2020)   Page **2**

Schedule B	Other Information

		Yes	No
1	What type of entity is filing this return? Check the applicable box:		

a ☐ Domestic general partnership   **b** ☐ Domestic limited partnership

c ☐ Domestic limited liability company   **d** ☐ Domestic limited liability partnership

e ☐ Foreign partnership   **f** ☐ Other ▶

2 At the end of the tax year:

a Did any foreign or domestic corporation, partnership (including any entity treated as a partnership), trust, or tax-exempt organization, or any foreign government own, directly or indirectly, an interest of 50% or more in the profit, loss, or capital of the partnership? For rules of constructive ownership, see instructions. If "Yes," attach Schedule B-1, Information on Partners Owning 50% or More of the Partnership

b Did any individual or estate own, directly or indirectly, an interest of 50% or more in the profit, loss, or capital of the partnership? For rules of constructive ownership, see instructions. If "Yes," attach Schedule B-1, Information on Partners Owning 50% or More of the Partnership . . . .

3 At the end of the tax year, did the partnership:

a Own directly 20% or more, or own, directly or indirectly, 50% or more of the total voting power of all classes of stock entitled to vote of any foreign or domestic corporation? For rules of constructive ownership, see instructions. If "Yes," complete (i) through (iv) below . . . .

(i) Name of Corporation	(ii) Employer Identification Number (if any)	(iii) Country of Incorporation	(iv) Percentage Owned in Voting Stock

b Own directly an interest of 20% or more, or own, directly or indirectly, an interest of 50% or more in the profit, loss, or capital in any foreign or domestic partnership (including an entity treated as a partnership) or in the beneficial interest of a trust? For rules of constructive ownership, see instructions. If "Yes," complete (i) through (v) below . .

(i) Name of Entity	(ii) Employer Identification Number (if any)	(iii) Type of Entity	(iv) Country of Organization	(v) Maximum Percentage Owned in Profit, Loss, or Capital

		Yes	No
4	Does the partnership satisfy **all four** of the following conditions?		

a The partnership's total receipts for the tax year were less than $250,000.

b The partnership's total assets at the end of the tax year were less than $1 million.

c Schedules K-1 are filed with the return and furnished to the partners on or before the due date (including extensions) for the partnership return.

d The partnership is not filing and is not required to file Schedule M-3 . . . .

If "Yes," the partnership is not required to complete Schedules L, M-1, and M-2; item F on page 1 of Form 1065; or item L on Schedule K-1.

5 Is this partnership a publicly traded partnership, as defined in section 469(k)(2)? . . . .

6 During the tax year, did the partnership have any debt that was canceled, was forgiven, or had the terms modified so as to reduce the principal amount of the debt? . . . .

7 Has this partnership filed, or is it required to file, Form 8918, Material Advisor Disclosure Statement, to provide information on any reportable transaction? . . . .

8 At any time during calendar year 2020, did the partnership have an interest in or a signature or other authority over a financial account in a foreign country (such as a bank account, securities account, or other financial account)? See instructions for exceptions and filing requirements for FinCEN Form 114, Report of Foreign Bank and Financial Accounts (FBAR). If "Yes," enter the name of the foreign country ▶

9 At any time during the tax year, did the partnership receive a distribution from, or was it the grantor of, or transferor to, a foreign trust? If "Yes," the partnership may have to file Form 3520, Annual Return To Report Transactions With Foreign Trusts and Receipt of Certain Foreign Gifts. See instructions . . . .

10a Is the partnership making, or had it previously made (and not revoked), a section 754 election? . . . . . . See instructions for details regarding a section 754 election.

b Did the partnership make for this tax year an optional basis adjustment under section 743(b) or 734(b)? If "Yes," attach a statement showing the computation and allocation of the basis adjustment. See instructions . . . .

Form **1065** (2020)

Form 1065 (2020)   Page **3**

Schedule B	Other Information *(continued)*	Yes	No
c	Is the partnership required to adjust the basis of partnership assets under section 743(b) or 734(b) because of a substantial built-in loss (as defined under section 743(d)) or substantial basis reduction (as defined under section 734(d))? If "Yes," attach a statement showing the computation and allocation of the basis adjustment. See instructions		
11	Check this box if, during the current or prior tax year, the partnership distributed any property received in a like-kind exchange or contributed such property to another entity (other than disregarded entities wholly owned by the partnership throughout the tax year) . . . . ▶ ☐		
12	At any time during the tax year, did the partnership distribute to any partner a tenancy-in-common or other undivided interest in partnership property?		
13	If the partnership is required to file Form 8858, Information Return of U.S. Persons With Respect To Foreign Disregarded Entities (FDEs) and Foreign Branches (FBs), enter the number of Forms 8858 attached. See instructions . . . . ▶		
14	Does the partnership have any foreign partners? If "Yes," enter the number of Forms 8805, Foreign Partner's Information Statement of Section 1446 Withholding Tax, filed for this partnership . . . ▶		
15	Enter the number of Forms 8865, Return of U.S. Persons With Respect to Certain Foreign Partnerships, attached to this return . . . . ▶		
16a	Did you make any payments in 2020 that would require you to file Form(s) 1099? See instructions		
b	If "Yes," did you or will you file required Form(s) 1099?		
17	Enter the number of Forms 5471, Information Return of U.S. Persons With Respect To Certain Foreign Corporations, attached to this return . . . . ▶		
18	Enter the number of partners that are foreign governments under section 892 . . . . ▶		
19	During the partnership's tax year, did the partnership make any payments that would require it to file Form 1042 and 1042-S under chapter 3 (sections 1441 through 1464) or chapter 4 (sections 1471 through 1474)?		
20	Was the partnership a specified domestic entity required to file Form 8938 for the tax year? See the Instructions for Form 8938		
21	Is the partnership a section 721(c) partnership, as defined in Regulations section 1.721(c)-1(b)(14)?		
22	During the tax year, did the partnership pay or accrue any interest or royalty for which one or more partners are not allowed a deduction under section 267A? See instructions . . . . If "Yes," enter the total amount of the disallowed deductions . . . . ▶ $		
23	Did the partnership have an election under section 163(j) for any real property trade or business or any farming business in effect during the tax year? See instructions		
24	Does the partnership satisfy one or more of the following? See instructions		
a	The partnership owns a pass-through entity with current, or prior year carryover, excess business interest expense.		
b	The partnership's aggregate average annual gross receipts (determined under section 448(c)) for the 3 tax years preceding the current tax year are more than $26 million and the partnership has business interest.		
c	The partnership is a tax shelter (see instructions) and the partnership has business interest expense. If "Yes" to any, complete and attach Form 8990.		
25	Is the partnership electing out of the centralized partnership audit regime under section 6221(b)? See instructions. If "Yes," the partnership must complete Schedule B-2 (Form 1065). Enter the total from Schedule B-2, Part III, line 3 . . . . ▶ _____ If "No," complete Designation of Partnership Representative below.		

Designation of Partnership Representative (see instructions)

Enter below the information for the partnership representative (PR) for the tax year covered by this return.

Name of PR ▶ _____

U.S. address of PR ▶		U.S. phone number of PR ▶

If the PR is an entity, name of the designated individual for the PR ▶ _____

U.S. address of designated individual ▶		U.S. phone number of designated individual ▶

26	Is the partnership attaching Form 8996 to certify as a Qualified Opportunity Fund? . . . . If "Yes," enter the amount from Form 8996, line 16 . . . . ▶ $		
27	Enter the number of foreign partners subject to section 864(c)(8) as a result of transferring all or a portion of an interest in the partnership or of receiving a distribution from the partnership . . . . . . ▶		
28	At any time during the tax year, were there any transfers between the partnership and its partners subject to the disclosure requirements of Regulations section 1.707-8?		
29	Since December 22, 2017, did a foreign corporation directly or indirectly acquire substantially all of the properties constituting a trade or business of your partnership, and was the ownership percentage (by vote or value) for purposes of section 7874 greater than 50% (for example, the partners held more than 50% of the stock of the foreign corporation)? If "Yes," list the ownership percentage by vote and by value. See instructions. Percentage: By Vote By Value		

Form **1065** (2020)

Form 1065 (2020)   Page **4**

Schedule K		Partners' Distributive Share Items		Total amount

Income (Loss)

	1	Ordinary business income (loss) (page 1, line 22)	**1**	
	2	Net rental real estate income (loss) (attach Form 8825)	**2**	
	3a	Other gross rental income (loss)	**3a**		
	b	Expenses from other rental activities (attach statement)	**3b**		
	c	Other net rental income (loss). Subtract line 3b from line 3a	**3c**	
	4	Guaranteed payments: **a** Services **4a**	**b** Capital **4b**		
		c Total. Add lines 4a and 4b	**4c**	
	5	Interest income	**5**	
	6	Dividends and dividend equivalents: **a** Ordinary dividends	**6a**	
		b Qualified dividends **6b**	**c** Dividend equivalents **6c**		
	7	Royalties	**7**	
	8	Net short-term capital gain (loss) (attach Schedule D (Form 1065))	**8**	
	9a	Net long-term capital gain (loss) (attach Schedule D (Form 1065))	**9a**	
	b	Collectibles (28%) gain (loss)	**9b**		
	c	Unrecaptured section 1250 gain (attach statement)	**9c**		
	10	Net section 1231 gain (loss) (attach Form 4797)	**10**	
	11	Other income (loss) (see instructions) Type ▶	**11**	

Deductions

	12	Section 179 deduction (attach Form 4562)	**12**	
	13a	Contributions	**13a**	
	b	Investment interest expense	**13b**	
	c	Section 59(e)(2) expenditures: **(1)** Type ▶_____ **(2)** Amount ▶	**13c(2)**	
	d	Other deductions (see instructions) Type ▶	**13d**	

Self-Employment

	14a	Net earnings (loss) from self-employment	**14a**	
	b	Gross farming or fishing income	**14b**	
	c	Gross nonfarm income	**14c**	

Credits

	15a	Low-income housing credit (section 42(j)(5))	**15a**	
	b	Low-income housing credit (other)	**15b**	
	c	Qualified rehabilitation expenditures (rental real estate) (attach Form 3468, if applicable) . .	**15c**	
	d	Other rental real estate credits (see instructions) Type ▶	**15d**	
	e	Other rental credits (see instructions) Type ▶	**15e**	
	f	Other credits (see instructions) Type ▶	**15f**	

Foreign Transactions

	16a	Name of country or U.S. possession ▶		
	b	Gross income from all sources	**16b**	
	c	Gross income sourced at partner level	**16c**	
		Foreign gross income sourced at partnership level		
	d	Reserved for future use ▶_____ **e** Foreign branch category . . . . . ▶	**16e**	
	f	Passive category ▶_____ **g** General category ▶_____ **h** Other (attach statement) ▶	**16h**	
		Deductions allocated and apportioned at partner level		
	i	Interest expense ▶_____ **j** Other _____ ▶	**16j**	
		Deductions allocated and apportioned at partnership level to foreign source income		
	k	Reserved for future use ▶_____ **l** Foreign branch category . . . . . ▶	**16l**	
	m	Passive category ▶_____ **n** General category ▶_____ **o** Other (attach statement) ▶	**16o**	
	p	Total foreign taxes (check one): ▶ Paid ☐ Accrued ☐	**16p**	
	q	Reduction in taxes available for credit (attach statement)	**16q**	
	r	Other foreign tax information (attach statement)		

Alternative Minimum Tax (AMT) Items

	17a	Post-1986 depreciation adjustment	**17a**	
	b	Adjusted gain or loss	**17b**	
	c	Depletion (other than oil and gas)	**17c**	
	d	Oil, gas, and geothermal properties—gross income	**17d**	
	e	Oil, gas, and geothermal properties—deductions	**17e**	
	f	Other AMT items (attach statement)	**17f**	

Other Information

	18a	Tax-exempt interest income	**18a**	
	b	Other tax-exempt income	**18b**	
	c	Nondeductible expenses	**18c**	
	19a	Distributions of cash and marketable securities	**19a**	
	b	Distributions of other property	**19b**	
	20a	Investment income	**20a**	
	b	Investment expenses	**20b**	
	c	Other items and amounts (attach statement)		

Form **1065** (2020)

Form 1065 (2020) Page **5**

Analysis of Net Income (Loss)

| 1 | Net income (loss). Combine Schedule K, lines 1 through 11. From the result, subtract the sum of Schedule K, lines 12 through 13d, and 16p . . . . | **1** | |

2	Analysis by partner type:	**(i)** Corporate	**(ii)** Individual (active)	**(iii)** Individual (passive)	**(iv)** Partnership	**(v)** Exempt Organization	**(vi)** Nominee/Other
a	General partners						
b	Limited partners						

Schedule L — Balance Sheets per Books

	Assets	Beginning of tax year (a)	(b)	End of tax year (c)	(d)
1	Cash				
2a	Trade notes and accounts receivable				
b	Less allowance for bad debts				
3	Inventories				
4	U.S. government obligations				
5	Tax-exempt securities				
6	Other current assets (attach statement)				
7a	Loans to partners (or persons related to partners) .				
b	Mortgage and real estate loans				
8	Other investments (attach statement) . .				
9a	Buildings and other depreciable assets . .				
b	Less accumulated depreciation				
10a	Depletable assets				
b	Less accumulated depletion				
11	Land (net of any amortization)				
12a	Intangible assets (amortizable only) . . .				
b	Less accumulated amortization . . .				
13	Other assets (attach statement)				
14	Total assets				
	Liabilities and Capital				
15	Accounts payable				
16	Mortgages, notes, bonds payable in less than 1 year				
17	Other current liabilities (attach statement)				
18	All nonrecourse loans				
19a	Loans from partners (or persons related to partners) .				
b	Mortgages, notes, bonds payable in 1 year or more .				
20	Other liabilities (attach statement)				
21	Partners' capital accounts				
22	Total liabilities and capital				

Schedule M-1 — Reconciliation of Income (Loss) per Books With Income (Loss) per Return

Note: The partnership may be required to file Schedule M-3. See instructions.

1	Net income (loss) per books		6	Income recorded on books this year not included on Schedule K, lines 1 through 11 (itemize):	
2	Income included on Schedule K, lines 1, 2, 3c, 5, 6a, 7, 8, 9a, 10, and 11, not recorded on books this year (itemize): _____		a	Tax-exempt interest $ _____	
3	Guaranteed payments (other than health insurance)		7	Deductions included on Schedule K, lines 1 through 13d, and 16p, not charged against book income this year (itemize):	
4	Expenses recorded on books this year not included on Schedule K, lines 1 through 13d, and 16p (itemize):		a	Depreciation $ _____	
a	Depreciation $ _____		8	Add lines 6 and 7	
b	Travel and entertainment $ _____		9	Income (loss) (Analysis of Net Income (Loss), line 1. Subtract line 8 from line 5	
5	Add lines 1 through 4				

Schedule M-2 — Analysis of Partners' Capital Accounts

1	Balance at beginning of year . . .		6	Distributions: **a** Cash	
2	Capital contributed: **a** Cash . .			**b** Property	
	b Property . .		7	Other decreases (itemize): _____	
3	Net income (loss) per books				
4	Other increases (itemize): _____		8	Add lines 6 and 7	
5	Add lines 1 through 4		9	Balance at end of year. Subtract line 8 from line 5	

Form **1065** (2020)

651119

☐ Final K-1   ☐ Amended K-1   OMB No. 1545-0123

Schedule K-1
(Form 1065)
Department of the Treasury
Internal Revenue Service

20**20**

For calendar year 2020, or tax year

beginning ☐ / / 2020 ending ☐ / /

Partner's Share of Income, Deductions, Credits, etc. ▶ See separate instructions.

DRAFT AS OF July 7, 2020 DO NOT FILE

Part I	**Information About the Partnership**
A	Partnership's employer identification number
B	Partnership's name, address, city, state, and ZIP code
C	IRS Center where partnership filed return ▶
D	☐ Check if this is a publicly traded partnership (PTP)

Part II	**Information About the Partner**
E	Partner's SSN or TIN (Do not use TIN of a disregarded entity. See instructions.)
F	Name, address, city, state, and ZIP code for partner entered in E. See instructions.

G ☐ General partner or LLC member-manager   ☐ Limited partner or other LLC member

H1 ☐ Domestic partner   ☐ Foreign partner

H2 ☐ If the partner is a disregarded entity (DE), enter the partner's:
TIN _____ Name _____

I1 What type of entity is this partner? _____

I2 If this partner is a retirement plan (IRA/SEP/Keogh/etc.), check here ☐

J Partner's share of profit, loss, and capital (see instructions):

	Beginning	**Ending**
Profit	%	%
Loss	%	%
Capital	%	%

Check if decrease is due to sale or exchange of partnership interest . . ☐

K Partner's share of liabilities:

	Beginning	**Ending**
Nonrecourse . .	$	$
Qualified nonrecourse financing . . .	$	$
Recourse . . .	$	$

☐ Check this box if Item K includes liability amounts from lower tier partnerships.

L   **Partner's Capital Account Analysis**

Beginning capital account . . . $ _____
Capital contributed during the year . . $ _____
Current year net income (loss) . . . $ _____
Other increase (decrease) (attach explanation) $ _____
Withdrawals & distributions . . . $ (_____)
Ending capital account . . . . $ _____

M Did the partner contribute property with a built-in gain or loss?
☐ Yes   ☐ No   If "Yes," attach statement. See instructions.

N   **Partner's Share of Net Unrecognized Section 704(c) Gain or (Loss)**
Beginning . . . . $ _____
Ending . . . . $ _____

Part III	**Partner's Share of Current Year Income, Deductions, Credits, and Other Items**		
1	Ordinary business income (loss)	15	Credits
2	Net rental real estate income (loss)		
3	Other net rental income (loss)	16	Foreign transactions
4a	Guaranteed payments for services		
4b	Guaranteed payments for capital		
4c	Total guaranteed payments		
5	Interest income		
6a	Ordinary dividends		
6b	Qualified dividends		
6c	Dividend equivalents	17	Alternative minimum tax (AMT) items
7	Royalties		
8	Net short-term capital gain (loss)		
9a	Net long-term capital gain (loss)	18	Tax-exempt income and nondeductible expenses
9b	Collectibles (28%) gain (loss)		
9c	Unrecaptured section 1250 gain		
10	Net section 1231 gain (loss)		
11	Other income (loss)	19	Distributions
12	Section 179 deduction	20	Other information
13	Other deductions		
14	Self-employment earnings (loss)		

21 ☐ More than one activity for at-risk purposes*
22 ☐ More than one activity for passive activity purposes*

*See attached statement for additional information.

For IRS Use Only

For Paperwork Reduction Act Notice, see Instructions for Form 1065.   www.irs.gov/Form1065   Cat. No. 11394R   **Schedule K-1 (Form 1065) 2020**

Schedule K-1 (Form 1065) 2019   Page **2**

This list identifies the codes used on Schedule K-1 for all partners and provides summarized reporting information for partners who file Form 1040 or 1040-SR. For detailed reporting and filing information, see the separate Partner's Instructions for Schedule K-1 and the instructions for your income tax return.

1. **Ordinary business income (loss).** Determine whether the income (loss) is passive or nonpassive and enter on your return as follows.

	Report on
Passive loss	See the Partner's Instructions
Passive income	Schedule E, line 28, column (h)
Nonpassive loss	See the Partner's Instructions
Nonpassive income	Schedule E, line 28, column (k)

2. **Net rental real estate income (loss)** — See the Partner's Instructions
3. **Other net rental income (loss)**
   Net income — Schedule E, line 28, column (h)
   Net loss — See the Partner's Instructions
4a. **Guaranteed payment Services** — See the Partner's Instructions
4b. **Guaranteed payment Capital** — See the Partner's Instructions
4c. **Guaranteed payment Total** — See the Partner's Instructions
5. **Interest income** — Form 1040 or 1040-SR, line 2b
6a. **Ordinary dividends** — Form 1040 or 1040-SR, line 3b
6b. **Qualified dividends** — Form 1040 or 1040-SR, line 3a
6c. **Dividend equivalents** — See the Partner's Instructions
7. **Royalties** — Schedule E, line 4
8. **Net short-term capital gain (loss)** — Schedule D, line 5
9a. **Net long-term capital gain (loss)** — Schedule D, line 12
9b. **Collectibles (28%) gain (loss)** — 28% Rate Gain Worksheet, line 4 (Schedule D instructions)
9c. **Unrecaptured section 1250 gain** — See the Partner's Instructions
10. **Net section 1231 gain (loss)** — See the Partner's Instructions
11. **Other income (loss)**

Code		Report on
A	Other portfolio income (loss)	See the Partner's Instructions
B	Involuntary conversions	See the Partner's Instructions
C	Sec. 1256 contracts & straddles	Form 6781, line 1
D	Mining exploration costs recapture	See Pub. 535
E	Cancellation of debt	
F	Section 743(b) positive adjustments	
G	Section 965(a) inclusion	
H	Income under subpart F (other than inclusions under sections 951A and 965)	See the Partner's Instructions
I	Other income (loss)	

12. **Section 179 deduction** — See the Partner's Instructions
13. **Other deductions**

A	Cash contributions (60%)	
B	Cash contributions (30%)	
C	Noncash contributions (50%)	
D	Noncash contributions (30%)	
E	Capital gain property to a 50% organization (30%)	See the Partner's Instructions
F	Capital gain property (20%)	
G	Contributions (100%)	
H	Investment interest expense	Form 4952, line 1
I	Deductions—royalty income	Schedule E, line 19
J	Section 59(e)(2) expenditures	See the Partner's Instructions
K	Excess business interest expense	See the Partner's Instructions
L	Deductions—portfolio (other)	Schedule A, line 16
M	Amounts paid for medical insurance	Schedule A, line 1, or Schedule 1 (Form 1040 or 1040-SR), line 16
N	Educational assistance benefits	See the Partner's Instructions
O	Dependent care benefits	Form 2441, line 12
P	Preproductive period expenses	See the Partner's Instructions
Q	Commercial revitalization deduction from rental real estate activities	See Form 8582 instructions
R	Pensions and IRAs	See the Partner's Instructions
S	Reforestation expense deduction	See the Partner's Instructions
T	through U	Reserved for future use
V	Section 743(b) negative adjustments	
W	Other deductions	See the Partner's Instructions
X	Section 965(c) deduction	

14. **Self-employment earnings (loss)**

Note: If you have a section 179 deduction or any partner-level deductions, see the Partner's Instructions before completing Schedule SE.

A	Net earnings (loss) from self-employment	Schedule SE, Section A or B
B	Gross farming or fishing income	See the Partner's Instructions
C	Gross non-farm income	See the Partner's Instructions

15. **Credits**

A	Low-income housing credit (section 42(j)(5)) from pre-2008 buildings	
B	Low-income housing credit (other) from pre-2008 buildings	
C	Low-income housing credit (section 42(j)(5)) from post-2007 buildings	
D	Low-income housing credit (other) from post-2007 buildings	See the Partner's Instructions
E	Qualified rehabilitation expenditures (rental real estate)	
F	Other rental real estate credits	
G	Other rental credits	

Code		Report on
H	Undistributed capital gains credit	Schedule 3 (Form 1040 or 1040-SR), line 13, box a
I	Biofuel producer credit	See the Partner's Instructions
J	Work opportunity credit	
K	Disabled access credit	
L	Empowerment zone employment credit	
M	Credit for increasing research activities	See the Partner's Instructions
N	Credit for employer social security and Medicare taxes	
O	Backup withholding	
P	Other credits	

16. **Foreign transactions**

A	Name of country or U.S. possession	
B	Gross income from all sources	Form 1116, Part I
C	Gross income sourced at partner level	

Foreign gross income sourced at partnership level

D	Reserved for future use	
E	Foreign branch category	
F	Passive category	Form 1116, Part I
G	General category	
H	Other	

Deductions allocated and apportioned at partner level

I	Interest expense	Form 1116, Part I
J	Other	Form 1116, Part I

Deductions allocated and apportioned at partnership level to foreign source income

K	Reserved for future use	
L	Foreign branch category	
M	Passive category	Form 1116, Part I
N	General category	
O	Other	

Other information

P	Total foreign taxes paid	Form 1116, Part II
Q	Total foreign taxes accrued	Form 1116, Part II
R	Reduction in taxes available for credit	Form 1116, line 12
S	Foreign trading gross receipts	Form 8873
T	Extraterritorial income exclusion	Form 8873
U	through V	Reserved for future use
W	Section 965 information	See the Partner's Instructions
X	Other foreign transactions	

17. **Alternative minimum tax (AMT) items**

A	Post-1986 depreciation adjustment	
B	Adjusted gain or loss	See the Partner's Instructions and the Instructions for Form 6251
C	Depletion (other than oil & gas)	
D	Oil, gas, & geothermal—gross income	
E	Oil, gas, & geothermal—deductions	
F	Other AMT items	

18. **Tax-exempt income and nondeductible expenses**

A	Tax-exempt interest income	Form 1040 or 1040-SR, line 2a
B	Other tax-exempt income	See the Partner's Instructions
C	Nondeductible expenses	See the Partner's Instructions

19. **Distributions**

A	Cash and marketable securities	
B	Distribution subject to section 737	See the Partner's Instructions
C	Other property	

20. **Other information**

A	Investment income	Form 4952, line 4a
B	Investment expenses	Form 4952, line 5
C	Fuel tax credit information	Form 4136
D	Qualified rehabilitation expenditures (other than rental real estate)	
E	Basis of energy property	See the Partner's Instructions
F	through G	
H	Recapture of investment credit	See Form 4255
I	Recapture of other credits	See the Partner's Instructions
J	Look-back interest—completed long-term contracts	See Form 8697
K	Look-back interest—income forecast method	See Form 8866
L	Dispositions of property with section 179 deductions	
M	Recapture of section 179 deduction	
N	Interest expense for corporate partners	
O	through Y	
Z	Section 199A information	
AA	Section 704(c) information	
AB	Section 751 gain (loss)	See the Partner's Instructions
AC	Section 1(h)(5) gain (loss)	
AD	Deemed section 1250 unrecaptured gain	
AE	Excess taxable income	
AF	Excess business interest income	
AG	Gross receipts for section 59A(e)	
AH	Other information	

Page 2 of Schedule K-1 is from 2019. 2020 not available when we went to print.

Schedule K-1
(Form 1065)
Department of the Treasury
Internal Revenue Service

20**20**

For calendar year 2020, or tax year

beginning ___ / ___ / 2020   ending ___ / ___ / ___

Partner's Share of Income, Deductions, Credits, etc.   ▶ See separate instructions.

651119

OMB No. 1545-0123

☐ Final K-1   ☐ Amended K-1

Part III   Partner's Share of Current Year Income, Deductions, Credits, and Other Items

1 Ordinary business income (loss)		**15** Credits	
2 Net rental real estate income (loss)			
3 Other net rental income (loss)		**16** Foreign transactions	
4a Guaranteed payments for services			
4b Guaranteed payments for capital			
4c Total guaranteed payments			
5 Interest income			
6a Ordinary dividends			
6b Qualified dividends			
6c Dividend equivalents		**17** Alternative minimum tax (AMT) items	
7 Royalties			
8 Net short-term capital gain (loss)			
9a Net long-term capital gain (loss)		**18** Tax-exempt income and nondeductible expenses	
9b Collectibles (28%) gain (loss)			
9c Unrecaptured section 1250 gain			
10 Net section 1231 gain (loss)			
11 Other income (loss)		**19** Distributions	
12 Section 179 deduction		**20** Other information	
13 Other deductions			
14 Self-employment earnings (loss)			

Part I   Information About the Partnership

A Partnership's employer identification number

B Partnership's name, address, city, state, and ZIP code

C IRS Center where partnership filed return ▶
D ☐ Check if this is a publicly traded partnership (PTP)

Part II   Information About the Partner

E Partner's SSN or TIN (Do not use TIN of a disregarded entity. See instructions.)

F Name, address, city, state, and ZIP code for partner entered in E. See instructions.

G ☐ General partner or LLC member-manager   ☐ Limited partner or other LLC member

H1 ☐ Domestic partner   ☐ Foreign partner
H2 ☐ If the partner is a disregarded entity (DE), enter the partner's:
TIN _____ Name _____

I1 What type of entity is this partner? _____
I2 If this partner is a retirement plan (IRA/SEP/Keogh/etc.), check here ☐
J Partner's share of profit, loss, and capital (see instructions):

	Beginning	Ending
Profit	%	%
Loss	%	%
Capital	%	%

Check if decrease is due to sale or exchange of partnership interest   ☐

K Partner's share of liabilities:

	Beginning	Ending
Nonrecourse	$	$
Qualified nonrecourse financing	$	$
Recourse	$	$

☐ Check this box if Item K includes liability amounts from lower tier partnerships.

L   **Partner's Capital Account Analysis**

Beginning capital account $_____
Capital contributed during the year $_____
Current year net income (loss) $_____
Other increase (decrease) (attach explanation) $_____
Withdrawals & distributions $(_____)
Ending capital account $_____

M Did the partner contribute property with a built-in gain or loss?
☐ Yes   ☐ No   If "Yes," attach statement. See instructions.

N Partner's Share of Net Unrecognized Section 704(c) Gain or (Loss)

21 ☐ More than one activity for at-risk purposes*
22 ☐ More than one activity for passive activity purposes*

*See attached statement for additional information.

For IRS Use Only

This list identifies the codes used on Schedule K-1 for all partners and provides summarized reporting information for partners who file Form 1040 or 1040-SR. For detailed reporting and filing information, see the separate Partner's Instructions for Schedule K-1 and the instructions for your income tax return.

1. Ordinary business income (loss). Determine whether the income (loss) is passive or nonpassive and enter on your return as follows.

	Report on
Passive loss	See the Partner's Instructions
Passive income	Schedule E, line 28, column (h)
Nonpassive loss	See the Partner's Instructions
Nonpassive income	Schedule E, line 28, column (k)

2. Net rental real estate income (loss) — See the Partner's Instructions

3. Other net rental income (loss)

Net income	Schedule E, line 28, column (h)
Net loss	See the Partner's Instructions

4a. Guaranteed payment Services — See the Partner's Instructions
4b. Guaranteed payment Capital — See the Partner's Instructions
4c. Guaranteed payment Total — See the Partner's Instructions
5. Interest income — Form 1040 or 1040-SR, line 2b
6a. Ordinary dividends — Form 1040 or 1040-SR, line 3b
6b. Qualified dividends — Form 1040 or 1040-SR, line 3a
6c. Dividend equivalents — See the Partner's Instructions
7. Royalties — Schedule E, line 4
8. Net short-term capital gain (loss) — Schedule D, line 5
9a. Net long-term capital gain (loss) — Schedule D, line 12
9b. Collectibles (28%) gain (loss) — 28% Rate Gain Worksheet, line 4 (Schedule D instructions)
9c. Unrecaptured section 1250 gain — See the Partner's Instructions
10. Net section 1231 gain (loss) — See the Partner's Instructions
11. Other income (loss)

Code
A	Other portfolio income (loss)	See the Partner's Instructions
B	Involuntary conversions	See the Partner's Instructions
C	Sec. 1256 contracts & straddles	Form 6781, line 1
D	Mining exploration costs recapture	See Pub. 535
E	Cancellation of debt	
F	Section 743(b) positive adjustments	
G	Section 965(a) inclusion	
H	Income under subpart F (other than inclusions under sections 951A and 965)	See the Partner's Instructions
I	Other income (loss)	

12. Section 179 deduction — See the Partner's Instructions

13. Other deductions

A	Cash contributions (60%)	
B	Cash contributions (30%)	
C	Noncash contributions (50%)	
D	Noncash contributions (30%)	
E	Capital gain property to a 50% organization (30%)	See the Partner's Instructions
F	Capital gain property (20%)	
G	Contributions (100%)	
H	Investment interest expense	Form 4952, line 1
I	Deductions—royalty income	Schedule E, line 19
J	Section 59(e)(2) expenditures	See the Partner's Instructions
K	Excess business interest expense	See the Partner's Instructions
L	Deductions—portfolio (other)	Schedule A, line 16
M	Amounts paid for medical insurance	Schedule A, line 1, or Schedule 1 (Form 1040 or 1040-SR), line 16
N	Educational assistance benefits	See the Partner's Instructions
O	Dependent care benefits	Form 2441, line 12
P	Preproductive period expenses	See the Partner's Instructions
Q	Commercial revitalization deduction from rental real estate activities	See Form 8582 instructions
R	Pensions and IRAs	See the Partner's Instructions
S	Reforestation expense deduction	See the Partner's Instructions
T	through U	Reserved for future use
V	Section 743(b) negative adjustments	
W	Other deductions	See the Partner's Instructions
X	Section 965(c) deduction	

14. Self-employment earnings (loss)

Note: If you have a section 179 deduction or any partner-level deductions, see the Partner's Instructions before completing Schedule SE.

A	Net earnings (loss) from self-employment	Schedule SE, Section A or B
B	Gross farming or fishing income	See the Partner's Instructions
C	Gross non-farm income	See the Partner's Instructions

15. Credits

A	Low-income housing credit (section 42(j)(5)) from pre-2008 buildings	
B	Low-income housing credit (other) from pre-2008 buildings	
C	Low-income housing credit (section 42(j)(5)) from post-2007 buildings	See the Partner's Instructions
D	Low-income housing credit (other) from post-2007 buildings	
E	Qualified rehabilitation expenditures (rental real estate)	
F	Other rental real estate credits	
G	Other rental credits	

Code		Report on
H	Undistributed capital gains credit	Schedule 3 (Form 1040 or 1040-SR), line 13, box a
I	Biofuel producer credit	See the Partner's Instructions
J	Work opportunity credit	
K	Disabled access credit	
L	Empowerment zone employment credit	
M	Credit for increasing research activities	See the Partner's Instructions
N	Credit for employer social security and Medicare taxes	
O	Backup withholding	
P	Other credits	

16. Foreign transactions

A	Name of country or U.S. possession	
B	Gross income from all sources	Form 1116, Part I
C	Gross income sourced at partner level	

Foreign gross income sourced at partnership level

D	Reserved for future use	
E	Foreign branch category	
F	Passive category	Form 1116, Part I
G	General category	
H	Other	

Deductions allocated and apportioned at partner level

I	Interest expense	Form 1116, Part I
J	Other	Form 1116, Part I

Deductions allocated and apportioned at partnership level to foreign source income

K	Reserved for future use	
L	Foreign branch category	
M	Passive category	Form 1116, Part I
N	General category	
O	Other	

Other information

P	Total foreign taxes paid	Form 1116, Part II
Q	Total foreign taxes accrued	Form 1116, Part II
R	Reduction in taxes available for credit	Form 1116, line 12
S	Foreign trading gross receipts	Form 8873
T	Extraterritorial income exclusion	Form 8873
U	through V	Reserved for future use
W	Section 965 information	
X	Other foreign transactions	See the Partner's Instructions

17. Alternative minimum tax (AMT) items

A	Post-1986 depreciation adjustment	
B	Adjusted gain or loss	See the Partner's Instructions and the Instructions for Form 6251
C	Depletion (other than oil & gas)	
D	Oil, gas, & geothermal—gross income	
E	Oil, gas, & geothermal—deductions	
F	Other AMT items	

18. Tax-exempt income and nondeductible expenses

A	Tax-exempt interest income	Form 1040 or 1040-SR, line 2a
B	Other tax-exempt income	See the Partner's Instructions
C	Nondeductible expenses	See the Partner's Instructions

19. Distributions

A	Cash and marketable securities	
B	Distribution subject to section 737	See the Partner's Instructions
C	Other property	

20. Other information

A	Investment income	Form 4952, line 4a
B	Investment expenses	Form 4952, line 5
C	Fuel tax credit information	Form 4136
D	Qualified rehabilitation expenditures (other than rental real estate)	
E	Basis of energy property	See the Partner's Instructions
F	through G	
H	Recapture of investment credit	See Form 4255
I	Recapture of other credits	See the Partner's Instructions
J	Look-back interest—completed long-term contracts	See Form 8697
K	Look-back interest—income forecast method	See Form 8866
L	Dispositions of property with section 179 deductions	
M	Recapture of section 179 deduction	
N	Interest expense for corporate partners	
O	through Y	
Z	Section 199A information	
AA	Section 704(c) information	
AB	Section 751 gain (loss)	See the Partner's Instructions
AC	Section 1(h)(5) gain (loss)	
AD	Deemed section 1250 unrecaptured gain	
AE	Excess taxable income	
AF	Excess business interest income	
AG	Gross receipts for section 59A(e)	
AH	Other information	

Page 2 of Schedule K-1 is from 2019. 2020 not available when we went to print.

Student Name _____

Class/Section _____

Date _____

KEY NUMBER TAX RETURN SUMMARY

CHAPTER 10

Comprehensive Problem

Ordinary Business Income (Loss) (Page 1, Line 22) _____

Net Income (Loss) (Page 5, Line 1) _____

Net Short-Term Capital Gain (Loss) (Page 4, Line 8) _____

Contributions (Page 4, Line 13a) _____

Nondeductible expenses (Page 4, Line 18c) _____

Net Income (Loss) per Books (Schedule M-2, Line 3) _____

The Corporate Income Tax

LEARNING OBJECTIVES

After completing this chapter, you should be able to:

LO 11.1 Employ the corporate tax rates to calculate corporate tax liability.

LO 11.2 Compute basic gains and losses for corporations.

LO 11.3 Apply special corporate deductions to corporate taxable income.

LO 11.4 Identify the components of Schedule M-1 and how they are reported to the IRS.

LO 11.5 Describe the corporate tax return filing and estimated tax payment requirements.

LO 11.6 Explain how an S corporation operates and is taxed.

LO 11.7 Describe the basic tax rules for the formation of a corporation.

LO 11.8 Describe the rules for the accumulated earnings tax and the personal holding company tax.

LO 11.9 Describe tax issues associated with the repeal of the alternative minimum tax.

OVERVIEW

There are many forms of organization which may be used by taxpayers to operate a business. These include the sole proprietorship (Form 1040, Schedule C, covered in Chapter 3); the partnership, LLC, and LLP (Form 1065 covered in Chapter 10); and the regular C corporation and S corporation (covered in this chapter). Regular C corporations are taxed as separate legal taxpaying entities, and S corporations are taxed as flow-through entities similar to partnerships.

This chapter covers corporate tax rates, capital gains and losses, special deductions, the Schedule M-1, filing requirements, corporate formations, and corporate earnings accumulations. Additionally, basic coverage of the S corporation election and operating requirements are presented in this chapter.

This chapter provides a summary of corporate taxation and the tax forms (Form 1120, Form 1120S, and related schedules) associated with reporting C or S corporation income or loss.

11-1 CORPORATE TAX RATES

Starting in 2018, corporations are subject to a flat income tax rate of 21 percent.

EXAMPLE   Jasmine Corporation has taxable income of $175,000 for 2020. The corporation's tax liability for the year is calculated as follows:

Taxable income	$ 175,000
Corporate tax rate	21%
Tax liability	$ 36,750

◆

Personal service corporations are taxed at the same 21 percent tax rate on all taxable income. A personal service corporation is substantially employee-owned and engages in one of the following activities:

- Health
- Law
- Engineering
- Architecture

- Accounting
- Actuarial science
- Performing arts
- Consulting

EXAMPLE   Elm & Ash, Inc., is a professional service corporation of CPAs. For the current tax year, the corporation has taxable income of $175,000. Elm & Ash will have a 21 percent tax rate like any other corporation and thus a tax liability of $36,750 (21% × $175,000). ◆

Self-Study Problem 11.1   *See Appendix E for Solutions to Self-Study Problems*

Maple Corporation has taxable income of $335,000 for the current tax year. Calculate the corporation's tax liability, before tax credits.

Tax liability $_____

11-2 CORPORATE GAINS AND LOSSES

If a corporation generates a net capital gain, the net gain is included in ordinary income and the tax is computed at the regular rate except under very rare circumstances. The tax law provides for a maximum rate of 21 percent on corporate capital gains. Thus, Congress intends the ordinary income and capital gains rates to be the same for corporations, so there is no tax rate benefit to having long-term capital gains in a corporation. Net short-term capital gains of a corporation are taxed as ordinary income.

11-2a Capital Losses

Corporations are not allowed to deduct capital losses against ordinary income. Capital losses may be used only to offset capital gains. If capital losses cannot be used in the year they occur, they may be carried back 3 years and forward 5 years to offset capital gains in those years. When a long-term capital loss is carried to another year, it is treated as a short-term capital loss, and may be offset against either long-term or short-term capital gains.

EXAMPLE   In 2020, Eucalyptus Corporation incurs a long-term capital loss of $8,000, none of which may be deducted in that year. The loss is carried back to tax years 2017, 2018, and 2019, in that order. If the loss is not entirely used to offset capital gains in those years, it may be carried forward to 2021, 2022, 2023, 2024, and 2025, in that order. When the long-term loss is carried to another year, it is considered to be short-term, and may offset against either long-term or short-term capital gains. ♦

11-2b Net Operating Losses

As discussed in Chapter 3, corporations—similar to individuals—may also carryforward net operating losses (NOLs) to offset future taxable income. The TCJA made significant changes to the carryback and carryforward of NOLs after 2017, but most of these changes were temporarily suspended by the CARES Act in 2020 due to the COVID-19 pandemic. As a result, careful attention needs to be paid to when an NOL was created so that it can be tracked appropriately and afforded the proper treatment. An NOL created before 2018 had a two-year carryback and then a twenty-year carryforward (a taxpayer could elect out of the carryback) and the NOL could be used to offset 100 percent of the future year's taxable income.

EXAMPLE In 2017, Dez Corporation has a net operating loss of $10,000. Dez elects to forego any carryback and instead carries the NOL forward to 2018. In 2018, Dez generates taxable income of $12,000 eligible to be offset by 100 percent of the 2017 NOL. Dez's 2018 taxable income is $2,000, after the carryforward of the 2017 NOL. ♦

Under the TCJA, the use of an NOL generated after December 31, 2017, may only be carried forward (indefinitely) and was limited to 80 percent of the current year's taxable income (without regard to the NOL deduction) when used.

EXAMPLE Before the advent of the CARES Act, Fez Corporation has a net operating loss of $10,000 in 2018. Fez may only carry the NOL forward to 2019. In 2019, Fez generates taxable income of $12,000. Fez may only offset $9,600 ($12,000 × 80%) of its 2019 income and will have taxable income of $2,400. Fez may carryforward the remaining $400 2018 NOL to 2020. ♦

The CARES Act of 2020 suspended both the TCJA's 80 percent income limit rules and the carryforward only rule. Under the current rules, the 80 percent income limitation rule does not apply to a NOL created in 2018, 2019, or 2020, and those same NOLs may be carried back five years (unless carryback is waived). The carryforward remains indefinite. The TCJA rules are reinstated for years after 2020, thus an NOL carried forward into 2021 will be subject to the 80 percent limitation.

EXAMPLE Pez Corporation has the following taxable income/(loss) over the previous six years:

Year	2015	2016	2017	2018	2019	2020
Income/(loss)	$10,000	$14,000	$3,000	$14,000	$15,000	$(68,000)

Under the current rules, Pez can carryback the current year's $68,000 NOL loss to 2015, 2016, 2017, 2018, and 2019, effectively eliminating any taxable income for all five years. The remaining $12,000 NOL can be carried forward indefinitely and can offset 80 percent of a future year's income. ♦

For a company that experienced losses in previous years, the tracking of NOLs can be even more complicated.

EXAMPLE Nez Corporation has the following taxable income/(loss) over the previous six years:

Year	2015	2016	2017	2018	2019	2020
Income/(loss)	$10,000	$14,000	$(30,000)	$7,000	$(4,000)	$(30,000)

In 2017, Nez would have carried back the $30,000 NOL to offset 2015 and 2016 income leaving a $6,000 NOL to carryforward. In 2018, the 2017 NOL was not subject to the 80 percent income limitation as it was generated prior to 2018; thus, Nez would have offset $6,000 of the 2018 income leaving taxable income of $1,000 for 2018. In 2019, the NOL generated was not eligible for carryback but could be carried forward indefinitely (and would be subject to the 80 percent income limitation). However, in 2020, due to the CARES Act suspension of the NOL rules, Nez can now carryback $1,000 of the 2019 loss to 2018 and the remaining $3,000 NOL from 2019 can be carried forward indefinitely but will be subject to the 80 percent limitation starting again in 2021. ◆

EXAMPLE Continuing on from the previous example, Nez generates taxable income of $35,000 in 2021. Nez will first use the remaining 2019 NOL of $3,000 and then will use the $25,000 of the 2020 NOL to offset the 2021 taxable income. This will leave $7,000 of taxable income in 2021. Note that the 2019 and 2020 NOLs are subject to the 80 percent income limitation for the income generated in 2021.

The following table describes the treatment of NOLs after the CARES Act:

NOL Year Generated	Carryback	Carryforward	Limitation on use against future income
Pre-2018	2 years	20 years	None
2018-2020	5 years	Indefinite	80% starting 2021
After 2020	None	Indefinite	80%

◆

Self-Study Problem 11.2   *See Appendix E for Solutions to Self-Study Problems*

a. During the current tax year, Taxus Corporation has ordinary income of $110,000, a long-term capital loss of $20,000, and a short-term capital loss of $5,000. Calculate Taxus Corporation's tax liability.

$_____

b. Maxus Corporation generated taxable income/(loss) of $10,000, ($40,000), $45,000, and ($70,000) in 2017, 2018, 2019 and 2020, respectively. What is the NOL carryforward to 2021, if any?

$_____

Learning Objective 11.3

Apply special corporate deductions to corporate taxable income.

11-3 SPECIAL DEDUCTIONS AND LIMITATIONS

Corporations are allowed certain "special deductions," including the dividends received deduction and the deduction for organizational expenditures and start-up costs. In addition, corporations are subject to limitations on the deduction of charitable contributions.

11-3a Dividends Received Deduction

When a corporation owns stock in another corporation, income earned by the first corporation could be taxed at least three times in the absence of a special provision. The income would be taxed to the first corporation when earned by the first corporation. Then it would be taxed to the corporation owning the stock in the first corporation when the income is distributed as dividend income. Finally, the income would be taxed to the shareholders of the second corporation when that corporation in turn distributes the earnings to its stockholders as dividends. To mitigate this potential for triple taxation of corporate earnings, corporations are allowed a deduction for all or a portion of dividends received from domestic corporations. Corporations are entitled to a dividends received deduction based on their percentage of ownership in the corporation paying the dividend. The deduction percentages are described below:

Percent Ownership	Dividends Received Percentage
Less than 20 percent	50%
20 percent or more, but less than 80 percent	65%
80 percent or more	100%

The dividends received deduction is limited to the applicable deduction percentage times the corporation's taxable income calculated before the dividends received deduction, the net operating loss deduction, and capital loss carrybacks. This taxable income limitation, however, does not apply if the receiving corporation has a net operating loss after reducing taxable income by the dividends received deduction. In other words, there is no taxable income limit if the dividends received deduction creates or increases a net operating loss.

EXAMPLE During the current year, Hackberry Corporation has the following income and expenses:

Gross income from operations	$240,000
Expenses from operations	200,000
Dividend received from a 30 percent-owned domestic corporation	100,000

The dividends received deduction is equal to the lesser of $65,000 (65% × $100,000) or 65 percent of taxable income before the dividends received deduction. Since taxable income (for computing this limitation) is $140,000 ($240,000 − $200,000 + $100,000) and 65 percent of $140,000 is $91,000, the full $65,000 is allowed as a deduction. ◆

EXAMPLE Assume the same facts as in the previous example, except Hackberry Corporation's gross income from operations is $190,000 (instead of $240,000). The dividends received deduction is equal to the lesser of $65,000 or 65 percent of $90,000 ($190,000 − $200,000 + $100,000), $58,500. Therefore, the dividends received deduction is limited to $58,500. Note that deducting the potential $65,000 dividends received deduction from taxable income does not generate a net operating loss. Accordingly, the taxable income limit is not avoided. ◆

11-3b Organizational Expenditures and Start-Up Costs

New businesses may incur organizational expenditures or start-up costs, or both, prior to starting a business. Organizational expenditures are incurred by partnerships, LLCs, and corporations in the process of forming an entity in which to operate a business. Start-up costs may be incurred by any business, including sole proprietorships reported on Schedule C, as well as the entities listed above.

Corporations amortize qualifying *organizational* costs over 180 months, and there is no upper limit to the amount of qualifying costs that can be amortized. Corporations can elect to deduct up to $5,000 of organizational costs in the year they begin business.

The $5,000 amount is reduced by each dollar of organizational expenses exceeding $50,000. Costs not expensed as part of the first-year election to expense are amortized ratably over the 180-month period beginning with the month the corporation begins business. Generally, organizational expenditures that qualify for amortization include legal and accounting services incident to organization, expenses of temporary directors and organizational meetings, and fees paid to the state for incorporation. Expenses such as the cost of transferring assets to the corporation and expenses connected with selling the corporation's stock are not organizational expenditures and, therefore, are not subject to amortization.

EXAMPLE In 2020, Coco Bola Corporation, an accrual-basis, calendar-year taxpayer, incurred $500 in fees to the state for incorporation, legal and accounting fees incident to the incorporation of $1,000, and temporary directors' expenses of $300. Assuming the corporation does not make an election to expense in the first year, the total $1,800 ($500 + $1,000 + $300) may be amortized over 15 years at a rate of $10 per month ($1,800/180 months). If the corporation began operations on June 1, 2020, $70 ($10 per month × 7 months) may be deducted for organizational expenditures for 2020. Alternatively, the corporation could elect to deduct the full $1,800 of organization costs in the first year of business. ◆

The *start-up costs* of a new business are given the same tax treatment as organizational costs, as illustrated in the previous paragraph and example. Start-up costs include both investigatory expenses and preopening costs. Investigatory expenses are expenses to investigate the potential success of a new business before the decision is made to actually pursue the business. Preopening costs are incurred after the taxpayer decides to start a new business but prior to the date the business actually begins. These expenses may include the training of new employees, advertising, and fees paid to consultants and professionals for advisory services.

11-3c Charitable Contributions

Corporations are allowed a deduction for contributions to qualified charitable organizations. Generally, a deduction is allowed in the year in which a payment is made. If, however, the directors of a corporation which maintains its books on the accrual basis make a pledge before year-end and the payment is made on or before the fifteenth day of the third month after the close of the tax year, the deduction may be claimed in the year of the pledge.

Typically, a corporation's charitable contribution deduction is limited to 10 percent of taxable income, computed before the deduction for charitable contributions, net operating loss carrybacks, capital loss carrybacks, and the dividends received deduction. Any excess contributions may be carried forward to the 5 succeeding tax years, but carryforward amounts are subject to the 10 percent annual limitation in the carryover years, with the current year's contributions deducted first. As part of the COVID-related stimulus, the 10 percent limit is increased to 25 percent for cash contributions made in 2020. The limit returns to 10 percent after 2020.

EXAMPLE Zircote Corporation had net operating income of $40,000 for the 2020 tax year and made a cash charitable contribution of $16,000 (not included in the operating income amount). Also not included in the operating income were dividends received of $10,000. The corporation's charitable contribution deduction is limited to 25 percent of $50,000 ($40,000 + $10,000), or $12,500. Note that the dividends received deduction is not used in calculating taxable income for purposes of determining the limitation on the charitable contribution deduction. The $3,500 ($16,000 − $12,500) of the charitable contribution that is disallowed in the current year is carried forward for up to 5 years. ◆

Self-Study Problem 11.3   *See Appendix E for Solutions to Self-Study Problems*

a. During 2020, Fraxinia Corporation has the following income and expenses:

Gross income from operations, excluding dividends	$ 90,000
Expenses from operations	100,000
Dividends received from a 25 percent-owned	
domestic corporation	70,000

Calculate the amount of Fraxinia Corporation's dividends received deduction.

$_____

b. Boyce Inc., a calendar year corporation, incurred organizational costs of $13,000 and start-up costs of $52,000 in 2020. Boyce started business on August 3, 2020. What is the maximum deduction for organizational and start-up costs for Boyce in 2020 and what is Boyce's 2021 deduction for the same costs?

c. Gant Corporation has income in 2020 of $95,000 before a dividends received deduction of $15,000 and a cash charitable contribution of $25,000. What is the deductible amount of the charitable contribution?

11-4 SCHEDULE M-1

11.4 Learning Objective

Identify the components of Schedule M-1 and how they are reported to the IRS.

A corporation is required to report its income and other items on Form 1120, U.S. Corporation Income Tax Return. Because of various provisions in the tax law, a corporation's taxable income seldom is the same as its accounting income (commonly referred to as "book income"). The purpose of Schedule M-1 of the Form 1120 corporate tax return is to reconcile a corporation's book income to its taxable income, computed before the net operating loss and special deductions such as the dividends received deduction. On the left side of Schedule M-1 are adjustments that must be added to book income, and on the right side of the schedule are adjustments that must be subtracted from book income to arrive at the amount of taxable income. The amounts that must be added to book income include the amount of federal income tax expense, net capital losses deducted for book purposes, income recorded on the tax return but not on the books, and expenses recorded on the books but not deducted on the tax return. Alternatively, the amounts that must be deducted from book income are income recorded on the books but not included on the tax return, and deductions on the return not deducted on the books.

EXAMPLE For the current tax year, Wisteria Corporation, an accrual-basis taxpayer, has net income reported on its books of $44,975. Included in this figure are the following items:

Net capital loss	$ 5,000
Interest income on tax-exempt bonds	9,000
Federal income tax expense	11,025
Depreciation deducted on the tax return, not deducted on the books	3,500
Interest deducted on the books, not deductible for tax purposes	4,000

Wisteria Corporation's Schedule M-1, Form 1120, is illustrated below.

Schedule M-1	Reconciliation of Income (Loss) per Books With Income per Return				
	Note: The corporation may be required to file Schedule M-3. See instructions.				
1	Net income (loss) per books	44,975	7	Income recorded on books this year not included on this return (itemize):	
2	Federal income tax per books	11,025		Tax-exempt interest $ 9,000	
3	Excess of capital losses over capital gains .	5,000			
4	Income subject to tax not recorded on books this year (itemize): _____				9,000
5	Expenses recorded on books this year not deducted on this return (itemize):		8	Deductions on this return not charged against book income this year (itemize):	
a	Depreciation . . . . $ _____		a	Depreciation . . $ 3,500	
b	Charitable contributions . $ _____		b	Charitable contributions $ _____	
c	Travel and entertainment . $ _____				
	_____ interest	4,000			3,500
6	Add lines 1 through 5	65,000	9	Add lines 7 and 8	12,500
			10	Income (page 1, line 28)—line 6 less line 9	52,500

◆

Self-Study Problem 11.4   *See Appendix E for Solutions to Self-Study Problems*

Redwood Corporation has net income reported on its books of $115,600. For the current year, the corporation had federal income tax expense of $29,400, a net capital loss of $9,100, and tax-exempt interest income of $4,700. The company deducted depreciation of $17,000 on its tax return and $13,000 on its books. Using Schedule M-1 below, calculate Redwood Corporation's taxable income, before any net operating loss or special deductions, for the current year.

Schedule M-1	Reconciliation of Income (Loss) per Books With Income per Return				
	Note: The corporation may be required to file Schedule M-3. See instructions.				
1	Net income (loss) per books		7	Income recorded on books this year not included on this return (itemize):	
2	Federal income tax per books			Tax-exempt interest $ _____	
3	Excess of capital losses over capital gains .				
4	Income subject to tax not recorded on books this year (itemize): _____				
5	Expenses recorded on books this year not deducted on this return (itemize):		8	Deductions on this return not charged against book income this year (itemize):	
a	Depreciation . . . . $ _____		a	Depreciation . . $ _____	
b	Charitable contributions . $ _____		b	Charitable contributions $ _____	
c	Travel and entertainment . $ _____				
6	Add lines 1 through 5		9	Add lines 7 and 8	
			10	Income (page 1, line 28)—line 6 less line 9	

Learning Objective 11.5

Describe the corporate tax return filing and estimated tax payment requirements.

11-5 FILING REQUIREMENTS AND ESTIMATED TAX

For all tax year-ends except for June 30, the due date for filing a corporate tax return is the fifteenth day of the fourth month after year-end. For June 30 year-end corporations, the filing due date is September 15 (fifteenth day of the third month). An extension provides an additional 6 months; thus, a calendar year-end corporation has an initial filing deadline of April 15 and an extended deadline of October 15 (6 month extension). However, corporations with tax years ending on June 30 will have an extended filing deadline of April 15 (7 month extension). When the due date falls on a weekend or holiday, the due date is the next business day. To avoid penalties, a corporation must pay any tax liability by the original due date of the return.

Corporations must make estimated tax payments in a manner similar to those made by self-employed individual taxpayers. The payments are made in four installments due on the fifteenth day of the fourth, sixth, ninth, and twelfth months of the corporation's tax year.

TAX BREAK

Small corporations with less than $250,000 in gross receipts and less than $250,000 in assets do not have to complete Schedule L (Balance Sheet) or Schedules M-1 and M-2. The rule applies to both S and C corporations, and allows small businesses to keep records based on their checkbook or cash receipts and disbursements journal. This makes the reporting requirements for a small corporation similar to the reporting requirements for a Schedule C sole proprietorship.

Self-Study Problem 11.5   *See Appendix E for Solutions to Self-Study Problems*

Aspen Corporation was formed and began operations on January 1, 2020. Aspen is located at 470 Rio Grande Place, Aspen, CO 81611 and the EIN is 92-2222222.

Aspen Corporation
Income Statement
for the Year Ended December 31, 2020

Gross income from operations		$ 285,000
Qualified dividends received from a 10 percent-		
owned domestic corporation		10,000
Total gross income		295,000
Cost of goods sold		(80,000)
Total income		215,000
Other expenses:		
Compensation of officers	$90,000	
Salaries and wages	82,000	
Repairs	8,000	
Depreciation expense for book and tax purposes	5,000	
Payroll taxes	11,000	
Total other expenses		(196,000)
Net income (before federal income tax expense)		$ 19,000

Aspen Corporation
Balance Sheet
as of December 31, 2020

Assets:		
Cash	$ 35,000	
Accounts receivable	10,000	
Land	18,000	
Building	125,000	
Less: accumulated depreciation	(5,000)	
Total assets		$ 183,000
Liabilities and owners' equity:		
Accounts payable	$ 26,940	
Common stock	140,000	
Retained earnings	16,060	
Total liabilities and owners' equity		$ 183,000

Aspen Corporation made estimated tax payments of $3,000.

Based on the above information, complete Form 1120 on Pages 11-11 through 11-16. Assume the corporation's book federal income tax expense is equal to its 2020 federal income tax liability and that any tax overpayment is to be applied to the next year's estimated tax. Schedule UTP, Form 4562, Form 1125-A, and Form 1125-E are not required. Make reasonable assumptions for any missing data.

Self-Study Problem 11.5

Form 1120
Department of the Treasury
Internal Revenue Service

U.S. Corporation Income Tax Return

For calendar year 2020 or tax year beginning _____ , 2020, ending _____ , 20 _____

▶ Go to *www.irs.gov/Form1120* for instructions and the latest information.

OMB No. 1545-0123

2020

A Check if:

1a Consolidated return (attach Form 851) ☐

  b Life/nonlife consolidated return . ☐

2 Personal holding co. (attach Sch. PH) . ☐

3 Personal service corp. (see instructions) . ☐

4 Schedule M-3 attached ☐

TYPE OR PRINT

Name

Number, street, and room or suite no. If a P.O. box, see instructions.

City or town, state or province, country, and ZIP or foreign postal code

B Employer identification number

C Date incorporated

D Total assets (see instructions)
$

E Check if: **(1)** ☐ Initial return   **(2)** ☐ Final return   **(3)** ☐ Name change   **(4)** ☐ Address change

Income	1a	Gross receipts or sales	1a	
	b	Returns and allowances	1b	
	c	Balance. Subtract line 1b from line 1a		1c
	2	Cost of goods sold (attach Form 1125-A)		2
	3	Gross profit. Subtract line 2 from line 1c		3
	4	Dividends and inclusions (Schedule C, line 23)		4
	5	Interest		5
	6	Gross rents		6
	7	Gross royalties		7
	8	Capital gain net income (attach Schedule D (Form 1120))		8
	9	Net gain or (loss) from Form 4797, Part II, line 17 (attach Form 4797)		9
	10	Other income (see instructions—attach statement)		10
	11	**Total income.** Add lines 3 through 10	▶	11

Deductions (See instructions for limitations on deductions.)	12	Compensation of officers (see instructions—attach Form 1125-E)	▶	12
	13	Salaries and wages (less employment credits)		13
	14	Repairs and maintenance		14
	15	Bad debts		15
	16	Rents		16
	17	Taxes and licenses		17
	18	Interest (see instructions)		18
	19	Charitable contributions		19
	20	Depreciation from Form 4562 not claimed on Form 1125-A or elsewhere on return (attach Form 4562)		20
	21	Depletion		21
	22	Advertising		22
	23	Pension, profit-sharing, etc., plans		23
	24	Employee benefit programs		24
	25	Reserved for future use		25
	26	Other deductions (attach statement)		26
	27	**Total deductions.** Add lines 12 through 26	▶	27
	28	Taxable income before net operating loss deduction and special deductions. Subtract line 27 from line 11.		28
	29a	Net operating loss deduction (see instructions)	29a	
	b	Special deductions (Schedule C, line 24)	29b	
	c	Add lines 29a and 29b		29c

Tax, Refundable Credits, and Payments	30	**Taxable income.** Subtract line 29c from line 28. See instructions		30
	31	Total tax (Schedule J, Part I, line 11)		31
	32	2020 net 965 tax liability paid (Schedule J, Part II, line 12)		32
	33	Total payments, credits, and section 965 net tax liability (Schedule J, Part III, line 23)		33
	34	Estimated tax penalty. See instructions. Check if Form 2220 is attached	▶ ☐	34
	35	**Amount owed.** If line 33 is smaller than the total of lines 31, 32, and 34, enter amount owed		35
	36	**Overpayment.** If line 33 is larger than the total of lines 31, 32, and 34, enter amount overpaid		36
	37	Enter amount from line 36 you want: **Credited to 2021 estimated tax ▶** _____ Refunded ▶		37

Sign Here

▶

Under penalties of perjury, I declare that I have examined this return, including accompanying schedules and statements, and to the best of my knowledge and belief, it is true, correct, and complete. Declaration of preparer (other than taxpayer) is based on all information of which preparer has any knowledge.

_____   _____   _____
Signature of officer   Date   Title

May the IRS discuss this return with the preparer shown below? See instructions. ☐ Yes ☐ No

Paid Preparer Use Only

Print/Type preparer's name	Preparer's signature	Date	Check ☐ if self-employed	PTIN

Firm's name ▶

Firm's address ▶

Firm's EIN ▶

Phone no.

For Paperwork Reduction Act Notice, see separate instructions.   Cat. No. 11450Q   Form **1120** (2020)

Form 1120 (2020)   Page **2**

Schedule C	Dividends, Inclusions, and Special Deductions (see instructions)	(a) Dividends and inclusions	(b) %	(c) Special deductions (a) × (b)
1	Dividends from less-than-20%-owned domestic corporations (other than debt-financed stock)		50	
2	Dividends from 20%-or-more-owned domestic corporations (other than debt-financed stock)		65	
3	Dividends on certain debt-financed stock of domestic and foreign corporations		See instructions	
4	Dividends on certain preferred stock of less-than-20%-owned public utilities		23.3	
5	Dividends on certain preferred stock of 20%-or-more-owned public utilities		26.7	
6	Dividends from less-than-20%-owned foreign corporations and certain FSCs		50	
7	Dividends from 20%-or-more-owned foreign corporations and certain FSCs		65	
8	Dividends from wholly owned foreign subsidiaries		100	
9	**Subtotal.** Add lines 1 through 8. See instructions for limitations		See instructions	
10	Dividends from domestic corporations received by a small business investment company operating under the Small Business Investment Act of 1958		100	
11	Dividends from affiliated group members		100	
12	Dividends from certain FSCs		100	
13	Foreign-source portion of dividends received from a specified 10%-owned foreign corporation (excluding hybrid dividends) (see instructions)		100	
14	Dividends from foreign corporations not included on line 3, 6, 7, 8, 11, 12, or 13 (including any hybrid dividends)			
15	Section 965(a) inclusion		See instructions	
16a	Subpart F inclusions derived from the sale by a controlled foreign corporation (CFC) of the stock of a lower-tier foreign corporation treated as a dividend (attach Form(s) 5471) (see instructions)		100	
b	Subpart F inclusions derived from hybrid dividends of tiered corporations (attach Form(s) 5471) (see instructions)			
c	Other inclusions from CFCs under subpart F not included on line 15, 16a, 16b, or 17 (attach Form(s) 5471) (see instructions)			
17	Global Intangible Low-Taxed Income (GILTI) (attach Form(s) 5471 and Form 8992)			
18	Gross-up for foreign taxes deemed paid			
19	IC-DISC and former DISC dividends not included on line 1, 2, or 3			
20	Other dividends			
21	Deduction for dividends paid on certain preferred stock of public utilities			
22	Section 250 deduction (attach Form 8993)			
23	**Total dividends and inclusions.** Add column (a), lines 9 through 20. Enter here and on page 1, line 4			
24	**Total special deductions.** Add column (c), lines 9 through 22. Enter here and on page 1, line 29b			

Form **1120** (2020)

Form 1120 (2020)   Page **3**

Schedule J	**Tax Computation and Payment** (see instructions)		

Part I—Tax Computation

1	Check if the corporation is a member of a controlled group (attach Schedule O (Form 1120)). See instructions ▶ ☐		
2	Income tax. See instructions		**2**	
3	Base erosion minimum tax amount (attach Form 8991)		**3**	
4	Add lines 2 and 3		**4**	
5a	Foreign tax credit (attach Form 1118)	**5a**		
b	Credit from Form 8834 (see instructions)	**5b**		
c	General business credit (attach Form 3800)	**5c**		
d	Credit for prior year minimum tax (attach Form 8827)	**5d**		
e	Bond credits from Form 8912	**5e**		
6	**Total credits.** Add lines 5a through 5e		**6**	
7	Subtract line 6 from line 4		**7**	
8	Personal holding company tax (attach Schedule PH (Form 1120))		**8**	
9a	Recapture of investment credit (attach Form 4255)	**9a**		
b	Recapture of low-income housing credit (attach Form 8611) . . .	**9b**		
c	Interest due under the look-back method—completed long-term contracts (attach Form 8697)	**9c**		
d	Interest due under the look-back method—income forecast method (attach Form 8866)	**9d**		
e	Alternative tax on qualifying shipping activities (attach Form 8902)	**9e**		
f	Interest/tax due under Section 453A(c) and/or Section 453(l)	**9f**		
g	Other (see instructions—attach statement)	**9g**		
10	**Total.** Add lines 9a through 9g		**10**	
11	**Total tax.** Add lines 7, 8, and 10. Enter here and on page 1, line 31		**11**	

Part II—Section 965 Payments (see instructions)

12	2020 net 965 tax liability paid from Form 965-B, Part II, column (k), line 4. Enter here and on page 1, line 32 . .	**12**	

Part III—Payments, Refundable Credits, and Section 965 Net Tax Liability

13	2019 overpayment credited to 2020		**13**	
14	2020 estimated tax payments		**14**	
15	2020 refund applied for on Form 4466		**15** (	)
16	Combine lines 13, 14, and 15		**16**	
17	Tax deposited with Form 7004		**17**	
18	Withholding (see instructions)		**18**	
19	**Total payments.** Add lines 16, 17, and 18		**19**	
20	Refundable credits from:			
a	Form 2439	**20a**		
b	Form 4136	**20b**		
c	Reserved for future use	**20c**		
d	Other (attach statement—see instructions)	**20d**		
21	**Total credits.** Add lines 20a through 20d		**21**	
22	2020 net 965 tax liability from Form 965-B, Part I, column (d), line 4. See instructions . . .		**22**	
23	**Total payments, credits, and section 965 net tax liability.** Add lines 19, 21, and 22. Enter here and on page 1, line 33		**23**	

Form **1120** (2020)

Form 1120 (2020)   Page **4**

Schedule K	**Other Information** (see instructions)			Yes	No

1 Check accounting method: **a** ☐ Cash   **b** ☐ Accrual   **c** ☐ Other (specify) ▶ _____

2 See the instructions and enter the:

a Business activity code no. ▶ _____

b Business activity ▶ _____

c Product or service ▶ _____

3 Is the corporation a subsidiary in an affiliated group or a parent–subsidiary controlled group? . . . . .

If "Yes," enter name and EIN of the parent corporation ▶ _____

_____

4 At the end of the tax year:

a Did any foreign or domestic corporation, partnership (including any entity treated as a partnership), trust, or tax-exempt organization own directly 20% or more, or own, directly or indirectly, 50% or more of the total voting power of all classes of the corporation's stock entitled to vote? If "Yes," complete Part I of Schedule G (Form 1120) (attach Schedule G)

b Did any individual or estate own directly 20% or more, or own, directly or indirectly, 50% or more of the total voting power of all classes of the corporation's stock entitled to vote? If "Yes," complete Part II of Schedule G (Form 1120) (attach Schedule G)

5 At the end of the tax year, did the corporation:

a Own directly 20% or more, or own, directly or indirectly, 50% or more of the total voting power of all classes of stock entitled to vote of any foreign or domestic corporation not included on **Form 851,** Affiliations Schedule? For rules of constructive ownership, see instructions. If "Yes," complete (i) through (iv) below.

(i) Name of Corporation	**(ii)** Employer Identification Number (if any)	**(iii)** Country of Incorporation	**(iv)** Percentage Owned in Voting Stock

b Own directly an interest of 20% or more, or own, directly or indirectly, an interest of 50% or more in any foreign or domestic partnership (including an entity treated as a partnership) or in the beneficial interest of a trust? For rules of constructive ownership, see instructions. If "Yes," complete (i) through (iv) below.

(i) Name of Entity	**(ii)** Employer Identification Number (if any)	**(iii)** Country of Organization	**(iv)** Maximum Percentage Owned in Profit, Loss, or Capital

6 During this tax year, did the corporation pay dividends (other than stock dividends and distributions in exchange for stock) in excess of the corporation's current and accumulated earnings and profits? See sections 301 and 316 . . . .

If "Yes," file **Form 5452,** Corporate Report of Nondividend Distributions. See the instructions for Form 5452.

If this is a consolidated return, answer here for the parent corporation and on Form 851 for each subsidiary.

7 At any time during the tax year, did one foreign person own, directly or indirectly, at least 25% of the total voting power of all classes of the corporation's stock entitled to vote or at least 25% of the total value of all classes of the corporation's stock?   .

For rules of attribution, see section 318. If "Yes," enter:

(a) Percentage owned ▶ _____ and **(b)** Owner's country ▶ _____

(c) The corporation may have to file **Form 5472,** Information Return of a 25% Foreign-Owned U.S. Corporation or a Foreign Corporation Engaged in a U.S. Trade or Business. Enter the number of Forms 5472 attached ▶ _____

8 Check this box if the corporation issued publicly offered debt instruments with original issue discount . . . . . . ▶ ☐

If checked, the corporation may have to file **Form 8281,** Information Return for Publicly Offered Original Issue Discount Instruments.

9 Enter the amount of tax-exempt interest received or accrued during the tax year ▶ $ _____

10 Enter the number of shareholders at the end of the tax year (if 100 or fewer) ▶ _____

11 If the corporation has an NOL for the tax year and is electing to forego the carryback period, check here (see instructions) ▶ ☐

If the corporation is filing a consolidated return, the statement required by Regulations section 1.1502-21(b)(3) must be attached or the election will not be valid.

12 Enter the available NOL carryover from prior tax years (do not reduce it by any deduction reported on page 1, line 29a.) . . . . ▶ $ _____

Form **1120** (2020)

Form 1120 (2020) Page **5**

	Schedule K	Other Information *(continued from page 4)*		Yes	No

13 Are the corporation's total receipts (page 1, line 1a, plus lines 4 through 10) for the tax year **and** its total assets at the end of the tax year less than $250,000? . . . .

    If "Yes," the corporation is not required to complete Schedules L, M-1, and M-2. Instead, enter the total amount of cash distributions and the book value of property distributions (other than cash) made during the tax year ▶ $ _____

14 Is the corporation required to file Schedule UTP (Form 1120), Uncertain Tax Position Statement? See instructions . . . .

    If "Yes," complete and attach Schedule UTP.

15a Did the corporation make any payments in 2020 that would require it to file Form(s) 1099? . . . .

  b If "Yes," did or will the corporation file required Form(s) 1099? . . . .

16 During this tax year, did the corporation have an 80%-or-more change in ownership, including a change due to redemption of its own stock? . . . .

17 During or subsequent to this tax year, but before the filing of this return, did the corporation dispose of more than 65% (by value) of its assets in a taxable, non-taxable, or tax deferred transaction? . . . .

18 Did the corporation receive assets in a section 351 transfer in which any of the transferred assets had a fair market basis or fair market value of more than $1 million? . . . .

19 During the corporation's tax year, did the corporation make any payments that would require it to file Forms 1042 and 1042-S under chapter 3 (sections 1441 through 1464) or chapter 4 (sections 1471 through 1474) of the Code? . . . .

20 Is the corporation operating on a cooperative basis? . . . .

21 During the tax year, did the corporation pay or accrue any interest or royalty for which the deduction is not allowed under section 267A? See instructions . . . .

    If "Yes," enter the total amount of the disallowed deductions ▶ $ _____

22 Does the corporation have gross receipts of at least $500 million in any of the 3 preceding tax years? (See sections 59A(e)(2) and (3)) . . . .

    If "Yes," complete and attach Form 8991.

23 Did the corporation have an election under section 163(j) for any real property trade or business or any farming business in effect during the tax year? See instructions . . . .

24 Does the corporation satisfy one or more of the following? See instructions . . . .

  a The corporation owns a pass-through entity with current, or prior year carryover, excess business interest expense.

  b The corporation's aggregate average annual gross receipts (determined under section 448(c)) for the 3 tax years preceding the current tax year are more than $26 million and the corporation has business interest expense.

  c The corporation is a tax shelter and the corporation has business interest expense.

    If "Yes," complete and attach Form 8990.

25 Is the corporation attaching Form 8996 to certify as a Qualified Opportunity Fund? . . . .

    If "Yes," enter amount from Form 8996, line 15 . . . . ▶ $

26 Since December 22, 2017, did a foreign corporation directly or indirectly acquire substantially all of the properties held directly or indirectly by the corporation, and was the ownership percentage (by vote or value) for purposes of section 7874 greater than 50% (for example, the shareholders held more than 50% of the stock of the foreign corporation)? If "Yes," list the ownership percentage by vote and by value. See instructions . . . .

    Percentage: By Vote   By Value

Form **1120** (2020)

Form 1120 (2020)   Page **6**

Schedule L	Balance Sheets per Books	Beginning of tax year		End of tax year	
	Assets	**(a)**	**(b)**	**(c)**	**(d)**
1	Cash				
2a	Trade notes and accounts receivable				
b	Less allowance for bad debts	( )		( )	
3	Inventories				
4	U.S. government obligations				
5	Tax-exempt securities (see instructions)				
6	Other current assets (attach statement)				
7	Loans to shareholders				
8	Mortgage and real estate loans				
9	Other investments (attach statement)				
10a	Buildings and other depreciable assets				
b	Less accumulated depreciation	( )		( )	
11a	Depletable assets				
b	Less accumulated depletion	( )		( )	
12	Land (net of any amortization)				
13a	Intangible assets (amortizable only)				
b	Less accumulated amortization	( )		( )	
14	Other assets (attach statement)				
15	Total assets				
	Liabilities and Shareholders' Equity				
16	Accounts payable				
17	Mortgages, notes, bonds payable in less than 1 year				
18	Other current liabilities (attach statement)				
19	Loans from shareholders				
20	Mortgages, notes, bonds payable in 1 year or more				
21	Other liabilities (attach statement)				
22	Capital stock: **a** Preferred stock				
	b Common stock				
23	Additional paid-in capital				
24	Retained earnings—Appropriated (attach statement)				
25	Retained earnings—Unappropriated				
26	Adjustments to shareholders' equity (attach statement)				
27	Less cost of treasury stock		( )		( )
28	Total liabilities and shareholders' equity				

Schedule M-1	Reconciliation of Income (Loss) per Books With Income per Return

Note: The corporation may be required to file Schedule M-3. See instructions.

1	Net income (loss) per books		7	Income recorded on books this year not included on this return (itemize):	
2	Federal income tax per books			Tax-exempt interest $ _____	
3	Excess of capital losses over capital gains				
4	Income subject to tax not recorded on books this year (itemize): _____				
	_____		8	Deductions on this return not charged against book income this year (itemize):	
5	Expenses recorded on books this year not deducted on this return (itemize):		a	Depreciation . . $ _____	
a	Depreciation . . . . $ _____		b	Charitable contributions $ _____	
b	Charitable contributions . $ _____			_____	
c	Travel and entertainment . $ _____				
	_____		9	Add lines 7 and 8	
6	Add lines 1 through 5		10	Income (page 1, line 28)—line 6 less line 9	

Schedule M-2	Analysis of Unappropriated Retained Earnings per Books (Schedule L, Line 25)

1	Balance at beginning of year		5	Distributions: **a** Cash	
2	Net income (loss) per books			**b** Stock	
3	Other increases (itemize): _____			**c** Property	
	_____		6	Other decreases (itemize): _____	
			7	Add lines 5 and 6	
4	Add lines 1, 2, and 3		8	Balance at end of year (line 4 less line 7)	

Form **1120** (2020)

11-6 S CORPORATIONS

Qualified corporations may elect to be taxed under Subchapter S of the Internal Revenue Code in a manner similar to partnerships. An S corporation does not generally pay tax, and each shareholder reports his or her share of corporate income. The S corporation election is designed to relieve corporations of certain corporate tax disadvantages, such as the double taxation of income.

To elect S corporation status, a corporation must have the following characteristics:

1. The corporation must be a domestic corporation;
2. The corporation must have 100 or fewer shareholders who are either individuals, estates, certain trusts, certain financial institutions, or certain exempt organizations;
3. The corporation must have only one class of stock; and
4. All shareholders must be U.S. citizens or resident aliens.

The S corporation election must be made during the prior year or the first two months and 15 days of the current tax year to obtain the status for the current year. Relief provisions may apply for elections that are filed late.

EXAMPLE Laurel Corporation is a calendar-year corporation that makes an S corporation election on November 2, 2020. The corporation does not qualify for any of the relief provisions for late S corporation elections for the 2020 tax year. The corporation is not an S corporation until the 2021 tax year; it is a regular C corporation for 2020. ◆

After electing S corporation status, the corporation retains the status until the election is voluntarily revoked or statutorily terminated. If the corporation ceases to qualify as an S corporation (e.g., it has 102 shareholders during the year), the election is statutorily terminated. Also, the election is terminated when a corporation receives 25 percent or more of its gross income from passive investments for 3 consecutive tax years and the corporation has accumulated earnings and profits at the end of each of those years. If a corporation experiences an involuntary termination of S corporation status, the election is terminated on the day the status changes. For example, the loss of S corporation status on June 1 causes the corporation to be a regular C corporation from that day on.

Upon consent of shareholders owning a majority of the voting stock, an S corporation election can be voluntarily revoked. If the consent to revoke the election is made during the first two months and 15 days of the tax year, the S corporation status will be considered voluntarily terminated effective at the beginning of that year. Shareholders may specify a date on or after the date of the revocation as the effective date for the voluntary termination of the S corporation election. If a prospective revocation date is not specified, and the consent to revoke the election is made after two months and 15 days of the tax year, the earliest that the S corporation status can be terminated is the first day of the following tax year.

EXAMPLE On January 20, 2020, Juniper Corporation, a calendar-year corporation, files a consent to revoke its S corporation election. No date is specified in the consent as the effective date of the revocation. The corporation is no longer an S corporation effective January 1, 2020. If the election were made after March 15, the corporation would not become a regular C corporation until the 2021 tax year. ◆

11-6a Reporting Income

An S corporation is required to report its income and other items on Form 1120S, U.S. Income Tax Return for an S Corporation, even though the corporate entity does not pay federal income tax. The tax return is due on the fifteenth day of the third month following the close of the corporation's tax year. S corporations may request a 6-month extension for filing its tax return. Each shareholder of an S corporation reports his or her share of corporate income based on his or her stock ownership during the year. The taxable income of an S corporation is computed in the same manner as a partnership.

Each shareholder of an S corporation takes into account separately his or her share of items of income, deductions, and credits on a per share per day basis. Schedule K-1 of Form 1120S is used to report the allocation of ordinary income or loss, plus all separately stated items of income or loss, to each of the shareholders. Each shareholder's share of these items is included in the shareholder's computation of taxable income for the tax year during which the corporation's year ends. In the case of the death of a shareholder, the shareholder's portion of S corporation items will be taken into account on the shareholder's final tax return.

EXAMPLE   Freda is the sole shareholder of the Freda Corporation, which has an S corporation election in effect. During calendar year 2020, the corporation has ordinary taxable income of $100,000. Freda must report $100,000 on her individual income tax return for 2020 as income from the Freda Corporation. ♦

11-6b S Corporation Losses

Losses from an S corporation also pass through to the shareholders. However, the amount of loss from an S corporation that a shareholder may report is limited to his or her adjusted basis in the corporation's stock plus the amount of any loans from the shareholder to the corporation. Any loss in excess of the shareholder's basis in the stock of the corporation plus loans is disallowed and becomes a carryforward loss. If a shareholder was not a shareholder for the entire tax year, losses must be allocated to the shareholder on a daily basis (the seller gets credit for the date of sale). This prevents a shareholder from selling losses late in the year to another taxpayer by selling the stock of an S corporation.

EXAMPLE   Lawson and Mary are equal shareholders in L&M Corporation, an S corporation. On December 1, 2020, Mary sells her interest to Connley for $15,000. Lawson's basis in his L&M Corporation stock is $10,000. For the 2020 tax year, the corporation has a loss of $24,000. Lawson can deduct only $10,000 of his half of the loss ($12,000), since that is the amount of his stock basis. Even though she is not a shareholder at year-end, Mary may deduct $11,016 of the loss, which is 336/366 of $12,000, assuming her basis was at least that amount. Connley may deduct $984, 30/366 of $12,000. In non-leap years, the amounts would be $11,014 (335/365 × $12,000) and $986 (30/365 × $12,000) for Mary and Connley, respectively. ♦

11-6c Pass-Through Items

Certain items pass through from an S corporation to the shareholders and retain their tax attributes on the shareholders' tax returns. The following are examples of pass-through items that are separately stated on the shareholders' Schedule K-1:

- Capital gains and losses
- Section 1231 gains and losses
- Dividend income
- Charitable contributions
- Tax-exempt interest
- Most credits

11-6d Qualified Business Income Deduction

Similar to partnerships, S corporations are flow-through entities that may generate qualified business income (QBI) and thus individual shareholders may be eligible for the QBI deduction. The same wage and service business limits apply as with other flow-through entities.

S corporations have a unique interaction between wages and qualified business income. The wages paid to an S corporation shareholder are not considered part of qualified business income; however, the wages count toward the wage limit, to the extent one applies to the taxpayer:

EXAMPLE Hogarth is a single taxpayer and the sole shareholder of Giant Corporation, which is an S corporation for tax purposes. Giant pays reasonable wages to Hogarth, the only employee, of $80,000 and allocates $100,000 of income. Hogarth's taxable income is above the threshold for a single taxpayer and he is required to apply the wage limitation to his QBI deduction. Hogarth can include $40,000 ($80,000 × 50%) of wages in computing the wage limit for the QBI deduction but may not consider the $80,000 of wages as QBI, only the $100,000 of income allocated. ♦

11-6e **Special Taxes**

S corporations are not subject to the corporate income tax on their regular taxable income. Under certain circumstances, an S corporation may be liable for tax at the corporate level. An S corporation may be subject to a tax on gains attributable to appreciation in the value of assets held by the corporation prior to the S corporation election, the built-in gains tax. In addition, a tax may be imposed on certain S corporations that have large amounts of passive investment income, such as income from dividends and interest. The rules for the application of these taxes are complex.

Self-Study Problem 11.6	*See Appendix E for Solutions to Self-Study Problems*

Assume that Aspen Corporation in Self-Study Problem 11.5 is owned by Ava Mendes, who owns all 100 shares outstanding. Ava lives at 1175 Delaware St., Denver, CO 80204 and her Social Security number is 411-41-4141. Also, assume that the corporation has a valid S corporation election in effect for 2020 and is not subject to any special taxes. Assume no wages are included in Aspen's cost of goods sold. Using the relevant information given in Self-Study Problem 11.5 and assuming the corporation's retained earnings are $19,000, instead of $16,060, accounts payable are $24,000, rather than $26,940, and no estimated tax payments are made, complete Form 1120S on Pages 11–21 through 11–25 for Aspen Corporation, and complete Schedule K-1 on Pages 11–27 and 11–28 for Ava. Assume there were no cash distributions to Ava during the year.

11-7 **CORPORATE FORMATION**

11.7 Learning Objective

Describe the basic tax rules for the formation of a corporation.

When a taxpayer incorporates a business and transfers high-value, low-basis property to the corporation in exchange for corporate stock, a substantial gain is realized. This gain is measured at the value of the shares received less the basis of the property transferred. Favorable tax treatment is available in certain cases, which allows many taxpayers to defer the recognition of the gain in the year of formation. To defer the gain, the taxpayer must meet certain requirements, including:

1. The taxpayer must transfer property or money to the corporation,
2. The transfer must be solely in exchange for stock of the corporation, and
3. The shareholder(s) qualifying for nonrecognition must own at least 80 percent of the corporation's stock after the transfer.

When the above requirements are met, gains and losses are not recognized on the formation of the corporation.

The shareholder must transfer property or cash to the corporation; performing services for corporate stock does not qualify for nonrecognition treatment. The shareholder performing services must recognize income in an amount equal to the value of the stock received. If the shareholder receives other property (boot) in addition to stock of the corporation in exchange for the transfer of cash or other property, the transaction may still qualify for partial nonrecognition treatment, provided the control requirement is met. However, realized gain must be recognized to the extent of the boot received.

11-7a Liabilities

As a general rule, the assumption of shareholder liabilities by the corporation is not considered boot. For example, if a shareholder transfers land to the corporation for stock and the land is subject to a liability that is assumed by the corporation, no gain would normally be recognized on the transfer. However, if there is no business purpose for transfer of the liability, or tax avoidance appears to be involved, the recognition of any realized gain is required. Also, when the total liabilities transferred to the corporation by a shareholder exceed the total basis of the property transferred by the shareholder, the excess amount is a gain that must be recognized without regard to whether gain is realized.

EXAMPLE Robusta Corporation is formed by Max, who contributes property with a basis of $12,000 in exchange for 100 percent of the company's stock. On the date of the contribution, the property contributed has a fair market value of $120,000 and is subject to a liability of $20,000. Max must recognize a gain of $8,000 on the transfer of the property to the corporation since the liability transferred to the corporation exceeds his basis in the property transferred. ◆

11-7b Shareholder's Stock Basis

After the transfer, the shareholder's basis in his or her stock is determined by the following formula:

Basis of the property transferred	$ xxxx
Less: boot received	(xxxx)
Plus: gain recognized	xxxx
Less: liabilities transferred	(xxxx)
Basis in the stock	$ xxxx

11-7c Corporation's Basis in Property Contributed

The corporation's basis in the property received from a shareholder in a transaction to which nonrecognition treatment applies is the same as the basis of the property to the shareholder, increased by any gain recognized by the shareholder on the transfer.

EXAMPLE A, B, and C form Hornbeam Corporation. A contributes property with a basis of $25,000 in exchange for 40 shares of stock worth $40,000. B performs services for the corporation in exchange for 10 shares of stock worth $10,000. C contributes property with a basis of $10,000 in exchange for 45 shares of stock worth $45,000 and $5,000 cash. The stock described above is all of the outstanding stock of the corporation. A and C qualify for complete or partial nonrecognition treatment, since together they own

Self-Study Problem 11.6

Form **1120-S**	**U.S. Income Tax Return for an S Corporation**	OMB No. 1545-0123

Department of the Treasury
Internal Revenue Service

▶ Do not file this form unless the corporation has filed or
is attaching Form 2553 to elect to be an S corporation.
▶ Go to *www.irs.gov/Form1120S* for instructions and the latest information.

2020

For calendar year 2020 or tax year beginning _____ , 2020, ending _____ , 20____

A S election effective date		Name	D Employer identification number
B Business activity code number (see instructions)	TYPE OR PRINT	Number, street, and room or suite no. If a P.O. box, see instructions.	E Date incorporated
C Check if Sch. M-3 attached ☐		City or town, state or province, country, and ZIP or foreign postal code	F Total assets (see instructions) $

G Is the corporation electing to be an S corporation beginning with this tax year? ☐ Yes ☐ No   If "Yes," attach Form 2553 if not already filed
H Check if: **(1)** ☐ Final return **(2)** ☐ Name change **(3)** ☐ Address change **(4)** ☐ Amended return **(5)** ☐ S election termination or revocation
I Enter the number of shareholders who were shareholders during any part of the tax year . . . . ▶ _____
J Check if corporation: **(1)** ☐ Aggregated activities for section 465 at-risk purposes **(2)** ☐ Grouped activities for section 469 passive activity purposes

Caution: Include **only** trade or business income and expenses on lines 1a through 21. See the instructions for more information.

Income

1a	Gross receipts or sales	1a	
b	Returns and allowances	1b	
c	Balance. Subtract line 1b from line 1a	1c	
2	Cost of goods sold (attach Form 1125-A)	2	
3	Gross profit. Subtract line 2 from line 1c	3	
4	Net gain (loss) from Form 4797, line 17 (attach Form 4797) . .	4	
5	Other income (loss) (see instructions—attach statement) . . .	5	
6	**Total income (loss).** Add lines 3 through 5 . . . . . . ▶	6	

Deductions (see instructions for limitations)

7	Compensation of officers (see instructions—attach Form 1125-E) . .	7	
8	Salaries and wages (less employment credits)	8	
9	Repairs and maintenance	9	
10	Bad debts	10	
11	Rents	11	
12	Taxes and licenses	12	
13	Interest (see instructions)	13	
14	Depreciation not claimed on Form 1125-A or elsewhere on return (attach Form 4562)	14	
15	Depletion **(Do not deduct oil and gas depletion.)**	15	
16	Advertising	16	
17	Pension, profit-sharing, etc., plans	17	
18	Employee benefit programs	18	
19	Other deductions (attach statement)	19	
20	**Total deductions.** Add lines 7 through 19 . . . . . . ▶	20	
21	**Ordinary business income (loss).** Subtract line 20 from line 6 . .	21	

Tax and Payments

22a	Excess net passive income or LIFO recapture tax (see instructions) . . .	22a	
b	Tax from Schedule D (Form 1120-S)	22b	
c	Add lines 22a and 22b (see instructions for additional taxes)		22c
23a	2020 estimated tax payments and 2019 overpayment credited to 2020	23a	
b	Tax deposited with Form 7004	23b	
c	Credit for federal tax paid on fuels (attach Form 4136) . . .	23c	
d	Reserved for future use	23d	
e	Add lines 23a through 23d		23e
24	Estimated tax penalty (see instructions). Check if Form 2220 is attached . . ▶ ☐		24
25	**Amount owed.** If line 23e is smaller than the total of lines 22c and 24, enter amount owed . . .		25
26	**Overpayment.** If line 23e is larger than the total of lines 22c and 24, enter amount overpaid . . .		26
27	Enter amount from line 26: **Credited to 2021 estimated tax** ▶ _____ Refunded ▶		27

Sign Here

Under penalties of perjury, I declare that I have examined this return, including accompanying schedules and statements, and to the best of my knowledge and belief, it is true, correct, and complete. Declaration of preparer (other than taxpayer) is based on all information of which preparer has any knowledge.

▶ _____   _____   ▶ _____
Signature of officer   Date   Title

May the IRS discuss this return with the preparer shown below? See instructions. ☐ Yes ☐ No

Paid Preparer Use Only

Print/Type preparer's name	Preparer's signature	Date	Check ☐ if self-employed	PTIN
Firm's name ▶			Firm's EIN ▶	
Firm's address ▶			Phone no.	

For Paperwork Reduction Act Notice, see separate instructions.   Cat. No. 11510H   Form **1120-S** (2020)

Form 1120-S (2020)   Page **2**

Schedule B   **Other Information** (see instructions)

		Yes	No
1	Check accounting method: **a** ☐ Cash **b** ☐ Accrual **c** ☐ Other (specify) ▶ _____		
2	See the instructions and enter the: **a** Business activity ▶ _____ **b** Product or service ▶ _____		
3	At any time during the tax year, was any shareholder of the corporation a disregarded entity, a trust, an estate, or a nominee or similar person? If "Yes," attach Schedule B-1, Information on Certain Shareholders of an S Corporation . .		
4	At the end of the tax year, did the corporation:		
a	Own directly 20% or more, or own, directly or indirectly, 50% or more of the total stock issued and outstanding of any foreign or domestic corporation? For rules of constructive ownership, see instructions. If "Yes," complete (i) through (v) below		

(i) Name of Corporation	(ii) Employer Identification Number (if any)	(iii) Country of Incorporation	(iv) Percentage of Stock Owned	(v) If Percentage in (iv) Is 100%, Enter the Date (if any) a Qualified Subchapter S Subsidiary Election Was Made

		Yes	No
b	Own directly an interest of 20% or more, or own, directly or indirectly, an interest of 50% or more in the profit, loss, or capital in any foreign or domestic partnership (including an entity treated as a partnership) or in the beneficial interest of a trust? For rules of constructive ownership, see instructions. If "Yes," complete (i) through (v) below		

(i) Name of Entity	(ii) Employer Identification Number (if any)	(iii) Type of Entity	(iv) Country of Organization	(v) Maximum Percentage Owned in Profit, Loss, or Capital

		Yes	No
5a	At the end of the tax year, did the corporation have any outstanding shares of restricted stock? . . . . If "Yes," complete lines (i) and (ii) below.		
	(i) Total shares of restricted stock . . . . ▶ _____		
	(ii) Total shares of non-restricted stock . . . . ▶ _____		
b	At the end of the tax year, did the corporation have any outstanding stock options, warrants, or similar instruments? . If "Yes," complete lines (i) and (ii) below.		
	(i) Total shares of stock outstanding at the end of the tax year . ▶		
	(ii) Total shares of stock outstanding if all instruments were executed ▶ _____		
6	Has this corporation filed, or is it required to file, **Form 8918,** Material Advisor Disclosure Statement, to provide information on any reportable transaction?		
7	Check this box if the corporation issued publicly offered debt instruments with original issue discount . . . . ▶ ☐ If checked, the corporation may have to file **Form 8281,** Information Return for Publicly Offered Original Issue Discount Instruments.		
8	If the corporation **(a)** was a C corporation before it elected to be an S corporation **or** the corporation acquired an asset with a basis determined by reference to the basis of the asset (or the basis of any other property) in the hands of a C corporation, **and** **(b)** has net unrealized built-in gain in excess of the net recognized built-in gain from prior years, enter the net unrealized built-in gain reduced by net recognized built-in gain from prior years. See instructions . . . . . ▶ $ _____		
9	Did the corporation have an election under section 163(j) for any real property trade or business or any farming business in effect during the tax year? See instructions		
10	Does the corporation satisfy one or more of the following? See instructions		
a	The corporation owns a pass-through entity with current, or prior year carryover, excess business interest expense.		
b	The corporation's aggregate average annual gross receipts (determined under section 448(c)) for the 3 tax years preceding the current tax year are more than $26 million and the corporation has business interest expense.		
c	The corporation is a tax shelter and the corporation has business interest expense. If "Yes," complete and attach Form 8990.		
11	Does the corporation satisfy **both** of the following conditions?		
a	The corporation's total receipts (see instructions) for the tax year were less than $250,000.		
b	The corporation's total assets at the end of the tax year were less than $250,000. If "Yes," the corporation is not required to complete Schedules L and M-1.		

Form **1120-S** (2020)

Form 1120-S (2020)   Page **3**

Schedule B	Other Information (see instructions) (continued)			Yes	No
12	During the tax year, did the corporation have any non-shareholder debt that was canceled, was forgiven, or had the terms modified so as to reduce the principal amount of the debt?				
	If "Yes," enter the amount of principal reduction . . . . ▶ $_____				
13	During the tax year, was a qualified subchapter S subsidiary election terminated or revoked? If "Yes," see instructions .				
14a	Did the corporation make any payments in 2020 that would require it to file Form(s) 1099?				
b	If "Yes," did the corporation file or will it file required Form(s) 1099?				
15	Is the corporation attaching Form 8996 to certify as a Qualified Opportunity Fund?				
	If "Yes," enter the amount from Form 8996, line 15 . . . . ▶ $_____				

Schedule K		Shareholders' Pro Rata Share Items			Total amount
Income (Loss)	1	Ordinary business income (loss) (page 1, line 21)		**1**	
	2	Net rental real estate income (loss) (attach Form 8825)		**2**	
	3a	Other gross rental income (loss)	3a		
	b	Expenses from other rental activities (attach statement)	3b		
	c	Other net rental income (loss). Subtract line 3b from line 3a		**3c**	
	4	Interest income		**4**	
	5	Dividends: **a** Ordinary dividends		**5a**	
		b Qualified dividends	5b		
	6	Royalties		**6**	
	7	Net short-term capital gain (loss) (attach Schedule D (Form 1120-S))		**7**	
	8a	Net long-term capital gain (loss) (attach Schedule D (Form 1120-S))		**8a**	
	b	Collectibles (28%) gain (loss)	8b		
	c	Unrecaptured section 1250 gain (attach statement)	8c		
	9	Net section 1231 gain (loss) (attach Form 4797)		**9**	
	10	Other income (loss) (see instructions) Type ▶		**10**	
Deductions	11	Section 179 deduction (attach Form 4562)		**11**	
	12a	Charitable contributions		**12a**	
	b	Investment interest expense		**12b**	
	c	Section 59(e)(2) expenditures . . . . . . Type ▶		**12c**	
	d	Other deductions (see instructions) . . . . . Type ▶		**12d**	
Credits	13a	Low-income housing credit (section 42(j)(5))		**13a**	
	b	Low-income housing credit (other)		**13b**	
	c	Qualified rehabilitation expenditures (rental real estate) (attach Form 3468, if applicable)		**13c**	
	d	Other rental real estate credits (see instructions) Type ▶		**13d**	
	e	Other rental credits (see instructions) . . . Type ▶		**13e**	
	f	Biofuel producer credit (attach Form 6478)		**13f**	
	g	Other credits (see instructions) . . . . . Type ▶		**13g**	
Foreign Transactions	14a	Name of country or U.S. possession ▶			
	b	Gross income from all sources		**14b**	
	c	Gross income sourced at shareholder level		**14c**	
		Foreign gross income sourced at corporate level			
	d	Reserved for future use		**14d**	
	e	Foreign branch category		**14e**	
	f	Passive category		**14f**	
	g	General category		**14g**	
	h	Other (attach statement)		**14h**	
		Deductions allocated and apportioned at shareholder level			
	i	Interest expense		**14i**	
	j	Other		**14j**	
		Deductions allocated and apportioned at corporate level to foreign source income			
	k	Reserved for future use		**14k**	
	l	Foreign branch category		**14l**	
	m	Passive category		**14m**	
	n	General category		**14n**	
	o	Other (attach statement)		**14o**	
		Other information			
	p	Total foreign taxes (check one): ☐ Paid ☐ Accrued . . . . ▶		**14p**	
	q	Reduction in taxes available for credit (attach statement)		**14q**	
	r	Other foreign tax information (attach statement)			

Form **1120-S** (2020)

Form 1120-S (2020)   Page **4**

Schedule K		Shareholders' Pro Rata Share Items *(continued)*		Total amount
Alternative Minimum Tax (AMT) Items	**15a**	Post-1986 depreciation adjustment	**15a**	
	b	Adjusted gain or loss	**15b**	
	c	Depletion (other than oil and gas)	**15c**	
	d	Oil, gas, and geothermal properties—gross income	**15d**	
	e	Oil, gas, and geothermal properties—deductions	**15e**	
	f	Other AMT items (attach statement)	**15f**	
Items Affecting Shareholder Basis	**16a**	Tax-exempt interest income	**16a**	
	b	Other tax-exempt income	**16b**	
	c	Nondeductible expenses	**16c**	
	d	Distributions (attach statement if required) (see instructions)	**16d**	
	e	Repayment of loans from shareholders	**16e**	
Other Information	**17a**	Investment income	**17a**	
	b	Investment expenses	**17b**	
	c	Dividend distributions paid from accumulated earnings and profits	**17c**	
	d	Other items and amounts (attach statement)		
Reconciliation	**18**	**Income (loss) reconciliation.** Combine the amounts on lines 1 through 10 in the far right column. From the result, subtract the sum of the amounts on lines 11 through 12d and 14p	**18**	

Schedule L	Balance Sheets per Books	Beginning of tax year		End of tax year	
	Assets	**(a)**	**(b)**	**(c)**	**(d)**
1	Cash				
2a	Trade notes and accounts receivable				
b	Less allowance for bad debts	( )		( )	
3	Inventories				
4	U.S. government obligations				
5	Tax-exempt securities (see instructions)				
6	Other current assets (attach statement)				
7	Loans to shareholders				
8	Mortgage and real estate loans				
9	Other investments (attach statement)				
10a	Buildings and other depreciable assets				
b	Less accumulated depreciation	( )		( )	
11a	Depletable assets				
b	Less accumulated depletion	( )		( )	
12	Land (net of any amortization)				
13a	Intangible assets (amortizable only)				
b	Less accumulated amortization	( )		( )	
14	Other assets (attach statement)				
15	Total assets				
	Liabilities and Shareholders' Equity				
16	Accounts payable				
17	Mortgages, notes, bonds payable in less than 1 year				
18	Other current liabilities (attach statement)				
19	Loans from shareholders				
20	Mortgages, notes, bonds payable in 1 year or more				
21	Other liabilities (attach statement)				
22	Capital stock				
23	Additional paid-in capital				
24	Retained earnings				
25	Adjustments to shareholders' equity (attach statement)				
26	Less cost of treasury stock		( )		( )
27	Total liabilities and shareholders' equity				

Form **1120-S** (2020)

Form 1120-S (2020)   Page **5**

Schedule M-1	Reconciliation of Income (Loss) per Books With Income (Loss) per Return

Note: The corporation may be required to file Schedule M-3. See instructions.

1	Net income (loss) per books		**5**	Income recorded on books this year not included on Schedule K, lines 1 through 10 (itemize):
2	Income included on Schedule K, lines 1, 2, 3c, 4, 5a, 6, 7, 8a, 9, and 10, not recorded on books this year (itemize) _____		**a**	Tax-exempt interest $ _____
3	Expenses recorded on books this year not included on Schedule K, lines 1 through 12 and 14p (itemize):		**6**	Deductions included on Schedule K, lines 1 through 12 and 14p, not charged against book income this year (itemize):
a	Depreciation $ _____		**a**	Depreciation $ _____
b	Travel and entertainment $ _____		**7**	Add lines 5 and 6 . . . .
4	Add lines 1 through 3		**8**	Income (loss) (Schedule K, line 18). Subtract line 7 from line 4

Schedule M-2	Analysis of Accumulated Adjustments Account, Shareholders' Undistributed Taxable Income Previously Taxed, Accumulated Earnings and Profits, and Other Adjustments Account

(see instructions)

		(a) Accumulated adjustments account	(b) Shareholders' undistributed taxable income previously taxed	(c) Accumulated earnings and profits	(d) Other adjustments account
1	Balance at beginning of tax year				
2	Ordinary income from page 1, line 21 . . .				
3	Other additions				
4	Loss from page 1, line 21	( )			
5	Other reductions	( )			( )
6	Combine lines 1 through 5				
7	Distributions				
8	Balance at end of tax year. Subtract line 7 from line 6				

Form **1120-S** (2020)

Self-Study Problem 11.6

671120

Schedule K-1 (Form 1120-S) Department of the Treasury Internal Revenue Service	20**20**		☐ Final K-1 ☐ Amended K-1 OMB No. 1545-0123

Schedule K-1 (Form 1120-S) 2020

For calendar year 2020, or tax year

beginning / / 2020 ending / /

Shareholder's Share of Income, Deductions, Credits, etc. ▶ See separate instructions.

Part I Information About the Corporation
A Corporation's employer identification number
B Corporation's name, address, city, state, and ZIP code
C IRS Center where corporation filed return

Part II Information About the Shareholder
D Shareholder's identifying number
E Shareholder's name, address, city, state, and ZIP code
F Current year allocation percentage . . . _____ %
G Shareholder's number of shares Beginning of tax year . . . . . _____ End of tax year . . . . _____
H Loans from shareholder Beginning of tax year . . . . . $ _____ End of tax year . . . . $ _____

For IRS Use Only

	Part III Shareholder's Share of Current Year Income, Deductions, Credits, and Other Items		
1	Ordinary business income (loss)	**13**	Credits
2	Net rental real estate income (loss)		
3	Other net rental income (loss)		
4	Interest income		
5a	Ordinary dividends		
5b	Qualified dividends	**14**	Foreign transactions
6	Royalties		
7	Net short-term capital gain (loss)		
8a	Net long-term capital gain (loss)		
8b	Collectibles (28%) gain (loss)		
8c	Unrecaptured section 1250 gain		
9	Net section 1231 gain (loss)		
10	Other income (loss)	**15**	Alternative minimum tax (AMT) items
11	Section 179 deduction	**16**	Items affecting shareholder basis
12	Other deductions		
		17	Other information
18	☐ More than one activity for at-risk purposes*		
19	☐ More than one activity for passive activity purposes*		
	* See attached statement for additional information.		

Schedule K-1 (Form 1120-S) 2019   Page **2**

This list identifies the codes used on Schedule K-1 for all shareholders and provides summarized reporting information for shareholders who file Form 1040 or 1040-SR. For detailed reporting and filing information, see the separate Shareholder's Instructions for Schedule K-1 and the instructions for your income tax return.

1. **Ordinary business income (loss).** Determine whether the income (loss) is passive or nonpassive and enter on your return as follows:

	Report on
Passive loss	See the Shareholder's Instructions
Passive income	Schedule E, line 28, column (h)
Nonpassive loss	See the Shareholder's Instructions
Nonpassive income	Schedule E, line 28, column (k)

2. **Net rental real estate income (loss)**   See the Shareholder's Instructions
3. **Other net rental income (loss)**
   | Net income | Schedule E, line 28, column (h) |
   | Net loss | See the Shareholder's Instructions |
4. **Interest income**   Form 1040 or 1040-SR, line 2b
5a. **Ordinary dividends**   Form 1040 or 1040-SR, line 3b
5b. **Qualified dividends**   Form 1040 or 1040-SR, line 3a
6. **Royalties**   Schedule E, line 4
7. **Net short-term capital gain (loss)**   Schedule D, line 5
8a. **Net long-term capital gain (loss)**   Schedule D, line 12
8b. **Collectibles (28%) gain (loss)**   28% Rate Gain Worksheet, line 4 (Schedule D instructions)
8c. **Unrecaptured section 1250 gain**   See the Shareholder's Instructions
9. **Net section 1231 gain (loss)**   See the Shareholder's Instructions
10. **Other income (loss)**
   Code
   A Other portfolio income (loss)   See the Shareholder's Instructions
   B Involuntary conversions   See the Shareholder's Instructions
   C Sec. 1256 contracts & straddles   Form 6781, line 1
   D Mining exploration costs recapture   See Pub. 535
   E Reserved for future use
   F Section 965(a) inclusion
   G Income under subpart F (other than inclusions under sections 951A and 965)   } See the Shareholder's Instructions
   H Other income (loss)
11. **Section 179 deduction**   See the Shareholder's Instructions
12. **Other deductions**
   A Cash contributions (60%)
   B Cash contributions (30%)
   C Noncash contributions (50%)
   D Noncash contributions (30%)
   E Capital gain property to a 50% organization (30%)   } See the Shareholder's Instructions
   F Capital gain property (20%)
   G Contributions (100%)
   H Investment interest expense   Form 4952, line 1
   I Deductions—royalty income   Schedule E, line 19
   J Section 59(e)(2) expenditures   See the Shareholder's Instructions
   K Section 965(c) deduction   See the Shareholder's Instructions
   L Deductions—portfolio (other)   Schedule A, line 16
   M Preproductive period expenses   See the Shareholder's Instructions
   N Commercial revitalization deduction from rental real estate activities   See Form 8582 instructions
   O Reforestation expense deduction   See the Shareholder's Instructions
   P through **R**   Reserved for future use
   S Other deductions   See the Shareholder's Instructions
13. **Credits**
   A Low-income housing credit (section 42(j)(5)) from pre-2008 buildings
   B Low-income housing credit (other) from pre-2008 buildings
   C Low-income housing credit (section 42(j)(5)) from post-2007 buildings
   D Low-income housing credit (other) from post-2007 buildings   } See the Shareholder's Instructions
   E Qualified rehabilitation expenditures (rental real estate)
   F Other rental real estate credits
   G Other rental credits
   H Undistributed capital gains credit   Schedule 3 (Form 1040 or 1040-SR), line 13, box a
   I Biofuel producer credit
   J Work opportunity credit
   K Disabled access credit   } See the Shareholder's Instructions
   L Empowerment zone employment credit
   M Credit for increasing research activities

Code		Report on
N	Credit for employer social security and Medicare taxes	} See the Shareholder's Instructions
O	Backup withholding	
P	Other credits	

14. **Foreign transactions**
   A Name of country or U.S. possession
   B Gross income from all sources   } Form 1116, Part I
   C Gross income sourced at shareholder level
   Foreign gross income sourced at corporate level
   D Reserved for future use
   E Foreign branch category
   F Passive category   } Form 1116, Part I
   G General category
   H Other
   Deductions allocated and apportioned at shareholder level
   I Interest expense   Form 1116, Part I
   J Other   Form 1116, Part I
   Deductions allocated and apportioned at corporate level to foreign source income
   K Reserved for future use
   L Foreign branch category
   M Passive category   } Form 1116, Part I
   N General category
   O Other
   Other information
   P Total foreign taxes paid   Form 1116, Part II
   Q Total foreign taxes accrued   Form 1116, Part II
   R Reduction in taxes available for credit   Form 1116, line 12
   S Foreign trading gross receipts   Form 8873
   T Extraterritorial income exclusion   Form 8873
   U Section 965 information   See the Shareholder's Instructions
   V Other foreign transactions   See the Shareholder's Instructions
15. **Alternative minimum tax (AMT) items**
   A Post-1986 depreciation adjustment
   B Adjusted gain or loss
   C Depletion (other than oil & gas)   See the Shareholder's Instructions and the Instructions for Form 6251
   D Oil, gas, & geothermal—gross income
   E Oil, gas, & geothermal—deductions
   F Other AMT items
16. **Items affecting shareholder basis**
   A Tax-exempt interest income   Form 1040 or 1040-SR, line 2a
   B Other tax-exempt income
   C Nondeductible expenses
   D Distributions   } See the Shareholder's Instructions
   E Repayment of loans from shareholders
17. **Other information**
   A Investment income   Form 4952, line 4a
   B Investment expenses   Form 4952, line 5
   C Qualified rehabilitation expenditures (other than rental real estate)   See the Shareholder's Instructions
   D Basis of energy property   See the Shareholder's Instructions
   E Recapture of low-income housing credit (section 42(j)(5))   Form 8611, line 8
   F Recapture of low-income housing credit (other)   Form 8611, line 8
   G Recapture of investment credit   See Form 4255
   H Recapture of other credits   See the Shareholder's Instructions
   I Look-back interest—completed long-term contracts   See Form 8697
   J Look-back interest—income forecast method   See Form 8866
   K Dispositions of property with section 179 deductions
   L Recapture of section 179 deduction   } See the Shareholder's Instructions
   M through **U**
   V Section 199A information
   W through **Z**   Reserved for future use
   AA Excess taxable income
   AB Excess business interest income   } See the Shareholder's Instructions
   AC Other information

Page 2 of Schedule K-1 is from 2019. 2020 not available when we went to print.

89 percent (85 of 95 shares) of the stock after the transfer. B's stock is not considered because it was received in exchange for services.

1. A has a realized gain of $15,000 ($40,000 − $25,000), but no recognized gain since no boot was received.
2. B's recognized income is $10,000, since she performed services in exchange for the stock, and stock received for services does not fall within the nonrecognition provisions.
3. C's realized gain is $40,000 ($45,000 + $5,000 − $10,000), but only $5,000 of the gain is recognized, the amount of boot received.
4. A's basis in the stock is $25,000 ($25,000 − $0 + $0 − $0), B's basis in the stock is $10,000 ($0 − $0 + $10,000 − $0), and C's basis in the stock is $10,000 ($10,000 − $5,000 + $5,000 − $0).
5. Hornbeam Corporation's basis in the property contributed by A is $25,000 ($25,000 + $0). The corporation's basis in the property contributed by C is $15,000 ($10,000 + $5,000 gain recognized). ◆

Self-Study Problem 11.7   *See Appendix E for Solutions to Self-Study Problems*

Tammy has a business which she decides to incorporate. She transfers to the new corporation, real estate with a basis of $75,000 and subject to a $34,000 mortgage in exchange for all of its stock. The stock is worth $125,000.

What is Tammy's realized gain? $_____

What is Tammy's recognized gain? $_____

What is Tammy's basis in her stock? $_____

What is the corporation's basis in the real estate? $_____

11-8 CORPORATE ACCUMULATIONS

11.8 Learning Objective

Describe the rules for the accumulated earnings tax and the personal holding company tax.

In many cases, taxpayers have established corporations to avoid paying income taxes at the shareholder level by allowing earnings to be accumulated by the corporations, rather than paid out as taxable dividends. To prevent that practice, Congress has enacted two special taxes which may be applied to certain corporations: the accumulated earnings tax and the personal holding company tax.

11-8a Accumulated Earnings Tax

The accumulated earnings tax is designed to prevent the shareholders of a corporation from avoiding tax at the shareholder level by retaining earnings in the corporation. The tax is a penalty tax imposed in addition to the regular corporate income tax. The tax is imposed at a rate of 20 percent on amounts that are deemed to be unreasonable accumulations of earnings. For all corporations except service corporations, such as accounting, law, and health care corporations, the first $250,000 in accumulated earnings is exempt from tax. Service corporations will not be taxed on their first $150,000 of accumulated earnings. Even if the accumulated earnings of a corporation exceed the exemption amount, the tax will not be imposed on accumulations that can be shown to be necessary to meet the reasonable needs of the business.

EXAMPLE Alder Corporation is a manufacturing corporation that has accumulated earnings of $625,000. The corporation can establish reasonable needs for $450,000 of this accumulation. Alder Corporation would be subject to the accumulated earnings tax on $175,000 ($625,000 − $450,000). The amount of the accumulated earnings tax is $35,000 (20% of $175,000). ♦

11-8b Personal Holding Company Tax

Personal holding companies, which are corporations with few shareholders and with income primarily from investments, are subject to a 20 percent tax on their undistributed earnings. The tax is imposed in addition to the regular corporate income tax; however, a corporation cannot be subject to both the accumulated earnings tax and the personal holding company tax in the same year. If both taxes are imposed, the taxpayer pays only the personal holding company tax. The rules for the personal holding company tax are very complex.

Self-Study Problem 11.8 *See Appendix E for Solutions to Self-Study Problems*

Sugarbush Corporation, an accounting corporation, has accumulated earnings of $340,000, and the corporation cannot establish a reasonable need for any of that amount. Calculate the amount of accumulated earnings tax (if any) that will be imposed on Sugarbush Corporation.

$_____

Learning Objective 11.9

Describe tax issues associated with the repeal of the alternative minimum tax.

11-9 THE CORPORATE ALTERNATIVE MINIMUM TAX

Unlike the individual alternative minimum tax (AMT), which remains in force, the corporate AMT was repealed for tax years after 2017 by the TCJA. Under the prior corporate AMT regime, a corporation subject to AMT may have had unused AMT credits that can be carried over indefinitely to offset regular tax. Under the CARES Act, any remaining AMT credit carryover can be used as a refundable credit in 2019. Alternatively, an election can be made by December 31, 2020, to take the entire credit amount in 2018.

EXAMPLE Lloyd Corporation, a calendar year C corporation, has unused AMT credits of $10,000 at the end 2017. In 2018, Lloyd applied $2,000 of the AMT credits against the 2018 tax liability. In 2019, Lloyd's tax liability was $6,000 but Lloyd was able to claim the entire remaining $8,000 balance of the AMT credits. Alternatively, Lloyd could have elected to apply the AMT credits against 2018. ♦

Self-Study Problem 11.9 *See Appendix E for Solutions to Self-Study Problems*

In 2019, Plum Corporation has regular income tax liability of $12,500. Plum has AMT credit carryforwards of $20,000 from prior years. What is Plum Corporation's remaining AMT credit carryforward after applying the maximum credit against 2019?

$_____

KEY TERMS

corporate tax rate, 11-2
personal service corporation, 11-2
corporate capital gains and
    losses, 11-2
net operating losses, 11-3
special deductions, 11-4
dividends received deduction, 11-4
organizational expenditures, 11-5
start-up costs, 11-6
corporate charitable contributions
    deduction, 11-6

Form 1120, 11-7
Schedule M-1, 11-7
book income, 11-7
Schedule L (Balance Sheet), 11-8
S Corporation, 11-17
statutorily terminated, 11-17
Form 1120S, 11-17
Schedule K-1, 11-18
pass-through items, 11-18
Qualified business income
    deduction, 11-18

built-in gains tax, 11-19
nonrecognition treatment, 11-20
boot, 11-20
stock basis, 11-20
corporation's basis, 11-20
accumulated earnings tax, 11-29
personal holding company
    tax, 11-30
corporate alternative minimum
    tax, 11-30

KEY POINTS

Learning Objectives	Key Points
LO 11.1: Employ the corporate tax rates to calculate corporate tax liability.	• The U.S. corporate tax rate is a flat 21 percent regardless of income level. • Qualified personal service corporations (health, law, engineering, architecture, accounting, actuarial science, performing arts, and consulting) are taxed at the same 21 percent tax rate on all taxable income.
LO 11.2: Compute basic gains and losses for corporations.	• Corporate ordinary income and capital gains tax rates are the same, so there is no tax rate benefit to having long-term capital gains in a corporation. • Net short-term capital gains of a corporation are taxed as ordinary income. • Capital losses may be used only to offset capital gains. • If capital losses cannot be used in the year they occur, they may be carried back 3 years and forward 5 years to offset capital gains in those years. • When a long-term capital loss is carried to another year, it is treated as a short-term capital loss and may be offset against either long-term or short-term capital gains. • Net operating losses generated in 2018, 2019, and 2020 can be carried back 5 years and carried forward indefinitely.
LO 11.3: Apply special corporate deductions to corporate taxable income.	• Corporations are allowed a dividends received deduction based on their percentage of ownership in the corporation paying the dividend. • The dividends received deduction percentage is 50 percent (for ownership less than 20 percent), 65 percent (for ownership of 20 percent or more, but less than 80 percent), or 100 percent (for ownership of 80 percent or more). • Corporations amortize qualifying organizational costs over 180 months, and there is no upper limit to the amount of qualifying costs that can be amortized.

- Corporations can elect to deduct up to $5,000 of organizational costs and $5,000 of start-up costs in the year they begin business. The $5,000 amounts are reduced by each dollar of organizational expenses and start-up costs exceeding $50,000.
- A corporation's charitable contribution deduction is limited to 10 percent of taxable income, computed before the deduction for charitable contributions, net operating loss carrybacks, capital loss carrybacks, and the dividends received deduction.
- Excess charitable contributions are carried forward to the 5 succeeding tax years, subject to the 10 percent annual limitation in the carryover years, with the current year's contributions deducted first.
- As part of the COVID-related stimulus, in 2020 only, cash contributions are deductible up to 25 percent of taxable income.

LO 11.4: Identify the components of Schedule M-1 and how they are reported to the IRS.	- The purpose of Schedule M-1 of the corporate tax return is to reconcile a corporation's accounting "book" income to its taxable income. - On the left side of Schedule M-1 are adjustments that must be added to book income, and on the right side of the schedule are adjustments that must be subtracted from book income to arrive at the amount of taxable income. - The additions to book income include the amount of federal income tax expense, net capital losses deducted for book purposes, income recorded on the tax return but not on the books, and expenses recorded on the books but not deducted on the tax return. - The amounts that must be deducted from book income include income recorded on the books but not included on the tax return, and deductions included on the return but not deducted on the books.
LO 11.5: Describe the corporate tax return filing and estimated tax payment requirements.	- The due date for filing a corporate tax return is the fifteenth day of the fourth month after year-end. An extension provides an additional 6 months; thus a calendar year-end corporation has an initial deadline of April 15 and an extended deadline of October 15. - A corporation must pay any tax liability by the original due date of the return. - Corporations must make estimated tax payments similar to those made by self-employed individual taxpayers. The payments are due on the fifteenth day of the fourth, sixth, ninth, and twelfth months of the corporation's tax year.
LO 11.6: Explain how an S corporation operates and is taxed.	- Certain qualified corporations may elect to be taxed under Subchapter S of the Internal Revenue Code in a manner similar to partnerships. - To elect S corporation status, a corporation *must* have the following characteristics: (1) be a domestic corporation; (2) have 100 or fewer shareholders who are either individuals, estates, certain trusts, certain financial institutions, or certain exempt organizations; (3) have only one class of stock; and (4) all shareholders must be U.S. citizens or resident aliens. - Each shareholder of an S corporation reports his or her share of corporate income based on his or her stock ownership during the year. - Schedule K-1 of Form 1120S is used to report the allocation of ordinary income or loss, and all separately stated items of income or loss, to each of the shareholders. - Losses from an S corporation pass through to the shareholders, but the loss deduction is limited to the shareholders' adjusted basis in the corporation's stock plus the amount of any loans from the shareholder to the corporation. - S corporation shareholders are eligible for the qualified business income deduction.
LO 11.7: Describe the basic tax rules for the formation of a corporation.	- If property is exchanged for stock in a corporation, the shareholders are in "control" of the corporation after the transfer, and the shareholders receive no boot, gain on the transfer is not recognized. - Realized gain is recognized to the extent that the shareholder receives boot. - The basis of the stock received by the shareholder is equal to the basis of the property transferred plus any gain recognized by the shareholder, less the fair market value of any boot received by the shareholder, less liabilities assumed by the corporation. - The basis of property received by the corporation is equal to the basis in the hands of the transferor plus any gain recognized by the transferor.

| LO 11.8:

Describe the rules for the accumulated earnings tax and the personal holding company tax. | • The accumulated earnings tax is a penalty tax, imposed in addition to the regular corporate income tax, at a rate of 20 percent on amounts that are deemed to be unreasonable accumulations of earnings.
• For all corporations, except personal service corporations, the first $250,000 in accumulated earnings is exempt from tax. The first $150,000 in accumulated earnings is exempt for personal service corporations.
• Personal holding companies, which are corporations with few shareholders and income primarily from investments, are subject to a 20 percent tax on undistributed earnings. |
| LO 11.9:

Describe tax issues associated with the repeal of the alternative minimum tax. | • The corporate AMT was repealed for tax years after 2017.
• Any AMT credit carryforwards may be used in full in 2019 (or 2018, if elected). |

QUESTIONS and PROBLEMS

GROUP 1:
MULTIPLE CHOICE QUESTIONS

LO 11.1
1. Ironwood Corporation has ordinary taxable income of $25,000 in 2020, and a short-term capital loss of $15,000. What is the corporation's tax liability for 2020?
   a. $2,100
   b. $5,250
   c. $10,500
   d. $13,650
   e. None of the above

LO 11.1
2. Tayla Corporation generated $400,000 of taxable income in the 2020. What is Tayla's corporate tax liability?
   a. $71,400
   b. $84,000
   c. $115,600
   d. $136,000
   e. None of the above

LO 11.2
3. Which of the following statements is *false* regarding corporate capital losses?
   a. Corporations may deduct $3,000 of net capital loss each year until the loss is used up.
   b. Corporations may carry capital losses back 3 years and forward 5 years to offset capital gains in those years.
   c. Corporations are not allowed to deduct capital losses against ordinary income.
   d. A long-term capital loss carried to another year is treated as a short-term capital loss.

LO 11.2
4. Harrison Corporation generates capital gains/(losses) of ($2,000), $4,000, ($14,000) in 2018, 2019, and 2020, respectively. Harrison started operating in 2018. What is Harrison's capital loss carryforward into 2021?
   a. $0
   b. $10,000
   c. $12,000
   d. $14,000
   e. None of the above

LO 11.2

5. Mask Corporation generated a net operating loss of $24,000 in 2020 and taxable income of $10,000 in 2021. How much NOL can Mask use in 2021 to reduce taxable income (assume no carryback is possible)?
   a. $8,000
   b. $10,000
   c. $19,200
   d. $24,000

LO 11.3

6. Walnut Corporation owns 26 percent of Teak Corporation, a domestic corporation. During the current year, Walnut Corporation received $20,000 in dividends from Teak Corporation. Assuming that Walnut's taxable income for the current year before the dividends received deduction is $500,000, what is the amount of Walnut's dividends received deduction for the current year?
   a. $10,000
   b. $13,000
   c. $16,000
   d. $20,000
   e. None of the above

LO 11.3

7. Which of the following is *not* a corporate organizational expenditure that may be amortized?
   a. The cost of organizational meetings
   b. Fees paid to the state for incorporation
   c. Accounting fees incident to organization
   d. Legal fees incident to organization
   e. All of the above are organizational expenditures

LO 11.4

8. The purpose of Schedule M-1 on the corporate tax return is to:
   a. Reconcile accounting (book) income to taxable income.
   b. Summarize the dividends received deduction calculation.
   c. List the officers of the corporation and their compensation.
   d. Calculate the net operating loss deduction.

LO 11.4

9. Which of the following would *not* generally appear on the M-1 reconciliation?
   a. Federal income tax expense per books
   b. Tax-exempt interest income
   c. Excess tax over book depreciation
   d. Dividends received deduction

LO 11.5

10. Which of the following statements is *false* regarding corporate tax return due dates?
    a. Corporate tax returns for 2020 calendar-year corporations are due April 15, 2021.
    b. Corporate tax returns may receive an automatic 6-month extension.
    c. Corporate taxes due must be paid no later than the extended due date of the tax return.
    d. When an IRS due date falls on a weekend or holiday, the due date is the next business day.

LO 11.5

11. Mansfield Incorporated, a calendar year corporation, is expecting to have a current year tax liability of $100,000. Which best describes the tax payments Mansfield should make to avoid penalty?
    a. Make payments at the end of June and December of $40,000 each and $20,000 when filing the return on the original due date.
    b. Make no payments during the year but pay the entire balance on the extended due date.
    c. Make no payments during the year but pay the entire balance on the original due date.
    d. Make quarterly payments totaling $100,000, all during the current year.
    e. None of these will avoid penalty.

LO 11.6   12. Which of the following is *not* required for a corporation to be eligible to make an S corporation election?
   a. The corporation must have 100 or fewer shareholders.
   b. The corporation must be a domestic corporation.
   c. The corporation must have both common and preferred stock.
   d. The shareholders of the corporation must not be nonresident aliens.
   e. All shareholders must be either individuals, estates, certain trusts, or financial institutions.

LO 11.6   13. Which of the following items are passed through and separately stated on Schedule K-1 to shareholders of an S corporation?
   a. Wages paid
   b. Typical MACRS depreciation
   c. Net long-term capital gains
   d. Advertising expense
   e. All of the above retain their character when passed through

LO 11.6   14. Which of the following is *true* about S corporations?
   a. S corporations pay corporate taxes like other corporations.
   b. S corporations pay the alternative minimum tax for all income.
   c. S corporations cannot issue corporate stock.
   d. The S corporation status may be elected by stockholders only for corporations that meet certain qualifications.
   e. None of the above.

LO 11.7   15. Travis transfers land with a fair market value of $125,000 and basis of $25,000, to a corporation in exchange for 100 percent of the corporation's stock. What amount of gain must Travis recognize as a result of this transaction?
   a. $0   d. $125,000
   b. $25,000   e. None of the above
   c. $100,000

LO 11.7   16. Carl transfers land with a fair market value of $120,000 and basis of $30,000, to a new corporation in exchange for 85 percent of the corporation's stock. The land is subject to a $45,000 liability, which the corporation assumes. What amount of gain must Carl recognize as a result of this transaction?
   a. $0
   b. $15,000
   c. $30,000
   d. $45,000
   e. None of the above

LO 11.7   17. What is the shareholder's basis in stock of a corporation received as a result of the transfer of property to the corporation and as a result of which gain was recognized by the stockholder?
   a. The shareholder's basis is equal to the basis of the property transferred less the gain.
   b. The shareholder's basis is equal to the fair market value of the stock received, less any liabilities transferred by the stockholder.
   c. The shareholder's basis is equal to the basis of the property transferred to the corporation, minus any liabilities transferred by the shareholder, plus the gain.
   d. The shareholder's basis is equal to the basis of the property transferred to the corporation, plus any liabilities transferred by the shareholder.
   e. None of the above.

LO 11.8   18. Which of the following statements regarding personal holding companies is *false*?
   a. A personal holding company is one which has few shareholders.
   b. A personal holding company has income primarily from investments.
   c. A personal holding company operates a business which is a hobby for its owners.
   d. Personal holding companies are subject to a 20 percent tax on income that is left undistributed.

LO 11.8

19. Boyce Industries, a manufacturing corporation, has accumulated earnings of $325,000 and cannot show any reasonable need for the accumulated earnings. What is Boyce's accumulated earnings tax?
    a. $15,000
    b. $0
    c. $13,750
    d. $75,000

LO 11.9

20. Which of the following statements is *true* about the 2020 corporate alternative minimum tax?
    a. The corporate alternative minimum tax only applies to small corporations.
    b. The corporate alternative minimum tax preferences and adjustments are exactly the same as those for individuals.
    c. The corporate alternative minimum tax was repealed for tax years after 2017.
    d. Corporations with alternative minimum taxable income greater than $310,000 receive no exemption.

LO 11.9

21. Any corporate AMT credit carryovers that existed at the end of 2017:
    a. Can be used to offset tax liability generated in 2018 and thereafter
    b. Do not expire
    c. Can generate a refundable credit of any unused AMT credits in 2019
    d. All of the above

GROUP 2:
PROBLEMS

LO 11.1

1. Quince Corporation has taxable income of $285,000 for its calendar tax year. Calculate the corporation's income tax liability for 2020 before tax credits.

   $ _____

LO 11.1

2. Ulmus Corporation is an engineering consulting firm and has $1,400,000 in taxable income for 2020. Calculate the corporation's income tax liability for 2020.

   $ _____

LO 11.1
LO 11.2

3. For its current tax year, Ilex Corporation has ordinary income of $250,000, a short-term capital loss of $20,000 and a long-term capital gain of $60,000. Calculate Ilex Corporation's tax liability for 2020.

   $ _____

LO 11.2

4. DeMaria Corporation, a calendar year corporation, generates the following taxable income (net operating losses) since its inception in 2017:

Year	Taxable result
2017	$40,000
2018	(15,000)
2019	(5,000)
2020	6,000

   Assuming DeMaria makes no special elections with regard to NOLs, what is DeMaria's net operating loss carryforward into 2021?

LO 11.3

5. Fisafolia Corporation has gross income from operations of $210,000 and operating expenses of $160,000 for 2020. The corporation also has $30,000 in dividends from publicly-traded domestic corporations in which the ownership percentage was 45 percent.
    a. Calculate the corporation's dividends received deduction for 2020.

   $ _____

b. Assume that instead of $210,000, Fisafolia Corporation has gross income from operations of $135,000. Calculate the corporation's dividends received deduction for 2020.

$ _____

c. Assume that instead of $210,000, Fisafolia Corporation has gross income from operations of $158,000. Calculate the corporation's dividends received deduction for 2020.

$_____

LO 11.3

6. Beech Corporation, an accrual basis calendar year taxpayer, was organized and began business on July of the current calendar tax year. During the current year, the corporation incurred the following expenses:

State fees for incorporation	$ 500
Legal and accounting fees incident to organization	4,150
Expenses for the sale of stock	2,100
Organizational meeting expenses	750

Assuming that Beech Corporation does not elect to expense but chooses to amortize organizational expenditures over 15 years, calculate the corporation's deduction for its current calendar tax year.

$ _____

LO 11.3

7. In Year 1, Citradoria Corporation is a regular corporation that contributes $35,000 cash to qualified charitable organizations during the current tax year. The corporation has net operating income of $145,000, before deducting the contributions, and dividends received from domestic corporations (ownership in all corporations is less than 20 percent) in the amount of $25,000.

a. What is the amount of Citradoria Corporation's allowable deduction for charitable contributions for Year 1?

$ _____

b. In Year 2, Citradoria contributes $5,000 to charitable organizations. The corporation has net operating income of $150,000 before deducting the contributions, and no dividend income. What is the amount of Citradoria's allowable deduction for charitable contributions for Year 2?

$ _____

c. If there is any carryover of the charitable contribution deduction from Year 2, what year will it expire (e.g., Year 3)?

$ _____

LO 11.4

8. The Loquat Corporation has book net income of $50,000 for the current year. Included in this figure are the following items, which are reported on the corporation's Schedule M-1, Reconciliation of Income (Loss) per Books with Income per Return.

Federal income tax expense	$ 7,500
Depreciation deducted on the books which is not deductible for tax purposes	10,000
Deduction for 50 percent of meals expense which is not allowed for tax purposes	5,500
Deduction for entertainment not allowed for tax purposes	2,000
Tax-exempt interest income included in book income but not in tax income	4,200

Calculate Loquat Corporation's taxable income for the current year based on the information given. Show your calculations.

$ _____

LO 11.4

9. Caloundra Corporation has book income of $40,000. Included in the book income is $3,000 of tax-exempt interest, $7,000 of book income tax expense, and a $2,000 non-deductible fine. Also included in book income are $10,000 of dividends Caloundra received from a 30 percent owned corporation. Using this information and Form 1120, provide the amounts that go on each line on the form.
   a. Form 1120, Schedule M-1 Line 1 $_____
   b. Form 1120, Schedule M-1, Line 10 $_____
   c. Form 1120, page 1, Line 28 $_____
   d. Form 1120, Schedule C, Line 2(a) $_____ and 2(c) $_____
   e. Form 1120, Schedule C, Line 24 $_____
   f. Form 1120, page 1, Line 29b $_____
   g. Form 1120, page 1, Line 30 $_____

LO 11.5

10. Mallory Corporation has a calendar year-end. The corporation has paid estimated taxes of $10,000 during 2020 but still owes an additional $5,000 for its 2020 tax year.
   a. When is the 2020 tax return due?

   _____

   b. If an automatic extension of time to file is requested, when is the 2020 tax return due?

   _____

   c. If an extension of time to file is requested, when is the additional $5,000 of tax for 2020 due?

   _____

LO 11.6

11. Cedar Corporation has an S corporation election in effect. During the 2020 calendar tax year, the corporation had ordinary taxable income of $200,000, and on January 15, 2020, the corporation paid dividends to shareholders in the amount of $120,000. How much taxable income, in total, must the shareholders of the corporation report on their 2020 tax returns?

   $_____

   Explain your answer _____

   _____

LO 11.6

12. Bill and Guilda each own 50 percent of the stock of Radiata Corporation, an S corporation. Guilda's basis in her stock is $21,000. On May 26, 2020, Bill sells his stock, with a basis of $40,000, to Loraine for $50,000. For the 2020 tax year, Radiata Corporation has a loss of $104,000.
   a. Calculate the amount of the corporation's loss that may be deducted by Bill on his 2020 tax return.

   $_____

   b. Calculate the amount of the corporation's loss that may be deducted by Guilda on her 2020 tax return.

   $_____

   c. Calculate the amount of the corporation's loss that may be deducted by Loraine on her 2020 tax return.

   $_____

LO 11.7

13. Karen, in forming a new corporation, transfers land to the corporation in exchange for 100 percent of the stock of the corporation. Karen's basis in the land is $275,000, and the corporation assumes a liability on the property in the amount of $300,000. The stock received by Karen has a fair market value of $550,000.
   a. What is the amount of gain or loss that must be recognized by Karen on this transfer?

   $_____

b. What is the amount of Karen's basis in the corporation's stock?

$ _____

c. What is the amount of the corporation's basis in the land?

$ _____

LO 11.8 14. Grevilla Corporation is a manufacturing company. The corporation has accumulated earnings of $950,000, and it can establish reasonable needs for $400,000 of that amount. Calculate the amount of the accumulated earnings tax (if any) that Grevilla Corporation is subject to for this year.

$ _____

LO 11.9 15. Cypress Corporation, a calendar year end corporation, has an AMT credit carryforward from 2018 (the credit arose in 2017) in the amount of $43,000. In 2019, Cypress has $170,000 of taxable income. Assuming Cypress is not a personal service corporation, what is the amount of refund Cypress can expect to receive from its 2019 tax return filing?

$ _____

LO 11.9 16. Go to the IRS website (**www.irs.gov**) and determine which IRS publication addresses the topic of corporate taxation. Print out the page with the *Table of Contents* of this IRS publication.

GROUP 3:
COMPREHENSIVE PROBLEMS

1. Floyd Corporation was formed and began operations on January 1, 2020. The corporation is located at 210 N. Main St., Pearisburg, VA 24134 and the EIN is 91-1111111. The corporation's income statement for the year and the balance sheet at year-end are presented below.

The Floyd Corporation Income Statement
for the Year Ended December 31, 2020

Gross income from operations		$ 320,000
Qualified dividends received from a 15 percent-		
owned domestic corporation		20,000
Total gross income		340,000
Cost of goods sold		(70,000)
Total income		270,000
Other expenses:		
Compensation of officers	$80,000	
Salaries and wages	20,000	
Bad debts (direct charge-offs)	9,000	
Repairs	3,000	
Depreciation for book (tax depreciation = $90,000)	10,000	
Advertising	3,000	
Payroll taxes	15,000	
Total other expenses		(140,000)
Pretax book income		130,000
Income tax expense		25,200
Net income		$ 104,800

The Floyd Corporation Balance Sheet
as of December 31, 2020

Assets:		
Cash	$ 140,600	
Accounts receivable	20,000	
Inventory (at cost)	70,000	
Equipment	90,000	
Less: accumulated depreciation	(10,000)	
Total assets		$310,600
Liabilities and owners' equity:		
Accounts payable	$ 24,000	
Other liabilities	16,800	
Note payable (due in 10 years)	85,000	
Common stock	80,000	
Retained earnings	104,800	
Total liabilities and owners' equity		$310,600

The corporation made estimated tax payments of $9,000. Complete Form 1120 for Floyd Corporation on Pages 11-43 through 11-48.

2. George Corporation is an S corporation started on January 1, 2020, with 50 shares owned by Trey Martin and 50 shares owned by Brianna Tabor. The corporation is located at 15620 McMullen Hwy SW, Cumberland, MD 21502 and has EIN 94–8888888. The corporation is not subject to any special taxes and no wages are included in cost of goods sold. The corporation's income statement for the year and the balance sheet at year-end are presented below.

The George Corporation Income Statement
for the Year Ended December 31, 2020

Gross income from operations		$ 320,000
Qualified dividends received from a 15 percent- owned domestic corporation		20,000
Total gross income		340,000
Cost of goods sold		(70,000)
Total income		270,000
Other expenses:		
Compensation of officers	$ 80,000	
Salaries and wages	20,000	
Bad debts (direct charge-offs)	9,000	
Repairs	3,000	
Depreciation for book (tax depreciation = $90,000)	10,000	
Advertising	3,000	
Payroll taxes	15,000	
Total other expenses		(140,000)
Net income		$ 130,000

The George Corporation Balance Sheet
as of December 31, 2020

Assets:

Cash	$ 109,000	
Accounts receivable	20,000	
Inventory (at cost)	70,000	
Other assets	40,000	
Equipment	90,000	
Less: accumulated depreciation	(10,000)	
Total assets		$319,000

Liabilities and owners' equity:

Accounts payable	$ 24,000	
Note payable (due in 10 years)	85,000	
Common stock	80,000	
Retained earnings	130,000	
Total liabilities and owners' equity		$319,000

Using this information, complete Form 1120–S for George Corporation and Schedule K–1 for Brianna (who lives at 12 Bowery St., Frostburg, MD 21532 and has SSN 444-11–5555) on Pages 11–49 through 11–56. Assume there are no cash distributions during the year.

U.S. Corporation Income Tax Return

Form **1120**

Department of the Treasury
Internal Revenue Service

For calendar year 2020 or tax year beginning _____ , 2020, ending _____ , 20 _____

▶ Go to *www.irs.gov/Form1120* for instructions and the latest information.

OMB No. 1545-0123

2020

A Check if:

1a Consolidated return (attach Form 851) ☐
 b Life/nonlife consolidated return . . ☐
2 Personal holding co. (attach Sch. PH) . ☐
3 Personal service corp. (see instructions) . ☐
4 Schedule M-3 attached ☐

TYPE OR PRINT

Name

Number, street, and room or suite no. If a P.O. box, see instructions.

City or town, state or province, country, and ZIP or foreign postal code

B Employer identification number

C Date incorporated

D Total assets (see instructions)
$

E Check if: (1) ☐ Initial return   (2) ☐ Final return   (3) ☐ Name change   (4) ☐ Address change

Income

1a	Gross receipts or sales	1a
b	Returns and allowances	1b
c	Balance. Subtract line 1b from line 1a	1c
2	Cost of goods sold (attach Form 1125-A)	2
3	Gross profit. Subtract line 2 from line 1c	3
4	Dividends and inclusions (Schedule C, line 23)	4
5	Interest	5
6	Gross rents	6
7	Gross royalties	7
8	Capital gain net income (attach Schedule D (Form 1120))	8
9	Net gain or (loss) from Form 4797, Part II, line 17 (attach Form 4797)	9
10	Other income (see instructions—attach statement)	10
11	**Total income.** Add lines 3 through 10 ▶	11

Deductions (See instructions for limitations on deductions.)

12	Compensation of officers (see instructions—attach Form 1125-E) ▶	12
13	Salaries and wages (less employment credits)	13
14	Repairs and maintenance	14
15	Bad debts	15
16	Rents	16
17	Taxes and licenses	17
18	Interest (see instructions)	18
19	Charitable contributions	19
20	Depreciation from Form 4562 not claimed on Form 1125-A or elsewhere on return (attach Form 4562)	20
21	Depletion	21
22	Advertising	22
23	Pension, profit-sharing, etc., plans	23
24	Employee benefit programs	24
25	Reserved for future use	25
26	Other deductions (attach statement)	26
27	**Total deductions.** Add lines 12 through 26 ▶	27
28	Taxable income before net operating loss deduction and special deductions. Subtract line 27 from line 11.	28
29a	Net operating loss deduction (see instructions)	29a
b	Special deductions (Schedule C, line 24)	29b
c	Add lines 29a and 29b	29c

Tax, Refundable Credits, and Payments

30	**Taxable income.** Subtract line 29c from line 28. See instructions	30
31	Total tax (Schedule J, Part I, line 11)	31
32	2020 net 965 tax liability paid (Schedule J, Part II, line 12)	32
33	Total payments, credits, and section 965 net tax liability (Schedule J, Part III, line 23)	33
34	Estimated tax penalty. See instructions. Check if Form 2220 is attached ▶ ☐	34
35	**Amount owed.** If line 33 is smaller than the total of lines 31, 32, and 34, enter amount owed	35
36	**Overpayment.** If line 33 is larger than the total of lines 31, 32, and 34, enter amount overpaid	36
37	Enter amount from line 36 you want: **Credited to 2021 estimated tax** ▶ **Refunded** ▶	37

Sign Here

Under penalties of perjury, I declare that I have examined this return, including accompanying schedules and statements, and to the best of my knowledge and belief, it is true, correct, and complete. Declaration of preparer (other than taxpayer) is based on all information of which preparer has any knowledge.

▶ _____
Signature of officer   Date

▶ _____
Title

May the IRS discuss this return with the preparer shown below? See instructions. ☐ Yes ☐ No

Paid Preparer Use Only

Print/Type preparer's name	Preparer's signature	Date	Check ☐ if self-employed	PTIN

Firm's name ▶   Firm's EIN ▶

Firm's address ▶   Phone no.

For Paperwork Reduction Act Notice, see separate instructions.   Cat. No. 11450Q   Form **1120** (2020)

Form 1120 (2020)   Page **2**

Schedule C	Dividends, Inclusions, and Special Deductions (see instructions)	(a) Dividends and inclusions	(b) %	(c) Special deductions (a) × (b)
1	Dividends from less-than-20%-owned domestic corporations (other than debt-financed stock)		50	
2	Dividends from 20%-or-more-owned domestic corporations (other than debt-financed stock)		65	
3	Dividends on certain debt-financed stock of domestic and foreign corporations . .		See instructions	
4	Dividends on certain preferred stock of less-than-20%-owned public utilities . . .		23.3	
5	Dividends on certain preferred stock of 20%-or-more-owned public utilities		26.7	
6	Dividends from less-than-20%-owned foreign corporations and certain FSCs . .		50	
7	Dividends from 20%-or-more-owned foreign corporations and certain FSCs . .		65	
8	Dividends from wholly owned foreign subsidiaries		100	
9	**Subtotal.** Add lines 1 through 8. See instructions for limitations		See instructions	
10	Dividends from domestic corporations received by a small business investment company operating under the Small Business Investment Act of 1958		100	
11	Dividends from affiliated group members		100	
12	Dividends from certain FSCs		100	
13	Foreign-source portion of dividends received from a specified 10%-owned foreign corporation (excluding hybrid dividends) (see instructions)		100	
14	Dividends from foreign corporations not included on line 3, 6, 7, 8, 11, 12, or 13 (including any hybrid dividends)			
15	Section 965(a) inclusion		See instructions	
16a	Subpart F inclusions derived from the sale by a controlled foreign corporation (CFC) of the stock of a lower-tier foreign corporation treated as a dividend (attach Form(s) 5471) (see instructions)		100	
b	Subpart F inclusions derived from hybrid dividends of tiered corporations (attach Form(s) 5471) (see instructions)			
c	Other inclusions from CFCs under subpart F not included on line 15, 16a, 16b, or 17 (attach Form(s) 5471) (see instructions).			
17	Global Intangible Low-Taxed Income (GILTI) (attach Form(s) 5471 and Form 8992) . .			
18	Gross-up for foreign taxes deemed paid			
19	IC-DISC and former DISC dividends not included on line 1, 2, or 3			
20	Other dividends			
21	Deduction for dividends paid on certain preferred stock of public utilities			
22	Section 250 deduction (attach Form 8993)			
23	**Total dividends and inclusions.** Add column (a), lines 9 through 20. Enter here and on page 1, line 4			
24	**Total special deductions.** Add column (c), lines 9 through 22. Enter here and on page 1, line 29b			

Form **1120** (2020)

Form 1120 (2020) Page **3**

Schedule J	**Tax Computation and Payment** (see instructions)		

Part I—Tax Computation

1	Check if the corporation is a member of a controlled group (attach Schedule O (Form 1120)). See instructions ▶ ☐		
2	Income tax. See instructions	**2**	
3	Base erosion minimum tax amount (attach Form 8991)	**3**	
4	Add lines 2 and 3	**4**	
5a	Foreign tax credit (attach Form 1118)	**5a**	
b	Credit from Form 8834 (see instructions)	**5b**	
c	General business credit (attach Form 3800)	**5c**	
d	Credit for prior year minimum tax (attach Form 8827)	**5d**	
e	Bond credits from Form 8912	**5e**	
6	**Total credits.** Add lines 5a through 5e	**6**	
7	Subtract line 6 from line 4	**7**	
8	Personal holding company tax (attach Schedule PH (Form 1120))	**8**	
9a	Recapture of investment credit (attach Form 4255)	**9a**	
b	Recapture of low-income housing credit (attach Form 8611)	**9b**	
c	Interest due under the look-back method—completed long-term contracts (attach Form 8697)	**9c**	
d	Interest due under the look-back method—income forecast method (attach Form 8866)	**9d**	
e	Alternative tax on qualifying shipping activities (attach Form 8902)	**9e**	
f	Interest/tax due under Section 453A(c) and/or Section 453(l)	**9f**	
g	Other (see instructions—attach statement)	**9g**	
10	**Total.** Add lines 9a through 9g	**10**	
11	**Total tax.** Add lines 7, 8, and 10. Enter here and on page 1, line 31	**11**	

Part II—Section 965 Payments (see instructions)

12	2020 net 965 tax liability paid from Form 965-B, Part II, column (k), line 4. Enter here and on page 1, line 32	**12**	

Part III—Payments, Refundable Credits, and Section 965 Net Tax Liability

13	2019 overpayment credited to 2020	**13**	
14	2020 estimated tax payments	**14**	
15	2020 refund applied for on Form 4466	**15**	( )
16	Combine lines 13, 14, and 15	**16**	
17	Tax deposited with Form 7004	**17**	
18	Withholding (see instructions)	**18**	
19	**Total payments.** Add lines 16, 17, and 18	**19**	
20	Refundable credits from:		
a	Form 2439	**20a**	
b	Form 4136	**20b**	
c	Reserved for future use	**20c**	
d	Other (attach statement—see instructions)	**20d**	
21	**Total credits.** Add lines 20a through 20d	**21**	
22	2020 net 965 tax liability from Form 965-B, Part I, column (d), line 4. See instructions	**22**	
23	**Total payments, credits, and section 965 net tax liability.** Add lines 19, 21, and 22. Enter here and on page 1, line 33	**23**	

Form **1120** (2020)

Form 1120 (2020)   Page **4**

Schedule K	**Other Information** (see instructions)		Yes	No

1 Check accounting method: **a** ☐ Cash   **b** ☐ Accrual   **c** ☐ Other (specify) ▶ _____

2 See the instructions and enter the:

a Business activity code no. ▶ _____

b Business activity ▶ _____

c Product or service ▶ _____

3 Is the corporation a subsidiary in an affiliated group or a parent–subsidiary controlled group? . . . .

If "Yes," enter name and EIN of the parent corporation ▶ _____

4 At the end of the tax year:

a Did any foreign or domestic corporation, partnership (including any entity treated as a partnership), trust, or tax-exempt organization own directly 20% or more, or own, directly or indirectly, 50% or more of the total voting power of all classes of the corporation's stock entitled to vote? If "Yes," complete Part I of Schedule G (Form 1120) (attach Schedule G) . . . . .

b Did any individual or estate own directly 20% or more, or own, directly or indirectly, 50% or more of the total voting power of all classes of the corporation's stock to vote? If "Yes," complete Part II of Schedule G (Form 1120) (attach Schedule G) . .

5 At the end of the tax year, did the corporation:

a Own directly 20% or more, or own, directly or indirectly, 50% or more of the total voting power of all classes of stock entitled to vote of any foreign or domestic corporation not included on **Form 851,** Affiliations Schedule? For rules of constructive ownership, see instructions.

If "Yes," complete (i) through (iv) below.

(i) Name of Corporation	**(ii)** Employer Identification Number (if any)	**(iii)** Country of Incorporation	**(iv)** Percentage Owned in Voting Stock

b Own directly an interest of 20% or more, or own, directly or indirectly, an interest of 50% or more in any foreign or domestic partnership (including an entity treated as a partnership) or in the beneficial interest of a trust? For rules of constructive ownership, see instructions.

If "Yes," complete (i) through (iv) below.

(i) Name of Entity	**(ii)** Employer Identification Number (if any)	**(iii)** Country of Organization	**(iv)** Maximum Percentage Owned in Profit, Loss, or Capital

6 During this tax year, did the corporation pay dividends (other than stock dividends and distributions in exchange for stock) in excess of the corporation's current and accumulated earnings and profits? See sections 301 and 316 . . . .

If "Yes," file **Form 5452,** Corporate Report of Nondividend Distributions. See the instructions for Form 5452.

If this is a consolidated return, answer here for the parent corporation and on Form 851 for each subsidiary.

7 At any time during the tax year, did one foreign person own, directly or indirectly, at least 25% of the total voting power of all classes of the corporation's stock entitled to vote or at least 25% of the total value of all classes of the corporation's stock? .

For rules of attribution, see section 318. If "Yes," enter:

(a) Percentage owned ▶ _____ and **(b)** Owner's country ▶ _____

(c) The corporation may have to file **Form 5472,** Information Return of a 25% Foreign-Owned U.S. Corporation or a Foreign Corporation Engaged in a U.S. Trade or Business. Enter the number of Forms 5472 attached ▶ _____

8 Check this box if the corporation issued publicly offered debt instruments with original issue discount . . . . . . ▶ ☐

If checked, the corporation may have to file **Form 8281,** Information Return for Publicly Offered Original Issue Discount Instruments.

9 Enter the amount of tax-exempt interest received or accrued during the tax year ▶ $ _____

10 Enter the number of shareholders at the end of the tax year (if 100 or fewer) ▶ _____

11 If the corporation has an NOL for the tax year and is electing to forego the carryback period, check here (see instructions) ▶ ☐

If the corporation is filing a consolidated return, the statement required by Regulations section 1.1502-21(b)(3) must be attached or the election will not be valid.

12 Enter the available NOL carryover from prior tax years (do not reduce it by any deduction reported on page 1, line 29a.) . . . . ▶ $ _____

Form **1120** (2020)

Form 1120 (2020)   Page **5**

Schedule K	**Other Information** *(continued from page 4)*	Yes	No

13 Are the corporation's total receipts (page 1, line 1a, plus lines 4 through 10) for the tax year **and** its total assets at the end of the tax year less than $250,000? . . . .

If "Yes," the corporation is not required to complete Schedules L, M-1, and M-2. Instead, enter the total amount of cash distributions and the book value of property distributions (other than cash) made during the tax year ▶ $ _____

14 Is the corporation required to file Schedule UTP (Form 1120), Uncertain Tax Position Statement? See instructions . . . .

If "Yes," complete and attach Schedule UTP.

15a Did the corporation make any payments in 2020 that would require it to file Form(s) 1099? . . . .

b If "Yes," did or will the corporation file required Form(s) 1099? . . . .

16 During this tax year, did the corporation have an 80%-or-more change in ownership, including a change due to redemption of its own stock? . . . .

17 During or subsequent to this tax year, but before the filing of this return, did the corporation dispose of more than 65% (by value) of its assets in a taxable, non-taxable, or tax deferred transaction? . . . .

18 Did the corporation receive assets in a section 351 transfer in which any of the transferred assets had a fair market basis or fair market value of more than $1 million? . . . .

19 During the corporation's tax year, did the corporation make any payments that would require it to file Forms 1042 and 1042-S under chapter 3 (sections 1441 through 1464) or chapter 4 (sections 1471 through 1474) of the Code? . . . .

20 Is the corporation operating on a cooperative basis? . . . .

21 During the tax year, did the corporation pay or accrue any interest or royalty for which the deduction is not allowed under section 267A? See instructions . . . .

If "Yes," enter the total amount of the disallowed deductions ▶ $ _____

22 Does the corporation have gross receipts of at least $500 million in any of the 3 preceding tax years? (See sections 59A(e)(2) and (3)) . . . .

If "Yes," complete and attach Form 8991.

23 Did the corporation have an election under section 163(j) for any real property trade or business or any farming business in effect during the tax year? See instructions . . . .

24 Does the corporation satisfy one or more of the following? See instructions . . . .

a The corporation owns a pass-through entity with current, or prior year carryover, excess business interest expense.

b The corporation's aggregate average annual gross receipts (determined under section 448(c)) for the 3 tax years preceding the current tax year are more than $26 million and the corporation has business interest expense.

c The corporation is a tax shelter and the corporation has business interest expense.

If "Yes," complete and attach Form 8990.

25 Is the corporation attaching Form 8996 to certify as a Qualified Opportunity Fund? . . . .

If "Yes," enter amount from Form 8996, line 15 . . . . ▶ $

26 Since December 22, 2017, did a foreign corporation directly or indirectly acquire substantially all of the properties held directly or indirectly by the corporation, and was the ownership percentage (by vote or value) for purposes of section 7874 greater than 50% (for example, the shareholders held more than 50% of the stock of the foreign corporation)? If "Yes," list the ownership percentage by vote and by value. See instructions . . . .

Percentage: By Vote   By Value

Form **1120** (2020)

Form 1120 (2020)   Page **6**

Schedule L	Balance Sheets per Books	Beginning of tax year		End of tax year	
	Assets	**(a)**	**(b)**	**(c)**	**(d)**
1	Cash				
2a	Trade notes and accounts receivable				
b	Less allowance for bad debts	( )		( )	
3	Inventories				
4	U.S. government obligations				
5	Tax-exempt securities (see instructions)				
6	Other current assets (attach statement)				
7	Loans to shareholders				
8	Mortgage and real estate loans				
9	Other investments (attach statement)				
10a	Buildings and other depreciable assets				
b	Less accumulated depreciation	( )		( )	
11a	Depletable assets				
b	Less accumulated depletion	( )		( )	
12	Land (net of any amortization)				
13a	Intangible assets (amortizable only)				
b	Less accumulated amortization	( )		( )	
14	Other assets (attach statement)				
15	Total assets				
	Liabilities and Shareholders' Equity				
16	Accounts payable				
17	Mortgages, notes, bonds payable in less than 1 year				
18	Other current liabilities (attach statement)				
19	Loans from shareholders				
20	Mortgages, notes, bonds payable in 1 year or more				
21	Other liabilities (attach statement)				
22	Capital stock: **a** Preferred stock				
	b Common stock				
23	Additional paid-in capital				
24	Retained earnings—Appropriated (attach statement)				
25	Retained earnings—Unappropriated				
26	Adjustments to shareholders' equity (attach statement)				
27	Less cost of treasury stock		( )		( )
28	Total liabilities and shareholders' equity				

Schedule M-1	Reconciliation of Income (Loss) per Books With Income per Return

Note: The corporation may be required to file Schedule M-3. See instructions.

1	Net income (loss) per books		7	Income recorded on books this year not included on this return (itemize):	
2	Federal income tax per books			Tax-exempt interest $_____	
3	Excess of capital losses over capital gains			_____	
4	Income subject to tax not recorded on books this year (itemize): _____		8	Deductions on this return not charged against book income this year (itemize):	
	_____		a	Depreciation . . $_____	
5	Expenses recorded on books this year not deducted on this return (itemize):		b	Charitable contributions $_____	
a	Depreciation . . . . $_____			_____	
b	Charitable contributions . $_____			_____	
c	Travel and entertainment . $_____		9	Add lines 7 and 8	
	_____				
6	Add lines 1 through 5		10	Income (page 1, line 28)—line 6 less line 9	

Schedule M-2	Analysis of Unappropriated Retained Earnings per Books (Schedule L, Line 25)

1	Balance at beginning of year		5	Distributions: **a** Cash	
2	Net income (loss) per books			**b** Stock	
3	Other increases (itemize): _____			**c** Property	
	_____		6	Other decreases (itemize): _____	
	_____		7	Add lines 5 and 6	
4	Add lines 1, 2, and 3		8	Balance at end of year (line 4 less line 7)	

Form **1120** (2020)

Form **1120-S**

Department of the Treasury
Internal Revenue Service

U.S. Income Tax Return for an S Corporation

▶ Do not file this form unless the corporation has filed or
is attaching Form 2553 to elect to be an S corporation.
▶ Go to *www.irs.gov/Form1120S* for instructions and the latest information.

OMB No. 1545-0123

2020

For calendar year 2020 or tax year beginning , 2020, ending , 20

A S election effective date	**Name**	**D** Employer identification number
B Business activity code number (see instructions)	**TYPE OR PRINT** Number, street, and room or suite no. If a P.O. box, see instructions.	**E** Date incorporated
C Check if Sch. M-3 attached ☐	City or town, state or province, country, and ZIP or foreign postal code	**F** Total assets (see instructions) $

G Is the corporation electing to be an S corporation beginning with this tax year? ☐ Yes ☐ No   If "Yes," attach Form 2553 if not already filed

H Check if: **(1)** ☐ Final return   **(2)** ☐ Name change   **(3)** ☐ Address change   **(4)** ☐ Amended return   **(5)** ☐ S election termination or revocation

I Enter the number of shareholders who were shareholders during any part of the tax year . . . . . . ▶

J Check if corporation: **(1)** ☐ Aggregated activities for section 465 at-risk purposes   **(2)** ☐ Grouped activities for section 469 passive activity purposes

Caution: Include **only** trade or business income and expenses on lines 1a through 21. See the instructions for more information.

Income

1a	Gross receipts or sales	**1a**	
b	Returns and allowances	**1b**	
c	Balance. Subtract line 1b from line 1a	**1c**	
2	Cost of goods sold (attach Form 1125-A)	**2**	
3	Gross profit. Subtract line 2 from line 1c	**3**	
4	Net gain (loss) from Form 4797, line 17 (attach Form 4797)	**4**	
5	Other income (loss) (see instructions—attach statement)	**5**	
6	**Total income (loss).** Add lines 3 through 5 . . . . ▶	**6**	

Deductions (see instructions for limitations)

7	Compensation of officers (see instructions—attach Form 1125-E)	**7**	
8	Salaries and wages (less employment credits)	**8**	
9	Repairs and maintenance	**9**	
10	Bad debts	**10**	
11	Rents	**11**	
12	Taxes and licenses	**12**	
13	Interest (see instructions)	**13**	
14	Depreciation not claimed on Form 1125-A or elsewhere on return (attach Form 4562) . . .	**14**	
15	Depletion **(Do not deduct oil and gas depletion.)**	**15**	
16	Advertising	**16**	
17	Pension, profit-sharing, etc., plans	**17**	
18	Employee benefit programs	**18**	
19	Other deductions (attach statement)	**19**	
20	**Total deductions.** Add lines 7 through 19 . . . . ▶	**20**	
21	**Ordinary business income (loss).** Subtract line 20 from line 6	**21**	

Tax and Payments

22a	Excess net passive income or LIFO recapture tax (see instructions) . . .	**22a**		
b	Tax from Schedule D (Form 1120-S)	**22b**		
c	Add lines 22a and 22b (see instructions for additional taxes)		**22c**	
23a	2020 estimated tax payments and 2019 overpayment credited to 2020	**23a**		
b	Tax deposited with Form 7004	**23b**		
c	Credit for federal tax paid on fuels (attach Form 4136)	**23c**		
d	Reserved for future use	**23d**		
e	Add lines 23a through 23d		**23e**	
24	Estimated tax penalty (see instructions). Check if Form 2220 is attached . . . . ▶ ☐		**24**	
25	**Amount owed.** If line 23e is smaller than the total of lines 22c and 24, enter amount owed . . .		**25**	
26	**Overpayment.** If line 23e is larger than the total of lines 22c and 24, enter amount overpaid . . .		**26**	
27	Enter amount from line 26: **Credited to 2021 estimated tax** ▶ **Refunded** ▶		**27**	

Sign Here

Under penalties of perjury, I declare that I have examined this return, including accompanying schedules and statements, and to the best of my knowledge and belief, it is true, correct, and complete. Declaration of preparer (other than taxpayer) is based on all information of which preparer has any knowledge.

▶ _____   _____   ▶ _____
Signature of officer   Date   Title

May the IRS discuss this return with the preparer shown below? See instructions. ☐ Yes ☐ No

Paid Preparer Use Only

Print/Type preparer's name	Preparer's signature	Date	Check ☐ if self-employed	PTIN
Firm's name ▶			Firm's EIN ▶	
Firm's address ▶			Phone no.	

For Paperwork Reduction Act Notice, see separate instructions.   Cat. No. 11510H   Form **1120-S** (2020)

Form 1120-S (2020)   Page **2**

Schedule B	**Other Information** (see instructions)			Yes	No

1 Check accounting method: **a** ☐ Cash **b** ☐ Accrual

    c ☐ Other (specify) ▶ _____

2 See the instructions and enter the:

    a Business activity ▶ _____ **b** Product or service ▶ _____

3 At any time during the tax year, was any shareholder of the corporation a disregarded entity, a trust, an estate, or a nominee or similar person? If "Yes," attach Schedule B-1, Information on Certain Shareholders of an S Corporation .   .

4 At the end of the tax year, did the corporation:

    a Own directly 20% or more, or own, directly or indirectly, 50% or more of the total stock issued and outstanding of any foreign or domestic corporation? For rules of constructive ownership, see instructions. If "Yes," complete (i) through (v) below

(i) Name of Corporation	**(ii)** Employer Identification Number (if any)	**(iii)** Country of Incorporation	**(iv)** Percentage of Stock Owned	**(v)** If Percentage in (iv) Is 100%, Enter the Date (if any) a Qualified Subchapter S Subsidiary Election Was Made

    b Own directly an interest of 20% or more, or own, directly or indirectly, an interest of 50% or more in the profit, loss, or capital in any foreign or domestic partnership (including an entity treated as a partnership) or in the beneficial interest of a trust? For rules of constructive ownership, see instructions. If "Yes," complete (i) through (v) below . . . .

(i) Name of Entity	**(ii)** Employer Identification Number (if any)	**(iii)** Type of Entity	**(iv)** Country of Organization	**(v)** Maximum Percentage Owned in Profit, Loss, or Capital

5a At the end of the tax year, did the corporation have any outstanding shares of restricted stock? . . . .

    If "Yes," complete lines (i) and (ii) below.

    (i) Total shares of restricted stock . . . . ▶ _____

    (ii) Total shares of non-restricted stock . . . . . . ▶ _____

   b At the end of the tax year, did the corporation have any outstanding stock options, warrants, or similar instruments? .

    If "Yes," complete lines (i) and (ii) below.

    (i) Total shares of stock outstanding at the end of the tax year . ▶ _____

    (ii) Total shares of stock outstanding if all instruments were executed ▶ _____

6 Has this corporation filed, or is it required to file, **Form 8918,** Material Advisor Disclosure Statement, to provide information on any reportable transaction? . . . .

7 Check this box if the corporation issued publicly offered debt instruments with original issue discount . . . . ▶ ☐

    If checked, the corporation may have to file **Form 8281,** Information Return for Publicly Offered Original Issue Discount Instruments.

8 If the corporation **(a)** was a C corporation before it elected to be an S corporation **or** the corporation acquired an asset with a basis determined by reference to the basis of the asset (or the basis of any other property) in the hands of a C corporation, **and (b)** has net unrealized built-in gain in excess of the net recognized built-in gain from prior years, enter the net unrealized built-in gain reduced by net recognized built-in gain from prior years. See instructions . . . . . . ▶ $ _____

9 Did the corporation have an election under section 163(j) for any real property trade or business or any farming business in effect during the tax year? See instructions . . . .

10 Does the corporation satisfy one or more of the following? See instructions . . . .

   a The corporation owns a pass-through entity with current, or prior year carryover, excess business interest expense.

   b The corporation's aggregate average annual gross receipts (determined under section 448(c)) for the 3 tax years preceding the current tax year are more than $26 million and the corporation has business interest expense.

   c The corporation is a tax shelter and the corporation has business interest expense.

    If "Yes," complete and attach Form 8990.

11 Does the corporation satisfy **both** of the following conditions? . . . .

   a The corporation's total receipts (see instructions) for the tax year were less than $250,000.

   b The corporation's total assets at the end of the tax year were less than $250,000.

    If "Yes," the corporation is not required to complete Schedules L and M-1.

Form **1120-S** (2020)

Form 1120-S (2020)   Page **3**

Schedule B	Other Information (see instructions) (continued)	Yes	No
12	During the tax year, did the corporation have any non-shareholder debt that was canceled, was forgiven, or had the terms modified so as to reduce the principal amount of the debt?		
	If "Yes," enter the amount of principal reduction . . . . ▶ $_____		
13	During the tax year, was a qualified subchapter S subsidiary election terminated or revoked? If "Yes," see instructions .		
14a	Did the corporation make any payments in 2020 that would require it to file Form(s) 1099?		
b	If "Yes," did the corporation file or will it file required Form(s) 1099?		
15	Is the corporation attaching Form 8996 to certify as a Qualified Opportunity Fund?		
	If "Yes," enter the amount from Form 8996, line 15 . . . . ▶ $_____		

Schedule K	Shareholders' Pro Rata Share Items		Total amount
Income (Loss)	**1** Ordinary business income (loss) (page 1, line 21)	**1**	
	2 Net rental real estate income (loss) (attach Form 8825)	**2**	
	3a Other gross rental income (loss)	3a	
	b Expenses from other rental activities (attach statement) . .	3b	
	c Other net rental income (loss). Subtract line 3b from line 3a . . .	**3c**	
	4 Interest income	**4**	
	5 Dividends: **a** Ordinary dividends	**5a**	
	b Qualified dividends	5b	
	6 Royalties	**6**	
	7 Net short-term capital gain (loss) (attach Schedule D (Form 1120-S)) . .	**7**	
	8a Net long-term capital gain (loss) (attach Schedule D (Form 1120-S)) . .	**8a**	
	b Collectibles (28%) gain (loss)	8b	
	c Unrecaptured section 1250 gain (attach statement)	8c	
	9 Net section 1231 gain (loss) (attach Form 4797)	**9**	
	10 Other income (loss) (see instructions) . . . Type ▶	**10**	
Deductions	**11** Section 179 deduction (attach Form 4562)	**11**	
	12a Charitable contributions	**12a**	
	b Investment interest expense	**12b**	
	c Section 59(e)(2) expenditures . . . . . Type ▶	**12c**	
	d Other deductions (see instructions) . . . . Type ▶	**12d**	
Credits	**13a** Low-income housing credit (section 42(j)(5))	**13a**	
	b Low-income housing credit (other)	**13b**	
	c Qualified rehabilitation expenditures (rental real estate) (attach Form 3468, if applicable) . .	**13c**	
	d Other rental real estate credits (see instructions) Type ▶	**13d**	
	e Other rental credits (see instructions) . . . Type ▶	**13e**	
	f Biofuel producer credit (attach Form 6478)	**13f**	
	g Other credits (see instructions) . . . . . Type ▶	**13g**	
Foreign Transactions	**14a** Name of country or U.S. possession ▶		
	b Gross income from all sources	**14b**	
	c Gross income sourced at shareholder level	**14c**	
	Foreign gross income sourced at corporate level		
	d Reserved for future use	**14d**	
	e Foreign branch category	**14e**	
	f Passive category	**14f**	
	g General category	**14g**	
	h Other (attach statement)	**14h**	
	Deductions allocated and apportioned at shareholder level		
	i Interest expense	**14i**	
	j Other	**14j**	
	Deductions allocated and apportioned at corporate level to foreign source income		
	k Reserved for future use	**14k**	
	l Foreign branch category	**14l**	
	m Passive category	**14m**	
	n General category	**14n**	
	o Other (attach statement)	**14o**	
	Other information		
	p Total foreign taxes (check one): ☐ Paid ☐ Accrued . . . . ▶	**14p**	
	q Reduction in taxes available for credit (attach statement)	**14q**	
	r Other foreign tax information (attach statement)		

Form **1120-S** (2020)

Form 1120-S (2020)   Page **4**

Schedule K		Shareholders' Pro Rata Share Items *(continued)*		Total amount
Alternative Minimum Tax (AMT) Items	**15a**	Post-1986 depreciation adjustment	**15a**	
	b	Adjusted gain or loss	**15b**	
	c	Depletion (other than oil and gas)	**15c**	
	d	Oil, gas, and geothermal properties—gross income	**15d**	
	e	Oil, gas, and geothermal properties—deductions	**15e**	
	f	Other AMT items (attach statement)	**15f**	
Items Affecting Shareholder Basis	**16a**	Tax-exempt interest income	**16a**	
	b	Other tax-exempt income	**16b**	
	c	Nondeductible expenses	**16c**	
	d	Distributions (attach statement if required) (see instructions)	**16d**	
	e	Repayment of loans from shareholders	**16e**	
Other Information	**17a**	Investment income	**17a**	
	b	Investment expenses	**17b**	
	c	Dividend distributions paid from accumulated earnings and profits	**17c**	
	d	Other items and amounts (attach statement)		
Recon-ciliation	**18**	**Income (loss) reconciliation.** Combine the amounts on lines 1 through 10 in the far right column. From the result, subtract the sum of the amounts on lines 11 through 12d and 14p	**18**	

Schedule L	Balance Sheets per Books	Beginning of tax year		End of tax year	
	Assets	**(a)**	**(b)**	**(c)**	**(d)**
1	Cash				
2a	Trade notes and accounts receivable				
b	Less allowance for bad debts	( )		( )	
3	Inventories				
4	U.S. government obligations				
5	Tax-exempt securities (see instructions)				
6	Other current assets (attach statement)				
7	Loans to shareholders				
8	Mortgage and real estate loans				
9	Other investments (attach statement)				
10a	Buildings and other depreciable assets				
b	Less accumulated depreciation	( )		( )	
11a	Depletable assets				
b	Less accumulated depletion	( )		( )	
12	Land (net of any amortization)				
13a	Intangible assets (amortizable only)				
b	Less accumulated amortization	( )		( )	
14	Other assets (attach statement)				
15	Total assets				
	Liabilities and Shareholders' Equity				
16	Accounts payable				
17	Mortgages, notes, bonds payable in less than 1 year				
18	Other current liabilities (attach statement)				
19	Loans from shareholders				
20	Mortgages, notes, bonds payable in 1 year or more				
21	Other liabilities (attach statement)				
22	Capital stock				
23	Additional paid-in capital				
24	Retained earnings				
25	Adjustments to shareholders' equity (attach statement)				
26	Less cost of treasury stock		( )		( )
27	Total liabilities and shareholders' equity				

Form **1120-S** (2020)

Form 1120-S (2020)   Page **5**

Schedule M-1	**Reconciliation of Income (Loss) per Books With Income (Loss) per Return**

Note: The corporation may be required to file Schedule M-3. See instructions.

1	Net income (loss) per books		5	Income recorded on books this year not included on Schedule K, lines 1 through 10 (itemize):	
2	Income included on Schedule K, lines 1, 2, 3c, 4, 5a, 6, 7, 8a, 9, and 10, not recorded on books this year (itemize) _____		a	Tax-exempt interest $ _____	
3	Expenses recorded on books this year not included on Schedule K, lines 1 through 12 and 14p (itemize):		6	Deductions included on Schedule K, lines 1 through 12 and 14p, not charged against book income this year (itemize):	
a	Depreciation $ _____		a	Depreciation $ _____	
b	Travel and entertainment $ _____		7	Add lines 5 and 6	
			8	Income (loss) (Schedule K, line 18). Subtract line 7 from line 4	
4	Add lines 1 through 3				

Schedule M-2	**Analysis of Accumulated Adjustments Account, Shareholders' Undistributed Taxable Income Previously Taxed, Accumulated Earnings and Profits, and Other Adjustments Account** (see instructions)

		(a) Accumulated adjustments account	**(b)** Shareholders' undistributed taxable income previously taxed	**(c)** Accumulated earnings and profits	**(d)** Other adjustments account
1	Balance at beginning of tax year				
2	Ordinary income from page 1, line 21 . . .				
3	Other additions				
4	Loss from page 1, line 21	( )			
5	Other reductions	( )			( )
6	Combine lines 1 through 5				
7	Distributions				
8	Balance at end of tax year. Subtract line 7 from line 6				

Form **1120-S** (2020)

671120

☐ Final K-1   ☐ Amended K-1   OMB No. 1545-0123

Schedule K-1
(Form 1120-S)

20**20**

Department of the Treasury
Internal Revenue Service

For calendar year 2020, or tax year

beginning ___/___/ 2020   ending ___/___/___

Shareholder's Share of Income, Deductions, Credits, etc.   ▶ **See separate instructions.**

Part I	**Information About the Corporation**

A   Corporation's employer identification number

B   Corporation's name, address, city, state, and ZIP code

C   IRS Center where corporation filed return

Part II	**Information About the Shareholder**

D   Shareholder's identifying number

E   Shareholder's name, address, city, state, and ZIP code

F   Current year allocation percentage . . . _____ %

G   Shareholder's number of shares
   Beginning of tax year   . . . . . _____
   End of tax year   . . . . . . _____

H   Loans from shareholder
   Beginning of tax year   . . . . . $ _____
   End of tax year   . . . . $ _____

For IRS Use Only

Part III	**Shareholder's Share of Current Year Income, Deductions, Credits, and Other Items**

1	Ordinary business income (loss)	13	Credits
2	Net rental real estate income (loss)		
3	Other net rental income (loss)		
4	Interest income		
5a	Ordinary dividends		
5b	Qualified dividends	14	Foreign transactions
6	Royalties		
7	Net short-term capital gain (loss)		
8a	Net long-term capital gain (loss)		
8b	Collectibles (28%) gain (loss)		
8c	Unrecaptured section 1250 gain		
9	Net section 1231 gain (loss)		
10	Other income (loss)	15	Alternative minimum tax (AMT) items
11	Section 179 deduction	16	Items affecting shareholder basis
12	Other deductions		
		17	Other information

18	☐ More than one activity for at-risk purposes*	
19	☐ More than one activity for passive activity purposes*	

* See attached statement for additional information.

For Paperwork Reduction Act Notice, see the Instructions for Form 1120-S.   www.irs.gov/Form1120S   Cat. No. 11520D   **Schedule K-1 (Form 1120-S) 2020**

Schedule K-1 (Form 1120-S) 2019   Page **2**

This list identifies the codes used on Schedule K-1 for all shareholders and provides summarized reporting information for shareholders who file Form 1040 or 1040-SR. For detailed reporting and filing information, see the separate Shareholder's Instructions for Schedule K-1 and the instructions for your income tax return.

1. **Ordinary business income (loss).** Determine whether the income (loss) is passive or nonpassive and enter on your return as follows:

	Report on
Passive loss	See the Shareholder's Instructions
Passive income	Schedule E, line 28, column (h)
Nonpassive loss	See the Shareholder's Instructions
Nonpassive income	Schedule E, line 28, column (k)

2. **Net rental real estate income (loss)**   See the Shareholder's Instructions
3. **Other net rental income (loss)**
   Net income   Schedule E, line 28, column (h)
   Net loss   See the Shareholder's Instructions
4. **Interest income**   Form 1040 or 1040-SR, line 2b
5a. **Ordinary dividends**   Form 1040 or 1040-SR, line 3b
5b. **Qualified dividends**   Form 1040 or 1040-SR, line 3a
6. **Royalties**   Schedule E, line 4
7. **Net short-term capital gain (loss)**   Schedule D, line 5
8a. **Net long-term capital gain (loss)**   Schedule D, line 12
8b. **Collectibles (28%) gain (loss)**   28% Rate Gain Worksheet, line 4 (Schedule D instructions)
8c. **Unrecaptured section 1250 gain**   See the Shareholder's Instructions
9. **Net section 1231 gain (loss)**   See the Shareholder's Instructions
10. **Other income (loss)**
    Code
    A   Other portfolio income (loss)   See the Shareholder's Instructions
    B   Involuntary conversions   See the Shareholder's Instructions
    C   Sec. 1256 contracts & straddles   Form 6781, line 1
    D   Mining exploration costs recapture   See Pub. 535
    E   Reserved for future use
    F   Section 965(a) inclusion
    G   Income under subpart F (other than inclusions under sections 951A and 965)   } See the Shareholder's Instructions
    H   Other income (loss)
11. **Section 179 deduction**   See the Shareholder's Instructions
12. **Other deductions**
    A   Cash contributions (60%)
    B   Cash contributions (30%)
    C   Noncash contributions (50%)
    D   Noncash contributions (30%)
    E   Capital gain property to a 50% organization (30%)   } See the Shareholder's Instructions
    F   Capital gain property (20%)
    G   Contributions (100%)
    H   Investment interest expense   Form 4952, line 1
    I   Deductions—royalty income   Schedule E, line 19
    J   Section 59(e)(2) expenditures   See the Shareholder's Instructions
    K   Section 965(c) deduction   See the Shareholder's Instructions
    L   Deductions—portfolio (other)   Schedule A, line 16
    M   Preproductive period expenses   See the Shareholder's Instructions
    N   Commercial revitalization deduction from rental real estate activities   See Form 8582 instructions
    O   Reforestation expense deduction   See the Shareholder's Instructions
    P   through **R**   Reserved for future use
    S   Other deductions   See the Shareholder's Instructions
13. **Credits**
    A   Low-income housing credit (section 42(j)(5)) from pre-2008 buildings
    B   Low-income housing credit (other) from pre-2008 buildings
    C   Low-income housing credit (section 42(j)(5)) from post-2007 buildings
    D   Low-income housing credit (other) from post-2007 buildings   } See the Shareholder's Instructions
    E   Qualified rehabilitation expenditures (rental real estate)
    F   Other rental real estate credits
    G   Other rental credits
    H   Undistributed capital gains credit   Schedule 3 (Form 1040 or 1040-SR), line 13, box a
    I   Biofuel producer credit
    J   Work opportunity credit
    K   Disabled access credit
    L   Empowerment zone employment credit   } See the Shareholder's Instructions
    M   Credit for increasing research activities

Code		Report on
N	Credit for employer social security and Medicare taxes	
O	Backup withholding	See the Shareholder's Instructions
P	Other credits	

14. **Foreign transactions**
    A   Name of country or U.S. possession
    B   Gross income from all sources   } Form 1116, Part I
    C   Gross income sourced at shareholder level
    Foreign gross income sourced at corporate level
    D   Reserved for future use
    E   Foreign branch category
    F   Passive category   } Form 1116, Part I
    G   General category
    H   Other
    Deductions allocated and apportioned at shareholder level
    I   Interest expense   Form 1116, Part I
    J   Other   Form 1116, Part I
    Deductions allocated and apportioned at corporate level to foreign source income
    K   Reserved for future use
    L   Foreign branch category
    M   Passive category   } Form 1116, Part I
    N   General category
    O   Other
    Other information
    P   Total foreign taxes paid   Form 1116, Part II
    Q   Total foreign taxes accrued   Form 1116, Part II
    R   Reduction in taxes available for credit   Form 1116, line 12
    S   Foreign trading gross receipts   Form 8873
    T   Extraterritorial income exclusion   Form 8873
    U   Section 965 information   See the Shareholder's Instructions
    V   Other foreign transactions   See the Shareholder's Instructions
15. **Alternative minimum tax (AMT) items**
    A   Post-1986 depreciation adjustment
    B   Adjusted gain or loss
    C   Depletion (other than oil & gas)   See the Shareholder's Instructions
    D   Oil, gas, & geothermal—gross income   and the Instructions for Form 6251
    E   Oil, gas, & geothermal—deductions
    F   Other AMT items
16. **Items affecting shareholder basis**
    A   Tax-exempt interest income   Form 1040 or 1040-SR, line 2a
    B   Other tax-exempt income
    C   Nondeductible expenses
    D   Distributions   See the Shareholder's Instructions
    E   Repayment of loans from shareholders
17. **Other information**
    A   Investment income   Form 4952, line 4a
    B   Investment expenses   Form 4952, line 5
    C   Qualified rehabilitation expenditures (other than rental real estate)   See the Shareholder's Instructions
    D   Basis of energy property   See the Shareholder's Instructions
    E   Recapture of low-income housing credit (section 42(j)(5))   Form 8611, line 8
    F   Recapture of low-income housing credit (other)   Form 8611, line 8
    G   Recapture of investment credit   See Form 4255
    H   Recapture of other credits   See the Shareholder's Instructions
    I   Look-back interest—completed long-term contracts   See Form 8697
    J   Look-back interest—income forecast method   See Form 8866
    K   Dispositions of property with section 179 deductions
    L   Recapture of section 179 deduction   See the Shareholder's Instructions
    M   through **U**
    V   Section 199A information
    W   through **Z**   Reserved for future use
    AA   Excess taxable income
    AB   Excess business interest income   } See the Shareholder's Instructions
    AC   Other information

Page 2 of Schedule K-1 is from 2019. 2020 not available when we went to print.

Student Name _____

Class/Section _____

Date   _____

KEY NUMBER TAX RETURN SUMMARY

CHAPTER 11

Comprehensive Problem 1

Total Income (Line 11) _____

Dividends Received Deduction (Line 29b) _____

Taxable Income (Line 30) _____

Total Tax (Line 31) _____

Overpayment (Line 36) _____

Comprehensive Problem 2

Cost of Goods Sold (Line 2) _____

Total Income (Loss) (Line 6) _____

Ordinary Business Income (Loss) (Line 21) _____

Amount Owed (Line 25) _____

Qualified Dividends (Schedule K-1, Line 5b) _____

Tax Administration and Tax Planning

After completing this chapter, you should be able to:

LO 12.1   Identify the organizational structure of the Internal Revenue Service (IRS).

LO 12.2   Describe the IRS audit process.

LO 12.3   Define the common penalties for taxpayers and be able to apply them to specific situations.

LO 12.4   Apply the general rule for the statute of limitations on tax returns and the important exceptions to the general rule.

LO 12.5   Describe the rules and penalties that apply to tax practitioners.

LO 12.6   Describe the Taxpayer Bill of Rights.

LO 12.7   Explain the basic concepts of tax planning.

OVERVIEW

Knowing how the Internal Revenue Service (IRS) operates, and how and why the IRS audits certain tax returns, is extremely important to tax practitioners. This chapter covers these topics as well as tax penalties that apply to taxpayers and tax preparers, the statute of limitations on tax liabilities and refund claims, and rules applicable to tax practitioners (i.e., Circular 230). The Taxpayer Bill of Rights, also covered in this chapter, provides taxpayers with significant rights when dealing with the IRS, such as the ability to record an IRS interview.

Arranging one's financial affairs in order to maximize after-tax cash flows is referred to as tax planning. This chapter includes a discussion of basic tax-planning techniques that may be used by individual taxpayers. This final chapter is intended to give an appreciation for the process of dealing with the IRS and several of the many issues involved in conducting a tax practice.

12-1 THE INTERNAL REVENUE SERVICE

Identify the organizational structure of the Internal Revenue Service (IRS).

The tax laws of the United States are administered by the IRS. In administering the tax law, the IRS has the responsibility for determining, assessing, and collecting internal revenue taxes and enforcing other provisions of the tax law. The IRS is a bureau of the Treasury Department. The mission of the IRS is to provide America's taxpayers quality service by helping them understand and meet their tax responsibilities and enforce the law with integrity and fairness. Congress passes tax laws and requires taxpayers to comply. A taxpayer is expected to understand and meet his or her tax obligations. The role of the IRS is to help the majority of compliant taxpayers with the tax law, while ensuring that the minority who are unwilling to comply pay their fair share.

The IRS organization currently consists of a national office in Washington, D.C., IRS Campus Processing Sites, and various operational offices throughout the United States. The national office is the headquarters of the commissioner of internal revenue and various deputy and associate commissioners. The commissioner of internal revenue is appointed by the president of the United States with the advice and consent of the Senate. The responsibilities of the commissioner are to establish policy, to supervise the activities of the organization, and to act in an advisory capacity to the Treasury Department on legislative matters. In addition, the commissioner is responsible for the collection of income tax, auditing of tax returns, intelligence operations, and appellate procedures.

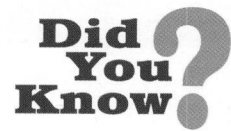

When the Form 1040 was introduced in 1914, it was 3 pages including the instructions. Today, the Form 1040 instructions are over 100 pages.

12-1a IRS Campus Processing Sites

In addition to the various operational offices discussed below, the IRS currently maintains IRS Campus Processing Sites. At these processing sites, the IRS computers process the information from tax documents such as tax returns, payroll tax forms, Forms 1099, and withholding forms.

Paper returns for individuals are processed at the Austin, Fresno, Kansas City, and Ogden offices while e-filings are processed at many sites. The IRS also maintains a national computer center in Martinsburg, West Virginia, where information from various processing sites is matched with records from other processing sites. This cross-matching of records helps to assure that taxpayers report all their income and do not file multiple refund claims.

"Tax day is the day that ordinary Americans send their money to Washington, D.C., and wealthy Americans send their money to the Cayman Islands." – Jimmy Kimmel

12-1b **The IRS Organizational Structure**

The Internal Revenue Service was completely reorganized under the 1998 IRS Restructuring Act (RRA 98), which provided the foundation for the current structure as shown in Figure 12.1.

FIGURE 12.1

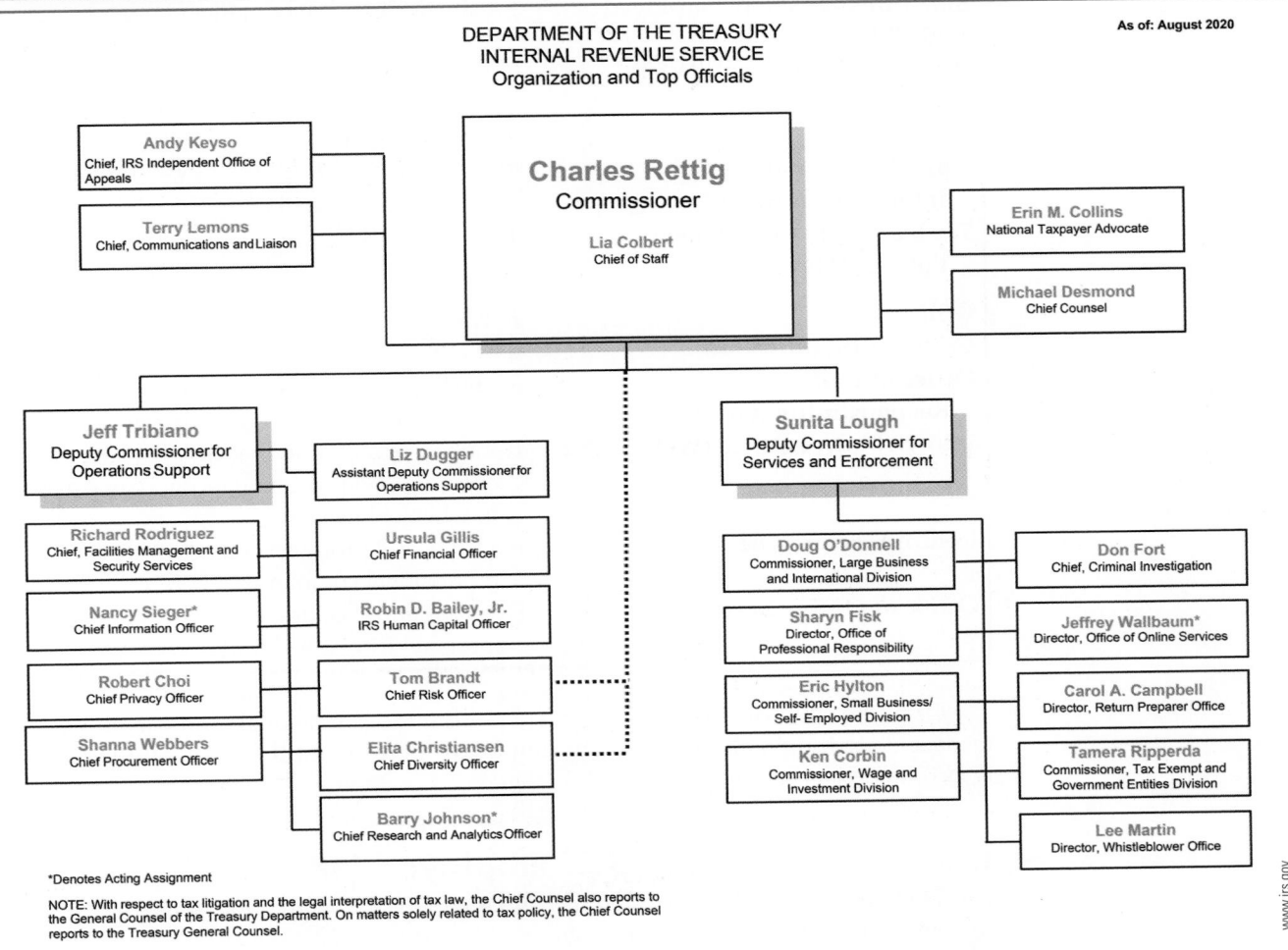

DEPARTMENT OF THE TREASURY
INTERNAL REVENUE SERVICE
Organization and Top Officials

As of: August 2020

Charles Rettig
Commissioner

Lia Colbert
Chief of Staff

Andy Keyso
Chief, IRS Independent Office of Appeals

Terry Lemons
Chief, Communications and Liaison

Erin M. Collins
National Taxpayer Advocate

Michael Desmond
Chief Counsel

Jeff Tribiano
Deputy Commissioner for Operations Support

Liz Dugger
Assistant Deputy Commissioner for Operations Support

Richard Rodriguez
Chief, Facilities Management and Security Services

Ursula Gillis
Chief Financial Officer

Nancy Sieger*
Chief Information Officer

Robin D. Bailey, Jr.
IRS Human Capital Officer

Robert Choi
Chief Privacy Officer

Tom Brandt
Chief Risk Officer

Shanna Webbers
Chief Procurement Officer

Elita Christiansen
Chief Diversity Officer

Barry Johnson*
Chief Research and Analytics Officer

Sunita Lough
Deputy Commissioner for Services and Enforcement

Doug O'Donnell
Commissioner, Large Business and International Division

Don Fort
Chief, Criminal Investigation

Sharyn Fisk
Director, Office of Professional Responsibility

Jeffrey Wallbaum*
Director, Office of Online Services

Eric Hylton
Commissioner, Small Business/ Self-Employed Division

Carol A. Campbell
Director, Return Preparer Office

Ken Corbin
Commissioner, Wage and Investment Division

Tamera Ripperda
Commissioner, Tax Exempt and Government Entities Division

Lee Martin
Director, Whistleblower Office

*Denotes Acting Assignment

NOTE: With respect to tax litigation and the legal interpretation of tax law, the Chief Counsel also reports to the General Counsel of the Treasury Department. On matters solely related to tax policy, the Chief Counsel reports to the Treasury General Counsel.

www.irs.gov

Note: In addition to Figure 12.1 above, more extensive information about the IRS organizational structure is available to the public at **www.irs.gov**.

The Services and Enforcement arm of the IRS, as shown in Figure 12.1, is now responsible for the collection of taxes and the auditing of tax returns, which is done through the following offices:

INTERNAL REVENUE SERVICE DIVISIONS AND PRINCIPAL OFFICES

Division	Responsibility
Small Business/Self-Employed (SB/SE)	Small business taxpayers including individuals who file business forms with their tax returns
Wage and Investment (W&I)	Taxpayers whose primary income is derived from wages and investments and who do not file business forms with their tax returns
Large Business and International (LB&I)	Taxpayers with assets of $10 million or more and the International Program
Tax Exempt & Government Entities (TE/GE)	Tax exempt and government entities

Office	Responsibility
Criminal Investigation	Law enforcement activities
Office of Professional Responsibility (OPR)	Regulating enrolled agents, attorneys, and CPAs who practice before the Service
Whistleblower Office (WO)	Handling information that helps uncover tax cheating and providing appropriate rewards to whistleblowers
Return Preparer Office	Registers and promotes a qualified tax professional community
Office of Online Services	Develops and executes strategies to update and integrate IRS Web services

---

Of these IRS divisions, the most significant to individual and small business taxpayers are the Small Business/Self-Employed (SB/SE) and the Wage and Investment (W&I) offices.

12-1c Small Business/Self-Employed (SB/SE) Division

The SB/SE headquarters are located in Lanham, Maryland, with a mission to serve SB/SE customers by educating and informing them of their tax obligations. The division develops educational products and services and helps the public to understand and comply with applicable laws. The SB/SE Division serves the following taxpayers:

- Individuals filing Forms 1040 and 1040-SR (U.S. Individual Income Tax Return), Schedules C, E, or F, and
- All other businesses with assets under $10 million.

The SB/SE Division serves this taxpayer segment through three organizations:

- Collection (specializing in delinquent taxes and tax returns)
- Examination (specializing in correspondence, office and field audits)
- Operations Support (provides support to other segments to ensure they are properly equipped)

12-1d **Wage and Investment (W&I) Division**

The mission of the W&I Division is to help taxpayers understand and comply with applicable tax laws and to protect the public interest by applying the tax law with integrity and fairness. The headquarters of the W&I office is in Atlanta, Georgia. The taxpayer profile of W&I is as follows:

- Most pay taxes through withholdings,
- More than half prepare their own returns,
- Most interact with the IRS once a year, and
- Most receive refunds.

Organizationally, the W&I Division is broken down into several operational administrative centers (offices). The key functional operations of the W&I offices include:

- Customer Assistance, Relationships, and Education (CARE)
- Customer Account Services (CAS)
- Return Integrity and Compliance Services (RICS)

12-1e **Examination of Records**

Federal tax law gives the IRS authority to examine a taxpayer's books and records to determine the correct amount of tax due. The IRS also has the right to summon taxpayers and to make them appear before the IRS and produce necessary accounting records. Taxpayers are required by law to maintain accounting records to facilitate an IRS audit.

The IRS may also issue a summons for taxpayer records from third parties such as banks, brokers, and CPAs. A third-party may not have the same incentives to protect the privacy of the taxpayers, and thus, the tax rules generally require that a taxpayer be notified prior to the summons being sent to the third-party.

Enforcement of summonses is one of the most litigated areas of tax compliance and has been for almost 15 years. A analysis prepared by the Taxpayer Advocates Office shows that the IRS is extremely successful in these cases, winning over 90 percent.

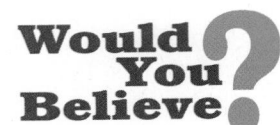

12-1f **Collections**

Taxpayers have several options when they are unable to pay the money they owe to the IRS as outlined in Publication 594. The IRS wants to help taxpayers move their issues toward resolution, and it has tools to help delinquent taxpayers pay the taxes they owe. Taxpayers may ask the IRS for a short-term administrative extension of time and then borrow money or sell assets to pay their tax debt. They may also enter into an installment agreement with the IRS, if their debt is below certain limits, and pay the debt within a 2-year or 3-year time frame. Another option for certain taxpayers is an *offer in compromise* where the IRS accepts a settlement less than the total amount of tax due. Generally, taxpayers who qualify for an offer in compromise are unlikely to ever be able to pay the amount they owe. Alternatively, sometimes the IRS will accept an offer in compromise when the tax liability is disputed, or to avert a costly and time-consuming legal battle.

If a taxpayer does not pay taxes that are due, ignores notices and demands for payment, and fails to make arrangements to pay the amount owed, the IRS will generally start a collection process. This process may include a tax levy that allows the IRS to take a portion of a taxpayer's wages or to seize property such as the taxpayer's house, car, bank account, or other financial accounts. The IRS may also put a tax lien on the taxpayer's property, which is a legal claim to the property. Liens will not be filed unless a taxpayer owes more than $10,000 in taxes. The IRS also has the power to assess significant penalties, some of which are covered later in this chapter.

Self-Study Problem 12.1   *See Appendix E for Solutions to Self-Study Problems*

Indicate whether the following statements are true or false in the current year by circling the appropriate letter.

T   F   1. The Wage and Investment Division deals with individuals filing a Form 1040.

T   F   2. Tax returns are processed at IRS Campus Processing Sites.

T   F   3. The commissioner of internal revenue is an elected position.

T   F   4. The IRS is part of the Justice Department.

T   F   5. The IRS has the right to summon a taxpayer's tax records.

Learning Objective 12.2

Describe the IRS audit process.

12-2 THE AUDIT PROCESS

A primary function of the IRS is to audit taxpayers' tax returns. After the service centers have checked the returns for accuracy, some returns are selected for audit. When a return is selected for examination, it may be subject to an "office audit" or a "field audit." An audit may also be conducted through the mail in what is called a "correspondence audit."

Correspondence audits now account for about 75 percent of the IRS examinations of individual returns each year. Correspondence audits are generally handled entirely by mail. The audit begins when the IRS sends a letter to a taxpayer requesting specific information about their tax return. Usually, the areas covered in correspondence audits relate to questions about Forms W-2 and 1099 that do not agree with the tax return, requests for information supporting charitable contributions, and information related to eligibility for claimed earned income credits.

The office audit is conducted in an IRS office and is typically used for individual taxpayers with little or no business activities. In an office audit, the taxpayer takes his or her records to the IRS office where they are reviewed by a revenue agent. The taxpayer is simply required to substantiate deductions, credits, or income items that appear on his or her tax return.

In a field audit, the IRS agent reviews a taxpayer's books and records at the taxpayer's place of business or at the office of the taxpayer's accountant. This type of audit is generally used when the accounting records are too extensive to take to the IRS office. Field audits are usually used for taxpayers with substantial trade or business activities. If a taxpayer can present a valid reason, he or she may have an office audit changed to a field audit.

12-2a **Selection of Returns for Audits**

The IRS selects returns for audit through a number of different methods:

- Identification of participants in abusive tax avoidance transactions
- Computer scoring (DIF)
- Large corporations
- Information matching
- Related examinations
- Other means

The estimated audit rate for individual tax returns in 2019 was 0.45 percent, the lowest level in over a decade. However, the higher the income, the more likely the audit. It is estimated that the IRS audited about 3 percent of returns that reported more than $1 million in income. Recent audit rates continue to be lower than historical levels. For example, in 1970, about 2.5 percent of individual returns were audited, and as recently as 2010, 6 percent of $1 million tax returns were audited.

The IRS uses information gleaned from other sources to identify taxpayers involved in abusive tax avoidance transactions. For example, the IRS may identify a promoter of abusive transactions and then use the promoter's records to identify taxpayers that may have engaged in the abusive planning. The IRS also may select a tax return for audit through a related examination. For example, if the IRS selects an entity or taxpayer for examination, they may also select business partners or other investors.

Most large corporations are involved with an IRS audit on a continuous basis and many have set aside permanent office space to house the IRS agents.

For computer scoring, the IRS uses the DIF (Discriminant Function System) and UIDIF (Unreported Income DIF) to select taxpayers for audit. Under the DIF system, the IRS uses mathematical formulas to assign a DIF score to each return. The DIF score represents the potential for discovery of improper treatment of items on the tax return. The higher the DIF score, the more likely the tax return is to be audited. The DIF score is designed to identify tax returns likely to contain errors because they contain amounts of income, deductions, or tax credits that fall outside "normal" ranges. For example, a tax return that contains unusually large charitable contribution claimed as a deduction will be assigned a high DIF score, and the chances of it being selected for audit are greater. The UIDIF scores returns for the likelihood of unreported income.

The IRS has operated a random audit selection process for many years under different program names such as the Taxpayer Compliance Measurement Program (TCMP) or, as currently more benignly named, the National Research Program (NRP). These programs are used to assist the IRS in determining which types of taxpayers should be audited and gather data to update the DIF system. These programs have not been without controversy and remain a sensitive issue for the IRS. The National Taxpayer Advocate has suggested providing compensation to taxpayers that are subjected to an NRP audit that results in no change to tax liability.

The old TCMP audits were sometimes so time-consuming and intrusive that one taxpayer referred to them as "an autopsy without the benefit of dying," according to a *Wall Street Journal*'s "Tax Report" column.

Other tax returns that are audited are selected due to matching problems between the information forms such as Forms W-2 and 1099 and the related taxpayer's return. From time to time, the IRS will also target special projects at a local or industry segment. For example, a "random" audit might reveal a tax issue with small auto repair shops. After required approvals from higher positions within the IRS, a number of small auto repair shops may be selected for audit to see if the issue is pervasive within the industry segment.

Lastly, the IRS can also select returns based on information obtained from other taxing jurisdictions, news sources, or whistleblowers. For example, the IRS and many state departments of revenue share tax information to assist in identification of returns for examination. Although the IRS has procedures in place to ensure that audits are not targeted at certain groups for political or other motivations, the history of such reported behavior continues to haunt the organization.

TAX BREAK Taxpayers selected for audit should consider hiring professionals to represent them. Lawyers say taxpayers confronted by IRS agents often tend to get nervous and talk too much, blurting out unnecessary details or becoming overly emotional and arousing needless suspicions.

12-2b The Appeals Process

After a return is selected for examination, an agent is assigned to perform the audit. There are three possible results arising from the agent's audit. First, the tax return may be found to require no adjustment, in which case the findings are reviewed and the tax return is sent to storage. A second possible outcome of the audit is an agreement between the agent and the taxpayer on a needed change in the tax liability on the tax return. Then, the tax is collected or the refund is paid, and after a review, the return is stored.

The final possible outcome of the audit is a disagreement between the agent and the taxpayer on the amount of the required adjustment to the tax return. In this situation, the appeals procedure begins with the IRS inviting the taxpayer to an informal conference with an appellate agent. If an agreement cannot be reached at the appeals level, then the matter is taken into the federal court system. The Federal Tax Court is open to the public. For tax professionals and tax students, watching the Tax Court in action can be an educational experience. Any group planning a court visit should contact the judge's chambers in advance since the courts are often small and cannot accommodate many spectators. Figures 12.2 and 12.3 on Pages 12-9 and 12-10, respectively, illustrate the audit process, beginning with the selection of a tax return for audit and ending with a decision of the federal courts.

The IRS considers the Appeals function to be highly successful, negotiating and settling 85 to 90 percent of the cases with taxpayers. If this high rate of settlement were not achieved, the number of disputed cases would soon overwhelm the courts hearing tax cases.

FIGURE 12.2

INCOME TAX AUDIT PROCEDURE
OF THE INTERNAL REVENUE SERVICE

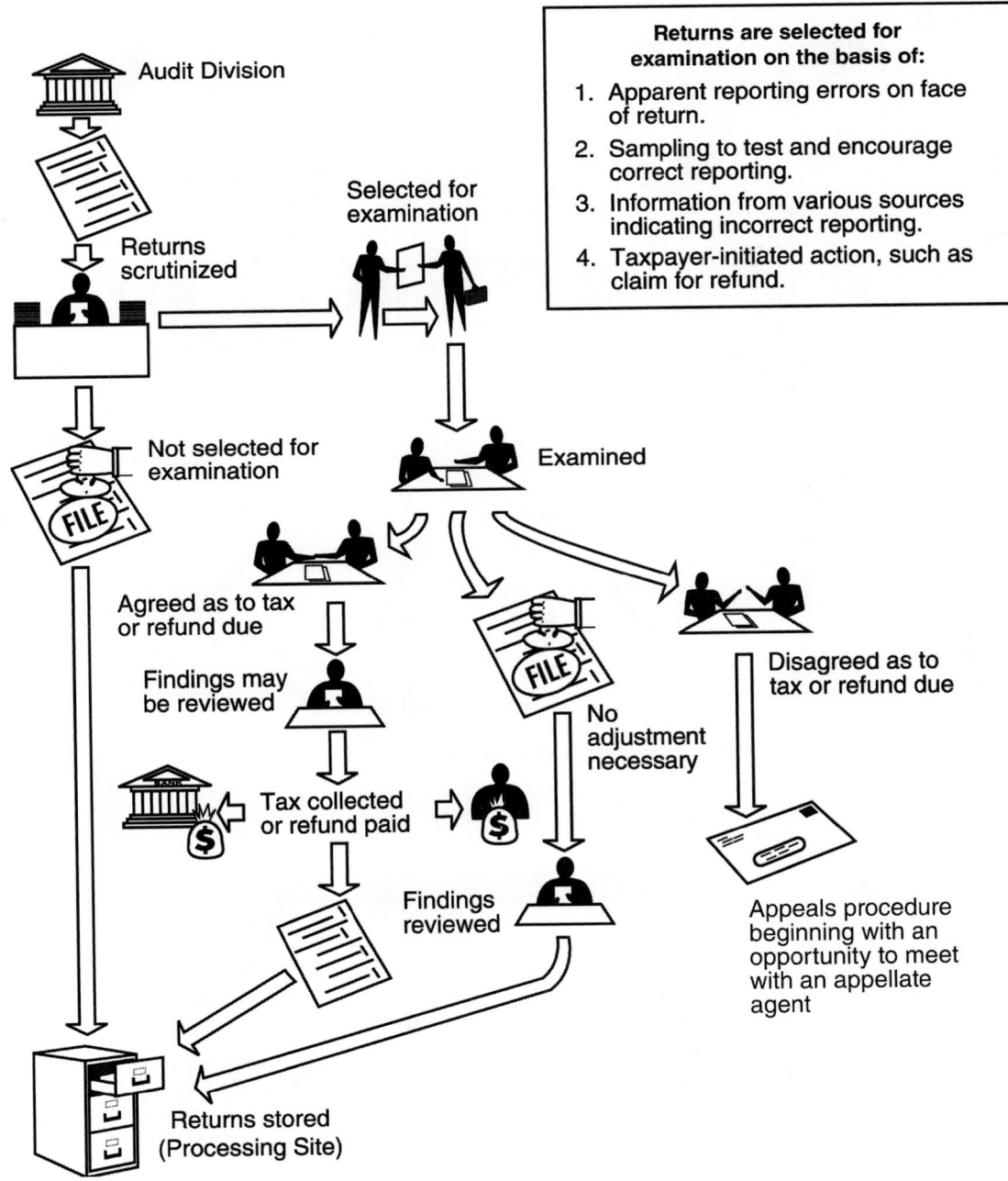

Audit Division

Returns scrutinized

Selected for examination

Returns are selected for examination on the basis of:

1. Apparent reporting errors on face of return.
2. Sampling to test and encourage correct reporting.
3. Information from various sources indicating incorrect reporting.
4. Taxpayer-initiated action, such as claim for refund.

Not selected for examination

Examined

Agreed as to tax or refund due

Findings may be reviewed

Tax collected or refund paid

No adjustment necessary

Disagreed as to tax or refund due

Findings reviewed

Appeals procedure beginning with an opportunity to meet with an appellate agent

Returns stored (Processing Site)

FIGURE 12.3

INCOME TAX APPEAL PROCEDURE
OF THE INTERNAL REVENUE SERVICE

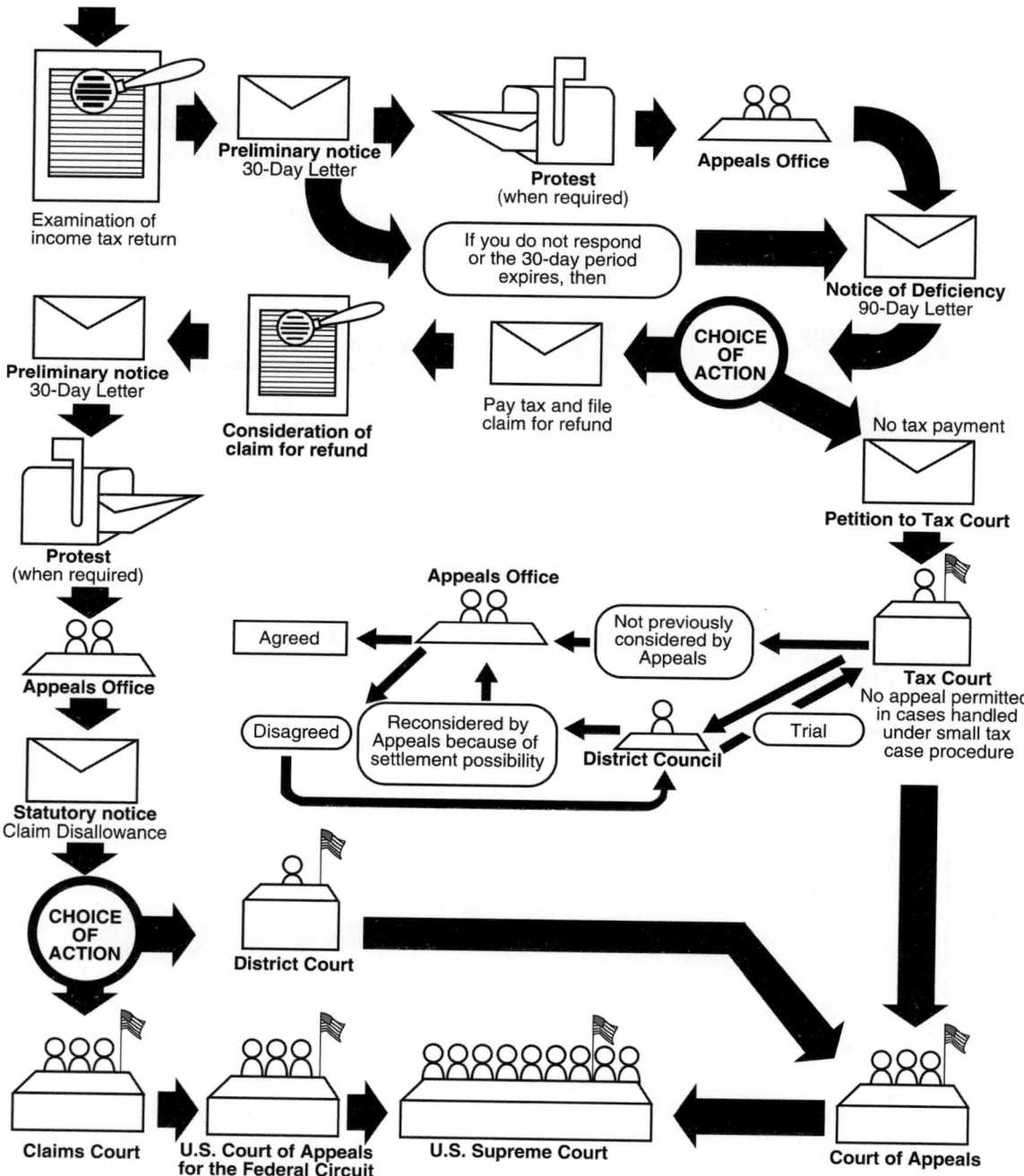

At any stage of procedure:
- You can agree and arrange to pay.
- You can ask the IRS to issue you a notice of deficiency
  so you can file a petition with the Tax Court.
- You can pay the tax and file a claim for a refund.

Self-Study Problem 12.2 — *See Appendix E for Solutions to Self-Study Problems*

Indicate whether the following statements are true or false by circling the appropriate letter.

T F 1. The IRS uses computers to select tax returns for most audits.

T F 2. An office audit is done at the taxpayer's office.

T F 3. NRP audits are selected randomly.

T F 4. An audit may result in a refund.

T F 5. A taxpayer cannot appeal the results of an IRS audit.

12-3 INTEREST AND PENALTIES

> **12.3 Learning Objective**
>
> Define the common penalties for taxpayers and be able to apply them to specific situations.

Taxpayers are charged interest on underpayments of taxes, and in some cases the IRS pays interest to taxpayers when they overpay their taxes. Usually, these interest charges or payments result from the settlement of a tax liability for a prior year's tax return. For example, when an IRS audit results in the taxpayer paying additional taxes for a prior tax year, the IRS will charge the taxpayer interest on the amount of additional taxes from the original due date to the date of payment of the tax. If the audit results in a refund, interest will be paid to the taxpayer based on the amount of the refund. The IRS also imposes a nondeductible penalty based on amounts of underpayments of estimated taxes for the current tax year (see Chapter 9), but a taxpayer is not paid interest on a refund arising from an overpayment of estimated taxes during the current tax year.

The interest rate applicable to underpayments and overpayments of taxes is adjusted each quarter based on the short-term federal rate. The rate is equal to the federal short-term rate plus 3 percentage points. Interest is compounded daily except when calculating the penalty for underpayment of estimated taxes by individuals and corporations. In calculating the penalty for underpayment of estimated taxes, the penalty is calculated as simple interest.

The rate of interest for selected recent periods is as follows:

2020	Rate
1st quarter	5%
2nd quarter	5%
3rd quarter	3%
4th quarter	3%

Tables are available from the IRS for performing the actual calculation of interest owed from or due to taxpayers. Interest paid on an underpayment of tax is considered consumer interest and, therefore, no deduction is allowed (see Chapter 5). The penalty for underpayment of estimated tax is calculated as interest but is a nondeductible penalty. Interest received on an overpayment is income in the year the payment is received. No interest is paid on a current year overpayment, unless the IRS takes more than 45 days to process the return.

EXAMPLE James pays $2,000 of interest in 2020 for an underpayment of taxes on his 2017 tax return. The $2,000 is not deductible since no deduction is allowed for consumer interest. ◆

EXAMPLE John receives $700 of interest income on the overpayment of his taxes resulting from an IRS audit on his 2017 tax return. The $700 interest is income in the year it is received by John. ◆

The tax law contains various penalties to ensure taxpayers accurately report and pay their taxes. Penalty payments are considered an addition to the amount of the taxes and, therefore, are not deductible. Several of the major taxpayer penalties are described in the following paragraphs.

Although the IRS is notoriously stingy about paying interest on refunds, due to delays in processing tax in 2020 as a result of the COVID-19 pandemic, the IRS took a taxpayer friendly position and will generally pay interest from April 15, 2020, until the date of the refund for individual tax returns filed by the temporarily extended July 15, 2020, due date.

12-3a The Failure-to-Pay and Failure-to-File Penalties

Taxpayers are subject to a penalty for failure to pay the amount of the taxes due on the due date of their tax return. The penalty for failure to pay is ½ of 1 percent of the amount of taxes due for every month or portion of a month that the payment is late, up to a maximum of 25 percent of the amount of taxes due. The penalty increases to 1 percent per month beginning 10 days after a notice of levy has been given to the taxpayer.

If a taxpayer does not file a tax return on the due date (including extensions), he or she is subject to a penalty equal to 5 percent of the tax due with the return for every month or portion of a month the return is late. The amount of the penalty for failure to file, however, is limited to a maximum of 25 percent of the amount of taxes due with the tax return. In the event the failure to file is fraudulent, the penalty is increased from 5 percent for each month or portion thereof to 15 percent, and the maximum penalty is increased from 25 percent to 75 percent. Also, if the taxpayer fails to file their tax return within 60 days of its due date, the minimum failure-to-file penalty is the lesser of $435 (in 2020) or the total amount of the taxes due with the tax return.

If both the failure-to-file and the failure-to-pay penalties apply, the failure-to-file penalty (5 percent) is reduced by the amount of the failure-to-pay penalty (½ of 1 percent) to 4.5 percent so the total combined penalty stays at 5 percent. The maximum combined penalty is 25 percent for the first 5 months. After 5 months, the failure-to-pay penalty continues at ½ of 1 percent per month for up to an additional 45 months. Thus, the maximum combined penalty could reach 47.5 percent.

Both the failure-to-file and the failure-to-pay penalties are zero if there is no tax due or if a refund is due from the IRS on the late tax return. The failure-to-file and the failure-to-pay penalty will not be assessed if the taxpayer can demonstrate that he or she had "reasonable cause" for failing to pay or file the tax return on time.

EXAMPLE Nancy filed her 2020 tax return 3½ months after the due date, and she had not requested an extension of time to file. The failure to file was not due to fraud. She included with her late return a check for $2,000, which was the balance of the tax she owed. Disregarding interest, her penalties are calculated as follows:

Failure-to-pay penalty		$ 40
(0.5% × $2,000) × 4 months		
Plus:		
Failure-to-file penalty	$400	
(5% × $2,000) × 4 months		
Less: Failure-to-pay penalty	(40)	
Net failure-to-file penalty	360	
Minimum failure to file after 60 days	$435	435
Total penalties		$475 ♦

The IRS has a first-time penalty abatement program which was meant to allow taxpayers who were assessed penalties for the first time to request a one-time penalty amnesty. The program applies to the failure-to-file and failure-to-pay penalties as well as several others, and can save taxpayers significant amounts of money in certain cases. The penalty abatement waiver must be requested by the taxpayer, but few taxpayers who qualify for the waiver request it or even know the program exists.

12-3b **Accuracy-Related Penalty**

The tax law imposes a penalty of 20 percent of the applicable underpayment due to (1) negligence of or disregard for rules or regulations, (2) a substantial understatement of income tax, or (3) a substantial valuation overstatement, as well as certain other understatements of income tax. Negligence includes the failure to make a reasonable attempt to comply with the tax law. For example, the penalty could be imposed on a taxpayer who deducts a personal expenditure as a business expense. A substantial understatement of income tax occurs where the required amount of tax exceeds the tax shown on the taxpayer's return by the greater of 10 percent (5 percent if claiming a qualified business income deduction) of the amount of tax that should be shown on the return or $5,000 ($10,000 for corporate taxpayers other than S corporations). A substantial valuation overstatement occurs when the value of property is 150 percent or more of the correct valuation. For example, a taxpayer who inflates the value of depreciable property to generate additional depreciation deductions may be subject to this penalty. The accuracy-related penalty applies only if the taxpayer has filed a return. In addition, if the taxpayer can demonstrate that he or she has reasonable cause for the understatement of tax and that he or she acted in good faith, the penalty will not be assessed.

EXAMPLE   Kim underpaid her taxes for the current year by $15,000 due to negligence. Kim's penalty for negligence under the accuracy-related penalty is calculated as follows:

Accuracy-related penalty (20% × $15,000)	$3,000 ♦

12-3c **Fraud Penalty**

The tax law also contains provisions for penalties for filing fraudulent tax returns. The fraud penalty is equal to 75 percent of the amount of underpayment of taxes attributable to fraud.

For the IRS to impose the fraud penalty, it must be shown by a "preponderance of evidence" that the taxpayer had an intent to evade taxes; however, once the IRS establishes that any portion of an underpayment of taxes is due to fraud, the entire underpayment is assumed to be attributable to fraud unless the taxpayer establishes otherwise. The tax law does not provide clear rules for what constitutes fraud; however, what is clearly mere negligence by a taxpayer will not cause this penalty to be imposed. When the fraud penalty is applicable, the accuracy-related penalty cannot be imposed. The fraud penalty will be applied only where the taxpayer has actually filed a return. Like the accuracy-related penalty, the fraud penalty will not be assessed if the taxpayer can demonstrate reasonable cause for the underpayment of tax and the taxpayer acted in good faith.

EXAMPLE   Jeff has a $20,000 tax deficiency because of civil fraud. Interest on this underpayment amounts to $8,000. Jeff's total amount due on this underpayment is calculated as follows:

Tax deficiency	$20,000
Fraud penalty (75% × $20,000)	15,000
Interest	8,000
Total due	$43,000

The interest is not deductible due to the disallowance of deductions for consumer interest. The fraud penalty is also not deductible. ♦

According to IRS data, 11 to 16 percent of Americans feel cheating on taxes is acceptable. Experts agree that tax cheating is a significant problem for the IRS, which must enforce the laws, and for honest taxpayers who pay more in taxes than they would otherwise have to. It is generally believed that tax evasion and noncompliance are costing the government more than $300 billion dollars in lost revenue each year.

Sign Here	Under penalties of perjury, I declare that I have examined this return and accompanying schedules and statements, and to the best of my knowledge and belief, they are true, correct, and complete. Declaration of preparer (other than taxpayer) is based on all information of which preparer has any knowledge.			
	Your signature	Date	Your occupation	If the IRS sent you an Identity Protection PIN, enter it here (see inst.) ▶
Joint return? See instructions. Keep a copy for your records.	Spouse's signature. If a joint return, **both** must sign.	Date	Spouse's occupation	If the IRS sent your spouse an Identity Protection PIN, enter it here (see inst.) ▶
	Phone no.		Email address	
Paid Preparer Use Only	Preparer's name	Preparer's signature		Date	PTIN	Check if: ☐ Self-employed
	Firm's name ▶				Phone no.	
	Firm's address ▶				Firm's EIN ▶	

Would You Sign This Tax Return?

Tim Trying, who is single, purchased a house on the beach in sunny Southern California 35 years ago. He is now retiring and moving to Hawaii for his golden years. Tim sold his house for $1,200,000 this year. Tim has been a client of yours for the past decade. He became a client when he was referred to you by your parents, who lived two houses away from Tim. When asked what his tax basis is in the house, Tim says it is $975,000. Your parents bought their house at about the same time, and you know they paid $100,000 for it. You have seen Tim's house many times and, although the house is well-maintained, you know it does not have any major improvements or betterments. You are reasonably certain that Tim is overstating his tax basis by hundreds of thousands of dollars in order to avoid reporting a taxable gain on the sale. Would you sign the Paid Preparer's declaration (see example above) on this return? Why or why not?

12-3d Miscellaneous Penalties

The tax law contains many other penalties applicable to taxpayers. The following are examples of such penalties:

- A civil penalty of $500 and a criminal penalty of $1,000 are imposed for filing false withholding information.
- An immediate $5,000 penalty can be assessed against a taxpayer who files a "frivolous" tax return (or document) as a tax protest.
- A tiered penalty system dependent on the timeliness of correction and filing of information returns (including payee information returns) is imposed for failing to file correct information returns. The penalties for information returns filed in 2020 are up to $280 per return, with an annual maximum of $3,392,000 ($1,130,500 for small businesses). If the failure to file is corrected or the information returns are filed closer to the due date, the penalties may be reduced. Exceptions to the information return penalties may be made for reasonable cause.
- Employers are subject to a penalty of 2, 5, or 10 percent of the amount of payroll taxes not deposited on time, depending on the number of days the taxes remain undeposited. A 15 percent penalty may apply where taxes remain undeposited after a delinquency notice has been presented to the taxpayer.
- Taxpayers are subject to a penalty for failure to pay estimated taxes. The penalty is calculated using the interest rates for the period of underpayment (but it is not deductible as interest).
- Taxpayers are subject to a penalty for issuing a "bad" check, unless the taxpayer can demonstrate that the check was issued in good faith. The penalty is equal to 2 percent of the amount of the check. If the check is less than $1,250, then the penalty is the lesser of $25 or the amount of the check.

Would You Believe?

In 2016, the European Commission levied taxes and interest due from Apple of €14.4 billion. Although Apple contests the charge, the $20 billion U.S. tax has been paid. In 2020 Apple won an appeal; however, the EU has the right to appeal to the highest EU court and the money remains in escrow.

3RD PARTY Vendors

Self-Study Problem 12.3 *See Appendix E for Solutions to Self-Study Problems*

Part a

Linda filed her tax return 43 days late. The tax paid with the return amounts to $3,000. What is Linda's total penalty for failure to file and failure to pay, assuming the failure to file is not fraudulent?

$_____

Part b

Using the same information as in Part a, what is Linda's total penalty if the tax return is 63 days late?

$_____

Part c

Kim underpaid her taxes by $10,000 due to negligence. What is Kim's penalty for negligence?

$_____

12-4 STATUTE OF LIMITATIONS

12.4 Learning Objective

Apply the general rule for the statute of limitations on tax returns and the important exceptions to the general rule.

The statute of limitations is the time period within which an action may be taken by the IRS and the taxpayer on a tax return. After the statute of limitations has run out on a given tax return, the government cannot assess additional taxes and the taxpayer cannot amend the return to request a refund. In general, the statute of limitations for a tax return runs for 3 years from the date the tax return was filed or the return due date (without extensions), whichever is later. For taxpayers seeking a refund, the statute of limitations is the later of 3 years from the time of filing or 2 years from the date that the taxes were actually paid. Due to the COVID-19 pandemic, recall that the deadline for filing 2019 individual tax returns was deferred until July 15, 2020.

EXAMPLE   Norm files his 2020 tax return on March 19, 2021. Unless an exception discussed below applies, the IRS has until April 15, 2024, to assess any additional taxes. ♦

12-4a Exceptions

The tax law contains several exceptions to the general rule of a 3-year statute of limitations. Several of these special rules are summarized below:

- If a fraudulent tax return is filed or no return is filed, there is no statute of limitations. The IRS may assess a tax deficiency at any time in the future.
- If a taxpayer omits an amount of gross income in excess of 25 percent of the gross income shown on the return, then the statute of limitations is increased to 6 years. For example, if a tax return with gross income of $40,000 contains an omission of over $10,000 (25 percent of $40,000) of gross income, the statute of limitations is increased to 6 years.
- The statute of limitations for the deduction of a bad debt or worthless securities is 7 years. This limitation applies only to the bad debt deduction or the worthless security deduction; all other items on the tax return would normally close out after 3 years.

Besides these exceptions, the statute of limitations may be extended by mutual consent of the IRS and the taxpayer. This extension is for a specific time period and is made by signing the appropriate form in the Form 872 series. An extension is generally used when the statute of limitations is about to lapse and an audit has not been completed.

If a tax deficiency has been assessed by the IRS within the period of the statute of limitations, then the government has 10 years from the date of assessment to collect the tax due.

An IRS study shows that many taxpayers lose refunds because they fail to file their returns within the statute of limitations for claiming a refund, which can be either 2 or 3 years depending on the circumstances. The IRS denies millions of dollars in refunds each year which were claimed in delinquent returns.

Self-Study Problem 12.4   *See Appendix E for Solutions to Self-Study Problems*

Indicate whether the following statements are true or false by circling the appropriate letter.

T F   1. The general statute of limitations for a tax return is 3 years.

T F   2. The statute of limitations for a bad debt deduction on a tax return is 6 years.

T F   3. The statute of limitations for a fraudulent tax return is 7 years.

T F   4. The special statute of limitations for a tax return that omits income greater than 25 percent of gross income is 6 years.

T F   5. For the deduction of worthless securities, the statute of limitations is 7 years.

Learning Objective 12.5

Describe the rules and penalties that apply to tax practitioners.

12-5 PREPARERS, PROOF, AND PRIVILEGE

12-5a Tax Practitioners

Many taxpayers find it desirable or necessary to have their tax returns prepared by a tax practitioner. Tax practitioners include commercial preparers, enrolled agents, attorneys, and certified public accountants (CPAs). Commercial preparers generally prepare non-complex returns of individuals, small corporations, and partnerships. Enrolled agents are individuals who have passed an IRS exam and are allowed to represent clients at IRS proceedings, as well as prepare tax returns. Attorneys and CPAs are individuals who have met education, examination, and experience requirements and are licensed to practice in their respective professions. CPAs and attorneys normally work with complex tax returns of individuals, corporations, partnerships, estates, and trusts. They also provide tax-planning advice to aid their clients in minimizing the amount of their taxes. Preparers that are enrolled agents, CPAs, and attorneys are sometimes referred to as enrolled preparers while other non-credentialed preparers are known as unenrolled preparers.

The IRS operated a program for taxpayers who failed to report offshore income known as the offshore voluntary disclosure program (OVDP). The Taxpayer Advocate's Office examined taxpayers who participated in the OVDP and found that those with the largest offshore accounts ($4.2 million or more) paid penalties of about three times the unpaid taxes. However, those with the smallest accounts (about $87,000 or less) paid nearly six times the unpaid tax. The OVDP closed in September 2018.

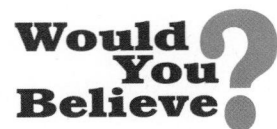

12-5b Annual Filing Season Program

All paid tax return preparers must sign up with the IRS and obtain a preparer tax identification number (PTIN). Every year, paid tax preparers must sign up or renew their PTIN online. There is no charge to obtain or renew a PTIN.

The IRS operates the Annual Filing Season Program (AFSP), a voluntary tax return preparer program designed to encourage preparers to participate in continuing education courses to help stay abreast of changes in tax law and help reduce the risk of using a preparer without professional credentials. The AFSP requires unenrolled preparers to obtain 18 hours of continuing education from an approved provider including at least 6 hours of an Annual Federal Tax Refresher (AFTR) course focused on filing season issues and tax updates and two hours of ethics. The AFTR must include a knowledge-based exam administered at the end of the course by the course provider.

In addition to being better prepared for the upcoming filing season, a list of tax preparers meeting the AFSP requirements is published at **www.irs.gov** to permit taxpayers to search for qualified tax return preparers. For additional information on the Annual Filing Season Program requirements, see the IRS website **(www.irs.gov)**.

12-5c Preparer Penalties

Under the tax law, any person who prepares a tax return, including nonincome tax returns (e.g., excise tax returns), for compensation is a "tax return preparer." The tax law has various penalty provisions applicable to tax return preparers. These penalties are designed to help the IRS regulate the preparation of tax returns. The more significant penalties are described below:

- $50 for failing to sign a tax return or failing to furnish the preparer's identifying number, $27,000 annual maximum
- $50 for each failure to keep a copy of the prepared return or include the return on a list of taxpayers for whom returns have been prepared, $27,000 annual maximum
- $50 for failing to provide a taxpayer a copy of the tax return prepared, $27,000 annual maximum
- $540 for endorsing or cashing a refund check issued to a taxpayer, or failing in due diligence for a taxpayer claiming the earned income credit
- Greater of $1,000 or 50 percent of the income derived (or to be derived) by the tax return preparer for an undisclosed unrealistic position on a return which does not meet a "substantial authority" standard, and which the preparer knew or reasonably should have known about

- Greater of $5,000 or 75 percent of the income derived (or to be derived) by the tax return preparer for each return in which the preparer willfully attempts to understate the amount of the taxpayer's tax liability, or each return in which an understatement is due to the preparer's reckless or intentional disregard of rules or regulations, reduced by the amount of the $1,000 (or 50 percent) penalty for unrealistic positions (discussed above)
- $1,000 ($10,000 for corporate returns) for each return or document filed in aiding or abetting a taxpayer in understating a tax liability
- For each separate activity (sale of an interest, organization of an entity, etc.), the lesser of $1,000 or 100 percent of the gross income derived by the promoter from promoting an "abusive tax shelter."

12-5d Burden of Proof

In most litigation, the party initiating the case has the burden of convincing the court that he or she is correct with respect to the issue. Historically, however, in most civil tax cases, the Internal Revenue Code (the Code) placed the burden of proof on the taxpayer, whether or not he or she initiated the case, except in cases involving such items as hobby losses, fraud with intent to evade tax, and the accumulated earnings tax.

In the IRS Restructuring and Reform Act of 1998, the tax law was changed to shift the burden of proof to the IRS in many situations. The IRS now has the burden of proof in any court proceeding on an income, gift, estate, or generation-skipping tax liability with respect to factual issues, provided the taxpayer (1) introduces credible evidence of the factual issue, (2) maintains records and substantiates items as presently required under the Code and Regulations, and (3) cooperates with reasonable IRS requests for meetings, interviews, witnesses, information, and documents. For corporations, trusts, and partnerships with net worth exceeding $7 million, the burden of proof remains on the taxpayer.

The burden of proof also automatically shifts to the IRS in two situations:

1. If the IRS uses statistics to reconstruct an individual's income, or
2. If the court proceeding against an individual taxpayer involves a penalty or addition to tax.

12-5e Tax Confidentiality Privilege

The 1998 Act also extended the existing attorney-client privilege of confidentiality in tax matters to nonattorneys authorized to practice before the IRS (e.g., CPAs and enrolled agents). The nonattorney-client privilege may be asserted only in a *noncriminal tax* proceeding before the IRS or federal courts. Also, the nonattorney-client privilege does not extend to written communications between a tax practitioner and a corporation in connection with the promotion of any tax shelter.

CPAs and enrolled agents need to understand the rules regarding tax confidentiality as they have been applied to lawyers to be aware of the tax privilege limits. For example, tax privileged communication usually does not apply to the preparation of tax returns, the giving of accounting or business advice, or to tax accrual workpapers. Also, unlike the general attorney-client privilege, the nonattorney-client privilege does not automatically apply to state tax situations.

Self-Study Problem 12.5 *See Appendix E for Solutions to Self-Study Problems*

Indicate whether the following statements are true or false by circling the appropriate letter.

T F 1. Only certified public accountants may represent taxpayers before the IRS.

T F 2. A college degree is required to prepare tax returns for compensation.

T F 3. Only attorneys may prepare corporate tax returns.

T F 4. The tax preparer penalty for filing a document aiding and abetting an individual taxpayer in the understatement of a tax liability is $1,000.

T F 5. The tax preparer penalty for endorsing a taxpayer's refund check is $520.

T F 6. The tax preparer penalty for failing to provide a copy of a tax return to a taxpayer is $50.

T F 7. For audits after 1998, if the IRS uses statistics to reconstruct an individual taxpayer's income, the burden of proof is on the taxpayer.

T F 8. For corporations, trusts, and partnerships with net worth over $7 million, the burden of proof is on the IRS in civil tax matters.

T F 9. CPAs and enrolled agents have tax privileged communication only in noncriminal proceedings before the IRS or federal courts.

T F 10. If an individual taxpayer does not cooperate with reasonable IRS requests for meetings, interviews, witnesses, information, and documents, the burden of proof in a tax matter is on the taxpayer.

T F 11. Commercial tax preparers must have a PTIN.

12-6 THE TAXPAYER BILL OF RIGHTS

12.6 Learning Objective

Describe the Taxpayer Bill of Rights.

Over the years, the news media carried many horror stories about taxpayers who claimed they had been abused by the IRS. As a result of this publicity, in 1988 Congress passed a set of provisions referred to as the Taxpayer Bill of Rights. The Taxpayer Bill of Rights has been amended several times since it was originally passed by Congress. This set of provisions requires the IRS to inform taxpayers of their rights in dealing with the IRS, and expands taxpayers' rights and remedies when they are involved in disputes with the IRS. The provisions of the Taxpayer Bill of Rights are summarized in IRS Publication 1, which is reproduced on Pages 12-20 and 12-21. Also note, Publication 1 directs taxpayers to other IRS publications with more details on specific taxpayer rights.

The first part of this publication explains some of the most important rights as a taxpayer. The second part explains the examination, appeal, collection, and refund processes.

Your Rights as a Taxpayer

Publication 1

This publication explains your rights as a taxpayer and the processes for examination, appeal, collection, and refunds. Also available in Spanish.

The Taxpayer Bill of Rights

1. The Right to Be Informed

Taxpayers have the right to know what they need to do to comply with the tax laws. They are entitled to clear explanations of the laws and IRS procedures in all tax forms, instructions, publications, notices, and correspondence. They have the right to be informed of IRS decisions about their tax accounts and to receive clear explanations of the outcomes.

2. The Right to Quality Service

Taxpayers have the right to receive prompt, courteous, and professional assistance in their dealings with the IRS, to be spoken to in a way they can easily understand, to receive clear and easily understandable communications from the IRS, and to speak to a supervisor about inadequate service.

3. The Right to Pay No More than the Correct Amount of Tax

Taxpayers have the right to pay only the amount of tax legally due, including interest and penalties, and to have the IRS apply all tax payments properly.

4. The Right to Challenge the IRS's Position and Be Heard

Taxpayers have the right to raise objections and provide additional documentation in response to formal IRS actions or proposed actions, to expect that the IRS will consider their timely objections and documentation promptly and fairly, and to receive a response if the IRS does not agree with their position.

5. The Right to Appeal an IRS Decision in an Independent Forum

Taxpayers are entitled to a fair and impartial administrative appeal of most IRS decisions, including many penalties, and have the right to receive a written response regarding the Office of Appeals' decision. Taxpayers generally have the right to take their cases to court.

6. The Right to Finality

Taxpayers have the right to know the maximum amount of time they have to challenge the IRS's position as well as the maximum amount of time the IRS has to audit a particular tax year or collect a tax debt. Taxpayers have the right to know when the IRS has finished an audit.

7. The Right to Privacy

Taxpayers have the right to expect that any IRS inquiry, examination, or enforcement action will comply with the law and be no more intrusive than necessary, and will respect all due process rights, including search and seizure protections, and will provide, where applicable, a collection due process hearing.

8. The Right to Confidentiality

Taxpayers have the right to expect that any information they provide to the IRS will not be disclosed unless authorized by the taxpayer or by law. Taxpayers have the right to expect appropriate action will be taken against employees, return preparers, and others who wrongfully use or disclose taxpayer return information.

9. The Right to Retain Representation

Taxpayers have the right to retain an authorized representative of their choice to represent them in their dealings with the IRS. Taxpayers have the right to seek assistance from a Low Income Taxpayer Clinic if they cannot afford representation.

10. The Right to a Fair and Just Tax System

Taxpayers have the right to expect the tax system to consider facts and circumstances that might affect their underlying liabilities, ability to pay, or ability to provide information timely. Taxpayers have the right to receive assistance from the Taxpayer Advocate Service if they are experiencing financial difficulty or if the IRS has not resolved their tax issues properly and timely through its normal channels.

The IRS Mission | Provide America's taxpayers top-quality service by helping them understand and meet their tax responsibilities and enforce the law with integrity and fairness to all.

Source: Internal Revenue Service (IRS)

Publication 1 (Rev. 9-2017) Catalog Number 64731W Department of the Treasury **Internal Revenue Service** www.irs.gov

Examinations, Appeals, Collections, and Refunds

Examinations (Audits)

We accept most taxpayers' returns as filed. If we inquire about your return or select it for examination, it does not suggest that you are dishonest. The inquiry or examination may or may not result in more tax. We may close your case without change; or, you may receive a refund.

The process of selecting a return for examination usually begins in one of two ways. First, we use computer programs to identify returns that may have incorrect amounts. These programs may be based on information returns, such as Forms 1099 and W-2, on studies of past examinations, or on certain issues identified by compliance projects. Second, we use information from outside sources that indicates that a return may have incorrect amounts. These sources may include newspapers, public records, and individuals. If we determine that the information is accurate and reliable, we may use it to select a return for examination.

Publication 556, Examination of Returns, Appeal Rights, and Claims for Refund, explains the rules and procedures that we follow in examinations. The following sections give an overview of how we conduct examinations.

By Mail

We handle many examinations and inquiries by mail. We will send you a letter with either a request for more information or a reason why we believe a change to your return may be needed. You can respond by mail or you can request a personal interview with an examiner. If you mail us the requested information or provide an explanation, we may or may not agree with you, and we will explain the reasons for any changes. Please do not hesitate to write to us about anything you do not understand.

By Interview

If we notify you that we will conduct your examination through a personal interview, or you request such an interview, you have the right to ask that the examination take place at a reasonable time and place that is convenient for both you and the IRS. If our examiner proposes any changes to your return, he or she will explain the reasons for the changes. If you do not agree with these changes, you can meet with the examiner's supervisor.

Repeat Examinations

If we examined your return for the same items in either of the 2 previous years and proposed no change to your tax liability, please contact us as soon as possible so we can see if we should discontinue the examination.

Appeals

If you do not agree with the examiner's proposed changes, you can appeal them to the Appeals Office of the IRS. Most differences can be settled without expensive and time-consuming court trials. Your appeal rights are explained in detail in both Publication 5, Your Appeal Rights and How To Prepare a Protest If You Don't Agree, and Publication 556, Examination of Returns, Appeal Rights, and Claims for Refund.

If you do not wish to use the Appeals Office or disagree with its findings, you may be able to take your case to the U.S. Tax Court, U.S. Court of Federal Claims, or the U.S. District Court where you live. If you take your case to court, the IRS will have the burden of proving certain facts if you kept adequate records to show your tax liability, cooperated with the IRS, and meet certain other conditions. If the court agrees with you on most issues in your case and finds that our position was largely unjustified, you may be able to recover some of your administrative and litigation costs. You will not be eligible to recover these costs unless you tried to resolve your case administratively, including going through the appeals system, and you gave us the information necessary to resolve the case.

Collections

Publication 594, The IRS Collection Process, explains your rights and responsibilities regarding payment of federal taxes. It describes:

- What to do when you owe taxes. It describes what to do if you get a tax bill and what to do if you think your bill is wrong. It also covers making installment payments, delaying collection action, and submitting an offer in compromise.

- IRS collection actions. It covers liens, releasing a lien, levies, releasing a levy, seizures and sales, and release of property.

- IRS certification to the State Department of a seriously delinquent tax debt, which will generally result in denial of a passport application and may lead to revocation of a passport.

Your collection appeal rights are explained in detail in Publication 1660, Collection Appeal Rights.

Innocent Spouse Relief

Generally, both you and your spouse are each responsible for paying the full amount of tax, interest, and penalties due on your joint return. However, if you qualify for innocent spouse relief, you may be relieved of part or all of the joint liability. To request relief, you must file Form 8857, Request for Innocent Spouse Relief. For more information on innocent spouse relief, see Publication 971, Innocent Spouse Relief, and Form 8857.

Potential Third Party Contacts

Generally, the IRS will deal directly with you or your duly authorized representative.

However, we sometimes talk with other persons if we need information that you have been unable to provide, or to verify information we have received. If we do contact other persons, such as a neighbor, bank, employer, or employees, we will generally need to tell them limited information, such as your name. The law prohibits us from disclosing any more information than is necessary to obtain or verify the information we are seeking. Our need to contact other persons may continue as long as there is activity in your case. If we do contact other persons, you have a right to request a list of those contacted. Your request can be made by telephone, in writing, or during a personal interview.

Refunds

You may file a claim for refund if you think you paid too much tax. You must generally file the claim within 3 years from the date you filed your original return or 2 years from the date you paid the tax, whichever is later. The law generally provides for interest on your refund if it is not paid within 45 days of the date you filed your return or claim for refund. Publication 556, Examination of Returns, Appeal Rights, and Claims for Refund, has more information on refunds.

If you were due a refund but you did not file a return, you generally must file your return within 3 years from the date the return was due (including extensions) to get that refund.

Taxpayer Advocate Service

TAS is an *independent* organization within the IRS that can help protect your taxpayer rights. We can offer you help if your tax problem is causing a hardship, or you've tried but haven't been able to resolve your problem with the IRS. If you qualify for our assistance, which is always free, we will do everything possible to help you. Visit *www.taxpayeradvocate.irs.gov* or call 1-877-777-4778.

Tax Information

The IRS provides the following sources for forms, publications, and additional information.

- *Tax Questions:* 1-800-829-1040 (1-800-829-4059 for TTY/TDD)
- *Forms and Publications:* 1-800-829-3676 (1-800-829-4059 for TTY/TDD)
- *Internet: www.irs.gov*
- *Small Business Ombudsman:* A small business entity can participate in the regulatory process and comment on enforcement actions of the IRS by calling 1-888-REG-FAIR.
- *Treasury Inspector General for Tax Administration:* You can confidentially report misconduct, waste, fraud, or abuse by an IRS employee by calling 1-800-366-4484 (1-800-877-8339 for TTY/TDD). You can remain anonymous.

Internal Revenue Service (IRS)

Self-Study Problem 12.6   *See Appendix E for Solutions to Self-Study Problems*

Indicate whether the following statements are true or false by circling the appropriate letter.

T F 1. Taxpayers have the right to represent themselves or, with proper written authorization, have someone else represent them.

T F 2. The IRS may contact a taxpayer's neighbor or employer to verify information.

T F 3. IRS Publication 594 explains a taxpayer's rights and responsibilities regarding payment of federal taxes.

T F 4. If a taxpayer is audited in the current year for an item that was audited in either of the 2 previous years and the IRS proposed no change to the tax liability, the taxpayer should contact the IRS as soon as possible to attempt to stop the repeat audit.

T F 5. Generally, both a taxpayer and his or her spouse are responsible, jointly and individually, for the tax and any interest or penalty due on a joint return.

T F 6. Taxpayers must file a claim for refund within 3 years of the date they filed their return or 2 years from the date they paid the tax if they think they paid too much tax.

Learning Objective 12.7

Explain the basic concepts of tax planning.

12-7 TAX PLANNING

The process of arranging one's financial affairs to maximize one's after-tax wealth is often referred to as tax planning. There is nothing wrong with tax planning to avoid tax, provided legal methods are used. Judge Learned Hand best stated the doctrine of tax planning in 1947 when he wrote:

"Over and over again, courts have said there is nothing sinister in so arranging one's affairs as to keep taxes as low as possible. Everybody does so, rich or poor, and all do right, for nobody owes any public duty to pay more than the law demands: taxes are enforced extractions, not voluntary contributions." *Commissioner v. Newman*, 159 F.2d 848 (CA-2, 1947).

When illegal methods are used to reduce tax liability, the process can no longer be considered tax planning, but instead becomes tax evasion. Tax evasion can subject the taxpayer and tax practitioner to fines, penalties, and incarceration. Illegal acts are outside the realm of tax-planning services offered by a professional tax practitioner.

Tax planning covers two basic categories of transactions, the "open transaction" and the "closed transaction." In an open transaction, all the events have not yet been completed; therefore, the taxpayer has some degree of control over the tax consequences. In a closed transaction, all material parts of the transaction have been completed. As a result, tax planning involving a closed transaction is limited to presentation of the facts to the IRS in the most favorable, legally acceptable manner possible.

EXAMPLE   Annie enters into an agreement with Erik to exchange real estate held as an investment. Escrow has not closed and the title of the property has not passed between the parties. Since all significant events (title passing) are not complete, the transaction is considered an open transaction. Once the title to the real estate passes, the tax planning involves a closed transaction. ◆

Tax planning cannot be considered in a void. Any tax-planning advice must consider the business goals of the taxpayer. Tax planning for a transaction should not override sound business judgment.

12-7a Tax Rate Terminology

Important to any tax-planning situation is an evaluation of the tax savings arising from increasing deductions or the tax cost of generating additional income. The tax consequences are dependent on the taxpayer's tax rate. The taxpayer's tax rate may be defined in several ways. For tax-planning purposes, the taxpayer needs to understand the difference between the "average" tax rate and the "marginal" tax rate. The average tax rate merely represents the average rate of tax applicable to the taxpayer's income and is calculated as the total tax paid divided by the total income of the taxpayer. The marginal tax rate represents the rate at which tax is imposed on the "next" dollar of income.

EXAMPLE Becky, a single taxpayer, has income of $41,200 during the current year on which she pays tax of $4,860. Her average tax rate is 11.80 percent ($4,860 ÷ $41,200). If Becky's income increases to $51,200, her tax liability will be $7,060. Thus, Becky's marginal rate is 22 percent [($7,060 − $4,860) ÷ ($51,200 − $41,200)]. ◆

When making tax-planning decisions, the taxpayer's marginal tax rate is the most important tax rate. For example, Jason has a 30 percent marginal tax rate and a 20 percent average tax rate and is considering making a tax-deductible expenditure of $2,000. His after-tax cost of the expenditure is calculated using his marginal tax rate, not his average tax rate. Jason's after-tax cost of the expenditure would be $1,400, calculated as follows: [$2,000 − ($2,000 × 30 percent)]. On the other hand, if Jason is to receive any additional income, he knows that he will pay tax at a rate of 30 percent on the next dollar of income.

12-7b Examples of Tax Planning

Tax planning opportunities can be classified into four categories: (1) timing, (2) jurisdiction, (3) entity, and (4) character. Most tax-planning techniques employ at least one of these characteristics in an attempt to save taxpayers money.

12-7c Timing

In its simplest form, timing implies deferring the payment of taxes to a future year and is generally achieved by either deferring income recognition or accelerating expense deduction.

EXAMPLE Karen operates a small cash basis, calendar year-end business. In order to lower her current year's income, Karen may prepay January's rent in December. She could also delay invoicing her customers in an attempt to defer the recognition of income. ◆

Most simple timing techniques work best when tax rates are not expected to change. If tax rates are expected to change across the periods in which the timing is being changed, a more thorough analysis is going to be required.

EXAMPLE If in the previous example Karen expects her tax rate to increase from 24 percent in the current year to 37 percent next year, she may want to consider accelerating the recognition of income into the current year at the lower rate and deferring the deduction of expenses until next year increasing the value of the deduction. ◆

One disadvantage of using the timing technique is that tax recognition frequently occurs simultaneously with cash transactions. For example, one way to defer income recognition might be to earn no income; however, that generally spells the end of the business as well.

12-7d Jurisdiction

Using jurisdiction for tax planning involves exploiting differences in tax rates or tax systems to lower tax liabilities.

EXAMPLE   Mark worked for the Lake Tahoe office of the state of California Department of Motor Vehicles for 35 years. In the current year, he starts his well-deserved retirement. Realizing that the individual tax rate in California can be over 10 percent, he moves to nearby Reno, Nevada, knowing that Nevada has no state income tax on individuals. He continues to collect his pension without paying state income tax. ◆

Jurisdiction, although simple in concept, can be difficult to implement for many taxpayers. Most individuals do not have the luxury to simply move to a new state to lower the state income tax rate. Larger businesses may have more flexibility than individuals or small businesses to implement a jurisdictional tax plan.

12-7e Entity

Entity-based tax planning involves making a choice about the type of entity a taxpayer chooses to operate as.

EXAMPLE   Raquel is starting a new small business and expects to operate at a loss for the first few years. In an attempt to take advantage of using the losses to offset her other forms of income, she establishes her new business as a flow-through entity such as an LLC in hopes of passing those losses through to her individual tax return. ◆

12-7f Character

Using character for tax planning often requires a deeper understanding of tax law than the other tax-planning techniques. Using character means the transaction will be designed to take advantage of the tax law or a taxpayer's current situation.

EXAMPLE   Axel owns stock purchased 11 months ago which has now doubled in value. Although Axel thinks the stock's value has peaked, he wishes to wait one additional month before selling to convert the short-term capital gain taxed at ordinary tax rates into a long-term capital gain taxed at preferential rates. Although this might also feel like a timing-based plan, the one-month deferral of taxes is not likely to be significant. ◆

EXAMPLE   Beck is a single taxpayer with a 24 percent marginal tax rate. Beck is debating between an investment in a taxable bond that pays 5 percent or a tax-exempt bond that pays 4.5 percent. Although the pre-tax return on the taxable bond of 5 percent is higher than the 4.5 percent exempt bond, the after-tax return of the taxable bond is only 3.8 percent [5% × (1 − 0.24 tax rate)]. ◆

Self-Study Problem 12.7   *See Appendix E for Solutions to Self-Study Problems*

During the current year, K's taxable income is $89,000 and he pays income tax of $15,446.00. K is single, has no dependents, and does not itemize his deductions. J, who files in *exactly* the same manner as K, has taxable income of $90,000 and pays income tax of $15,686.00.

1. What is K's average tax rate?   _____

2. What is J's average tax rate?   _____

3. If K's income increased to the same amount as J,
   what would K's marginal tax rate be?   _____

KEY TERMS

Internal Revenue Service (IRS), 12-2
commissioner of internal revenue, 12-2
IRS Campus Processing Sites, 12-2
IRS organizational structure, 12-3
Small Business/Self-Employed
   (SB/SE) Division, 12-4
Wage and Investment (W&I)
   Division, 12-5
offer in compromise, 12-5
office audit, 12-6
field audit, 12-6
correspondence audit, 12-6
Discriminant Function System
   (DIF), 12-7
Unreported Income DIF (UIDIF),
   12-7

appeals process of IRS, 12-8
Federal Tax Court, 12-8
audit procedure of IRS, 12-9
appeal procedure of IRS, 12-10
interest, 12-11
nondeductible penalty, 12-11
interest rate, 12-11
failure-to-pay penalty, 12-12
failure-to-file penalty, 12-12
accuracy-related penalty, 12-13
fraud penalty, 12-13
statute of limitations, 12-15
tax practitioners, 12-16
preparer tax identification number
   (PTIN), 12-17

Annual Filing Season Program
   (AFSP), 12-17
Annual Federal Tax Refresher (AFTR),
   12-17
tax return preparer, 12-17
burden of proof, 12-18
nonattorney-client privilege, 12-18
Taxpayer Bill of Rights, 12-19
tax planning, 12-22
tax evasion, 12-22
open transaction, 12-22
closed transaction, 12-22
average tax rate, 12-23
marginal tax rate, 12-23

KEY POINTS

Learning Objectives	Key Points
LO 12.1: Identify the organizational structure of the Internal Revenue Service (IRS).	• The IRS is a bureau of the Treasury Department, tasked with administering the tax laws of the United States. • The national IRS office is the headquarters of the commissioner of internal revenue. The commissioner of internal revenue is appointed by the president of the United States with the advice and consent of the Senate. • The IRS maintains Campus Processing Sites where the IRS computers process the information from tax documents such as tax returns, payroll tax forms, Forms 1099, and withholding forms. • The IRS maintains a national computer center in Martinsburg, West Virginia, where information from various processing sites is matched with records from other processing sites. • The IRS has the authority to examine a taxpayer's books and records to determine the correct amount of tax due. The IRS also has the right to summon taxpayers to appear before the IRS and produce necessary accounting records.

LO 12.2: Describe the IRS audit process.	• A primary function of the IRS is to audit taxpayers' tax returns. • Correspondence audits are generally handled entirely by mail and account for the majority of the individual tax returns examined each year. • The office audit is conducted in an IRS office and is typically used for individual taxpayers with little or no business activities. • In a field audit, the IRS agent reviews a taxpayer's books and records at the taxpayer's place of business or at the office of the taxpayer's accountant. • The IRS uses a computerized statistical sampling technique called the Discriminant Function System (DIF) to select tax returns for most audits of individuals. • Under the DIF system, the IRS uses mathematical formulas to assign a DIF score to each return, which represents the potential for discovery of improper treatment of items on the tax return. • The IRS also selects returns for audit using information from other sources such as informants, other governmental agencies, news items, and associated tax returns. • If an audit results in a disagreement between the agent and the taxpayer, the appeals procedure begins with the IRS inviting the taxpayer to an informal conference with an appellate agent.
LO 12.3: Define the common penalties for taxpayers and be able to apply them to specific situations.	• Taxpayers are charged interest on underpayments of taxes, and in some cases, the IRS pays interest to taxpayers when they overpay their taxes. • The interest rate applicable to underpayments and overpayments of taxes is adjusted each quarter and is equal to the federal short-term rate plus 3 percentage points. • The penalty for failure to pay is ½ of 1 percent of the amount of taxes due for every month or portion of a month that the payment is late (up to a maximum of 25 percent of the total taxes due). • The failure to file a tax return is subject to a penalty equal to 5 percent of the tax due with the return, for every month or portion of a month the return is late (up to a maximum of 25 percent). If filed more than 60 days from the due date, the minimum failure to file is the lesser of the tax due or $435. • The accuracy-related penalty is 20 percent of the applicable underpayment due to (1) negligence of or disregard for rules or regulations, (2) a substantial understatement of income tax, or (3) a substantial valuation overstatement, as well as certain other understatements of income tax. • When a taxpayer files a fraudulent tax return, there is a fraud penalty equal to 75 percent of the amount of underpayment of taxes attributable to fraud. • The tax law contains many other penalties applicable to taxpayers, including but not limited to a civil penalty of $500 and a criminal penalty of $1,000 imposed for filing false withholding information, and there is an immediate $5,000 penalty for filing a "frivolous" tax return (or document) as a tax protest.
LO 12.4: Apply the general rule for the statute of limitations on tax returns and the important exceptions to the general rule.	• In general, the statute of limitations for a tax return runs for 3 years from the date the tax return was filed or the return due date (without extensions), whichever is later. • If a fraudulent tax return is filed or no return is filed, there is no statute of limitations. • If a taxpayer omits an amount of gross income in excess of 25 percent of the gross income shown on the return, then the statute of limitations is increased to 6 years. • The statute of limitations for the deduction of a bad debt or worthless securities is 7 years (all other items on the tax return would normally be considered closed out after 3 years). • The statute of limitations may be extended by mutual consent of the IRS and the taxpayer.

LO 12.5: Describe the rules and penalties that apply to tax practitioners.	• Tax practitioners include commercial preparers, enrolled agents, attorneys, and certified public accountants (CPAs).
	• Unenrolled preparers can currently participate in the Annual Filing Season Program, a voluntary program created to encourage preparers to participate in continuing education.
	• Tax return preparer penalties include, but are not limited to, (1) $50 for failing to sign a tax return or failing to furnish the preparer's identifying number, (2) $50 for each failure to keep a copy of the prepared return or include the return on a list of taxpayers for whom returns have been prepared, or (3) $50 for failing to provide a taxpayer with a copy of the tax return prepared.
	• The IRS has the burden of proof in any court proceeding with respect to factual issues, provided the taxpayer (1) introduces credible evidence of the factual issue, (2) maintains records and substantiates items, and (3) cooperates with reasonable IRS requests for meetings, interviews, witnesses, information, and documents.
	• The tax law extends the attorney-client privilege of confidentiality in noncriminal tax matters to nonattorneys authorized to practice before the IRS (e.g., CPAs and enrolled agents).
LO 12.6: Describe the Taxpayer Bill of Rights.	• The Taxpayer Bill of Rights (IRS Publication 1) requires the IRS to inform taxpayers of their rights in dealing with the IRS, and expands taxpayers' rights and remedies when they are involved in disputes with the IRS.
LO 12.7: Explain the basic concepts of tax planning.	• Tax planning is the process of arranging one's financial affairs to minimize one's overall tax liability.
	• When illegal methods are used to reduce tax liability, the process can no longer be considered tax planning, but instead becomes tax evasion.
	• For making tax-planning decisions, the taxpayer's marginal tax rate is the most important tax rate to consider.

QUESTIONS and PROBLEMS

GROUP 1:
MULTIPLE CHOICE QUESTIONS

LO 12.1

1. Which of the following is a responsibility of a local office of the IRS?
   a. Advising the Treasury Department on legislation
   b. Intelligence operations
   c. Appellate procedures
   d. Developing IRS rules and regulations
   e. None of the above

LO 12.1

2. The IRS does *not* have the authority to:
   a. Examine a taxpayer's books and records
   b. Summon taxpayers to make them appear before the IRS
   c. Summon third parties for taxpayer records
   d. Place a lien on taxpayer property
   e. None of the above—the IRS has the authority to do all these

LO 12.2

3. Which of the following is the most common type of audit for an individual taxpayer?
   a. Office audit
   b. Correspondence audit
   c. Telephone audit
   d. Field audit
   e. Service center audit

LO 12.2 4. In which of the following ways are tax returns selected for audits?
   a. Through the Discriminant Function System
   b. Through informants
   c. Through news sources
   d. Through information matching
   e. All of the above

LO 12.3 5. Which of the following is *not* a penalty that may be imposed by the IRS?
   a. Failure-to-file penalty
   b. Failure-to-pay penalty
   c. Penalty for negligence
   d. Early filing penalty
   e. All of the above may be imposed by the IRS

LO 12.3 6. Martha inadvertently failed to file her tax return for 11 months. The tax due on the return was $1,000. Her failure to file penalty will be:
   a. 55 percent of the tax due
   b. 25 percent of the tax due
   c. $435
   d. $5,000

LO 12.4 7. If a taxpayer's 2020 individual income tax return was filed on March 3, 2021, the statute of limitations would normally run out on:
   a. April 15, 2023
   b. March 3, 2022
   c. April 15, 2024
   d. March 3, 2024
   e. None of the above

LO 12.4 8. Which of the following has a 6-year statute of limitations?
   a. Depreciation
   b. Salaries
   c. Travel and entertainment
   d. A return in which the taxpayer omitted gross income in excess of 25 percent of the gross income shown on the return
   e. Worthless securities

LO 12.5 9. Which of the following tax preparers may *not* represent their clients in all IRS proceedings?
   a. An enrolled agent
   b. A certified public accountant
   c. An attorney
   d. All of the above may represent their clients in IRS proceedings

LO 12.5 10. Which of the following is *not* required to participate in the Annual Filing Season Program?
   a. 18 total hours of continuing education from an approved provider
   b. An annual federal tax refresher course lasting at least 6 hours
   c. A comprehensive oral exam administered by the IRS that tests preparer knowledge
   d. A PTIN if the preparer wishes to prepare and file tax returns
   e. All of the above are required

LO 12.5 11. Which of the following does *not* result in a minimum $50 fine for an income tax preparer?
   a. Failure to provide a tax preparer identification number
   b. Cashing a refund check for a customer
   c. Failing to keep any record of the returns prepared
   d. Failing to provide a copy of their prepared return to a customer

LO 12.5 12. In which of the following situations does the burden of proof in a tax matter *not* automatically shift to the IRS?
   a. The IRS uses statistics to reconstruct an individual's income.
   b. A court proceeding against an individual taxpayer involves a penalty or addition to tax.
   c. A taxpayer who did not maintain records.
   d. a and b are correct.
   e. a, b, and c are correct.

LO 12.5   13. Which of the following have privileged communication with a client in a noncriminal tax matter?
   a. CPAs
   b. Enrolled agents
   c. Attorneys
   d. a and c
   e. a, b, and c

LO 12.5   14. The burden of proof remains on the taxpayer for corporations, trusts, and partnerships with net worth exceeding:
   a. $1 million
   b. $3 million
   c. $5 million
   d. $7 million
   e. Some other amount

LO 12.6   15. The IRS does *not* have to furnish the taxpayer with information concerning which of the following items?
   a. The way the taxpayer's return was selected for audit
   b. The procedures for appealing an IRS ruling
   c. The refund claims process
   d. The IRS collection process
   e. All of the above must be provided to the taxpayer

LO 12.6   16. Both spouses are responsible, jointly and individually, for paying the full amount of any tax, interest, or penalties due on a joint return. Which of the following is correct in reference to the preceding statement?
   a. This does not apply to spouses who have divorced after the return was filed.
   b. Spouses are responsible jointly but not individually.
   c. Spouses are responsible individually but not jointly.
   d. Innocent spouses may be relieved of the liability for tax, interest, and penalties.
   e. None of the above.

LO 12.6   17. A taxpayer's rights are explained in:
   a. Publication 5
   b. Publication 17
   c. Publication 556
   d. Publication 1
   e. None of the above

LO 12.6   18. Taxpayers have the right to have an IRS examination take place at:
   a. The IRS office
   b. Any city of the taxpayer's choosing
   c. A neutral site
   d. A reasonable time and place
   e. None of the above

LO 12.6   19. If a U.S. Tax Court agrees with the taxpayer on appeal that the IRS position was largely unjustified, which of the following is correct?
   a. The taxpayer must still pay administrative and litigation costs.
   b. The taxpayer may recover administrative but not litigation costs.
   c. The taxpayer may recover litigation but not administrative costs.
   d. To be eligible to recover some of the administrative and litigation costs, the taxpayer must have tried to resolve the case administratively, including going through the appeals process, and must have given the IRS the information necessary to resolve the case.
   e. None of the above.

LO 12.6   20. If the IRS owes a taxpayer a refund, the law generally provides that the IRS must pay interest on the refund if it is not paid within _____ days of the date the taxpayer filed his or her tax return or claim for refund.
   a. 30
   b. 45

c. 60
d. 90
e. None of the above

LO 12.7   21. Glen's taxable income is $50,000 and he pays income tax of $6,796. If his income were $60,000, he would pay taxes of $8,996. What is Glen's marginal tax rate?
a. 18.23%
b. 22.00%
c. 12.00%
d. 25.00%
e. Some other amount

LO 12.7   22. Melodie's taxable income is $39,000 and she pays income tax of $4,486. If Melodie's taxable income increases to $43,000, she would pay income taxes of $5,256. What is Melodie's marginal tax rate?
a. 17.00%
b. 22.00%
c. 19.25%
d. 12.00%
e. Some other amount

LO 12.7   23. Jim has a house payment of $2,000 per month of which $1,700 is deductible interest and real estate taxes with the remaining $300 representing a repayment of the principal balance of the note. Jim's marginal tax rate is 30 percent. What is Jim's after-tax cost of his house payment?
a. $600
b. $540
c. $1,490
d. $1,460
e. Some other amount

GROUP 2:
PROBLEMS

LO 12.1
LO 12.2   1. Indicate whether the following statements are true or false:

_____ The IRS is a division of the Treasury Department.
_____ The IRS has four major divisions.
_____ The IRS local offices process most individual tax returns.
_____ IRS Campus Processing Sites are the locations that taxpayers should call to obtain tax information.
_____ Taxpayers should have their CPAs keep their tax records to prevent the IRS from being able to summon their records.
_____ Most IRS audits are conducted through the mail.

LO 12.2
LO 12.3   2. Indicate whether the following statements are true or false:

_____ A field audit by the IRS is an audit conducted at the IRS field office.
_____ A low Discriminant Function System score for a tax return increases the possibility that the return will be selected for audit.
_____ The IRS charges interest on underpayments of taxes, but never pays interest on amounts of overpayments of taxes.
_____ If a taxpayer fails to file a tax return on its due date, he or she may be subject to a failure-to-file penalty.
_____ The tax law includes a penalty for preparing a tax return in a negligent manner.
_____ If a taxpayer fails to file a tax return, the IRS may impose both the failure-to-file penalty and the fraud penalty.

LO 12.3   3. a. Wilson filed his individual tax return on the original due date, but failed to pay $700 in taxes that were due with the return. If Wilson pays the taxes exactly 2 months late, calculate the amount of his failure-to-pay penalty.

$ _____

b. Joan filed her individual income tax return 4½ months after it was due. She did not request an extension of time for filing. Along with her return, Joan remitted a check for $750, which was the balance of the taxes she owed with her return. Disregarding interest, calculate the total penalty that Joan will be required to pay, assuming the failure to file was not fraudulent.

$ _____

c. Jack filed his tax return 2 months and 3 days late and did not request an extension of time for filing. Jack's return indicated that he is to receive a $50 refund in taxes. Calculate the amount of Jack's penalty for failure to file his tax return on time, assuming the failure to file was not fraudulent.

$ _____

LO 12.3

4. In the 2020 tax year, Michelle paid the following amounts relating to her 2018 tax return:

Tax deficiency	$5,000
Negligence penalty	1,000
Interest	500
Underpayment of estimated tax penalty	350

Which of the above items may be deducted on Michelle's 2020 individual income tax return?

$ _____

Explain _____

_____

LO 12.3

5. Linda underpaid her taxes for the current year by $4,000 due to negligence.
   a. Calculate Linda's accuracy-related penalty for negligence.

$ _____

   b. Assume that the underpayment of taxes by Linda was determined to be fraudulent, and calculate the total amount of Linda's fraud penalty.

$ _____

LO 12.3

6. For each of the following situations, indicate the nature and amount of the penalty that could be imposed.

	Description of the Penalty	*Penalty Amount*
a. Larry is a tax protester and files his tax return in the name of "Mickey Mouse."	_____	$ _____
b. Anne writes a check for $900 in payment of her taxes that she knows will not clear the bank due to insufficient funds in her account.	_____	$ _____
c. Gerald understated his tax liability by $10,000. The total amount of tax that should have been shown on his return was $70,000.	_____	$ _____

LO 12.3
LO 12.4
LO 12.5
LO 12.6

7. Indicate whether the following statements are true or false:

   _____ The tax law includes a penalty for writing a "bad" check in payment of the taxpayer's tax liability.
   _____ The statute of limitations for a tax return is normally 4 years.
   _____ If a fraudulent tax return is filed, the IRS may assess a deficiency at any time in the future.
   _____ Enrolled agents work for the IRS.

_____ A commercial tax preparer may represent tax clients in any proceeding with the IRS.

_____ The IRS is entitled to choose a place and time for an audit, without regard to the inconvenience to the taxpayer or the reasonableness of the request.

LO 12.4

8. Indicate the date that the statute of limitations would run out on each of the following 2020 individual tax returns:

a. A fraudulent tax return that was filed April 15, 2021   _____
b. A tax return that was filed May 19, 2021   _____
c. A tax return that was filed February 12, 2021   _____
d. A tax return that was filed March 1, 2021, and   _____
  omitted $15,000 in income. The total gross income
  shown on the tax return was $50,000

LO 12.5

9. For each of the following situations, indicate the amount of the penalty that could be imposed on the tax return preparer:

a. A tax return preparer understates the taxpayer's tax $ _____
  liability with a frivolous position and does not disclose
  the position.
b. A tax return preparer fails to furnish his identifying $ _____
  number.
c. A tax return preparer aids a taxpayer in understating a $ _____
  tax liability.
d. A tax return preparer endorses and cashes a client's tax $ _____
  refund check.

LO 12.5

10. Classify each of the following as an enrolled or unenrolled preparer:
a. Certified public accountant
b. Enrolled agent
c. A preparer that has completed the annual filing season program
d. An attorney

LO 12.6

11. The Taxpayer Bill of Rights lists 10 different rights. Name four of those rights.

_____
_____
_____
_____

LO 12.7

12. Indicate whether the following statements are true or false:

_____ Decreasing one's tax liability through legal methods is called tax planning, while illegally reducing taxes is called tax evasion.

_____ In a "closed" transaction, all tax-significant events have been completed.

_____ The marginal tax rate is computed as the total tax paid divided by the total income of the taxpayer.

_____ The marginal tax rate is the most important rate for decision making in tax planning situations.

_____ The timing tax planning technique usually takes advantage of deferring the payment of tax until a later year.

Tax Rate Schedules and Tax Table

CONTENTS

2020 Tax Rate Schedules

 CAUTION

The Tax Rate Schedules are shown so you can see the tax rate that applies to all levels of taxable income. Don't use them to figure your tax. Instead, see the instructions for line 16.

Schedule X—If your filing status is **Single**

If your taxable income is: Over—	But not over—	The tax is:	of the amount over—
$0	$9,875	---------- 10%	$0
9,875	40,125	$987.50 + 12%	9,875
40,125	85,525	4,617.50 + 22%	40,125
85,525	163,300	14,605.50 + 24%	85,525
163,300	207,350	33,271.50 + 32%	163,300
207,350	518,400	47,367.50 + 35%	207,350
518,400	----------	156,235.00 + 37%	518,400

Schedule Y-1—If your filing status is **Married filing jointly** or **Qualifying widow(er)**

If your taxable income is: Over—	But not over—	The tax is:	of the amount over—
$0	$19,750	---------- 10%	$0
19,750	80,250	$1,975.00 + 12%	19,750
80,250	171,050	9,235.00 + 22%	80,250
171,050	326,600	29,211.00 + 24%	171,050
326,600	414,700	66,543.00 + 32%	326,600
414,700	622,050	94,735.00 + 35%	414,700
622,050	----------	167,307.50 + 37%	622,050

Schedule Y-2—If your filing status is **Married filing separately**

If your taxable income is: Over—	But not over—	The tax is:	of the amount over—
$0	$9,875	---------- 10%	$0
9,875	40,125	$987.50 + 12%	9,875
40,125	85,525	4,617.50 + 22%	40,125
85,525	163,300	14,605.50 + 24%	85,525
163,300	207,350	33,271.50 + 32%	163,300
207,350	311,025	47,367.50 + 35%	207,350
311,025	----------	83,653.75 + 37%	311,025

Schedule Z—If your filing status is **Head of household**

If your taxable income is: Over—	But not over—	The tax is:	of the amount over—
$0	$14,100	---------- 10%	$0
14,100	53,700	$1,410.00 + 12%	14,100
53,700	85,500	6,162.00 + 22%	53,700
85,500	163,300	13,158.00 + 24%	85,500
163,300	207,350	31,830.00 + 32%	163,300
207,350	518,400	45,926.00 + 35%	207,350
518,400	----------	154,793.50 + 37%	518,400

Note: The tax rate schedules for income of at least $100,000 are presented in the traditional "additive" format on this page and in the somewhat lesser used "deductive" style on Page A-3. Both formats will compute the same tax amounts for taxable income of at least $100,000.

2020 Tax Computation Worksheet

Section A—Use if your filing status is **Single.** Complete the row below that applies to you.

Taxable income. If line 15 is—	(a) Enter the amount from line 15	(b) Multiplication amount	(c) Multiply (a) by (b)	(d) Subtraction amount	Tax. Subtract (d) from (c). Enter the result here and on the entry space on line 16.
At least $100,000 but not over $163,300	$	× 24% (0.24)	$	$ 5,920.50	$
Over $163,300 but not over $207,350	$	× 32% (0.32)	$	$ 18,984.50	$
Over $207,350 but not over $518,400	$	× 35% (0.35)	$	$ 25,205.00	$
Over $518,400	$	× 37% (0.37)	$	$ 35,573.00	$

Section B—Use if your filing status is **Married filing jointly** or **Qualifying widow(er).** Complete the row below that applies to you.

Taxable income. If line 15 is—	(a) Enter the amount from line 15	(b) Multiplication amount	(c) Multiply (a) by (b)	(d) Subtraction amount	Tax. Subtract (d) from (c). Enter the result here and on the entry space on line 16.
At least $100,000 but not over $171,050	$	× 22% (0.22)	$	$ 8,420.00	$
Over $171,050 but not over $326,600	$	× 24% (0.24)	$	$ 11,841.00	$
Over $326,600 but not over $414,700	$	× 32% (0.32)	$	$ 37,969.00	$
Over $414,700 but not over $622,050	$	× 35% (0.35)	$	$ 50,410.00	$
Over $622,050	$	× 37% (0.37)	$	$ 62,851.00	$

Section C—Use if your filing status is **Married filing separately.** Complete the row below that applies to you.

Taxable income. If line 15 is—	(a) Enter the amount from line 15	(b) Multiplication amount	(c) Multiply (a) by (b)	(d) Subtraction amount	Tax. Subtract (d) from (c). Enter the result here and on the entry space on line 16.
At least $100,000 but not over $163,300	$	× 24% (0.24)	$	$ 5,920.50	$
Over $163.300 but not over $207,350	$	× 32% (0.32)	$	$ 18,984.50	$
Over $207,350 but not over $311,025	$	× 35% (0.35)	$	$ 25,205.00	$
Over $311,025	$	× 37% (0.37)	$	$ 31,425.50	$

Section D—Use if your filing status is **Head of household.** Complete the row below that applies to you.

Taxable income. If line 15 is—	(a) Enter the amount from line 15	(b) Multiplication amount	(c) Multiply (a) by (b)	(d) Subtraction amount	Tax. Subtract (d) from (c). Enter the result here and on the entry space on line 16.
At least $100,000 but not over $163,300	$	× 24% (0.24)	$	$ 7,362.00	$
Over $163,300 but not over $207,350	$	× 32% (0.32)	$	$ 20,426.00	$
Over $207,350 but not over $518,400	$	× 35% (0.35)	$	$ 26,646.50	$
Over $518,400	$	× 37% (0.37)	$	$ 37,014.50	$

2020 Tax Table

See the instructions for line 16 to see if you must use the Tax Table below to figure your tax.

Example. Mr. and Mrs. Brown are filing a joint return. Their taxable income on Form 1040, line 15, is $25,300. First, they find the $25,300–25,350 taxable income line. Next, they find the column for married filing jointly and read down the column. The amount shown where the taxable income line and filing status column meet is $2,644. This is the tax amount they should enter in the entry space on Form 1040, line 16.

Sample Table

At Least	But Less Than	Single	Married filing jointly*	Married filing separately	Head of a house-hold
			Your tax is—		
25,200	25,250	2,830	2,632	2,830	2,745
25,250	25,300	2,836	2,638	2,836	2,751
25,300	25,350	2,842	(2,644)	2,842	2,757
25,350	25,400	2,848	2,650	2,848	2,763

If line 15 (taxable income) is—		And you are—			
At least	But less than	Single	Married filing jointly *	Married filing sepa-rately	Head of a house-hold
			Your tax is—		
0	5	0	0	0	0
5	15	1	1	1	1
15	25	2	2	2	2
25	50	4	4	4	4
50	75	6	6	6	6
75	100	9	9	9	9
100	125	11	11	11	11
125	150	14	14	14	14
150	175	16	16	16	16
175	200	19	19	19	19
200	225	21	21	21	21
225	250	24	24	24	24
250	275	26	26	26	26
275	300	29	29	29	29
300	325	31	31	31	31
325	350	34	34	34	34
350	375	36	36	36	36
375	400	39	39	39	39
400	425	41	41	41	41
425	450	44	44	44	44
450	475	46	46	46	46
475	500	49	49	49	49
500	525	51	51	51	51
525	550	54	54	54	54
550	575	56	56	56	56
575	600	59	59	59	59
600	625	61	61	61	61
625	650	64	64	64	64
650	675	66	66	66	66
675	700	69	69	69	69
700	725	71	71	71	71
725	750	74	74	74	74
750	775	76	76	76	76
775	800	79	79	79	79
800	825	81	81	81	81
825	850	84	84	84	84
850	875	86	86	86	86
875	900	89	89	89	89
900	925	91	91	91	91
925	950	94	94	94	94
950	975	96	96	96	96
975	1,000	99	99	99	99

1,000

If line 15 (taxable income) is—		And you are—			
At least	But less than	Single	Married filing jointly *	Married filing sepa-rately	Head of a house-hold
			Your tax is—		
1,000	1,025	101	101	101	101
1,025	1,050	104	104	104	104
1,050	1,075	106	106	106	106
1,075	1,100	109	109	109	109
1,100	1,125	111	111	111	111
1,125	1,150	114	114	114	114
1,150	1,175	116	116	116	116
1,175	1,200	119	119	119	119
1,200	1,225	121	121	121	121
1,225	1,250	124	124	124	124
1,250	1,275	126	126	126	126
1,275	1,300	129	129	129	129
1,300	1,325	131	131	131	131
1,325	1,350	134	134	134	134
1,350	1,375	136	136	136	136
1,375	1,400	139	139	139	139
1,400	1,425	141	141	141	141
1,425	1,450	144	144	144	144
1,450	1,475	146	146	146	146
1,475	1,500	149	149	149	149
1,500	1,525	151	151	151	151
1,525	1,550	154	154	154	154
1,550	1,575	156	156	156	156
1,575	1,600	159	159	159	159
1,600	1,625	161	161	161	161
1,625	1,650	164	164	164	164
1,650	1,675	166	166	166	166
1,675	1,700	169	169	169	169
1,700	1,725	171	171	171	171
1,725	1,750	174	174	174	174
1,750	1,775	176	176	176	176
1,775	1,800	179	179	179	179
1,800	1,825	181	181	181	181
1,825	1,850	184	184	184	184
1,850	1,875	186	186	186	186
1,875	1,900	189	189	189	189
1,900	1,925	191	191	191	191
1,925	1,950	194	194	194	194
1,950	1,975	196	196	196	196
1,975	2,000	199	199	199	199

2,000

If line 15 (taxable income) is—		And you are—			
At least	But less than	Single	Married filing jointly *	Married filing sepa-rately	Head of a house-hold
			Your tax is—		
2,000	2,025	201	201	201	201
2,025	2,050	204	204	204	204
2,050	2,075	206	206	206	206
2,075	2,100	209	209	209	209
2,100	2,125	211	211	211	211
2,125	2,150	214	214	214	214
2,150	2,175	216	216	216	216
2,175	2,200	219	219	219	219
2,200	2,225	221	221	221	221
2,225	2,250	224	224	224	224
2,250	2,275	226	226	226	226
2,275	2,300	229	229	229	229
2,300	2,325	231	231	231	231
2,325	2,350	234	234	234	234
2,350	2,375	236	236	236	236
2,375	2,400	239	239	239	239
2,400	2,425	241	241	241	241
2,425	2,450	244	244	244	244
2,450	2,475	246	246	246	246
2,475	2,500	249	249	249	249
2,500	2,525	251	251	251	251
2,525	2,550	254	254	254	254
2,550	2,575	256	256	256	256
2,575	2,600	259	259	259	259
2,600	2,625	261	261	261	261
2,625	2,650	264	264	264	264
2,650	2,675	266	266	266	266
2,675	2,700	269	269	269	269
2,700	2,725	271	271	271	271
2,725	2,750	274	274	274	274
2,750	2,775	276	276	276	276
2,775	2,800	279	279	279	279
2,800	2,825	281	281	281	281
2,825	2,850	284	284	284	284
2,850	2,875	286	286	286	286
2,875	2,900	289	289	289	289
2,900	2,925	291	291	291	291
2,925	2,950	294	294	294	294
2,950	2,975	296	296	296	296
2,975	3,000	299	299	299	299

* This column must also be used by a qualifying widow(er).

(Continued)

3,000

If line 15 (taxable income) is—		And you are—			
At least	But less than	Single	Married filing jointly *	Married filing separately	Head of a house-hold
		Your tax is—			
3,000	3,050	303	303	303	303
3,050	3,100	308	308	308	308
3,100	3,150	313	313	313	313
3,150	3,200	318	318	318	318
3,200	3,250	323	323	323	323
3,250	3,300	328	328	328	328
3,300	3,350	333	333	333	333
3,350	3,400	338	338	338	338
3,400	3,450	343	343	343	343
3,450	3,500	348	348	348	348
3,500	3,550	353	353	353	353
3,550	3,600	358	358	358	358
3,600	3,650	363	363	363	363
3,650	3,700	368	368	368	368
3,700	3,750	373	373	373	373
3,750	3,800	378	378	378	378
3,800	3,850	383	383	383	383
3,850	3,900	388	388	388	388
3,900	3,950	393	393	393	393
3,950	4,000	398	398	398	398

4,000

At least	But less than	Single	Married filing jointly *	Married filing separately	Head of a house-hold
4,000	4,050	403	403	403	403
4,050	4,100	408	408	408	408
4,100	4,150	413	413	413	413
4,150	4,200	418	418	418	418
4,200	4,250	423	423	423	423
4,250	4,300	428	428	428	428
4,300	4,350	433	433	433	433
4,350	4,400	438	438	438	438
4,400	4,450	443	443	443	443
4,450	4,500	448	448	448	448
4,500	4,550	453	453	453	453
4,550	4,600	458	458	458	458
4,600	4,650	463	463	463	463
4,650	4,700	468	468	468	468
4,700	4,750	473	473	473	473
4,750	4,800	478	478	478	478
4,800	4,850	483	483	483	483
4,850	4,900	488	488	488	488
4,900	4,950	493	493	493	493
4,950	5,000	498	498	498	498

5,000

At least	But less than	Single	Married filing jointly *	Married filing separately	Head of a house-hold
5,000	5,050	503	503	503	503
5,050	5,100	508	508	508	508
5,100	5,150	513	513	513	513
5,150	5,200	518	518	518	518
5,200	5,250	523	523	523	523
5,250	5,300	528	528	528	528
5,300	5,350	533	533	533	533
5,350	5,400	538	538	538	538
5,400	5,450	543	543	543	543
5,450	5,500	548	548	548	548
5,500	5,550	553	553	553	553
5,550	5,600	558	558	558	558
5,600	5,650	563	563	563	563
5,650	5,700	568	568	568	568
5,700	5,750	573	573	573	573
5,750	5,800	578	578	578	578
5,800	5,850	583	583	583	583
5,850	5,900	588	588	588	588
5,900	5,950	593	593	593	593
5,950	6,000	598	598	598	598

6,000

If line 15 (taxable income) is—		And you are—			
At least	But less than	Single	Married filing jointly *	Married filing separately	Head of a house-hold
		Your tax is—			
6,000	6,050	603	603	603	603
6,050	6,100	608	608	608	608
6,100	6,150	613	613	613	613
6,150	6,200	618	618	618	618
6,200	6,250	623	623	623	623
6,250	6,300	628	628	628	628
6,300	6,350	633	633	633	633
6,350	6,400	638	638	638	638
6,400	6,450	643	643	643	643
6,450	6,500	648	648	648	648
6,500	6,550	653	653	653	653
6,550	6,600	658	658	658	658
6,600	6,650	663	663	663	663
6,650	6,700	668	668	668	668
6,700	6,750	673	673	673	673
6,750	6,800	678	678	678	678
6,800	6,850	683	683	683	683
6,850	6,900	688	688	688	688
6,900	6,950	693	693	693	693
6,950	7,000	698	698	698	698

7,000

At least	But less than	Single	Married filing jointly *	Married filing separately	Head of a house-hold
7,000	7,050	703	703	703	703
7,050	7,100	708	708	708	708
7,100	7,150	713	713	713	713
7,150	7,200	718	718	718	718
7,200	7,250	723	723	723	723
7,250	7,300	728	728	728	728
7,300	7,350	733	733	733	733
7,350	7,400	738	738	738	738
7,400	7,450	743	743	743	743
7,450	7,500	748	748	748	748
7,500	7,550	753	753	753	753
7,550	7,600	758	758	758	758
7,600	7,650	763	763	763	763
7,650	7,700	768	768	768	768
7,700	7,750	773	773	773	773
7,750	7,800	778	778	778	778
7,800	7,850	783	783	783	783
7,850	7,900	788	788	788	788
7,900	7,950	793	793	793	793
7,950	8,000	798	798	798	798

8,000

At least	But less than	Single	Married filing jointly *	Married filing separately	Head of a house-hold
8,000	8,050	803	803	803	803
8,050	8,100	808	808	808	808
8,100	8,150	813	813	813	813
8,150	8,200	818	818	818	818
8,200	8,250	823	823	823	823
8,250	8,300	828	828	828	828
8,300	8,350	833	833	833	833
8,350	8,400	838	838	838	838
8,400	8,450	843	843	843	843
8,450	8,500	848	848	848	848
8,500	8,550	853	853	853	853
8,550	8,600	858	858	858	858
8,600	8,650	863	863	863	863
8,650	8,700	868	868	868	868
8,700	8,750	873	873	873	873
8,750	8,800	878	878	878	878
8,800	8,850	883	883	883	883
8,850	8,900	888	888	888	888
8,900	8,950	893	893	893	893
8,950	9,000	898	898	898	898

9,000

If line 15 (taxable income) is—		And you are—			
At least	But less than	Single	Married filing jointly *	Married filing separately	Head of a house-hold
		Your tax is—			
9,000	9,050	903	903	903	903
9,050	9,100	908	908	908	908
9,100	9,150	913	913	913	913
9,150	9,200	918	918	918	918
9,200	9,250	923	923	923	923
9,250	9,300	928	928	928	928
9,300	9,350	933	933	933	933
9,350	9,400	938	938	938	938
9,400	9,450	943	943	943	943
9,450	9,500	948	948	948	948
9,500	9,550	953	953	953	953
9,550	9,600	958	958	958	958
9,600	9,650	963	963	963	963
9,650	9,700	968	968	968	968
9,700	9,750	973	973	973	973
9,750	9,800	978	978	978	978
9,800	9,850	983	983	983	983
9,850	9,900	988	988	988	988
9,900	9,950	994	993	994	993
9,950	10,000	1,000	998	1,000	998

10,000

At least	But less than	Single	Married filing jointly *	Married filing separately	Head of a house-hold
10,000	10,050	1,006	1,003	1,006	1,003
10,050	10,100	1,012	1,008	1,012	1,008
10,100	10,150	1,018	1,013	1,018	1,013
10,150	10,200	1,024	1,018	1,024	1,018
10,200	10,250	1,030	1,023	1,030	1,023
10,250	10,300	1,036	1,028	1,036	1,028
10,300	10,350	1,042	1,033	1,042	1,033
10,350	10,400	1,048	1,038	1,048	1,038
10,400	10,450	1,054	1,043	1,054	1,043
10,450	10,500	1,060	1,048	1,060	1,048
10,500	10,550	1,066	1,053	1,066	1,053
10,550	10,600	1,072	1,058	1,072	1,058
10,600	10,650	1,078	1,063	1,078	1,063
10,650	10,700	1,084	1,068	1,084	1,068
10,700	10,750	1,090	1,073	1,090	1,073
10,750	10,800	1,096	1,078	1,096	1,078
10,800	10,850	1,102	1,083	1,102	1,083
10,850	10,900	1,108	1,088	1,108	1,088
10,900	10,950	1,114	1,093	1,114	1,093
10,950	11,000	1,120	1,098	1,120	1,098

11,000

At least	But less than	Single	Married filing jointly *	Married filing separately	Head of a house-hold
11,000	11,050	1,126	1,103	1,126	1,103
11,050	11,100	1,132	1,108	1,132	1,108
11,100	11,150	1,138	1,113	1,138	1,113
11,150	11,200	1,144	1,118	1,144	1,118
11,200	11,250	1,150	1,123	1,150	1,123
11,250	11,300	1,156	1,128	1,156	1,128
11,300	11,350	1,162	1,133	1,162	1,133
11,350	11,400	1,168	1,138	1,168	1,138
11,400	11,450	1,174	1,143	1,174	1,143
11,450	11,500	1,180	1,148	1,180	1,148
11,500	11,550	1,186	1,153	1,186	1,153
11,550	11,600	1,192	1,158	1,192	1,158
11,600	11,650	1,198	1,163	1,198	1,163
11,650	11,700	1,204	1,168	1,204	1,168
11,700	11,750	1,210	1,173	1,210	1,173
11,750	11,800	1,216	1,178	1,216	1,178
11,800	11,850	1,222	1,183	1,222	1,183
11,850	11,900	1,228	1,188	1,228	1,188
11,900	11,950	1,234	1,193	1,234	1,193
11,950	12,000	1,240	1,198	1,240	1,198

(Continued)

* This column must also be used by a qualifying widow(er).

12,000

At least	But less than	Single	Married filing jointly *	Married filing separately	Head of a household
				Your tax is—	
12,000	12,050	1,246	1,203	1,246	1,203
12,050	12,100	1,252	1,208	1,252	1,208
12,100	12,150	1,258	1,213	1,258	1,213
12,150	12,200	1,264	1,218	1,264	1,218
12,200	12,250	1,270	1,223	1,270	1,223
12,250	12,300	1,276	1,228	1,276	1,228
12,300	12,350	1,282	1,233	1,282	1,233
12,350	12,400	1,288	1,238	1,288	1,238
12,400	12,450	1,294	1,243	1,294	1,243
12,450	12,500	1,300	1,248	1,300	1,248
12,500	12,550	1,306	1,253	1,306	1,253
12,550	12,600	1,312	1,258	1,312	1,258
12,600	12,650	1,318	1,263	1,318	1,263
12,650	12,700	1,324	1,268	1,324	1,268
12,700	12,750	1,330	1,273	1,330	1,273
12,750	12,800	1,336	1,278	1,336	1,278
12,800	12,850	1,342	1,283	1,342	1,283
12,850	12,900	1,348	1,288	1,348	1,288
12,900	12,950	1,354	1,293	1,354	1,293
12,950	13,000	1,360	1,298	1,360	1,298

13,000

At least	But less than	Single	Married filing jointly *	Married filing separately	Head of a household
13,000	13,050	1,366	1,303	1,366	1,303
13,050	13,100	1,372	1,308	1,372	1,308
13,100	13,150	1,378	1,313	1,378	1,313
13,150	13,200	1,384	1,318	1,384	1,318
13,200	13,250	1,390	1,323	1,390	1,323
13,250	13,300	1,396	1,328	1,396	1,328
13,300	13,350	1,402	1,333	1,402	1,333
13,350	13,400	1,408	1,338	1,408	1,338
13,400	13,450	1,414	1,343	1,414	1,343
13,450	13,500	1,420	1,348	1,420	1,348
13,500	13,550	1,426	1,353	1,426	1,353
13,550	13,600	1,432	1,358	1,432	1,358
13,600	13,650	1,438	1,363	1,438	1,363
13,650	13,700	1,444	1,368	1,444	1,368
13,700	13,750	1,450	1,373	1,450	1,373
13,750	13,800	1,456	1,378	1,456	1,378
13,800	13,850	1,462	1,383	1,462	1,383
13,850	13,900	1,468	1,388	1,468	1,388
13,900	13,950	1,474	1,393	1,474	1,393
13,950	14,000	1,480	1,398	1,480	1,398

14,000

At least	But less than	Single	Married filing jointly *	Married filing separately	Head of a household
14,000	14,050	1,486	1,403	1,486	1,403
14,050	14,100	1,492	1,408	1,492	1,408
14,100	14,150	1,498	1,413	1,498	1,413
14,150	14,200	1,504	1,418	1,504	1,419
14,200	14,250	1,510	1,423	1,510	1,425
14,250	14,300	1,516	1,428	1,516	1,431
14,300	14,350	1,522	1,433	1,522	1,437
14,350	14,400	1,528	1,438	1,528	1,443
14,400	14,450	1,534	1,443	1,534	1,449
14,450	14,500	1,540	1,448	1,540	1,455
14,500	14,550	1,546	1,453	1,546	1,461
14,550	14,600	1,552	1,458	1,552	1,467
14,600	14,650	1,558	1,463	1,558	1,473
14,650	14,700	1,564	1,468	1,564	1,479
14,700	14,750	1,570	1,473	1,570	1,485
14,750	14,800	1,576	1,478	1,576	1,491
14,800	14,850	1,582	1,483	1,582	1,497
14,850	14,900	1,588	1,488	1,588	1,503
14,900	14,950	1,594	1,493	1,594	1,509
14,950	15,000	1,600	1,498	1,600	1,515

15,000

At least	But less than	Single	Married filing jointly *	Married filing separately	Head of a household
				Your tax is—	
15,000	15,050	1,606	1,503	1,606	1,521
15,050	15,100	1,612	1,508	1,612	1,527
15,100	15,150	1,618	1,513	1,618	1,533
15,150	15,200	1,624	1,518	1,624	1,539
15,200	15,250	1,630	1,523	1,630	1,545
15,250	15,300	1,636	1,528	1,636	1,551
15,300	15,350	1,642	1,533	1,642	1,557
15,350	15,400	1,648	1,538	1,648	1,563
15,400	15,450	1,654	1,543	1,654	1,569
15,450	15,500	1,660	1,548	1,660	1,575
15,500	15,550	1,666	1,553	1,666	1,581
15,550	15,600	1,672	1,558	1,672	1,587
15,600	15,650	1,678	1,563	1,678	1,593
15,650	15,700	1,684	1,568	1,684	1,599
15,700	15,750	1,690	1,573	1,690	1,605
15,750	15,800	1,696	1,578	1,696	1,611
15,800	15,850	1,702	1,583	1,702	1,617
15,850	15,900	1,708	1,588	1,708	1,623
15,900	15,950	1,714	1,593	1,714	1,629
15,950	16,000	1,720	1,598	1,720	1,635

16,000

At least	But less than	Single	Married filing jointly *	Married filing separately	Head of a household
16,000	16,050	1,726	1,603	1,726	1,641
16,050	16,100	1,732	1,608	1,732	1,647
16,100	16,150	1,738	1,613	1,738	1,653
16,150	16,200	1,744	1,618	1,744	1,659
16,200	16,250	1,750	1,623	1,750	1,665
16,250	16,300	1,756	1,628	1,756	1,671
16,300	16,350	1,762	1,633	1,762	1,677
16,350	16,400	1,768	1,638	1,768	1,683
16,400	16,450	1,774	1,643	1,774	1,689
16,450	16,500	1,780	1,648	1,780	1,695
16,500	16,550	1,786	1,653	1,786	1,701
16,550	16,600	1,792	1,658	1,792	1,707
16,600	16,650	1,798	1,663	1,798	1,713
16,650	16,700	1,804	1,668	1,804	1,719
16,700	16,750	1,810	1,673	1,810	1,725
16,750	16,800	1,816	1,678	1,816	1,731
16,800	16,850	1,822	1,683	1,822	1,737
16,850	16,900	1,828	1,688	1,828	1,743
16,900	16,950	1,834	1,693	1,834	1,749
16,950	17,000	1,840	1,698	1,840	1,755

17,000

At least	But less than	Single	Married filing jointly *	Married filing separately	Head of a household
17,000	17,050	1,846	1,703	1,846	1,761
17,050	17,100	1,852	1,708	1,852	1,767
17,100	17,150	1,858	1,713	1,858	1,773
17,150	17,200	1,864	1,718	1,864	1,779
17,200	17,250	1,870	1,723	1,870	1,785
17,250	17,300	1,876	1,728	1,876	1,791
17,300	17,350	1,882	1,733	1,882	1,797
17,350	17,400	1,888	1,738	1,888	1,803
17,400	17,450	1,894	1,743	1,894	1,809
17,450	17,500	1,900	1,748	1,900	1,815
17,500	17,550	1,906	1,753	1,906	1,821
17,550	17,600	1,912	1,758	1,912	1,827
17,600	17,650	1,918	1,763	1,918	1,833
17,650	17,700	1,924	1,768	1,924	1,839
17,700	17,750	1,930	1,773	1,930	1,845
17,750	17,800	1,936	1,778	1,936	1,851
17,800	17,850	1,942	1,783	1,942	1,857
17,850	17,900	1,948	1,788	1,948	1,863
17,900	17,950	1,954	1,793	1,954	1,869
17,950	18,000	1,960	1,798	1,960	1,875

18,000

At least	But less than	Single	Married filing jointly *	Married filing separately	Head of a household
				Your tax is—	
18,000	18,050	1,966	1,803	1,966	1,881
18,050	18,100	1,972	1,808	1,972	1,887
18,100	18,150	1,978	1,813	1,978	1,893
18,150	18,200	1,984	1,818	1,984	1,899
18,200	18,250	1,990	1,823	1,990	1,905
18,250	18,300	1,996	1,828	1,996	1,911
18,300	18,350	2,002	1,833	2,002	1,917
18,350	18,400	2,008	1,838	2,008	1,923
18,400	18,450	2,014	1,843	2,014	1,929
18,450	18,500	2,020	1,848	2,020	1,935
18,500	18,550	2,026	1,853	2,026	1,941
18,550	18,600	2,032	1,858	2,032	1,947
18,600	18,650	2,038	1,863	2,038	1,953
18,650	18,700	2,044	1,868	2,044	1,959
18,700	18,750	2,050	1,873	2,050	1,965
18,750	18,800	2,056	1,878	2,056	1,971
18,800	18,850	2,062	1,883	2,062	1,977
18,850	18,900	2,068	1,888	2,068	1,983
18,900	18,950	2,074	1,893	2,074	1,989
18,950	19,000	2,080	1,898	2,080	1,995

19,000

At least	But less than	Single	Married filing jointly *	Married filing separately	Head of a household
19,000	19,050	2,086	1,903	2,086	2,001
19,050	19,100	2,092	1,908	2,092	2,007
19,100	19,150	2,098	1,913	2,098	2,013
19,150	19,200	2,104	1,918	2,104	2,019
19,200	19,250	2,110	1,923	2,110	2,025
19,250	19,300	2,116	1,928	2,116	2,031
19,300	19,350	2,122	1,933	2,122	2,037
19,350	19,400	2,128	1,938	2,128	2,043
19,400	19,450	2,134	1,943	2,134	2,049
19,450	19,500	2,140	1,948	2,140	2,055
19,500	19,550	2,146	1,953	2,146	2,061
19,550	19,600	2,152	1,958	2,152	2,067
19,600	19,650	2,158	1,963	2,158	2,073
19,650	19,700	2,164	1,968	2,164	2,079
19,700	19,750	2,170	1,973	2,170	2,085
19,750	19,800	2,176	1,978	2,176	2,091
19,800	19,850	2,182	1,984	2,182	2,097
19,850	19,900	2,188	1,990	2,188	2,103
19,900	19,950	2,194	1,996	2,194	2,109
19,950	20,000	2,200	2,002	2,200	2,115

20,000

At least	But less than	Single	Married filing jointly *	Married filing separately	Head of a household
20,000	20,050	2,206	2,008	2,206	2,121
20,050	20,100	2,212	2,014	2,212	2,127
20,100	20,150	2,218	2,020	2,218	2,133
20,150	20,200	2,224	2,026	2,224	2,139
20,200	20,250	2,230	2,032	2,230	2,145
20,250	20,300	2,236	2,038	2,236	2,151
20,300	20,350	2,242	2,044	2,242	2,157
20,350	20,400	2,248	2,050	2,248	2,163
20,400	20,450	2,254	2,056	2,254	2,169
20,450	20,500	2,260	2,062	2,260	2,175
20,500	20,550	2,266	2,068	2,266	2,181
20,550	20,600	2,272	2,074	2,272	2,187
20,600	20,650	2,278	2,080	2,278	2,193
20,650	20,700	2,284	2,086	2,284	2,199
20,700	20,750	2,290	2,092	2,290	2,205
20,750	20,800	2,296	2,098	2,296	2,211
20,800	20,850	2,302	2,104	2,302	2,217
20,850	20,900	2,308	2,110	2,308	2,223
20,900	20,950	2,314	2,116	2,314	2,229
20,950	21,000	2,320	2,122	2,320	2,235

* This column must also be used by a qualifying widow(er).

(Continued)

2020 Tax Table — *Continued*

If line 15 (taxable income) is—		And you are—			
At least	But less than	Single	Married filing jointly *	Married filing separately	Head of a household
		Your tax is—			

21,000

At least	But less than	Single	Married filing jointly *	Married filing separately	Head of a household
21,000	21,050	2,326	2,128	2,326	2,241
21,050	21,100	2,332	2,134	2,332	2,247
21,100	21,150	2,338	2,140	2,338	2,253
21,150	21,200	2,344	2,146	2,344	2,259
21,200	21,250	2,350	2,152	2,350	2,265
21,250	21,300	2,356	2,158	2,356	2,271
21,300	21,350	2,362	2,164	2,362	2,277
21,350	21,400	2,368	2,170	2,368	2,283
21,400	21,450	2,374	2,176	2,374	2,289
21,450	21,500	2,380	2,182	2,380	2,295
21,500	21,550	2,386	2,188	2,386	2,301
21,550	21,600	2,392	2,194	2,392	2,307
21,600	21,650	2,398	2,200	2,398	2,313
21,650	21,700	2,404	2,206	2,404	2,319
21,700	21,750	2,410	2,212	2,410	2,325
21,750	21,800	2,416	2,218	2,416	2,331
21,800	21,850	2,422	2,224	2,422	2,337
21,850	21,900	2,428	2,230	2,428	2,343
21,900	21,950	2,434	2,236	2,434	2,349
21,950	22,000	2,440	2,242	2,440	2,355

22,000

At least	But less than	Single	Married filing jointly *	Married filing separately	Head of a household
22,000	22,050	2,446	2,248	2,446	2,361
22,050	22,100	2,452	2,254	2,452	2,367
22,100	22,150	2,458	2,260	2,458	2,373
22,150	22,200	2,464	2,266	2,464	2,379
22,200	22,250	2,470	2,272	2,470	2,385
22,250	22,300	2,476	2,278	2,476	2,391
22,300	22,350	2,482	2,284	2,482	2,397
22,350	22,400	2,488	2,290	2,488	2,403
22,400	22,450	2,494	2,296	2,494	2,409
22,450	22,500	2,500	2,302	2,500	2,415
22,500	22,550	2,506	2,308	2,506	2,421
22,550	22,600	2,512	2,314	2,512	2,427
22,600	22,650	2,518	2,320	2,518	2,433
22,650	22,700	2,524	2,326	2,524	2,439
22,700	22,750	2,530	2,332	2,530	2,445
22,750	22,800	2,536	2,338	2,536	2,451
22,800	22,850	2,542	2,344	2,542	2,457
22,850	22,900	2,548	2,350	2,548	2,463
22,900	22,950	2,554	2,356	2,554	2,469
22,950	23,000	2,560	2,362	2,560	2,475

23,000

At least	But less than	Single	Married filing jointly *	Married filing separately	Head of a household
23,000	23,050	2,566	2,368	2,566	2,481
23,050	23,100	2,572	2,374	2,572	2,487
23,100	23,150	2,578	2,380	2,578	2,493
23,150	23,200	2,584	2,386	2,584	2,499
23,200	23,250	2,590	2,392	2,590	2,505
23,250	23,300	2,596	2,398	2,596	2,511
23,300	23,350	2,602	2,404	2,602	2,517
23,350	23,400	2,608	2,410	2,608	2,523
23,400	23,450	2,614	2,416	2,614	2,529
23,450	23,500	2,620	2,422	2,620	2,535
23,500	23,550	2,626	2,428	2,626	2,541
23,550	23,600	2,632	2,434	2,632	2,547
23,600	23,650	2,638	2,440	2,638	2,553
23,650	23,700	2,644	2,446	2,644	2,559
23,700	23,750	2,650	2,452	2,650	2,565
23,750	23,800	2,656	2,458	2,656	2,571
23,800	23,850	2,662	2,464	2,662	2,577
23,850	23,900	2,668	2,470	2,668	2,583
23,900	23,950	2,674	2,476	2,674	2,589
23,950	24,000	2,680	2,482	2,680	2,595

24,000

At least	But less than	Single	Married filing jointly *	Married filing separately	Head of a household
24,000	24,050	2,686	2,488	2,686	2,601
24,050	24,100	2,692	2,494	2,692	2,607
24,100	24,150	2,698	2,500	2,698	2,613
24,150	24,200	2,704	2,506	2,704	2,619
24,200	24,250	2,710	2,512	2,710	2,625
24,250	24,300	2,716	2,518	2,716	2,631
24,300	24,350	2,722	2,524	2,722	2,637
24,350	24,400	2,728	2,530	2,728	2,643
24,400	24,450	2,734	2,536	2,734	2,649
24,450	24,500	2,740	2,542	2,740	2,655
24,500	24,550	2,746	2,548	2,746	2,661
24,550	24,600	2,752	2,554	2,752	2,667
24,600	24,650	2,758	2,560	2,758	2,673
24,650	24,700	2,764	2,566	2,764	2,679
24,700	24,750	2,770	2,572	2,770	2,685
24,750	24,800	2,776	2,578	2,776	2,691
24,800	24,850	2,782	2,584	2,782	2,697
24,850	24,900	2,788	2,590	2,788	2,703
24,900	24,950	2,794	2,596	2,794	2,709
24,950	25,000	2,800	2,602	2,800	2,715

25,000

At least	But less than	Single	Married filing jointly *	Married filing separately	Head of a household
25,000	25,050	2,806	2,608	2,806	2,721
25,050	25,100	2,812	2,614	2,812	2,727
25,100	25,150	2,818	2,620	2,818	2,733
25,150	25,200	2,824	2,626	2,824	2,739
25,200	25,250	2,830	2,632	2,830	2,745
25,250	25,300	2,836	2,638	2,836	2,751
25,300	25,350	2,842	2,644	2,842	2,757
25,350	25,400	2,848	2,650	2,848	2,763
25,400	25,450	2,854	2,656	2,854	2,769
25,450	25,500	2,860	2,662	2,860	2,775
25,500	25,550	2,866	2,668	2,866	2,781
25,550	25,600	2,872	2,674	2,872	2,787
25,600	25,650	2,878	2,680	2,878	2,793
25,650	25,700	2,884	2,686	2,884	2,799
25,700	25,750	2,890	2,692	2,890	2,805
25,750	25,800	2,896	2,698	2,896	2,811
25,800	25,850	2,902	2,704	2,902	2,817
25,850	25,900	2,908	2,710	2,908	2,823
25,900	25,950	2,914	2,716	2,914	2,829
25,950	26,000	2,920	2,722	2,920	2,835

26,000

At least	But less than	Single	Married filing jointly *	Married filing separately	Head of a household
26,000	26,050	2,926	2,728	2,926	2,841
26,050	26,100	2,932	2,734	2,932	2,847
26,100	26,150	2,938	2,740	2,938	2,853
26,150	26,200	2,944	2,746	2,944	2,859
26,200	26,250	2,950	2,752	2,950	2,865
26,250	26,300	2,956	2,758	2,956	2,871
26,300	26,350	2,962	2,764	2,962	2,877
26,350	26,400	2,968	2,770	2,968	2,883
26,400	26,450	2,974	2,776	2,974	2,889
26,450	26,500	2,980	2,782	2,980	2,895
26,500	26,550	2,986	2,788	2,986	2,901
26,550	26,600	2,992	2,794	2,992	2,907
26,600	26,650	2,998	2,800	2,998	2,913
26,650	26,700	3,004	2,806	3,004	2,919
26,700	26,750	3,010	2,812	3,010	2,925
26,750	26,800	3,016	2,818	3,016	2,931
26,800	26,850	3,022	2,824	3,022	2,937
26,850	26,900	3,028	2,830	3,028	2,943
26,900	26,950	3,034	2,836	3,034	2,949
26,950	27,000	3,040	2,842	3,040	2,955

27,000

At least	But less than	Single	Married filing jointly *	Married filing separately	Head of a household
27,000	27,050	3,046	2,848	3,046	2,961
27,050	27,100	3,052	2,854	3,052	2,967
27,100	27,150	3,058	2,860	3,058	2,973
27,150	27,200	3,064	2,866	3,064	2,979
27,200	27,250	3,070	2,872	3,070	2,985
27,250	27,300	3,076	2,878	3,076	2,991
27,300	27,350	3,082	2,884	3,082	2,997
27,350	27,400	3,088	2,890	3,088	3,003
27,400	27,450	3,094	2,896	3,094	3,009
27,450	27,500	3,100	2,902	3,100	3,015
27,500	27,550	3,106	2,908	3,106	3,021
27,550	27,600	3,112	2,914	3,112	3,027
27,600	27,650	3,118	2,920	3,118	3,033
27,650	27,700	3,124	2,926	3,124	3,039
27,700	27,750	3,130	2,932	3,130	3,045
27,750	27,800	3,136	2,938	3,136	3,051
27,800	27,850	3,142	2,944	3,142	3,057
27,850	27,900	3,148	2,950	3,148	3,063
27,900	27,950	3,154	2,956	3,154	3,069
27,950	28,000	3,160	2,962	3,160	3,075

28,000

At least	But less than	Single	Married filing jointly *	Married filing separately	Head of a household
28,000	28,050	3,166	2,968	3,166	3,081
28,050	28,100	3,172	2,974	3,172	3,087
28,100	28,150	3,178	2,980	3,178	3,093
28,150	28,200	3,184	2,986	3,184	3,099
28,200	28,250	3,190	2,992	3,190	3,105
28,250	28,300	3,196	2,998	3,196	3,111
28,300	28,350	3,202	3,004	3,202	3,117
28,350	28,400	3,208	3,010	3,208	3,123
28,400	28,450	3,214	3,016	3,214	3,129
28,450	28,500	3,220	3,022	3,220	3,135
28,500	28,550	3,226	3,028	3,226	3,141
28,550	28,600	3,232	3,034	3,232	3,147
28,600	28,650	3,238	3,040	3,238	3,153
28,650	28,700	3,244	3,046	3,244	3,159
28,700	28,750	3,250	3,052	3,250	3,165
28,750	28,800	3,256	3,058	3,256	3,171
28,800	28,850	3,262	3,064	3,262	3,177
28,850	28,900	3,268	3,070	3,268	3,183
28,900	28,950	3,274	3,076	3,274	3,189
28,950	29,000	3,280	3,082	3,280	3,195

29,000

At least	But less than	Single	Married filing jointly *	Married filing separately	Head of a household
29,000	29,050	3,286	3,088	3,286	3,201
29,050	29,100	3,292	3,094	3,292	3,207
29,100	29,150	3,298	3,100	3,298	3,213
29,150	29,200	3,304	3,106	3,304	3,219
29,200	29,250	3,310	3,112	3,310	3,225
29,250	29,300	3,316	3,118	3,316	3,231
29,300	29,350	3,322	3,124	3,322	3,237
29,350	29,400	3,328	3,130	3,328	3,243
29,400	29,450	3,334	3,136	3,334	3,249
29,450	29,500	3,340	3,142	3,340	3,255
29,500	29,550	3,346	3,148	3,346	3,261
29,550	29,600	3,352	3,154	3,352	3,267
29,600	29,650	3,358	3,160	3,358	3,273
29,650	29,700	3,364	3,166	3,364	3,279
29,700	29,750	3,370	3,172	3,370	3,285
29,750	29,800	3,376	3,178	3,376	3,291
29,800	29,850	3,382	3,184	3,382	3,297
29,850	29,900	3,388	3,190	3,388	3,303
29,900	29,950	3,394	3,196	3,394	3,309
29,950	30,000	3,400	3,202	3,400	3,315

(Continued)

* This column must also be used by a qualifying widow(er).

If line 15 (taxable income) is—		And you are—				If line 15 (taxable income) is—		And you are—				If line 15 (taxable income) is—		And you are—			
At least	But less than	Single	Married filing jointly *	Married filing separately	Head of a household	At least	But less than	Single	Married filing jointly *	Married filing separately	Head of a household	At least	But less than	Single	Married filing jointly *	Married filing separately	Head of a household
		Your tax is—						Your tax is—						Your tax is—			

30,000 / 33,000 / 36,000

At least	But less than	Single	MFJ	MFS	HoH	At least	But less than	Single	MFJ	MFS	HoH	At least	But less than	Single	MFJ	MFS	HoH
30,000	30,050	3,406	3,208	3,406	3,321	33,000	33,050	3,766	3,568	3,766	3,681	36,000	36,050	4,126	3,928	4,126	4,041
30,050	30,100	3,412	3,214	3,412	3,327	33,050	33,100	3,772	3,574	3,772	3,687	36,050	36,100	4,132	3,934	4,132	4,047
30,100	30,150	3,418	3,220	3,418	3,333	33,100	33,150	3,778	3,580	3,778	3,693	36,100	36,150	4,138	3,940	4,138	4,053
30,150	30,200	3,424	3,226	3,424	3,339	33,150	33,200	3,784	3,586	3,784	3,699	36,150	36,200	4,144	3,946	4,144	4,059
30,200	30,250	3,430	3,232	3,430	3,345	33,200	33,250	3,790	3,592	3,790	3,705	36,200	36,250	4,150	3,952	4,150	4,065
30,250	30,300	3,436	3,238	3,436	3,351	33,250	33,300	3,796	3,598	3,796	3,711	36,250	36,300	4,156	3,958	4,156	4,071
30,300	30,350	3,442	3,244	3,442	3,357	33,300	33,350	3,802	3,604	3,802	3,717	36,300	36,350	4,162	3,964	4,162	4,077
30,350	30,400	3,448	3,250	3,448	3,363	33,350	33,400	3,808	3,610	3,808	3,723	36,350	36,400	4,168	3,970	4,168	4,083
30,400	30,450	3,454	3,256	3,454	3,369	33,400	33,450	3,814	3,616	3,814	3,729	36,400	36,450	4,174	3,976	4,174	4,089
30,450	30,500	3,460	3,262	3,460	3,375	33,450	33,500	3,820	3,622	3,820	3,735	36,450	36,500	4,180	3,982	4,180	4,095
30,500	30,550	3,466	3,268	3,466	3,381	33,500	33,550	3,826	3,628	3,826	3,741	36,500	36,550	4,186	3,988	4,186	4,101
30,550	30,600	3,472	3,274	3,472	3,387	33,550	33,600	3,832	3,634	3,832	3,747	36,550	36,600	4,192	3,994	4,192	4,107
30,600	30,650	3,478	3,280	3,478	3,393	33,600	33,650	3,838	3,640	3,838	3,753	36,600	36,650	4,198	4,000	4,198	4,113
30,650	30,700	3,484	3,286	3,484	3,399	33,650	33,700	3,844	3,646	3,844	3,759	36,650	36,700	4,204	4,006	4,204	4,119
30,700	30,750	3,490	3,292	3,490	3,405	33,700	33,750	3,850	3,652	3,850	3,765	36,700	36,750	4,210	4,012	4,210	4,125
30,750	30,800	3,496	3,298	3,496	3,411	33,750	33,800	3,856	3,658	3,856	3,771	36,750	36,800	4,216	4,018	4,216	4,131
30,800	30,850	3,502	3,304	3,502	3,417	33,800	33,850	3,862	3,664	3,862	3,777	36,800	36,850	4,222	4,024	4,222	4,137
30,850	30,900	3,508	3,310	3,508	3,423	33,850	33,900	3,868	3,670	3,868	3,783	36,850	36,900	4,228	4,030	4,228	4,143
30,900	30,950	3,514	3,316	3,514	3,429	33,900	33,950	3,874	3,676	3,874	3,789	36,900	36,950	4,234	4,036	4,234	4,149
30,950	31,000	3,520	3,322	3,520	3,435	33,950	34,000	3,880	3,682	3,880	3,795	36,950	37,000	4,240	4,042	4,240	4,155

31,000 / 34,000 / 37,000

At least	But less than	Single	MFJ	MFS	HoH	At least	But less than	Single	MFJ	MFS	HoH	At least	But less than	Single	MFJ	MFS	HoH
31,000	31,050	3,526	3,328	3,526	3,441	34,000	34,050	3,886	3,688	3,886	3,801	37,000	37,050	4,246	4,048	4,246	4,161
31,050	31,100	3,532	3,334	3,532	3,447	34,050	34,100	3,892	3,694	3,892	3,807	37,050	37,100	4,252	4,054	4,252	4,167
31,100	31,150	3,538	3,340	3,538	3,453	34,100	34,150	3,898	3,700	3,898	3,813	37,100	37,150	4,258	4,060	4,258	4,173
31,150	31,200	3,544	3,346	3,544	3,459	34,150	34,200	3,904	3,706	3,904	3,819	37,150	37,200	4,264	4,066	4,264	4,179
31,200	31,250	3,550	3,352	3,550	3,465	34,200	34,250	3,910	3,712	3,910	3,825	37,200	37,250	4,270	4,072	4,270	4,185
31,250	31,300	3,556	3,358	3,556	3,471	34,250	34,300	3,916	3,718	3,916	3,831	37,250	37,300	4,276	4,078	4,276	4,191
31,300	31,350	3,562	3,364	3,562	3,477	34,300	34,350	3,922	3,724	3,922	3,837	37,300	37,350	4,282	4,084	4,282	4,197
31,350	31,400	3,568	3,370	3,568	3,483	34,350	34,400	3,928	3,730	3,928	3,843	37,350	37,400	4,288	4,090	4,288	4,203
31,400	31,450	3,574	3,376	3,574	3,489	34,400	34,450	3,934	3,736	3,934	3,849	37,400	37,450	4,294	4,096	4,294	4,209
31,450	31,500	3,580	3,382	3,580	3,495	34,450	34,500	3,940	3,742	3,940	3,855	37,450	37,500	4,300	4,102	4,300	4,215
31,500	31,550	3,586	3,388	3,586	3,501	34,500	34,550	3,946	3,748	3,946	3,861	37,500	37,550	4,306	4,108	4,306	4,221
31,550	31,600	3,592	3,394	3,592	3,507	34,550	34,600	3,952	3,754	3,952	3,867	37,550	37,600	4,312	4,114	4,312	4,227
31,600	31,650	3,598	3,400	3,598	3,513	34,600	34,650	3,958	3,760	3,958	3,873	37,600	37,650	4,318	4,120	4,318	4,233
31,650	31,700	3,604	3,406	3,604	3,519	34,650	34,700	3,964	3,766	3,964	3,879	37,650	37,700	4,324	4,126	4,324	4,239
31,700	31,750	3,610	3,412	3,610	3,525	34,700	34,750	3,970	3,772	3,970	3,885	37,700	37,750	4,330	4,132	4,330	4,245
31,750	31,800	3,616	3,418	3,616	3,531	34,750	34,800	3,976	3,778	3,976	3,891	37,750	37,800	4,336	4,138	4,336	4,251
31,800	31,850	3,622	3,424	3,622	3,537	34,800	34,850	3,982	3,784	3,982	3,897	37,800	37,850	4,342	4,144	4,342	4,257
31,850	31,900	3,628	3,430	3,628	3,543	34,850	34,900	3,988	3,790	3,988	3,903	37,850	37,900	4,348	4,150	4,348	4,263
31,900	31,950	3,634	3,436	3,634	3,549	34,900	34,950	3,994	3,796	3,994	3,909	37,900	37,950	4,354	4,156	4,354	4,269
31,950	32,000	3,640	3,442	3,640	3,555	34,950	35,000	4,000	3,802	4,000	3,915	37,950	38,000	4,360	4,162	4,360	4,275

32,000 / 35,000 / 38,000

At least	But less than	Single	MFJ	MFS	HoH	At least	But less than	Single	MFJ	MFS	HoH	At least	But less than	Single	MFJ	MFS	HoH
32,000	32,050	3,646	3,448	3,646	3,561	35,000	35,050	4,006	3,808	4,006	3,921	38,000	38,050	4,366	4,168	4,366	4,281
32,050	32,100	3,652	3,454	3,652	3,567	35,050	35,100	4,012	3,814	4,012	3,927	38,050	38,100	4,372	4,174	4,372	4,287
32,100	32,150	3,658	3,460	3,658	3,573	35,100	35,150	4,018	3,820	4,018	3,933	38,100	38,150	4,378	4,180	4,378	4,293
32,150	32,200	3,664	3,466	3,664	3,579	35,150	35,200	4,024	3,826	4,024	3,939	38,150	38,200	4,384	4,186	4,384	4,299
32,200	32,250	3,670	3,472	3,670	3,585	35,200	35,250	4,030	3,832	4,030	3,945	38,200	38,250	4,390	4,192	4,390	4,305
32,250	32,300	3,676	3,478	3,676	3,591	35,250	35,300	4,036	3,838	4,036	3,951	38,250	38,300	4,396	4,198	4,396	4,311
32,300	32,350	3,682	3,484	3,682	3,597	35,300	35,350	4,042	3,844	4,042	3,957	38,300	38,350	4,402	4,204	4,402	4,317
32,350	32,400	3,688	3,490	3,688	3,603	35,350	35,400	4,048	3,850	4,048	3,963	38,350	38,400	4,408	4,210	4,408	4,323
32,400	32,450	3,694	3,496	3,694	3,609	35,400	35,450	4,054	3,856	4,054	3,969	38,400	38,450	4,414	4,216	4,414	4,329
32,450	32,500	3,700	3,502	3,700	3,615	35,450	35,500	4,060	3,862	4,060	3,975	38,450	38,500	4,420	4,222	4,420	4,335
32,500	32,550	3,706	3,508	3,706	3,621	35,500	35,550	4,066	3,868	4,066	3,981	38,500	38,550	4,426	4,228	4,426	4,341
32,550	32,600	3,712	3,514	3,712	3,627	35,550	35,600	4,072	3,874	4,072	3,987	38,550	38,600	4,432	4,234	4,432	4,347
32,600	32,650	3,718	3,520	3,718	3,633	35,600	35,650	4,078	3,880	4,078	3,993	38,600	38,650	4,438	4,240	4,438	4,353
32,650	32,700	3,724	3,526	3,724	3,639	35,650	35,700	4,084	3,886	4,084	3,999	38,650	38,700	4,444	4,246	4,444	4,359
32,700	32,750	3,730	3,532	3,730	3,645	35,700	35,750	4,090	3,892	4,090	4,005	38,700	38,750	4,450	4,252	4,450	4,365
32,750	32,800	3,736	3,538	3,736	3,651	35,750	35,800	4,096	3,898	4,096	4,011	38,750	38,800	4,456	4,258	4,456	4,371
32,800	32,850	3,742	3,544	3,742	3,657	35,800	35,850	4,102	3,904	4,102	4,017	38,800	38,850	4,462	4,264	4,462	4,377
32,850	32,900	3,748	3,550	3,748	3,663	35,850	35,900	4,108	3,910	4,108	4,023	38,850	38,900	4,468	4,270	4,468	4,383
32,900	32,950	3,754	3,556	3,754	3,669	35,900	35,950	4,114	3,916	4,114	4,029	38,900	38,950	4,474	4,276	4,474	4,389
32,950	33,000	3,760	3,562	3,760	3,675	35,950	36,000	4,120	3,922	4,120	4,035	38,950	39,000	4,480	4,282	4,480	4,395

* This column must also be used by a qualifying widow(er).

(Continued)

2020 Tax Table — *Continued*

39,000

If line 15 (taxable income) is— At least	But less than	Single	Married filing jointly *	Married filing separately	Head of a household
			Your tax is—		
39,000	39,050	4,486	4,288	4,486	4,401
39,050	39,100	4,492	4,294	4,492	4,407
39,100	39,150	4,498	4,300	4,498	4,413
39,150	39,200	4,504	4,306	4,504	4,419
39,200	39,250	4,510	4,312	4,510	4,425
39,250	39,300	4,516	4,318	4,516	4,431
39,300	39,350	4,522	4,324	4,522	4,437
39,350	39,400	4,528	4,330	4,528	4,443
39,400	39,450	4,534	4,336	4,534	4,449
39,450	39,500	4,540	4,342	4,540	4,455
39,500	39,550	4,546	4,348	4,546	4,461
39,550	39,600	4,552	4,354	4,552	4,467
39,600	39,650	4,558	4,360	4,558	4,473
39,650	39,700	4,564	4,366	4,564	4,479
39,700	39,750	4,570	4,372	4,570	4,485
39,750	39,800	4,576	4,378	4,576	4,491
39,800	39,850	4,582	4,384	4,582	4,497
39,850	39,900	4,588	4,390	4,588	4,503
39,900	39,950	4,594	4,396	4,594	4,509
39,950	40,000	4,600	4,402	4,600	4,515

40,000

At least	But less than	Single	Married filing jointly *	Married filing separately	Head of a household
40,000	40,050	4,606	4,408	4,606	4,521
40,050	40,100	4,612	4,414	4,612	4,527
40,100	40,150	4,618	4,420	4,618	4,533
40,150	40,200	4,629	4,426	4,629	4,539
40,200	40,250	4,640	4,432	4,640	4,545
40,250	40,300	4,651	4,438	4,651	4,551
40,300	40,350	4,662	4,444	4,662	4,557
40,350	40,400	4,673	4,450	4,673	4,563
40,400	40,450	4,684	4,456	4,684	4,569
40,450	40,500	4,695	4,462	4,695	4,575
40,500	40,550	4,706	4,468	4,706	4,581
40,550	40,600	4,717	4,474	4,717	4,587
40,600	40,650	4,728	4,480	4,728	4,593
40,650	40,700	4,739	4,486	4,739	4,599
40,700	40,750	4,750	4,492	4,750	4,605
40,750	40,800	4,761	4,498	4,761	4,611
40,800	40,850	4,772	4,504	4,772	4,617
40,850	40,900	4,783	4,510	4,783	4,623
40,900	40,950	4,794	4,516	4,794	4,629
40,950	41,000	4,805	4,522	4,805	4,635

41,000

At least	But less than	Single	Married filing jointly *	Married filing separately	Head of a household
41,000	41,050	4,816	4,528	4,816	4,641
41,050	41,100	4,827	4,534	4,827	4,647
41,100	41,150	4,838	4,540	4,838	4,653
41,150	41,200	4,849	4,546	4,849	4,659
41,200	41,250	4,860	4,552	4,860	4,665
41,250	41,300	4,871	4,558	4,871	4,671
41,300	41,350	4,882	4,564	4,882	4,677
41,350	41,400	4,893	4,570	4,893	4,683
41,400	41,450	4,904	4,576	4,904	4,689
41,450	41,500	4,915	4,582	4,915	4,695
41,500	41,550	4,926	4,588	4,926	4,701
41,550	41,600	4,937	4,594	4,937	4,707
41,600	41,650	4,948	4,600	4,948	4,713
41,650	41,700	4,959	4,606	4,959	4,719
41,700	41,750	4,970	4,612	4,970	4,725
41,750	41,800	4,981	4,618	4,981	4,731
41,800	41,850	4,992	4,624	4,992	4,737
41,850	41,900	5,003	4,630	5,003	4,743
41,900	41,950	5,014	4,636	5,014	4,749
41,950	42,000	5,025	4,642	5,025	4,755

42,000

At least	But less than	Single	Married filing jointly *	Married filing separately	Head of a household
42,000	42,050	5,036	4,648	5,036	4,761
42,050	42,100	5,047	4,654	5,047	4,767
42,100	42,150	5,058	4,660	5,058	4,773
42,150	42,200	5,069	4,666	5,069	4,779
42,200	42,250	5,080	4,672	5,080	4,785
42,250	42,300	5,091	4,678	5,091	4,791
42,300	42,350	5,102	4,684	5,102	4,797
42,350	42,400	5,113	4,690	5,113	4,803
42,400	42,450	5,124	4,696	5,124	4,809
42,450	42,500	5,135	4,702	5,135	4,815
42,500	42,550	5,146	4,708	5,146	4,821
42,550	42,600	5,157	4,714	5,157	4,827
42,600	42,650	5,168	4,720	5,168	4,833
42,650	42,700	5,179	4,726	5,179	4,839
42,700	42,750	5,190	4,732	5,190	4,845
42,750	42,800	5,201	4,738	5,201	4,851
42,800	42,850	5,212	4,744	5,212	4,857
42,850	42,900	5,223	4,750	5,223	4,863
42,900	42,950	5,234	4,756	5,234	4,869
42,950	43,000	5,245	4,762	5,245	4,875

43,000

At least	But less than	Single	Married filing jointly *	Married filing separately	Head of a household
43,000	43,050	5,256	4,768	5,256	4,881
43,050	43,100	5,267	4,774	5,267	4,887
43,100	43,150	5,278	4,780	5,278	4,893
43,150	43,200	5,289	4,786	5,289	4,899
43,200	43,250	5,300	4,792	5,300	4,905
43,250	43,300	5,311	4,798	5,311	4,911
43,300	43,350	5,322	4,804	5,322	4,917
43,350	43,400	5,333	4,810	5,333	4,923
43,400	43,450	5,344	4,816	5,344	4,929
43,450	43,500	5,355	4,822	5,355	4,935
43,500	43,550	5,366	4,828	5,366	4,941
43,550	43,600	5,377	4,834	5,377	4,947
43,600	43,650	5,388	4,840	5,388	4,953
43,650	43,700	5,399	4,846	5,399	4,959
43,700	43,750	5,410	4,852	5,410	4,965
43,750	43,800	5,421	4,858	5,421	4,971
43,800	43,850	5,432	4,864	5,432	4,977
43,850	43,900	5,443	4,870	5,443	4,983
43,900	43,950	5,454	4,876	5,454	4,989
43,950	44,000	5,465	4,882	5,465	4,995

44,000

At least	But less than	Single	Married filing jointly *	Married filing separately	Head of a household
44,000	44,050	5,476	4,888	5,476	5,001
44,050	44,100	5,487	4,894	5,487	5,007
44,100	44,150	5,498	4,900	5,498	5,013
44,150	44,200	5,509	4,906	5,509	5,019
44,200	44,250	5,520	4,912	5,520	5,025
44,250	44,300	5,531	4,918	5,531	5,031
44,300	44,350	5,542	4,924	5,542	5,037
44,350	44,400	5,553	4,930	5,553	5,043
44,400	44,450	5,564	4,936	5,564	5,049
44,450	44,500	5,575	4,942	5,575	5,055
44,500	44,550	5,586	4,948	5,586	5,061
44,550	44,600	5,597	4,954	5,597	5,067
44,600	44,650	5,608	4,960	5,608	5,073
44,650	44,700	5,619	4,966	5,619	5,079
44,700	44,750	5,630	4,972	5,630	5,085
44,750	44,800	5,641	4,978	5,641	5,091
44,800	44,850	5,652	4,984	5,652	5,097
44,850	44,900	5,663	4,990	5,663	5,103
44,900	44,950	5,674	4,996	5,674	5,109
44,950	45,000	5,685	5,002	5,685	5,115

45,000

At least	But less than	Single	Married filing jointly *	Married filing separately	Head of a household
45,000	45,050	5,696	5,008	5,696	5,121
45,050	45,100	5,707	5,014	5,707	5,127
45,100	45,150	5,718	5,020	5,718	5,133
45,150	45,200	5,729	5,026	5,729	5,139
45,200	45,250	5,740	5,032	5,740	5,145
45,250	45,300	5,751	5,038	5,751	5,151
45,300	45,350	5,762	5,044	5,762	5,157
45,350	45,400	5,773	5,050	5,773	5,163
45,400	45,450	5,784	5,056	5,784	5,169
45,450	45,500	5,795	5,062	5,795	5,175
45,500	45,550	5,806	5,068	5,806	5,181
45,550	45,600	5,817	5,074	5,817	5,187
45,600	45,650	5,828	5,080	5,828	5,193
45,650	45,700	5,839	5,086	5,839	5,199
45,700	45,750	5,850	5,092	5,850	5,205
45,750	45,800	5,861	5,098	5,861	5,211
45,800	45,850	5,872	5,104	5,872	5,217
45,850	45,900	5,883	5,110	5,883	5,223
45,900	45,950	5,894	5,116	5,894	5,229
45,950	46,000	5,905	5,122	5,905	5,235

46,000

At least	But less than	Single	Married filing jointly *	Married filing separately	Head of a household
46,000	46,050	5,916	5,128	5,916	5,241
46,050	46,100	5,927	5,134	5,927	5,247
46,100	46,150	5,938	5,140	5,938	5,253
46,150	46,200	5,949	5,146	5,949	5,259
46,200	46,250	5,960	5,152	5,960	5,265
46,250	46,300	5,971	5,158	5,971	5,271
46,300	46,350	5,982	5,164	5,982	5,277
46,350	46,400	5,993	5,170	5,993	5,283
46,400	46,450	6,004	5,176	6,004	5,289
46,450	46,500	6,015	5,182	6,015	5,295
46,500	46,550	6,026	5,188	6,026	5,301
46,550	46,600	6,037	5,194	6,037	5,307
46,600	46,650	6,048	5,200	6,048	5,313
46,650	46,700	6,059	5,206	6,059	5,319
46,700	46,750	6,070	5,212	6,070	5,325
46,750	46,800	6,081	5,218	6,081	5,331
46,800	46,850	6,092	5,224	6,092	5,337
46,850	46,900	6,103	5,230	6,103	5,343
46,900	46,950	6,114	5,236	6,114	5,349
46,950	47,000	6,125	5,242	6,125	5,355

47,000

At least	But less than	Single	Married filing jointly *	Married filing separately	Head of a household
47,000	47,050	6,136	5,248	6,136	5,361
47,050	47,100	6,147	5,254	6,147	5,367
47,100	47,150	6,158	5,260	6,158	5,373
47,150	47,200	6,169	5,266	6,169	5,379
47,200	47,250	6,180	5,272	6,180	5,385
47,250	47,300	6,191	5,278	6,191	5,391
47,300	47,350	6,202	5,284	6,202	5,397
47,350	47,400	6,213	5,290	6,213	5,403
47,400	47,450	6,224	5,296	6,224	5,409
47,450	47,500	6,235	5,302	6,235	5,415
47,500	47,550	6,246	5,308	6,246	5,421
47,550	47,600	6,257	5,314	6,257	5,427
47,600	47,650	6,268	5,320	6,268	5,433
47,650	47,700	6,279	5,326	6,279	5,439
47,700	47,750	6,290	5,332	6,290	5,445
47,750	47,800	6,301	5,338	6,301	5,451
47,800	47,850	6,312	5,344	6,312	5,457
47,850	47,900	6,323	5,350	6,323	5,463
47,900	47,950	6,334	5,356	6,334	5,469
47,950	48,000	6,345	5,362	6,345	5,475

(Continued)

* This column must also be used by a qualifying widow(er).

48,000

At least	But less than	Single	Married filing jointly *	Married filing separately	Head of a household
48,000	48,050	6,356	5,368	6,356	5,481
48,050	48,100	6,367	5,374	6,367	5,487
48,100	48,150	6,378	5,380	6,378	5,493
48,150	48,200	6,389	5,386	6,389	5,499
48,200	48,250	6,400	5,392	6,400	5,505
48,250	48,300	6,411	5,398	6,411	5,511
48,300	48,350	6,422	5,404	6,422	5,517
48,350	48,400	6,433	5,410	6,433	5,523
48,400	48,450	6,444	5,416	6,444	5,529
48,450	48,500	6,455	5,422	6,455	5,535
48,500	48,550	6,466	5,428	6,466	5,541
48,550	48,600	6,477	5,434	6,477	5,547
48,600	48,650	6,488	5,440	6,488	5,553
48,650	48,700	6,499	5,446	6,499	5,559
48,700	48,750	6,510	5,452	6,510	5,565
48,750	48,800	6,521	5,458	6,521	5,571
48,800	48,850	6,532	5,464	6,532	5,577
48,850	48,900	6,543	5,470	6,543	5,583
48,900	48,950	6,554	5,476	6,554	5,589
48,950	49,000	6,565	5,482	6,565	5,595

49,000

At least	But less than	Single	Married filing jointly *	Married filing separately	Head of a household
49,000	49,050	6,576	5,488	6,576	5,601
49,050	49,100	6,587	5,494	6,587	5,607
49,100	49,150	6,598	5,500	6,598	5,613
49,150	49,200	6,609	5,506	6,609	5,619
49,200	49,250	6,620	5,512	6,620	5,625
49,250	49,300	6,631	5,518	6,631	5,631
49,300	49,350	6,642	5,524	6,642	5,637
49,350	49,400	6,653	5,530	6,653	5,643
49,400	49,450	6,664	5,536	6,664	5,649
49,450	49,500	6,675	5,542	6,675	5,655
49,500	49,550	6,686	5,548	6,686	5,661
49,550	49,600	6,697	5,554	6,697	5,667
49,600	49,650	6,708	5,560	6,708	5,673
49,650	49,700	6,719	5,566	6,719	5,679
49,700	49,750	6,730	5,572	6,730	5,685
49,750	49,800	6,741	5,578	6,741	5,691
49,800	49,850	6,752	5,584	6,752	5,697
49,850	49,900	6,763	5,590	6,763	5,703
49,900	49,950	6,774	5,596	6,774	5,709
49,950	50,000	6,785	5,602	6,785	5,715

50,000

At least	But less than	Single	Married filing jointly *	Married filing separately	Head of a household
50,000	50,050	6,796	5,608	6,796	5,721
50,050	50,100	6,807	5,614	6,807	5,727
50,100	50,150	6,818	5,620	6,818	5,733
50,150	50,200	6,829	5,626	6,829	5,739
50,200	50,250	6,840	5,632	6,840	5,745
50,250	50,300	6,851	5,638	6,851	5,751
50,300	50,350	6,862	5,644	6,862	5,757
50,350	50,400	6,873	5,650	6,873	5,763
50,400	50,450	6,884	5,656	6,884	5,769
50,450	50,500	6,895	5,662	6,895	5,775
50,500	50,550	6,906	5,668	6,906	5,781
50,550	50,600	6,917	5,674	6,917	5,787
50,600	50,650	6,928	5,680	6,928	5,793
50,650	50,700	6,939	5,686	6,939	5,799
50,700	50,750	6,950	5,692	6,950	5,805
50,750	50,800	6,961	5,698	6,961	5,811
50,800	50,850	6,972	5,704	6,972	5,817
50,850	50,900	6,983	5,710	6,983	5,823
50,900	50,950	6,994	5,716	6,994	5,829
50,950	51,000	7,005	5,722	7,005	5,835

51,000

At least	But less than	Single	Married filing jointly *	Married filing separately	Head of a household
51,000	51,050	7,016	5,728	7,016	5,841
51,050	51,100	7,027	5,734	7,027	5,847
51,100	51,150	7,038	5,740	7,038	5,853
51,150	51,200	7,049	5,746	7,049	5,859
51,200	51,250	7,060	5,752	7,060	5,865
51,250	51,300	7,071	5,758	7,071	5,871
51,300	51,350	7,082	5,764	7,082	5,877
51,350	51,400	7,093	5,770	7,093	5,883
51,400	51,450	7,104	5,776	7,104	5,889
51,450	51,500	7,115	5,782	7,115	5,895
51,500	51,550	7,126	5,788	7,126	5,901
51,550	51,600	7,137	5,794	7,137	5,907
51,600	51,650	7,148	5,800	7,148	5,913
51,650	51,700	7,159	5,806	7,159	5,919
51,700	51,750	7,170	5,812	7,170	5,925
51,750	51,800	7,181	5,818	7,181	5,931
51,800	51,850	7,192	5,824	7,192	5,937
51,850	51,900	7,203	5,830	7,203	5,943
51,900	51,950	7,214	5,836	7,214	5,949
51,950	52,000	7,225	5,842	7,225	5,955

52,000

At least	But less than	Single	Married filing jointly *	Married filing separately	Head of a household
52,000	52,050	7,236	5,848	7,236	5,961
52,050	52,100	7,247	5,854	7,247	5,967
52,100	52,150	7,258	5,860	7,258	5,973
52,150	52,200	7,269	5,866	7,269	5,979
52,200	52,250	7,280	5,872	7,280	5,985
52,250	52,300	7,291	5,878	7,291	5,991
52,300	52,350	7,302	5,884	7,302	5,997
52,350	52,400	7,313	5,890	7,313	6,003
52,400	52,450	7,324	5,896	7,324	6,009
52,450	52,500	7,335	5,902	7,335	6,015
52,500	52,550	7,346	5,908	7,346	6,021
52,550	52,600	7,357	5,914	7,357	6,027
52,600	52,650	7,368	5,920	7,368	6,033
52,650	52,700	7,379	5,926	7,379	6,039
52,700	52,750	7,390	5,932	7,390	6,045
52,750	52,800	7,401	5,938	7,401	6,051
52,800	52,850	7,412	5,944	7,412	6,057
52,850	52,900	7,423	5,950	7,423	6,063
52,900	52,950	7,434	5,956	7,434	6,069
52,950	53,000	7,445	5,962	7,445	6,075

53,000

At least	But less than	Single	Married filing jointly *	Married filing separately	Head of a household
53,000	53,050	7,456	5,968	7,456	6,081
53,050	53,100	7,467	5,974	7,467	6,087
53,100	53,150	7,478	5,980	7,478	6,093
53,150	53,200	7,489	5,986	7,489	6,099
53,200	53,250	7,500	5,992	7,500	6,105
53,250	53,300	7,511	5,998	7,511	6,111
53,300	53,350	7,522	6,004	7,522	6,117
53,350	53,400	7,533	6,010	7,533	6,123
53,400	53,450	7,544	6,016	7,544	6,129
53,450	53,500	7,555	6,022	7,555	6,135
53,500	53,550	7,566	6,028	7,566	6,141
53,550	53,600	7,577	6,034	7,577	6,147
53,600	53,650	7,588	6,040	7,588	6,153
53,650	53,700	7,599	6,046	7,599	6,159
53,700	53,750	7,610	6,052	7,610	6,168
53,750	53,800	7,621	6,058	7,621	6,179
53,800	53,850	7,632	6,064	7,632	6,190
53,850	53,900	7,643	6,070	7,643	6,201
53,900	53,950	7,654	6,076	7,654	6,212
53,950	54,000	7,665	6,082	7,665	6,223

54,000

At least	But less than	Single	Married filing jointly *	Married filing separately	Head of a household
54,000	54,050	7,676	6,088	7,676	6,234
54,050	54,100	7,687	6,094	7,687	6,245
54,100	54,150	7,698	6,100	7,698	6,256
54,150	54,200	7,709	6,106	7,709	6,267
54,200	54,250	7,720	6,112	7,720	6,278
54,250	54,300	7,731	6,118	7,731	6,289
54,300	54,350	7,742	6,124	7,742	6,300
54,350	54,400	7,753	6,130	7,753	6,311
54,400	54,450	7,764	6,136	7,764	6,322
54,450	54,500	7,775	6,142	7,775	6,333
54,500	54,550	7,786	6,148	7,786	6,344
54,550	54,600	7,797	6,154	7,797	6,355
54,600	54,650	7,808	6,160	7,808	6,366
54,650	54,700	7,819	6,166	7,819	6,377
54,700	54,750	7,830	6,172	7,830	6,388
54,750	54,800	7,841	6,178	7,841	6,399
54,800	54,850	7,852	6,184	7,852	6,410
54,850	54,900	7,863	6,190	7,863	6,421
54,900	54,950	7,874	6,196	7,874	6,432
54,950	55,000	7,885	6,202	7,885	6,443

55,000

At least	But less than	Single	Married filing jointly *	Married filing separately	Head of a household
55,000	55,050	7,896	6,208	7,896	6,454
55,050	55,100	7,907	6,214	7,907	6,465
55,100	55,150	7,918	6,220	7,918	6,476
55,150	55,200	7,929	6,226	7,929	6,487
55,200	55,250	7,940	6,232	7,940	6,498
55,250	55,300	7,951	6,238	7,951	6,509
55,300	55,350	7,962	6,244	7,962	6,520
55,350	55,400	7,973	6,250	7,973	6,531
55,400	55,450	7,984	6,256	7,984	6,542
55,450	55,500	7,995	6,262	7,995	6,553
55,500	55,550	8,006	6,268	8,006	6,564
55,550	55,600	8,017	6,274	8,017	6,575
55,600	55,650	8,028	6,280	8,028	6,586
55,650	55,700	8,039	6,286	8,039	6,597
55,700	55,750	8,050	6,292	8,050	6,608
55,750	55,800	8,061	6,298	8,061	6,619
55,800	55,850	8,072	6,304	8,072	6,630
55,850	55,900	8,083	6,310	8,083	6,641
55,900	55,950	8,094	6,316	8,094	6,652
55,950	56,000	8,105	6,322	8,105	6,663

56,000

At least	But less than	Single	Married filing jointly *	Married filing separately	Head of a household
56,000	56,050	8,116	6,328	8,116	6,674
56,050	56,100	8,127	6,334	8,127	6,685
56,100	56,150	8,138	6,340	8,138	6,696
56,150	56,200	8,149	6,346	8,149	6,707
56,200	56,250	8,160	6,352	8,160	6,718
56,250	56,300	8,171	6,358	8,171	6,729
56,300	56,350	8,182	6,364	8,182	6,740
56,350	56,400	8,193	6,370	8,193	6,751
56,400	56,450	8,204	6,376	8,204	6,762
56,450	56,500	8,215	6,382	8,215	6,773
56,500	56,550	8,226	6,388	8,226	6,784
56,550	56,600	8,237	6,394	8,237	6,795
56,600	56,650	8,248	6,400	8,248	6,806
56,650	56,700	8,259	6,406	8,259	6,817
56,700	56,750	8,270	6,412	8,270	6,828
56,750	56,800	8,281	6,418	8,281	6,839
56,800	56,850	8,292	6,424	8,292	6,850
56,850	56,900	8,303	6,430	8,303	6,861
56,900	56,950	8,314	6,436	8,314	6,872
56,950	57,000	8,325	6,442	8,325	6,883

* This column must also be used by a qualifying widow(er).

(Continued)

2020 Tax Table — Continued

57,000

At least	But less than	Single	Married filing jointly *	Married filing separately	Head of a household
					Your tax is—
57,000	57,050	8,336	6,448	8,336	6,894
57,050	57,100	8,347	6,454	8,347	6,905
57,100	57,150	8,358	6,460	8,358	6,916
57,150	57,200	8,369	6,466	8,369	6,927
57,200	57,250	8,380	6,472	8,380	6,938
57,250	57,300	8,391	6,478	8,391	6,949
57,300	57,350	8,402	6,484	8,402	6,960
57,350	57,400	8,413	6,490	8,413	6,971
57,400	57,450	8,424	6,496	8,424	6,982
57,450	57,500	8,435	6,502	8,435	6,993
57,500	57,550	8,446	6,508	8,446	7,004
57,550	57,600	8,457	6,514	8,457	7,015
57,600	57,650	8,468	6,520	8,468	7,026
57,650	57,700	8,479	6,526	8,479	7,037
57,700	57,750	8,490	6,532	8,490	7,048
57,750	57,800	8,501	6,538	8,501	7,059
57,800	57,850	8,512	6,544	8,512	7,070
57,850	57,900	8,523	6,550	8,523	7,081
57,900	57,950	8,534	6,556	8,534	7,092
57,950	58,000	8,545	6,562	8,545	7,103

58,000

At least	But less than	Single	Married filing jointly *	Married filing separately	Head of a household
58,000	58,050	8,556	6,568	8,556	7,114
58,050	58,100	8,567	6,574	8,567	7,125
58,100	58,150	8,578	6,580	8,578	7,136
58,150	58,200	8,589	6,586	8,589	7,147
58,200	58,250	8,600	6,592	8,600	7,158
58,250	58,300	8,611	6,598	8,611	7,169
58,300	58,350	8,622	6,604	8,622	7,180
58,350	58,400	8,633	6,610	8,633	7,191
58,400	58,450	8,644	6,616	8,644	7,202
58,450	58,500	8,655	6,622	8,655	7,213
58,500	58,550	8,666	6,628	8,666	7,224
58,550	58,600	8,677	6,634	8,677	7,235
58,600	58,650	8,688	6,640	8,688	7,246
58,650	58,700	8,699	6,646	8,699	7,257
58,700	58,750	8,710	6,652	8,710	7,268
58,750	58,800	8,721	6,658	8,721	7,279
58,800	58,850	8,732	6,664	8,732	7,290
58,850	58,900	8,743	6,670	8,743	7,301
58,900	58,950	8,754	6,676	8,754	7,312
58,950	59,000	8,765	6,682	8,765	7,323

59,000

At least	But less than	Single	Married filing jointly *	Married filing separately	Head of a household
59,000	59,050	8,776	6,688	8,776	7,334
59,050	59,100	8,787	6,694	8,787	7,345
59,100	59,150	8,798	6,700	8,798	7,356
59,150	59,200	8,809	6,706	8,809	7,367
59,200	59,250	8,820	6,712	8,820	7,378
59,250	59,300	8,831	6,718	8,831	7,389
59,300	59,350	8,842	6,724	8,842	7,400
59,350	59,400	8,853	6,730	8,853	7,411
59,400	59,450	8,864	6,736	8,864	7,422
59,450	59,500	8,875	6,742	8,875	7,433
59,500	59,550	8,886	6,748	8,886	7,444
59,550	59,600	8,897	6,754	8,897	7,455
59,600	59,650	8,908	6,760	8,908	7,466
59,650	59,700	8,919	6,766	8,919	7,477
59,700	59,750	8,930	6,772	8,930	7,488
59,750	59,800	8,941	6,778	8,941	7,499
59,800	59,850	8,952	6,784	8,952	7,510
59,850	59,900	8,963	6,790	8,963	7,521
59,900	59,950	8,974	6,796	8,974	7,532
59,950	60,000	8,985	6,802	8,985	7,543

60,000

At least	But less than	Single	Married filing jointly *	Married filing separately	Head of a household
60,000	60,050	8,996	6,808	8,996	7,554
60,050	60,100	9,007	6,814	9,007	7,565
60,100	60,150	9,018	6,820	9,018	7,576
60,150	60,200	9,029	6,826	9,029	7,587
60,200	60,250	9,040	6,832	9,040	7,598
60,250	60,300	9,051	6,838	9,051	7,609
60,300	60,350	9,062	6,844	9,062	7,620
60,350	60,400	9,073	6,850	9,073	7,631
60,400	60,450	9,084	6,856	9,084	7,642
60,450	60,500	9,095	6,862	9,095	7,653
60,500	60,550	9,106	6,868	9,106	7,664
60,550	60,600	9,117	6,874	9,117	7,675
60,600	60,650	9,128	6,880	9,128	7,686
60,650	60,700	9,139	6,886	9,139	7,697
60,700	60,750	9,150	6,892	9,150	7,708
60,750	60,800	9,161	6,898	9,161	7,719
60,800	60,850	9,172	6,904	9,172	7,730
60,850	60,900	9,183	6,910	9,183	7,741
60,900	60,950	9,194	6,916	9,194	7,752
60,950	61,000	9,205	6,922	9,205	7,763

61,000

At least	But less than	Single	Married filing jointly *	Married filing separately	Head of a household
61,000	61,050	9,216	6,928	9,216	7,774
61,050	61,100	9,227	6,934	9,227	7,785
61,100	61,150	9,238	6,940	9,238	7,796
61,150	61,200	9,249	6,946	9,249	7,807
61,200	61,250	9,260	6,952	9,260	7,818
61,250	61,300	9,271	6,958	9,271	7,829
61,300	61,350	9,282	6,964	9,282	7,840
61,350	61,400	9,293	6,970	9,293	7,851
61,400	61,450	9,304	6,976	9,304	7,862
61,450	61,500	9,315	6,982	9,315	7,873
61,500	61,550	9,326	6,988	9,326	7,884
61,550	61,600	9,337	6,994	9,337	7,895
61,600	61,650	9,348	7,000	9,348	7,906
61,650	61,700	9,359	7,006	9,359	7,917
61,700	61,750	9,370	7,012	9,370	7,928
61,750	61,800	9,381	7,018	9,381	7,939
61,800	61,850	9,392	7,024	9,392	7,950
61,850	61,900	9,403	7,030	9,403	7,961
61,900	61,950	9,414	7,036	9,414	7,972
61,950	62,000	9,425	7,042	9,425	7,983

62,000

At least	But less than	Single	Married filing jointly *	Married filing separately	Head of a household
62,000	62,050	9,436	7,048	9,436	7,994
62,050	62,100	9,447	7,054	9,447	8,005
62,100	62,150	9,458	7,060	9,458	8,016
62,150	62,200	9,469	7,066	9,469	8,027
62,200	62,250	9,480	7,072	9,480	8,038
62,250	62,300	9,491	7,078	9,491	8,049
62,300	62,350	9,502	7,084	9,502	8,060
62,350	62,400	9,513	7,090	9,513	8,071
62,400	62,450	9,524	7,096	9,524	8,082
62,450	62,500	9,535	7,102	9,535	8,093
62,500	62,550	9,546	7,108	9,546	8,104
62,550	62,600	9,557	7,114	9,557	8,115
62,600	62,650	9,568	7,120	9,568	8,126
62,650	62,700	9,579	7,126	9,579	8,137
62,700	62,750	9,590	7,132	9,590	8,148
62,750	62,800	9,601	7,138	9,601	8,159
62,800	62,850	9,612	7,144	9,612	8,170
62,850	62,900	9,623	7,150	9,623	8,181
62,900	62,950	9,634	7,156	9,634	8,192
62,950	63,000	9,645	7,162	9,645	8,203

63,000

At least	But less than	Single	Married filing jointly *	Married filing separately	Head of a household
63,000	63,050	9,656	7,168	9,656	8,214
63,050	63,100	9,667	7,174	9,667	8,225
63,100	63,150	9,678	7,180	9,678	8,236
63,150	63,200	9,689	7,186	9,689	8,247
63,200	63,250	9,700	7,192	9,700	8,258
63,250	63,300	9,711	7,198	9,711	8,269
63,300	63,350	9,722	7,204	9,722	8,280
63,350	63,400	9,733	7,210	9,733	8,291
63,400	63,450	9,744	7,216	9,744	8,302
63,450	63,500	9,755	7,222	9,755	8,313
63,500	63,550	9,766	7,228	9,766	8,324
63,550	63,600	9,777	7,234	9,777	8,335
63,600	63,650	9,788	7,240	9,788	8,346
63,650	63,700	9,799	7,246	9,799	8,357
63,700	63,750	9,810	7,252	9,810	8,368
63,750	63,800	9,821	7,258	9,821	8,379
63,800	63,850	9,832	7,264	9,832	8,390
63,850	63,900	9,843	7,270	9,843	8,401
63,900	63,950	9,854	7,276	9,854	8,412
63,950	64,000	9,865	7,282	9,865	8,423

64,000

At least	But less than	Single	Married filing jointly *	Married filing separately	Head of a household
64,000	64,050	9,876	7,288	9,876	8,434
64,050	64,100	9,887	7,294	9,887	8,445
64,100	64,150	9,898	7,300	9,898	8,456
64,150	64,200	9,909	7,306	9,909	8,467
64,200	64,250	9,920	7,312	9,920	8,478
64,250	64,300	9,931	7,318	9,931	8,489
64,300	64,350	9,942	7,324	9,942	8,500
64,350	64,400	9,953	7,330	9,953	8,511
64,400	64,450	9,964	7,336	9,964	8,522
64,450	64,500	9,975	7,342	9,975	8,533
64,500	64,550	9,986	7,348	9,986	8,544
64,550	64,600	9,997	7,354	9,997	8,555
64,600	64,650	10,008	7,360	10,008	8,566
64,650	64,700	10,019	7,366	10,019	8,577
64,700	64,750	10,030	7,372	10,030	8,588
64,750	64,800	10,041	7,378	10,041	8,599
64,800	64,850	10,052	7,384	10,052	8,610
64,850	64,900	10,063	7,390	10,063	8,621
64,900	64,950	10,074	7,396	10,074	8,632
64,950	65,000	10,085	7,402	10,085	8,643

65,000

At least	But less than	Single	Married filing jointly *	Married filing separately	Head of a household
65,000	65,050	10,096	7,408	10,096	8,654
65,050	65,100	10,107	7,414	10,107	8,665
65,100	65,150	10,118	7,420	10,118	8,676
65,150	65,200	10,129	7,426	10,129	8,687
65,200	65,250	10,140	7,432	10,140	8,698
65,250	65,300	10,151	7,438	10,151	8,709
65,300	65,350	10,162	7,444	10,162	8,720
65,350	65,400	10,173	7,450	10,173	8,731
65,400	65,450	10,184	7,456	10,184	8,742
65,450	65,500	10,195	7,462	10,195	8,753
65,500	65,550	10,206	7,468	10,206	8,764
65,550	65,600	10,217	7,474	10,217	8,775
65,600	65,650	10,228	7,480	10,228	8,786
65,650	65,700	10,239	7,486	10,239	8,797
65,700	65,750	10,250	7,492	10,250	8,808
65,750	65,800	10,261	7,498	10,261	8,819
65,800	65,850	10,272	7,504	10,272	8,830
65,850	65,900	10,283	7,510	10,283	8,841
65,900	65,950	10,294	7,516	10,294	8,852
65,950	66,000	10,305	7,522	10,305	8,863

(Continued)

* This column must also be used by a qualifying widow(er).

If line 15 (taxable income) is—		And you are—			
At least	But less than	Single	Married filing jointly *	Married filing separately	Head of a household
		Your tax is—			

66,000

At least	But less than	Single	MFJ	MFS	HoH
66,000	66,050	10,316	7,528	10,316	8,874
66,050	66,100	10,327	7,534	10,327	8,885
66,100	66,150	10,338	7,540	10,338	8,896
66,150	66,200	10,349	7,546	10,349	8,907
66,200	66,250	10,360	7,552	10,360	8,918
66,250	66,300	10,371	7,558	10,371	8,929
66,300	66,350	10,382	7,564	10,382	8,940
66,350	66,400	10,393	7,570	10,393	8,951
66,400	66,450	10,404	7,576	10,404	8,962
66,450	66,500	10,415	7,582	10,415	8,973
66,500	66,550	10,426	7,588	10,426	8,984
66,550	66,600	10,437	7,594	10,437	8,995
66,600	66,650	10,448	7,600	10,448	9,006
66,650	66,700	10,459	7,606	10,459	9,017
66,700	66,750	10,470	7,612	10,470	9,028
66,750	66,800	10,481	7,618	10,481	9,039
66,800	66,850	10,492	7,624	10,492	9,050
66,850	66,900	10,503	7,630	10,503	9,061
66,900	66,950	10,514	7,636	10,514	9,072
66,950	67,000	10,525	7,642	10,525	9,083

67,000

At least	But less than	Single	MFJ	MFS	HoH
67,000	67,050	10,536	7,648	10,536	9,094
67,050	67,100	10,547	7,654	10,547	9,105
67,100	67,150	10,558	7,660	10,558	9,116
67,150	67,200	10,569	7,666	10,569	9,127
67,200	67,250	10,580	7,672	10,580	9,138
67,250	67,300	10,591	7,678	10,591	9,149
67,300	67,350	10,602	7,684	10,602	9,160
67,350	67,400	10,613	7,690	10,613	9,171
67,400	67,450	10,624	7,696	10,624	9,182
67,450	67,500	10,635	7,702	10,635	9,193
67,500	67,550	10,646	7,708	10,646	9,204
67,550	67,600	10,657	7,714	10,657	9,215
67,600	67,650	10,668	7,720	10,668	9,226
67,650	67,700	10,679	7,726	10,679	9,237
67,700	67,750	10,690	7,732	10,690	9,248
67,750	67,800	10,701	7,738	10,701	9,259
67,800	67,850	10,712	7,744	10,712	9,270
67,850	67,900	10,723	7,750	10,723	9,281
67,900	67,950	10,734	7,756	10,734	9,292
67,950	68,000	10,745	7,762	10,745	9,303

68,000

At least	But less than	Single	MFJ	MFS	HoH
68,000	68,050	10,756	7,768	10,756	9,314
68,050	68,100	10,767	7,774	10,767	9,325
68,100	68,150	10,778	7,780	10,778	9,336
68,150	68,200	10,789	7,786	10,789	9,347
68,200	68,250	10,800	7,792	10,800	9,358
68,250	68,300	10,811	7,798	10,811	9,369
68,300	68,350	10,822	7,804	10,822	9,380
68,350	68,400	10,833	7,810	10,833	9,391
68,400	68,450	10,844	7,816	10,844	9,402
68,450	68,500	10,855	7,822	10,855	9,413
68,500	68,550	10,866	7,828	10,866	9,424
68,550	68,600	10,877	7,834	10,877	9,435
68,600	68,650	10,888	7,840	10,888	9,446
68,650	68,700	10,899	7,846	10,899	9,457
68,700	68,750	10,910	7,852	10,910	9,468
68,750	68,800	10,921	7,858	10,921	9,479
68,800	68,850	10,932	7,864	10,932	9,490
68,850	68,900	10,943	7,870	10,943	9,501
68,900	68,950	10,954	7,876	10,954	9,512
68,950	69,000	10,965	7,882	10,965	9,523

69,000

At least	But less than	Single	MFJ	MFS	HoH
69,000	69,050	10,976	7,888	10,976	9,534
69,050	69,100	10,987	7,894	10,987	9,545
69,100	69,150	10,998	7,900	10,998	9,556
69,150	69,200	11,009	7,906	11,009	9,567
69,200	69,250	11,020	7,912	11,020	9,578
69,250	69,300	11,031	7,918	11,031	9,589
69,300	69,350	11,042	7,924	11,042	9,600
69,350	69,400	11,053	7,930	11,053	9,611
69,400	69,450	11,064	7,936	11,064	9,622
69,450	69,500	11,075	7,942	11,075	9,633
69,500	69,550	11,086	7,948	11,086	9,644
69,550	69,600	11,097	7,954	11,097	9,655
69,600	69,650	11,108	7,960	11,108	9,666
69,650	69,700	11,119	7,966	11,119	9,677
69,700	69,750	11,130	7,972	11,130	9,688
69,750	69,800	11,141	7,978	11,141	9,699
69,800	69,850	11,152	7,984	11,152	9,710
69,850	69,900	11,163	7,990	11,163	9,721
69,900	69,950	11,174	7,996	11,174	9,732
69,950	70,000	11,185	8,002	11,185	9,743

70,000

At least	But less than	Single	MFJ	MFS	HoH
70,000	70,050	11,196	8,008	11,196	9,754
70,050	70,100	11,207	8,014	11,207	9,765
70,100	70,150	11,218	8,020	11,218	9,776
70,150	70,200	11,229	8,026	11,229	9,787
70,200	70,250	11,240	8,032	11,240	9,798
70,250	70,300	11,251	8,038	11,251	9,809
70,300	70,350	11,262	8,044	11,262	9,820
70,350	70,400	11,273	8,050	11,273	9,831
70,400	70,450	11,284	8,056	11,284	9,842
70,450	70,500	11,295	8,062	11,295	9,853
70,500	70,550	11,306	8,068	11,306	9,864
70,550	70,600	11,317	8,074	11,317	9,875
70,600	70,650	11,328	8,080	11,328	9,886
70,650	70,700	11,339	8,086	11,339	9,897
70,700	70,750	11,350	8,092	11,350	9,908
70,750	70,800	11,361	8,098	11,361	9,919
70,800	70,850	11,372	8,104	11,372	9,930
70,850	70,900	11,383	8,110	11,383	9,941
70,900	70,950	11,394	8,116	11,394	9,952
70,950	71,000	11,405	8,122	11,405	9,963

71,000

At least	But less than	Single	MFJ	MFS	HoH
71,000	71,050	11,416	8,128	11,416	9,974
71,050	71,100	11,427	8,134	11,427	9,985
71,100	71,150	11,438	8,140	11,438	9,996
71,150	71,200	11,449	8,146	11,449	10,007
71,200	71,250	11,460	8,152	11,460	10,018
71,250	71,300	11,471	8,158	11,471	10,029
71,300	71,350	11,482	8,164	11,482	10,040
71,350	71,400	11,493	8,170	11,493	10,051
71,400	71,450	11,504	8,176	11,504	10,062
71,450	71,500	11,515	8,182	11,515	10,073
71,500	71,550	11,526	8,188	11,526	10,084
71,550	71,600	11,537	8,194	11,537	10,095
71,600	71,650	11,548	8,200	11,548	10,106
71,650	71,700	11,559	8,206	11,559	10,117
71,700	71,750	11,570	8,212	11,570	10,128
71,750	71,800	11,581	8,218	11,581	10,139
71,800	71,850	11,592	8,224	11,592	10,150
71,850	71,900	11,603	8,230	11,603	10,161
71,900	71,950	11,614	8,236	11,614	10,172
71,950	72,000	11,625	8,242	11,625	10,183

72,000

At least	But less than	Single	MFJ	MFS	HoH
72,000	72,050	11,636	8,248	11,636	10,194
72,050	72,100	11,647	8,254	11,647	10,205
72,100	72,150	11,658	8,260	11,658	10,216
72,150	72,200	11,669	8,266	11,669	10,227
72,200	72,250	11,680	8,272	11,680	10,238
72,250	72,300	11,691	8,278	11,691	10,249
72,300	72,350	11,702	8,284	11,702	10,260
72,350	72,400	11,713	8,290	11,713	10,271
72,400	72,450	11,724	8,296	11,724	10,282
72,450	72,500	11,735	8,302	11,735	10,293
72,500	72,550	11,746	8,308	11,746	10,304
72,550	72,600	11,757	8,314	11,757	10,315
72,600	72,650	11,768	8,320	11,768	10,326
72,650	72,700	11,779	8,326	11,779	10,337
72,700	72,750	11,790	8,332	11,790	10,348
72,750	72,800	11,801	8,338	11,801	10,359
72,800	72,850	11,812	8,344	11,812	10,370
72,850	72,900	11,823	8,350	11,823	10,381
72,900	72,950	11,834	8,356	11,834	10,392
72,950	73,000	11,845	8,362	11,845	10,403

73,000

At least	But less than	Single	MFJ	MFS	HoH
73,000	73,050	11,856	8,368	11,856	10,414
73,050	73,100	11,867	8,374	11,867	10,425
73,100	73,150	11,878	8,380	11,878	10,436
73,150	73,200	11,889	8,386	11,889	10,447
73,200	73,250	11,900	8,392	11,900	10,458
73,250	73,300	11,911	8,398	11,911	10,469
73,300	73,350	11,922	8,404	11,922	10,480
73,350	73,400	11,933	8,410	11,933	10,491
73,400	73,450	11,944	8,416	11,944	10,502
73,450	73,500	11,955	8,422	11,955	10,513
73,500	73,550	11,966	8,428	11,966	10,524
73,550	73,600	11,977	8,434	11,977	10,535
73,600	73,650	11,988	8,440	11,988	10,546
73,650	73,700	11,999	8,446	11,999	10,557
73,700	73,750	12,010	8,452	12,010	10,568
73,750	73,800	12,021	8,458	12,021	10,579
73,800	73,850	12,032	8,464	12,032	10,590
73,850	73,900	12,043	8,470	12,043	10,601
73,900	73,950	12,054	8,476	12,054	10,612
73,950	74,000	12,065	8,482	12,065	10,623

74,000

At least	But less than	Single	MFJ	MFS	HoH
74,000	74,050	12,076	8,488	12,076	10,634
74,050	74,100	12,087	8,494	12,087	10,645
74,100	74,150	12,098	8,500	12,098	10,656
74,150	74,200	12,109	8,506	12,109	10,667
74,200	74,250	12,120	8,512	12,120	10,678
74,250	74,300	12,131	8,518	12,131	10,689
74,300	74,350	12,142	8,524	12,142	10,700
74,350	74,400	12,153	8,530	12,153	10,711
74,400	74,450	12,164	8,536	12,164	10,722
74,450	74,500	12,175	8,542	12,175	10,733
74,500	74,550	12,186	8,548	12,186	10,744
74,550	74,600	12,197	8,554	12,197	10,755
74,600	74,650	12,208	8,560	12,208	10,766
74,650	74,700	12,219	8,566	12,219	10,777
74,700	74,750	12,230	8,572	12,230	10,788
74,750	74,800	12,241	8,578	12,241	10,799
74,800	74,850	12,252	8,584	12,252	10,810
74,850	74,900	12,263	8,590	12,263	10,821
74,900	74,950	12,274	8,596	12,274	10,832
74,950	75,000	12,285	8,602	12,285	10,843

* This column must also be used by a qualifying widow(er).

(Continued)

2020 Tax Table — *Continued*

If line 15 (taxable income) is—		And you are—				If line 15 (taxable income) is—		And you are—				If line 15 (taxable income) is—		And you are—			
At least	But less than	Single	Married filing jointly *	Married filing sepa-rately	Head of a house-hold	At least	But less than	Single	Married filing jointly *	Married filing sepa-rately	Head of a house-hold	At least	But less than	Single	Married filing jointly *	Married filing sepa-rately	Head of a house-hold
		Your tax is—						Your tax is—						Your tax is—			

75,000 / 78,000 / 81,000

At least	But less than	Single	MFJ	MFS	HoH	At least	But less than	Single	MFJ	MFS	HoH	At least	But less than	Single	MFJ	MFS	HoH
75,000	75,050	12,296	8,608	12,296	10,854	78,000	78,050	12,956	8,968	12,956	11,514	81,000	81,050	13,616	9,406	13,616	12,174
75,050	75,100	12,307	8,614	12,307	10,865	78,050	78,100	12,967	8,974	12,967	11,525	81,050	81,100	13,627	9,417	13,627	12,185
75,100	75,150	12,318	8,620	12,318	10,876	78,100	78,150	12,978	8,980	12,978	11,536	81,100	81,150	13,638	9,428	13,638	12,196
75,150	75,200	12,329	8,626	12,329	10,887	78,150	78,200	12,989	8,986	12,989	11,547	81,150	81,200	13,649	9,439	13,649	12,207
75,200	75,250	12,340	8,632	12,340	10,898	78,200	78,250	13,000	8,992	13,000	11,558	81,200	81,250	13,660	9,450	13,660	12,218
75,250	75,300	12,351	8,638	12,351	10,909	78,250	78,300	13,011	8,998	13,011	11,569	81,250	81,300	13,671	9,461	13,671	12,229
75,300	75,350	12,362	8,644	12,362	10,920	78,300	78,350	13,022	9,004	13,022	11,580	81,300	81,350	13,682	9,472	13,682	12,240
75,350	75,400	12,373	8,650	12,373	10,931	78,350	78,400	13,033	9,010	13,033	11,591	81,350	81,400	13,693	9,483	13,693	12,251
75,400	75,450	12,384	8,656	12,384	10,942	78,400	78,450	13,044	9,016	13,044	11,602	81,400	81,450	13,704	9,494	13,704	12,262
75,450	75,500	12,395	8,662	12,395	10,953	78,450	78,500	13,055	9,022	13,055	11,613	81,450	81,500	13,715	9,505	13,715	12,273
75,500	75,550	12,406	8,668	12,406	10,964	78,500	78,550	13,066	9,028	13,066	11,624	81,500	81,550	13,726	9,516	13,726	12,284
75,550	75,600	12,417	8,674	12,417	10,975	78,550	78,600	13,077	9,034	13,077	11,635	81,550	81,600	13,737	9,527	13,737	12,295
75,600	75,650	12,428	8,680	12,428	10,986	78,600	78,650	13,088	9,040	13,088	11,646	81,600	81,650	13,748	9,538	13,748	12,306
75,650	75,700	12,439	8,686	12,439	10,997	78,650	78,700	13,099	9,046	13,099	11,657	81,650	81,700	13,759	9,549	13,759	12,317
75,700	75,750	12,450	8,692	12,450	11,008	78,700	78,750	13,110	9,052	13,110	11,668	81,700	81,750	13,770	9,560	13,770	12,328
75,750	75,800	12,461	8,698	12,461	11,019	78,750	78,800	13,121	9,058	13,121	11,679	81,750	81,800	13,781	9,571	13,781	12,339
75,800	75,850	12,472	8,704	12,472	11,030	78,800	78,850	13,132	9,064	13,132	11,690	81,800	81,850	13,792	9,582	13,792	12,350
75,850	75,900	12,483	8,710	12,483	11,041	78,850	78,900	13,143	9,070	13,143	11,701	81,850	81,900	13,803	9,593	13,803	12,361
75,900	75,950	12,494	8,716	12,494	11,052	78,900	78,950	13,154	9,076	13,154	11,712	81,900	81,950	13,814	9,604	13,814	12,372
75,950	76,000	12,505	8,722	12,505	11,063	78,950	79,000	13,165	9,082	13,165	11,723	81,950	82,000	13,825	9,615	13,825	12,383

76,000 / 79,000 / 82,000

At least	But less than	Single	MFJ	MFS	HoH	At least	But less than	Single	MFJ	MFS	HoH	At least	But less than	Single	MFJ	MFS	HoH
76,000	76,050	12,516	8,728	12,516	11,074	79,000	79,050	13,176	9,088	13,176	11,734	82,000	82,050	13,836	9,626	13,836	12,394
76,050	76,100	12,527	8,734	12,527	11,085	79,050	79,100	13,187	9,094	13,187	11,745	82,050	82,100	13,847	9,637	13,847	12,405
76,100	76,150	12,538	8,740	12,538	11,096	79,100	79,150	13,198	9,100	13,198	11,756	82,100	82,150	13,858	9,648	13,858	12,416
76,150	76,200	12,549	8,746	12,549	11,107	79,150	79,200	13,209	9,106	13,209	11,767	82,150	82,200	13,869	9,659	13,869	12,427
76,200	76,250	12,560	8,752	12,560	11,118	79,200	79,250	13,220	9,112	13,220	11,778	82,200	82,250	13,880	9,670	13,880	12,438
76,250	76,300	12,571	8,758	12,571	11,129	79,250	79,300	13,231	9,118	13,231	11,789	82,250	82,300	13,891	9,681	13,891	12,449
76,300	76,350	12,582	8,764	12,582	11,140	79,300	79,350	13,242	9,124	13,242	11,800	82,300	82,350	13,902	9,692	13,902	12,460
76,350	76,400	12,593	8,770	12,593	11,151	79,350	79,400	13,253	9,130	13,253	11,811	82,350	82,400	13,913	9,703	13,913	12,471
76,400	76,450	12,604	8,776	12,604	11,162	79,400	79,450	13,264	9,136	13,264	11,822	82,400	82,450	13,924	9,714	13,924	12,482
76,450	76,500	12,615	8,782	12,615	11,173	79,450	79,500	13,275	9,142	13,275	11,833	82,450	82,500	13,935	9,725	13,935	12,493
76,500	76,550	12,626	8,788	12,626	11,184	79,500	79,550	13,286	9,148	13,286	11,844	82,500	82,550	13,946	9,736	13,946	12,504
76,550	76,600	12,637	8,794	12,637	11,195	79,550	79,600	13,297	9,154	13,297	11,855	82,550	82,600	13,957	9,747	13,957	12,515
76,600	76,650	12,648	8,800	12,648	11,206	79,600	79,650	13,308	9,160	13,308	11,866	82,600	82,650	13,968	9,758	13,968	12,526
76,650	76,700	12,659	8,806	12,659	11,217	79,650	79,700	13,319	9,166	13,319	11,877	82,650	82,700	13,979	9,769	13,979	12,537
76,700	76,750	12,670	8,812	12,670	11,228	79,700	79,750	13,330	9,172	13,330	11,888	82,700	82,750	13,990	9,780	13,990	12,548
76,750	76,800	12,681	8,818	12,681	11,239	79,750	79,800	13,341	9,178	13,341	11,899	82,750	82,800	14,001	9,791	14,001	12,559
76,800	76,850	12,692	8,824	12,692	11,250	79,800	79,850	13,352	9,184	13,352	11,910	82,800	82,850	14,012	9,802	14,012	12,570
76,850	76,900	12,703	8,830	12,703	11,261	79,850	79,900	13,363	9,190	13,363	11,921	82,850	82,900	14,023	9,813	14,023	12,581
76,900	76,950	12,714	8,836	12,714	11,272	79,900	79,950	13,374	9,196	13,374	11,932	82,900	82,950	14,034	9,824	14,034	12,592
76,950	77,000	12,725	8,842	12,725	11,283	79,950	80,000	13,385	9,202	13,385	11,943	82,950	83,000	14,045	9,835	14,045	12,603

77,000 / 80,000 / 83,000

At least	But less than	Single	MFJ	MFS	HoH	At least	But less than	Single	MFJ	MFS	HoH	At least	But less than	Single	MFJ	MFS	HoH
77,000	77,050	12,736	8,848	12,736	11,294	80,000	80,050	13,396	9,208	13,396	11,954	83,000	83,050	14,056	9,846	14,056	12,614
77,050	77,100	12,747	8,854	12,747	11,305	80,050	80,100	13,407	9,214	13,407	11,965	83,050	83,100	14,067	9,857	14,067	12,625
77,100	77,150	12,758	8,860	12,758	11,316	80,100	80,150	13,418	9,220	13,418	11,976	83,100	83,150	14,078	9,868	14,078	12,636
77,150	77,200	12,769	8,866	12,769	11,327	80,150	80,200	13,429	9,226	13,429	11,987	83,150	83,200	14,089	9,879	14,089	12,647
77,200	77,250	12,780	8,872	12,780	11,338	80,200	80,250	13,440	9,232	13,440	11,998	83,200	83,250	14,100	9,890	14,100	12,658
77,250	77,300	12,791	8,878	12,791	11,349	80,250	80,300	13,451	9,241	13,451	12,009	83,250	83,300	14,111	9,901	14,111	12,669
77,300	77,350	12,802	8,884	12,802	11,360	80,300	80,350	13,462	9,252	13,462	12,020	83,300	83,350	14,122	9,912	14,122	12,680
77,350	77,400	12,813	8,890	12,813	11,371	80,350	80,400	13,473	9,263	13,473	12,031	83,350	83,400	14,133	9,923	14,133	12,691
77,400	77,450	12,824	8,896	12,824	11,382	80,400	80,450	13,484	9,274	13,484	12,042	83,400	83,450	14,144	9,934	14,144	12,702
77,450	77,500	12,835	8,902	12,835	11,393	80,450	80,500	13,495	9,285	13,495	12,053	83,450	83,500	14,155	9,945	14,155	12,713
77,500	77,550	12,846	8,908	12,846	11,404	80,500	80,550	13,506	9,296	13,506	12,064	83,500	83,550	14,166	9,956	14,166	12,724
77,550	77,600	12,857	8,914	12,857	11,415	80,550	80,600	13,517	9,307	13,517	12,075	83,550	83,600	14,177	9,967	14,177	12,735
77,600	77,650	12,868	8,920	12,868	11,426	80,600	80,650	13,528	9,318	13,528	12,086	83,600	83,650	14,188	9,978	14,188	12,746
77,650	77,700	12,879	8,926	12,879	11,437	80,650	80,700	13,539	9,329	13,539	12,097	83,650	83,700	14,199	9,989	14,199	12,757
77,700	77,750	12,890	8,932	12,890	11,448	80,700	80,750	13,550	9,340	13,550	12,108	83,700	83,750	14,210	10,000	14,210	12,768
77,750	77,800	12,901	8,938	12,901	11,459	80,750	80,800	13,561	9,351	13,561	12,119	83,750	83,800	14,221	10,011	14,221	12,779
77,800	77,850	12,912	8,944	12,912	11,470	80,800	80,850	13,572	9,362	13,572	12,130	83,800	83,850	14,232	10,022	14,232	12,790
77,850	77,900	12,923	8,950	12,923	11,481	80,850	80,900	13,583	9,373	13,583	12,141	83,850	83,900	14,243	10,033	14,243	12,801
77,900	77,950	12,934	8,956	12,934	11,492	80,900	80,950	13,594	9,384	13,594	12,152	83,900	83,950	14,254	10,044	14,254	12,812
77,950	78,000	12,945	8,962	12,945	11,503	80,950	81,000	13,605	9,395	13,605	12,163	83,950	84,000	14,265	10,055	14,265	12,823

(Continued)

* This column must also be used by a qualifying widow(er).

2020 Tax Table — *Continued*

84,000

If line 15 (taxable income) is—		And you are—			
At least	But less than	Single	Married filing jointly *	Married filing separately	Head of a household
		Your tax is—			
84,000	84,050	14,276	10,066	14,276	12,834
84,050	84,100	14,287	10,077	14,287	12,845
84,100	84,150	14,298	10,088	14,298	12,856
84,150	84,200	14,309	10,099	14,309	12,867
84,200	84,250	14,320	10,110	14,320	12,878
84,250	84,300	14,331	10,121	14,331	12,889
84,300	84,350	14,342	10,132	14,342	12,900
84,350	84,400	14,353	10,143	14,353	12,911
84,400	84,450	14,364	10,154	14,364	12,922
84,450	84,500	14,375	10,165	14,375	12,933
84,500	84,550	14,386	10,176	14,386	12,944
84,550	84,600	14,397	10,187	14,397	12,955
84,600	84,650	14,408	10,198	14,408	12,966
84,650	84,700	14,419	10,209	14,419	12,977
84,700	84,750	14,430	10,220	14,430	12,988
84,750	84,800	14,441	10,231	14,441	12,999
84,800	84,850	14,452	10,242	14,452	13,010
84,850	84,900	14,463	10,253	14,463	13,021
84,900	84,950	14,474	10,264	14,474	13,032
84,950	85,000	14,485	10,275	14,485	13,043

85,000

At least	But less than	Single	Married filing jointly *	Married filing separately	Head of a household
85,000	85,050	14,496	10,286	14,496	13,054
85,050	85,100	14,507	10,297	14,507	13,065
85,100	85,150	14,518	10,308	14,518	13,076
85,150	85,200	14,529	10,319	14,529	13,087
85,200	85,250	14,540	10,330	14,540	13,098
85,250	85,300	14,551	10,341	14,551	13,109
85,300	85,350	14,562	10,352	14,562	13,120
85,350	85,400	14,573	10,363	14,573	13,131
85,400	85,450	14,584	10,374	14,584	13,142
85,450	85,500	14,595	10,385	14,595	13,153
85,500	85,550	14,606	10,396	14,606	13,164
85,550	85,600	14,618	10,407	14,618	13,176
85,600	85,650	14,630	10,418	14,630	13,188
85,650	85,700	14,642	10,429	14,642	13,200
85,700	85,750	14,654	10,440	14,654	13,212
85,750	85,800	14,666	10,451	14,666	13,224
85,800	85,850	14,678	10,462	14,678	13,236
85,850	85,900	14,690	10,473	14,690	13,248
85,900	85,950	14,702	10,484	14,702	13,260
85,950	86,000	14,714	10,495	14,714	13,272

86,000

At least	But less than	Single	Married filing jointly *	Married filing separately	Head of a household
86,000	86,050	14,726	10,506	14,726	13,284
86,050	86,100	14,738	10,517	14,738	13,296
86,100	86,150	14,750	10,528	14,750	13,308
86,150	86,200	14,762	10,539	14,762	13,320
86,200	86,250	14,774	10,550	14,774	13,332
86,250	86,300	14,786	10,561	14,786	13,344
86,300	86,350	14,798	10,572	14,798	13,356
86,350	86,400	14,810	10,583	14,810	13,368
86,400	86,450	14,822	10,594	14,822	13,380
86,450	86,500	14,834	10,605	14,834	13,392
86,500	86,550	14,846	10,616	14,846	13,404
86,550	86,600	14,858	10,627	14,858	13,416
86,600	86,650	14,870	10,638	14,870	13,428
86,650	86,700	14,882	10,649	14,882	13,440
86,700	86,750	14,894	10,660	14,894	13,452
86,750	86,800	14,906	10,671	14,906	13,464
86,800	86,850	14,918	10,682	14,918	13,476
86,850	86,900	14,930	10,693	14,930	13,488
86,900	86,950	14,942	10,704	14,942	13,500
86,950	87,000	14,954	10,715	14,954	13,512

87,000

If line 15 (taxable income) is—		And you are—			
At least	But less than	Single	Married filing jointly *	Married filing separately	Head of a household
		Your tax is—			
87,000	87,050	14,966	10,726	14,966	13,524
87,050	87,100	14,978	10,737	14,978	13,536
87,100	87,150	14,990	10,748	14,990	13,548
87,150	87,200	15,002	10,759	15,002	13,560
87,200	87,250	15,014	10,770	15,014	13,572
87,250	87,300	15,026	10,781	15,026	13,584
87,300	87,350	15,038	10,792	15,038	13,596
87,350	87,400	15,050	10,803	15,050	13,608
87,400	87,450	15,062	10,814	15,062	13,620
87,450	87,500	15,074	10,825	15,074	13,632
87,500	87,550	15,086	10,836	15,086	13,644
87,550	87,600	15,098	10,847	15,098	13,656
87,600	87,650	15,110	10,858	15,110	13,668
87,650	87,700	15,122	10,869	15,122	13,680
87,700	87,750	15,134	10,880	15,134	13,692
87,750	87,800	15,146	10,891	15,146	13,704
87,800	87,850	15,158	10,902	15,158	13,716
87,850	87,900	15,170	10,913	15,170	13,728
87,900	87,950	15,182	10,924	15,182	13,740
87,950	88,000	15,194	10,935	15,194	13,752

88,000

At least	But less than	Single	Married filing jointly *	Married filing separately	Head of a household
88,000	88,050	15,206	10,946	15,206	13,764
88,050	88,100	15,218	10,957	15,218	13,776
88,100	88,150	15,230	10,968	15,230	13,788
88,150	88,200	15,242	10,979	15,242	13,800
88,200	88,250	15,254	10,990	15,254	13,812
88,250	88,300	15,266	11,001	15,266	13,824
88,300	88,350	15,278	11,012	15,278	13,836
88,350	88,400	15,290	11,023	15,290	13,848
88,400	88,450	15,302	11,034	15,302	13,860
88,450	88,500	15,314	11,045	15,314	13,872
88,500	88,550	15,326	11,056	15,326	13,884
88,550	88,600	15,338	11,067	15,338	13,896
88,600	88,650	15,350	11,078	15,350	13,908
88,650	88,700	15,362	11,089	15,362	13,920
88,700	88,750	15,374	11,100	15,374	13,932
88,750	88,800	15,386	11,111	15,386	13,944
88,800	88,850	15,398	11,122	15,398	13,956
88,850	88,900	15,410	11,133	15,410	13,968
88,900	88,950	15,422	11,144	15,422	13,980
88,950	89,000	15,434	11,155	15,434	13,992

89,000

At least	But less than	Single	Married filing jointly *	Married filing separately	Head of a household
89,000	89,050	15,446	11,166	15,446	14,004
89,050	89,100	15,458	11,177	15,458	14,016
89,100	89,150	15,470	11,188	15,470	14,028
89,150	89,200	15,482	11,199	15,482	14,040
89,200	89,250	15,494	11,210	15,494	14,052
89,250	89,300	15,506	11,221	15,506	14,064
89,300	89,350	15,518	11,232	15,518	14,076
89,350	89,400	15,530	11,243	15,530	14,088
89,400	89,450	15,542	11,254	15,542	14,100
89,450	89,500	15,554	11,265	15,554	14,112
89,500	89,550	15,566	11,276	15,566	14,124
89,550	89,600	15,578	11,287	15,578	14,136
89,600	89,650	15,590	11,298	15,590	14,148
89,650	89,700	15,602	11,309	15,602	14,160
89,700	89,750	15,614	11,320	15,614	14,172
89,750	89,800	15,626	11,331	15,626	14,184
89,800	89,850	15,638	11,342	15,638	14,196
89,850	89,900	15,650	11,353	15,650	14,208
89,900	89,950	15,662	11,364	15,662	14,220
89,950	90,000	15,674	11,375	15,674	14,232

90,000

If line 15 (taxable income) is—		And you are—			
At least	But less than	Single	Married filing jointly *	Married filing separately	Head of a household
		Your tax is—			
90,000	90,050	15,686	11,386	15,686	14,244
90,050	90,100	15,698	11,397	15,698	14,256
90,100	90,150	15,710	11,408	15,710	14,268
90,150	90,200	15,722	11,419	15,722	14,280
90,200	90,250	15,734	11,430	15,734	14,292
90,250	90,300	15,746	11,441	15,746	14,304
90,300	90,350	15,758	11,452	15,758	14,316
90,350	90,400	15,770	11,463	15,770	14,328
90,400	90,450	15,782	11,474	15,782	14,340
90,450	90,500	15,794	11,485	15,794	14,352
90,500	90,550	15,806	11,496	15,806	14,364
90,550	90,600	15,818	11,507	15,818	14,376
90,600	90,650	15,830	11,518	15,830	14,388
90,650	90,700	15,842	11,529	15,842	14,400
90,700	90,750	15,854	11,540	15,854	14,412
90,750	90,800	15,866	11,551	15,866	14,424
90,800	90,850	15,878	11,562	15,878	14,436
90,850	90,900	15,890	11,573	15,890	14,448
90,900	90,950	15,902	11,584	15,902	14,460
90,950	91,000	15,914	11,595	15,914	14,472

91,000

At least	But less than	Single	Married filing jointly *	Married filing separately	Head of a household
91,000	91,050	15,926	11,606	15,926	14,484
91,050	91,100	15,938	11,617	15,938	14,496
91,100	91,150	15,950	11,628	15,950	14,508
91,150	91,200	15,962	11,639	15,962	14,520
91,200	91,250	15,974	11,650	15,974	14,532
91,250	91,300	15,986	11,661	15,986	14,544
91,300	91,350	15,998	11,672	15,998	14,556
91,350	91,400	16,010	11,683	16,010	14,568
91,400	91,450	16,022	11,694	16,022	14,580
91,450	91,500	16,034	11,705	16,034	14,592
91,500	91,550	16,046	11,716	16,046	14,604
91,550	91,600	16,058	11,727	16,058	14,616
91,600	91,650	16,070	11,738	16,070	14,628
91,650	91,700	16,082	11,749	16,082	14,640
91,700	91,750	16,094	11,760	16,094	14,652
91,750	91,800	16,106	11,771	16,106	14,664
91,800	91,850	16,118	11,782	16,118	14,676
91,850	91,900	16,130	11,793	16,130	14,688
91,900	91,950	16,142	11,804	16,142	14,700
91,950	92,000	16,154	11,815	16,154	14,712

92,000

At least	But less than	Single	Married filing jointly *	Married filing separately	Head of a household
92,000	92,050	16,166	11,826	16,166	14,724
92,050	92,100	16,178	11,837	16,178	14,736
92,100	92,150	16,190	11,848	16,190	14,748
92,150	92,200	16,202	11,859	16,202	14,760
92,200	92,250	16,214	11,870	16,214	14,772
92,250	92,300	16,226	11,881	16,226	14,784
92,300	92,350	16,238	11,892	16,238	14,796
92,350	92,400	16,250	11,903	16,250	14,808
92,400	92,450	16,262	11,914	16,262	14,820
92,450	92,500	16,274	11,925	16,274	14,832
92,500	92,550	16,286	11,936	16,286	14,844
92,550	92,600	16,298	11,947	16,298	14,856
92,600	92,650	16,310	11,958	16,310	14,868
92,650	92,700	16,322	11,969	16,322	14,880
92,700	92,750	16,334	11,980	16,334	14,892
92,750	92,800	16,346	11,991	16,346	14,904
92,800	92,850	16,358	12,002	16,358	14,916
92,850	92,900	16,370	12,013	16,370	14,928
92,900	92,950	16,382	12,024	16,382	14,940
92,950	93,000	16,394	12,035	16,394	14,952

* This column must also be used by a qualifying widow(er).

(Continued)

2020 Tax Table — Continued

If line 15 (taxable income) is—		And you are—			
At least	But less than	Single	Married filing jointly *	Married filing separately	Head of a house-hold
		Your tax is—			

93,000

At least	But less than	Single	Married filing jointly	Married filing separately	Head of a household
93,000	93,050	16,406	12,046	16,406	14,964
93,050	93,100	16,418	12,057	16,418	14,976
93,100	93,150	16,430	12,068	16,430	14,988
93,150	93,200	16,442	12,079	16,442	15,000
93,200	93,250	16,454	12,090	16,454	15,012
93,250	93,300	16,466	12,101	16,466	15,024
93,300	93,350	16,478	12,112	16,478	15,036
93,350	93,400	16,490	12,123	16,490	15,048
93,400	93,450	16,502	12,134	16,502	15,060
93,450	93,500	16,514	12,145	16,514	15,072
93,500	93,550	16,526	12,156	16,526	15,084
93,550	93,600	16,538	12,167	16,538	15,096
93,600	93,650	16,550	12,178	16,550	15,108
93,650	93,700	16,562	12,189	16,562	15,120
93,700	93,750	16,574	12,200	16,574	15,132
93,750	93,800	16,586	12,211	16,586	15,144
93,800	93,850	16,598	12,222	16,598	15,156
93,850	93,900	16,610	12,233	16,610	15,168
93,900	93,950	16,622	12,244	16,622	15,180
93,950	94,000	16,634	12,255	16,634	15,192

94,000

At least	But less than	Single	Married filing jointly	Married filing separately	Head of a household
94,000	94,050	16,646	12,266	16,646	15,204
94,050	94,100	16,658	12,277	16,658	15,216
94,100	94,150	16,670	12,288	16,670	15,228
94,150	94,200	16,682	12,299	16,682	15,240
94,200	94,250	16,694	12,310	16,694	15,252
94,250	94,300	16,706	12,321	16,706	15,264
94,300	94,350	16,718	12,332	16,718	15,276
94,350	94,400	16,730	12,343	16,730	15,288
94,400	94,450	16,742	12,354	16,742	15,300
94,450	94,500	16,754	12,365	16,754	15,312
94,500	94,550	16,766	12,376	16,766	15,324
94,550	94,600	16,778	12,387	16,778	15,336
94,600	94,650	16,790	12,398	16,790	15,348
94,650	94,700	16,802	12,409	16,802	15,360
94,700	94,750	16,814	12,420	16,814	15,372
94,750	94,800	16,826	12,431	16,826	15,384
94,800	94,850	16,838	12,442	16,838	15,396
94,850	94,900	16,850	12,453	16,850	15,408
94,900	94,950	16,862	12,464	16,862	15,420
94,950	95,000	16,874	12,475	16,874	15,432

95,000

At least	But less than	Single	Married filing jointly	Married filing separately	Head of a household
95,000	95,050	16,886	12,486	16,886	15,444
95,050	95,100	16,898	12,497	16,898	15,456
95,100	95,150	16,910	12,508	16,910	15,468
95,150	95,200	16,922	12,519	16,922	15,480
95,200	95,250	16,934	12,530	16,934	15,492
95,250	95,300	16,946	12,541	16,946	15,504
95,300	95,350	16,958	12,552	16,958	15,516
95,350	95,400	16,970	12,563	16,970	15,528
95,400	95,450	16,982	12,574	16,982	15,540
95,450	95,500	16,994	12,585	16,994	15,552
95,500	95,550	17,006	12,596	17,006	15,564
95,550	95,600	17,018	12,607	17,018	15,576
95,600	95,650	17,030	12,618	17,030	15,588
95,650	95,700	17,042	12,629	17,042	15,600
95,700	95,750	17,054	12,640	17,054	15,612
95,750	95,800	17,066	12,651	17,066	15,624
95,800	95,850	17,078	12,662	17,078	15,636
95,850	95,900	17,090	12,673	17,090	15,648
95,900	95,950	17,102	12,684	17,102	15,660
95,950	96,000	17,114	12,695	17,114	15,672

If line 15 (taxable income) is—		And you are—			
At least	But less than	Single	Married filing jointly *	Married filing separately	Head of a house-hold
		Your tax is—			

96,000

At least	But less than	Single	Married filing jointly	Married filing separately	Head of a household
96,000	96,050	17,126	12,706	17,126	15,684
96,050	96,100	17,138	12,717	17,138	15,696
96,100	96,150	17,150	12,728	17,150	15,708
96,150	96,200	17,162	12,739	17,162	15,720
96,200	96,250	17,174	12,750	17,174	15,732
96,250	96,300	17,186	12,761	17,186	15,744
96,300	96,350	17,198	12,772	17,198	15,756
96,350	96,400	17,210	12,783	17,210	15,768
96,400	96,450	17,222	12,794	17,222	15,780
96,450	96,500	17,234	12,805	17,234	15,792
96,500	96,550	17,246	12,816	17,246	15,804
96,550	96,600	17,258	12,827	17,258	15,816
96,600	96,650	17,270	12,838	17,270	15,828
96,650	96,700	17,282	12,849	17,282	15,840
96,700	96,750	17,294	12,860	17,294	15,852
96,750	96,800	17,306	12,871	17,306	15,864
96,800	96,850	17,318	12,882	17,318	15,876
96,850	96,900	17,330	12,893	17,330	15,888
96,900	96,950	17,342	12,904	17,342	15,900
96,950	97,000	17,354	12,915	17,354	15,912

97,000

At least	But less than	Single	Married filing jointly	Married filing separately	Head of a household
97,000	97,050	17,366	12,926	17,366	15,924
97,050	97,100	17,378	12,937	17,378	15,936
97,100	97,150	17,390	12,948	17,390	15,948
97,150	97,200	17,402	12,959	17,402	15,960
97,200	97,250	17,414	12,970	17,414	15,972
97,250	97,300	17,426	12,981	17,426	15,984
97,300	97,350	17,438	12,992	17,438	15,996
97,350	97,400	17,450	13,003	17,450	16,008
97,400	97,450	17,462	13,014	17,462	16,020
97,450	97,500	17,474	13,025	17,474	16,032
97,500	97,550	17,486	13,036	17,486	16,044
97,550	97,600	17,498	13,047	17,498	16,056
97,600	97,650	17,510	13,058	17,510	16,068
97,650	97,700	17,522	13,069	17,522	16,080
97,700	97,750	17,534	13,080	17,534	16,092
97,750	97,800	17,546	13,091	17,546	16,104
97,800	97,850	17,558	13,102	17,558	16,116
97,850	97,900	17,570	13,113	17,570	16,128
97,900	97,950	17,582	13,124	17,582	16,140
97,950	98,000	17,594	13,135	17,594	16,152

98,000

At least	But less than	Single	Married filing jointly	Married filing separately	Head of a household
98,000	98,050	17,606	13,146	17,606	16,164
98,050	98,100	17,618	13,157	17,618	16,176
98,100	98,150	17,630	13,168	17,630	16,188
98,150	98,200	17,642	13,179	17,642	16,200
98,200	98,250	17,654	13,190	17,654	16,212
98,250	98,300	17,666	13,201	17,666	16,224
98,300	98,350	17,678	13,212	17,678	16,236
98,350	98,400	17,690	13,223	17,690	16,248
98,400	98,450	17,702	13,234	17,702	16,260
98,450	98,500	17,714	13,245	17,714	16,272
98,500	98,550	17,726	13,256	17,726	16,284
98,550	98,600	17,738	13,267	17,738	16,296
98,600	98,650	17,750	13,278	17,750	16,308
98,650	98,700	17,762	13,289	17,762	16,320
98,700	98,750	17,774	13,300	17,774	16,332
98,750	98,800	17,786	13,311	17,786	16,344
98,800	98,850	17,798	13,322	17,798	16,356
98,850	98,900	17,810	13,333	17,810	16,368
98,900	98,950	17,822	13,344	17,822	16,380
98,950	99,000	17,834	13,355	17,834	16,392

If line 15 (taxable income) is—		And you are—			
At least	But less than	Single	Married filing jointly *	Married filing separately	Head of a house-hold
		Your tax is—			

99,000

At least	But less than	Single	Married filing jointly	Married filing separately	Head of a household
99,000	99,050	17,846	13,366	17,846	16,404
99,050	99,100	17,858	13,377	17,858	16,416
99,100	99,150	17,870	13,388	17,870	16,428
99,150	99,200	17,882	13,399	17,882	16,440
99,200	99,250	17,894	13,410	17,894	16,452
99,250	99,300	17,906	13,421	17,906	16,464
99,300	99,350	17,918	13,432	17,918	16,476
99,350	99,400	17,930	13,443	17,930	16,488
99,400	99,450	17,942	13,454	17,942	16,500
99,450	99,500	17,954	13,465	17,954	16,512
99,500	99,550	17,966	13,476	17,966	16,524
99,550	99,600	17,978	13,487	17,978	16,536
99,600	99,650	17,990	13,498	17,990	16,548
99,650	99,700	18,002	13,509	18,002	16,560
99,700	99,750	18,014	13,520	18,014	16,572
99,750	99,800	18,026	13,531	18,026	16,584
99,800	99,850	18,038	13,542	18,038	16,596
99,850	99,900	18,050	13,553	18,050	16,608
99,900	99,950	18,062	13,564	18,062	16,620
99,950	100,000	18,074	13,575	18,074	16,632

**$100,000
or over
use the Tax
Computation
Worksheet**

* This column must also be used by a qualifying widow(er).

Earned Income Credit Table

CONTENTS

Worksheet **A**—2020 EIC—Line 27*

Keep for Your Records

Before you begin: √ Be sure you are using the correct worksheet. Use this worksheet only if you answered "No" to Step 5, question 2. Otherwise, use Worksheet B.

Part 1

All Filers Using Worksheet A

1. Enter your earned income from Step 5.
   Wages, salaries

   1 _____

2. Look up the amount on line 1 above in the EIC Table (right after Worksheet B) to find the credit. Be sure you use the correct column for your filing status and the number of children you have. Enter the credit here.
   If line 2 is zero, (STOP) You can't take the credit.
   Enter "No" on the dotted line next to Form 1040 or 1040-SR, line 27.

   2 _____

3. Enter the amount from Form 1040 or 1040-SR, line 11.
   Adjusted gross income

   3 _____

4. Are the amounts on lines 3 and 1 the same?

   ☐ **Yes.** Skip line 5; enter the amount from line 2 on line 6.

   ☐ **No.**   Go to line 5.

Part 2

Filers Who Answered "No" on Line 4

5. If you have:
   ● No qualifying children, is the amount on line 3 less than $8,800 ($14,700 if married filing jointly)?
   ● 1 or more qualifying children, is the amount on line 3 less than $19,350 ($25,250 if married filing jointly)?

   ☐ **Yes.** Leave line 5 blank; enter the amount from line 2 on line 6.

   ☐ **No.**   Look up the amount on line 3 in the EIC Table to find the credit. Be sure you use the correct column for your filing status and the number of children you have. Enter the credit here.
   Look at the amounts on lines 5 and 2.
   Then, enter the **smaller** amount on line 6.

   5 _____

Part 3

Your Earned Income Credit

6. **This is your earned income credit.**

   6 _____

   Enter this amount on
   Form 1040 or 1040-SR,
   line 27.

   Reminder—

   √ If you have a qualifying child, complete and attach Schedule EIC.

   ⚠ **CAUTION** If your EIC for a year after 1996 was reduced or disallowed, see Form 8862, who must file, *earlier*, to find out if you must file Form 8862 to take the credit for 2020.

---

*Download the latest version of this worksheet from the Form 1040 Instructions available at www.irs.gov. The 2020 worksheet was not available as we went to print. This worksheet is adapted from the 2019 version.

2020 Earned Income Credit (EIC) Table
Caution. This is **not** a tax table.

1. To find your credit, read down the "At least - But less than" columns and find the line that includes the amount you were told to look up from your EIC Worksheet.

2. Then, go to the column that includes your filing status and the number of qualifying children you have. Enter the credit from that column on your EIC Worksheet.

Example. If your filing status is single, you have one qualifying child, and the amount you are looking up from your EIC Worksheet is $2,455, you would enter $842.

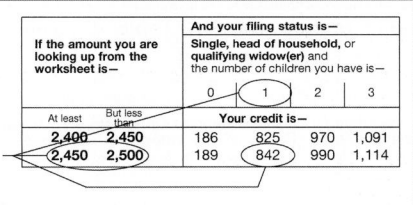

If the amount you are looking up from the worksheet is—	And your filing status is— Single, head of household, or qualifying widow(er) and the number of children you have is—			
At least	But less than	0	1	2	3
		Your credit is—			
2,400	2,450	186	825	970	1,091
2,450	2,500	189	842	990	1,114

If the amount you are looking up from the worksheet is–		And your filing status is–							
		Single, head of household, or qualifying widow(er) and you have–				Married filing jointly and you have–			
At least	But less than	0	1	2	3	0	1	2	3
		Your credit is–				Your credit is–			
$1	$50	$2	$9	$10	$11	$2	$9	$10	$11
50	100	6	26	30	34	6	26	30	34
100	150	10	43	50	56	10	43	50	56
150	200	13	60	70	79	13	60	70	79
200	250	17	77	90	101	17	77	90	101
250	300	21	94	110	124	21	94	110	124
300	350	25	111	130	146	25	111	130	146
350	400	29	128	150	169	29	128	150	169
400	450	33	145	170	191	33	145	170	191
450	500	36	162	190	214	36	162	190	214
500	550	40	179	210	236	40	179	210	236
550	600	44	196	230	259	44	196	230	259
600	650	48	213	250	281	48	213	250	281
650	700	52	230	270	304	52	230	270	304
700	750	55	247	290	326	55	247	290	326
750	800	59	264	310	349	59	264	310	349
800	850	63	281	330	371	63	281	330	371
850	900	67	298	350	394	67	298	350	394
900	950	71	315	370	416	71	315	370	416
950	1,000	75	332	390	439	75	332	390	439
1,000	1,050	78	349	410	461	78	349	410	461
1,050	1,100	82	366	430	484	82	366	430	484
1,100	1,150	86	383	450	506	86	383	450	506
1,150	1,200	90	400	470	529	90	400	470	529
1,200	1,250	94	417	490	551	94	417	490	551
1,250	1,300	98	434	510	574	98	434	510	574
1,300	1,350	101	451	530	596	101	451	530	596
1,350	1,400	105	468	550	619	105	468	550	619
1,400	1,450	109	485	570	641	109	485	570	641
1,450	1,500	113	502	590	664	113	502	590	664
1,500	1,550	117	519	610	686	117	519	610	686
1,550	1,600	120	536	630	709	120	536	630	709
1,600	1,650	124	553	650	731	124	553	650	731
1,650	1,700	128	570	670	754	128	570	670	754
1,700	1,750	132	587	690	776	132	587	690	776
1,750	1,800	136	604	710	799	136	604	710	799
1,800	1,850	140	621	730	821	140	621	730	821
1,850	1,900	143	638	750	844	143	638	750	844
1,900	1,950	147	655	770	866	147	655	770	866
1,950	2,000	151	672	790	889	151	672	790	889
2,000	2,050	155	689	810	911	155	689	810	911
2,050	2,100	159	706	830	934	159	706	830	934
2,100	2,150	163	723	850	956	163	723	850	956
2,150	2,200	166	740	870	979	166	740	870	979
2,200	2,250	170	757	890	1,001	170	757	890	1,001
2,250	2,300	174	774	910	1,024	174	774	910	1,024
2,300	2,350	178	791	930	1,046	178	791	930	1,046
2,350	2,400	182	808	950	1,069	182	808	950	1,069
2,400	2,450	186	825	970	1,091	186	825	970	1,091
2,450	2,500	189	842	990	1,114	189	842	990	1,114
2,500	2,550	193	859	1,010	1,136	193	859	1,010	1,136
2,550	2,600	197	876	1,030	1,159	197	876	1,030	1,159
2,600	2,650	201	893	1,050	1,181	201	893	1,050	1,181
2,650	2,700	205	910	1,070	1,204	205	910	1,070	1,204
2,700	2,750	208	927	1,090	1,226	208	927	1,090	1,226
2,750	2,800	212	944	1,110	1,249	212	944	1,110	1,249

If the amount you are looking up from the worksheet is–		And your filing status is–							
		Single, head of household, or qualifying widow(er) and you have–				Married filing jointly and you have–			
At least	But less than	0	1	2	3	0	1	2	3
		Your credit is–				Your credit is–			
2,800	2,850	216	961	1,130	1,271	216	961	1,130	1,271
2,850	2,900	220	978	1,150	1,294	220	978	1,150	1,294
2,900	2,950	224	995	1,170	1,316	224	995	1,170	1,316
2,950	3,000	228	1,012	1,190	1,339	228	1,012	1,190	1,339
3,000	3,050	231	1,029	1,210	1,361	231	1,029	1,210	1,361
3,050	3,100	235	1,046	1,230	1,384	235	1,046	1,230	1,384
3,100	3,150	239	1,063	1,250	1,406	239	1,063	1,250	1,406
3,150	3,200	243	1,080	1,270	1,429	243	1,080	1,270	1,429
3,200	3,250	247	1,097	1,290	1,451	247	1,097	1,290	1,451
3,250	3,300	251	1,114	1,310	1,474	251	1,114	1,310	1,474
3,300	3,350	254	1,131	1,330	1,496	254	1,131	1,330	1,496
3,350	3,400	258	1,148	1,350	1,519	258	1,148	1,350	1,519
3,400	3,450	262	1,165	1,370	1,541	262	1,165	1,370	1,541
3,450	3,500	266	1,182	1,390	1,564	266	1,182	1,390	1,564
3,500	3,550	270	1,199	1,410	1,586	270	1,199	1,410	1,586
3,550	3,600	273	1,216	1,430	1,609	273	1,216	1,430	1,609
3,600	3,650	277	1,233	1,450	1,631	277	1,233	1,450	1,631
3,650	3,700	281	1,250	1,470	1,654	281	1,250	1,470	1,654
3,700	3,750	285	1,267	1,490	1,676	285	1,267	1,490	1,676
3,750	3,800	289	1,284	1,510	1,699	289	1,284	1,510	1,699
3,800	3,850	293	1,301	1,530	1,721	293	1,301	1,530	1,721
3,850	3,900	296	1,318	1,550	1,744	296	1,318	1,550	1,744
3,900	3,950	300	1,335	1,570	1,766	300	1,335	1,570	1,766
3,950	4,000	304	1,352	1,590	1,789	304	1,352	1,590	1,789
4,000	4,050	308	1,369	1,610	1,811	308	1,369	1,610	1,811
4,050	4,100	312	1,386	1,630	1,834	312	1,386	1,630	1,834
4,100	4,150	316	1,403	1,650	1,856	316	1,403	1,650	1,856
4,150	4,200	319	1,420	1,670	1,879	319	1,420	1,670	1,879
4,200	4,250	323	1,437	1,690	1,901	323	1,437	1,690	1,901
4,250	4,300	327	1,454	1,710	1,924	327	1,454	1,710	1,924
4,300	4,350	331	1,471	1,730	1,946	331	1,471	1,730	1,946
4,350	4,400	335	1,488	1,750	1,969	335	1,488	1,750	1,969
4,400	4,450	339	1,505	1,770	1,991	339	1,505	1,770	1,991
4,450	4,500	342	1,522	1,790	2,014	342	1,522	1,790	2,014
4,500	4,550	346	1,539	1,810	2,036	346	1,539	1,810	2,036
4,550	4,600	350	1,556	1,830	2,059	350	1,556	1,830	2,059
4,600	4,650	354	1,573	1,850	2,081	354	1,573	1,850	2,081
4,650	4,700	358	1,590	1,870	2,104	358	1,590	1,870	2,104
4,700	4,750	361	1,607	1,890	2,126	361	1,607	1,890	2,126
4,750	4,800	365	1,624	1,910	2,149	365	1,624	1,910	2,149
4,800	4,850	369	1,641	1,930	2,171	369	1,641	1,930	2,171
4,850	4,900	373	1,658	1,950	2,194	373	1,658	1,950	2,194
4,900	4,950	377	1,675	1,970	2,216	377	1,675	1,970	2,216
4,950	5,000	381	1,692	1,990	2,239	381	1,692	1,990	2,239
5,000	5,050	384	1,709	2,010	2,261	384	1,709	2,010	2,261
5,050	5,100	388	1,726	2,030	2,284	388	1,726	2,030	2,284
5,100	5,150	392	1,743	2,050	2,306	392	1,743	2,050	2,306
5,150	5,200	396	1,760	2,070	2,329	396	1,760	2,070	2,329
5,200	5,250	400	1,777	2,090	2,351	400	1,777	2,090	2,351
5,250	5,300	404	1,794	2,110	2,374	404	1,794	2,110	2,374
5,300	5,350	407	1,811	2,130	2,396	407	1,811	2,130	2,396
5,350	5,400	411	1,828	2,150	2,419	411	1,828	2,150	2,419
5,400	5,450	415	1,845	2,170	2,441	415	1,845	2,170	2,441
5,450	5,500	419	1,862	2,190	2,464	419	1,862	2,190	2,464
5,500	5,550	423	1,879	2,210	2,486	423	1,879	2,210	2,486
5,550	5,600	426	1,896	2,230	2,509	426	1,896	2,230	2,509

(Continued)

Earned Income Credit (EIC) Table - *Continued* (**Caution.** This is **not** a tax table.)

If the amount you are looking up from the worksheet is–		And your filing status is– Single, head of household, or qualifying widow(er) and you have–				Married filing jointly and you have–			
At least	But less than	0	1	2	3	0	1	2	3
		Your credit is–				Your credit is–			
5,600	5,650	430	1,913	2,250	2,531	430	1,913	2,250	2,531
5,650	5,700	434	1,930	2,270	2,554	434	1,930	2,270	2,554
5,700	5,750	438	1,947	2,290	2,576	438	1,947	2,290	2,576
5,750	5,800	442	1,964	2,310	2,599	442	1,964	2,310	2,599
5,800	5,850	446	1,981	2,330	2,621	446	1,981	2,330	2,621
5,850	5,900	449	1,998	2,350	2,644	449	1,998	2,350	2,644
5,900	5,950	453	2,015	2,370	2,666	453	2,015	2,370	2,666
5,950	6,000	457	2,032	2,390	2,689	457	2,032	2,390	2,689
6,000	6,050	461	2,049	2,410	2,711	461	2,049	2,410	2,711
6,050	6,100	465	2,066	2,430	2,734	465	2,066	2,430	2,734
6,100	6,150	469	2,083	2,450	2,756	469	2,083	2,450	2,756
6,150	6,200	472	2,100	2,470	2,779	472	2,100	2,470	2,779
6,200	6,250	476	2,117	2,490	2,801	476	2,117	2,490	2,801
6,250	6,300	480	2,134	2,510	2,824	480	2,134	2,510	2,824
6,300	6,350	484	2,151	2,530	2,846	484	2,151	2,530	2,846
6,350	6,400	488	2,168	2,550	2,869	488	2,168	2,550	2,869
6,400	6,450	492	2,185	2,570	2,891	492	2,185	2,570	2,891
6,450	6,500	495	2,202	2,590	2,914	495	2,202	2,590	2,914
6,500	6,550	499	2,219	2,610	2,936	499	2,219	2,610	2,936
6,550	6,600	503	2,236	2,630	2,959	503	2,236	2,630	2,959
6,600	6,650	507	2,253	2,650	2,981	507	2,253	2,650	2,981
6,650	6,700	511	2,270	2,670	3,004	511	2,270	2,670	3,004
6,700	6,750	514	2,287	2,690	3,026	514	2,287	2,690	3,026
6,750	6,800	518	2,304	2,710	3,049	518	2,304	2,710	3,049
6,800	6,850	522	2,321	2,730	3,071	522	2,321	2,730	3,071
6,850	6,900	526	2,338	2,750	3,094	526	2,338	2,750	3,094
6,900	6,950	530	2,355	2,770	3,116	530	2,355	2,770	3,116
6,950	7,000	534	2,372	2,790	3,139	534	2,372	2,790	3,139
7,000	7,050	538	2,389	2,810	3,161	538	2,389	2,810	3,161
7,050	7,100	538	2,406	2,830	3,184	538	2,406	2,830	3,184
7,100	7,150	538	2,423	2,850	3,206	538	2,423	2,850	3,206
7,150	7,200	538	2,440	2,870	3,229	538	2,440	2,870	3,229
7,200	7,250	538	2,457	2,890	3,251	538	2,457	2,890	3,251
7,250	7,300	538	2,474	2,910	3,274	538	2,474	2,910	3,274
7,300	7,350	538	2,491	2,930	3,296	538	2,491	2,930	3,296
7,350	7,400	538	2,508	2,950	3,319	538	2,508	2,950	3,319
7,400	7,450	538	2,525	2,970	3,341	538	2,525	2,970	3,341
7,450	7,500	538	2,542	2,990	3,364	538	2,542	2,990	3,364
7,500	7,550	538	2,559	3,010	3,386	538	2,559	3,010	3,386
7,550	7,600	538	2,576	3,030	3,409	538	2,576	3,030	3,409
7,600	7,650	538	2,593	3,050	3,431	538	2,593	3,050	3,431
7,650	7,700	538	2,610	3,070	3,454	538	2,610	3,070	3,454
7,700	7,750	538	2,627	3,090	3,476	538	2,627	3,090	3,476
7,750	7,800	538	2,644	3,110	3,499	538	2,644	3,110	3,499
7,800	7,850	538	2,661	3,130	3,521	538	2,661	3,130	3,521
7,850	7,900	538	2,678	3,150	3,544	538	2,678	3,150	3,544
7,900	7,950	538	2,695	3,170	3,566	538	2,695	3,170	3,566
7,950	8,000	538	2,712	3,190	3,589	538	2,712	3,190	3,589
8,000	8,050	538	2,729	3,210	3,611	538	2,729	3,210	3,611
8,050	8,100	538	2,746	3,230	3,634	538	2,746	3,230	3,634
8,100	8,150	538	2,763	3,250	3,656	538	2,763	3,250	3,656
8,150	8,200	538	2,780	3,270	3,679	538	2,780	3,270	3,679
8,200	8,250	538	2,797	3,290	3,701	538	2,797	3,290	3,701
8,250	8,300	538	2,814	3,310	3,724	538	2,814	3,310	3,724
8,300	8,350	538	2,831	3,330	3,746	538	2,831	3,330	3,746
8,350	8,400	538	2,848	3,350	3,769	538	2,848	3,350	3,769
8,400	8,450	538	2,865	3,370	3,791	538	2,865	3,370	3,791
8,450	8,500	538	2,882	3,390	3,814	538	2,882	3,390	3,814
8,500	8,550	538	2,899	3,410	3,836	538	2,899	3,410	3,836
8,550	8,600	538	2,916	3,430	3,859	538	2,916	3,430	3,859
8,600	8,650	538	2,933	3,450	3,881	538	2,933	3,450	3,881
8,650	8,700	538	2,950	3,470	3,904	538	2,950	3,470	3,904
8,700	8,750	538	2,967	3,490	3,926	538	2,967	3,490	3,926
8,750	8,800	538	2,984	3,510	3,949	538	2,984	3,510	3,949
8,800	8,850	535	3,001	3,530	3,971	538	3,001	3,530	3,971
8,850	8,900	531	3,018	3,550	3,994	538	3,018	3,550	3,994
8,900	8,950	527	3,035	3,570	4,016	538	3,035	3,570	4,016
8,950	9,000	524	3,052	3,590	4,039	538	3,052	3,590	4,039
9,000	9,050	520	3,069	3,610	4,061	538	3,069	3,610	4,061
9,050	9,100	516	3,086	3,630	4,084	538	3,086	3,630	4,084
9,100	9,150	512	3,103	3,650	4,106	538	3,103	3,650	4,106
9,150	9,200	508	3,120	3,670	4,129	538	3,120	3,670	4,129
9,200	9,250	505	3,137	3,690	4,151	538	3,137	3,690	4,151
9,250	9,300	501	3,154	3,710	4,174	538	3,154	3,710	4,174
9,300	9,350	497	3,171	3,730	4,196	538	3,171	3,730	4,196
9,350	9,400	493	3,188	3,750	4,219	538	3,188	3,750	4,219
9,400	9,450	489	3,205	3,770	4,241	538	3,205	3,770	4,241
9,450	9,500	485	3,222	3,790	4,264	538	3,222	3,790	4,264
9,500	9,550	482	3,239	3,810	4,286	538	3,239	3,810	4,286
9,550	9,600	478	3,256	3,830	4,309	538	3,256	3,830	4,309
9,600	9,650	474	3,273	3,850	4,331	538	3,273	3,850	4,331
9,650	9,700	470	3,290	3,870	4,354	538	3,290	3,870	4,354
9,700	9,750	466	3,307	3,890	4,376	538	3,307	3,890	4,376
9,750	9,800	462	3,324	3,910	4,399	538	3,324	3,910	4,399
9,800	9,850	459	3,341	3,930	4,421	538	3,341	3,930	4,421
9,850	9,900	455	3,358	3,950	4,444	538	3,358	3,950	4,444
9,900	9,950	451	3,375	3,970	4,466	538	3,375	3,970	4,466
9,950	10,000	447	3,392	3,990	4,489	538	3,392	3,990	4,489
10,000	10,050	443	3,409	4,010	4,511	538	3,409	4,010	4,511
10,050	10,100	439	3,426	4,030	4,534	538	3,426	4,030	4,534
10,100	10,150	436	3,443	4,050	4,556	538	3,443	4,050	4,556
10,150	10,200	432	3,460	4,070	4,579	538	3,460	4,070	4,579
10,200	10,250	428	3,477	4,090	4,601	538	3,477	4,090	4,601
10,250	10,300	424	3,494	4,110	4,624	538	3,494	4,110	4,624
10,300	10,350	420	3,511	4,130	4,646	538	3,511	4,130	4,646
10,350	10,400	417	3,528	4,150	4,669	538	3,528	4,150	4,669
10,400	10,450	413	3,545	4,170	4,691	538	3,545	4,170	4,691
10,450	10,500	409	3,562	4,190	4,714	538	3,562	4,190	4,714
10,500	10,550	405	3,584	4,210	4,736	538	3,584	4,210	4,736
10,550	10,600	401	3,584	4,230	4,759	538	3,584	4,230	4,759
10,600	10,650	397	3,584	4,250	4,781	538	3,584	4,250	4,781
10,650	10,700	394	3,584	4,270	4,804	538	3,584	4,270	4,804
10,700	10,750	390	3,584	4,290	4,826	538	3,584	4,290	4,826
10,750	10,800	386	3,584	4,310	4,849	538	3,584	4,310	4,849
10,800	10,850	382	3,584	4,330	4,871	538	3,584	4,330	4,871
10,850	10,900	378	3,584	4,350	4,894	538	3,584	4,350	4,894
10,900	10,950	374	3,584	4,370	4,916	538	3,584	4,370	4,916
10,950	11,000	371	3,584	4,390	4,939	538	3,584	4,390	4,939
11,000	11,050	367	3,584	4,410	4,961	538	3,584	4,410	4,961
11,050	11,100	363	3,584	4,430	4,984	538	3,584	4,430	4,984
11,100	11,150	359	3,584	4,450	5,006	538	3,584	4,450	5,006
11,150	11,200	355	3,584	4,470	5,029	538	3,584	4,470	5,029
11,200	11,250	352	3,584	4,490	5,051	538	3,584	4,490	5,051
11,250	11,300	348	3,584	4,510	5,074	538	3,584	4,510	5,074
11,300	11,350	344	3,584	4,530	5,096	538	3,584	4,530	5,096
11,350	11,400	340	3,584	4,550	5,119	538	3,584	4,550	5,119
11,400	11,450	336	3,584	4,570	5,141	538	3,584	4,570	5,141
11,450	11,500	332	3,584	4,590	5,164	538	3,584	4,590	5,164
11,500	11,550	329	3,584	4,610	5,186	538	3,584	4,610	5,186
11,550	11,600	325	3,584	4,630	5,209	538	3,584	4,630	5,209
11,600	11,650	321	3,584	4,650	5,231	538	3,584	4,650	5,231
11,650	11,700	317	3,584	4,670	5,254	538	3,584	4,670	5,254
11,700	11,750	313	3,584	4,690	5,276	538	3,584	4,690	5,276
11,750	11,800	309	3,584	4,710	5,299	538	3,584	4,710	5,299
11,800	11,850	306	3,584	4,730	5,321	538	3,584	4,730	5,321
11,850	11,900	302	3,584	4,750	5,344	538	3,584	4,750	5,344
11,900	11,950	298	3,584	4,770	5,366	538	3,584	4,770	5,366
11,950	12,000	294	3,584	4,790	5,389	538	3,584	4,790	5,389
12,000	12,050	290	3,584	4,810	5,411	538	3,584	4,810	5,411
12,050	12,100	286	3,584	4,830	5,434	538	3,584	4,830	5,434
12,100	12,150	283	3,584	4,850	5,456	538	3,584	4,850	5,456
12,150	12,200	279	3,584	4,870	5,479	538	3,584	4,870	5,479
12,200	12,250	275	3,584	4,890	5,501	538	3,584	4,890	5,501
12,250	12,300	271	3,584	4,910	5,524	538	3,584	4,910	5,524
12,300	12,350	267	3,584	4,930	5,546	538	3,584	4,930	5,546
12,350	12,400	264	3,584	4,950	5,569	538	3,584	4,950	5,569
12,400	12,450	260	3,584	4,970	5,591	538	3,584	4,970	5,591
12,450	12,500	256	3,584	4,990	5,614	538	3,584	4,990	5,614
12,500	12,550	252	3,584	5,010	5,636	538	3,584	5,010	5,636
12,550	12,600	248	3,584	5,030	5,659	538	3,584	5,030	5,659
12,600	12,650	244	3,584	5,050	5,681	538	3,584	5,050	5,681
12,650	12,700	241	3,584	5,070	5,704	538	3,584	5,070	5,704
12,700	12,750	237	3,584	5,090	5,726	538	3,584	5,090	5,726
12,750	12,800	233	3,584	5,110	5,749	538	3,584	5,110	5,749

(Continued)

Earned Income Credit (EIC) Table - *Continued*

(**Caution.** This is **not** a tax table.)

Left section

If the amount you are looking up from the worksheet is— At least	But less than	Single, head of household, or qualifying widow(er) and you have— 0	1	2	3	Married filing jointly and you have— 0	1	2	3
		Your credit is—				Your credit is—			
12,800	12,850	229	3,584	5,130	5,771	538	3,584	5,130	5,771
12,850	12,900	225	3,584	5,150	5,794	538	3,584	5,150	5,794
12,900	12,950	221	3,584	5,170	5,816	538	3,584	5,170	5,816
12,950	13,000	218	3,584	5,190	5,839	538	3,584	5,190	5,839
13,000	13,050	214	3,584	5,210	5,861	538	3,584	5,210	5,861
13,050	13,100	210	3,584	5,230	5,884	538	3,584	5,230	5,884
13,100	13,150	206	3,584	5,250	5,906	538	3,584	5,250	5,906
13,150	13,200	202	3,584	5,270	5,929	538	3,584	5,270	5,929
13,200	13,250	199	3,584	5,290	5,951	538	3,584	5,290	5,951
13,250	13,300	195	3,584	5,310	5,974	538	3,584	5,310	5,974
13,300	13,350	191	3,584	5,330	5,996	538	3,584	5,330	5,996
13,350	13,400	187	3,584	5,350	6,019	538	3,584	5,350	6,019
13,400	13,450	183	3,584	5,370	6,041	538	3,584	5,370	6,041
13,450	13,500	179	3,584	5,390	6,064	538	3,584	5,390	6,064
13,500	13,550	176	3,584	5,410	6,086	538	3,584	5,410	6,086
13,550	13,600	172	3,584	5,430	6,109	538	3,584	5,430	6,109
13,600	13,650	168	3,584	5,450	6,131	538	3,584	5,450	6,131
13,650	13,700	164	3,584	5,470	6,154	538	3,584	5,470	6,154
13,700	13,750	160	3,584	5,490	6,176	538	3,584	5,490	6,176
13,750	13,800	156	3,584	5,510	6,199	538	3,584	5,510	6,199
13,800	13,850	153	3,584	5,530	6,221	538	3,584	5,530	6,221
13,850	13,900	149	3,584	5,550	6,244	538	3,584	5,550	6,244
13,900	13,950	145	3,584	5,570	6,266	538	3,584	5,570	6,266
13,950	14,000	141	3,584	5,590	6,289	538	3,584	5,590	6,289
14,000	14,050	137	3,584	5,610	6,311	538	3,584	5,610	6,311
14,050	14,100	133	3,584	5,630	6,334	538	3,584	5,630	6,334
14,100	14,150	130	3,584	5,650	6,356	538	3,584	5,650	6,356
14,150	14,200	126	3,584	5,670	6,379	538	3,584	5,670	6,379
14,200	14,250	122	3,584	5,690	6,401	538	3,584	5,690	6,401
14,250	14,300	118	3,584	5,710	6,424	538	3,584	5,710	6,424
14,300	14,350	114	3,584	5,730	6,446	538	3,584	5,730	6,446
14,350	14,400	111	3,584	5,750	6,469	538	3,584	5,750	6,469
14,400	14,450	107	3,584	5,770	6,491	538	3,584	5,770	6,491
14,450	14,500	103	3,584	5,790	6,514	538	3,584	5,790	6,514
14,500	14,550	99	3,584	5,810	6,536	538	3,584	5,810	6,536
14,550	14,600	95	3,584	5,830	6,559	538	3,584	5,830	6,559
14,600	14,650	91	3,584	5,850	6,581	538	3,584	5,850	6,581
14,650	14,700	88	3,584	5,870	6,604	538	3,584	5,870	6,604
14,700	14,750	84	3,584	5,890	6,626	534	3,584	5,890	6,626
14,750	14,800	80	3,584	5,910	6,649	531	3,584	5,910	6,649
14,800	14,850	76	3,584	5,920	6,660	527	3,584	5,920	6,660
14,850	14,900	72	3,584	5,920	6,660	523	3,584	5,920	6,660
14,900	14,950	68	3,584	5,920	6,660	519	3,584	5,920	6,660
14,950	15,000	65	3,584	5,920	6,660	515	3,584	5,920	6,660
15,000	15,050	61	3,584	5,920	6,660	511	3,584	5,920	6,660
15,050	15,100	57	3,584	5,920	6,660	508	3,584	5,920	6,660
15,100	15,150	53	3,584	5,920	6,660	504	3,584	5,920	6,660
15,150	15,200	49	3,584	5,920	6,660	500	3,584	5,920	6,660
15,200	15,250	46	3,584	5,920	6,660	496	3,584	5,920	6,660
15,250	15,300	42	3,584	5,920	6,660	492	3,584	5,920	6,660
15,300	15,350	38	3,584	5,920	6,660	488	3,584	5,920	6,660
15,350	15,400	34	3,584	5,920	6,660	485	3,584	5,920	6,660
15,400	15,450	30	3,584	5,920	6,660	481	3,584	5,920	6,660
15,450	15,500	26	3,584	5,920	6,660	477	3,584	5,920	6,660
15,500	15,550	23	3,584	5,920	6,660	473	3,584	5,920	6,660
15,550	15,600	19	3,584	5,920	6,660	469	3,584	5,920	6,660
15,600	15,650	15	3,584	5,920	6,660	466	3,584	5,920	6,660
15,650	15,700	11	3,584	5,920	6,660	462	3,584	5,920	6,660
15,700	15,750	7	3,584	5,920	6,660	458	3,584	5,920	6,660
15,750	15,800	3	3,584	5,920	6,660	454	3,584	5,920	6,660
15,800	15,850	*	3,584	5,920	6,660	450	3,584	5,920	6,660
15,850	15,900	0	3,584	5,920	6,660	446	3,584	5,920	6,660
15,900	15,950	0	3,584	5,920	6,660	443	3,584	5,920	6,660
15,950	16,000	0	3,584	5,920	6,660	439	3,584	5,920	6,660

Right section

If the amount you are looking up from the worksheet is— At least	But less than	Single, head of household, or qualifying widow(er) and you have— 0	1	2	3	Married filing jointly and you have— 0	1	2	3
		Your credit is—				Your credit is—			
16,000	16,050	0	3,584	5,920	6,660	435	3,584	5,920	6,660
16,050	16,100	0	3,584	5,920	6,660	431	3,584	5,920	6,660
16,100	16,150	0	3,584	5,920	6,660	427	3,584	5,920	6,660
16,150	16,200	0	3,584	5,920	6,660	423	3,584	5,920	6,660
16,200	16,250	0	3,584	5,920	6,660	420	3,584	5,920	6,660
16,250	16,300	0	3,584	5,920	6,660	416	3,584	5,920	6,660
16,300	16,350	0	3,584	5,920	6,660	412	3,584	5,920	6,660
16,350	16,400	0	3,584	5,920	6,660	408	3,584	5,920	6,660
16,400	16,450	0	3,584	5,920	6,660	404	3,584	5,920	6,660
16,450	16,500	0	3,584	5,920	6,660	400	3,584	5,920	6,660
16,500	16,550	0	3,584	5,920	6,660	397	3,584	5,920	6,660
16,550	16,600	0	3,584	5,920	6,660	393	3,584	5,920	6,660
16,600	16,650	0	3,584	5,920	6,660	389	3,584	5,920	6,660
16,650	16,700	0	3,584	5,920	6,660	385	3,584	5,920	6,660
16,700	16,750	0	3,584	5,920	6,660	381	3,584	5,920	6,660
16,750	16,800	0	3,584	5,920	6,660	378	3,584	5,920	6,660
16,800	16,850	0	3,584	5,920	6,660	374	3,584	5,920	6,660
16,850	16,900	0	3,584	5,920	6,660	370	3,584	5,920	6,660
16,900	16,950	0	3,584	5,920	6,660	366	3,584	5,920	6,660
16,950	17,000	0	3,584	5,920	6,660	362	3,584	5,920	6,660
17,000	17,050	0	3,584	5,920	6,660	358	3,584	5,920	6,660
17,050	17,100	0	3,584	5,920	6,660	355	3,584	5,920	6,660
17,100	17,150	0	3,584	5,920	6,660	351	3,584	5,920	6,660
17,150	17,200	0	3,584	5,920	6,660	347	3,584	5,920	6,660
17,200	17,250	0	3,584	5,920	6,660	343	3,584	5,920	6,660
17,250	17,300	0	3,584	5,920	6,660	339	3,584	5,920	6,660
17,300	17,350	0	3,584	5,920	6,660	335	3,584	5,920	6,660
17,350	17,400	0	3,584	5,920	6,660	332	3,584	5,920	6,660
17,400	17,450	0	3,584	5,920	6,660	328	3,584	5,920	6,660
17,450	17,500	0	3,584	5,920	6,660	324	3,584	5,920	6,660
17,500	17,550	0	3,584	5,920	6,660	320	3,584	5,920	6,660
17,550	17,600	0	3,584	5,920	6,660	316	3,584	5,920	6,660
17,600	17,650	0	3,584	5,920	6,660	313	3,584	5,920	6,660
17,650	17,700	0	3,584	5,920	6,660	309	3,584	5,920	6,660
17,700	17,750	0	3,584	5,920	6,660	305	3,584	5,920	6,660
17,750	17,800	0	3,584	5,920	6,660	301	3,584	5,920	6,660
17,800	17,850	0	3,584	5,920	6,660	297	3,584	5,920	6,660
17,850	17,900	0	3,584	5,920	6,660	293	3,584	5,920	6,660
17,900	17,950	0	3,584	5,920	6,660	290	3,584	5,920	6,660
17,950	18,000	0	3,584	5,920	6,660	286	3,584	5,920	6,660
18,000	18,050	0	3,584	5,920	6,660	282	3,584	5,920	6,660
18,050	18,100	0	3,584	5,920	6,660	278	3,584	5,920	6,660
18,100	18,150	0	3,584	5,920	6,660	274	3,584	5,920	6,660
18,150	18,200	0	3,584	5,920	6,660	270	3,584	5,920	6,660
18,200	18,250	0	3,584	5,920	6,660	267	3,584	5,920	6,660
18,250	18,300	0	3,584	5,920	6,660	263	3,584	5,920	6,660
18,300	18,350	0	3,584	5,920	6,660	259	3,584	5,920	6,660
18,350	18,400	0	3,584	5,920	6,660	255	3,584	5,920	6,660
18,400	18,450	0	3,584	5,920	6,660	251	3,584	5,920	6,660
18,450	18,500	0	3,584	5,920	6,660	247	3,584	5,920	6,660
18,500	18,550	0	3,584	5,920	6,660	244	3,584	5,920	6,660
18,550	18,600	0	3,584	5,920	6,660	240	3,584	5,920	6,660
18,600	18,650	0	3,584	5,920	6,660	236	3,584	5,920	6,660
18,650	18,700	0	3,584	5,920	6,660	232	3,584	5,920	6,660
18,700	18,750	0	3,584	5,920	6,660	228	3,584	5,920	6,660
18,750	18,800	0	3,584	5,920	6,660	225	3,584	5,920	6,660
18,800	18,850	0	3,584	5,920	6,660	221	3,584	5,920	6,660
18,850	18,900	0	3,584	5,920	6,660	217	3,584	5,920	6,660
18,900	18,950	0	3,584	5,920	6,660	213	3,584	5,920	6,660
18,950	19,000	0	3,584	5,920	6,660	209	3,584	5,920	6,660
19,000	19,050	0	3,584	5,920	6,660	205	3,584	5,920	6,660
19,050	19,100	0	3,584	5,920	6,660	202	3,584	5,920	6,660
19,100	19,150	0	3,584	5,920	6,660	198	3,584	5,920	6,660
19,150	19,200	0	3,584	5,920	6,660	194	3,584	5,920	6,660

* If the amount you are looking up from the worksheet is at least $15,800 but less than $15,820, and you have no qualifying children, your credit is $1.
  If the amount you are looking up from the worksheet is $15,820 or more, and you have no qualifying children, you can't take the credit.

(Continued)

Earned Income Credit (EIC) Table - *Continued* (**Caution.** This is **not** a tax table.)

If the amount you are looking up from the worksheet is—		Single, head of household, or qualifying widow(er) and you have—				Married filing jointly and you have—			
At least	But less than	0	1	2	3	0	1	2	3
		Your credit is—				Your credit is—			
19,200	19,250	0	3,584	5,920	6,660	190	3,584	5,920	6,660
19,250	19,300	0	3,584	5,920	6,660	186	3,584	5,920	6,660
19,300	19,350	0	3,584	5,920	6,660	182	3,584	5,920	6,660
19,350	19,400	0	3,576	5,911	6,651	179	3,584	5,920	6,660
19,400	19,450	0	3,568	5,900	6,640	175	3,584	5,920	6,660
19,450	19,500	0	3,560	5,889	6,629	171	3,584	5,920	6,660
19,500	19,550	0	3,552	5,879	6,619	167	3,584	5,920	6,660
19,550	19,600	0	3,544	5,868	6,608	163	3,584	5,920	6,660
19,600	19,650	0	3,536	5,858	6,598	160	3,584	5,920	6,660
19,650	19,700	0	3,528	5,847	6,587	156	3,584	5,920	6,660
19,700	19,750	0	3,520	5,837	6,577	152	3,584	5,920	6,660
19,750	19,800	0	3,512	5,826	6,566	148	3,584	5,920	6,660
19,800	19,850	0	3,504	5,816	6,556	144	3,584	5,920	6,660
19,850	19,900	0	3,497	5,805	6,545	140	3,584	5,920	6,660
19,900	19,950	0	3,489	5,795	6,535	137	3,584	5,920	6,660
19,950	20,000	0	3,481	5,784	6,524	133	3,584	5,920	6,660
20,000	20,050	0	3,473	5,774	6,514	129	3,584	5,920	6,660
20,050	20,100	0	3,465	5,763	6,503	125	3,584	5,920	6,660
20,100	20,150	0	3,457	5,753	6,493	121	3,584	5,920	6,660
20,150	20,200	0	3,449	5,742	6,482	117	3,584	5,920	6,660
20,200	20,250	0	3,441	5,732	6,472	114	3,584	5,920	6,660
20,250	20,300	0	3,433	5,721	6,461	110	3,584	5,920	6,660
20,300	20,350	0	3,425	5,710	6,450	106	3,584	5,920	6,660
20,350	20,400	0	3,417	5,700	6,440	102	3,584	5,920	6,660
20,400	20,450	0	3,409	5,689	6,429	98	3,584	5,920	6,660
20,450	20,500	0	3,401	5,679	6,419	94	3,584	5,920	6,660
20,500	20,550	0	3,393	5,668	6,408	91	3,584	5,920	6,660
20,550	20,600	0	3,385	5,658	6,398	87	3,584	5,920	6,660
20,600	20,650	0	3,377	5,647	6,387	83	3,584	5,920	6,660
20,650	20,700	0	3,369	5,637	6,377	79	3,584	5,920	6,660
20,700	20,750	0	3,361	5,626	6,366	75	3,584	5,920	6,660
20,750	20,800	0	3,353	5,616	6,356	72	3,584	5,920	6,660
20,800	20,850	0	3,345	5,605	6,345	68	3,584	5,920	6,660
20,850	20,900	0	3,337	5,595	6,335	64	3,584	5,920	6,660
20,900	20,950	0	3,329	5,584	6,324	60	3,584	5,920	6,660
20,950	21,000	0	3,321	5,574	6,314	56	3,584	5,920	6,660
21,000	21,050	0	3,313	5,563	6,303	52	3,584	5,920	6,660
21,050	21,100	0	3,305	5,553	6,293	49	3,584	5,920	6,660
21,100	21,150	0	3,297	5,542	6,282	45	3,584	5,920	6,660
21,150	21,200	0	3,289	5,531	6,271	41	3,584	5,920	6,660
21,200	21,250	0	3,281	5,521	6,261	37	3,584	5,920	6,660
21,250	21,300	0	3,273	5,510	6,250	33	3,584	5,920	6,660
21,300	21,350	0	3,265	5,500	6,240	29	3,584	5,920	6,660
21,350	21,400	0	3,257	5,489	6,229	26	3,584	5,920	6,660
21,400	21,450	0	3,249	5,479	6,219	22	3,584	5,920	6,660
21,450	21,500	0	3,241	5,468	6,208	18	3,584	5,920	6,660
21,500	21,550	0	3,233	5,458	6,198	14	3,584	5,920	6,660
21,550	21,600	0	3,225	5,447	6,187	10	3,584	5,920	6,660
21,600	21,650	0	3,217	5,437	6,177	7	3,584	5,920	6,660
21,650	21,700	0	3,209	5,426	6,166	3	3,584	5,920	6,660
21,700	21,750	0	3,201	5,416	6,156	*	3,584	5,920	6,660
21,750	21,800	0	3,193	5,405	6,145	0	3,584	5,920	6,660
21,800	21,850	0	3,185	5,395	6,135	0	3,584	5,920	6,660
21,850	21,900	0	3,177	5,384	6,124	0	3,584	5,920	6,660
21,900	21,950	0	3,169	5,373	6,113	0	3,584	5,920	6,660
21,950	22,000	0	3,161	5,363	6,103	0	3,584	5,920	6,660
22,000	22,050	0	3,153	5,352	6,092	0	3,584	5,920	6,660
22,050	22,100	0	3,145	5,342	6,082	0	3,584	5,920	6,660
22,100	22,150	0	3,137	5,331	6,071	0	3,584	5,920	6,660
22,150	22,200	0	3,129	5,321	6,061	0	3,584	5,920	6,660
22,200	22,250	0	3,121	5,310	6,050	0	3,584	5,920	6,660
22,250	22,300	0	3,113	5,300	6,040	0	3,584	5,920	6,660
22,300	22,350	0	3,105	5,289	6,029	0	3,584	5,920	6,660
22,350	22,400	0	3,097	5,279	6,019	0	3,584	5,920	6,660

If the amount you are looking up from the worksheet is—		Single, head of household, or qualifying widow(er) and you have—				Married filing jointly and you have—			
At least	But less than	0	1	2	3	0	1	2	3
		Your credit is—				Your credit is—			
22,400	22,450	0	3,089	5,268	6,008	0	3,584	5,920	6,660
22,450	22,500	0	3,081	5,258	5,998	0	3,584	5,920	6,660
22,500	22,550	0	3,073	5,247	5,987	0	3,584	5,920	6,660
22,550	22,600	0	3,065	5,237	5,977	0	3,584	5,920	6,660
22,600	22,650	0	3,057	5,226	5,966	0	3,584	5,920	6,660
22,650	22,700	0	3,049	5,216	5,956	0	3,584	5,920	6,660
22,700	22,750	0	3,041	5,205	5,945	0	3,584	5,920	6,660
22,750	22,800	0	3,033	5,194	5,934	0	3,584	5,920	6,660
22,800	22,850	0	3,025	5,184	5,924	0	3,584	5,920	6,660
22,850	22,900	0	3,017	5,173	5,913	0	3,584	5,920	6,660
22,900	22,950	0	3,009	5,163	5,903	0	3,584	5,920	6,660
22,950	23,000	0	3,001	5,152	5,892	0	3,584	5,920	6,660
23,000	23,050	0	2,993	5,142	5,882	0	3,584	5,920	6,660
23,050	23,100	0	2,985	5,131	5,871	0	3,584	5,920	6,660
23,100	23,150	0	2,977	5,121	5,861	0	3,584	5,920	6,660
23,150	23,200	0	2,969	5,110	5,850	0	3,584	5,920	6,660
23,200	23,250	0	2,961	5,100	5,840	0	3,584	5,920	6,660
23,250	23,300	0	2,953	5,089	5,829	0	3,584	5,920	6,660
23,300	23,350	0	2,945	5,079	5,819	0	3,584	5,920	6,660
23,350	23,400	0	2,937	5,068	5,808	0	3,584	5,920	6,660
23,400	23,450	0	2,929	5,058	5,798	0	3,584	5,920	6,660
23,450	23,500	0	2,921	5,047	5,787	0	3,584	5,920	6,660
23,500	23,550	0	2,913	5,037	5,777	0	3,584	5,920	6,660
23,550	23,600	0	2,905	5,026	5,766	0	3,584	5,920	6,660
23,600	23,650	0	2,897	5,015	5,755	0	3,584	5,920	6,660
23,650	23,700	0	2,889	5,005	5,745	0	3,584	5,920	6,660
23,700	23,750	0	2,881	4,994	5,734	0	3,584	5,920	6,660
23,750	23,800	0	2,873	4,984	5,724	0	3,584	5,920	6,660
23,800	23,850	0	2,865	4,973	5,713	0	3,584	5,920	6,660
23,850	23,900	0	2,857	4,963	5,703	0	3,584	5,920	6,660
23,900	23,950	0	2,849	4,952	5,692	0	3,584	5,920	6,660
23,950	24,000	0	2,841	4,942	5,682	0	3,584	5,920	6,660
24,000	24,050	0	2,833	4,931	5,671	0	3,584	5,920	6,660
24,050	24,100	0	2,825	4,921	5,661	0	3,584	5,920	6,660
24,100	24,150	0	2,817	4,910	5,650	0	3,584	5,920	6,660
24,150	24,200	0	2,809	4,900	5,640	0	3,584	5,920	6,660
24,200	24,250	0	2,801	4,889	5,629	0	3,584	5,920	6,660
24,250	24,300	0	2,793	4,879	5,619	0	3,584	5,920	6,660
24,300	24,350	0	2,785	4,868	5,608	0	3,584	5,920	6,660
24,350	24,400	0	2,777	4,858	5,598	0	3,584	5,920	6,660
24,400	24,450	0	2,769	4,847	5,587	0	3,584	5,920	6,660
24,450	24,500	0	2,761	4,836	5,576	0	3,584	5,920	6,660
24,500	24,550	0	2,753	4,826	5,566	0	3,584	5,920	6,660
24,550	24,600	0	2,745	4,815	5,555	0	3,584	5,920	6,660
24,600	24,650	0	2,737	4,805	5,545	0	3,584	5,920	6,660
24,650	24,700	0	2,729	4,794	5,534	0	3,584	5,920	6,660
24,700	24,750	0	2,721	4,784	5,524	0	3,584	5,920	6,660
24,750	24,800	0	2,713	4,773	5,513	0	3,584	5,920	6,660
24,800	24,850	0	2,705	4,763	5,503	0	3,584	5,920	6,660
24,850	24,900	0	2,698	4,752	5,492	0	3,584	5,920	6,660
24,900	24,950	0	2,690	4,742	5,482	0	3,584	5,920	6,660
24,950	25,000	0	2,682	4,731	5,471	0	3,584	5,920	6,660
25,000	25,050	0	2,674	4,721	5,461	0	3,584	5,920	6,660
25,050	25,100	0	2,666	4,710	5,450	0	3,584	5,920	6,660
25,100	25,150	0	2,658	4,700	5,440	0	3,584	5,920	6,660
25,150	25,200	0	2,650	4,689	5,429	0	3,584	5,920	6,660
25,200	25,250	0	2,642	4,679	5,419	0	3,584	5,920	6,660
25,250	25,300	0	2,634	4,668	5,408	0	3,575	5,908	6,648
25,300	25,350	0	2,626	4,657	5,397	0	3,567	5,898	6,638
25,350	25,400	0	2,618	4,647	5,387	0	3,559	5,887	6,627
25,400	25,450	0	2,610	4,636	5,376	0	3,551	5,877	6,617
25,450	25,500	0	2,602	4,626	5,366	0	3,543	5,866	6,606
25,500	25,550	0	2,594	4,615	5,355	0	3,535	5,856	6,596
25,550	25,600	0	2,586	4,605	5,345	0	3,527	5,845	6,585

* If the amount you are looking up from the worksheet is at least $21,700 but less than $21,710, and you have no qualifying children, your credit is $0.
  If the amount you are looking up from the worksheet is $21,710 or more, and you have no qualifying children, you can't take the credit.

(Continued)

Earned Income Credit (EIC) Table - *Continued*

(Caution. This is not a tax table.)

If the amount you are looking up from the worksheet is— At least	But less than	Single, head of household, or qualifying widow(er) and you have— 0	1	2	3	Married filing jointly and you have— 0	1	2	3
25,600	25,650	0	2,578	4,594	5,334	0	3,519	5,835	6,575
25,650	25,700	0	2,570	4,584	5,324	0	3,511	5,824	6,564
25,700	25,750	0	2,562	4,573	5,313	0	3,503	5,814	6,554
25,750	25,800	0	2,554	4,563	5,303	0	3,495	5,803	6,543
25,800	25,850	0	2,546	4,552	5,292	0	3,487	5,793	6,533
25,850	25,900	0	2,538	4,542	5,282	0	3,479	5,782	6,522
25,900	25,950	0	2,530	4,531	5,271	0	3,471	5,772	6,512
25,950	26,000	0	2,522	4,521	5,261	0	3,463	5,761	6,501
26,000	26,050	0	2,514	4,510	5,250	0	3,455	5,750	6,490
26,050	26,100	0	2,506	4,500	5,240	0	3,447	5,740	6,480
26,100	26,150	0	2,498	4,489	5,229	0	3,439	5,729	6,469
26,150	26,200	0	2,490	4,478	5,218	0	3,431	5,719	6,459
26,200	26,250	0	2,482	4,468	5,208	0	3,423	5,708	6,448
26,250	26,300	0	2,474	4,457	5,197	0	3,415	5,698	6,438
26,300	26,350	0	2,466	4,447	5,187	0	3,407	5,687	6,427
26,350	26,400	0	2,458	4,436	5,176	0	3,399	5,677	6,417
26,400	26,450	0	2,450	4,426	5,166	0	3,391	5,666	6,406
26,450	26,500	0	2,442	4,415	5,155	0	3,383	5,656	6,396
26,500	26,550	0	2,434	4,405	5,145	0	3,375	5,645	6,385
26,550	26,600	0	2,426	4,394	5,134	0	3,367	5,635	6,375
26,600	26,650	0	2,418	4,384	5,124	0	3,359	5,624	6,364
26,650	26,700	0	2,410	4,373	5,113	0	3,351	5,614	6,354
26,700	26,750	0	2,402	4,363	5,103	0	3,343	5,603	6,343
26,750	26,800	0	2,394	4,352	5,092	0	3,335	5,593	6,333
26,800	26,850	0	2,386	4,342	5,082	0	3,327	5,582	6,322
26,850	26,900	0	2,378	4,331	5,071	0	3,319	5,571	6,311
26,900	26,950	0	2,370	4,320	5,060	0	3,311	5,561	6,301
26,950	27,000	0	2,362	4,310	5,050	0	3,303	5,550	6,290
27,000	27,050	0	2,354	4,299	5,039	0	3,295	5,540	6,280
27,050	27,100	0	2,346	4,289	5,029	0	3,287	5,529	6,269
27,100	27,150	0	2,338	4,278	5,018	0	3,279	5,519	6,259
27,150	27,200	0	2,330	4,268	5,008	0	3,271	5,508	6,248
27,200	27,250	0	2,322	4,257	4,997	0	3,263	5,498	6,238
27,250	27,300	0	2,314	4,247	4,987	0	3,255	5,487	6,227
27,300	27,350	0	2,306	4,236	4,976	0	3,247	5,477	6,217
27,350	27,400	0	2,298	4,226	4,966	0	3,239	5,466	6,206
27,400	27,450	0	2,290	4,215	4,955	0	3,231	5,456	6,196
27,450	27,500	0	2,282	4,205	4,945	0	3,223	5,445	6,185
27,500	27,550	0	2,274	4,194	4,934	0	3,215	5,435	6,175
27,550	27,600	0	2,266	4,184	4,924	0	3,207	5,424	6,164
27,600	27,650	0	2,258	4,173	4,913	0	3,199	5,414	6,154
27,650	27,700	0	2,250	4,163	4,903	0	3,191	5,403	6,143
27,700	27,750	0	2,242	4,152	4,892	0	3,183	5,392	6,132
27,750	27,800	0	2,234	4,141	4,881	0	3,175	5,382	6,122
27,800	27,850	0	2,226	4,131	4,871	0	3,167	5,371	6,111
27,850	27,900	0	2,218	4,120	4,860	0	3,159	5,361	6,101
27,900	27,950	0	2,210	4,110	4,850	0	3,151	5,350	6,090
27,950	28,000	0	2,202	4,099	4,839	0	3,143	5,340	6,080
28,000	28,050	0	2,194	4,089	4,829	0	3,135	5,329	6,069
28,050	28,100	0	2,186	4,078	4,818	0	3,127	5,319	6,059
28,100	28,150	0	2,178	4,068	4,808	0	3,119	5,308	6,048
28,150	28,200	0	2,170	4,057	4,797	0	3,111	5,298	6,038
28,200	28,250	0	2,162	4,047	4,787	0	3,103	5,287	6,027
28,250	28,300	0	2,154	4,036	4,776	0	3,095	5,277	6,017
28,300	28,350	0	2,146	4,026	4,766	0	3,087	5,266	6,006
28,350	28,400	0	2,138	4,015	4,755	0	3,079	5,256	5,996
28,400	28,450	0	2,130	4,005	4,745	0	3,071	5,245	5,985
28,450	28,500	0	2,122	3,994	4,734	0	3,063	5,234	5,974
28,500	28,550	0	2,114	3,984	4,724	0	3,055	5,224	5,964
28,550	28,600	0	2,106	3,973	4,713	0	3,047	5,213	5,953
28,600	28,650	0	2,098	3,962	4,702	0	3,039	5,203	5,943
28,650	28,700	0	2,090	3,952	4,692	0	3,031	5,192	5,932
28,700	28,750	0	2,082	3,941	4,681	0	3,024	5,182	5,922
28,750	28,800	0	2,074	3,931	4,671	0	3,016	5,171	5,911
28,800	28,850	0	2,066	3,920	4,660	0	3,008	5,161	5,901
28,850	28,900	0	2,058	3,910	4,650	0	3,000	5,150	5,890
28,900	28,950	0	2,050	3,899	4,639	0	2,992	5,140	5,880
28,950	29,000	0	2,042	3,889	4,629	0	2,984	5,129	5,869
29,000	29,050	0	2,034	3,878	4,618	0	2,976	5,119	5,859
29,050	29,100	0	2,026	3,868	4,608	0	2,968	5,108	5,848
29,100	29,150	0	2,018	3,857	4,597	0	2,960	5,098	5,838
29,150	29,200	0	2,010	3,847	4,587	0	2,952	5,087	5,827
29,200	29,250	0	2,002	3,836	4,576	0	2,944	5,077	5,817
29,250	29,300	0	1,994	3,826	4,566	0	2,936	5,066	5,806
29,300	29,350	0	1,986	3,815	4,555	0	2,928	5,055	5,795
29,350	29,400	0	1,978	3,805	4,545	0	2,920	5,045	5,785
29,400	29,450	0	1,970	3,794	4,534	0	2,912	5,034	5,774
29,450	29,500	0	1,962	3,783	4,523	0	2,904	5,024	5,764
29,500	29,550	0	1,954	3,773	4,513	0	2,896	5,013	5,753
29,550	29,600	0	1,946	3,762	4,502	0	2,888	5,003	5,743
29,600	29,650	0	1,938	3,752	4,492	0	2,880	4,992	5,732
29,650	29,700	0	1,930	3,741	4,481	0	2,872	4,982	5,722
29,700	29,750	0	1,922	3,731	4,471	0	2,864	4,971	5,711
29,750	29,800	0	1,914	3,720	4,460	0	2,856	4,961	5,701
29,800	29,850	0	1,906	3,710	4,450	0	2,848	4,950	5,690
29,850	29,900	0	1,899	3,699	4,439	0	2,840	4,940	5,680
29,900	29,950	0	1,891	3,689	4,429	0	2,832	4,929	5,669
29,950	30,000	0	1,883	3,678	4,418	0	2,824	4,919	5,659
30,000	30,050	0	1,875	3,668	4,408	0	2,816	4,908	5,648
30,050	30,100	0	1,867	3,657	4,397	0	2,808	4,898	5,638
30,100	30,150	0	1,859	3,647	4,387	0	2,800	4,887	5,627
30,150	30,200	0	1,851	3,636	4,376	0	2,792	4,876	5,616
30,200	30,250	0	1,843	3,626	4,366	0	2,784	4,866	5,606
30,250	30,300	0	1,835	3,615	4,355	0	2,776	4,855	5,595
30,300	30,350	0	1,827	3,604	4,344	0	2,768	4,845	5,585
30,350	30,400	0	1,819	3,594	4,334	0	2,760	4,834	5,574
30,400	30,450	0	1,811	3,583	4,323	0	2,752	4,824	5,564
30,450	30,500	0	1,803	3,573	4,313	0	2,744	4,813	5,553
30,500	30,550	0	1,795	3,562	4,302	0	2,736	4,803	5,543
30,550	30,600	0	1,787	3,552	4,292	0	2,728	4,792	5,532
30,600	30,650	0	1,779	3,541	4,281	0	2,720	4,782	5,522
30,650	30,700	0	1,771	3,531	4,271	0	2,712	4,771	5,511
30,700	30,750	0	1,763	3,520	4,260	0	2,704	4,761	5,501
30,750	30,800	0	1,755	3,510	4,250	0	2,696	4,750	5,490
30,800	30,850	0	1,747	3,499	4,239	0	2,688	4,740	5,480
30,850	30,900	0	1,739	3,489	4,229	0	2,680	4,729	5,469
30,900	30,950	0	1,731	3,478	4,218	0	2,672	4,719	5,459
30,950	31,000	0	1,723	3,468	4,208	0	2,664	4,708	5,448
31,000	31,050	0	1,715	3,457	4,197	0	2,656	4,697	5,437
31,050	31,100	0	1,707	3,447	4,187	0	2,648	4,687	5,427
31,100	31,150	0	1,699	3,436	4,176	0	2,640	4,676	5,416
31,150	31,200	0	1,691	3,425	4,165	0	2,632	4,666	5,406
31,200	31,250	0	1,683	3,415	4,155	0	2,624	4,655	5,395
31,250	31,300	0	1,675	3,404	4,144	0	2,616	4,645	5,385
31,300	31,350	0	1,667	3,394	4,134	0	2,608	4,634	5,374
31,350	31,400	0	1,659	3,383	4,123	0	2,600	4,624	5,364
31,400	31,450	0	1,651	3,373	4,113	0	2,592	4,613	5,353
31,450	31,500	0	1,643	3,362	4,102	0	2,584	4,603	5,343
31,500	31,550	0	1,635	3,352	4,092	0	2,576	4,592	5,332
31,550	31,600	0	1,627	3,341	4,081	0	2,568	4,582	5,322
31,600	31,650	0	1,619	3,331	4,071	0	2,560	4,571	5,311
31,650	31,700	0	1,611	3,320	4,060	0	2,552	4,561	5,301
31,700	31,750	0	1,603	3,310	4,050	0	2,544	4,550	5,290
31,750	31,800	0	1,595	3,299	4,039	0	2,536	4,540	5,280
31,800	31,850	0	1,587	3,289	4,029	0	2,528	4,529	5,269
31,850	31,900	0	1,579	3,278	4,018	0	2,520	4,518	5,258
31,900	31,950	0	1,571	3,267	4,007	0	2,512	4,508	5,248
31,950	32,000	0	1,563	3,257	3,997	0	2,504	4,497	5,237
32,000	32,050	0	1,555	3,246	3,986	0	2,496	4,487	5,227
32,050	32,100	0	1,547	3,236	3,976	0	2,488	4,476	5,216
32,100	32,150	0	1,539	3,225	3,965	0	2,480	4,466	5,206
32,150	32,200	0	1,531	3,215	3,955	0	2,472	4,455	5,195
32,200	32,250	0	1,523	3,204	3,944	0	2,464	4,445	5,185
32,250	32,300	0	1,515	3,194	3,934	0	2,456	4,434	5,174
32,300	32,350	0	1,507	3,183	3,923	0	2,448	4,424	5,164
32,350	32,400	0	1,499	3,173	3,913	0	2,440	4,413	5,153
32,400	32,450	0	1,491	3,162	3,902	0	2,432	4,403	5,143
32,450	32,500	0	1,483	3,152	3,892	0	2,424	4,392	5,132
32,500	32,550	0	1,475	3,141	3,881	0	2,416	4,382	5,122
32,550	32,600	0	1,467	3,131	3,871	0	2,408	4,371	5,111
32,600	32,650	0	1,459	3,120	3,860	0	2,400	4,361	5,101
32,650	32,700	0	1,451	3,110	3,850	0	2,392	4,350	5,090
32,700	32,750	0	1,443	3,099	3,839	0	2,384	4,339	5,079
32,750	32,800	0	1,435	3,088	3,828	0	2,376	4,329	5,069

(Continued)

Earned Income Credit (EIC) Table - *Continued*

(**Caution.** This is **not** a tax table.)

If the amount you are looking up from the worksheet is— At least	But less than	Single, head of household, or qualifying widow(er) and you have— 0	1	2	3	Married filing jointly and you have— 0	1	2	3
32,800	32,850	0	1,427	3,078	3,818	0	2,368	4,318	5,058
32,850	32,900	0	1,419	3,067	3,807	0	2,360	4,308	5,048
32,900	32,950	0	1,411	3,057	3,797	0	2,352	4,297	5,037
32,950	33,000	0	1,403	3,046	3,786	0	2,344	4,287	5,027
33,000	33,050	0	1,395	3,036	3,776	0	2,336	4,276	5,016
33,050	33,100	0	1,387	3,025	3,765	0	2,328	4,266	5,006
33,100	33,150	0	1,379	3,015	3,755	0	2,320	4,255	4,995
33,150	33,200	0	1,371	3,004	3,744	0	2,312	4,245	4,985
33,200	33,250	0	1,363	2,994	3,734	0	2,304	4,234	4,974
33,250	33,300	0	1,355	2,983	3,723	0	2,296	4,224	4,964
33,300	33,350	0	1,347	2,973	3,713	0	2,288	4,213	4,953
33,350	33,400	0	1,339	2,962	3,702	0	2,280	4,203	4,943
33,400	33,450	0	1,331	2,952	3,692	0	2,272	4,192	4,932
33,450	33,500	0	1,323	2,941	3,681	0	2,264	4,181	4,921
33,500	33,550	0	1,315	2,931	3,671	0	2,256	4,171	4,911
33,550	33,600	0	1,307	2,920	3,660	0	2,248	4,160	4,900
33,600	33,650	0	1,299	2,909	3,649	0	2,240	4,150	4,890
33,650	33,700	0	1,291	2,899	3,639	0	2,232	4,139	4,879
33,700	33,750	0	1,283	2,888	3,628	0	2,225	4,129	4,869
33,750	33,800	0	1,275	2,878	3,618	0	2,217	4,118	4,858
33,800	33,850	0	1,267	2,867	3,607	0	2,209	4,108	4,848
33,850	33,900	0	1,259	2,857	3,597	0	2,201	4,097	4,837
33,900	33,950	0	1,251	2,846	3,586	0	2,193	4,087	4,827
33,950	34,000	0	1,243	2,836	3,576	0	2,185	4,076	4,816
34,000	34,050	0	1,235	2,825	3,565	0	2,177	4,066	4,806
34,050	34,100	0	1,227	2,815	3,555	0	2,169	4,055	4,795
34,100	34,150	0	1,219	2,804	3,544	0	2,161	4,045	4,785
34,150	34,200	0	1,211	2,794	3,534	0	2,153	4,034	4,774
34,200	34,250	0	1,203	2,783	3,523	0	2,145	4,024	4,764
34,250	34,300	0	1,195	2,773	3,513	0	2,137	4,013	4,753
34,300	34,350	0	1,187	2,762	3,502	0	2,129	4,002	4,742
34,350	34,400	0	1,179	2,752	3,492	0	2,121	3,992	4,732
34,400	34,450	0	1,171	2,741	3,481	0	2,113	3,981	4,721
34,450	34,500	0	1,163	2,730	3,470	0	2,105	3,971	4,711
34,500	34,550	0	1,155	2,720	3,460	0	2,097	3,960	4,700
34,550	34,600	0	1,147	2,709	3,449	0	2,089	3,950	4,690
34,600	34,650	0	1,139	2,699	3,439	0	2,081	3,939	4,679
34,650	34,700	0	1,131	2,688	3,428	0	2,073	3,929	4,669
34,700	34,750	0	1,123	2,678	3,418	0	2,065	3,918	4,658
34,750	34,800	0	1,115	2,667	3,407	0	2,057	3,908	4,648
34,800	34,850	0	1,107	2,657	3,397	0	2,049	3,897	4,637
34,850	34,900	0	1,100	2,646	3,386	0	2,041	3,887	4,627
34,900	34,950	0	1,092	2,636	3,376	0	2,033	3,876	4,616
34,950	35,000	0	1,084	2,625	3,365	0	2,025	3,866	4,606
35,000	35,050	0	1,076	2,615	3,355	0	2,017	3,855	4,595
35,050	35,100	0	1,068	2,604	3,344	0	2,009	3,845	4,585
35,100	35,150	0	1,060	2,594	3,334	0	2,001	3,834	4,574
35,150	35,200	0	1,052	2,583	3,323	0	1,993	3,823	4,563
35,200	35,250	0	1,044	2,573	3,313	0	1,985	3,813	4,553
35,250	35,300	0	1,036	2,562	3,302	0	1,977	3,802	4,542
35,300	35,350	0	1,028	2,551	3,291	0	1,969	3,792	4,532
35,350	35,400	0	1,020	2,541	3,281	0	1,961	3,781	4,521
35,400	35,450	0	1,012	2,530	3,270	0	1,953	3,771	4,511
35,450	35,500	0	1,004	2,520	3,260	0	1,945	3,760	4,500
35,500	35,550	0	996	2,509	3,249	0	1,937	3,750	4,490
35,550	35,600	0	988	2,499	3,239	0	1,929	3,739	4,479
35,600	35,650	0	980	2,488	3,228	0	1,921	3,729	4,469
35,650	35,700	0	972	2,478	3,218	0	1,913	3,718	4,458
35,700	35,750	0	964	2,467	3,207	0	1,905	3,708	4,448
35,750	35,800	0	956	2,457	3,197	0	1,897	3,697	4,437
35,800	35,850	0	948	2,446	3,186	0	1,889	3,687	4,427
35,850	35,900	0	940	2,436	3,176	0	1,881	3,676	4,416
35,900	35,950	0	932	2,425	3,165	0	1,873	3,666	4,406
35,950	36,000	0	924	2,415	3,155	0	1,865	3,655	4,395
36,000	36,050	0	916	2,404	3,144	0	1,857	3,644	4,384
36,050	36,100	0	908	2,394	3,134	0	1,849	3,634	4,374
36,100	36,150	0	900	2,383	3,123	0	1,841	3,623	4,363
36,150	36,200	0	892	2,372	3,112	0	1,833	3,613	4,353
36,200	36,250	0	884	2,362	3,102	0	1,825	3,602	4,342
36,250	36,300	0	876	2,351	3,091	0	1,817	3,592	4,332
36,300	36,350	0	868	2,341	3,081	0	1,809	3,581	4,321
36,350	36,400	0	860	2,330	3,070	0	1,801	3,571	4,311

If the amount you are looking up from the worksheet is— At least	But less than	Single, head of household, or qualifying widow(er) and you have— 0	1	2	3	Married filing jointly and you have— 0	1	2	3
36,400	36,450	0	852	2,320	3,060	0	1,793	3,560	4,300
36,450	36,500	0	844	2,309	3,049	0	1,785	3,550	4,290
36,500	36,550	0	836	2,299	3,039	0	1,777	3,539	4,279
36,550	36,600	0	828	2,288	3,028	0	1,769	3,529	4,269
36,600	36,650	0	820	2,278	3,018	0	1,761	3,518	4,258
36,650	36,700	0	812	2,267	3,007	0	1,753	3,508	4,248
36,700	36,750	0	804	2,257	2,997	0	1,745	3,497	4,237
36,750	36,800	0	796	2,246	2,986	0	1,737	3,487	4,227
36,800	36,850	0	788	2,236	2,976	0	1,729	3,476	4,216
36,850	36,900	0	780	2,225	2,965	0	1,721	3,465	4,205
36,900	36,950	0	772	2,214	2,954	0	1,713	3,455	4,195
36,950	37,000	0	764	2,204	2,944	0	1,705	3,444	4,184
37,000	37,050	0	756	2,193	2,933	0	1,697	3,434	4,174
37,050	37,100	0	748	2,183	2,923	0	1,689	3,423	4,163
37,100	37,150	0	740	2,172	2,912	0	1,681	3,413	4,153
37,150	37,200	0	732	2,162	2,902	0	1,673	3,402	4,142
37,200	37,250	0	724	2,151	2,891	0	1,665	3,392	4,132
37,250	37,300	0	716	2,141	2,881	0	1,657	3,381	4,121
37,300	37,350	0	708	2,130	2,870	0	1,649	3,371	4,111
37,350	37,400	0	700	2,120	2,860	0	1,641	3,360	4,100
37,400	37,450	0	692	2,109	2,849	0	1,633	3,350	4,090
37,450	37,500	0	684	2,099	2,839	0	1,625	3,339	4,079
37,500	37,550	0	676	2,088	2,828	0	1,617	3,329	4,069
37,550	37,600	0	668	2,078	2,818	0	1,609	3,318	4,058
37,600	37,650	0	660	2,067	2,807	0	1,601	3,308	4,048
37,650	37,700	0	652	2,057	2,797	0	1,593	3,297	4,037
37,700	37,750	0	644	2,046	2,786	0	1,585	3,286	4,026
37,750	37,800	0	636	2,035	2,775	0	1,577	3,276	4,016
37,800	37,850	0	628	2,025	2,765	0	1,569	3,265	4,005
37,850	37,900	0	620	2,014	2,754	0	1,561	3,255	3,995
37,900	37,950	0	612	2,004	2,744	0	1,553	3,244	3,984
37,950	38,000	0	604	1,993	2,733	0	1,545	3,234	3,974
38,000	38,050	0	596	1,983	2,723	0	1,537	3,223	3,963
38,050	38,100	0	588	1,972	2,712	0	1,529	3,213	3,953
38,100	38,150	0	580	1,962	2,702	0	1,521	3,202	3,942
38,150	38,200	0	572	1,951	2,691	0	1,513	3,192	3,932
38,200	38,250	0	564	1,941	2,681	0	1,505	3,181	3,921
38,250	38,300	0	556	1,930	2,670	0	1,497	3,171	3,911
38,300	38,350	0	548	1,920	2,660	0	1,489	3,160	3,900
38,350	38,400	0	540	1,909	2,649	0	1,481	3,150	3,890
38,400	38,450	0	532	1,899	2,639	0	1,473	3,139	3,879
38,450	38,500	0	524	1,888	2,628	0	1,465	3,128	3,868
38,500	38,550	0	516	1,878	2,618	0	1,457	3,118	3,858
38,550	38,600	0	508	1,867	2,607	0	1,449	3,107	3,847
38,600	38,650	0	500	1,856	2,596	0	1,441	3,097	3,837
38,650	38,700	0	492	1,846	2,586	0	1,433	3,086	3,826
38,700	38,750	0	484	1,835	2,575	0	1,426	3,076	3,816
38,750	38,800	0	476	1,825	2,565	0	1,418	3,065	3,805
38,800	38,850	0	468	1,814	2,554	0	1,410	3,055	3,795
38,850	38,900	0	460	1,804	2,544	0	1,402	3,044	3,784
38,900	38,950	0	452	1,793	2,533	0	1,394	3,034	3,774
38,950	39,000	0	444	1,783	2,523	0	1,386	3,023	3,763
39,000	39,050	0	436	1,772	2,512	0	1,378	3,013	3,753
39,050	39,100	0	428	1,762	2,502	0	1,370	3,002	3,742
39,100	39,150	0	420	1,751	2,491	0	1,362	2,992	3,732
39,150	39,200	0	412	1,741	2,481	0	1,354	2,981	3,721
39,200	39,250	0	404	1,730	2,470	0	1,346	2,971	3,711
39,250	39,300	0	396	1,720	2,460	0	1,338	2,960	3,700
39,300	39,350	0	388	1,709	2,449	0	1,330	2,949	3,689
39,350	39,400	0	380	1,699	2,439	0	1,322	2,939	3,679
39,400	39,450	0	372	1,688	2,428	0	1,314	2,928	3,668
39,450	39,500	0	364	1,677	2,417	0	1,306	2,918	3,658
39,500	39,550	0	356	1,667	2,407	0	1,298	2,907	3,647
39,550	39,600	0	348	1,656	2,396	0	1,290	2,897	3,637
39,600	39,650	0	340	1,646	2,386	0	1,282	2,886	3,626
39,650	39,700	0	332	1,635	2,375	0	1,274	2,876	3,616
39,700	39,750	0	324	1,625	2,365	0	1,266	2,865	3,605
39,750	39,800	0	316	1,614	2,354	0	1,258	2,855	3,595
39,800	39,850	0	308	1,604	2,344	0	1,250	2,844	3,584
39,850	39,900	0	301	1,593	2,333	0	1,242	2,834	3,574
39,900	39,950	0	293	1,583	2,323	0	1,234	2,823	3,563
39,950	40,000	0	285	1,572	2,312	0	1,226	2,813	3,553

(Continued)

Earned Income Credit (EIC) Table - *Continued*

(Caution. This is not a tax table.)

If the amount you are looking up from the worksheet is–		Single, head of household, or qualifying widow(er) and you have–				Married filing jointly and you have–			
At least	But less than	0	1	2	3	0	1	2	3
		Your credit is–				Your credit is–			
40,000	40,050	0	277	1,562	2,302	0	1,218	2,802	3,542
40,050	40,100	0	269	1,551	2,291	0	1,210	2,792	3,532
40,100	40,150	0	261	1,541	2,281	0	1,202	2,781	3,521
40,150	40,200	0	253	1,530	2,270	0	1,194	2,770	3,510
40,200	40,250	0	245	1,520	2,260	0	1,186	2,760	3,500
40,250	40,300	0	237	1,509	2,249	0	1,178	2,749	3,489
40,300	40,350	0	229	1,498	2,238	0	1,170	2,739	3,479
40,350	40,400	0	221	1,488	2,228	0	1,162	2,728	3,468
40,400	40,450	0	213	1,477	2,217	0	1,154	2,718	3,458
40,450	40,500	0	205	1,467	2,207	0	1,146	2,707	3,447
40,500	40,550	0	197	1,456	2,196	0	1,138	2,697	3,437
40,550	40,600	0	189	1,446	2,186	0	1,130	2,686	3,426
40,600	40,650	0	181	1,435	2,175	0	1,122	2,676	3,416
40,650	40,700	0	173	1,425	2,165	0	1,114	2,665	3,405
40,700	40,750	0	165	1,414	2,154	0	1,106	2,655	3,395
40,750	40,800	0	157	1,404	2,144	0	1,098	2,644	3,384
40,800	40,850	0	149	1,393	2,133	0	1,090	2,634	3,374
40,850	40,900	0	141	1,383	2,123	0	1,082	2,623	3,363
40,900	40,950	0	133	1,372	2,112	0	1,074	2,613	3,353
40,950	41,000	0	125	1,362	2,102	0	1,066	2,602	3,342
41,000	41,050	0	117	1,351	2,091	0	1,058	2,591	3,331
41,050	41,100	0	109	1,341	2,081	0	1,050	2,581	3,321
41,100	41,150	0	101	1,330	2,070	0	1,042	2,570	3,310
41,150	41,200	0	93	1,319	2,059	0	1,034	2,560	3,300
41,200	41,250	0	85	1,309	2,049	0	1,026	2,549	3,289
41,250	41,300	0	77	1,298	2,038	0	1,018	2,539	3,279
41,300	41,350	0	69	1,288	2,028	0	1,010	2,528	3,268
41,350	41,400	0	61	1,277	2,017	0	1,002	2,518	3,258
41,400	41,450	0	53	1,267	2,007	0	994	2,507	3,247
41,450	41,500	0	45	1,256	1,996	0	986	2,497	3,237
41,500	41,550	0	37	1,246	1,986	0	978	2,486	3,226
41,550	41,600	0	29	1,235	1,975	0	970	2,476	3,216
41,600	41,650	0	21	1,225	1,965	0	962	2,465	3,205
41,650	41,700	0	13	1,214	1,954	0	954	2,455	3,195
41,700	41,750	0	5	1,204	1,944	0	946	2,444	3,184
41,750	41,800	0	*	1,193	1,933	0	938	2,434	3,174
41,800	41,850	0	0	1,183	1,923	0	930	2,423	3,163
41,850	41,900	0	0	1,172	1,912	0	922	2,412	3,152
41,900	41,950	0	0	1,161	1,901	0	914	2,402	3,142
41,950	42,000	0	0	1,151	1,891	0	906	2,391	3,131
42,000	42,050	0	0	1,140	1,880	0	898	2,381	3,121
42,050	42,100	0	0	1,130	1,870	0	890	2,370	3,110
42,100	42,150	0	0	1,119	1,859	0	882	2,360	3,100
42,150	42,200	0	0	1,109	1,849	0	874	2,349	3,089
42,200	42,250	0	0	1,098	1,838	0	866	2,339	3,079
42,250	42,300	0	0	1,088	1,828	0	858	2,328	3,068
42,300	42,350	0	0	1,077	1,817	0	850	2,318	3,058
42,350	42,400	0	0	1,067	1,807	0	842	2,307	3,047
42,400	42,450	0	0	1,056	1,796	0	834	2,297	3,037
42,450	42,500	0	0	1,046	1,786	0	826	2,286	3,026
42,500	42,550	0	0	1,035	1,775	0	818	2,276	3,016
42,550	42,600	0	0	1,025	1,765	0	810	2,265	3,005
42,600	42,650	0	0	1,014	1,754	0	802	2,255	2,995
42,650	42,700	0	0	1,004	1,744	0	794	2,244	2,984
42,700	42,750	0	0	993	1,733	0	786	2,233	2,973
42,750	42,800	0	0	982	1,722	0	778	2,223	2,963
42,800	42,850	0	0	972	1,712	0	770	2,212	2,952
42,850	42,900	0	0	961	1,701	0	762	2,202	2,942
42,900	42,950	0	0	951	1,691	0	754	2,191	2,931
42,950	43,000	0	0	940	1,680	0	746	2,181	2,921
43,000	43,050	0	0	930	1,670	0	738	2,170	2,910
43,050	43,100	0	0	919	1,659	0	730	2,160	2,900
43,100	43,150	0	0	909	1,649	0	722	2,149	2,889
43,150	43,200	0	0	898	1,638	0	714	2,139	2,879
43,200	43,250	0	0	888	1,628	0	706	2,128	2,868
43,250	43,300	0	0	877	1,617	0	698	2,118	2,858
43,300	43,350	0	0	867	1,607	0	690	2,107	2,847
43,350	43,400	0	0	856	1,596	0	682	2,097	2,837
43,400	43,450	0	0	846	1,586	0	674	2,086	2,826
43,450	43,500	0	0	835	1,575	0	666	2,075	2,815
43,500	43,550	0	0	825	1,565	0	658	2,065	2,805
43,550	43,600	0	0	814	1,554	0	650	2,054	2,794
43,600	43,650	0	0	803	1,543	0	642	2,044	2,784
43,650	43,700	0	0	793	1,533	0	634	2,033	2,773
43,700	43,750	0	0	782	1,522	0	627	2,023	2,763
43,750	43,800	0	0	772	1,512	0	619	2,012	2,752
43,800	43,850	0	0	761	1,501	0	611	2,002	2,742
43,850	43,900	0	0	751	1,491	0	603	1,991	2,731
43,900	43,950	0	0	740	1,480	0	595	1,981	2,721
43,950	44,000	0	0	730	1,470	0	587	1,970	2,710
44,000	44,050	0	0	719	1,459	0	579	1,960	2,700
44,050	44,100	0	0	709	1,449	0	571	1,949	2,689
44,100	44,150	0	0	698	1,438	0	563	1,939	2,679
44,150	44,200	0	0	688	1,428	0	555	1,928	2,668
44,200	44,250	0	0	677	1,417	0	547	1,918	2,658
44,250	44,300	0	0	667	1,407	0	539	1,907	2,647
44,300	44,350	0	0	656	1,396	0	531	1,896	2,636
44,350	44,400	0	0	646	1,386	0	523	1,886	2,626
44,400	44,450	0	0	635	1,375	0	515	1,875	2,615
44,450	44,500	0	0	624	1,364	0	507	1,865	2,605
44,500	44,550	0	0	614	1,354	0	499	1,854	2,594
44,550	44,600	0	0	603	1,343	0	491	1,844	2,584
44,600	44,650	0	0	593	1,333	0	483	1,833	2,573
44,650	44,700	0	0	582	1,322	0	475	1,823	2,563
44,700	44,750	0	0	572	1,312	0	467	1,812	2,552
44,750	44,800	0	0	561	1,301	0	459	1,802	2,542
44,800	44,850	0	0	551	1,291	0	451	1,791	2,531
44,850	44,900	0	0	540	1,280	0	443	1,781	2,521
44,900	44,950	0	0	530	1,270	0	435	1,770	2,510
44,950	45,000	0	0	519	1,259	0	427	1,760	2,500
45,000	45,050	0	0	509	1,249	0	419	1,749	2,489
45,050	45,100	0	0	498	1,238	0	411	1,739	2,479
45,100	45,150	0	0	488	1,228	0	403	1,728	2,468
45,150	45,200	0	0	477	1,217	0	395	1,717	2,457
45,200	45,250	0	0	467	1,207	0	387	1,707	2,447
45,250	45,300	0	0	456	1,196	0	379	1,696	2,436
45,300	45,350	0	0	445	1,185	0	371	1,686	2,426
45,350	45,400	0	0	435	1,175	0	363	1,675	2,415
45,400	45,450	0	0	424	1,164	0	355	1,665	2,405
45,450	45,500	0	0	414	1,154	0	347	1,654	2,394
45,500	45,550	0	0	403	1,143	0	339	1,644	2,384
45,550	45,600	0	0	393	1,133	0	331	1,633	2,373
45,600	45,650	0	0	382	1,122	0	323	1,623	2,363
45,650	45,700	0	0	372	1,112	0	315	1,612	2,352
45,700	45,750	0	0	361	1,101	0	307	1,602	2,342
45,750	45,800	0	0	351	1,091	0	299	1,591	2,331
45,800	45,850	0	0	340	1,080	0	291	1,581	2,321
45,850	45,900	0	0	330	1,070	0	283	1,570	2,310
45,900	45,950	0	0	319	1,059	0	275	1,560	2,300
45,950	46,000	0	0	309	1,049	0	267	1,549	2,289
46,000	46,050	0	0	298	1,038	0	259	1,538	2,278
46,050	46,100	0	0	288	1,028	0	251	1,528	2,268
46,100	46,150	0	0	277	1,017	0	243	1,517	2,257
46,150	46,200	0	0	266	1,006	0	235	1,507	2,247
46,200	46,250	0	0	256	996	0	227	1,496	2,236
46,250	46,300	0	0	245	985	0	219	1,486	2,226
46,300	46,350	0	0	235	975	0	211	1,475	2,215
46,350	46,400	0	0	224	964	0	203	1,465	2,205

* If the amount you are looking up from the worksheet is at least $41,750 but less than $41,756, and you have one qualifying child, your credit is $0.
If the amount you are looking up from the worksheet is $41,756 or more, and you have one qualifying child, you can't take the credit.

(Continued)

Earned Income Credit (EIC) Table - *Continued*

(Caution. This is not a tax table.)

If the amount you are looking up from the worksheet is—		Single, head of household, or qualifying widow(er) and you have—				Married filing jointly and you have—			
At least	But less than	0	1	2	3	0	1	2	3
		Your credit is—				Your credit is—			
46,400	46,450	0	0	214	954	0	195	1,454	2,194
46,450	46,500	0	0	203	943	0	187	1,444	2,184
46,500	46,550	0	0	193	933	0	179	1,433	2,173
46,550	46,600	0	0	182	922	0	171	1,423	2,163
46,600	46,650	0	0	172	912	0	163	1,412	2,152
46,650	46,700	0	0	161	901	0	155	1,402	2,142
46,700	46,750	0	0	151	891	0	147	1,391	2,131
46,750	46,800	0	0	140	880	0	139	1,381	2,121
46,800	46,850	0	0	130	870	0	131	1,370	2,110
46,850	46,900	0	0	119	859	0	123	1,359	2,099
46,900	46,950	0	0	108	848	0	115	1,349	2,089
46,950	47,000	0	0	98	838	0	107	1,338	2,078
47,000	47,050	0	0	87	827	0	99	1,328	2,068
47,050	47,100	0	0	77	817	0	91	1,317	2,057
47,100	47,150	0	0	66	806	0	83	1,307	2,047
47,150	47,200	0	0	56	796	0	75	1,296	2,036
47,200	47,250	0	0	45	785	0	67	1,286	2,026
47,250	47,300	0	0	35	775	0	59	1,275	2,015
47,300	47,350	0	0	24	764	0	51	1,265	2,005
47,350	47,400	0	0	14	754	0	43	1,254	1,994
47,400	47,450	0	0	*	743	0	35	1,244	1,984
47,450	47,500	0	0	0	733	0	27	1,233	1,973
47,500	47,550	0	0	0	722	0	19	1,223	1,963
47,550	47,600	0	0	0	712	0	11	1,212	1,952
47,600	47,650	0	0	0	701	0	**	1,202	1,942
47,650	47,700	0	0	0	691	0	0	1,191	1,931
47,700	47,750	0	0	0	680	0	0	1,180	1,920
47,750	47,800	0	0	0	669	0	0	1,170	1,910
47,800	47,850	0	0	0	659	0	0	1,159	1,899
47,850	47,900	0	0	0	648	0	0	1,149	1,889
47,900	47,950	0	0	0	638	0	0	1,138	1,878
47,950	48,000	0	0	0	627	0	0	1,128	1,868
48,000	48,050	0	0	0	617	0	0	1,117	1,857
48,050	48,100	0	0	0	606	0	0	1,107	1,847
48,100	48,150	0	0	0	596	0	0	1,096	1,836
48,150	48,200	0	0	0	585	0	0	1,086	1,826
48,200	48,250	0	0	0	575	0	0	1,075	1,815
48,250	48,300	0	0	0	564	0	0	1,065	1,805
48,300	48,350	0	0	0	554	0	0	1,054	1,794
48,350	48,400	0	0	0	543	0	0	1,044	1,784
48,400	48,450	0	0	0	533	0	0	1,033	1,773
48,450	48,500	0	0	0	522	0	0	1,022	1,762
48,500	48,550	0	0	0	512	0	0	1,012	1,752
48,550	48,600	0	0	0	501	0	0	1,001	1,741
48,600	48,650	0	0	0	490	0	0	991	1,731
48,650	48,700	0	0	0	480	0	0	980	1,720
48,700	48,750	0	0	0	469	0	0	970	1,710
48,750	48,800	0	0	0	459	0	0	959	1,699
48,800	48,850	0	0	0	448	0	0	949	1,689
48,850	48,900	0	0	0	438	0	0	938	1,678
48,900	48,950	0	0	0	427	0	0	928	1,668
48,950	49,000	0	0	0	417	0	0	917	1,657
49,000	49,050	0	0	0	406	0	0	907	1,647
49,050	49,100	0	0	0	396	0	0	896	1,636
49,100	49,150	0	0	0	385	0	0	886	1,626
49,150	49,200	0	0	0	375	0	0	875	1,615

If the amount you are looking up from the worksheet is—		Single, head of household, or qualifying widow(er) and you have—				Married filing jointly and you have—			
At least	But less than	0	1	2	3	0	1	2	3
		Your credit is—				Your credit is—			
49,200	49,250	0	0	0	364	0	0	865	1,605
49,250	49,300	0	0	0	354	0	0	854	1,594
49,300	49,350	0	0	0	343	0	0	843	1,583
49,350	49,400	0	0	0	333	0	0	833	1,573
49,400	49,450	0	0	0	322	0	0	822	1,562
49,450	49,500	0	0	0	311	0	0	812	1,552
49,500	49,550	0	0	0	301	0	0	801	1,541
49,550	49,600	0	0	0	290	0	0	791	1,531
49,600	49,650	0	0	0	280	0	0	780	1,520
49,650	49,700	0	0	0	269	0	0	770	1,510
49,700	49,750	0	0	0	259	0	0	759	1,499
49,750	49,800	0	0	0	248	0	0	749	1,489
49,800	49,850	0	0	0	238	0	0	738	1,478
49,850	49,900	0	0	0	227	0	0	728	1,468
49,900	49,950	0	0	0	217	0	0	717	1,457
49,950	50,000	0	0	0	206	0	0	707	1,447
50,000	50,050	0	0	0	196	0	0	696	1,436
50,050	50,100	0	0	0	185	0	0	686	1,426
50,100	50,150	0	0	0	175	0	0	675	1,415
50,150	50,200	0	0	0	164	0	0	664	1,404
50,200	50,250	0	0	0	154	0	0	654	1,394
50,250	50,300	0	0	0	143	0	0	643	1,383
50,300	50,350	0	0	0	132	0	0	633	1,373
50,350	50,400	0	0	0	122	0	0	622	1,362
50,400	50,450	0	0	0	111	0	0	612	1,352
50,450	50,500	0	0	0	101	0	0	601	1,341
50,500	50,550	0	0	0	90	0	0	591	1,331
50,550	50,600	0	0	0	80	0	0	580	1,320
50,600	50,650	0	0	0	69	0	0	570	1,310
50,650	50,700	0	0	0	59	0	0	559	1,299
50,700	50,750	0	0	0	48	0	0	549	1,289
50,750	50,800	0	0	0	38	0	0	538	1,278
50,800	50,850	0	0	0	27	0	0	528	1,268
50,850	50,900	0	0	0	17	0	0	517	1,257
50,900	50,950	0	0	0	6	0	0	507	1,247
50,950	51,000	0	0	0	***	0	0	496	1,236
51,000	51,050	0	0	0	0	0	0	485	1,225
51,050	51,100	0	0	0	0	0	0	475	1,215
51,100	51,150	0	0	0	0	0	0	464	1,204
51,150	51,200	0	0	0	0	0	0	454	1,194
51,200	51,250	0	0	0	0	0	0	443	1,183
51,250	51,300	0	0	0	0	0	0	433	1,173
51,300	51,350	0	0	0	0	0	0	422	1,162
51,350	51,400	0	0	0	0	0	0	412	1,152
51,400	51,450	0	0	0	0	0	0	401	1,141
51,450	51,500	0	0	0	0	0	0	391	1,131
51,500	51,550	0	0	0	0	0	0	380	1,120
51,550	51,600	0	0	0	0	0	0	370	1,110
51,600	51,650	0	0	0	0	0	0	359	1,099
51,650	51,700	0	0	0	0	0	0	349	1,089
51,700	51,750	0	0	0	0	0	0	338	1,078
51,750	51,800	0	0	0	0	0	0	328	1,068
51,800	51,850	0	0	0	0	0	0	317	1,057
51,850	51,900	0	0	0	0	0	0	306	1,046
51,900	51,950	0	0	0	0	0	0	296	1,036
51,950	52,000	0	0	0	0	0	0	285	1,025

* If the amount you are looking up from the worksheet is at least $47,400 but less than $47,440, and you have two qualifying children, your credit is $4.
If the amount you are looking up from the worksheet is $47,440 or more, and you have two qualifying children, you can't take the credit.

** If the amount you are looking up from the worksheet is at least $47,600 but less than $47,646, and you have one qualifying child, your credit is $4.
If the amount you are looking up from the worksheet is $47,646 or more, and you have one qualifying child, you can't take the credit.

*** If the amount you are looking up from the worksheet is at least $50,950 but less than $50,954, and you have three qualifying children, your credit is $0.
If the amount you are looking up from the worksheet is $50,954 or more, and you have three qualifying children, you can't take the credit.

(Continued)

Earned Income Credit (EIC) Table - Continued

(**Caution.** This is **not** a tax table.)

If the amount you are looking up from the worksheet is–		Single, head of household, or qualifying widow(er) and you have–				Married filing jointly and you have–			
At least	But less than	0	1	2	3	0	1	2	3
		Your credit is–				Your credit is–			
52,000	52,050	0	0	0	0	0	0	275	1,015
52,050	52,100	0	0	0	0	0	0	264	1,004
52,100	52,150	0	0	0	0	0	0	254	994
52,150	52,200	0	0	0	0	0	0	243	983
52,200	52,250	0	0	0	0	0	0	233	973
52,250	52,300	0	0	0	0	0	0	222	962
52,300	52,350	0	0	0	0	0	0	212	952
52,350	52,400	0	0	0	0	0	0	201	941
52,400	52,450	0	0	0	0	0	0	191	931
52,450	52,500	0	0	0	0	0	0	180	920
52,500	52,550	0	0	0	0	0	0	170	910
52,550	52,600	0	0	0	0	0	0	159	899
52,600	52,650	0	0	0	0	0	0	149	889
52,650	52,700	0	0	0	0	0	0	138	878
52,700	52,750	0	0	0	0	0	0	127	867
52,750	52,800	0	0	0	0	0	0	117	857
52,800	52,850	0	0	0	0	0	0	106	846
52,850	52,900	0	0	0	0	0	0	96	836
52,900	52,950	0	0	0	0	0	0	85	825
52,950	53,000	0	0	0	0	0	0	75	815
53,000	53,050	0	0	0	0	0	0	64	804
53,050	53,100	0	0	0	0	0	0	54	794
53,100	53,150	0	0	0	0	0	0	43	783
53,150	53,200	0	0	0	0	0	0	33	773
53,200	53,250	0	0	0	0	0	0	22	762
53,250	53,300	0	0	0	0	0	0	12	752
53,300	53,350	0	0	0	0	0	0	*	741
53,350	53,400	0	0	0	0	0	0	0	731
53,400	53,450	0	0	0	0	0	0	0	720
53,450	53,500	0	0	0	0	0	0	0	709
53,500	53,550	0	0	0	0	0	0	0	699
53,550	53,600	0	0	0	0	0	0	0	688
53,600	53,650	0	0	0	0	0	0	0	678
53,650	53,700	0	0	0	0	0	0	0	667
53,700	53,750	0	0	0	0	0	0	0	657
53,750	53,800	0	0	0	0	0	0	0	646
53,800	53,850	0	0	0	0	0	0	0	636
53,850	53,900	0	0	0	0	0	0	0	625
53,900	53,950	0	0	0	0	0	0	0	615
53,950	54,000	0	0	0	0	0	0	0	604
54,000	54,050	0	0	0	0	0	0	0	594
54,050	54,100	0	0	0	0	0	0	0	583
54,100	54,150	0	0	0	0	0	0	0	573
54,150	54,200	0	0	0	0	0	0	0	562
54,200	54,250	0	0	0	0	0	0	0	552
54,250	54,300	0	0	0	0	0	0	0	541
54,300	54,350	0	0	0	0	0	0	0	530
54,350	54,400	0	0	0	0	0	0	0	520
54,400	54,450	0	0	0	0	0	0	0	509
54,450	54,500	0	0	0	0	0	0	0	499
54,500	54,550	0	0	0	0	0	0	0	488
54,550	54,600	0	0	0	0	0	0	0	478
54,600	54,650	0	0	0	0	0	0	0	467
54,650	54,700	0	0	0	0	0	0	0	457
54,700	54,750	0	0	0	0	0	0	0	446
54,750	54,800	0	0	0	0	0	0	0	436

If the amount you are looking up from the worksheet is–		Single, head of household, or qualifying widow(er) and you have–				Married filing jointly and you have–			
At least	But less than	0	1	2	3	0	1	2	3
		Your credit is–				Your credit is–			
54,800	54,850	0	0	0	0	0	0	0	425
54,850	54,900	0	0	0	0	0	0	0	415
54,900	54,950	0	0	0	0	0	0	0	404
54,950	55,000	0	0	0	0	0	0	0	394
55,000	55,050	0	0	0	0	0	0	0	383
55,050	55,100	0	0	0	0	0	0	0	373
55,100	55,150	0	0	0	0	0	0	0	362
55,150	55,200	0	0	0	0	0	0	0	351
55,200	55,250	0	0	0	0	0	0	0	341
55,250	55,300	0	0	0	0	0	0	0	330
55,300	55,350	0	0	0	0	0	0	0	320
55,350	55,400	0	0	0	0	0	0	0	309
55,400	55,450	0	0	0	0	0	0	0	299
55,450	55,500	0	0	0	0	0	0	0	288
55,500	55,550	0	0	0	0	0	0	0	278
55,550	55,600	0	0	0	0	0	0	0	267
55,600	55,650	0	0	0	0	0	0	0	257
55,650	55,700	0	0	0	0	0	0	0	246
55,700	55,750	0	0	0	0	0	0	0	236
55,750	55,800	0	0	0	0	0	0	0	225
55,800	55,850	0	0	0	0	0	0	0	215
55,850	55,900	0	0	0	0	0	0	0	204
55,900	55,950	0	0	0	0	0	0	0	194
55,950	56,000	0	0	0	0	0	0	0	183
56,000	56,050	0	0	0	0	0	0	0	172
56,050	56,100	0	0	0	0	0	0	0	162
56,100	56,150	0	0	0	0	0	0	0	151
56,150	56,200	0	0	0	0	0	0	0	141
56,200	56,250	0	0	0	0	0	0	0	130
56,250	56,300	0	0	0	0	0	0	0	120
56,300	56,350	0	0	0	0	0	0	0	109
56,350	56,400	0	0	0	0	0	0	0	99
56,400	56,450	0	0	0	0	0	0	0	88
56,450	56,500	0	0	0	0	0	0	0	78
56,500	56,550	0	0	0	0	0	0	0	67
56,550	56,600	0	0	0	0	0	0	0	57
56,600	56,650	0	0	0	0	0	0	0	46
56,650	56,700	0	0	0	0	0	0	0	36
56,700	56,750	0	0	0	0	0	0	0	25
56,750	56,800	0	0	0	0	0	0	0	15
56,800	56,844	0	0	0	0	0	0	0	**

* If the amount you are looking up from the worksheet is at least $53,300 but less than $53,330, and you have two qualifying children, your credit is $3.
If the amount you are looking up from the worksheet is $53,330 or more, and you have two qualifying children, you can't take the credit.

** If the amount you are looking up from the worksheet is at least $56,800 but less than $56,844, and you have three qualifying children, your credit is $5.
If the amount you are looking up from the worksheet is $56,844 or more, and you have three qualifying children, you can't take the credit.

Withholding Tables

CONTENTS

2020 Percentage Method Tables for Manual Payroll Systems With Forms W-4 From 2019 or Earlier

WEEKLY Payroll Period

MARRIED Persons					SINGLE Persons				
If the Adjusted Wage Amount (line 1d) is		The tentative amount to withhold is...	Plus this percentage ...	of the amount that the wage exceeds...	If the Adjusted Wage Amount (line 1d) is		The tentative amount to withhold is...	Plus this percentage ...	of the amount that the wage exceeds...
at least...	But less than...				at least...	But less than...			
A	B	C	D	E	A	B	C	D	E
$0	$229	$0.00	0%	$0	$0	$73	$0.00	0%	$0
$229	$609	$0.00	10%	$229	$73	$263	$0.00	10%	$73
$609	$1,772	$38.00	12%	$609	$263	$845	$19.00	12%	$263
$1,772	$3,518	$177.56	22%	$1,772	$845	$1,718	$88.84	22%	$845
$3,518	$6,510	$561.68	24%	$3,518	$1,718	$3,213	$280.90	24%	$1,718
$6,510	$8,204	$1,279.76	32%	$6,510	$3,213	$4,061	$639.70	32%	$3,213
$8,204	$12,191	$1,821.84	35%	$8,204	$4,061	$10,042	$911.06	35%	$4,061
$12,191		$3,217.29	37%	$12,191	$10,042		$3,004.41	37%	$10,042

BIWEEKLY Payroll Period

MARRIED Persons					SINGLE Persons				
If the Adjusted Wage Amount (line 1d) is		The tentative amount to withhold is...	Plus this percentage ...	of the amount that the wage exceeds...	If the Adjusted Wage Amount (line 1d) is		The tentative amount to withhold is...	Plus this percentage ...	of the amount that the wage exceeds...
at least...	But less than...				at least...	But less than...			
A	B	C	D	E	A	B	C	D	E
$0	$458	$0.00	0%	$0	$0	$146	$0.00	0%	$0
$458	$1,217	$0.00	10%	$458	$146	$526	$0.00	10%	$146
$1,217	$3,544	$75.90	12%	$1,217	$526	$1,689	$38.00	12%	$526
$3,544	$7,037	$355.14	22%	$3,544	$1,689	$3,436	$177.56	22%	$1,689
$7,037	$13,019	$1,123.60	24%	$7,037	$3,436	$6,427	$561.90	24%	$3,436
$13,019	$16,408	$2,559.28	32%	$13,019	$6,427	$8,121	$1,279.74	32%	$6,427
$16,408	$24,383	$3,643.76	35%	$16,408	$8,121	$20,085	$1,821.82	35%	$8,121
$24,383		$6,435.01	37%	$24,383	$20,085		$6,009.22	37%	$20,085

SEMIMONTHLY Payroll Period

MARRIED Persons					SINGLE Persons				
If the Adjusted Wage Amount (line 1d) is		The tentative amount to withhold is...	Plus this percentage ...	of the amount that the wage exceeds...	If the Adjusted Wage Amount (line 1d) is		The tentative amount to withhold is...	Plus this percentage ...	of the amount that the wage exceeds...
at least...	But less than...				at least...	But less than...			
A	B	C	D	E	A	B	C	D	E
$0	$496	$0.00	0%	$0	$0	$158	$0.00	0%	$0
$496	$1,319	$0.00	10%	$496	$158	$570	$0.00	10%	$158
$1,319	$3,840	$82.30	12%	$1,319	$570	$1,830	$41.20	12%	$570
$3,840	$7,623	$384.82	22%	$3,840	$1,830	$3,722	$192.40	22%	$1,830
$7,623	$14,104	$1,217.08	24%	$7,623	$3,722	$6,963	$608.64	24%	$3,722
$14,104	$17,775	$2,772.52	32%	$14,104	$6,963	$8,798	$1,386.48	32%	$6,963
$17,775	$26,415	$3,947.24	35%	$17,775	$8,798	$21,758	$1,973.68	35%	$8,798
$26,415		$6,971.24	37%	$26,415	$21,758		$6,509.68	37%	$21,758

2020 Percentage Method Tables for Manual Payroll Systems With Forms W-4 From 2019 or Earlier

MONTHLY Payroll Period

MARRIED Persons					SINGLE Persons				
If the Adjusted Wage Amount (line 1d) is		The tentative amount to withhold is...	Plus this percentage ...	of the amount that the wage exceeds...	If the Adjusted Wage Amount (line 1d) is		The tentative amount to withhold is...	Plus this percentage ...	of the amount that the wage exceeds...
at least...	But less than...				at least...	But less than...			
A	B	C	D	E	A	B	C	D	E
$0	$992	$0.00	0%	$0	$0	$317	$0.00	0%	$0
$992	$2,638	$0.00	10%	$992	$317	$1,140	$0.00	10%	$317
$2,638	$7,679	$164.60	12%	$2,638	$1,140	$3,660	$82.30	12%	$1,140
$7,679	$15,246	$769.52	22%	$7,679	$3,660	$7,444	$384.70	22%	$3,660
$15,246	$28,208	$2,434.26	24%	$15,246	$7,444	$13,925	$1,217.18	24%	$7,444
$28,208	$35,550	$5,545.14	32%	$28,208	$13,925	$17,596	$2,772.62	32%	$13,925
$35,550	$52,829	$7,894.58	35%	$35,550	$17,596	$43,517	$3,947.34	35%	$17,596
$52,829		$13,942.23	37%	$52,829	$43,517		$13,019.69	37%	$43,517

QUARTERLY Payroll Period

MARRIED Persons					SINGLE Persons				
If the Adjusted Wage Amount (line 1d) is		The tentative amount to withhold is...	Plus this percentage ...	of the amount that the wage exceeds...	If the Adjusted Wage Amount (line 1d) is		The tentative amount to withhold is...	Plus this percentage ...	of the amount that the wage exceeds...
at least...	But less than...				at least...	But less than...			
A	B	C	D	E	A	B	C	D	E
$0	$2,975	$0.00	0%	$0	$0	$950	$0.00	0%	$0
$2,975	$7,913	$0.00	10%	$2,975	$950	$3,419	$0.00	10%	$950
$7,913	$23,038	$493.80	12%	$7,913	$3,419	$10,981	$246.90	12%	$3,419
$23,038	$45,738	$2,308.80	22%	$23,038	$10,981	$22,331	$1,154.34	22%	$10,981
$45,738	$84,625	$7,302.80	24%	$45,738	$22,331	$41,775	$3,651.34	24%	$22,331
$84,625	$106,650	$16,635.68	32%	$84,625	$41,775	$52,788	$8,317.90	32%	$41,775
$106,650	$158,488	$23,683.68	35%	$106,650	$52,788	$130,550	$11,842.06	35%	$52,788
$158,488		$41,826.98	37%	$158,488	$130,550		$39,058.76	37%	$130,550

SEMIANNUAL Payroll Period

MARRIED Persons					SINGLE Persons				
If the Adjusted Wage Amount (line 1d) is		The tentative amount to withhold is...	Plus this percentage ...	of the amount that the wage exceeds...	If the Adjusted Wage Amount (line 1d) is		The tentative amount to withhold is...	Plus this percentage ...	of the amount that the wage exceeds...
at least...	But less than...				at least...	But less than...			
A	B	C	D	E	A	B	C	D	E
$0	$5,950	$0.00	0%	$0	$0	$1,900	$0.00	0%	$0
$5,950	$15,825	$0.00	10%	$5,950	$1,900	$6,838	$0.00	10%	$1,900
$15,825	$46,075	$987.50	12%	$15,825	$6,838	$21,963	$493.80	12%	$6,838
$46,075	$91,475	$4,617.50	22%	$46,075	$21,963	$44,663	$2,308.80	22%	$21,963
$91,475	$169,250	$14,605.50	24%	$91,475	$44,663	$83,550	$7,302.80	24%	$44,663
$169,250	$213,300	$33,271.50	32%	$169,250	$83,550	$105,575	$16,635.68	32%	$83,550
$213,300	$316,975	$47,367.50	35%	$213,300	$105,575	$261,100	$23,683.68	35%	$105,575
$316,975		$83,653.75	37%	$316,975	$261,100		$78,117.43	37%	$261,100

2020 Percentage Method Tables for Manual Payroll Systems With Forms W-4 From 2019 or Earlier

ANNUAL Payroll Period

MARRIED Persons					SINGLE Persons				
If the Adjusted Wage Amount (line 1d) is		The tentative amount to withhold is...	Plus this percentage ...	of the amount that the wage exceeds...	If the Adjusted Wage Amount (line 1d) is		The tentative amount to withhold is...	Plus this percentage ...	of the amount that the wage exceeds...
at least...	But less than...				at least...	But less than...			
A	B	C	D	E	A	B	C	D	E
$0	$11,900	$0.00	0%	$0	$0	$3,800	$0.00	0%	$0
$11,900	$31,650	$0.00	10%	$11,900	$3,800	$13,675	$0.00	10%	$3,800
$31,650	$92,150	$1,975.00	12%	$31,650	$13,675	$43,925	$987.50	12%	$13,675
$92,150	$182,950	$9,235.00	22%	$92,150	$43,925	$89,325	$4,617.50	22%	$43,925
$182,950	$338,500	$29,211.00	24%	$182,950	$89,325	$167,100	$14,605.50	24%	$89,325
$338,500	$426,600	$66,543.00	32%	$338,500	$167,100	$211,150	$33,271.50	32%	$167,100
$426,600	$633,950	$94,735.00	35%	$426,600	$211,150	$522,200	$47,367.50	35%	$211,150
$633,950		$167,307.50	37%	$633,950	$522,200		$156,235.00	37%	$522,200

DAILY Payroll Period

MARRIED Persons					SINGLE Persons				
If the Adjusted Wage Amount (line 1d) is		The tentative amount to withhold is...	Plus this percentage ...	of the amount that the wage exceeds...	If the Adjusted Wage Amount (line 1d) is		The tentative amount to withhold is...	Plus this percentage ...	of the amount that the wage exceeds...
at least...	But less than...				at least...	But less than...			
A	B	C	D	E	A	B	C	D	E
$0.00	$45.80	$0.00	0%	$0.00	$0.00	$14.60	$0.00	0%	$0.00
$45.80	$121.70	$0.00	10%	$45.80	$14.60	$52.60	$0.00	10%	$14.60
$121.70	$354.40	$7.59	12%	$121.70	$52.60	$168.90	$3.80	12%	$52.60
$354.40	$703.70	$35.51	22%	$354.40	$168.90	$343.60	$17.76	22%	$168.90
$703.70	$1,301.90	$112.36	24%	$703.70	$343.60	$642.70	$56.19	24%	$343.60
$1,301.90	$1,640.80	$255.93	32%	$1,301.90	$642.70	$812.10	$127.97	32%	$642.70
$1,640.80	$2,438.30	$364.38	35%	$1,640.80	$812.10	$2,008.50	$182.18	35%	$812.10
$2,438.30		$643.50	37%	$2,438.30	$2,008.50		$600.92	37%	$2,008.50

2020 Percentage Method Tables for Manual Payroll Systems With Forms W-4 From 2020 or Later

WEEKLY Payroll Period

STANDARD Withholding Rate Schedules (Use these if the box in Step 2 of Form W-4 is **NOT** checked)					Form W-4, Step 2, Checkbox, Withholding Rate Schedules (Use these if the box in Step 2 of Form W-4 **IS** checked)				
If the Adjusted Wage Amount (line 1h) is:		The tentative amount to withhold is:	Plus this percentage—	of the amount that the Adjusted Wage exceeds—	If the Adjusted Wage Amount (line 1h) is:		The tentative amount to withhold is:	Plus this percentage—	of the amount that the Adjusted Wage exceeds—
At least—	But less than—				At least—	But less than—			
A	B	C	D	E	A	B	C	D	E
Married Filing Jointly					**Married Filing Jointly**				
$0	$477	$0.00	0%	$0	$0	$238	$0.00	0%	$0
$477	$857	$0.00	10%	$477	$238	$428	$0.00	10%	$238
$857	$2,020	$38.00	12%	$857	$428	$1,010	$19.00	12%	$428
$2,020	$3,766	$177.56	22%	$2,020	$1,010	$1,883	$88.84	22%	$1,010
$3,766	$6,758	$561.68	24%	$3,766	$1,883	$3,379	$280.90	24%	$1,883
$6,758	$8,452	$1,279.76	32%	$6,758	$3,379	$4,226	$639.94	32%	$3,379
$8,452	$12,439	$1,821.84	35%	$8,452	$4,226	$6,220	$910.98	35%	$4,226
$12,439		$3,217.29	37%	$12,439	$6,220		$1,608.88	37%	$6,220
Single or Married Filing Separately					**Single or Married Filing Separately**				
$0	$238	$0.00	0%	$0	$0	$119	$0.00	0%	$0
$238	$428	$0.00	10%	$238	$119	$214	$0.00	10%	$119
$428	$1,010	$19.00	12%	$428	$214	$505	$9.50	12%	$214
$1,010	$1,883	$88.84	22%	$1,010	$505	$942	$44.42	22%	$505
$1,883	$3,379	$280.90	24%	$1,883	$942	$1,689	$140.56	24%	$942
$3,379	$4,226	$639.94	32%	$3,379	$1,689	$2,113	$319.84	32%	$1,689
$4,226	$10,208	$910.98	35%	$4,226	$2,113	$5,104	$455.52	35%	$2,113
$10,208		$3,004.68	37%	$10,208	$5,104		$1,502.37	37%	$5,104
Head of Household					**Head of Household**				
$0	$359	$0.00	0%	$0	$0	$179	$0.00	0%	$0
$359	$630	$0.00	10%	$359	$179	$315	$0.00	10%	$179
$630	$1,391	$27.10	12%	$630	$315	$696	$13.60	12%	$315
$1,391	$2,003	$118.42	22%	$1,391	$696	$1,001	$59.32	22%	$696
$2,003	$3,499	$253.06	24%	$2,003	$1,001	$1,750	$126.42	24%	$1,001
$3,499	$4,346	$612.10	32%	$3,499	$1,750	$2,173	$306.18	32%	$1,750
$4,346	$10,328	$883.14	35%	$4,346	$2,173	$5,164	$441.54	35%	$2,173
$10,328		$2,976.84	37%	$10,328	$5,164		$1,488.39	37%	$5,164

2020 Percentage Method Tables for Manual Payroll Systems With Forms W-4 From 2020 or Later

BIWEEKLY Payroll Period

STANDARD Withholding Rate Schedules (Use these if the box in Step 2 of Form W-4 is **NOT** checked)					Form W-4, Step 2, Checkbox, Withholding Rate Schedules (Use these if the box in Step 2 of Form W-4 **IS** checked)				
If the Adjusted Wage Amount (line 1h) is:		The tentative amount to withhold is:	Plus this percentage—	of the amount that the Adjusted Wage exceeds—	If the Adjusted Wage Amount (line 1h) is:		The tentative amount to withhold is:	Plus this percentage—	of the amount that the Adjusted Wage exceeds—
At least—	But less than—				At least—	But less than—			
A	B	C	D	E	A	B	C	D	E
Married Filing Jointly					**Married Filing Jointly**				
$0	$954	$0.00	0%	$0	$0	$477	$0.00	0%	$0
$954	$1,713	$0.00	10%	$954	$477	$857	$0.00	10%	$477
$1,713	$4,040	$75.90	12%	$1,713	$857	$2,020	$38.00	12%	$857
$4,040	$7,533	$355.14	22%	$4,040	$2,020	$3,766	$177.56	22%	$2,020
$7,533	$13,515	$1,123.60	24%	$7,533	$3,766	$6,758	$561.68	24%	$3,766
$13,515	$16,904	$2,559.28	32%	$13,515	$6,758	$8,452	$1,279.76	32%	$6,758
$16,904	$24,879	$3,643.76	35%	$16,904	$8,452	$12,439	$1,821.84	35%	$8,452
$24,879		$6,435.01	37%	$24,879	$12,439		$3,217.29	37%	$12,439
Single or Married Filing Separately					**Single or Married Filing Separately**				
$0	$477	$0.00	0%	$0	$0	$238	$0.00	0%	$0
$477	$857	$0.00	10%	$477	$238	$428	$0.00	10%	$238
$857	$2,020	$38.00	12%	$857	$428	$1,010	$19.00	12%	$428
$2,020	$3,766	$177.56	22%	$2,020	$1,010	$1,883	$88.84	22%	$1,010
$3,766	$6,758	$561.68	24%	$3,766	$1,883	$3,379	$280.90	24%	$1,883
$6,758	$8,452	$1,279.76	32%	$6,758	$3,379	$4,226	$639.94	32%	$3,379
$8,452	$20,415	$1,821.84	35%	$8,452	$4,226	$10,208	$910.98	35%	$4,226
$20,415		$6,008.89	37%	$20,415	$10,208		$3,004.68	37%	$10,208
Head of Household					**Head of Household**				
$0	$717	$0.00	0%	$0	$0	$359	$0.00	0%	$0
$717	$1,260	$0.00	10%	$717	$359	$630	$0.00	10%	$359
$1,260	$2,783	$54.30	12%	$1,260	$630	$1,391	$27.10	12%	$630
$2,783	$4,006	$237.06	22%	$2,783	$1,391	$2,003	$118.42	22%	$1,391
$4,006	$6,998	$506.12	24%	$4,006	$2,003	$3,499	$253.06	24%	$2,003
$6,998	$8,692	$1,224.20	32%	$6,998	$3,499	$4,346	$612.10	32%	$3,499
$8,692	$20,656	$1,766.28	35%	$8,692	$4,346	$10,328	$883.14	35%	$4,346
$20,656		$5,953.68	37%	$20,656	$10,328		$2,976.84	37%	$10,328

2020 Percentage Method Tables for Manual Payroll Systems With Forms W-4 From 2020 or Later

SEMIMONTHLY Payroll Period

STANDARD Withholding Rate Schedules (Use these if the box in Step 2 of Form W-4 is **NOT** checked)					Form W-4, Step 2, Checkbox, Withholding Rate Schedules (Use these if the box in Step 2 of Form W-4 **IS** checked)				
If the Adjusted Wage Amount (line 1h) is:		The tentative amount to withhold is:	Plus this percentage—	of the amount that the Adjusted Wage exceeds—	If the Adjusted Wage Amount (line 1h) is:		The tentative amount to withhold is:	Plus this percentage—	of the amount that the Adjusted Wage exceeds—
At least—	But less than—				At least—	But less than—			
A	B	C	D	E	A	B	C	D	E
Married Filing Jointly					**Married Filing Jointly**				
$0	$1,033	$0.00	0%	$0	$0	$517	$0.00	0%	$0
$1,033	$1,856	$0.00	10%	$1,033	$517	$928	$0.00	10%	$517
$1,856	$4,377	$82.30	12%	$1,856	$928	$2,189	$41.10	12%	$928
$4,377	$8,160	$384.82	22%	$4,377	$2,189	$4,080	$192.42	22%	$2,189
$8,160	$14,642	$1,217.08	24%	$8,160	$4,080	$7,321	$608.44	24%	$4,080
$14,642	$18,313	$2,772.76	32%	$14,642	$7,321	$9,156	$1,386.28	32%	$7,321
$18,313	$26,952	$3,947.48	35%	$18,313	$9,156	$13,476	$1,973.48	35%	$9,156
$26,952		$6,971.13	37%	$26,952	$13,476		$3,485.48	37%	$13,476
Single or Married Filing Separately					**Single or Married Filing Separately**				
$0	$517	$0.00	0%	$0	$0	$258	$0.00	0%	$0
$517	$928	$0.00	10%	$517	$258	$464	$0.00	10%	$258
$928	$2,189	$41.10	12%	$928	$464	$1,094	$20.60	12%	$464
$2,189	$4,080	$192.42	22%	$2,189	$1,094	$2,040	$96.20	22%	$1,094
$4,080	$7,321	$608.44	24%	$4,080	$2,040	$3,660	$304.32	24%	$2,040
$7,321	$9,156	$1,386.28	32%	$7,321	$3,660	$4,578	$693.12	32%	$3,660
$9,156	$22,117	$1,973.48	35%	$9,156	$4,578	$11,058	$986.88	35%	$4,578
$22,117		$6,509.83	37%	$22,117	$11,058		$3,254.88	37%	$11,058
Head of Household					**Head of Household**				
$0	$777	$0.00	0%	$0	$0	$389	$0.00	0%	$0
$777	$1,365	$0.00	10%	$777	$389	$682	$0.00	10%	$389
$1,365	$3,015	$58.80	12%	$1,365	$682	$1,507	$29.30	12%	$682
$3,015	$4,340	$256.80	22%	$3,015	$1,507	$2,170	$128.30	22%	$1,507
$4,340	$7,581	$548.30	24%	$4,340	$2,170	$3,791	$274.16	24%	$2,170
$7,581	$9,417	$1,326.14	32%	$7,581	$3,791	$4,708	$663.20	32%	$3,791
$9,417	$22,377	$1,913.66	35%	$9,417	$4,708	$11,189	$956.64	35%	$4,708
$22,377		$6,449.66	37%	$22,377	$11,189		$3,224.99	37%	$11,189

2020 Percentage Method Tables for Manual Payroll Systems With Forms W-4 From 2020 or Later

MONTHLY Payroll Period

STANDARD Withholding Rate Schedules (Use these if the box in Step 2 of Form W-4 is **NOT** checked)

Form W-4, Step 2, Checkbox, Withholding Rate Schedules (Use these if the box in Step 2 of Form W-4 **IS** checked)

Married Filing Jointly

If the Adjusted Wage Amount (line 1h) is: At least—	But less than—	The tentative amount to withhold is:	Plus this percentage—	of the amount that the Adjusted Wage exceeds—	If the Adjusted Wage Amount (line 1h) is: At least—	But less than—	The tentative amount to withhold is:	Plus this percentage—	of the amount that the Adjusted Wage exceeds—
A	B	C	D	E	A	B	C	D	E
$0	$2,067	$0.00	0%	$0	$0	$1,033	$0.00	0%	$0
$2,067	$3,713	$0.00	10%	$2,067	$1,033	$1,856	$0.00	10%	$1,033
$3,713	$8,754	$164.60	12%	$3,713	$1,856	$4,377	$82.30	12%	$1,856
$8,754	$16,321	$769.52	22%	$8,754	$4,377	$8,160	$384.82	22%	$4,377
$16,321	$29,283	$2,434.26	24%	$16,321	$8,160	$14,642	$1,217.08	24%	$8,160
$29,283	$36,625	$5,545.14	32%	$29,283	$14,642	$18,313	$2,772.76	32%	$14,642
$36,625	$53,904	$7,894.58	35%	$36,625	$18,313	$26,952	$3,947.48	35%	$18,313
$53,904		$13,942.23	37%	$53,904	$26,952		$6,971.13	37%	$26,952

Single or Married Filing Separately

A	B	C	D	E	A	B	C	D	E
$0	$1,033	$0.00	0%	$0	$0	$517	$0.00	0%	$0
$1,033	$1,856	$0.00	10%	$1,033	$517	$928	$0.00	10%	$517
$1,856	$4,377	$82.30	12%	$1,856	$928	$2,189	$41.10	12%	$928
$4,377	$8,160	$384.82	22%	$4,377	$2,189	$4,080	$192.42	22%	$2,189
$8,160	$14,642	$1,217.08	24%	$8,160	$4,080	$7,321	$608.44	24%	$4,080
$14,642	$18,313	$2,772.76	32%	$14,642	$7,321	$9,156	$1,386.28	32%	$7,321
$18,313	$44,233	$3,947.48	35%	$18,313	$9,156	$22,117	$1,973.48	35%	$9,156
$44,233		$13,019.48	37%	$44,233	$22,117		$6,509.83	37%	$22,117

Head of Household

A	B	C	D	E	A	B	C	D	E
$0	$1,554	$0.00	0%	$0	$0	$777	$0.00	0%	$0
$1,554	$2,729	$0.00	10%	$1,554	$777	$1,365	$0.00	10%	$777
$2,729	$6,029	$117.50	12%	$2,729	$1,365	$3,015	$58.80	12%	$1,365
$6,029	$8,679	$513.50	22%	$6,029	$3,015	$4,340	$256.80	22%	$3,015
$8,679	$15,163	$1,096.50	24%	$8,679	$4,340	$7,581	$548.30	24%	$4,340
$15,163	$18,833	$2,652.66	32%	$15,163	$7,581	$9,417	$1,326.14	32%	$7,581
$18,833	$44,754	$3,827.06	35%	$18,833	$9,417	$22,377	$1,913.66	35%	$9,417
$44,754		$12,899.41	37%	$44,754	$22,377		$6,449.66	37%	$22,377

2020 Percentage Method Tables for Manual Payroll Systems With Forms W-4 From 2020 or Later

DAILY Payroll Period

STANDARD Withholding Rate Schedules (Use these if the box in Step 2 of Form W-4 is **NOT** checked)					Form W-4, Step 2, Checkbox, Withholding Rate Schedules (Use these if the box in Step 2 of Form W-4 **IS** checked)				
If the Adjusted Wage Amount (line 1h) is:		The tentative amount to withhold is:	Plus this percentage—	of the amount that the Adjusted Wage exceeds—	If the Adjusted Wage Amount (line 1h) is:		The tentative amount to withhold is:	Plus this percentage—	of the amount that the Adjusted Wage exceeds—
At least—	But less than—				At least—	But less than—			
A	B	C	D	E	A	B	C	D	E
Married Filing Jointly					**Married Filing Jointly**				
$0.00	$95.40	$0.00	0%	$0.00	$0.00	$47.70	$0.00	0%	$0.00
$95.40	$171.30	$0.00	10%	$95.40	$47.70	$85.70	$0.00	10%	$47.70
$171.30	$404.00	$7.59	12%	$171.30	$85.70	$202.00	$3.80	12%	$85.70
$404.00	$753.30	$35.51	22%	$404.00	$202.00	$376.60	$17.76	22%	$202.00
$753.30	$1,351.50	$112.36	24%	$753.30	$376.60	$675.80	$56.17	24%	$376.60
$1,351.50	$1,690.40	$255.93	32%	$1,351.50	$675.80	$845.20	$127.98	32%	$675.80
$1,690.40	$2,487.90	$364.38	35%	$1,690.40	$845.20	$1,243.90	$182.18	35%	$845.20
$2,487.90		$643.50	37%	$2,487.90	$1,243.90		$321.73	37%	$1,243.90
Single or Married Filing Separately					**Single or Married Filing Separately**				
$0.00	$47.70	$0.00	0%	$0.00	$0.00	$23.80	$0.00	0%	$0.00
$47.70	$85.70	$0.00	10%	$47.70	$23.80	$42.80	$0.00	10%	$23.80
$85.70	$202.00	$3.80	12%	$85.70	$42.80	$101.00	$1.90	12%	$42.80
$202.00	$376.60	$17.76	22%	$202.00	$101.00	$188.30	$8.88	22%	$101.00
$376.60	$675.80	$56.17	24%	$376.60	$188.30	$337.90	$28.09	24%	$188.30
$675.80	$845.20	$127.98	32%	$675.80	$337.90	$422.60	$63.99	32%	$337.90
$845.20	$2,041.50	$182.18	35%	$845.20	$422.60	$1,020.80	$91.10	35%	$422.60
$2,041.50		$600.89	37%	$2,041.50	$1,020.80		$300.47	37%	$1,020.80
Head of Household					**Head of Household**				
$0.00	$71.70	$0.00	0%	$0.00	$0.00	$35.90	$0.00	0%	$0.00
$71.70	$126.00	$0.00	10%	$71.70	$35.90	$63.00	$0.00	10%	$35.90
$126.00	$278.30	$5.43	12%	$126.00	$63.00	$139.10	$2.71	12%	$63.00
$278.30	$400.60	$23.71	22%	$278.30	$139.10	$200.30	$11.84	22%	$139.10
$400.60	$699.80	$50.61	24%	$400.60	$200.30	$349.90	$25.31	24%	$200.30
$699.80	$869.20	$122.42	32%	$699.80	$349.90	$434.60	$61.21	32%	$349.90
$869.20	$2,065.60	$176.63	35%	$869.20	$434.60	$1,032.80	$88.31	35%	$434.60
$2,065.60		$595.37	37%	$2,065.60	$1,032.80		$297.68	37%	$1,032.80

2020 Wage Bracket Method Tables for Manual Payroll Systems With Forms W-4 From 2019 or Earlier

MONTHLY Payroll Period

If the Wage Amount (line 1a) is		MARRIED Persons And the number of allowances is:										
At least	But less than	0	1	2	3	4	5	6	7	8	9	10
		The Tentative Withholding Amount is:										
$0	$995	$0	$0	$0	$0	$0	$0	$0	$0	$0	$0	$0
$995	$1,015	$1	$0	$0	$0	$0	$0	$0	$0	$0	$0	$0
$1,015	$1,035	$3	$0	$0	$0	$0	$0	$0	$0	$0	$0	$0
$1,035	$1,055	$5	$0	$0	$0	$0	$0	$0	$0	$0	$0	$0
$1,055	$1,075	$7	$0	$0	$0	$0	$0	$0	$0	$0	$0	$0
$1,075	$1,095	$9	$0	$0	$0	$0	$0	$0	$0	$0	$0	$0
$1,095	$1,145	$13	$0	$0	$0	$0	$0	$0	$0	$0	$0	$0
$1,145	$1,195	$18	$0	$0	$0	$0	$0	$0	$0	$0	$0	$0
$1,195	$1,245	$23	$0	$0	$0	$0	$0	$0	$0	$0	$0	$0
$1,245	$1,295	$28	$0	$0	$0	$0	$0	$0	$0	$0	$0	$0
$1,295	$1,345	$33	$0	$0	$0	$0	$0	$0	$0	$0	$0	$0
$1,345	$1,395	$38	$2	$0	$0	$0	$0	$0	$0	$0	$0	$0
$1,395	$1,445	$43	$7	$0	$0	$0	$0	$0	$0	$0	$0	$0
$1,445	$1,495	$48	$12	$0	$0	$0	$0	$0	$0	$0	$0	$0
$1,495	$1,545	$53	$17	$0	$0	$0	$0	$0	$0	$0	$0	$0
$1,545	$1,595	$58	$22	$0	$0	$0	$0	$0	$0	$0	$0	$0
$1,595	$1,645	$63	$27	$0	$0	$0	$0	$0	$0	$0	$0	$0
$1,645	$1,695	$68	$32	$0	$0	$0	$0	$0	$0	$0	$0	$0
$1,695	$1,745	$73	$37	$1	$0	$0	$0	$0	$0	$0	$0	$0
$1,745	$1,795	$78	$42	$6	$0	$0	$0	$0	$0	$0	$0	$0
$1,795	$1,845	$83	$47	$11	$0	$0	$0	$0	$0	$0	$0	$0
$1,845	$1,895	$88	$52	$16	$0	$0	$0	$0	$0	$0	$0	$0
$1,895	$1,945	$93	$57	$21	$0	$0	$0	$0	$0	$0	$0	$0
$1,945	$1,995	$98	$62	$26	$0	$0	$0	$0	$0	$0	$0	$0
$1,995	$2,045	$103	$67	$31	$0	$0	$0	$0	$0	$0	$0	$0
$2,045	$2,095	$108	$72	$36	$0	$0	$0	$0	$0	$0	$0	$0
$2,095	$2,145	$113	$77	$41	$5	$0	$0	$0	$0	$0	$0	$0
$2,145	$2,195	$118	$82	$46	$10	$0	$0	$0	$0	$0	$0	$0
$2,195	$2,245	$123	$87	$51	$15	$0	$0	$0	$0	$0	$0	$0
$2,245	$2,295	$128	$92	$56	$20	$0	$0	$0	$0	$0	$0	$0
$2,295	$2,345	$133	$97	$61	$25	$0	$0	$0	$0	$0	$0	$0
$2,345	$2,395	$138	$102	$66	$30	$0	$0	$0	$0	$0	$0	$0
$2,395	$2,445	$143	$107	$71	$35	$0	$0	$0	$0	$0	$0	$0
$2,445	$2,495	$148	$112	$76	$40	$5	$0	$0	$0	$0	$0	$0
$2,495	$2,545	$153	$117	$81	$45	$10	$0	$0	$0	$0	$0	$0
$2,545	$2,595	$158	$122	$86	$50	$15	$0	$0	$0	$0	$0	$0
$2,595	$2,645	$163	$127	$91	$55	$20	$0	$0	$0	$0	$0	$0
$2,645	$2,705	$169	$133	$97	$61	$25	$0	$0	$0	$0	$0	$0
$2,705	$2,765	$176	$139	$103	$67	$31	$0	$0	$0	$0	$0	$0
$2,765	$2,825	$183	$145	$109	$73	$37	$1	$0	$0	$0	$0	$0
$2,825	$2,885	$191	$151	$115	$79	$43	$7	$0	$0	$0	$0	$0
$2,885	$2,945	$198	$157	$121	$85	$49	$13	$0	$0	$0	$0	$0
$2,945	$3,005	$205	$163	$127	$91	$55	$19	$0	$0	$0	$0	$0
$3,005	$3,065	$212	$169	$133	$97	$61	$25	$0	$0	$0	$0	$0
$3,065	$3,125	$219	$176	$139	$103	$67	$31	$0	$0	$0	$0	$0
$3,125	$3,185	$227	$184	$145	$109	$73	$37	$1	$0	$0	$0	$0
$3,185	$3,245	$234	$191	$151	$115	$79	$43	$7	$0	$0	$0	$0
$3,245	$3,305	$241	$198	$157	$121	$85	$49	$13	$0	$0	$0	$0
$3,305	$3,365	$248	$205	$163	$127	$91	$55	$19	$0	$0	$0	$0
$3,365	$3,425	$255	$212	$169	$133	$97	$61	$25	$0	$0	$0	$0
$3,425	$3,485	$263	$220	$177	$139	$103	$67	$31	$0	$0	$0	$0

2020 Wage Bracket Method Tables for Manual Payroll Systems With Forms W-4 From 2019 or Earlier

MONTHLY Payroll Period

If the **Wage Amount** (line 1a) is		MARRIED Persons										
		And the number of allowances is:										
At least	But less than	0	1	2	3	4	5	6	7	8	9	10
		The Tentative Withholding Amount is:										
$3,485	$3,545	$270	$227	$184	$145	$109	$73	$37	$2	$0	$0	$0
$3,545	$3,605	$277	$234	$191	$151	$115	$79	$43	$8	$0	$0	$0
$3,605	$3,665	$284	$241	$198	$157	$121	$85	$49	$14	$0	$0	$0
$3,665	$3,725	$291	$248	$205	$163	$127	$91	$55	$20	$0	$0	$0
$3,725	$3,785	$299	$256	$213	$170	$133	$97	$61	$26	$0	$0	$0
$3,785	$3,845	$306	$263	$220	$177	$139	$103	$67	$32	$0	$0	$0
$3,845	$3,905	$313	$270	$227	$184	$145	$109	$73	$38	$2	$0	$0
$3,905	$3,965	$320	$277	$234	$191	$151	$115	$79	$44	$8	$0	$0
$3,965	$4,025	$327	$284	$241	$198	$157	$121	$85	$50	$14	$0	$0
$4,025	$4,085	$335	$292	$249	$206	$163	$127	$91	$56	$20	$0	$0
$4,085	$4,145	$342	$299	$256	$213	$170	$133	$97	$62	$26	$0	$0
$4,145	$4,205	$349	$306	$263	$220	$177	$139	$103	$68	$32	$0	$0
$4,205	$4,265	$356	$313	$270	$227	$184	$145	$109	$74	$38	$2	$0
$4,265	$4,325	$363	$320	$277	$234	$191	$151	$115	$80	$44	$8	$0
$4,325	$4,385	$371	$328	$285	$242	$199	$157	$121	$86	$50	$14	$0
$4,385	$4,445	$378	$335	$292	$249	$206	$163	$127	$92	$56	$20	$0
$4,445	$4,505	$385	$342	$299	$256	$213	$170	$133	$98	$62	$26	$0
$4,505	$4,565	$392	$349	$306	$263	$220	$177	$139	$104	$68	$32	$0
$4,565	$4,625	$399	$356	$313	$270	$227	$184	$145	$110	$74	$38	$2
$4,625	$4,685	$407	$364	$321	$278	$235	$192	$151	$116	$80	$44	$8
$4,685	$4,745	$414	$371	$328	$285	$242	$199	$157	$122	$86	$50	$14
$4,745	$4,805	$421	$378	$335	$292	$249	$206	$163	$128	$92	$56	$20
$4,805	$4,865	$428	$385	$342	$299	$256	$213	$170	$134	$98	$62	$26
$4,865	$4,925	$435	$392	$349	$306	$263	$220	$177	$140	$104	$68	$32
$4,925	$4,985	$443	$400	$357	$314	$271	$228	$185	$146	$110	$74	$38
$4,985	$5,045	$450	$407	$364	$321	$278	$235	$192	$152	$116	$80	$44
$5,045	$5,105	$457	$414	$371	$328	$285	$242	$199	$158	$122	$86	$50
$5,105	$5,165	$464	$421	$378	$335	$292	$249	$206	$164	$128	$92	$56
$5,165	$5,225	$471	$428	$385	$342	$299	$256	$213	$170	$134	$98	$62
$5,225	$5,285	$479	$436	$393	$350	$307	$264	$221	$178	$140	$104	$68
$5,285	$5,345	$486	$443	$400	$357	$314	$271	$228	$185	$146	$110	$74
$5,345	$5,405	$493	$450	$407	$364	$321	$278	$235	$192	$152	$116	$80
$5,405	$5,465	$500	$457	$414	$371	$328	$285	$242	$199	$158	$122	$86
$5,465	$5,525	$507	$464	$421	$378	$335	$292	$249	$206	$164	$128	$92
$5,525	$5,585	$515	$472	$429	$386	$343	$300	$257	$214	$171	$134	$98
$5,585	$5,645	$522	$479	$436	$393	$350	$307	$264	$221	$178	$140	$104
$5,645	$5,705	$529	$486	$443	$400	$357	$314	$271	$228	$185	$146	$110
$5,705	$5,765	$536	$493	$450	$407	$364	$321	$278	$235	$192	$152	$116
$5,765	$5,825	$543	$500	$457	$414	$371	$328	$285	$242	$199	$158	$122
$5,825	$5,885	$551	$508	$465	$422	$379	$336	$293	$250	$207	$164	$128
$5,885	$5,945	$558	$515	$472	$429	$386	$343	$300	$257	$214	$171	$134
$5,945	$6,005	$565	$522	$479	$436	$393	$350	$307	$264	$221	$178	$140
$6,005	$6,065	$572	$529	$486	$443	$400	$357	$314	$271	$228	$185	$146
$6,065	$6,125	$579	$536	$493	$450	$407	$364	$321	$278	$235	$192	$152
$6,125	$6,185	$587	$544	$501	$458	$415	$372	$329	$286	$243	$200	$158
$6,185	$6,245	$594	$551	$508	$465	$422	$379	$336	$293	$250	$207	$164
$6,245	$6,305	$601	$558	$515	$472	$429	$386	$343	$300	$257	$214	$171
$6,305	$6,365	$608	$565	$522	$479	$436	$393	$350	$307	$264	$221	$178
$6,365	$6,425	$615	$572	$529	$486	$443	$400	$357	$314	$271	$228	$185
$6,425	$6,485	$623	$580	$537	$494	$451	$408	$365	$322	$279	$236	$193
$6,485	$6,545	$630	$587	$544	$501	$458	$415	$372	$329	$286	$243	$200

2020 Wage Bracket Method Tables for Manual Payroll Systems With Forms W-4 From 2019 or Earlier
MONTHLY Payroll Period

If the Wage Amount (line 1a) is		MARRIED Persons										
At least	But less than	And the number of allowances is:										
		0	1	2	3	4	5	6	7	8	9	10
		The Tentative Withholding Amount is:										
$6,545	$6,605	$637	$594	$551	$508	$465	$422	$379	$336	$293	$250	$207
$6,605	$6,665	$644	$601	$558	$515	$472	$429	$386	$343	$300	$257	$214
$6,665	$6,725	$651	$608	$565	$522	$479	$436	$393	$350	$307	$264	$221
$6,725	$6,785	$659	$616	$573	$530	$487	$444	$401	$358	$315	$272	$229
$6,785	$6,845	$666	$623	$580	$537	$494	$451	$408	$365	$322	$279	$236
$6,845	$6,905	$673	$630	$587	$544	$501	$458	$415	$372	$329	$286	$243
$6,905	$6,965	$680	$637	$594	$551	$508	$465	$422	$379	$336	$293	$250
$6,965	$7,025	$687	$644	$601	$558	$515	$472	$429	$386	$343	$300	$257
$7,025	$7,085	$695	$652	$609	$566	$523	$480	$437	$394	$351	$308	$265
$7,085	$7,145	$702	$659	$616	$573	$530	$487	$444	$401	$358	$315	$272
$7,145	$7,205	$709	$666	$623	$580	$537	$494	$451	$408	$365	$322	$279
$7,205	$7,265	$716	$673	$630	$587	$544	$501	$458	$415	$372	$329	$286
$7,265	$7,325	$723	$680	$637	$594	$551	$508	$465	$422	$379	$336	$293
$7,325	$7,385	$731	$688	$645	$602	$559	$516	$473	$430	$387	$344	$301
$7,385	$7,445	$738	$695	$652	$609	$566	$523	$480	$437	$394	$351	$308
$7,445	$7,505	$745	$702	$659	$616	$573	$530	$487	$444	$401	$358	$315
$7,505	$7,565	$752	$709	$666	$623	$580	$537	$494	$451	$408	$365	$322
$7,565	$7,625	$759	$716	$673	$630	$587	$544	$501	$458	$415	$372	$329
$7,625	$7,685	$767	$724	$681	$638	$595	$552	$509	$466	$423	$380	$337
$7,685	$7,765	$780	$732	$689	$646	$603	$560	$517	$474	$431	$388	$345
$7,765	$7,845	$797	$742	$699	$656	$613	$570	$527	$484	$441	$398	$355
$7,845	$7,925	$815	$751	$708	$665	$622	$579	$536	$493	$450	$407	$364
$7,925	$8,005	$832	$761	$718	$675	$632	$589	$546	$503	$460	$417	$374
$8,005	$8,085	$850	$771	$727	$684	$641	$598	$555	$512	$469	$426	$383
$8,085	$8,165	$868	$789	$737	$694	$651	$608	$565	$522	$479	$436	$393
$8,165	$8,245	$885	$806	$747	$704	$661	$618	$575	$532	$489	$446	$403
$8,245	$8,325	$903	$824	$756	$713	$670	$627	$584	$541	$498	$455	$412
$8,325	$8,405	$920	$842	$766	$723	$680	$637	$594	$551	$508	$465	$422

2020 Wage Bracket Method Tables for Manual Payroll Systems With Forms W-4 From 2019 or Earlier

MONTHLY Payroll Period

If the **Wage Amount** (line 1a) is		SINGLE Persons										
		And the number of allowances is:										
At least	But less than	0	1	2	3	4	5	6	7	8	9	10
		The Tentative Withholding Amount is:										
$0	$320	$0	$0	$0	$0	$0	$0	$0	$0	$0	$0	$0
$320	$340	$1	$0	$0	$0	$0	$0	$0	$0	$0	$0	$0
$340	$360	$3	$0	$0	$0	$0	$0	$0	$0	$0	$0	$0
$360	$380	$5	$0	$0	$0	$0	$0	$0	$0	$0	$0	$0
$380	$400	$7	$0	$0	$0	$0	$0	$0	$0	$0	$0	$0
$400	$420	$9	$0	$0	$0	$0	$0	$0	$0	$0	$0	$0
$420	$470	$13	$0	$0	$0	$0	$0	$0	$0	$0	$0	$0
$470	$520	$18	$0	$0	$0	$0	$0	$0	$0	$0	$0	$0
$520	$570	$23	$0	$0	$0	$0	$0	$0	$0	$0	$0	$0
$570	$620	$28	$0	$0	$0	$0	$0	$0	$0	$0	$0	$0
$620	$670	$33	$0	$0	$0	$0	$0	$0	$0	$0	$0	$0
$670	$720	$38	$2	$0	$0	$0	$0	$0	$0	$0	$0	$0
$720	$770	$43	$7	$0	$0	$0	$0	$0	$0	$0	$0	$0
$770	$820	$48	$12	$0	$0	$0	$0	$0	$0	$0	$0	$0
$820	$870	$53	$17	$0	$0	$0	$0	$0	$0	$0	$0	$0
$870	$920	$58	$22	$0	$0	$0	$0	$0	$0	$0	$0	$0
$920	$970	$63	$27	$0	$0	$0	$0	$0	$0	$0	$0	$0
$970	$1,020	$68	$32	$0	$0	$0	$0	$0	$0	$0	$0	$0
$1,020	$1,070	$73	$37	$1	$0	$0	$0	$0	$0	$0	$0	$0
$1,070	$1,120	$78	$42	$6	$0	$0	$0	$0	$0	$0	$0	$0
$1,120	$1,170	$83	$47	$11	$0	$0	$0	$0	$0	$0	$0	$0
$1,170	$1,230	$90	$53	$17	$0	$0	$0	$0	$0	$0	$0	$0
$1,230	$1,290	$97	$59	$23	$0	$0	$0	$0	$0	$0	$0	$0
$1,290	$1,350	$104	$65	$29	$0	$0	$0	$0	$0	$0	$0	$0
$1,350	$1,410	$111	$71	$35	$0	$0	$0	$0	$0	$0	$0	$0
$1,410	$1,470	$118	$77	$41	$5	$0	$0	$0	$0	$0	$0	$0
$1,470	$1,530	$126	$83	$47	$11	$0	$0	$0	$0	$0	$0	$0
$1,530	$1,590	$133	$90	$53	$17	$0	$0	$0	$0	$0	$0	$0
$1,590	$1,650	$140	$97	$59	$23	$0	$0	$0	$0	$0	$0	$0
$1,650	$1,710	$147	$104	$65	$29	$0	$0	$0	$0	$0	$0	$0
$1,710	$1,770	$154	$111	$71	$35	$0	$0	$0	$0	$0	$0	$0
$1,770	$1,830	$162	$119	$77	$41	$5	$0	$0	$0	$0	$0	$0
$1,830	$1,890	$169	$126	$83	$47	$11	$0	$0	$0	$0	$0	$0
$1,890	$1,950	$176	$133	$90	$53	$17	$0	$0	$0	$0	$0	$0
$1,950	$2,010	$183	$140	$97	$59	$23	$0	$0	$0	$0	$0	$0
$2,010	$2,070	$190	$147	$104	$65	$29	$0	$0	$0	$0	$0	$0
$2,070	$2,130	$198	$155	$112	$71	$35	$0	$0	$0	$0	$0	$0
$2,130	$2,190	$205	$162	$119	$77	$41	$5	$0	$0	$0	$0	$0
$2,190	$2,250	$212	$169	$126	$83	$47	$11	$0	$0	$0	$0	$0
$2,250	$2,310	$219	$176	$133	$90	$53	$17	$0	$0	$0	$0	$0
$2,310	$2,370	$226	$183	$140	$97	$59	$23	$0	$0	$0	$0	$0
$2,370	$2,430	$234	$191	$148	$105	$65	$29	$0	$0	$0	$0	$0
$2,430	$2,490	$241	$198	$155	$112	$71	$35	$0	$0	$0	$0	$0
$2,490	$2,550	$248	$205	$162	$119	$77	$41	$5	$0	$0	$0	$0
$2,550	$2,610	$255	$212	$169	$126	$83	$47	$11	$0	$0	$0	$0
$2,610	$2,670	$262	$219	$176	$133	$90	$53	$17	$0	$0	$0	$0
$2,670	$2,730	$270	$227	$184	$141	$98	$59	$23	$0	$0	$0	$0
$2,730	$2,790	$277	$234	$191	$148	$105	$65	$29	$0	$0	$0	$0
$2,790	$2,850	$284	$241	$198	$155	$112	$71	$35	$0	$0	$0	$0
$2,850	$2,910	$291	$248	$205	$162	$119	$77	$41	$6	$0	$0	$0
$2,910	$2,970	$298	$255	$212	$169	$126	$83	$47	$12	$0	$0	$0

2020 Wage Bracket Method Tables for Manual Payroll Systems With Forms W-4 From 2019 or Earlier

MONTHLY Payroll Period

If the Wage Amount (line 1a) is		SINGLE Persons										
		And the number of allowances is:										
At least	But less than	0	1	2	3	4	5	6	7	8	9	10
		The Tentative Withholding Amount is:										
$2,970	$3,030	$306	$263	$220	$177	$134	$91	$53	$18	$0	$0	$0
$3,030	$3,090	$313	$270	$227	$184	$141	$98	$59	$24	$0	$0	$0
$3,090	$3,150	$320	$277	$234	$191	$148	$105	$65	$30	$0	$0	$0
$3,150	$3,210	$327	$284	$241	$198	$155	$112	$71	$36	$0	$0	$0
$3,210	$3,270	$334	$291	$248	$205	$162	$119	$77	$42	$6	$0	$0
$3,270	$3,330	$342	$299	$256	$213	$170	$127	$84	$48	$12	$0	$0
$3,330	$3,390	$349	$306	$263	$220	$177	$134	$91	$54	$18	$0	$0
$3,390	$3,450	$356	$313	$270	$227	$184	$141	$98	$60	$24	$0	$0
$3,450	$3,510	$363	$320	$277	$234	$191	$148	$105	$66	$30	$0	$0
$3,510	$3,570	$370	$327	$284	$241	$198	$155	$112	$72	$36	$0	$0
$3,570	$3,630	$378	$335	$292	$249	$206	$163	$120	$78	$42	$6	$0
$3,630	$3,690	$385	$342	$299	$256	$213	$170	$127	$84	$48	$12	$0
$3,690	$3,770	$400	$350	$307	$264	$221	$178	$135	$92	$55	$19	$0
$3,770	$3,850	$418	$360	$317	$274	$231	$188	$145	$102	$63	$27	$0
$3,850	$3,930	$435	$369	$326	$283	$240	$197	$154	$111	$71	$35	$0
$3,930	$4,010	$453	$379	$336	$293	$250	$207	$164	$121	$79	$43	$7
$4,010	$4,090	$471	$392	$346	$303	$260	$217	$174	$131	$88	$51	$15
$4,090	$4,170	$488	$409	$355	$312	$269	$226	$183	$140	$97	$59	$23
$4,170	$4,250	$506	$427	$365	$322	$279	$236	$193	$150	$107	$67	$31
$4,250	$4,330	$523	$444	$374	$331	$288	$245	$202	$159	$116	$75	$39
$4,330	$4,410	$541	$462	$384	$341	$298	$255	$212	$169	$126	$83	$47
$4,410	$4,490	$559	$480	$401	$351	$308	$265	$222	$179	$136	$93	$55
$4,490	$4,570	$576	$497	$418	$360	$317	$274	$231	$188	$145	$102	$63
$4,570	$4,650	$594	$515	$436	$370	$327	$284	$241	$198	$155	$112	$71
$4,650	$4,730	$611	$532	$454	$379	$336	$293	$250	$207	$164	$121	$79
$4,730	$4,810	$629	$550	$471	$392	$346	$303	$260	$217	$174	$131	$88
$4,810	$4,890	$647	$568	$489	$410	$356	$313	$270	$227	$184	$141	$98
$4,890	$4,970	$664	$585	$506	$428	$365	$322	$279	$236	$193	$150	$107
$4,970	$5,050	$682	$603	$524	$445	$375	$332	$289	$246	$203	$160	$117
$5,050	$5,130	$699	$620	$542	$463	$384	$341	$298	$255	$212	$169	$126
$5,130	$5,210	$717	$638	$559	$480	$402	$351	$308	$265	$222	$179	$136
$5,210	$5,290	$735	$656	$577	$498	$419	$361	$318	$275	$232	$189	$146
$5,290	$5,370	$752	$673	$594	$516	$437	$370	$327	$284	$241	$198	$155
$5,370	$5,450	$770	$691	$612	$533	$454	$380	$337	$294	$251	$208	$165
$5,450	$5,530	$787	$708	$630	$551	$472	$393	$346	$303	$260	$217	$174
$5,530	$5,610	$805	$726	$647	$568	$490	$411	$356	$313	$270	$227	$184
$5,610	$5,690	$823	$744	$665	$586	$507	$428	$366	$323	$280	$237	$194
$5,690	$5,770	$840	$761	$682	$604	$525	$446	$375	$332	$289	$246	$203
$5,770	$5,850	$858	$779	$700	$621	$542	$464	$385	$342	$299	$256	$213
$5,850	$5,930	$875	$796	$718	$639	$560	$481	$402	$351	$308	$265	$222
$5,930	$6,010	$893	$814	$735	$656	$578	$499	$420	$361	$318	$275	$232
$6,010	$6,090	$911	$832	$753	$674	$595	$516	$438	$371	$328	$285	$242
$6,090	$6,170	$928	$849	$770	$692	$613	$534	$455	$380	$337	$294	$251
$6,170	$6,250	$946	$867	$788	$709	$630	$552	$473	$394	$347	$304	$261
$6,250	$6,330	$963	$884	$806	$727	$648	$569	$490	$411	$356	$313	$270
$6,330	$6,410	$981	$902	$823	$744	$666	$587	$508	$429	$366	$323	$280
$6,410	$6,490	$999	$920	$841	$762	$683	$604	$526	$447	$376	$333	$290
$6,490	$6,570	$1,016	$937	$858	$780	$701	$622	$543	$464	$385	$342	$299
$6,570	$6,650	$1,034	$955	$876	$797	$718	$640	$561	$482	$403	$352	$309
$6,650	$6,730	$1,051	$972	$894	$815	$736	$657	$578	$499	$421	$361	$318
$6,730	$6,810	$1,069	$990	$911	$832	$754	$675	$596	$517	$438	$371	$328

2020 Wage Bracket Method Tables for Manual Payroll Systems With Forms W-4 From 2019 or Earlier

MONTHLY Payroll Period

If the **Wage Amount** (line 1a) is		SINGLE Persons										
		And the number of allowances is:										
At least	But less than	0	1	2	3	4	5	6	7	8	9	10
		The Tentative Withholding Amount is:										
$6,810	$6,890	$1,087	$1,008	$929	$850	$771	$692	$614	$535	$456	$381	$338
$6,890	$6,970	$1,104	$1,025	$946	$868	$789	$710	$631	$552	$473	$395	$347
$6,970	$7,050	$1,122	$1,043	$964	$885	$806	$728	$649	$570	$491	$412	$357
$7,050	$7,130	$1,139	$1,060	$982	$903	$824	$745	$666	$587	$509	$430	$366
$7,130	$7,210	$1,157	$1,078	$999	$920	$842	$763	$684	$605	$526	$447	$376
$7,210	$7,290	$1,175	$1,096	$1,017	$938	$859	$780	$702	$623	$544	$465	$386
$7,290	$7,370	$1,192	$1,113	$1,034	$956	$877	$798	$719	$640	$561	$483	$404
$7,370	$7,450	$1,210	$1,131	$1,052	$973	$894	$816	$737	$658	$579	$500	$421
$7,450	$7,530	$1,228	$1,148	$1,070	$991	$912	$833	$754	$675	$597	$518	$439
$7,530	$7,610	$1,247	$1,166	$1,087	$1,008	$930	$851	$772	$693	$614	$535	$457
$7,610	$7,690	$1,267	$1,184	$1,105	$1,026	$947	$868	$790	$711	$632	$553	$474
$7,690	$7,770	$1,286	$1,201	$1,122	$1,044	$965	$886	$807	$728	$649	$571	$492
$7,770	$7,850	$1,305	$1,219	$1,140	$1,061	$982	$904	$825	$746	$667	$588	$509
$7,850	$7,930	$1,324	$1,238	$1,158	$1,079	$1,000	$921	$842	$763	$685	$606	$527
$7,930	$8,010	$1,343	$1,257	$1,175	$1,096	$1,018	$939	$860	$781	$702	$623	$545
$8,010	$8,090	$1,363	$1,277	$1,193	$1,114	$1,035	$956	$878	$799	$720	$641	$562
$8,090	$8,170	$1,382	$1,296	$1,210	$1,132	$1,053	$974	$895	$816	$737	$659	$580
$8,170	$8,250	$1,401	$1,315	$1,229	$1,149	$1,070	$992	$913	$834	$755	$676	$597
$8,250	$8,330	$1,420	$1,334	$1,248	$1,167	$1,088	$1,009	$930	$851	$773	$694	$615
$8,330	$8,410	$1,439	$1,353	$1,267	$1,184	$1,106	$1,027	$948	$869	$790	$711	$633

2020 Wage Bracket Method Tables for Manual Payroll Systems With Forms W-4 From 2020 or Later
MONTHLY Payroll Period

If the Adjusted Wage Amount (line 1h) is		Married Filing Jointly		Head of Household		Single or Married Filing Separately	
At least	But less than	Standard withholding	Form W-4, Step 2, Checkbox withholding	Standard withholding	Form W-4, Step 2, Checkbox withholding	Standard withholding	Form W-4, Step 2, Checkbox withholding
		The Tentative Withholding Amount is:					
$0	$520	$0	$0	$0	$0	$0	$0
$520	$530	$0	$0	$0	$0	$0	$1
$530	$540	$0	$0	$0	$0	$0	$2
$540	$550	$0	$0	$0	$0	$0	$3
$550	$560	$0	$0	$0	$0	$0	$4
$560	$570	$0	$0	$0	$0	$0	$5
$570	$580	$0	$0	$0	$0	$0	$6
$580	$590	$0	$0	$0	$0	$0	$7
$590	$600	$0	$0	$0	$0	$0	$8
$600	$610	$0	$0	$0	$0	$0	$9
$610	$620	$0	$0	$0	$0	$0	$10
$620	$630	$0	$0	$0	$0	$0	$11
$630	$640	$0	$0	$0	$0	$0	$12
$640	$650	$0	$0	$0	$0	$0	$13
$650	$660	$0	$0	$0	$0	$0	$14
$660	$670	$0	$0	$0	$0	$0	$15
$670	$680	$0	$0	$0	$0	$0	$16
$680	$690	$0	$0	$0	$0	$0	$17
$690	$700	$0	$0	$0	$0	$0	$18
$700	$710	$0	$0	$0	$0	$0	$19
$710	$720	$0	$0	$0	$0	$0	$20
$720	$730	$0	$0	$0	$0	$0	$21
$730	$740	$0	$0	$0	$0	$0	$22
$740	$750	$0	$0	$0	$0	$0	$23
$750	$760	$0	$0	$0	$0	$0	$24
$760	$770	$0	$0	$0	$0	$0	$25
$770	$780	$0	$0	$0	$0	$0	$26
$780	$790	$0	$0	$0	$1	$0	$27
$790	$800	$0	$0	$0	$2	$0	$28
$800	$810	$0	$0	$0	$3	$0	$29
$810	$820	$0	$0	$0	$4	$0	$30
$820	$830	$0	$0	$0	$5	$0	$31
$830	$840	$0	$0	$0	$6	$0	$32
$840	$850	$0	$0	$0	$7	$0	$33
$850	$860	$0	$0	$0	$8	$0	$34
$860	$870	$0	$0	$0	$9	$0	$35
$870	$880	$0	$0	$0	$10	$0	$36
$880	$890	$0	$0	$0	$11	$0	$37
$890	$900	$0	$0	$0	$12	$0	$38
$900	$910	$0	$0	$0	$13	$0	$39
$910	$920	$0	$0	$0	$14	$0	$40
$920	$930	$0	$0	$0	$15	$0	$41
$930	$955	$0	$0	$0	$17	$0	$43
$955	$980	$0	$0	$0	$19	$0	$46
$980	$1,005	$0	$0	$0	$22	$0	$49
$1,005	$1,030	$0	$0	$0	$24	$0	$52
$1,030	$1,055	$0	$1	$0	$27	$1	$55
$1,055	$1,080	$0	$3	$0	$29	$3	$58
$1,080	$1,105	$0	$6	$0	$32	$6	$61
$1,105	$1,130	$0	$8	$0	$34	$8	$64
$1,130	$1,155	$0	$11	$0	$37	$11	$67
$1,155	$1,180	$0	$13	$0	$39	$13	$70
$1,180	$1,205	$0	$16	$0	$42	$16	$73
$1,205	$1,230	$0	$18	$0	$44	$18	$76
$1,230	$1,255	$0	$21	$0	$47	$21	$79
$1,255	$1,280	$0	$23	$0	$49	$23	$82
$1,280	$1,305	$0	$26	$0	$52	$26	$85
$1,305	$1,330	$0	$28	$0	$54	$28	$88
$1,330	$1,355	$0	$31	$0	$57	$31	$91
$1,355	$1,380	$0	$33	$0	$59	$33	$94
$1,380	$1,405	$0	$36	$0	$62	$36	$97
$1,405	$1,430	$0	$38	$0	$65	$38	$100
$1,430	$1,455	$0	$41	$0	$68	$41	$103
$1,455	$1,480	$0	$43	$0	$71	$43	$106
$1,480	$1,505	$0	$46	$0	$74	$46	$109

2020 Wage Bracket Method Tables for Manual Payroll Systems With Forms W-4 From 2020 or Later
MONTHLY Payroll Period

If the Adjusted Wage Amount (line 1h) is		Married Filing Jointly		Head of Household		Single or Married Filing Separately	
		Standard withholding	Form W-4, Step 2, Checkbox withholding	Standard withholding	Form W-4, Step 2, Checkbox withholding	Standard withholding	Form W-4, Step 2, Checkbox withholding
At least	But less than	The Tentative Withholding Amount is:					
$1,505	$1,530	$0	$48	$0	$77	$48	$112
$1,530	$1,555	$0	$51	$0	$80	$51	$115
$1,555	$1,580	$0	$53	$1	$83	$53	$118
$1,580	$1,605	$0	$56	$4	$86	$56	$121
$1,605	$1,630	$0	$58	$6	$89	$58	$124
$1,630	$1,655	$0	$61	$9	$92	$61	$127
$1,655	$1,680	$0	$63	$11	$95	$63	$130
$1,680	$1,705	$0	$66	$14	$98	$66	$133
$1,705	$1,730	$0	$68	$16	$101	$68	$136
$1,730	$1,755	$0	$71	$19	$104	$71	$139
$1,755	$1,780	$0	$73	$21	$107	$73	$142
$1,780	$1,805	$0	$76	$24	$110	$76	$145
$1,805	$1,830	$0	$78	$26	$113	$78	$148
$1,830	$1,855	$0	$81	$29	$116	$81	$151
$1,855	$1,880	$0	$84	$31	$119	$84	$154
$1,880	$1,905	$0	$87	$34	$122	$87	$157
$1,905	$1,930	$0	$90	$36	$125	$90	$160
$1,930	$1,955	$0	$93	$39	$128	$93	$163
$1,955	$1,980	$0	$96	$41	$131	$96	$166
$1,980	$2,005	$0	$99	$44	$134	$99	$169
$2,005	$2,030	$0	$102	$46	$137	$102	$172
$2,030	$2,055	$0	$105	$49	$140	$105	$175
$2,055	$2,080	$0	$108	$51	$143	$108	$178
$2,080	$2,105	$3	$111	$54	$146	$111	$181
$2,105	$2,130	$5	$114	$56	$149	$114	$184
$2,130	$2,155	$8	$117	$59	$152	$117	$187
$2,155	$2,180	$10	$120	$61	$155	$120	$190
$2,180	$2,205	$13	$123	$64	$158	$123	$193
$2,205	$2,255	$16	$127	$68	$163	$127	$202
$2,255	$2,305	$21	$133	$73	$169	$133	$213
$2,305	$2,355	$26	$139	$78	$175	$139	$224
$2,355	$2,405	$31	$145	$83	$181	$145	$235
$2,405	$2,455	$36	$151	$88	$187	$151	$246
$2,455	$2,505	$41	$157	$93	$193	$157	$257
$2,505	$2,555	$46	$163	$98	$199	$163	$268
$2,555	$2,605	$51	$169	$103	$205	$169	$279
$2,605	$2,655	$56	$175	$108	$211	$175	$290
$2,655	$2,705	$61	$181	$113	$217	$181	$301
$2,705	$2,755	$66	$187	$118	$223	$187	$312
$2,755	$2,805	$71	$193	$124	$229	$193	$323
$2,805	$2,855	$76	$199	$130	$235	$199	$334
$2,855	$2,905	$81	$205	$136	$241	$205	$345
$2,905	$2,955	$86	$211	$142	$247	$211	$356
$2,955	$3,005	$91	$217	$148	$253	$217	$367
$3,005	$3,055	$96	$223	$154	$260	$223	$378
$3,055	$3,105	$101	$229	$160	$271	$229	$389
$3,105	$3,155	$106	$235	$166	$282	$235	$400
$3,155	$3,205	$111	$241	$172	$293	$241	$411
$3,205	$3,255	$116	$247	$178	$304	$247	$422
$3,255	$3,305	$121	$253	$184	$315	$253	$433
$3,305	$3,355	$126	$259	$190	$326	$259	$444
$3,355	$3,405	$131	$265	$196	$337	$265	$455
$3,405	$3,455	$136	$271	$202	$348	$271	$466
$3,455	$3,505	$141	$277	$208	$359	$277	$477
$3,505	$3,555	$146	$283	$214	$370	$283	$488
$3,555	$3,605	$151	$289	$220	$381	$289	$499
$3,605	$3,655	$156	$295	$226	$392	$295	$510
$3,655	$3,705	$161	$301	$232	$403	$301	$521
$3,705	$3,755	$167	$307	$238	$414	$307	$532
$3,755	$3,805	$173	$313	$244	$425	$313	$543
$3,805	$3,855	$179	$319	$250	$436	$319	$554
$3,855	$3,905	$185	$325	$256	$447	$325	$565
$3,905	$3,955	$191	$331	$262	$458	$331	$576
$3,955	$4,005	$197	$337	$268	$469	$337	$587
$4,005	$4,055	$203	$343	$274	$480	$343	$598

2020 Wage Bracket Method Tables for Manual Payroll Systems With Forms W-4 From 2020 or Later
MONTHLY Payroll Period

If the Adjusted Wage Amount (line 1h) is		Married Filing Jointly		Head of Household		Single or Married Filing Separately	
At least	But less than	Standard withholding	Form W-4, Step 2, Checkbox withholding	Standard withholding	Form W-4, Step 2, Checkbox withholding	Standard withholding	Form W-4, Step 2, Checkbox withholding
			The Tentative Withholding Amount is:				
$4,055	$4,105	$209	$349	$280	$491	$349	$609
$4,105	$4,180	$216	$357	$287	$505	$357	$624
$4,180	$4,255	$225	$366	$296	$521	$366	$642
$4,255	$4,330	$234	$375	$305	$538	$375	$660
$4,330	$4,405	$243	$384	$314	$555	$384	$678
$4,405	$4,480	$252	$399	$323	$573	$399	$696
$4,480	$4,555	$261	$416	$332	$591	$416	$714
$4,555	$4,630	$270	$432	$341	$609	$432	$732
$4,630	$4,705	$279	$449	$350	$627	$449	$750
$4,705	$4,780	$288	$465	$359	$645	$465	$768
$4,780	$4,855	$297	$482	$368	$663	$482	$786
$4,855	$4,930	$306	$498	$377	$681	$498	$804
$4,930	$5,005	$315	$515	$386	$699	$515	$822
$5,005	$5,080	$324	$531	$395	$717	$531	$840
$5,080	$5,155	$333	$548	$404	$735	$548	$858
$5,155	$5,230	$342	$564	$413	$753	$564	$876
$5,230	$5,305	$351	$581	$422	$771	$581	$894
$5,305	$5,380	$360	$597	$431	$789	$597	$912
$5,380	$5,455	$369	$614	$440	$807	$614	$930
$5,455	$5,530	$378	$630	$449	$825	$630	$948
$5,530	$5,605	$387	$647	$458	$843	$647	$966
$5,605	$5,680	$396	$663	$467	$861	$663	$984
$5,680	$5,755	$405	$680	$476	$879	$680	$1,002
$5,755	$5,830	$414	$696	$485	$897	$696	$1,020
$5,830	$5,905	$423	$713	$494	$915	$713	$1,038
$5,905	$5,980	$432	$729	$503	$933	$729	$1,056
$5,980	$6,055	$441	$746	$512	$951	$746	$1,074
$6,055	$6,130	$450	$762	$527	$969	$762	$1,092
$6,130	$6,205	$459	$779	$544	$987	$779	$1,110
$6,205	$6,280	$468	$795	$560	$1,005	$795	$1,128
$6,280	$6,355	$477	$812	$577	$1,023	$812	$1,146
$6,355	$6,430	$486	$828	$593	$1,041	$828	$1,164
$6,430	$6,505	$495	$845	$610	$1,059	$845	$1,182
$6,505	$6,580	$504	$861	$626	$1,077	$861	$1,200
$6,580	$6,655	$513	$878	$643	$1,095	$878	$1,218
$6,655	$6,730	$522	$894	$659	$1,113	$894	$1,236
$6,730	$6,805	$531	$911	$676	$1,131	$911	$1,254
$6,805	$6,880	$540	$927	$692	$1,149	$927	$1,272
$6,880	$6,955	$549	$944	$709	$1,167	$944	$1,290
$6,955	$7,030	$558	$960	$725	$1,185	$960	$1,308
$7,030	$7,105	$567	$977	$742	$1,203	$977	$1,326
$7,105	$7,180	$576	$993	$758	$1,221	$993	$1,344
$7,180	$7,255	$585	$1,010	$775	$1,239	$1,010	$1,362
$7,255	$7,330	$594	$1,026	$791	$1,257	$1,026	$1,380
$7,330	$7,430	$605	$1,045	$811	$1,278	$1,045	$1,405
$7,430	$7,530	$617	$1,067	$833	$1,302	$1,067	$1,437
$7,530	$7,630	$629	$1,089	$855	$1,326	$1,089	$1,469
$7,630	$7,730	$641	$1,111	$877	$1,358	$1,111	$1,501
$7,730	$7,830	$653	$1,133	$899	$1,390	$1,133	$1,533
$7,830	$7,930	$665	$1,155	$921	$1,422	$1,155	$1,565
$7,930	$8,030	$677	$1,177	$943	$1,454	$1,177	$1,597
$8,030	$8,130	$689	$1,199	$965	$1,486	$1,199	$1,629
$8,130	$8,230	$701	$1,222	$987	$1,518	$1,222	$1,661
$8,230	$8,330	$713	$1,246	$1,009	$1,550	$1,246	$1,693

Additional Comprehensive Tax Return Problems

CONTENTS

*Please note: Additional tax forms can be printed by going to the IRS website at **www.irs.gov**.

Comprehensive Problem One

Noah and Joan Arc's Tax Return

Noah and Joan Arc live with their family in Dayton, OH. Noah's Social Security number is 434-11-3311. Noah was born on February 22, 1985 and Joan was born on July 1, 1986. Both enjoy good health and eyesight. Noah owns and operates a pet store and Joan is a firefighter for the city of Dayton.

1. The Arcs have two children, a son named Shem (Social Security number 598-01-2345), born on March 21, 2013, and a daughter named Nora (Social Security number 554-33-2411), born on December 3, 2016.
2. Joan and Noah brought a folder of tax documents located on Pages D-3 to D-5.
3. Noah's pet store is located at 1415 S. Patterson Blvd, Dayton, OH 45409. The name of the store is "The Arc," and its taxpayer identification number is 95-9876556. Since you handle Noah's bookkeeping, you have printed the income statement from your Quickbooks software, shown on Page D-5. The Arc did not claim the COVID-related provisions for the employee retention credit or sick and family leave credits but Noah did defer his self-employment taxes related to The Arc. He estimates 77.5 percent of the profits can be allocated to the period March 27, 2020 through December 31, 2020.
4. Detail of The Arc's meals and entertainment:

$ 400	Meals associated with business travel
300	Arc employee holiday party
100	Overtime meals for employees
600	Sports tickets for entertaining large customers
$ 1,400	

5. Travel costs are business related and do not include meals.

6. Noah and Joan paid the following amounts during the year (all by check):

Political contributions	$ 250
Church donations (for which a written acknowledgment was received)	5,025
Real estate taxes on their home	2,400
Medical co-pays for doctor visits	700
Mortgage interest for purchase of home	See Form 1098 (Page D-4)
Tax return preparation fees	350
Credit card interest	220
Automobile insurance premiums	600
Uniforms for Joan	125
Contribution to Noah's individual retirement account (made on April 1, 2021)	6,000

7. Noah has a long-term capital loss carryover from last year of $2,313.
8. Noah and Joan own a condo and use it as a rental property. The condo is located at 16 Oakwood Ave, Unit A, Dayton, OH 45409. Noah provides the management services for the rental including selection of tenants, maintenance, repairs, rent collection, and other services as needed. On average, Noah spends about 2 hours per week on the rental activity. The revenue and expenses for the year are as follows:

Rental income	$14,000
Insurance	600
Interest expense	5,700
Property taxes	1,000
Miscellaneous expenses	700

The home was acquired for $82,500 in 2004. No improvements have been made to the property.

9. The Arcs paid Ohio general sales tax of $1,076 during the year.

10. The Arcs received a $3,400 EIP in 2020.

Required: You are to prepare the Arc's federal income tax return in good form, signing the return as the preparer. Do not complete an Ohio state income tax return. Make realistic assumptions about any missing data that you may need. The following forms and schedules are required:

Form 1040	Schedule SE
Schedule 1	Form 2441
Schedule 2	Form 4562
Schedule 3	Form 8812
Schedule A	Form 8949
Schedule B	Form 8995
Schedule C	Child Tax Credit Worksheet
Schedule D	Qualified Dividends and Capital Gain Tax Worksheet
Schedule E	

Note: The forms included in Appendix D are provided for the student to work on only one of the two additional comprehensive problems. If desired, additional tax forms may be obtained from the IRS website at **www.irs.gov**.

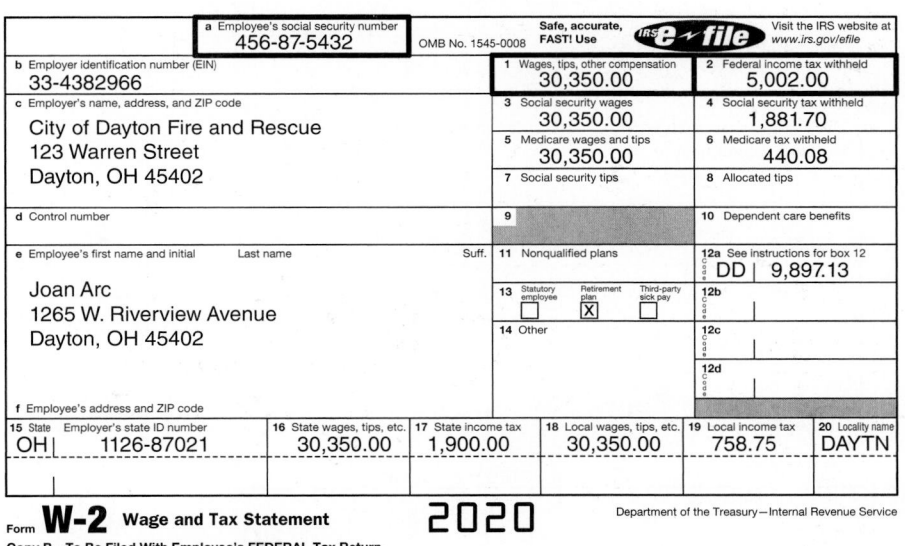

Substitute 1099 Statement

Charlotte Squab Financial Services

123 Wall Street
New York, NY 10005

Joan and Noah Arc
1265 W. Riverview Avenue
Dayton, OH 45402
SSN: 456-87-5432

Date

December 31, 2020

Dividends						
Payor	Box 1a Ordinary Dividends	Box 1b Qualified Dividends	Box 2a Cap Gain Distrib	Box 4 Federal Income Tax withheld	Box 7 Foreign Tax Paid	Box 11 Tax-exempt Dividends
ExxonMobil	322.00	322.00	0.00	0.00	0.00	0.00
Texas Util.	1,200.00	1,200.00	0.00	0.00	0.00	0.00
CS Growth Fund	400.00	400.00	250.00	0.00	20.00	0.00

Stock Transactions				
Description	Date Acq.	Date Sold	Net Proceeds	Basis (reported to IRS)
100 shs. Blue Corp.	02/11/2010	08/15/2020	4,545.00	2,580.00
50 shs. Yellow Corp.	01/13/2020	06/05/2020	6,100.00	5,375.00
25 shs. Red Co.	10/02/2011	10/07/2020	12,200.00	1,650.00

☐ CORRECTED (if checked)

RECIPIENT'S/LENDER'S name, street address, city or town, state or province, country, ZIP or foreign postal code, and telephone no.	*Caution: The amount shown may not be fully deductible by you. Limits based on the loan amount and the cost and value of the secured property may apply. Also, you may only deduct interest to the extent it was incurred by you, actually paid by you, and not reimbursed by another person.	OMB No. 1545-1380 2020 Form 1098	Mortgage Interest Statement
Chase Mortgage 100 Park Avenue New York, NY 10017	1 Mortgage interest received from payer(s)/borrower(s)* $ 10,105.00		Copy B For Payer/ Borrower

RECIPIENT'S/LENDER'S TIN	PAYER'S/BORROWER'S TIN	2 Outstanding mortgage principal	3 Mortgage origination date
13-4296127	434-11-3311	$ 274,700.00	03/13/2011

The information in boxes 1 through 9 and 11 is important tax information and is being furnished to the IRS. If you are required to file a return, a negligence penalty or other sanction may be imposed on you if the IRS determines that an underpayment of tax results because you overstated a deduction for this mortgage interest or for these points, reported in boxes 1 and 6; or because you didn't report the refund of interest (box 4); or because you claimed a nondeductible item.

		4 Refund of overpaid interest $	5 Mortgage insurance premiums $
PAYER'S/BORROWER'S name Noah and Joan Arc		6 Points paid on purchase of principal residence $	
Street address (including apt. no.) 1265 W. Riverview Avenue		7 ☒ If address of property securing mortgage is the same as PAYER'S/BORROWER'S address, the box is checked, or the address or description is entered in box 8.	
City or town, state or province, country, and ZIP or foreign postal code Dayton, OH 45402		8 Address or description of property securing mortgage (see instructions)	
9 Number of properties securing the mortgage 1	10 Other		
Account number (see instructions)			11 Mortgage acquisition date

Form **1098**   (Keep for your records)   www.irs.gov/Form1098   Department of the Treasury - Internal Revenue Service

ROUNDUP DAY CARE CENTER
245 N. WILKINSON STREET
DAYTON, OH 45402

January 12, 2021

Joan and Noah Arc
1265 W. Riverview Avenue
Dayton, OH 45402

Dear Joan and Noah,

Thank you for a great 2020 at Roundup! We appreciate your patronage during the year and hope to continue to provide excellent service for Nora in 2020. We have provided the tax information for calendar year 2020 below. Please let us know if you need any additional information.

Sincerely,

Charles F. Burgundian

Charles F. Burgundian
Executive Director, Roundup Day Care
EIN 54-0983456

Date of service	Amount Paid	Child
January 1, 2020 – December 31, 2020	$3,000.00	Nora Arc

The Arc
95-9876556
Income Statement
For the Year Ended December 31, 2020

Revenue:		
Gross Sales		$ 143,500.00
Less: Sales Returns and Allowances		-
Net Sales		143,500.00
Cost of Goods Sold:		
Beginning Inventory	$ 10,250.00	
Add: Purchases	62,150.00	
	72,400.00	
Less: Ending Inventory	10,000.00	
Cost of Goods Sold		62,400.00
Gross Profit (Loss)		81,100.00
Expenses:		
Dues and Subscriptions	-	
Estimated Federal Tax Payments	7,500.00	
Estimated State Tax Payments	3,800.00	
Insurance	3,950.00	
Meals and Entertainment	1,400.00	
Miscellaneous	-	
Payroll Taxes	3,830.00	
Professional Fees	1,710.00	
Rent	8,420.00	
Travel	1,230.00	
Utilities	1,250.00	
Vehicle Expenses	-	
Wages	25,110.00	
Total Expenses		58,200.00
Net Operating Income		$ 22,900.00

Comprehensive Problem Two

Michael and Jeanette Boyd's Tax Return

Michael D. and Jeanette S. Boyd live with their family at the Rock Glen House Bed & Breakfast, which Michael operates. The Bed & Breakfast (B&B) is located at 33333 Fume Blanc Way, Temecula, CA 92591. Michael (born May 4, 1977) and Jeanette (born June 12, 1978) enjoy good health and eyesight.

1. The Boyds have three sons. Maxwell was born April 16, 2003, Seve was born December 2, 2008, and Denzel was born January 13, 2010. All three boys live at home and the Boyds provide more than 50 percent of their support.

2. The Rock Glen House B&B is operated as a sole proprietorship and had the following income and expenses for the year:

Room rental income	$137,900
Vending machine income	2,000
Advertising expense	4,800
Depreciation for book and tax purposes	18,000
Mortgage interest on the B&B	23,000
Wages of cleaning people	17,540
Taxes and licenses	6,420
Supplies consumed	19,000
Business insurance	6,300
Laundry expenses	4,300
Accounting fees	1,800
Office expenses	2,400
Utilities	6,300

All of the above amounts relate to the business portion of the Bed & Breakfast; the personal portion is accounted for separately. The Rock Glen House B&B uses the cash method of accounting and has no inventory. The employer tax ID number is 95-1234567. Michael contracted the coronavirus in 2020 and the bed and breakfast was forced to close for 24 days. Shortly after recovering, Michael was required to close the bed and breakfast for another 15 days while he cared for his son Denzel, who was unable to attend school. Michael elects to take any sick and family leave credits associated with this leave, but does not defer his self-employment tax payments.

a Employee's social security number 256-43-8819	OMB No. 1545-0008	Safe, accurate, FAST! Use	IRS e-file	Visit the IRS website at www.irs.gov/efile

b Employer identification number (EIN) 43-7654321		1 Wages, tips, other compensation 13,850.00	2 Federal income tax withheld 1,700.00
c Employer's name, address, and ZIP code Temecula Valley Unified School District 31350 Rancho Vista Road Temecula, CA 92592		3 Social security wages 13,850.00	4 Social security tax withheld 858.70
		5 Medicare wages and tips 13,850.00	6 Medicare tax withheld 200.83
		7 Social security tips	8 Allocated tips
d Control number		9	10 Dependent care benefits
e Employee's first name and initial Last name Suff. Jeanette Boyd 33333 Fume Blanc Way Temecula, CA 92591		11 Nonqualified plans	12a See instructions for box 12
		13 Statutory employee ☐ Retirement plan ☐ Third-party sick pay ☐	12b
		14 Other	12c
			12d
f Employee's address and ZIP code			

15 State	Employer's state ID number	16 State wages, tips, etc.	17 State income tax	18 Local wages, tips, etc.	19 Local income tax	20 Locality name
CA	3990-1832	13,850.00	402.00			

Form **W-2** Wage and Tax Statement   **2020**   Department of the Treasury—Internal Revenue Service

Copy B—To Be Filed With Employee's FEDERAL Tax Return.
This information is being furnished to the Internal Revenue Service.

3. The Boyds made estimated federal income tax payments of $2,000 and estimated state income tax payments of $6,000 (all made during 2020).

4. Jeanette worked about 1,000 hours as a substitute schoolteacher with the local school district. She also spent $246 out-of-pocket for various supplies for her classroom. For the current year, Jeanette's Form W-2 from the school district is presented on the previous page.

5. Michael is retired from the U.S. Navy. His annual statement from the Navy, Form 1099-R, is shown on Page D-12.

6. Michael and Jeanette paid (and can substantiate) the following amounts during the year:

Mastercard interest	$1,480
Dental expenses (orthodontics for Maxwell)	5,457
California state income tax (for 2019)	2,130
Charitable contributions	875
Life insurance premiums	845
Automobile registration fees (deductible portion)	45
Tax return preparation fee	475
Contributions to the president's re-election campaign	1,000

The Boyds are taking the standard deduction in 2020.

7. During the year, Michael and Jeanette received the following qualifying dividends and interest:

Interest:

Bob's Big Bank	$ 390
Bank of England	290
City of Temecula Tax-Exempt Bonds	1,500
Vintage Bank	See 1099-INT (Page D-12)

Qualified dividends:

Southwest Airlines	$ 250
Heinz Foods	550

Also, Jeanette owns Series EE U.S. savings bonds. During the year, the bond redemption value increased by $1,300. Jeanette has not elected the accrual method for these bonds. There were no British taxes paid on the interest from the Bank of England. All the above stocks, bonds, and bank accounts are community property.

8. Jeanette has a stock portfolio. During the year, she sold the following stock, shown on her Forms 1099-B as follows (basis was provided to the IRS in all cases):

	Orange Co.	*Gold Co.*	*Green Co.*
Sales price	$8,100	See	$1,500
Basis	3,775	Form	2,600
Date acquired	02/11/20	1099-B	10/31/18
Date sold	06/19/20	(Page D-12)	10/23/20

9. Jeanette paid her ex-husband $4,600 alimony in the current year, as required under the 2003 divorce decree. Her ex-husband's name is Hector Leach and his Social Security number is 566-23-5431.

10. Michael does all the significant work in the Bed & Breakfast and therefore he pays self-employment tax on 100 percent of the earnings from the B&B.

11. During the year, Michael's uncle Boris died. Boris had a $50,000 life insurance policy that named Michael as the beneficiary. Michael received the check for the benefits payable under the policy on November 30 of the current year. Boris also left Michael a parcel of land with an appraised value of $120,000.

12. Michael is a general partner in a partnership that owns a boutique hotel in northern California and leases the property to a hotel management company. Michael does not materially participate in the partnership activity but the partnership activity does rise to the level of a trade or business. The Schedule K-1 from the partnership is shown on Page D-9.

13. Jeanette was not eligible for health care benefits due to the part-time nature of her job, thus health insurance for the Boyd household was purchased through the Covered California program and the Boyds received the Form 1095-A shown on Page D-11. They had no other health insurance during 2020. Assume that the self-employed health insurance deduction is $1,472. The Boyds did not claim an advance premium tax credit.

14. The Boyds received a $3,400 EIP in 2020.

Required: Michael and Jeanette have come to you to prepare their 2020 federal income tax return. Do not complete a California state income tax return. Michael and Jeanette have given you several IRS forms (see Pages D-9 to D-12). Make realistic assumptions about any missing data that you need. Do not file a federal Form 4952. The following is a list of the forms and schedules that you will need to complete the tax return:

Form 1040	Schedule SE
Schedule 1	Form 7202
Schedule 2	Form 8812
Schedule 3	Form 8949
Schedule B	Form 8962
Schedule C	Form 8995
Schedule D	Child Tax Credit Worksheet
Schedule E	Qualified Dividends and Capital Gain Tax Worksheet

Note: The forms included in Appendix D are provided for the student to work on only one of the two additional comprehensive problems. If desired, additional tax forms may be obtained from the IRS website at **www.irs.gov**.

651119

☐ Final K-1   ☐ Amended K-1   OMB No. 1545-0123

Schedule K-1 **(Form 1065)**	20**20**

Department of the Treasury
Internal Revenue Service

For calendar year 2020, or tax year

beginning ___ / ___ / 2020   ending ___ / ___ / ___

Partner's Share of Income, Deductions, Credits, etc.

▶ See separate instructions.

Part I	**Information About the Partnership**

A Partnership's employer identification number
11-2343212

B Partnership's name, address, city, state, and ZIP code
Wine Acres Partners
581 Coombs Street
Napa, CA 94559

C IRS Center where partnership filed return ▶ Ogden, UT

D ☐ Check if this is a publicly traded partnership (PTP)

Part II	**Information About the Partner**

E Partner's SSN or TIN (Do not use TIN of a disregarded entity. See instructions.)
543-88-9756

F Name, address, city, state, and ZIP code for partner entered in E. See instructions.

Michael Boyd
33333 Fume Blanc Way
Temecula, CA 92591

G ☒ General partner or LLC member-manager   ☐ Limited partner or other LLC member

H1 ☒ Domestic partner   ☐ Foreign partner

H2 ☐ If the partner is a disregarded entity (DE), enter the partner's:
TIN _____ Name _____

I1 What type of entity is this partner? _____

I2 If this partner is a retirement plan (IRA/SEP/Keogh/etc.), check here ☐

J Partner's share of profit, loss, and capital (see instructions):

	Beginning	Ending
Profit	2 %	2 %
Loss	2 %	2 %
Capital	2 %	2 %

Check if decrease is due to sale or exchange of partnership interest . . ☐

K Partner's share of liabilities:

	Beginning	Ending
Nonrecourse . . $	4,679	$ 4,679
Qualified nonrecourse financing . . $		$
Recourse . . $		$

☐ Check this box if Item K includes liability amounts from lower tier partnerships.

L **Partner's Capital Account Analysis**

Beginning capital account . . . $	13,256
Capital contributed during the year . . $	
Current year net income (loss) . . . $	720
Other increase (decrease) (attach explanation) $	
Withdrawals & distributions . . . $ (	350)
Ending capital account . . . . $	13,626

M Did the partner contribute property with a built-in gain or loss?
☐ Yes ☒ No If "Yes," attach statement. See instructions.

N **Partner's Share of Net Unrecognized Section 704(c) Gain or (Loss)**
Beginning . . . . $ _____
Ending . . . . $ _____

Part III	**Partner's Share of Current Year Income, Deductions, Credits, and Other Items**

1	Ordinary business income (loss)	15	Credits
2	Net rental real estate income (loss) 1,600		
3	Other net rental income (loss)	16	Foreign transactions
4a	Guaranteed payments for services		
4b	Guaranteed payments for capital		
4c	Total guaranteed payments		
5	Interest income		
6a	Ordinary dividends 10		
6b	Qualified dividends 10		
6c	Dividend equivalents	17	Alternative minimum tax (AMT) items
7	Royalties		
8	Net short-term capital gain (loss)		
9a	Net long-term capital gain (loss) (890)	18	Tax-exempt income and nondeductible expenses
9b	Collectibles (28%) gain (loss)		
9c	Unrecaptured section 1250 gain		
10	Net section 1231 gain (loss)	19	Distributions
11	Other income (loss)	A	350
		20	Other information
12	Section 179 deduction	Z	1,600
13	Other deductions		
14	Self-employment earnings (loss)		
A	1,600		

21 ☐ More than one activity for at-risk purposes*
22 ☐ More than one activity for passive activity purposes*
*See attached statement for additional information.

(left margin, vertical) For IRS Use Only

For Paperwork Reduction Act Notice, see Instructions for Form 1065.   www.irs.gov/Form1065   Cat. No. 11394R   **Schedule K-1 (Form 1065) 2020**

Form **1095-A**

Department of the Treasury
Internal Revenue Service

Health Insurance Marketplace Statement

▶ Do not attach to your tax return. Keep for your records.
▶ Go to *www.irs.gov/Form1095A* for instructions and the latest information.

☐ VOID
☐ CORRECTED

OMB No. 1545-2232

2020

Part I   Recipient Information

1 Marketplace identifier 31-1234567	**2** Marketplace-assigned policy number A1000HT	**3** Policy issuer's name Covered California
4 Recipient's name Michael Boyd	**5** Recipient's SSN 543-88-9756	**6** Recipient's date of birth 05/04/1977
7 Recipient's spouse's name Jeanette Boyd	**8** Recipient's spouse's SSN 256-43-8819	**9** Recipient's spouse's date of birth 06/12/1978
10 Policy start date 05/01/2020	**11** Policy termination date 12/31/2020	**12** Street address (including apartment no.) 33333 Fume Blanc Way
13 City or town Temecula	**14** State or province CA	**15** Country and ZIP or foreign postal code 92591

Part II   Covered Individuals

	A. Covered individual name	**B.** Covered individual SSN	**C.** Covered individual date of birth	**D.** Coverage start date	**E.** Coverage termination date
16	Michael Boyd	543-88-9756	05/04/1977	05/01/2020	12/31/2020
17	Jeanette Boyd	256-43-8819	06/12/1978	05/01/2020	12/31/2020
18	Maxwell Boyd	466-74-1131	04/16/2003	05/01/2020	12/31/2020
19	Seve Boyd	465-76-8375	12/02/2008	05/01/2020	12/31/2020
20	Denzel Boyd	475-23-1426	01/13/2010	05/01/2020	12/31/2020

Part III   Coverage Information

Month	**A.** Monthly enrollment premiums	**B.** Monthly second lowest cost silver plan (SLCSP) premium	**C.** Monthly advance payment of premium tax credit
21 January			
22 February			
23 March			
24 April			
25 May	1,540	1,625	0
26 June	1,540	1,625	0
27 July	1,540	1,625	0
28 August	1,540	1,625	0
29 September	1,540	1,625	0
30 October	1,540	1,625	0
31 November	1,540	1,625	0
32 December	1,540	1,625	0
33 Annual Totals	12,320	13,000	0

For Privacy Act and Paperwork Reduction Act Notice, see separate instructions.   Cat. No. 60703Q   Form **1095-A** (2020)

☐ CORRECTED (if checked)

Form 1099-R

PAYER'S name, street address, city or town, state or province, country, ZIP or foreign postal code, and phone no. United States Navy Retired Benefits Center Cleveland, OH 43267	1 Gross distribution $ 14,600.00	OMB No. 1545-0119 20**20** Form **1099-R**	Distributions From Pensions, Annuities, Retirement or Profit-Sharing Plans, IRAs, Insurance Contracts, etc.
	2a Taxable amount $ 14,600.00		
	2b Taxable amount not determined ☐	Total distribution ☐	**Copy B**
PAYER'S TIN 11-4662891	RECIPIENT'S TIN 543-88-9756	3 Capital gain (included in box 2a) $	4 Federal income tax withheld $ 1,500.00	**Report this income on your federal tax return. If this form shows federal income tax withheld in box 4, attach this copy to your return.**
RECIPIENT'S name Michael D. Boyd	5 Employee contributions/ Designated Roth contributions or insurance premiums $	6 Net unrealized appreciation in employer's securities $	
Street address (including apt. no.) 33333 Fume Blanc Way	7 Distribution code(s)　7	IRA/ SEP/ SIMPLE ☐	8 Other $　　　%	This information is being furnished to the IRS.
City or town, state or province, country, and ZIP or foreign postal code Temecula, CA 92591	9a Your percentage of total distribution　%	9b Total employee contributions $	
10 Amount allocable to IRR within 5 years $	11 1st year of desig. Roth contrib.	12 FATCA filing requirement ☐	14 State tax withheld $ 350.00	15 State/Payer's state no. CA	16 State distribution $ 14,600.00
Account number (see instructions)		13 Date of payment	17 Local tax withheld $	18 Name of locality	19 Local distribution $

Form **1099-R**　　　www.irs.gov/Form1099R　　　Department of the Treasury - Internal Revenue Service

☐ CORRECTED (if checked)

Form 1099-B

PAYER'S name, street address, city or town, state or province, country, ZIP or foreign postal code, and telephone no. Bear Stearns 269 Wall Street New York, NY 10001	Applicable checkbox on Form 8949 A	OMB No. 1545-0715 20**20** Form **1099-B**	Proceeds From Broker and Barter Exchange Transactions
	1a Description of property (Example: 100 sh. XYZ Co.) Gold Company		
	1b Date acquired 03/27/2020	1c Date sold or disposed 09/18/2020	
PAYER'S TIN 11-4396782	RECIPIENT'S TIN 256-43-8819	1d Proceeds $ 12,100.00	1e Cost or other basis $ 14,200.00	**Copy B** **For Recipient**
	1f Accrued market discount $	1g Wash sale loss disallowed $	
RECIPIENT'S name Jeanette Boyd	2 Short-term gain or loss ☒ Long-term gain or loss ☐ Ordinary ☐	3 If checked, proceeds from: Collectibles ☐ QOF ☐	This is important tax information and is being furnished to the IRS. If you are required to file a return, a negligence penalty or other sanction may be imposed on you if this income is taxable and the IRS determines that it has not been reported.
Street address (including apt. no.) 33333 Fume Blanc Way	4 Federal income tax withheld $	5 If checked, noncovered security ☐	
City or town, state or province, country, and ZIP or foreign postal code Temecula, CA 92591	6 Reported to IRS: Gross proceeds ☐ Net proceeds ☒	7 If checked, loss is not allowed based on amount in 1d ☐	
Account number (see instructions)	8 Profit or (loss) realized in 2020 on closed contracts $	9 Unrealized profit or (loss) on open contracts—12/31/2019 $	
CUSIP number	FATCA filing requirement ☐	10 Unrealized profit or (loss) on open contracts—12/31/2020 $	11 Aggregate profit or (loss) on contracts $	
14 State name	15 State identification no.	16 State tax withheld $ $	12 If checked, basis reported to IRS ☒	13 Bartering $	

Form **1099-B**　　(Keep for your records)　　www.irs.gov/Form1099B　　Department of the Treasury - Internal Revenue Service

☐ CORRECTED (if checked)

Form 1099-INT

PAYER'S name, street address, city or town, state or province, country, ZIP or foreign postal code, and telephone no. Vintage Bank 6792 Main Street Temecula, CA 92591	Payer's RTN (optional)	OMB No. 1545-0112 20**20** Form **1099-INT**	**Interest Income**
	1 Interest income 1,411.58		
	2 Early withdrawal penalty $		**Copy B**
PAYER'S TIN 96-8724390	RECIPIENT'S TIN 543-88-9756	3 Interest on U.S. Savings Bonds and Treas. obligations $	**For Recipient**
RECIPIENT'S name Michael Boyd	4 Federal income tax withheld $	5 Investment expenses $	This is important tax information and is being furnished to the IRS. If you are required to file a return, a negligence penalty or other sanction may be imposed on you if this income is taxable and the IRS determines that it has not been reported.
Street address (including apt. no.) 33333 Fume Blanc Way	6 Foreign tax paid $	7 Foreign country or U.S. possession	
City or town, state or province, country, and ZIP or foreign postal code Temecula, CA 92591	8 Tax-exempt interest $	9 Specified private activity bond interest $	
	FATCA filing requirement ☐	10 Market discount $	11 Bond premium $	
		12 Bond premium on Treasury obligations $	13 Bond premium on tax-exempt bond $	
Account number (see instructions)		14 Tax-exempt and tax credit bond CUSIP no.	15 State	16 State identification no.	17 State tax withheld $ $

Form **1099-INT**　　(keep for your records)　　www.irs.gov/Form1099INT　　Department of the Treasury - Internal Revenue Service

Form **1040** Department of the Treasury—Internal Revenue Service (99)
U.S. Individual Income Tax Return **2020** OMB No. 1545-0074 IRS Use Only—Do not write or staple in this space.

Filing Status
Check only one box.

☐ Single ☐ Married filing jointly ☐ Married filing separately (MFS) ☐ Head of household (HOH) ☐ Qualifying widow(er) (QW)

If you checked the MFS box, enter the name of your spouse. If you checked the HOH or QW box, enter the child's name if the qualifying person is a child but not your dependent ▶

Your first name and middle initial	Last name		Your social security number
If joint return, spouse's first name and middle initial	Last name		Spouse's social security number

Home address (number and street). If you have a P.O. box, see instructions.		Apt. no.
City, town, or post office. If you have a foreign address, also complete spaces below.	State	ZIP code
Foreign country name	Foreign province/state/county	Foreign postal code

Presidential Election Campaign
Check here if you, or your spouse if filing jointly, want $3 to go to this fund. Checking a box below will not change your tax or refund.
☐ You ☐ Spouse

At any time during 2020, did you receive, sell, send, exchange, or otherwise acquire any financial interest in any virtual currency? ☐ Yes ☐ No

Standard Deduction
Someone can claim: ☐ You as a dependent ☐ Your spouse as a dependent
☐ Spouse itemizes on a separate return or you were a dual-status alien

Age/Blindness You: ☐ Were born before January 2, 1956 ☐ Are blind **Spouse:** ☐ Was born before January 2, 1956 ☐ Is blind

Dependents (see instructions):
If more than four dependents, see instructions and check here ▶ ☐

(1) First name Last name	(2) Social security number	(3) Relationship to you	(4) ✔ if qualifies for (see instructions):	
			Child tax credit	Credit for other dependents
			☐	☐
			☐	☐
			☐	☐
			☐	☐

Attach Sch. B if required.

1	Wages, salaries, tips, etc. Attach Form(s) W-2	**1**
2a	Tax-exempt interest . . . 2a	**b** Taxable interest **2b**
3a	Qualified dividends . . . 3a	**b** Ordinary dividends **3b**
4a	IRA distributions . . . 4a	**b** Taxable amount **4b**
5a	Pensions and annuities . . 5a	**b** Taxable amount . **5b**
6a	Social security benefits . . 6a	**b** Taxable amount . . . **6b**
7	Capital gain or (loss). Attach Schedule D if required. If not required, check here . . . . . ▶ ☐	**7**
8	Other income from Schedule 1, line 9	**8**
9	Add lines 1, 2b, 3b, 4b, 5b, 6b, 7, and 8. This is your **total income** . . . . ▶	**9**
10	Adjustments to income:	
a	From Schedule 1, line 22 . . . . **10a**	
b	Charitable contributions if you take the standard deduction. See instructions **10b**	
c	Add lines 10a and 10b. These are your **total adjustments to income** . . . . ▶	**10c**
11	Subtract line 10c from line 9. This is your **adjusted gross income** . . . . ▶	**11**
12	**Standard deduction or itemized deductions** (from Schedule A)	**12**
13	Qualified business income deduction. Attach Form 8995 or Form 8995-A	**13**
14	Add lines 12 and 13	**14**
15	**Taxable income.** Subtract line 14 from line 11. If zero or less, enter -0-	**15**

Standard Deduction for—
- Single or Married filing separately, $12,400
- Married filing jointly or Qualifying widow(er), $24,800
- Head of household, $18,650
- If you checked any box under *Standard Deduction,* see instructions.

For Disclosure, Privacy Act, and Paperwork Reduction Act Notice, see separate instructions. Cat. No. 11320B Form **1040** (2020)

Form 1040 (2020)   Page **2**

16	**Tax** (see instructions). Check if any from Form(s): 1 ☐ 8814 2 ☐ 4972 3 ☐ _____	16	
17	Amount from Schedule 2, line 3	17	
18	Add lines 16 and 17	18	
19	Child tax credit or credit for other dependents	19	
20	Amount from Schedule 3, line 7	20	
21	Add lines 19 and 20	21	
22	Subtract line 21 from line 18. If zero or less, enter -0-	22	
23	Other taxes, including self-employment tax, from Schedule 2, line 10	23	
24	Add lines 22 and 23. This is your **total tax** ▶	24	
25	Federal income tax withheld from:		
a	Form(s) W-2	25a	
b	Form(s) 1099	25b	
c	Other forms (see instructions)	25c	
d	Add lines 25a through 25c	25d	
26	2020 estimated tax payments and amount applied from 2019 return	26	

• If you have a qualifying child, attach Sch. EIC.
• If you have nontaxable combat pay, see instructions.

27	Earned income credit (EIC)	27	
28	Additional child tax credit. Attach Schedule 8812	28	
29	American opportunity credit from Form 8863, line 8	29	
30	Recovery rebate credit. See instructions	30	
31	Amount from Schedule 3, line 13	31	
32	Add lines 27 through 31. These are your **total other payments and refundable credits** ▶	32	
33	Add lines 25d, 26, and 32. These are your **total payments** ▶	33	

Refund

Direct deposit? See instructions.

34	If line 33 is more than line 24, subtract line 24 from line 33. This is the amount you **overpaid**	34	
35a	Amount of line 34 you want **refunded to you.** If Form 8888 is attached, check here ▶ ☐	35a	
▶b	Routing number ____ ▶c Type: ☐ Checking ☐ Savings		
▶d	Account number ____		
36	Amount of line 34 you want **applied to your 2021 estimated tax** ▶	36	

Amount You Owe

For details on how to pay, see instructions.

37	Subtract line 33 from line 24. This is the **amount you owe now** ▶	37	

Note: Schedule H and Schedule SE filers, line 37 may not represent all of the taxes you owe for 2020. See Schedule 3, line 12e, and its instructions for details.

38	Estimated tax penalty (see instructions) ▶	38	

Third Party Designee

Do you want to allow another person to discuss this return with the IRS? See instructions ▶ ☐ **Yes.** Complete below. ☐ **No**

Designee's name ▶   Phone no. ▶   Personal identification number (PIN) ▶

Sign Here

Under penalties of perjury, I declare that I have examined this return and accompanying schedules and statements, and to the best of my knowledge and belief, they are true, correct, and complete. Declaration of preparer (other than taxpayer) is based on all information of which preparer has any knowledge.

Joint return? See instructions. Keep a copy for your records.

Your signature | Date | Your occupation | If the IRS sent you an Identity Protection PIN, enter it here (see inst.) ▶

Spouse's signature. If a joint return, **both** must sign. | Date | Spouse's occupation | If the IRS sent your spouse an Identity Protection PIN, enter it here (see inst.) ▶

Phone no. | Email address

Paid Preparer Use Only

Preparer's name | Preparer's signature | Date | PTIN | Check if: ☐ Self-employed

Firm's name ▶   Phone no. ▶

Firm's address ▶   Firm's EIN ▶

Go to *www.irs.gov/Form1040* for instructions and the latest information.   Form **1040** (2020)

SCHEDULE 1
(Form 1040)

Department of the Treasury
Internal Revenue Service

Additional Income and Adjustments to Income

▶ **Attach to Form 1040, 1040-SR, or 1040-NR.**
▶ **Go to www.irs.gov/Form1040 for instructions and the latest information.**

OMB No. 1545-0074

20**20**

Attachment
Sequence No. **01**

Name(s) shown on Form 1040, 1040-SR, or 1040-NR | Your social security number

Part I   Additional Income

1	Taxable refunds, credits, or offsets of state and local income taxes	**1**
2a	Alimony received	**2a**
b	Date of original divorce or separation agreement (see instructions) ▶ _____	
3	Business income or (loss). Attach Schedule C	**3**
4	Other gains or (losses). Attach Form 4797	**4**
5	Rental real estate, royalties, partnerships, S corporations, trusts, etc. Attach Schedule E	**5**
6	Farm income or (loss). Attach Schedule F	**6**
7	Unemployment compensation	**7**
8	Other income. List type and amount ▶	
	_____	**8**
9	Combine lines 1 through 8. Enter here and on Form 1040, 1040-SR, or 1040-NR, line 8	**9**

Part II   Adjustments to Income

10	Educator expenses	**10**
11	Certain business expenses of reservists, performing artists, and fee-basis government officials. Attach Form 2106	**11**
12	Health savings account deduction. Attach Form 8889	**12**
13	Moving expenses for members of the Armed Forces. Attach Form 3903	**13**
14	Deductible part of self-employment tax. Attach Schedule SE	**14**
15	Self-employed SEP, SIMPLE, and qualified plans	**15**
16	Self-employed health insurance deduction	**16**
17	Penalty on early withdrawal of savings	**17**
18a	Alimony paid	**18a**
b	Recipient's SSN . . . . ▶ _____	
c	Date of original divorce or separation agreement (see instructions) ▶ _____	
19	IRA deduction	**19**
20	Student loan interest deduction	**20**
21	Tuition and fees deduction. Attach Form 8917	**21**
22	Add lines 10 through 21. These are your **adjustments to income.** Enter here and on Form 1040, 1040-SR, or 1040-NR, line 10a	**22**

For Paperwork Reduction Act Notice, see your tax return instructions.   Cat. No. 71479F   Schedule 1 (Form 1040) 2020

SCHEDULE 2
(Form 1040)

Department of the Treasury
Internal Revenue Service

Additional Taxes

▶ Attach to Form 1040, 1040-SR, or 1040-NR.
▶ Go to *www.irs.gov/Form1040* for instructions and the latest information.

OMB No. 1545-0074

2020

Attachment
Sequence No. **02**

Name(s) shown on Form 1040, 1040-SR, or 1040-NR

Your social security number

Part I	Tax	
1	Alternative minimum tax. Attach Form 6251	**1**
2	Excess advance premium tax credit repayment. Attach Form 8962	**2**
3	Add lines 1 and 2. Enter here and on Form 1040, 1040-SR, or 1040-NR, line 17 . .	**3**

Part II	Other Taxes	
4	Self-employment tax. Attach Schedule SE	**4**
5	Unreported social security and Medicare tax from Form: **a** ☐ 4137 **b** ☐ 8919 .	**5**
6	Additional tax on IRAs, other qualified retirement plans, and other tax-favored accounts. Attach Form 5329 if required	**6**
7a	Household employment taxes. Attach Schedule H	**7a**
b	Repayment of first-time homebuyer credit from Form 5405. Attach Form 5405 if required	**7b**
8	Taxes from: **a** ☐ Form 8959 **b** ☐ Form 8960	
	c ☐ Instructions; enter code(s)_____	**8**
9	Section 965 net tax liability installment from Form 965-A . . . **9**	
10	Add lines 4 through 8. These are your **total other taxes.** Enter here and on Form 1040 or 1040-SR, line 23, or Form 1040-NR, line 23b	**10**

For Paperwork Reduction Act Notice, see your tax return instructions.   Cat. No. 71478U   **Schedule 2 (Form 1040) 2020**

SCHEDULE 3
(Form 1040)

Department of the Treasury
Internal Revenue Service

Additional Credits and Payments

▶ Attach to Form 1040, 1040-SR, or 1040-NR.
▶ Go to *www.irs.gov/Form1040* for instructions and the latest information.

OMB No. 1545-0074

2020

Attachment
Sequence No. **03**

Name(s) shown on Form 1040, 1040-SR, or 1040-NR | Your social security number

DRAFT AS OF August 18, 2020 DO NOT FILE

Part I   Nonrefundable Credits

1	Foreign tax credit. Attach Form 1116 if required	**1**	
2	Credit for child and dependent care expenses. Attach Form 2441	**2**	
3	Education credits from Form 8863, line 19	**3**	
4	Retirement savings contributions credit. Attach Form 8880	**4**	
5	Residential energy credits. Attach Form 5695	**5**	
6	Other credits from Form: **a** ☐ 3800 **b** ☐ 8801 **c** ☐ ____	**6**	
7	Add lines 1 through 6. Enter here and on Form 1040, 1040-SR, or 1040-NR, line 20	**7**	

Part II   Other Payments and Refundable Credits

8	Net premium tax credit. Attach Form 8962	**8**	
9	Amount paid with request for extension to file (see instructions)	**9**	
10	Excess social security and tier 1 RRTA tax withheld	**10**	
11	Credit for federal tax on fuels. Attach Form 4136	**11**	
12	Other payments or refundable credits:		
a	Form 2439	**12a**	
b	Qualified sick and family leave credits from Schedule(s) H and Form(s) 7202	**12b**	
c	Health coverage tax credit from Form 8885	**12c**	
d	Other: ____	**12d**	
e	Deferral for certain Schedule H or SE filers (see instructions) .	**12e**	
f	Add lines 12a through 12e	**12f**	
13	Add lines 8 through 12f. Enter here and on Form 1040, 1040-SR, or 1040-NR, line 31	**13**	

For Paperwork Reduction Act Notice, see your tax return instructions.   Cat. No. 71480G   **Schedule 3 (Form 1040) 2020**

SCHEDULE A
(Form 1040)

Department of the Treasury
Internal Revenue Service (99)

Itemized Deductions

▶ Go to *www.irs.gov/ScheduleA* for instructions and the latest information.
▶ Attach to Form 1040 or 1040-SR.

Caution: If you are claiming a net qualified disaster loss on Form 4684, see the instructions for line 16.

OMB No. 1545-0074

2020

Attachment
Sequence No. **07**

Name(s) shown on Form 1040 or 1040-SR

Your social security number

Medical and Dental Expenses	**Caution:** Do not include expenses reimbursed or paid by others.	
	1 Medical and dental expenses (see instructions)	**1**
	2 Enter amount from Form 1040 or 1040-SR, line 11 **2**	
	3 Multiply line 2 by 7.5% (0.075)	**3**
	4 Subtract line 3 from line 1. If line 3 is more than line 1, enter -0-	**4**
Taxes You Paid	**5** State and local taxes.	
	a State and local income taxes or general sales taxes. You may include either income taxes or general sales taxes on line 5a, but not both. If you elect to include general sales taxes instead of income taxes, check this box . . . . ▶ ☐	**5a**
	b State and local real estate taxes (see instructions)	**5b**
	c State and local personal property taxes	**5c**
	d Add lines 5a through 5c	**5d**
	e Enter the smaller of line 5d or $10,000 ($5,000 if married filing separately)	**5e**
	6 Other taxes. List type and amount ▶ _____	**6**
	7 Add lines 5e and 6	**7**
Interest You Paid **Caution:** Your mortgage interest deduction may be limited (see instructions).	**8** Home mortgage interest and points. If you didn't use all of your home mortgage loan(s) to buy, build, or improve your home, see instructions and check this box . . . . ▶ ☐	
	a Home mortgage interest and points reported to you on Form 1098. See instructions if limited	**8a**
	b Home mortgage interest not reported to you on Form 1098. See instructions if limited. If paid to the person from whom you bought the home, see instructions and show that person's name, identifying no., and address . . . . ▶ _____ _____	**8b**
	c Points not reported to you on Form 1098. See instructions for special rules	**8c**
	d Mortgage insurance premiums (see instructions)	**8d**
	e Add lines 8a through 8d	**8e**
	9 Investment interest. Attach Form 4952 if required. See instructions .	**9**
	10 Add lines 8e and 9	**10**
Gifts to Charity **Caution:** If you made a gift and got a benefit for it, see instructions.	**11** Gifts by cash or check. If you made any gift of $250 or more, see instructions	**11**
	12 Other than by cash or check. If you made any gift of $250 or more, see instructions. You **must** attach Form 8283 if over $500. . . .	**12**
	13 Carryover from prior year	**13**
	14 Add lines 11 through 13	**14**
Casualty and Theft Losses	**15** Casualty and theft loss(es) from a federally declared disaster (other than net qualified disaster losses). Attach Form 4684 and enter the amount from line 18 of that form. See instructions	**15**
Other Itemized Deductions	**16** Other—from list in instructions. List type and amount ▶ _____ _____	**16**
Total Itemized Deductions	**17** Add the amounts in the far right column for lines 4 through 16. Also, enter this amount on Form 1040 or 1040-SR, line 12	**17**
	18 If you elect to itemize deductions even though they are less than your standard deduction, check this box . . . . ▶ ☐	

For Paperwork Reduction Act Notice, see the Instructions for Forms 1040 and 1040-SR.   Cat. No. 17145C   **Schedule A (Form 1040) 2020**

DRAFT AS OF July 13, 2020 DO NOT FILE

SCHEDULE B
(Form 1040)

Department of the Treasury
Internal Revenue Service (99)

Interest and Ordinary Dividends

▶ Go to *www.irs.gov/ScheduleB* for instructions and the latest information.
▶ Attach to Form 1040 or 1040-SR.

OMB No. 1545-0074

2020

Attachment
Sequence No. **08**

Name(s) shown on return

Your social security number

Part I Interest		Amount

Part I

Interest

(See instructions and the instructions for Forms 1040 and 1040-SR, line 2b.)

Note: If you received a Form 1099-INT, Form 1099-OID, or substitute statement from a brokerage firm, list the firm's name as the payer and enter the total interest shown on that form.

1 List name of payer. If any interest is from a seller-financed mortgage and the buyer used the property as a personal residence, see the instructions and list this interest first. Also, show that buyer's social security number and address ▶

2 Add the amounts on line 1 . . . . **2**

3 Excludable interest on series EE and I U.S. savings bonds issued after 1989. Attach Form 8815 . . . . **3**

4 Subtract line 3 from line 2. Enter the result here and on Form 1040 or 1040-SR, line 2b . . . . ▶ **4**

Note: If line 4 is over $1,500, you must complete Part III.

Part II

Ordinary Dividends

(See instructions and the instructions for Forms 1040 and 1040-SR, line 3b.)

Note: If you received a Form 1099-DIV or substitute statement from a brokerage firm, list the firm's name as the payer and enter the ordinary dividends shown on that form.

5 List name of payer ▶

6 Add the amounts on line 5. Enter the total here and on Form 1040 or 1040-SR, line 3b . . . . ▶ **6**

Note: If line 6 is over $1,500, you must complete Part III.

Part III

Foreign Accounts and Trusts

Caution: If required, failure to file FinCEN Form 114 may result in substantial penalties. See instructions.

You must complete this part if you **(a)** had over $1,500 of taxable interest or ordinary dividends; **(b)** had a foreign account; or **(c)** received a distribution from, or were a grantor of, or a transferor to, a foreign trust.

		Yes	No
7a	At any time during 2020, did you have a financial interest in or signature authority over a financial account (such as a bank account, securities account, or brokerage account) located in a foreign country? See instructions		
	If "Yes," are you required to file FinCEN Form 114, Report of Foreign Bank and Financial Accounts (FBAR), to report that financial interest or signature authority? See FinCEN Form 114 and its instructions for filing requirements and exceptions to those requirements		
b	If you are required to file FinCEN Form 114, enter the name of the foreign country where the financial account is located ▶		
8	During 2020, did you receive a distribution from, or were you the grantor of, or transferor to, a foreign trust? If "Yes," you may have to file Form 3520. See instructions		

For Paperwork Reduction Act Notice, see your tax return instructions.   Cat. No. 17146N   Schedule B (Form 1040) 2020

SCHEDULE C
(Form 1040)

Department of the Treasury
Internal Revenue Service (99)

Profit or Loss From Business
(Sole Proprietorship)

▶ Go to *www.irs.gov/ScheduleC* for instructions and the latest information.
▶ **Attach to Form 1040, 1040-SR, 1040-NR, or 1041; partnerships generally must file Form 1065.**

OMB No. 1545-0074

2020

Attachment
Sequence No. **09**

Name of proprietor

Social security number (SSN)

A Principal business or profession, including product or service (see instructions)

B Enter code from instructions ▶

C Business name. If no separate business name, leave blank.

D Employer ID number (EIN) (see instr.)

E Business address (including suite or room no.) ▶

City, town or post office, state, and ZIP code

F Accounting method: **(1)** ☐ Cash   **(2)** ☐ Accrual   **(3)** ☐ Other (specify) ▶

G Did you "materially participate" in the operation of this business during 2020? If "No," see instructions for limit on losses   ☐ Yes   ☐ No

H If you started or acquired this business during 2020, check here   ▶ ☐

I Did you make any payments in 2020 that would require you to file Form(s) 1099? See instructions   ☐ Yes   ☐ No

J If "Yes," did you or will you file required Form(s) 1099?   ☐ Yes   ☐ No

Part I   Income

1	Gross receipts or sales. See instructions for line 1 and check the box if this income was reported to you on Form W-2 and the "Statutory employee" box on that form was checked ▶ ☐	1
2	Returns and allowances	2
3	Subtract line 2 from line 1	3
4	Cost of goods sold (from line 42)	4
5	**Gross profit.** Subtract line 4 from line 3	5
6	Other income, including federal and state gasoline or fuel tax credit or refund (see instructions)	6
7	**Gross income.** Add lines 5 and 6 ▶	7

Part II   Expenses. Enter expenses for business use of your home **only** on line 30.

8	Advertising	8	18	Office expense (see instructions)	18
9	Car and truck expenses (see instructions)	9	19	Pension and profit-sharing plans	19
10	Commissions and fees	10	20	Rent or lease (see instructions):	
11	Contract labor (see instructions)	11	a	Vehicles, machinery, and equipment	20a
12	Depletion	12	b	Other business property	20b
13	Depreciation and section 179 expense deduction (not included in Part III) (see instructions)	13	21	Repairs and maintenance	21
			22	Supplies (not included in Part III)	22
			23	Taxes and licenses	23
14	Employee benefit programs (other than on line 19)	14	24	Travel and meals:	
15	Insurance (other than health)	15	a	Travel	24a
16	Interest (see instructions):		b	Deductible meals (see instructions)	24b
a	Mortgage (paid to banks, etc.)	16a	25	Utilities	25
b	Other	16b	26	Wages (less employment credits)	26
17	Legal and professional services	17	27a	Other expenses (from line 48)	27a
			b	**Reserved for future use**	27b

28	**Total expenses** before expenses for business use of home. Add lines 8 through 27a ▶	28
29	Tentative profit or (loss). Subtract line 28 from line 7	29
30	Expenses for business use of your home. Do not report these expenses elsewhere. Attach Form 8829 unless using the simplified method. See instructions. **Simplified method filers only:** Enter the total square footage of (a) your home: _____ and (b) the part of your home used for business: _____ . Use the Simplified Method Worksheet in the instructions to figure the amount to enter on line 30	30
31	**Net profit or (loss).** Subtract line 30 from line 29. • If a profit, enter on both **Schedule 1 (Form 1040), line 3,** and on **Schedule SE, line 2.** (If you checked the box on line 1, see instructions). Estates and trusts, enter on **Form 1041, line 3.** • If a loss, you **must** go to line 32.	31

32 If you have a loss, check the box that describes your investment in this activity. See instructions.

• If you checked 32a, enter the loss on both **Schedule 1 (Form 1040), line 3,** and on **Schedule SE, line 2.** (If you checked the box on line 1, see the line 31 instructions). Estates and trusts, enter on **Form 1041, line 3.**

• If you checked 32b, you **must** attach **Form 6198.** Your loss may be limited.

32a ☐ All investment is at risk.
32b ☐ Some investment is not at risk.

For Paperwork Reduction Act Notice, see the separate instructions.   Cat. No. 11334P   Schedule C (Form 1040) 2020

Part III   **Cost of Goods Sold** (see instructions)

33	Method(s) used to value closing inventory: **a** ☐ Cost **b** ☐ Lower of cost or market **c** ☐ Other (attach explanation)	
34	Was there any change in determining quantities, costs, or valuations between opening and closing inventory? If "Yes," attach explanation . . . . ☐ Yes ☐ No	
35	Inventory at beginning of year. If different from last year's closing inventory, attach explanation . . .	35
36	Purchases less cost of items withdrawn for personal use	36
37	Cost of labor. Do not include any amounts paid to yourself	37
38	Materials and supplies	38
39	Other costs	39
40	Add lines 35 through 39	40
41	Inventory at end of year	41
42	**Cost of goods sold.** Subtract line 41 from line 40. Enter the result here and on line 4	42

Part IV   **Information on Your Vehicle.** Complete this part **only** if you are claiming car or truck expenses on line 9 and are not required to file Form 4562 for this business. See the instructions for line 13 to find out if you must file Form 4562.

43   When did you place your vehicle in service for business purposes? (month/day/year) ▶ _____ / _____ / _____

44   Of the total number of miles you drove your vehicle during 2020, enter the number of miles you used your vehicle for:

a Business _____   **b** Commuting (see instructions) _____   **c** Other _____

45	Was your vehicle available for personal use during off-duty hours? . . . . ☐ Yes ☐ No	
46	Do you (or your spouse) have another vehicle available for personal use? . . . . ☐ Yes ☐ No	
47a	Do you have evidence to support your deduction? . . . . ☐ Yes ☐ No	
b	If "Yes," is the evidence written? . . . . ☐ Yes ☐ No	

Part V   **Other Expenses.** List below business expenses not included on lines 8–26 or line 30.

_____	
_____	
_____	
_____	
_____	
_____	
_____	
_____	
48 **Total other expenses.** Enter here and on line 27a	48

SCHEDULE D
(Form 1040)

Department of the Treasury
Internal Revenue Service (99)

Capital Gains and Losses

► Attach to Form 1040, 1040-SR, or 1040-NR.
► Go to *www.irs.gov/ScheduleD* for instructions and the latest information.
► Use Form 8949 to list your transactions for lines 1b, 2, 3, 8b, 9, and 10.

OMB No. 1545-0074

2020

Attachment
Sequence No. **12**

Name(s) shown on return | Your social security number

Did you dispose of any investment(s) in a qualified opportunity fund during the tax year? ☐ **Yes** ☐ **No**
If "Yes," attach Form 8949 and see its instructions for additional requirements for reporting your gain or loss.

Part I   **Short-Term Capital Gains and Losses—Generally Assets Held One Year or Less** (see instructions)

See instructions for how to figure the amounts to enter on the lines below. This form may be easier to complete if you round off cents to whole dollars.	(d) Proceeds (sales price)	(e) Cost (or other basis)	(g) Adjustments to gain or loss from Form(s) 8949, Part I, line 2, column (g)	(h) Gain or (loss) Subtract column (e) from column (d) and combine the result with column (g)
1a Totals for all short-term transactions reported on Form 1099-B for which basis was reported to the IRS and for which you have no adjustments (see instructions). However, if you choose to report all these transactions on Form 8949, leave this line blank and go to line 1b .				
1b Totals for all transactions reported on Form(s) 8949 with **Box A** checked .				
2 Totals for all transactions reported on Form(s) 8949 with **Box B** checked				
3 Totals for all transactions reported on Form(s) 8949 with **Box C** checked				

4 Short-term gain from Form 6252 and short-term gain or (loss) from Forms 4684, 6781, and 8824 . .	**4**	
5 Net short-term gain or (loss) from partnerships, S corporations, estates, and trusts from Schedule(s) K-1	**5**	
6 Short-term capital loss carryover. Enter the amount, if any, from line 8 of your **Capital Loss Carryover Worksheet** in the instructions	**6** ( )
7 **Net short-term capital gain or (loss).** Combine lines 1a through 6 in column (h). If you have any long-term capital gains or losses, go to Part II below. Otherwise, go to Part III on the back	**7**	

Part II   **Long-Term Capital Gains and Losses—Generally Assets Held More Than One Year** (see instructions)

See instructions for how to figure the amounts to enter on the lines below. This form may be easier to complete if you round off cents to whole dollars.	(d) Proceeds (sales price)	(e) Cost (or other basis)	(g) Adjustments to gain or loss from Form(s) 8949, Part II, line 2, column (g)	(h) Gain or (loss) Subtract column (e) from column (d) and combine the result with column (g)
8a Totals for all long-term transactions reported on Form 1099-B for which basis was reported to the IRS and for which you have no adjustments (see instructions). However, if you choose to report all these transactions on Form 8949, leave this line blank and go to line 8b .				
8b Totals for all transactions reported on Form(s) 8949 with **Box D** checked				
9 Totals for all transactions reported on Form(s) 8949 with **Box E** checked				
10 Totals for all transactions reported on Form(s) 8949 with **Box F** checked.				

11 Gain from Form 4797, Part I; long-term gain from Forms 2439 and 6252; and long-term gain or (loss) from Forms 4684, 6781, and 8824	**11**	
12 Net long-term gain or (loss) from partnerships, S corporations, estates, and trusts from Schedule(s) K-1	**12**	
13 Capital gain distributions. See the instructions	**13**	
14 Long-term capital loss carryover. Enter the amount, if any, from line 13 of your **Capital Loss Carryover Worksheet** in the instructions	**14** ( )
15 **Net long-term capital gain or (loss).** Combine lines 8a through 14 in column (h). Then, go to Part III on the back	**15**	

For Paperwork Reduction Act Notice, see your tax return instructions.   Cat. No. 11338H   **Schedule D (Form 1040) 2020**

Part III	Summary

16 Combine lines 7 and 15 and enter the result **16**

- If line 16 is a **gain,** enter the amount from line 16 on Form 1040, 1040-SR, or 1040-NR, line 7. Then, go to line 17 below.
- If line 16 is a **loss,** skip lines 17 through 20 below. Then, go to line 21. Also be sure to complete line 22.
- If line 16 is **zero,** skip lines 17 through 21 below and enter -0- on Form 1040, 1040-SR, or 1040-NR, line 7. Then, go to line 22.

17 Are lines 15 and 16 **both** gains?
  ☐ **Yes.** Go to line 18.
  ☐ **No.** Skip lines 18 through 21, and go to line 22.

18 If you are required to complete the **28% Rate Gain Worksheet** (see instructions), enter the amount, if any, from line 7 of that worksheet . . . . ▶ **18**

19 If you are required to complete the **Unrecaptured Section 1250 Gain Worksheet** (see instructions), enter the amount, if any, from line 18 of that worksheet . . . . ▶ **19**

20 Are lines 18 and 19 **both** zero or blank?
  ☐ **Yes.** Complete the **Qualified Dividends and Capital Gain Tax Worksheet** in the instructions for Forms 1040 and 1040-SR, line 16. **Don't** complete lines 21 and 22 below.

  ☐ **No.** Complete the **Schedule D Tax Worksheet** in the instructions. **Don't** complete lines 21 and 22 below.

21 If line 16 is a loss, enter here and on Form 1040, 1040-SR, or 1040-NR, line 7, the **smaller** of:

- The loss on line 16; or
- ($3,000), or if married filing separately, ($1,500)   } . . . . **21** (   )

Note: When figuring which amount is smaller, treat both amounts as positive numbers.

22 Do you have qualified dividends on Form 1040, 1040-SR, or 1040-NR, line 3a?

  ☐ **Yes.** Complete the **Qualified Dividends and Capital Gain Tax Worksheet** in the instructions for Forms 1040 and 1040-SR, line 16.

  ☐ **No.** Complete the rest of Form 1040, 1040-SR, or 1040-NR.

Form **8949**

Department of the Treasury
Internal Revenue Service

Sales and Other Dispositions of Capital Assets

▶ Go to *www.irs.gov/Form8949* for instructions and the latest information.

▶ File with your Schedule D to list your transactions for lines 1b, 2, 3, 8b, 9, and 10 of Schedule D.

OMB No. 1545-0074

2020

Attachment
Sequence No. **12A**

Name(s) shown on return

Social security number or taxpayer identification number

Before you check Box A, B, or C below, see whether you received any Form(s) 1099-B or substitute statement(s) from your broker. A substitute statement will have the same information as Form 1099-B. Either will show whether your basis (usually your cost) was reported to the IRS by your broker and may even tell you which box to check.

Part I   **Short-Term.** Transactions involving capital assets you held 1 year or less are generally short-term (see instructions). For long-term transactions, see page 2.

Note: You may aggregate all short-term transactions reported on Form(s) 1099-B showing basis was reported to the IRS and for which no adjustments or codes are required. Enter the totals directly on Schedule D, line 1a; you aren't required to report these transactions on Form 8949 (see instructions).

You *must* check Box A, B, *or* C below. Check only one box. If more than one box applies for your short-term transactions, complete a separate Form 8949, page 1, for each applicable box. If you have more short-term transactions than will fit on this page for one or more of the boxes, complete as many forms with the same box checked as you need.

- ☐ **(A)** Short-term transactions reported on Form(s) 1099-B showing basis was reported to the IRS (see **Note** above)
- ☐ **(B)** Short-term transactions reported on Form(s) 1099-B showing basis **wasn't** reported to the IRS
- ☐ **(C)** Short-term transactions not reported to you on Form 1099-B

1 (a) Description of property (Example: 100 sh. XYZ Co.)	(b) Date acquired (Mo., day, yr.)	(c) Date sold or disposed of (Mo., day, yr.)	(d) Proceeds (sales price) (see instructions)	(e) Cost or other basis. See the **Note** below and see *Column (e)* in the separate instructions	Adjustment, if any, to gain or loss. If you enter an amount in column (g), enter a code in column (f). See the separate instructions. (f) Code(s) from instructions	(g) Amount of adjustment	(h) Gain or (loss). Subtract column (e) from column (d) and combine the result with column (g)

2 Totals. Add the amounts in columns (d), (e), (g), and (h) (subtract negative amounts). Enter each total here and include on your Schedule D, **line 1b** (if **Box A** above is checked), **line 2** (if **Box B** above is checked), or **line 3** (if **Box C** above is checked) ▶

Note: If you checked Box A above but the basis reported to the IRS was incorrect, enter in column (e) the basis as reported to the IRS, and enter an adjustment in column (g) to correct the basis. See *Column (g)* in the separate instructions for how to figure the amount of the adjustment.

For Paperwork Reduction Act Notice, see your tax return instructions.   Cat. No. 37768Z   Form **8949** (2020)

Form 8949 (2020)   Attachment Sequence No. **12A**   Page **2**

Name(s) shown on return. Name and SSN or taxpayer identification no. not required if shown on other side	Social security number or taxpayer identification number

Before you check Box D, E, or F below, see whether you received any Form(s) 1099-B or substitute statement(s) from your broker. A substitute statement will have the same information as Form 1099-B. Either will show whether your basis (usually your cost) was reported to the IRS by your broker and may even tell you which box to check.

Part II   **Long-Term.** Transactions involving capital assets you held more than 1 year are generally long-term (see instructions). For short-term transactions, see page 1.

Note: You may aggregate all long-term transactions reported on Form(s) 1099-B showing basis was reported to the IRS and for which no adjustments or codes are required. Enter the totals directly on Schedule D, line 8a; you aren't required to report these transactions on Form 8949 (see instructions).

You _must_ check Box D, E, _or_ F below. Check only one box. If more than one box applies for your long-term transactions, complete a separate Form 8949, page 2, for each applicable box. If you have more long-term transactions than will fit on this page for one or more of the boxes, complete as many forms with the same box checked as you need.

- ☐ **(D)** Long-term transactions reported on Form(s) 1099-B showing basis was reported to the IRS (see **Note** above)
- ☐ **(E)** Long-term transactions reported on Form(s) 1099-B showing basis **wasn't** reported to the IRS
- ☐ **(F)** Long-term transactions not reported to you on Form 1099-B

1 (a) Description of property (Example: 100 sh. XYZ Co.)	(b) Date acquired (Mo., day, yr.)	(c) Date sold or disposed of (Mo., day, yr.)	(d) Proceeds (sales price) (see instructions)	(e) Cost or other basis. See the **Note** below and see *Column (e)* in the separate instructions	(f) Code(s) from instructions	(g) Amount of adjustment	(h) Gain or (loss). Subtract column (e) from column (d) and combine the result with column (g)

Adjustment, if any, to gain or loss. If you enter an amount in column (g), enter a code in column (f). See the separate instructions. (spans columns (f) and (g))

2 Totals. Add the amounts in columns (d), (e), (g), and (h) (subtract negative amounts). Enter each total here and include on your Schedule D, **line 8b** (if **Box D** above is checked), **line 9** (if **Box E** above is checked), or **line 10** (if **Box F** above is checked) ▶

Note: If you checked Box D above but the basis reported to the IRS was incorrect, enter in column (e) the basis as reported to the IRS, and enter an adjustment in column (g) to correct the basis. See *Column (g)* in the separate instructions for how to figure the amount of the adjustment.

Form **8949** (2020)

SCHEDULE E (Form 1040) Department of the Treasury Internal Revenue Service (99)	**Supplemental Income and Loss** (From rental real estate, royalties, partnerships, S corporations, estates, trusts, REMICs, etc.) ▶ **Attach to Form 1040, 1040-SR, 1040-NR, or 1041.** ▶ **Go to** *www.irs.gov/ScheduleE* **for instructions and the latest information.**	OMB No. 1545-0074 **2020** Attachment Sequence No. **13**

Name(s) shown on return | Your social security number

Part I — Income or Loss From Rental Real Estate and Royalties   Note: If you are in the business of renting personal property, use **Schedule C.** See instructions. If you are an individual, report farm rental income or loss from **Form 4835** on page 2, line 40.

A Did you make any payments in 2020 that would require you to file Form(s) 1099? See instructions . . . . . ☐ Yes ☐ No
B If "Yes," did you or will you file required Form(s) 1099? . . . . ☐ Yes ☐ No

1a Physical address of each property (street, city, state, ZIP code)

A
B
C

1b Type of Property (from list below)	2 For each rental real estate property listed above, report the number of fair rental and personal use days. Check the **QJV** box only if you meet the requirements to file as a qualified joint venture. See instructions.		Fair Rental Days	Personal Use Days	QJV
A		**A**			☐
B		**B**			☐
C		**C**			☐

Type of Property:
1 Single Family Residence   3 Vacation/Short-Term Rental   5 Land   7 Self-Rental
2 Multi-Family Residence   4 Commercial   6 Royalties   8 Other (describe)

Income:	Properties:		A	B	C
3 Rents received	**3**				
4 Royalties received	**4**				
Expenses:					
5 Advertising	**5**				
6 Auto and travel (see instructions)	**6**				
7 Cleaning and maintenance	**7**				
8 Commissions.	**8**				
9 Insurance	**9**				
10 Legal and other professional fees	**10**				
11 Management fees	**11**				
12 Mortgage interest paid to banks, etc. (see instructions)	**12**				
13 Other interest.	**13**				
14 Repairs.	**14**				
15 Supplies	**15**				
16 Taxes	**16**				
17 Utilities.	**17**				
18 Depreciation expense or depletion . . .	**18**				
19 Other (list) ▶ _____	**19**				
20 Total expenses. Add lines 5 through 19	**20**				
21 Subtract line 20 from line 3 (rents) and/or 4 (royalties). If result is a (loss), see instructions to find out if you must file **Form 6198**	**21**				
22 Deductible rental real estate loss after limitation, if any, on **Form 8582** (see instructions)	**22**	(	)(	)(	)

23a Total of all amounts reported on line 3 for all rental properties	**23a**	
b Total of all amounts reported on line 4 for all royalty properties	**23b**	
c Total of all amounts reported on line 12 for all properties	**23c**	
d Total of all amounts reported on line 18 for all properties	**23d**	
e Total of all amounts reported on line 20 for all properties	**23e**	
24 **Income.** Add positive amounts shown on line 21. **Do not** include any losses	**24**	
25 **Losses.** Add royalty losses from line 21 and rental real estate losses from line 22. Enter total losses here .	**25** (	)
26 **Total rental real estate and royalty income or (loss).** Combine lines 24 and 25. Enter the result here. If Parts II, III, IV, and line 40 on page 2 do not apply to you, also enter this amount on Schedule 1 (Form 1040), line 5. Otherwise, include this amount in the total on line 41 on page 2 .	**26**	

For Paperwork Reduction Act Notice, see the separate instructions.   Cat. No. 11344L   **Schedule E (Form 1040) 2020**

Schedule E (Form 1040) 2020   Attachment Sequence No. **13**   Page **2**

Name(s) shown on return. Do not enter name and social security number if shown on other side. | Your social security number

Caution: The IRS compares amounts reported on your tax return with amounts shown on Schedule(s) K-1.

| **Part II** | **Income or Loss From Partnerships and S Corporations — Note:** If you report a loss, receive a distribution, dispose of stock, or receive a loan repayment from an S corporation, you **must** check the box in column **(e)** on line 28 and attach the required basis computation. If you report a loss from an at-risk activity for which **any** amount is **not** at risk, you **must** check the box in column **(f)** on line 28 and attach **Form 6198**. See instructions. |

27   Are you reporting any loss not allowed in a prior year due to the at-risk or basis limitations, a prior year unallowed loss from a passive activity (if that loss was not reported on Form 8582), or unreimbursed partnership expenses? If you answered "Yes," see instructions before completing this section   ☐ **Yes**   ☐ **No**

28

	(a) Name	**(b)** Enter **P** for partnership; **S** for S corporation	**(c)** Check if foreign partnership	**(d)** Employer identification number	**(e)** Check if basis computation is required	**(f)** Check if any amount is not at risk
A			☐		☐	☐
B			☐		☐	☐
C			☐		☐	☐
D			☐		☐	☐

	Passive Income and Loss		Nonpassive Income and Loss		
	(g) Passive loss allowed (attach **Form 8582** if required)	**(h)** Passive income from **Schedule K-1**	**(i)** Nonpassive loss allowed (see **Schedule K-1**)	**(j)** Section 179 expense deduction from **Form 4562**	**(k)** Nonpassive income from **Schedule K-1**
A					
B					
C					
D					
29a Totals					
b Totals					

30   Add columns (h) and (k) of line 29a.   **30**

31   Add columns (g), (i), and (j) of line 29b.   **31** ( )

32   **Total partnership and S corporation income or (loss).** Combine lines 30 and 31   **32**

| **Part III** | **Income or Loss From Estates and Trusts** |

33

	(a) Name	**(b)** Employer identification number
A		
B		

	Passive Income and Loss		Nonpassive Income and Loss	
	(c) Passive deduction or loss allowed (attach **Form 8582** if required)	**(d)** Passive income from **Schedule K-1**	**(e)** Deduction or loss from **Schedule K-1**	**(f)** Other income from **Schedule K-1**
A				
B				
34a Totals				
b Totals				

35   Add columns (d) and (f) of line 34a   **35**

36   Add columns (c) and (e) of line 34b   **36** ( )

37   **Total estate and trust income or (loss).** Combine lines 35 and 36   **37**

| **Part IV** | **Income or Loss From Real Estate Mortgage Investment Conduits (REMICs)—Residual Holder** |

38

	(a) Name	**(b)** Employer identification number	**(c)** Excess inclusion from **Schedules Q,** line 2c (see instructions)	**(d)** Taxable income (net loss) from **Schedules Q,** line 1b	**(e)** Income from **Schedules Q,** line 3b

39   Combine columns (d) and (e) only. Enter the result here and include in the total on line 41 below   **39**

| **Part V** | **Summary** |

40   Net farm rental income or (loss) from **Form 4835.** Also, complete line 42 below   **40**

41   **Total income or (loss).** Combine lines 26, 32, 37, 39, and 40. Enter the result here and on Schedule 1 (Form 1040), line 5 ▶   **41**

42   **Reconciliation of farming and fishing income.** Enter your **gross** farming and fishing income reported on Form 4835, line 7; Schedule K-1 (Form 1065), box 14, code B; Schedule K-1 (Form 1120-S), box 17, code AD; and Schedule K-1 (Form 1041), box 14, code F. See instructions   **42**

43   **Reconciliation for real estate professionals.** If you were a real estate professional (see instructions), enter the net income or (loss) you reported anywhere on Form 1040, Form 1040-SR, or Form 1040-NR from all rental real estate activities in which you materially participated under the passive activity loss rules   **43**

Schedule E (Form 1040) 2020

Form **4562**	**Depreciation and Amortization** **(Including Information on Listed Property)** ▶ Attach to your tax return. ▶ Go to *www.irs.gov/Form4562* for instructions and the latest information.	OMB No. 1545-0172 20**20** Attachment Sequence No. **179**
Department of the Treasury Internal Revenue Service (99)		

Name(s) shown on return | Business or activity to which this form relates | Identifying number

Part I — Election To Expense Certain Property Under Section 179
Note: If you have any listed property, complete Part V before you complete Part I.

1	Maximum amount (see instructions)	**1**
2	Total cost of section 179 property placed in service (see instructions)	**2**
3	Threshold cost of section 179 property before reduction in limitation (see instructions)	**3**
4	Reduction in limitation. Subtract line 3 from line 2. If zero or less, enter -0-	**4**
5	Dollar limitation for tax year. Subtract line 4 from line 1. If zero or less, enter -0-. If married filing separately, see instructions	**5**

6	(a) Description of property	(b) Cost (business use only)	(c) Elected cost

7	Listed property. Enter the amount from line 29 .... **7**	
8	Total elected cost of section 179 property. Add amounts in column (c), lines 6 and 7	**8**
9	Tentative deduction. Enter the **smaller** of line 5 or line 8	**9**
10	Carryover of disallowed deduction from line 13 of your 2019 Form 4562	**10**
11	Business income limitation. Enter the smaller of business income (not less than zero) or line 5. See instructions	**11**
12	Section 179 expense deduction. Add lines 9 and 10, but don't enter more than line 11	**12**
13	Carryover of disallowed deduction to 2021. Add lines 9 and 10, less line 12 ▶ **13**	

Note: Don't use Part II or Part III below for listed property. Instead, use Part V.

Part II — Special Depreciation Allowance and Other Depreciation (Don't include listed property. See instructions.)

14	Special depreciation allowance for qualified property (other than listed property) placed in service during the tax year. See instructions	**14**
15	Property subject to section 168(f)(1) election	**15**
16	Other depreciation (including ACRS)	**16**

Part III — MACRS Depreciation (Don't include listed property. See instructions.)

Section A

17	MACRS deductions for assets placed in service in tax years beginning before 2020	**17**
18	If you are electing to group any assets placed in service during the tax year into one or more general asset accounts, check here ▶ ☐	

Section B—Assets Placed in Service During 2020 Tax Year Using the General Depreciation System

(a) Classification of property	(b) Month and year placed in service	(c) Basis for depreciation (business/investment use only—see instructions)	(d) Recovery period	(e) Convention	(f) Method	(g) Depreciation deduction
19a 3-year property						
b 5-year property						
c 7-year property						
d 10-year property						
e 15-year property						
f 20-year property						
g 25-year property			25 yrs.		S/L	
h Residential rental property			27.5 yrs.	MM	S/L	
			27.5 yrs.	MM	S/L	
i Nonresidential real property			39 yrs.	MM	S/L	
				MM	S/L	

Section C—Assets Placed in Service During 2020 Tax Year Using the Alternative Depreciation System

20a Class life					S/L	
b 12-year			12 yrs.		S/L	
c 30-year			30 yrs.	MM	S/L	
d 40-year			40 yrs.	MM	S/L	

Part IV — Summary (See instructions.)

21	Listed property. Enter amount from line 28	**21**
22	**Total.** Add amounts from line 12, lines 14 through 17, lines 19 and 20 in column (g), and line 21. Enter here and on the appropriate lines of your return. Partnerships and S corporations—see instructions	**22**
23	For assets shown above and placed in service during the current year, enter the portion of the basis attributable to section 263A costs **23**	

For Paperwork Reduction Act Notice, see separate instructions.   Cat. No. 12906N   Form **4562** (2020)

Form 4562 (2020)   Page **2**

Part V Listed Property (Include automobiles, certain other vehicles, certain aircraft, and property used for entertainment, recreation, or amusement.)

Note: For any vehicle for which you are using the standard mileage rate or deducting lease expense, complete **only** 24a, 24b, columns (a) through (c) of Section A, all of Section B, and Section C if applicable.

Section A—Depreciation and Other Information (Caution: See the instructions for limits for passenger automobiles.)

24a Do you have evidence to support the business/investment use claimed? ☐ Yes ☐ No   **24b** If "Yes," is the evidence written? ☐ Yes ☐ No

(a) Type of property (list vehicles first)	(b) Date placed in service	(c) Business/investment use percentage	(d) Cost or other basis	(e) Basis for depreciation (business/investment use only)	(f) Recovery period	(g) Method/ Convention	(h) Depreciation deduction	(i) Elected section 179 cost
25 Special depreciation allowance for qualified listed property placed in service during the tax year and used more than 50% in a qualified business use. See instructions . **25**								
26 Property used more than 50% in a qualified business use:								
		%						
		%						
		%						
27 Property used 50% or less in a qualified business use:								
		%				S/L –		
		%				S/L –		
		%				S/L –		

28 Add amounts in column (h), lines 25 through 27. Enter here and on line 21, page 1 . **28**

29 Add amounts in column (i), line 26. Enter here and on line 7, page 1 . . . . **29**

Section B—Information on Use of Vehicles

Complete this section for vehicles used by a sole proprietor, partner, or other "more than 5% owner," or related person. If you provided vehicles to your employees, first answer the questions in Section C to see if you meet an exception to completing this section for those vehicles.

	(a) Vehicle 1		(b) Vehicle 2		(c) Vehicle 3		(d) Vehicle 4		(e) Vehicle 5		(f) Vehicle 6	
30 Total business/investment miles driven during the year (**don't** include commuting miles) .												
31 Total commuting miles driven during the year												
32 Total other personal (noncommuting) miles driven												
33 Total miles driven during the year. Add lines 30 through 32												
34 Was the vehicle available for personal use during off-duty hours?	Yes	No	Yes	No	Yes	No	Yes	No	Yes	No	Yes	No
35 Was the vehicle used primarily by a more than 5% owner or related person? . .												
36 Is another vehicle available for personal use?												

Section C—Questions for Employers Who Provide Vehicles for Use by Their Employees

Answer these questions to determine if you meet an exception to completing Section B for vehicles used by employees who **aren't** more than 5% owners or related persons. See instructions.

		Yes	No
37	Do you maintain a written policy statement that prohibits all personal use of vehicles, including commuting, by your employees?		
38	Do you maintain a written policy statement that prohibits personal use of vehicles, except commuting, by your employees? See the instructions for vehicles used by corporate officers, directors, or 1% or more owners . .		
39	Do you treat all use of vehicles by employees as personal use?		
40	Do you provide more than five vehicles to your employees, obtain information from your employees about the use of the vehicles, and retain the information received?		
41	Do you meet the requirements concerning qualified automobile demonstration use? See instructions.		

Note: If your answer to 37, 38, 39, 40, or 41 is "Yes," don't complete Section B for the covered vehicles.

Part VI Amortization

(a) Description of costs	(b) Date amortization begins	(c) Amortizable amount	(d) Code section	(e) Amortization period or percentage	(f) Amortization for this year
42 Amortization of costs that begins during your 2020 tax year (see instructions):					
43 Amortization of costs that began before your 2020 tax year **43**					
44 Total. Add amounts in column (f). See the instructions for where to report **44**					

Form **4562** (2020)

SCHEDULE SE (Form 1040) Department of the Treasury Internal Revenue Service (99)	**Self-Employment Tax** ▶ Go to *www.irs.gov/ScheduleSE* for instructions and the latest information. ▶ Attach to Form 1040, 1040-SR, or 1040-NR.	OMB No. 1545-0074 20**20** Attachment Sequence No. **17**

Name of person with self-employment income (as shown on Form 1040, 1040-SR, or 1040-NR)	Social security number of person with **self-employment** income ▶

Part I   **Self-Employment Tax**

Note: If your only income subject to self-employment tax is **church employee income,** see instructions for how to report your income and the definition of church employee income.

A   If you are a minister, member of a religious order, or Christian Science practitioner **and** you filed Form 4361, but you had $400 or more of **other** net earnings from self-employment, check here and continue with Part I . . . . ▶ ☐

Skip lines 1a and 1b if you use the farm optional method in Part II. See instructions.

1a	Net farm profit or (loss) from Schedule F, line 34, and farm partnerships, Schedule K-1 (Form 1065), box 14, code A . . .	**1a**	
b	If you received social security retirement or disability benefits, enter the amount of Conservation Reserve Program payments included on Schedule F, line 4b, or listed on Schedule K-1 (Form 1065), box 20, code AH	**1b** (	)

Skip line 2 if you use the nonfarm optional method in Part II. See instructions.

2	Net profit or (loss) from Schedule C, line 31; and Schedule K-1 (Form 1065), box 14, code A (other than farming). See instructions for other income to report or if you are a minister or member of a religious order	**2**	
3	Combine lines 1a, 1b, and 2	**3**	
4a	If line 3 is more than zero, multiply line 3 by 92.35% (0.9235). Otherwise, enter amount from line 3 .	**4a**	
	Note: If line 4a is less than $400 due to Conservation Reserve Program payments on line 1b, see instructions.		
b	If you elect one or both of the optional methods, enter the total of lines 15 and 17 here	**4b**	
c	Combine lines 4a and 4b. If less than $400, **stop;** you don't owe self-employment tax. **Exception:** If less than $400 and you had **church employee income,** enter -0- and continue . . . . . . ▶	**4c**	
5a	Enter your **church employee income** from Form W-2. See instructions for definition of church employee income **5a**		
b	Multiply line 5a by 92.35% (0.9235). If less than $100, enter -0-	**5b**	
6	Add lines 4c and 5b	**6**	
7	Maximum amount of combined wages and self-employment earnings subject to social security tax or the 6.2% portion of the 7.65% railroad retirement (tier 1) tax for 2020	**7**	137,700
8a	Total social security wages and tips (total of boxes 3 and 7 on Form(s) W-2) and railroad retirement (tier 1) compensation. If $137,700 or more, skip lines 8b through 10, and go to line 11 . . . . **8a**		
b	Unreported tips subject to social security tax from Form 4137, line 10 . . . **8b**		
c	Wages subject to social security tax from Form 8919, line 10 . . . . . **8c**		
d	Add lines 8a, 8b, and 8c	**8d**	
9	Subtract line 8d from line 7. If zero or less, enter -0- here and on line 10 and go to line 11 . . ▶	**9**	
10	Multiply the **smaller** of line 6 or line 9 by 12.4% (0.124)	**10**	
11	Multiply line 6 by 2.9% (0.029)	**11**	
12	**Self-employment tax.** Add lines 10 and 11. Enter here and on **Schedule 2 (Form 1040), line 4** . .	**12**	
13	**Deduction for one-half of self-employment tax.** Multiply line 12 by 50% (0.50). Enter here and on **Schedule 1 (Form 1040), line 14** **13**		

Part II   **Optional Methods To Figure Net Earnings**   (see instructions)

Farm Optional Method. You may use this method **only** if **(a)** your gross farm income[1] wasn't more than $8,460, **or (b)** your net farm profits[2] were less than $6,107.

14	Maximum income for optional methods	**14**	5,640
15	Enter the **smaller** of: two-thirds (2/3) of gross farm income[1] (not less than zero) **or** $5,640. Also, include this amount on line 4b above	**15**	

Nonfarm Optional Method. You may use this method **only** if **(a)** your net nonfarm profits[3] were less than $6,107 and also less than 72.189% of your gross nonfarm income,[4] **and (b)** you had net earnings from self-employment of at least $400 in 2 of the prior 3 years. **Caution:** You may use this method no more than five times.

16	Subtract line 15 from line 14	**16**	
17	Enter the **smaller** of: two-thirds (2/3) of gross nonfarm income[4] (not less than zero) **or** the amount on line 16. Also, include this amount on line 4b above	**17**	

[1] From Sch. F, line 9; and Sch. K-1 (Form 1065), box 14, code B.
[2] From Sch. F, line 34; and Sch. K-1 (Form 1065), box 14, code A—minus the amount you would have entered on line 1b had you not used the optional method.
[3] From Sch. C, line 31; and Sch. K-1 (Form 1065), box 14, code A.
[4] From Sch. C, line 7; and Sch. K-1 (Form 1065), box 14, code C.

For Paperwork Reduction Act Notice, see your tax return instructions.   Cat. No. 11358Z   **Schedule SE (Form 1040) 2020**

Schedule SE (Form 1040) 2020   Attachment Sequence No. **17**   Page **2**

Part III	Maximum Deferral of Self-Employment Tax Payments		

If line 4c is zero, skip lines 18 through 20, and enter -0- on line 21.

18	Enter the portion of line 3 that can be attributed to March 27, 2020, through December 31, 2020	18	
19	If line 18 is more than zero, multiply line 18 by 92.35% (0.9235); otherwise, enter the amount from line 18	19	
20	Enter the portion of lines 15 and 17 that can be attributed to March 27, 2020, through December 31, 2020	20	
21	Combine lines 19 and 20	21	

If line 5b is zero, skip line 22 and enter -0- on line 23.

22	Enter the portion of line 5a that can be attributed to March 27, 2020, through December 31, 2020	22	
23	Multiply line 22 by 92.35% (0.9235)	23	
24	Add lines 21 and 23	24	
25	Enter the smaller of line 9 or line 24	25	
26	Multiply line 25 by 6.2% (0.062). Enter here and see the instructions for line 12e of Schedule 3 (Form 1040)	26	

Schedule SE (Form 1040) 2020

Form 2441

Child and Dependent Care Expenses

► Attach to Form 1040, 1040-SR, or 1040-NR.

► Go to *www.irs.gov/Form2441* for instructions and the latest information.

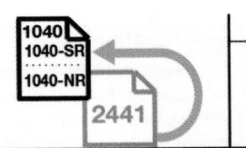

OMB No. 1545-0074

2020

Attachment Sequence No. **21**

Department of the Treasury
Internal Revenue Service (99)

Name(s) shown on return

Your social security number

You cannot claim a credit for child and dependent care expenses if your filing status is married filing separately unless you meet the requirements listed in the instructions under "Married Persons Filing Separately." If you meet these requirements, check this box. ☐

Part I   Persons or Organizations Who Provided the Care—You **must** complete this part.
(If you have more than two care providers, see the instructions.)

1	**(a)** Care provider's name	**(b)** Address (number, street, apt. no., city, state, and ZIP code)	**(c)** Identifying number (SSN or EIN)	**(d)** Amount paid (see instructions)

Did you receive **dependent care benefits?**   No ──────► Complete only Part II below.
Yes ──────► Complete Part III on the back next.

Caution: If the care was provided in your home, you may owe employment taxes. For details, see the instructions for Schedule 2 (Form 1040), line 7a.

Part II   Credit for Child and Dependent Care Expenses

2   Information about your **qualifying person(s)**. If you have more than two qualifying persons, see the instructions.

(a) Qualifying person's name		**(b)** Qualifying person's social security number	**(c)** Qualified expenses you incurred and paid in 2020 for the person listed in column (a)
First	Last		

3	Add the amounts in column (c) of line 2. **Don't** enter more than $3,000 for one qualifying person or $6,000 for two or more persons. If you completed Part III, enter the amount from line 31 . .	**3**
4	Enter your **earned income.** See instructions	**4**
5	If married filing jointly, enter your spouse's earned income (if you or your spouse was a student or was disabled, see the instructions); **all others,** enter the amount from line 4	**5**
6	Enter the **smallest** of line 3, 4, or 5	**6**
7	Enter the amount from Form 1040, 1040-SR, or 1040-NR, line 11 . **7**	
8	Enter on line 8 the decimal amount shown below that applies to the amount on line 7.	

If line 7 is:			If line 7 is:		
Over	**But not over**	**Decimal amount is**	**Over**	**But not over**	**Decimal amount is**
$0—15,000		.35	$29,000—31,000		.27
15,000—17,000		.34	31,000—33,000		.26
17,000—19,000		.33	33,000—35,000		.25
19,000—21,000		.32	35,000—37,000		.24
21,000—23,000		.31	37,000—39,000		.23
23,000—25,000		.30	39,000—41,000		.22
25,000—27,000		.29	41,000—43,000		.21
27,000—29,000		.28	43,000—No limit		.20

8		**X .**
9	Multiply line 6 by the decimal amount on line 8. If you paid 2019 expenses in 2020, see the instructions	**9**
10	Tax liability limit. Enter the amount from the Credit Limit Worksheet in the instructions **10**	
11	**Credit for child and dependent care expenses.** Enter the **smaller** of line 9 or line 10 here and on Schedule 3 (Form 1040), line 2	**11**

For Paperwork Reduction Act Notice, see your tax return instructions.   Cat. No. 11862M   Form **2441** (2020)

Form 2441 (2020)   Page **2**

Part III	Dependent Care Benefits

12 Enter the total amount of **dependent care benefits** you received in 2020. Amounts you received as an employee should be shown in box 10 of your Form(s) W-2. **Don't** include amounts reported as wages in box 1 of Form(s) W-2. If you were self-employed or a partner, include amounts you received under a dependent care assistance program from your sole proprietorship or partnership . **12**

13 Enter the amount, if any, you carried over from 2019 and used in 2020 during the grace period. See instructions . **13**

14 Enter the amount, if any, you forfeited or carried forward to 2021. See instructions . **14** ( )

15 Combine lines 12 through 14. See instructions . **15**

16 Enter the total amount of **qualified expenses** incurred in 2020 for the care of the **qualifying person(s)** . **16**

17 Enter the **smaller** of line 15 or 16 . **17**

18 Enter your **earned income.** See instructions . **18**

19 Enter the amount shown below that applies to you.

- If married filing jointly, enter your spouse's earned income (if you or your spouse was a student or was disabled, see the instructions for line 5).
- If married filing separately, see instructions.
- All others, enter the amount from line 18.

  19

20 Enter the **smallest** of line 17, 18, or 19 . **20**

21 Enter $5,000 ($2,500 if married filing separately **and** you were required to enter your spouse's earned income on line 19) . **21**

22 Is any amount on line 12 from your sole proprietorship or partnership?

☐ **No.** Enter -0-.

☐ **Yes.** Enter the amount here . **22**

23 Subtract line 22 from line 15 . **23**

24 **Deductible benefits.** Enter the **smallest** of line 20, 21, or 22. Also, include this amount on the appropriate line(s) of your return. See instructions . **24**

25 **Excluded benefits.** If you checked "No" on line 22, enter the smaller of line 20 or 21. Otherwise, subtract line 24 from the smaller of line 20 or line 21. If zero or less, enter -0- . **25**

26 **Taxable benefits.** Subtract line 25 from line 23. If zero or less, enter -0-. Also, include this amount on Form 1040 or 1040-SR, line 1; or Form 1040-NR, line 1a. On the dotted line next to Form 1040 or 1040-SR, line 1; or Form 1040-NR, line 1a, enter "DCB" . **26**

To claim the child and dependent care
credit, complete lines 27 through 31 below.

27 Enter $3,000 ($6,000 if two or more qualifying persons) . **27**

28 Add lines 24 and 25 . **28**

29 Subtract line 28 from line 27. If zero or less, **stop.** You can't take the credit. **Exception.** If you paid 2019 expenses in 2020, see the instructions for line 9 . **29**

30 Complete line 2 on the front of this form. **Don't** include in column (c) any benefits shown on line 28 above. Then, add the amounts in column (c) and enter the total here . **30**

31 Enter the **smaller** of line 29 or 30. Also, enter this amount on line 3 on the front of this form and complete lines 4 through 11 . **31**

Form **2441** (2020)

SCHEDULE 8812	**Additional Child Tax Credit**		OMB No. 1545-0074

SCHEDULE 8812
(Form 1040)

Additional Child Tax Credit

► Attach to Form 1040, 1040-SR, or 1040-NR.
► Go to *www.irs.gov/Schedule8812* for instructions and the latest information.

Department of the Treasury
Internal Revenue Service (99)

OMB No. 1545-0074

20**20**

Attachment
Sequence No. **47**

Name(s) shown on return

Your social security number

Part I	**All Filers**

Caution: If you file Form 2555, **stop here;** you cannot claim the additional child tax credit.

1   If you are required to use the worksheet in Pub. 972, enter the amount from line 10 of the Child Tax Credit and Credit for Other Dependents Worksheet in the publication. Otherwise, enter the amount from line 8 of your Child Tax Credit and Credit for Other Dependents Worksheet. (See the instructions for Forms 1040 and 1040-SR, line 19, or the instructions for Form 1040-NR, line 19.)   **1**

2   Enter the amount from line 19 of your Form 1040, Form 1040-SR, or Form 1040-NR   **2**

3   Subtract line 2 from line 1. If zero, **stop here;** you cannot claim this credit   **3**

4   Number of qualifying children under 17 with the required social security number: _____ x $1,400.
Enter the result. If zero, **stop here;** you cannot claim this credit   **4**

TIP: The number of children you use for this line is the same as the number of children you used for line 1 of the Child Tax Credit and Credit for Other Dependents Worksheet.

5   Enter the **smaller** of line 3 or line 4   **5**

6a   Earned income (see instructions)   **6a**

 b   Nontaxable combat pay (see instructions)   **6b**

7   Is the amount on line 6a more than $2,500?
☐ **No.**   Leave line 7 blank and enter -0- on line 8.
☐ **Yes.**   Subtract $2,500 from the amount on line 6a. Enter the result   **7**

8   Multiply the amount on line 7 by 15% (0.15) and enter the result   **8**
Next. On line 4, is the amount $4,200 or more?
☐ **No.**   If line 8 is zero, **stop here;** you cannot claim this credit. Otherwise, skip Part II and enter the **smaller** of line 5 or line 8 on line 15.
☐ **Yes.**   If line 8 is equal to or more than line 5, skip Part II and enter the amount from line 5 on line 15. Otherwise, go to line 9.

Part II	**Certain Filers Who Have Three or More Qualifying Children**

9   Withheld social security, Medicare, and Additional Medicare taxes from Form(s) W-2, boxes 4 and 6. If married filing jointly, include your spouse's amounts with yours. If your employer withheld or you paid Additional Medicare Tax or tier 1 RRTA taxes, see instructions   **9**

10   Enter the total of the amounts from Schedule 1 (Form 1040), line 14, and Schedule 2 (Form 1040), line 5, plus any taxes that you identified using code "UT" and entered on Schedule 2 (Form 1040), line 8   **10**

11   Add lines 9 and 10   **11**

12   **1040 and**   Enter the total of the amounts from Form 1040 or 1040-SR, line 27,
1040-SR filers: and Schedule 3 (Form 1040), line 10.
1040-NR filers: Enter the amount from Schedule 3 (Form 1040), line 10.   **12**

13   Subtract line 12 from line 11. If zero or less, enter -0-   **13**

14   Enter the **larger** of line 8 or line 13   **14**
Next, enter the **smaller** of line 5 or line 14 on line 15.

Part III	**Additional Child Tax Credit**

15   **This is your additional child tax credit**   **15**

Enter this amount on
Form 1040, line 28;
Form 1040-SR, line 28; or
Form 1040-NR, line 28.

For Paperwork Reduction Act Notice, see your tax return instructions.   Cat. No. 59761M   **Schedule 8812 (Form 1040) 2020**

DRAFT AS OF AUGUST 10, 2020 DO NOT FILE

Form **7202**

Department of the Treasury
Internal Revenue Service

**Credits for Sick Leave and Family Leave
for Certain Self-Employed Individuals**
▶ Attach to Form 1040 or 1040-SR.
▶ Go to *www.irs.gov/Form7202* for instructions and the latest information.

OMB No. 1545-0074

2020

Attachment
Sequence No. **202**

Name of person with self-employment income (as shown on Form 1040 or 1040-SR)

Social security number of person with
self-employment income

Part I	Credit for Sick Leave for Certain Self-Employed Individuals	
1	Number of days you were unable to perform services as a self-employed individual because of certain coronavirus-related care you required. See instructions	1
2	Number of days you were unable to perform services as a self-employed individual because of certain coronavirus-related care you provided to another. (Do not include days you included in line 1.) See instructions	2
3	If you are filing a fiscal year return, see instructions; otherwise enter 10	3
4	Enter the smaller of line 1 or line 3	4
5	Subtract line 4 from line 3	5
6	Enter the smaller of line 2 or line 5	6
7	Net earnings from self-employment (see instructions)	7
8	Divide line 7 by 260 (round to nearest whole number)	8
9	Enter the smaller of line 8 or $511	9
10	Multiply line 4 by line 9	10
11	Multiply line 8 by 67% (0.67)	11
12	Enter the smaller of line 11 or $200	12
13	Multiply line 6 by line 12	13
14	Add lines 10 and 13	14
15	Amount of emergency paid sick leave subject to the $511 per day limit you received from an employer (see instructions)	15
16	Amount of emergency paid sick leave subject to the $200 per day limit you received from an employer (see instructions)	16
	If line 15 and line 16 are both zero, skip to line 24 and enter the amount from line 14.	
17	Add line 13 and line 16	17
18	Enter the smaller of line 17 or $2,000	18
19	Subtract line 18 from line 17	19
20	Add lines 10, 15, and 18	20
21	Enter the smaller of line 20 or $5,110	21
22	Subtract line 21 from line 20	22
23	Add line 19 and line 22	23
24	Subtract line 23 from line 14. If zero or less, enter -0-. Enter here and include on Schedule 3 (Form 1040), line 12b	24

Part II	Credit for Family Leave for Certain Self-Employed Individuals	
25	Number of days you were unable to perform services as a self-employed individual because of certain coronavirus-related care you provided to a son or daughter under the age of 18. (Do not enter more than 50 days.) See instructions	25
26	Net earnings from self-employment (see instructions)	26
27	Divide line 26 by 260 (round to nearest whole number)	27
28	Multiply line 27 by 67% (0.67)	28
29	Enter the smaller of line 28 or $200	29
30	Multiply line 25 by line 29	30
31	Amount of emergency family leave wages you received from an employer (see instructions)	31
	If line 31 is zero, skip to line 35 and enter the amount from line 30.	
32	Add line 30 and line 31	32
33	Enter the smaller of line 32 or $10,000	33
34	Subtract line 33 from line 32	34
35	Subtract line 34 from line 30. If zero or less, enter -0-. Enter here and include on Schedule 3 (Form 1040), line 12b	35

For Privacy Act and Paperwork Reduction Act Notice, see your tax return instructions.   Cat. No. 56395K   Form **7202** (2020)

Form **8962**

Department of the Treasury
Internal Revenue Service

Premium Tax Credit (PTC)

▶ Attach to Form 1040, 1040-SR, or 1040-NR.
▶ Go to *www.irs.gov/Form8962* for instructions and the latest information.

OMB No. 1545-0074

2020

Attachment
Sequence No. **73**

Name shown on your return

Your social security number

You cannot take the PTC if your filing status is married filing separately unless you qualify for an exception. See instructions. If you qualify, check the box ▶ ☐

Part I   Annual and Monthly Contribution Amount

1	Tax family size. Enter your tax family size. See instructions	**1**
2a	Modified AGI. Enter your modified AGI. See instructions	**2a**
b	Enter the total of your dependents' modified AGI. See instructions	**2b**
3	Household income. Add the amounts on lines 2a and 2b. See instructions	**3**
4	Federal poverty line. Enter the federal poverty line amount from Table 1-1, 1-2, or 1-3. See instructions. Check the appropriate box for the federal poverty table used. **a** ☐ Alaska **b** ☐ Hawaii **c** ☐ Other 48 states and DC	**4**
5	Household income as a percentage of federal poverty line (see instructions)	**5** %
6	Did you enter 401% on line 5? (See instructions if you entered less than 100%.)	

☐ **No.** Continue to line 7.

☐ **Yes.** You are not eligible to take the PTC. If advance payment of the PTC was made, see the instructions for how to report your excess advance PTC repayment amount.

7	Applicable figure. Using your line 5 percentage, locate your "applicable figure" on the table in the instructions	**7**
8a	Annual contribution amount. Multiply line 3 by line 7. Round to nearest whole dollar amount	**8a**
8b	Monthly contribution amount. Divide line 8a by 12. Round to nearest whole dollar amount	**8b**

Part II   Premium Tax Credit Claim and Reconciliation of Advance Payment of Premium Tax Credit

9 Are you allocating policy amounts with another taxpayer or do you want to use the alternative calculation for year of marriage? See instructions.

☐ **Yes.** Skip to Part IV, Allocation of Policy Amounts, or Part V, Alternative Calculation for Year of Marriage. ☐ **No.** Continue to line 10.

10 See the instructions to determine if you can use line 11 or must complete lines 12 through 23.

☐ **Yes.** Continue to line 11. Compute your annual PTC. Then skip lines 12–23 and continue to line 24. ☐ **No.** Continue to lines 12–23. Compute your monthly PTC and continue to line 24.

Annual Calculation	**(a)** Annual enrollment premiums (Form(s) 1095-A, line 33A)	**(b)** Annual applicable SLCSP premium (Form(s) 1095-A, line 33B)	**(c)** Annual contribution amount (line 8a)	**(d)** Annual maximum premium assistance (subtract (c) from (b); if zero or less, enter -0-)	**(e)** Annual premium tax credit allowed (smaller of (a) or (d))	**(f)** Annual advance payment of PTC (Form(s) 1095-A, line 33C)
11 Annual Totals						

Monthly Calculation	**(a)** Monthly enrollment premiums (Form(s) 1095-A, lines 21–32, column A)	**(b)** Monthly applicable SLCSP premium (Form(s) 1095-A, lines 21–32, column B)	**(c)** Monthly contribution amount (amount from line 8b or alternative marriage monthly calculation)	**(d)** Monthly maximum premium assistance (subtract (c) from (b); if zero or less, enter -0-)	**(e)** Monthly premium tax credit allowed (smaller of (a) or (d))	**(f)** Monthly advance payment of PTC (Form(s) 1095-A, lines 21–32, column C)
12 January						
13 February						
14 March						
15 April						
16 May						
17 June						
18 July						
19 August						
20 September						
21 October						
22 November						
23 December						

24	Total premium tax credit. Enter the amount from line 11(e) or add lines 12(e) through 23(e) and enter the total here	**24**
25	Advance payment of PTC. Enter the amount from line 11(f) or add lines 12(f) through 23(f) and enter the total here	**25**
26	Net premium tax credit. If line 24 is greater than line 25, subtract line 25 from line 24. Enter the difference here and on Schedule 3 (Form 1040), line 8. If line 24 equals line 25, enter -0-. Stop here. If line 25 is greater than line 24, leave this line blank and continue to line 27	**26**

Part III   Repayment of Excess Advance Payment of the Premium Tax Credit

27	Excess advance payment of PTC. If line 25 is greater than line 24, subtract line 24 from line 25. Enter the difference here	**27**
28	Repayment limitation (see instructions)	**28**
29	Excess advance premium tax credit repayment. Enter the smaller of line 27 or line 28 here and on Schedule 2 (Form 1040), line 2	**29**

For Paperwork Reduction Act Notice, see your tax return instructions.   Cat. No. 37784Z   Form **8962** (2020)

DRAFT AS OF August 19, 2020 DO NOT FILE

Form **8995**

Department of the Treasury
Internal Revenue Service

Qualified Business Income Deduction
Simplified Computation

▶ Attach to your tax return.
▶ Go to *www.irs.gov/Form8995* for instructions and the latest information.

OMB No. 1545-0123

20**20**

Attachment
Sequence No. **55**

Name(s) shown on return

Your taxpayer identification number

Note. *You can claim the qualified business income deduction **only** if you have qualified business income from a qualified trade or business, real estate investment trust dividends, publicly traded partnership income, or a domestic production activities deduction passed through from an agricultural or horticultural cooperative. See instructions.*
Use this form if your taxable income, before your qualified business income deduction, is at or below $163,300 ($326,600 if married filing jointly), and you aren't a patron of an agricultural or horticultural cooperative.

1	(a) Trade, business, or aggregation name	(b) Taxpayer identification number	(c) Qualified business income or (loss)
i			
ii			
iii			
iv			
v			

2	Total qualified business income or (loss). Combine lines 1i through 1v, column (c)	2	
3	Qualified business net (loss) carryforward from the prior year	3 ( )	
4	Total qualified business income. Combine lines 2 and 3. If zero or less, enter -0-	4	
5	Qualified business income component. Multiply line 4 by 20% (0.20)		5
6	Qualified REIT dividends and publicly traded partnership (PTP) income or (loss) (see instructions)	6	
7	Qualified REIT dividends and qualified PTP (loss) carryforward from the prior year	7 ( )	
8	Total qualified REIT dividends and PTP income. Combine lines 6 and 7. If zero or less, enter -0-	8	
9	REIT and PTP component. Multiply line 8 by 20% (0.20)		9
10	Qualified business income deduction before the income limitation. Add lines 5 and 9		10
11	Taxable income before qualified business income deduction	11	
12	Net capital gain (see instructions)	12	
13	Subtract line 12 from line 11. If zero or less, enter -0-	13	
14	Income limitation. Multiply line 13 by 20% (0.20)		14
15	Qualified business income deduction. Enter the lesser of line 10 or line 14. Also enter this amount on the applicable line of your return . . . . ▶		15
16	Total qualified business (loss) carryforward. Combine lines 2 and 3. If greater than zero, enter -0- . .		16 ( )
17	Total qualified REIT dividends and PTP (loss) carryforward. Combine lines 6 and 7. If greater than zero, enter -0-		17 ( )

For Privacy Act and Paperwork Reduction Act Notice, see instructions.   Cat. No. 37806C   Form **8995** (2020)

2020 Child Tax Credit and Credit for Other Dependents Worksheet—Line 19 *

Keep for Your Records

1. To be a qualifying child for the child tax credit, the child must be your dependent, **under age 17** at the end of 2020, and meet all the conditions in Steps 1 through 3 under *Who Qualifies as Your Dependent*. Make sure you checked the "child tax credit" box in column (4) of the *Dependents* section on Form 1040 or 1040-SR for each qualifying child.

2. If you don't have a qualifying child, you can't claim the child tax credit; but you may be able to claim the credit for other dependents for that child. See Step 3 under *Who Qualifies as Your Dependent*.

3. To see if your qualifying relative qualifies you to take the credit for other dependents, see Step 5 under *Who Qualifies as Your Dependent*.

4. Be sure to see *Social security number* under *Who Qualifies as Your Dependent*.

5. Do **not** use this worksheet, but use Pub. 972 instead, if:

   a. You are claiming the adoption credit, mortgage interest credit, District of Columbia first-time homebuyer credit, or residential energy efficient property credit*;

   b. You are excluding income from Puerto Rico; or

   c. You are filing Form 2555 or 4563.

   * If applicable.

Part 1

1. Number of qualifying children under age 17 with the required social security number: _____ × $2,000. Enter the result.
   1 [ ]

2. Number of other dependents, including qualifying children without the required social security number: _____ × $500. Enter the result.
   2 [ ]

   Caution. Don't include yourself, your spouse, or anyone who is not a U.S. citizen, U.S. national, or U.S. resident alien. Also, don't include anyone you included on line 1.

3. Add lines 1 and 2.
   3 [ ]

4. Enter the amount from Form 1040 or 1040-SR, line 11.
   4 [ ]

5. Enter the amount shown below for your filing status.

   ● Married filing jointly — $400,000

   ● All other filing statuses — $200,000
   5 [ ]

6. Is the amount on line 4 more than the amount on line 5?

   [ ] **No.** Leave line 6 blank. Enter -0- on line 7, and go to line 8.

   [ ] **Yes.** Subtract line 5 from line 4.
   6 [ ]

   If the result isn't a multiple of $1,000, increase it to the next multiple of $1,000. For example, increase $425 to $1,000, increase $1,025 to $2,000, etc.

7. Multiply the amount on line 6 by 5% (0.05). Enter the result.
   7 [ ]

8. Is the amount on line 3 more than the amount on line 7?

   [ ] **No.** (STOP) You can't take the child tax credit on Form 1040 or 1040-SR, line 19. You also can't take the additional child tax credit on Form 1040 or 1040-SR, line 28. Complete the rest of your Form 1040 or 1040-SR.

   [ ] **Yes.** Subtract line 7 from line 3. Enter the result. *Go to Part 2.*
   8 [ ]

---

* Download the latest version of this worksheet from the Form 1040 Instructions available at www.irs.gov. The 2020 worksheet was not available as we went to print. This worksheet is adapted from the 2019 version.

2020 Child Tax Credit and Credit for Other Dependents
Worksheet—*Continued* *

Keep for Your Records

Before you begin Part 2: √ Figure the amount of any credits you are claiming on Schedule 3; Form 5695, Part II*; Form 8910; Form 8936; or Schedule R.

Part 2

9. Enter the amount from Form 1040 or 1040-SR, line 16.   **9** _____

10. Add any amounts from:

Schedule 3, line 1   _____

Schedule 3, line 2 + _____

Schedule 3, line 3 + _____

Schedule 3, line 4 + _____

Form 5695, line 30* + _____

Form 8910, line 15* + _____

Form 8936, line 23 + _____

Schedule R, line 22 + _____

Enter the total.   **10** _____

11. Are the amounts on lines 9 and 10 the same?

☐ **Yes.** (STOP)
You can't take this credit because there is no tax to reduce. However, you may be able to take the **additional child tax credit** if line 1 is more than zero. See the **TIP** below.

☐ **No.** Subtract line 10 from line 9.   **11** _____

12. Is the amount on line 8 more than the amount on line 11?

☐ **Yes.** Enter the amount from line 11.
Also, you may be able to take the **additional child tax credit** if line 1 is more than zero. See the **TIP** below.

☐ **No.** Enter the amount from line 8.

This is your child tax credit and credit for other dependents.

12 _____

Enter this amount on Form 1040 or 1040-SR, line 19.

1040 or 1040-SR ◄ . . . .

TIP *You may be able to take the **additional child tax credit** on Form 1040 or 1040-SR, line 28, if you answered "Yes" on line 11 **or** line 12 above.*

- *First, complete your Form 1040 or 1040-SR through line 27 (also complete Schedule 3, line 10).*
- *Then, use Schedule 8812 to figure any additional child tax credit.*

⚠ CAUTION *If your child tax credit or additional child tax credit for a year after 2015 was reduced or disallowed, see Form 8862, who must file to find out if you must file Form 8862 to take the credit for 2020.*

*If applicable.

---

* Download the latest version of this worksheet from the Form 1040 Instructions available at www.irs.gov. The 2020 worksheet was not available as we went to print. This worksheet is adapted from the 2019 version.

Qualified Dividends and Capital Gain Tax Worksheet—Line 16

Before you begin:
 ✓ See the earlier instructions for line 16 to see if you can use this worksheet to figure your tax.
 ✓ Before completing this worksheet, complete Form 1040 or 1040-SR through line 15.
 ✓ If you don't have to file Schedule D and you received capital gain distributions, be sure you checked the box on Form 1040 or 1040-SR, line 7.

1. Enter the amount from Form 1040 or 1040-SR, line 15. However, if you are filing Form 2555 (relating to foreign earned income), enter the amount from line 3 of the Foreign Earned Income Tax Worksheet .... **1.** _____

2. Enter the amount from Form 1040 or 1040-SR, line 3a* .... **2.** _____

3. Are you filing Schedule D?*
   ☐ **Yes.** Enter the **smaller** of line 15 or 16 of Schedule D. If either line 15 or 16 is blank or a loss, enter -0-.
   ☐ **No.** Enter the amount from Form 1040 or 1040-SR, line 7.   **3.** _____

4. Add lines 2 and 3 .... **4.** _____

5. If filing Form 4952 (used to figure investment interest expense deduction), enter any amount from line 4g of that form. Otherwise, enter -0- .... **5.** _____

6. Subtract line 5 from line 4. If zero or less, enter -0- .... **6.** _____

7. Subtract line 6 from line 1. If zero or less, enter -0- .... **7.** _____

8. Enter:
   $40,000 if single or married filing separately,
   $80,000 if married filing jointly or qualifying widow(er),
   $53,600 if head of household.   .... **8.** _____

9. Enter the smaller of line 1 or line 8 .... **9.** _____

10. Enter the smaller of line 7 or line 9 .... **10.** _____

11. Subtract line 10 from line 9. This amount is taxed at 0% .... **11.** _____

12. Enter the smaller of line 1 or line 6 .... **12.** _____

13. Enter the amount from line 11 .... **13.** _____

14. Subtract line 13 from line 12 .... **14.** _____

15. Enter:
    $441,450 if single,
    $248,300 if married filing separately,
    $496,600 if married filing jointly or qualifying widow(er),
    $469,050 if head of household.   .... **15.** _____

16. Enter the smaller of line 1 or line 15 .... **16.** _____

17. Add lines 7 and 11 .... **17.** _____

18. Subtract line 17 from line 16. If zero or less, enter -0- .... **18.** _____

19. Enter the smaller of line 14 or line 18 .... **19.** _____

20. Multiply line 19 by 15% (0.15) .... **20.** _____

21. Add lines 11 and 19 .... **21.** _____

22. Subtract line 21 from line 12 .... **22.** _____

23. Multiply line 22 by 20% (0.20) .... **23.** _____

24. Figure the tax on the amount on line 7. If the amount on line 7 is less than $100,000, use the Tax Table to figure the tax. If the amount on line 7 is $100,000 or more, use the Tax Computation Worksheet .... **24.** _____

25. Add lines 20, 23, and 24 .... **25.** _____

26. Figure the tax on the amount on line 1. If the amount on line 1 is less than $100,000, use the Tax Table to figure the tax. If the amount on line 1 is $100,000 or more, use the Tax Computation Worksheet .... **26.** _____

27. **Tax on all taxable income.** Enter the **smaller** of line 25 or 26. Also include this amount on the entry space on Form 1040 or 1040-SR, line 16. If you are filing Form 2555, don't enter this amount on the entry space on Form 1040 or 1040-SR, line 16. Instead, enter it on line 4 of the Foreign Earned Income Tax Worksheet .... **27.** _____

* If you are filing Form 2555, see the footnote in the Foreign Earned Income Tax Worksheet before completing this line.

Solutions to Self-Study Problems

CHAPTER 1   THE INDIVIDUAL INCOME TAX RETURN

Self-Study Problem 1.1

Answer is d. Answers a, b, and c are goals of the U.S. income tax system.

Self-Study Problem 1.2

1. Schedule B, Forms 1040 and 1040-SR.
2. Schedule D, Forms 1040 and 1040-SR.
3. Schedule 1 and Schedule F, Forms 1040 and 1040-SR.
4. Form 1041 is used to report the income of estates and trusts.
5. Schedule K-1, Form 1065.
6. Form 1040.
7. Schedule 1 and Schedule C, Forms 1040 and 1040-SR.
8. Schedule 1 and Schedule E, Forms 1040 and 1040-SR.
9. Schedule B, Forms 1040 and 1040-SR.
10. Form 1120 or Form 1120S if making an S election.
11. Form 1065.
12. Schedule A, Forms 1040 and 1040-SR.
13. Form 1040-SR (can always also use Form 1040).

Self-Study Problem 1.3

1. Gross income = $29,000 + $1,500 = $30,500
2. Adjusted gross income = $30,500 − $2,200 = $28,300
3. Standard deduction = $12,400 (exceeds his itemized deduction amount of $6,500)
4. Taxable income = $28,300 − $12,400 = $15,900

Self-Study Problem 1.4

Refer to Figures 1.1, 1.2, and 1.3 in Chapter 1.

1. No Income is below single under 65 threshold. See Figure 1.1.
2. No Income is below MFJ with one spouse 65 or older limit. See Figure 1.1.
3. No Standard deduction is earned income plus $350 up to $12,400 for single dependent. See Figure 1.2.
4. Yes Self-employment income is greater than $400. See Figure 1.3.

5. No   Income is below MFJ threshold; however, the taxpayers should file to obtain a refund. See Figure 1.1.
6. Yes Social Security taxes are due on the tip income. See Figure 1.3.
7. No   Income is below threshold for qualifying widow for under 65 with dependent. See Figure 1.1.

Self-Study Problem 1.5

1. B or C
2. D
3. A
4. C
5. D
6. E

Self-Study Problem 1.6

1. Yes. A baby born on or before December 31 may be a dependent.
2. No.   The brother is not a qualifying child (he is older than Charlie) and fails the gross income test for qualifying relative.
3. Yes. The mother is a qualifying relative under the multiple support agreement rules.
4. Yes. The son qualifies as a qualifying child and the daughter-in-law is a qualifying relative. The joint return was only filed to claim a refund.
5. Yes. The daughter is a full-time student under the age of 24 and Gary provides more than 50 percent of her support. Scholarships are exluded and do not count toward support.
6. Yes. The mother is a qualifying relative. Non-taxable Social Security benefits are not counted toward the gross income test.

Self-Study Problem 1.7

1. $0
2. $1,200 RRC
3. $500 RRC

Self-Study Problem 1.8

1. $12,400
2. $26,100 = $24,800 + $1,300
3. $15,700 = $12,400 + $1,650 + $1,650
4. $18,650
5. $1,100
6. $24,800

Self-Study Problem 1.9

1. $12,600 = $12,800 − $200
2. $8,750
3. $3,850 = $12,800 − $200 − $8,750
4. $3,850 = $12,800 − $200 − $8,750
5. Because the stock has been held for more than a year, the gain is a long-term capital gain. The long-term capital gain will be taxed at 0, 15, or 20 percent, depending on the taxpayer's income. A net investment income tax of 3.8 percent may also apply to certain high income taxpayers.

Self-Study Problem 1.10

1. True
2. True
3. True

Self-Study Problem 1.11

1. True
2. False
3. True
4. False

CHAPTER 2   GROSS INCOME AND EXCLUSIONS

Self-Study Problem 2.1

1. Included
2. Included
3. Excluded
4. Included (pre-2019), excluded (2019 and after)
5. Included
6. Excluded
7. Excluded
8. Excluded
9. Included
10. Included
11. Excluded
12. Included
13. Included
14. Included
15. Excluded
16. Excluded
17. Included
18. Included
19. Excluded

Self-Study Problem 2.2

a. $56,000
b. $3,456
c. $5,000

Self-Study Problem 2.3

None.   Neither the premiums nor the reimbursement are included in gross income.

Self-Study Problem 2.4

1. Excluded
2. Included
3. Excluded
4. Included
5. Excluded

Self-Study Problem 2.5

1. Excluded
2. Included (the excess discount over 15%)
3. Excluded
4. Excluded
5. Included
6. Included
7. Excluded

Self-Study Problem 2.6

1. $2,000
2. $10,000
3. $2,500
4. $5,000
5. $0. A service award less than $400 may be excluded from income.

Self-Study Problem 2.7

Part a

$14,645   The amount excluded from income will be $16,500 × [$42,500 ÷ ($1,500 × 12 months × 21 years)] = $1,855. Therefore, Phil will have taxable income of $14,645 ($16,500 − $1,855).

Part b

SIMPLIFIED METHOD WORKSHEET

1. Enter total amount received this year.	1.	$ 16,500.00
2. Enter cost in the plan at the annuity starting date.	2.	$ 42,500.00
3. Age at annuity starting date:		

	Enter
55 or under	360
56–60	310
61–65	260
66–70	210
71 or older	160

3. _____ 260

4. Divide line 2 by line 3.	4. $	163.46
5. Multiply line 4 by the number of monthly payments this year. If the annuity starting date was before 1987, also enter this amount on line 8; and skip lines 6 and 7. Otherwise, go to line 6.	5. $	1,798.06
6. Enter the amount, if any, recovered tax free in prior years.	6.	0.00
7. Subtract line 6 from line 2.	7.	$ 42,500.00
8. Enter the smaller of line 5 or 7.	8.	$ 1,798.06
9. Taxable amount this year: Subtract line 8 from line 1. Do not enter less than 0.	9.	$ 14,701.94

Self-Study Problem 2.8

Amount received	$ 13,250
Less: 1/10 of $100,000	(10,000)
Taxable interest	$ 3,250

Self-Study Problem 2.9

See Schedule B and the Qualifying Dividends and Capital Gain Tax Worksheet on Pages E-5 and E-6.

Self-Study Problem 2.10

1. $\dfrac{7\%}{1 - 0.24} = 9.21\%$

2. $\dfrac{6.5\%}{1 - 0.32} = 9.56\%$

Self-Study Problem 2.11

$40,000   Gifts in a business setting are taxable income, even if there was no obligation to make the payment. This problem is similar to the facts of a court case (*Duberstein*) in which the Supreme Court held that the value of the automobile was income, even where there was no legal obligation to make the gift.

Self-Study Problem 2.9

SCHEDULE B **(Form 1040)** Department of the Treasury Internal Revenue Service (99)	**Interest and Ordinary Dividends** ▶ Go to *www.irs.gov/ScheduleB* for instructions and the latest information. ▶ Attach to Form 1040 or 1040-SR.	OMB No. 1545-0074 20**20** Attachment Sequence No. **08**

Name(s) shown on return
Victor and Grace Alito

Your social security number
313-44-5454

Part I **Interest** (See instructions and the instructions for Forms 1040 and 1040-SR, line 2b.) **Note:** If you received a Form 1099-INT, Form 1099-OID, or substitute statement from a brokerage firm, list the firm's name as the payer and enter the total interest shown on that form.	1	List name of payer. If any interest is from a seller-financed mortgage and the buyer used the property as a personal residence, see the instructions and list this interest first. Also, show that buyer's social security number and address ▶ Mango Savings and Loan			**Amount**
				1	1,780
	2	Add the amounts on line 1		2	1,780
	3	Excludable interest on series EE and I U.S. savings bonds issued after 1989. Attach Form 8815		3	
	4	Subtract line 3 from line 2. Enter the result here and on Form 1040 or 1040-SR, line 2b . . . . ▶		4	1,780

Note: If line 4 is over $1,500, you must complete Part III.

Part II **Ordinary Dividends** (See instructions and the instructions for Forms 1040 and 1040-SR, line 3b.) **Note:** If you received a Form 1099-DIV or substitute statement from a brokerage firm, list the firm's name as the payer and enter the ordinary dividends shown on that form.	5	List name of payer ▶ Grape Large Cap Index Fund		**Amount**
				1,658
			5	
	6	Add the amounts on line 5. Enter the total here and on Form 1040 or 1040-SR, line 3b . . . . ▶	6	1,658

Note: If line 6 is over $1,500, you must complete Part III.

Part III **Foreign Accounts and Trusts** **Caution:** If required, failure to file FinCEN Form 114 may result in substantial penalties. See instructions.		You must complete this part if you **(a)** had over $1,500 of taxable interest or ordinary dividends; **(b)** had a foreign account; or **(c)** received a distribution from, or were a grantor of, or a transferor to, a foreign trust.	Yes	No
	7a	At any time during 2020, did you have a financial interest in or signature authority over a financial account (such as a bank account, securities account, or brokerage account) located in a foreign country? See instructions		✓
		If "Yes," are you required to file FinCEN Form 114, Report of Foreign Bank and Financial Accounts (FBAR), to report that financial interest or signature authority? See FinCEN Form 114 and its instructions for filing requirements and exceptions to those requirements		
	b	If you are required to file FinCEN Form 114, enter the name of the foreign country where the financial account is located ▶		
	8	During 2020, did you receive a distribution from, or were you the grantor of, or transferor to, a foreign trust? If "Yes," you may have to file Form 3520. See instructions		✓

For Paperwork Reduction Act Notice, see your tax return instructions.   Cat. No. 17146N   **Schedule B (Form 1040) 2020**

Self-Study Problem 2.9

Qualified Dividends and Capital Gain Tax Worksheet—Line 16

Before you begin:	✓ See the earlier instructions for line 16 to see if you can use this worksheet to figure your tax.
	✓ Before completing this worksheet, complete Form 1040 or 1040-SR through line 15.
	✓ If you don't have to file Schedule D and you received capital gain distributions, be sure you checked the box on Form 1040 or 1040-SR, line 7.

1.	Enter the amount from Form 1040 or 1040-SR, line 15. However, if you are filing Form 2555 (relating to foreign earned income), enter the amount from line 3 of the Foreign Earned Income Tax Worksheet .... **1.**		42,000
2.	Enter the amount from Form 1040 or 1040-SR, line 3a* .... **2.**	1,600	
3.	Are you filing Schedule D?*		
	☐ **Yes.** Enter the **smaller** of line 15 or 16 of Schedule D. If either line 15 or 16 is blank or a loss, enter -0-.		
	☒ **No.** Enter the amount from Form 1040 or 1040-SR, line 7. } **3.**	200	
4.	Add lines 2 and 3 .... **4.**	1,800	
5.	If filing Form 4952 (used to figure investment interest expense deduction), enter any amount from line 4g of that form. Otherwise, enter -0- .... **5.**		
6.	Subtract line 5 from line 4. If zero or less, enter -0- .... **6.**		1,800
7.	Subtract line 6 from line 1. If zero or less, enter -0- .... **7.**		40,200
8.	Enter:		
	$40,000 if single or married filing separately, $80,000 if married filing jointly or qualifying widow(er), $53,600 if head of household. } .... **8.**		80,000
9.	Enter the smaller of line 1 or line 8 .... **9.**		42,000
10.	Enter the smaller of line 7 or line 9 .... **10.**		40,200
11.	Subtract line 10 from line 9. This amount is taxed at 0% .... **11.**		1,800
12.	Enter the smaller of line 1 or line 6 .... **12.**		1,800
13.	Enter the amount from line 11 .... **13.**		1,800
14.	Subtract line 13 from line 12 .... **14.**		0
15.	Enter:		
	$441,450 if single, $248,300 if married filing separately, $496,600 if married filing jointly or qualifying widow(er), $469,050 if head of household. } .... **15.**		496,600
16.	Enter the smaller of line 1 or line 15 .... **16.**		42,000
17.	Add lines 7 and 11 .... **17.**		42,000
18.	Subtract line 17 from line 16. If zero or less, enter -0- .... **18.**		0
19.	Enter the smaller of line 14 or line 18 .... **19.**		0
20.	Multiply line 19 by 15% (0.15) .... **20.**		0
21.	Add lines 11 and 19 .... **21.**	1,800	
22.	Subtract line 21 from line 12 .... **22.**	0	
23.	Multiply line 22 by 20% (0.20) .... **23.**		0
24.	Figure the tax on the amount on line 7. If the amount on line 7 is less than $100,000, use the Tax Table to figure the tax. If the amount on line 7 is $100,000 or more, use the Tax Computation Worksheet .... **24.**		4,432
25.	Add lines 20, 23, and 24 .... **25.**		4,432
26.	Figure the tax on the amount on line 1. If the amount on line 1 is less than $100,000, use the Tax Table to figure the tax. If the amount on line 1 is $100,000 or more, use the Tax Computation Worksheet .... **26.**		4,648
27.	**Tax on all taxable income.** Enter the **smaller** of line 25 or 26. Also include this amount on the entry space on Form 1040 or 1040-SR, line 16. If you are filing Form 2555, don't enter this amount on the entry space on Form 1040 or 1040-SR, line 16. Instead, enter it on line 4 of the Foreign Earned Income Tax Worksheet .... **27.**		4,432

* If you are filing Form 2555, see the footnote in the Foreign Earned Income Tax Worksheet before completing this line.

This worksheet adapted from the 2019 worksheet.

Self-Study Problem 2.12

1. Excluded
2. Included

3. Included

4. Included
5. Included and Excluded. The $7,600 used for qualifying expenses is excluded but the excess scholarship of $2,400 in included in taxable income.
6. Included

Self-Study Problem 2.13

Deductible by payer	Includable by recipient
a. $ 0	$ 0
b. 12,000	12,000
c. 0	0

Self-Study Problem 2.14

a. $0
b. $2,000. Henry's AGI is under $95,000 so there is no phase-out.
c. $2,000. Esther's AGI is greater than $65,000 but less than $80,000.

Self-Study Problem 2.15

$3,000 Unemployment compensation is fully taxable.

Self-Study Problem 2.16

Simplified Taxable Social Security Worksheet (for most people)

1. Enter the total amount of Social Security income.	1.	$13,000
2. Enter one-half of line 1.	2.	6,500
3. Enter the total of taxable income items on Form 1040 except Social Security income.	3.	20,000
4. Enter the amount of tax-exempt interest income.	4.	30,000
5. Add lines 2, 3, and 4.	5.	56,500
6. Enter all adjustments for AGI except for student loan interest, the domestic production activities deduction, and the tuition and fees deduction.	6.	0
7. Subtract line 6 from line 5. If 0 or less, stop here, none of the Social Security benefits are taxable.	7.	56,500
8. Enter $25,000 ($32,000 if married filing jointly; $0 if married filing separately and living with spouse at any time during the year).	8.	32,000
9. Subtract line 8 from line 7. If 0 or less, enter -0-.	9.	24,500

Note: If line 9 is 0 or less, stop here; none of your benefits are taxable. Otherwise, go on to line 10.

10. Enter $9,000 ($12,000 if married filing jointly; $0 if married filing separately and living with spouse at any time during the year).	10.	12,000
11. Subtract line 10 from line 9. If 0 or less, enter -0-.	11.	12,500
12. Enter the **smaller of line 9 or line 10.**	12.	12,000
13. Enter one-half of line 12.	13.	6,000
14. Enter the **smaller of line 2 or line 13.**	14.	6,000
15. Multiply line 11 by 85% (.85). If line 11 is 0, enter -0-.	15.	10,625
16. Add lines 14 and 15.	16.	16,625
17. Multiply line 1 by 85% (.85).	17.	11,050
18. **Taxable benefits. Enter the smaller of line 16 or line 17.**	18.	$11,050

Self-Study Problem 2.17

a. Tom's salary (50 percent)	$20,000
Rachel's salary (50 percent)	15,000
Dividends, Rachel's property (100 percent)	3,000
Interest (50 percent)	2,000
Total	$40,000

b. Tom's salary (50 percent) $20,000
   Rachel's salary (50 percent)   15,000
   Dividends, Tom's property (50 percent)   2,500
   Dividends, Rachel's property (50 percent)   1,500
   Interest (50 percent)   2,000
   Total $41,000

Self-Study Problem 2.18

a. $0   Stuart may exclude the cancellation of debt income.
b. $160,000. The original basis of $200,000 is reduced by the excluded
   cancellation of debt income of $40,000.

CHAPTER 3   BUSINESS INCOME AND EXPENSES

Self-Study Problem 3.1

See Schedule C on Pages E-9 and E-10.

Self-Study Problem 3.2

Part III   **Cost of Goods Sold** (see instructions)

33	Method(s) used to value closing inventory: a ☑ Cost b ☐ Lower of cost or market c ☐ Other (attach explanation)	
34	Was there any change in determining quantities, costs, or valuations between opening and closing inventory? If "Yes," attach explanation . . . . ☐ Yes ☑ No	
35	Inventory at beginning of year. If different from last year's closing inventory, attach explanation . . **35**	62,500
36	Purchases less cost of items withdrawn for personal use **36**	178,750
37	Cost of labor. Do not include any amounts paid to yourself **37**	
38	Materials and supplies **38**	
39	Other costs **39**	
40	Add lines 35 through 39 . . . . **40**	241,250
41	Inventory at end of year **41**	68,400
42	**Cost of goods sold.** Subtract line 41 from line 40. Enter the result here and on line 4 . . . . . **42**	172,850

Self-Study Problem 3.3

Marc's transportation deduction is the greater of his actual costs or his deduction using the standard mileage method.

Actual Cost Calculation:

Cash Outlays	$ 4,028
Depreciation	4,000
	8,028
Business percentage (13,120/16,000)	×82%
Subtotal	6,583
Tolls & Fees	327
Actual Costs	$ 6,910

Standard Mileage Calculation:

13,120 miles @ 57.5¢	$ 7,544
Tolls & Fees	327
Marc's deduction for 2020 is	$ 7,871

Self-Study Problem 3.1

SCHEDULE C **(Form 1040)** Department of the Treasury Internal Revenue Service (99)	**Profit or Loss From Business** (Sole Proprietorship) ▶ Go to *www.irs.gov/ScheduleC* for instructions and the latest information. ▶ Attach to Form 1040, 1040-SR, 1040-NR, or 1041; partnerships generally must file Form 1065.

OMB No. 1545-0074

20**20**

Attachment Sequence No. **09**

Name of proprietor   Teri Kataoka

Social security number (SSN)   466-47-8833

A   Principal business or profession, including product or service (see instructions)   Golf Instructor

B Enter code from instructions ▶ 8 1 2 9 9 0

C   Business name. If no separate business name, leave blank.

D Employer ID number (EIN) (see instr.)

E   Business address (including suite or room no.) ▶ 1234 Pinecrest Drive
City, town or post office, state, and ZIP code   Kennesaw, GA 30152

F   Accounting method: **(1)** ☑ Cash   **(2)** ☐ Accrual   **(3)** ☐ Other (specify) ▶

G   Did you "materially participate" in the operation of this business during 2020? If "No," see instructions for limit on losses   ☑ Yes   ☐ No

H   If you started or acquired this business during 2020, check here   ▶ ☐

I   Did you make any payments in 2020 that would require you to file Form(s) 1099? See instructions   ☐ Yes   ☑ No

J   If "Yes," did you or will you file required Form(s) 1099?   ☐ Yes   ☐ No

Part I   Income

1	Gross receipts or sales. See instructions for line 1 and check the box if this income was reported to you on Form W-2 and the "Statutory employee" box on that form was checked ▶ ☐	1	40,125
2	Returns and allowances	2	
3	Subtract line 2 from line 1	3	40,125
4	Cost of goods sold (from line 42)	4	
5	**Gross profit.** Subtract line 4 from line 3	5	40,125
6	Other income, including federal and state gasoline or fuel tax credit or refund (see instructions)	6	
7	**Gross income.** Add lines 5 and 6 ▶	7	40,125

Part II   Expenses. Enter expenses for business use of your home **only** on line 30.

8	Advertising	8		18	Office expense (see instructions)	18	660
9	Car and truck expenses (see instructions)	9	3,036	19	Pension and profit-sharing plans	19	
10	Commissions and fees	10		20	Rent or lease (see instructions):		
11	Contract labor (see instructions)	11		a	Vehicles, machinery, and equipment	20a	
12	Depletion	12		b	Other business property	20b	2,700
13	Depreciation and section 179 expense deduction (not included in Part III) (see instructions)	13		21	Repairs and maintenance	21	
				22	Supplies (not included in Part III)	22	
				23	Taxes and licenses	23	250
14	Employee benefit programs (other than on line 19)	14		24	Travel and meals:		
15	Insurance (other than health)	15	475	a	Travel	24a	3,000
16	Interest (see instructions):			b	Deductible meals (see instructions)	24b	985
a	Mortgage (paid to banks, etc.)	16a		25	Utilities	25	515
b	Other	16b		26	Wages (less employment credits)	26	
17	Legal and professional services	17		27a	Other expenses (from line 48)	27a	500
				b	**Reserved for future use**	27b	

28	**Total expenses** before expenses for business use of home. Add lines 8 through 27a ▶	28	12,121
29	Tentative profit or (loss). Subtract line 28 from line 7	29	28,004
30	Expenses for business use of your home. Do not report these expenses elsewhere. Attach Form 8829 unless using the simplified method. See instructions. **Simplified method filers only:** Enter the total square footage of (a) your home: _____ and (b) the part of your home used for business: _____ . Use the Simplified Method Worksheet in the instructions to figure the amount to enter on line 30	30	
31	**Net profit or (loss).** Subtract line 30 from line 29. • If a profit, enter on both **Schedule 1 (Form 1040), line 3,** and on **Schedule SE, line 2.** (If you checked the box on line 1, see instructions). Estates and trusts, enter on **Form 1041, line 3.** • If a loss, you **must** go to line 32.	31	28,004
32	If you have a loss, check the box that describes your investment in this activity. See instructions. • If you checked 32a, enter the loss on both **Schedule 1 (Form 1040), line 3,** and on **Schedule SE, line 2.** (If you checked the box on line 1, see the line 31 instructions). Estates and trusts, enter on **Form 1041, line 3.** • If you checked 32b, you **must** attach **Form 6198.** Your loss may be limited.	32a ☐ All investment is at risk. 32b ☐ Some investment is not at risk.	

For Paperwork Reduction Act Notice, see the separate instructions.   Cat. No. 11334P   Schedule C (Form 1040) 2020

DRAFT AS OF July 13, 2020 DO NOT FILE

Self-Study Problem 3.1

Schedule C (Form 1040) 2020   Page **2**

Part III   **Cost of Goods Sold** (see instructions)

33   Method(s) used to
     value closing inventory: **a** ☐ Cost   **b** ☐ Lower of cost or market   **c** ☐ Other (attach explanation)

34   Was there any change in determining quantities, costs, or valuations between opening and closing inventory?
     If "Yes," attach explanation . . . . ☐ Yes   ☐ No

35   Inventory at beginning of year. If different from last year's closing inventory, attach explanation . . | **35** |

36   Purchases less cost of items withdrawn for personal use . . . . | **36** |

37   Cost of labor. Do not include any amounts paid to yourself . . . . | **37** |

38   Materials and supplies . . . . | **38** |

39   Other costs . . . . | **39** |

40   Add lines 35 through 39 . . . . | **40** |

41   Inventory at end of year . . . . | **41** |

42   **Cost of goods sold.** Subtract line 41 from line 40. Enter the result here and on line 4 . . . . . . | **42** |

Part IV   **Information on Your Vehicle.** Complete this part **only** if you are claiming car or truck expenses on line 9 and are not required to file Form 4562 for this business. See the instructions for line 13 to find out if you must file Form 4562.

43   When did you place your vehicle in service for business purposes? (month/day/year)   ▶   01 / 01 / 2020

44   Of the total number of miles you drove your vehicle during 2020, enter the number of miles you used your vehicle for:

a Business ___5,280___   **b** Commuting (see instructions) ___1,200___   **c** Other ___5,000___

45   Was your vehicle available for personal use during off-duty hours? . . . . ☑ Yes   ☐ No

46   Do you (or your spouse) have another vehicle available for personal use?. . . . . ☐ Yes   ☑ No

47a Do you have evidence to support your deduction? . . . . ☑ Yes   ☐ No

 b   If "Yes," is the evidence written? . . . . ☑ Yes   ☐ No

Part V   **Other Expenses.** List below business expenses not included on lines 8–26 or line 30.

Membership in professional golfers' association	500

48	**Total other expenses.** Enter here and on line 27a	**48**	500

Schedule C (Form 1040) 2020

Self-Study Problem 3.4

Deductible expenses:

Airfare	$ 480
Hotel while working on the audit	825
Meals while working on the audit	168
Laundry	22
Taxi	72
Total travel deduction	$1,567

Self-Study Problem 3.5

Business meals ($500 + $600) × 50% = $550. Entertainment, dues, and personal expenses are not generally deductible.

Self-Study Problem 3.6

Lodging	$1,200
Transportation	350
Meals (50% of $200)	100
Books	175
Tuition	550
Total Deduction	$2,375

The cost of the weekend trip to the Grand Canyon is not deductible.

Self-Study Problem 3.7

1. Deductible
2. Not Deductible
3. Not Deductible
4. Not Deductible
5. Not Deductible

Self-Study Problem 3.8

Safety shoes and orange vest	$ 650
Climbing equipment, etc.	275
Total special clothing deduction	$ 925

Self-Study Problem 3.9

1. Mr. Jones	$ 20
2. Mr. Brown	25
3. Mrs. and Mr. Green	25
4. Ms. Gray	0
5. Mr. Edwards	75
6. Various customers	140
Total business gift deduction	$ 285

Self-Study Problem 3.10

1. Business
2. Nonbusiness
3. Nonbusiness
4. Business
5. Nonbusiness

Self-Study Problem 3.11

Gross income	$ 2,900
Less: interest and taxes	(2,100)
Balance	$ 800
Less: maintenance, utilities, and cleaning ($1,400) limited to	(800)
Net income	$ 0

Note: The excess expenses of $600 may be carried forward.

Self-Study Problem 3.12

Income $250.   The hobby income must be recognized.
Deduction $0.   No deduction is permitted.

CHAPTER 4   ADDITIONAL INCOME AND THE QUALIFIED BUSINESS INCOME DEDUCTION

Self-Study Problem 4.1

1. No   Inventory is specifically excluded from the definition of a capital asset.
2. Yes
3. No   Property held by the creator is specifically excluded from the definition of a capital asset.
4. No   Accounts receivable are specifically excluded from the definition of a capital asset.
5. Yes   The copyright is not held by the creator.
6. No   Section 1231 assets (depreciable property and real estate used in a trade or business) are specifically excluded from the definition of a capital asset.
7. Yes
8. Yes
9. Yes
10. Yes
11. No   Inventory is specifically excluded from the definition of a capital asset.
12. Yes

Self-Study Problem 4.2

1. Short-term
2. Long-term
3. Short-term
4. Long-term

Self-Study Problem 4.3

1. Adjusted basis = $11,000
2. Capital improvements = $2,000
3. Accumulated depreciation = $15,000
4. Original cost = $23,000

Self-Study Problem 4.4

Net long-term ($12,000 − $4,000) +	
($14,000 − $17,500) =	$ 4,500
Net short-term	(1,800)
Net capital gains	2,700
Capital gains rate	× 15%
Tax	$ 405

Self-Study Problem 4.5

See Schedule D, Form 8949, and the Qualified Dividends and Capital Gain Tax Worksheet on Pages E-14 through E-18.

Self-Study Problem 4.6

a. Sales price	$350,000
Basis	(30,000)
Realized gain	320,000
Exclusion	(250,000)
Recognized gain	$ 70,000

b. $0. The $500,000 exclusion for joint filers exceeds the $320,000 realized gain.

c. $25,000 = ($350,000 − $200,000) − (½ × $250,000)

Self-Study Problem 4.7

See Schedule E on Page E-19.

Self-Study Problem 4.8

See Form 8582 on Page E-20.

Self-Study Problem 4.9

1. F   NOLs for the year 2020 can be carried back 5 years and forward indefinitely.
2. F   Generally, NOLs are only from the operation of a trade or business or casualty and theft losses.
3. F   Individual NOLs require an analysis of business and nonbusiness income and deductions to determine the business portion that compose the NOL.
4. F   Due to the suspension of the overall business loss rules resulting from the CARES Act, the limit no longer applies in 2020.
5. F   NOLs generated after 2017 can only offset 80 percent of the taxable income starting again in 2021

Self-Study Problem 4.5

SCHEDULE D (Form 1040)	**Capital Gains and Losses**	OMB No. 1545-0074
Department of the Treasury Internal Revenue Service (99)	▶ Attach to Form 1040, 1040-SR, or 1040-NR. ▶ Go to *www.irs.gov/ScheduleD* for instructions and the latest information. ▶ Use Form 8949 to list your transactions for lines 1b, 2, 3, 8b, 9, and 10.	20**20** Attachment Sequence No. **12**

Name(s) shown on return	Your social security number
Louis Winthorp	123-44-3214

Did you dispose of any investment(s) in a qualified opportunity fund during the tax year? ☐ Yes ☑ No
If "Yes," attach Form 8949 and see its instructions for additional requirements for reporting your gain or loss.

Part I   Short-Term Capital Gains and Losses—Generally Assets One Year or Less (see instructions)

See instructions for how to figure the amounts to enter on the lines below. This form may be easier to complete if you round off cents to whole dollars.	**(d)** Proceeds (sales price)	**(e)** Cost (or other basis)	**(g)** Adjustments to gain or loss from Form(s) 8949, Part I, line 2, column (g)	**(h) Gain or (loss)** Subtract column (e) from column (d) and combine the result with column (g)
1a Totals for all short-term transactions reported on Form 1099-B for which basis was reported to the IRS and for which you have no adjustments (see instructions). However, if you choose to report all these transactions on Form 8949, leave this line blank and go to line 1b .				
1b Totals for all transactions reported on Form(s) 8949 with **Box A** checked	12,000	19,200		(7,200)
2 Totals for all transactions reported on Form(s) 8949 with **Box B** checked				
3 Totals for all transactions reported on Form(s) 8949 with **Box C** checked				

4 Short-term gain from Form 6252 and short-term gain or (loss) from Forms 4684, 6781, and 8824 . .	**4**	
5 Net short-term gain or (loss) from partnerships, S corporations, estates, and trusts from Schedule(s) K-1	**5**	
6 Short-term capital loss carryover. Enter the amount, if any, from line 8 of your **Capital Loss Carryover Worksheet** in the instructions	**6** ( )	
7 **Net short-term capital gain or (loss).** Combine lines 1a through 6 in column (h). If you have any long-term capital gains or losses, go to Part II below. Otherwise, go to Part III on the back	**7**	(7,200)

Part II   Long-Term Capital Gains and Losses—Generally Assets Held More Than One Year (see instructions)

See instructions for how to figure the amounts to enter on the lines below. This form may be easier to complete if you round off cents to whole dollars.	**(d)** Proceeds (sales price)	**(e)** Cost (or other basis)	**(g)** Adjustments to gain or loss from Form(s) 8949, Part II, line 2, column (g)	**(h) Gain or (loss)** Subtract column (e) from column (d) and combine the result with column (g)
8a Totals for all long-term transactions reported on Form 1099-B for which basis was reported to the IRS and for which you have no adjustments (see instructions). However, if you choose to report all these transactions on Form 8949, leave this line blank and go to line 8b .				
8b Totals for all transactions reported on Form(s) 8949 with **Box D** checked	43,000	33,500		9,500
9 Totals for all transactions reported on Form(s) 8949 with **Box E** checked				
10 Totals for all transactions reported on Form(s) 8949 with **Box F** checked				

11 Gain from Form 4797, Part I; long-term gain from Forms 2439 and 6252; and long-term gain or (loss) from Forms 4684, 6781, and 8824	**11**	
12 Net long-term gain or (loss) from partnerships, S corporations, estates, and trusts from Schedule(s) K-1	**12**	
13 Capital gain distributions. See the instructions	**13**	
14 Long-term capital loss carryover. Enter the amount, if any, from line 13 of your **Capital Loss Carryover Worksheet** in the instructions	**14** ( )	
15 **Net long-term capital gain or (loss).** Combine lines 8a through 14 in column (h). Then, go to Part III on the back	**15**	9,500

For Paperwork Reduction Act Notice, see your tax return instructions.   Cat. No. 11338H   Schedule D (Form 1040) 2020

Self-Study Problem 4.5

Schedule D (Form 1040) 2020   Page **2**

Part III	**Summary**

16 Combine lines 7 and 15 and enter the result . . . . | **16** | 2,300

- If line 16 is a **gain,** enter the amount from line 16 on Form 1040, 1040-SR, or 1040-NR, line 7. Then, go to line 17 below.
- If line 16 is a **loss,** skip lines 17 through 20 below. Then, go to line 21. Also be sure to complete line 22.
- If line 16 is **zero,** skip lines 17 through 21 below and enter -0- on Form 1040, 1040-SR, or 1040-NR, line 7. Then, go to line 22.

17 Are lines 15 and 16 **both** gains?
☑ **Yes.** Go to line 18.
☐ **No.** Skip lines 18 through 21, and go to line 22.

18 If you are required to complete the **28% Rate Gain Worksheet** (see instructions), enter the amount, if any, from line 7 of that worksheet . . . . ▶ | **18** | 0

19 If you are required to complete the **Unrecaptured Section 1250 Gain Worksheet** (see instructions), enter the amount, if any, from line 18 of that worksheet . . . . ▶ | **19** | 0

20 Are lines 18 and 19 **both** zero or blank?
☑ **Yes.** Complete the **Qualified Dividends and Capital Gain Tax Worksheet** in the instructions for Forms 1040 and 1040-SR, line 16. **Don't** complete lines 21 and 22 below.

☐ **No.** Complete the **Schedule D Tax Worksheet** in the instructions. **Don't** complete lines 21 and 22 below.

21 If line 16 is a loss, enter here and on Form 1040, 1040-SR, or 1040-NR, line 7, the **smaller** of:

- The loss on line 16; or
- ($3,000), or if married filing separately, ($1,500) . . . . | **21** | ( )

Note: When figuring which amount is smaller, treat both amounts as positive numbers.

22 Do you have qualified dividends on Form 1040, 1040-SR, or 1040-NR, line 3a?

☐ **Yes.** Complete the **Qualified Dividends and Capital Gain Tax Worksheet** in the instructions for Forms 1040 and 1040-SR, line 16.

☐ **No.** Complete the rest of Form 1040, 1040-SR, or 1040-NR.

Schedule D (Form 1040) 2020

Self-Study Problem 4.5

Form **8949**	**Sales and Other Dispositions of Capital Assets**	OMB No. 1545-0074
Department of the Treasury Internal Revenue Service	▶ Go to *www.irs.gov/Form8949* for instructions and the latest information. ▶ File with your Schedule D to list your transactions for lines 1b, 2, 3, 8b, 9, and 10 of Schedule D.	20**20** Attachment Sequence No. **12A**

Name(s) shown on return	Social security number or taxpayer identification number
Louis Winthorp	123-44-3214

Before you check Box A, B, or C below, see whether you received any Form(s) 1099-B or substitute statement(s) from your broker. A substitute statement will have the same information as Form 1099-B. Either will show whether your basis (usually your cost) was reported to the IRS by your broker and may even tell you which box to check.

Part I **Short-Term.** Transactions involving capital assets you held 1 year or less are generally short-term (see instructions). For long-term transactions, see page 2.

Note: You may aggregate all short-term transactions reported on Form(s) 1099-B showing basis was reported to the IRS and for which no adjustments or codes are required. Enter the totals directly on Schedule D, line 1a; you aren't required to report these transactions on Form 8949 (see instructions).

You *must* check Box A, B, *or* C below. Check only one box. If more than one box applies for your short-term transactions, complete a separate Form 8949, page 1, for each applicable box. If you have more short-term transactions than will fit on this page for one or more of the boxes, complete as many forms with the same box checked as you need.

- ☑ **(A)** Short-term transactions reported on Form(s) 1099-B showing basis was reported to the IRS (see **Note** above)
- ☐ **(B)** Short-term transactions reported on Form(s) 1099-B showing basis **wasn't** reported to the IRS
- ☐ **(C)** Short-term transactions not reported to you on Form 1099-B

1 **(a)** Description of property (Example: 100 sh. XYZ Co.)	**(b)** Date acquired (Mo., day, yr.)	**(c)** Date sold or disposed of (Mo., day, yr.)	**(d)** Proceeds (sales price) (see instructions)	**(e)** Cost or other basis. See the **Note** below and see *Column (e)* in the separate instructions	Adjustment, if any, to gain or loss. If you enter an amount in column (g), enter a code in column (f). See the separate instructions. **(f)** Code(s) from instructions	**(g)** Amount of adjustment	**(h)** **Gain or (loss).** Subtract column (e) from column (d) and combine the result with column (g)
100 shs. Rose Corp	04/18/2020	12/07/2020	12,000	19,200			(7,200)
2 Totals. Add the amounts in columns (d), (e), (g), and (h) (subtract negative amounts). Enter each total here and include on your Schedule D, **line 1b** (if **Box A** above is checked), **line 2** (if **Box B** above is checked), or **line 3** (if **Box C** above is checked) ▶			12,000	19,200			(7,200)

Note: If you checked Box A above but the basis reported to the IRS was incorrect, enter in column (e) the basis as reported to the IRS, and enter an adjustment in column (g) to correct the basis. See *Column (g)* in the separate instructions for how to figure the amount of the adjustment.

For Paperwork Reduction Act Notice, see your tax return instructions.   Cat. No. 37768Z   Form **8949** (2020)

Self-Study Problem 4.5

Form 8949 (2020)   Attachment Sequence No. **12A**   Page **2**

Name(s) shown on return. Name and SSN or taxpayer identification no. not required if shown on other side	Social security number or taxpayer identification number
Louis Winthorp	123-44-3214

Before you check Box D, E, or F below, see whether you received any Form(s) 1099-B or substitute statement(s) from your broker. A substitute statement will have the same information as Form 1099-B. Either will show whether your basis (usually your cost) was reported to the IRS by your broker and may even tell you which box to check.

Part II   **Long-Term.** Transactions involving capital assets you held more than 1 year are generally long-term (see instructions). For short-term transactions, see page 1.

Note: You may aggregate all long-term transactions reported on Form(s) 1099-B showing basis was reported to the IRS and for which no adjustments or codes are required. Enter the totals directly on Schedule D, line 8a; you aren't required to report these transactions on Form 8949 (see instructions).

You *must* **check Box D, E,** *or* **F below. Check only one box.** If more than one box applies for your long-term transactions, complete a separate Form 8949, page 2, for each applicable box. If you have more long-term transactions than will fit on this page for one or more of the boxes, complete as many forms with the same box checked as you need.

- ☑ **(D)** Long-term transactions reported on Form(s) 1099-B showing basis was reported to the IRS (see **Note** above)
- ☐ **(E)** Long-term transactions reported on Form(s) 1099-B showing basis **wasn't** reported to the IRS
- ☐ **(F)** Long-term transactions not reported to you on Form 1099-B

1 (a) Description of property (Example: 100 sh. XYZ Co.)	(b) Date acquired (Mo., day, yr.)	(c) Date sold or disposed of (Mo., day, yr.)	(d) Proceeds (sales price) (see instructions)	(e) Cost or other basis. See the **Note** below and see *Column (e)* in the separate instructions	Adjustment, if any, to gain or loss. If you enter an amount in column (g), enter a code in column (f). See the separate instructions. (f) Code(s) from instructions	(g) Amount of adjustment	(h) Gain or (loss). Subtract column (e) from column (d) and combine the result with column (g)
50 shs. Blue	12/18/2012	10/02/2020	25,000	21,000			4,000
100 shs. Purple	06/21/2011	08/15/2020	18,000	12,500			5,500
2 Totals. Add the amounts in columns (d), (e), (g), and (h) (subtract negative amounts). Enter each total here and include on your Schedule D, **line 8b** (if **Box D** above is checked), **line 9** (if **Box E** above is checked), or **line 10** (if **Box F** above is checked) ▶			43,000	33,500			9,500

Note: If you checked Box D above but the basis reported to the IRS was incorrect, enter in column (e) the basis as reported to the IRS, and enter an adjustment in column (g) to correct the basis. See *Column (g)* in the separate instructions for how to figure the amount of the adjustment.

Form **8949** (2020)

Self-Study Problem 4.5

Qualified Dividends and Capital Gain Tax Worksheet—Line 16

Before you begin:	✓ See the earlier instructions for line 16 to see if you can use this worksheet to figure your tax. ✓ Before completing this worksheet, complete Form 1040 or 1040-SR through line 15. ✓ If you don't have to file Schedule D and you received capital gain distributions, be sure you checked the box on Form 1040 or 1040-SR, line 7.

1. Enter the amount from Form 1040 or 1040-SR, line 15. However, if you are filing Form 2555 (relating to foreign earned income), enter the amount from line 3 of the Foreign Earned Income Tax Worksheet .... **1.** _____59,000_____

2. Enter the amount from Form 1040 or 1040-SR, line 3a* .... **2.** _____

3. Are you filing Schedule D?*
   ☒ **Yes.** Enter the **smaller** of line 15 or 16 of Schedule D. If either line 15 or 16 is blank or a loss, enter -0-.
   ☐ **No.** Enter the amount from Form 1040 or 1040-SR, line 7. } **3.** _____2,300_____

4. Add lines 2 and 3 .... **4.** _____2,300_____

5. If filing Form 4952 (used to figure investment interest expense deduction), enter any amount from line 4g of that form. Otherwise, enter -0- .... **5.** _____

6. Subtract line 5 from line 4. If zero or less, enter -0- .... **6.** _____2,300_____

7. Subtract line 6 from line 1. If zero or less, enter -0- .... **7.** _____56,700_____

8. Enter:
   $40,000 if single or married filing separately,
   $80,000 if married filing jointly or qualifying widow(er),
   $53,600 if head of household. } .... **8.** _____40,000_____

9. Enter the smaller of line 1 or line 8 .... **9.** _____40,000_____

10. Enter the smaller of line 7 or line 9 .... **10.** _____40,000_____

11. Subtract line 10 from line 9. This amount is taxed at 0% .... **11.** _____0_____

12. Enter the smaller of line 1 or line 6 .... **12.** _____2,300_____

13. Enter the amount from line 11 .... **13.** _____0_____

14. Subtract line 13 from line 12 .... **14.** _____2,300_____

15. Enter:
    $441,450 if single,
    $248,300 if married filing separately,
    $496,600 if married filing jointly or qualifying widow(er),
    $469,050 if head of household. } .... **15.** _____441,450_____

16. Enter the smaller of line 1 or line 15 .... **16.** _____59,000_____

17. Add lines 7 and 11 .... **17.** _____56,700_____

18. Subtract line 17 from line 16. If zero or less, enter -0- .... **18.** _____2,300_____

19. Enter the smaller of line 14 or line 18 .... **19.** _____2,300_____

20. Multiply line 19 by 15% (0.15) .... **20.** _____345_____

21. Add lines 11 and 19 .... **21.** _____2,300_____

22. Subtract line 21 from line 12 .... **22.** _____0_____

23. Multiply line 22 by 20% (0.20) .... **23.** _____0_____

24. Figure the tax on the amount on line 7. If the amount on line 7 is less than $100,000, use the Tax Table to figure the tax. If the amount on line 7 is $100,000 or more, use the Tax Computation Worksheet .... **24.** _____8,270_____

25. Add lines 20, 23, and 24 .... **25.** _____8,615_____

26. Figure the tax on the amount on line 1. If the amount on line 1 is less than $100,000, use the Tax Table to figure the tax. If the amount on line 1 is $100,000 or more, use the Tax Computation Worksheet .... **26.** _____8,776_____

27. **Tax on all taxable income.** Enter the **smaller** of line 25 or 26. Also include this amount on the entry space on Form 1040 or 1040-SR, line 16. If you are filing Form 2555, don't enter this amount on the entry space on Form 1040 or 1040-SR, line 16. Instead, enter it on line 4 of the Foreign Earned Income Tax Worksheet .... **27.** _____8,615_____

*If you are filing Form 2555, see the footnote in the Foreign Earned Income Tax Worksheet before completing this line.

This worksheet adapted from the 2019 worksheet.

Self-Study Problem 4.7

SCHEDULE E (Form 1040) Department of the Treasury Internal Revenue Service (99)	**Supplemental Income and Loss** (From rental real estate, royalties, partnerships, S corporations, estates, trusts, REMICs, etc.) ▶ Attach to Form 1040, 1040-SR, 1040-NR, or 1041. ▶ Go to *www.irs.gov/ScheduleE* for instructions and the latest information.	OMB No. 1545-0074 20**20** Attachment Sequence No. **13**

Name(s) shown on return: Nancy Valentino | Your social security number

Part I **Income or Loss From Rental Real Estate and Royalties**   Note: If you are in the business of renting personal property, use **Schedule C.** See instructions. If you are an individual, report farm rental income or loss from **Form 4835** on page 2, line 40.

A Did you make any payments in 2020 that would require you to file Form(s) 1099? See instructions . . . . . ☐ Yes ☑ No
B If "Yes," did you or will you file required Form(s) 1099? . . . . ☐ Yes ☐ No

1a Physical address of each property (street, city, state, ZIP code)
A 14 Lancaster Dr., Salem, OR 97305
B
C

1b	Type of Property (from list below)	2 For each rental real estate property listed above, report the number of fair rental and personal use days. Check the **QJV** box only if you meet the requirements to file as a qualified joint venture. See instructions.		Fair Rental Days	Personal Use Days	QJV
A	2		A	365		☐
B			B			☐
C			C			☐

Type of Property:
1 Single Family Residence   3 Vacation/Short-Term Rental   5 Land   7 Self-Rental
2 Multi-Family Residence   4 Commercial   6 Royalties   8 Other (describe)

Income:	Properties:		A	B	C
3 Rents received	3		6,000		
4 Royalties received	4				
Expenses:					
5 Advertising	5				
6 Auto and travel (see instructions)	6				
7 Cleaning and maintenance	7				
8 Commissions.	8				
9 Insurance	9		225		
10 Legal and other professional fees . . .	10				
11 Management fees	11				
12 Mortgage interest paid to banks, etc. (see instructions)	12		1,700		
13 Other interest.	13				
14 Repairs.	14				
15 Supplies	15				
16 Taxes	16		600		
17 Utilities	17		900		
18 Depreciation expense or depletion	18		545		
19 Other (list) ▶ _____	19				
20 Total expenses. Add lines 5 through 19	20		3,970		
21 Subtract line 20 from line 3 (rents) and/or 4 (royalties). If result is a (loss), see instructions to find out if you must file **Form 6198**	21		2,030		
22 Deductible rental real estate loss after limitation, if any, on **Form 8582** (see instructions)	22	(	)(	)(	)

23a Total of all amounts reported on line 3 for all rental properties	23a	6,000		
b Total of all amounts reported on line 4 for all royalty properties	23b			
c Total of all amounts reported on line 12 for all properties	23c	1,700		
d Total of all amounts reported on line 18 for all properties	23d	545		
e Total of all amounts reported on line 20 for all properties	23e	3,970		
24 **Income.** Add positive amounts shown on line 21. **Do not** include any losses	24			2,030
25 **Losses.** Add royalty losses from line 21 and rental real estate losses from line 22. Enter total losses here .	25	(		)
26 **Total rental real estate and royalty income or (loss).** Combine lines 24 and 25. Enter the result here. If Parts II, III, IV, and line 40 on page 2 do not apply to you, also enter this amount on Schedule 1 (Form 1040), line 5. Otherwise, include this amount in the total on line 41 on page 2 .	26			2,030

For Paperwork Reduction Act Notice, see the separate instructions.   Cat. No. 11344L   Schedule E (Form 1040) 2020

Self-Study Problem 4.8

Form **8582**	**Passive Activity Loss Limitations**	OMB No. 1545-1008
Department of the Treasury Internal Revenue Service (99)	▶ See separate instructions. ▶ Attach to Form 1040, 1040-SR, or 1041. ▶ Go to *www.irs.gov/Form8582* for instructions and the latest information.	**2020** Attachment Sequence No. **858**

Name(s) shown on return
Sherry Lockey

Identifying number

Part I — 2020 Passive Activity Loss

Caution: Complete Worksheets 1, 2, and 3 before completing Part I.

Rental Real Estate Activities With Active Participation (For the definition of active participation, see **Special Allowance for Rental Real Estate Activities** in the instructions.)

1a	Activities with net income (enter the amount from Worksheet 1, column (a))	**1a**	
b	Activities with net loss (enter the amount from Worksheet 1, column (b))	**1b** (9,000)	
c	Prior years' unallowed losses (enter the amount from Worksheet 1, column (c))	**1c** ( )	
d	Combine lines 1a, 1b, and 1c		**1d** (9,000)

Commercial Revitalization Deductions From Rental Real Estate Activities

2a	Commercial revitalization deductions from Worksheet 2, column (a)	**2a** ( )	
b	Prior year unallowed commercial revitalization deductions from Worksheet 2, column (b)	**2b** ( )	
c	Add lines 2a and 2b		**2c** ( )

All Other Passive Activities

3a	Activities with net income (enter the amount from Worksheet 3, column (a))	**3a**	
b	Activities with net loss (enter the amount from Worksheet 3, column (b))	**3b** (15,000)	
c	Prior years' unallowed losses (enter the amount from Worksheet 3, column (c))	**3c** ( )	
d	Combine lines 3a, 3b, and 3c		**3d** (15,000)

4	Combine lines 1d, 2c, and 3d. If this line is zero or more, stop here and include this form with your return; all losses are allowed, including any prior year unallowed losses entered on line 1c, 2b, or 3c. Report the losses on the forms and schedules normally used	**4**	(24,000)

If line 4 is a loss and: • Line 1d is a loss, go to Part II.
• Line 2c is a loss (and line 1d is zero or more), skip Part II and go to Part III.
• Line 3d is a loss (and lines 1d and 2c are zero or more), skip Parts II and III and go to line 15.

Caution: If your filing status is married filing separately and you lived with your spouse at any time during the year, **do not** complete Part II or Part III. Instead, go to line 15.

Part II — Special Allowance for Rental Real Estate Activities With Active Participation

Note: Enter all numbers in Part II as positive amounts. See instructions for an example.

5	Enter the **smaller** of the loss on line 1d or the loss on line 4		**5**	9,000
6	Enter $150,000. If married filing separately, see instructions	**6** 150,000		
7	Enter modified adjusted gross income, but not less than zero. See instructions	**7** 138,000		
	Note: If line 7 is greater than or equal to line 6, skip lines 8 and 9, enter -0- on line 10. Otherwise, go to line 8.			
8	Subtract line 7 from line 6	**8** 12,000		
9	Multiply line 8 by 50% (0.50). **Do not** enter more than $25,000. If married filing separately, see instructions		**9**	6,000
10	Enter the **smaller** of line 5 or line 9		**10**	6,000

If line 2c is a loss, go to Part III. Otherwise, go to line 15.

Part III — Special Allowance for Commercial Revitalization Deductions From Rental Real Estate Activities

Note: Enter all numbers in Part III as positive amounts. See the example for Part II in the instructions.

11	Enter $25,000 reduced by the amount, if any, on line 10. If married filing separately, see instructions	**11**	
12	Enter the loss from line 4	**12**	
13	Reduce line 12 by the amount on line 10	**13**	
14	Enter the **smallest** of line 2c (treated as a positive amount), line 11, or line 13	**14**	

Part IV — Total Losses Allowed

15	Add the income, if any, on lines 1a and 3a and enter the total	**15**	
16	**Total losses allowed from all passive activities for 2020.** Add lines 10, 14, and 15. See instructions to find out how to report the losses on your tax return	**16**	6,000

For Paperwork Reduction Act Notice, see instructions.   Cat. No. 63704F   Form **8582** (2020)

Self-Study Problem 4.10a

Taxpayer	Eligible for QBI deduction (Y/N)?	QBI deduction amount
a.	No. Corporations are not eligible for the QBI deduction and Aretha's dividend income from the corporation is not considered QBI income.	$0
b.	Yes. Terri's business likely falls into the special services category that would subject her to the wage limitation; however, because Terri's taxable income is below the threshold of $163,300, she is not subject to the wage or special service limits.	See Form 8995 below.
c.	Yes. Alice's restaurant business is not subject to the special service limitation; however, her joint taxable income exceeds the $326,600 threshold. As a result, her QBI deduction is subject to the wage limitation.	See Form 8995-A on Pages E-22 and E-23

Self-Study Problem 4.10b

Form **8995**

Department of the Treasury
Internal Revenue Service

Qualified Business Income Deduction
Simplified Computation

▶ Attach to your tax return.
▶ Go to *www.irs.gov/Form8995* for instructions and the latest information.

OMB No. 1545-0123

20**20**

Attachment
Sequence No. **55**

Name(s) shown on return
Terri Jones

Your taxpayer identification number
317-65-4321

Note. *You can claim the qualified business income deduction **only** if you have qualified business income from a qualified trade or business, real estate investment trust dividends, publicly traded partnership income, or a domestic production activities deduction passed through from an agricultural or horticultural cooperative. See instructions.*
Use this form if your taxable income, before your qualified business income deduction, is at or below $163,300 ($326,600 if married filing jointly), and you aren't a patron of an agricultural or horticultural cooperative.

1	(a) Trade, business, or aggregation name	(b) Taxpayer identification number	(c) Qualified business income or (loss)
i	The Bee Hive	317-65-4321	120,000
ii			
iii			
iv			
v			

2	Total qualified business income or (loss). Combine lines 1i through 1v, column (c)	2	120,000	
3	Qualified business net (loss) carryforward from the prior year	3	( )	
4	Total qualified business income. Combine lines 2 and 3. If zero or less, enter -0-	4	120,000	
5	Qualified business income component. Multiply line 4 by 20% (0.20)			5 24,000
6	Qualified REIT dividends and publicly traded partnership (PTP) income or (loss) (see instructions)	6		
7	Qualified REIT dividends and qualified PTP (loss) carryforward from the prior year	7	( )	
8	Total qualified REIT dividends and PTP income. Combine lines 6 and 7. If zero or less, enter -0-	8		
9	REIT and PTP component. Multiply line 8 by 20% (0.20)			9
10	Qualified business income deduction before the income limitation. Add lines 5 and 9			10 24,000
11	Taxable income before qualified business income deduction	11	132,500	
12	Net capital gain (see instructions)	12		
13	Subtract line 12 from line 11. If zero or less, enter -0-	13	132,500	
14	Income limitation. Multiply line 13 by 20% (0.20)			14 26,500
15	Qualified business income deduction. Enter the lesser of line 10 or line 14. Also enter this amount on the applicable line of your return ▶			15 24,000
16	Total qualified business (loss) carryforward. Combine lines 2 and 3. If greater than zero, enter -0-			16 ( )
17	Total qualified REIT dividends and PTP (loss) carryforward. Combine lines 6 and 7. If greater than zero, enter -0-			17 ( )

For Privacy Act and Paperwork Reduction Act Notice, see instructions.   Cat. No. 37806C   Form **8995** (2020)

Self-Study Problem 4.10c

Form **8995-A**	**Qualified Business Income Deduction**	OMB No. 1545-0123
Department of the Treasury Internal Revenue Service	▶ **Attach to your tax return.** ▶ **Go to** *www.irs.gov/Form8995A* **for instructions and the latest information.**	**2019** Attachment Sequence No. **55A**

Name(s) shown on return	Your taxpayer identification number
Alice Delvecchio	565-22-4321

Part I   Trade, Business, or Aggregation Information

Complete Schedules A, B, and/or C (Form 8995-A), as applicable, before starting Part I. Attach additional worksheets when needed. See instructions.

1	(a) Trade, business, or aggregation name	(b) Check if specified service	(c) Check if aggregation	(d) Taxpayer identification number	(e) Check if patron
A	D's Pizza	☐	☐	565-22-4321	☐
B		☐	☐		☐
C		☐	☐		☐

Part II   Determine Your Adjusted Qualified Business Income

			A	B	C
2	Qualified business income from the trade, business, or aggregation. See instructions	2	100,000		
3	Multiply line 2 by 20% (0.20). If your taxable income is $160,700 or less ($160,725 if married filing separately; $321,400 if married filing jointly), skip lines 4 through 12 and enter the amount from line 3 on line 13	3	20,000	see note below	
4	Allocable share of W-2 wages from the trade, business, or aggregation	4	36,000		
5	Multiply line 4 by 50% (0.50)	5	18,000		
6	Multiply line 4 by 25% (0.25)	6	9,000		
7	Allocable share of the unadjusted basis immediately after acquisition (UBIA) of all qualified property	7	67,000		
8	Multiply line 7 by 2.5% (0.025)	8	1,675		
9	Add lines 6 and 8	9	10,675		
10	Enter the greater of line 5 or line 9	10	18,000		
11	W-2 wage and qualified property limitation. Enter the smaller of line 3 or line 10	11	18,000		
12	Phased-in reduction. Enter the amount from line 26, if any. See instructions	12	19,252		
13	Qualified business income deduction before patron reduction. Enter the greater of line 11 or line 12	13	19,252		
14	Patron reduction. Enter the amount from Schedule D (Form 8995-A), line 6, if any. See instructions	14			
15	Qualified business income component. Subtract line 14 from line 13	15	19,252		
16	Total qualified business income component. Add all amounts reported on line 15 . . . . ▶	16	19,252		

For Privacy Act and Paperwork Reduction Act Notice, see separate instructions.   Cat. No. 71661B   Form **8995-A** (2019)

*Please go to www.irs.gov to download the latest Form 8995-A. The 2020 version of Form 8995-A was not available as we went to print. If using the prior year form included in the textbook, be sure and use updated income limits on Line 3 and Line 21 ($326,600 for married filing jointly and $163,300 for all other).

Part III   Phased-in Reduction*

Complete Part III only if your taxable income is more than $160,700 but not $210,700 ($160,725 and $210,725 if married filing separately; $321,400 and $421,400 if married filing jointly) and line 10 is less than line 3. Otherwise, skip Part III.

			A	B	C
17	Enter the amounts from line 3	**17**	20,000		
18	Enter the amounts from line 10	**18**	18,000		
19	Subtract line 18 from line 17	**19**	2,000		
20	Taxable income before qualified business income deduction	**20** 364,000			
21	Threshold. Enter $160,700 ($160,725 if married filing separately; $321,400 if married filing jointly)	**21** see note below 326,600			
22	Subtract line 21 from line 20	**22** 37,400			
23	Phase-in range. Enter $50,000 ($100,000 if married filing jointly)	**23** 100,000			
24	Phase-in percentage. Divide line 22 by line 23	**24** 37.4%			
25	Total phase-in reduction. Multiply line 19 by line 24	**25**	748		
26	Qualified business income after phase-in reduction. Subtract line 25 from line 17. Enter this amount here and on line 12, for the corresponding trade or business	**26**	19,252		

Part IV   Determine Your Qualified Business Income Deduction

27	Total qualified business income component from all qualified trades, businesses, or aggregations. Enter the amount from line 16	**27**	19,252	
28	Qualified REIT dividends and publicly traded partnership (PTP) income or (loss). See instructions	**28**		
29	Qualified REIT dividends and PTP (loss) carryforward from prior years	**29** (	)	
30	Total qualified REIT dividends and PTP income. Combine lines 28 and 29. If less than zero, enter -0-	**30**		
31	REIT and PTP component. Multiply line 30 by 20% (0.20)	**31**		
32	Qualified business income deduction before the income limitation. Add lines 27 and 31 ▶	**32**	19,252	
33	Taxable income before qualified business income deduction	**33**	364,000	
34	Net capital gain. See instructions	**34**	12,000	
35	Subtract line 34 from line 33. If zero or less, enter -0-	**35**	352,000	
36	Income limitation. Multiply line 35 by 20% (0.20)	**36**	70,400	
37	Qualified business income deduction before the domestic production activities deduction (DPAD) under section 199A(g). Enter the smaller of line 32 or line 36 ▶	**37**	19,252	
38	DPAD under section 199A(g) allocated from an agricultural or horticultural cooperative. Don't enter more than line 33 minus line 37	**38**		
39	Total qualified business income deduction. Add lines 37 and 38 ▶	**39**	19,252	
40	Total qualified REIT dividends and PTP (loss) carryforward. Combine lines 28 and 29. If zero or greater, enter -0-	**40** (	)	

Form **8995-A** (2019)

*Please go to www.irs.gov to download the latest Form 8995-A. The 2020 version of Form 8995-A was not available as we went to print. If using the prior year form included in the textbook, be sure and use updated income limits on Line 3 and Line 21 ($326,600 for married filing jointly and $163,300 for all other).

CHAPTER 5   DEDUCTIONS FOR AND FROM AGI

Self-Study Problem 5.1

a.   1. $7,100
2. $0 A plan with no deductible does not qualify.
3. $2,000
4. $0 Individuals are not allowed to make contributions to an HSA after age 65 and qualify for Medicare.

b.   HSA Deduction is $2,750 and taxable distribution is $0. See Form 8889 on Page E-24.

Self-Study Problem 5.1b

Form **8889** Department of the Treasury Internal Revenue Service	**Health Savings Accounts (HSAs)** ▶ Attach to Form 1040, 1040-SR, or 1040-NR. ▶ Go to *www.irs.gov/Form8889* for instructions and the latest information.	OMB No. 1545-0074 20**20** Attachment Sequence No. **52**

Name(s) shown on Form 1040, 1040-SR, or 1040-NR Alex Morton	Social security number of HSA beneficiary. If both spouses have HSAs, see instructions ▶	213-21-3121

Before you begin: Complete Form 8853, Archer MSAs and Long-Term Care Insurance Contracts, if required.

Part I   HSA Contributions and Deduction. See the instructions before completing this part. If you are filing jointly and both you and your spouse each have separate HSAs, complete a separate Part I for each spouse.

1	Check the box to indicate your coverage under a high-deductible health plan (HDHP) during 2020. See instructions . . . . ▶		☑ Self-only ☐ Family
2	HSA contributions you made for 2020 (or those made on your behalf), including those made from January 1, 2021, through April 15, 2021, that were for 2020. **Do not** include employer contributions, contributions through a cafeteria plan, or rollovers. See instructions	**2**	2,750
3	If you were under age 55 at the end of 2020 and, on the first day of **every** month during 2020, you were, or were considered, an eligible individual with the **same** coverage, enter $3,550 ($7,100 for family coverage). **All others,** see the instructions for the amount to enter	**3**	3,550
4	Enter the amount you and your employer contributed to your Archer MSAs for 2020 from Form 8853, lines 1 and 2. If you or your spouse had family coverage under an HDHP at any time during 2020, also include any amount contributed to your spouse's Archer MSAs	**4**	0
5	Subtract line 4 from line 3. If zero or less, enter -0-	**5**	3,550
6	Enter the amount from line 5. But if you and your spouse each have separate HSAs and had family coverage under an HDHP at any time during 2020, see the instructions for the amount to enter . .	**6**	3,550
7	If you were age 55 or older at the end of 2020, married, and you or your spouse had family coverage under an HDHP at any time during 2020, enter your additional contribution amount. See instructions	**7**	
8	Add lines 6 and 7	**8**	3,550
9	Employer contributions made to your HSAs for 2020	**9**	300	
10	Qualified HSA funding distributions	**10**		
11	Add lines 9 and 10	**11**	300
12	Subtract line 11 from line 8. If zero or less, enter -0-	**12**	3,250
13	**HSA deduction.** Enter the **smaller** of line 2 or line 12 here and on Schedule 1 (Form 1040), Part II, line 12	**13**	2,750
	Caution: If line 2 is more than line 13, you may have to pay an additional tax. See instructions.		

Part II   HSA Distributions. If you are filing jointly and both you and your spouse each have separate HSAs, complete a separate Part II for each spouse.

14a	Total distributions you received in 2020 from all HSAs (see instructions)	**14a**	1,783
b	Distributions included on line 14a that you rolled over to another HSA. Also include any excess contributions (and the earnings on those excess contributions) included on line 14a that were withdrawn by the due date of your return. See instructions	**14b**	
c	Subtract line 14b from line 14a	**14c**	1,783
15	Qualified medical expenses paid using HSA distributions (see instructions)	**15**	2,500
16	**Taxable HSA distributions.** Subtract line 15 from line 14c. If zero or less, enter -0-. Also, include this amount in the total on Schedule 1 (Form 1040), Part I, line 8, and enter "HSA" and the amount on the dotted line	**16**	0
17a	If any of the distributions included on line 16 meet any of the **Exceptions to the Additional 20% Tax** (see instructions), check here . . . . ▶ ☐		
b	**Additional 20% tax** (see instructions). Enter 20% (0.20) of the distributions included on line 16 that are subject to the additional 20% tax. Also, include this amount in the total on Schedule 2 (Form 1040), Part II, line 8; check box c and enter "HSA" and the amount on the line next to the box	**17b**	

Part III   Income and Additional Tax for Failure To Maintain HDHP Coverage. See the instructions before completing this part. If you are filing jointly and both you and your spouse each have separate HSAs, complete a separate Part III for each spouse.

18	Last-month rule	**18**	
19	Qualified HSA funding distribution	**19**	
20	**Total income.** Add lines 18 and 19. Include this amount on Schedule 1 (Form 1040), Part I, line 8, and enter "HSA" and the amount on the dotted line	**20**	
21	**Additional tax.** Multiply line 20 by 10% (0.10). Include this amount in the total on Schedule 2 (Form 1040), Part II, line 8; check box c and enter "HDHP" and the amount on the line next to the box . .	**21**	

For Paperwork Reduction Act Notice, see your tax return instructions.   Cat. No. 37621P   Form **8889** (2020)

Self-Study Problem 5.2

$20,810 = $15,000 + $2,000 + $3,000 + $810 (limited by age)

Self-Study Problem 5.3

a. $4,800 = $6,000 \times \dfrac{\$75,000 - \$67,000}{\$10,000}$

b. $5,400 = $6,000 \times \dfrac{\$139,000 - \$125,500}{\$15,000}$

Self-Study Problem 5.4

a. $10,000, the lesser of (0.25/1.25) × $50,000 or $57,000
b. i. $10,000, lesser of 25% × $40,000 or $19,500 (annual dollar limit effective for 2020)
   ii. $19,500 (annual dollar limit effective for 2020)

Self-Study Problem 5.5

a. No. Professor Hill is not a K-12 educator.
b. Yes. Jackie worked for two employers, both of which paid her more than $200; her expenses exceeded 10 percent of the gross income from performing artist work ($1,100 > $8,000 × 10%); and her AGI was below $16,000.
c. Yes.

Self-Study Problems 5.6 through 5.10

See Schedule A and Form 4684 on Pages E-26 and E-27.
Line 1 of Schedule A is computed as follows:

Medical insurance	$ 425
Prescription medicines and drugs	364
Hospital bills	2,424
Doctor bills	725
Eyeglasses for Frank's dependent mother	75
Doctor bills for Betty's sister, who is claimed as a dependent by Frank and Betty	220
Medical transportation in personal vehicle (700 miles * $0.17)	119
Total	4,352
Less reimbursement	(1,420)
Medical and dental expenses	$2,932

Line 5 of Schedule A—The $225 refund is included on Line 1 of Schedule 1 of Form 1040 as gross income.
Line 11 of Schedule A—$11,075 is subject to the 60 percent limitation for cash donations and is deductible ($21,000 × 60% = $12,600). The clothing is subject to the 50 percent limit. Since $21,000 × 50% = $10,500, Eric has utilized all of his permitted deduction with his $11,075 deduction; thus the $150 must be carried over to 2020. The Mexican Red Cross is not a qualified organization and there is no deduction for sports tickets.
Line 16 of Schedule A—Only the gambling losses are deductible subject to the limit of gambling winnings.

Continued on Page E-28

Self-Study Problems 5.6, 5.7, 5.8, 5.9, and 5.10

SCHEDULE A
(Form 1040)

Department of the Treasury
Internal Revenue Service (99)

Itemized Deductions

▶ Go to *www.irs.gov/ScheduleA* for instructions and the latest information.
▶ Attach to Form 1040 or 1040-SR.

Caution: If you are claiming a net qualified disaster loss on Form 4684, see the instructions for line 16.

OMB No. 1545-0074

2020

Attachment
Sequence No. **07**

Name(s) shown on Form 1040 or 1040-SR

Your social security number

Medical and Dental Expenses	**Caution:** Do not include expenses reimbursed or paid by others.			
	1 Medical and dental expenses (see instructions)	**1** 2,932		
	2 Enter amount from Form 1040 or 1040-SR, line 11	**2** 25,400		
	3 Multiply line 2 by 7.5% (0.075)	**3** 1,905		
	4 Subtract line 3 from line 1. If line 3 is more than line 1, enter -0-		**4**	1,027
Taxes You Paid	**5** State and local taxes.			
	a State and local income taxes or general sales taxes. You may include either income taxes or general sales taxes on line 5a, but not both. If you elect to include general sales taxes instead of income taxes, check this box ▶ ☐	**5a** 1,050		
	b State and local real estate taxes (see instructions)	**5b** 825		
	c State and local personal property taxes	**5c** 85		
	d Add lines 5a through 5c	**5d** 1,960		
	e Enter the smaller of line 5d or $10,000 ($5,000 if married filing separately)	**5e** 1,960		
	6 Other taxes. List type and amount ▶	**6**		
	7 Add lines 5e and 6		**7**	1,960
Interest You Paid **Caution:** Your mortgage interest deduction may be limited (see instructions).	**8** Home mortgage interest and points. If you didn't use all of your home mortgage loan(s) to buy, build, or improve your home, see instructions and check this box ▶ ☐			
	a Home mortgage interest and points reported to you on Form 1098. See instructions if limited	**8a** 9,250		
	b Home mortgage interest not reported to you on Form 1098. See instructions if limited. If paid to the person from whom you bought the home, see instructions and show that person's name, identifying no., and address ▶	**8b**		
	c Points not reported to you on Form 1098. See instructions for special rules	**8c**		
	d Mortgage insurance premiums (see instructions)	**8d**		
	e Add lines 8a through 8d	**8e** 9,250		
	9 Investment interest. Attach Form 4952 if required. See instructions	**9** 1,000		
	10 Add lines 8e and 9		**10**	10,250
Gifts to Charity **Caution:** If you made a gift and got a benefit for it, see instructions.	**11** Gifts by cash or check. If you made any gift of $250 or more, see instructions	**11** 11,075		
	12 Other than by cash or check. If you made any gift of $250 or more, see instructions. You **must** attach Form 8283 if over $500.	**12** 0		
	13 Carryover from prior year	**13**		
	14 Add lines 11 through 13		**14**	11,075
Casualty and Theft Losses	**15** Casualty and theft loss(es) from a federally declared disaster (other than net qualified disaster losses). Attach Form 4684 and enter the amount from line 18 of that form. See instructions		**15**	5,400
Other Itemized Deductions	**16** Other—from list in instructions. List type and amount ▶ Gambling losses (limited to gambling winnings)		**16**	1,400
Total Itemized Deductions	**17** Add the amounts in the far right column for lines 4 through 16. Also, enter this amount on Form 1040 or 1040-SR, line 12		**17**	
	18 If you elect to itemize deductions even though they are less than your standard deduction, check this box ▶ ☐			

For Paperwork Reduction Act Notice, see the Instructions for Forms 1040 and 1040-SR.   Cat. No. 17145C   Schedule A (Form 1040) 2020

DRAFT AS OF JULY 13, 2020 DO NOT FILE

Self-Study Problem 5.10

Form **4684**	**Casualties and Thefts**	OMB No. 1545-0177
Department of the Treasury Internal Revenue Service	▶ Go to *www.irs.gov/Form4684* for instructions and the latest information. ▶ Attach to your tax return. ▶ Use a separate Form 4684 for each casualty or theft.	**20****20** Attachment Sequence No. **26**

Name(s) shown on tax return	Identifying number
Robert	

SECTION A—Personal Use Property (Use this section to report casualties and thefts of property **not** used in a trade or business or for income-producing purposes. You must use a separate Form 4684 (through line 12) for each casualty or theft event involving personal use property. **If reporting a qualified disaster loss, see the instructions for special rules that apply before completing this section.**)

If the casualty or theft loss is attributable to a federally declared disaster, check here ☑ and enter the DR-_____ or EM- 5566 _____ declaration number assigned by FEMA. (See instructions.)

1. Description of properties (show type, location (city, state, and ZIP code), and date acquired for each property). Use a separate line for each property lost or damaged from the same casualty or theft. If you checked the box and entered the FEMA disaster declaration number above, enter the ZIP code for the property most affected on the line for Property **A**.

	Type of Property	City and State	ZIP Code	Date Acquired
Property **A**	Automobile	Jupiter, FL	33477	July 2017
Property **B**				
Property **C**				
Property **D**				

			Properties			
			A	**B**	**C**	**D**
2	Cost or other basis of each property	2	18,500			
3	Insurance or other reimbursement (whether or not you filed a claim) (see instructions) **Note:** If line 2 is **more** than line 3, skip line 4.	3	5,000			
4	Gain from casualty or theft. If line 3 is **more** than line 2, enter the difference here and skip lines 5 through 9 for that column. See instructions if line 3 includes insurance or other reimbursement you did not claim, or you received payment for your loss in a later tax year	4				
5	Fair market value **before** casualty or theft	5	14,000			
6	Fair market value **after** casualty or theft	6	0			
7	Subtract line 6 from line 5	7	14,000			
8	Enter the **smaller** of line 2 or line 7	8	14,000			
9	Subtract line 3 from line 8. If zero or less, enter -0-	9	9,000			

10	Casualty or theft loss. Add the amounts on line 9 in columns A through D	10	9,000
11	Enter $100 ($500 if qualified disaster loss rules apply; see instructions)	11	100
12	Subtract line 11 from line 10. If zero or less, enter -0-	12	8,900

Caution: Use only one Form 4684 for lines 13 through 18.

13	Add the amounts on line 4 of all Forms 4684	13	
14	Add the amounts on line 12 of all Forms 4684. If you have losses not attributable to a federally declared disaster, see the instructions	14	8,900

Caution: See instructions before completing line 15.

15. • If line 13 is **more** than line 14, enter the difference here and on Schedule D. **Do not** complete the rest of this section.

• If line 13 is **equal** to line 14, enter -0- here. **Do not** complete the rest of this section.

• If line 13 is **less** than line 14, and you have no qualified disaster losses subject to the $500 reduction on line 11 on any Form(s) 4684, enter -0- here and go to line 16. If you have qualified disaster losses subject to the $500 reduction, subtract line 13 from line 14 and enter the smaller of this difference or the amount on line 12 of the Form(s) 4684 reporting those losses. Enter that result here and on Schedule A (Form 1040), line 16, or Form 1040-NR, Schedule A, line 7. If you claim the standard deduction, also include on Schedule A (Form 1040), line 16, the amount of your standard deduction (see the Instructions for Forms 1040 and 1040-SR). Do not complete the rest of this section if all of your casualty or theft losses are subject to the $500 reduction.

15		0

16	Add lines 13 and 15. Subtract the result from line 14	16	8,900
17	Enter 10% of your adjusted gross income from Form 1040, 1040-SR, or 1040-NR, line 11. Estates and trusts, see instructions	17	3,500
18	Subtract line 17 from line 16. If zero or less, enter -0-. Also, enter the result on Schedule A (Form 1040), line 15, or Form 1040-NR, Schedule A, line 6. Estates and trusts, enter the result on the "Other deductions" line of your tax return	18	5,400

For Paperwork Reduction Act Notice, see instructions.   Cat. No. 12997O   Form **4684** (2020)

Self-Study Problems 5.6 through 5.10

See Schedule A of Page E-26 for reporting of interest under Problem 5.8 Part a.

	Total	Part a.	Part b.	Part c.
Interest on her home mortgage	$9,250	$ 9,250	$ 9,250	$ 9,250
Service charges on her checking account	48	0	0	0
Credit card interest	168	0	0	0
Auto loan interest	675	0	0	0
Interest from a home equity line of credit (HELOC)	2,300	0	2,300	0
Interest from a loan used to purchase stock	1,600	1,000	1,000	1,000
Credit investigation fee for loan	75	0	0	0
Deductible amount		$10,250	$12,550	$10,250

Dorothie's mortgage interest is from qualified mortgage debt (secured by residence, less than $1,000,000) and is deductible in parts a–c. Because Dorothie's mortgage originated prior to December 16, 2017, the $1 million threshold continues to apply in 2020. The home equity interest is deductible in part a under the pre-TCJA tax law. It is not deductible in part a in 2020 as generally home equity interest is not deductible under TCJA. In part b, the home equity debt is treated as acquisition debt which continues to qualify as deductible post-TCJA (subject to the $1 million limitation for grandfathered debt). The investment interest remains deductible after TCJA but also remains limited to net investment income ($1,000 in this example). The other forms of interest are nondeductible personal interest.

CHAPTER 6 ACCOUNTING PERIODS AND OTHER TAXES

Self-Study Problem 6.1

Taxpayer	Calendar year-end	Fiscal year-end	Fiscal year-end but some restrictions
1. Individual with no separate books and records	X		
2. Partnership for which all the partners are calendar year-end individuals	X		X
3. A corporation that keeps its book and records on a fiscal year ending June 30		X	
4. An S corporation for which all shareholders are calendar year-end individuals	X		X

Self-Study Problem 6.2A

Business income	$ 63,000
Less: business expenses	(42,000)
Operating income	21,000
Add: rent received	9,000
Add: prepaid interest received	12,000
Less: rent expense for one month ($7,200/6)	(1,200)
Net income	$ 40,800

Self-Study Problem 6.2B

1. Yes
2. Yes
3. No, annual receipts exceed $26 million
4. Yes, assuming this is a personal service corporation.

Self-Study Problem 6.3

1. 56%; 40% owned directly and 16% (80% × 20%) through X Corporation.
2. 40%; 20% owned directly plus 20% as Gene's brother.
3. 40%; 20% owned directly plus 20% as Frank's brother.
4. $0; since they are related parties, the loss would be disallowed.

Self-Study Problem 6.4

a. See Form 8615 on Page E-30.
b. See Form 8814 on Page E-31.

Self-Study Problem 6.5

See Form 6251 on Page E-32.

Self-Study Problem 6.6

See Schedule SE on Pages E-33 and E-34 and Form 7202 on Page E-35.

Self-Study Problem 6.7

See Schedule H on Pages E-36 and E-37.

Self-Study Problem 6.8

See Form 8960 on Page E-38 and Form 8959 on Page E-39.

Self-Study Problem 6.4

Form **8615**	Tax for Certain Children Who Have Unearned Income	OMB No. 1545-0074

Department of the Treasury
Internal Revenue Service (99)

▶ **Attach only to the child's Form 1040 or Form 1040-NR.**
▶ **Go to** *www.irs.gov/Form8615* **for instructions and the latest information.**

2020

Attachment
Sequence No. **33**

Child's name shown on return	Child's social security number
Robert	

Before you begin: If the child, the parent, or any of the parent's other children for whom Form 8615 must be filed must use the Schedule D Tax Worksheet or has income from farming or fishing, see Pub. 929, Tax Rules for Children and Dependents. It explains how to figure the child's tax using the **Schedule D Tax Worksheet** or **Schedule J** (Form 1040).

A Parent's name (first, initial, and last). **Caution:** See instructions before completing.	**B** Parent's social security number
Bill and Janet	

C Parent's filing status (check one):

☐ Single   ☑ Married filing jointly   ☐ Married filing separately   ☐ Head of household   ☐ Qualifying widow(er)

Part I   Child's Net Unearned Income

1	Enter the child's unearned income. See Instructions	1	3,000
2	If the child **did not** itemize deductions on **Schedule A** (Form 1040 or Form 1040-NR), enter $2,200. Otherwise, see instructions	2	2,200
3	Subtract line 2 from line 1. If zero or less, **stop;** do not complete the rest of this form but **do** attach it to the child's return	3	800
4	Enter the child's **taxable income** from Form 1040 or 1040-NR, line 15. If the child files Form 2555, see the instructions	4	1,900 (a)
5	Enter the **smaller** of line 3 or line 4. If zero, **stop;** do not complete the rest of this form but **do** attach it to the child's return	5	800

Part II   Tentative Tax Based on the Tax Rate of the Parent

6	Enter the parent's **taxable income** from Form 1040 or 1040-NR, line 15. If zero or less, enter -0-. If the parent files Form 2555, see the instructions	6	46,000 (b)
7	Enter the total, if any, from Forms 8615, line 5, of **all other** children of the parent named above. **Do not** include the amount from line 5 above	7	
8	Add lines 5, 6, and 7. See instructions	8	46,800
9	Enter the tax on the amount on line 8 based on the **parent's** filing status above. See instructions. If the Qualified Dividends and Capital Gain Tax Worksheet, Schedule D Tax Worksheet, or Schedule J (Form 1040) is used to figure the tax, check here ▶ ☐	9	5,224 (c)
10	Enter the parent's tax from Form 1040 or 1040-NR, line 16, minus any alternative minimum tax. **Do not** include any tax from **Form 4972, 8814,** or **8885** or any tax from recapture of an education credit. If the parent files Form 2555, see the instructions. If the Qualified Dividends and Capital Gain Tax Worksheet, Schedule D Tax Worksheet, or Schedule J (Form 1040) was used to figure the tax, check here ▶ ☐	10	5,128 (c)
11	Subtract line 10 from line 9 and enter the result. If line 7 is blank, also enter this amount on line 13 and go to Part III	11	96
12a	Add lines 5 and 7 **12a**		
b	Divide line 5 by line 12a. Enter the result as a decimal (rounded to at least three places)	12b	× .
13	Multiply line 11 by line 12b	13	96

Part III   Child's Tax—If lines 4 and 5 above are the same, enter -0- on line 15 and go to line 16.

14	Subtract line 5 from line 4 **14** 1,100		
15	Enter the tax on the amount on line 14 based on the **child's** filing status. See instructions. If the Qualified Dividends and Capital Gain Tax Worksheet, Schedule D Tax Worksheet, or Schedule J (Form 1040) is used to figure the tax, check here ▶ ☐	15	111 (c)
16	Add lines 13 and 15	16	207
17	Enter the tax on the amount on line 4 based on the **child's** filing status. See instructions. If the Qualified Dividends and Capital Gain Tax Worksheet, Schedule D Tax Worksheet, or Schedule J (Form 1040) is used to figure the tax, check here ▶ ☐	17	191 (c)
18	Enter the **larger** of line 16 or line 17 here and on the **child's** Form 1040 or 1040-NR, line 16. If the child files Form 2555, see the instructions	18	207

For Paperwork Reduction Act Notice, see your tax return instructions.   Cat. No. 64113U   Form **8615** (2020)

(a) $3,000 less $1,100, the standard deduction for someone claimed as a dependent.
(b) $70,800 less $24,800 standard deduction.
(c) Tax is from tax tables for income less than $100,000 in Appendix A.

Self-Study Problem 6.4

Form **8814**	**Parents' Election To Report Child's Interest and Dividends**	OMB No. 1545-0074
Department of the Treasury Internal Revenue Service (99)	▶ Go to *www.irs.gov/Form8814* for the latest information. ▶ Attach to parents' Form 1040, 1040-SR, or 1040-NR.	**2020** Attachment Sequence No. **40**

Name(s) shown on your return
Bill and Janet

Your social security number

Caution: The federal income tax on your child's income, including qualified dividends and capital gain distributions, may be less if you file a separate tax return for the child instead of making this election. This is because you cannot take certain tax benefits that your child could take on his or her own return. For details, see *Tax benefits you cannot take* in the instructions.

A Child's name (first, initial, and last)
Robert

B Child's social security number

C If more than one Form 8814 is attached, check here . . . . ▶ ☐

Part I   Child's Interest and Dividends To Report on Your Return

1a	Enter your child's **taxable** interest. If this amount is different from the amounts shown on the child's Forms 1099-INT and 1099-OID, see the instructions	**1a**	3,000
b	Enter your child's **tax-exempt** interest. **Do not** include this amount on line 1a **1b**		
2a	Enter your child's ordinary dividends, including any Alaska Permanent Fund dividends. If your child received any ordinary dividends as a nominee, see the instructions	**2a**	0
b	Enter your child's qualified dividends included on line 2a. See the instructions **2b**		
3	Enter your child's capital gain distributions. If your child received any capital gain distributions as a nominee, see the instructions	**3**	0
4	Add lines 1a, 2a, and 3. If the total is $2,200 or less, skip lines 5 through 12 and go to line 13. If the total is $11,000 or more, **do not** file this form. Your child **must** file his or her own return to report the income	**4**	3,000
5	Base amount. Enter 2,200	**5**	2,200
6	Subtract line 5 from line 4	**6**	800

If both lines 2b and 3 are zero or blank, skip lines 7 through 10, enter -0- on line 11, and go to line 12. Otherwise, go to line 7.

7	Divide line 2b by line 4. Enter the result as a decimal (rounded to at least three places)	**7**	.
8	Divide line 3 by line 4. Enter the result as a decimal (rounded to at least three places)	**8**	.
9	Multiply line 6 by line 7. Enter the result here. See the instructions for where to report this amount on your return	**9**	
10	Multiply line 6 by line 8. Enter the result here. See the instructions for where to report this amount on your return	**10**	
11	Add lines 9 and 10	**11**	0
12	Subtract line 11 from line 6. Include this amount in the total on Schedule 1 (Form 1040), line 8. In the space next to that line, enter "Form 8814" and show the amount. If you checked the box on line C above, see the instructions. Go to line 13 below	**12**	800

Part II   Tax on the First $2,200 of Child's Interest and Dividends

13	Amount not taxed. Enter 1,100	**13**	1,100
14	Subtract line 13 from line 4. If the result is zero or less, enter -0-	**14**	1,900
15	**Tax.** Is the amount on line 14 less than $1,100? ☑ **No.** Enter $110 here and see the **Note** below. ☐ **Yes.** Multiply line 14 by 10% (0.10). Enter the result here and see the **Note** below. }	**15**	110

Note: If you checked the box on line C above, see the instructions. Otherwise, include the amount from line 15 in the tax you enter on Form 1040, 1040-SR, or 1040-NR, line 16. Be sure to check box 1 on Form 1040, 1040-SR, or 1040-NR, line 16.

For Paperwork Reduction Act Notice, see your tax return instructions.   Cat. No. 10750J   Form **8814** (2020)

Self-Study Problem 6.5

Form **6251**	**Alternative Minimum Tax—Individuals**	OMB No. 1545-0074
Department of the Treasury Internal Revenue Service (99)	▶ Go to *www.irs.gov/Form6251* for instructions and the latest information. ▶ Attach to Form 1040, 1040-SR, or 1040-NR.	**20**20 Attachment Sequence No. **32**

Name(s) shown on Form 1040, 1040-SR, or 1040-NR
Harold Brown

Your social security number

Part I — Alternative Minimum Taxable Income (See instructions for how to complete each line.)

1	Enter the amount from Form 1040 or 1040-SR, line 15, if more than zero. If Form 1040 or 1040-SR, line 15, is zero, subtract lines 12 and 13 of Form 1040 or 1040-SR from line 11 of Form 1040 or 1040-SR and enter the result here. (If less than zero, enter as a negative amount.)	**1**	556,000
2a	If filing Schedule A (Form 1040), enter the taxes from Schedule A, line 7; otherwise, enter the amount from Form 1040 or 1040-SR, line 12	**2a**	10,000
b	Tax refund from Schedule 1 (Form 1040), line 1 or line 8	**2b**	( )
c	Investment interest expense (difference between regular tax and AMT)	**2c**	
d	Depletion (difference between regular tax and AMT)	**2d**	
e	Net operating loss deduction from Schedule 1 (Form 1040), line 8. Enter as a positive amount	**2e**	
f	Alternative tax net operating loss deduction	**2f**	( )
g	Interest from specified private activity bonds exempt from the regular tax	**2g**	100,000
h	Qualified small business stock, see instructions	**2h**	
i	Exercise of incentive stock options (excess of AMT income over regular tax income)	**2i**	
j	Estates and trusts (amount from Schedule K-1 (Form 1041), box 12, code A)	**2j**	
k	Disposition of property (difference between AMT and regular tax gain or loss)	**2k**	
l	Depreciation on assets placed in service after 1986 (difference between regular tax and AMT)	**2l**	
m	Passive activities (difference between AMT and regular tax income or loss)	**2m**	
n	Loss limitations (difference between AMT and regular tax income or loss)	**2n**	
o	Circulation costs (difference between regular tax and AMT)	**2o**	
p	Long-term contracts (difference between AMT and regular tax income)	**2p**	
q	Mining costs (difference between regular tax and AMT)	**2q**	
r	Research and experimental costs (difference between regular tax and AMT)	**2r**	
s	Income from certain installment sales before January 1, 1987	**2s**	( )
t	Intangible drilling costs preference	**2t**	
3	Other adjustments, including income-based related adjustments	**3**	
4	**Alternative minimum taxable income.** Combine lines 1 through 3. (If married filing separately and line 4 is more than $745,200, see instructions.)	**4**	666,000

Part II — Alternative Minimum Tax (AMT)

5	Exemption.		

IF your filing status is . . .	AND line 4 is not over . . .	THEN enter on line 5 . . .
Single or head of household	$ 518,400	$ 72,900
Married filing jointly or qualifying widow(er)	1,036,800	113,400
Married filing separately	518,400	56,700

If line 4 is **over** the amount shown above for your filing status, see instructions.

		5	36,000 (a)
6	Subtract line 5 from line 4. If more than zero, go to line 7. If zero or less, enter -0- here and on lines 7, 9, and 11, and go to line 10.	**6**	630,000
7	• If you are filing Form 2555, see instructions for the amount to enter. • If you reported capital gain distributions directly on Form 1040 or 1040-SR, line 7; you reported qualified dividends on Form 1040 or 1040-SR, line 3a; **or** you had a gain on both lines 15 and 16 of Schedule D (Form 1040) (as refigured for the AMT, if necessary), complete Part III on the back and enter the amount from line 40 here. • **All others:** If line 6 is $197,900 or less ($98,950 or less if married filing separately), multiply line 6 by 26% (0.26). Otherwise, multiply line 6 by 28% (0.28) and subtract $3,958 ($1,979 if married filing separately) from the result.	**7**	172,442
8	Alternative minimum tax foreign tax credit (see instructions)	**8**	
9	Tentative minimum tax. Subtract line 8 from line 7	**9**	172,442
10	Add Form 1040 or 1040-SR, line 16 (minus any tax from Form 4972), and Schedule 2 (Form 1040), line 2. Subtract from the result any foreign tax credit from Schedule 3 (Form 1040), line 1. If you used Schedule J to figure your tax on Form 1040 or 1040-SR, line 16, refigure that tax without using Schedule J before completing this line (see instructions)	**10**	170,147
11	**AMT.** Subtract line 10 from line 9. If zero or less, enter -0-. Enter here and on Schedule 2 (Form 1040), line 1	**11**	2,295

For Paperwork Reduction Act Notice, see your tax return instructions.   Cat. No. 13600G   Form **6251** (2020)

(a) $36,000 = $72,900 − [($666,000 − $518,400) × 25%]

Self-Study Problem 6.6

SCHEDULE SE	Self-Employment Tax	OMB No. 1545-0074
(Form 1040)	▶ Go to *www.irs.gov/ScheduleSE* for instructions and the latest information.	**2020**
Department of the Treasury Internal Revenue Service (99)	▶ Attach to Form 1040, 1040-SR, or 1040-NR.	Attachment Sequence No. **17**

Name of person with self-employment income (as shown on Form 1040, 1040-SR, or 1040-NR)	Social security number of person with **self-employment** income ▶
Joanne Plummer	

Part I — Self-Employment Tax

Note: If your only income subject to self-employment tax is **church employee income,** see instructions for how to report your income and the definition of church employee income.

A If you are a minister, member of a religious order, or Christian Science practitioner **and** you filed Form 4361, but you had $400 or more of **other** net earnings from self-employment, check here and continue with Part I . . . . ▶ ☐

Skip lines 1a and 1b if you use the farm optional method in Part II. See instructions.

1a	Net farm profit or (loss) from Schedule F, line 34, and farm partnerships, Schedule K-1 (Form 1065), box 14, code A . . .	**1a**	
b	If you received social security retirement or disability benefits, enter the amount of Conservation Reserve Program payments included on Schedule F, line 4b, or listed on Schedule K-1 (Form 1065), box 20, code AH	**1b**	( )

Skip line 2 if you use the nonfarm optional method in Part II. See instructions.

2	Net profit or (loss) from Schedule C, line 31; and Schedule K-1 (Form 1065), box 14, code A (other than farming). See instructions for other income to report or if you are a minister or member of a religious order	**2**	36,600
3	Combine lines 1a, 1b, and 2	**3**	36,600
4a	If line 3 is more than zero, multiply line 3 by 92.35% (0.9235). Otherwise, enter amount from line 3 .	**4a**	33,800
	Note: If line 4a is less than $400 due to Conservation Reserve Program payments on line 1b, see instructions.		
b	If you elect one or both of the optional methods, enter the total of lines 15 and 17 here	**4b**	
c	Combine lines 4a and 4b. If less than $400, **stop;** you don't owe self-employment tax. **Exception:** If less than $400 and you had **church employee income,** enter -0- and continue . . . . ▶	**4c**	33,800
5a	Enter your **church employee income** from Form W-2. See instructions for definition of church employee income **5a**	**5b**	
b	Multiply line 5a by 92.35% (0.9235). If less than $100, enter -0-	**5b**	
6	Add lines 4c and 5b	**6**	33,800
7	Maximum amount of combined wages and self-employment earnings subject to social security tax or the 6.2% portion of the 7.65% railroad retirement (tier 1) tax for 2020	**7**	137,700
8a	Total social security wages and tips (total of boxes 3 and 7 on Form(s) W-2) and railroad retirement (tier 1) compensation. If $137,700 or more, skip lines 8b through 10, and go to line 11 . . . . **8a**	4,400	
b	Unreported tips subject to social security tax from Form 4137, line 10 . . . **8b**		
c	Wages subject to social security tax from Form 8919, line 10 . . . . . . **8c**		
d	Add lines 8a, 8b, and 8c	**8d**	4,400
9	Subtract line 8d from line 7. If zero or less, enter -0- here and on line 10 and go to line 11 . . . ▶	**9**	133,300
10	Multiply the **smaller** of line 6 or line 9 by 12.4% (0.124)	**10**	4,191
11	Multiply line 6 by 2.9% (0.029)	**11**	980
12	**Self-employment tax.** Add lines 10 and 11. Enter here and on **Schedule 2 (Form 1040), line 4** . .	**12**	5,171
13	**Deduction for one-half of self-employment tax.** Multiply line 12 by 50% (0.50). Enter here and on **Schedule 1 (Form 1040), line 14** **13**	2,586	

Part II — Optional Methods To Figure Net Earnings (see instructions)

Farm Optional Method. You may use this method **only** if **(a)** your gross farm income[1] wasn't more than $8,460, **or (b)** your net farm profits[2] were less than $6,107.

14	Maximum income for optional methods	**14**	5,640
15	Enter the **smaller** of: two-thirds (⅔) of gross farm income[1] (not less than zero) or $5,640. Also, include this amount on line 4b above	**15**	

Nonfarm Optional Method. You may use this method **only** if **(a)** your net nonfarm profits[3] were less than $6,107 and also less than 72.189% of your gross nonfarm income,[4] **and (b)** you had net earnings from self-employment of at least $400 in 2 of the prior 3 years. **Caution:** You may use this method no more than five times.

16	Subtract line 15 from line 14	**16**	
17	Enter the **smaller** of: two-thirds (⅔) of gross nonfarm income[4] (not less than zero) **or** the amount on line 16. Also, include this amount on line 4b above	**17**	

[1] From Sch. F, line 9; and Sch. K-1 (Form 1065), box 14, code B.
[2] From Sch. F, line 34; and Sch. K-1 (Form 1065), box 14, code A—minus the amount you would have entered on line 1b had you not used the optional method.
[3] From Sch. C, line 31; and Sch. K-1 (Form 1065), box 14, code A.
[4] From Sch. C, line 7; and Sch. K-1 (Form 1065), box 14, code C.

For Paperwork Reduction Act Notice, see your tax return instructions.   Cat. No. 11358Z   **Schedule SE (Form 1040) 2020**

Self-Study Problem 6.6

Schedule SE (Form 1040) 2020   Attachment Sequence No. **17**   Page **2**

Part III	Maximum Deferral of Self-Employment Tax Payments		
	If line 4c is zero, skip lines 18 through 20, and enter -0- on line 21.		
18	Enter the portion of line 3 that can be attributed to March 27, 2020, through December 31, 2020 . .	**18**	28,365
19	If line 18 is more than zero, multiply line 18 by 92.35% (0.9235); otherwise, enter the amount from line 18	**19**	26,195
20	Enter the portion of lines 15 and 17 that can be attributed to March 27, 2020, through December 31, 2020	**20**	
21	Combine lines 19 and 20	**21**	26,195
	If line 5b is zero, skip line 22 and enter -0- on line 23.		
22	Enter the portion of line 5a that can be attributed to March 27, 2020, through December 31, 2020	**22**	
23	Multiply line 22 by 92.35% (0.9235)	**23**	
24	Add lines 21 and 23	**24**	26,195
25	Enter the smaller of line 9 or line 24	**25**	26,195
26	Multiply line 25 by 6.2% (0.062). Enter here and see the instructions for line 12e of Schedule 3 (Form 1040)	**26**	1,624

Schedule SE (Form 1040) 2020

Self-Study Problem 6.6

Form **7202**	**Credits for Sick Leave and Family Leave for Certain Self-Employed Individuals** ► Attach to Form 1040 or 1040-SR. ► Go to *www.irs.gov/Form7202* for instructions and the latest information.	OMB No. 1545-0074 **2020**
Department of the Treasury Internal Revenue Service		Attachment Sequence No. **202**

Name of person with self-employment income (as shown on Form 1040 or 1040-SR)

Joanne Plummer

Social security number of person with self-employment income

Part I — Credit for Sick Leave for Certain Self-Employed Individuals

1	Number of days you were unable to perform services as a self-employed individual because of certain coronavirus-related care you required. See instructions	**1**	10
2	Number of days you were unable to perform services as a self-employed individual because of certain coronavirus-related care you provided to another. (Do not include days you included in line 1.) See instructions	**2**	0
3	If you are filing a fiscal year return, see instructions; otherwise enter 10	**3**	10
4	Enter the smaller of line 1 or line 3	**4**	10
5	Subtract line 4 from line 3	**5**	0
6	Enter the smaller of line 2 or line 5	**6**	0
7	Net earnings from self-employment (see instructions)	**7**	34,014 (a)
8	Divide line 7 by 260 (round to nearest whole number)	**8**	131
9	Enter the smaller of line 8 or $511	**9**	131
10	Multiply line 4 by line 9	**10**	1,310
11	Multiply line 8 by 67% (0.67)	**11**	88
12	Enter the smaller of line 11 or $200	**12**	88
13	Multiply line 6 by line 12	**13**	0
14	Add lines 10 and 13	**14**	1,310
15	Amount of emergency paid sick leave subject to the $511 per day limit you received from an employer (see instructions)	**15**	0
16	Amount of emergency paid sick leave subject to the $200 per day limit you received from an employer (see instructions)	**16**	0
	If line 15 and line 16 are both zero, skip to line 24 and enter the amount from line 14.		
17	Add line 13 and line 16	**17**	
18	Enter the smaller of line 17 or $2,000	**18**	
19	Subtract line 18 from line 17	**19**	
20	Add lines 10, 15, and 18	**20**	
21	Enter the smaller of line 20 or $5,110	**21**	
22	Subtract line 21 from line 20	**22**	
23	Add line 19 and line 22	**23**	
24	Subtract line 23 from line 14. If zero or less, enter -0-. Enter here and include on Schedule 3 (Form 1040), line 12b	**24**	1,310

Part II — Credit for Family Leave for Certain Self-Employed Individuals

25	Number of days you were unable to perform services as a self-employed individual because of certain coronavirus-related care you provided to a son or daughter under the age of 18. (Do not enter more than 50 days.) See instructions	**25**	21
26	Net earnings from self-employment (see instructions)	**26**	34,014 (a)
27	Divide line 26 by 260 (round to nearest whole number)	**27**	131
28	Multiply line 27 by 67% (0.67)	**28**	88
29	Enter the smaller of line 28 or $200	**29**	88
30	Multiply line 25 by line 29	**30**	1,848
31	Amount of emergency family leave wages you received from an employer (see instructions)	**31**	0
	If line 31 is zero, skip to line 35 and enter the amount from line 30.		
32	Add line 30 and line 31	**32**	
33	Enter the smaller of line 32 or $10,000	**33**	
34	Subtract line 33 from line 32	**34**	
35	Subtract line 34 from line 30. If zero or less, enter -0-. Enter here and include on Schedule 3 (Form 1040), line 12b	**35**	1,848

For Privacy Act and Paperwork Reduction Act Notice, see your tax return instructions.   Cat. No. 56395K   Form **7202** (2020)

(a) $34,014. Net earnings from self-employment after self-employment tax deduction. (Schedule SE, line 2: $36,600 - Schedule SE deduction - line 11: $2,586)

Self-Study Problem 6.7

SCHEDULE H (Form 1040) Department of the Treasury Internal Revenue Service (99)	**Household Employment Taxes** (For Social Security, Medicare, Withheld Income, and Federal Unemployment (FUTA) Taxes) ▶ **Attach to Form 1040, 1040-SR, 1040-NR, 1040-SS, or 1041.** ▶ **Go to www.irs.gov/ScheduleH for instructions and the latest information.**	OMB No. 1545-1971 20**20** Attachment Sequence No. **44**

Name of employer

Susan Green

Social security number

Employer identification number

Calendar year taxpayers having no household employees in 2020 don't have to complete this form for 2020.

A   Did you pay **any one** household employee cash wages of $2,200 or more in 2020? (If any household employee was your spouse, your child under age 21, your parent, or anyone under age 18, see the line A instructions before you answer this question.)

☑ **Yes.** Skip lines B and C and go to line 1a.
☐ **No.** Go to line B.

B   Did you withhold federal income tax during 2020 for any household employee?

☐ **Yes.** Skip line C and go to line 7.
☐ **No.** Go to line C.

C   Did you pay **total** cash wages of $1,000 or more in **any** calendar **quarter** of 2019 or 2020 to **all** household employees? (**Don't** count cash wages paid in 2019 or 2020 to your spouse, your child under age 21, or your parent.)

☐ **No.** Stop. Don't file this schedule.
☐ **Yes.** Skip lines 1a–9 and go to line 10.

Part I   Social Security, Medicare, and Federal Income Taxes

1a	Total cash wages subject to social security tax	**1a**	3,600	
b	Qualified sick and family wages included on line 1a	**1b**		
2a	Social security tax. Multiply line 1a by 12.4% (0.124)		**2a**	446
b	Employer share of social security tax on qualified sick and family leave wages. Multiply line 1b by 6.2% (0.062)		**2b**	
c	Total social security tax. Subtract line 2b from line 2a		**2c**	446
3	Total cash wages subject to Medicare tax	**3**	3,600	
4	Medicare tax. Multiply line 3 by 2.9% (0.029)		**4**	104
5	Total cash wages subject to Additional Medicare Tax withholding	**5**		
6	Additional Medicare Tax withholding. Multiply line 5 by 0.9% (0.009)		**6**	
7	Federal income tax withheld, if any		**7**	0
8a	Total social security, Medicare, and federal income taxes. Add lines 2c, 4, 6, and 7.		**8a**	550
b	Nonrefundable portion of credit for qualified sick and family leave wages from Worksheet 3		**8b**	
c	Total social security, Medicare, and federal income taxes after nonrefundable credit. Subtract line 8b from line 8a		**8c**	550
d	Maximum amount of the employer share of social security tax that can be deferred; see instructions		**8d**	223
e	Refundable portion of credit for qualified sick and family leave wages from Worksheet 3		**8e**	
f	Qualified sick leave wages		**8f**	
g	Qualified health plan expenses allocable to qualified sick leave wages		**8g**	
h	Qualified family leave wages		**8h**	
i	Qualified health plan expenses allocable to qualified family leave wages		**8i**	

9   Did you pay **total** cash wages of $1,000 or more in **any** calendar **quarter** of 2019 or 2020 to **all** household employees? (**Don't** count cash wages paid in 2019 or 2020 to your spouse, your child under age 21, or your parent.)

☐ **No.** Stop. Include the amount from line 8c above on Schedule 2 (Form 1040), line 7a. Include the amount, if any, from line 8e, on Schedule 3 (Form 1040), line 12b. If you're not required to file Form 1040, see the line 9 instructions.
☑ **Yes.** Go to line 10.

For Privacy Act and Paperwork Reduction Act Notice, see the instructions.   Cat. No. 12187K   Schedule H (Form 1040) 2020

Self-Study Problem 6.7

Part II   Federal Unemployment (FUTA) Tax

		Yes	No
10	Did you pay unemployment contributions to only one state? If you paid contributions to a credit reduction state, see instructions and check **"No"**	10 ✓	
11	Did you pay all state unemployment contributions for 2020 by April 15, 2021? Fiscal year filers, see instructions	11 ✓	
12	Were all wages that are taxable for FUTA tax also taxable for your state's unemployment tax?	12 ✓	

Next: If you checked the **"Yes"** box on **all** the lines above, complete Section A.
If you checked the **"No"** box on **any** of the lines above, skip Section A and complete Section B.

Section A

13	Name of the state where you paid unemployment contributions ▶ Virginia		
14	Contributions paid to your state unemployment fund	**14**	194
15	Total cash wages subject to FUTA tax	**15**	3,600
16	**FUTA tax.** Multiply line 15 by 0.6% (0.006). Enter the result here, skip Section B, and go to line 25 .	**16**	22

Section B

17 Complete all columns below that apply (if you need more space, see instructions):

(a) Name of state	(b) Taxable wages (as defined in state act)	(c) State experience rate period From	To	(d) State experience rate	(e) Multiply col. (b) by 0.054	(f) Multiply col. (b) by col. (d)	(g) Subtract col. (f) from col. (e). If zero or less, enter -0-.	(h) Contributions paid to state unemployment fund

18	Totals	**18**		
19	Add columns (g) and (h) of line 18	**19**		
20	Total cash wages subject to FUTA tax (see the line 15 instructions)	**20**		
21	Multiply line 20 by 6.0% (0.06)	**21**		
22	Multiply line 20 by 5.4% (0.054)	**22**		
23	Enter the **smaller** of line 19 or line 22 . . . . (If you paid state unemployment contributions late or you're in a credit reduction state, see instructions and check here) . . . . ☐	**23**	
24	**FUTA tax.** Subtract line 23 from line 21. Enter the result here and go to line 25	**24**	

Part III   Total Household Employment Taxes

25	Enter the amount from line 8c. If you checked the **"Yes"** box on line C of page 1, enter -0-	**25**	550
26	Add line 16 (or line 24) and line 25	**26**	572
27	Are you required to file Form 1040?		

☑ **Yes. Stop.** Include the amount from line 26 above on Schedule 2 (Form 1040), line 7a. Include the amount, if any, from line 8e, on Schedule 3 (Form 1040), line 12b. **Don't** complete Part IV below.

☐ **No.** You may have to complete Part IV. See instructions for details.

Part IV   Address and Signature — Complete this part **only** if required. See the line 27 instructions.

Address (number and street) or P.O. box if mail isn't delivered to street address	Apt., room, or suite no.

City, town or post office, state, and ZIP code

Under penalties of perjury, I declare that I have examined this schedule, including accompanying statements, and to the best of my knowledge and belief, it is true, correct, and complete. No part of any payment made to a state unemployment fund claimed as a credit was, or is to be, deducted from the payments to employees. Declaration of preparer (other than taxpayer) is based on all information of which preparer has any knowledge.

▶ Employer's signature	▶ Date		

Paid Preparer Use Only	Print/Type preparer's name	Preparer's signature	Date	Check ☐ if self-employed	PTIN
	Firm's name ▶			Firm's EIN ▶	
	Firm's address ▶			Phone no.	

Schedule H (Form 1040) 2020

Self-Study Problem 6.8

Form **8960**	**Net Investment Income Tax—**	OMB No. 1545-2227

Net Investment Income Tax—Individuals, Estates, and Trusts

Form **8960**

Department of the Treasury
Internal Revenue Service (99)

► Attach to your tax return.
► Go to *www.irs.gov/Form8960* for instructions and the latest information.

2020

OMB No. 1545-2227

Attachment
Sequence No. **72**

Name(s) shown on your tax return
Ronald Trunk

Your social security number or EIN

Part I   Investment Income

☐ Section 6013(g) election (see instructions)
☐ Section 6013(h) election (see instructions)
☐ Regulations section 1.1411-10(g) election (see instructions)

1	Taxable interest (see instructions)	**1**	110,000
2	Ordinary dividends (see instructions)	**2**	
3	Annuities (see instructions)	**3**	
4a	Rental real estate, royalties, partnerships, S corporations, trusts, etc. (see instructions)	**4a**	
b	Adjustment for net income or loss derived in the ordinary course of a non-section 1411 trade or business (see instructions)	**4b**	
c	Combine lines 4a and 4b	**4c**	
5a	Net gain or loss from disposition of property (see instructions)	**5a**	
b	Net gain or loss from disposition of property that is not subject to net investment income tax (see instructions)	**5b**	
c	Adjustment from disposition of partnership interest or S corporation stock (see instructions)	**5c**	
d	Combine lines 5a through 5c	**5d**	
6	Adjustments to investment income for certain CFCs and PFICs (see instructions)	**6**	
7	Other modifications to investment income (see instructions)	**7**	
8	Total investment income. Combine lines 1, 2, 3, 4c, 5d, 6, and 7	**8**	110,000

Part II   Investment Expenses Allocable to Investment Income and Modifications

9a	Investment interest expenses (see instructions)	**9a**	
b	State, local, and foreign income tax (see instructions)	**9b**	
c	Miscellaneous investment expenses (see instructions)	**9c**	
d	Add lines 9a, 9b, and 9c	**9d**	
10	Additional modifications (see instructions)	**10**	
11	Total deductions and modifications. Add lines 9d and 10	**11**	0

Part III   Tax Computation

12	Net investment income. Subtract Part II, line 11, from Part I, line 8. Individuals, complete lines 13–17. Estates and trusts, complete lines 18a–21. If zero or less, enter -0-	**12**	110,000
	Individuals:		
13	Modified adjusted gross income (see instructions) **13** 380,000		
14	Threshold based on filing status (see instructions) **14** 200,000		
15	Subtract line 14 from line 13. If zero or less, enter -0- **15** 180,000		
16	Enter the smaller of line 12 or line 15	**16**	110,000
17	Net investment income tax for individuals. Multiply line 16 by 3.8% (0.038). **Enter here and include on your tax return** (see instructions)	**17**	4,180
	Estates and Trusts:		
18a	Net investment income (line 12 above) **18a**		
b	Deductions for distributions of net investment income and deductions under section 642(c) (see instructions) **18b**		
c	Undistributed net investment income. Subtract line 18b from 18a (see instructions). If zero or less, enter -0- **18c**		
19a	Adjusted gross income (see instructions) **19a**		
b	Highest tax bracket for estates and trusts for the year (see instructions) **19b**		
c	Subtract line 19b from line 19a. If zero or less, enter -0- **19c**		
20	Enter the smaller of line 18c or line 19c	**20**	
21	Net investment income tax for estates and trusts. Multiply line 20 by 3.8% (0.038). **Enter here and include on your tax return** (see instructions)	**21**	

For Paperwork Reduction Act Notice, see your tax return instructions.   Cat. No. 59474M   Form **8960** (2020)

Self-Study Problem 6.8

Form **8959**	**Additional Medicare Tax**	OMB No. 1545-0074

Form **8959**

Department of the Treasury
Internal Revenue Service

Additional Medicare Tax

▶ If any line does not apply to you, leave it blank. See separate instructions.
▶ Attach to Form 1040, 1040-SR, 1040-NR, 1040-PR, or 1040-SS.
▶ Go to *www.irs.gov/Form8959* for instructions and the latest information.

OMB No. 1545-0074

20**20**

Attachment
Sequence No. **71**

Name(s) shown on return

Meng and Eang Ung

Your social security number

Part I   Additional Medicare Tax on Medicare Wages

1	Medicare wages and tips from Form W-2, box 5. If you have more than one Form W-2, enter the total of the amounts from box 5	**1**	265,000
2	Unreported tips from Form 4137, line 6	**2**	
3	Wages from Form 8919, line 6	**3**	
4	Add lines 1 through 3	**4**	265,000
5	Enter the following amount for your filing status:		
	Married filing jointly $250,000		
	Married filing separately $125,000		
	Single, Head of household, or Qualifying widow(er) $200,000	**5**	250,000
6	Subtract line 5 from line 4. If zero or less, enter -0-	**6**	15,000
7	Additional Medicare Tax on Medicare wages. Multiply line 6 by 0.9% (0.009). Enter here and go to Part II	**7**	135

Part II   Additional Medicare Tax on Self-Employment Income

8	Self-employment income from Schedule SE (Form 1040), Part I, line 6. If you had a loss, enter -0- (Form 1040-PR or 1040-SS filers, see instructions.)	**8**	130,000
9	Enter the following amount for your filing status:		
	Married filing jointly $250,000		
	Married filing separately $125,000		
	Single, Head of household, or Qualifying widow(er) $200,000	**9**	250,000
10	Enter the amount from line 4	**10**	265,000
11	Subtract line 10 from line 9. If zero or less, enter -0-	**11**	0
12	Subtract line 11 from line 8. If zero or less, enter -0-	**12**	130,000
13	Additional Medicare Tax on self-employment income. Multiply line 12 by 0.9% (0.009). Enter here and go to Part III	**13**	1,170

Part III   Additional Medicare Tax on Railroad Retirement Tax Act (RRTA) Compensation

14	Railroad retirement (RRTA) compensation and tips from Form(s) W-2, box 14 (see instructions)	**14**	
15	Enter the following amount for your filing status:		
	Married filing jointly $250,000		
	Married filing separately $125,000		
	Single, Head of household, or Qualifying widow(er) $200,000	**15**	
16	Subtract line 15 from line 14. If zero or less, enter -0-	**16**	
17	Additional Medicare Tax on railroad retirement (RRTA) compensation. Multiply line 16 by 0.9% (0.009). Enter here and go to Part IV	**17**	

Part IV   Total Additional Medicare Tax

18	Add lines 7, 13, and 17. Also include this amount on Schedule 2 (Form 1040), line 8 (check box a) (Form 1040-PR or 1040-SS filers, see instructions), and go to Part V	**18**	1,305

Part V   Withholding Reconciliation

19	Medicare tax withheld from Form W-2, box 6. If you have more than one Form W-2, enter the total of the amounts from box 6	**19**	4,428
20	Enter the amount from line 1	**20**	265,000
21	Multiply line 20 by 1.45% (0.0145). This is your regular Medicare tax withholding on Medicare wages	**21**	3,843
22	Subtract line 21 from line 19. If zero or less, enter -0-. This is your Additional Medicare Tax withholding on Medicare wages	**22**	585
23	Additional Medicare Tax withholding on railroad retirement (RRTA) compensation from Form W-2, box 14 (see instructions)	**23**	
24	**Total Additional Medicare Tax withholding.** Add lines 22 and 23. Also include this amount with federal income tax withholding on Form 1040, 1040-SR, or 1040-NR, line 25c (Form 1040-PR or 1040-SS filers, see instructions)	**24**	585

For Paperwork Reduction Act Notice, see your tax return instructions.   Cat. No. 59475X   Form **8959** (2020)

CHAPTER 7   TAX CREDITS

Self-Study Problem 7.1

a. $4,500. See Child Tax Credit Worksheet on Pages E-41 and E-42.

b. $4,200. Total possible credit is $4,500. Income of $405,600 exceeds $400,000 threshold by $5,600 which is rounded up to $6,000. $6,000/$1,000 = 6. 6 × $50 = phase out of $300. $4,500 less $300 = $4,200

c. Child tax credit = $383
   Additional child tax credit = $4,200. See Child Tax Credit Worksheet on Pages E-43 and E-44 and Schedule 8812 on Page E-45.

Self-Study Problem 7.2

$3,584. See Worksheet A—EIC Worksheet on Page E-46.

Self-Study Problem 7.3

$380. See Form 2441 on Pages E-47 and E-48.

Self-Study Problem 7.4

1. $3,974
2. Excess advance credit of $1,870.
3. Repayment of $1,600.
See Form 8962 on Page E-49.

Self-Study Problem 7.5

a. $500. Refundable American Opportunity tax credit, Line 8 of Form 8863. $750. Nonrefundable American Opportunity tax credit, Line 19 of Form 8863. See Form 8863 on Pages E-50 and E-51.

b. $1,040 = 20% × $5,200 ($10,000 maximum)

Self-Study Problem 7.6

Overall limitation:

$$\frac{\$1,500}{\$58,000} \times \$8,556 = \$221$$

The foreign tax credit is limited to $221. The remaining balance of $211 can be carried back one year or carried forward 10 years.

Self-Study Problem 7.7

See Form 8839 on Pages E-52 and E-53.

Self-Study Problem 7.1a

2020 Child Tax Credit and Credit for Other Dependents Worksheet—Line 19 *

Keep for Your Records

CAUTION

1. To be a qualifying child for the child tax credit, the child must be your dependent, **under age 17** at the end of 2020, and meet all the conditions in Steps 1 through 3 under *Who Qualifies as Your Dependent*. Make sure you checked the "child tax credit" box in column (4) of the *Dependents* section on Form 1040 or 1040-SR for each qualifying child.

2. If you don't have a qualifying child, you can't claim the child tax credit; but you may be able to claim the credit for other dependents for that child. See Step 3 under *Who Qualifies as Your Dependent*.

3. To see if your qualifying relative qualifies you to take the credit for other dependents, see Step 5 under *Who Qualifies as Your Dependent*.

4. Be sure to see *Social security number* under *Who Qualifies as Your Dependent*.

5. Do **not** use this worksheet, but use Pub. 972 instead, if:

   a. You are claiming the adoption credit, mortgage interest credit, District of Columbia first-time homebuyer credit, or residential energy efficient property credit*;

   b. You are excluding income from Puerto Rico; or

   c. You are filing Form 2555 or 4563.

   * If applicable.

Part 1

1. Number of qualifying children under age 17 with the required social security number: __2__ × \$2,000. Enter the result. | **1** | 4,000 |

2. Number of other dependents, including qualifying children without the required social security number: __1__ × \$500. Enter the result. | **2** | 500 |

   Caution. Don't include yourself, your spouse, or anyone who is not a U.S. citizen, U.S. national, or U.S. resident alien. Also, don't include anyone you included on line 1.

3. Add lines 1 and 2. | **3** | 4,500 |

4. Enter the amount from Form 1040 or 1040-SR, line 11. | **4** | 125,400 |

5. Enter the amount shown below for your filing status.

   ● Married filing jointly — \$400,000

   ● All other filing statuses — \$200,000 | **5** | 400,000 |

6. Is the amount on line 4 more than the amount on line 5?

   [X] **No.** Leave line 6 blank. Enter -0- on line 7, and go to line 8.

   [ ] **Yes.** Subtract line 5 from line 4.

   If the result isn't a multiple of \$1,000, increase it to the next multiple of \$1,000. For example, increase \$425 to \$1,000, increase \$1,025 to \$2,000, etc. | **6** | |

7. Multiply the amount on line 6 by 5% (0.05). Enter the result. | **7** | 0 |

8. Is the amount on line 3 more than the amount on line 7?

   [ ] **No.** (STOP) You can't take the child tax credit on Form 1040 or 1040-SR, line 19. You also can't take the additional child tax credit on Form 1040 or 1040-SR, line 28. Complete the rest of your Form 1040 or 1040-SR.

   [X] **Yes.** Subtract line 7 from line 3. Enter the result. *Go to Part 2.* | **8** | 4,500 |

---

* Download the latest version of this worksheet from the Form 1040 Instructions available at www.irs.gov. The 2020 worksheet was not available as we went to print. This worksheet is adapted from the 2019 version.

Self-Study Problem 7.1a

2020 Child Tax Credit and Credit for Other Dependents
Worksheet—*Continued* *

Keep for Your Records

Before you begin Part 2: √ Figure the amount of any credits you are claiming on Schedule 3; Form 5695, Part II*;
Form 8910; Form 8936; or Schedule R.

Part 2

9. Enter the amount from Form 1040 or 1040-SR, line 16.

| 9 | 13,712 |

10. Add any amounts from:

Schedule 3, line 1 _____

Schedule 3, line 2 + _____

Schedule 3, line 3 + _____

Schedule 3, line 4 + _____

Form 5695, line 30* + _____

Form 8910, line 15* + _____

Form 8936, line 23 + _____

Schedule R, line 22 + _____

Enter the total.

| 10 | 0 |

11. Are the amounts on lines 9 and 10 the same?

☐ **Yes.** (STOP)
You can't take this credit because there is no tax to reduce.
However, you may be able to take the **additional child tax
credit** if line 1 is more than zero. See the **TIP** below.

☒ **No.** Subtract line 10 from line 9.

| 11 | 13,712 |

12. Is the amount on line 8 more than the amount on line 11?

☐ **Yes.** Enter the amount from line 11.
Also, you may be able to take the
additional child tax credit if line 1
is more than zero. See the **TIP** below.

☒ **No.** Enter the amount from line 8.

} **This is your child tax
credit and credit for
other dependents.**

| 12 | 4,500 |

Enter this amount on
Form 1040 or 1040-SR,
line 19.

TIP
*You may be able to take the **additional child tax credit**
on Form 1040 or 1040-SR, line 28, if you answered "Yes" on
line 11 **or** line 12 above.*

● *First, complete your Form 1040 or 1040-SR through line
27 (also complete Schedule 3, line 10).*

● *Then, use Schedule 8812 to figure any additional child tax
credit.*

CAUTION
*If your child tax credit or additional child tax credit for a year after
2015 was reduced or disallowed, see* Form 8862, who must file *to
find out if you must file Form 8862 to take the credit for 2020.*

*If applicable.

* Download the latest version of this worksheet from the Form 1040 Instructions available at www.irs.gov. The 2020 worksheet was not available
as we went to print. This worksheet is adapted from the 2019 version.

Self-Study Problem 7.1c

2020 Child Tax Credit and Credit for Other Dependents Worksheet—Line 19 *

Keep for Your Records

1. To be a qualifying child for the child tax credit, the child must be your dependent, **under age 17** at the end of 2020, and meet all the conditions in Steps 1 through 3 under *Who Qualifies as Your Dependent*. Make sure you checked the "child tax credit" box in column (4) of the *Dependents* section on Form 1040 or 1040-SR for each qualifying child.

2. If you don't have a qualifying child, you can't claim the child tax credit; but you may be able to claim the credit for other dependents for that child. See Step 3 under *Who Qualifies as Your Dependent*.

3. To see if your qualifying relative qualifies you to take the credit for other dependents, see Step 5 under *Who Qualifies as Your Dependent*.

4. Be sure to see *Social security number* under *Who Qualifies as Your Dependent*.

5. Do **not** use this worksheet, but use Pub. 972 instead, if:

   a. You are claiming the adoption credit, mortgage interest credit, District of Columbia first-time homebuyer credit, or residential energy efficient property credit*;

   b. You are excluding income from Puerto Rico; or

   c. You are filing Form 2555 or 4563.

   * If applicable.

Part 1

1. Number of qualifying children under age 17 with the required social security number: ___3___ × $2,000. Enter the result.

   1   6,000

2. Number of other dependents, including qualifying children without the required social security number: _____ × $500. Enter the result.

   2   0

   Caution. Don't include yourself, your spouse, or anyone who is not a U.S. citizen, U.S. national, or U.S. resident alien. Also, don't include anyone you included on line 1.

3. Add lines 1 and 2.

   3   6,000

4. Enter the amount from Form 1040 or 1040-SR, line 11.

   4   36,400

5. Enter the amount shown below for your filing status.

   ● Married filing jointly — $400,000

   ● All other filing statuses — $200,000

   5   400,000

6. Is the amount on line 4 more than the amount on line 5?

   [X] **No.** Leave line 6 blank. Enter -0- on line 7, and go to line 8.

   [ ] **Yes.** Subtract line 5 from line 4.

     If the result isn't a multiple of $1,000, increase it to the next multiple of $1,000. For example, increase $425 to $1,000, increase $1,025 to $2,000, etc.

   6

7. Multiply the amount on line 6 by 5% (0.05). Enter the result.

   7   0

8. Is the amount on line 3 more than the amount on line 7?

   [ ] **No.** (STOP) You can't take the child tax credit on Form 1040 or 1040-SR, line 19. You also can't take the additional child tax credit on Form 1040 or 1040-SR, line 28. Complete the rest of your Form 1040 or 1040-SR.

   [X] **Yes.** Subtract line 7 from line 3. Enter the result.
     Go to Part 2.

   8   6,000

---

* Download the latest version of this worksheet from the Form 1040 Instructions available at www.irs.gov. The 2020 worksheet was not available as we went to print. This worksheet is adapted from the 2019 version.

Self-Study Problem 7.1c

2020 Child Tax Credit and Credit for Other Dependents
Worksheet—*Continued* *

Keep for Your Records

Before you begin Part 2: ✓ Figure the amount of any credits you are claiming on Schedule 3; Form 5695, Part II*; Form 8910; Form 8936; or Schedule R.

Part 2		

9. Enter the amount from Form 1040 or 1040-SR, line 16.

9	383

10. Add any amounts from:

Schedule 3, line 1 _____

Schedule 3, line 2 + _____

Schedule 3, line 3 + _____

Schedule 3, line 4 + _____

Form 5695, line 30* + _____

Form 8910, line 15* + _____

Form 8936, line 23 + _____

Schedule R, line 22 + _____

Enter the total.

10	0

11. Are the amounts on lines 9 and 10 the same?

☐ **Yes.** (STOP)
You can't take this credit because there is no tax to reduce. However, you may be able to take the **additional child tax credit** if line 1 is more than zero. See the **TIP** below.

☒ **No.** Subtract line 10 from line 9.

11	383

12. Is the amount on line 8 more than the amount on line 11?

☒ **Yes.** Enter the amount from line 11.
Also, you may be able to take the **additional child tax credit** if line 1 is more than zero. See the **TIP** below.

} **This is your child tax credit and credit for other dependents.**

☐ **No.** Enter the amount from line 8.

12	383

Enter this amount on Form 1040 or 1040-SR, line 19.

1040 or 1040-SR ◄····

TIP *You may be able to take the **additional child tax credit** on Form 1040 or 1040-SR, line 28, if you answered "Yes" on line 11 **or** line 12 above.*

● *First, complete your Form 1040 or 1040-SR through line 27 (also complete Schedule 3, line 10).*

● *Then, use Schedule 8812 to figure any additional child tax credit.*

CAUTION *If your child tax credit or additional child tax credit for a year after 2015 was reduced or disallowed, see Form 8862, who must file to find out if you must file Form 8862 to take the credit for 2020.*

*If applicable.

* Download the latest version of this worksheet from the Form 1040 Instructions available at www.irs.gov. The 2020 worksheet was not available as we went to print. This worksheet is adapted from the 2019 version.

Self-Study Problem 7.1c

SCHEDULE 8812
(Form 1040)

Department of the Treasury
Internal Revenue Service (99)

Additional Child Tax Credit

► **Attach to Form 1040, 1040-SR, or 1040-NR.**
► **Go to** *www.irs.gov/Schedule8812* **for instructions and the latest information.**

1040
1040-SR
1040-NR   8812

OMB No. 1545-0074

20**20**

Attachment
Sequence No. **47**

Name(s) shown on return
Marie and Pierre Curry

Your social security number

Part I	All Filers		

Caution: If you file Form 2555, **stop here;** you cannot claim the additional child tax credit.

1	If you are required to use the worksheet in Pub. 972, enter the amount from line 10 of the Child Tax Credit and Credit for Other Dependents Worksheet in the publication. Otherwise, enter the amount from line 8 of your Child Tax Credit and Credit for Other Dependents Worksheet. (See the instructions for Forms 1040 and 1040-SR, line 19, or the instructions for Form 1040-NR, line 19.)	**1**	6,000
2	Enter the amount from line 19 of your Form 1040, Form 1040-SR, or Form 1040-NR	**2**	383
3	Subtract line 2 from line 1. If zero, **stop here;** you cannot claim this credit	**3**	5,617
4	Number of qualifying children under 17 with the required social security number: 3 x $1,400. Enter the result. If zero, **stop here;** you cannot claim this credit	**4**	4,200
	TIP: The number of children you use for this line is the same as the number of children you used for line 1 of the Child Tax Credit and Credit for Other Dependents Worksheet.		
5	Enter the **smaller** of line 3 or line 4	**5**	4,200

6a	Earned income (see instructions)	**6a**	36,400	
b	Nontaxable combat pay (see instructions)	**6b**		
7	Is the amount on line 6a more than $2,500?			
	☐ **No.** Leave line 7 blank and enter -0- on line 8.			
	☑ **Yes.** Subtract $2,500 from the amount on line 6a. Enter the result	**7**	33,900	
8	Multiply the amount on line 7 by 15% (0.15) and enter the result	**8**		5,085
	Next. On line 4, is the amount $4,200 or more?			
	☐ **No.** If line 8 is zero, **stop here;** you cannot claim this credit. Otherwise, skip Part II and enter the **smaller** of line 5 or line 8 on line 15.			
	☑ **Yes.** If line 8 is equal to or more than line 5, skip Part II and enter the amount from line 5 on line 15. Otherwise, go to line 9.			

Part II	Certain Filers Who Have Three or More Qualifying Children		

9	Withheld social security, Medicare, and Additional Medicare taxes from Form(s) W-2, boxes 4 and 6. If married filing jointly, include your spouse's amounts with yours. If your employer withheld or you paid Additional Medicare Tax or tier 1 RRTA taxes, see instructions	**9**		
10	Enter the total of the amounts from Schedule 1 (Form 1040), line 14, and Schedule 2 (Form 1040), line 5, plus any taxes that you identified using code "UT" and entered on Schedule 2 (Form 1040), line 8	**10**		
11	Add lines 9 and 10	**11**		
12	**1040 and 1040-SR filers:** Enter the total of the amounts from Form 1040 or 1040-SR, line 27, and Schedule 3 (Form 1040), line 10.	**12**		
	1040-NR filers: Enter the amount from Schedule 3 (Form 1040), line 10.			
13	Subtract line 12 from line 11. If zero or less, enter -0-	**13**		
14	Enter the **larger** of line 8 or line 13	**14**		
	Next, enter the **smaller** of line 5 or line 14 on line 15.			

Part III	Additional Child Tax Credit		

15	This is your additional child tax credit	**15**	4,200

1040
1040-SR
1040-NR

Enter this amount on
Form 1040, line 28;
Form 1040-SR, line 28; or
Form 1040-NR, line 28.

For Paperwork Reduction Act Notice, see your tax return instructions.   Cat. No. 59761M   **Schedule 8812 (Form 1040) 2020**

Self-Study Problem 7.2

Worksheet A—2020 EIC—Line 27*

Keep for Your Records

Before you begin: √ Be sure you are using the correct worksheet. Use this worksheet only if you answered "No" to Step 5, question 2. Otherwise, use Worksheet B.

Part 1

All Filers Using Worksheet A

1. Enter your earned income from Step 5.

Wages, salaries

| 1 | 15,800 |

2. Look up the amount on line 1 above in the EIC Table (right after Worksheet B) to find the credit. Be sure you use the correct column for your filing status and the number of children you have. Enter the credit here.

If line 2 is zero, (STOP) You can't take the credit. Enter "No" on the dotted line next to Form 1040 or 1040-SR, line 27.

| 2 | 3,584 |

3. Enter the amount from Form 1040 or 1040-SR, line 11. Adjusted gross income

| 3 | 15,900 |

4. Are the amounts on lines 3 and 1 the same?

☐ **Yes.** Skip line 5; enter the amount from line 2 on line 6.

☒ **No.** Go to line 5.

Part 2

Filers Who Answered "No" on Line 4

5. If you have:
- No qualifying children, is the amount on line 3 less than $8,800 ($14,700 if married filing jointly)?
- 1 or more qualifying children, is the amount on line 3 less than $19,350 ($25,250 if married filing jointly)?

☒ **Yes.** Leave line 5 blank; enter the amount from line 2 on line 6.

☐ **No.** Look up the amount on line 3 in the EIC Table to find the credit. Be sure you use the correct column for your filing status and the number of children you have. Enter the credit here.
Look at the amounts on lines 5 and 2.
Then, enter the **smaller** amount on line 6.

| 5 | |

Part 3

Your Earned Income Credit

6. This is your earned income credit.

| 6 | 3,584 |

Enter this amount on Form 1040 or 1040-SR, line 27.

Reminder—

√ If you have a qualifying child, complete and attach Schedule EIC.

⚠ **CAUTION** *If your EIC for a year after 1996 was reduced or disallowed, see Form 8862, who must file, earlier, to find out if you must file Form 8862 to take the credit for 2020.*

Self-Study Problem 7.3

Form **2441**	**Child and Dependent Care Expenses**		OMB No. 1545-0074
	▶ Attach to Form 1040, 1040-SR, or 1040-NR.		**2020**
Department of the Treasury Internal Revenue Service (99)	▶ Go to *www.irs.gov/Form2441* for instructions and the latest information.	2441	Attachment Sequence No. **21**

Name(s) shown on return

Julie Brown

Your social security number

456-23-6543

You cannot claim a credit for child and dependent care expenses if your filing status is married filing separately unless you meet the requirements listed in the instructions under "Married Persons Filing Separately." If you meet these requirements, check this box. ☐

Part I   **Persons or Organizations Who Provided the Care—You must complete this part.**
(If you have more than two care providers, see the instructions.)

1	(a) Care provider's name	(b) Address (number, street, apt. no., city, state, and ZIP code)	(c) Identifying number (SSN or EIN)	(d) Amount paid (see instructions)
	Ivy Childcare	1 Sunflower Street Terre Haute, IN 47803	56-7654321	1,500
	De Anza Adult Care	13 Fort Harrison Rd. Dewey, IN 47805	43-1234567	2,400

Did you receive dependent care benefits?	**No** ▶ Complete only Part II below.
	Yes ▶ Complete Part III on the back next.

Caution: If the care was provided in your home, you may owe employment taxes. For details, see the instructions for Schedule 2 (Form 1040), line 7a.

Part II   **Credit for Child and Dependent Care Expenses**

2   Information about your **qualifying person(s)**. If you have more than two qualifying persons, see the instructions.

(a) Qualifying person's name		(b) Qualifying person's social security number	(c) **Qualified expenses** you incurred and paid in 2020 for the person listed in column (a)
First	Last		
Chuck	Brown	123-33-4444	0*
Devona	Neuporte	214-55-6666	1,900*

3	Add the amounts in column (c) of line 2. **Don't** enter more than $3,000 for one qualifying person or $6,000 for two or more persons. If you completed Part III, enter the amount from line 31 . .	**3**	1,900
4	Enter your **earned income.** See instructions	**4**	90,000
5	If married filing jointly, enter your spouse's earned income (if you or your spouse was a student or was disabled, see the instructions); **all others**, enter the amount from line 4	**5**	90,000
6	Enter the **smallest** of line 3, 4, or 5	**6**	1,900
7	Enter the amount from Form 1040, 1040-SR, or 1040-NR, line 11 **7** 90,000		
8	Enter on line 8 the decimal amount shown below that applies to the amount on line 7.		

If line 7 is:			If line 7 is:		
Over	But not over	Decimal amount is	Over	But not over	Decimal amount is
$0—15,000		.35	$29,000—31,000		.27
15,000—17,000		.34	31,000—33,000		.26
17,000—19,000		.33	33,000—35,000		.25
19,000—21,000		.32	35,000—37,000		.24
21,000—23,000		.31	37,000—39,000		.23
23,000—25,000		.30	39,000—41,000		.22
25,000—27,000		.29	41,000—43,000		.21
27,000—29,000		.28	43,000—No limit		.20

8			X . .2

9	Multiply line 6 by the decimal amount on line 8. If you paid 2019 expenses in 2020, see the instructions	**9**	380
10	Tax liability limit. Enter the amount from the Credit Limit Worksheet in the instructions **10** 5,181		
11	**Credit for child and dependent care expenses.** Enter the **smaller** of line 9 or line 10 here and on Schedule 3 (Form 1040), line 2	**11**	380

For Paperwork Reduction Act Notice, see your tax return instructions.   Cat. No. 11862M   Form **2441** (2020)

*$2,000 of Dependent Care Flexible Spending Amount that is withheld from Julie's salary for the reimbursement of qualified dependent care expenses. $2,000 − $1,500 of son's care − $500 (limited) for mother's care.

Self-Study Problem 7.3

Form 2441 (2020)   Page **2**

Part III	Dependent Care Benefits

12 Enter the total amount of **dependent care benefits** you received in 2020. Amounts you received as an employee should be shown in box 10 of your Form(s) W-2. **Don't** include amounts reported as wages in box 1 of Form(s) W-2. If you were self-employed or a partner, include amounts you received under a dependent care assistance program from your sole proprietorship or partnership.   **12**   2,000

13 Enter the amount, if any, you carried over from 2019 and used in 2020 during the grace period. See instructions   **13**

14 Enter the amount, if any, you forfeited or carried forward to 2021. See instructions   **14** (   )

15 Combine lines 12 through 14. See instructions   **15**   2,000

16 Enter the total amount of **qualified expenses** incurred in 2020 for the care of the **qualifying person(s)**   **16**   3,900

17 Enter the **smaller** of line 15 or 16   **17**   2,000

18 Enter your **earned income.** See instructions   **18**   90,000

19 Enter the amount shown below that applies to you.
  • If married filing jointly, enter your spouse's earned income (if you or your spouse was a student or was disabled, see the instructions for line 5).
  • If married filing separately, see instructions.
  • All others, enter the amount from line 18.   **19**   90,000

20 Enter the **smallest** of line 17, 18, or 19   **20**   2,000

21 Enter $5,000 ($2,500 if married filing separately **and** you were required to enter your spouse's earned income on line 19)   **21**   5,000

22 Is any amount on line 12 from your sole proprietorship or partnership?
  ☑ **No.** Enter -0-.
  ☐ **Yes.** Enter the amount here   **22**   0

23 Subtract line 22 from line 15   **23**   2,000

24 **Deductible benefits.** Enter the **smallest** of line 20, 21, or 22. Also, include this amount on the appropriate line(s) of your return. See instructions   **24**   0

25 **Excluded benefits.** If you checked "No" on line 22, enter the smaller of line 20 or line 21. Otherwise, subtract line 24 from the smaller of line 20 or line 21. If zero or less, enter -0-   **25**   2,000

26 **Taxable benefits.** Subtract line 25 from line 23. If zero or less, enter -0-. Also, include this amount on Form 1040 or 1040-SR, line 1; or Form 1040-NR, line 1a. On the dotted line next to Form 1040 or 1040-SR, line 1; or Form 1040-NR, line 1a, enter "DCB"   **26**   0

To claim the child and dependent care
credit, complete lines 27 through 31 below.

27 Enter $3,000 ($6,000 if two or more qualifying persons)   **27**   6,000

28 Add lines 24 and 25   **28**   2,000

29 Subtract line 28 from line 27. If zero or less, **stop.** You can't take the credit. **Exception.** If you paid 2019 expenses in 2020, see the instructions for line 9   **29**   4,000

30 Complete line 2 on the front of this form. **Don't** include in column (c) any benefits shown on line 28 above. Then, add the amounts in column (c) and enter the total here   **30**   1,900

31 Enter the **smaller** of line 29 or 30. Also, enter this amount on line 3 on the front of this form and complete lines 4 through 11   **31**   1,900

Form **2441** (2020)

Self-Study Problem 7.4

Form **8962**	**Premium Tax Credit (PTC)**	OMB No. 1545-0074
Department of the Treasury Internal Revenue Service	▶ Attach to Form 1040, 1040-SR, or 1040-NR. ▶ Go to *www.irs.gov/Form8962* for instructions and the latest information.	**2020** Attachment Sequence No. **73**

Name shown on your return	Your social security number
Tracy and Marco Brigantine	123-44-5555

You cannot take the PTC if your filing status is married filing separately unless you qualify for an exception. See instructions. If you qualify, check the box . . ▶ ☐

Part I   Annual and Monthly Contribution Amount

1	Tax family size. Enter your tax family size. See instructions	**1**	4
2a	Modified AGI. Enter your modified AGI. See instructions **2a** 68,040		
b	Enter the total of your dependents' modified AGI. See instructions **2b** 0		
3	Household income. Add the amounts on lines 2a and 2b. See instructions	**3**	68,040
4	Federal poverty line. Enter the federal poverty line amount from Table 1-1, 1-2, or 1-3. See instructions. Check the appropriate box for the federal poverty table used. **a** ☐ Alaska **b** ☐ Hawaii **c** ☑ Other 48 states and DC	**4**	25,750
5	Household income as a percentage of federal poverty line (see instructions)	**5**	264 %*
6	Did you enter 401% on line 5? (See instructions if you entered less than 100%.)		
	☑ **No.** Continue to line 7.		
	☐ **Yes.** You are not eligible to take the PTC. If advance payment of the PTC was made, see the instructions for how to report your excess advance PTC repayment amount.		
7	Applicable figure. Using your line 5 percentage, locate your "applicable figure" on the table in the instructions	**7**	.0871
8a	Annual contribution amount. Multiply line 3 by line 7. Round to nearest whole dollar amount **8a** 5,926	**b** Monthly contribution amount. Divide line 8a by 12. Round to nearest whole dollar amount	**8b** 494

Part II   Premium Tax Credit Claim and Reconciliation of Advance Payment of Premium Tax Credit

9 Are you allocating policy amounts with another taxpayer or do you want to use the alternative calculation for year of marriage? See instructions.
   ☐ **Yes.** Skip to Part IV, Allocation of Policy Amounts, or Part V, Alternative Calculation for Year of Marriage. ☑ **No.** Continue to line 10.

10 See the instructions to determine if you can use line 11 or must complete lines 12 through 23.
   ☑ **Yes.** Continue to line 11. Compute your annual PTC. Then skip lines 12–23 and continue to line 24. ☐ **No.** Continue to lines 12–23. Compute your monthly PTC and continue to line 24.

Annual Calculation	(a) Annual enrollment premiums (Form(s) 1095-A, line 33A)	(b) Annual applicable SLCSP premium (Form(s) 1095-A, line 33B)	(c) Annual contribution amount (line 8a)	(d) Annual maximum premium assistance (subtract (c) from (b); if zero or less, enter -0-)	(e) Annual premium tax credit allowed (smaller of (a) or (d))	(f) Annual advance payment of PTC (Form(s) 1095-A, line 33C)
11 Annual Totals	11,484	9,900	5,926	3,974	3,974	5,844

Monthly Calculation	(a) Monthly enrollment premiums (Form(s) 1095-A, lines 21–32, column A)	(b) Monthly applicable SLCSP premium (Form(s) 1095-A, lines 21–32, column B)	(c) Monthly contribution amount (amount from line 8b or alternative marriage monthly calculation)	(d) Monthly maximum premium assistance (subtract (c) from (b); if zero or less, enter -0-)	(e) Monthly premium tax credit allowed (smaller of (a) or (d))	(f) Monthly advance payment of PTC (Form(s) 1095-A, lines 21–32, column C)
12 January						
13 February						
14 March						
15 April						
16 May						
17 June						
18 July						
19 August						
20 September						
21 October						
22 November						
23 December						

24	Total premium tax credit. Enter the amount from line 11(e) or add lines 12(e) through 23(e) and enter the total here	**24**	3,974
25	Advance payment of PTC. Enter the amount from line 11(f) or add lines 12(f) through 23(f) and enter the total here	**25**	5,844
26	Net premium tax credit. If line 24 is greater than line 25, subtract line 25 from line 24. Enter the difference here and on Schedule 3 (Form 1040), line 8. If line 24 equals line 25, enter -0-. Stop here. If line 25 is greater than line 24, leave this line blank and continue to line 27	**26**	

Part III   Repayment of Excess Advance Payment of the Premium Tax Credit

27	Excess advance payment of PTC. If line 25 is greater than line 24, subtract line 24 from line 25. Enter the difference here	**27**	1,870
28	Repayment limitation (see instructions)	**28**	1,600
29	Excess advance premium tax credit repayment. Enter the smaller of line 27 or line 28 here and on Schedule 2 (Form 1040), line 2	**29**	1,600

For Paperwork Reduction Act Notice, see your tax return instructions.   Cat. No. 37784Z   Form **8962** (2020)

*Per Form 8962 instructions, this amount is not rounded. Instead, multiply the result by 100 and drop any amounts after the decimal.

Self-Study Problem 7.5a

Form **8863**	**Education Credits**	OMB No. 1545-0074
	(American Opportunity and Lifetime Learning Credits)	**2020**
Department of the Treasury Internal Revenue Service (99)	▶ Attach to Form 1040 or 1040-SR. ▶ Go to *www.irs.gov/Form8863* for instructions and the latest information.	Attachment Sequence No. **50**

Name(s) shown on return	Your social security number
Santiago and Sophia Estudiante	

> **CAUTION** Complete a separate Part III on page 2 for each student for whom you're claiming either credit before you complete Parts I and II.

Part I   Refundable American Opportunity Credit

1	After completing Part III for each student, enter the total of all amounts from all Parts III, line 30 . .	**1**	2,500
2	Enter: $180,000 if married filing jointly; $90,000 if single, head of household, or qualifying widow(er)	**2**	180,000
3	Enter the amount from Form 1040 or 1040-SR, line 11. If you're filing Form 2555 or 4563, or you're excluding income from Puerto Rico, see Pub. 970 for the amount to enter	**3**	170,000
4	Subtract line 3 from line 2. If zero or less, **stop**; you can't take any education credit	**4**	10,000
5	Enter: $20,000 if married filing jointly; $10,000 if single, head of household, or qualifying widow(er)	**5**	20,000
6	If line 4 is: • Equal to or more than line 5, enter 1.000 on line 6 . . . . • Less than line 5, divide line 4 by line 5. Enter the result as a decimal (rounded to at least three places)	**6**	0.5000
7	Multiply line 1 by line 6. **Caution:** If you were under age 24 at the end of the year **and** meet the conditions described in the instructions, you **can't** take the refundable American opportunity credit; skip line 8, enter the amount from line 7 on line 9, and check this box . . . . . . ▶ ☐	**7**	1,250
8	**Refundable American opportunity credit.** Multiply line 7 by 40% (0.40). Enter the amount here and on Form 1040 or 1040-SR, line 29. Then go to line 9 below.	**8**	500

Part II   Nonrefundable Education Credits

9	Subtract line 8 from line 7. Enter here and on line 2 of the Credit Limit Worksheet (see instructions) .	**9**	750
10	After completing Part III for each student, enter the total of all amounts from all Parts III, line 31. If zero, skip lines 11 through 17, enter -0- on line 18, and go to line 19	**10**	0
11	Enter the smaller of line 10 or $10,000	**11**	
12	Multiply line 11 by 20% (0.20)	**12**	
13	Enter: $138,000 if married filing jointly; $69,000 if single, head of household, or qualifying widow(er)	**13**	
14	Enter the amount from Form 1040, line 11. If you're filing Form 2555 or 4563, or you're excluding income from Puerto Rico, see Pub. 970 for the amount to enter	**14**	
15	Subtract line 14 from line 13. If zero or less, skip lines 16 and 17, enter -0- on line 18, and go to line 19	**15**	
16	Enter: $20,000 if married filing jointly; $10,000 if single, head of household, or qualifying widow(er)	**16**	
17	If line 15 is: • Equal to or more than line 16, enter 1.000 on line 17 and go to line 18 • Less than line 16, divide line 15 by line 16. Enter the result as a decimal (rounded to at least three places)	**17**	.
18	Multiply line 12 by line 17. Enter here and on line 1 of the Credit Limit Worksheet (see instructions) ▶	**18**	0
19	**Nonrefundable education credits.** Enter the amount from line 7 of the Credit Limit Worksheet (see instructions) here and on Schedule 3 (Form 1040), line 3	**19**	750

For Paperwork Reduction Act Notice, see your tax return instructions.	Cat. No. 25379M	Form **8863** (2020)

Note: The taxpayers have a large tax liability relative to the AOTC. As a result, the nonrefundable AOTC will not be limited.

Self-Study Problem 7.5a

Form 8863 (2020)   Page **2**

Name(s) shown on return	Your social security number
Santiago and Sophia Estudiante	

⚠️ **CAUTION** *Complete Part III for each student for whom you're claiming either the American opportunity credit or lifetime learning credit. Use additional copies of page 2 as needed for each student.*

Part III **Student and Educational Institution Information.** See instructions.

20 Student name (as shown on page 1 of your tax return)	**21** Student social security number (as shown on page 1 of your tax return)
Judy Estudiante	434 11 7812

22 Educational institution information (see instructions)

a. Name of first educational institution	**b.** Name of second educational institution (if any)
Southwest University	
(1) Address. Number and street (or P.O. box). City, town or post office, state, and ZIP code. If a foreign address, see instructions. 1234 Cleveland Ave. El Paso, TX 79925	**(1)** Address. Number and street (or P.O. box). City, town or post office, state, and ZIP code. If a foreign address, see instructions.
(2) Did the student receive Form 1098-T from this institution for 2020? ☑ Yes ☐ No	**(2)** Did the student receive Form 1098-T from this institution for 2020? ☐ Yes ☐ No
(3) Did the student receive Form 1098-T from this institution for 2019 with box 7 checked? ☐ Yes ☑ No	**(3)** Did the student receive Form 1098-T from this institution for 2019 with box 7 checked? ☐ Yes ☐ No
(4) Enter the institution's employer identification number (EIN) if you're claiming the American opportunity credit or if you checked "Yes" in **(2)** or **(3)**. You can get the EIN from Form 1098-T or from the institution. 1 2 - 7 6 5 2 3 1 1	**(4)** Enter the institution's employer identification number (EIN) if you're claiming the American opportunity credit or if you checked "Yes" in **(2)** or **(3)**. You can get the EIN from Form 1098-T or from the institution. ___ ___ - ___ ___ ___ ___ ___ ___ ___

23 Has the Hope Scholarship Credit or American opportunity credit been claimed for this student for any 4 tax years before 2020?   ☐ Yes — **Stop!** Go to line 31 for this student.   ☑ No — Go to line 24.

24 Was the student enrolled at least half-time for at least one academic period that began or is treated as having begun in 2020 at an eligible educational institution in a program leading towards a postsecondary degree, certificate, or other recognized postsecondary educational credential? See instructions.   ☑ Yes — Go to line 25.   ☐ No — **Stop!** Go to line 31 for this student.

25 Did the student complete the first 4 years of postsecondary education before 2020? See instructions.   ☐ Yes — **Stop!** Go to line 31 for this student.   ☑ No — Go to line 26.

26 Was the student convicted, before the end of 2020, of a felony for possession or distribution of a controlled substance?   ☐ Yes — **Stop!** Go to line 31 for this student.   ☑ No — Complete lines 27 through 30 for this student.

⚠️ **CAUTION** *You **can't** take the American opportunity credit and the lifetime learning credit for the **same student** in the same year. If you complete lines 27 through 30 for this student, don't complete line 31.*

American Opportunity Credit

27	Adjusted qualified education expenses (see instructions). **Don't enter more than $4,000**	**27**	4,000
28	Subtract $2,000 from line 27. If zero or less, enter -0-	**28**	2,000
29	Multiply line 28 by 25% (0.25)	**29**	500
30	If line 28 is zero, enter the amount from line 27. Otherwise, add $2,000 to the amount on line 29 and enter the result. Skip line 31. Include the total of all amounts from all Parts III, line 30, on Part I, line 1 .	**30**	2,500

Lifetime Learning Credit

31	Adjusted qualified education expenses (see instructions). Include the total of all amounts from all Parts III, line 31, on Part II, line 10	**31**	0

Form **8863** (2020)

Self-Study Problem 7.7

Form **8839**		**Qualified Adoption Expenses**		OMB No. 1545-0074
Department of the Treasury Internal Revenue Service (99)		► Attach to Form 1040, 1040-SR, or 1040-NR. ► Go to *www.irs.gov/Form8839* for instructions and the latest information.		**2020** Attachment Sequence No. **38**

Name(s) shown on return
James and Michael Bass

Your social security number

Part I Information About Your Eligible Child or Children—You **must** complete this part. See instructions for details, including what to do if you need more space.

1	(a) Child's name		(b) Child's year of birth	Check if child was— (c) born **before 2003** and disabled	(d) a child with special needs	(e) a foreign child	(f) Child's identifying number	(g) Check if adoption became final in 2020 or earlier
	First	Last						
Child 1	Allison	Bass	2020	☐	☐	☐	466-47-3311	✔
Child 2				☐	☐	☐		☐
Child 3				☐	☐	☐		☐

Caution: If the child was a foreign child, see **Special rules** in the instructions for line 1, column (e), before you complete Part II or Part III. If you received **employer-provided adoption benefits,** complete Part III on the back next.

Part II Adoption Credit

			Child 1	Child 2	Child 3		
2	Maximum adoption credit per child. Enter $14,300 (see instructions)	2	14,300				
3	Did you file Form 8839 for a prior year for the same child? ☑ **No.** Enter -0-. ☐ **Yes.** See instructions for the amount to enter.	3	0				
4	Subtract line 3 from line 2	4	14,300				
5	**Qualified adoption expenses** (see instructions) . .	5	17,000				
	Caution: Your qualified adoption expenses may not be equal to the adoption expenses you paid in 2020.						
6	Enter the **smaller** of line 4 or line 5	6	14,300				
7	Enter modified adjusted gross income (see instructions)				7	222,520	
8	Is line 7 more than $214,520? ☐ **No.** Skip lines 8 and 9, and enter -0- on line 10. ☑ **Yes.** Subtract $214,520 from line 7				8	8,000	
9	Divide line 8 by $40,000. Enter the result as a decimal (rounded to at least three places). Do not enter more than 1.000				9	× .200	
10	Multiply each amount on line 6 by line 9	10	2,860				
11	Subtract line 10 from line 6	11	11,440				
12	Add the amounts on line 11				12	11,440	
13	Credit carryforward, if any, from prior years. See your Adoption Credit Carryforward Worksheet in the 2019 Form 8839 instructions				13		
14	Add lines 12 and 13				14	11,440	
15	Enter the amount from line 5 of the Credit Limit Worksheet in the instructions				15	27,343	
16	**Adoption Credit.** Enter the smaller of line 14 or line 15 here and on Schedule 3 (Form 1040), line 6. Check box **c** on that line and enter "**8839**" in the space next to box **c**. If line 15 is smaller than line 14, you may have a credit carryforward (see instructions)				16	11,440	

For Paperwork Reduction Act Notice, see your tax return instructions.   Cat. No. 22843L   Form **8839** (2020)

Self-Study Problem 7.7

Form 8839 (2020)   Page **2**

Part III	**Employer-Provided Adoption Benefits**		Child 1	Child 2	Child 3		
17	Maximum exclusion per child. Enter $14,300 (see instructions)	**17**	14,300				
18	Did you receive employer-provided adoption benefits for a prior year for the same child? ☑ **No.** Enter -0-. ☐ **Yes.** See instructions for the amount to enter.	**18**	0				
19	Subtract line 18 from line 17	**19**	14,300				
20	Employer-provided adoption benefits you received in 2020. This amount should be shown in box 12 of your 2020 Form(s) W-2 with code **T**	**20**	4,000				
21	Add the amounts on line 20					**21**	4,000
22	Enter the **smaller** of line 19 or line 20. But if the child was a child with special needs and the adoption became final in 2020, enter the amount from line 19 .	**22**	4,000				
23	Enter modified adjusted gross income (from the worksheet in the instructions)	**23**	222,520				
24	Is line 23 more than $214,520? ☐ **No.** Skip lines 24 and 25, and enter -0- on line 26. ☑ **Yes.** Subtract $214,520 from line 23	**24**	8,000				
25	Divide line 24 by $40,000. Enter the result as a decimal (rounded to at least three places). Do not enter more than 1.000	**25**	× .20				
26	Multiply each amount on line 22 by line 25	**26**	800				
27	**Excluded benefits.** Subtract line 26 from line 22 . .	**27**	3,200				
28	Add the amounts on line 27					**28**	3,200
29	**Taxable benefits.** Is line 28 more than line 21? ☑ **No.** Subtract line 28 from line 21. Also, include this amount, if more than zero, on line 1 of Form 1040 or 1040-SR or line 1a of Form 1040-NR. On the dotted line next to line 1 of Form 1040 or 1040-SR or line 1a of Form 1040-NR, enter "AB." ☐ **Yes.** Subtract line 21 from line 28. Enter the result as a negative number. Reduce the total you would enter on line 1 of Form 1040 or 1040-SR or line 1a of Form 1040-NR by the amount on Form 8839, line 29. Enter the result on line 1 of Form 1040 or 1040-SR or line 1a of Form 1040-NR. Enter "SNE" on the dotted line next to the entry line.	**29**					800

You may be able to claim the adoption credit in Part II on the front of this form if any of the following apply.

- You paid adoption expenses in 2019, those expenses were not fully reimbursed by your employer or otherwise, and the adoption was not final by the end of 2019.

- The total adoption expenses you paid in 2020 were not fully reimbursed by your employer or otherwise, and the adoption became final in 2020 or earlier.

- You adopted a child with special needs and the adoption became final in 2020.

Form **8839** (2020)

Self-Study Problem 7.8

a. $7,500. The Nissan Leaf qualifies for the full $7,500 credit.

b. $2,600 (26% × $10,000). The solar system for the hot tub is not an allowed cost for the credit.

Self-Study Problem 7.9

See Form 8880 below.

Form 8880

Credit for Qualified Retirement Savings Contributions

OMB No. 1545-0074

2020

Department of the Treasury
Internal Revenue Service

▶ Attach to Form 1040, 1040-SR, or 1040-NR.
▶ Go to *www.irs.gov/Form8880* for the latest information.

Attachment Sequence No. **54**

Name(s) shown on return: Robin and Steve Harrington

Your social security number

⚠ **CAUTION**

You **cannot** take this credit if **either** of the following applies.
- The amount on Form 1040, 1040-SR, or 1040-NR, line 11, is more than $32,500 ($48,750 if head of household; $65,000 if married filing jointly).
- The person(s) who made the qualified contribution or elective deferral **(a)** was born after January 1, 2003; **(b)** is claimed as a dependent on someone else's 2020 tax return; or **(c)** was a **student** (see instructions).

			(a) You	(b) Your spouse
1	Traditional and Roth IRA contributions, and ABLE account contributions by the designated beneficiary for 2020. **Do not** include rollover contributions	1	6,000	6,000
2	Elective deferrals to a 401(k) or other qualified employer plan, voluntary employee contributions, and 501(c)(18)(D) plan contributions for 2020 (see instructions)	2		
3	Add lines 1 and 2	3	6,000	6,000
4	Certain distributions received **after** 2017 and **before** the due date (including extensions) of your 2020 tax return (see instructions). If married filing jointly, include **both** spouses' amounts in **both** columns. See instructions for an exception	4		
5	Subtract line 4 from line 3. If zero or less, enter -0-	5	6,000	6,000
6	In each column, enter the **smaller** of line 5 or $2,000	6	2,000	2,000

7	Add the amounts on line 6. If zero, **stop**; you can't take this credit	7	4,000
8	Enter the amount from Form 1040, 1040-SR, or 1040-NR, line 11*	8	39,500
9	Enter the applicable decimal amount from the table below.		

If line 8 is—		And your filing status is—		
Over—	But not over—	Married filing jointly	Head of household	Single, Married filing separately, or Qualifying widow(er)
		Enter on line 9—		
---	$19,500	0.5	0.5	0.5
$19,500	$21,250	0.5	0.5	0.2
$21,250	$29,250	0.5	0.5	0.1
$29,250	$31,875	0.5	0.2	0.1
$31,875	$32,500	0.5	0.1	0.1
$32,500	$39,000	0.5	0.1	0.0
$39,000	$42,500	0.2	0.1	0.0
$42,500	$48,750	0.1	0.1	0.0
$48,750	$65,000	0.1	0.0	0.0
$65,000	---	0.0	0.0	0.0

(line 9: × 0.2)

Note: If line 9 is zero, **stop**; you can't take this credit.

10	Multiply line 7 by line 9	10	800
11	Limitation based on tax liability. Enter the amount from the Credit Limit Worksheet in the instructions	11	1,473
12	**Credit for qualified retirement savings contributions.** Enter the **smaller** of line 10 or line 11 here and on Schedule 3 (Form 1040), line 4	12	800

* See Pub. 590-A for the amount to enter if you claim any exclusion or deduction for foreign earned income, foreign housing, or income from Puerto Rico or for bona fide residents of American Samoa.

For Paperwork Reduction Act Notice, see your tax return instructions.   Cat. No. 33394D   Form **8880** (2020)

CHAPTER 8   DEPRECIATION AND SALE OF BUSINESS PROPERTY

Self-Study Problem 8.1

Year	Depreciation Deduction
20X1	$ 583
20X2	700
20X3	700
20X4	700
20X5	700
20X6	117
Total	$3,500

Self-Study Problem 8.2

a. Bonus on 7-year property: $16,000 ($12,000 + $4,000)
   Real estate: $175,000 × 0.02033 = $3,558
   See Form 4562 on Page E-56.
b. MACRS: $12,000 × 0.1429 = $1,715
   MACRS: $4,000 × 0.1429 = $572
   Total 7-year property = $2,287
   Real estate: $175,000 × 0.02033 = $3,558
c. 7-year property: $0 (cost fully recovered through bonus depreciation in year 1)
   Real estate: $175,000 × 0.02564 = $4,487

Self-Study Problem 8.3

a. $405,407. $2,837,000 × 0.1429 (MACRS depreciation factor for the first year for 7-year property using the half-year convention).
b. $1,085,088. Chang's eligible §179 property exceeds the $2,590,000 threshold by $247,000; thus, she must reduce the 2020 Section 179 $1,040,000 annual limit to $793,000. The $2,044,000 remaining balance of the property ($2,837,000 − $793,000) is depreciated using the MACRS: $2,044,000 × 0.1429 = $292,088. The total cost recovery is $793,000 + $292,088 = $1,085,088.
c. $2,837,000. Chang is eligible for 100% bonus depreciation on the equipment and there are no taxable income limits or thresholds associated with bonus depreciation. Chang will generate a $337,000 net operating loss.

Self-Study Problem 8.4

1. Yes   Qualified business use is 50 percent or less; therefore, Alvarez must use the straight-line method of depreciation for the auto.
2. No   Qualified business use is more than 50 percent; therefore, Laura may use the accelerated method of depreciation.

Self-Study Problem 8.5

	2020	2021	2022
Original cost	$56,000	$56,000	$56,000
Business use percentage	0.90	0.9	0.9
Basis for depreciation	$ 50,400	$ 50,400	$ 50,400
Depreciation factor	20%	32%	19.2%
MACRS depreciation	$10,080	$ 16,128	$ 9,677
Annual depreciation limit × 90%	$ 9,090	$14,490	$ 8,730

Self-Study Problem 8.2

Form 4562

Department of the Treasury
Internal Revenue Service   (99)

Depreciation and Amortization
(Including Information on Listed Property)
▶ Attach to your tax return.
▶ Go to *www.irs.gov/Form4562* for instructions and the latest information.

OMB No. 1545-0172

2020

Attachment
Sequence No. **179**

Name(s) shown on return
Mary Moser

Business or activity to which this form relates

Identifying number

Part I — **Election To Expense Certain Property Under Section 179**
Note: If you have any listed property, complete Part V before you complete Part I.

1	Maximum amount (see instructions)	1
2	Total cost of section 179 property placed in service (see instructions)	2
3	Threshold cost of section 179 property before reduction in limitation (see instructions)	3
4	Reduction in limitation. Subtract line 3 from line 2. If zero or less, enter -0-	4
5	Dollar limitation for tax year. Subtract line 4 from line 1. If zero or less, enter -0-. If married filing separately, see instructions	5

6	(a) Description of property	(b) Cost (business use only)	(c) Elected cost

7	Listed property. Enter the amount from line 29	7
8	Total elected cost of section 179 property. Add amounts in column (c), lines 6 and 7	8
9	Tentative deduction. Enter the **smaller** of line 5 or line 8	9
10	Carryover of disallowed deduction from line 13 of your 2019 Form 4562	10
11	Business income limitation. Enter the smaller of business income (not less than zero) or line 5. See instructions	11
12	Section 179 expense deduction. Add lines 9 and 10, but don't enter more than line 11	12
13	Carryover of disallowed deduction to 2021. Add lines 9 and 10, less line 12 ▶	13

Note: Don't use Part II or Part III below for listed property. Instead, use Part V.

Part II — **Special Depreciation Allowance and Other Depreciation (Don't** include listed property. See instructions.)

14	Special depreciation allowance for qualified property (other than listed property) placed in service during the tax year. See instructions	14	16,000
15	Property subject to section 168(f)(1) election	15	
16	Other depreciation (including ACRS)	16	

Part III — **MACRS Depreciation (Don't** include listed property. See instructions.)

Section A

17	MACRS deductions for assets placed in service in tax years beginning before 2020	17	
18	If you are electing to group any assets placed in service during the tax year into one or more general asset accounts, check here .... ▶ ☐		

Section B—Assets Placed in Service During 2020 Tax Year Using the General Depreciation System

(a) Classification of property	(b) Month and year placed in service	(c) Basis for depreciation (business/investment use only—see instructions)	(d) Recovery period	(e) Convention	(f) Method	(g) Depreciation deduction
19a 3-year property						
b 5-year property						
c 7-year property						
d 10-year property						
e 15-year property						
f 20-year property						
g 25-year property			25 yrs.		S/L	
h Residential rental property			27.5 yrs.	MM	S/L	
			27.5 yrs.	MM	S/L	
i Nonresidential real property	03/30/2020	175,000	39 yrs.	MM	S/L	3,558
				MM	S/L	

Section C—Assets Placed in Service During 2020 Tax Year Using the Alternative Depreciation System

20a Class life					S/L	
b 12-year			12 yrs.		S/L	
c 30-year			30 yrs.	MM	S/L	
d 40-year			40 yrs.	MM	S/L	

Part IV — **Summary** (See instructions.)

21	Listed property. Enter amount from line 28	21	
22	**Total.** Add amounts from line 12, lines 14 through 17, lines 19 and 20 in column (g), and line 21. Enter here and on the appropriate lines of your return. Partnerships and S corporations—see instructions	22	19,558
23	For assets shown above and placed in service during the current year, enter the portion of the basis attributable to section 263A costs	23	

For Paperwork Reduction Act Notice, see separate instructions.   Cat. No. 12906N   Form **4562** (2020)

Self-Study Problem 8.6

1. 15-year Amortization.	5. 15-year Amortization.
2. Useful Life.	6. Not Amortizable.
3. Useful Life.	7. 15-year Amortization.
4. 15-year Amortization.	8. Not Amortizable.

Self-Study Problem 8.7

	Land	Computer	Equipment
Proceeds	$37,000	$14,000	$16,000
Adjusted Basis:			
Cost	$24,000	$25,875	$25,000
Cost Recovery	0	5,175	4,300
Adjusted Basis	24,000	20,700	20,700
Selling Costs	500	0	1,600
Gain/(Loss)	$12,500	$ (6,700)	$ (6,300)

The land and the computer are both Section 1231 properties and thus, the gain and loss is netted resulting in a $5,800 net Section 1231 gain. As a result, both the gain on the land and the loss on the computer will be treated as long-term capital gains. The equipment was not held for more than one year and thus, is an ordinary asset (depreciable business property is not a capital asset—see Chapter 4) and the loss will be treated as an ordinary loss.

Self-Study Problem 8.8

See Form 4797 on Pages E-58 and E-59.

Self-Study Problem 8.9

	Furniture (completely destroyed)	Machinery (partially destroyed)
Insurance proceeds	$ 0	$10,000
Adjusted basis	5,000	**14,000**
Decrease in FMV	n/a	15,000
Loss	$(5,000)	$ (4,000)

Since both result in a casualty loss, the losses are excluded from Section 1231 treatment and are treated as ordinary losses. The gain on the sale of the land would be treated as a Section 1231 long-term capital gain.

Self-Study Problem 8.8

Form **4797**	**Sales of Business Property**	OMB No. 1545-0184
	(Also Involuntary Conversions and Recapture Amounts Under Sections 179 and 280F(b)(2))	**2020**
Department of the Treasury Internal Revenue Service	▶ **Attach to your tax return.** ▶ Go to *www.irs.gov/Form4797* for instructions and the latest information.	Attachment Sequence No. **27**

Name(s) shown on return: Serena

Identifying number: 74-8976432

1 Enter the gross proceeds from sales or exchanges reported to you for 2020 on Form(s) 1099-B or 1099-S (or substitute statement) that you are including on line 2, 10, or 20. See instructions **1**

Part I Sales or Exchanges of Property Used in a Trade or Business and Involuntary Conversions From Other Than Casualty or Theft—Most Property Held More Than 1 Year (see instructions)

2 (a) Description of property	(b) Date acquired (mo., day, yr.)	(c) Date sold (mo., day, yr.)	(d) Gross sales price	(e) Depreciation allowed or allowable since acquisition	(f) Cost or other basis, plus improvements and expense of sale	(g) Gain or (loss) Subtract (f) from the sum of (d) and (e)
Land	12/03/2009	01/05/2020	37,000		24,500	12,500
Computer	04/05/2017	05/02/2020	14,000	5,175	25,875	(6,700)

3 Gain, if any, from Form 4684, line 39	**3**	
4 Section 1231 gain from installment sales from Form 6252, line 26 or 37	**4**	
5 Section 1231 gain or (loss) from like-kind exchanges from Form 8824	**5**	
6 Gain, if any, from line 32, from other than casualty or theft	**6**	146,050
7 Combine lines 2 through 6. Enter the gain or (loss) here and on the appropriate line as follows	**7**	151,850

Partnerships and S corporations. Report the gain or (loss) following the instructions for Form 1065, Schedule K, line 10, or Form 1120-S, Schedule K, line 9. Skip lines 8, 9, 11, and 12 below.

Individuals, partners, S corporation shareholders, and all others. If line 7 is zero or a loss, enter the amount from line 7 on line 11 below and skip lines 8 and 9. If line 7 is a gain and you didn't have any prior year section 1231 losses, or they were recaptured in an earlier year, enter the gain from line 7 as a long-term capital gain on the Schedule D filed with your return and skip lines 8, 9, 11, and 12 below.

8 Nonrecaptured net section 1231 losses from prior years. See instructions	**8**	
9 Subtract line 8 from line 7. If zero or less, enter -0-. If line 9 is zero, enter the gain from line 7 on line 12 below. If line 9 is more than zero, enter the amount from line 8 on line 12 below and enter the gain from line 9 as a long-term capital gain on the Schedule D filed with your return. See instructions	**9**	

Part II Ordinary Gains and Losses (see instructions)

10 Ordinary gains and losses not included on lines 11 through 16 (include property held 1 year or less):

Equipment	10/21/2019	7/22/2020	16,000	4,300	26,600	(6,300)

11 Loss, if any, from line 7	**11** (	)
12 Gain, if any, from line 7 or amount from line 8, if applicable	**12**	
13 Gain, if any, from line 31	**13**	7,600
14 Net gain or (loss) from Form 4684, lines 31 and 38a	**14**	
15 Ordinary gain from installment sales from Form 6252, line 25 or 36	**15**	
16 Ordinary gain or (loss) from like-kind exchanges from Form 8824	**16**	
17 Combine lines 10 through 16	**17**	1,300

18 For all except individual returns, enter the amount from line 17 on the appropriate line of your return and skip lines a and b below. For individual returns, complete lines a and b below.

a If the loss on line 11 includes a loss from Form 4684, line 35, column (b)(ii), enter that part of the loss here. Enter the loss from income-producing property on Schedule A (Form 1040), line 16. (Do not include any loss on property used as an employee.) Identify as from "Form 4797, line 18a." See instructions	**18a**	
b Redetermine the gain or (loss) on line 17 excluding the loss, if any, on line 18a. Enter here and on Schedule 1 (Form 1040), Part I, line 4	**18b**	1,300

For Paperwork Reduction Act Notice, see separate instructions.   Cat. No. 13086I   Form **4797** (2020)

Self-Study Problem 8.8

Form 4797 (2020)   Page **2**

Part III	**Gain From Disposition of Property Under Sections 1245, 1250, 1252, 1254, and 1255** (see instructions)

19	(a) Description of section 1245, 1250, 1252, 1254, or 1255 property:		**(b)** Date acquired (mo., day, yr.)	**(c)** Date sold (mo., day, yr.)
A	Building		12/03/2009	10/07/2020
B	Furniture		12/03/2009	10/07/2020
C				
D				

	These columns relate to the properties on lines 19A through 19D. ▶		**Property A**	**Property B**	**Property C**	**Property D**
20	Gross sales price (**Note:** *See line 1 before completing.*) .	**20**	355,000	7,600		
21	Cost or other basis plus expense of sale	**21**	335,000	15,000		
22	Depreciation (or depletion) allowed or allowable. .	**22**	126,050	15,000		
23	Adjusted basis. Subtract line 22 from line 21. . .	**23**	208,950	0		
24	Total gain. Subtract line 23 from line 20	**24**	146,050	7,600		
25	**If section 1245 property:**					
a	Depreciation allowed or allowable from line 22 . .	**25a**		15,000		
b	Enter the **smaller** of line 24 or 25a.	**25b**		7,600		
26	**If section 1250 property:** If straight line depreciation was used, enter -0- on line 26g, except for a corporation subject to section 291.					
a	Additional depreciation after 1975. See instructions .	**26a**				
b	Applicable percentage multiplied by the **smaller** of line 24 or line 26a. See instructions.	**26b**				
c	Subtract line 26a from line 24. If residential rental property **or** line 24 isn't more than line 26a, skip lines 26d and 26e	**26c**				
d	Additional depreciation after 1969 and before 1976. .	**26d**				
e	Enter the **smaller** of line 26c or 26d	**26e**				
f	Section 291 amount (corporations only)	**26f**				
g	Add lines 26b, 26e, and 26f	**26g**	0			
27	**If section 1252 property:** Skip this section if you didn't dispose of farmland or if this form is being completed for a partnership.					
a	Soil, water, and land clearing expenses	**27a**				
b	Line 27a multiplied by applicable percentage. See instructions	**27b**				
c	Enter the **smaller** of line 24 or 27b	**27c**				
28	**If section 1254 property:**					
a	Intangible drilling and development costs, expenditures for development of mines and other natural deposits, mining exploration costs, and depletion. See instructions	**28a**				
b	Enter the **smaller** of line 24 or 28a.	**28b**				
29	**If section 1255 property:**					
a	Applicable percentage of payments excluded from income under section 126. See instructions	**29a**				
b	Enter the **smaller** of line 24 or 29a. See instructions .	**29b**				

Summary of Part III Gains. Complete property columns A through D through line 29b before going to line 30.

30	Total gains for all properties. Add property columns A through D, line 24	**30**	153,650
31	Add property columns A through D, lines 25b, 26g, 27c, 28b, and 29b. Enter here and on line 13	**31**	7,600
32	Subtract line 31 from line 30. Enter the portion from casualty or theft on Form 4684, line 33. Enter the portion from other than casualty or theft on Form 4797, line 6	**32**	146,050

Part IV	**Recapture Amounts Under Sections 179 and 280F(b)(2) When Business Use Drops to 50% or Less** (see instructions)

			(a) Section 179	**(b)** Section 280F(b)(2)
33	Section 179 expense deduction or depreciation allowable in prior years.	**33**		
34	Recomputed depreciation. See instructions	**34**		
35	Recapture amount. Subtract line 34 from line 33. See the instructions for where to report . .	**35**		

Form **4797** (2020)

Self-Study Problem 8.10

Cash	$ 20,000
Add: buyer's note	100,000
Selling price	120,000
Less: the adjusted basis ($80,000 − $26,000)	(54,000)
Total gain realized	$ 66,000
Contract price ($20,000 + $100,000)	$120,000
Taxable gain in 2020 = $66,000 / $120,000 × $20,000	$ 11,000

Self-Study Problem 8.11

Calculation of gain recognized:

Fair market value of new land	$ 22,000
Add: liability assumed by the buyer	8,000
Total amount realized	30,000
Less: the adjusted basis of the old land	(18,000)
Gain realized	$ 12,000
Boot received (liability assumed by the buyer)	$ 8,000
Gain recognized (the lesser of the gain realized or the boot received)	$ 8,000

Basis of the new land:

Basis of old land	$ 18,000
Less: boot received	(8,000)
Add: the gain recognized	8,000
Basis of the new land received	$ 18,000

Self-Study Problem 8.12

1.

Insurance proceeds	$150,000
Less: the adjusted basis of the property	(70,000)
Gain realized	$ 80,000
Insurance proceeds	$150,000
Less: the cost of the replacement store	(135,000)
Proceeds not reinvested	$ 15,000
Gain recognized (the lesser of the gain realized or the proceeds not reinvested)	$ 15,000

2.

Cost of the new store	$135,000
Less: the gain deferred ($80,000 − $15,000)	(65,000)
Basis of the new store	$ 70,000

CHAPTER 9 PAYROLL, ESTIMATED PAYMENTS, AND RETIREMENT PLANS

Self-Study Problem 9.1

1. See Form W-4 on Page E-62.
2. Percentage Method:
   Adjusted Wage Amount: $3,498.33 [$3,290 + ($6,500 ÷ 12) − ($4,000 ÷ 12)]
   Tentative Withholding Amount: $279.38 [$82.30 + (($3,498.33 − $1,856) × 12%)].
   Be sure and use the table for employees that checked the box in Step 2(c) of the
   Form W-4.
   Tax Credits: $208.33 ($2,500 ÷ 12)
   Final withholding: $71.05 ($279.38 − $208.33)

   Wage Bracket Method:

   Adjusted Wage Amount: $3,498.33 [$3,290 + ($6,500 ÷ 12) − ($4,000 ÷ 12)]
   Tentative Withholding Amount: $277.00. Be sure and use the colum for
   employees that checked the box in Step 2(c) of the Form W-4.
   Tax Credits: $208.33 ($2,500 ÷ 12)
   Final withholding: $68.67 ($277.00 − $208.33)

Self-Study Problem 9.2

Form **1040-ES** Department of the Treasury Internal Revenue Service	20**20** Estimated Tax	**Payment Voucher 1** OMB No. 1545-0074

		Calendar year—**Due April 15, 2020**
File only if you are making a payment of estimated tax by check or money order. Mail this voucher with your check or money order payable to **"United States Treasury."** Write your social security number and "2020 Form 1040-ES" on your check or money order. Do not send cash. Enclose, but do not staple or attach, your payment with this voucher.		Amount of estimated tax you are paying by check or money order. Dollars **1,645** Cents **00** *

Pay online at www.irs.gov/etpay

Simple. Fast. Secure.

Print or type

Your first name and middle initial	Your last name	Your social security number
Ray	Adams	466-47-1131

If joint payment, complete for spouse

Spouse's first name and middle initial	Spouse's last name	Spouse's social security number

Address (number, street, and apt. no.)

City, state, and ZIP code. (If a foreign address, enter city, also complete spaces below.)

Foreign country name	Foreign province/county	Foreign postal code

For Privacy Act and Paperwork Reduction Act Notice, see instructions.   Form 1040-ES (2020)

*$1,645 = ($7,600/4) − $255

Form **W-4**	**Employee's Withholding Certificate**	OMB No. 1545-0074
Department of the Treasury Internal Revenue Service	▶ Complete Form W-4 so that your employer can withhold the correct federal income tax from your pay. ▶ Give Form W-4 to your employer. ▶ Your withholding is subject to review by the IRS.	2020

Step 1:

Enter Personal Information

(a) First name and middle initial	Last name	(b) Social security number
Lillian	Miles	

Address

456 Peachtree Court

City or town, state, and ZIP code

Atlanta, GA 30310

▶ **Does your name match the name on your social security card?** If not, to ensure you get credit for your earnings, contact SSA at 800-772-1213 or go to *www.ssa.gov*.

(c)   ☐   Single or Married filing separately

☑   Married filing jointly (or Qualifying widow(er))

☐   Head of household (Check only if you're unmarried and pay more than half the costs of keeping up a home for yourself and a qualifying individual.)

Complete Steps 2–4 ONLY if they apply to you; otherwise, skip to Step 5. See page 2 for more information on each step, who can claim exemption from withholding, when to use the online estimator, and privacy.

Step 2:

Multiple Jobs or Spouse Works

Complete this step if you (1) hold more than one job at a time, or (2) are married filing jointly and your spouse also works. The correct amount of withholding depends on income earned from all of these jobs.

Do **only one** of the following.

(a) Use the estimator at *www.irs.gov/W4App* for most accurate withholding for this step (and Steps 3–4); **or**

(b) Use the Multiple Jobs Worksheet on page 3 and enter the result in Step 4(c) below for roughly accurate withholding; **or**

(c) If there are only two jobs total, you may check this box. Do the same on Form W-4 for the other job. This option is accurate for jobs with similar pay; otherwise, more tax than necessary may be withheld . . . . . ▶ ☑

TIP: To be accurate, submit a 2020 Form W-4 for all other jobs. If you (or your spouse) have self-employment income, including as an independent contractor, use the estimator.

Complete Steps 3–4(b) on Form W-4 for only ONE of these jobs. Leave those steps blank for the other jobs. (Your withholding will be most accurate if you complete Steps 3–4(b) on the Form W-4 for the highest paying job.)

Step 3:

Claim Dependents

If your income will be $200,000 or less ($400,000 or less if married filing jointly):

Multiply the number of qualifying children under age 17 by $2,000 ▶ $ 2,000

Multiply the number of other dependents by $500   . . . . ▶ $ 500

Add the amounts above and enter the total here   . . . . **3** $ 2,500

Step 4 (optional):

Other Adjustments

(a) **Other income (not from jobs).** If you want tax withheld for other income you expect this year that won't have withholding, enter the amount of other income here. This may include interest, dividends, and retirement income   . . . . **4(a)** $ 6,500

(b) **Deductions.** If you expect to claim deductions other than the standard deduction and want to reduce your withholding, use the Deductions Worksheet on page 3 and enter the result here   . . . . **4(b)** $ 4,000

(c) **Extra withholding.** Enter any additional tax you want withheld each **pay period**   .   **4(c)** $

Step 5:

Sign Here

Under penalties of perjury, I declare that this certificate, to the best of my knowledge and belief, is true, correct, and complete.

▶ _____   ▶ _____

    Employee's signature (This form is not valid unless you sign it.)   Date

Employers Only	Employer's name and address	First date of employment	Employer identification number (EIN)

For Privacy Act and Paperwork Reduction Act Notice, see page 3.   Cat. No. 10220Q   Form **W-4** (2020)

Note: Lillian will not complete the Multiple Jobs Worksheet because her wages and John's wages are similar. Instead, she will check the box under 2(c) on page 1 of the Form W-4.

Form W-4 (2020)   Page **3**

Step 2(b)—Multiple Jobs Worksheet *(Keep for your records.)*

If you choose the option in Step 2(b) on Form W-4, complete this worksheet (which calculates the total extra tax for all jobs) on **only ONE** Form W-4. Withholding will be most accurate if you complete the worksheet and enter the result on the Form W-4 for the highest paying job.

Note: If more than one job has annual wages of more than $120,000 or there are more than three jobs, see Pub. 505 for additional tables; or, you can use the online withholding estimator at *www.irs.gov/W4App.*

1   **Two jobs.** If you have two jobs or you're married filing jointly and you and your spouse each have one job, find the amount from the appropriate table on page 4. Using the "Higher Paying Job" row and the "Lower Paying Job" column, find the value at the intersection of the two household salaries and enter that value on line 1. Then, **skip** to line 3 . . . .   **1** $ _____

2   **Three jobs.** If you and/or your spouse have three jobs at the same time, complete lines 2a, 2b, and 2c below. Otherwise, skip to line 3.

    a   Find the amount from the appropriate table on page 4 using the annual wages from the highest paying job in the "Higher Paying Job" row and the annual wages for your next highest paying job in the "Lower Paying Job" column. Find the value at the intersection of the two household salaries and enter that value on line 2a . . . .   **2a** $ _____

    b   Add the annual wages of the two highest paying jobs from line 2a together and use the total as the wages in the "Higher Paying Job" row and use the annual wages for your third job in the "Lower Paying Job" column to find the amount from the appropriate table on page 4 and enter this amount on line 2b . . . .   **2b** $ _____

    c   Add the amounts from lines 2a and 2b and enter the result on line 2c . . . .   **2c** $ _____

3   Enter the number of pay periods per year for the highest paying job. For example, if that job pays weekly, enter 52; if it pays every other week, enter 26; if it pays monthly, enter 12, etc. . . . . . .   **3** _____

4   **Divide** the annual amount on line 1 or line 2c by the number of pay periods on line 3. Enter this amount here and in **Step 4(c)** of Form W-4 for the highest paying job (along with any other additional amount you want withheld) . . . .   **4** $ _____

Step 4(b)—Deductions Worksheet *(Keep for your records.)*

1   Enter an estimate of your 2020 itemized deductions (from Schedule A (Form 1040 or 1040-SR)). Such deductions may include qualifying home mortgage interest, charitable contributions, state and local taxes (up to $10,000), and medical expenses in excess of 7.5% of your income . . . .   **1** $ _____

2   Enter: { • $24,800 if you're married filing jointly or qualifying widow(er)
           • $18,650 if you're head of household
           • $12,400 if you're single or married filing separately } . . . .   **2** $ _____

3   If line 1 is greater than line 2, subtract line 2 from line 1. If line 2 is greater than line 1, enter "-0-" . .   **3** $ _____

4   Enter an estimate of your student loan interest, deductible IRA contributions, and certain other adjustments (from Part II of Schedule 1 (Form 1040 or 1040-SR)). See Pub. 505 for more information   **4** $ 4,000

5   **Add** lines 3 and 4. Enter the result here and in **Step 4(b)** of Form W-4 . . . .   **5** $ 4,000

Privacy Act and Paperwork Reduction Act Notice. We ask for the information on this form to carry out the Internal Revenue laws of the United States. Internal Revenue Code sections 3402(f)(2) and 6109 and their regulations require you to provide this information; your employer uses it to determine your federal income tax withholding. Failure to provide a properly completed form will result in your being treated as a single person with no other entries on the form; providing fraudulent information may subject you to penalties. Routine uses of this information include giving it to the Department of Justice for civil and criminal litigation; to cities, states, the District of Columbia, and U.S. commonwealths and possessions for use in administering their tax laws; and to the Department of Health and Human Services for use in the National Directory of New Hires. We may also disclose this information to other countries under a tax treaty, to federal and state agencies to enforce federal nontax criminal laws, or to federal law enforcement and intelligence agencies to combat terrorism.

You are not required to provide the information requested on a form that is subject to the Paperwork Reduction Act unless the form displays a valid OMB control number. Books or records relating to a form or its instructions must be retained as long as their contents may become material in the administration of any Internal Revenue law. Generally, tax returns and return information are confidential, as required by Code section 6103.

The average time and expenses required to complete and file this form will vary depending on individual circumstances. For estimated averages, see the instructions for your income tax return.

If you have suggestions for making this form simpler, we would be happy to hear from you. See the instructions for your income tax return.

Self-Study Problem 9.3

1. a. Employee's portion: Social Security tax $8,475.40 [$140,000 − ($141,000 − $137,700)] × 6.2%. Note that Juliette's year-to-date pay exceeds the 2020 FICA cap of $137,700.

    b. Hills' portion: Social Security tax $8,475.40 [$140,000 − ($141,000 − $137,700)] × 6.2%

    c. Employee's portion: Medicare tax $2,030.00 ($140,000 × 1.45%)

    d. Hills' portion: Medicare tax $2,030.00 ($140,000 × 1.45%)

2. ai. Health care costs allocated to sick pay is $777.77. Yvette's allocation of health care costs to sick pay is $333.33 ($2,500 sick pay ÷ $15,000 total pay × $2,000 health care costs). Juan's allocation of health care costs to sick pay is $444.44 ($2,000 sick pay ÷ $9,000 total × $2,000 health care costs)

    aii. Health care costs allocated to family leave pay is $1,333.33. Yvette's allocation of health care costs to family leave pay is $1,333.33 ($10,000 family leave pay ÷ $15,000 total pay × $2,000 health care costs)

    aiii. Health care costs allocated to the employee retention credit is $9,888.90. Total health care costs of $12,000 (6 employees × $2,000 per employee) less amounts allocated to sick ($777.77) and family leave pay ($1,333.33). Note that only $8,000 of wages were allocated to the ERC for Juliette, Yan and Sai; since otherwise, ERC wages plus health care costs would exceed the $10,000 per employee limit for the ERC.

    b. Hills' sick pay credit is $5,343.02. The sum of qualified wages $4,500 plus $777.77 in health care costs plus $65.25 ($4,500 × 1.45%) of employer's Medicare tax costs

    c. Hills' family leave pay credit is $11,478.33. The sum of qualified wages of $10,000 plus $1,333.33 in health care costs plus $145.00 ($10,000 × 1.45%) of employer's Medicare tax costs.

    d. Hills' employee retention credit is $24,694.45. [($39,500 wages + $9,888.90 health care costs allocated) × 50%]

Self-Study Problem 9.4

1. See Form 941 on Pages E-65 to E-66.
2. See Form 941 and Worksheet 1 on Pages E-67 to E-70.

Self-Study Problem 9.4, part 1

Form 941 for 2020: Employer's QUARTERLY Federal Tax Return
(Rev. April 2020)   Department of the Treasury — Internal Revenue Service

950120

OMB No. 1545-0029

Employer identification number (EIN) 3 3 – 4 4 3 4 4 3 2

Name (not your trade name) Hills Scientific Corporation

Trade name (if any)

Address
Number   Street   Suite or room number

City   State   ZIP code

Foreign country name   Foreign province/county   Foreign postal code

Report for this Quarter of 2020
(Check one.)

☐ **1:** January, February, March

☒ **2:** April, May, June

☐ **3:** July, August, September

☐ **4:** October, November, December

Go to *www.irs.gov/Form941* for instructions and the latest information.

Read the separate instructions before you complete Form 941. Type or print within the boxes.

Part 1:   Answer these questions for this quarter.

1	Number of employees who received wages, tips, or other compensation for the pay period including: *June 12* (Quarter 2), *Sept. 12* (Quarter 3), or *Dec. 12* (Quarter 4) . . .	1	6
2	Wages, tips, and other compensation	2	140,000 . 00
3	Federal income tax withheld from wages, tips, and other compensation	3	33,630 . 00
4	If no wages, tips, and other compensation are subject to social security or Medicare tax	☐ Check and go to line 6.	

		Column 1		Column 2
5a	Taxable social security wages . .	136,700 . 00	× 0.124 =	16,950 . 80
5a (i)	Qualified sick leave wages . .	.	× 0.062 =	.
5a (ii)	Qualified family leave wages .	.	× 0.062 =	.
5b	Taxable social security tips . . .	.	× 0.124 =	.
5c	Taxable Medicare wages & tips .	140,000 . 00	× 0.029 =	4,060 . 00
5d	Taxable wages & tips subject to Additional Medicare Tax withholding	.	× 0.009 =	.

5e	Total social security and Medicare taxes. Add Column 2 from lines 5a, 5a(i), 5a(ii), 5b, 5c, and 5d	5e	21,010 . 80
5f	Section 3121(q) Notice and Demand—Tax due on unreported tips (see instructions) . .	5f	.
6	Total taxes before adjustments. Add lines 3, 5e, and 5f	6	54,640 . 80
7	Current quarter's adjustment for fractions of cents	7	.
8	Current quarter's adjustment for sick pay	8	.
9	Current quarter's adjustments for tips and group-term life insurance	9	.
10	Total taxes after adjustments. Combine lines 6 through 9	10	54,640 . 80
11a	Qualified small business payroll tax credit for increasing research activities. Attach Form 8974	11a	.
11b	Nonrefundable portion of credit for qualified sick and family leave wages from Worksheet 1	11b	.
11c	Nonrefundable portion of employee retention credit from Worksheet 1	11c	.

▶ **You MUST complete all three pages of Form 941 and SIGN it.**

Next ▶

For Privacy Act and Paperwork Reduction Act Notice, see the back of the Payment Voucher.   Cat. No. 17001Z   Form **941** (Rev. 4-2020)

Self-Study Problem 9.4, part 1

950220

Name *(not your trade name)*	Employer identification number (EIN)
Hills Scientific Corporation	33-4434432

Part 1:   Answer these questions for this quarter. *(continued)*

11d **Total nonrefundable credits.** Add lines 11a, 11b, and 11c . . . . **11d** [.   ]

12 **Total taxes after adjustments and nonrefundable credits.** Subtract line 11d from line 10 . **12** [54,640 . 80]

13a **Total deposits for this quarter, including overpayment applied from a prior quarter and overpayments applied from Form 941-X, 941-X (PR), 944-X, or 944-X (SP) filed in the current quarter** **13a** [40,000 . 00]

13b **Deferred amount of the employer share of social security tax** . . . . **13b** [8,475 . 40] *

13c **Refundable portion of credit for qualified sick and family leave wages from Worksheet 1** **13c** [.   ]

13d **Refundable portion of employee retention credit from Worksheet 1** . . . . **13d** [.   ]

13e **Total deposits, deferrals, and refundable credits.** Add lines 13a, 13b, 13c, and 13d . . . **13e** [48,475 . 40]

13f **Total advances received from filing Form(s) 7200 for the quarter** . . . . **13f** [.   ]

13g **Total deposits, deferrals, and refundable credits less advances.** Subtract line 13f from line 13e . **13g** [48,475 . 40]

14 **Balance due.** If line 12 is more than line 13g, enter the difference and see instructions . . . **14** [6,165 . 40]

15 **Overpayment.** If line 13g is more than line 12, enter the difference [.   ] Check one: ☐ Apply to next return.   ☐ Send a refund.

Part 2:   Tell us about your deposit schedule and tax liability for this quarter.

If you're unsure about whether you're a monthly schedule depositor or a semiweekly schedule depositor, see section 11 of Pub. 15.

16 **Check one:** ☐   Line 12 on this return is less than $2,500 or line 12 on the return for the prior quarter was less than $2,500, and you didn't incur a $100,000 next-day deposit obligation during the current quarter. If line 12 for the prior quarter was less than $2,500 but line 12 on this return is $100,000 or more, you must provide a record of your federal tax liability. If you're a monthly schedule depositor, complete the deposit schedule below; if you're a semiweekly schedule depositor, attach Schedule B (Form 941). Go to Part 3.

☐   **You were a monthly schedule depositor for the entire quarter.** Enter your tax liability for each month and total liability for the quarter, then go to Part 3.

Tax liability: Month 1 [.   ]

Month 2 [.   ]

Month 3 [.   ]

Total liability for quarter [.   ]   **Total must equal line 12.**

☐   **You were a semiweekly schedule depositor for any part of this quarter.** Complete Schedule B (Form 941), Report of Tax Liability for Semiweekly Schedule Depositors, and attach it to Form 941. Go to Part 3.

▶ **You MUST complete all three pages of Form 941 and SIGN it.**   Next ■▶

*Column 2 of Line 5a × 50%

Self-Study Problem 9.4, part 2

Form 941 for 2020: Employer's QUARTERLY Federal Tax Return
(Rev. April 2020)   Department of the Treasury — Internal Revenue Service

950120

OMB No. 1545-0029

Employer identification number (EIN) 3 3 – 4 4 3 4 4 3 2

Name (not your trade name) Hills Scientific Corporation

Trade name (if any)

Address
Number   Street   Suite or room number

City   State   ZIP code

Foreign country name   Foreign province/county   Foreign postal code

Report for this Quarter of 2020
(Check one.)

☐ 1: January, February, March

☒ 2: April, May, June

☐ 3: July, August, September

☐ 4: October, November, December

Go to *www.irs.gov/Form941* for instructions and the latest information.

Read the separate instructions before you complete Form 941. Type or print within the boxes.

Part 1:   Answer these questions for this quarter.

1	Number of employees who received wages, tips, or other compensation for the pay period including: *June 12* (Quarter 2), *Sept. 12* (Quarter 3), or *Dec. 12* (Quarter 4) . . .	1	6
2	Wages, tips, and other compensation	2	140,000 . 00
3	Federal income tax withheld from wages, tips, and other compensation	3	33,630 . 00

4   If no wages, tips, and other compensation are subject to social security or Medicare tax ☐ **Check and go to line 6.**

		Column 1		Column 2
5a	Taxable social security wages *. .	122,200 . 00	× 0.124 =	15,152 . 80
5a	(i) Qualified sick leave wages . .	4,500 . 00	× 0.062 =	279 . 00
5a	(ii) Qualified family leave wages .	10,000 . 00	× 0.062 =	620 . 00
5b	Taxable social security tips . . .	.	× 0.124 =	.
5c	Taxable Medicare wages & tips. .	140,000 . 00	× 0.029 =	4,060 . 00
5d	Taxable wages & tips subject to Additional Medicare Tax withholding	.	× 0.009 =	.

5e	Total social security and Medicare taxes. Add Column 2 from lines 5a, 5a(i), 5a(ii), 5b, 5c, and 5d	5e	20,111 . 80
5f	Section 3121(q) Notice and Demand—Tax due on unreported tips (see instructions) . .	5f	.
6	Total taxes before adjustments. Add lines 3, 5e, and 5f	6	53,741 . 80
7	Current quarter's adjustment for fractions of cents	7	.
8	Current quarter's adjustment for sick pay	8	.
9	Current quarter's adjustments for tips and group-term life insurance	9	.
10	Total taxes after adjustments. Combine lines 6 through 9	10	53,741 . 80
11a	Qualified small business payroll tax credit for increasing research activities. Attach Form 8974	11a	.
11b	Nonrefundable portion of credit for qualified sick and family leave wages from Worksheet 1	11b	7,576 . 40
11c	Nonrefundable portion of employee retention credit from Worksheet 1	11c	0 . 00

Next ▶

▶ **You MUST complete all three pages of Form 941 and SIGN it.**

For Privacy Act and Paperwork Reduction Act Notice, see the back of the Payment Voucher.   Cat. No. 17001Z   Form **941** (Rev. 4-2020)

*$140,000 − $4,500 (sick pay) − $10,000 (family leave pay) − $3,300 (Juliette's year-to-date pay in excess of FICA cap of $137,700)

Self-Study Problem 9.4, part 2

950220

Name *(not your trade name)*	Employer identification number (EIN)
Hills Scientific Corporation	33-4434432

Part 1:   Answer these questions for this quarter. *(continued)*

11d   Total nonrefundable credits. Add lines 11a, 11b, and 11c . . . .   **11d**   7,576 . 40

12   Total taxes after adjustments and nonrefundable credits. Subtract line 11d from line 10 .   **12**   46,165 . 40

13a   Total deposits for this quarter, including overpayment applied from a prior quarter and overpayments applied from Form 941-X, 941-X (PR), 944-X, or 944-X (SP) filed in the current quarter   **13a**   40,000 . 00

13b   Deferred amount of the employer share of social security tax . . . .   **13b**   0 .

13c   Refundable portion of credit for qualified sick and family leave wages from Worksheet 1   **13c**   9,244 . 95

13d   Refundable portion of employee retention credit from Worksheet 1 . . . .   **13d**   24,694 . 45

13e   Total deposits, deferrals, and refundable credits. Add lines 13a, 13b, 13c, and 13d . . .   **13e**   73,939 . 40

13f   Total advances received from filing Form(s) 7200 for the quarter . . . .   **13f**   .

13g   Total deposits, deferrals, and refundable credits less advances. Subtract line 13f from line 13e .   **13g**   73,939 . 40

14   Balance due. If line 12 is more than line 13g, enter the difference and see instructions . . .   **14**   .

15   Overpayment. If line 13g is more than line 12, enter the difference   27,774 . 40   Check one: ☐ Apply to next return. ☒ Send a refund.

Part 2:   Tell us about your deposit schedule and tax liability for this quarter.

If you're unsure about whether you're a monthly schedule depositor or a semiweekly schedule depositor, see section 11 of Pub. 15.

16   Check one: ☐   Line 12 on this return is less than $2,500 or line 12 on the return for the prior quarter was less than $2,500, and you didn't incur a $100,000 next-day deposit obligation during the current quarter. If line 12 for the prior quarter was less than $2,500 but line 12 on this return is $100,000 or more, you must provide a record of your federal tax liability. If you're a monthly schedule depositor, complete the deposit schedule below; if you're a semiweekly schedule depositor, attach Schedule B (Form 941). Go to Part 3.

☐   **You were a monthly schedule depositor for the entire quarter.** Enter your tax liability for each month and total liability for the quarter, then go to Part 3.

Tax liability: **Month 1**   .

Month 2   .

Month 3   .

Total liability for quarter   .   **Total must equal line 12.**

☐   **You were a semiweekly schedule depositor for any part of this quarter.** Complete Schedule B (Form 941), Report of Tax Liability for Semiweekly Schedule Depositors, and attach it to Form 941. Go to Part 3.

▶ **You MUST complete all three pages of Form 941 and SIGN it.**   Next ▶

Form **941** (Rev. 4-2020)

Self-Study Problem 9.4, part 2

950920

Name *(not your trade name)*	Employer identification number (EIN)
Hills Scientific Corporation	33-4434432

Part 3: Tell us about your business. If a question does NOT apply to your business, leave it blank.

17 If your business has closed or you stopped paying wages . . . . ☐ Check here, and

enter the final date you paid wages [/ /] ; also attach a statement to your return. See instructions.

18 If you're a seasonal employer and you don't have to file a return for every quarter of the year . . . ☐ Check here.

19 Qualified health plan expenses allocable to qualified sick leave wages . . . . . . **19** | 777 . 77

20 Qualified health plan expenses allocable to qualified family leave wages . . . . . . **20** | 1,333 . 33

21 Qualified wages for the employee retention credit . . . . **21** | 39,500 . 00

22 Qualified health plan expenses allocable to wages reported on line 21 . . . . . . **22** | 9,888 . 90

23 Credit from Form 5884-C, line 11, for this quarter . . . . **23** | .

24 Qualified wages paid March 13 through March 31, 2020, for the employee retention credit (use this line only for the second quarter filing of Form 941) . . . . **24** | .

25 Qualified health plan expenses allocable to wages reported on line 24 (use this line only for the second quarter filing of Form 941) . . . . **25** | .

Part 4: May we speak with your third-party designee?

Do you want to allow an employee, a paid tax preparer, or another person to discuss this return with the IRS? See the instructions for details.

☐ **Yes.** Designee's name and phone number

Select a 5-digit personal identification number (PIN) to use when talking to the IRS. ☐ ☐ ☐ ☐ ☐

☐ **No.**

Part 5: Sign here. You MUST complete all three pages of Form 941 and SIGN it.

Under penalties of perjury, I declare that I have examined this return, including accompanying schedules and statements, and to the best of my knowledge and belief, it is true, correct, and complete. Declaration of preparer (other than taxpayer) is based on all information of which preparer has any knowledge.

✗ **Sign your name here**

Print your name here

Print your title here

Date [/ /]

Best daytime phone

Paid Preparer Use Only   Check if you're self-employed . . . ☐

Preparer's name

PTIN

Preparer's signature

Date [/ /]

Firm's name (or yours if self-employed)

EIN

Address

Phone

City

State

ZIP code

Self-Study Problem 9.4, part 2

Worksheet 1. Credit for Qualified Sick and Family Leave Wages and the Employee Retention Credit

Keep for Your Records

Determine how you will complete this worksheet

If you paid both qualified sick and family leave wages and qualified wages for purposes of the employee retention credit this quarter, complete Step 1, Step 2, and Step 3. If you paid qualified sick and family leave wages this quarter but you didn't pay any qualified wages for purposes of the employee retention credit this quarter, complete Step 1 and Step 2. If you paid qualified wages for purposes of the employee retention credit this quarter but you didn't pay any qualified sick and family leave wages this quarter, complete Step 1 and Step 3.

Step 1.   **Determine the employer share of social security tax this quarter after it is reduced by any credit claimed on Form 8974 and any credit to be claimed on Form 5884-C**

1a	Enter the amount of social security tax from Form 941, Part 1, line 5a, column 2	1a	15,152.80
1b	Enter the amount of social security tax from Form 941, Part 1, line 5b, column 2	1b	0
1c	Add lines 1a and 1b	1c	15,152.80
1d	Multiply line 1c by 50% (0.50)	1d	7,576.40
1e	If you're a third-party payer of sick pay that isn't an agent and you're claiming credits for amounts paid to your employees, enter the employer share of social security tax included on Form 941, Part 1, line 8 (enter as a positive number)	1e	
1f	Subtract line 1e from line 1d	1f	7,576.40
1g	If you received a Section 3121(q) Notice and Demand during the quarter, enter the amount of the employer share of social security tax from the notice	1g	
1h	**Employer share of social security tax.** Add lines 1f and 1g	1h	7,576.40
1i	Enter the amount from Form 941, Part 1, line 11a (credit from Form 8974)	1i	
1j	Enter the amount to be claimed on Form 5884-C, line 11, for this quarter	1j	
1k	**Total nonrefundable credits already used against the employer share of social security tax.** Add lines 1i and 1j	1k	
1l	**Employer share of social security tax remaining.** Subtract line 1k from line 1h	1l	7,576.40

Step 2.   **Figure the sick and family leave credit**

2a	Qualified sick leave wages reported on Form 941, Part 1, line 5a(i), column 1	2a	4,500
2a(i)	Qualified sick leave wages included on Form 941, Part 1, line 5c, but not included on Form 941, Part 1, line 5a(i), column 1, because the wages reported on that line were limited by the social security wage base	2a(i)	
2a(ii)	Total qualified sick leave wages. Add lines 2a and 2a(i)	2a(ii)	4,500
2b	Qualified health plan expenses allocable to qualified sick leave wages (Form 941, Part 3, line 19)	2b	777.77
2c	Employer share of Medicare tax on qualified sick leave wages. Multiply line 2a(ii) by 1.45% (0.0145)	2c	65.25
2d	**Credit for qualified sick leave wages.** Add lines 2a(ii), 2b, and 2c	2d	5,343.02
2e	Qualified family leave wages reported on Form 941, Part 1, line 5a(ii), column 1	2e	10,000
2e(i)	Qualified family leave wages included on Form 941, Part 1, line 5c, but not included on Form 941, Part 1, line 5a(ii), column 1, because the wages reported on that line were limited by the social security wage base	2e(i)	
2e(ii)	Total qualified family leave wages. Add lines 2e and 2e(i)	2e(ii)	10,000
2f	Qualified health plan expenses allocable to qualified family leave wages (Form 941, Part 3, line 20)	2f	1,333.33
2g	Employer share of Medicare tax on qualified family leave wages. Multiply line 2e(ii) by 1.45% (0.0145)	2g	145
2h	**Credit for qualified family leave wages.** Add lines 2e(ii), 2f, and 2g	2h	11,478.33
2i	**Credit for qualified sick and family leave wages.** Add lines 2d and 2h	2i	16,821.35
2j	**Nonrefundable portion of credit for qualified sick and family leave wages.** Enter the smaller of line 1l or line 2i. Enter this amount on Form 941, Part 1, line 11b	2j	7,576.40
2k	**Refundable portion of credit for qualified sick and family leave wages.** Subtract line 2j from line 2i and enter this amount on Form 941, Part 1, line 13c	2k	9,244.95

Step 3.   **Figure the employee retention credit**

3a	Qualified wages (excluding qualified health plan expenses) for the employee retention credit (Form 941, Part 3, line 21)	3a	39,500
3b	Qualified health plan expenses allocable to qualified wages for the employee retention credit (Form 941, Part 3, line 22)	3b	9,888.90
3c	Qualified wages (excluding qualified health plan expenses) paid March 13, 2020, through March 31, 2020, for the employee retention credit (Form 941, Part 3, line 24). Enter an amount here only for the second quarter Form 941	3c	
3d	Qualified health plan expenses allocable to qualified wages paid March 13, 2020, through March 31, 2020, for the employee retention credit (Form 941, Part 3, line 25). Enter an amount here only for the second quarter Form 941	3d	
3e	Add lines 3a, 3b, 3c, and 3d	3e	49,388.90
3f	**Retention credit.** Multiply line 3e by 50% (0.50)	3f	24,694.45
3g	Enter the amount of the employer share of social security tax from Step 1, line 1l	3g	7,576.40
3h	Enter the amount of the nonrefundable portion of the credit for qualified sick and family leave wages from Step 2, line 2j	3h	7,576.40
3i	Subtract line 3h from line 3g	3i	0
3j	**Nonrefundable portion of employee retention credit.** Enter the smaller of line 3f or line 3i. Enter this amount on Form 941, Part 1, line 11c	3j	0
3k	**Refundable portion of employee retention credit.** Subtract line 3j from line 3f and enter this amount on Form 941, Part 1, line 13d	3k	24,694.45

Caution: Only complete lines 3c and 3d for your second quarter 2020 Form 941.

Note: See solution to Self-Study Problem 9.3, part 2 on Page E-64 for additional calculations.

Self-Study Problem 9.5

a Employee's social security number 464-74-1132 OMB No. 1545-0008	Safe, accurate, FAST! Use IRS e-file Visit the IRS website at www.irs.gov/efile

b Employer identification number (EIN) 95-1234567	**1** Wages, tips, other compensation 16,150.00	**2** Federal income tax withheld 2,422.00
c Employer's name, address, and ZIP code Big Bank PO Box 12344 San Diego, CA 92101	**3** Social security wages 16,150.00	**4** Social security tax withheld 1,001.30
	5 Medicare wages and tips 16,150.00	**6** Medicare tax withheld 234.18
	7 Social security tips	**8** Allocated tips
d Control number	**9**	**10** Dependent care benefits
e Employee's first name and initial Last name Suff. Mary Jones 6431 Gary Street San Diego, CA 92115	**11** Nonqualified plans	**12a** See instructions for box 12
	13 Statutory employee ☐ Retirement plan ☐ Third-party sick pay ☐	**12b**
	14 Other	**12c**
		12d
f Employee's address and ZIP code		

15 State Employer's state ID number	**16** State wages, tips, etc.	**17** State income tax	**18** Local wages, tips, etc.	**19** Local income tax	**20** Locality name
CA 800 4039 250 092	16,150.00	969.00			

Form **W-2** Wage and Tax Statement   2020   Department of the Treasury—Internal Revenue Service

Copy B—To Be Filed With Employee's FEDERAL Tax Return.
This information is being furnished to the Internal Revenue Service.

☐ CORRECTED (if checked)

PAYER'S name, street address, city or town, state or province, country, ZIP or foreign postal code, and telephone no. Big Bank PO Box 12344 San Diego, CA 92101 800-555-1212	Payer's RTN (optional) OMB No. 1545-0112 20**20** **1** Interest income 461.00 $ Form **1099-INT** **Interest Income**

PAYER'S TIN 95-1234567	RECIPIENT'S TIN 464-74-1132	**2** Early withdrawal penalty $	**Copy B** **For Recipient**
		3 Interest on U.S. Savings Bonds and Treas. obligations $	

RECIPIENT'S name Mary Jones	**4** Federal income tax withheld $	**5** Investment expenses $	This is important tax information and is being furnished to the IRS. If you are required to file a return, a negligence penalty or other sanction may be imposed on you if this income is taxable and the IRS determines that it has not been reported.
Street address (including apt. no.) 6431 Gary Street	**6** Foreign tax paid $	**7** Foreign country or U.S. possession	
City or town, state or province, country, and ZIP or foreign postal code San Diego, CA 92115	**8** Tax-exempt interest $	**9** Specified private activity bond interest $	
	10 Market discount $	**11** Bond premium $	
FATCA filing requirement ☐	**12** Bond premium on Treasury obligations $	**13** Bond premium on tax-exempt bond $	
Account number (see instructions)	**14** Tax-exempt and tax credit bond CUSIP no.	**15** State **16** State identification no. **17** State tax withheld $ $	

Form **1099-INT**   (keep for your records)   www.irs.gov/Form1099INT   Department of the Treasury - Internal Revenue Service

Self-Study Problem 9.6

See Form 940 on Pages E-72 and E-73.

Self-Study Problem 9.6

Form **940 for 2020:** Employer's Annual Federal Unemployment (FUTA) Tax Return   850113

Department of the Treasury — Internal Revenue Service

OMB No. 1545-0028

Employer identification number (EIN)   9 4 – 0 0 0 1 1 1 2

Name *(not your trade name)*   Anatolian Corporation

Trade name *(if any)*

Address   400 8th Street N.

Number   Street   Suite or room number

La Crosse   WI   54601

City   State   ZIP code

Foreign country name   Foreign province/county   Foreign postal code

Type of Return
(Check all that apply.)

☐ **a.** Amended

☐ **b.** Successor employer

☐ **c.** No payments to employees in 2020

☐ **d.** Final: Business closed or stopped paying wages

Go to *www.irs.gov/Form940* for instructions and the latest information.

Read the separate instructions before you complete this form. Please type or print within the boxes.

Part 1:   Tell us about your return. If any line does NOT apply, leave it blank. See instructions before completing Part 1.

1a If you had to pay state unemployment tax in one state only, enter the state abbreviation .   **1a**   W   I

1b If you had to pay state unemployment tax in more than one state, you are a multi-state employer . . . .   **1b** ☐ Check here. Complete Schedule A (Form 940).

2 If you paid wages in a state that is subject to CREDIT REDUCTION . . . .   **2** ☐ Check here. Complete Schedule A (Form 940).

Part 2:   Determine your FUTA tax before adjustments. If any line does NOT apply, leave it blank.

3	Total payments to all employees		**3**	113,000 ▪ 00
4	Payments exempt from FUTA tax	**4**		▪

Check all that apply: **4a** ☐ Fringe benefits   **4c** ☐ Retirement/Pension   **4e** ☐ Other
4b ☐ Group-term life insurance   **4d** ☐ Dependent care

5	Total of payments made to each employee in excess of $7,000	**5**	22,000 ▪ 00	
6	Subtotal (line 4 + line 5 = line 6)		**6**	22,000 ▪ 00
7	Total taxable FUTA wages (line 3 – line 6 = line 7). See instructions		**7**	91,000 ▪ 00
8	FUTA tax before adjustments (line 7 x 0.006 = line 8)		**8**	546 ▪ 00

Part 3:   Determine your adjustments. If any line does NOT apply, leave it blank.

9	If ALL of the taxable FUTA wages you paid were excluded from state unemployment tax, multiply line 7 by 0.054 (line 7 x 0.054 = line 9). Go to line 12	**9**	▪
10	If SOME of the taxable FUTA wages you paid were excluded from state unemployment tax, OR you paid ANY state unemployment tax late (after the due date for filing Form 940), complete the worksheet in the instructions. Enter the amount from line 7 of the worksheet . .	**10**	▪
11	If credit reduction applies, enter the total from Schedule A (Form 940)	**11**	▪

Part 4:   Determine your FUTA tax and balance due or overpayment. If any line does NOT apply, leave it blank.

12	Total FUTA tax after adjustments (lines 8 + 9 + 10 + 11 = line 12)	**12**	546 ▪ 00
13	FUTA tax deposited for the year, including any overpayment applied from a prior year . .	**13**	546 ▪ 00
14	Balance due. If line 12 is more than line 13, enter the excess on line 14. • If line 14 is more than $500, you must deposit your tax. • If line 14 is $500 or less, you may pay with this return. See instructions	**14**	0 ▪ 00
15	Overpayment. If line 13 is more than line 12, enter the excess on line 15 and check a box below	**15**	0 ▪ 00

▶ You **MUST** complete both pages of this form and **SIGN** it.   Check one: ☐ Apply to next return.   ☐ Send a refund.

Next ▶

For Privacy Act and Paperwork Reduction Act Notice, see the back of the Payment Voucher.   Cat. No. 11234O   Form **940** (2020)

Self-Study Problem 9.6

850212

Name (not your trade name)	Employer identification number (EIN)
Anatolian Corporation	94-0001112

Part 5: Report your FUTA tax liability by quarter only if line 12 is more than $500. If not, go to Part 6.

16 Report the amount of your FUTA tax liability for each quarter; do NOT enter the amount you deposited. If you had no liability for a quarter, leave the line blank.

16a	1st quarter (January 1 – March 31)	16a	150 . 00
16b	2nd quarter (April 1 – June 30)	16b	156 . 00
16c	3rd quarter (July 1 – September 30)	16c	96 . 00
16d	4th quarter (October 1 – December 31)	16d	144 . 00

17 Total tax liability for the year (lines 16a + 16b + 16c + 16d = line 17) **17**   546 . 00   Total must equal line 12.

Part 6: May we speak with your third-party designee?

Do you want to allow an employee, a paid tax preparer, or another person to discuss this return with the IRS? See the instructions for details.

☐ **Yes.**   Designee's name and phone number

Select a 5-digit personal identification number (PIN) to use when talking to the IRS.

☐ **No.**

Part 7: Sign here. You MUST complete both pages of this form and SIGN it.

Under penalties of perjury, I declare that I have examined this return, including accompanying schedules and statements, and to the best of my knowledge and belief, it is true, correct, and complete, and that no part of any payment made to a state unemployment fund claimed as a credit was, or is to be, deducted from the payments made to employees. Declaration of preparer (other than taxpayer) is based on all information of which preparer has any knowledge.

✗ Sign your name here

Print your name here

Print your title here

Date   /   /

Best daytime phone

Paid Preparer Use Only

Check if you are self-employed ☐

Preparer's name		PTIN	
Preparer's signature		Date	/ /
Firm's name (or yours if self-employed)		EIN	
Address		Phone	
City	State	ZIP code	

Self-Study Problem 9.7

    a. $12,500, lesser of 25% × $50,000 or $57,000 (annual limit effective for 2020)
    b. $57,000 (annual dollar limit effective for 2020)

Self-Study Problem 9.8

    a. $150,000
    b. $120,000 ($150,000 − 20% × $150,000)
    c. August 30, 20XX, which is the 60th day after the day the distribution was received, unless the hardship waiver provisions apply.
    d. $150,000

CHAPTER 10   PARTNERSHIP TAXATION

Self-Study Problem 10.1

1.	Yes	
2.	No	A corporation is not a partnership, but a separate type of entity.
3.	No	The mere joint ownership of property does not constitute a partnership; the owners must engage in some type of business activity.
4.	Yes	The marketing of oil qualifies the venture as a partnership.
5.	Yes and No	The married couple has the choice to operate as a qualified joint venture or as a partnership.

Self-Study Problem 10.2

1.	$0	
2.	$36,000	The amount of cash contributed.
3.	$0	
4.	$17,500	The same as Linda's basis in the equipment contributed to the partnership.
5.	$17,500	The same as Linda's basis in the equipment contributed.

Self-Study Problem 10.3

See Form 1065 and Schedule K-1 on Pages E-76 to E-80.

Self-Study Problem 10.4

1.	Partnership income before guaranteed payments	$ 32,000
	Less: guaranteed payments	(36,000)
	Partnership loss after guaranteed payments	$ (4,000)
	Jim's income:	
	Guaranteed payments	$ 36,000
	50% of the $4,000 partnership loss	(2,000)
	Total income	$ 34,000
2.	Jack's income (loss): 50% of the $4,000 partnership loss	$(2,000)

Self-Study Problem 10.3

Form **1065**		U.S. Return of Partnership Income		OMB No. 1545-0123	

Department of the Treasury
Internal Revenue Service

For calendar year 2020, or tax year beginning _____, 2020, ending _____, 20_____

▶ Go to *www.irs.gov/Form1065* for instructions and the latest information.

2020

A Principal business activity		Name of partnership		**D** Employer identification number
		Cahokia Partnership		44-4444444
B Principal product or service	**Type or Print**	Number, street, and room or suite no. If a P.O. box, see instructions.		**E** Date business started
		40 Rainy Street		01/01/20
C Business code number		City or town, state or province, country, and ZIP or foreign postal code		**F** Total assets (see instructions)
		Collinsville, IL 62234		$ 257,750

G Check applicable boxes: **(1)** ☑ Initial return **(2)** ☐ Final return **(3)** ☐ Name change **(4)** ☐ Address change **(5)** ☐ Amended return

H Check accounting method: **(1)** ☐ Cash **(2)** ☑ Accrual **(3)** ☐ Other (specify) ▶ _____

I Number of Schedules K-1. Attach one for each person who was a partner at any time during the tax year ▶ 2

J Check if Schedules C and M-3 are attached ▶ ☐

K Check if partnership: **(1)** ☐ Aggregated activities for section 465 at-risk purposes **(2)** ☐ Grouped activities for section 469 passive activity purposes

Caution: Include **only** trade or business income and expenses on lines 1a through 22 below. See instructions for more information.

Income

1a	Gross receipts or sales	**1a**	255,600	
b	Returns and allowances	**1b**		
c	Balance. Subtract line 1b from line 1a			**1c** 255,600
2	Cost of goods sold (attach Form 1125-A)			**2**
3	Gross profit. Subtract line 2 from line 1c			**3** 255,600
4	Ordinary income (loss) from other partnerships, estates, and trusts (attach statement)			**4**
5	Net farm profit (loss) (attach Schedule F (Form 1040))			**5**
6	Net gain (loss) from Form 4797, Part II, line 17 (attach Form 4797)			**6**
7	Other income (loss) (attach statement)			**7**
8	**Total income (loss).** Combine lines 3 through 7			**8** 255,600

Deductions (see instructions for limitations)

9	Salaries and wages (other than to partners) (less employment credits)			**9** 168,000
10	Guaranteed payments to partners			**10**
11	Repairs and maintenance			**11**
12	Bad debts			**12**
13	Rent			**13** 12,000
14	Taxes and licenses			**14** 6,100
15	Interest (see instructions)			**15**
16a	Depreciation (if required, attach Form 4562)	**16a**	9,250	
b	Less depreciation reported on Form 1125-A and elsewhere on return	**16b**		**16c** 9,250
17	Depletion (**Do not deduct oil and gas depletion.**)			**17**
18	Retirement plans, etc.			**18**
19	Employee benefit programs			**19**
20	Other deductions (attach statement)			**20**
21	**Total deductions.** Add the amounts shown in the far right column for lines 9 through 20			**21** 195,350
22	**Ordinary business income (loss).** Subtract line 21 from line 8			**22** 60,250

Tax and Payment

23	Interest due under the look-back method—completed long-term contracts (attach Form 8697)		**23**
24	Interest due under the look-back method—income forecast method (attach Form 8866)		**24**
25	BBA AAR imputed underpayment (see instructions)		**25**
26	Other taxes (see instructions)		**26**
27	**Total balance due.** Add lines 23 through 26		**27**
28	Payment (see instructions)		**28**
29	**Amount owed.** If line 28 is smaller than line 27, enter amount owed		**29**
30	**Overpayment.** If line 28 is larger than line 27, enter overpayment		**30**

Sign Here

Under penalties of perjury, I declare that I have examined this return, including accompanying schedules and statements, and to the best of my knowledge and belief, it is true, correct, and complete. Declaration of preparer (other than partner or limited liability company member) is based on all information of which preparer has any knowledge.

▶ _____ Signature of partner or limited liability company member ▶ _____ Date

May the IRS discuss this return with the preparer shown below? See instructions. ☑ Yes ☐ No

Paid Preparer Use Only

Print/Type preparer's name	Preparer's signature	Date	Check ☐ if self-employed	PTIN
Firm's name ▶			Firm's EIN ▶	
Firm's address ▶			Phone no.	

For Paperwork Reduction Act Notice, see separate instructions.   Cat. No. 11390Z   Form **1065** (2020)

Self-Study Problem 10.3

Form 1065 (2020)   Page **2**

Schedule B	**Other Information**				

				Yes	**No**
1	What type of entity is filing this return? Check the applicable box:				
a	☑ Domestic general partnership	**b** ☐ Domestic limited partnership			
c	☐ Domestic limited liability company	**d** ☐ Domestic limited liability partnership			
e	☐ Foreign partnership	**f** ☐ Other ▶			
2	At the end of the tax year:				
a	Did any foreign or domestic corporation, partnership (including any entity treated as a partnership), trust, or tax-exempt organization, or any foreign government own, directly or indirectly, an interest of 50% or more in the profit, loss, or capital of the partnership? For rules of constructive ownership, see instructions. If "Yes," attach Schedule B-1, Information on Partners Owning 50% or More of the Partnership				✓
b	Did any individual or estate own, directly or indirectly, an interest of 50% or more in the profit, loss, or capital of the partnership? For rules of constructive ownership, see instructions. If "Yes," attach Schedule B-1, Information on Partners Owning 50% or More of the Partnership			✓	
3	At the end of the tax year, did the partnership:				
a	Own directly 20% or more, or own, directly or indirectly, 50% or more of the total voting power of all classes of stock entitled to vote of any foreign or domestic corporation? For rules of constructive ownership, see instructions. If "Yes," complete (i) through (iv) below				✓

(i) Name of Corporation	(ii) Employer Identification Number (if any)	(iii) Country of Incorporation	(iv) Percentage Owned in Voting Stock

				Yes	No
b	Own directly an interest of 20% or more, or own, directly or indirectly, an interest of 50% or more in the profit, loss, or capital in any foreign or domestic partnership (including an entity treated as a partnership) or in the beneficial interest of a trust? For rules of constructive ownership, see instructions. If "Yes," complete (i) through (v) below . .				✓

(i) Name of Entity	(ii) Employer Identification Number (if any)	(iii) Type of Entity	(iv) Country of Organization	(v) Maximum Percentage Owned in Profit, Loss, or Capital

			Yes	No
4	Does the partnership satisfy **all four** of the following conditions?			
a	The partnership's total receipts for the tax year were less than $250,000.			
b	The partnership's total assets at the end of the tax year were less than $1 million.			
c	Schedules K-1 are filed with the return and furnished to the partners on or before the due date (including extensions) for the partnership return.			
d	The partnership is not filing and is not required to file Schedule M-3			✓
	If "Yes," the partnership is not required to complete Schedules L, M-1, and M-2; item F on page 1 of Form 1065; or item L on Schedule K-1.			
5	Is this partnership a publicly traded partnership, as defined in section 469(k)(2)?			✓
6	During the tax year, did the partnership have any debt that was canceled, was forgiven, or had the terms modified so as to reduce the principal amount of the debt?			✓
7	Has this partnership filed, or is it required to file, Form 8918, Material Advisor Disclosure Statement, to provide information on any reportable transaction?			✓
8	At any time during calendar year 2020, did the partnership have an interest in or a signature or other authority over a financial account in a foreign country (such as a bank account, securities account, or other financial account)? See instructions for exceptions and filing requirements for FinCEN Form 114, Report of Foreign Bank and Financial Accounts (FBAR). If "Yes," enter the name of the foreign country ▶			✓
9	At any time during the tax year, did the partnership receive a distribution from, or was it the grantor of, or transferor to, a foreign trust? If "Yes," the partnership may have to file Form 3520, Annual Return To Report Transactions With Foreign Trusts and Receipt of Certain Foreign Gifts. See instructions			✓
10a	Is the partnership making, or had it previously made (and not revoked), a section 754 election? . . . . . . See instructions for details regarding a section 754 election.			✓
b	Did the partnership make for this tax year an optional basis adjustment under section 743(b) or 734(b)? If "Yes," attach a statement showing the computation and allocation of the basis adjustment. See instructions			✓

Form **1065** (2020)

Self-Study Problem 10.3

Schedule B	Other Information *(continued)*	Yes	No
c	Is the partnership required to adjust the basis of partnership assets under section 743(b) or 734(b) because of a substantial built-in loss (as defined under section 743(d)) or substantial basis reduction (as defined under section 734(d))? If "Yes," attach a statement showing the computation and allocation of the basis adjustment. See instructions		✓
11	Check this box if, during the current or prior tax year, the partnership distributed any property received in a like-kind exchange or contributed such property to another entity (other than disregarded entities wholly owned by the partnership throughout the tax year) . . . . ▶ ☐		
12	At any time during the tax year, did the partnership distribute to any partner a tenancy-in-common or other undivided interest in partnership property?		✓
13	If the partnership is required to file Form 8858, Information Return of U.S. Persons With Respect To Foreign Disregarded Entities (FDEs) and Foreign Branches (FBs), enter the number of Forms 8858 attached. See instructions . . . . ▶		
14	Does the partnership have any foreign partners? If "Yes," enter the number of Forms 8805, Foreign Partner's Information Statement of Section 1446 Withholding Tax, filed for this partnership . . . ▶		✓
15	Enter the number of Forms 8865, Return of U.S. Persons With Respect to Certain Foreign Partnerships, attached to this return . . . . ▶		
16a	Did you make any payments in 2020 that would require you to file Form(s) 1099? See instructions	✓	
b	If "Yes," did you or will you file required Form(s) 1099?	✓	
17	Enter the number of Forms 5471, Information Return of U.S. Persons With Respect To Certain Foreign Corporations, attached to this return . . . . ▶		
18	Enter the number of partners that are foreign governments under section 892 . . . . ▶		
19	During the partnership's tax year, did the partnership make any payments that would require it to file Form 1042 and 1042-S under chapter 3 (sections 1441 through 1464) or chapter 4 (sections 1471 through 1474)?		✓
20	Was the partnership a specified domestic entity required to file Form 8938 for the tax year? See the Instructions for Form 8938		✓
21	Is the partnership a section 721(c) partnership, as defined in Regulations section 1.721(c)-1(b)(14)?		✓
22	During the tax year, did the partnership pay or accrue any interest or royalty for which one or more partners are not allowed a deduction under section 267A? See instructions		✓
	If "Yes," enter the total amount of the disallowed deductions . . . . ▶ $		
23	Did the partnership have an election under section 163(j) for any real property trade or business or any farming business in effect during the tax year? See instructions		✓
24	Does the partnership satisfy one or more of the following? See instructions		✓
a	The partnership owns a pass-through entity with current, or prior year carryover, excess business interest expense.		
b	The partnership's aggregate average annual gross receipts (determined under section 448(c)) for the 3 tax years preceding the current tax year are more than $26 million and the partnership has business interest.		
c	The partnership is a tax shelter (see instructions) and the partnership has business interest expense. If "Yes" to any, complete and attach Form 8990.		
25	Is the partnership electing out of the centralized partnership audit regime under section 6221(b)? See instructions. If "Yes," the partnership must complete Schedule B-2 (Form 1065). Enter the total from Schedule B-2, Part III, line 3 . . . . ▶ _____ If "No," complete Designation of Partnership Representative below.		✓

Designation of Partnership Representative (see instructions)

Enter below the information for the partnership representative (PR) for the tax year covered by this return.

Name of PR ▶

U.S. address of PR ▶ _____	U.S. phone number of ▶ PR

If the PR is an entity, name of the designated individual for the PR ▶

U.S. address of ▶ _____ designated individual	U.S. phone number of ▶ designated individual

26	Is the partnership attaching Form 8996 to certify as a Qualified Opportunity Fund? . . . . If "Yes," enter the amount from Form 8996, line 16 . . . . ▶ $		✓
27	Enter the number of foreign partners subject to section 864(c)(8) as a result of transferring all or a portion of an interest in the partnership or of receiving a distribution from the partnership . . . . . ▶		
28	At any time during the tax year, were there any transfers between the partnership and its partners subject to the disclosure requirements of Regulations section 1.707-8?		✓
29	Since December 22, 2017, did a foreign corporation directly or indirectly acquire substantially all of the properties constituting a trade or business of your partnership, and was the ownership percentage (by vote or value) for purposes of section 7874 greater than 50% (for example, the partners held more than 50% of the stock of the foreign corporation)? If "Yes," list the ownership percentage by vote and by value. See instructions. Percentage: By Vote By Value		✓

Form **1065** (2020)

Self-Study Problem 10.3

Schedule K		Partners' Distributive Share Items		Total amount
Income (Loss)	1	Ordinary business income (loss) (page 1, line 22)	1	60,250
	2	Net rental real estate income (loss) (attach Form 8825)	2	
	3a	Other gross rental income (loss) **3a**		
	b	Expenses from other rental activities (attach statement) **3b**		
	c	Other net rental income (loss). Subtract line 3b from line 3a	3c	
	4	Guaranteed payments: **a** Services **4a** **b** Capital **4b**		
		c Total. Add lines 4a and 4b	4c	
	5	Interest income	5	
	6	Dividends and dividend equivalents: **a** Ordinary dividends	6a	
		b Qualified dividends **6b** **c** Dividend equivalents **6c**		
	7	Royalties	7	
	8	Net short-term capital gain (loss) (attach Schedule D (Form 1065))	8	
	9a	Net long-term capital gain (loss) (attach Schedule D (Form 1065))	9a	
	b	Collectibles (28%) gain (loss) **9b**		
	c	Unrecaptured section 1250 gain (attach statement) **9c**		
	10	Net section 1231 gain (loss) (attach Form 4797)	10	
	11	Other income (loss) (see instructions) Type ▶	11	
Deductions	12	Section 179 deduction (attach Form 4562)	12	
	13a	Contributions	13a	1,500
	b	Investment interest expense	13b	
	c	Section 59(e)(2) expenditures: **(1)** Type ▶ **(2)** Amount ▶	13c(2)	
	d	Other deductions (see instructions) Type ▶	13d	
Self-Employ-ment	14a	Net earnings (loss) from self-employment	14a	60,250
	b	Gross farming or fishing income	14b	
	c	Gross nonfarm income	14c	
Credits	15a	Low-income housing credit (section 42(j)(5))	15a	
	b	Low-income housing credit (other)	15b	
	c	Qualified rehabilitation expenditures (rental real estate) (attach Form 3468, if applicable)	15c	
	d	Other rental real estate credits (see instructions) Type ▶	15d	
	e	Other rental credits (see instructions) Type ▶	15e	
	f	Other credits (see instructions) Type ▶	15f	
Foreign Transactions	16a	Name of country or U.S. possession ▶		
	b	Gross income from all sources	16b	
	c	Gross income sourced at partner level	16c	
		Foreign gross income sourced at partnership level		
	d	Reserved for future use ▶ **e** Foreign branch category ▶	16e	
	f	Passive category ▶ **g** General category ▶ **h** Other (attach statement) ▶	16h	
		Deductions allocated and apportioned at partner level		
	i	Interest expense ▶ **j** Other ▶	16j	
		Deductions allocated and apportioned at partnership level to foreign source income		
	k	Reserved for future use ▶ **l** Foreign branch category ▶	16l	
	m	Passive category ▶ **n** General category ▶ **o** Other (attach statement) ▶	16o	
	p	Total foreign taxes (check one): ▶ Paid ☐ Accrued ☐	16p	
	q	Reduction in taxes available for credit (attach statement)	16q	
	r	Other foreign tax information (attach statement)		
Alternative Minimum Tax (AMT) Items	17a	Post-1986 depreciation adjustment	17a	
	b	Adjusted gain or loss	17b	
	c	Depletion (other than oil and gas)	17c	
	d	Oil, gas, and geothermal properties—gross income	17d	
	e	Oil, gas, and geothermal properties—deductions	17e	
	f	Other AMT items (attach statement)	17f	
Other Information	18a	Tax-exempt interest income	18a	
	b	Other tax-exempt income	18b	
	c	Nondeductible expenses	18c	
	19a	Distributions of cash and marketable securities	19a	50,000
	b	Distributions of other property	19b	
	20a	Investment income	20a	
	b	Investment expenses	20b	
	c	Other items and amounts (attach statement)		

DRAFT AS OF September 1, 2020 DO NOT FILE

Self-Study Problem 10.3

Form 1065 (2020)   Page **5**

Analysis of Net Income (Loss)

1	Net income (loss). Combine Schedule K, lines 1 through 11. From the result, subtract the sum of Schedule K, lines 12 through 13d, and 16p					**1**	58,750

2	Analysis by partner type:	(i) Corporate	(ii) Individual (active)	(iii) Individual (passive)	(iv) Partnership	(v) Exempt Organization	(vi) Nominee/Other
a	General partners		58,750				
b	Limited partners						

Schedule L — Balance Sheets per Books

	Assets	Beginning of tax year (a)	(b)	End of tax year (c)	(d)
1	Cash		Initial Return		27,000
2a	Trade notes and accounts receivable			10,000	
b	Less allowance for bad debts				10,000
3	Inventories				
4	U.S. government obligations				
5	Tax-exempt securities				
6	Other current assets (attach statement)				
7a	Loans to partners (or persons related to partners) .				
b	Mortgage and real estate loans				
8	Other investments (attach statement)				
9a	Buildings and other depreciable assets			115,000	
b	Less accumulated depreciation			9,250	105,750
10a	Depletable assets				
b	Less accumulated depletion				
11	Land (net of any amortization)				115,000
12a	Intangible assets (amortizable only)				
b	Less accumulated amortization				
13	Other assets (attach statement)				
14	Total assets				257,750
	Liabilities and Capital				
15	Accounts payable				29,750
16	Mortgages, notes, bonds payable in less than 1 year				
17	Other current liabilities (attach statement)				
18	All nonrecourse loans				
19a	Loans from partners (or persons related to partners) .				
b	Mortgages, notes, bonds payable in 1 year or more .				187,750
20	Other liabilities (attach statement)				
21	Partners' capital accounts				40,250
22	Total liabilities and capital				257,750

Schedule M-1 — Reconciliation of Income (Loss) per Books With Income (Loss) per Return

Note: The partnership may be required to file Schedule M-3. See instructions.

1	Net income (loss) per books	58,750	6	Income recorded on books this year not included on Schedule K, lines 1 through 11 (itemize):	
2	Income included on Schedule K, lines 1, 2, 3c, 5, 6a, 7, 8, 9a, 10, and 11, not recorded on books this year (itemize): _____		a	Tax-exempt interest $_____	
3	Guaranteed payments (other than health insurance)		7	Deductions included on Schedule K, lines 1 through 13d, and 16p, not charged against book income this year (itemize):	
4	Expenses recorded on books this year not included on Schedule K, lines 1 through 13d, and 16p (itemize):		a	Depreciation $_____	
a	Depreciation $_____		8	Add lines 6 and 7	
b	Travel and entertainment $_____		9	Income (loss) (Analysis of Net Income (Loss), line 1). Subtract line 8 from line 5	58,750
5	Add lines 1 through 4	58,750			

Schedule M-2 — Analysis of Partners' Capital Accounts

1	Balance at beginning of year . . .	0	6	Distributions: **a** Cash	50,000
2	Capital contributed: **a** Cash . . .	31,500		**b** Property	
	b Property . .		7	Other decreases (itemize): _____	
3	Net income (loss) per books	58,750			
4	Other increases (itemize): _____		8	Add lines 6 and 7	50,000
5	Add lines 1 through 4	90,250	9	Balance at end of year. Subtract line 8 from line 5	40,250

Form **1065** (2020)

Self-Study Problem 10.3

651119

☐ Final K-1 ☐ Amended K-1	OMB No. 1545-0123

Schedule K-1
(Form 1065)
Department of the Treasury
Internal Revenue Service

For calendar year 2020, or tax year

beginning ___/___/ 2020   ending ___/___/___

2020

Part III   Partner's Share of Current Year Income, Deductions, Credits, and Other Items

1	Ordinary business income (loss)	15	Credits
	30,125		
2	Net rental real estate income (loss)		
3	Other net rental income (loss)	16	Foreign transactions
4a	Guaranteed payments for services		
4b	Guaranteed payments for capital		
4c	Total guaranteed payments		
5	Interest income		
6a	Ordinary dividends		
6b	Qualified dividends		
6c	Dividend equivalents	17	Alternative minimum tax (AMT) items
7	Royalties		
8	Net short-term capital gain (loss)		
9a	Net long-term capital gain (loss)	18	Tax-exempt income and nondeductible expenses
9b	Collectibles (28%) gain (loss)		
9c	Unrecaptured section 1250 gain		
10	Net section 1231 gain (loss)		
11	Other income (loss)	19	Distributions
		A	25,000
12	Section 179 deduction	20	Other information
		Z*	30,125
13	Other deductions		
A	750	Z**	84,000
14	Self-employment earnings (loss)		
A	30,125		

**Partner's Share of Income, Deductions,
Credits, etc.** ▶ See separate instructions.

Part I   Information About the Partnership

A   Partnership's employer identification number
44-4444444

B   Partnership's name, address, city, state, and ZIP code
Cahokia Partnership 40 Rainy Street, Collinsville, IL 62234

C   IRS Center where partnership filed return ▶ Ogden, UT
D   ☐ Check if this is a publicly traded partnership (PTP)

Part II   Information About the Partner

E   Partner's SSN or TIN (Do not use TIN of a disregarded entity. See instructions.)
444-14-1414

F   Name, address, city, state, and ZIP code for partner entered in E. See instructions.
Sapat Illiniwek

G   ☒ General partner or LLC member-manager   ☐ Limited partner or other LLC member

H1   ☒ Domestic partner   ☐ Foreign partner
H2   ☐ If the partner is a disregarded entity (DE), enter the partner's:
   TIN _____ Name _____

I1   What type of entity is this partner?   Individual
I2   If this partner is a retirement plan (IRA/SEP/Keogh/etc.), check here ☐

J   Partner's share of profit, loss, and capital (see instructions):

	Beginning	Ending
Profit	%	50 %
Loss	%	50 %
Capital	%	50 %

Check if decrease is due to sale or exchange of partnership interest . . ☐

K   Partner's share of liabilities:

	Beginning	Ending
Nonrecourse . . $		$
Qualified nonrecourse financing . . . $		$
Recourse . . . $		$ 108,750

☐ Check this box if Item K includes liability amounts from lower tier partnerships.

L   **Partner's Capital Account Analysis**

Beginning capital account . . . $	0
Capital contributed during the year . $	15,750
Current year net income (loss) . . . $	29,375
Other increase (decrease) (attach explanation) $	
Withdrawals & distributions . . $(	25,000)
Ending capital account . . . . $	20,125

M   Did the partner contribute property with a built-in gain or loss?
☐ Yes   ☒ No   If "Yes," attach statement. See instructions.

N   **Partner's Share of Net Unrecognized Section 704(c) Gain or (Loss)**
Beginning . . . . $
Ending . . . . $

| 21 | ☐ More than one activity for at-risk purposes* |
| 22 | ☐ More than one activity for passive activity purposes* |

*See attached statement for additional information.

For IRS Use Only

The IRS uses code Z for QBI deduction reporting and recommends use of Statement A from the Form 1065 Instructions (which is not presented in this solution). Z is qualified business income and Z** is allocated W-2 wages.

Self-Study Problem 10.5

12 months × $1,000 per month guaranteed payment	$12,000
Add: Robert's distributive share of income	21,000
Total income	$33,000

The $1,500 per month received in September, October, November, and December of 2020 will be reported on Robert's 2021 income tax return. The guaranteed payments received are reported for the partnership tax year that ends with or within the partner's tax year, in the same manner as a distributive share of the partnership income.

Self-Study Problem 10.6

1. Maxwell has a $5,000 realized loss ($70,000 − $75,000), but the loss is not recognized since he is a more-than-50 percent partner, 50 percent directly and 50 percent indirectly from his daughter.
2. The daughter has a $15,000 gain ($40,000 − $25,000). Since she is a more-than-50 percent partner (50 percent directly and 50 percent indirectly), and the car is not a capital asset to the partnership, the gain is ordinary income.

Self-Study Problem 10.7

a. Marla's QBI deduction with no limitation is $200,000 × 20% = $40,000. The guaranteed payments and the capital gains are not part of QBI income. Because Marla's income exceeds the phase-out range for taxable income (starts at $163,300 and is completely phased out by $213,300 in 2020), the W-2 wage limitation applies.

    a. W-2 Wages allocated to Marla are $46,000 ($230,000 × 20% interest). Qualified property allocated to Marla is $240,000 ($1,200,000 × 20%). The limit is the greater of:

        i. $46,000 × 50% = $23,000
        ii. ($46,000 × 25%) + ($240,000 × 2.5%) = $17,500

    The W-2 wages limit of $23,000 is less than $40,000; thus the QBI deduction is $23,000 (note that the taxable income limit of $155,200 ($776,000 × 20%) exceeds the QBI deduction).

    b. If Salem is a service business, because Marla's income exceeds the phase-out range for taxable income (starts at $163,300 and completely phased out by $213,300 in 2020), she is not eligible for any QBI deduction.

Self-Study Problem 10.8

1. $45,000, his amount at risk in the activity.

2. Profit	$ 31,000
Less: carryover of disallowed loss from the prior year ($60,000 − $45,000)	(15,000)
Taxable income for next year	$ 16,000

Self-Study Problem 10.9

1. False   An election must be made to be treated like a corporation for tax purposes.
2. False
3. True
4. True
5. False

CHAPTER 11   THE CORPORATE INCOME TAX

Self-Study Problem 11.1

$335,000 × 21% = $70,350

Self-Study Problem 11.2

a. $110,000 × 21% = $23,100

None of the capital losses may be used to offset current year ordinary income. The capital losses may be carried back 3 years and forward 5 years to offset capital gains, if any, recognized during those years.

b. Maxus would have utilized $36,000 ($45,000 × 80%) of the 2018 NOL in 2019, leaving 2019 taxable income of $9,000, and a 2018 NOL carryforward of $4,000. Note that the 2018 NOL was at that time not eligible for carryback. Under the changes imposed by the CARES Act in 2020, Maxus would now first carryback $10,000 of the 2018 NOL to offset 2017 taxable income. The remaining $30,000 2018 NOL would be carried forward to 2019 and can be used in its entirety, leaving $15,000 of taxable income in 2019. The 2020 NOL can be first carried back to offset the $15,000 of 2019 taxable income, leaving $55,000 of NOL to be carried forward. Note that the 2020 NOL will be subject to the 80 percent income limitation in years 2021 and after.

Self-Study Problem 11.3

a. The dividends received deduction is equal to the lesser of $45,500 = 65% × $70,000; or $39,000 = 65% × $60,000 ($90,000 + $70,000 − $100,000). Therefore, $39,000 is the amount of the deduction.

b. Organization costs of $5,222.22 can be deducted in 2020. Boyce is eligible to expense $5,000 organization costs. The balance of $8,000 ($13,000 − $5,000) is amortized over 180 months for 5 months of 2020 for a deduction of $222.22 ($8,000 ÷ 180 × 5 months). In 2021, Boyce will deduct $533.33 ($8,000 ÷ 180 × 12 months).

Start-up costs exceed $50,000, thus Boyce is not eligible to deduct the entire $5,000 of start-up costs. The $5,000 is reduced by $2,000 (the start-up costs in excess of $50,000) to $3,000. The remaining balance of $49,000 ($52,000 − $3,000) is amortized over 180 months × 5 months in 2020 or $1,361.11 for a total 2020 deduction of $4,361.11. In 2021, Boyce will deduct $3,266.67 ($49,000 ÷ 180 × 12).

c. Gant's modified taxable income for purposes of the charitable contribution deduction limit of 25% is $95,000 ($55,000 + $15,000 + $25,000). Thus the charitable contribution limit is $23,750 ($95,000 × 25%). The remaining $1,250 can be carried forward for up to 5 years.

Self-Study Problem 11.4

Schedule M-1	Reconciliation of Income (Loss) per Books With Income per Return						
	Note: The corporation may be required to file Schedule M-3. See instructions.						
1	Net income (loss) per books	115,600		7	Income recorded on books this year not included on this return (itemize):		
2	Federal income tax per books	29,400					
3	Excess of capital losses over capital gains .	9,100			Tax-exempt interest $_____4,700		
4	Income subject to tax not recorded on books this year (itemize):_____				_____		
	_____				_____		4,700
				8	Deductions on this return not charged against book income this year (itemize):		
5	Expenses recorded on books this year not deducted on this return (itemize):			a	Depreciation . . $_____4,000		
a	Depreciation . . . . $_____			b	Charitable contributions $_____		
b	Charitable contributions . $_____						
c	Travel and entertainment . $_____				_____		
					_____		4,000
	_____			9	Add lines 7 and 8		8,700
6	Add lines 1 through 5	154,100		10	Income (page 1, line 28)—line 6 less line 9		145,400

Self-Study Problem 11.5

See Form 1120 on Pages E-84 to E-89. The calculation of tax for Aspen Corporation is as follows: 21% × $14,000 = $2,940. Net income per the books is equal to $16,060, $19,000 net income before income tax expense − $2,940 income tax expense.

Self-Study Problem 11.6

See Form 1120S and Schedule K-1 on Pages E-90 to E-96.

Self-Study Problem 11.7

Tammy's realized gain is $125,000 + $34,000 − $75,000 = $84,000.
    Tammy's recognized gain is $0.
    Tammy's basis in her stock is $75,000 − $0 + $0 − $34,000 = $41,000.
    The corporation's basis in the real estate is $75,000 + $0 = $75,000.

Self-Study Problem 11.5

Form 1120
Department of the Treasury
Internal Revenue Service

U.S. Corporation Income Tax Return
For calendar year 2020 or tax year beginning _____, 2020, ending _____, 20 ___
▶ Go to www.irs.gov/Form1120 for instructions and the latest information.

OMB No. 1545-0123

2020

A Check if:
1a Consolidated return (attach Form 851) ☐
b Life/nonlife consolidated return ☐
2 Personal holding co. (attach Sch. PH) ☐
3 Personal service corp. (see instructions) ☐
4 Schedule M-3 attached ☐

TYPE OR PRINT

Name: Aspen Corporation
Number, street, and room or suite no. If a P.O. box, see instructions.
470 Rio Grande Place
City or town, state or province, country, and ZIP or foreign postal code
Aspen, CO 81611

B Employer identification number
92-2222222

C Date incorporated
01/01/2020

D Total assets (see instructions)
$ 183,000

E Check if: (1) ☑ Initial return (2) ☐ Final return (3) ☐ Name change (4) ☐ Address change

Income

1a	Gross receipts or sales	1a 285,000	
b	Returns and allowances	1b	
c	Balance. Subtract line 1b from line 1a	1c	285,000
2	Cost of goods sold (attach Form 1125-A)	2	80,000
3	Gross profit. Subtract line 2 from line 1c	3	205,000
4	Dividends and inclusions (Schedule C, line 23)	4	10,000
5	Interest	5	
6	Gross rents	6	
7	Gross royalties	7	
8	Capital gain net income (attach Schedule D (Form 1120))	8	
9	Net gain or (loss) from Form 4797, Part II, line 17 (attach Form 4797)	9	
10	Other income (see instructions—attach statement)	10	
11	**Total income.** Add lines 3 through 10 ▶	11	215,000

Deductions (See instructions for limitations on deductions.)

12	Compensation of officers (see instructions—attach Form 1125-E) ▶	12	90,000
13	Salaries and wages (less employment credits)	13	82,000
14	Repairs and maintenance	14	8,000
15	Bad debts	15	
16	Rents	16	
17	Taxes and licenses	17	11,000
18	Interest (see instructions)	18	
19	Charitable contributions	19	
20	Depreciation from Form 4562 not claimed on Form 1125-A or elsewhere on return (attach Form 4562)	20	5,000
21	Depletion	21	
22	Advertising	22	
23	Pension, profit-sharing, etc., plans	23	
24	Employee benefit programs	24	
25	Reserved for future use	25	
26	Other deductions (attach statement)	26	
27	**Total deductions.** Add lines 12 through 26 ▶	27	196,000
28	Taxable income before net operating loss deduction and special deductions. Subtract line 27 from line 11.	28	19,000
29a	Net operating loss deduction (see instructions)	29a	
b	Special deductions (Schedule C, line 24)	29b 5,000	
c	Add lines 29a and 29b	29c	

Tax, Refundable Credits, and Payments

30	**Taxable income.** Subtract line 29c from line 28. See instructions	30	14,000
31	Total tax (Schedule J, Part I, line 11)	31	2,940
32	2020 net 965 tax liability paid (Schedule J, Part II, line 12)	32	
33	Total payments, credits, and section 965 net tax liability (Schedule J, Part III, line 23)	33	3,000
34	Estimated tax penalty. See instructions. Check if Form 2220 is attached ▶ ☐	34	
35	**Amount owed.** If line 33 is smaller than the total of lines 31, 32, and 34, enter amount owed	35	
36	**Overpayment.** If line 33 is larger than the total of lines 31, 32, and 34, enter amount overpaid	36	60
37	Enter amount from line 36 you want: **Credited to 2021 estimated tax** ▶ 60 **Refunded** ▶	37	0

Sign Here

Under penalties of perjury, I declare that I have examined this return, including accompanying schedules and statements, and to the best of my knowledge and belief, it is true, correct, and complete. Declaration of preparer (other than taxpayer) is based on all information of which preparer has any knowledge.

▶ Signature of officer ___ Date ___ ▶ Title ___

May the IRS discuss this return with the preparer shown below? See instructions. ☑ Yes ☐ No

Paid Preparer Use Only

Print/Type preparer's name	Preparer's signature	Date	Check ☐ if self-employed	PTIN
Firm's name ▶			Firm's EIN ▶	
Firm's address ▶			Phone no.	

For Paperwork Reduction Act Notice, see separate instructions.　Cat. No. 11450Q　Form **1120** (2020)

Self-Study Problem 11.5

Form 1120 (2020)   Aspen Corporation

Page **2**

Schedule C	Dividends, Inclusions, and Special Deductions (see instructions)	(a) Dividends and inclusions	(b) %	(c) Special deductions (a) × (b)
1	Dividends from less-than-20%-owned domestic corporations (other than debt-financed stock)	10,000	50	5,000
2	Dividends from 20%-or-more-owned domestic corporations (other than debt-financed stock)		65	
3	Dividends on certain debt-financed stock of domestic and foreign corporations . . .		See instructions	
4	Dividends on certain preferred stock of less-than-20%-owned public utilities . . .		23.3	
5	Dividends on certain preferred stock of 20%-or-more-owned public utilities		26.7	
6	Dividends from less-than-20%-owned foreign corporations and certain FSCs . .		50	
7	Dividends from 20%-or-more-owned foreign corporations and certain FSCs . . .		65	
8	Dividends from wholly owned foreign subsidiaries		100	
9	**Subtotal.** Add lines 1 through 8. See instructions for limitations	10,000	See instructions	5,000
10	Dividends from domestic corporations received by a small business investment company operating under the Small Business Investment Act of 1958		100	
11	Dividends from affiliated group members		100	
12	Dividends from certain FSCs		100	
13	Foreign-source portion of dividends received from a specified 10%-owned foreign corporation (excluding hybrid dividends) (see instructions)		100	
14	Dividends from foreign corporations not included on line 3, 6, 7, 8, 11, 12, or 13 (including any hybrid dividends)			
15	Section 965(a) inclusion		See instructions	
16a	Subpart F inclusions derived from the sale by a controlled foreign corporation (CFC) of the stock of a lower-tier foreign corporation treated as a dividend (attach Form(s) 5471) (see instructions)		100	
b	Subpart F inclusions derived from hybrid dividends of tiered corporations (attach Form(s) 5471) (see instructions)			
c	Other inclusions from CFCs under subpart F not included on line 15, 16a, 16b, or 17 (attach Form(s) 5471) (see instructions).			
17	Global Intangible Low-Taxed Income (GILTI) (attach Form(s) 5471 and Form 8992) . .			
18	Gross-up for foreign taxes deemed paid			
19	IC-DISC and former DISC dividends not included on line 1, 2, or 3			
20	Other dividends			
21	Deduction for dividends paid on certain preferred stock of public utilities			
22	Section 250 deduction (attach Form 8993)			
23	**Total dividends and inclusions.** Add column (a), lines 9 through 20. Enter here and on page 1, line 4	10,000		
24	**Total special deductions.** Add column (c), lines 9 through 22. Enter here and on page 1, line 29b			5,000

Form **1120** (2020)

Self-Study Problem 11.5

Form 1120 (2020)   Aspen Corporation   Page **3**

Schedule J	Tax Computation and Payment (see instructions)		
Part I—Tax Computation			

1	Check if the corporation is a member of a controlled group (attach Schedule O (Form 1120)). See instructions ▶ ☐		
2	Income tax. See instructions	2	2,940
3	Base erosion minimum tax amount (attach Form 8991)	3	
4	Add lines 2 and 3	4	2,940
5a	Foreign tax credit (attach Form 1118)	5a	
b	Credit from Form 8834 (see instructions)	5b	
c	General business credit (attach Form 3800)	5c	
d	Credit for prior year minimum tax (attach Form 8827)	5d	
e	Bond credits from Form 8912	5e	
6	**Total credits.** Add lines 5a through 5e	6	
7	Subtract line 6 from line 4	7	2,940
8	Personal holding company tax (attach Schedule PH (Form 1120))	8	
9a	Recapture of investment credit (attach Form 4255)	9a	
b	Recapture of low-income housing credit (attach Form 8611)	9b	
c	Interest due under the look-back method—completed long-term contracts (attach Form 8697)	9c	
d	Interest due under the look-back method—income forecast method (attach Form 8866)	9d	
e	Alternative tax on qualifying shipping activities (attach Form 8902)	9e	
f	Interest/tax due under Section 453A(c) and/or Section 453(l)	9f	
g	Other (see instructions—attach statement)	9g	
10	**Total.** Add lines 9a through 9g	10	
11	**Total tax.** Add lines 7, 8, and 10. Enter here and on page 1, line 31	11	2,940
Part II—Section 965 Payments (see instructions)			
12	2020 net 965 tax liability paid from Form 965-B, Part II, column (k), line 4. Enter here and on page 1, line 32	12	
Part III—Payments, Refundable Credits, and Section 965 Net Tax Liability			
13	2019 overpayment credited to 2020	13	
14	2020 estimated tax payments	14	3,000
15	2020 refund applied for on Form 4466	15	( )
16	Combine lines 13, 14, and 15	16	3,000
17	Tax deposited with Form 7004	17	
18	Withholding (see instructions)	18	
19	**Total payments.** Add lines 16, 17, and 18	19	3,000
20	Refundable credits from:		
a	Form 2439	20a	
b	Form 4136	20b	
c	Reserved for future use	20c	
d	Other (attach statement—see instructions)	20d	
21	**Total credits.** Add lines 20a through 20d	21	
22	2020 net 965 tax liability from Form 965-B, Part I, column (d), line 4. See instructions	22	
23	**Total payments, credits, and section 965 net tax liability.** Add lines 19, 21, and 22. Enter here and on page 1, line 33	23	3,000

Form **1120** (2020)

Self-Study Problem 11.5

Form 1120 (2020)   Aspen Corporation   Page **4**

Schedule K	**Other Information** (see instructions)			Yes	No

1 Check accounting method: **a** ☐ Cash   **b** ☑ Accrual   **c** ☐ Other (specify) ▶ _____

2 See the instructions and enter the:

a Business activity code no. ▶ _____

b Business activity ▶ _____

c Product or service ▶ _____

3 Is the corporation a subsidiary in an affiliated group or a parent–subsidiary controlled group? . . . .   ✓ (No)

If "Yes," enter name and EIN of the parent corporation ▶ _____

4 At the end of the tax year:

a Did any foreign or domestic corporation, partnership (including any entity treated as a partnership), trust, or tax-exempt organization own directly 20% or more, or own, directly or indirectly, 50% or more of the total voting power of all classes of the corporation's stock entitled to vote? If "Yes," complete Part I of Schedule G (Form 1120) (attach Schedule G) . . . .   ✓ (No)

b Did any individual or estate own directly 20% or more, or own, directly or indirectly, 50% or more of the total voting power of all classes of the corporation's stock entitled to vote? If "Yes," complete Part II of Schedule G (Form 1120) (attach Schedule G) .   ✓ (No)

5 At the end of the tax year, did the corporation:

a Own directly 20% or more, or own, directly or indirectly, 50% or more of the total voting power of all classes of stock entitled to vote of any foreign or domestic corporation not included on **Form 851,** Affiliations Schedule? For rules of constructive ownership, see instructions.   ✓ (No)

If "Yes," complete (i) through (iv) below.

(i) Name of Corporation	**(ii)** Employer Identification Number (if any)	**(iii)** Country of Incorporation	**(iv)** Percentage Owned in Voting Stock

b Own directly an interest of 20% or more, or own, directly or indirectly, an interest of 50% or more in any foreign or domestic partnership (including an entity treated as a partnership) or in the beneficial interest of a trust? For rules of constructive ownership, see instructions.   ✓ (No)

If "Yes," complete (i) through (iv) below.

(i) Name of Entity	**(ii)** Employer Identification Number (if any)	**(iii)** Country of Organization	**(iv)** Maximum Percentage Owned in Profit, Loss, or Capital

6 During this tax year, did the corporation pay dividends (other than stock dividends and distributions in exchange for stock) in excess of the corporation's current and accumulated earnings and profits? See sections 301 and 316 . . . .   ✓ (No)

If "Yes," file **Form 5452,** Corporate Report of Nondividend Distributions. See the instructions for Form 5452.

If this is a consolidated return, answer here for the parent corporation and on Form 851 for each subsidiary.

7 At any time during the tax year, did one foreign person own, directly or indirectly, at least 25% of the total voting power of all classes of the corporation's stock entitled to vote or at least 25% of the total value of all classes of the corporation's stock? .   ✓ (No)

For rules of attribution, see section 318. If "Yes," enter:

(a) Percentage owned ▶ _____   and **(b)** Owner's country ▶ _____

(c) The corporation may have to file **Form 5472,** Information Return of a 25% Foreign-Owned U.S. Corporation or a Foreign Corporation Engaged in a U.S. Trade or Business. Enter the number of Forms 5472 attached ▶ _____

8 Check this box if the corporation issued publicly offered debt instruments with original issue discount . . . . . ▶ ☐

If checked, the corporation may have to file **Form 8281,** Information Return for Publicly Offered Original Issue Discount Instruments.

9 Enter the amount of tax-exempt interest received or accrued during the tax year ▶ $ _____

10 Enter the number of shareholders at the end of the tax year (if 100 or fewer) ▶ _____

11 If the corporation has an NOL for the tax year and is electing to forego the carryback period, check here (see instructions) ▶ ☐

If the corporation is filing a consolidated return, the statement required by Regulations section 1.1502-21(b)(3) must be attached or the election will not be valid.

12 Enter the available NOL carryover from prior tax years (do not reduce it by any deduction reported on page 1, line 29a.) . . . . ▶ $ _____

Form **1120** (2020)

Self-Study Problem 11.5

Schedule K	Other Information (continued from page 4)		

		Yes	No
13	Are the corporation's total receipts (page 1, line 1a, plus lines 4 through 10) for the tax year **and** its total assets at the end of the tax year less than $250,000?		✓
	If "Yes," the corporation is not required to complete Schedules L, M-1, and M-2. Instead, enter the total amount of cash distributions and the book value of property distributions (other than cash) made during the tax year ▶ $ _____		
14	Is the corporation required to file Schedule UTP (Form 1120), Uncertain Tax Position Statement? See instructions		✓
	If "Yes," complete and attach Schedule UTP.		
15a	Did the corporation make any payments in 2020 that would require it to file Form(s) 1099?	✓	
b	If "Yes," did or will the corporation file required Form(s) 1099?	✓	
16	During this tax year, did the corporation have an 80%-or-more change in ownership, including a change due to redemption of its own stock?		✓
17	During or subsequent to this tax year, but before the filing of this return, did the corporation dispose of more than 65% (by value) of its assets in a taxable, non-taxable, or tax deferred transaction?		✓
18	Did the corporation receive assets in a section 351 transfer in which any of the transferred assets had a fair market basis or fair market value of more than $1 million?		✓
19	During the corporation's tax year, did the corporation make any payments that would require it to file Forms 1042 and 1042-S under chapter 3 (sections 1441 through 1464) or chapter 4 (sections 1471 through 1474) of the Code?		✓
20	Is the corporation operating on a cooperative basis?		✓
21	During the tax year, did the corporation pay or accrue any interest or royalty for which the deduction is not allowed under section 267A? See instructions		✓
	If "Yes," enter the total amount of the disallowed deductions ▶ $ _____		
22	Does the corporation have gross receipts of at least $500 million in any of the 3 preceding tax years? (See sections 59A(e)(2) and (3))		✓
	If "Yes," complete and attach Form 8991.		
23	Did the corporation have an election under section 163(j) for any real property trade or business or any farming business in effect during the tax year? See instructions		✓
24	Does the corporation satisfy one or more of the following? See instructions		✓
a	The corporation owns a pass-through entity with current, or prior year carryover, excess business interest expense.		
b	The corporation's aggregate average annual gross receipts (determined under section 448(c)) for the 3 tax years preceding the current tax year are more than $26 million and the corporation has business interest expense.		
c	The corporation is a tax shelter and the corporation has business interest expense.		
	If "Yes," complete and attach Form 8990.		
25	Is the corporation attaching Form 8996 to certify as a Qualified Opportunity Fund?		✓
	If "Yes," enter amount from Form 8996, line 15 . . . . . ▶ $		
26	Since December 22, 2017, did a foreign corporation directly or indirectly acquire substantially all of the properties held directly or indirectly by the corporation, and was the ownership percentage (by vote or value) for purposes of section 7874 greater than 50% (for example, the shareholders held more than 50% of the stock of the foreign corporation)? If "Yes," list the ownership percentage by vote and by value. See instructions		✓
	Percentage: By Vote By Value		

Self-Study Problem 11.5

Form 1120 (2020)   Aspen Corporation   Page **6**

Schedule L — Balance Sheets per Books

		Beginning of tax year		End of tax year	
	Assets	**(a)**	**(b)**	**(c)**	**(d)**
1	Cash		Initial Return		35,000
2a	Trade notes and accounts receivable			10,000	
b	Less allowance for bad debts	( )		(0)	10,000
3	Inventories				
4	U.S. government obligations				
5	Tax-exempt securities (see instructions)				
6	Other current assets (attach statement)				
7	Loans to shareholders				
8	Mortgage and real estate loans				
9	Other investments (attach statement)				
10a	Buildings and other depreciable assets			125,000	
b	Less accumulated depreciation	( )		(5,000)	120,000
11a	Depletable assets				
b	Less accumulated depletion	( )		( )	
12	Land (net of any amortization)				18,000
13a	Intangible assets (amortizable only)				
b	Less accumulated amortization	( )		( )	
14	Other assets (attach statement)				
15	Total assets				183,000
	Liabilities and Shareholders' Equity				
16	Accounts payable				26,940
17	Mortgages, notes, bonds payable in less than 1 year				
18	Other current liabilities (attach statement)				
19	Loans from shareholders				
20	Mortgages, notes, bonds payable in 1 year or more				
21	Other liabilities (attach statement)				
22	Capital stock: **a** Preferred stock				
	b Common stock			140,000	140,000
23	Additional paid-in capital				
24	Retained earnings—Appropriated (attach statement)				
25	Retained earnings—Unappropriated				16,060
26	Adjustments to shareholders' equity (attach statement)				
27	Less cost of treasury stock		( )		( )
28	Total liabilities and shareholders' equity				183,000

Schedule M-1 — Reconciliation of Income (Loss) per Books With Income per Return

Note: The corporation may be required to file Schedule M-3. See instructions.

1	Net income (loss) per books		7	Income recorded on books this year not included on this return (itemize):	
2	Federal income tax per books	16,060			
3	Excess of capital losses over capital gains	2,940		Tax-exempt interest $ _____	
4	Income subject to tax not recorded on books this year (itemize): _____				
	_____		8	Deductions on this return not charged against book income this year (itemize):	
5	Expenses recorded on books this year not deducted on this return (itemize):		a	Depreciation $ _____	
a	Depreciation $ _____		b	Charitable contributions $ _____	
b	Charitable contributions $ _____			_____	
c	Travel and entertainment $ _____		9	Add lines 7 and 8	
6	Add lines 1 through 5	19,000	10	Income (page 1, line 28)—line 6 less line 9	19,000

Schedule M-2 — Analysis of Unappropriated Retained Earnings per Books (Schedule L, Line 25)

1	Balance at beginning of year	0	5	Distributions: **a** Cash	
2	Net income (loss) per books	16,060		**b** Stock	
3	Other increases (itemize): _____			**c** Property	
	_____		6	Other decreases (itemize): _____	
	_____		7	Add lines 5 and 6	0
4	Add lines 1, 2, and 3	16,060	8	Balance at end of year (line 4 less line 7)	16,060

Form **1120** (2020)

Self-Study Problem 11.6

Form **1120-S**		**U.S. Income Tax Return for an S Corporation**			OMB No. 1545-0123

▶ Do not file this form unless the corporation has filed or is attaching Form 2553 to elect to be an S corporation.
▶ Go to *www.irs.gov/Form1120S* for instructions and the latest information.

Department of the Treasury
Internal Revenue Service

2020

For calendar year 2020 or tax year beginning _____, 2020, ending _____, 20____

A S election effective date		Name		**D** Employer identification number
01/01/20	**TYPE OR PRINT**	Aspen Corporation		92-2222222
B Business activity code number (see instructions)		Number, street, and room or suite no. If a P.O. box, see instructions.		**E** Date incorporated
		470 Rio Grande Place		01/01/2020
		City or town, state or province, country, and ZIP or foreign postal code		**F** Total assets (see instructions)
C Check if Sch. M-3 attached ☐		Aspen, CO 81611		$ 183,000

G Is the corporation electing to be an S corporation beginning with this tax year? ☑ Yes ☐ No   If "Yes," attach Form 2553 if not already filed

H Check if: **(1)** ☐ Final return **(2)** ☐ Name change **(3)** ☐ Address change **(4)** ☐ Amended return **(5)** ☐ S election termination or revocation

I Enter the number of shareholders who were shareholders during any part of the tax year . . . . ▶

J Check if corporation: **(1)** ☐ Aggregated activities for section 465 at-risk purposes **(2)** ☐ Grouped activities for section 469 passive activity purposes

Caution: Include **only** trade or business income and expenses on lines 1a through 21. See the instructions for more information.

Income

1a	Gross receipts or sales	**1a**	285,000	
b	Returns and allowances	**1b**		
c	Balance. Subtract line 1b from line 1a	**1c**		285,000
2	Cost of goods sold (attach Form 1125-A)	**2**		80,000
3	Gross profit. Subtract line 2 from line 1c	**3**		205,000
4	Net gain (loss) from Form 4797, line 17 (attach Form 4797) . . .	**4**		
5	Other income (loss) (see instructions—attach statement)	**5**		
6	**Total income (loss).** Add lines 3 through 5 . . . . ▶	**6**		205,000

Deductions (see instructions for limitations)

7	Compensation of officers (see instructions—attach Form 1125-E) . .	**7**	90,000
8	Salaries and wages (less employment credits)	**8**	82,000
9	Repairs and maintenance	**9**	8,000
10	Bad debts	**10**	
11	Rents	**11**	
12	Taxes and licenses	**12**	11,000
13	Interest (see instructions)	**13**	
14	Depreciation not claimed on Form 1125-A or elsewhere on return (attach Form 4562)	**14**	5,000
15	Depletion **(Do not deduct oil and gas depletion.)**	**15**	
16	Advertising	**16**	
17	Pension, profit-sharing, etc., plans	**17**	
18	Employee benefit programs	**18**	
19	Other deductions (attach statement)	**19**	
20	**Total deductions.** Add lines 7 through 19 . . . . ▶	**20**	196,000
21	**Ordinary business income (loss).** Subtract line 20 from line 6 . .	**21**	9,000

Tax and Payments

22a	Excess net passive income or LIFO recapture tax (see instructions) . .	**22a**		
b	Tax from Schedule D (Form 1120-S)	**22b**		
c	Add lines 22a and 22b (see instructions for additional taxes)	**22c**		0
23a	2020 estimated tax payments and 2019 overpayment credited to 2020 .	**23a**		
b	Tax deposited with Form 7004	**23b**		
c	Credit for federal tax paid on fuels (attach Form 4136) .	**23c**		
d	Reserved for future use	**23d**		
e	Add lines 23a through 23d	**23e**		0
24	Estimated tax penalty (see instructions). Check if Form 2220 is attached . . . . . . ▶ ☐	**24**		
25	**Amount owed.** If line 23e is smaller than the total of lines 22c and 24, enter amount owed . . .	**25**		
26	**Overpayment.** If line 23e is larger than the total of lines 22c and 24, enter amount overpaid . . .	**26**		0
27	Enter amount from line 26: **Credited to 2021 estimated tax** ▶ _____ **Refunded** ▶	**27**		

Sign Here

Under penalties of perjury, I declare that I have examined this return, including accompanying schedules and statements, and to the best of my knowledge and belief, it is true, correct, and complete. Declaration of preparer (other than taxpayer) is based on all information of which preparer has any knowledge.

▶ _____   ▶ _____
Signature of officer   Date   Title

May the IRS discuss this return with the preparer shown below? See instructions. ☑ Yes ☐ No

Paid Preparer Use Only

Print/Type preparer's name	Preparer's signature	Date	Check ☐ if self-employed	PTIN
Firm's name ▶			Firm's EIN ▶	
Firm's address ▶			Phone no.	

For Paperwork Reduction Act Notice, see separate instructions.   Cat. No. 11510H   Form **1120-S** (2020)

Self-Study Problem 11.6

Form 1120-S (2020) Aspen Corporation   Page **2**

Schedule B	Other Information (see instructions)	Yes	No

1 Check accounting method: **a** ☐ Cash   **b** ☑ Accrual
    c ☐ Other (specify) ▶ _____

2 See the instructions and enter the:
    a Business activity ▶ _____   **b** Product or service ▶ _____

3 At any time during the tax year, was any shareholder of the corporation a disregarded entity, a trust, an estate, or a nominee or similar person? If "Yes," attach Schedule B-1, Information on Certain Shareholders of an S Corporation   .   .   **No: ✓**

4 At the end of the tax year, did the corporation:

   a Own directly 20% or more, or own, directly or indirectly, 50% or more of the total stock issued and outstanding of any foreign or domestic corporation? For rules of constructive ownership, see instructions. If "Yes," complete (i) through (v) below . . . . .   **No: ✓**

(i) Name of Corporation	(ii) Employer Identification Number (if any)	(iii) Country of Incorporation	(iv) Percentage of Stock Owned	(v) If Percentage in (iv) Is 100%, Enter the Date (if any) a Qualified Subchapter S Subsidiary Election Was Made

   b Own directly an interest of 20% or more, or own, directly or indirectly, an interest of 50% or more in the profit, loss, or capital in any foreign or domestic partnership (including an entity treated as a partnership) or in the beneficial interest of a trust? For rules of constructive ownership, see instructions. If "Yes," complete (i) through (v) below   .   .   .   .   .   .   **No: ✓**

(i) Name of Entity	(ii) Employer Identification Number (if any)	(iii) Type of Entity	(iv) Country of Organization	(v) Maximum Percentage Owned in Profit, Loss, or Capital

5a At the end of the tax year, did the corporation have any outstanding shares of restricted stock?   .   .   .   .   .   .   **No: ✓**
    If "Yes," complete lines (i) and (ii) below.
    (i)   Total shares of restricted stock   .   .   .   .   ▶ _____
    (ii)   Total shares of non-restricted stock   .   .   .   .   ▶ _____

   b At the end of the tax year, did the corporation have any outstanding stock options, warrants, or similar instruments?   .   **No: ✓**
    If "Yes," complete lines (i) and (ii) below.
    (i)   Total shares of stock outstanding at the end of the tax year   ▶ _____
    (ii)   Total shares of stock outstanding if all instruments were executed ▶ _____

6 Has this corporation filed, or is it required to file, **Form 8918,** Material Advisor Disclosure Statement, to provide information on any reportable transaction?   .   .   .   .   **No: ✓**

7 Check this box if the corporation issued publicly offered debt instruments with original issue discount   .   .   .   . ▶ ☐
    If checked, the corporation may have to file **Form 8281,** Information Return for Publicly Offered Original Issue Discount Instruments.

8 If the corporation **(a)** was a C corporation before it elected to be an S corporation **or** the corporation acquired an asset with a basis determined by reference to the basis of the asset (or the basis of any other property) in the hands of a C corporation, **and (b)** has net unrealized built-in gain in excess of the net recognized built-in gain from prior years, enter the net unrealized built-in gain reduced by net recognized built-in gain from prior years. See instructions   .   .   .   .   .   ▶ $ _____

9 Did the corporation have an election under section 163(j) for any real property trade or business or any farming business in effect during the tax year? See instructions   .   .   .   .   **No: ✓**

10 Does the corporation satisfy one or more of the following? See instructions   .   .   .   .   **No: ✓**
   a The corporation owns a pass-through entity with current, or prior year carryover, excess business interest expense.
   b The corporation's aggregate average annual gross receipts (determined under section 448(c)) for the 3 tax years preceding the current tax year are more than $26 million and the corporation has business interest expense.
   c The corporation is a tax shelter and the corporation has business interest expense.
    If "Yes," complete and attach Form 8990.

11 Does the corporation satisfy **both** of the following conditions?   .   .   .   .   **No: ✓**
   a The corporation's total receipts (see instructions) for the tax year were less than $250,000.
   b The corporation's total assets at the end of the tax year were less than $250,000.
    If "Yes," the corporation is not required to complete Schedules L and M-1.

Form **1120-S** (2020)

Self-Study Problem 11.6

Form 1120-S (2020)   Aspen Corporation   Page **3**

Schedule B	**Other Information** (see instructions) *(continued)*	Yes	No
12	During the tax year, did the corporation have any non-shareholder debt that was canceled, was forgiven, or had the terms modified so as to reduce the principal amount of the debt?		✓
	If "Yes," enter the amount of principal reduction ▶ $		
13	During the tax year, was a qualified subchapter S subsidiary election terminated or revoked? If "Yes," see instructions		✓
14a	Did the corporation make any payments in 2020 that would require it to file Form(s) 1099?	✓	
b	If "Yes," did the corporation file or will it file required Form(s) 1099?	✓	
15	Is the corporation attaching Form 8996 to certify as a Qualified Opportunity Fund?		✓
	If "Yes," enter the amount from Form 8996, line 15 ▶ $		

Schedule K		**Shareholders' Pro Rata Share Items**			Total amount
Income (Loss)	1	Ordinary business income (loss) (page 1, line 21)		**1**	9,000
	2	Net rental real estate income (loss) (attach Form 8825)		**2**	
	3a	Other gross rental income (loss)	**3a**		
	b	Expenses from other rental activities (attach statement)	**3b**		
	c	Other net rental income (loss). Subtract line 3b from line 3a		**3c**	
	4	Interest income		**4**	
	5	Dividends: **a** Ordinary dividends		**5a**	10,000
		b Qualified dividends	**5b**	10,000	
	6	Royalties		**6**	
	7	Net short-term capital gain (loss) (attach Schedule D (Form 1120-S))		**7**	
	8a	Net long-term capital gain (loss) (attach Schedule D (Form 1120-S))		**8a**	
	b	Collectibles (28%) gain (loss)	**8b**		
	c	Unrecaptured section 1250 gain (attach statement)	**8c**		
	9	Net section 1231 gain (loss) (attach Form 4797)		**9**	
	10	Other income (loss) (see instructions) Type ▶		**10**	
Deductions	11	Section 179 deduction (attach Form 4562)		**11**	
	12a	Charitable contributions		**12a**	
	b	Investment interest expense		**12b**	
	c	Section 59(e)(2) expenditures Type ▶		**12c**	
	d	Other deductions (see instructions) Type ▶		**12d**	
Credits	13a	Low-income housing credit (section 42(j)(5))		**13a**	
	b	Low-income housing credit (other)		**13b**	
	c	Qualified rehabilitation expenditures (rental real estate) (attach Form 3468, if applicable)		**13c**	
	d	Other rental real estate credits (see instructions) Type ▶		**13d**	
	e	Other rental credits (see instructions) Type ▶		**13e**	
	f	Biofuel producer credit (attach Form 6478)		**13f**	
	g	Other credits (see instructions) Type ▶		**13g**	
Foreign Transactions	14a	Name of country or U.S. possession ▶			
	b	Gross income from all sources		**14b**	
	c	Gross income sourced at shareholder level		**14c**	
		Foreign gross income sourced at corporate level			
	d	Reserved for future use		**14d**	
	e	Foreign branch category		**14e**	
	f	Passive category		**14f**	
	g	General category		**14g**	
	h	Other (attach statement)		**14h**	
		Deductions allocated and apportioned at shareholder level			
	i	Interest expense		**14i**	
	j	Other		**14j**	
		Deductions allocated and apportioned at corporate level to foreign source income			
	k	Reserved for future use		**14k**	
	l	Foreign branch category		**14l**	
	m	Passive category		**14m**	
	n	General category		**14n**	
	o	Other (attach statement)		**14o**	
		Other information			
	p	Total foreign taxes (check one): ☐ Paid ☐ Accrued ▶		**14p**	
	q	Reduction in taxes available for credit (attach statement)		**14q**	
	r	Other foreign tax information (attach statement)			

Form **1120-S** (2020)

Self-Study Problem 11.6

Form 1120-S (2020)   Aspen Corporation   Page **4**

Schedule K   Shareholders' Pro Rata Share Items (continued)

			Total amount
Alternative Minimum Tax (AMT) Items	15a	Post-1986 depreciation adjustment	15a	
	b	Adjusted gain or loss	15b	
	c	Depletion (other than oil and gas)	15c	
	d	Oil, gas, and geothermal properties—gross income	15d	
	e	Oil, gas, and geothermal properties—deductions	15e	
	f	Other AMT items (attach statement)	15f	
Items Affecting Shareholder Basis	16a	Tax-exempt interest income	16a	
	b	Other tax-exempt income	16b	
	c	Nondeductible expenses	16c	
	d	Distributions (attach statement if required) (see instructions)	16d	
	e	Repayment of loans from shareholders	16e	
Other Information	17a	Investment income	17a	
	b	Investment expenses	17b	
	c	Dividend distributions paid from accumulated earnings and profits	17c	
	d	Other items and amounts (attach statement)		
Reconciliation	18	**Income (loss) reconciliation.** Combine the amounts on lines 1 through 10 in the far right column. From the result, subtract the sum of the amounts on lines 11 through 12d and 14p	18	19,000

Schedule L   Balance Sheets per Books

	Assets	Beginning of tax year (a)	(b)	End of tax year (c)	(d)
1	Cash		Initial Return		35,000
2a	Trade notes and accounts receivable			10,000	
b	Less allowance for bad debts	( )		(0)	10,000
3	Inventories				
4	U.S. government obligations				
5	Tax-exempt securities (see instructions)				
6	Other current assets (attach statement)				
7	Loans to shareholders				
8	Mortgage and real estate loans				
9	Other investments (attach statement)				
10a	Buildings and other depreciable assets			125,000	
b	Less accumulated depreciation	( )		(5,000)	120,000
11a	Depletable assets				
b	Less accumulated depletion	( )		( )	
12	Land (net of any amortization)				18,000
13a	Intangible assets (amortizable only)				
b	Less accumulated amortization	( )		( )	
14	Other assets (attach statement)				
15	Total assets				183,000
	Liabilities and Shareholders' Equity				
16	Accounts payable				24,000
17	Mortgages, notes, bonds payable in less than 1 year				
18	Other current liabilities (attach statement)				
19	Loans from shareholders				
20	Mortgages, notes, bonds payable in 1 year or more				
21	Other liabilities (attach statement)				
22	Capital stock				140,000
23	Additional paid-in capital				
24	Retained earnings				19,000
25	Adjustments to shareholders' equity (attach statement)				
26	Less cost of treasury stock		( )		( )
27	Total liabilities and shareholders' equity				183,000

Form **1120-S** (2020)

Self-Study Problem 11.6

Form 1120-S (2020)   Aspen Corporation   Page **5**

Schedule M-1	**Reconciliation of Income (Loss) per Books With Income (Loss) per Return**		
	Note: The corporation may be required to file Schedule M-3. See instructions.		

1	Net income (loss) per books	19,000	**5**	Income recorded on books this year not included on Schedule K, lines 1 through 10 (itemize):		
2	Income included on Schedule K, lines 1, 2, 3c, 4, 5a, 6, 7, 8a, 9, and 10, not recorded on books this year (itemize) _____		**a**	Tax-exempt interest $ _____		
3	Expenses recorded on books this year not included on Schedule K, lines 1 through 12 and 14p (itemize):		**6**	Deductions included on Schedule K, lines 1 through 12 and 14p, not charged against book income this year (itemize):		
a	Depreciation $ _____		**a**	Depreciation $ _____		
b	Travel and entertainment $ _____		**7**	Add lines 5 and 6		0
			8	Income (loss) (Schedule K, line 18).		
4	Add lines 1 through 3	19,000		Subtract line 7 from line 4		19,000

Schedule M-2	**Analysis of Accumulated Adjustments Account, Shareholders' Undistributed Taxable Income Previously Taxed, Accumulated Earnings and Profits, and Other Adjustments Account** (see instructions)			

		(a) Accumulated adjustments account	**(b)** Shareholders' undistributed taxable income previously taxed	**(c)** Accumulated earnings and profits	**(d)** Other adjustments account
1	Balance at beginning of tax year	0			
2	Ordinary income from page 1, line 21 . . .	9,000			
3	Other additions	10,000			
4	Loss from page 1, line 21	( )			
5	Other reductions	( )			( )
6	Combine lines 1 through 5	19,000			
7	Distributions				
8	Balance at end of tax year. Subtract line 7 from line 6	19,000			

Form **1120-S** (2020)

Self-Study Problem 11.6

671120

☐ Final K-1	☐ Amended K-1	OMB No. 1545-0123

**Schedule K-1
(Form 1120-S)**
Department of the Treasury
Internal Revenue Service

2020

For calendar year 2020, or tax year

beginning ___ / ___ / 2020   ending ___ / ___ / ___

Shareholder's Share of Income, Deductions, Credits, etc.   ▶ See separate instructions.

DRAFT AS OF July 2, 2020 DO NOT FILE

Part I Information About the Corporation

A Corporation's employer identification number
92-2222222

B Corporation's name, address, city, state, and ZIP code

Aspen Corp
470 Rio Grande Place
Aspen, CO 81611

C IRS Center where corporation filed return
Ogden, UT

Part II Information About the Shareholder

D Shareholder's identifying number
411-41-4141

E Shareholder's name, address, city, state, and ZIP code

Ava Mendes
1175 Delaware St.
Denver, CO 80204

F Current year allocation percentage . . . 100 %

G Shareholder's number of shares
Beginning of tax year 100
End of tax year 100

H Loans from shareholder
Beginning of tax year . . . . . . $ _____
End of tax year . . . . $ _____

For IRS Use Only

Part III Shareholder's Share of Current Year Income, Deductions, Credits, and Other Items

1	Ordinary business income (loss) 9,000		**13**	Credits
2	Net rental real estate income (loss)			
3	Other net rental income (loss)			
4	Interest income			
5a	Ordinary dividends 10,000			
5b	Qualified dividends 10,000		**14**	Foreign transactions
6	Royalties			
7	Net short-term capital gain (loss)			
8a	Net long-term capital gain (loss)			
8b	Collectibles (28%) gain (loss)			
8c	Unrecaptured section 1250 gain			
9	Net section 1231 gain (loss)			
10	Other income (loss)		**15**	Alternative minimum tax (AMT) items
11	Section 179 deduction		**16**	Items affecting shareholder basis
12	Other deductions			
			17	Other information
			A	10,000
			V*	9,000
			V**	172,000
			V***	125,000
18	☐ More than one activity for at-risk purposes*			
19	☐ More than one activity for passive activity purposes*			

* See attached statement for additional information.

For Paperwork Reduction Act Notice, see the Instructions for Form 1120-S.   www.irs.gov/Form1120S   Cat. No. 11520D   **Schedule K-1 (Form 1120-S) 2020**

The IRS uses code V for QBI deduction reporting and recommends use of Statement A from the Form 1120-S Instructions (which is not presented in this solution). V* is qualified business income, V** is allocated W-2 wages, and V*** is qualified property.

Schedule K-1 (Form 1120-S) 2019   Page **2**

This list identifies the codes used on Schedule K-1 for all shareholders and provides summarized reporting information for shareholders who file Form 1040 or 1040-SR. For detailed reporting and filing information, see the separate Shareholder's Instructions for Schedule K-1 and the instructions for your income tax return.

1. Ordinary business income (loss). Determine whether the income (loss) is passive or nonpassive and enter on your return as follows:

	Report on
Passive loss	See the Shareholder's Instructions
Passive income	Schedule E, line 28, column (h)
Nonpassive loss	See the Shareholder's Instructions
Nonpassive income	Schedule E, line 28, column (k)

2. Net rental real estate income (loss) See the Shareholder's Instructions

3. Other net rental income (loss)
Net income	Schedule E, line 28, column (h)
Net loss	See the Shareholder's Instructions

4. Interest income Form 1040 or 1040-SR, line 2b
5a. Ordinary dividends Form 1040 or 1040-SR, line 3b
5b. Qualified dividends Form 1040 or 1040-SR, line 3a
6. Royalties Schedule E, line 4
7. Net short-term capital gain (loss) Schedule D, line 5
8a. Net long-term capital gain (loss) Schedule D, line 12
8b. Collectibles (28%) gain (loss) 28% Rate Gain Worksheet, line 4 (Schedule D instructions)
8c. Unrecaptured section 1250 gain See the Shareholder's Instructions
9. Net section 1231 gain (loss) See the Shareholder's Instructions

10. Other income (loss)
Code
A	Other portfolio income (loss)	See the Shareholder's Instructions
B	Involuntary conversions	See the Shareholder's Instructions
C	Sec. 1256 contracts & straddles	Form 6781, line 1
D	Mining exploration costs recapture	See Pub. 535
E	Reserved for future use	
F	Section 965(a) inclusion	
G	Income under subpart F (other than inclusions under sections 951A and 965)	See the Shareholder's Instructions
H	Other income (loss)	

11. Section 179 deduction See the Shareholder's Instructions

12. Other deductions
A	Cash contributions (60%)	
B	Cash contributions (30%)	
C	Noncash contributions (50%)	
D	Noncash contributions (30%)	
E	Capital gain property to a 50% organization (30%)	See the Shareholder's Instructions
F	Capital gain property (20%)	
G	Contributions (100%)	
H	Investment interest expense	Form 4952, line 1
I	Deductions—royalty income	Schedule E, line 19
J	Section 59(e)(2) expenditures	See the Shareholder's Instructions
K	Section 965(c) deduction	See the Shareholder's Instructions
L	Deductions—portfolio (other)	Schedule A, line 16
M	Preproductive period expenses	See the Shareholder's Instructions
N	Commercial revitalization deduction from rental real estate activities	See Form 8582 instructions
O	Reforestation expense deduction	See the Shareholder's Instructions
P	through **R**	Reserved for future use
S	Other deductions	See the Shareholder's Instructions

13. Credits
A	Low-income housing credit (section 42(j)(5)) from pre-2008 buildings	
B	Low-income housing credit (other) from pre-2008 buildings	
C	Low-income housing credit (section 42(j)(5)) from post-2007 buildings	
D	Low-income housing credit (other) from post-2007 buildings	See the Shareholder's Instructions
E	Qualified rehabilitation expenditures (rental real estate)	
F	Other rental real estate credits	
G	Other rental credits	
H	Undistributed capital gains credit	Schedule 3 (Form 1040 or 1040-SR), line 13, box a
I	Biofuel producer credit	
J	Work opportunity credit	
K	Disabled access credit	See the Shareholder's Instructions
L	Empowerment zone employment credit	
M	Credit for increasing research activities	

Code		Report on
N	Credit for employer social security and Medicare taxes	
O	Backup withholding	See the Shareholder's Instructions
P	Other credits	

14. Foreign transactions
A	Name of country or U.S. possession	
B	Gross income from all sources	Form 1116, Part I
C	Gross income sourced at shareholder level	

Foreign gross income sourced at corporate level
D	Reserved for future use	
E	Foreign branch category	
F	Passive category	Form 1116, Part I
G	General category	
H	Other	

Deductions allocated and apportioned at shareholder level
I	Interest expense	Form 1116, Part I
J	Other	Form 1116, Part I

Deductions allocated and apportioned at corporate level to foreign source income
K	Reserved for future use	
L	Foreign branch category	
M	Passive category	
N	General category	Form 1116, Part I
O	Other	

Other information
P	Total foreign taxes paid	Form 1116, Part II
Q	Total foreign taxes accrued	Form 1116, Part II
R	Reduction in taxes available for credit	Form 1116, line 12
S	Foreign trading gross receipts	Form 8873
T	Extraterritorial income exclusion	Form 8873
U	Section 965 information	See the Shareholder's Instructions
V	Other foreign transactions	See the Shareholder's Instructions

15. Alternative minimum tax (AMT) items
A	Post-1986 depreciation adjustment	
B	Adjusted gain or loss	
C	Depletion (other than oil & gas)	See the Shareholder's Instructions
D	Oil, gas, & geothermal—gross income	and the Instructions for Form 6251
E	Oil, gas, & geothermal—deductions	
F	Other AMT items	

16. Items affecting shareholder basis
A	Tax-exempt interest income	Form 1040 or 1040-SR, line 2a
B	Other tax-exempt income	
C	Nondeductible expenses	
D	Distributions	See the Shareholder's Instructions
E	Repayment of loans from shareholders	

17. Other information
A	Investment income	Form 4952, line 4a
B	Investment expenses	Form 4952, line 5
C	Qualified rehabilitation expenditures (other than rental real estate)	See the Shareholder's Instructions
D	Basis of energy property	See the Shareholder's Instructions
E	Recapture of low-income housing credit (section 42(j)(5))	Form 8611, line 8
F	Recapture of low-income housing credit (other)	Form 8611, line 8
G	Recapture of investment credit	See Form 4255
H	Recapture of other credits	See the Shareholder's Instructions
I	Look-back interest—completed long-term contracts	See Form 8697
J	Look-back interest—income forecast method	See Form 8866
K	Dispositions of property with section 179 deductions	
L	Recapture of section 179 deduction	See the Shareholder's Instructions
M	through **U**	
V	Section 199A information	
W	through **Z**	Reserved for future use
AA	Excess taxable income	
AB	Excess business interest income	See the Shareholder's Instructions
AC	Other information	

Page 2 of Schedule K-1 is from 2019. 2020 not available when we went to print.

Self-Study Problem 11.8

20% × $190,000 = $38,000

Only $190,000 ($340,000 − $150,000) is subject to the accumulated earnings tax.

Self-Study Problem 11.9

Under the CARES Act, Plum can utilize all of the AMT credits in 2019; thus, there is no carryforward.

CHAPTER 12   TAX ADMINISTRATION AND TAX PLANNING

Self-Study Problem 12.1

1. True
2. True
3. False   The commissioner of internal revenue is appointed by the president of the United States.
4. False   The IRS is part of the Treasury Department.
5. True

Self-Study Problem 12.2

1. True
2. False   An office audit is conducted at the IRS office.
3. True
4. True
5. False   Audits can be appealed to an appellate agent.

Self-Study Problem 12.3

Part a.	Failure-to-pay penalty:		
	$3,000 × 0.5% × 2 months		$ 30
	Failure-to-file penalty:		
	$3,000 × 5% × 2 months	$ 300	
	Less: failure-to-pay penalty	(30)	
			270
	Total		$300

The minimum failure-to-file penalty does not apply since the return was filed within 60 days of the due date.

Part b.	Failure-to-pay penalty:		
	$3,000 × 0.5% × 3 months		$ 45
	Failure-to-file penalty:		
	$3,000 × 5% × 3 months	$ 450	
	Less: failure-to-pay penalty	(45)	
		405	
	Minimum failure-to-file penalty		435
	Total		$480

Part c.	20% × $10,000	$2,000

Self-Study Problem 12.4

1. True
2. False   For bad debts, the statute of limitations is 7 years.
3. False   There is no statute of limitations for fraudulent returns.
4. True
5. True

Self-Study Problem 12.5

1. False   Lawyers and enrolled agents may also represent
              taxpayers before the IRS.
2. False   A college degree is not required.
3. False   Anyone may prepare corporate tax returns.
4. True
5. False   The penalty is $540 for tax returns filed in 2020.
6. True
7. False   The burden of proof is on the IRS.
8. False   The burden of proof remains on the taxpayer.
9. True
10. True
11. True

Self-Study Problem 12.6

1. True
2. True
3. True   Publication 1 directs the
              reader to Publication 594.
4. True
5. True
6. True

Self-Study Problem 12.7

1. 17.36% = $15,446 / $89,000
2. 17.43% = $15,686 / $90,000
3. 24% = ($15,686 − $15,446) /
         ($90,000 − $89,000)

GLOSSARY OF TAX TERMS

NOTE: The words and phrases appearing below have been defined to reflect their conventional use in the field of taxation. Such definitions may, therefore, be incomplete for other purposes.

0.9 percent Medicare tax

For tax years after 2012, the Affordable Care Act (ACA) imposed an additional Medicare tax on high-income taxpayers, at a rate of 0.9 percent applicable to wages, compensation, and self-employment income above an annual threshold amount.

Accelerated Cost Recovery System (ACRS)

For tax years after 1980, a rapid write-off of the cost of a capital asset is allowed by this system, which was later modified in 1986 and renamed Modified Accelerated Cost Recovery System (MACRS). The minimum number of years over which the asset may be depreciated and the applicable percentage of the asset's cost that may be deducted each year depend on the class of the property.

Accelerated death benefits

Early payouts of life insurance, also called accelerated death benefits or viatical settlements, are excluded from gross income for certain terminally or chronically ill taxpayers. The taxpayer may either collect an early payout from the insurance company or sell or assign the policy to a viatical settlement provider. See *Viatical settlements*.

Accident and health benefits

Employee fringe benefits provided by employers through the payment of health and accident insurance premiums, or the establishment of employer-funded medical reimbursement plans. Employers generally are entitled to a deduction for such payments, whereas employees generally exclude the fringe benefits from gross income.

Accrual method

A method of accounting that reflects expenses incurred and income earned for any one tax year. In contrast to the cash basis of accounting, expenses do not have to be paid to be deductible, nor does income have to be received to be taxable.

Adjusted basis

The cost or other basis of property reduced by depreciation allowed or allowable and increased by capital improvements. See *Basis*.

Adjusted gross income (AGI)

A determination unique to individual taxpayers used as the basis to calculate limitations on the amount of certain expenses which may be deductible, including medical expenses, charitable contributions, certain personal casualty losses, and certain other itemized deductions. Generally, AGI represents gross income minus specific deductions such as certain trade or business expenses (deductions *for* AGI) but before itemized deductions or the standard deduction (deductions *from* AGI).

Adoption expenses

Adoption fees, court costs, attorney fees, and other expenses directly related to the legal adoption of an eligible child.

Affordable Care Act (ACA)

Also referred to as Obamacare, ACA is a federal law providing for a fundamental reform of the U.S. healthcare and health insurance system, signed by President Barack Obama in 2010.

Alimony payments

Payments from one spouse or former spouse, to the other, required as a result of a divorce or separation agreement, which meet certain statutory requirements. Alimony and separate maintenance payments, but not child support payments, are included in the gross income of the recipient and are deducted by the payor for divorces occurring before 2019. The TCJA has repealed both the deduction of and inclusion of alimony for tax years beginning in 2019. See also *Child support payments*.

Alternative minimum tax (AMT)

Designed to prevent wealthy taxpayers (but now applicable to many taxpayers) from taking advantage of tax write-offs to pay little or no tax. Computed by calculating both regular tax and AMT and generally paying whichever tax is larger.

American Opportunity tax credit

Previously referred to as the Hope credit, a tax credit available for the first 4 years of postsecondary education expenses for students who meet specific requirements.

Amortization

The allocation (and charge to expense) of the cost or other basis of an intangible asset over its estimated useful life. Examples of amortizable intangibles include patents, copyrights, and goodwill.

Amount realized

The amount received by a taxpayer on the sale or exchange of property less the cost incurred to transfer the property. The measure of the amount received is the sum of the cash and the fair market value of any property or services plus any relieved liability of the taxpayer. Determining the amount realized is the starting point for arriving at a realized gain or loss.

AMT exemption allowance

Statutory deduction reducing AMT income for taxpayers with taxable income below an annually specified dollar amount.

AMT preferences

Items excluded from the computation of regular taxable income but required to be added to compute alternative minimum taxable income.

Annuity

A fixed sum payable at specified intervals for a specific period of time or for life. Payments represent a partial return of capital and a return (e.g., interest income) on the capital investment. An exclusion ratio is generally used to compute the amounts of nontaxable and taxable income.

Automobile expenses

Automobile expenses are generally deductible only to the extent the automobile is used in business or for the production of income. Personal commuting expenses are not deductible. The taxpayer may deduct actual expenses (including depreciation and insurance), or choose to use the standard mileage rate.

Backup withholding

Certain situations in which the issuer of payment such as dividends or interest is required to withhold income tax at the time of payment. Designed to ensure that income tax is paid on payments to certain taxpayers (generally, non-U.S. tax residents).

Bad debts

An ordinary deduction is permitted if a business debt, such as an account receivable, subsequently becomes worthless (uncollectible), provided the income arising from the debt was previously included in taxable income. The deduction is allowed only in the year of worthlessness. A nonbusiness bad debt deduction is allowed as a short-term capital loss when a debt which did not arise in connection with the creditor's trade or business activities becomes worthless. Loans between related parties (family members) generally are classified as nonbusiness debts.

Basis

The amount assigned to an asset for income tax purposes. For assets acquired by purchase, the basis would be the cost of the asset plus any direct costs incidental to the purchase. Special rules govern the basis of property received as a result of another's death or by gift. See also *Adjusted basis.*

Bona fide

Authentic and genuine. In the context of tax law, serving a specific business purpose.

Bonus depreciation

The immediate deduction of all or some of the cost of otherwise slowly depreciated property.

Boot

Cash or property of a type other than that permitted to be received tax-free in a nontaxable like-kind exchange. The receipt of boot will cause an otherwise tax-free transfer to become taxable to the extent of the lesser of the fair market value of such boot or the realized gain on the transfer.

Business gifts

Business gifts are deductible only to the extent that each gift does not exceed $25 per person per year. Exceptions are made for promotional gifts and for certain employee awards.

Cancellation of debt income

Also referred to as forgiveness of debt income. When a lender forgives or cancels all or some of the taxpayer's outstanding loans or other credit account. In general, the amount of debt that has been forgiven is considered taxable income unless specifically excluded.

Capital asset

All assets are capital assets except those specifically excluded by the tax law. Major categories of noncapital assets include property held for sale in the normal course of business (i.e., inventory), trade accounts and notes receivable, depreciable property, and real estate used in a trade or business.

Capital expenditure

An expenditure, the amount of which should be added to the basis of the property improved. For income tax purposes, this generally precludes a deduction for the full amount of the expenditure in the year paid or incurred. Any tax deduction has to come in the form of cost recovery or depreciation.

Capital gain

The gain from the sale or exchange of a capital asset. Gain from a property held 12 months or less is deemed to be a short-term capital gain. If the property is held more than 12 months, the gain is deemed to be long-term. See *Capital asset and Holding period.*

Capital loss

The loss from the sale or exchange of a capital asset. A loss from a property held 12 months or less is deemed to be a short-term capital loss. If the property is held more than 12 months, the loss is deemed to be long-term. See *Capital asset and Holding period.*

Capital loss carryovers

A net capital loss that is not deducted in the current tax year but is eligible to be carried forward into future taxable years.

Cash basis

A method of accounting under which income is reported when received and expenses are deductible when paid by the taxpayer. Prepaid rent and prepaid interest must be deducted using the accrual method.

Casualty loss

A casualty is defined as the complete or partial destruction of property resulting from an identifiable event of a sudden, unexpected or unusual nature (e.g., floods, shipwrecks, storms, fires, automobile accidents). Beginning in the 2018 tax year, personal casualty losses are only eligible for deduction when resulting from a federally declared disaster area. Personal casualty losses are deductible as itemized deductions subject to a $100 nondeductible floor and only to the extent that the taxpayer's total losses from personal-use property (net of the $100 floor) exceed 10 percent of adjusted gross income. Special rules are provided for the combining (netting) of certain casualty gains and losses.

Change in accounting method

A change in the taxpayer's method of accounting (e.g., from the FIFO to the LIFO inventory method) generally requires prior approval from the IRS. In some instances, the permission for change will not be granted unless the taxpayer agrees to certain adjustments prescribed by the IRS.

Change in accounting period

A taxpayer must obtain the consent of the IRS before changing his or her tax year. Income for the short period created by the change must be annualized.

Charitable contributions

Contributions are deductible (subject to various restrictions and ceiling limitations) if made to qualified nonprofit charitable organizations. A cash-basis taxpayer is entitled to a deduction in the year of payment. Accrual-basis corporations may accrue contributions at year-end under certain circumstances.

Child and dependent care credit

This credit is available to individuals who are employed on a full-time basis and maintain a household for a dependent child or disabled spouse or dependent. The amount of the credit is equal to a percentage of the cost of employment-related child and dependent care expenses, up to a stated maximum amount.

Child support payments

Payments for child support do not constitute alimony, and are, therefore, not included in gross income by the recipient or deducted as alimony by the payor to the extent permitted otherwise. See also *Alimony.*

Child and other dependent tax credit

A direct reduction in tax liability granted for each qualifying child under age 17 and other qualifying dependents. The child and other dependent tax credit is phased out based on the level of modified adjusted gross income.

Community property

Community property is all property, other than separate property, owned by a married couple. The income from community property is generally split equally between spouses. The classification of property as community property is important in determining the separate taxable income of married taxpayers.

Consumer interest

Not deductible for tax purposes, consumer interest is interest expense generated from personal loans, credit cards or other debt used for personal purposes.

Cost of goods sold

The amount equal to the cost of inventory sold during the period. Generally, beginning inventory plus purchases of inventory (or the cost to create inventory) less ending inventory. Cost of goods sold is deducted from gross receipts on Schedule C.

Deferred compensation

Compensation which will be taxed when received or upon the removal of certain restrictions, not when earned. An example would be contributions by an employer to a qualified pension or profit-sharing plan on behalf of an employee. Such contributions will not be taxed to the employee until the funds are made available or distributed to the employee (e.g., upon retirement). See *Qualified pension or profit-sharing plan.*

Defined benefit plan

A type of pension plan in which the plan specifies the pension payment amounts payable to an employee upon retirement, based on the employee's earnings history, tenure of service and age.

Defined contribution plan

A type of pension plan in which the plan specifies the regular contributions made by the employer and employee in which the pension benefits are based on the contribution amounts and the returns of the plan's investments.

Depreciation recapture

The recharacterizing of gain on the sale of certain property used in a trade or business to ordinary income to the extent of depreciation previously allowed.

Discriminant Function System (DIF)

One process by which the IRS selects tax returns for audits. The DIF is a computerized statistical sampling technique.

Dividends received deduction

A special deduction for corporations that receive dividend income distributions from a domestic corporation that it has an ownership interest in. Generally designed to prevent double-taxation of corporate dividends paid by a corporate subsidiary to its parent.

Earned income

Income from personal services as distinguished from income generated by property.

Earned income credit

The earned income credit is a refundable credit available to qualifying individuals with income and AGI below certain levels.

Economic Income Payment (EIP)

In 2020 in response to the COVID-19 pandemic, eligible taxpayers, based on adjusted gross income, received an EIP of up to $1,200 for individuals or $2,400 for married couples and up to $500 for each qualifying child in the form of a recovery rebate. See *Recovery rebate credit (RRC)*.

Education expenses

Employees may deduct education expenses if such items are incurred either (1) to maintain or improve existing job-related skills or (2) to meet the express requirements of the employer or the requirements imposed by law to retain employment status. Such expenses are not deductible if the education is required to meet the minimum educational requirements for the taxpayer's job or the education qualifies the individual for a new trade or business.

Educational assistance program

A fringe benefit that provides that tax-free educational assistance may be paid to an employee or prior employee for a specific dollar amount provided annually. Requires a written plan to allow employees to receive tax-free payments for tuition, fees, books, course-related supplies and equipment, but not payments for meals, lodging or entertainment.

Election to expense (Section 179)

The tax code Section 179 allows a taxpayer to elect to immediately expense and deduct the cost of certain property when placed in service, up to a certain limit, rather than capitalizing and depreciating such property.

Employee Stock Ownership Plan (ESOP)

A type of defined contribution pension plan in which employers provide their employees with ownership in the employer's stock.

Entertainment expenses

Starting with the 2018 tax year, the TCJA has disallowed the deductibility of entertainment expenses.

Fair market value

The amount at which property would change hands between a willing buyer and a willing seller, neither being under any compulsion to buy or sell, and both having reasonable knowledge of the relevant facts.

Federal Insurance Contributions Act (FICA)

FICA imposes social taxes on forms of earned income to provide benefits for retired and disabled workers. Referred to as FICA taxes, Social Security and Medicare taxes are withheld using a specific percentage from an employee's wages. Both the employer, the employee, and the self-employed are responsible for the payment of FICA taxes.

First in, first out (FIFO)

An accounting method for determining the cost of inventories. Under this method, the first merchandise acquired is the first to be sold. Thus, the cost of inventory on hand is deemed to be the cost of the most recently acquired merchandise.

Fiscal year-end

An annual accounting period which does not end on December 31, a calendar year-end. An example of a fiscal year is July 1 through June 30.

Foreign tax credit or deduction

Both U.S. individual taxpayers and U.S. corporations may claim a foreign tax credit on income earned and subject to tax in a foreign country or U.S. possession. As an alternative to the credit, a deduction may be taken for the foreign taxes paid. The purpose of this credit is to eliminate double taxation on income earned in a foreign country.

Forgiveness of debt

See *Cancellation of debt*.

Fringe benefits

Non-wage benefits or perquisites (perks) provided to employees in addition to their normal wages and salaries. Most fringe benefits are required to be included in the employee's gross income; however, certain *qualified* fringe benefits such as employee-paid health insurance premiums may be excluded from the employee's gross income but remain deductible by the business.

Gift

A transfer of property for less than adequate consideration. Gifts usually occur in a personal setting (such as between members of the same family) and are generally excluded from taxable income.

Goodwill

The ability of a business to generate income in excess of a normal rate on assets due to superior managerial skills, market position, new product technology, etc. In the purchase of a business, goodwill is the difference between the purchase price and the value of the net assets. Goodwill is an intangible asset which possesses an indefinite life; however, it is amortized over a 15-year period for federal income tax purposes.

Gross income

All income from whatever source derived except that which is specifically excluded by tax law. Gross income does not include income such as interest on municipal bonds. In the case of a manufacturing or merchandising business, gross income means gross profit (i.e., gross sales or gross receipts less cost of goods sold).

Guaranteed payments

Payments made to a partner for services rendered or for use of the partner's capital, that are made without regard to the income of the partnership (similar to wages). The payments are generally ordinary income to the partner and deductible by the partnership.

Head of household

An unmarried individual who maintains a household for another and satisfies certain conditions. Such status enables the taxpayer to use income tax rates lower than those applicable to other unmarried individuals (single) but higher than those applicable to surviving spouses (widow(er)) and married persons filing a joint return.

Health savings accounts (HSA)

A type of savings account established by an employer to pay unreimbursed medical expenses by taxpayers with certain high-deductible medical insurance. Contributions to HSAs are deductible for AGI and are subject to limitations.

Hobby loss

A nondeductible loss arising from a personal hobby as contrasted with an activity engaged in for profit. Generally, the law provides a presumption that an activity is engaged in for profit if profits are earned during any 3 or more years in a 5-year period.

Household workers

Employees hired to work at specific tasks within a household, including child care, cleaning, meal preparation, and household administration. The payment of household workers generally subjects the taxpayer to a requirement to withhold or pay related payroll taxes. See *Nanny tax*.

Holding period

The period of time that property has been held by a taxpayer. The holding period is of significance in determining whether gains or losses from the sale or exchange of capital assets are classified as long-term or short-term. See *capital asset*.

Hybrid method

A method of accounting that involves the use of both the cash and accrual methods of accounting. The tax law permits the use of a hybrid method, provided the taxpayer's income is clearly reflected by the method.

Independent contractor

Classification of a worker that provides goods or services via a written contract or verbal agreement. Independent contractors differ from employees based on a number of criteria and are classified by law not by choice by the worker or the employer. The distinguishment between an independent contractor and an employee is important as the costs for business owners to maintain employees are often significantly higher due to federal and state requirements for employers to pay employment taxes and other employee benefits.

Installment method

A method of accounting enabling a taxpayer to spread the recognition of gain on the sale of property over the payment period. Under this procedure, the seller computes the gross profit percentage from the sale (i.e., the gain divided by the contract price) and applies the percentage to each payment received to arrive at the gain to be recognized for each accounting period.

Installment sales

A sale in which part of the proceeds will be received in a tax year or years following the year of sale and permits the partial deferral of gain to future tax years. See *Installment method*.

Intangible assets

An asset that does not have a physical presence but has value. Some examples of intangible assets include copyrights, goodwill, patents, trademarks, etc.

Internal Revenue Code

Sometimes referred to as the Tax Code or the Code, the comprehensive set of tax laws enacted as Title 26 of the United States Code of Congress. The Code is organized according to topic, and covers all relevant rules pertaining to income, gift, estate sales, payroll, and excise taxes. The IRS is the implementing agency of the Internal Revenue Code.

Internal Revenue Service (IRS)

A United States government agency that is responsible for the enforcement of the Internal Revenue Code and collection of taxes. The IRS was established in 1862 by President Lincoln and operates under the authority of the United States Department of the Treasury.

Inventory

The goods and raw materials used to produce goods, held for sale by a business, to be sold to produce a profit.

Involuntary conversion

The loss or destruction of property through theft, casualty, or condemnation. If the owner reinvests any proceeds received within a prescribed period of time in property that is similar or related in service or use, any gain realized on an involuntary conversion can, at the taxpayer's election, be deferred for federal income tax purposes.

Kiddie tax

The amount of tax on the unearned income of certain dependent children.

Last in, first out (LIFO)

An accounting method for determining the cost of inventories. Under this method, the most recently acquired goods are sold first and the cost of inventory on hand is deemed to consist of the earliest purchased merchandise (goods).

Life insurance proceeds

Generally, life insurance proceeds paid to a beneficiary upon the death of the insured are exempt from federal income tax. An exception exists when a life insurance contract has been transferred for valuable consideration to another individual who assumes ownership rights. In such a case, the proceeds are income to the assignee to the extent that the proceeds exceed the amount paid for the policy (cash surrender value at the time of transfer) plus any subsequent premiums paid.

Lifetime learning credit

The lifetime learning credit may be used in any tax year the American Opportunity tax credit is not used for expenses paid for education. Unlike the American Opportunity tax credit, the lifetime learning credit may be claimed for an unlimited number of tax years.

Like-kind exchange

An exchange of property held for productive use in a trade or business or for investment (except inventory and stocks and bonds) for property of the same type. Unless different property is received (i.e., "boot"), the exchange will be nontaxable.

Like-kind property

See *Like-kind exchange*.

Limited Liability Company (LLC)

Business organizations usually treated as partnerships for tax purposes but offering the limited liability of a corporate stockholder to all members.

Medical expenses

Medical expenses of an individual, spouse, and dependents are allowed as an itemized deduction to the extent that total medical expenses, less insurance reimbursements, exceed limitations based on the taxpayer's AGI.

Medical flexible spending account (FSA)

A medical flexible spending account is a fringe benefit that allows employees to be reimbursed for medical expenses tax-free up to a certain dollar limit when incurred and claimed within a specific time period. FSAs are usually funded through an employee's voluntary salary reduction agreement with their employer.

Moving expenses

A deduction in arriving at adjusted gross income available to employees and self-employed individuals provided certain tests are met (e.g., the taxpayer's new job must be at least 50 miles farther from the former residence than the former residence was from the former place of work). The TCJA has suspended the deduction of moving expenses for all taxpayers except members of the U.S. Armed Services beginning in the 2018 tax year and ending in 2025.

Nanny tax

Payroll taxes paid by a taxpayer that employs certain household workers. See *Household workers*.

Necessary

Appropriate and helpful in furthering the taxpayer's business or income-producing activity. See *Ordinary*.

Net investment income

Income such as dividends and interest from investment assets such as stocks, bonds, mutual funds and other investment assets, less investment expenses other than interest expense.

Net investment income tax

The ACA imposed a 3.8 percent Medicare tax on certain net investment income of individuals that have net investment income or modified adjusted gross income above the annual statutory threshold amounts.

Net operating loss

To mitigate the effect of the annual accounting period, taxpayers are allowed to use a net loss resulting from operations, as a deduction from net income in past or future years. A carryback period of 2 years and a carryforward period of 20 years are allowed.

Nonbusiness bad debts

A bad debt loss not incurred in connection with a taxpayer's trade or business. Such loss is deductible subject to annual limitations, as a short-term capital loss and will only be allowed in the year the debt becomes entirely worthless. Many investor losses fall into the classification of nonbusiness bad debts.

Nonrecourse debt

An obligation for which the endorser is not personally liable. An example of a nonrecourse debt is a mortgage on real estate acquired by a partnership without the assumption of any liability on the mortgage by the partnership or any of the partners. The acquired property generally is pledged as collateral for the loan.

Office-in-the-home expenses

Business-related expenses attributable to the use of a residence (e.g., den or office) are allowed only if the portion of the residence is used exclusively and on a regular basis as the taxpayer's place of business or as a place of business which is used by patients, clients, or customers.

Ordinary

Common, accepted, and legitimate in the general industry or type of activity in which the taxpayer is engaged. It comprises one of the tests for the deductibility of expenses incurred or paid in connection with a trade or business: for the production or collection of income; for the management, conservation, or maintenance of property held for the production of income; or in connection with the determination, collection, or refund of any tax. See *Necessary*.

Organizational expenses

Organizational expenses (also known as organizational costs) are associated with the formation of a business prior to the beginning of operation. A corporation may amortize organizational expenses over a period of 180 months. Certain expenses related to starting a company do not qualify for amortization (e.g., expenses connected with issuing or selling stock or other securities).

Partnerships

Partnerships are conduit, reporting entities, that engage in some type of business or financial activity, and are not subject to taxation. Various items of partnership income, expenses, gains, and losses flow through to the partners and are reported on their respective individual income tax returns.

Passive losses

Passive losses are deductible only to the extent of passive income. Losses from actively managed rental real estate may be deducted up to $25,000 annually. Unused passive losses carry forward indefinitely (until the activity which generated the losses is disposed of) and can be used by taxpayers to offset passive income in future years.

Patents

A patent is an intangible asset which may be amortized over its life. The sale of a patent usually results in long-term capital gain treatment.

Per diem

An alternative to reporting actual expenses, a per diem allows for a daily allowance for travel expenses including lodging, meals, and incidentals to be reimbursed to employees. Per diem reporting is designed to eliminate the record keeping usually associated with travel expenses.

Personal expenses

Expenses of an individual incurred for personal reasons which are not deductible unless specifically allowed under the tax law.

Personal property

Generally, all property other than real estate. Personal property is sometimes designated as "personalty" while real estate is termed "realty." Personal property can also refer to property not used in a taxpayer's trade or business or held for the production or collection of income. When used in this sense, personal property could include both realty (e.g., a personal residence) and personalty (e.g., personal effects such as clothing and furniture).

Personal residence

The sale of a personal residence may result in the recognition of capital gain (but not loss). Taxpayers may permanently exclude $250,000 ($500,000 if married) of gain on the sale of their personal residence from income provided certain requirements are met, but generally not more than once every two years.

Points

Loan origination fees paid generally deductible as interest expense by a buyer of property.

Portfolio income

Portfolio income includes dividends, interest, royalties, annuities, and realized gains or losses on the sale of assets producing portfolio income.

Premium tax credit

Lower income individuals who obtain health insurance coverage may be eligible for the premium tax credit to assist in covering the cost of health care premiums. Eligible individuals can choose to receive the credit paid in advance or claim the total credit when filing their tax return. If an individual chooses to have the credit paid in advance, the individual will reconcile the amount paid in advance with the actual credit computed when filing their tax return.

Private mortgage insurance (PMI)

Mortgage insurance is an additional expense charged to a borrower that is often required when the borrower makes only a small investment (down payment) on their home at time of purchase.

Prizes and awards

The fair market value of a prize or award generally is included in gross income.

Qualified business income (QBI)

The income attributed to individual taxpayers by a pass-through entity such as a sole proprietorship, partnership, or S corporation that excludes capital gains, most dividends, interest, and other nonbusiness income.

Qualified business income (QBI) deduction

A deduction in the amount of 20 percent of the qualified business income, subject to certain limitations such as the taxable income limit, the wage limitation and the specified service business limitation. The limitations are computed before considering the QBI deduction.

Qualified business property

Tangible property subject to depreciation (i.e., not inventory or land) for which the depreciable period has not ended before the close of the taxable year, held by the business at year-end, and used at any point during the year in the production of QBI. Qualified business property is an element of the wage and capital limitation, which is a component of the wage limitation.

Qualified improvement property (QIP)

Any improvement to a building's interior with the exception of improvements relating to enlarging the building, any elevator or escalator, or the internal structural framework of the building.

Qualified pension or profit-sharing plan

An employer-sponsored plan that meets certain requirements. If these requirements are met, none of the employer's contributions to the plan will be taxed to the employee until distributed to him or her. The employer will be allowed a deduction in the year the contributions are made.

Qualified tuition program

See *Section 529 tuition plan*.

Qualified trade or business

Any trade or business other than a specified service trade or business, or the trade or business of performing services as an employee.

Qualifying widow(er)

A tax filing status available to widows or widowers for two years after their spouse's death. To claim this status, the taxpayer must also have a dependent child who lives in the household and for which the taxpayer pays over half the cost of maintaining the household.

Realized gain or loss

The difference between the amount realized upon the sale or other disposition of property and the adjusted basis of such property.

Recognized gain or loss

The portion of realized gain or loss that is subject to income taxation. See *Realized gain or loss*.

Recovery period

The amount of time in which a business asset is depreciated and thereby creating a tax deduction, under the useful life requirements established by the Internal Revenue Service.

Recovery rebate credit (RRC)

A refundable tax credit against 2020 federal income taxes in response to the COVID-19 pandemic. Based on their adjusted gross income, eligible taxpayers are entitled to a RRC amount of up to $1,200 for individuals or $2,400 for married couples and up to $500 for each qualifying child. Many taxpayers will have received an EIP in 2020 for their recovery rebate. For those taxpayers that did not receive an EIP or whose EIP was underfunded based on their AGI or family size, they will record their RRC on their 2020 Form 1040. See *Economic impact payment (EIC)*.

Required minimum distributions (RMDs)

The minimum amount of money that must be withdrawn each year from a traditional IRA, SEP or SIMPLE IRA by owners and qualified retirement plan participants of retirement age. The retiree must withdraw the RMD amount annually, starting in the year the retiree turns age 72, (70 1/2 years old before

January 1, 2020). Roth IRAs do not require withdrawals until after the death of the owner.

Rollover

Transfer of pension funds from one plan or trustee to another. The transfer may be a direct transfer or a rollover distribution.

Roth Individual Retirement Accounts (IRAs)

The Roth IRA allows nondeductible contributions. Although the contributions to a Roth IRA are not deductible, earnings accumulate tax-free, and qualified distributions are generally not included in income when received.

S corporation

A small business corporation whose shareholders have filed an election permitting the corporation to be treated in a manner similar to partnerships for income tax purposes. Of major significance are the facts that S corporations usually avoid the corporate income tax and that corporate losses can be claimed by the shareholders, limited to individual shareholder's adjusted basis.

Saver's Credit

A tax credit designed to give low-to-moderate-income taxpayers a tax credit for part of a contribution to a qualified retirement plan.

Scholarships

Scholarships are generally taxable income to the recipient except for amounts received for tuition, fees, books, and course-required supplies and equipment.

Section 179

See *Election to Expense (Section 179)*.

Section 401(k) plan

A Section 401(k) plan is a qualified retirement plan which grants employee participants a deferral of income for employer contributions to the plan. The plan allows taxpayers to elect to receive compensation or to have the employer make a contribution to the retirement plan. The plan may be structured as a salary reduction plan. There is a maximum annual dollar limitation, as well as a limitation based on the employee's compensation. Some employers match employee contributions up to a certain limit in order to encourage participation.

Section 1231 assets

Section 1231 assets include depreciable assets and real estate used in a trade or business, held for the long-term holding period. Under certain circumstances, the classification also includes timber, coal, domestic iron ore, livestock (held for draft, breeding, dairy, or sporting purposes), and unharvested crops. Gains may be treated as long-term capital gains while losses in some cases may be deducted as ordinary losses.

Section 1245 recapture

See *depreciation recapture*.

Section 1250 recapture

See *depreciation recapture*.

Self-employment income

Self-employment income is the taxpayer's net earnings from self-employment, which includes gross income from a taxpayer's trade or business, less trade or business deductions. Self-employment income also includes the taxpayer's share of income from a partnership trade or business.

Simplified Employee Pension (SEP) IRA

A form of qualified retirement plan for certain small businesses. See *SEP*.

Separate property

Separate property is property, other than community property, acquired by a spouse before marriage or after marriage as a gift or inheritance.

SEP

A retirement plan that any employer or self-employed individual can establish. SEPs are simple to establish and have flexible funding arrangements with contributions that are limited on an annual basis.

SIMPLE IRA

A form of qualified retirement plan for small businesses with 100 or fewer employees. Unlike a SEP, employers are required to make certain contributions.

Simplified method

A specific calculation used by individual taxpayers to calculate the taxable amount of a payment from an annuity after November 18, 1996.

Social Security number

A unique 9-digit number provided by the U.S. Social Security Administration to identify each person and track Social Security benefits. Most taxpayers use the Social Security number as their taxpayer identification number. See *Taxpayer identification number*.

Social Security tax

A component of FICA (see *Federal Insurance Contributions Act [FICA]*), Social Security taxes refer to Old Age, Survivors, and Disability Insurance (OASDI) and are applied to all wages, up to an annual limitation.

Specified service trade or business

Used in the context of qualified business income as being excluded from a qualified trade or business, it involves the performance of services where the principal asset of such trade or business is based on the reputation or skill of one or more of its employees, such as accounting, actuarial science, consulting, financial and brokerage services, health, law, performing arts, and professional athletes.

Standard deduction

Taxpayers can deduct the larger of the standard deduction or their itemized deductions in calculating taxable income. An extra standard deduction amount is allowed for elderly and blind taxpayers. The standard deduction amounts are set by the IRS and may change annually.

Statute of limitations

A time period within which an action may be taken by the IRS or a taxpayer on a tax return. In general, the statute of limitations for a tax return runs for 3 years from the date the tax return was filed or the return extended due date, whichever is later.

Tax home

Since travel expenses of a taxpayer are deductible only if the taxpayer is away from home, the deductibility of such expenses rests upon the definition of "tax home." The IRS position is that the "tax home" is the business location, post, or station of the taxpayer. If the taxpayer is temporarily reassigned to a new post for a period of 1 year or less, the taxpayer's home should be his or her personal residence and the travel expenses should be deductible.

Taxpayer Bill of Rights

Passed by Congress in 1988 and amended several times, this set of provisions requires that the IRS informs taxpayers of their rights when dealing with the IRS and it expands taxpayers' rights and remedies when involved in disputes with the IRS. The provisions of the Taxpayer Bill of Rights are summarized in IRS Publication 1.

Taxpayer identification number

A unique number of a taxpayer used by the IRS in the administration of tax laws. For individuals, it is generally a Social Security number, but can also be an Individual Taxpayer Identification Number (ITIN) which is issued by the IRS to individuals who are not eligible to receive a Social Security number. For employers, it is an IRS-issued number known as an Employer Identification Number (EIN). See *Social Security number*.

TCJA

The Tax Cuts and Jobs Act (TCJA) of 2017 was signed into law resulting in the most dramatic change to the tax code since 1986.

Trade or business expenses

Deductions for AGI which are attributable to a taxpayer's business or profession. The expenses must be ordinary and necessary to that business.

Traditional IRA

An individual retirement account (IRA) for taxpayers. The traditional IRA often permits a deduction for contributions and deferred taxation of earnings until withdrawals.

Transportation expenses

Transportation expenses for a taxpayer include only the costs of transportation (taxi fares, automobile expenses, etc.) in the course of employment where the taxpayer is not "away from home" in a travel status. Commuting expenses are not deductible.

Travel expenses

Travel expenses include meals (50 percent deductible), lodging, and transportation expenses while away from home in the pursuit of a trade or business (including that as an employee).

Trustee-to-trustee transfer

When a trustee of a retirement plan transfers assets to the trustee of a different retirement plan, upon instruction from the taxpayer. There are no tax implications nor are there any restrictions on amounts or number of transfer occurrences in a given year.

Unearned income

For tax purposes, unearned income (e.g., rent) is taxable in the year of receipt. In certain cases involving advance payments for goods and services, income may be deferred.

Vacation home

The Internal Revenue Code places restrictions upon taxpayers who rent their residence or vacation home for part of the tax year. The restrictions may result in the limitation of certain expenses related to the vacation home.

Viatical settlements

An early payout resulting from the sale of a life insurance policy often due to the insured being terminally or chronically ill. A viatical settlement is a way to extract value from the policy while the policy holder is still alive. See *Accelerated death benefits*.

Wage and capital limitation

A limitation on the qualified business income deduction of 25 percent of wages and 2.5 percent of qualified business property.

Wage limitation

A limitation on the qualified business income deduction of 50 percent of wages.

Withholding

The amount of tax deducted (withheld) by a payer and ultimately remitted to the tax authority as a tax payment on behalf of the payment recipient. For example, income taxes are often withheld from an employee's wages and then remitted on behalf of the employee as a tax payment to the IRS.

LIST OF SCHEDULES

LIST OF WORKSHEETS